I0214401

MODERN HUMANITIES RESEARCH ASSOCIATION
BIBLIOGRAPHIES
VOLUME 4 (I)

EDITOR
DAVID GILLESPIE

AN INTERNATIONAL ANNOTATED BIBLIOGRAPHY OF STRINDBERG STUDIES 1870–2005

AN INTERNATIONAL ANNOTATED BIBLIOGRAPHY OF STRINDBERG STUDIES 1870–2005

COMPILED, ANNOTATED, AND EDITED BY

MICHAEL ROBINSON

VOLUME ONE: GENERAL STUDIES

MODERN HUMANITIES RESEARCH ASSOCIATION

2008

Published by
The Modern Humanities Research Association
1 Carlton House Terrace
London SW1Y 5AF

First published 2008

ISBN 978-0-947623-81-4

Copies may be ordered from www.bibliographies.mhra.org.uk

CONTENTS

Volume Two

E. Individual Plays

Volume Three

F. Autobiographies

ACKNOWLEDGEMENTS

I am grateful to the Modern Humanities Research Association for supporting this project, and for the confidence in its merits evidenced by the Association's decision to include it in its series of scholarly bibliographies. I am particularly grateful to its Secretary, Professor David Gillespie, and the Association's Publishing Manager, Gerard Lowe, for their advice and help in preparing these volumes. I also owe an immense debt to Christopher Smith, without whom it is unlikely that this link with the MHRA would have occurred. Meanwhile, the Research Fund of the University of East Anglia's School of English and American Studies, and its successor School of Literature, has provided financial means for furthering the project on several occasions.

I have received practical assistance of various kinds in numerous countries and concerning several languages from Maria Alexandru, Sanda Tomescu Baciu, Elena Balzamo, Sirkka Betts, Janet Birkett, Anna Höök, Veronika Bowker, Katarina Brennan, Margareta Brundin, Piotr Bukowski, Jo Catling, Zbyněk Černík, Don Chapman, Massimo Ciaravalo, Gunnel Engwall, Olof Eriksson, Vera Gantjeva, Martin Hampál, Sally Harrower, Nina di Ponziano Hatt, Richard Hibbitt, Eric Homberger, Erik Höök, Marion Houssart, George Hyde, Henrik Johnsson, Carl Lavery, Henk van der Liet, Polina Lisovskaia, Eugenia Lofredo, Björn Meidal, Nola Merckel, Fritz Paul, Freddie Rokem, Sven Hakon Rossel, Bess Ryder, Clive Scott, Siv, Lech Sokół, Per Stam, Eszter Szalczer, Alice Tonzig, Egil Törnqvist, Irena Tsimbal, Gonçalo Vilas-Boas, Louise Vinge, Anthony Vivis, and Clas Zilliacus. Elena Smirnova provided me with transliterations of many of the Russian proper names and titles. Hieronim Chojnacki generously shared the material in his bibliography of Swedish Literature in Poland with me when it was still in typescript, and Franco Perrelli made available a considerable amount of Italian material with comparable generosity. Alex Noel-Tod advised me on bibliographical principles, and his advice and encouragement have been of great help. I stand in particular debt to David Harris, Rebecca Coleman, and Tracey Wells of the sadly defunct Interlibrary Loan Department at the University of East Anglia, through whose agency and patience a great deal of the material listed here eventually found its way into my hands. Meanwhile, both at its inception and in preparing the text for publication, I have received much encouragement, assistance, and true scholarly generosity from Barbro Ståhle Sjönell and Hans-Göran Ekman. I am exceedingly grateful for the informed and detailed scrutiny which they gave to portions of the typescript; their observations, corrections, and advice have been of great value in considering both the principles on which these volumes are based, as well as their organisation and the accuracy of the data they contain. Needless to say, whatever errors remain are entirely my responsibility.

Several other debts are of a less personal nature, but no less deeply felt on that account. Boris Erkhov's exemplary Russian bibliography, *Strindberg: Biobibliograficheskii ukazatel* (**A1:18**), from 1981 renders any attempt to reassemble the material listed there an act of pointless repetition, and I have consequently redeployed his documentation here, where the Russian proper names and book and journal titles are transliterated according to the Library of Congress system (without diacritics). All such entries are identified by the inclusion of the number they were originally accorded in Erkhov's bibliography in a final parenthesis in square brackets at the end of an entry, thus [E.681]. This enables anyone who wishes to consult the original to do so with ease. Likewise, much of the early material of relevance to Strindberg's reception in Serbia and Croatia has been assembled by Mirko Rumac in his 'Bibliografija: prijevoda Strindbergovih djela, prikaza izvedaba njegovih drama napisa of A. Strindbergu na hrvatskom odnosno srpskom jezičnom području', published in a special Strindberg issue of the Belgrade journal *Prolog*, 55-56 (1983), pp. 103-127 (**A1:86**). Cross-reference to the source of an entry in Rumac's bibliography is likewise facilitated by the inclusion of the number assigned to an article there in a final parenthesis, thus [R.367]. In several cases an essay or other title in Russian is given only in English, but then always within square brackets.

MR

INTRODUCTION

Strindberg's passion for books and their importance for his writing in numerous genres is well-documented, not least by Hans Lindström's invaluable two-volume bibliographical study *Strindberg och böckerna* (**A2:57**). So, too, is his appreciation of the values of bibliography which he imbibed, in part at least, during the period he spent as an assistant librarian at the Royal Library in Stockholm during the late 1870s and early 1880s. But alongside such positive responses to books and bibliography, Strindberg's bibliographer cannot ignore the scepticism with which he also regarded such labours as the one published here. Thus, in commenting on the apparent retirement of the Swedish Signature poet, Count Carl Snoilsky, from the socially concerned poetry with which he had recently toyed, Sg portrayed him as turning away from an engagement with direct experience to 'the distinguished morphinism of bibliomania and numismatics', and, notwithstanding his own mania for classification in numerous fields, it is impossible for his bibliographer to forget that it was Strindberg who coined the Swedish word 'knappologi' (lit. 'buttonology') to describe precisely the sort of obsessive pedantry that sustains the compilation of a work such as this. But, allowing for certain geographical black holes that remain (for example, there is little or nothing here from Central and South America, Australia, or New Zealand, omissions that it will, I hope, prove possible to remedy in a subsequent Addenda), it became clear as work progressed and material accumulated that these volumes are in many respects as much a study in reception as a straightforward bibliography. Indeed, the relevance of what is being written about, or in relation to, Strindberg, as well as when, where, and by whom, is apparent in almost every entry, and, underlying both the organisation and the annotation of the bibliography as a whole, is an interest in charting developments in Strindberg's reception, both at home in Sweden and abroad, as well as during his life and after his death.

Since this bibliography is published in several volumes, it is helpful to provide an overview of its scope and organisation here, at the outset. For the most part, it is organised generically, and moves from the general to the particular, both as a whole and within the various categories into which Strindberg's works have been arranged. But a conscious decision to counteract what might otherwise seem to endorse a misleading emphasis on the kind of biographical or anecdotal material that has dominated a great deal of Strindberg studies to date has led me to place the section devoted to Biography towards the end, along with many other Miscellaneous items, rather than to present this material at the outset, in Volume One. Consequently, the bibliography takes the following form:

A1. (Bibliographies) provides a listing of previous primary and secondary bibliographical sources, published as books or articles, with some annotation on their accuracy and usefulness. As well as bibliographies devoted specifically to Strindberg and his works, several other catalogues and bibliographies devoted to Swedish or Scandinavian literature in general are also listed here where they include a substantial number of items of direct relevance to Strindberg studies. So, too, are a few national bibliographies and several bibliographical works devoted to critics or scholars who have frequently concerned themselves with Strindberg and his writings. However, any bibliographies or bibliographical discussions of the critical literature on individual works are listed under the relevant title as appropriate.

A2 (Strindberg's Manuscripts and Book Collections) lists essays on, and catalogues of, his writings and the three personal libraries that he amassed at different periods of his life, while **A3 (Strindberg Editions)** is concerned with the various editions of his work that have appeared in Sweden and elsewhere, the controversies they have often provoked, and the editorial principles on which they have been based. Reviews of more than one volume of works in different genres in the National Edition of Strindberg's *Samlade Verk* are also listed here. However, reviews of individual volumes which are dedicated to a single work in what has now become the standard Swedish edition of Strindberg's writings are to be found in the section on the play, novel, or collection of verse in question. Meanwhile, reviews of volumes containing more than one of the plays are recorded in Section **D2**. Section **A4** contains studies of different critical approaches to Strindberg as well as general essay reviews and surveys of the literature on his life and work, including reference works. A number of archive sources, themselves the subject of occasional commentary, are catalogued in **A5**.

B:1-2 (General Studies). The first part of this section is largely concerned with book-length studies which discuss several works by Strindberg in more than a single genre, and where the overall perspective does not, as in some of the 'Life-and-Letters' studies by e.g. Gunnar Brandell, Erik Hedén, or Olof Lagercrantz place the principal stress on the relationship of the works to the life. Since their approach is essentially biographical in form and method, such studies are listed under section **R** (Biography) even though they may contain perceptive commentary on the works as well as on Strindberg's practice as a creative writer. Given the history of Strindberg criticism with its emphasis, especially in Sweden, on the biographical dimension of his work, the same may often be said of some items included in **B:1-2**, but their focus nevertheless remains primarily on Strindberg's writing as opposed to an account of his life, or to an elucidation of the former mainly in terms of the latter.

This section also lists collections of essays devoted entirely to Strindberg or which otherwise include two or more items on his work, again in more than a single genre. The essays themselves are annotated and listed individually in the relevant section elsewhere in the bibliography but, as with the collections of theatre reviews and miscellaneous material on the dramas listed in sections **D1** and **D2**, providing details of their source volumes here sometimes helps to place these essays in their original context and serves both as a means of cross-referencing and as an indication of their authors' general contribution to Strindberg studies. Hence, volumes which contain the proceedings of the various International Strindberg conferences, generally held biennially, are also listed here, as are publications related to other conferences devoted wholly or in part to Strindberg. In keeping with the practice adopted throughout this bibliography, reviews of all such works are also included in this section, immediately following the work in question.

As well as substantial essays in books and journals in which several of Strindberg's works in different genres and periods are the subject of discussion, **Part 2** of this section includes a number of brief comments by eminent critics, such as Georg Lukács, who have otherwise not concerned themselves with Strindberg to any great extent. It also lists some unassuming early articles by non-Scandinavian critics in which his writings are presented for the first time to a new readership, and includes both a number of reviews and longer discussions of his work by major Scandinavian critics, whose accounts were sometimes instrumental in establishing and confirming his reputation as a writer rather than as a mere polemicist or controversialist. There is, consequently, some overlap here with studies of Strindberg's reception in section **B3** and with the mainly biographically inflected material which extrapolates his image in Sweden, both before and after his death, that forms a substantial part of the biographical material presented in section **R**. However, genre specific studies of the plays, novels, poetry, essays, historical studies, and other works are to be found in the general section devoted to the relevant genre in turn.

B3 (Reception). The majority of entries in this section concern studies in literary reception, a significant research field particularly where Strindberg studies in German and Poland are concerned. It also includes a number of slight but pertinent early pieces, such as the essay by his earliest Polish translator, Ignacy Suesser (**B3:402**), which first brought Strindberg's work to the attention of readers in another language area. In this respect, Ola Hansson's role as an intermediary between late 19th-Century Scandinavian literature and its reception in France, Germany, and Russia is also of relevance here, as are several books or essays which played a significant role in establishing the way in which Strindberg was initially received in a particular country or language, sometimes even as a consequence of a specific incident, like the furore surrounding the staging of *Dödsdansen* in Bulgaria in 1920. Such events, reviews, or essays thus came to define Strindberg's initial impact on a country and coloured much subsequent discussion there concerning his work and its significance. But the same might be said of many of the earliest discussions of his work and personality in Sweden and numerous, sometimes polemical, accounts of his misogyny or religious views, of the kind separately listed in sections **B8** and **B9**, often performed a similar role in establishing his reputation abroad.

B4 (Translation). As well as theoretical discussions which address particular aspects of translation theory or practice in relation to versions of Strindberg's works in different languages, this section also includes evaluations of his translators and assessments of Strindberg's translations of his own and other people's work. Thus, as well as his own French translation of *Fadren*, his competence as a writer of French in those texts originally written in that language, including *En dåres försvarstal* and *Inferno*, is also a frequent issue here. Since, for non-Scandinavian readers, initial access to Strindberg's literary works is usually via translation, many items listed here inevitably impinge closely on material covered in the section on Reception, **B3**, and vice versa: which works are translated as well as how and when is naturally a factor in any discussion of Strindberg's international reputation. Translation is thus a frequent concern in discussions of non-Swedish editions of his works, including many initial responses to early collections of his plays and, though largely neglected, this is sometimes also an issue in reviews of their performance and the text on which a production has been based. Indeed, it is also of relevance to the editorial principles adopted in Swedish editions of certain of his works, and this applies particularly to their translation into Swedish by another author from the French, German, or Danish in which they first appeared, as several items listed here demonstrate.

B5 (General Histories of Swedish, Scandinavian, and European Literature; Textbooks; and Selected Works of Reference). As well as several frequently reprinted and influential literary histories, this section also contains both a number of works, including several by Swedish authors, in which an account of Swedish literature and Strindberg's place in it, was conveyed to a non-Swedish readership in translation, and a number of Swedish school textbooks, which performed a similar function for generations of young Swedes. Many of these works appeared in numerous editions, either reprinted verbatim or sometimes in a significantly revised form. This latter process is discussed in detail by Sten-Olof Ullström in *Likt och olikt. Strindbergsbildens förvandlingar i gymnasiet*, **B3:466**, in which he charts Strindberg's heavily contested assimilation into the Swedish secondary-school curriculum and considers the changes made over many years to the account of his life and works presented in several of the most widely read textbooks listed here. A limited number of encyclopaedic reference works are also noted in this section especially where, as in the case of Russia, such treatments have played a culturally significant role.

B6 (Conference Reports). The greater part of this section lists reports on the series of International Strindberg Conferences, initiated in Stockholm in 1973 and held subsequently at different venues, usually on a biennial basis. It also includes reports on a number of other, more occasional, symposia devoted to Strindberg and his work.

B7 (Special Issues of Academic, Theatre, and Literary Journals). This section catalogues the wide range of journals in several languages that have devoted special issues to Strindberg and his work, including the Yearbook, *Strindbergiana*, published annually in Stockholm since 1985.

Sections **B8 (Religion)** and **B9 (The Woman Question)** are thematically based in their focus on two aspects of Strindberg's life and work that played a prominent role in establishing his early reputation, most particularly in Germany during the opening decades of the 20th Century. It is this, often defining, role which these two aspects of his work played in Strindberg's early reception, whether cast in an antithetical role to the 'feminist' Ibsen or as the freethinker who opened up an exemplary route to Damascus in what was, for many, a period of religious turmoil and challenge, that governed the way in which his work was often first read and perceived, and accounts for their presence as separate categories in the organisation of this bibliography. Significantly, while his sexual politics continues to compel a great deal of attention, his religious beliefs are very much less the burden of a notable amount of new work. Indeed, other themes (for example, the nature of the self, madness, or the role of dreams and dreaming) might be considered to have supplanted the latter in interest, but it is the relevance of these two dominant topics in the recuperation of Strindberg's image and the presumed significance of his work in the period before and during the First World War that commends them to the kind of prominence they are given here.

Although Strindberg's portrayal of women and his views on marriage and gender relationships are often discussed at length, both in many general evaluations of his work and in accounts of his life, as well as in many reviews of individual novels, stories, and plays, the first of these sections brings together specific items in the abundant literature devoted to his attitude to women, as they are expressed in the essays he dedicated specifically to the topic and those literary works in which he (mis)represents them. This was one of the principal ways in which Strindberg impacted most immediately upon his contemporaries, and some of their, often equally polemical, responses feature here. But the topic is also relevant to comparative studies of the literature and writers of the Scandinavian Modern Breakthrough which are listed in section **C1**, and his reputation as a woman-hater and anti-Ibsenite misogynist frequently coloured his early reception outside Sweden. Indeed, this was one way in which the, often idle, pairing of Strindberg with Ibsen first operated. Likewise, his reputation for misogyny was noted in many of the obituaries and other reflections on his life and work which appeared in the months immediately after his death. These are to be found grouped together in section **U4**, and only a very small proportion of such cross-references have been noted here.

In addition to discussions of Strindberg's religious beliefs, the section on **Religion** includes several items in which his life and work is interpreted in religious terms, including those that Strindberg himself provided for his readers when he structured his experience in the form of a Calvary or a journey to Damascus, or by assuming the role of Jacob or Job and employing the terminology of Theosophy, Anthroposophy, Swedenborg, or Buddhism, rather than the language and imagery that he had inherited from Christianity, in order to recuperate the details of his life in what appeared to him a meaningful and artistically fruitful form. Similar issues are often discussed in general studies of his work, of course, especially those which, like Gunnar Brandell's *Strindbergs Infernokris* (**B1:55**) or Göran Stockenström's *Ismael i öknen* (**B1:437**), are concerned with the Inferno Crisis and the works of art and literature most immediately related to it, but the same is also true of many studies, both of early plays like *Fritänkaren* and *Mäster Olof* or numerous later works in different genres, including *Ett drömspel*, *Spöksonaten*, *Svarta fanor*, and *En blå bok*.

C1 (Comparative Studies). As well as books and essays in which Strindberg and his works are compared with those of other writers in the manner generally associated with comparative literary criticism, this section contains critical articles, reviews, and statements about Strindberg by major authors, including Aleksandr Blok, Knut Hamsun, Franz Kafka, Maksim Gor'kii, and Thomas Mann, which sometimes reveal more about their authors than they do about Strindberg. It also lists books and articles which study Strindberg in the context of those literary movements such as Naturalism and Symbolism with which he was involved, as well as works which seek to place him in terms of the development of Scandinavian literature, such as Gunnar Ahlström's *Det moderna genombrottet i Nordens litteratur* (**C1:13**), or relate him to a major theme or topos, such as Charles Dédéyan's *Le Thème de Faust dans la littérature européenne* (**C1:305**). But comparisons between Strindberg and other writers regarding particular novels, plays, or other works (e.g. the relevance of Alphonse Daudet and Zola for *Röda rummet*, or of Joris-Karl Huysmans for *Inferno*) are listed in the section devoted to the work in question.

Some comparisons or studies in influence such as those which relate Strindberg's literary works to the plays of Ibsen or Eugene O'Neill are recurring topics in Strindberg studies. Others, e.g. the coupling of Strindberg with Friedrich Dürrenmatt apropos the latter's adaptation of *Dödsdansen* as *Play Strindberg* in 1969, are the prolific preoccupation of a brief period only. Indeed, it could be argued that it was Dürrenmatt's play rather than

Strindberg's own texts which served for a brief period to mediate his image to a speculative public in performances from New York to Moscow just as, six years later, Per Olov Enquist's biographical drama, *Tribadernas natt*, about Strindberg's relationship with Siri von Essen, represented him to audiences that were often unfamiliar with his works, let alone with the life that Enquist's play purported to dramatise. The widespread discussion which these plays provoked motivates the grouping of a selection of this material in two sub-sections (**C3** and **C4**) at the end of what is, even so, an extensive list of comparative material. The length and range of this section as a whole is hardly surprising, however, since it derives from the work of an author who read widely and willingly acknowledged the inspiration that his writing frequently derived from his study of other authors.
Finally, the majority of the numerous items concerned with the much explored artistic and temperamental affinity between Strindberg and Ingmar Bergman are also listed here rather than in **D2**, since they are generally concerned as much with Strindberg's influence on Bergman the film director as with Bergman's work as a theatre director. Hence, they are also grouped in a separate Section (**C2**).

D1 (General Studies of Modern Drama and Theatre). This section is devoted to histories of the theatre and studies of modern drama in which Strindberg features, either at length, in a particular chapter, or more diffusely as a seminal presence. Occasionally, he is accorded only brief mention but, in the case of many of the earliest of these items, this is itself significant for an appreciation of the initial reception accorded his theatre. Indeed, the lack, or brevity, of serious comment is sometimes eloquent; likewise, the date and focus of any discussion may also be revealing.
This section includes collections of republished reviews which often bring together numerous items that are listed elsewhere in the bibliography in the sections devoted to the respective plays discussed, and lists the autobiographies or biographies of actors and directors, like Max Reinhardt and Karol Adwentowicz, whose careers were closely associated with Strindberg's work. Many of the discussions concerning Strindberg's impact on the modern theatre also assess his influence on later dramatists and thus cover ground which might sometimes have been classified along with the comparative studies in **C1**, but the element of theatrical history or dramatic theory involved has led to their inclusion here. Nevertheless, many comparable studies in which Strindberg's work for the theatre is compared with plays by other dramatists such as Albee, Dürrenmatt, Ibsen, O'Neill, or H.-R. Lenormand are to be found under that heading.

D2 (Monographs, Collections of Essays and Reviews, Essays, and Longer Studies on Strindberg's Plays and Work in the Theatre). As well as book-length studies of the plays and discussions of Strindberg's engagement with theatre practice and his place in theatre history, this section lists collections of essays or books which include several items on more than one of the plays, with the exception of the Chamber Plays of 1907. These are frequently discussed, and sometimes even staged, as a self-contained and thematically linked group. Consequently, books or essays in which more than one of these plays is treated together are listed in a separate section (**E48**). Meanwhile, the second section of **D2** lists essays, articles, and reviews devoted wholly or substantially to Strindberg's theatre in general, or to at least two or more of plays.

D3 (Surveys or Reviews of Two or More of Strindberg's Plays in Separate Performance).

E1 through **E59 (Individual Plays).** Each of these sections provides details of critical commentaries and theatre reviews concerning one of Strindberg's published and performed plays, listed in the order of their composition, from *Fritänkaren* in 1869 to *Stora landsvägen* in 1909, and including the posthumously published fragments. Monographs, critical essays, reviews on publication, and other discussions of the play texts are listed at the start of each section, organised alphabetically by their author's name. In the remainder of the section, devoted to performance reviews, the organisation is somewhat different. Where several reviews of the same production are concerned, these have normally been grouped together under a single annotational heading which gives details of one or more of the following: the theatre, première date, and – wherever possible – the names of the director together with the principal roles and actors. Thus, for example, Ingmar Bergman's production of *Fröken Julie* in 1985 has the following heading: 'Dramaten, Stockholm, 7 December 1985, Dir. Ingmar Bergman; Julie: Marie Göranzon; Jean: Peter Stormare; Kristin: Gerthi Kulle; Design: Gunilla Palmstierna-Weiss'. Productions singled out in this way are listed chronologically following on from the section devoted to the literary critical and other discussions of the relevant play text. Where the reviewer is unknown and not anonymous the entry is indexed merely by the title of the paper or journal and the publication date, and, even where it is known, no title is given since the review frequently appeared only under a general heading. Moreover, where fewer than four reviews of a production are concerned (and always where only one review has been identified), entries are listed alphabetically according to the reviewer's name at the end of the section, under the general heading 'Other'. Except for premières, such reviews normally have minimal or no annotation. Indeed, where reviews of the plays in performance are concerned, any annotation is usually limited to identifying merely the theatre, director, and principal actors, and comment is restricted to the reception accorded the play rather than to the performers, however eminent, or the acting, however distinguished or mundane. In noting a play's reception, more attention has been paid to the impression that a play made on its earliest outings rather than to subsequent revivals, however numerous or prestigious.

Sections F1-10 and **G1-19.** Following a distinction which Strindberg himself often made, these two sections divide his prose fiction into the sequence of autobiographical narratives from *Tjänstekvinnans son* to *Ensam* and including *En dåres försvarstal* and *Inferno* that encompass an account of his personal history, on the one hand, and his less personal novels and collections of short stories, on the other. Each section in which these works are treated individually, in order of composition, is prefaced by a separate section (**F1** and **G1**) which lists general treatments of Strindberg's work as an autobiographer or novelist respectively. All adaptations for the stage of Strindberg's novels and autobiographical fictions are listed here under the work in question, except for *Hemsöborna* which was originally adapted for the stage by Sg himself (see **E.16**).
Similar coverage is given in Section **H** to his three collections of poetry, and in Section **J** to a genre in which he was not only prolific but also excelled, namely his more than 9.000 extant letters. Meanwhile, sections **K1** to **K7** apply the same principles to Strindberg's

works of non-fiction, including *Bland franska bönder*, the two collections of *Vivisektioner*, and *En blå bok*, and in **L1** to **L6** to the several substantial works of historiography that he produced at different stages of his life, including *Gamla Stockholm, Svenska folket*, and the theoretical essay 'Världshistoriens mystik' (The Mysticism of World History).

Sections M and **N** document two other aspects of Strindberg's multifaceted project, and are relatively straightforward in their scope and organisation although, since it is often impossible to discriminate precisely between the two, Section **M (Science),** includes discussions of his ventures into occultism alongside assessments of his scientific speculations in astronomy, biology, chemistry, and geology, etc. A number of items in the contemporary French press concerning his (al)chemical experiments are also listed here, indicating the interest which they already aroused during the 1890s, although in many of these items he is the subject of only brief reference. Specific discussions of *Inferno, En blå bok*, and several of the items in the section on his other non-fictional writings also address this aspect of Strindberg's project, which is likewise of relevance to his activity as a photographer and commented on in several items in Section **P2**. This is again frequently the case with several general discussions of his ideas and writings, particularly those concerned with the Inferno crisis, such as Gunnar Brandell's *Strindbergs Infernokris*, **B1:55**, and Göran Stockenström's *Ismael i öknen*, **B1:437**. But Strindberg's, often equally speculative, ventures into linguistics during the 1900s are the subject of Section **N**.

Strindberg's activities as a painter and photographer and the relationship between his writing and the other arts (most notably music, but also film and ballet) are covered by the next five sections, of which the most substantial is:

P1 (Painting), This section includes several items on the iconography of Strindberg, including portraits, busts, and satirical sketches, but is primarily concerned with documenting the gradual recognition accorded his own painting and art criticism, and the significance of his engagement with the visual arts for his literary work. Articles on his painting tend to come in waves to coincide with successive exhibitions (e.g. in 1892, 1911, 1922, 1949, 1960, 1962, 1974, and 2001), and they frequently catch one another's tone, as in the reflex association of Strindberg's aleatory art with contemporary Spontanism in 1962. However, although Strindberg's opinion of the painting of other artists is of relevance here, some further material concerning his personal relationships with painters and sculptors is listed under Section **R** (Biography), since he associated with a number of distinguished artists, including Carl Larsson, Per Ekström, Carl Eldh, Edvard Munch, and Paul Gauguin. Likewise, comments on Strindberg's acute visual imagination and the relevance of his painting for his writing are to be found in many of the discussions of his literary works recorded throughout the bibliography, although it might be argued that some of these studies, e.g. Harry G. Carlson's *Out of Inferno. Strindberg's Reawakening as an Artist*, **B1:93**, are as relevant here as in the place assigned them elsewhere in this bibliography.

P2 (Photography) pays similar attention to those books and essays in which his experimental photography and theories of vision have gained increasing recognition, both in themselves and for what they may contribute to the aesthetics of his literary works.

P3 (Music) includes books and essays which take account of Strindberg's lifelong interest in music. Apart from discussions of his admiration for various composers and their significance for his work, this interest becomes of special relevance for his post-Inferno dramaturgy, where a plot-centred drama is replaced by one that is organised thematically, as in music. Similarly, several of his works have been set to music by (among others) Ture Rangström, Julius Weismann, Ingvar Lidholm, Antonio Bibalo, Philippe Boesman, Ned Rorem, Malcolm Williamson, and Aribert Reimann, all of whom have composed operas based on one or more of Strindberg's texts. Hence material on some of these works is included here.

P4 (Ballet) is largely concerned with Birgit Cullberg's ballet, based on *Fröken Julie.*

P5 (Film) lists critical discussions of adaptations of several of Strindberg's plays and novels for the cinema or for television, and notes reviews of televisual adaptations of several of the novels and autobiographical fictions, including *Röda rummet, I havsbandet, Syndabocken, En dåres försvarstal.* Cinematic versions of the plays are also included here, but reviews of productions of the plays screened on television are listed in the section devoted to the relevant play in chronological order of writing, in **E1-E59**. Likewise, reviews and critical commentary concerning Per Olov Enquist's biographical film of Strindberg's life, broadcast by Swedish Television in 1984-85, are listed along with the book of the series in section **R**.

Of the remaining sections:

R (Biographies, Memoirs, and Reminiscences) offers an extensive list of biographical sources, published as books, articles, chapters, interviews, and essays. A writer as intensely autobiographical as Strindberg invites, and has received, criticism which often shades into biography as well as biographies that sometimes treat his works with critical rigour. Indeed, several of the studies listed here comment on the works *in extenso*, but considered mainly from the perspective of the life which they supposedly document or illuminate. Like the General Studies in **B1** and **B2**, some of the items listed among the studies of Strindberg's individual plays and novels in Sections **E1-59**, **F2-10**, and **G2-19** are also preoccupied with Strindberg's life as well as the works which their authors often associate so directly and readily with it. Thus, for example, in the case of Allan Hagsten's *Den Unge Strindberg. Studier kring Tjänstekvinnans son och ungdomsverken*, **B1:151**, which examines the circumstances underlying both the autobiographical fiction of the 1880s and the early works written during the period it describes, or Göran Söderström's study of Strindberg's life-long relationship with painting and painters, *Strindberg och bildkonsten*, **P1:455**, classification is neither easy nor clear cut in this respect.

This section also includes pen-portraits, character sketches, and general reflections on Strindberg's personality and beliefs where these do not involve a close examination of his writings. Some articles listed here, like Ola Hansson's 'Ein Brief von August Strindberg', **R:937**, published in *Die Zukunft* in 1892, impacted directly on his life at the time and what is, given the history of Strindberg studies, a significantly long section also encompasses documentary material other than letters, as well as essays or memoirs depicting places like

Grez-sur-Loing or the Berlin tavern, Zum schwarzen Ferkel, with which he was closely associated, or people, such as Edvard Munch and Stanisław Przybyszewski, with whom he associated intensely during a particular period of his life. Such individuals sometimes feature more prominently than they may actually have done in Strindberg's life because of their subsequent renown while the prominence accorded certain periods in later studies of his life is often a response to the colourful, sometimes mythologising accounts that he provides of his experiences in his autobiographical fictions and correspondence. Indeed, places figure prominently in much of the literature listed here and rightly so, since certain cities and landscapes like Lund, Paris, the Danube, and the Stockholm archipelago feature prominently in the works while a change of place that relocates Strindberg's private life to another setting, often entailed his adopting a new artistic or philosophical point of view. Nevertheless, much of this literature is anecdotal and trivial, and numerous such accounts of his association with (say) the island of Kymmendö or Stockholm are also listed among the miscellaneous entries in Section U.

S (Psycho-Pathological Studies). Dominated by the work of Karl Jaspers and other, mainly German, studies of Strindberg's psyche, which emerged in the wake of the First World War, this section brings together a range of largely ill-informed studies, some of which have nevertheless played an important role in establishing an enduring image of Strindberg as a variously classified madman, an image which, as Ulf Olsson has shown in *Jag blir galen*, **S:233**, was already frequently employed during Strindberg's lifetime, not least in his own early attempts to heighten the impact of his work. However, the numerous psychological and psychoanalytically inflected readings of many of Strindberg's works, including several of the most artistically achieved like *Ett drömspel*, *Fröken Julie*, or *En dåres försvarstal*, are listed in the section on the work in question.

T (Politics), contains a great deal of contemporary material, including much that is seemingly of only local or passing interest. The bulk of it is concerned with the Strindberg Feud of 1910-12, but it also includes several studies attuned to his interest in anarchism during the 1880s, and the impact which the ideas of Rousseau, Tolstoi, or the Swedish utopian radical, Nils Herman Quiding, exerted on him, as well as his relationship with Hjalmar Branting and the growth of Swedish socialism.

U (Miscellaneous) is less a repository for items otherwise unclassified by a desperate bibliographer than a listing of numerous fugitive items in which Strindberg and his image have been established and nurtured, not least by the work of the Strindberg Society and Museum. Often indicative of his reception in Sweden as well as abroad, the section includes many of the obituaries and commemorative articles that were written to mark one or other of the anniversaries of his birth or death in 1899, 1909, 1912, 1949, 1962, 1999, etc. Some of these items, particularly those published in the aftermath of his death in 1912, are quite substantial, and were sometimes penned by a major writer or critic; many, however, merely rehearse his received reputation at a particular date and repeat the associated clichés. Commemorative tributes to Strindberg and comments on his achievement by major authors such as Maksim Gor'kii, Knut Hamsun, Hermann Hesse, Karl Kraus, Thomas Mann, and Bernard Shaw are listed in the section with Comparative Studies, **C1**.

Some of these miscellaneous items have only the most tenuous connection with either the man or his work, others are occasional pieces on what become familiar themes such as Strindberg's association with Stockholm or Kymmendö, his fear of dogs or his interest in food or fishing. For all (or sometimes precisely because of) their naiveté and quaint banality, the earlier items from non-Scandinavian sources are frequently indicative of Strindberg's current reception in their respective countries while the titles suggest many of the subjects and discourses with which Strindberg has often been associated. Hence they provide an insight into how his image and reputation have been fashioned over the years. However, given the relatively insubstantial nature of many of the items in this section as well as the often self-explanatory nature of their titles, annotation of these miscellaneous entries has been kept to a minimum.

V (Dissertations). This section lists dissertations which have not been published and made available in the same form elsewhere. Many other dissertations concerned wholly or in part with Strindberg have often been revised and published or, as is the case with virtually all Swedish theses, have been published simultaneously with their doctoral defence. Where this has occurred, such theses are listed in the bibliography in the appropriate section, and are consequently not normally listed again here. The majority of items recorded here are doctoral theses, but I have also noted some MA dissertations and other such items. Thus, a few Swedish *C betygsuppsatser* and similar studies are also included, particularly where, like Olof Lagercrantz's examination of *Strindbergs satiriska och polemiska diktning mellan Röda rummet och utresan 1883* (1941), **V:126**, they feature in the critical literature on Strindberg.

N.B. English translations of the titles of all Strindberg's major works and their dates are given in the comprehensive table of contents to all three volumes of the bibliography at the head of Volume One.

*

The following general principles and conventions have been observed throughout this bibliography.

In the **annotation** in square brackets which accompanies a majority of the entries, I have, except in titles or translations of titles, used 'Sg' to denote Strindberg's surname and 'Strindbergian' (Sgian) for its adjectival form, but used the full forms when translating the titles of books and essays to English from all other languages. Quotations indicated within the annotations are from the work annotated unless otherwise attributed. Such quotations are intended to be of relevance to the reception accorded Strindberg or the specific work under discussion and, in reviews of stage performances, it is a critic's response to the play rather than the quality of the acting or directing that has generally been of interest. Likewise, early performances have often been documented in greater detail than revivals.
For the most part, the annotation I have supplied seeks to indicate the area of relevance explored by an item rather than its quality, although some judgements, both positive and negative, are also included with reference to key works in the development of Strindberg

studies or to those which contain misleading errors and exemplify demonstrably perverse judgements. The length of the annotation accorded an entry is sometimes an indication of its interest or importance, but not always so. Those works by Strindberg alluded to of listed in the annotation are normally those with which the book or essay in question is primarily concerned, but unlike the kind of annotation that accompanies many electronic databases, it does not list every text or figure mentioned. The aim has nevertheless been to allow readers to judge sensibly what is likely to be of particular relevance for the purpose of their field of research in any item listed; hence the annotation distinguishes between those works by Strindberg with which an entry is principally concerned, and those to which it refers rather more than merely in passing. Where an item contains illustrations, whether these are reproductions, sketches, photographs, facsimiles or other forms of pictorial matter, this is merely indicated by 'Illus'. (However, this does not extend to reviews of the plays in performance which may often be accompanied by a production photograph; this is not noted here.) Finally, formulations such as 'Notes' or 'Comments on' indicate a relatively modest account of whatever topic is referred to; 'discusses' or 'examines' or 'studies', indicates a more elaborate treatment. Moreover, only the titles of Strindberg's works which figure at all significantly are listed, and then sometimes to indicate the scope of the treatment offered rather than to confirm any really detailed discussion. Finally, the bibliography has been organised to include a separate entry for each item of reprinted material since the ubiquity of certain articles or reviews, often appearing in different forms over a considerable period of time in later collections and anthologies, clearly indicates not only their regular availability but the continuing impact which they may have exerted on Strindberg's developing reception.

Given the unfamiliarity of many of Strindberg's works to readers of English and the frequent variations in the **titles** they have sometimes been given when they have been translated, I have identified the works throughout with their original Swedish or French titles. This also makes for ease of reference across the bibliography as a whole, since there is often little comparability between the names his works have been given in English and the titles they appear under in French, German, or Russian. Every individual section is prefaced with bibliographical details concerning the relevant work in the National Edition of Strindberg's *Samlade Verk* under the general editorship of Lars Dahlbäck. However, other editions of Strindberg's works, either in the original or in translation, are not listed unless they include an introduction, afterword, or other editorial commentary.

In keeping with the underlying concern of the bibliography, which has been to document Strindberg's reception both in Sweden and abroad, the **place** of publication of all serials and newspapers has been identified wherever possible, when it is not self-evident from a version of the place name in the title of the journal or paper. Although this inevitably entails considerable repetition, immediate identification has been deemed preferable to cross-referencing between volumes. Likewise, the multiplicity of primary sources in several languages makes it preferable to provide the full title of journals and newspapers throughout rather than in the algebra of numerous abbreviations. The titles of journals are not translated. Nor are the titles of programme books issued in conjunction with a specific production. The publication date for the latter is that of the première.

I have included only a small amount of **cross-referencing** in order (1) to direct the reader to a main entry citing a work or collection from which a particular title has been extracted, (2) in the headnotes to each section, or (3) where an entry is specifically engaged in a polemic with another item located elsewhere in the bibliography. Such references are noted in bold text. Otherwise, I have been sparing in making cross-references to entries of a general nature at the end of the sections on individual works. In the case of *Röda rummet*, *Hemsöborna*, *Fröken Julie*, or *Ett drömspel*, for example, this would have entailed a copious interchange of references to numerous items distributed throughout all three volumes. I have therefore assumed a willingness on the part of readers to seek references to, for example, a particular play, in many of the general works listed in Section **D2** on Strindberg's dramas, or to works of a general nature in **B1,** as well as in the section devoted solely to the work in question.

Except in a very few cases where no confusion is possible, a **translation** in square brackets is supplied as part of the annotation for the title of each non-English entry. Although sometimes pedantic, this approach frequently summarises the content and often indicates the register in which the original is written. However, 'strap' lines, or the regular titles of the columns under which a writer contributes theatre reviews or book reviews to a paper or journal, have not been translated, but remain in their impersonal original, e.g. 'Litteratur och konst', 'Teater och musik', or 'Echo der Bühnen'. Likewise, where numerous reviews of the same production are listed, the perfunctory heading provided as an alternative by the title of the play under review has often been omitted entirely, thus restricting the entry to the names of the reviewer, newspaper or journal, and the date. Similarly, where reviewers (or their editors) post-1945 have often made of their titles a frequently meaningless, self-indulgent play on words in order to draw attention to their own cleverness rather than the substance of the book or play under review, I have sometimes followed the same conventions as elsewhere in the extensive lists of newspaper reviews of theatre productions, and excluded such titles altogether.

Book reviews of titles listed in the bibliography are recorded immediately after the book in question, generally without annotation or a repetition of the title of the volume reviewed. Such items are distinguished from other entries by a single em dash — between the entry number and the author's name where known. Thus, a review of Ulf Boëthius, *Strindberg och kvinnofrågan: Till och med Giftas I*, appears merely as **[B9:32]** — Ekenwall, Asta, *Göteborgs Handels- och Sjöfartstidning*, 12 November 1969.

**

Seeming discrepancies in the dates ascribed to some items regarding Strindberg's last years and death, especially in Section **U**, may be accounted for by the fact that, prior to 1918, Russia used the Julian ('Old Style') calendar, which was thirteen days behind the Gregorian ('New Style') calendar.

Otherwise, abbreviations have been kept to a minimum. 'Editor' or 'Edited by' is denoted by 'Red.' where Swedish titles are concerned, 'Hrsg.' in the case of works in German, and 'Ed.' where English, French, Italian, Polish, Russian, and other titles are concerned. Sp. denotes column in those journals published in that format and Rpr. denotes 'Reprint'. Otherwise, page references in books and yearbooks (e.g. *Samlaren*) are designated by 'pp.', but this practice is not extended to journals unless there is some possibility of confusion, in which case 'pp.' is retained.

Items in daily newspapers are normally identified by their date (day, month, year) except where many Serbo-Croat, Polish, and other East European daily newspapers are concerned. These have often been identified in the format in which I acquired the information. Hence, when my source followed local custom in the earlier part of the 20th Century and identified an edition of a newspaper only by its issue number in a particular year rather than the date, I have done likewise. Consequently, I have followed the custom of distinguishing them by (sometimes) the page as well as the issue number and year, but not the day, month, and year. Finally, for newspapers and journals published in the Finnish capital, 'Helsingfors' in parenthesis after the title serves to indicate that the item is in Finland Swedish, 'Helsinki' that it is in Finnish. For brevity's sake, I have generally called the Stockholm Royal Dramatic Theatre by its popular diminutive, Dramaten, even when a reference applies to one of those periods when this was not necessarily the name by which it was familiarly known. Likewise, 'Indra's Daughter' normally features as 'Agnes'. * beside a date or word, especially among the theatre reviews, indicates questionable information.

January 2005 serves as the point at which the recording of entries generally ends but the vicissitudes of publishing means that a number of items, especially books, from after that period until December 2007 have also been included.

Several published works have been of inestimable value in helping me to establish the underlying direction of Strindberg's reception in various countries and languages. Amongst the most useful have been the accounts of Strindberg's impact on France by Stellan Ahlström and Anthony Swerling in *Strindbergs erövring av Paris. Strindberg och Frankrike 1884-1895*, and *Strindberg's Impact in France 1920-60*, respectively. I have benefited from information in both Hans-Peter Bayerdörfer's invaluable collection of articles related to Strindberg's early impact on Germany, *Strindberg auf der deutschen Bühne. Eine exemplarische Rezeptionsgeschichte der Moderne in Dokumenten (1890 bis 1925)*, and Wilhelm Friese's collection of essays *Strindberg und die deutschsprachigen Länder. Internationale Beiträge zum Tübinger Strindberg-Symposium 1977.* I also derived a great deal of valuable material in Robert Fallenstein and Christian Hennig's *Rezeption skandinavischer Literatur in Deutschland 1870-1914: Quellenbibliographie*, and Christian Hennig, Jens Heese, and Kirsten Kopiske's *Rezeption skandinavischer Literatur in den deutschsprachigen Ländern 1915 bis 1980*. For Russia, apart from Boris Erkhov's excellent Strindberg bibliography, *Strindberg: Biobibliograficheskii ukazatel*, and the two complementary volumes, *Khudozhestvennaia literatura skandinavskikh stran v russkoi pechati. Bibliograficheski ukazatel*, I gained much from Maria Nikolajeva's illuminating examination of Strindberg's early Russian reception in *När Sverige erövrade Ryssland. En studie i kulturernas samspel*, as well as from the essays of Nils Åke Nilsson, while, for Denmark, Harry Jacobsen's account of Strindberg's impact on Copenhagen in the 1880s in *Strindberg i Firsernes København* was inavaluable. Likewise, as well as Hieronim Chojnacki's invaluable bibliography, *Szwedzka literatura piękna w polsce 1939-1996*, I have benefited considerably from Andrzej Nils Uggla's *Strindberg och den polska teatern 1890-*

1970. En studie i reception and the various studies of Marian Lewko. For Strindberg's early impact on England and the United States, Esther H. Rapp's lightly annotated bibliography remains an invaluable tool, but apart from two brief articles by Margery M. Morgan, there is little else to hand on his reception in England, where his general reputation continues to lag well behind the respect he is accorded in North America, the recent exhibition of his paintings at Tate Modern notwithstanding. An exception to the otherwise under-representation of information on Strindberg's impact on Central and South America has been filled for one place, Montevideo, thanks to Louise von Bergen's *Nordisk teater i Montevideo. Kontextrelaterad reception av Henrik Ibsen och August Strindberg.*

Where Strindberg's Swedish reputation as a dramatist is concerned, meanwhile, Gunnar Ollén's *Strindbergs dramatik* and his contributions to *Meddelanden från Strindbergssäll-skapet* and *Strindbergiana* on performances of the plays have been especially useful (as have those by Richard Bark), while his early reception and image formation during much of his own lifetime is covered by the four-volume catalogue of articles and excerpts, *Strindberg i offentligheten*, edited by Björn Meidal in 1980. But the bibliography lists numerous other works of Swedish scholarship which have charted the national response, both to the man and his writings. Needless to say, however, any errors, whether of fact, misreading, or transcription from these volumes are, of course, my responsibility.

***

In due course, and with some recasting, this bibliography will appear in electronic form, a development that will clearly facilitate its use in response to a range of scholarly questions less shaped by its present format. But having utilised numerous printed, as well as electronic, resources while compiling this work, I find there are still numerous things which books can reveal and convey as well as, or even better than, an electronic database. These extend from an appreciation of the critical mass of the corpus involved to its reshaping and adaptation in the serendipity of personal browsing. Marginalia in the white frame to a page are more personal and charged with potential than electronic bookmarks; fresh patterns may emerge in the material as it is sifted and revisited, thus permitting innovative trajectories from one part of the corpus to another in pursuit of answers to questions which the compiler of an on-line bibliography may not have framed or allowed for in selecting key words and hyperlinks. Both modes of bibliography are valid, of course; neither, on its own, exhausts the possibilities of the genre, particularly in relation to a writer as fecund as Strindberg, whose project extends so significantly to several of the other arts, as well as to science, the occult, linguistics, and historiography. Hence the sheer extent and variety of the present work; hence, too, the way in which one section frequently overlaps with another, which is wholly in keeping with a writer who deliberately blurred boundaries, both between the lived and the written, and the various genres in which he recuperated his experience. During his Inferno crisis, Strindberg frequently played with the notion that the world he inhabited was characterised by a great disorder and yet was also endowed with an infinite coherence. It would be surprising if, in seeking to map the multifarious responses that his works have elicited, this bibliography did not share something of this duality.

A1-A5. Bibliographies, Indexes, Bibliographical Essays and Surveys of Criticism, Strindberg Editions, and Archival Material

A1. Bibliographies and Bibliographical Articles devoted entirely or in part to Strindberg and his Work.

[*N.B. bibliographies or bibliographical discussions of the critical literature on individual works by Strindberg are listed under the relevant title*]

[A1:1] Adelman, Irving, and Rita Dworkin, 'Strindberg', in *Modern Drama: A Checklist of Critical Literature on 20th-Century Plays*, Metuchen, N.J.: The Scarecrow Press, Inc., 1967, pp. 293-305. [Even for the period, the section on Sg is quite basic and deals exclusively with material in English]

[A1:2] Åhlen, Bengt, *Svenskt författarlexikon*, 7 vols, *1900-1940*, *1941-1950*, *1951-1955*, *1956-1960*, Under medverkan av C.-T. Friss, P. Harnesk, A. Lonberg, B. Lundblad, and L. Hook, Stockholm: Rabén & Sjögren, 1942-63. [A cumulative bibliography of Swedish literature which includes bibliographical information about new Swedish editions of Sg's works, as well as a selection of biographical and critical books and articles]

[A1:3] Anon, '60.Todestag des schwedischen Schriftstellers August Strindberg', *Bibliograph Kalenderblätter der Berliner Stadtbibliothek*, 1972:2, pp. 24-28. ['The 60th Anniversary of the Death of the Swedish Writer August Strindberg'. A commemorative chronology of Sg's life together with a bibliography of his writings]

[A1:4] Anon, 'Förteckning öfver en boksamling som tillhört litteratören August Strindberg och hvilken säljes å Stockholms Bokauktionskammare…den 13 mars', Stockholm, 1886. 12 pp. ['A Catalogue of Items in a Collection of Books which Belonged to the Man of Letters August Strindberg, To be Sold at Stockholm's Book Auction, 13 March'. An invaluable source of information concerning Sg's early interests and reading, assembled in conjunction with the sale of his first book collection by his brother Axel on Sg's instructions, and utilised by Hans Lindström when compiling **A2:57**, *Strindberg och böckerna*, where the items listed here are catalogued anew]

[A1:5] Arvidsson, Rolf, *Fredrik Bööks bibliografi 1898-1967*, Stockholm: P. A. Norstedt & Söners Förlag, 1970. 353 pp. [Includes bibliographical details about Böök's numerous articles and books in which he discusses Sg and his works]

[A1:6] Ballu, Denis, 'Au fil du temps: Strindberg en français', in Olof Eriksson, red., *Strindberg och det franska språket: Föredrag från ett symposium vid Växjö universitet 22-23 maj 2003*, Acta Wexionensia, Humaniora, Växjö: Växjö University Press, 2004, pp. 11-20. [A bibliographical essay on Sg's works in French translation, together with two bibliographies, 'Strindberg en français', p. 29, and a chronological bibliography of the relevant secondary literature, 'A propos d'August Strindberg', pp. 29-34]

[A1:7] Berendsohn, Walter, A[rthur], 'Register över Strindbergs manuskript', 1–4, *Meddelanden från Strindbergssällskapet* (Stockholm), No. 10 (1951), pp. 3-7; No. 11 (1951), pp. 2-8; No. 12 (1952), pp. 3-9; No. 18 (1955), pp. 9-10. ['A Catalogue of Strindberg's Manuscripts'.

Berendsohn lists and identifies the location of all the known extant manuscripts of Sg's published works, together with a selection of preliminary sketches, corrected proofs, and published copies with annotations in Sg's hand. Uses John Landquist's edition of *Samlade Skrifter* in 55 volumes as a point of published reference]

[A1:8] Berendsohn, Walter A[rthur], 'Register till Strindberg', *Stockholms-Tidningen*, 3 February 1947. ['Index to Strindberg'. Discusses the need for an index to John Landquist's edition of Sg's *Samlade Skrifter* and the principles on which this might be based]

[A1:9] Birr, Ewald, *Nordeuropäische Literatur. Prosa – Lyrik – Dramatik. Bibliographie*, Rostock: Willi-Bredel-Bibliothek, Stadt- und Bezirksbilbiothek, 1979. 104 pp.

[A1:10] Böök, [Martin] Fredrik [Christofferson], 'August Strindberg', in *Sveriges moderna litteratur*, Stockholm: P. A. Norstedt & Söners Förlag, 1921, pp. 375-381. [A relatively full and scholarly bibliography for the period, published in conjunction with a substantial, if not always sympathetic, critical survey of Sg's writings, pp. 86-127, 332-346]

[A1:11] Boyer, Robert D., '[Johan] August Strindberg', in *Realism in European Theatre and Drama, 1870-1920: A Bibliography*, Westport, Connecticut; London, England: Greenwood Press, 1979, pp. 175-183. [An inaccurate and exceedingly incomplete listing of secondary material on Sg as a dramatist. Boyer's bibliography also includes some general items of limited relevance, pp. [3]-17]

[A1:12] Breed, Paul F., and Florence M. Sniderman, eds, *Dramatic Criticism Index: A Bibliography of Commentaries on Playwrights from Ibsen to the Avant-Garde*, Detroit: Gale Research Company, 1972, pp. 670-682. [The section on Sg includes some interesting material but is concerned exclusively with items published in English]

[A1:13] Brøndsted, Mogens, *Bibliografisk vejledning til studiet af nordisk litteratur og sprog*, 6. ajouførte udg., Odense: Center for nordiske studier, Odense Universitet, 1992. 45 pp. ['A Bibliographical Guide to the Study of Nordic Literature and Languages'. Includes some general references of relevance to Sg]

[A1:14] Bryer, Jackson R., 'Strindberg 1951-62: A Bibliography', *Modern Drama* (Lawrence, Kansas), 5:3 (1963), 269-275. [A useful supplement to Rapp's bibliography, **A1:80-82**. Bryer brings her listing up-to-date, again with the focus primarily on Anglo-Saxon material]

[A1:15] Chojnacki, Hieronim, *Szwedzka literatura piękna w polsce 1939-1996 / Den svenska skönlitteraturen i Polen 1939-1996. Bibliografia prsekładów i opracowań krytycznych*, Gdańska: Wydawnictwo Uniwersytetu Gdańskiego, 2003. 312 pp. ['Swedish Literature in Poland, 1939-1996. A Bibliography of Translations and Critical Works'. An impressively detailed bibliography of Swedish literature in Polish translation which also covers its critical reception in Poland. The volume includes theatre reviews and Sg features prominently throughout. There is also an introduction in both Polish and Swedish by Hieronim Chojnacki which surveys the history of Swedish literature in Polish translation, and a foreword by Andrzej Nils Uggla]

[A1:16] Edwardson, Erik, *Jan Myrdal. En kronologisk bibliography: 1943-1992*, Stockholm: Hägglund, 1999. 325 pp. ['Jan Myrdal. A Chronological Bibliography, 1943-1992'. A comprehensive bibliography of Myrdal's diverse writings, which provides details of his many articles on Sg and related subjects over a fifty-year period]

[A1:17] Engel, Ann Mari, *Swedish Plays in English Translation from Strindberg to the Present*, Stockholm: Swedish Institute, 1985. 24 pp. [The section on Sg is compiled by Ann Sonnerman]

[A1:18] Erkhov, B[oris] A[leksandrovich], *Avgust Strindberg: Biobibliograficheskii ukazatel'*, otvetstvennyi redaktor E. V. Pereslegina, Moskva: "Kniga", 1981. [118] pp. ['August Strindberg. A Bibliography'. Includes an invaluable bibliography of Russian material devoted to Sg's life and work, and organised chronologically, pp. 65-93. This exemplary volume also contains an introduction with an account of Sg's life, pp. 5-18, as well as extensive bibliographies of Sg's works in Swedish, the principal literature on his life and work in other languages, details of Russian editions of his complete and selected works, and a guide to the titling of his writings in Russian translation]

[A1:19] Erkhov, B[oris] A[leksandrovich], *Khudozhestvennaia literatura skandinavskikh stran v russkoi pechati. Bibliograficheskii ukazatel'*, Moskva: VGBIL, 1986. [120] pp. ['A Bibliography of Scandinavian Literature Published in Russian'. Includes some material on Sg supplementary to **A1:18**]

[A1:20] Erkhov, B[oris] A[leksandrovich], *Khudozhestvennaia literatura skandinavskikh stran v russkoi pechati. Bibliograficheski ukazatel'*, Otvetsstvennyi redaktor E. V. Pereslegina, Moskva: Vses. gs. biblioteka inostrannoi lit-ry, 1995, [128] pp. ['A Bibliography of Scandinavian Literature Published in Russian'. Brings Erkhov's previous bibliographies (**A1:18** and **A1:19**) up to date for the period 1984-1994, with additional items on Sg listed pp. 71-77]

[A1:21] Fallenstein, Robert, and Christian Hennig, *Rezeption skandinavischer Literatur in Deutschland 1870-1914: Quellenbibliographie*, Skandinavistische Studien 7, Neumünster: Karl Wachholtz Verlag, 1977. ['The Reception of Scandinavian Literature in Germany, 1870-1914'. Includes extensive bibliographical details of publications about Sg published in Germany during the period of his early reception there, pp. 389-426, 454-457]

[A1:22] Garagulay, Brita von, *Walter A. Berendsohn. Verzeichnis seiner 1908-1978 erschienenen Veröffentlichungen anlässlich seines 94. Geburtstages am 10. September 1978. Mit einem Vorwort von Gustav Korlén*, Acta Bibliothecæ Regiæ Stockholmiensis 31, Stockholm: Kungliga Biblioteket, 1978. 103 pp. [A bibliography published to commemorate Berendsohn's 94th birthday which includes details of the publications of one of the most prolific Strindberg scholars during the three decades immediately following the Second World War]

[A1:23] Gentikow, Barbara, ed., *Skandinavische und deutsche Literatur. Bibliographie der Schriften zu den literarischen, historischen und kulturgeschichtlichen Wechselbeziehungen*, Skandinavistische Studien 3, Neumünster: Karl Wachholtz Verlag, 1975. 213 pp. ['Scandinavian and German Literature. A Bibliography of Writings about their Literary, Historical, and Cultural Interdependence'. Bibliographical entries related to the impact of Sg on German literature prior to 1970 are listed, pp. 89-95]

[A1:24] Górski, Ryszard, 'A. Strindberg na scenach polskich (Próba bibliografii)', in *Panna Julia*, Warszawa, 1957. ['August Strindberg on the Polish Stage: A Bibliography'. In the programme book for a production of *Fröken Julie* at the Teatru Ludowy (Mała Scena)]

[**A1:25**] Gruszczyńska, Ewa, 'Literatura szwedzka w Polsce', *Acta Sueco-Polonica* (Uppsala), No. 1 (1993), pp. 55-68. ['Swedish Literature in Polish']

[**A1:26**] Gustafson, Alrik, *A Bibliographical Guide to Swedish Literature*, Stockholm: The Swedish Institute, 1961. 80 pp. [An offprint of the bibliography in **B5:63**. Includes a lightly annotated survey of the academic literature on Sg, pp. 37-45]

[**A1:27**] Gustavsson, Bodil, *C. G. Bjurström. En bibliografi*, Acta Bibliothecæ Regiæ Stockholmiensis LXI, Stockholm: Kungl. Biblioteket, 1999. 100 pp. [A bibliography which includes details of Carl Gustaf Bjurström's numerous translations of, and articles about, Sg and his works, generally published in France and in French]

[**A1:28**] Hagström, Tore, *Svensk litteraturhistorisk bibliografi intill år 1900*, Skrifter utg. av Svenska litteratursällskapet, 34:1-12, Uppsala: Svenska litteratursällskapet, 1964-1989. ['A Bibliography of Swedish Literature to the Year 1900']

[**A1:29**] Hedvall, Anders, *Sven Rinman. Tryckta skrifter 1922-1969. Bibliografi utg. till 65-årsdagen 1 april 1970*, Stockholm: Acta Bibliothecæ Regiæ Stockholmiensis, 1970. XIII+56 pp. [A bibliographical *festschrift* presented to the head librarian at Kungliga Biblioteket, Stockholm, himself a significant bibliographer of the critical literature on Sg (see **A1:84**) and a frequent reviewer of books by and about Sg]

[**A1:30**] Helsztynski, Stanisław, *Bibliografia pism Stanisław Przybyszewski: w 100 rocznice urodzin, 1868 7.V.*, Warszawa: Towarzystwo przyjaciol ksiazki, 1968. 48 pp. [Includes details of several of Przybyszewski's publications of relevance to Sg and the period when the two writers associated in Berlin during the early 1890s]

[**A1:31**] Henderson, Archibald, 'August Strindberg (1849-1912): A Bibliography', *Bulletin of Bibliography* (Boston, Mass.), 7:2 (July 1912), 41-42. [Principally concerned with documenting early English translations of Sg's works]

[**A1:32**] Henderson, Archibald, 'Strindberg: A Bibliography, Translators, Productions and Criticism in English', in *Modern Drama and Opera*, Vol. 2, Boston: The Boston Book Company, 1915, pp. 116-126. [See **A1:31**]

[**A1:33**] Hennig, Christian, Jens Heese, and Kirsten Kopiske, *Rezeption skandinavischer Literatur in den deutschsprachigen Ländern 1915 bis 1980*, Quellenbibliographie. Skandinavische Studien 19, 2 vols, Neumünster: Karl Wachholtz Verlag, 1988. 1066 pp. ['The Reception of Scandinavian Literature in the German-Speaking Countries, 1915 to 1980'. An invaluable source of information for material published in German during the designated period. Specific entries on Sg are included in Volume Two from item No. 15394 (p. 750) to item No. 17038 (p. 849)]

[**A1:34**] Horn-Monval, Madeleine, *Répertoire bibliographique des traductions et adaptations françaises du théâtre étranger du 15e siècle a nos jours*, T. VII, 'Théâtre scandinave', Paris, 1965. 84 pp. ['A Bibliographical Catalogue of French Translations and Adaptations of Foreign Theatre from the 15th Century until Our Time'. Provides details of French translations of Sg's plays to date]

[**A1:35**] Jacobsen, Harry, 'Bidrag till Strindberg-Bibliografien. Dansk Afdelning 1880-1889', in *Strindberg i Firsernes København* (**R:1044**), København: Gyldendal, 1948, pp. 165-180. ['Contribution to a Strindberg Bibliography. The Danish Section, 1880-1889'. Provides detailed information about the publication of Sg's works in Danish translation as well as reviews, interviews, and other articles published about Sg and his writings in the Danish press during the 1880s, when he was sometimes in close epistolary contact with several prominent Danish writers, including Edvard and Georg Brandes. From late 1887 to early 1889 Sg was based in Denmark where he completed *En dåres försvarstal*, witnessed the première of *Fadren*, wrote *Fröken Julie*, *Paria*, *Fordringsägare*, *Den starkare*, *Hemsöborna*, and 'Tschandala', established his Scandinavian Experimental Theatre which gave the first performances of many of these plays, and entered into polemics about the Woman Question. In this context, Jacobsen's bibliographical essay is an invaluable resource which facilitates a close analysis of Sg's relationship with Danish culture and his reception in Denmark in the 1880s during one of the most colourful and productive periods of his life, when he emerged as the most notable contemporary Scandinavian dramatists alongside Ibsen]

[A1:36] Järv, Harry, *Victor Svanberg. Tryckta skrifter 1918-1976. Bibliografi utg. till 80-årsdagen den 24 maj 1976. Förord av Thure Stenström*, Stockholm: Acta Bibliothecæ Regiæ Stockholmiensis, 1976. 186 pp. [A commemorative bibliography which lists the publications of a Swedish critic whose writings on Sg were frequently critical. Published in honour of Svanberg's 80th birthday]

[A1:37] Johansson, Carl Olof, 'Register över Strindbergssällskapets publikationer 1945-2005, *Strindbergiana* (Stockholm), 20 (2005), pp. 159-167. ['An Index to the Publications of the Strindberg Society, 1945-2005'. Comprises an index established by B. I. B. Lindahl to the sixty-eight issues of *Meddelanden från Strindbergssällskapet*, published between 1945 and 1984, and an index to the first twenty volumes of the Yearbook *Strindbergiana*, established by Carl Olof Johansson, who also provides a brief introduction]

[A1:38] Johansson, J. Viktor, *Svenska diktare från Karl XIV:s och Oscar II:s tid. Original-upplagor ur en göteborgsprivatsamling*, Göteborg, 1965. 50 pp. ['Swedish Writers from the Age of Karl XIV and Oscar II. First Editions from a Private Collection in Gothenburg'. Includes bibliographical data concerning the author's book collection which includes numerous items by Sg, currently on exhibition at Göteborgs Universitetsbibliotek. Also incorporates a detailed summary of the publishing history of the various early works grouped together by Sg in the collection *I vårbrytningen*]

[A1:39] Kalderén, Gudrun, *Schwedische Literatur in deutscher Übersetzung 1950-1967. Ein bibliografisches Verzeichnis*, Stockholm: Svenska Institutet, 1968. 84 pp. ['Swedish Literature in German Translation, 1950-1967. A Bibliographical Catalogue']

[A1:40] Kärnell, Karl-Åke, and Per Erik Lindahl, *August Strindberg 1849-1949*, Lunds studenters bibliofila klubb, Skrifter 1, Malmö: Sydsvenska Dagbladets Aktiebolaget, 1949. Illus. 103 pp. [The catalogue for an exhibition in Lund to mark the centenary of Sg's birth. Contains an introduction, 'August Strindberg 1849-1949', by Algot Werin, pp. 5-9; a bibliography of primary and secondary material together with commentary by the editors, pp. 11-70; a further essay by the editors on Sg's connections with Lund ('Strindberg och Lund') accompanied by a bibliography which documents his residence there, pp. 71-78; and two essays by John Landquist, 'Strindberg och psykiat-erna' (Strindberg and the Psychiatrists), pp. 79-83, and Knut Lundmark, 'Att samla Strindberg' (Collecting Strindberg), pp. 85-103. Also published in an edition for bibliophiles in 99 numbered copies]

[A1:41] Klemmings Antikvariat, *August Strindberg. Meddelanden för bokvänner*, Katalog (Klemmings Antikvariat) 176, Stockholm, 1927. 45 pp. ['August Strindberg. Information for Bibliophiles'. A descriptive catalogue covering editions of Sg's works by a leading antiquarian bookseller in Stockholm]

[A1:42] Kloeden, Wolfdietrich von, 'August Strindberg', in *Biographisch-Bibliographisches Kirchenlexikon*, Vol. 11, Herzberg: Verlag Traugott Bautz, 1996, Sp. 57-83. [Offers an overview of Sg's life and career as a writer together with quite detailed but sometimes erratic bibliographical data regarding German translations and general secondary literature]

[A1:43] Knapp, Winifred, 'Select List of Books in English about Scandinavians or by Scandinavians', *Bulletin of Bibliography* (Boston, Mass.), 8 (1915), 187-192. [Titles relevant to Sg, p. 191]

[A1:44] Kvamme, Janet, and Edwin Brownrigg, eds, *Index Nordicus. A Cumulative Index to English-language Periodicals on Scandinavian Studies*, Boston, Mass.: Hall, 1980. [Covers the period 1911-1976 but lists comparatively little on Sg]

[A1:45] Lahad, Ezra, 'Strindberg ba-teatron ha-yivri', *Bama* (Jerusalem), No. 71 (1976), pp. 40-47. [For a bibliography of Sg's works and Sg criticism in Hebrew by Yerushalmi]

[A1:46] Lilliestam, Olof Åke, red., 'Uno Willers tryckta skrifter 1930-30/10 1971', in *Biblioteket och historia. Festskrift till Uno Willers*, Acta Bibliothecæ Regiæ Stockholmiensis 12, Stockholm: Kungliga Biblioteket, 1971. [384] pp. and 20 Plates. [Includes **N:33**: John Rohnström, 'Strindbergs mongoliska studier. Ett nyfunnet Strindbergsmanuskript', and the miscellaneous article, **U1:188**, 'Jenny Lind, Kristina Nilsson, August Strindberg. Fakta och önsketänkande kring de första svenska ljudinspelningarna' by Claes M. Cnattingius (Jenny Lind, Kristina Nilsson, August Strindberg. Facts and Wishful Thinking Concerning the First Swedish Sound Recordings), as well as a bibliography of Willer's publications from 1930 to 30 October 1971, pp. 350-376]

[A1:47] Lindström, Hans, *Att samla Strindberg*, Bokvännens småskrifter 1, Stockholm, 1980. 57 pp. ['Collecting Strindberg'. A bibliographical essay on collecting Sg and Sgiana. Contains short chapters concerning Sg's life-long interest in books ('Strindberg och böckerna'), a history of his relationships with publishers ('Förläggarhistoria'), collecting Sg editions ('Att samla Strindberg'), and a brief guide to the biographical and critical literature about Sg ('Litteraturen om Strindberg')]

[A1:48] Litteraturhistoriska institutionen i Lund, *Register till August Strindbergs Samlade Skrifter 1-55 (1912-19)*, Lund: Lundensiska litteratursällskapet, 1964. 53 pp. ['An Index to August Strindberg's *Samlade Skrifter, Vols 1-55 (1912-1919)*. Index compiled and disseminated by the Department of Literature at Lund University]

[A1:49] Lundblad, Bengt, *August Strindberg. Ett urval litteratur 1900-1961*, Sveriges Allmänna Biblioteksförenings Småskrifter 62, Lund: Bibliotekstjänst, 1962. 35 pp. [Contains bibliographic details of a selection of the literature concerning Sg's life and works, focusing mainly on those published in Sweden between 1900-1961]

[A1:50] Lundmark, Knut, 'En Strindbergsbibliografi', *Meddelanden från Strindbergssällskapet* (Stockholm), 10 (1951), pp. 1-3. ['A Strindberg Bibliography'. Outlines Lundmark's plans for a comprehensive Sg bibliography, together with some of the criteria on which it should be based]

[A1:51] [Meidal, Björn], red., *Strindberg i offentligheten*, 4 del., Uppsala: Litteraturvetenskapliga institutionen, 1980. Vol. 1, '1879-1884', XVII+199 pp.; Vol. 2, '1884-1885', VI+209 pp.; Vol. 3, '1887-1892', V+191 pp.; Vol. 4, '1899-1906', VIII+426 pp. ['Strindberg

Before the Public'. An invaluable, annotated 'Excerpt-Catalogue' of articles about Sg published in the Swedish daily press and elsewhere during the greater part of his active career as a writer. It blends the trivial with the significant and not only illustrates the chequered history of Sg's reception in Sweden but also indicates how his image was constructed and altered during his lifetime. A brief introduction by Meidal (Vol. 1, pp. i-xi) outlines the basis of a project which reveals how the figure we now refer to as 'Strindberg' is both the product of his own works and the compound dramatic creation of his contemporaries in the literary field they shared and fought over]

[**A1:52**] — Johnson, Walter [Gilbert], *Scandinavian Studies* (Lawrence, Kansas), 53:2 (1981), 237-238.

[**A1:53**] — Robinson, Michael, *Scandinavica* (Norwich), 26:1 (1987), 57-59.

[**A1:54**] [Meidal, Björn], 'Projektet "Strindberg i offentligheten"', *Litterarium* (Uppsala), 1979:2, pp. 53-57. ['The Project "Strindberg Before the Public"'. Presents the research project ultimately published in four volumes as **A1:51**]

[**A1:55**] Nordisk Kulturkommisjon, *Oversettelse til engelsk av nordisk skjønnlitteratur*, Innstilling (med bilag I–V), Oslo: Oscar Andersens boktrykkeri, 1954. ['Translations of Nordic Literature into English'. Includes a list of translations with bibliographical details of existing English versions of Sg's works together with the publisher and name of the translator where known, pp. 121-131]

[**A1:56**] Øksnevad, Reidar, *Sverige i Norsk Litteratur*, Oslo: Gyldendal Norsk Forlag, 1951. ['Sweden in Norwegian Literature'. A bibliography which contains works on Swedish subjects by Norwegian authors. Of limited specific relevance to Sg]

[**A1:57**] Ollfors, Anders, 'August Strindbergs arbeten under Bonniertiden – några bibliografiska och bibliofila anteckningar', *Bokvännen* (Stockholm), 30 (1985), pp. 81-88. ['August Strindberg's Works during the Bonnier Period – Some Bibliographical and Bibliophile Notes']

[**A1:58**] Ollfors, Anders, *August Strindberg i bibliografisk och bibliofil belysning*, Borås: Norma Bokförlag, 1987. Illus. 114 pp. ['August Strindberg in a Bibliographical and Bibliophile Light'. Regards Sg's work from a bibliographical perspective and, using the author's own extensive collection of Sgiana as a basis, from the point of view of an enthusiastic book collector. Includes a reprint of **A1:57**, **G2:30**: 'Om publiceringsgången av skrifterna i Strindbergs *I vårbrytningen*', and **R:1725**: 'Klas Fåhreus och August Strindberg', in a revised form]

[**A1:59**] — Andrén, Sigvard, *Vestmanlands Läns Tidning* (Västerås), 28 July 1987.

[**A1:60**] — Ekbrant, I., *Smålandsposten* (Växjö), 9 June 1987.

[**A1:61**] — Ekerwald, Carl-Göran, *Dagens Nyheter* (Stockholm), 21 May 1987.

[**A1:62**] — Jacobsson, Roger, *Västerbottens Kuriren* (Umeå), 4 August 1987.

[**A1:63**] — Jacobsson, Roger, 'Bibliografisk och bibliofilt hos Strindberg', *Horisont* (Vasa), 39:6 (1992), pp. 2-4. [Also reviews Ollfors, *Strindbergs dedikationer*, **R:1732**]

[**A1:65**] — Lindström, Hans, *Nordisk Tidskrift för Bok- och Biblioteksväsen* (Stockholm), 74 (1987), 118-119.

[**A1:65**] — Morelius, I., *DAST-Magazin* (Bromma), 20:3 (1987), p. 18.

[**A1:66**] — Ollén, Gunnar, *Sydsvenska Dagbladet* (Malmö), 24 June 1987.

[**A1:67**] — Rinman, Sven, *Upsala Nya Tidning*, 8 July 1987.

[A1:68] — Robinson, Michael, *Scandinavica* (Norwich), 32:2 (1993), 239-240. [Also reviews Ollfors, *Strindbergs dedikationer*, **R:1732**]

[A1:69] — Sommar, Carl Olof, *Östgöta Correspondenten* (Linköping), 2 June 1987.

[A1:70] — Sommar, Carl Olof, *Bokvännen* (Stockholm), 93 (1988), 70-71.

[A1:71] — Stolpe, Sven, *Arbetet* (Malmö), 14 August 1987.

[A1:72] — Stolpe, Sven, *Kvällsposten* (Malmö), 30 August 1987.

[A1:73] Ollfors, Anders, 'Tillägg och rättelser till *August Strindberg i bibliografisk och bibliofil belysning*', in *Litterärt och bibliofilt. Om böcker och boksamlande*, Borås: Norma, pp. 84-93. ['Addenda and Corrections to *August Strindberg in a Bibliographical and Bibliophile Light*', **A1:58**]

[A1:74] Olsson, Lesley M., 'Strindberg's Plays in English Translation: A Select Bibliography', *Swedish Book Review* (Lampeter), 1986 (Supplement), pp. 48-52.

[A1:75] Palmer, Helen H., 'August Strindberg', in *European Drama Criticism*, 2nd edition, Dawson: The Shoe String Press, Inc., 1977, pp. 517-525. [The subjects may be European but the focus is almost exclusively on material in English, for the most part published in North America. Lists a few performance reviews, identified mainly by journal title only]

[A1:76] Palmqvist, Arne, and Odd Grandin, *Svenska författare. Bibliografisk handbok*, Stockholm: Almqvist & Wiksell, 1967. 243 pp. ['Swedish Authors. A Bibliographic Guide'. Lists critical studies of Sg's works, focusing mainly on books and scholarly essays published in Swedish, pp. 204-216. The selection of titles for detailed reference helps confirm those accorded the greatest attention in Sweden in the half-century following his death]

[A1:77] Paul, Fritz, 'Auswahlbibliographie', in *August Strindberg*, Sammlung Metzler 178, Stuttgart: J. B. Metzlersche Verlagsbuchhandlung, 1979, pp. IX-XXIV. ['Selected Bibliography'. A good, basic bibliography of editions and secondary literature to date. Each subject and section about Sg's writing in different genres and on various themes, as well as every work discussed in the main body of the book is also accompanied by a succinct but useful listing of the most relevant literature]

[A1:78] Paul, Fritz, and Heinz-Georg Halbe, Hrsg., *Schwedische Literatur in deutscher Übersetzung 1830-1980. Eine Bibliographie*, bearbeitet von Regina Quandt, 7 Bde, Abhandlung der Akademie der Wißenschaften in Göttingen, Göttingen: Vandenhoeck & Ruprecht, 1987-1988. ['Swedish Literature in German Translation, 1830-1980. A Bibliography'. A comprehensive, seven-volume bibliography of Swedish literature in German translation. Sg's works are listed in entries 8759 to 9272.2 in Volume 5, pp. 2099-2332]

[A1:79] Raabe, Paul, Hrsg., *Index Expressionismus. Bibliographie der Beiträge in den Zeitschriften und Jahrbüchern des literarischen Expressionismus 1910 bis 1925*, Band 9, Nendeln: Kraus-Thomsen, 1972, pp. 3552-3563. [A bibliography of literary expressionism in journals and yearbooks for a period that coincides with Sg's preeminence in the German theatre]

[A1:80] Rapp, Esther H., 'Strindberg Bibliography. Strindberg's Reception in England and America: Part A: Strindberg in England', *Scandinavian Studies* (Menasha, Wisconsin), 23:1 (1951), 1-22. [A lightly annotated survey which draws on newspapers, journals, and books, including translations and some general histories of drama and culture. With some quotation and in spite of a primarily East-Coast bias in its North-American coverage, it remains a very useful source of information on Sg's early reception in both Britain (mainly London) and the United States (mainly New York). Based on Rapp's doctoral thesis, **V:172**]

[A1:81] Rapp, Esther H., 'Strindberg Bibliography. Strindberg's Reception in England and America: Part B: Criticism in America', *Scandinavian Studies* (Menasha, Wisconsin), 23:2 (1951), 49-59. [See **A1:80**]

[A1:82] Rapp, Esther H., 'Strindberg Bibliography. Strindberg's Reception in England and America: Part C: Criticism in America', *Scandinavian Studies* (Menasha, Wisconsin), 23:3 (1951), 109-137. [See **A1:80**]

[A1:83] Rinman, Sven, *Deutsche Bücher über Schweden und schwedishe Dichtung in deutscher Übersetzung. Ein bibliographisches Verzeichnis*, Stockholm: Schwedisches Institut, 1952. 64 pp. ['German Books on Sweden and Swedish literature in German Translation. A Bibliographic Index']

[A1:84] Rinman, Sven, 'Strindberg', in E[ugène] N[apoleon] Tigerstedt, red., *Ny Illustrerad Svensk Literaturhistoria*, Andra bearbetade upplagan, 4 vols, Stockholm: Natur och Kultur, Vol. 4, 'Åttiotal, Nittiotal', 1967, pp. 415-425. [A useful bibliography of mainly Swedish material, accompanying an excellent, discerning overview of Sg's achievement as a writer in what was, for many years, the standard and most authoritative history of Swedish literature. See **B5:117**]

[A1:85] Rokem, Freddie, *Scandinavian Literatures in Hebrew Translation 1894-1980*, Studies in Translation Theory 2, Ramat Aviv: Tel Aviv University, 1982. XX+75 pp. [In English and Hebrew with an introduction]

[A1:86] Rumac, Mirko, 'Bibliografija: prijevoda Strindbergovih djela, prikaza izvedaba njegovih drama napisa of A. Strindbergu na hrvatskom odnosno srpskom jezičnom području', *Prolog* (Zagreb), 55-56 (1983), pp. 103-127. [A bibliography which covers material published mainly in Croatia and Serbia between 1895 and 1983. Rumac lists not only critical essays in journals and books but also translations of his works and book and theatre reviews]

[A1:87] Samzelius, Jonas L:son, *Svensk litteraturhistorisk bibiografi 1900-1935*, Skrifter utgivna av Svenska litteratursällskapet 29, Uppsala: Svenska litteratursällskapet, 1939-1950. [A rolling bibliography of Swedish literary history, listing many, often ephemeral, biographical items, as well as more substantial works of literary criticism]

[A1:88] [Samzelius, Jonas L:son], *Svensk litteraturhistorisk bibiografi 1936-1965*, Skrifter utgivna av Svenska litteratursällskapet 38, Uppsala: Almqvist & Wicksell, 1985ff. [See **A1:87**]

[A1:89] Schröder, Stephan Michael, Hrsg., *Studienbibliographie zur Neuskandinavistik*, Berliner Beiträge zue Skandinavistik 7, Berlin: Humboldt-Universität zu Berlin, 1997. 193 pp. [A guide to archives and resources for the study of Scandinavian literature in both print and electronic form]

[A1:90] Steene, Birgitta, 'August Strindberg in America, 1963-1979. A Bibliographical Assessment', in Marilyn Johns Blackwell, **C1:142**, *Structures of Influence*, pp. 256-276. [A lightly annnotated listing which brings the American sections of the bibliographical articles by Rapp, **A1:80, A1:81,** and **A1:82**, as well as Bryer, **A1:14**, up to date and includes some information about translations and doctoral dissertations as well as books and articles]

[A1:91] Steene, Birgitta, 'Bibliography', *Scandinavian Studies* (Madison), 62:1 (1990), [130]-132. [A list of scholarly books and articles with the emphasis placed on Sg's interest in history and his history plays, in a special issue devoted to Sg's achievement as a historical dramatist. See **B7:39**]

[A1:92] Suchodolska, Ewa, *Översättningar av svensk litteratur till polska*, Warszawa: Bibl. Narodowa, 1969. 28 pp. ['Translations of Swedish Literature into Polish'. A bibliographical listing]

[A1:93] Suchodolska, Ewa, and Zofia Żydanowicz, *Bibliografia polskich przekladów z literatury pięknej krajów skandynawskich do roku 1969 włącznie*, Poznań: Wydawnictwo Poznańskie, 1971. 326 pp. ['A Bibliography of Polish Translations from the Literatures of the Scandinavian Countries up to and Including 1969']

[A1:94] — Ciesielski, Zenon, 'Nad bibliografią literatury skandynawskiej w Polsce', *Miesięcznik Literacki* (Warsaw), 1972:8, pp. 136-137. ['A Bibliography of Scandinavian Literature in Polish']

[A1:95] — W. N. [Witold Nawrocki], 'Literatury skandynawskie', *Twórczo* (Warsaw), 1971:11, pp. 156-157. ['Scandinavian Literature']

[A1:96] Svanfeldt, Henrik, *Katalog över en samling August Strindberg i första upplagor jämte tidningsklipp och några mer betydande arbeten om Strindberg, tillhörande Henrik Svanfeldt*, [Privately printed], 1957. 27 pp. ['Catalogue of a Collection of August Strindberg in First Editions together with Newspaper Cuttings and some more Important Works about Strindberg, Belonging to Henrik Svanfeldt'. See also **A2:3, A5:20**, and **U1:780**]

[A1:97] — Rinman, Sven, 'En Strindbergskatalog', *Göteborgs Handels- och Sjöfarts Tidning*, 4 July 1957. ['A Strindberg Catalogue'. Presents Henrik Svanfeldt's catalogue of Strindbergiana and presscuttings, **A1:96**]

[A1:98] Svenska Institutet, *Schwedischen Stücke in deutscher Übersetzung von Strindberg bis zur Gegenwart*, Stockholm: Svenska Institutet, 1983. 37 pp. ['Swedish Plays in German Translation from Strindberg to the Present'. The most substantial number of works listed are by Sg]

[A1:99] Swan, Gustaf N[ilsson], 'August Strindberg i Amerika. Bibliografiska anteckningar för *Nordstjernan*', 1-2, *Nordstjernan* (New York), 14 and 17 October 1913. ['August Strindberg in America. Bibliographical Notes for *Nordstjernan*'. A bibliographical essay which identifies early articles on Sg in the English and (mainly) North-American press, and comments on his initial reception there]

[A1:100] Uggla, Andrzej Nils, 'Dwei bibliografie Strindberga', *Acta Sueco-Polonica* (Uppsala), 5 (1996), [181]-191. ['Two Strindberg Bibliographies'. Presents two Polish bibliographies, one listing Polish translations of his works, the other listing the titles as organised in *Samlade Verk*]

[A1:101] Volz, Ruprecht, 'Projekt einer internationalen Strindberg-Bibliographie', in Heiko Uecker, Hrsg., *Akten der Fünften Arbeitstagung der Skandinavisten des deutschen Sprachgebiets* 16-22 August 1981 in Kungälv, St. Augustin: Verlag Dr. Bernd Kretschmer, 1983, pp. 305-306. ['Project for an International Strindberg Bibliography']

[**A1:102**] Willers, Uno, *Anders Österling. En bibliografi 1964-1974*, Acta Bibliothecæ regiæ Stockholmiensis 20, Stockholm: Kungliga Biblioteket, 1974. 36 pp. [Includes details of Österling's critical journalism about Sg]

[**A1:103**] Wingren, Gottfrid Erland, *Svensk dramatisk litteratur under åren 1840-1913. Bibliografisk förteckning*, Uppsala: F. C. Askerberg, 1914. XIV+265 pp. ['Swedish Dramatic Literature during the Years 1840-1913. A Bibliographical Listing']

[**A1:104**] Yeroshalmi, Joseph, 'Al Strindberg be-yivrit: Bivli-ographi-a', *Bama* (Jerusalem), No. 71 (1976), pp. 41-45. [A bibliography of Sg's works and some critical studies]

[**A1:105**] Zetterlund, Rune, *Bibliografiska anteckningar om August Strindberg*, Stockholm: Albert Bonniers Förlag, 1913. 325 pp. ['Bibliographical Notes on August Strindberg'. An enthusiast's indispensable, if occasionally inaccurate, chronological bibliography of Sg's published works to date, together with a bibliography of early, mainly Swedish, essays, reviews, and polemical articles provoked both by his life and work. Zetterlund also lists by date a selection of the numerous newspaper articles relating to the Strindberg Feud as well as many others concerned with his final illness and death]

[**A1:106**] — F. V. [Fredrik Vetterlund], *Aftonbladet* (Stockholm), 7 July 1913 (Landsorts upplaga).

[**A1:107**] — Landquist, John, *Dagens Nyheter* (Stockholm), 27 June 1913.

[**A1:108**] — O. R-s [Olof Rabenius], *Stockholms Dagblad*, 24* July 1913.

[**A1:109**] Zetterlund, Rune, *Bibliografiska anteckningar om August Strindberg*, Burt Franklin: Bibliography and Reference Series #195, New York: Burt Franklin, 1968. [Facsimile Rpr. of **A1:105**]

See also Denis Ballu, *Lettres nordiques en traduction française 1720-1995*, **B3:78**, and the subject-specific bibliographies devoted to aspects of Sg's work by Nina di Ponziano Hatt, **V:168**, *Bildkonstnären August Strindberg i svensk press 1892-1996. Ett bibliografiskt utkast*, Krzysztof Rózycki, **V:182**, *August Strindberg – bibliografia przedmiotowa za lata 1970-1990*, Karin Johnsson, **V:115**, *Bibliografi över Vilhelm Carlheim-Gyllenskölds Samling av Strindbergiana på Kungliga Biblioteket i Stockholm*, **V:139**, Marie H. Malmin, *Annotated Bibliography of the Translations of Scandinavian Literature in England and America*, and **T:509**, 'Strindbergsfejden', by Barbro Svensson, Göran Hassler, Johan af Sandeberg, and Carl-Johan Sjögren on the many articles and pamphlets pertaining to the Strindberg Feud. See also Per Åsberg, **G12:2**, for *Sagor*, **U1:670**, Alice Rasmussen, 'Strindbergs verk som följetong och tjuvtryck i Amerika' and **N:10a** and **N:10a** for discussions of Sg's bibliographical work and publications as a librarian by Bo Bennich-Björkman.

A2. Strindberg's Manuscripts and Book Collections

[**A2:1**] Afzelius, Nils, 'Selma Lagerlöfs manuskript och något om August Strindbergs', *Biblis* (Stockholm), 3 (1959-60), 135-156. ['Selma Lagerlöf's Manuscripts and something about August Strindberg's']

[**A2:2**] Afzelius, Nils, 'Selma Lagerlöfs manuskript och något om August Strindbergs', in *Selma Lagerlöf – den förargelseväckande*, Lund: Gleerups, 1969, pp. 20–37. Illus. ['Selma Lagerlöf's Manuscripts and something about August Strindberg's'. Rpr. of **A2:1**]

[A2:3] Åhlén, Bengt, 'Strindberg och boksamlarna. Randanteckningar till Henrik Svanfeldts Strindbergssamling', *Upsala Nya Tidning*, 21 January 1949. ['Strindberg and the Book Collectors. Marginalia to Henrik Svanfeldt's Strindberg Collection'. See **A1:96** and **A5:20**]

[A2:4] Anon, 'Gyllensköldska arkivaffären ännu oförklarad', *Dagens Nyheter* (Stockholm), 1 February 1922. ['The Gyllensköld Archive Affair still Unexplained'. Reflections on the long-running furore concerning Vilhelm Carlheim-Gyllensköld's much criticised custodianship of Sg's literary remains]

[A2:5] Anon, 'Inventeringen av de Strindbergska arkivsamlingarna', *Stockholms-Tidningen*, 1 February 1922. ['The Inventory of the Strindberg Archives and Collections']

[A2:6] Anon, 'Khronika', *Internatsional'naia literatura* (Moscow), 1940:9-10, p. 292. [Introduces Sg's unpublished essay on the poet of the Swedish Enlightnment, Thomas Thorild (1759-1808). E.954]

[A2:7] Anon, 'Nyfunna Strindbergsmanuskript', *Bonniers Litterära Magasin* (Stockholm), 18:5 (1949), p. 419. ['Newly Discovered Strindberg Manuscripts'. Reports the recent acquisition by Kungliga Biblioteket in Stockholm of the manuscript of *Ensam*, as well as several other shorter items, including holographs of the prose poem 'Solrök' (Heat Haze, 1881), the story 'Silverträsket' (The Silver Marsh, 1898), and Sg's speculative essay in optics, 'En blick mot rymden' (A Glance into Space, 1897)]

[A2:8] Anon, 'Prof. Carlheim-Gyllensköld och Strindbergs papper', *Aftonbladet* (Stockholm), 12 December 1913. ['Professor Carlheim-Gyllensköld and Strindberg's Papers']

[A2:9] Anon, 'Striden om Strindbergsarkivet', *Stockholms Dagblad*, 20 November 1912. ['The Conflict over the Strindberg Archive']

[A2:10] Anon, 'Strindberg och den gröna säcken', *Östgöta Correspondenten* (Linköping), 1 March 1949. ['Strindberg and the Green Bag'. Reports on a lecture by Oscar Wieselgren on the current state of Sg's literary remains and their preservation in the Royal Library, Stockholm, which was delivered at the annual meeting of Samfundet Linköping stiftsbiblioteks vänner]

[A2:11] Anon, 'Strindbergs efterlämnade kvarlåtenskap – allvarlig konflikt med skaldens tyske översättare', *Dagens Nyheter* (Stockholm), 30 October 1912. ['Strindberg's Literary Remains – A Serious Conflict with the Poet's German Translator'. Reports a developing dispute concerning Emil Schering's claims to the rights to those manuscripts and original copies of his works which Sg had sent him for translation, as well as to the numerous letters that he had addressed to Schering in Germany during the last twelve years of his (Sg's) life. See **A2:12**, **A2:67**, **A2:68**, and **A2:70**]

[A2:12] Anon, 'Strindbergsarvet i Tyskland. Emil Schering uppställer orimliga anspråk', *Dagens Nyheter* (Stockholm), 20 December 1912. ['Strindberg's Legacy in Germany. Emil Schering has Unreasonable Pretensions'. Comments on Schering's ambtious plans for the manuscript material by Sg, including letters, which he has in his keeping. See **A2:11**, **A2:67**, **A2:68**, and **A2:70**]

[A2:13] Anon, 'Strindbergs' literaire nalatenschap', *Het Handelsblad van Antwerpen*, 19 January 1914. ['Strindberg's Literary Remains']

[A2:14] Anon, 'Strindbergsarkivet får donationer för kompletteringsköp', *Stockholms-Tidningen*, 5 February 1922. ['The Strindberg Archive Receives Donations for Supplementing the Collection'. On measures taken to supplement the collections comprising Sg's manuscripts and other papers then (1922) held in Nordiska Museet, Stockholm]

[A2:15] Anon, 'Strindbergsarkivets vanvård avslöjas', *Aftonbladet* (Stockholm), 29 January 1922. ['The Mismanagement of the Strindberg Archive Uncovered'. Accuses Vilhelm Carlheim-Gyllensköld of mismanaging the archive of Sg's literary remains entrusted to him as his executor]

[A2:16] Anon, 'Strindbergsbrev och dokument som vanvårdas', *Dagens Nyheter* (Stockholm), 30 January 1922. ['Strindberg's Letters and Documents Neglected'. See **A3:15**]

[A2:17] Anon, 'Strindbergsdokument och brev som vanvårdas', *Dagens Nyheter* (Stockholm), 30 January 1922. ['Strindberg's Documents and Letters Neglected'. A further contribution to the ongoing controversy concerning Vilhelm Carlheim-Gyllensköld's custodianship of Sg's literary remains and personal papers. See **A3:15**]

[A2:18] Anon, 'Strindbergsrelikerna', *Afton-Tidningen* (Stockholm), 21 November 1922. ['The Strindberg Relics']

[A2:19] Anon, 'Svenska öden och äventyr', *Stockholms-Dagblad*, 30 January 1922. ['Swedish Destinies and Adventures'. Comments on the current controversy concerning Vilhelm Carlheim-Gyllensköld's custodianship of Sg's literary remains and personal papers]

[A2:20] Anon, 'Uppgörelse om Strindbergsarkivet', *Dagens Nyheter* (Stockholm), 5 February 1922. ['Agreement about the Strindberg Archive'. Reports a resolution to the controversy concerning Vilhelm Carlheim-Gyllensköld's custodianship of Sg's papers]

[A2:21] Berendsohn, Walter, A[rthur], 'Fynd i Strindbergs bibliotek', *Dagens Nyheter* (Stockholm), 12 July 1948. ['Discoveries in Strindberg's Library'. Draws attention to several volumes in Sg's final book collection, including some items with his marginalia]

[A2:22] Berendsohn, Walter, A[rthur], 'Registrierung der Manuskripte August Strindbergs', *Nachrichten für wissenschaftliche Bibliotheken* (Frankfurt am Main), 3 (1950), p. 78. ['Cataloguing August Strindberg's Manuscripts']

[A2:23] Berendsohn, Walter A[rthur], 'Strindbergiana. Fynd i Strindbergsmanuskript', *Bonniers Litterära Magasin* (Stockholm), 19:10 (1950), 807-808. ['Strindbergiana. Discoveries among Strindberg's Manuscripts'. Reports the recent discovery of several manuscripts in Göteborg, Stockholm, and Berlin, including both original material and variants to published texts in Sg's hand]

[A2:24] Berendsohn, Walter A[rthur], 'Strindbergiana. Nyfunna brev och manuskript', *Bonniers Litterära Magasin* (Stockholm), 21:1 (1952), 75-76. ['Strindbergiana. Newly Discovered Letters and Manuscripts'. Reports on recent discoveries among Sg's manuscripts in the archives of Albert Bonniers Förlag in Stockholm, including some original material, variants on published texts, and a number of previously unpublished letters]

[A2:25] Berendsohn, Walter, A[rthur], 'Strindbergs manuskript', *Dagens Nyheter* (Stockholm), 5 May 1950. ['Strindberg's Manuscripts']

[A2:26] Böök, Fredrik, 'De nya Strindbergsdokumenten. Randglossor och reflexioner', *Svenska Dagbladet* (Stockholm), 8 July 1910. ['The New Strindberg Documents. Marginalia and Reflections']

[A2:27] Brundin, Margareta, 'Diktaren vid skrivbordet', in **B1:86**, *August Strindberg. Diktare som mångfrestare*, pp. 31-44. Illus. ['The Writer at His Desk'. Describes Sg's working methods as a writer, as reflected in 'Gröna säcken' (The Green Bag), i.e. the manuscript material, notes, and drafts deposited in Kungliga Biblioteket, Stockholm]

[A2:28] Brundin, Margareta, 'Hur förvarade Strindberg sina manuskript?', *Kungliga bibliotekets årsberättelse 1981* (Stockholm), pp. 61-97. Illus. ['How did Strindberg Preserve His Manuscripts?' Provides invaluable insights into how Sg kept his manuscripts and the way in which his extant papers were deposited in Nordiska Museet and arranged, provisionally catalogued, and sometimes published by his executor, Vilhelm Carlheim-Gyllensköld. Brundin describes their subsequent removal to Kungliga Biblioteket and the methods adopted for their preservation and cataloguing by the Royal librarians Oscar Wieselgren and Arvid Bæckström. She largely exonerates Carlheim-Gyllensköld from the accusations of mismanagement that have frequently been levelled against his custodianship of Sg's manuscripts and other material. It is possible that, when arranging his papers, Sg employed an organic structure which was peculiar to the work in hand, rather than the kind of traditional, systematic methods which conventionally trained archivists might wish to impose, and Carlheim-Gyllensköld, who recognised that Sg was an artist even in his seemingly aberrant scientific experiments, may well have been closer than most to understanding how his mind worked and how he arranged his papers. Brundin utilises significant unpublished, as well as published material]

[A2:29] Brundin, Margareta, 'Kungliga Bibliotekets Strindbergssamlingar', *Strindbergiana* (Stockholm), 1 (1985), pp. 50-70. ['The Royal Library's Strindberg Collections'. A useful overview which presents the various collections of material by, and pertaining to, Sg currently held by Kungliga Biblioteket, Stockholm]

[A2:30] Brundin, Margareta, 'The Royal Library's Strindberg Collections', *Nordic Theatre Studies* (Copenhagen), 6:1-2 (1993), 68-70. [An account of the various collections of material by, and pertaining to, Sg in Kungliga Biblioteket, Stockholm, and their organisation]

[A2:31] Brundin, Margareta, 'Strindbergssamlingar i KB', in **B1:86**, *August Strindberg. Diktare som mångfrestare*, pp. 27-28. Illus. ['Strindberg Collections in the Royal Library'. Surveys the material in the Sg archive of Kungliga Biblioteket, Stockholm]

[A2:32] Brunius, Teddy, 'Bibliografiska epistlar', *Upsala Nya Tidning*, 23 December 1983. ['Bibliographical Epistles']

[A2:33] Carlheim-Gyllensköld, Monika, 'Ordning eller oordning i Strindbergs bibliotek. Vilhelm Carlheim-Gyllenskölds insats', *Strindbergiana* (Stockholm), 1 (1985), pp. 71-80. ['Order or Disorder in Strindberg's Library. Vilhelm Carlheim-Gyllensköld's Contribution'. Concludes that, contrary to received opinion, Carlheim-Gyllensköld made an important contribution to the way in which Sg's papers and books were preserved, catalogued, and organised after his death, not least through his close personal knowledge of Sg and his own scientific training, which also led him to make a careful and convincing record of many of his conversations with Sg. Far from neglecting his responsibilities as Sg's executor, his close familiarity with Sg's working methods and manner of thinking meant that he could preserve the material in something approaching its original form]

[A2:34] Catalogue, *"Mina skrifter är jag". En utställning med böcker ur August Strindbergs bibliotek. 18 nov 1992-19 jan 1993*, Stockholm: Strindbergsmuseet, 1992. Illus. 12 pp. ['"My Writings Are Myself". An Exhibition of Books from August Strindberg's

Library'. The catalogue for an exhibition of books from Sg's final book collection, now preserved in its original order at 85 Drottninggatan, Stockholm. Includes extracts from Hans Lindström, **A2:57**, *Strindberg och böckerna*]

[A2:35] Dahlbäck, Lars, 'Strindbergs Samlade Oskrivna Verk', in Margareta Brundin, red., **B1:86**, *August Strindberg. Diktare som mångfrestare*, pp. 45-49; illus. pp. 50-55. ['Strindberg's Collected Unwritten Works'. Surveys the many uncompleted or unwritten projects among the manuscripts in the Sg archives now housed in the Royal Library, Stockholm]

[A2:36] Florin, Magnus, and Ulf Olsson, '[Förord]' to *Köra och vända. Strindbergs efterlämnade papper i urval*, Stockholm: Albert Bonniers Förlag, 1999, pp. 5-[9]. ['*Out and Turn*'. A Selection of Strindberg's Posthumous Papers'. Introduces an anthology of items selected from the notes and manuscripts in Sg's so-called 'Gröna säcken' (Green Bag), many of them previously unpublished]

[A2:37] — Andersson, Gunder, *Aftonbladet* (Stockholm), 21 January 1999. [What is of interest about the collection is the way that these pieces reveal Sg as continuously on the offensive, and almost never as self-pitying or sentimental]

[A2:38] — Berg, Aase, *Dagens Nyheter* (Stockholm), 24 January 1999.

[A2:39] — Bergström, Ulf, *Aftonbladet Kultur* (Stockholm), 1993:8, pp. 18-19.

[A2:40] — Bladh, Curt, *Sundsvalls Tidning*, 25 January 1999.

[A2:41] — Dahlman, Inger, *Norrköpings Tidningar-Östergötlands Dagblad*, 22 January 1999.

[A2:42] — Ehnmark, Anders, *Expressen* (Stockholm), 22 January 1999.

[A2:43] — Erlandsson, Daniel, *Östgöta Correspondenten* (Linköping), 28 January 1999.

[A2:44] — Gunnarsson, Björn, *LO-tidningen* (Stockholm), 78:8 (1999), p. 19.

[A2:45] — Gustafsson, Lars, *Nerikes Allehanda* (Örebro), 22 January 1999.

[A2:46] — Kronqvist, Dan, *Hufvudstadsbladet* (Helsingfors), 22 January 1999.

[A2:47] — Lundstedt, Göran, *Sydsvenska Dagbladet* (Malmö), 22 January 1999.

[A2:48] — Sommelius, Sören, *Helsingborgs Dagblad*, 22 January 1999.

[A2:49] — Svedjedal, Johan, *Svenska Dagbladet* (Stockholm), 28 January 1999.

[A2:50] — Tjäder, Per Arne, *Göteborgs-Posten*, 22 January 1999.

[A2:51] — Wittrock, Ulf, *Upsala Nya Tidning*, 22 January 1999.

[A2:52] Jakobsson, Arvid, 'Strindberg's bibliotek', *Nordisk tidskrift för bok- och bibliotekshistoria* (Stockholm), 86:1 (2002), 105-114. ['Strindberg's Libraries']

[A2:53] Johansson, Gotthard, 'Skandalen kring Strindbergsarkivet: Strindbergsarkivets vanvård avslöjad', *Aftonbladet* (Stockholm), 29 January 1922. ['The Scandal Concerning the Strindberg Archive. The Strindberg Archive's Neglect Revealed'. Publicises the apparently scandalous way in which Sg's old friend and executor, Vilhelm Carlheim-Gyllensköld, is supposed to have cared for his literary remains and personal papers]

[A2:54] Landquist, John, 'Strindbergsarkivet har blivit utsatt för upprörande vanvård', *Stockholms-Tidningen*, 30 January 1922. ['The Strindberg Archive has been Exposed to Shocking Negligence'. Using his authority as the editor of Sg's *Samlade Skrifter*, Landquist upbraids Vilhelm Carlheim-Gyllensköld for the incompetence he has displayed during his stewardship of Sg's extant papers in Nordiska Museet and comments critically on the obstacles that have been placed in the way of reputable scholars seeking access to the collection]

[**A2:55**] Landquist, John, 'Strindbergsarkivet har blivit utsatt för upprörande vanvård', in Solveig Landquist, red., **B1:248**, *John Landquist om Strindberg, personen och diktaren*, pp. 85-88. [Rpr. of **A2:54**]

[**A2:56**] Landqvist, Marianne, 'SESAM-projektet'. Strindbergs anteckningar i bibliotekets böcker', in *Litterære museer i Skandinavia*, Oslo: Ibsen Museet, 1999, pp. 93-95. ['The SESAM Project. Strindberg's Annotations in the Books in His Library'. Presents current plans for cataloguing Sg's marginalia in his final book collection, which is now preserved in as close as possible a format to its original organisation as an adjunct to the Strindberg Museum at Blå Tornet, Stockholm]

[**A2:57**] Lindström, Hans, *Strindberg och böckerna*, 2 vols, Del I: Biblioteken 1883, 1892 och 1912. Förteckningar och kommentarer; Del II: Boklån och läsning. Förteckning och kommentarer, Skrifter utgivna av svenska litteratursällskapet 36 & 42, Uppsala: Svenska Litteratursällskapet, 1977-1990. Illus. 231, 244 pp. ['Strindberg and His Books'. Two indispensable volumes containing (I) a catalogue of Sg's three book collections from 1883, 1892, and 1912, and (II) detailed information concerning his borrowings from libraries in Uppsala, Stockholm, and Lund, together with references to authors and their books in both his works and letters. Along with their introductions, annotation, and commentary, these meticulously assembled catalogues are invaluable for the insight they afford into the works and practice of an author whose writing is permeated profoundly by his reading and richly intertextual in its composition. Lindström establishes the fourteen titles that were to be found in all three collections, including Shakespeare's works in Carl Hagberg's Swedish translation, Plato's *Republic*, Alexis de Tocqueville's *De la Démocratie en Amerique*, Georg Brandes's biography of *Ferdinand Lassalle*, Gunnar Olof Hyltén-Cavallius's ethnographic study, *Wärend och wirdarne*, the *Edda* translated by Arvid Afzelius, Anders Fryxell's *Berättelser ur svenska historien* (Stories from Swedish History), Geijer and Afzelius's *Svenska folkvisor* (Swedish Folk Songs), Arvid Ahnfeldt's *Verldslitteraturens historia* (A History of World Literature), and C. E. Smith's *Om båtar och båtsegling* (On Boats and Sailing). He outlines the variations between the three collections according to the spread of material in different subject areas, which highlight differences that largely reflect Sg's several ideological transformations and the shifts in direction of his literary aims at different stages of his career. He also notes examples of Sg's often deeply engaged marginalia and argues the importance that books held for him as a writer for whom they were essential tools. Apart from those books in Sg's possession at his death in 1912, the other two collections are dated, and their contents determined, with reference to the catalogues that were drawn up prior to their sale in periods of hardship. See **A1:4**]

See also **A2:69**

[**A2:58**] — Dahlbäck, Lars, *Nordisk tidskrift för Bok- och Biblioteksväsen* (Stockholm), 66:2 (1979), 56-61.

[**A2:59**] — Ekman, Hans-Göran, *Samlaren* (Uppsala), 112 (1991), pp. 130-131.

[**A2:60**] — Johansson, U. R., *Kvällsposten* (Malmö), 4 March 1978.

[**A2:61**] — Johnson, Walter [Gilbert], *Scandinavian Studies* (Lawrence, Kansas), 52:1 (1980), 93-94.

[A2:62] — Lindström, Göran, *Sydsvenska Dagbladet* (Stockholm), 14 February 1978.

[A2:63] — Rinman, Sven, *Upsala Nya Tidning*, 6 April 1978.

[A2:64] — Uggla, Andrzej Nils, 'Biblioteki Strindberga', *Życie Literacki* (Kraków), No. 1378 (1978), p. 12. ['Strindberg's Library']

[A2:65] — Wästberg, Per, *Dagens Nyheter* (Stockholm), 2 June 1978.

[A2:66] Lindström, Hans, 'Strindbergs bibliotek', *Bokvännen* (Stockholm), 3 (1948), 178-180. ['Strindberg's Library']

[A2:67] Marcus, C[arl] D[avid], 'Strindbergsarvet och Emil Schering', *Dagens Nyheter* (Stockholm), 26 October 1912. ['Strindberg's Legacy and Emil Schering'. A response to Schering's remarks in **A2:70**]

[A2:68] Marcus, C[arl] D[avid], 'Strindbergs litterära kvarlåtenskap i Tyskland', *Dagens Nyheter* (Stockholm), 19 October 1912. ['Strindberg's Literary Remains in Germany'. Considers the current position regarding the rights to Sg's literary remains in Germany, which are now mainly, and dubiously, in the hands of his German translator, Emil Schering]

[A2:69] Robinson, Michael, 'Something from Nothing: Strindberg's Reading', *Scandinavica* (Norwich), 31:2 (1992), 221-229. [Discusses Sg's reading apropos Hans Lindström's *Strindberg och böckerna*, **A2:57**, and Barbro Ståhle Sjönell's annotated catalogue of his extant papers, **A2:73**, both of which afford important insights into his creative processes]

[A2:70] Schering, Emil, 'Strindbergs litterära kvarlåtenskap i Tyskland', *Dagens Nyheter* (Stockholm), 19 October 1912. ['Strindberg's Literary Remains in Germany'. See Marcus, **A2:67** and **A2:68**]

[A2:71] 'Sive' [Siv Österberg], 'Affisch om häst-debut bland Strindbergstryck', *Dagens Nyheter* (Stockholm), 18 January 1949. ['Poster on a Horse's Debut among Strindberg Papers'. Reviews an exhibition of Henrik Svanfeldt's collection of Sgiana in Uppsala. See **A1:96**]

[A2:72] Söderström, Göran, 'Strindbergssällskapets och Strindbergsmuseets pressklippsamling', *Strindbergiana* (Stockholm), 9 (1994), pp. 176-182. ['The Press-Cutting Collection of the Strindberg Society and Strindberg Museum'. A useful guide to the Museum's archive of press-cuttings, including the general collections originally assembled by Knut Lundmark, Hilmer Lundquist, and Rune Zetterlund. Söderström also provides details of A. F. W. Lindwall's collection of material pertaining to the furore which surrounded the publication of *Giftas* and the proceedings brought against Sg for blasphemy in 1884, as well as Adolf Björk's collection of articles on Sg in German newspapers between 1885 and 1919]

[A2:73] Ståhle Sjönell, Barbro, *Katalog över "Gröna säcken". Strindbergs efterlämnade papper i Kungl. biblioteket*, Acta Bibliothecae Regiæ Stockholmiensis, Stockholm, 1991. 372 pp. ['Catalogue of "The Green Bag". Strindberg's Literary Remains in the Royal Library'. An indispensable, descriptive catalogue of the first nine box-files containing Sg's literary remains in the Royal Library, Stockholm, with extensive quotation from many of the notes and drafts, and presented in a manner that affords invaluable insight into Sg's working methods, as well as to the genesis of many of his later works. This covers virtually all the post-Inferno history plays, *Ett drömspel*, *Advent*, *Brott och brott*, *Till Damaskus*, *Dödsdansen*, *Stora landsvägen*, the Chamber Plays, *Abu Casems* *tofflor*, and *Svanevit*, as well as several works in prose or verse from different periods, including 'Den romantiske klockaren på Rånö' (The Romantic Sexton on Rånö), *Tjänstekvinnans son*, *Sagor*, *Klostret*, *Fagervik och Skamsund*, *Götiska rummen*, *Svarta fanor*, *Taklagsöl*, *Ordalek och småkonst*, and *En blå bok*. These papers also document Sg's reading of Swedenborg during the Inferno years, as well as his familiarity with Maeterlinck, Péladan, and others. The material also includes the fragmentary germs of numerous unfulfilled, or aborted, ideas for sometimes named but never published works. The editor's clear and meticulous summaries, as well as facsimile reproductions of some of the manuscript material, is an invaluable resource, particularly for scholars working away from Stockholm]

[**A2:74**] — Ekman, Hans-Göran, *Samlaren* (Uppsala), 116 (1995), p. 255.

[**A2:75**] — Florin, Magnus, *Bonniers Litterära Magasin* (Stockholm), 61:6 (1992), 64-65.

[**A2:76**] — Sommar, Carl Olov, *Östgöta Correspondenten* (Linköping), 13 February 1992.

[**A2:77**] — Westholm, Carl Axel, *Vestmanlands Läns Tidning* (Västerås), 6 December 1992.

[**A2:78**] — Wirmark, Margareta, *Tidskrift för litteraturvetenskap* (Stockholm), 21:2-3 (1992), 142-143.

See also **A2:69**

[**A2:79**] Ståhle Sjönell, Barbro, 'Strindbergs litterära förarbeten i "Gröna säcken"', *Tidskrift för litteraturvetenskap* (Lund), 13:2-3 (1984), 19-32. Illus. ['Strindberg's Literary Drafts in "The Green Bag"'. Presents an overview of the drafts and manuscript material in Box Files 1-9 of the Sg archive in Kungliga Biblioteket, Stockholm, i.e. those most immediately concerned with his literary works, both published and unpublished]

[**A2:80**] Sturzenbecker, Robert, 'Strindbergs litterära kvarlåtenskap', *Aftonbladet* (Stockholm), 18 May 1912. ['Strindberg's Literary Remains']

[**A2:81**] Svidén, Åke, 'Strindbergs arbetsverktyg', *Arbetarbladet* (Gävle), 20 February 1993. ['Strindberg's Work Tools'. Argues that Sg's various book collections were the essential tools which underpinned much of his best work as a writer]

[**A2:82**] Wieselgren, Oscar, 'Nya Strindbergspapper i Kungliga Biblioteket', *Svenska Dagbladet* (Stockholm), 20 July 1941. ['New Strindberg Papers in the Royal Library'. Reports on recent acquisitions in Kungliga Biblioteket's Sg archive, including four letters addressed in 1888 to the Danish journalist Viggo Adler and several manuscript chapters of *Blomstermålningar och djurstycken*]

[**A2:83**] Wieselgren, Oscar, 'Strindbergs gröna säck en diktares skattgömma', *Eskilstuna-Kuriren*, 15 February 1941. ['Strindberg's Green Bag a Writer's Hidden Treasure'. Presents the manuscript material in Sg's so-called 'Green Bag', which Wieselgren describes as a writer's concealed treasure]

[**A2:84**] Wieselgren, Oscar, 'Strindbergssamlingarna i Kungl. Biblioteket', *Nordisk familjeboks månadskrönika* (Stockholm), 2:10 (1939), 715-722. ['The Strindberg Collections in the Royal Library']

[**A2:85**] Wieslander, Henning, 'Matsedlar för vintern. Ett Strindbergsmanuskript', *Samfundet Örebro stads- och biblioteks vänner, Meddelanden* (Örebro), 29 (1961-62), pp. 122-126. ['Menus for Winter. A Strindberg Manuscript']

[A2:86] Willers, Uno, 'Forskarmotiv till KB:s begären', *Dagens Nyheter* (Stockholm), 24 August 1968. ['Research Motivates the Royal Library's Demands']

[A2:87] Wirde, Karl Gustav, 'Birger Mörner och hans samlingar i Örebro stadsbiblioteket', *Samfundet Örebro- stads- och länsbibliotek, Meddelande* (Örebro), 34 (1967), pp. 9-16. ['Birger Mörner and His Collections in Örebro City Library'. Gives details of Count Birger Mörner's valuable collection of Sgiana, acquired during a friendship which lasted from 1890 until Sg's death. Wirde confirms that, as well as literary manuscripts, the collection includes several important personal items that have been previously published, sometimes in facsimile, in Mörner's memoir *Den Strindberg jag känt*, **R:1586**]

A3. Strindberg Editions

[*With the exception of the Eklund-Meidal edition of Sg's letters in 22 Volumes, almost every published collection of his works in both Sweden and abroad has provoked controversy, and been fraught with often hotly debated difficulties, both theoretical and organisational. As well as the composition of these editions, and the works which they might or might not include, there have been controversies regarding issues of translation (see also* **B4**), *and particularly the status of those works originally written by Sg in French which were subsequently translated into Swedish by another hand. In addition to scholarly reflections on their underlying principles, these debates, for example over the protracted publication of* Samlade Verk, *in 77 volumes or the assertion that Vilhelm Carlheim-Gyllensköld's mismanagement of Sg's literary estate is evident in his truncated two-volume edition of the* Samlade otryckta skrifter, *have given rise to numerous, usually short, articles, many of which are listed here. Other comments, including the criticism directed against John Landquist's Swedish translation of* Le Plaidoyer d'un fou *for* Samlade Skrifter, *are listed in section* **B4**, *on Translation, as are a few judgements on Emil Schering's influential German edition. Reviews of the dramatic fragments in Volume One of* Samlade otryckta skrifter *(*Collected Unpublished Writings*) are listed in section* **D2**, *devoted to general studies of the plays, but comments on the miscellaneous pieces in Volume Two are listed here. Reviews of more than one volume of works in different genres in* Samlade Verk *are also listed here, but reviews of individual volumes containing a single work are located in the section devoted to the relevant play, novel, or collection of verse. Reviews of volumes that contain more than one play are listed in* **D2**]

[A3:1] 'Abbé Coignard' [Pseudonym of Hjalmar Lundgren], 'Med anledning av - - -', *Göteborgs Handels- och Sjöfartstidning*, 4 February 1922. ['In View Of - - -'. Discusses Vilhelm Carlheim-Gyllensköld's controversial stewardship of Sg's literary remains and the publication of his unpublished writings]

[A3:2] Abendroth, Walter, 'Das Werk des Giganten. Eine notwendige deutsch Neuausgabe Strindbergs beginnt zu erscheinen', *Die Zeit* (Hamburg), 11 (1956), No. 26, p. 4. ['The Work of a Giant. A Necessary New German Edition of Strindberg has Begun to Appear'. On the 1955-59 German edition in nine volumes]

[A3:3] Ackerknecht, E[rwin], 'Das Inselmeer', *Bücherei und Bildungspflege* (Leipzig), 2 (1922), p. 181. ['Life in the Skerries'. Discusses Emil Schering's German edition of Sg's works, apropos the publication of a volume of short stories from *Skärkarlsliv*]

[A3:4] Ahlzén, R., 'Strindberg. *Samlade Verk*', *Nya Wermlands Tidningen* (Karlstad), 4 March 1987. [Reviews a newly published facsimile edition of John Landquist's edition of Sg's *Samlade Skrifter* (1912-20) in 55 volumes, together with its editorial apparatus including notes, commentary, and the description of Sg's, then, extant manuscripts]

[A3:5] A. J., 'Strindbergs samlade skrifter. Några anmärkningar', *Nya Dagligt Allehanda* (Stockholm), 20 October 1917. ['Strindberg's Collected Works. Some Comments'. Reflections on the editorial principles adopted by John Landquist in *Samlade Skrifter*]

[A3:6] Anderberg, Rolf, 'Strindberg. *Samlade Verk*', *Göteborgs-Posten*, 4 June 1981. [Reviews Volumes 2 (*I vårbrytningen*) and 6 (*Röda rummet*) in *Samlade Verk*]

[A3:7] Andersson, G., 'Strindberg. *Samlade Verk*', *Aftonbladet* (Stockholm), 7 November 1988. [Reviews Volumes 28 (*Kamraterna*), 44 (*Dödsdansen*), 46 (*Ett drömspel*), 48 (*Kristina* and *Gustav III*), and 68 (*Tal till svenska nationen*) in *Samlade Verk*]

[A3:8] Anon, 'Die neue Strindberg-Ausgabe', *Bücherschiff* (Frankfurt am Main), 8:9-9a (1958), p. 30. ['The New Strindberg Edition'. Reviews Volumes 6 to 8 in the nine-volume German edition of 1955-59]

[A3:9] Anon, 'His Countrymen Honor Strindberg', *The Book Buyer* (New York), 37 (February 1912), 6-8. [Reports on negotiations for an authoritative edition of Sg's works in Swedish have now been concluded. An authorised translation, including some of the best of the plays, is about to be published in America by Chas. Scribner's Sons (i.e. Edwin Björkman's edition)]

[A3:10] Anon, 'Strindberg', *Die Bücherkommentare* (Stuttgart), 8:1 (1959), p. 24. [Reviews Volumes 5 to 8 in the nine-volume, 1955-59, German edition]

[A3:11] Anon, 'Strindberg. *Samlade Verk*', *Aftonbladet* (Stockholm), 22 February 1990. [Reviews Volumes 20 (*Tjänstekvinnans son, I-II*) and 51 (*Ordalek och småkonst*) in *Samlade Verk*]

[A3:12] Anon, 'Strindberg. *Samlade Verk*', *Sydsvenska Dagbladet* (Malmö), 1 December 1983. [Reviews Volumes 12 (*Det nya riket*) and 40 (*Vid högre rätt*) in *Samlade Verk*]

[A3:13] Anon, 'Strindberg, A., *Sobranie sochinenii*, *Obrazovanie* (St Petersburg), 1908:5, pp. 112-114. [Reviews Volume One of *Polnoe sobranie sochinenii v 12 tomakh*, the uncompleted Sablin edition of Sg's collected works in twelve volumes, published in Moscow, 1908-1912. Comments on Sg's personal and intellectual links with Stanisław Przybyszewski and Nietzsche. E.783]

[A3:14] Anon, 'Strindberg, A., *Sobranie sochinenii*, *Russkoe bogatstvo* (St Petersburg), 1908:6, pp. 179-182. [Reviews Volume One of *Polnoe sobranie sochinenii v 15 tomakh*, the fifteen-volume Sovremennye problemy edition of Sg's collected works published in Moscow. Observes that Sg is of interest in that he has undergone a continuous process of development; he is always seeking something, is inspired by something. A gifted man and one of our time's most tendentious writers, he lacks his own ideas, continually changes his *Weltanschauung*, and is no genius. E.784]

[A3:15] Anon, 'Strindberg, A., *Sobranie sochinenii*, *Damskii mir* (St Petersburg), 1911:2, p. 39. [Reviews Volume 10 of *Polnoe sobranie sochinenii v 15 tomakh*, the fifteen-volume Sovremennye problemy edition of Sg's collected works, published in Moscow. E.823]

[A3:16] Anon, 'Strindberg, A., *Sobranie sochinenii*, *Russkoe bogatstvo* (St Petersburg), 1909:8, pp. 104-106. [Reviews Volume 3 of *Polnoe sobranie sochinenii v 12 tomakh*, the uncompleted Sablin edition of Sg's collected works in twelve volumes, published in Moscow, 1908-1912. E.805]

[A3:17] Attius, H., 'Strindberg. *Samlade Verk*', *Västerbottens Kuriren* (Umeå), 20 April 1989. [Reviews Volumes 28 (*Kamraterna*), 44 (*Dödsdansen*), 46 (*Ett drömspel*), 48 (*Kristina* and *Gustaf III*), and 68 (*Tal till svenska nationen*) in *Samlade Verk*]

[A3:18] Becher, H[ubert], 'Strindberg. Deutsche Ausgabe', *Stimmen der Zeit* (Freiburg), 164 (1958-59), p. 158. [Reviews Volumes 3 and 4 in the nine-volume German edition of 1955-59]

[A3:19] Berendsohn, Walter A[rthur], 'August Strindbergs Nachlass', *Neue Zürcher Zeitung* (Zürich), 13 February 1966. ['August Strindberg's Literary Remains']

[A3:20] Berendsohn, Walter A[rthur], 'Början till en ny tysk Strindbergsupplaga', *Meddelanden från Strindbergssällskapet* (Stockholm), 17 (1955), pp. 6-7. ['The Start of a New German Strindberg Edition'. Gives the background to a new German edition of Sg's principal works, to be published in Munich by Albert Langen-Georg Müller in nine-volumes]

[A3:21] Berendsohn, Walter A[rthur], 'Nya Strindbergsupplaga behövs. Men räcker århundradet till? Volym med textkritik!', *Svenska Dagbladet* (Stockholm), 13 March 1955. ['New Strindberg Edition Needed. But will the Century be Long Enough? Text Critical Volumes!']

[A3:22] Berendsohn, Walter A[rthur], 'Texten i Strindbergs Samlade Skrifter. Förslag till revision på grundval av bevarade manuskript', *Nysvenska studier* (Uppsala), 43:1 (1963), [5]-15. ['The Text of Strindberg's Collected Works. Suggestions for a Revision on the Basis of the Extant Manuscripts'. Outlines the principles which might form the basis for a new edition of Sg's *Samlade Skrifter*, taking newly available holographs into account. Discusses problems raised by punctuation, old pre-reform spellings, deletions, misreadings, and dubious passages with reference to manuscript material, and lists those works translated into Swedish by another hand from the original Danish, French, or German, which raise different, but equally difficult, questions]

[A3:23] Bergsten, Staffan, 'August Strindberg. *Legender* och *Svenska folket*', *Vestmanlands Läns Tidning* (Västerås), 15 October 2001. [Reviews Volumes 9 (*Svenska Folket I*) and 38 (*Legender*) in *Samlade Verk*]

[A3:24] Björck, Staffan, 'Strindberg. *Samlade Verk*', *Sydsvenska Dagbladet* (Malmö), 26 July 1981. [Reviews Volumes 2 (*I vårbrytningen*) and 6 (*Röda rummet*) in *Samlade Verk*]

[A3:25] Bladh, Curt, 'Strindberg. *Samlade Verk*', *Sundsvalls Tidning*, 9 February 1997. [Reviews Volumes 20 (*Tjänstekvinnans son I-II*), 22 (*Han och hon*), and 63 (*Den världshistoriska trilogin*) in *Samlade Verk*]

[A3:26] Boekhoff, Hermann, 'Zwei neue Strindberg-Band', *Westermanns Monatshefte* (Braunschweig), 98:4 (1957), p. 96. ['Two New Strindberg Volumes'. Reviews Volumes 3 and 4 in the nine-volume German edition of 1955-59]

[A3:27] Böök, Fredrik, '*Samlade otryckta skrifter. Del 2. Berättelser och dikter*', *Stockholms Dagblad*, 28 December 1919. [Reviews Volume Two of Vilhelm Carlheim-Gyllensköld's edition of Sg's posthumous works]

[A3:28] Böök, Fredrik, *Till ägarna av Strindbergs samlade skrifter*, Stockholm: Albert Bonniers Förlag, [1925], [4] pp. ['To the Owners of Strindberg's Collected Works'. A critique of John Landquist's editorial practice in his edition of Sg's *Samlade Skrifter*]

[A3:29] Brandell, Gunnar, 'Utgåvor av Strindberg', *Svenska Dagbladet* (Stockholm), 25 October 1966. ['Editions of Strindberg']

[A3:30] Brunius, Teddy, 'Strindberg. *Samlade Verk*', *Upsala Nya Tidning*, 10 January 1984. [Criticises several of the principles adopted for Sg's *Samlade Verk* under Lars Dahlbäck's general editorship]

[A3:31] Carlheim-Gyllensköld, Vilhelm, 'August Strindbergs otryckta skrifter', *Svenska Dagbladet* (Stockholm), 16 January 1920. ['August Strindberg's Unpublished Writings'. A response by Carlheim-Gyllensköld to John Landquist's criticism of his edition of Volume Two of Sg's posthumous works in **A3:101**]

[A3:32] Carlsson, Anni, 'Klassikerausgaben – kritisch betrachtet. Nur am Schreibtisch lebendig. August Strindberg: Dramatiker, Romancier, Lyriker, Soziologe, Maler', *Die Zeit* (Hamburg), 29 (1974), No. 47, p. 7. ['Editions of the Classics – Critically Examined. Only Alive when at his Desk. August Strindberg: Playwright, Novelist, Poet, Sociologist, Painter']

[A3:33] Chesnokova, T., '[Rebellious Magician]', *Literaturnoe obozrenie* (Moscow), 1987:1, pp. 74-76. [Reviews Volume One in a new two-volume Russian edition of Sg's selected works. See **B1:394**. E.1784]

[A3:34] Ciesielski, Zenon, 'Głos w dyskusji na konferencji w sprawie wydania pism zbiorowych Augusta Strindberga', *Acta Sueco-Polonica* (Uppsala), 5 (1996), [175]-176. [Sums up the discussion of a colloquium devoted to planning a ten-volume edition of Sg's works in Polish translation]

[A3:35] Cohn, Alfons Fedor, 'Strindbergs-Nachlass', *Deutsche allgemeine Zeitung*, 30 November 1920. ['Strindberg's Literary Remains'. Reviews Volume Two of Vilhelm Carlheim-Gyllensköld's edition of Sg's *Samlade otryckta skrifter*]

[A3:36] Dahlbäck, Lars, 'Enquist skjuter över målet', *Expressen* (Stockholm), 28 January 1986. ['Enquist Misses the Target'. A response to Per Olov Enquist in **A3:65**]

[A3:37] Dahlbäck, Lars, 'Konsten skall upplevas direkt', *Dagens Nyheter* (Stockholm), 12 November 1985. ['Art Should be Experienced Live'. Responds negatively to Douglas Feuk's suggestion that a volume of Sg's *Samlade Verk* should be devoted to reproductions of his paintings, **A3:68**]

[A3:38] Dahlbäck, Lars, 'The National Edition. A Presentation', in Kela Kvam, ed., **D2:158**, *Strindberg's Post-Inferno Plays*, pp. 9-18. [On the ongoing edition of Sg's *Samlade Verk*]

[A3:39] [Dahlbäck, Lars], 'The National Edition of Strindberg's Collected Works', *Nordic Theatre Studies* (Copenhagen), 6:1-2 (1993), p. 71. [A progress report on the publication of the ongoing edition of Sg's *Samlade Verk* by its general editor]

[A3:40] Dahlbäck, Lars, 'Nya upplagan av Samlade Skrifter', *Meddelanden från Strindbergssällskapet* (Stockholm), 57-58 (1977), pp. 14-21. ['New Edition of Collected Works'. Outlines the scope and editorial principles to be employed in the new edition of Sg's *Samlade Verk* and compares them with John Landquist's methods and achievement in *Samlade Skrifter*, not least where a work had to be translated from the French in which Sg originally wrote it]

[A3:41] Dahlbäck, Lars, 'Presentation av den nya Strindbergsupplagan på Strindbergssymposiet den 22 maj 1981', *Meddelanden från Strindbergssällskapet* (Stockholm), 66 (1982), pp. 19-24. ['A Presentation of the New Strindberg Edition at the Strindberg

Conference, 22 May 1981'. Outlines plans for the publication of the new edition of Sg's *Samlade Verk* and some of the text-critical principles on which it is based]

[A3:42] Dahlbäck, Lars, 'Presentation av Nationalupplagan och redogörelse för redigeringsprinciperna', in *Samlade Verk*, Stockholm: Norstedts, 1989, Vol. 1, pp. [275]-333. ['Presentation of the National Edition and an Account of its Editorial Principles'. Outlines the scope of the new edition of Sg's *Samlade Verk* and presents the editorial principles informing its approach to spelling, punctuation, and typography. Dahlbäck also explains the grounds for establishing what is an 'original' Strindberg text, as well as the nature of the editorial material which is to be included in each text volume as well as its supplementary companion volume]

[A3:43] Dahlbäck, Lars, 'Presentation av Nationalupplagan och redogörelse för redigeringsprinciperna', Särtryck ur del 1 (*Ungdomsdramer*), Stockholm: Norstedts, pp. 277-336. ['Presentation of the National Edition and an Account of its Editorial Principles'. Offprint of **A3:42**]

[A3:44] Dahlbäck, Lars, '[Strindbergs *Samlade Verk*]', *Expressen* (Stockholm), 19 November 1985. [Defends the scholarly principles underlying *Samlade Verk* and its necessarily slow rate of publication against Per Olov Enquist's attack on his editorship in **A3:65**]

[A3:45] Dahlbäck, Lars, 'Utgivningen av Strindbergs Samlade Verk. En lägesrapport våren 1984', *Meddelanden från Strindbergssällskapet* (Stockholm), 68 (1984), pp. 20-22. ['The Publication of Strindberg's Collected Works. A Progress Report, Spring 1984']

[A3:46] Dahlbäck, Lars, 'Strindberg au complet', Traduit du suédois par Régis Boyer, *Europe* (Paris), No. 858 (October 2000), pp. 218-223. ['The Complete Strindberg'. Presents the ongoing edition of Sg's *Samlade Verk* and highlights particular problems posed in the editing of his work]

[A3:47] Dahlbäck, Lars, 'Strindberg i nationalupplagan', *Tidskrift för litteraturvetenskap* (Lund), 13:2-3 (1984), 2-14. ['Strindberg in the National Edition'. Outlines the editorial principles employed in the new edition of Sg's *Samlade Verk* and comments on its aims and scope in comparison with John Landquist's edition of *Samlade Skrifter*]

[A3:48] Dahlbäck, Lars, 'Strindbergs ordvärld i Nationalupplagan', *Strindbergiana* (Stockholm), 8 (1993), pp. 30-47. ['Strindberg's Vocabulary in the National Edition'. Illustrates the extraordinary, polymathic breadth of Sg's vocabulary and the conclusions which may be drawn from this, as evidenced by the glossaries established in the course of editing the new edition of his *Samlade Verk*, and as regards the demands he placed on his readers concerning complex and sometimes obscure forms of expression, his continually shifting frames of reference, favourite expressions, and phrases in his works that have assumed proverbial status]

[A3:49] Dahlbäck, Lars, '"Trrrrrrrrrrrrrrrrrrrrrrrrrrråm!" Rapportering om August Strindbergs Samlade Verk och resonemang kring frågan: "Är det Strindbergs egen text som etableras i nationalupplagan?"', in Barbro Ståhle Sjönell, red., *Textkritik. Teori och praktik vid edering av litterära texter*, Stockholm: Svenska Vitterhetssamfundet/Almqvist & Wiksell International, 1991, pp. 99-112. ['"Trrrrrrrrrrrrrrrrrrrrrrrrrrrråm!" A Report on August Strindberg's Collected Works and the Arguments Regarding the Question: "Is it Strindberg's own Text which is Established in the National Edition?"' Examines the status of the text published in the ongoing edition of *Samlade Verk* and the extent to which it really is Sg's 'own', given its normalisation in the light of subsequent spelling reforms and the difficulty which editors sometimes encounter in referring to an 'original' source manuscript. Dahlbäck concludes that, in spite of numerous apparent compromises, the method adopted comes closest than any other to establishing Sg's 'own text' in an optimum fashion as regards not only the language but the punctuation and deviations between the manuscript and the first published edition, with or without any extant alterations in Sg's hand]

[**A3:50**] Delblanc, Sven, 'Riv inte upp en god grund! Om utgivningen av Strindberg's *Samlade Verk*', *Expressen* (Stockholm), 22 November 1985. ['Don't Destroy a Good Foundation! On the Publication of Strindberg's *Collected Works*'. Refutes criticisms levelled against the ongoing National Edition of Sg's works by Per Olov Enquist (see **A3:65**) and others]

[**A3:51**] Delblanc, Sven, 'Riv inte upp en god grund! Om utgivningen av Strindberg's *Samlade Verk*', in Lars Ahlbom and Björn Meidal, red., *Strindberg – urtida, samtida, framtida*, **B1:119**, pp. 236-237. ['Don't Destroy a Good Foundation! On the Publication of Strindberg's *Collected Works*'. Rpr. of **A3:50**]

[**A3:52**] Diederichsen, Diedrich, 'Deutsche Strindberg-Ausgabe', *Bücherei und Bildung* (Bremen), 14 (1962), Teil B, pp. 158-159. ['German Strindberg Edition'. Reviews Volumes Four to Nine in the nine-volume German edition of 1955-59]

[**A3:53**] Drews, Wolfgang, 'Er machte die Bühne zum Filmatelier. Zu einer neuen Strindberg-Ausgabe', *Sonntagsblatt* (Hannover), 2 June 1957, p. 8. ['He Made the Stage Into a Film Studio. On a New Strindberg Edition'. Reviews Volumes One to Four in the nine-volume German edition of 1955-59]

[**A3:54**] Ek, Sverker, '*Samlade otryckta skrifter. I-II*', *Ny tid* (Göteborg), 6 December 1919. [Reviews Vilhelm Carlheim-Gyllensköld's two-volume collection of Sg's unpublished writings]

[**A3:55**] Ek. Hn. [Erik Hedén], 'En stor Strindbergsupplaga. Första häftet utkommet', *Social-Demokraten* (Stockholm), 31 May 1912. ['A Major Strindberg Edition. The First Part Has Appeared'. Reviews the first volume in John Landquist's edition of *Samlade Skrifter*]

[**A3:56**] Ek. Hn. [Erik Hedén], 'Hur utges Strindbergs samlade skrifter?', *Social-Demokraten* (Stockholm), 12 October 1912. ['How are Strindberg's Collected Works being Published?' Questions several of the principles on which John Landquist has based his edition of Sg's *Samlade Skrifter*. See Landquist's response, **A3:106**]

[**A3:57**] Ek. Hn. [Erik Hedén], 'Litteraturen: Strindbergslitteraturen 3. Bortglömt och återupplivat. Samlade Skrifter del 54', *Social-Demokraten* (Stockholm), 19 July 1920. ['Strindberg Literature 3. Forgotten and Brought Back to Life'. Reviews *Efterslåtter*, a collection of previously uncollected or unpublished pieces published as Volume 55 in John Landquist's edition of Sg's *Samlade Skrifter*]

[**A3:58**] Ek. Hn. [Erik Hedén], 'Litteraturen: Strindbergslitteraturen 4', *Social-Demokraten* (Stockholm), 20 July 1920.

[**A3:59**] Ek. Hn. [Erik Hedén], 'Svar på John Landquist', *Social-Demokraten* (Stockholm), 21 October 1912. ['Reply to John Landquist'. A response to Landquist's comments in **A3:106** on his previous criticism of the latter's editorial practice]

[**A3:60**] Ekman, Hans-Göran, 'Reflexioner inför den polska Strindbergsupplagan', *Acta Sueco-Polonica* (Uppsala), 5 (1996), [167]-170. ['Reflections on the Forthcoming Polish

Strindberg Edition'. Considers problems of translation and selection confronting the planned Polish edition of Sg's works in ten volumes]

[**A3:61**] Elschenbroich, Adalbert, 'Deutsche Strindberg-Ausgabe', *Bücherei und Bildung* (Bremen), 11 (1959), Teil B, pp. 11-12. ['German Strindberg Edition'. Reviews two volumes in the nine-volume German edition of 1955-59]

[**A3:62**] Engström, Albert, 'Ett inlägg', *Strix* (Stockholm), 8 February 1922. ['A Contribution'. Defends Vilhelm Carlheim-Gyllensköld against the criticism he has received from John Landquist and others about his stewardship of Sg's extant manuscripts and other literary remains]

[**A3:63**] Engwall, Gunnel, 'Litteraturen och kulturarvet: bokens roll', in *Forskningens roll i offensiv kulturarvsvård: rapport från ett seminarium 14 november 1996*, Stockholm: Riksbankens jubileumsfond, 1997, pp. 67-88. ['Literature and Our Cultural Heritage: The Role of the Book'. Discusses the publication of the 'National Edition' of Sg's works, or *Samlade Verk*, and its cultural significance]

[**A3:64**] Enquist, Per Olov, 'Farhågår inför beslutet i dag om nationalutgåvan', *Expressen* (Stockholm), 20 February 1986. ['Misgivings Concerning Today's Impending Decision about the National Edition']

[**A3:65**] Enquist, Per Olov, 'Om ämbetsverk för utgivandet av August Strindbergs nationalutgåva: en skandal', *Expressen* (Stockholm), 14 November 1985. ['On the Official Department for the Publication of August Strindberg's National Edition'. Using a title derived from Sg's satire of bureaucracy in *Röda rummet*, Enquist declares the ongoing edition of *Samlade Verk* to be both a scholarly and a financial scandal, thus initiating a long and acrimonious debate about the (lack of) progress and principles of the edition in the Swedish press. His article prompts immediate responses in *Expressen* and elsewhere from (among others) Lars Dahlbäck, **A3:36**, Gunnar Ollén, **A3:133**, Sven Delblanc, **A3:50**, Lars Forsell, **A3:69**, Lars-Olof Franzén, **A3:70**, Hans Lindström, **A3:120**, Anders Isaksson, **A3:92**, Harry Järv, **A3:93**, Bengt Landgren, **A3:98**, Björn Håkonsson, **A3:84**, Lotta Meurling, **A3:128**, Barbro Ståhle Sjönell, **A3:155**, and Sven Axel Holm, **A3:89**, as well as leading articles in *Dagens Nyheter* (15/12/85) and *Svenska Dagbladet* (3/2 and 18/2/86)]

[**A3:66**] Erkhov, B[oris] A[leksandrovich], 'Strindberg v Rossii', *Diapazon: Vesti inostrannoi literatury*, 1995:1, pp. 99-112. ['Strindberg in Russia'. Reviews Aleksandra Aleksandrovna Afinogenova's translation of *Ett drömspel* and other works, published by Start in Moscow, in 1994. E.17980]

[**A3:67**] Felner, Karl von, 'August Strindbergs Werke. Deutsche Gesamtausgabe', *Der Merker* (Vienna), 7 (1916), 142-145. ['August Strindberg's Works. German Collected Edition'. Reviews Emil Schering's edition of Sg's works]

[**A3:68**] Feuk, Douglas, 'Om nationalutgåvan av Strindbergs verk. In med målningarna!', *Dagens Nyheter* (Stockholm), 12 October 1985. ['On the National Edition of Strindberg's Works. In with the Paintings!' Maintains that a volume containing reproductions of Sg's paintings ought to included in *Samlade Verk* if the new edition of his works is to be truly complete. See Lars Dahlbäck's response, **A3:37**]

[**A3:69**] Forssell, Lars, '[Strindbergs *Samlade Verk*]', *Expressen* (Stockholm), 29 November 1985. [Rebuts academic criticism of Per Olov Enquist for his attack on the pedantry and lack of urgency afflicting publication of the National Edition of Sg's works in **A3:65**]

[A3:70] Franzén, Lars-Olof, '[Strindbergs *Samlade Verk*]', *Dagens Nyheter* (Stockholm), 20 January 1986. [Criticises what Franzén considers is the excessive scholarship in the National Edition of Sg's *Samlade Verk*, and applauds Per Olov Enquist's critique in **A3:65**]

[A3:71] Fritje [or Friche] V., 'A. Strindberg, '*Sobranie sochinenii*, *Sovremennyi mir* (St Petersburg), 1910:2, pp. 127-129. [Reviews Volume 8 of *Polnoe sobranie sochinenii v 15 tomakh*, the fifteen-volume edition of Sg's works published in Moscow by Sovremennye problemy. E.818]

[A3:72] G. C. [Gunnar Castrén], 'Ur Strindbergs kvarlåtenskap', *Nya Argus* (Helsingfors), 13:4 (16 February 1920), 39-41. ['From Strindberg's Literary Remains'. Reviews Volume Two of Vilhelm Carlheim-Gyllensköld's edition of Sg's 'only modestly interesting' posthumous works, as well as the appearance in *Samlade Skrifter* of the previously unpublished epistolary novel, *Han och hon*, which is closely based on Sg's correspondence with Siri von Essen. Castrén finds this somewhat tiresome reading, even though it bears traces of the Sg one knows from his later works and fortunes]

[A3:73] Geiger, Hannsludwig, 'Das Bleibende', *Evangelische Literarturbeobachter* (Düsseldorf), 1955, p. 387. ['What Lasts'. Reviews Volumes One and Two in the nine-volume German edition of 1955-59]

[A3:74] Gellerstam, Martin, and Sven-Göran Malmgren, 'Strindbergska fingeravtryck i anonyma tidningsartiklar från 1870-talet', in Barbro Ståhle Sjönell, red., *Textkritik. Teori och praktik vid edering av litterära texter*, Stockholm: Svenska Vitterhetssamfundet / Almqvist & Wiksell International, 1991, pp. 138-155. ['Strindbergian Fingerprints in Anonymous Newspaper Articles from the 1870s'. Presents the principles underlying the linguistic analysis of anonymous articles in the Swedish press during the 1870s in order to determine if they might be attributed to Sg and hence included in *Samlade Verk*. Discusses the problems this entails and includes two samples from *Morgonbladet* and *Dagens Nyheter*]

[A3:75] Go., 'Ahnherr der Moderne', *Bücherkommentare* (Stuttgart), 4:4 (1955), p. 16. ['Forefather of the Modern'. Reviews Volumes One and Two in the nine-volume German edition of 1955-59]

[A3:76] Gofman, V., 'Strindberg, A., *Sobranie sochinenii*, *Rech*' (St Petersburg), No. 147 (1 June 1909), p. 3. [Reviews Volume 6 in the *Polnoe sobranie sochinenii v 15 tomakh* edition of Sg's works, published in Moscow by Sovremennye problemy. E.796]

[A3:77] Victor G., [Viktor Gofman], 'Strindberg, A., *Sobranie sochinenii*, *Rech* (St Petersburg), No. 203 (27 July 1909), p. 3. [Reviews Volume Seven in the *Polnoe sobranie sochinenii v 15 tomakh* edition of Sg's works, published in Moscow by Sovremennye problemy. E.795]

[A3:78] Gofman, V., 'Strindberg, A., *Sobranie sochinenii*' *Rech*' (St Petersburg), 22 March 1910, p. 3. [Reviews Volume Ten in the *Polnoe sobranie sochinenii v 15 tomakh* edition of Sg's works, published in Moscow by Sovremennye problemy. E.813]

[A3:79] Granberg, Nils, 'Strindberg förvanskas', *Aftonbladet* (Stockholm), 27 November 1994. ['Strindberg Mutilated'. Criticises the editorial principles underlying Volumes 5 (*Mäster Olof*) and 50 (*Klostret*) in the National Edition of Sg's *Samlade Verk*]

[A3:80] Granberg, Nils, 'Strindberg förvanskas', *Folket i bild/Kulturfront* (Stockholm), 1994:11-12, p. 29. [Rpr. of **A3:79**]

[A3:81] Granvik, Margot, 'Forskare och poliser letar äkta Strindberg', *Grafia* (Malmö), 1991:9, pp. 10-11. ['Researchers and Police Seek a Genuine Strindberg'. Interviews Lars Dahlbäck about some of the methods employed in establishing an authentic text for Sg's works in *Samlade Verk*, including the use of infra-red techniques normally employed in police investigations in order to determine the identity of the handwriting in which alterations have sometimes been made to Sg's original manuscript]

[A3:82] Gruszczyńska, Ewa, 'Głos w dyskusji', *Acta Sueco-Polonica* (Uppsala), 5 (1996), [177]-180. [Sums up the conclusions of contributors to a conference about a projected Polish edition of Sg's works in ten volumes]

[A3:83] Gustafsson, Lars, 'Strindberg', *Nerikes Allehanda* (Örebro), 30 January 1990. [Reviews Volumes 20 (*Tjänstekvinnans son, I-II*) and 51 (*Ordalek och småkonst*) in *Samlade Verk*]

[A3:84] Håkanson, Björn, 'Befria oss från Strindbergsterrorn!', *Aftonbladet* (Stockholm), 28 January 1986. ['Free Us from the Strindberg Terror!' An irritated comment regarding the debate provoked by Per Olov Enquist's critique of the ongoing edition of Sg's *Samlade Verk*. According to Håkanson, Sweden needs worthwhile editions of many other authors, apart from Sg]

[A3:85] Hartmann, Jacob W., 'August Strindberg – *Samlade Skrifter*', *American-Scandinavian Review* (New York), 2 (1914), p. 50. ['August Strindberg – Collected Works'. Comments on John Landquist's ongoing edition of Sg's *Samlade Skrifter*]

[A3:86] Hedén, Erik, 'Hur utges Strindbergs Samlade Skrifter?', in Solveig Landquist, red., **B1:248**, *John Landquist om Strindberg, personen och diktaren*, pp. 70-72. ['How are Strindberg's Collected Works being Published?' Rpr. of **A3:56**]

[A3:87] Hermann, Rudolf, 'Kleines format – gute Prosa', *Die Zeit* (Hamburg), 12 (1957), No. 39, p. 8. ['Small Format – Fine Prose'. Reviews Volume Five in the nine-volume German edition of 1955-59]

[A3:88] Hohenberg, Volker, 'Eine neue Strindberg-Ausgabe', *Westermanns Monatshefte* (Braunschweig), 97:3 (1956), pp. 90, 92. ['A New Strindberg Edition'. Reviews Volumes One and Two in the nine-volume German edition of 1955-59]

[A3:89] Holm, Sven Axel, '[Strindbergs *Samlade Verk*]', *Dagens Nyheter* (Stockholm), 26 February 1986. [A news report concerning a letter to the Minister of Culture from a group of German professors and lecturers which argues for the continuation of *Samlade Verk* in its present form. See **A3:65**]

[A3:90] Holmqvist, Ivo, *Östgöta Correspondenten* (Linköping), 18 February 1987. [Reviews a new facsimile impression of John Landquist's edition of *Samlade Skrifter* (1912-20) in 55 volumes]

[A3:91] Ilovlev, N., 'Strindberg, A., *Ispoved' gluptsa*', *Sovremennyi mir* (St Petersburg), 1908:5, pp. 105-107. [Reviews Volume One in the *Polnoe sobranie sochinenii* edition of Sg's works *v 15 tomakh*, published in Moscow by Sovremennye problemy. Compares Sg with Dostoevskii and displays unusual perception in recognising the existence, rarely observed in Sweden, of a distinction between Sg's narrator and his narrative in the apparently autobiographical *En dåres försvarstal*. E.779]

[A3:92] Isaksson, Anders, '[Strindbergs *Samlade Verk*]', *Expressen* (Stockholm), 20 December 1985. [Prompted by Per Olov Enquist in **A3:65**]

[A3:93] Järv, Harry, 'Strindbergs *Samlade Verk*', *Expressen* (Stockholm), 20 December1985. [Defends Lars Dahlbäck against Per Olov Enquist's critique in **A3:65**. He is 'clearly the only person capable of carrying out this ill-fated enterprise']

[A3:94] Johansson, Gotthard, '*Samlade otryckta skrifter. Del 2. Berättelser och dikter*', *Afton-Tidningen* (Stockholm), 1 February 1920. [Reviews the second part of Vilhelm Carlheim-Gyllensköld's two-volume collection of Sg's unpublished works]

[A3:95] Johansson, Gotthard, 'Strindbergs Samlade Skrifter. Prosabitar från 1890-talet. Några anmärkningar om utgivandet', *Göteborgs Handels- och Sjöfartstidning*, 6 March 1918. ['Strindberg's Collected Works. Prose Pieces from the 1890s. Some Remarks on the Edition'. Discusses the format of a volume which contains numerous miscellaneous essays and short prose pieces, including several examples of Sg's occult and scientific writings, most of them originally published in French and gathered together here in book form in Swedish for the first time]

[A3:96] Johnson, Walter [Gilbert], 'August Strindberg, *I vårbrytningen*, *Röda rummet*, *Svenska öden och äventyr*', *Scandinavica* (Norwich), 22:1 (1983), 84-85. [Reviews the first volumes to be published in the new edition of Sg's *Samlade Verk*, under the general editorship of Lars Dahbäck]

[A3:97] Jönsson, U., 'Strindbergs Samlade Skrifter', *Arbetarbladet* (Gävle), 2 December 1982. [Reviews Volumes 16 (*Giftas*) and 31 (*I havsbandet*) in *Samlade Verk*]

[A3:98] Landgren, Bengt, 'Strindbergsutgåvans kvalitet måste bibehållas!', *Upsala Nya Tidning*, 27 January 1986. ['The Quality of the Strindberg Edition must be Retained!'. Counters Hans Lindström's critique of *Samlade Verk* in **A3:121**, and argues in favour of retaining scrupulous scholarly standards in the new National Edition of Sg's works]

[A3:99] Landquist, John, 'Anmärkningar', in *Ungdomsdramer*, Stockholm: Albert Bonniers Förlag, 1912, pp. 329–330. [Comments on the general editorial principles observed by Landquist in Volume One of his edition of Sg's *Samlade Skrifter*]

[A3:100] Landquist, John, 'Anmärkningar', in *Ungdomsdramer*, Stockholm: Albert Bonniers Förlag, 1919, pp. 329–335. [An extended comment in the 1919 reprint of Volume One of Sg's *Samlade Skrifter*, which clarifies the general editorial principles Landquist has observed in editing Sg's texts. Retained in the second edition of 1924]

[A3:101] Landquist, John, 'August Strindbergs "Otryckta" skrifter – tryckta? En kuriös edition av prof. Carlheim-Gyllensköld', *Stockholms-Tidningen*, 21 December 1919. ['August Strindberg's "Unpublished" Writings – Published? A Curious Edition from Prof. Carlheim-Gyllensköld'. Criticises Volume Two of Carlheim-Gyllensköld's edition of Sg's literary remains. See the latter's response in **A3:31**]

[A3:102] Landquist, John, 'August Strindbergs "Otryckta" skrifter – tryckta? En kuriös edition av prof. Carlheim-Gyllensköld', in Solveig Landquist, red., **B1:248**, *John Landquist om Strindberg, personen och diktaren*, pp. 79-84. [Rpr. of **A3:101**]

[A3:103] Landquist, John, 'Den fiktiva Strindbergsmuseet. Prof. V. Carlheim-Gyllensköld hindrar studium av papperen', *Dagens Nyheter* (Stockholm), 26 March 1918. ['The Fictional Strindberg Museum. Prof. V. Carlheim-Gyllensköld Obstructs the Study of the Papers'. Criticises Carlheim-Gyllensköld's stewardship of Sg's literary remains and the obstacles which, according to Landquist, he has placed in the way of those who require access to them for purposes of research]

[A3:104] Landquist, John, 'Liv och ord hörde samman för Strindberg – men han förblev en dålig korrekturläsare', *Aftonbladet* (Stockholm), 9 May 1962. ['Life and Words Belonged Together for Strindberg, But He Remained a Poor Proofreader'. Landquist considers the consequences which Sg's often inadequate proofreading of the original editions of his works have had for the editing of his *Samlade Skrifter*, with examples. He also comments on the decorative additions and marginalia with which he decorated some of his manuscripts]

[A3:105] Landquist, John, 'Liv och ord hörde samman för Strindberg – men han förblev en dålig korrekturläsare', in Solveig Landquist, red., **B1:248**, *John Landquist om Strindberg, personen och diktaren*, pp. 101-104. ['Life and Words Belonged Together for Strindberg, But He Remained a Poor Proofreader'. Rpr. of **A3:104** above]

[A3:106] Landquist, John, 'Om utgivningen av Strindbergs Samlade Skrifter. Ett svar från dr John Landquist', *Social-Demokraten* (Stockholm), 21 October 1912. ['On the Publication of Strindberg's Collected Works. A Reply from Dr. John Landquist'. A response to Erik Hedin, **A3:56**, who replies in turn with **A3:59**]

[A3:107] Landquist, John, 'Om utgivningen av Strindbergs Samlade Skrifter. Ett svar från dr John Landquist', in Solveig Landquist, red., **B1:248**, *John Landquist om Strindberg, personen och diktaren*, pp. 73-76. [Rpr. of **A3:106** together with the text of Hedén's response, **A3:56**, pp. 76-78]

[A3:108] Landquist, John, 'Strindbergs posthuma dramer', *Litteraturen. Nordens kritiske revue* (Copenhagen), 1 (1918-19), 716-719. ['Strindberg's Posthumous Plays'. Reviews Volume One of Vilhelm Carlheim-Gyllensköld's collection of Sg's unpublished works, implicitly critical of its editor whom Landquist refers to as merely 'the keeper of the papers' (papperens vårdare)]

[A3:109] Landquist, John, 'Strindbergs posthuma dramer, in Solveig Landquist, red., **B1:248**, *John Landquist om Strindberg, personen och diktaren*, pp. 217-221. ['Strindberg's Posthumous Plays'. Rpr. of **A3:108**]

[A3:110] Landsträsser, Ludwig, 'Neue Strindberg-Bände', *Westermanns Monatshefte* (Braunschweig), 99:12 (1958), pp. 96, 98. [Reviews Volumes Five to Eight in the nine-volume German edition of 1955-59]

[A3:111] Langer, Felix, 'Literarischer Unfug', *Die Wage* (Vienna), 22 (1919), 769-771. ['Literary Nonsense'. Comments on a dispute between the Georg Müller Verlag and Hyperion Verlag over a collected edition of Sg's works in German and compares their respective publications]

[A3:112] Levander, Hans, 'Strindberg', *Svenska Dagbladet* (Stockholm), 23 July 1981. [Reviews Volumes 2 (*I vårbrytningen*) and 6 (*Röda rummet*) in *Samlade Verk*]

[A3:113] Levander, Hans, 'Strindberg', *Svenska Dagbladet* (Stockholm), 3 June 1984. [Reviews Volumes 27 (*Fadren*, *Fröken Julie*, and *Fordringsägare*), 40 (*Advent* and *Brott och brott*), and 55 (*Taklagsöl* and *Syndabocken*) in *Samlade Verk*]

[A3:114] Levander, Hans, 'Strindberg', *Svenska Dagbladet* (Stockholm), 6 February 1985. [Reviews Volumes 26 (*Skärkarlsliv*) and 33 (*Nio enaktare* – Nine One-Acters) in *Samlade Verk*]

[A3:115] Levander, Hans, 'Strindberg', *Svenska Dagbladet* (Stockholm), 27 December 1988. [Reviews Volumes 28 (*Kamraterna*), 44 (*Dödsdansen*), 46 (*Ett drömspel*), 48 (*Kristina* and *Gustav III*), and 68 (*Tal till svenska nationen*) in *Samlade Verk*]

[A3:116] Levander, Hans, 'Strindberg', *Svenska Dagbladet* (Stockholm), 14 May 1990. [Reviews Volumes 20 (*Tjänstekvinnans son, I-II*) and 51 (*Ordalek och småkonst*) in *Samlade Verk* and Erik Wijk's selection from Sg's correspondence, **J:379**]

[A3:117] Levinson, A., 'Strindberg, A., *Sobranie sochinenii*, *Sovremennyi mir* (St Petersburg), 1911:7, pp. 336-339. [Reviews Volume Nine in the *Polnoe sobranie sochinenii v 15 tomakh* edition of Sg's works, published in Moscow by Sovremennye problemy. E.821]

[A3:118] Lindstedt, Torvald, 'Anteckningar om Strindberg som korrekturläsare', *Nysvenska studier* (Uppsala), 8 (1928), [30]-42. ['Observations on Strindberg as a Proof Reader'. Exemplifies Sg's occasional lack of care as a proof reader, with detailed reference to manuscript material. Lindstedt discusses the nature of the changes introduced by Sg in proof, notably his concern to avoid lexical repetition and the numerous alterations he made to grammatical structures, word order, and diction. He concludes that Sg evidently paid much greater attention to small details and grammatical correctness than has hitherto been supposed]

[A3:119] Lindström, Hans, 'Att ge ut Strindberg', *Tvärsnitt* (Uppsala), 1983:3, pp. 10-17. ['Publishing Strindberg']

[A3:120] Lindström, Hans, '[*Samlade Verk*]', *Expressen* (Stockholm), 11 December 1985. [Declares the lack of progress in publishing the National Edition to be 'nothing short of catastrophic'. Apropos Per Olov Enquist's attack on Lars Dahlbäck in **A3:65**]

[A3:121] Lindström, Hans, '[*Samlade Verk*]', *Upsala Nya Tidning*, 23 January 1986. [Takes issue with an open letter from Sweden's professors of literary history, Nordic languages, and Swedish to Kulturrådet in Stockholm, in which they voice their unease at the possibility of a reduction in the scholarly standards presently employed in editing the National Edition of Sg's *Samlade Verk*. See **A3:98**]

[A3:122] Lippold, M., 'Strindbergs *Samlade Skrifter*', *Kvällsposten* (Malmö), 9 March 1987. [Reviews a new, facsimile impression of John Landquist's edition of *Samlade Skrifter*]

[A3:123] Lisinski, Stewfan, 'Slitsamt bearbeta Strindberg. Stormig strid inför nyutgivning', *Bohuslänningen* (Uddevalla), 28 June 1986. ['Tough-Going Reworking Strindberg. Violent Conflict Over the New Edition'. Surveys the controversy surrounding the publication of the new Swedish edition of Sg's *Samlade Verk* initiated by Per Olov Enquist in **A3:65**]

[A3:124] Lundberg, E., 'Ny Strindberg', *Hallandsposten* (Halmstad), 16 November 1988. [Reviews Volumes 28 (*Kamraterna*), 44 (*Dödsdansen*), 46 (*Ett drömspel*), 48 (*Kristina* and *Gustav III*), and 68 (*Tal till svenska nationen*) in *Samlade Verk*]

[A3:125] Malakhieva-Mirovich, V., 'Strindberg, A., *Sobranie sochinenii*, *Russkaia mysl'* (Moscow), 1909:7, pp. 163-164. [Reviews Volume 3 of *Polnoe sobranie sochinenii v 12 tomakh*, published in Moscow by Sablin, and Volumes 5-6 of *Polnoe sobranie sochinenii v 15 tomakh*, also published in Moscow by Sovremennye problemy. E.800]

[A3:126] Mortensen, Johan [Martin], '*Samlade otryckta skrifter. Del 2. Berättelser och dikter*', *Sydsvenska Dagbladet* (Malmö), 5 January 1920. [Reviews Volume Two of Vilhelm Carlheim-Gyllensköld's edition of Sg's posthumous works]

[A3:127] Mortensen, Johan [Martin], '*Samlade otryckta skrifter. Del 2. Berättelser och dikter*', *Forum* (Stockholm), 7 (1920), 49-59. [Reviews Volume Two of Vilhelm Carlheim-Gyllensköld's edition of Sg's unpublished works and the previously unpublished epistolary novel, *Han och hon*, which draws upon Sg's correspondence with Siri von Essen in *Samlade Skrifter*]

[A3:128] Meurling, Lotta, and Nils Gärdegård, 'Strindbergs *Samlade Verk*', *Sundsvalls Tidning*, 19 November 1985. [A response to Per Olov Enquist's critique in **A3:65**. 'We suspect that P. O. Enquist himself...is the real threat to serious work on Sg. First P.O.E. uses his television series to try and convince Swedes that Sg's primary achievement was as a womaniser, and now he tries to shunt critical authority [i.e. Lars Dahlbäck] aside, thus mangling both the National Edition and Sg's texts']

[A3:129] Muradian, K[atarin], '[Despite Madness and Delusions]', *Inostrannaia literatura* (Moscow), 1 (1987), pp. 237-239. [Reviews the first in a new two-volume Russian edition of Sg's selected works. See **B1:394**. E.1780]

[A3:130] Muradian, K[atarin], *Obshchestvennye nauki v SSSR RZh. Seriia 7. Literaturovedenie* (Moscow), 2, (1987), 116-121. [Reviews the first in a new two-volume Russian edition of Sg's selected works. See **B1:394**. E.1782]

[A3:131] N. E. [Nils Erdmann], '*Samlade otryckta skrifter. Del 2. Berättelser och dikter*', *Nya Dagligt Allehanda* (Stockholm), 24 December 1919. [Reviews Volume Two of Vilhelm Carlheim-Gyllensköld's edition of Sg's posthumous works]

[A3:132] Neuger, Leonard, 'Zamknięcie i otwarcie. Refleksje na temat 10-tomowej edycji *Dzieł wybranych* Strindberga', *Acta Sueco-Polonica* (Uppsala), 5 (1996), [141]-150. ['Closing and Opening Remarks'. Summary reflections on the scope and editorial principles for adoption in a proposed ten-volume collection of Sg's works in Polish translation]

[A3:133] Ollén, Gunnar, 'Strindberg *Samlade Verk*', *Expressen* (Stockholm), 19 November 1985. [Defends the editorial principles underlying the National Edition of Sg's Collected Works and consequently the necessarily slow pace with which it has been published, in response to the criticism expressed by Per Olov Enquist in **A3:65**]

[A3:134] Österling, Anders, 'Neue Strindberg-Dokument, *Frankfurter Zeitung*, 28 March 1920. ['New Strindberg Documents'. Translation of **A3:135** by Marie Franzos]

[A3:135] Österling, Anders, 'Nya Strindbergs dokument', *Svenska Dagbladet* (Stockholm), 14 December 1919. ['New Strindberg Documents'. Reviews Volume Two of Vilhelm Carlheim-Gyllensköld's edition of Sg's posthumous works and the belated first publication of Sg's correspondence with Siri von Essen as the epistolary novel, *Han och hon*, in *Samlade Skrifter*]

[A3:136] Ottelin, Odal, 'Utgifvandet af bortgångna författares verk', *Svenska Dagbladet* (Stockholm), 2 October 1912. ['The Publication of Deceased Writers' Works']

[A3:137] Palmqvist, Bertil, 'Strindberg, *Samlade* Verk', *Arbetet* (Malmö), 21 January 1999. [Reviews Volumes 42 and 56 in *Samlade Verk*, and Magnus Florin, red., *Köra och vända*, **A2:36**]

[A3:138] Paul, Fritz, 'August Strindberg, *Werke in zeitlicher Folge, Frankfurter Ausgabe*, Hg. A. Gundlach, 12 Bde, 1984ff., Bde. 4, 5, 10', *Skandinavistik* (Kiel), 18:2 (1988), 147-152. [Reviews three volumes in the Frankfurt edition of Sg's collected works under the general editorship of Angelica Gundlach]

[A3:139] Paul, Fritz, 'August Strindberg, *Werke in zeitlicher Folge. Frankfurter Ausgabe*. 1984-1992', *Skandinavistik* (Kiel), 25:2 (1995), 166-168. [Reviews Volume Eight of the

Frankfurt edition of Sg's collected works, edited in two parts by Wolfgang Pasche, **B2:306**. Paul also extends a valedictory comment on this aborted project as a whole]

[A3:140] Persson, Anita, 'Strindberg återerövrad', *Socialistisk debatt* (Stockholm), 1982:3-4. ['Strindberg Reclaimed'. On the publication of Sg's *Samlade Verk*]

[A3:141] 'Qvidam Qvidamsson' [Pseudonym of Nils Peter Svensson], 'Strindbergs Efterladenskaber', *Politiken* (Copenhagen), 27 August 1920. ['Strindberg's Literary Remains'. Reviews Vilhelm Carlheim-Gyllensköld's two-volume edition of Sg's posthumously published works]

[A3:142] R. E. [P. D. Ettinger], '[Strindberg's Posthumous Works]', *Vestnik teatra* (Moscow), 1919:6 (15-16 February), p. 6. [Reviews Volume One of Vilhelm Carlheim-Gyllensköld's edition of Sg's unpublished writings. E.888]

[A3:143] Retz, Rolf E. Du, 'Några synpunkter på Strindbergs-projektet', *Text* (Uppsala), 2:4 (1983), 202-220. ['Some Views on the Strindberg Project'. Scrutinises the text-critical principles adopted in the ongoing edition of Sg's *Samlade Verk*]

[A3:144] Rismondo, Piero, 'Strindbergs Leben – ein Drama von Strindberg', *Wort und Wahrheit* (Freiburg im Breisgau), 12 (1957), 476-477. ['Strindberg's Life – A Drama By Strindberg'. Reviews Volumes Three and Four in the nine-volume German edition of 1955-59 in progress]

[A3:145] 'Rosidor' [Gösta Langenfelt], 'Strindbergspapperen nu på bordet', *Social-Demokraten* (Stockholm), 1 February 1922. ['Strindberg's Papers now Out'. On Vilhelm Carlheim-Gyllensköld's management of Sg's literary remains and the publication of Volume Two of his edition of Sg's unpublished works]

[A3:146] Rüdiger, Horst, 'Pflege der Tradition', *Schweizer Monatshefte* (Zürich), 37 (1957-58), 425-431. ['Maintaining Tradition'. Reviews two volumes in the nine-volume German edition of 1955-59]

[A3:147] Scheffer, Thassilo von, 'Strindbergs Werke', *Xenien* (Leipzig), 1:2 (1908), 370-372. ['Strindberg's Works'. On Volumes One to Four of Emil Schering's German edition of Sg's collected works]

[A3:148] Seekamp, Hans-Jürgen, 'Deutsche Strindberg-Ausgabe', *Die neue Schau* (Kassel), 18 (1957), p. 26. ['German Strindberg Edition'. Reviews Volumes One and Two in the nine-volume German edition of 1955-59]

[A3:149] Shevelev, I., '[The Son of the End of the Century: Our Predecessor In Human Passion]', *Nezavisimaia gazeta* (Moscow), 11 June 1994. [Reviews Aleksandra Aleksandrovna Afinogenova's new translation of *Ett drömspel* and other works, with an introduction by Lars Kleberg, one in a two-volume selection published by Start in Moscow]

[A3:150] Sokół, Lech, 'Uwagi na temat planowanego wydania dziel Augusta Strindberga', *Acta Sueco-Polonica* (Uppsala), 5 (1996), [171]-174. [Reflections on a projected Polish edition of Sg's works in ten volumes]

[A3:151] Spens, James, 'Ordförklaringar. Om teori och praktik i Strindbergsutgivningen', in Johnny Kondrup og Karsten Kynde, red., *Megen viden i forskellige hoveder*, Nordisk Nätverk för Editionsfilologer Skrifter 2, København: C. A. Reitzels Forlag, 2000, 188-201. ['Definitions. On Theory and Practice in the Strindberg Edition'. Presents the arguments for and against the practice adopted by the editors of *Samlade Verk* in establishing the list of words which qualify for explicatory definition in every one of the edition's volumes. These include proper nouns of a biographical, historical, or geographical nature, as well as words in dialect and other languages or unfamiliar terms, specialised scientific vocabulary, and dialectal and archaic forms]

[A3:152] St., 'Strindberg, A., *Sobranie sochinenii*, *Bessarabskaia zhizn*' (Kishinev), No. 148 (9 July 1911), p. 5. [Reviews the last two volumes of the Russian edition, *Polnoe sobranie sochinenii v 15 tomakh*, published in Moscow by Sovremennye problemy. E.824]

[A3:153] Ståhle Sjönell, Barbro, 'Att ge ut noveller', Anförande vid Svenska Vitterhetssamfundets årsmöte den 2 maj 2001, Stockholm, 2001, pp. 3-23. ['Publishing Short Stories'. Discusses issues raised in the scholarly editing of short stories with reference to the fiction of Selma Lagerlöf, Anna Maria Lenngren, C. J. L. Almquist, and several other Swedish writers, including Sg. The text of a lecture delivered at the annual meeting of the Swedish Society of Literature]

[A3:154] Ståhle Sjönell, Barbro, 'August Strindberg, *Tjänstekvinnans son 3-4*, *Han och hon*, *Historiska miniatyrer*, *Den världshistoriska trilogin*', *Samlaren* (Uppsala), 118 (1997), pp. 306-312. [Reviews Volumes 21 (*Tjänstekvinnans son, III-IV*), 22 (*Han och hon*), 54 (*Historiska miniatyrer*), and 63 (*Den världshistoriska trilogin*) in *Samlade Verk*]

[A3:155] Ståhle Sjönell, Barbro, 'Kvalitet åt folket!', *Dagens Nyheter* (Stockholm), 27 January 1986. ['Quality for the People!' A contribution to the ongoing debate concerning the principles to be adopted in publishing the new edition of Sg's *Samlade Verk*]

[A3:156] Stenström, Thure, 'Något av hans mest fnoskiga', *Svenska Dagbladet* (Stockholm), 7 April 2002. ['Amongst His Dottiest'. Reviews Volumes 53 (*Götiska rummen*) and 11 (*Tidiga 80-talsdramer*) in *Samlade Verk*]

[A3:157] Strandh, A. S., 'Strindberg. *Samlade Verk*', *Örebro-Kuriren*, 3 February 1989. [Reviews Volumes 28 (*Kamraterna*), 44 (*Dödsdansen*), 46 (*Ett drömspel*), 48 (*Kristina* and *Gustaf III*), and 68 (*Tal till svenska nationen*) in *Samlade Verk*]

[A3:158] Svedjedal, Johan, '*Samlade Verk – Svarta fanor*', *Svenska Dagbladet* (Stockholm), 11 December 1995. [Questions the text-critical principles underlying *Samlade Verk* with reference to Volume 57. Response by Lars Dahlbäck, 21 December]

[A3:159] Svedjedal, Johan, 'Strindberg som han verkligen skrev', *Svenska Dagbladet* (Stockholm), 29 January 1994. ['Strindberg as He really Wrote'. Questions the text-critical principles underlying the National Edition of Sg's *Samlade Verk*]

[A3:160] Svenson, Lars, 'Strindberg. *Samlade Verk*', *Helsingborgs Dagblad*, 3 June 1990. [Reviews Volumes 20 (*Tjänstekvinnans son, I-II*) and 51 (*Ordalek och småkonst*) in *Samlade Verk*]

[A3:161] Svenson, Lars, 'Strindberg *Samlade Verk*', *Helsingborgs Dagblad*, 14 May 1992. [Reviews Volumes 4 (*Ungdomsjournalistik*), 39 (*Till Damaskus*), and 58 (*Kammarspel*) in *Samlade Verk*]

[A3:162] T. F-t [Torsten Fogelqvist], '*Samlade otryckta skrifter. Del 2. Berättelser och dikter*', *Dagens Nyheter* (Stockholm), 16 January 1920. [Reviews Volume Two of Vilhelm Carlheim Gyllensköld's two-volume edition of Sg's posthumous works]

[A3:163] Tagger, Theodor, 'Gesamtausgaben', *Wieland* (Berlin), 2:10 (1916-17), p. 24. [On Emil Schering's collected edition of Sg's works, published by Müller in Munich]

[A3:164] Thompson, Laurie, 'The National Edition of Strindberg: Triumph or Scandal?', *Swedish Book Review* (Lampeter), 1986 (Supplement), pp. 39-47. [Discusses the hotly debated edition of Sg's *Samlade Verk* and the textual principles on which it is based.

Reprints translated extracts from contributions to the debate by several Swedish writers and critics both for and against Enquist's critique and Lars Dahlbäck's editorship]

[A3:165] Upmark, G., 'Tvisten om Strindbergsarkivet', *Dagens Nyheter* (Stockholm), 27 March 1918. ['The Dispute over the Strindberg Archive'. Apropos John Landquist's criticism of Carlheim-Gyllensköld in **A3:103**]

[A3:166] Wahlin, Claes, 'August Strindberg', *Aftonbladet* (Stockholm), 20 January 2000. [Reviews Volumes 25 (*En dåres försvarstal*) and 64 (*Teater och Intima teatern*) in *Samlade Verk*]

[A3:167] Wahlin, Claes, 'Strindberg, *Samlade Verk*', *Aftonbladet* (Stockholm), 22 July 2002. [Reviews Volumes 11 (*Tidiga 80-talsdramer*) and 53 (*Götiska rummen*) in *Samlade Verk*]

[A3:168] Warmland, Knut, 'Strindberg. *Samlade Verk*', *Nya Wermlands Tidningen* (Karlstad), 4 April 1985. [Reviews Volumes 26, (*Skärkarlsliv*) and 33 (*Nio enaktare* – Nine One-Acters) in *Samlade Verk*]

[A3:169] Warmland, Knut, 'Strindberg. *Samlade Verk*', *Nya Wermlands Tidningen* (Karlstad), 21 April 1998. [Reviews Volumes 54 (*Historiska miniatyrer*) and 65 (*En blå bok I*) in *Samlade Verk*]

[A3:170] Warmland, Knut, 'Strindberg. *Samlade Verk*', *Nya Wermlands Tidningen* (Karlstad), 28 January 1989. [Reviews Volumes 28 (*Kamraterna*), 44 (*Dödsdansen*), 46 (*Ett drömspel*), 48 (*Kristina* and *Gustaf III*), and 68 (*Tal till svenska nationen*) in *Samlade Verk*]

[A3:171] Westholm, Carl Axel, 'Strindberg. *Samlade Verk*', *Vestmanlands Läns Tidning* (Västerås), 19 February 1990. [Reviews Volumes 20 (*Tjänstekvinnans son, I-II*) and 51 (*Ordalek och småkonst*) in *Samlade Verk*]

[A3:172] Wieselgren, Oscar, '*Samlade otryckta skrifter. Del 2. Berättelser och dikter*', *Göteborgs Dagblad*, 14 February 1920. [Reviews Volume Two of Vilhelm Carlheim-Gyllensköld's edition of Sg's posthumous works]

[A3:173] Wieselgren, Oscar, '*Samlade otryckta skrifter. Del 2. Berättelser och dikter*', *Svensk Tidskrift* (Stockholm), 10 (1920), 40-42. [Reviews Volume Two of Vilhelm Carlheim-Gyllensköld's edition of Sg's posthumous works]

[A3:174] Wittrock, Ulf, '*Nationalupplagan av August Strindbergs Samlade Verk. Presentation och redigeringsprinciper. 15. Dikter på vers och prosa, 20. Tjänstekvinnans son I-II, 37. Inferno, 57. Svarta fanor*', *Samlaren* (Uppsala), 117 (1996), pp. 129-133. [Examines the efficacy and validity of the editorial principles on which four recent volumes in the ongoing edition of the National Edition of Sg's *Samlade Verk* are based]

[A3:175] I. V., [I. Veselovskii], 'Strindberg, A., *Sobranie sochinenii*, *Russkie vedomosti* (Moscow), 29 July 1908. [Reviews Volume One of *Polnoe sobranie sochinenii v 12 tomakh*, published in Moscow by Sablin, and Volume One of *Polnoe sobranie sochinenii v 15 tomakh*, also published in Moscow by Sovremennye problemy. E.777]

[A3:176] I. V., [I. Veselovskii], 'Strindberg, A., *Sobranie sochinenii*, *Russkie vedomosti* (Moscow), No. 226 (30 September 1908), p. 4. [Reviews Volume Three of *Polnoe sobranie sochinenii v 15 tomakh*, published in Moscow by Sovremennye problemy. E.778]

[A3:177] I. V., [I. Veselovskii], 'Strindberg, A., *Sobranie sochinenii*, *Russkie vedomosti*, (Moscow), No. 291 (16 December 1908), p. 5. [Reviews Volume Two of *Polnoe sobranie sochinenii v 15 tomakh*, published in Moscow by Sovremennye problemy. E.778a]

[A3:178] I. V., [I. Veselovskii], 'Strindberg, A., *Sobranie sochinenii*, *Russkie vedomosti* (Moscow), No. 258 (10 November 1909), p.5. [Reviews Volumes Five to Eight of *Polnoe sobranie sochinenii v 15 tomakh*, published in Moscow by Sovremennye problemy. E.793]

[A3:179] I. V., [I. Veselovskii], 'Strindberg, A., *Sobranie sochinenii*, *Russkie vedomosti* (Moscow), No. 177 (3 August 1910), p.4. [Reviews Volume Nine of *Sobranie sochinenii v 12 tomakh*, published in Moscow by Sablin, and Volume Ten of *Polnoe sobranie sochinenii v 15 tomakh*, also published in Moscow by Sovremennye problemy. E.811]

[A3:180] I. V., [I. Veselovskii], 'Strindberg, A., *Sobranie sochinenii*, *Russkie vedomosti* (Moscow), No. 188 (17 August 1911), p. 6. [Reviews Volume Thirteen of *Polnoe sobranie sochinenii v 15 tomakh*, published in Moscow by Sovremennye problemy. E.820]

See also:

[A3:181] Projekt Runeberg. John Landquist's edition of *Samlade Skrifter* with Landquist's original editorial apparatus scanned in as part of *Project Runeberg* at http://www.lysator.liu.se/runeberg/strindbg/

A4. Critical Approaches to Strindberg and General Surveys of Strindberg Literature, including works of reference.

[*As well as essay reviews which survey the current state of Sg criticism, this section lists both theoretical assessments of the application of different critical methods to Sg and his works, and a number of reviews and review essays which discuss more than a single book on Sg. Full details of these books and their titles in translation are given against their listing in the relevant section of the bibliography*]

[A4:1] Ahlenius, Holger, 'Om Strindberg', *Bonniers Litterära Magasin* (Stockholm), 22:3 (1953), 224-225. ['On Strindberg'. Reviews Carl Reinhold Smedmark, *Mäster Olof och Röda rummet*, **B1:395**, and Hans Lindström, *Hjärnornas kamp*, **C1:782**]

[A4:2] Ahlström, Stellan, 'Strindbergshyllningar', *Samtid och framtid* (Stockholm), 6 (1949), 27-31. ['Tributes to Strindberg'. A round-up of the principal books and essays devoted to Sg during his centennial year]

[A4:3] Alker, Ernst, 'Neues schwedisches Schriftum', *Literarisches Zentralblatt für Deutschland* (Leipzig), 76 (1925), 1221-1226. ['New Swedish Writing'. Comments on Volume One of Martin Lamm's study of Sg's plays, **D2:169**, and Göran Lindblad's pioneering thesis on his early prose fiction, **G1:54**]

[A4:4] Anderberg, Rolf, 'En utställning och tre böcker. Strindbergsnyheter', *Göteborgs-Posten*, 4 June 1981. ['An Exhibition and Three Books. New on Strindberg']

[A4:5] Anon [Arthur Calder-Marshall], 'Genius Versus Ambition', *The Times Literary Supplement* (London), 1 February 1968. [Reviews Evert Sprinchorn's translation of

Volume One of *Tjänstekvinnans son*, **F2:93**, Elizabeth Sprigge's translation of *Röda rummet* in Everyman's Library, and Walter Johnson's University of Washington Press English edition of *Memorandum till medlemmarne af Intima Teatern*, **D2:797**. 'The publication of these three works in so short a space of time leads one to hope that the time is ripe at last for us to accept this strange and fecund genius']

[**A4:6**] Anon [Harold Hannyngton Child], 'August Strindberg', *The Times Literary Supplement* (London), 16 January 1913. [Reviews *Fröken Julie* and *Den starkare* in translations by Edwin Björkman, *En dåres försvarstal*, translated by Ellie Schleusser, and *Inferno* and *Legender*, both translated from the German by Claud Field. The article also offers a survey of the career of someone who is described here as a Swedish author known until recently only as one 'with no very savoury reputation']

[**A4:7**] Anon [James Walter McFarlane], 'Illuminating the Dark World of Strindberg', *The Times Literary Supplement* (London), 25 January 1963. [Reviews Børge Gedsø Madsen's analysis of Sg's naturalistic dramas, **D2:206**, Walter Berendsohn's study of Sg's style, *August Strindbergs skärgårds och Stockholmsskildringar*, **B1:25**, and *Inferno* in Mary Sandbach's English translation]

[**A4:8**] Anon [Michael Meyer?], 'Black Comedies and Perpetual Roses', *The Times Literary Supplement* (London), 10 September 1971. [Reviews the English edition of Martin Lamm's account of Sg's life and works, **B1:241**, and Anthony Swerling's study of Sg's impact on France, **B3:420**. Prompts a dissenting letter, 29 October]

[**A4:9**] Anon [Orlando Cyprian Williams], 'The Burning Heart', *The Times Literary Supplement* (London), 19 February 1949. [Reviews Elizabeth Sprigge's biography, **R:2066**, and Walter Berendsohn's study of Sg's final years in Blå Tornet, **R:223**. Concludes that 'It is difficult to pin Sg down to any classification']

[**A4:10**] Anon, 'The Madness of Strindberg', *The Nation and Athenaeum* (London), 13:9 (31 May 1913), 357-358. [Uses a review of Lizzie Lind-af-Hageby's biographical study, *Strindberg: The Spirit of Revolt*, **R:1361**, and Volumes One and Two in Edwin Björkman's series of translations of the plays to reflect more generally upon Sg's achievement as a writer. The author suggests that 'Sg laid hold on life through an exceptional excitability – even an exceptional irritability....His genius was the genius of frank and destructive criticism rather than the genius of creation.... [Yet] as a writer of personal literature, he was indeed one of the boldest and most original men of his time']

[**A4:11**] Bark, Richard, '*Strindbergs Dramen im Lichte neuerer Methodendiskussionen*, Hrsg. von Oskar Bandle; *Structures of Influence. A Comparative Approach to August Strindberg*. Edited by Marilyn Johns Blackwell, *Samlaren* (Uppsala), 104 (1983), pp. 124-127. [Reviews **D2:8** and **C1:142**]

[**A4:12**] Berendsohn, Walter A[rthur], 'Der Stand der Strindbergforschung', *Forschungen und Fortschritte* (Berlin), 24:3-4 (1948), 27-28. ['The Present State of Strindberg Research'. Surveys the current situation regarding the critical reception of Sg prior to his centenary in 1849, with particular reference to Martin Lamm's revised life and letters study in one volume, **B1:231**, and Torsten Eklund's Adlerian analysis of Sg's personality and some of his works, *Tjänstekvinnans son*, **S:85**]

[**A4:13**] Berendsohn, Walter A[rthur], 'Die Strindberg-Literatur wächst und entwickelt neue Formen', *Ausblick* (Lübeck), 17 (1966), 17-18. ['The Literature on Strindberg is Growing and Taking New Forms'. Examines the changing nature of Sg research]

[A4:14] Berendsohn, Walter A[rthur], 'Forschungsbericht. Neuerscheinungen über August Strindberg', *Deutsche Literaturzeitung* (Berlin), 70:6 (1949), Sp. 241-254. ['Research Report. New Publications on August Strindberg'. Surveys the literature on Sg published during the 1940s, up to and including his centenary in 1949]

[A4:15] Berendsohn, Walter A[rthur], 'Något om Strindbergsforskningen', *Värld och vetande* (Göteborg), 2 (1952), 21-25. Illus. ['On Strindberg Research']

[A4:16] Berendsohn, Walter A[rthur], 'Neue Strindberg-Literatur', *Ausblick* (Lübeck), 14 (1963), 13-14. ['New Literature on Strindberg'. Surveys recent Sg scholarship, published in conjunction with the 50th anniversary of his death]

[A4:17] Berendsohn, Walter A[rthur], 'Neues von und über August Strindberg', *Ausblick* (Lübeck), 15 (1964), 30-31. ['New Literature by and about August Strindberg'. Covers Hanno Lunin's *Strindbergs Dramen*, **D2:205**, Torsten Eklund's conflation of a selection from Sg's Occult Diary and his correspondence with Harriet Bosse in *Ur Ockulta dagboken*, **F10:14**, Harald Svensson, red., *Dikterna om Strindberg* (The Poets on Strindberg), and Per Hemmingsson's study of Sg as a photographer, **P2:40**]

[A4:18] Berendsohn, Walter A[rthur], 'Problemet liv-verk i den svenska Strindbergsforskningen', *Bonniers Litterära Magasin* (Stockholm), 13:10 (1944), 869-874. ['The Problem of the Relationship between the Life and the Works in Swedish Strindberg Research'. Considers the problems inherent in the biographical approach that has been widely adopted in Swedish studies of Sg and his works, and highlights the kind of reductive controversies to which such an approach readily leads. They are exemplified here by contributions from Adolf Paul and Fredrik Böök. Berendsohn maintains that Sg's works need to be studied on their own terms, and consequently have to be set apart from the minutiae of the life that informs them]

[A4:19] Berendsohn, Walter A[rthur], 'Problemet liv-verk i den svenska Strindbergsforskningen', in **B1:42**, *Strindbergsproblem*, pp. 15-25. ['The Problem of the Relationship between the Life and the Works in Swedish Strindberg Research'. Rpr. of **A4:18**]

[A4:20] Berendsohn, Walter A[rthur], 'Gunnar Brandell, *Strindbergs Infernokris*', *Erasmus* (Darmstadt), 5 (1952), Sp. 505-511. [A review of **B1:55** in which Berendsohn also discusses Torsten Eklund's Adlerian study of Sg's life and work, *Tjänstekvinnans son*, **S:85**]

[A4:21] Berendsohn, Walter A[rthur], 'Strindbergssällskapets andra årtionde', *Meddelanden från Strindbergssällskapet* (Stockholm), 19 (1956), pp. 15-16. ['The Strindberg Society's Second Decade'. Considers the priorities facing Sg scholarship in 1956]

[A4:22] Berendsohn, Walter A[rthur], 'Struktur- och stilanalysen – ett nödvändigt komplement til den svenska Strindbergsforskningen', *Horisont* (Vasa), 10:6 (1963), 34-45. ['Structure and Stylistic Analysis – A Necessary Complement to Swedish Strindberg Research'. Berendsohn argues that a structural and stylistic analysis of Sg's texts which stresses their conscious artistry is a much needed complement to the customary biographical tendency in Swedish Sg research]

[A4:23] Berendsohn, Walter A[rthur], *Struktur- och stilanalysen – ett nödvändigt komplement till den svenska Strindbergsforskningen*, Horisonts småskrifter 5, Vasa (Finland), 1964. 12 pp. [Offprint of **A4:22**]

[A4:24] Berendsohn, Walter A[rthur], 'Zur Strindberg-Forschung', *Zeitschrift für deutsche Philologie* (Berlin), 52 (1927), 232-235. ['On Strindberg Research'. Discusses recent literary biographies of Sg's life and work by Nils Erdmann, **R:736** (*August Strindberg. En kämpande och lidande själs historia*), and Erik Hedén, **R:942** (*Strindberg. En ledtråd vid studiet av hans verk*), as well as the studies of Sg's psychopathology by Karl Jaspers, **S:162** (*Strindberg und Van Gogh*), and Alfred Storch, **S:274** (*August Strindberg im Lichte seiner Selbstbiographie*)]

[A4:25] Björck, Staffan, '*August Strindbergs dramer*, Vol. 4', *Dagens Nyheter* (Stockholm), 5 April 1971. [Reviews Volume Four of Carl Reinhold Smedmark's text-critical edition of the Plays and Volume Twelve in the Eklund-Meidal edition of the letters]

[A4:26] Boëthius, Ulf, 'Att använda Strindberg', *Bonniers Litterära Magasin* (Stockholm), 46:5 (1977), 263-270. ['Using Strindberg'. Examines the relationship between Sg's life, his works, and the issues raised by the way in which the latter represents the former, in the critical response to the recently published facsmile edition of *Ockulta dagboken*. Boëthius also discusses how Sg's own mythic projection of himself easily imposes itself on the unwary critic]

[A4:27] Boëthius, Ulf, 'Strindberg, Micawber, och Lagercrantz', *Bonniers Litterära Magasin* (Stockholm), 49:1 (1980), 48-50. [A review of Olof Lagercrantz's biography, **R:1171**, which suggests there is an affinity between Sg and Dickens's fictional character from *David Copperfield*. Boëthius also discusses Sven Delblanc's essays on Sg in *Stormhatten*, **B1:105**]

[A4:28] Boëthius, Ulf, 'Strindbergs bibliotek anno 1892', *Upsala Nya Tidning*, 14 August 1971. ['Strindberg's Library in 1892'. Discusses an essay by Hans Lindström in *Lyrik i tid och otid* on Sg's second book collection, sold at auction in 1892]

[A4:29] Boyer, Régis, 'Repères bibliographiques', *Europe* (Paris), No. 858 (October 2000), pp. 224-228. [A superficial survey of biographies and critical works on Sg which is restricted almost exclusively to publications in, or translated into, French]

[A4:30] Brandell, Gunnar, '*Drömspelets* Strindberg', *Bonniers Litterära Magasin* (Stockholm), 12:2 (1943), 167-169. ['*The Dream Play's* Strindberg'. Reviews Volume Two of Martin Lamm's biographically inflected study, **B1:205b**, which, with its broad and deep knowledge of Sg's texts, has redeemed him from the worst excesses of his many German commentators, and Vagn Børge's monograph on Sg's post-Inferno theatre, **D2:29**, which, in some respects, compounds them. Brandell concludes that Lamm's volumes represent an Olympian achievement]

[A4:31] Brandell, Gunnar, 'Stand und Aufgaben der heutigen Strindbergforschung', in Wilhelm Friese, Hrsg., **B3:168**, *Strindberg und die deutschsprachigen Länder*, pp. 9-21. ['The Current Situation and Aims of Strindberg Research'. Surveys trends in contemporary Sg research and comments on recent demands for a paradigm shift away from the biographical approach associated primarily with Martin Lamm. Brandell points out that Børge misreads *Ett drömspel* with his insistence in his study of Sg's mystical theatre, **D2:29**, that the play is entirely a dream dreamt by Indra's Daughter]

[A4:32] Brandmeyer, Carl, 'Ausländische Literatur der Buchgemeinde', *Büchergemeinde* (Berlin), 8 (1931-32), 395-401.

[A4:33] Braun, Robert, 'Eingebildetes Unglück. Strindberg in seinen Krisen', *Rheinischer Merkur* (Koblenz), 12:29 (1957), 7-8. ['Imaginary Misfortune. Strindberg During His Crises'. Reviews Gunnar Brandell's *Strindbergs Infernokris*, **B1:55**. Braun also discusses

Karin Smirnoff's biographical study of Sg and her mother, Siri von Essen, *Så var det i verkligheten*, **R:1977**]

[**A4:34**] Braun, Robert, 'Neues über Strindberg', *Rheinischer Merkur* (Koblenz), 15:12 (1960), p. 8. ['New on Strindberg']

[**A4:35**] Braun, Robert, 'Zur neuesten schwedischen Strindberg-Literatur', *Frankfurter Hefte*, 13:2 (1958), 152-154. ['On the Most Recent Literature in Swedish about Strindberg'. Reviews Volume Five of *August Strindbergs brev* and Karin Smirnoff's recollections in *Så var det i verkligheten*, **R:1977**]

[**A4:36**] Budtz-Jørgensen, Jørgen, 'Dramæt August Strindberg', *Nationaltidende* (Copenhagen), 22 January 1949. ['The Drama of August Strindberg'. Surveys recent publications on Sg, in conjunction with the centenary of his birth]

[**A4:37**] Bullough, Geoffrey, 'Recent Scandinavian Studies in Italy', *Skandinavistik* (Kiel), 13:2 (1983), 141-144. [Comments on Iselin Maria Gabrieli's essay, 'Strindberg il precursore', **D2:650**]

[**A4:38**] Carlson, Harry G., 'Evert Sprinchorn, *Strindberg as Dramatist*', *Modern Drama* (Toronto), 27:2 (1984), 269-272. [Reviews Birgitta Steene, *August Strindberg. An Introduction to his Major Works*, **B1:430**, as well as the Sprinchorn volume, **B1:421**]

[**A4:39**] Carlson, Harry G., 'Several Unknown Strindbergs', *Scandinavian Review* (New York), 64:3 (1976), 5-6. [Introduces a special issue on Sg. Challenges the prevailing biographical approach in Sg criticism which has tended to dominate the criticism of his works to the detriment of new insights, particularly in Sweden]

[**A4:40**] Dahlbäck, Lars, 'Inledning', in Solveig Landquist, red., **B1:248**, *John Landquist om Strindberg, personen och diktaren*, pp. 11-26. [An appreciation of Landquist's major contribution to Sg studies and his work as the sole editor of *Samlade Skrifter* which also discusses his participation in the Strindberg Feud and his long-standing conflict concerning Sg's reputation with Fredrik Böök over the publication of *En dåres försvarstal* and other issues]

[**A4:41**] Delblanc, Sven, 'Om Strindbergsstudier', *Bonniers Litterära Magasin* (Stockholm), 38:6 (1969), p. 406. ['On Strindberg Studies'. Interprets the Inferno crisis as an active rather than a passive process, a half unconscious, morally meaningful, and aesthetically fruitful act of will. Sg poses relevant questions; the time has now come to ask the right questions of him]

[**A4:42**] Delblanc, Sven, 'Om Strindbergsstudier', in Lars Ahlbom and Björn Meidal, red., *Strindberg – urtida, samtida, framtida*, **B1:119**, pp. 148-150. [Rpr. of **A4:41**]

[**A4:43**] Delblanc, Sven, 'På väg mot nya och fruktbara metoder inom strindbergsforskningen', *Samlaren* (Uppsala), 88 (1967), pp. 224-231. ['On the Way to New and Fruitful Methods in Strindberg Research'. Reviews Carl Reinhold Smedmark, ed., *Essays on Strindberg*, **B1:405**, and Pavel Fraenkl, *Strindbergs dramatiske fantasi i Spöksonaten'*, **E51:41**. Delblanc also criticises the 'chaos' of the badly organised Sg archive in Nordiska Museet, where much primary material still requires attention. Otherwise he is critical of Fraenkel's method and generally positve regarding the essays in **B1:405**]

[**A4:44**] Delblanc, Sven, 'På väg mot nya och fruktbara metoder inom strindbergsforskningen', in Lars Ahlbom and Björn Meidal, red., *Strindberg – urtida, samtida, framtida*, **B1:119**, pp. 54-70. [Rpr. of **A4:43**]

[A4:45] Dinnage, Rosemary, 'On Life's Terrible Stage', *The Times Literary Supplement* (London), 9 November 1984. [Reviews Olof Lagercrantz's biography, **R:1232**, and Mary Sandbach's translation of *I havsbandet*, **G10:51**. For Dinnage, the latter is 'a poor novel, but a powerful document of psychopathology' while, in its English guise, Lagercrantz's book emerges as 'a rather pedestrian chronicle of a far from pedestrian life']

[A4:45a] Ekman, Hans-Göran, 'Egil Törnqvist och Barry Jacobs: *Strindberg's Miss Julie. A Play and its Transpositions*; Göran Stockenström (red.): *Strindberg's Dramaturgy*', *Samlaren* (Uppsala), 110 (1989), pp. 155-158. [Reviews **E12:274** and **D2:288**]

[A4:46] Elovson, Harald, 'Strindberg, mystikern. En litteraturöversikt', *Folklig kultur* (Stockholm), 1 (1936), 138-141. ['Strindberg the Mystic. A Survey of the Literature'. Discusses Sg's post-Inferno outlook with reference especially to Martin Lamm's *Strindberg och makterna*, **B8:70**]

[A4:46a] Erdmann, Michael, 'Der eine Strindberg und der andere Strindberg', *Theater heute* (Hannover), 22:6 (1981), 52-57. Illus. ['Strindberg the One and the Other'. Surveys recent German publications on Sg as a dramatist, painter, and photographer, and reflects on the new image they present of him]

[A4:47] Erdmann, Nils, 'Nyare dokument om August Strindberg. Refererade och kommenterade', *Ord och Bild* (Stockholm), 27:3 (1918), 166-176. ['Recent Documents on August Strindberg. Reviewed and Discussed'. Reviews recent personal or psychological material concerned with Sg's life and personality, including Carl Ludwig Schleich's memoir of Sg, **R:1925**, Sigismund Rahmer's *August Strindberg. Eine pathologische Studie*, **S:245**, and Adolf Paul's recollections, *Strindberg-Erinnerungen und Briefe*, **R:1770**, two of which are primarily concerned with his sojourn in Berlin in the early 1890s]

[A4:48] Ewbank, Inga-Stina, 'Michael Robinson, *Studies in Strindberg*; Michael Robinson, ed., *Strindberg: The Moscow Papers*', *New Theatre Quarterly* (Cambridge), 16:3 (2000), 300-301. [Reviews **B1:380** and **B1:379**]

[A4:49] Franke, Jan-Gunnar, 'Strindberg!', *Norrøna* (Kiel), No. 28 (2000), pp. 83-85. [Reviews Strindberg, *Ich dichte nie*, Hrsg. von Renate Bleibtreu, and new translations of his experimental prose work 'Sensations détraquées' (Deranged Impressions) in Amsterdam and *Röda rummet* in Berlin]

[A4:50] Fraser, Catherine C., 'August Strindberg as Novelist, Autobiographer, and Constructive Social Critic', *Scandinavian Studies* (Lawrence, Kansas), 61:1 (1989), 68-72. [Reviews Michael Robinson's thesis, *Strindberg and Autobiography*, **F1:49**, Martin Kylhammar's monograph on the pastoral response of Sg and Verner von Heidenstam to late 19th-Century technology, **C1:715**, and a translation into English of Sg's novella, *Taklagsöl*, and the story 'Silverträsket' (The Silver Marsh) by David and Margareta Paul]

[A4:51] Garibova, O., '[New Publications on Strindberg]', *Sovremennaia khudozhestvennaia literature za rubezhom* (Moscow), 1977:6, pp. 154-158. [Reviews Walter Berendsohn's *August Strindberg: Der Mensch und seine Umwelt*, **B1:20**, Lars Dahlbäck's monograph on *Hemsöborna*, **G8:28**, Kela Kvam's thesis on Sg and Max Reinhardt, **D2:166**, and Egil Törnqvist's documentary analysis of Ingmar Bergman's 1973 production of *Spöksonaten*, **E51:143**. E.1097]

[A4:52] Gerloff, Hans, 'Strindberg', *Deutsch-Swedische Blätter* (Berlin), 3 (1922-23), 97-104. [Reviews Arthur Liebert's *August Strindberg. Seine Weltanschauung und seine Kunst*, **B1:264**, and Karl Möhlig's *Strindbergs Weltanschauung. I: Strindberg und der Katholizismus*, **B8:115**]

[A4:53] Goldschmidt, Kurt Walter, 'Strindberg und kein Ende', *Die Flöte: Monatschrift für neue Dichtung* (Coburg), 4:10 (1921-22), 291-296. ['Strindberg without End'. Surveys the 'recent flood' of literature about Sg, most notably Arthur Liebert's *August Strindberg. Seine Weltanschauung und seine Kunst*, **B1:264**]

[A4:54] Gravier, Maurice, 'Etudes strindbergiennes', *Etudes Germaniques* (Paris), 26:4 (1971), 573-577. [Discusses the French edition of Torsten Eklund's selection from *Ockulta dagboken* and Sg's letters to Harriet Bosse, **F10:14**, Ulf Boëthius's thesis on Sg and the Woman Question, **B9:30**, and Anthony Swerling's study of Sg's impact in France, **B3:420**]

[A4:55] Gravier, Maurice, 'Etudes strindbergiennes', *Etudes Germaniques* (Paris), 28:4 (1973), 467-471. [Discusses Göran Söderström's *Strindberg och bildkonsten*, **P1:463**, Göran Stockenström's thesis *Ismael i öknen*, **B1:437**, and Anthony Swerling's *Strindberg's Impact in France*, **B3:420**]

[A4:56] Gravier, Maurice, 'Etudes strindbergiennes', *Etudes Germaniques* (Paris), 30:3 (1975), 301-304. [Discusses Egil Törnqvist's study of Ingmar Bergman's 1973 production of *Spöksonaten*, **E51:143**, Gunnar Brandell's study of Sg's Inferno crisis in both Swedish and English, **B1:55** and **B1:77**, and Lars Dahlbäck's monograph on *Hemsöborna*, **G8:28**]

[A4:57] Gravier, Maurice, 'Etudes strindbergiennes', *Etudes Germaniques* (Paris), 32:4 (1977), 407-410. [On *En dåres försvarstal* apropos Hans Levander's Swedish translation of the newly discovered original French manuscript, the facsimile edition of *Ockulta dagboken*, and Vagn Børge's monograph on Sg's post-Inferno theatre, **D2:29**. The latter fails to establish whether it is a biography, an account of Sg's successive relationships with his three wives, or a study of his plays as a whole]

[A4:58] Gravier, Maurice, 'Etudes strindbergiennes', *Etudes Germaniques* (Paris), 40:4 (1985), 491-495. [Discusses recent German and French editions of the plays, a new edition of Arthur Adamov's study of Sg as a dramatist, **D2:1**, Björn Meidal's thesis on the Strindberg Feud, *Från profet till folktribun. Strindberg och Strindbergsfejden 1910-12*, **T:339**, Donald Weaver, ed., *Strindberg on Stage*, **D2:321**, and the life and letters biographies by Olof Lagercrantz, **R:1171**, and Gunnar Brandell, **R:333**. Gravier also comments on the first volumes in the National Edition of Sg's *Samlade Verk*]

[A4:59] Gravier, Maurice, 'Publications récentes concernant la vie et l'œuvre de Strindberg', *Etudes Germaniques* (Paris), 22:3 (1967), 477-482. ['Recent Publications on the Life and Work of Strindberg'. Discusses French editions of *Inferno*, *Legender*, *Ensam*, *Han och hon*, and *Klostret*, Jenny Hortenbach's, *Freiheitsstreben und Destruktivität. Frauen in den Dramen August Strindbergs und Gerhart Hauptmanns*, **B9:140**, Helmut Müssener's stilistic and structural study of *Ett drömspel*, **E41:121**, and Carl Reinhold Smedmark, ed., *Essays on Strindberg*, **B1:405**]

[A4:60] Gravier, Maurice, 'Etudes Strindbergiennes', *Etudes Germaniques* (Paris), 24:3 (1969), 481-485. [Discusses Walter Berendsohn's German anthology of letters to Sg, *Briefe an Sg*, **J:25**, Harry Järv's two-volume anthology of documents relating to the

Strindberg Feud, **T:220**, Pavel Fraenkel's monograph on *Spöksonaten*, **E51:41**, and monographs on *Fröken Julie* by Lennart Josephson, **E12:142**, and Carl-Olof Gierow, **E12:105**]

[**A4:61**] Gravier, Maurice, 'Publications récentes sur Strindberg', *Etudes Germaniques* (Paris), 18:3 (1963), 353-359. ['Recent Publications on Strindberg'. Discusses Hedenberg, *Strindberg i skärselden*, **S:134**, Uno Willers, *Från slottsflygeln till Humlegården. August Strindberg som biblioteksman*, **R:2411**, Carl Öhman's, *August Strindberg and the Origins of Scenic Expressionism* **D2:233** (not as yet identified as an ingenious forgery), Børge Gedsø Madsen's *Strindberg's Naturalistic Theatre*, **D2:206**, Elie Poulenard's monograph on Sg's prose fiction, **G1:96**, his comparative study *Strindberg et Rousseau*, **C1:1040**, and Walter Berendsohn's *August Strindbergs skärgårds och Stockholmsskildringar. Struktur- och stilstudier*, **B1:25**, as well as new editions of the plays in Swedish, English, and German, many published in conjunction with the 50th anniversary of Sg's death]

[**A4:62**] Gravier, Maurice, 'Publications récentes sur Strindberg', *Etudes Germaniques* (Paris), 20:3 (1965), 441-446. ['Recent Publications on Strindberg'. Discusses the German edition of Sg's *Briefe an seine Tochter Kerstin*, Torsten Eklund's selection from *Ockulta dagboken*, **F10:14**, Per Hemmingsson's study of Sg as a photographer, **P2:40**, Walter Johnson's monograph on the history plays, **D2:139**, new French and German editions of *En dåres försvarstal*, and Volume Three of Carl-Reinhold Smedmark's text-critical edition of the plays]

[**A4:63**] Gregori, Ferdinand, 'Aus der Strindberg-Literatur', *Die Scene* (Berlin), 11:12 (1921), 59-63. ['Recent Literature on Strindberg'. Reviews Otto Kaus, *Strindberg. Eine Kritik*, **B3:241**, C. D. Marcus, *Strindbergs Dramatik*, **D2:213**, and Leopold von Wiese, *Strindberg. Ein Beitrag zur Soziologie der Geschlechter*, **B9:257**]

[**A4:64**] Groß, Edgar, 'Strindbergprobleme und andere Literaturkritik', *Das literarische Echo* (Berlin), 24 (1921-22), Sp. 915-918. ['Strindberg Problems and other Literary Criticism'. Reviews studies of Sg's personality and ideas by Leopold von Wiese, **B9:257**, and Herbert Oczeret, **S:228**]

[**A4:65**] Groß, Edgar, 'Karl Strecker, *Strindbergs Kindheit*', *Die Literatur* (Berlin), 28 (1925-26), p. 119. [Reviews Strecker's psychoanalytical study, **S:276**, together with Karl Möhlig's *Strindbergs Weltanschauung. I: Strindberg und der Katholizismus*, **B8:115**]

[**A4:66**] Groß, Edgar, 'Zwei Strindbergbücher', *Das literarische Echo* (Berlin), 23:11 (1920-21), Sp. 654-656. ['Two Books on Strindberg'. Reviews Hermann Esswein, *August Strindberg im Lichte seines Lebens und seiner Werke*, **B1:134**, and C. D. Marcus, *Strindbergs Dramatik*, **D2:213**]

[**A4:67**] Gustafson, Alrik, 'Recent Developments and Future Prospects in Strindberg Studies', *Modern Philology* (Chicago), 46:1 (1948), 49-62. [Discusses recent Sg scholarship, including Martin Lamm, *August Strindberg*, **B1:231**, Gunnar Ollén's study of Sg's later poetry, *Strindbergs 1900-tals lyrik*, **H4:26**, Walter Berendsohn's collection of essays, *Strindbergs problem*, **B1:42**, Vagn Børge's study of Strindberg's post-Inferno theatre, **D2:29**, Harry Jacobsen's account of Sg in Denmark, *Digteren og Fantasten*, **R:1028**, Hans Taub's *Strindberg als Traumdichter*, **B1:470**, and Torsten Eklund's collection of Sg's early journalism from the 1870s, *Före Röda rummet*, **K1:13**]

[A4:68] Gustafson, Alrik, 'Six Recent Doctoral Dissertations on Strindberg', *Modern Philology* (Chicago), 52:1 (1954), 52-56. [Discusses Torsten Eklund, *Tjänstekvinnans son*, **S:85**, Gunnar Brandell, *Strindbergs Infernokris*, **B1:55**, Allan Hagsten, *Den unge Strindberg*, **B1:151**, Carl Reinhold Smedmark, *Mäster Olof och Röda rummet*, **B1:395**, Nils Norman, *Den unge Strindberg och väckelserörelsen*, **B8:119**, and Hans Lindström, *Hjärnornas kamp. Psykologiska idéer och motiv i Strindbergs åttiotalsdiktning*, **C1:782**]

[A4:69] Gustafson, Alrik, 'Strindberg Criticism', *American-Scandinavian Review* (New York), 38 (1950), 256-257. [A survey of publications issued in conjunction with the centenary of Sg's birth in 1849]

[A4:70] Heppenstall, Rayner, 'Playing With Fire', *The Spectator* (London), 16 June 1967, pp. 711, 714. [Reviews Walter Johnson's translation of *Memorandum till medlemmarne af Intima Teatern* and Evert Sprinchorn's English edition of Volume One of *Tjänstekvinnans son*, **F2:93**]

[A4:71] Holmqvist, Ivo, *Femtio artiklar om svensk (och annan) litteratur*, Stockholm: Svenska Institutet, 1981. 200 pp. [Reprints two articles on Olof Lagercrantz's biographical studies, **R:1171** and **R:1249**, as well as Sg's posthumously translated and published account of Swedish society in the 1880s, *I Bernadottes land*, and an article on *Röda rummet*, **G3:70**, pp. 20-28]

[A4:72] Hornby, Richard, 'Three Modern Playwrights', *Sewanee Review* (Sewanee, Tennessee), 105:4 (1997), 595-599. [Praises Harry Carlson's *Out of Inferno*, **B1:93**, for eschewing the usual biographical approach to Sg, and for placing him instead in the context of the major European artistic movements of the later 19th century]

[A4:73] Josephson, Lennart, 'August Strindberg', *Sydsvenska Dagbladet* (Malmö), 23 January 1949. [Surveys works on Sg published in the latter half of 1948, in association with the centenary of his birth]

[A4:74] Kärnell, Karl-Åke, 'Bilder och syner', *Bonniers Litterära Magasin* (Stockholm), 33:3 (1964), 214-216. [Reviews Per Hemmingsson, *August Strindberg som fotograf*, **P2:40**, Torsten Eklund's selection *Ur Ockulta dagboken*, **F10:14**, and Tage Aurell's Swedish translation of *Le Plaidoyer d'un fou*]

[A4:75] Kärnell, Karl-Åke, 'La ricerca strindberghiana in Svezia', traduzione dallo svedese di Birgit Selén Del Buono, in Franco Perrelli, ed., **B1:365**, *Omaggio a Strindberg. Strindberg nella cultura moderna. Colloquio Italiano*, Biblioteca di Cultura 239, Roma: Bulzoni editore, 1983, pp. 11-20. ['Strindberg Studies in Sweden'. A chronological survey of past and current research on Sg in Sweden, with additional comments on Landquist's edition of *Samlade Skrifter*, the function of the Strindberg Society, and Torsten Eklund's ongoing edition of the letters]

[A4:76] Kärnell, Karl-Åke, *Strindbergslexikon. Figurer, titlar, bevingade ord m.m. i Strindbergs verk*, Sammanställt av Karl-Åke Kärnell, Andra upplagan, Stockholm: Liber Förlag, 1985. 152 pp. [Revised and enlarged edition of **A4:77**]

[A4:77] Kärnell, Karl-Åke, *Strindbergslexikon. Figurer, titlar, bevingade ord m.m. i Strindbergs verk*, Stockholm: Almqvist & Wiksell, 1969. 106 pp. [A guide in dictionary form to the characters, titles, familiar quotations, and other aspects of Sg's works, designed as much for the general reader as for the scholar]

[A4:78] — Boëthius, Ulf, 'En ofullständigt Strindbergs-lexikon', *Vestmanlands Läns Tidning* (Västerås), 2 July 1971. ['An Incomplete Strindberg Dictionary']

[**A4:79**] — Swahn, Sigbrit, *Edda* (Oslo), 70:2 (1970), 122-123.

[**A4:80**] Kunnas, Maria-Liisa, 'Strindberg ruotslaisen kulttuurikeskustelun virittäjänä. Henkilö-Strindberg vastaan kirjailija Strindberg', *Kanava* (Helsinki), 9 (1981), 26-29. ['Strindberg as an Instigator of Swedish Cultural Debate: Strindberg the Man versus Strindberg the Writer'. Discusses two biographical studies of Sg and his works by Olof Lagercrantz, **R:1171**, and Sven Stolpe, **B1:457**]

[**A4:81**] Kvam, Kela, 'Strindberg', *Nordic Theatre Studies* (Copenhagen), 4 (1991), pp. 190-192. [Reviews Margareta Wirmark's monograph on *Dödsdansen*, **E35:129**, her study of women in Sg's plays, **D2:332**, *Den kluvna scenen*, and Egil Törnqvist and Barry Jacobs's monograph on *Fröken Julie*, **E12:274**]

[**A4:82**] Landquist, John, 'Nytt om Strindberg', *Aftonbladet* (Stockholm), 3 June 1962. ['New on Strindberg'. Reviews a new edition of Gunnar Ollén's *Strindbergs dramatik*, **D2:251**, and Atos Wirtanen's biographical study, **R:2440**]

[**A4:83**] Landquist, John, 'Strindberg i ny belysning', *Aftonbladet* (Stockholm), 24 November 1961. ['Strindberg in a New Light'. Reviews Sg's *Brev till min dotter Kerstin* in Swedish translation, Sven Hedenberg, *Strindberg i skärselden*, **S:134**, and Sven-Gustaf Edqvist, *Samhällets fiende. En studie i Strindbergs anarkism till och med Tjänstekvinnans son*, **T:107**]

[**A4:84**] Landquist, John, 'Två nya Strindbergsböcker', *Aftonbladet* (Stockholm), 1 July 1924. ['Two New Strindberg Books'. Reviews Birger Mörner's recollections of Sg, *Den Strindberg jag känt*, **R:1586**, and Göran Lindblad's pioneering thesis on the early prose fiction, *Strindberg som berättaren*, **G1:54**]

[**A4:85**] Levander, Hans, 'Är Strindbergs geni oupptäckt?', *Stockholms-Tidningen*, 2 June 1962. ['Is Strindberg's Genius Undiscovered?' Suggests that Swedish Sg scholarship takes two forms, biographical (including psychology) and intellectual history. Ultimately, however, one does Sg an injustice by repeatedly commenting on the genesis of his works and their basis in his biographical experience; for Levander, his linguistic style and creativity deserve far greater attention than they are generally accorded. Republished as '*Spöksonaten* eller Röda huset', **A4:87**]

[**A4:86**] Levander, Hans, 'Skomakaren och hans sko', *Morgon-Tidningen* (Stockholm), 13 September 1955. ['The Shoemaker and His Shoe'. Reflections on the current state of Sg research in Sweden, which continues to be dominated by the biographical approach of Martin Lamm that also underlies the stage productions of Olof Molander]

[**A4:87**] Levander, Hans, '*Spöksonaten* eller Röda huset', in *Tur och retur 1800-talet. Litterär orientering*, Stockholm: LiberFörlag, 1979, pp. 161-165. ['*The Ghost Sonata* or The Red House'. Rpr. of **A4:85**]

[**A4:88**] Levander, Hans, 'Strindbergsforskning: skomakaren och hans sko', in *Tur och retur 1800-talet. Litterär orientering*, Stockholm: LiberFörlag, 1979, pp. 157-161. [Rpr. of **A4:84** and **A4:86**]

[**A4:89**] Linder, Eric Hjalmar, 'Blev Strindberg omvänd?', *Stockholms-Tidningen*, 8 March 1951. ['Was Strindberg Converted?' Reviews Gunnar Brandell, **B1:55**, *Strindbergs Infernokris*, and Jacob Kulling, **B8:60**, *Att spjärna mot udden. En studie om Kristus-gestaltens betydelse i Strindbergs religiösa utveckling*. For Linder, these two studies of the Inferno period and Sg's religious leanings in general both prompt the question of whether or not he actually underwent a religious conversion during the Inferno crisis in the 1890s and, if so, precisely to what form of Christianity]

[A4:90] Lindström, Göran, 'Strindbergsforskning 1915-1962', *Svensk Litteraturtidskrift* (Stockholm), 25:2 (1962), 60-81. ['Strindberg Research, 1915-1962'. A valuable discussion of the history and current situation of Sg studies fifty years after his death. Lindström focuses primarily on work in Sweden but includes some reference to Germany and developments elsewhere. He concludes by welcoming the way in which recent criticism has begun to supplant more traditional, predominantly biographically based, approaches with a new concern for Sg as a conscious (rather than naive) artist and craftsman. See John Landquist's comments on the response to Lindström's essay, **U1:452**]

[A4:91] Lindström, Göran, 'Strindberg Studies 1915-1962', *Scandinavica* (London), 2:1 (1963), 27-50. [English version of **A4:90**]

[A4:92] Lindvåg, Alf, 'Strindbergiana', *Nya Argus* (Helsingfors), 56 (1963), 50-52. [Surveys recent publications on Sg, several published to mark the 50th anniversary of his death]

[A4:93] Linnér, Sven, 'Tre om Strindberg', *Årsbok för kristen humanism* (Uppsala), 42 (1980), 94-103. ['Three on Strindberg'. Reviews Harry Carlson's *Strindberg och myterna*, **D2:44**, Olof Lagercrantz's biography, **R:1171**, and Sven Delblanc's three essays on Sg in *Stormhatten*, **B1:105**]

[A4:94] Lundblad, Bengt, *Strindberg*, *Vandringar med böcker*, 1953:1 (Lund), 1953, 4 pp. [A brief survey of the critical literature on Sg to date]

[A4:95] Lundgren, Solveig, 'Brita Mortensen and Brian Downs, *Strindberg: An Introduction to His Life and Work*; Elizabeth Sprigge, *The Strange Life of August Strindberg*', *Stockholms-Tidningen*, 6 February 1950. [Reviews two English studies, **B1:306** and **R:2066**]

[A4:96] Marcus, Carl David, 'Strindberg och den tyska vetenskapen', *Nordisk Tidskrift* (Stockholm), 27 (1924), 435-441. ['Strindberg and German Scholarship'. Examines early Sg studies in German by Gustav Landauer, *Der werdende Mensch*, **B1:245**, Bernhard Diebold, *Anarchie im Drama*, **D1:108**, Arthur Liebert, *August Strindberg. Seine Weltanschauung und seine Kunst*, **B1:264**, Ludwig Marcuse, *Strindberg: Das Leben einer tragischen Seele*, **R:1466**, Alfred Storch, *August Strindberg im Lichte seiner Selbstbiographie. Eine psychopathologische Persönlichkeitsanalyse*, **S:274**, and Karl Jaspers, *Strindberg und Van Gogh. Versuch einer pathographischen Analyse*, **S:159**. Marcus concludes that, overall, Sg has fallen victim to a very German tendency to approach literature in philosophical rather than literary or theatrical terms, and to judge his works on slender evidence, often only in translation. Nevertheless, he praises Landauer for his model essays on *Ett drömspel*, **E41:88**, and *Spöksonaten*, **E51:70**]

[A4:97] Martens, Kurt, 'Neues über Strindberg', *Illustrierte Zeitung* (Leipzig), 154 (1920), No. 4013, p. 700. [Reviews Herman Esswein, *August Strindberg im Lichte seines Lebens und seiner Werke*, **B1:134**, and C. D. Marcus, *Strindbergs Dramatik*, **D2:213**]

[A4:98] Martinoir, Francine de, 'Strindberg', *La Quinzaine littéraire* (Paris), 15-16 January 2001, pp. 15-16. [Presents two French collections of essays on Sg by international scholars, published by *L'Herne*, **B1:7**, and *Europe*, **B7:15**. Between them they afford French readers a new and broader understanding of Sg]

[A4:99] Meckauer, Walter, 'Methodisches zur Strindberg-Forschung', *Nord und Süd* (Breslau), 174 (1920), 314-316. ['Methodology in Strindberg Research']

[A4:100] Meckauer, Walter, 'Methodisches zur Strindbergforschung', *Freie deutsche Bühne* (Berlin), 2 (1920-21), 256-258. [Identical with **A4:99**]

[A4:101] Mellgren, Thomas, '2 x Strindberg', *entré* (Norsborg), 7:2 (1980), p. 39. [Reviews Olof Lagercrantz's biography of Sg, **R:1171**, and Sven Delblanc's collection of essays, *Stormhatten*, **B1:105**]

[A4:102] Müller-Lauterbach, M., 'Olof Lagercrantz, *Strindberg*, Aus dem Schwedischen von Angelika Gundlach; Fritz Paul, *August Strindberg*', *Referatedienst zur Literaturwissenschaft* (Berlin), 14 (1982), 117-120. [Reviews **R:1171** and **B1:360**]

[A4:103] Myrdal, Jan, 'Några bilder till liket vid August Strindbergs tredje död', *Förr och nu* (Stockholm), 1984:3, pp. 31-43. ['Some Images of the Corpse at August Strindberg's Third Death'. Compares various aspects of contemporary Sg scholarship, in which Myrdal observes academics swarming over his texts like worms devouring a corpse in the grave]

[A4:104] Myrdal, Jan, 'Några bilder till liket vid August Strindbergs tredje död', in *En annan ordning. Litterärt och Personligt*, Stockholm: Norstedts, 1988, pp. 87-99. Illus. ['Some Images of the Corpse at August Strindberg's Third Death'. Rpr. of **A4:103**]

[A4:105] Olsson, Ulf, 'Korrekta texter, korrekt forskning och bristen på förnyelse – ett samtal om Strindberg och litteraturvetenskapen', *Tidskrift för litteraturvetenskap* (Stockholm), 23:2 (1994), 73-80. ['Correct Texts, Correct Research, and the Absence of Renewal: A Conversation on Strindberg and Literary Criticism'. A discussion between Olsson, Björn Meidal, and Lars Dahlbäck on the current situation of Sg studies which considers what lies behind the worrying absence of new scholarship. Also comments on the progress of the ongoing edition of Sg's *Samlade Verk*]

[A4:106] Örnkloo, Ulf, 'Till flydda tider. Literaturen i Sverige 1979', *Nordisk Tidskrift* (Stockholm), 56 (1980), 173-187. [Comments on Olof Lagercrantz, **R:1171**, Sven Delblanc's *Stormhatten*, **B1:105**, and Harry Carlson's *Strindberg och myterna*, **D2:44**]

[A4:107] Poritzky, J[akob] E[lias], 'Neues von und über Strindberg', *Das literarische Echo* (Berlin), 12 (1909-10), Sp. 1672-1675. ['New Literature by and about Strindberg'. Reviews Arthur Babillotte, *August Strindberg. Das hohe Lied seines Lebens*, **B1:4**, and Hermann Esswein, *August Strindberg im Lichte seines Lebens und seiner Werke*, **B1:134**, as well as recent German translations of *Tjänstekvinnans son* and *Ensam*]

[A4:108] Printz-Påhlson, Göran, '*Strindbergsfejden. 465 debattinlägg och kommentarer utgivna av Harry Järv*', *Scandinavica* (London), 8:1 (1969), 57-60. [Reviews Harry Järv's two-volume anthology of documents relating to the Strindberg Feud, **T:220**, and comments on Gunnar Axberger's psychoanalytically based discussion of Sg's imagination in *Diktarfantasi och eld. En litteraturvetenskaplig undersökning under jämförelser med ett rättspsykiatriskt material*, **S:16**]

[A4:109] 'Qvidam Qvidamsson' [Pseudonym of Nils Peter Svensson], 'Strindbergslitteratur', *Tidens Tegn* (Oslo), 3 August 1918. [Reviews recent books on Sg by Gustaf Uddgren, Hermann Esswein, and the Swedish edition of Carl Ludwig Schleich's recollections of Sg, **R:1934**]

[A4:110] Ratcliffe, Michael, 'Fugitive Swede', *The Observer* (London), 28 October 1984. [Reviews the English edition of Olof Lagercrantz's biography of Sg, **R:1232**, and Mary Sandbach's translation of *I havsbandet*, **G10:48**]

[A4:111] Rinman, Sven, 'Av och om Strindberg', *Göteborgs Handels- och Sjöfarts Tidning*, 9 February 1967. ['By and About Strindberg'. Reviews C. G. Bjurström's pioneering edition of *Klostret* and *Essays on Strindberg*, **B1:405**, edited by Carl Reinhold Smedmark]

[A4:112] Rinman, Sven, 'Birgitta Steene, *The Greatest Fire. A Study of August Strindberg*; Vagn Albeck Börge: *Strindberg, Prometheus des Theaters*', *Samlaren* (Uppsala), 97 (1976), pp. 218-220. [Reviews **B1:429** and **D2:26**]

[A4:113] Rinman, Sven, 'Femton års Strindbergsforskning', *Strindbergiana* (Stockholm), 1 (1985), pp. 81-108. ['Fifteen Years' Research on Strindberg'. An invaluable survey of critical and biographical studies devoted to Sg during the period 1968-1983. Updates the annotated bibliography in **A4:116**]

[A4:114] Rinman, Sven, 'Mera Strindberg *Göteborgs Handels- och Sjöfartstidning*, 11 July 1962. ['More Strindberg'. Reviews Uno Willers, *Från slottsflygeln till Humlegården. August Strindberg som biblioteksman*, **R:2411**, and Atos Wirtanen's biographical study, **R:2439**, two among many publications which marked the 50th anniversary of Sg's death]

[A4:115] Rinman, Sven, 'Strindbergiana', *Göteborgs Handels- och Sjöfartstidning*, 9 March 1965. [Reviews two collections of essays on Sg: Gunnar Brandell, red., *Synpunkter på Strindberg*, **B1:82**, and Göran Lindström, red., *Strindbergs språk och stil*, **B1:291**]

[A4:116] Rinman, Sven, 'Tio års Strindbergsforskning', *Meddelanden från Strindbergssällskapet* (Stockholm), 40-41 (1968), pp. 24-29. ['Ten Years' Research on Strindberg'. Updates the annotated bibliography in **A1:83** with a judicious survey of Sg research during the last ten years]

[A4:117] Rinman, Sven, 'Tre års Strindbergsforskning', *Strindbergiana* (Stockholm), 4 (1989), pp. 172-179. ['Three Years' Research on Strindberg'. Updates the survey in **A4:113**, with an overview of recent Sg scholarship covering the period 1984-1986]

[A4:118] Rinman, Sven, 'Walter Johnson: *August Strindberg*; Hans Lindström: *Strindberg och böckerna. I. Biblioteken 1883, 1892 och 1912*', *Samlaren* (Uppsala), 99 (1978), pp. 202-204. [Review of **B1:171** and **A2:57**]

[A4:119] Robinson, Michael, 'Sesquicentennial Strindberg: An Anglo-Swedish Editorial Note', *Scandinavica* (Norwich), 38:1 (1999), 5-12. [Introduces a special Sg issue of *Scandinavica*. Discusses the present state of Sg studies and comments briefly on numerous works of scholarship published subsequent to Göran Lindström's survey in *Scandinavica*, **A4:91**]

[A4:120] Robinson, Michael, 'Strindberg – A Life Thrice Taken', *Scandinavica* (Norwich), 25:2 (1986), 203-216. [Examines the problems inherent in writing Strindberg's biography as recently exemplified in accounts of his life by Per Olov Enquist, **R:665**, Olof Lagercrantz, **R:1232**, and Michael Meyer, **R:1516**. Not only is Sg's biographer confronted by a life that his subject has already converted into a series of literary texts; he is also dealing with someone who challenged the very notion of a single essential self and problematised both narrative and plot-making as direct modes of cognition. Robinson concludes that, while Gunnar Brandell's life and letters survey in four volumes, **R:333**, is factually the most dependable source among recent accounts of Sg's life, it is Lagercrantz who best conveys a sense of Sg's extraordinary creative vitality and the diverse nature of his multi-faceted project. He also includes a brief discussion of Enquist's biography for television, as well as its publication as a biography in novel form]

[A4:121] Robinson, Michael, '"Tror Ni, att någon annan kan stryka ut, vad Ni skriver?": Strindberg Old and New', *Scandinavica* (Norwich), 34:1 (1995), 97-118. ['"Do You Believe that Anyone Else can Cross Out what You Write?"' Reflects on the present state of Sg scholarship, discussing new editions of *Inferno* and *Klostret* in *Samlade Verk* and recent studies of Sg's personality and work by Clarence Crafoord, *Barndomens återkomst. En psykoanalytisk och litterär studie*, **S:52**, Thomas Millroth, *Molards salong*, **R:1556**, Margaretha Fahlgren, *Kvinnans ekvation. Kön, makt och rationalitet i Strindbergs författarskap*, **B9:95**, and Kerstin Dahlbäck, *Ändå tycks allt vara osagt. August Strindberg som brevskrivare*, **J:122**. Robinson also comments on Volume XIX of *August Strindbergs brev*, and a special issue of *Tidskrift för litteraturvetenskap*, **B7:145**]

[A4:122] Rönnerstrand, T., 'Harry Carlson, *Strindberg och myterna*; Sven Delblanc, *Stormhatten*', *Svenskläraren* (Stockholm), 25:1 (1980), 12-14. [Reviews **D2:44** and **B1:105**]

[A4:123] Rosén, Sven, 'Strindberg i den nya litteraturforskningen', *Det nya Sverige*, 1922:2, pp. 91-94. ['Strindberg in the New Literary Criticism'. Considers Fredrik Böök's treatment of Sg in *Sveriges moderna literatur*, **B5:21**, and Erik Hedén's biography, **R:942**, which Rosén regards as the best published to date in Sweden]

[A4:124] Sandbach, Mary, 'Recent Books on Strindberg', *Swedish Book Review*, (Lampeter), 1983:2, pp. 30-33. Illus. [Reviews three studies in English: Harry Carlson, *Strindberg and the Poetry of Myth*, **D2:40**, Evert Sprinchorn, *Strindberg as Dramatist*, **B1:421**, and Egil Törnqvist, *Strindbergian Drama*, **D2:310**]

[A4:125] Schimmelpfung, Hans, 'Neues über August Strindberg', *Die christliche Welt* (Marburg), 41 (1927), 516-523. ['New on August Strindberg'. Reviews studies of Sg's life and work by Hermann Esswein, **B1:134**, *Strindberg im Lichte seines Lebens und seiner Werke*, Nils Erdmann, **R:742**, *August Strindberg, Die Geschichte einer kämpfenden und leidenden Seele*, Erik Hedén, **R:942**, *Strindberg. En ledtråd vid studiet av hans verk*, and Karl Jaspers, **S:162**, *Strindberg und Van Gogh. Versuch einer pathographischen Analyse unter vergleichender Heranziehung von Swedenborg und Hölderlin*]

[A4:126] Sjöberg, Leif, 'Strategier för den svenska skönlitteraturens (Strindbergs) överlevnad', *Artes* (Stockholm), 1984:4, pp. 92-100. ['Strategies for the Survival of Swedish (Strindberg's) Literature'. Discusses current Sg research, the 1988 Sg symposium in Seattle, Michael Robinson's scholarship in his two-volume English edition of Sg's letters, **J:311**, and strategies for the survival of Swedish literature abroad and the development of Sg studies in the U.S.A.]

[A4:127] Smedmark, Carl Reinhold, 'Walter A. Berendsohn, *Strindbergs sista levnadsår*. Gunnar Ollén, *Strindbergs dramatik*', *Bonniers Litterära Magasin* (Stockholm), 18:1 (1949), 72-73. [Reviews **R:223** and the first edition of Ollén's study of the dramas, **D2:239**]

[A4:128] Sprengel, David, 'Vår Strindbergs entreprenörer', 1-3, *Nya Dagligt Allehanda* (Stockholm), 16, 18, and 27 February 1915. ['Our Strindberg Entrepreneurs'. A three-part discussion of John Landquist and Erik Hedén as critics of Sg. Also comments on the controversy provoked by Landquist's translation of *Le Plaidoyer d'un fou*]

[A4:129] St. [Carl Stang], 'Otto Kaus *Strindberg. Eine Kritik*; C. D. Marcus, *Strindbergs Dramatik*; Leopold von Wiese, *Strindberg. Ein Beitrag zur Soziologie der Geschlechter*', *Die Flöte* (Coburg), 1 (1918-19), 163-164. [Reviews **B3:231**, **D2:213**, and **B9:257**]

[A4:130] Stern, A., 'Neues über Strindberg', *Davoser Revue* (Davos), 12 (1940), 97-102. ['New on Strindberg']

[A4:131] Stockenström, Göran, 'Strindberg i Amerika 1988', *Strindbergiana* (Stockholm), 4 (1989), pp. 73-99. [A survey article which covers translations, critical studies, and theatre productions. 'Amerika' here means the United States. Stockenström comments on Sg's recent reception there and provides a bibliographical survey]

[A4:132] Stounbjerg, Per, 'Konservatoren og nissen. Nogle strategier i de seneste års forskning i Strindbergs dramatik', *Edda* (Oslo), 90:2 (1990), 65-74. ['The Curator and the Goblin. Some Strategies in Recent Research into Strindberg's Plays'. An essay review which discusses the study of *Fröken Julie*, **E12:266**, by Egil Törnqvist and Barry Jacobs, Margareta Wirmark's monograph *Kampen med döden*, **E35:129**, on *Dödsdansen*, Ola Kindstedt's thesis on *Kristina*, **E40:22**, and *Strindberg's Dramaturgy*, **D2:288**. edited by Göran Stockenström. Stounbjerg also reflects on the state of contemporary Sg research, as well as the melancholic patterns inherent his writing, which are approachable via the theories of Julia Kristeva and would possibly become more discernable via a closer scrutiny of his language than is customary in many traditional critical approaches]

[A4:133] Sundberg, Björn, 'Fokus på texten förnyar forskningen om Strindberg', *Svenska Dagbladet* (Stockholm), 16 June 2000. ['Focusing on the Text Renews Research into Strindberg'. Considers the renewal of Swedish Sg criticism which has been brought about by textual, rather than more traditional, biographical approaches]

[A4:134] Sundberg, Björn, 'Gunnar Brandell: *Strindberg – ett författarliv. Första delen*; Michael Robinson: *Strindberg and Autobiography*', *Samlaren* (Uppsala), 109 (1988), pp. 150-152. [Reviews **R:324** and **F1:44**]

[A4:135] Sundberg, Björn, 'Gunnar Ollén: *Strindbergs dramatik*', *Samlaren* (Uppsala), 104 (1983), pp. 127-130. [Reviews the last edition of Gunnar Ollén's *Strindbergs dramatik*, **D2:266**, and Hans-Peter Bayerdörfer, Hrsg., *Strindberg auf der deutschen Bühne. Eine exemplarische Rezeptionsgeschichte der Moderne in Dokumenten (1890 bis 1925)*, **B3:85**]

[A4:136] Sundberg, Björn, 'Michael Meyer: *Strindberg. A Biography*'; Gunnar Brandell: *Strindberg – ett författarliv. Andra delen*'; John Eric Bellquist: *Strindberg as a Modern Poet*', *Samlaren* (Uppsala), 107 (1986), pp. 134-137. [Reviews **R:1516**, Volume Two of Brandell's life and letters study in four volumes, **R:350**, and Bellquist's monograph on Sg's poetry, **H1:3**]

[A4:137] Svanberg, Victor, 'Tyskt och danskt om Strindberg', *Stockholms-Tidningen*, 25 January 1947. ['German and Danish on Strindberg'. Reviews Walter Berendsohn's collection of essays, *Strindbergsproblem*, **B1:42**, and Harry Jacobsen's account of Sg's first marriage, *Strindberg og hans første hustru*, **R:1060**]

[A4:138] Svensson, Conny, 'Ny litteratur om Strindberg', *Hufvudstadsbladet* (Helsingfors), 20 April 1986. ['New Literature about Strindberg'. Reviews Volume Two of Gunnar Brandell's biography, **R:333**, and Barbro Ståhle Sjönell's thesis, *Strindbergs Taklagsöl*, **G16:50**]

[A4:139] Uecker, Heiko, '*Die Strindberg-Fehde*, Hrsg. von Klaus von See; *Strindbergs Dramen im Lichte neuerer Methodendiskussionen*, Hrsg. von Oskar Bandle, Walter Baumgartner, und Jürg Glauser', *Arcadia* (West Berlin), 23:2 (1988), 198-203. [Reviews Oskar Bandle **D2:8**, Hans-Peter Bayerdörfer, **B3:85**, and Klaus von See's well-documented study of the Strindberg Feud, **T:461**]

[A4:140] Vallette, Jacques, 'Libres propos sur Strindberg', *Cahiers du monde nouveau* (Paris), 5:8-9 (1949), 88-90. [Discusses publications arising from the centenary of Sg's birth]

[A4:141] Vendelft, Erik, 'Göran Stockenström: *Ismael i öknen*; Göran Söderström, *Strindberg och bildkonsten*', *Judisk krönika* (Stockholm), 40 (1972), p. 195. [Reviews two recent doctoral theses, one on Sg's mysticism and his Inferno philosophy, **B1:437**, and the other on his painting and interest in the fine arts, **P1:463**]

[A4:142] Vowles, Richard B., 'A Cook's Tour of Strindberg Scholarship', *Modern Drama* (Lawrence, Kansas), 5:3 (1962), 256-268. [A 50th anniversary overview of the state of Sg studies. Vowles summarises substantial books by Sven-Gustaf Edqvist, *Samhällets fiende. En studie i Strindbergs anarkism till och med Tjänstekvinnans son*, **T:107**, Elie Poulenard, *Strindberg romancier*, **G1:96**, and Karl-Åke Kärnell, *Strindbergs bildspråk*, **B1:179**, for English readers, samples recent trends in Sg studies, and laments that the bulk of significant research remains in the Scandinavian languages, and is thus inaccessible to so many scholars]

[A4:143] Waal, Carla, '*Open Letters* and *The Occult Diary*', *Quarterly Journal of Speech* (Annandale, VA), 53 (1967), p. 198. [Reviews recent translations of *Memorandum till medlemmarne af Intima Teatern* and *Ur Ockulta dagboken* by Walter Johnson and Mary Sandbach respectively]

[A4:144] Williams, Raymond, 'Torches for Superman', *London Review of Books*, 21 November 1985. [Reviews Mary Sandbach's translation of *I havsbandet*, **G10:48**, and the biographies of Sg by Olof Lagercrantz, **R:1232**, and Michael Meyer, **R:1516**. Williams is especially interested by the complex links these books suggest were forged between the oppositional, suffering modernist and the Swedish working-class which celebrated Sg's 63rd birthday with a public demonstration. He concludes that 'Sg remains important because, more clearly – at once more powerfully and more analytically – than any other writer of this phase he both embodied and illuminated this dynamically influential structure']

[A4:145] Wirtanen, Atos, 'Den första doktorsdissertationen om Strindberg', *Göteborgs-Posten*, 12 July 1962. ['The First Doctoral Thesis on Strindberg'. Rpr. of **A4:146**]

[A4:146] Wirtanen, Atos, 'Den första doktorsdissertationen om Strindberg', *Hufvudstadsbladet* (Helsingfors), 10 February 1962. ['The First Doctoral Thesis on Strindberg'. On A. W. Burjam's pioneering dissertation of 1912. See **V:37**]

[A4:147] Wittrock, Ulf, *Svensk litteraturvetenskap 1970-1977. En forskningsöversikt med de nya doktorsavhandlingarna i fokus*, Uppsala, 1979, pp. 53-58. [Surveys recent Swedish doctoral theses, including those by Andrzej Uggla, *Strindberg och den polska teatern 1890-1970*, **B3:444**, Bruno Liljestrand, *Strindbergs Mäster Olof-dramer. En studie i 1800-talets dramaspråk*, **E5:61**, Lars Dahlbäck, *Hemsöborna. En monografi*, **G8:28**, and Göran Stockenström, *Ismael i öknen: Strindberg som mystiker*, **B1:437**]

[**A4:148**] Wittrock, Ulf, '*August Strindbergs dramer*, Vol. 4', *Upsala Nya Tidning*, 21 July 1971. [Reviews Volume Four of Carl-Reinhold Smedmark's incomplete text-critical edition of the plays and Volume XII of *August Strindbergs brev*]

[**A4:149**] Zennström, Per-Olov, 'Strindbergsbilden 1949', *Vår Tid* (Stockholm), 5:1 (1949), 11-13. ['Strindberg's Image in 1949'. Reviews works published around the centenary of Sg's birth, including Torsten Eklund, *Tjänstekvinnans son*, **S:85**, Gunnar Ollén, *Strindbergs dramatik*, **D2:239**, Walter Berendsohn, *Strindbergs sista levnadsår*, **R:223**, and Torsten Svedfelt, *Strindbergs ansikte*, **P1:506**]

[**A4:150**] Zennström, Per-Olov, 'Strindberg', *Kommunistisk kritik*, 2 vols (Vol. 2: 'Krig och fred'), Staffanstorp: Bo Cavefors Bokförlag, 1975, pp. 93-96. [Rpr. of **A4:149**]

A5. Other Sources:

[**A5:1**] Anon, 'En Strindbergssamling i Landskrona', *Stockholms Dagblad*, 7 March 1918. [On a private collection of Sgiana, comprising 6,000 press cuttings]

[**A5:2**] Gunnar Lagerstedts Klippsamling, Kungliga Biblioteket, Stockholm. [A collection of cuttings mainly comprising articles in the Swedish press between 1942 and 1960. Signum SgKB Lagerstedt. Handskriftssignum: acc.nr 1981/91]

[**A5:3**] Hilmer Lundquists Klippsamling, Strindberg Museum, Stockholm.

[**A5:4**] *Hilmerska samlingen av Strindbergsklipp*, Uppsala University Library. [Ernst Hilmer's collection of Sg cuttings, covering the period 1881-1916, with a preponderance of material from the last five years. Includes many occasional pieces and ephemera by way of advertisements for books and forthcoming performances of the plays as well as news reports of Sg's birthdays, his last sickness, death, and burial, and the affairs of the Intimate Theatre, the National collection on his behalf, the Strindberg Feud, the publication of his collected works by Bonniers, and plans for the performance of *Gustav Adolf*. There are also a number of more substantial items and some (at times dubiously dated) reviews of productions in Skåne as well as in Stockholm and Copenhagen. A microfilm copy exists in the British Library, London, 5 reels, Mic. A. 6512-6516]

[**A5:5**] *Höglundska klippsamlingen*, Uppsala University Library. [Zeth Höglund's collection of press cuttings, including many related to Sg. A microfilm copy exists in the British Library, London, 9 reels, Mic. A. 6517-6525]

[**A5:6**] Karin Smirnoffs kvårlåtenskap, Kungliga Biblioteket, Stockholm. [Includes mainly family material relating to Sg's marriage with Siri von Essen and their children, utilised in Smirnoff's books *Så var det i verkligheten*, **R:1977**, and *Strindbergs första fru*, **R:2009**. Signum SgKB Smirnoff]

[**A5:7**] Kungliga Biblioteket, *A Collection of Swedish and Foreign Newspaper Cuttings Relating to August Strindberg*, 1 Reel, British Library, London, Mic A. 6502. [From material in Kungliga Biblioteket, Stockholm]

[**A5:8**] Lindvall Samlingen, *Tidningspressen angående Strindbergs Giftas och därmed sammanhängande tryckfrihetsmålet, 1884*. Strindberg Museum, Stockholm. [A. F. W. Lindvall's collection of press cuttings pertaining to Sg's trial for blasphemy in 1884, bound in four volumes with a handwritten introduction]

[A5:9] Knut Lundmarks Klippsamling, Strindberg Museum, Stockholm. [Mainly journal and newspaper articles, often separately bound, and sometimes utilised by the Sg enthusiast Lundmark in *Strindberg. Geniet – Sökaren - Människan*, **B1:296**]

[A5:10] Michal, E., *Tal- och sångpjeser uppförde å Stockholms samtliga teatrar och öfriga lokaler spelåren 1863-1913*, Stockholm. ['Spoken Dramas and Lyrical Dramas Performed in All the Theatres of Stockholm and Other Venues, 1863-1913'. Includes details of performances of Sg's plays in Stockholm during his lifetime. Unpublished, but copies are in circulation for examination at Drottningholms Teatermuseum and elsewhere]

[A5:11] Mörner Samlingen, Örebro Stadsbibliotek. [Count Birger Mörner's archive. Includes Sg's correspondence with Nietzsche. See Walter Berendsohn's article, 'Strindberg och Nietzsche', **C1:105**, and Mörner's reminiscences of Sg, **R:1586**]

[A5:12] Nylinska Samlingen, Kungliga Biblioteket, Stockholm. [Vilhelm Nylin's archive. See **A5:16**. SgKB Nylin. Handskriftssignum: Vf 196d.]

[A5:13] — Anon, 'En samling omfattande allt av och om August Strindberg', *Svenska Dagbladet* (Stockholm), 14 September 1919. ['A Collection Embracing everything by and about August Strindberg'. Reports on Nylin's archive]

[A5:14] — Boëthius, Jacob, 'Okänd Strindberg', *Aftonbladet* (Stockholm), 2 April 1945. ['Unknown Strindberg'. On Nylin's archive]

[A5:15] — 'Bo Grip', 'En sällsynt rik samling Strindbergiana. Bankokommissarie V. Nylin äger i sitt privatbibliotek ett imponerande material till belysning av vår störste dramatiker', *Stockholms-Tidningen*, 25 November 1923 (Söndags bilaga). ['An Unusually Rich Collection of Strindbergiana. Bank Commisioner V. Nylin's Library Contains an Impressive Amount of Material that Sheds Light on Our Greatest Dramatist']

[A5:16] — Thulin, Petrus, *Katalog över en Strindbergssamling som tillhört framliden bankokommissarien Vilhelm Nylin*, Lidingö: P. Thulin, 1957. 88 pp. [The privately published catalogue of Nylin's collection of Sgiana (see **A5:12**), subsequently acquired by Kungliga biblioteket. The catalogue lists 576 items, many in several parts since e.g. reviews are grouped together with the book reviewed. Pages 1-7 provide an historical account of the collection which includes some manuscript material, many first editions, numerous cuttings, and a good deal of material on Sg's life and works]

[A5:17] Rune Zetterlunds Klippsamling, Strindberg Museum, Stockholm. [Press cuttings assembled by Sg's first bibliographer. See **A1:105**, *Bibliografiska anteckningar om August Strindberg*]

[A5:18] Signum T36. *Strindberg och Intima teatern*, Kungliga Biblioteket, Stockholm. [August Falck's archive. Contains material relating to his and Sg's collaboration over the Intimate Theatre, 1907-1910]

[A5:19] Kristoph Sultzbach Deposition, Kungliga Biblioteket, Stockholm. [Includes many of Frida Uhl's papers. Signum Dep. 146]

[A5:20] Svanfeldt Samlingen, Uppsala University Library, 1957. 6 vols + 1 konvolut. [Henrik Svanfeldt's [i.e. William Lengertz's] archive. Contains press cuttings of articles by and about Sg for the period 1910-1930. See also **A1:96**]

[A5:21] Ulrich Samlingen, Kungliga Biblioteket, Stockholm. [Arvid Ulrich's archive. Includes certified copies of documents relating to Sg's genealogy, biographical data, and information concerning his wives, children, and residences. Also includes material on the trial for blasphemy brought against *Giftas* in 1884. Signum SgKB Ulrich]

[**A5:22**] Vilhelm Carlheim-Gyllenskölds Kvarlåtenskap. Kungliga Biblioteket, Stockholm. [A collection of manuscript material, hand-written copies, and biographical documents and data, assembled by Sg's literary executor. See **A2:28** and **A2:33**. Signum SgKB Carlheim-Gyllensköld]

Other relevant sources in Kungliga Biblioteket include the papers of Strindberg's French translator, Georges Loiseau, and those of the Strindberg scholars Walter A. Berendsohn, Martin Lamm, and John Landquist.

B1 – B2. *General Studies*

[Part I of this section lists critical studies in which several works by Sg in more than a single genre are discussed, and where the overall perspective does not, as in some of the 'Life and Letters' studies listed in section **R** *on Biography by e.g. Gunnar Brandell, Erik Hedén, or Olof Lagercrantz, place the principal stress on the relationship of the works to the life. The latter often contain much perceptive commentary on the works as well as on Sg's practice as a creative writer, but their approach is essentially biographical, or at least chronological, in structure and method. Given the history of Sg criticism with its emphasis, especially in Sweden, on the biographical dimension, the same may often be said of some items included here, but their focus remains primarily on Sg's writing as opposed to an account of his life, or to elucidations of the former primarily in terms of the latter.*

This section also lists collections of essays devoted entirely to Sg or which include two or more items on his work, again in more than a single genre. The essays themselves are annotated and listed individually in the relevant section elsewhere in this bibliography but, as with the collections of theatre reviews and miscellaneous material on the dramas in sections **D1** *and* **D2**, *listing them in their source volumes here helps place these essays in their original context. It also serves both as a means of cross-referencing and as an indication of an author's overall engagement in Sg studies. Hence volumes containing the proceedings of the various international Sg conferences are also listed here. In keeping with the practice adopted throughout this bibliography, reviews of these works are included in this section.*

As well as substantial essays in books and journals which discuss several works in different genres, and which often encompass more than a single period in Sg's career, Part II of this section includes a number of brief comments by eminent critics, e.g. Georg Lukács, who have otherwise not concerned themselves with Sg to any great extent. It also lists some early articles by non-Scandinavian critics, in which his writings were introduced to a new readership. So, too, are a number of reviews and longer discussions of Sg's work by major Scandinavian critics, some of which were instrumental in establishing his reputation as a writer rather than a mere polemicist or controversialist. There is consequently some overlap here with studies of Sg's reception in section **B3** *and the mainly biographically inflected material which extrapolates his image in Sweden, both before and after his death, in section* **R**. *Genre specific studies of the plays, novels, poetry, and other works are to be found in the general section devoted to each genre,* **F1**, **G1**, *and* **H1**]

B1. Books and Collections of Essays

[B1:1] Aalto, Väinö, *Naturalisticheskii period v tvorchestve A. Strindberga*, Moscow and Leningrad: Izd-vo Akademii Nauk, 1936. 7 pp. ['On the Naturalistic Period in the Work of A[ugust] Strindberg'. An academic thesis, published in an edition of 250 copies. E.940]

[B1:2] Adams, Ann-Charlotte Gavel, and Terje L. Leiren, eds, *Stage and Screen: Studies in Scandinavian Drama and Film. Essays in Honor of Birgitta Steene*, Seattle: DreamPlay Press Northwest, 2000. XIV+265 pp. [Includes **B2:334**: Matthew M. Roy, 'History Revisited and Rewritten: August Strindberg, Magnus Smek, and Heliga Birgitta'; **C1:380**: Inga-Stina Ewbank, 'Ibsen, Strindberg and Exile'; **E38:18**: Anne Charlotte Hanes Harvey, 'The Theatrical Compulsion of Strindberg's *Carl II*'; **E38:26**: Otto

Reinert, 'Meaning Compounded: Strindberg's *Charles XII* and the Question of Genre'; and **F6:7**: Lotta Gavel Adams, 'Delacroix's Murals in Église Saint-Sulpice and Strindberg's *Jacob Wrestles* and *To Damaskus I*'. The volume also includes an appreciation of Steene as a scholar by Terje L. Leiren (pp. 1-5), a Tabula Gratulatoria, a bibliography of her publications (pp. 245-260), and further essays on Ibsen, Victor Sjöström, Alf Sjöberg, and Ingmar Bergman]

[B1:3] Anwand, Oskar, *Strindberg. Wege zum Wissen*, Berlin: Verlag Ullstein, [1924]. [139] pp. ['Strindberg. Roads to Knowledge'. A largely life and letters but partly thematic study with brief chapters on the social revolutionary of *Röda rummet, Giftas, Utopier i verkligheten, Hemsöborna,* and *En dåres försvarstal*, as well as the naturalistic dramas, *Inferno, Till Damaskus*, the history plays, and the development of Sg's dramaturgy from *Till Damaskus* in 1898 to the Chamber Plays of 1907. Anwand also includes a brief account of the year which Sg spent partly in Berlin during 1892-93, and of his last years in Blå Tornet. Among other individual conclusions, Anwand argues that *Näktergalen i Wittenberg* is Sg's highest achievement, for in it he attains a synthesis of the divine and the human]

[B1:4] Babillotte, Arthur, *August Strindberg. Das hohe Lied seines Lebens*, Leipzig: Xenien-Verlag, 1910. [136] pp. ['August Strindberg. The High Song of his Life'. Contains chapters on the development of a national literature in Sweden, *Mäster Olof* and Sg's apprentice years, *Inferno, En blå bok*. and his road to *Svarta fanor*, as well as general surveys of the plays and poetry. Babillotte concludes with an assessment of his 'volcanic' nature and the primary driving force of this religious revolutionary: 'He is no John the Baptist who paves the way for the saviour in art, but he is not yet the Messiah either'. Nevertheless, he is full of admiration for Sg's personality and his overall achievement, even if it is based on an erratic and very partial reading of his works]

[B1:5] — K. B., *Weimarer Schriftsteller-Zeitung* (Weimar), 2 (1918-19), p. 182.

[B1:6] — Meyer, Richard M[oritz], *Deutsche Literaturzeitung* (Berlin), 32 (1911), 738-739.

[B1:7] Balzamo, Elena, ed., *August Strindberg*, Paris: L'Herne, 2000. Illus. 476 pp. [Contains critical essays on Sg as a dramatist, novelist, autobiographer, poet, thinker, and letter writer by an international group of scholars whose contributions are often translated from Swedish or other languages. Also contains a chronology of Sg's life and work, **R:183**, selections from his works in translation, his correspondence with Nietzsche, a bibliography, and extracts in French from memoirs of Sg by Karl-Otto Bonnier, August Falck, and Bengt Lidforss. Includes **B2:76**: Harry G. Carlson, 'Réflexions sur le processus créatif chez Strindberg: le rôle des références visuelles'; **B9:85**: E. B. [Elena Balzamo], 'Strindberg et les femmes'; **B9:148**: Marc-Vincent Howlett, 'Tekla au miroir des femmes'; **C1:1026**: Franco Perrelli, 'Strindberg: l'expérience du surhomme'; **D2:106**: August Falck, 'Cinq ans avec Strindberg'; **D2:1141**: Jean-Pierre Sarrazac, 'Dramaturgie de l'impersonnel'; **E12:38**: Carl-Gustaf Bjurström, 'Au sujet de *Mademoiselle Julie*'; **E51:36**: Sverker Ek, 'Voyage de l'Ile de la vie à l'Ile des morts. Structures visuelles et verbales dans *La Sonate des spectres*'; **F1:44**: Michael Robinson, 'L'écriture autobiographique: le cas Strindberg'; **F10:79**: Göran Stockenström, 'Le *Journal occulte*: secrets de la création. Le grand chaos et l'ordre infini'; **G1:18**: Elena Balzamo, 'Trois nouvelles historiques de Strindberg'; **G12:29**: Boel Westin, '"Des arts nouveaux!" Strindberg conteur'; **G15:51**: Ulf Olsson, 'Le signe ensanglanté. Sens et sexualité dans *Drapeaux noirs*'; **H1:8**: E. B. 'Poète. . .'; **J:19**: Elena Balzamo, 'Dichtung oder Wahrheit?' Une analyse de quelques lettres de Strindberg'; **J:163**: Kerstin Dahlbäck, 'Lettres et lettres: August Strindberg épistolier'; **K7:52**: Sophie Grimal, '*Un livre bleu*: le testament spirituel d'August Strindberg'; **M:3**: Ann-Charlotte Gavel Adams, 'Strindberg et l'occultisme en France'; **S:239**: Ulf Olsson, 'Simulacres. L'histoire de la folie chez Strindberg'; **T:127:** Sven-Gustaf Edqvist, 'L'ennemi de la société. Strindberg et l'anarchisme'; and Göran Stockenström on *Ockulta dagboken*]

[B1:8] Balzamo, Elena, *August Strindberg; visages et destin*, Paris: Viviane Hamy, 1999. Illus. [320] pp. ['August Strindberg: Aspects and Career'. A thematic rather than chronological study of Sg's life and work, which moves back and forth between genres in pursuit of a series of themes, including 'Strindberg and History', 'Strindberg and Geography', 'Strindberg and Society', 'Strindberg and Women', 'Strindberg and the Individual', 'Strindberg and Madness', 'Strindberg and the Visible World', 'Strindberg and Authority', 'Strindberg and the Invisible World', and 'Strindberg and Jesus'. Relying heavily on the correspondence in order to relate Sg's work to his life, what emerges unusually from the multifarious nature of his project is an extraordinary coherence, the astonishing facility with which the real is absorbed by an individual consciousness, and the prodigious skill with which, depending on the subject, genre, or style he chooses, Sg is able to remodel a reality that, as early as his first works, is constantly "recast" in order to fit within the "matrix moulds" he imposes on it. Balzamo discusses a wide range of Sg's works, including many essays and short stories not normally given great prominence, and relates them suggestively to the work of other writers and thinkers. Consequently, she opens numerous intriguing vistas upon his work as a whole]

[B1:9] — Cyprien, M., 'Lectures', *Le Généraliste* (Paris), 19 February 1999.

[B1:10] — Decker, Jacques de, 'Strindberg, médium multimédia', *Le Soir* (Paris), 3 February 1999.

[B1:11] — Perrier, Jean Louis, 'Le labyrinthe Strindberg', *Le Monde* (Paris), 29 January 1999. ['Strindberg the Labyrinth'. Also reviews Balzamo's translation of 'Den romantiske klockaren på Rånö' (The Romantic Sexton on Rånö) from *Skärkarlsliv*]

[B1:12] — Lapouge, Gilles, *La Quinzaine Littéraire* (Paris), 16-28 February 1999, p. 15. [Also reviews Balzamo's translation of 'Den romantiske klockaren på Rånö']

[B1:13] — Marcabru, Pierre, 'Strindberg: Le génie de déplaire', *Le Figaro littéraire* (Paris), 11 February 1999. ['Strindberg: The Disagreeable Genius'. Sg emerges as both actor and prophet, anarchist and mystic, and is revealed here as a monstrous compendium of contradictions]

[B1:14] — Pagnard, Rose-Marie, '"L'énorme Strindberg". C'est bien plus que le théâtre!', *Le Temps* (Paris), 13 February 1999 (Supplement culturel au samedi). ['"The Prodigious Strindberg". There's Far More than the Theatre!' Also comments on Balzamo's translation of 'Den romantiske klockaren på Rånö' (The Romantic Sexton on Rånö), which provides a summary of Sg's universe *in nuce*]

[B1:15] — Perrier, Jean-Louis, '*August Strindberg: Visages et destins*', *Biography: An Interdisciplinary Quarterly* (Honolulu), 22:4 (1999), p. 667. [Summary of **B1:16**]

[B1:16] — Perrier, Jean-Louis, 'Strindberg', *Le Monde des Livres* (Paris), 21 January 1999.

[B1:17] — Voilley, Pascale, '*August Strindberg: Visages et destins*', *Europe* (Paris), Nos 844-845 (August-September 1999), pp. 288-289.

[B1:18] Barrios Peña, Jaime, 'August Strindberg', in *Strindberg, Bergman y Norén. La Tragedia de la restitución*, Bromma/Stockholm: Fénix, n.d., pp. 23-60. Illus. ['Strindberg, Bergman, and [Lars] Norén'. A study of three Swedish creative personalities whose work often invites comparison and is related to one another's achievements in the theatre or the cinema. Includes **C2:49**: 'Strindberg-Bergman. *Sueño*' (a study of Bergman's association as a director with *Ett drömspel*), and **F10:2**: 'Del diario intimo di Strindberg', on *Ockulta dagboken*]

[B1:19] Baumgartner, Walter, and Thomas Fechner-Smarsly, Hrsg., *August Strindberg: Der Dichter und die Medien*, München: Wilhelm Fink Verlag, 2003. Illus. 285 pp. ['August Strindberg: The Writer and the Media'. Contains the proceedings of an inter-disciplinary colloquium devoted to Sg's interest in, and forays into, other media apart from writing (most notably photography and painting), and which considers their relevance for his work as an autobiographer and dramatist. Substantial contributions also examine television as a medium for his plays, the nature of his theatrical naturalism, his experimental prose texts of the mid-1890s, and the discourse of insanity applied to, and developed within, his writing. Includes **B2:147**: Thomas Fechner-Smarsly, 'Von der Suggestion zur Projektion. Die Laterna Magica als Medium und Mittel der Analyse in August Strindbergs *Fräulein Julie* und *Tschandala*'; **B2:176**: Thomas Götselius, 'Die Hölle ist los: Strindberg schreibt'; **B2:194**: Vreni Hockenjos, 'Phantom, Schein, Traumbild. Zur visuellen Wahrnehmung bei August Strindberg'; **B2:303**: Ulf Olsson, 'Simulakren. Die Geschichte des Wahnsinns bei Strindberg'; **C1:448**: Erik Gloßmann, 'Die Apollobrüder am Musenhof. Ein Versuch über Künstler und Überlebenskunstler' – Ola Hansson, August Strindberg und der "Friedrichshagener Dichterkreis"; **C1:874**: András Masát, 'Die Insel und das Paradies. Zu Utopie und Utopieverlust bei Strindberg und Gauguin'; **D2:421**: Michael Astroh, 'Strindbergs theatralischer Naturalismus'; **F1:4**: Wolfgang Behschnitt, 'Auto(r)porträts. Strindbergs Selbstdarstellung in Wort und Bild'; **G1:26:** Sophie Grimal, 'Brücken zum Unbekannten. Eine Einführung in Strindberg's experimentelle französische Schriften'; **P1:365**: Grischka Petri, 'August Strindbergs moderne Malerei und der Zufall im Kunsthistorischen Schaffen'; **P2:88**: Bernd Stiegler, 'August Strindbergs Theorie der Photographie. Versuch einer Rekonstruktion'; **P5:61**: Stephan Michael Schröder, 'Distraktion statt Wesensschau. Strindbergs Diskurs über das Kino'; and **P5:81**: Egil Törnqvist, '"Die zartesten Regungen der Seele", Strindberg als Fernsehdramatiker'; together with a Foreword by the editors, pp. 7-8. See the article by Astrid Söderbergh Widding, **P2:96**]

[B1:20] Berendsohn, Walter A[rthur], *August Strindberg: Der Mensch und seine Umwelt – Das Werk – Der schöpferische Künstler*, Amsterdamer Publikationen zur Sprache und Literatur 4, Amsterdam: Rodopi N. V., 1974. Illus. XVIII+473 pp. ['August Strindberg: The Man and His World – The Works – The Creative Artist'. A mainly generic overview of all the plays and (though 'Sg is not a born novelist') his prose fiction, poetry and autobiographical writings. Reviews the critical literature on Sg in Swedish and German, assesses his personality and the course of his life, and comments on his painting, photography, and musical interests. Berendsohn concludes by stressing the need to regard Sg as a creative artist and hence to approach his works not biographically, as merely the transposition of lived events into literature, but as artistic artefacts, hence placing the emphasis on their style and structure. Utilises some material previously published in both Swedish and German]

[B1:21] — Bergengren, Kurt, *Aftonbladet* (Stockholm), 2 August 1974.

[B1:22] — [Jessen, Karsten], *Ausblick* (Lübeck), 28 (1977), p. 18.

[B1:23] — Lindström, Göran, *Sydsvenska Dagbladet* (Malmö), 10 September 1974.

[B1:24] — Oster, Rose-Marie, *Books Abroad* (Norman, Oklahoma), 49 (1975), p. 563.

See also **A4:51**

[B1:25] Berendsohn, Walter A[rthur], *August Strindbergs skärgårds och Stockholmsskildringar. Struktur- och stilstudier*, Stockholm: Rabén & Sjögren, 1962. 578 pp. ['August Strindberg's Depictions of the Archipelago and Stockholm. Studies in Structure and Style'. Focuses on Sg's portrayal of Stockholm and its archipelago, with copious linguistic analysis and detailed textual reference. Exemplifies Sg's artistry in terms of his diction, imagery, syntax, and rhetorical strategies, and deliberately eschews the prevailing genetic approach to his works in a detailed structural and stylistic analysis of a wide range of texts in several genres. Discusses the prose narratives *Röda rummet*, *Svenska öden och äventyr*, *Giftas*, *Hemsöborna*, *Skärkarlsliv*, *I havsbandet*, *Götiska rummen*, *Svarta fanor*, *Fagervik och Skamsund*, and *Ensam*, the essays and historical studies, including *Svenska folket*, *Gamla Stockholm*, and *Blomstermålningar och djurstycken*, all three volumes of poetry (*Dikter på vers och prosa*, *Sömngångarnätter*, and *Ordalek och småkonst*), and the dramas, including *Dödsdansen*, *Mäster Olof*, *Bjälbo-Jarlen*, *Gustav Vasa*, *Erik XIV*, *Kristina*, *Gustav III*, and the Chamber Plays of 1907, as well as a number of Sg's shorter journalistic pieces. Berendsohn places the emphasis on Sg's style and artistry rather than his biography, and stresses the degree of conscious artistry that underlies his writing in those works concerned with Stockholm and its environs, treating what he regards as Sg's most accomplished works (*Hemsöborna*, *I havsbandet*, *Dödsdansen*, and several of the stories and poems) in greatest detail, on the assumption that style represents the secret fusion of the personal with the factual and is consequently in that sense most revealing of the individual writer's emotional life and imagination]

[B1:26] — Ahlström, Stellan, *Svenska Dagbladet* (Stockholm), 4 March 1963.

[B1:27] — Bergmann S[ven]-Å[rne], *Scandinavica* (London), 2:1 (1963), 60-62. [Recognises that Berendsohn's exhaustive and penetrating analysis of Sg's style sets out to destroy the dogma that he is one of the world's most egocentric writers. Furthermore, only a study of this scope could do justice to the stupendous fertility and complexity of Sg's mind]

[B1:28] — Edqvist, Sven-Gustaf, *Östersunds-Posten*, 12 December 1963.

[B1:29] — Fröier, Lennart, *Arbetet* (Malmö), 10 October 1962.

[B1:30] — Holmberg, Olle, *Dagens Nyheter* (Stockholm), 2 May 1963.

[B1:31] — Johannesson, Eric O., *Scandinavian Studies* (Lawrence, Kansas), 35:3 (1963), p. 249.

[B1:32] — Kärnell, Karl-Åke, *Kvällsposten* (Malmö), 25 October 1962.

[B1:33] — Landquist, John, 'Självständig Strindberg forskare', *Aftonbladet* (Stockholm), 10 June 1963. ['Independent Strindberg Scholar']

[B1:34] — Lindström, Göran, *Sydsvenska Dagbladet* (Malmö), 10 January 1963.

[B1:35] — Loos, Viggo, *Norrköpings Tidningar*, 12 October 1962.

[B1:36] — N. B-n [Nils Berman], *Östergötlands Folkblad* (Norrköping), 29 October 1962.

[B1:37] — Nils Ludvig [Nils Ludvig Olsson], *Ystads Allehanda*, 23 March 1963.

[B1:38] — Nils Ludvig [Nils Ludvig Olsson], *Helsingborgs Dagblad*, 19 March 1963.

[B1:39] — Poulenard, Elie, *Orbis Litterarum* (Copenhagen), 19 (1964), 239-240.

[B1:40] — Rinman, Sven, *Göteborgs Handels- och Sjöfartstidning*, 24 January 1963.

[B1:41] See also **A4:7**, **A4:61**

[B1:42] Berendsohn, Walter A[rthur], *Strindbergsproblem. Essäer och studier*, Från det tyska manuskriptet av Knut Stubbendorff, Stockholm: Kooperativa Förbundets Bokförlag, 1946. 239 pp. ['Strindberg Problems. Essays and Studies'. Brings together Berendsohn's essays on a range of topics, most of them previously published. Contains **A4:19**: 'Problemet liv-verk i den svenska Strindbergsforskningen'; **B2:32**: 'Människokunskap'; **B3:94**: 'Strindberg och Frankrike'; **D2:466**: 'Strindberg och teatern'; **F5:43**: '*Inferno*'; **G3:22**: 'Dramatisk mellanspel i *Röda rummet*'; **G3:24**: 'Inledningen till *Röda rummet*'; **G18:1**: '"Armageddon"'; **J:34**: 'Strindbergs brev'; **P3:10**: 'Musikskildringar'; **R:212**: 'I tidsproblemets ström'; and **R:215**: 'Några grunddrag i Strindbergs andliga struktur']

[B1:43] — Andersson, Elis, *Göteborgs-Posten*, 28 August 1946.

[B1:44] — Anon [Orlando Cyprian Williams], 'Strindberg Re-Examined', *The Times Literary Supplement* (London), 4 January 1947, p. 7.

[B1:45] — Boman, John, *Tidning för Sveriges läroverk* (Stockholm), 46 (1946), p. 385.

[B1:46] — Børup, Marinus, *Jyllandsposten* (Viby), 9 November 1946.

[B1:47] — Elmquist, Carl Johan, *Politiken* (Copenhagen), 27 September 1946.

[B1:48] — Lagercrantz, Olof, *Svenska Dagbladet* (Stockholm), 24 February 1947.

[B1:49] — Lindberger, Örjan, *Nordisk Tidskrift* (Stockholm), 22:7 (1946), p. 494.

[B1:50] — Schiller, Harald, *Sydsvenska Dagbladet* (Malmö), 6 September 1946. [Also comments on the reception of Sg in Germany and compares the enthusiasm for his later work there with his reputation in Sweden. Berendsohn's book is observant but all too ingenious]

[B1:51] — Schiller, Harald, 'Strindbergsforskning', in **D1:397**, *Thalia i Malmö och andra essayer*, pp. 138-[143]. ['Strindberg Research'. Rpr. of **B1:50**]

[B1:52] — Smedmark, Carl Reinhold, *Bonniers Litterära Magasin* (Stockholm), 15:8 (1946), 703-704. [With his psychological approach, Berendsohn has the advantage of standing apart from the Swedish Sg tradition; this is sometimes helpful, sometimes not]

[B1:53] — Taub, Hans, *Erasmus* (Darmstadt), 1 (1947), Sp. 859-863.

[B1:54] Berg, Ruben G:son, *Litteraturbilder*, andra samlingen, Stockholm: P. A. Norstedt & Söners Förlag, 1919, pp. 159-224. [Includes the essays **B2:37**: 'August Strindberg'; **G2:2**: 'Strindbergs första roman'; and **G5:25**: 'Dygdens lön' (The Reward of Virtue)]

[B1:55] Brandell, Gunnar, *Strindbergs Infernokris*, Stockholm: Alb. Bonniers Boktryckeri, 1950. 304 pp. ['Strindberg's Inferno Crisis'. One of the most significant works in the development of Sg studies. Brandell analyses the background to the Inferno crisis of the mid-1890s by tracing Sg's religious thinking and his concern with guilt and nemesis in vivisections such as 'Mystik – tills vidare' and 'Nemesis divina' from 1887, as well as plays like *Gillets hemlighet* (1880). He also charts the course of the psychotic attacks which Sg suffered in 1894-96 with insight and psychological acumen, casting doubt on Karl Jaspers's diagnosis in his influential pathography of Sg and Van Gogh, **S:162**, and offers the most thorough account to date of the ferment of scientific, religious, literary, occult, and aesthetic ideas which preceded and accompanied the crisis. Brandell is thus able to explain how Sg remade himself as a writer during the seemingly fallow period between 1892 and 1898. The role of established influences, including Kierkegaard, Schopenhauer, and Eduard von Hartmann, is clarified and account is taken of the impact on Sg's thinking of Swedenborg, Carl du Prel, Bernardin de Saint-Pierre, and Francis Bacon, as well as the impulses he received from numerous *fin-de-siècle* occultists, theosophists, and alchemists, among whom 'Papus', Allan Kardec, Stanislas de Guaita, and Ch. Théodore (also Henri) Tiffereau are prominent. Brandell analyses Sg's scientific and alchemical ideas in *Antibarbarus* and the essays of *Jardin des Plantes* and *Sylva Sylvarum* in relation to the ideas of Linnaeus, Darwin, Haeckel, and Bengt Lidforss, while 'På kyrkogården' (In the Cemetery, 1896), *Inferno*, *Legender*, 'Sensations détraquées' (Deranged Sensations, 1894), and (particularly) *Till Damaskus I* are read and evaluated in the context of the post-naturalist writings of Maeterlinck, Huysmans, Rimbaud, Verlaine, Mallarmé, and Parisian symbolism in general. He also reassesses Sg's personal relationships with Frida Uhl, Stanisław Przybyszewski, Paul Gauguin, Torsten Hedlund, and Carl Gustaf Wrangel, and includes an invaluable descriptive catalogue of his writings, both published and unpublished, covering the period 1893-98. Doctoral dissertation]

[B1:56] — Ahlström, Stellan, *Göteborgs Handels- och Sjöfartstidning*, 23 October 1950.

[B1:57] — Amenius, Ragnar, *Expressen* (Stockholm), 23 October 1950.

[B1:58] — Bengtson, Nils A., *Perspektiv* (Stockholm), 2 (1951), p. 373.

[B1:59] — Fehrman, Carl, *Sydsvenska Dagbladet* (Malmö), 29 January 1951.

[B1:60] — Fredén, Gustaf, *Årsbok för kristen humanism* (Uppsala), 13 (1951), 148-149.

[B1:61] — Fredén, Gustaf, *Svenska Morgonbladet* (Stockholm), 23 February 1951.

[B1:62] — Hallsten, Olof, *Folklig kultur* (Stockholm), 16 (1951), 12-14.

[B1:63] — Hallsten, Olof, *Lantarbetaren* (Stockholm), 35:50-52 (1950), p. 8.

[B1:64] — Holmberg, Olle, *Dagens Nyheter* (Stockholm), 13 November 1950.

[B1:65] — Kulling, Jacob, and Gustaf Fredén, *Svenska Morgonbladet* (Stockholm), 9 July 1951.

[B1:66] — Landquist, John, 'Strindberg och elementalerna', *Aftonbladet* (Stockholm), 20 October 1950. ['Strindberg and the Elementals'. Criticises the psychoanalytical aspects of Brandell's otherwise praiseworthy study. Landquist wonders why good literary historians have to adopt psychoanalytical methods when they don't need to, and when, as here, they have an inadequate grasp of them]

[B1:67] — Landquist, John, 'Strindberg och elementalerna', in Solveig Landquist, *John Landquist om Strindberg personen och diktaren*, red. **B1:248**, pp. 170-174. [Rpr. of **B1:66**]

[B1:68] — Levander, Hans, *Morgon-Tidningen* (Stockholm), 14 December 1950.

[B1:69] — Linnér, Sven, *Vår lösen* (Sigtuna), 42 (1951), 88-89.

[B1:70] — Myrdal, Jan, 'Religiöst om Strindberg och religion', *Arbetaren* (Stockholm), 12 July 1951. ['Religiously about Strindberg and Religion']

[B1:71] — Ollén, Gunnar, *Samlaren* (Uppsala), 31 (1950), pp. 129-130.

[B1:72] — P[eter] R[ohde], *Information* (Copenhagen), 14 February 1951.

[B1:73] — Rössel, James, *Afton-Tidningen* (Stockholm), 21 October 1950.

[B1:74] — Selander, Sven, *Svenska Dagbladet* (Stockholm), 4 November 1950.

[B1:75] — Svanberg, Victor, 'Omvändelsesjuka', *Tidsbilden* (Stockholm), 1951:1, p. 9. ['Conversion Sickness']

[B1:76] — T. B-s [Teddy Brunius], *Upsala Nya Tidning*, 26 October 1950.

[B1:77] Brandell, Gunnar, *Strindberg in Inferno*, Translated by Barry Jacobs, Cambridge, Mass.: Harvard University Press, 1974. XX+336 pp. [A finely translated English edition of **B1:55** with a Foreword by Evert Sprinchorn, pp. [v]-ix, and a Preface by Jacobs, pp. [xi]-xviii, as well as numerous revisions by Brandell to his original text]

[B1:78] — Bergholtz, Harry, *Books Abroad* (Norman, Oklahoma), 49 (1975), p. 135.

[B1:79] — Johnson, Walter [Gilbert], *Scandinavian Studies* (Lawrence, Kansas), 47:2 (1975), 261-263.

[B1:80] — Meyer, Michael, 'The Multitudinous Strindberg', *The Times Literary Supplement* (London), 20 December 1974.

[B1:81] — Williams, Simon, *Scandinavica* (London), 14:2 (1975), 153-157. [A substantial essay review]

See also **A4:20, A4:33, A4:56, A4:68, A4:89**

[B1:82] Brandell, Gunnar, red., *Synpunkter på Strindberg*, Stockholm: Aldus, 1964. 246 pp. ['Standpoints on Strindberg'. A useful paperback anthology of previously published, mainly Swedish, criticism of Sg's works, sometimes excerpted from longer studies. Contains **B2:126**: Torsten Eklund, 'Strindberg och diktarkallet'; **B2:213**: Karl-Åke Kärnell, 'Strindbergs bildkretsar'; **B3:415**: Victor Svanberg, 'Strindbergskulten'; **B8:157**: Nathan Söderblom, 'Skuld och försoning'; **C1:795**: Hans Lindström, 'Strindberg och kriminalpsykologien'; **D2:692**: Maurice Gravier, 'Karaktären och själen'; **D2:861**: John Landquist, 'Strindberg och hans härskargestalter'; **E5:55**: Martin Lamm, '*Mäster Olof*'; **E25:23**: Gunnar Brandell, '*Till Damaskus*, första delen'; **E41:176**: Evert Sprinchorn, 'Logiken i *Ett drömspel*'; **G3:160**: Algot Werin, 'Karaktärer i *Röda rummet*'; and **G4:39**: Göran Lindblad, '*Det nya riket*'; together with an essay by Henry Olsson on *Sömngångarnätter*, **H3:33**; and an introduction by Brandell, pp. [7]-8]

[B1:83] — Ahlström, Gunnar, *Sydsvenska Dagbladet* (Malmö), 8 January 1965.

[B1:84] — Jørgensen, Aage, *Jyllands Tidende* (Aarhus), 31 March 1965.

[B1:85] — Lundqvist, Åke, *Dagens Nyheter* (Stockholm), 21 August 1965.

[B1:86] Brundin, Margareta, red., *August Strindberg. Diktare och mångfrestare*, Stockholm: Kungliga Biblioteket, 1999. Illus. 160 pp. ['Strindberg. Writer and Jack of All Trades'. The catalogue for an exhibition mounted at the Royal Library, Stockholm, to commemorate the 150th anniversary of Sg's birth and comprising a collection of short essays and presentations of different aspects of his life, writings, and multiple interests by several Swedish authors, all finely illustrated with numerous photographs of his manuscripts and papers. Contains: **A2:27**, **A2:31**, **A2:35**, **D2:611**, **F10:63**, **J:274**, **K1:9**, **L1:2**, **M:2**, **M:41**, **M:152**, **N:11**, **P1:284**, **P2:61**, **P3:82**, **R:445**, and **T:338**]

[B1:87] — Svedjedal, Johan, *Svenska Dagbladet* (Stockholm), 25 June 1999.

[B1:88] Brundin, Margareta, *et al.*, red., *20 x Strindberg. Vänbok till Lars Dahlbäck*, Acta universitatis stockholmiensis, Stockholm Studies in History of Literature 48, Stockholm: Almqvist & Wiksell International, 2003. Illus. 290 pp. [A Festschrift presented to Lars Dahlbäck, the editor of the National Edition of Sg's *Samlade Verk*, at 65. Contains 20 essays by editors and other contributors to *Samlade Verk*: **B2:27**: Bo Bennich-Björkman, 'Strindbergs optiska lekar'; **B2:120**: Sven-Gustaf Edqvist, 'Den grönskande ön. Ett motiv hos Strindberg'; **B2:152**: Sigurd Fries, 'Strindbergs *men*'; **B2:211**: Olle Josephson, 'Räkna *att* och gå vidare. Om formord in Strindbergs prosa'; **B2:371**: Björn Sundberg, 'Tecken ristade av Skaparens hand'; **B3:248**: Bengt Landgren, '"En förvirrad intelligens och ett sjukt känsloliv". Strindberg i svensk akademisk litteraturundervisning 1915-1946'; **B4:127**: Anders Ollfors, 'De tidiga översättningarna av Strindbergs verk till tyska'; **C1:353**: Hans-Göran Ekman, 'Humor, dubbelmoral och Strindbergs kritik av Bellman'; **C1:416**: Lars Furuland, 'Strindberg, Ivar Lo och statarna'; **C1:1067**: Magnus Röhl, 'Inte bara Strindberg. Om nordisk litteratur och om Strindberg i en kosmopolitisk 1800-talskulturtidskrift'; **E12:219**: Carin Östman, '"I kväll är fröken Julie galen igen; komplett galen!", Om Strindbergs dialogteknik i *Fröken Julie*'; **E12:257**: Göran Stockenström, 'The Dilemma of Naturalistic Tragedy: Strindberg's *Miss Julie*'; **E36:3**: Katarina Ek-Nilsson, 'En krona dejligare än en dronnings. Motiv i *Kronbruden* utifrån etnologiska perspektiv'; **F8:12**: Barbro Ståhle Sjönell, 'Novellerna i *Fagervik och Skamsund* – löstagbart fyllnadsgods?'; **F10:3**: Margareta Brundin, '*Ockulta dagbokens bilagor*'; **G2:33**: Conny Svensson, '*Från Fjärdingen och Svartbäcken*'; **M:61**: Gunnar Brusewitz, 'Strindberg och fåglarnas språk'; **M:167**: Per Stam, 'Det Stora Verket. Perspektiv på naturvetenskap, alkemi och ockultism i *Inferno* och *Legender*'; **P3:80**: Erik Höök, 'Med musiken som förebild. Några reflektioner kring musiktermernas betydelse i *Öppna brev till Intima teatern*'; and **R:1071**: Ritva Maria Jacobsson, 'Klostret Maredsous – något om en bakgrund för Strindbergs klosterdrömmar']

[**B1:89**] — Johnsson, Henrik, *Tidskrift för litteraturvetenskap* (Stockholm), 33:1 (2004), 179-80.

[**B1:90**] — Lotass, Lotta, '20 x Strindberg', *Dagens Nyheter* (Stockholm), 30 July 2004.

[**B1:91**] Bryfonski, Dedria, and Phyllis Carmel Mendelson, eds, '(Johan) August Strindberg', in *Twentieth-Century Literary Criticism*, Vol. 1, Detroit: Gale Research Inc., 1978, pp. 443-464. [Reprints articles and extracts from critical studies including, pp. 443-444, Martin Lamm, **E12:175**, '*Miss Julie*'; pp. 444-445, Archibald Henderson, **D1:190**, 'August Strindberg'; pp. 445-446, Oscar Cargill, **B2:74**, *Intellectual America*; pp. 446-448, Eric Bentley, **D1:48**, *The Playwright as Thinker*; pp. 448-449, Alrik Gustafson, **D1:182**, 'The Scandinavian Countries'; p. 450, Allardyce Nicoll, **D1:330**, *World Drama*; pp. 450-451, Joseph Wood Krutch, **D1:240**, *Modernism in Modern Drama*; p. 451, J. B. Priestly, **B5:115**, *Literature and Western Man*; pp. 451-454, Robert Brustein, **D1:75**, *The Theatre of Revolt*; pp. 454-456, R. J. Kaufman, **B2:214**, 'Strindberg: The Absence of Irony'; pp. 456-457, Pär Lagerqvist, **D1:604**, 'Modern Theatre: Points of View and Attack'; pp. 457-458, Raymond Williams, **D1:490**, *Modern Tragedy*; pp. 458-460, Otto Reinert, **B1:371**, *Strindberg*; pp. 460-461, John Gassner, **D2:657**, 'Strindberg the Expressionist'; pp. 461-464, Richard Gilman, **D1:170**, *The Making of Modern Drama*]

[**B1:92**] Carlson, Harry G[ilbert], *Genom Inferno. Bildens magi och Strindbergs förnyelse*, Översättning Gun R. Bengtsson, Stockholm: Carlssons, 1995. Illus. 373 pp. ['Out of Inferno. The Magic of Visual Images and Strindberg's Renewal'. A lightly modified Swedish edition of **B1:93**]

[**B1:93**] Carlson, Harry G[ilbert], *Out of Inferno. Strindberg's Reawakening as an Artist*, Seattle & London: University of Washington Press, 1996. Illus. XII+390 pp. [A wide-ranging study of the way in which Sg renewed himself and his work in the mid-1890s, stressing the crucial role played by his visual imagination, his association with Edvard Munch and Paul Gauguin in Berlin and Paris, and the inspiration he derived from a variety of occult and alchemical tendencies, not least their techniques for rendering the invisible visible or transforming matter from one form into another. Carlson also considers the widespread medievalism of *fin-de-siècle* Paris, including its newly discovered interest in the medieval theatre, and traces the complex association in Sg of the naturalist and the romantic, as well as the development of the aleatory theories of art that he formulated in the vivisection 'Des arts nouveaux!' (1894), where he anticipates the modernist techniques of Paul Klee, Wassily Kandinsky, and Max Ernst. Carlson discusses both the autobiographical fictions *Inferno* and *Legender*, the scientific essays in *Jardin des Plantes* and *Sylva Sylvarum*, 'På kyrkogården' (In the Cemetery), and several plays, including *Fadren*, *Fröken Julie*, *Mäster Olof*, *Till Damaskus*, *Ett drömspel*, and *Spöksonaten*, as well as a number of short stories, including 'Samvetskval' (Remorse), 'Den romantiske klockaren på Rånö' (The Romantic Sexton on Rånö), 'Mot betalning' (For Payment), 'En häxa' (A Witch), and 'Utveckling' (Evolution). Carlson's study links disparate aspects of Sg's project in a suggestive synthesis that illuminates both the sources and the autotherapeutic resources of his creative imagination]

[B1:94] — Ekerwald, Carl-Göran, *Dagens Nyheter* (Stockholm), 7 June 1995.

[B1:95] — Ekman, Hans-Göran, *Samlaren* (Uppsala), 116 (1995), p. 258.

[B1:96] — Gustafsson, Lars, *Nerikes Allehanda* (Örebro), 28 August 1995.

[B1:97] — Karlsson, Lena S., *Aftonbladet* (Stockholm), 2 September 1995.

[B1:98] — Lewin, Jan, 'Fantasin som Strindbergs frälsare', *entré* (Norsborg), 22:4 (1995), p. 60. ['Imagination as Strindberg's Saviour']

[B1:99] — Lindvåg, Alf, *Smålandsposten* (Växjö), 30 May 1995.

[B1:100] — Lundstedt, Göran, *Sydsvenska Dagbladet* (Malmö), 10 July 1995.

[B1:101] — Sommar, Carl Olov, *Östgöta Correspondenten* (Linköping), 21 August 1995.

[B1:102] — Wittrock, Ulf, *Upsala Nya Tidning*, 27 August 1996.

[B1:103] Carlsson, Anni, *Ibsen, Strindberg, Hamsun: Essays zur skandinavischen Literatur*, Kronberg/Ts.: Athenäum, 1978. Illus. 103 pp. [Includes **B3:128**: 'Forderungen an ein neues Strindberg-Bild. Zur Monographie Vagn Albeck Börges'; **C1:262**: 'Der Sohn der Magd und der Dovre-Alte'; **C1:263**: 'Die Tragödie Gustaf af Geijerstams'; **E51:28**: '*Spöksonaten* – Strindbergs *Når vi døde vågner*'; and **T:90**: 'Die Strindberg-Fehde – Schwedens Dreyfus-Affäre']

[B1:104] Codignola, Luciano, *Strindberg o La forza di contraddirsi*, Venezia: Marsilio Editori, 1979. 159 pp. ['Strindberg or The Power of Contradictions'. A dialectical study which focuses primarily on *Till Damaskus* in a chapter entitled 'Mimesi e tempo in *Verso Damasco*' (Mimesis and Time in *To Damascus*) and the Chamber Plays, in 'Alcune immagini ricorrenti nei drammi da camera' (Some Recurrent Images in the Chamber Plays'). But Codignola also analyses the narrative method of *Inferno* as well as its biographical and intellectual background, and extends his discussion to *Ensam*, *Påsk*, *Holländaren*, and *Stora landsvägen*. In a chapter on 'Il Naturalismo di Sg et la "questione femminile"' (Strindberg's Naturalism and the "Woman Question") he discusses *Herr Bengts hustru* and the *Vivisektioner* of 1887, as well as *Kamraterna*, *Fadren*, *Fröken Julie*, and *Fordringsägare*, while Sg is linked throughout with numerous intertextual figures, including Rousseau, Zola, Swedenborg, Kierkegaard, Edgar Allan

Poe, Balzac, and Schopenhauer. But Codignola, who demonstrates an awareness of the secondary literature on Sg in several languages, including Swedish, prefers to approach his work and personality via the writings of Gaston Bachelard and Carl Gustav Jung]

[B1:105] Delblanc, Sven, *Stormhatten. Tre Strindbergsstudier*, Stockholm: Alba, 1979. 107 pp. ['The Monk's Hood. Three Strindberg Studies'. Contains Delblanc's three most substantial and perceptive essays on Sg: **E41:33**: '*Ett drömspel*'; **E48:9**: 'Kärlekens föda. Ett motiv i Strindbergs kammerspel - bakgrund och innebörd'; and **G10:16**: 'Demiurgen. En läsning av Strindbergs *I havsbandet*']

[B1:106] — Brevinge, V. *Örebro Kuriren*, 25 September 1979.

[B1:107] — Falck, J., *Helsingborgs Dagblad*, 28 October 1979.

[B1:108] — Fischer, W., *Västerbottens-Kuriren* (Umeå), 18 December 1979.

[B1:109] — Hägg, Göran, *Aftonbladet* (Stockholm), 18 September 1979.

[B1:110] — Hamberg, L., *Vasabladet* (Vasa), 19 July 1980.

[B1:111] — Johnson, Walter [Gilbert], *Scandinavian Studies* (Lawrence, Kansas), 52:4 (1980), 473-474.

[B1:112] — Lindgren, R. E., *World Literature* (Norman, Oklahoma), 55 (1981), p. 122.

[B1:113] — Randver, Gunnel W., *Östgöta Correspondenten* (Linköping), 28 September 1979.

[B1:114] — Rönnerstrand, T., *Göteborgs-Tidningen*, 1 November 1979.

[B1:115] — Stenström, Thure, *Svenska Dagbladet* (Stockholm), 29 November 1979.

[B1:116] — Svedjedal, Johan, *Västerbottens Folkblad* (Umeå), 18 September 1979.

[B1:117] — Zern, Leif, *Dagens Nyheter* (Stockholm), 18 September 1979.

See also **A4:27**

[B1:118] Delblanc, Sven, *Stormhatten*, in Lars Ahlbom and Björn Meidal, red., *Strindberg – urtida, samtida, framtida*, **B1:119**, pp. 76-144. [Rpr. of **B1:105**]

[B1:119] Delblanc, Sven, *Strindberg – urtida, samtida, framtida*, red. Lars Ahlbom and Björn Meidal, Stockholm: Carlssons, 2007. 337 pp. [Collects discussions of Sg and Sgiana by the Swedish novelist and critic (1931-1992), together with essays on Delblanc's contribution to Sg research by Björn Meidal ('Strindbergforskaren Sven Delblanc, pp. 304-316) and Sg's relevance for Delblanc as a creative writer ('Författaren Delblanc och August Strindberg', pp. 317-330) by Lars Ahlbom. As well as the fugitive pieces 'Jean på ålderdomshemmet – en radiointervju', pp. 160-163, 'Tafsa inte på Strindberg, vad ni gör! (see **U1:411**), 'På Tages tid, då var himmelen vid', 'Författarnas intåg i intimsfären', 'Hur mycket minns Guds änka?', and Delblanc's discussions of Sg in *Den svenska litteraturen* (see **B5:44**), the collection contains **A3:51**: 'Riv inte upp en god grund! Om utgivningen av Strindberg's *Samlade Verk*'; **A4:44**: 'På väg mot nya och fruktbara metoder inom strindbergsforskningen'; **A4:42**; 'Om Strindbergsstudier'; **B1:118**: *Stormhatten*; **B1:441**: 'August Strindberg i Swedenborgs landskap. Göran Stockenströms avhandling om Strindbergs "swedenborgianism"'; **B2:113**: 'Den giftiga blomman. Erotiska motiv i Strindbergs ålderdomsdiktning'; **B2:115**: 'Humanisten Strindberg'; **F10:22**: 'Vansinnigt och sublimt'; **G1:40**: 'Fräscha och okonventionella analyser av Strindberg's romaner'; **E34:11**: 'Svårspelad passion – att spela *Påsk* i dag'; **E40:12**: 'Drottning Kristina – historiens redskap'; **F10:23**: 'Vansinnigt och sublimt'; **G8:41**: 'Korngudinnan madam Flod och den falske samhällsbyggaren Carlsson'; **G16:20**: 'Bortglömd vara av prima sort ur Strindbergs diversehandel'; **H1:6**: 'Poeten Strindberg'; **J:170**: 'Obehagliga frågor om Strindbergs brev'; **R:75**: 'Johan August Strindberg tränger på god'; **J:518**: 'Johan August Strindberg tränger sig på'; **K7:37**: 'Slagghög med rent guld', **R:581**: 'Fotnot till August och Frida'; **R:583**: 'Visst var Strindberg konsekvent'; **R:678**: 'Då uppenbarade sig Strindbergs ande'; **R:1185**: 'Lagercrantz' Strindbergsbok markerar geniet'; **R:1526**: 'Om Strindberg åtminstone varit fransos!'; **R:2446**: 'Stimulerande bok om Strindberg'; **U1:207**: 'En ungdomsvän på besök'; **U1:209**: 'Gör som Strindberg – fila, stryck och lägg till!'; **U1:211**: 'Strindberg – en framtida'; **U1:213**: 'Förtruppernas eftersnack. Svenska författarroller från Strindberg till i dag']

[B1:120] Ekerwald, Carl-Göran, *Dagsmeja. Artiklar och marginalanteckningar 1979-1989*, Stockholm: Carlssons, 1990. 223 pp. [Contains republished reviews and other journalism, including a discussion of Sg's correspondence and a review of *Syndabocken*, **G16:23**]

[B1:121] Engwall, Gunnel, *Strindberg et La France. Douze essais édités par Gunnel Engwall*, Acta Universitatis Stockholmiensis, Romanica Stockholmiensis 15, Stockholm: Almqvist & Wicksell International, 1994. 144 pp. ['Strindberg and France. Twelve Essays'. Contains **B3:2**: Eva Ahlstedt, 'L'accueil critique des *Mariés* en France en 1885 et cent ans plus tard'; **B3:197**: Sophie Grimal, 'Strindberg dans la presse française 1894-1902'; **B3:356**: Jean-François de Ramond, 'Strindberg actuel et intempestif'; **B4:33**: Philippe Bouquet, 'Boris Vian, traducteur de *Mademoiselle Julie*'; **C1:3**: Ann-Charlotte Gavel Adams, 'Strindberg et Huysmans: un cas de plagiat?'; **C1:759**: Hans Levander, '*Séraphita*: le roman de Balzac et son importance pour Strindberg'; **C1:1098**: Jean-Pierre Sarrazac, 'Adamov devant Strindberg: la dramaturgie de l'aveu'; **D2:694**: Maurice Gravier, 'Les Drames oniriques (Drömspel) de Strindberg et leur représentation en France'; **D2:1079**: Francis Pruner, 'Strindberg et Antoine'; **E51:59**: Sven Åke Heed, '*La Sonate des spectres* et le théâtre d'avant-garde français': **K3:25**: Régis Boyer, 'En lisant *Bland franska bönder*: en français dans le texte'; and **L4:21**: Magnus Röhl, 'Les liaisons avantageuses: Strindberg et Les Relations de la France avec la Suède'. Also contains an introduction by Engwall, pp. 7-10]

[B1:122] — Auchet, Marc, *Orbis Litterarum* (Copenhagen), 51 (1996), [129]-130.

[B1:123] Eriksson, Olof, red., *Strindberg och det franska språket: Föredrag från ett symposium vid Växjö universitet 22-23 maj 2003*, Acta Wexionensia, Humaniora, Växjö: Växjö University Press, 2004. 204 pp. [Contains the greater part of the proceedings of a conference on 'Strindberg and the French Language', with an introduction by the editor, pp. 2-9. Includes **A1:6**: Denis Ballu, 'Au fil du temps: Strindberg en français'; **B4:54**: Olof Eriksson, 'Strindbergs franska: en språklig paradox'; **B4:108**: Roger Marmus, 'Réinventer le paysage. La traduction des descriptions de paysages dans *Au bord de la vaste mer*'; **B4:170**: Elisabeth Tegelberg, 'Översättningarna av *Hemsöborna* till franska – några reflektioner kring svårigheter, strategier och strykningar'; **E12:86**: Gunnel Engwall, '*Mademoiselle Julie* à quatre mains'; **F5:61**: Mickaëlle Cedergren, 'Le réécriture des citations bibliques dans *Inferno*'; **G1:34**: Kristina Jansson, 'La traduction du discours indirect libre dans l'œuvre d'August Strindberg'; **G6:17**: Elena Balzamo, 'Le substrat français dans *Utopies dans la réalité*'; and **K4:10**: Philippe Bouquet, 'Les *Vivisections* ou le noeud strindbergien franco-suédois']

[B1:124] Esswein, Hermann, *August Strindberg. Ein psychologischer Versuch*, München: Piper & Co., 1907. 66 pp. ['August Strindberg. A Psychological Sketch'. A psychologically inflected reading of Sg's life and personality deduced from a perusal of his works which regards them as faithful transcriptions of his lived experience. Published in respect of his 60th birthday and focusing on his childhood and youth as portrayed in *Tjänstekvinnans son* and his social criticism in *Röda rummet*, as well as *I havsbandet*, *En dåres försvarstal* (see also **F4:33**), *Gustav Adolf*, and 'Tschandala', Esswein interprets his characters in light of Sg's own character and life, and relates them directly to his opinions on women, history, science, and religion. He also comments on Sg's pessimism, the conflict between ideal and reality in his writings, and his portrayal of women, although none of the works is analysed in any detail. This first monograph on Sg regards him as a modern Faust]

[B1:125] — A. S., *Dagens Nyheter* (Stockholm), 22 September 1907.

[B1:126] — Belfrage, Sixten, *Svenska Dagbladet* (Stockholm), 17 July 1907.

[B1:127] — Schering, Emil, *Die Zukunft* (Berlin), 61 (1907), 211-212.

[B1:128] — *Stockholms-Tidningen*, 1 November 1907.

[B1:129] — Z. V. [Z. Vengerova], *Vestnik Evropy* (Moscow), 1907:7, pp. 406-414. [E.767]

[B1:130] Esswein, Hermann, *August Strindberg. En studie och en öfverblick*, auktoriserad öfversättning af Erik Thyselius, Stockholm: Björck & Börjesson, 1909. Illus. 189 pp. ['August Strindberg. A Study and a Profile'. Authorised Swedish translation of **B1:134**]

[B1:131] — C. D. M[arcus], *Aftonbladet* (Stockholm), 14 November 1909.

[B1:132] — Erdmann, Nils, *Nya Dagligt Allehanda* (Stockholm), 7 June 1909.

[B1:133] — Landquist, John, *Svenska Dagbladet* (Stockholm), 27 July 1909.

[B1:134] Esswein, Hermann, *August Strindberg im Lichte seines Lebens und seiner Werke*, Mit 27 Bildbeilagen, München und Leipzig: Georg Müller, 1909. Illus. 212 pp. ['August Strindberg in the Light of His Life and His Works'. This pioneering book-length study of Sg's work, the second to be published during his lifetime, is organised in eight chapters: 'Der Bekenner' (concerned with the autobiographical writings but focusing only on the first three volumes of *Tjänstekvinnans son* and setting aside the existing German translation of *En dåres försvarstal*, on the grounds that it is faulty and incomplete), 'Der Ankläger' (subtitled 'Strindberg und die Gesellschaft' and focusing mainly on *Röda rummet*, *I havsbandet*, 'Tschandala', and Sg's notion of the superman), 'Strindbergs Menschen und der Mensch Strindberg' (which considers a range of Sg's fictional characters and analyses his notion of character in general), 'Strindberg und die Frauen', 'Strindberg und die Naturwissenschaften', 'Biographisches', 'Strindberg und die Historie', and 'Strindbergs Verhältnis zur Religion'. Provides one of the first book-length overviews of Sg's project, focusing primarily on the themes and issues which frequently preoccupied his early critics in Germany]

[B1:135] — Langer, Felix, *Der Merker* (Vienna), 2 (1910-11), 887-888.

[B1:136] — Rosén, Sven, *Stockholms Dagblad*, 3 April 1909.

[B1:137] — Sprengler, Joseph, 'August Strindberg', *Hochland* (München), 9:2 (1911-12), 126-128.

See also **A4:66, A4:107, A4:125**

[B1:138] Esswein, Hermann, *August Strindberg im Lichte seines Lebens und seiner Werke*, München und Leipzig: Georg Müller, 1919. Illus. 315 pp. [An expanded edition of **B1:134**]

[B1:139] — Knudsen, Hans, 'Strindbergs Weg', *Die Scene* (Berlin), 11 (1921), 20-22. ['Strindberg's Path']

[B1:140] Esswein, Hermann, 'Avgust Strindberg', Translated from the German by V. M. Friche [or Fritje], in A. Strindberg, *Sobranie sochinenii*, Vol. 6, Moscow: Sovremennye problemy, 1909, pp. 5-89. [Russian edition of **B1:134**, published together with a translation of 'Tschandala' in *Polnoe sobranie sochinenii v 15 tomakh*. E.789]

[B1:141] Faggi, Vico, *August Strindberg*, Il Castoro 142, Firenze: La Nuova Italia, 1978. 118 pp. [Contains short chapters on the novels, poetry, politics, and paintings, as well as on *Inferno* and *Ensam*. The plays are considered chronologically, focusing especially on *Fadren*, *Fröken Julie*, *Till Damaskus*, *Dödsdansen*, *Ett drömspel*, *Påsk*, *Gustav Vasa*, *Svanevit*, and the Chamber Plays of 1907. Also includes an Italian translation of Sg's responses to a questionnaire by the Danish journalist Georg Brøchner (see **R:225**)]

[B1:142] [Fröding, Gustaf, and Birger Mörner], red., *En bok om Strindberg*, Med porträtt utfördt af J. Segelcke, Karlstadt: Forssells Boktryckeri, 1894. 211 pp. ['A Book about Strindberg'. A pioneering collection of essays whose assembly, often extracted from already published sources, was encouraged and monitored by Sg himself. Contains contributions by Holger Drachmann (a poem); Georg Brandes, **B2:67**; Laura Marholm, **B9:172**; Arne Garborg, **C1:433**; Knut Hamsun, **C1:512**; Justin Huntly M'Carthy [sic], **D2:924**; Adolf Paul, **E13:42**; Gustaf Fröding, **H1:14**; Anton Nyström, **L1:30**; Ad. Hansen (a poem); Bjørnstjerne Bjørnson, **R:279**; and Jonas Lie, **R:1357**]

[B1:143] Gabrieli, Mario, *August Strindberg. Uno studio*, Göteborg: Elanders boktryckeri, 1945. 137 pp. ['August Strindberg. A Study'. Contains a short biography together with chapters on Sg's moral and intellectual significance, his work as an autobiographer, and the conflict in his prose writings between polemics and poetry. Gabrieli also devotes separate chapters to what he calls 'The Drama of Decadent Eroticism' (primarily *Fadren, Fröken Julie*, and *Dödsdansen*), 'Strindberg the Visionary' (i.e. *Till Damaskus* and the post-Inferno dramas), and the history plays]

[B1:144] — [Bach, Giovanni], *Rivista di letterature moderne* (Asti), 1 (1946), 235-236.

[B1:145] — Sjöstedt, Nils Åke, *Götheborgske spionen* (Gothenburg), 11:1 (1946), pp. 8-10. [See Gabrieli's response in **B1:146**]

[B1:146] Gabrieli, Mario, 'Öppet brev till Nils Åke Sjöstedt', *Götheborgske spionen* (Gothenburg), 11:3 (1946), 9-10. ['Open Letter to Nils Åke Sjöstedt'. Includes a response by Sjöstedt, p. 10]

[B1:147] Gherasim, Vasile, A. *Strindberg als Künstler und Philosoph*, *Cernauti* (Czernowitz), 1927. 32 pp. ['Strindberg as Artist and Philosopher']

[B1:148] Gitel'man, L[ev], and V[alentina] Dianova, eds, *Avgust Strindberg i mirovaia kul'tura. Materialy mezhvyzovskoi nauchnoi konferentsii. Stat'i. Soobshcheniia*, St Petersburg: Levsha, 1999. Illus. 156 pp. [Contains the proceedings of a conference held in the Tsar's Hall of the Pushkin State Drama Theatre (Aleksandrinskii Teatr), St Petersburg, 17-19 March 1999, to commemorate the 150th anniversary of Sg's birth. Contains **B2:117**: V. Dianova, '[The Philosophy in Strindberg's Life and Creative Activities]'; **B2:221**: A. Kolesnikov, '[The Problem of a Subject in Strindberg's Work]'; **B2:356**: E. Sokolov, '[The Reserve Fund of Local Apocalypses]'; **C1:454**: N. Golik, '[The Tragedy of Human Existence (Kierkegaard – Strindberg)]'; **C1:685**: G. Kovalenko, '[A. Strindberg & E. Albee]'; **C1:758**: V. Letsovich, '[Strindberg in the Misogynist Tradition of European Culture]'; **C1:945**: I. Nekrasova, 'A. Strindberg i P. Claudel'; **C1:1397**: Andrei Alekseevich Iur'ev, 'H. Ibsen i A. Strindberg'; **D2:667**: L[ev] Gitel'man, 'A. Strindberg i A. Antuan'; **D2:837**: D. Kumakova, '[The Musical Structure of Strindberg's "Late Sonatas"]'; **E11:166**: Irina Tsimbal, '[*The Father*: The History of the Play on the Russian Stage]'; **E25:137**: N. Tishunina, '[Strindberg's Dramatic Trilogy *To Damascus* and the French Symbolist Tradition]'; and **E51:83**: V. Maksimov, '[*The Spook Sonata* by Strindberg and the French Symbolist Tradition]'. Also includes an English summary, pp. 5-7, an editor's introduction by Gitel'man '[A Word about Strindberg]', pp. 11-12, in which he comments on the importance of Sg and the controversial attitude adopted towards his works in Soviet Russia, and a popular guide to '[The Monuments to August Strindberg in Stockholm]' by Anita Persson, **P1:361**, pp. 142-149]

[B1:149] Gundlach, Angelika, *August Strindberg: nichts als Dichter*, Insel Almanach auf das Jahr 1980, Frankfurt am Main: Insel Verlag, 1980. Illus. 91 pp. ['August Strindberg: Not Only a Writer'. Presents Sg as a painter and photographer in order to challenge the received image of him in Germany as merely a writer]

[B1:150] Gundlach, Angelika, Hrsg., *Der andere Strindberg. Materialien zu Malerei, Photographie und Theaterpraxis*, Aus dem Schwedischen von Birgitta Hofmann-Mella, Astrid Walter, Susanne Seul, Frankfurt am Mein: Insel Verlag, 1981. Illus. [343] pp. ['The Other Strindberg. On His Painting, Photography, and Theatre Practice'. A collection of essays designed to make several lesser known aspects of Sg's life and work more familiar to German readers. The most substantial contribution is Göran Söderström's account of Sg's life, **P1:443** ('Biographie eines modernen Künstlers'), in which his painting and relationships with artists are given special prominence, but the volume also contains essays on the painting, (**P1:458**: 'Strindbergs malerei'), photography (**P2:76**: 'Photogenie – Photogenique. August Strindberg und die Photographie'), and the reception accorded the plays in Germany, (**B3:337**:Wolfgang Pasche, 'Wer hat Angst vor August Strindberg? Autor- und Dramenrezeption in Deutschland 1890-1980'), all prefaced by a Foreword by Gundlach, pp. 11-16]

[B1:151] Hagsten, Allan, *Den Unge Strindberg. Studier kring Tjänstekvinnans son och ungdomsverken*, 2 vols, Stockholm: Albert Bonniers Förlag, 1951. 516 and 183 pp. ['The Young Strindberg. Studies on *The Son of a Servant* and the Works of His Youth'. Although Hagsten discusses *Mäster Olof* in detail and comments on many other early works, including *Röda rummet*, *Den fredlöse*, *Fritänkaren*, *Blotsven*, *Början av Ån Bogsveigs saga*, 'Konstens martyrer', *Det sjunkande Hellas*, and the early journalism, his approach is essentially biographical, based on exhaustive (and exhausting) documentary research which aims to verify the accuracy of Sg's own account of these years in *Tjänstekvinnans son*. Hagsten reviews his family circumstances, schooldays, educational, and religious influences, and documents his reading in great detail. He also clarifies the relevance for *Mäster Olof* and *Röda rummet* of Sg's response to the Paris Commune, and is, for the period, illuminating on Sg's politics in general, but his intellectual development, and especially his writing, is often submerged in an approach which relies on a positivistic accumulation of minute detail and where *Tjänstekvinnans son* is treated as a documentary source and never as a work of literature. Vol. II contains a series of Appendices on Johan Ludvig and Carl Oscar Strindberg, the latter's diary, Sg's schooldays, a catalogue of Sg's library loans between 1867 and 1871, his earliest short story set in the Stockholm archipelago, a detailed summary of the draft material for *Mäster*

Olof and its historical sources, the dating of several early works, his socialism, and his relationship with Verner von Heidenstam as portrayed in *Författeren*. Doctoral dissertation]

[B1:152] — Ahlenius, Holger, *Bonniers Litterära Magasin* (Stockholm), 21:2 (1952), 143-144.

[B1:153] — Björck, Staffan, *Dagens Nyheter* (Stockholm), 31 August 1951.

[B1:154] — Brandell, Gunnar, *Svenska Dagbladet* (Stockholm), 15 June 1951.

[B1:155] — Brunius, Teddy, *Expressen* (Stockholm), 15 September 1951.

[B1:156] — Eklund, Torsten, *Samlaren* (Uppsala), 32 (1951), pp. 130-140. [Critical reflections on Hagsten's thesis which, in Eklund's view, offers no truly original understanding of its subject but presents numerous new facts and is based on a thorough investigation of personal documents and other archival material. Eklund assesses Hagsten's biographical studies in some detail, and not uncritically, reserving special praise for the discussion of *Fritänkaren* and (particularly) *Mäster Olof*. See Hagsten's response in **B1:164**]

[B1:157] — Hallsten, Olof, *Lantarbetaren* (Stockholm), 36:44 (1951), 12-13.

[B1:158] — Ivre, Ivar, *Afton-Tidningen* (Stockholm), 26 August 1951.

[B1:159] — J. L. [John Landquist], 'Strindbergs far, förmögen men snål', *Aftonbladet* (Stockholm), 27 August 1951. ['Strindberg's Father, Wealthy but Mean'. Uses Hagsten's biographical study to condemn Sg's father for his 'meanness' and considers the impact this had on Sg]

[B1:160] — Landquist, John, 'Strindbergs far, förmögen men snål', in Solveig Landquist, red. **B1:248**, *John Landquist om Strindberg personen och diktaren*, pp. 175-179. ['Strindberg's Father, Wealthy but Mean'. Rpr. of **B1:159**]

[B1:161] — Levander, Hans, *Morgon-Tidningen* (Stockholm), 30 August 1952.

[B1:162] — Rinman, Sven, 'Strindbergs ungdom', *Göteborgs Handels- och Sjöfartstidning*, 10 October 1951. ['Strindberg's Youth']

[B1:163] — Thomasson, Carl-Gustaf, *Svensk Tidskrift* (Stockholm), 39 (1952), 478-480.

See also **A4:68**

[B1:164] Hagsten, Allan, 'Strindberg och hans fader än en gång', *Tiden* (Stockholm), 44:2 (1952), 93-98. ['Strindberg and His Father Revisited'. Offers further evidence in support of his portrayal of Sg's father in **B1:151**, in response to criticism by Eklund in **B1:156**]

[B1:165] Hall, Sharon K., ed., '(Johan) August Strindberg', in *Twentieth-Century Literary Criticism*, Vol. 8, Detroit-London: Gale Research Inc., 1984, pp. 404-421. [Reprints articles and extracts from critical studies, including, p. 406, Justin Huntly McCarthy, **B2:264**, 'August Strindberg'; pp. 406-407, H. L. Mencken, **D1:634**, 'The Drama and Some Dramatists'; pp. 407-408, Desmond McCarthy, **E12:1394**, '*Miss Julie* and the *Pariah*'; pp. 408-411, Brita Mortensen and Brian Downes, **B1:306**, *Strindberg: An Introduction to his Life and Work*; p. 411, Colin Wilson, **C1:1377**, 'Shaw and Strindberg'; pp. 411-413, Raymond Williams, **D1:489**, *Drama: From Ibsen to Brecht*; pp. 413-416, Birgitta Steene, **B1:429**, *The Greatest Fire*; pp. 417-418, Walter Johnson, **B1:171**, *August Strindberg*; p. 416, Marilyn Johns, **C2:35**, 'Kindred Spirits: Strindberg and Bergman'; pp, 418-420, John Eric Bellquist, **H3:12**, 'Strindberg's "femte natten"'; Clive Barnes, **E11:793**, 'Maddening *Father* at Circle in Square']

[B1:166] Hedberg, Oscar, *August Strindberg. En urolig Tids urolige Aand. Biografi og Studievekledning*, Hellerup: Olson, 1924. 17 pp. ['August Strindberg. A Restless Time's Restless Spirit'. A basic, generally banal, study guide which divides the works into four periods, 1849-1978, 1879-1890, 1891-1899, and 1900-1912. Hedberg also presents a superficial account of Sg's life. Originally published in *Læsning*, 1924:4]

[B1:167] Hedberg, Tor, *Ett decenium*, Del I: Litteratur, Stockholm: Albert Bonniers Förlag, 1912. [Reprints several articles and reviews originally published in *Svenska Dagbladet* during the preceding decade. Includes **D2:737** on *Ett drömspel* and *Kronbruden*; **F2:48**: on *Författaren*; **F8:8** on *Fagervik och Skamsund*; and **G15:28** on *Svarta fanor*. Also includes a commemorative article, 'På femtioårsdagen', **U2:7**]

[B1:168] Hedén, Erik, 'Strindbergsstudier', in *Eros och Polemos. Litterära hyllnings- och stridsartiklar*, Stockholm: Frams Förlag, 1916, pp. 20-71. ['Strindberg Studies'. Reprints several of Hedén's articles on Sg and his works previously published in the Swedish press. Includes reviews of *Gustav Adolf*, **E31:19**, and *Svarta fanor* and *En blå bok*, **G15:29**, on publication, as well as several commemorative or polemical articles including 'Från seger- och dödsåret: 1. Titanen; 2. Vid Strindbergs bår', **T:175**; and 'Från Strindbergs-striden 1910: 1. Vad striden gäller; 2. Strindberg och den svenska diktens framtid', **T:176**]

[B1:169] Herzfeld, Marie, 'Strindbergiana', in *Menschen und Bücher*, Wien: Verlag von Leopold Weiss, 1893, pp. 104-137. [Includes **B9:139**: 'Die Emanzipation des Mannes'; **G3:65**: '*Das rothe Zimmer*'; and **G10:28**: 'Der Roman von Übermenschen']

[B1:170] Houe, Poul, Sven Hakon Rossel, and Göran Stockenström, eds, *August Strindberg and the Other: New Critical Approaches*, Amsterdam – New York: Rodopi, 2002. XV+187 pp. [Publishes the papers from a colloquium in Minneapolis. Contains **B2:1**: Ann-Charlotte Gavel Adams, 'Strindberg and Paris 1894-1898: Barbarian, Initiate, and Self'; **B2:75**: Harry G. Carlson, 'Landscape as Mediator in Strindberg's Search for the Other'; **C1:1203**: Evert Sprinchorn, 'Strindberg Among the Prophets'; **C4:27**: Gunnar Syréhn, 'The Phenomenon of "Otherness" in P. O. Enquist's View of Strindberg in *The Night* of *the Tribades*'; **D2:1230**: Eszter Szalczer, 'Theosophy as Catalyst – Strindberg's Theatre of the Self and the Other'; **E25:15**: Jon M. Berry, 'The Alchemical Regeneration of Souls in Strindberg's *To Damascus, III*'; **F1:71**: Per Stounbjerg, '"To Eat or Be Eaten – that Is the Question" – Incorporations and Rejections of the Other in Strindberg's Autobiographical Prose'; **F4:48**: Poul Houe, 'Writing with a Vengeance: *A Madman's Defence* – an "Otherness" Called Suspense'; **M:164**: Göran Stockenström, 'The World that Strindberg Found: Deciphering the Palimpsest of Nature'; **N:34**: Freddie Rokem, 'Secret Codes: Strindberg and the Dead Languages'; **P1:239**: Ingvar Holm, 'On the Road to Damascus: Strindberg as a Painter'; and **S:232**: Ulf Olsson, 'Going Crazy: Strindberg and the Construction of Literary Madness'. Also contains an editorial Foreword, 'August Strindberg and the Other', pp. [ix]-[xv], and a summatory Afterword, 'An-Other August Strindberg' by Poul Houe, which considers and compares contemporary perspectives on Sg as articulated by contributors in a concluding discussion, pp. [177]-180]

[B1:171] Johnson, Walter [Gilbert], *August Strindberg*, New York: Twayne, 1976. 221 pp. [A concise study of Sg's multi-faceted achievement, with chapters on the man as well as the autobiographer, essayist, poet, novelist, scholar, and scientist. The dramatist is discussed in three chapters, with brief comments on each of the plays in turn. The series format is unhelpful in dealing with a writer as various and prolific as Sg and, though well-informed and informative, the volume is in many respects an extended, reliable footnote to Johnson's long career as a Sg scholar]

[B1:172] — Butt, Wolfgang, *Skandinavistik* (Kiel), 8:2 (1978), 159-160.

[B1:173] — Carlson, Harry G[ilbert], *Modern Language Journal* (Madison, Wisconsin), 62:4 (1976), 203.

[B1:174] — Jarvi, Raymond, *Scandinavian Studies* (Lawrence, Kansas), 49:3 (1977), 362-363.

[B1:175] — Knapp, Bettina L., *Comparative Drama* (Kalamazoo, Michigan), 12:2 (1978), 178-180.

[B1:176] Kärnell, Karl-Åke, *Strindbergs bildspråk*, Stockholm: Geber, 1969. 175 pp. [An abridged, paperback edition of **B1:179**]

[B1:177] — Rinman, Sven, *Göteborgs Handels- och Sjöfartstidning*, 26 June 1970. [Also reviews Kärnell's *Strindbergs lexikon*, **A4:77**]

[B1:178] — Swahn, Sigbrit, *Edda* (Oslo), 70 (1970), 122-123.

[B1:179] Kärnell, Karl-Åke, *Strindbergs bildspråk. En studie i prosastil*, Stockholm: Almqvist & Wicksell, 1962. 320 pp. ['Strindberg's Imagery. A Study in Prose Style'. A consistently illuminating study of Sg's language, style, and imagery in his prose works, which affords great insight into his associational mind, creative imagination, and delight in metaphor. Kärnell gives an account of the place of imagery in the theory and practice of Naturalism and reflects on Sg's early, utilitarian distrust of fiction. He also reviews the syntax of the Sgian image and compares his metaphors with Shakespeare's and demonstrates how many of his most effective formulations are taken from fields of experience that had previously been more or less untouched, including several developing technologies (e.g. photography). How he employs metaphor to illuminate inner experience, to psychologise people, and to give substance to spiritual action is a major concern of Kärnell's thesis, and *Röda rummet*, *Hemsöborna*, *Svarta fanor*, and *I havsbandet* are analysed to establish how Sg's imagery is adapted to the various settings he depicts, as well as to the intellectual and social conditions of his characters. Kärnell also reveals how, with the scientific studies that he conducted during the 1890s, metaphor becomes a means of interpreting the universe, where likenesses (or correspondences) became a way of conferring order on the great confusion and endless continuity of nature and experience. This applies in his chemistry, botany, and linguistics, and became a central feature of his post-Inferno world view and the writing which represents it. He also compares Sg's practice with the theories of Swedenborg and contemporary French Symbolism; discusses 'Den romantiske klockaren på Ranö', *Inferno*, *Jardin des Plantes*, *Sylva Sylvarum*, and 'Hjärnornas kamp', and refers to numerous other works throughout. This remains one of the abiding works of Sg scholarship. Summary in English. Doctoral Dissertation]

[B1:180] — Berendsohn, Walter A[rthur], *Erasmus* (Darmstadt), 15 (1963), Sp. 278-279.

[B1:181] — Björck, Staffan, *Dagens Nyheter* (Stockholm), 25 May 1962.

[B1:182] — Fröier, Lennart, *Arbetet* (Malmö), 13 May 1962.

[B1:183] — Johannesson, Eric O., *Scandinavian Studies* (Lawrence, Kansas), 35:4 (1963), 349-351.

[B1:184] — K. P. [Karl Persson], *Borås Tidning*, 30 August 1962.

[B1:185] — Jonsson, Inge, *Bonniers Litterära Magasin* (Stockholm), 31:6 (1962), 486-489.

[B1:186] — Lagerroth, Erland, *Stockholms-Tidningen*, 26 June 1962.

[B1:187] — Landquist, John, *Aftonbladet* (Stockholm), 1 July 1962.

[B1:188] — Lindström, Göran, *Sydsvenska Dagbladet* (Malmö), 11 May 1962.

[B1:189] — Lindvåg, Alf, *Nya Argus* (Helsingfors), 56 (1963), p. 52.

[B1:190] — Nils Ludvig [Nils Ludvig Olsson], *Ystads Allehanda*, 9 June 1962.

[B1:191] — Palmlund, E., *Kvällsposten* (Malmö), 11 May 1962.

[B1:192] — Poulenard, Elie, *Orbis Litterarum* (Copenhagen), 23 (1968), 325-326.

[B1:193] — Qvarnström, Gunnar, *Samlaren* (Uppsala), 85 (1964), pp. 247-255.

[B1:194] — Rinman, Sven, 'Strindberg – femtio år död och levande', *Göteborgs Handels- och Sjöfartstidning*, 14 May 1962. ['Strindberg – Fifty Years Dead and Still Alive']

[B1:195] — Wittrock, Ulf, *Perspektiv* (Stockholm), 14 (1963), 316-317.

[B1:196] — Wittrock, Ulf, *Upsala Nya Tidning*, 24 July 1962.

[B1:197] Kjær, Nils, 'Strindberg, 1-3', in *Profiler*, Kristiania: Gyldendal, 1922. 280 pp. [Includes three essays on Sg originally published in Norwegian journals (**F5:112** and **F5:113** on *Inferno*, **E49:195** on *Oväder*), and the text of an essay marking Sg's 60th birthday, published in *Verdens Gang* in 1909]

[B1:198] Kjær, Nils, 'Strindberg, 1-3', in *Profiler*, Oslo: Gyldendal Norsk Forlag, 1969. pp. 220. [Rpr. of **B1:197**]

[B1:199] Kjær, Nils, 'August Strindberg', in Nils Kjær, *Essays og Epistler*, Oslo: Dreyer, 1990, pp. 112-[118].

[B1:200] Kullenberg, Annette, *Strindberg – murveln. En bok om journalisten August Strindberg*, Stockholm: Wahlström & Widstrand, 1997. Illus. 364 pp. ['Strindberg the Hack. A Book about August Strindberg the Journalist'. Presents Sg as an exemplary journalist who commanded a range of registers and techniques which are illustrated here by extracts from his works, selected to exemplify his style, polemical strategies, expressions of feeling, and how he describes different milieux, reports various social, political, and artistic events, and portrays a wide range of individuals.]

[B1:201] — Elam, Ingrid, *Aftonbladet* (Stockholm), 14 August 1997.

[B1:202] — Kärnborg, Ulrika, *Dagens Nyheter* (Stockholm), 14 August 1997.

[B1:202a] — Linnel, Björn, 'Två murvlar som kan knepen', *LO-Tidningen* (Stockholm), 76:25 (1997), p. 19. ['Two Hacks who Know their Tricks']

[B1:203] — Littberger, Inger, 'Journalisten Strindberg', *Årsbok för kristen humanism och samhällsyn* (Uppsala), 60 (1997), pp. 169-170. ['Strindberg the Journalist']

[B1:204] — Svedjedal, Johan, *Svenska Dagbladet* (Stockholm), 2 September 1997.

[B1:205] — Wittrock, Ulf, *Upsala Nya Tidning*, 16 August 1997.

[B1:205a/B1:205b] Lamm, Martin, *August Strindberg*, 2 vols, Vol. 1: 'Före infernokrisen', Stockholm: Albert Bonniers Förlag, 1940. Illus. 468 pp; Vol. 2: 'Efter omvändelsen', Stockholm: Albert Bonniers Förlag, 1942. Illus. 410 pp. ['August Strindberg, I. Before the Inferno Crisis'; II. 'After His Conversion'. A defining work in Swedish Sg scholarship which discusses his *œuvre* in its entirety and was responsible for establishing an image of Sg as man and writer which came to dominate not only scholarly practice in Sweden for several decades but also exerted a powerful influence on the staging of his plays there through the stress it placed on an indissoluble link between Sg's life and his works. Based on scrupulous scholarship but adopting a biographical approach to the occasional detriment of its judgement of Sg's artistic achievements, few works on any major writer, particularly one as protean as Sg, have been as influential as Lamm's, which helped to rehabilitate him from much local prejudice and yet retarded the application of alternative, potentially more productive, approaches to both the plays and the novels by the next generation of Swedish scholars. Nevertheless, its scope remains impressive, dealing as it does with all the plays, prose fiction, and poetry. Its insights into their genesis remain perspicacious and relevant, and Lamm's achievement is all the more remarkable for the fact that it predates the scholarly publication of Sg's correspondence and much other source material on which it draws extensively, and he had consequently to rely upon a wealth of disparate manuscript sources]

Reviews of Volume I – *Före infernokrisen*:

[B1:206] — Ahlenius, Holger, *Bonniers Litterära Magasin* (Stockholm), 10 (1941), 144-145.

[B1:207] — Amenius, Ragnar, *Folklig kultur* (Stockholm), 6 (1941), 25-27.

[B1:208] — B. B-m [Birger Bæckström], *Göteborgs Handels- och Sjöfartstidning*, 11 January 1941.

[B1:209] — Beyer, Nils, *Social-Demokraten* (Stockholm), 23 December 1940.

[B1:210] — E. Ek [E. Ehnmark], *Upsala Nya Tidning*, 21 December 1940.

[B1:211] — Elmquist, Carl Johan, *Aarhus Stiftstidende*, 13 January 1941.

[B1:212] — Grevenius, Herbert, *Stockholms-Tidningen*, 20 December 1940.

[B1:213] — J. L. [John Landquist], *Aftonbladet* (Stockholm), 17 December 1940.

[B1:214] — Landquist, John, 'Lamms Strindbergsbok', in Solveig Landquist, red., *John Landquist om Strindberg personen och diktaren*, **B1:248**, pp. 159-161. [Rpr. of **B1:213**]

[B1:215] — P. F[roberg], *Tidning för Sveriges läroverket* (Stockholm), 41 (1941), pp. 63, 81.

[B1:216] — R[afael] K[oskimies], *Valvoja Aika* (Helsinki), 20 (1942), 309-312.

[B1:217] — Schiller, Harald, *Sydsvenska Dagbladet* (Malmö), 2 December 1940.

[B1:218] — Schyberg, Frederik, *Politiken* (Copenhagen), 14 January 1941.

[B1:219] — Söderberg, Karl, *Studiekamraten* (Tollarp), 24:9-10 (1942)

[B1:220] — Wizelius, Ingemar, *Gaudeamus* (Stockholm), 18:1 (1941), p. 6.

Reviews of Volume II – *Efter omvändelsen*:

[B1:221] — Amenius, Ragnar, *Folklig kultur* (Stockholm), 8 (1943), 243-245.

[B1:222] — Beyer, Nils, *Social-Demokraten* (Stockholm), 21 December 1942.

[B1:223] — E. E-d [Erik Ekelund], *Nya Argus* (Helsingfors), 36 (1943), 105-106.

[B1:224] — Elmquist, Carl Johan, *Politiken* (Copenhagen), 9 July 1943.

[B1:225] — Grevenius, Herbert, *Stockholms-Tidningen*, 14 December 1942.

[B1:226] — Grevenius, Herbert, 'Strindberg efter krisen', in *Offentliga nöjen. Premiärer och mellanspel 1939-1944*, Stockholm: Fritzes Bokförlag, 1946, pp. 194-198. ['Strindberg after the Crisis'. Rpr. of **B1:225**]

[B1:227] — J. L. [John Landquist], 'Lamms Strindbergsbok', *Aftonbladet* (Stockholm), 15 December 1942.

[B1:228] — Landquist, John, 'Lamms Strindbergsbok', in Solveig Landquist, red., *John Landquist om Strindberg personen och diktaren*, **B1:248**, pp. 162-164. [Rpr. of **B1:227**]

[B1:229] — O. H-g [Olle Holmberg], *Dagens Nyheter* (Stockholm), 8 December 1942.

[B1:230] — Wieselgren, Oscar, *Svenska Dagbladet* (Stockholm), 30 January 1943.

See also **A4:30**

[B1:231] Lamm, Martin, *August Strindberg*, Andra reviderade upplagan, Stockholm: Albert Bonniers Förlag, 1948. Illus. 418 pp. [Revised, one-volume edition of **B1:205a** and **B1:205b**]

[B1:232] Lamm, Martin, *August Strindberg*, Stockholm: Aldus, 1968. Illus. 450 pp. [Rpr. of **B1:231** in paperback]

Reviews of the One Volume Edition:

[B1:233] — Ahlenius, Holger, *Bonniers Litterära Magasin* (Stockholm), 18 (1949), 258-259.

[B1:234] — B. B-m [Birger Bæckström], *Göteborgs Handels- och Sjöfartstidning*, 9 July 1949.

[B1:235] — Berendsohn, Walter A[rthur], *Erasmus* (Darmstadt), 1 (1947), Sp. 420-424.

[B1:236] — B. H-t [Bengt Holmqvist], *Nya Argus* (Helsingfors), 42 (1949), 86-89.

[B1:237] — Dahlström, Carl E. W. L., *Scandinavian Studies* (Menasha, Wisconsin), 22:3 (1950), 136-139.

[B1:238] — E. Ek [Elof Ehnmark], *Upsala Nya Tidning*, 13 March 1943.

[B1:239] — Linneballe, Paul, *Aarhus Stiftstidende*, 6 December 1949.

[B1:240] — Sjöstedt, Nils Åke, *Götheborgske spionen* (Gothenburg) 14:1 (1949), 7-8.

[B1:240a] — T. Hln [T. Hallén], *Dagens Nyheter* (Stockholm), 21 February 1949.

[B1:241] Lamm, Martin, *August Strindberg*, Translated by Harry Carlson, New York: Benjamin Blom, 1971. Illus. XXI+561 pp. [A translation of **B1:231**, considerably adapted by the translator for an English language readership]

[B1:242] — Johnson, Walter [Gilbert], *Journal of English and Germanic Philology* (Urbana, Illinois), 71:1 (1972), 104-106.

[B1:243] — Sandstroem, Yvonne, *Scandinavian Studies* (Lawrence, Kansas), 44:1 (1972), p. 147.

[B1:244] — Sprinchorn, Evert, *Modern Drama* (Lawrence, Kansas), 15:2 (1972), 209-211.

See also **A4:8**

[B1:245] Landauer, Gustav, *Der werdende Mensch*, Aufsätze über Leben und Schrifttum, Hrsg. von Martin Büber, Potsdam: Gustav Kiepenheuer, 1921, pp. 259-341. ['The Coming Man'. Includes a general assessment, **B2:229**, together with essays on *Historiska miniatyrer*, **G14:22**, *Ett drömspel*, **E41:88**, and *Spöksonaten*, **E51:70** (See **A4:96**)]

[B1:246] Landauer, Gustav, *Der werdende Mensch*, Aufsätze über Leben und Schrifttum, Hrsg. von Martin Büber, Telgte-Westbevern: Büchse der Pandora, 1921. X+263 pp. [Rpr. of the Potsdam edition, **B1:245**]

[B1:247] Landauer, Gustav, *Der werdende Mensch*, Aufsätze zur Literatur, Mit einem Essay von Arnold Zweig, Leipzig und Weimar: Gustav Kiepenheuer Verlag, 1980. [208] pp. [An abridged edition of **B1:245**. Includes the essays on *Historiska miniatyrer*, **G14:22**, and *Spöksonaten*, **E51:70**. See also **E51:71** and **E51:72**]

[B1:248] Landquist, Solveig, red., *John Landquist om Strindberg personen och diktaren*, Inledning av Lars Dahlbäck, Stockholm: Legenda, 1984. Illus. 379 pp. ['John Landquist on Strindberg the Man and Writer'. Contains a selection from Landquist's writings about Sg, including both his contributions to the Sg Feud and the controversies surrounding publication of *Samlade Skrifter*, of which he was sole editor. The collection also includes numerous reviews of critical and other works about Sg, theatre reviews, personal recollections of Sg, and analyses of his personality and philosophy. See **A2:55**, **A3:86**, **A3:102**, **A3:105**, **A3:107**, **A3:109**, **B1:214**, **B1:228**, **B2:231**, **B2:233**, **B2:237**, **B2:239**, **B4:99**, **B8:129**, **B9:164**, **C1:790**, **D2:119**, **D2:145**, **D2:187**, **D2:189**, **D2:862**, **E11:109**, **E12:150**, **E26:13**, **E30:23**, **E30:155**, **E31:86**, **E35:209**, **E41:359**, **E42:160**, **G7:60**, **G15:31**, **J:571**, **R:661**, **R:1286**, **R:1290**, **R:1295**, **R:1300**, **R:1302**, **R:1303**, **S:199**, and **U1:449**. There is also an introduction by Lars Dahlbäck, **A4:40**, pp. 11-26, a bibliography of Landquist's writings on Sg, and an account of his work as a cultural journalist in general]

[B1:249] — Battail, Jean-François, *Etudes Germaniques* (Paris), 41:1 (1986), 67-69.

[B1:250] — Fehrman, Carl, 'Landquist fick rätt', *Svenska Dagbladet* (Stockholm), 8 November 1984. ['Landquist was Right']

[B1:251] — Forser, Tomas, *Arbetarbladet* (Gävle), 6 December 1984.

[B1:252] — Granberg, Nils, *Aftonbladet* (Stockholm), 11 January 1985.

[B1:253] — Lång, Helmer, *Skånska Dagbladet* (Malmö), 28 November 1984.

[B1:254] — Lundh, Trygve, *Folket* (Eskilstuna), 5 December 1984.

[B1:255] — Magnusson, Bo, *Eskilstuna-Kuriren*, 22 November 1984.

[B1:256] — Myrdal, Jan, 'Nå! Vad med de döda? Apropå Landquists Strindbergsbok', *Folket i Bild* (Stockholm), 14:2 (1985), p. 27. ['Well! What of the Dead? Apropos Landquist's Strindberg Book']

[B1:257] — Myrdal, Jan, 'Nå! Vad med de döda? Apropå Landquists Strindbergsbok', in *En annann ordning. Litterärt och Personligt*, Stockholm: Norstedts, 1988, pp. 104-113. ['Well! What of the Dead? Apropos Landquist's Strindberg Book'. Rpr. of **B1:256**]

[B1:258] — Ollén, Gunnar, *Sydsvenska Dagbladet* (Malmö), 11 January 1985.

[B1:259] — Rinman, Sven, *Upsala Nya Tidning*, 15 May 1985.

[B1:260] — Sommar, Carl-Olof, *Östgöta Correspondenten* (Linköping), 18 December 1984.

[B1:261] — Stolpe, Sven, *Nya Wermlands Tidningen* (Karlstad), 26 November 1984.

[B1:262] — Vejde, E., *Hufvudstadsbladet* (Helsingfors), 10 December 1984.

[B1:263] — Widegren, Björn, *Gefle Dagblad* (Gävle), 19 November 1984.

[B1:264] Liebert, Arthur, *August Strindberg. Seine Weltanschauung und seine Kunst*, Sammlung Collignon 5, Berlin: Arthur Collignon, 1920. Illus. 155 pp. ['August Strindberg. His *Weltanschauung* and his Art'. Unlike many other German studies of the period, Liebert's neo-Kantian approach places greater emphasis on Sg the writer than the psychological case and relates him interestingly to the trend in modern thought that links naturalistic determinism with more recent mystical and semi-mystical tendencies. Incorporates Liebert's essay on Sg's philosophy of history, **L1:21**, originally published in 1918 in *Preußiche Jahrbücher*]

[**B1:265**] — Ahlberg, Alf, 'En Strindbergsstudie', *Svenska Dagbladet* (Stockholm), 26 March 1921. [Praises a book which Ahlström would himself translate into Swedish (see **B1:277**), calling it 'Among the most stimulating and lucid studies of Sg yet published']

[**B1:266**] — Israel, Walter, *Die Glocke* (München), 6:1 (1920-21), 448-449.

[**B1:267**] — Metz, Rudolf, *Literaturblatt für germanische und romanische Philologie* (Leipzig), 43 (1922), 17-20.

[**B1:268**] — Mortensen, Johan [Martin], *Stockholms-Tidningen*, 22 August 1920.

[**B1:269**] — Mortensen, Johan [Martin], *Sydsvenska Dagbladet* (Malmö), 4 November 1920.

[**B1:270**] — N. E. [Nils Erdmann], *Nya Dagligt Allehanda* (Stockholm), 17 April 1921.

[**B1:271**] — Nilsson, Albert, *Göteborgs Handels- och Sjöfartstidning*, 9 October 1920.

[**B1:272**] — Pieth, W., *Bücherei und Bildungspflege* (Berlin), 1 (1921), p. 183.

[**B1:273**] — Sternberg, Kurt, 'Unsere Zeit und August Strindberg. Mit besonderer Rücksicht auf Arthur Lieberts neues Strindberg-Buch', *Die Glocke* (München), 6 (1920-21), Sp. 1176-1184. ['Our Time and August Strindberg. With Particular Reference to Arthur Liebert's New Strindberg Book']

See also **A4:52, A4:53, A4:96**

[**B1:274**] Liebert, Arthur, *August Strindberg*, Berlin: Pan-Verlag Rolf Heise, 1923. 155 pp. [A new edition of **B1:264**]

[**B1:275**] — Banfi, Antonio, 'August Strindberg', *Rivista di filosofia* (Modena), 14:4 (1923), 384-387. [Surveys recent publications by Liebert, including the 1923 edition of **B1:264**]

[**B1:276**] — E. S., *Hellweg* (Essen), 4 (1924), p. 560.

[**B1:277**] Liebert, Arthur, *Strindberg och nutidens andliga problem*, Till Svenska och med förord av fil. d:r. Alf Ahlberg, Stockholm: Bokförlaget Natur och Kultur, 1925. 136 pp. ['Strindberg and Contemporary Spiritual Problems'. Swedish edition of **B1:264** with a Foreword by the translator]

[**B1:278**] — G. A. [G. Aspelin], *Lundagård* (Lund), 6:5 (1925), 10-11.

[**B1:279**] — H. G-s [Herbert Grevenius], *Stockholms Dagblad*, 11 April 1925.

[**B1:280**] — K. H. [K. Hagberg], *Nya Dagligt Allehanda* (Stockholm), 13 September 1925.

[**B1:281**] Linder, Sten, *August Strindberg*, Studentföreningen Verdandis småskrifter 445, Stockholm: Albert Bonniers Förlag, 1942. 79 pp. [A short, well-informed, introductory survey of Sg's principal works in a popular series aimed at the general reader. Given the date, it accords *Ett drömspel*, as Sg's 'most singular and beautiful post-conversion work', an unusually prominent place in the context of his work as a whole]

[**B1:282**] — Amenius, Ragnar, *Folklig kultur* (Stockholm), 7 (1942), 246-247.

[**B1:283**] — Beyer, Nils, *Bonniers Litterära Magasin* (Stockholm), 11 (1942), 478-479.

[**B1:284**] — Brandell, Gunnar, *Göteborgs Handels- och Sjöfartstidning*, 28 August 1942.

[**B1:285**] — Cederblad, Carl, *Folklig kultur* (Stockholm), 8 (1943), p. 165.

[**B1:286**] — E. Ek [E. Ehnmark], *Upsala Nya Tidning*, 5 June 1942.

[**B1:287**] — G. A. [Gösta Attorps], *Svenska Dagbladet* (Stockholm), 13 July 1942.

[**B1:288**] — G. J. [Gabriel Jönsson], *Sydsvenska Dagbladet* (Malmö), 13 July 1942.

[**B1:289**] — O. Hg [Olle Holmberg], *Dagens Nyheter* (Stockholm), 1 June 1942.

[**B1:290**] — Wizelius, Ingemar, *Tiden* (Stockholm), 34 (1942), 508-509.

[B1:291] Lindström, Göran, red., *Strindbergs språk och stil: valda studier*, Lund: C. W. K. Gleerups Förlag, 1965. 180 pp. ['Strindberg's Laguage and Style. Selected Studies'. A useful collection of republished early essays on Sg's style and language, with an introduction by Lindström, pp. 7-10. Contains **B2:217**: Bengt Kinnander, 'Ordstudier i Strindbergs prosa'; **B2:378**: Nils,Svanberg, 'Ur Strindbergs prosautveckling'; **E48:43**: Göran Lindström, 'Dialog och bildspråk i Strindbergs kammarspel'; **G1:109**: Nils Svanberg, 'Ur Strindbergs prosautvecking'; **G1:124**: Eva Wennerström, 'Expressiva anföringsverb'; **G2:32**: Nils Svanberg, '*Från Fjärdingen och Svartbäcken*'; **G3:25**: Walter A. Berendsohn, 'Inledningen till *Röda rummet*'; **G8:20**: Staffan Björck, 'I marginalen till *Hemsöborna*'; **G8:61**: Karl-Åke Kärnell, 'Metafor och fiktion i *Hemsöborna*'; **G8:76**: Gösta Lundberg, 'Fackmässig och konstnärlig exakthet i Strindbergs *Hemsöborna*'; **H2:20**: Gunnar Brandell, 'Strindbergs monologer'; and **H4:25**: Gunnar Ollén, 'Stilen i *Ordalek och småkonst*']

[B1:292] — Lundqvist, Åke, *Dagens Nyheter* (Stockholm), 22 February 1965.

[B1:293] — Rinman, Sven, *Göteborgs Handels- och Sjöfartstidning*, 14 April 1964.

[B1:294] — Swahn, Sigbrit, *Sydsvenska Dagbladet* (Malmö), 6 July 1965.

[B1:295] Ludvig, Nils [Nils Ludvig Olsson], *På vandring i Skåne*, Lund: C. W. K. Gleerups Förlag, 1967. 155 pp. [Includes **B8:102**: 'Nemesis Divina'; **R:1421**: 'På vägen till Inferno'; **M:149**: 'I Linnés fotspår'; and **R:1422**: 'Efter Legender'. Also contains an essay on Sg's friend, the Lawyer 'Nils Andersson från Hofterup', pp. 54-59]

[B1:296] Lundmark, Knut, *Strindberg. Geniet - Sökaren - Människan,* Stockholm: Nordisk Rotogravyr, 1948. Illus. 325 pp. ['Strindberg. Genius - Seeker - Man'. Lundmark's volume is the work of an enthusiast who sometimes appears to be still embroiled in many of the controversies initiated by Sg during his own lifetime. It incorporates material from several previously published essays and treats a wide range of topics, including Sg's personality, his religious beliefs, *Hemsöborna* (which is subjected to a useful genetic analysis of the published text vis-à-vis the original manuscript), and his work as a cultural historian in *Svenska folket* and elsewhere. Lundmark contextualises Sg's life and conflicts, both personal and political, but his reflections are most relevant where his scientific conjectures are concerned, not least for presenting the reflections of a professional astronomer on his astronomical speculations. Lundmark also discusses *Spöksonaten*, *Götiska rummen*, and *Svarta fanor* in some detail]

[B1:297] — E. A-n [Elis Andersson], *Göteborgs-Posten*, 29 December 1948.

[B1:298] — Elovson, Harald, *Arbetet* (Malmö), 16 April 1949.

[B1:299] — O. H-g [Olle Holmberg], *Dagens Nyheter* (Stockholm), 15 January 1949.

[B1:300] — T. B-s [Teddy Brunius], *Upsala Nya Tidning*, 12 January 1949.

[B1:301] — Uppvall, Axel Johan, *Scandinavian Studies* (Menasha, Wisconsin), 21:3 (1949), 164-166.

[B1:302] Lux, Joseph Aug[ust], 'Brief an eine Dame über den Dichter und Mystiker August Strindberg', *Kunstrat und Kulturrat. Blätter für die neue Zeit* (Salzburg), 1 (1919-20), pp. 21-23, 54-55, 80-82, 116-118, 145-147, 182-184. ['Letters to a Lady on the Writer and Mystic August Strindberg'. Includes I: Strindbergs Metaphysik; II: Leitsätze aus Strindbergs Ethos; III: Seine innere Personlichkeit; IV: Sein Verhältnis zum Weibe]

[B1:303] Maury, Lucien, 'August Strindberg', in *L'Imagination scandinave: études et portraits*, Paris: Perrin et Cie, 1929, pp. 114-153. ['The Scandinavian Imagination: Studies and Portraits'. Brings together several shorter pieces on Sg: **F2:67**: 'Les Confessions' and **F2:66**: 'Fermentation' on the first two volumes of *Tjänstekvinnans son* in French translation; **F1:33**: 'Strindberg et la Suisse'; **B3:290**: 'Strindberg et nous'; and **T:336**: 'Strindberg et la démocratie']

[B1:304] Meyer, Michael (Compiler), *File on Strindberg*, London: Methuen, 1986. 61 pp. [A chronology of Sg's life and work is followed by summaries of, and comments on, what Meyer considers are Sg's twenty most important plays. The non-dramatic writing is consigned to a mere two-thirds of a page. Also includes a selection of brief quotations by and about the writer and his work, mainly translated from Sg's own letters and *Ockulta dagboken*]

[B1:305] Moritzen, Julius, *August Strindberg. The Literary Enigma*, Little Blue Book 503, Girard, Kansas: Haldeman-Julius Co., 1924. 96 pp.

[B1:306] Mortensen, Brita M. E., and Brian W[esterdale] Downs, *Strindberg: An Introduction to his Life and Work*, Cambridge: Cambridge University Press, 1949. XII+234 pp. [A long-serving, level-headed, but ultimately inadequate and frustrating volume which provides an outline of Sg's life in four chapters and then deals cursorily with the works under five headings: plays, novels, short stories, autobiographical writings, and miscellaneous works. The authors find that Sg's 'most positive quality is his fluidity', the 'first and greatest of [his] misfortunes was his birth']

[B1:307] — Anon [Sir Peter F. D. Tennant], *The Times Literary Supplement* (London), 3 February 1950.

[B1:308] — Blanck, Anton, *Göteborgs Handels- och Sjöfartstidning*, 23 January 1950.

[B1:309] — Bredsdorff, Elias, *Cambridge Review*, 6 May 1950, pp. 500-501. ['An admirable and authoritative introduction to Sweden's greatest writer']

[B1:310] — Gustafson, Alrik, *Bulletin of the American Swedish Institute* (Minneapolis), 5:1 (1950), 29-30.

[B1:311] — Rothwell, Brian, *Moderna språk* (Stockholm), 59:4 (1965), p. 443. [Reviews the 2nd edition. The limitations of an introduction like this are clear, although the book might have overcome them in some extent if it had communicated a little more enthusiasm for Sg. It is completely unrevised (the bibliography mentions nothing published after 1948), and will hardly stimulate any serious reader]

[B1:312] — T. B-s [Teddy Brunius], *Upsala Nya Tidning*, 12 December 1949.

[B1:313] Muralt, Roland de, *Un regard si étrange. Traversées d'Auguste Strindberg*, Vevey: Editions Bertil Galland, 1981. Illus. 108 pp. ['So Strange a Gaze'. A short collection of Barthesian reflections on the body of Sg and the corpus of his work which, for Muralt, is that of a writer 'who reads with his body' and whose *œuvre* originates in 'an écriture based upon fear']

[B1:314] Myrdal, Jan, 'August Strindberg', in *I de svartare fanors tid. Texter om litteratur, lögn och förbannad dikt*, Skriftställning 18, Stockholm: Hägglunds Förlag, 1998, pp. 9-139. ['In the Time of the Blacker Banners. Texts on Literature, Lies, and Bloody Poetry'. A collection of Myrdal's literary journalism which includes a largely political analysis of Sg in **B3:312**: 'Lika normal som sill och potatis'; **E11:126**: '*Fadren*'; **E12:206**: 'På tal om Ranskan Jussi'; **E23:9**: '*Leka med elden*'; **F1:38**: 'August Strindberg och hans tradition i svensk litteratur. Bortom fiktion, självbiografi och den etablerade sanningens litteratur'; **R:1622**: 'Till ett modernt åttiotal'; **T:381**: 'Återta August Strindberg!'; **T:435**:

'Strindbergsgala för yttrandefriheten'; **T:432**: 'Strindberg och antisemitismen'; **T:426**: 'På balkongen'; **T:421**: 'Om icke politiskt korrekta åsikter'; **T:417**: 'En exemplarisk fasförskjutning: Strindbergs modernitet'; **T:386**: 'August Strindberg. Ett påpekande och ett förslag'; **T:411**: 'Förmörkelsen av August Strindberg'; and the miscellaneous piece, 'En skriftställare. En Svensk en; en karl', **U1:572**]

[B1:315] Myrdal, Jan, *Johan August Strindberg*, Stockholm: Natur och Kultur, 2000. Illus. 253 pp. [A personal and polemical reading, which utilises material from numerous previous articles. Myrdal discusses Sg's Swedishness and his role as a national author, as well as his language, family background, autobiographical writings, social criticism, letters, attitude to women, masculinity, and anti-Semitism. He also questions the values and conclusions of mainstream Swedish scholarship, relates Sg to the political issues and thought of his period, and discusses his personal and literary links with Verner von Heidenstam, Goethe, Shakespeare, Wedekind, Balzac, Hjalmar Branting, Georg and Edvard Brandes, Karl Otto Bonnier, Siri von Essen, Frida Uhl, Carl Ludwig Schleich, Jules Vallès, A. O. Wallenberg, and Carl David af Wirsén. Includes comments on a range of works, including, in some detail, *En dåres försvarstal*, *Tjänstekvinnans son*, *Ett drömspel*, *Fadren*, and *Mäster Olof*]

[B1:316] — Blackwell, Marilyn Johns, *Scandinavian Studies* (Provo), 73:4 (2001), 608-612. [Maintains that this is a book about Myrdal rather than Sg, many of whose dysfunctional attributes (e.g. his misogyny and adolescent rebelliousness) are common to both writers. Myrdal uses Sg to excoriate his own demons, applauding him as a kind of paradigm of rebellion, excusing his anti-Semitism, and explaining away his misogyny on the grounds that it is quite normal behaviour]

[B1:317] — Cullberg, Johan, 'Myrdals Strindberg: Är psykoser ointressanta?', *Svenska Dagbladet* (Stockholm), 28 August 2000. ['Myrdal's Strindberg: Are Psychoses Interesting?']

[B1:318] — Elam, Ingrid, 'Myrdal ser Strindberg i ögonen', *Dagens Nyheter* (Stockholm), 12 May 2000. ['Myrdal Looks Strindberg in the Eyes'. Stresses the extent of Jan Myrdal's self-identification with Sg in **B1:315**]

[B1:319] — Granberg, Nils, 'Bättre – och sämre än sitt rykte', *Aftonbladet* (Stockholm), 14 April 2000. ['Better – and Worse than His Reputation'. Points out that in writing about Sg Myrdal provides a double perspective; the book is as much about its author as his subject]

[B1:320] — Samuelsson, Marie Louise, 'Har du aldrig haft riktigt fel?', *Svenska Dagbladet* (Stockholm), 30 April 2000. ['Have You never been Really Mistaken?' The text of an interview with Myrdal about his presentation of Sg in **B1:315**]

[B1:321] — Zorn, Henrietta, 'Ett demokratiskt Myrdalprojekt', *Politikens, kulturens & idéernas arena*, 2000:3, pp. 58-59. ['A Democratic Myrdal Project']

[B1:322] Myrdal, Jan, *Johan August Strindberg*, Stockholm: Natur och kultur, 2003. Illus. 253 pp. [Paperback Rpr. of **B1:315**]

[B1:323] Myrdal, Jan, 'Kring verkan', in *Strindberg och Balzac. Essayer kring realismens problem*, Stockholm: P. A. Norstedt & Söners Förlag, 1981, pp. 50-77. ['Strindberg and Balzac. Essays on the Problem of Realism'. The collection also includes **B3:311**: 'En Strindbergspresentation för tyskar'; **C1:925**: 'Jules Vallès'; and previously published discussions of **E51:389**: *Spöksonaten*; **F2:77**: *Tjänstekvinnans son*; **F9:26**: *Ensam*; **G3:115**:

Röda rummet; **G4:43**: *Det nya riket*; **G5:96**: *Giftas*; **G7:69**: 'Tschandala'; **K3:46**: *Bland franska bönder*; as well as **T:385**: 'Bortom avfalet'; and **T:425**: 'Om Svanbergsproblemet i Strindbergsdiskussionen'. The collection is less a comparative study of Balzac and Sg, more a compendium of earlier essays on the two authors, which also includes an introduction in which Myrdal discusses Sg's reputation in Sweden, pp. 5-13]

[B1:324] — Andersson, Rolf, *Göteborgs-Posten*, 24 September 1981.

[B1:325] — Brandell, Gunnar, *Svenska Dagbladet* (Stockholm), 7 September 1981.

[B1:326] — Engdahl, Horace, *Expressen* (Stockholm), 7 September 1981.

[B1:327] — Fogelbäck, Jan, *Förr och nu* (Stockholm), 1981:4, p. 71.

[B1:328] — Hägg, Göran, *Aftonbladet* (Stockholm), 7 September 1981.

[B1:329] — Jerring, J., *Bokvännen* (Stockholm), 37 (1982), p. 68.

[B1:330] — Jonsson, Inge, *Bonniers Litterära Magasin* (Stockholm), 51 (1982), 80-82.

[B1:331] — Lång, Helmer, *Skånska Dagbladet* (Malmö), 30 September 1981.

[B1:332] — Liedman, S.-E., *Sydsvenska Dagbladet* (Malmö), 7 September 1981.

[B1:333] — Lundberg, E., *Hallandsposten* (Halmstad), 17 September 1981.

[B1:334] — Magnusson, Bo, *Eskilstuna-Kuriren*, 14 September 1981.

[B1:335] — Mellgren, Thomas, *entré* (Norsborg), 9:6 (1982), 27-28.

[B1:336] — Myrdal, Jan, *Svenska Dagbladet* (Stockholm), 12 October 1981.

[B1:337] — Pehrsson, G. *Örebro-Kuriren*, 8 September 1981.

[B1:338] — Polvall, T., *Helsingborgs Dagblad*, 21 September 1981.

[B1:339] — Stolpe, Sven, *Nya Wermlands Tidningen* (Karlstad), 24 August 1981.

[B1:340] — Sundberg, Björn, *Vår lösen* (Sigtuna), 73 (1982), 461-462.

[B1:341] — Tjäder, Per Arne, *Ny Dag* (Stockholm), 11 December 1981.

[B1:342] — Wolf, Lars, *Nerikes Allehanda* (Örebro), 14 October 1981.

[B1:343] — Zern, Leif, *Dagens Nyheter* (Stockholm), 7 September 1981.

[B1:344] Neuhaus, Johannes, *August Strindberg im Leben und Streben. Unterlage für die Strindberg-Vorlesung an der Berliner Universität*, 2. vermehrte Auflage, Halle: Buchdruckerei Wilhelm Hendrichs, 1916. 58 pp. ['August Strindberg's Life and Strife. Documents for the Strindberg Lecture at Berlin University']

[B1:345] Nilsson, Arne, *August Strindberg. Korta inblickar i hans liv och författarskap. Med en avslutande bibliografi*, Tryckt i 200 exemplar, Handbunden av författaren, Vinslöv: Br. Enroth Tryckeri, 1998. ['August Strindberg. Brief Impressions of his Life and Works. With a Concluding Bibliography'. Privately printed reflections on Sg's life and writings, published in an edition of 200 copies]

[B1:346] Nilsson, Skans Kersti, Sten Furhammar, Claes Lennartsson, red., *Strindberg i världen. Essäer med anledning av 150-årsjubiléet 1999*, Småtryck från Valfrid 23, Borås: Publiceringsföreningen VALFRID, 2000. 74 pp. ['Strindberg in the World. Essays Commemorating the 150th anniversary of Sg's Birth'. Contains **B9:93**: Margaretha Fahlgren, '"Jag har alltid tillbett kvinnorna, dessa förtjusande tokor" – kvinnan i Strindbergs författarskap'; **G12:32**: Boel Westin, 'Strindberg skriver sagor'; **R:1108**: Carl Olof Josephson, 'August Strindberg och Kungliga Biblioteket'; and **R:1339**: Jan Lewin, 'Strindbergs irrfäder i Europa'; as well as two miscellaneous pieces: **U1:505**: Helene

Lis, 'Strindberg i olika världar' and Lars-Inge Nilsson, 'Experimentet Augustivärlden', **U1:591**]

[**B1:347**] Ollén, Gunnar, *Forskarliv - sex decennier med Strindberg*, red. Catharina Söderberg and Anna Bodin, Stockholm: Strindbergssällskapet, 2004. Illus. 146 pp. [A collection of articles, reviews, and other pieces on Sg by Ollén republished to commemorate the latter's 90th birthday. Contains a Foreword by Björn Meidal, p. 7, and an introduction by Catharina Söderberg, 'Gunnar Ollén - sex decennier av Strindbergsforskning' (Gunnar Ollén - Six Decades of Strindberg research, **U1:724**), as well as the text of, or selections from, **B3:333**, **D1:650**, **D2:1027**, **D2:1029**, **E12:216**, **E12:218**, **E25:106**, **E29:13**, **E29:13**, **E59:22**, **K7:69**, **P5:49**, **R:1717**, **R:1718**, **R:1720**, and **U1:612**]

[**B1:348**] [Olsson, Folke], red., *Strindberg*, Stockholm: LiberFörlag, 1981. Illus. 208 pp. [The richly illustrated catalogue accompanying an exhibition on Sg's life and work at Kulturhuset, Stockholm. It includes a series of short essays, both biographical and technical, which are designed to introduce the general reader to different, often less familiar, aspects of his multifaceted project and contains **B2:212**: Karl-Åke Kärnell, 'På språng i verkligheten'; **B3:332**: Gunnar Ollén, 'Dramat erövrar världen'; **B9:191**: Karin Monié, 'Kvinnosyn i dikt och verklighet'; **D2:1074**: Agneta Pleijel and Lennart Hjulström, 'Han gör allt till dramatik'; **D2:756**: Kirsten Gram Holmström, 'Teatermannen'; **E53:35**: Per Verner-Carlsson and Lennart Mörk, 'Vita rum och andra' (on *Pelikanen*); **H2:57**: James Spens, 'De blottlagda känslornas poesi'; **J:175**: Torsten Eklund, 'En god och sann bok är ett brev'; **L1:31**: Per Nyström, 'Folkets historiker'; **M:138**: Hans Lindström, 'Konstnär och vetenkapsman'; **P1:441**: Göran Söderström, 'Att få bli målare...'; **P2:56**: Per Hemmingsson, 'Tänkt bli fotograf...'; **R:1280**: Olof Lagercrantz, 'Vår litterära superkändis'; **R:1338**: Hans Levander, 'Strindberg - liv och verk'; **T:218**: Harry Järv, 'Strindberg - Den reaktionäre radikalen'; **T:459**: Sven Rinman, 'Hyllningar och smädelser'; and **T:514**: Per-Arne, Tjäder, 'Det borgerliga samhällets fiende'. The volume also contains a causerie, 'Idag har jag gudamat...', by Torsten Eklund (**U1:236**) and a speculative essay by Ingela Josefson and Bo Göranzon, 'Automat eller människa', **U1:403**, as well as a chronology, a bibliography, and a biographical sketch in English by Harry G. Carlson, **R:477**]

[**B1:349**] — Anderberg, Rolf, *Göteborgs-Posten*, 4 June 1981.

[**B1:350**] — Andrén, Sigvard, *Vestmanlands Läns Tidning* (Västerås), 3 July 1981.

[**B1:351**] — Brennecke, Detlef, *Skandinavistik* (Kiel), 12:1 (1982), 68-70.

[**B1:352**] — Ekman, Hans-Göran, *Upsala Nya Tidning*, 23 July 1981.

[**B1:353**] — Johansson, Ulf R., *Kvällsposten* (Malmö), 5 July 1981.

[**B1:354**] — Nettervik, I., *Smålandsposten* (Växjö), 6 July 1981.

[**B1:355**] — Ohlson, Per-Ove, *Borås Tidning*, 16 July 1981.

[**B1:356**] — Sommelius, Sören, *Helsingborgs Dagblad*, 31 July 1981.

[**B1:357**] Olsson, Ulf, red., *Strindbergs förvandlingar*, Eslöv: Brutus Östlings Bokförlag Symposion, 1999. 233 pp. ['Strindberg's Transformations'. A frequently stimulating collection of ten essays on Sg's work, using the resources of contemporary literary theory to shed new light on different aspects of Sg's authorship. Contains **B2:2**: Eva Adolphson, 'Strindbergs början'; **B2:175**: Thomas Götselius, 'Helvetet lössläppt: Strindberg skriver'; **B2:278**: Arne Melberg, 'Barbaren i Paris'; **B2:368**: Per Stounbjerg, 'En melankolisk konstellation. Konstruktion av ett mönster i Strindbergs författarskap';

B9:119: Geneviève Fraisse, 'Strindbergs kvinnohat, mellan politisk och metafysik'; **C1:1308**: Birgitta Trotzig, 'En förvandlingskonstnär'; **D2:1046**: Fritz Paul, 'Strindbergs antimimetiska teater'; **F9:42**: Boel Westin, 'Vandraren, drömmen och dikten: *Ensam*'; **G15:49**: Ulf Olsson, 'Det blodiga tecknet. Sexualitet och mening i *Svarta fanor*'; and **G16:18**: Johan Dahlbäck, '*Syndabocken* vid gränserna', together with an introduction by Olsson, pp. 7-11]

[B1:358] — Zetterström, Margareta, *Folket i bild/Kulturfront* (Stockholm), 2000:4, p. 34.

[B1:359] Pallas, Gustav, *August Strindberg a naturalismus švédský*, Moderní literatura severská v hlavních predstavitelích a smerech, Sv. 3, V. Praze: Nakladatelstvi Julius Akbert, 1933, [72] pp. ['August Strindberg and Swedish Naturalism'. A study in Czech of Sg and Naturalism, including an outline of his career as a writer. Pallas concentrates mainly on the plays of the 1880s and the autobiographical fictions of the same period, and examines his quarrel with feminism along with other Swedish writing of the period]

[B1:360] Paul, Fritz, *August Strindberg*, Sammlung Metzler 178, Stuttgart: J. B. Metzlersche Verlagsbuchhandlung, 1979. XXIV+130 pp. [An informative and reliable introductory study which concentrates primarily on the dramas but also includes chapters on the autobiographical writings in relation to the life, the novels, and (very briefly) the poetry. Also includes useful bibliographical information on both primary and secondary sources]

[B1:361] Paul, Fritz, *Kleine Schriften zur Nordischen Philologie*, Hrsg. von Joachim Grage, Heinrich Detering, Wilhelm Heizmann, und Lutz Rühling, Wiener Studien zur Skandinavistik 9, Wien: Edition Praessens, 2003. 350 pp. [Includes three well-sourced essays on Sg's autobiographical self-image; his post-Inferno dramaturgy; and his place in the Berlin bohème of the 1890s: **C1:1013**: 'Die Bohème als subkultureller 'Salon'. Strindberg, Munch und Przybyszewski im Berliner Künstlerkreis des Schwarzen Ferkels'; **D2:1048**: 'Strindbergs Nachinfernodramatik und das lyrische Drama des Fin de Siècle'; and **F1:41**: 'Ismael, Hiob, Jakob: Alttestamentarische Typologie bei August Strindberg']

[B1:362] Pellegrini, Alessandro, *Il poeta del nichilismo: Strindberg*, Coll. Il pensiero. Critica, storia, filosofia, Milano: Rosa & Ballo Editori, 1944. [97] pp. ['The Poet of Nihilism: Strindberg'. Places Sg in an historical context defined by the dissolution of accepted values where personal experience emerges as a countervailing force set against a general disruption in meaning. Pellegrini sees Sg's career as a lifelong engagement with, and struggle against, nihilism, which reaches its crisis in the experiences described in *Inferno* and *Legender*]

[B1:363] Perrelli, Franco, *Introduzione a Strindberg*, Bari-Roma: Laterza, 1990. 164 pp. ['Introduction to Strindberg'. A reliable, well-informed general Italian introduction to Sg's writings]

[B1:364] Perrelli, Franco, *il teatro della vita*, Milano: Iperborea, 2003. 184 pp. [A new and substantially revised edition of **B1:363** which covers Sg's life and work in four periods, 1869-1885: 'Scrivere per colpire' (Writing for Effect), 1886-1893: 'Il combattimento dei cervelli' (The Battle of the Brains), 1894-1901: Uno scrittore religioso' (A Religious Writer), and 1902-1912: 'Il più moderno dei moderni' (The Most Modern of the Moderns)]

[B1:365] Perrelli, Franco, ed., *Omaggio a Strindberg. Strindberg nella cultura moderna. Colloquio Italiano*, Biblioteca di Cultura 239, Roma: Bulzoni editore, 1983. Illus. [184] pp. ['Homage to Strindberg. Strindberg in Modern Culture'. The Proceedings of an Italian Colloquium on Sg in 1982. Contains **A4:75**: Karl-Åke Kärnell, 'La ricerca strindberghiana in Svezia'; **C1:799**: Giuseppe Liotta, 'Strindberg e Zola (ovvero la questione del naturalismo)'; **C1:872**: Nicola Marrone, 'Strindberg/Moor'; **C1:1021**: Franco Perrelli, 'Strindberg e Weininger'; **D2:439**: Rosangela Barone, 'Alla ricerca di August Strindberg: Stretta strada verso il profondo nord'; **D2:446**: Pasquale Bellini, 'Giancarlo Nanni: il *suo* Strindberg'; **D2:1069**: Franco Perrelli, 'Tre atti unici di Strindberg'; **D3:220**: Ugo Volli, 'Strindberg: motivi di un'attualità'; **E22:2**: Ferdinando Gasparini, 'Una lettura psicanalitica di *Amor materno* di A. Strindberg'; **F4:34**: Vico Faggi, 'Strindberg: lo sguardo deformante (*Le Plaidoyer d'un fou*)'; **G10:9**: Gianmario Borio 'Elemente nietzscheani nei romanzi di Strindberg (in particolare riferimento a *In mare aperto*'; **H1:45**: Adamaria Terziani, 'Strindberg poeta'; **P2:18**: Carlo Crispolti, 'Strindberg e le arti figurative', and **R:1754**: Birgitta Ottosson-Pinna, 'Strindberg e l'Italia'; together with an introduction by Perrelli, pp. 7-9, a personal statement by Giancarlo Nanni, 'Il mio Strindberg', **U1:579**, and translations of the third of Sg's *Sömngångarnätter* and the poem 'Holländaren']

[B1:366] Persson, Anita, and Barbara Lide, *Ja, må han leva! 22 kvinnor skriver om August Strindberg*, Stockholm: Carlssons, 2000. 209 pp. ['Long may he Live! 22 Women Write about August Strindberg'. A collection of sixteen short, mainly personal, responses to Sg as a man and writer by contemporary female translators, performers, and enthusiasts. Includes **B2:382**: Eszter Szalczer, 'Strindberg – vår text'; **B3:157**: Solveiga Elsberga, 'Den tredje vågen i Lettland'; **B3:177**: Vera Gantjeva, 'Bulgarien: Strindbergs timma'; **B4:81**; Anne-Charlotte Hanes Harvey, 'Översättaren som Sparf'; **B9:167**: Barbara Lide, 'Kvinnan var din fiende...och modern var inte heller din vän'; **B9:184**: Eivor Martinus, 'Strindberg och kvinnorna'; **D2:613**: Agneta Elers-Jarleman, 'Varför Strindberg?'; **D2:640**: Debra L. Freeberg, 'Fem generationer Dramatenskådespelerskor talar om Strindberg'; **E41:159**: Vida Saviciunaité, 'Två versioner av *Ett drömspel* i litauisk Strindbergiana'; **E51:68**: Pirkko Koski, '*Spöksonaten* i kulturernas korsning. Jouko Turkkas iscensättning på Helsingfors Stadsteater'; and **P5:36**: Katrin Litsfeldt, 'Strindberg, Prokofjev och så jag'. It also includes the miscellaneous personal pieces **U1:274**, **U1:429**, **U1:545**, **U1:615**, **U1:642**, **U1:697**, and **U1:815**]

[B1:367] — Kessle, Gun, *Folket i bild/Kulturfront* (Stockholm), 2001:3, p. 39.

[B1:367a] — Petersson, Kerstin, *Swedish Book Review* (Norwich), 2001:2, pp. 58-59.

[B1:368] Poupard, Dennis, ed., '(Johan) August Strindberg', in *Twentieth-Century Literary Criticism*, Vol. 21, Detroit: Gale Research Inc., 1986, pp. 342-370. [Reprints articles and extracts from a range of Anglo-Saxon critical studies and reviews including, pp. 347-348, H. L. Mencken, **D2:966**, 'The Terrible Swede'; pp. 348-351, Edwin Björkman, **B2:48**, 'August Strindberg'; pp. 351-352, Ludwig Lewisohn, **E35:259**, 'Jangled Lives'; pp. 352-353, John Macy, **B2:265**, *The Critical Game*; p. 353, Eugene O'Neill, **C1:986**, 'Strindberg and Our Theatre'; p. 354, Joseph Wood Krutch, **E41:328**, 'Whips and Scorns'; pp. 354-355, Desmond MacCarthy, **D1:295**, 'Strindberg'; p. 356, Hermann Hesse, **C1:558**, 'August Strindberg, In Memoriam'; pp. 356-358, Carl E. W. Dahlström, **E11:53**, 'Strindberg's *The Father* as Tragedy'; pp. 358-361, Walter Johnson, **E35:51**, 'Strindberg and the Danse Macabre'; pp. 361-367, Richard Gilman, **C1:445**, 'Ibsen and Strindberg'; pp. 365-

366, Mary Sandbach, **G5:114**, '*Getting Married*'; pp. 366-368, V. S. Pritchett, **G5:108**, 'A Bolting Horse'; p. 368, Arthur Miller, **R:1234**, 'The Mad Inventor of Modern Drama'; p. 369, Vernon Young, 'Strindberg's Ghosts', **B2:401**]

[B1:369] Proost, K[arel] F[rederik], *August Strindberg. Zijn leven en werken. Een inleiding*, Zeist: J. Ploegsma, 1922. VII+305 pp. ['August Strindberg. His Life and Works. An Introduction'. The first book-length study of Sg's life and work to be published in the Netherlands. Proost relies heavily on Emil Schering's German edition for its source texts, as well as the biographies of Sg by Nils Erdmann, **R:742**, and Erik Hedén, **R:942**, for much personal data. The work of a theologian, this survey is characterised by a pronounced Christian perspective]

[B1:370] — Meester, B. J. de, *De Gids* (Amsterdam), 86:4 (1922), 162-164.

[B1:371] Reinert, Otto, ed., *Strindberg: A Collection of Critical Essays*, Englewood Cliffs N. J.: Prentice-Hall Inc., 1971. 178 pp. [A widely distributed anthology of previously published material that concentrates almost entirely on the plays. Contains **D1:609**: Pär Lagerkvist, 'Strindberg and the Theater of Tomorrow'; **B2:215**: R. J. Kaufman, 'Strindberg: The Absence of Irony'; **B3:416**: Victor Svanberg, 'The Strindberg Cult'; **D2:457**: Eric Bentley, 'Strindberg, the One and the Many'; **D2:537**: Robert Brustein, 'August Strindberg'; **D2:688**: Maurice Gravier, 'The Character and the Soul'; **D2:1207**: Birgitta Steene, 'Shakespearean Elements in the Historical Plays of Strindberg'; **D2:1304**: Raymond Williams, 'Private Tragedy: Strindberg'; **E12:175**: Martin Lamm, '*Miss Julie*'; **E35:52**: Walter Johnson, 'Strindberg and the Danse Macabre'; **E41:175**: Evert Sprinchorn, 'The Logic of *A Dream Play*'; and **E48:53**: Brian Rothwell, 'The Chamber Plays'. The volume also contains a lightly annotated bibliography and an introduction by Reinert, pp. 1-25, which maintains that 'Sg is the artist as neurotic and criticism must begin by coming to terms with the life and the personality'. Most of the essays are by well-informed Sg specialists, but the choice of material is conservative and not always judicious]

[B1:372] — Printz-Påhlson, Göran, *Scandinavica* (London), 12:2 (1973), 147-149.

[B1:373] Robinson, Michael, ed., *Strindberg and Genre*, Norwich: Norvik Press, 1991. 295 pp. [Publishes the proceedings of the 10th International Sg Conference, held in Norwich in 1990. Contains **B2:141**: Inga-Stina Ewbank, '"Tragical-Comical-Historical-Pastoral": Strindberg and the Absurdity of Categories'; **B2:360**: Barbro Ståhle Sjönell, 'Strindberg's Mixing of Genres'; **B4:47**: Gunnel Engwall, 'Frenchifying *Fordringsägare*: Strindberg as his own Translator'; **D2:775**: Barry Jacobs, 'Strindberg's *Advent* and *Brott och brott*: *Sagospel* and Comedy in a Higher Court'; **D2:845**: Kela Kvam, 'Strindberg as an Innovator of Dramatic and Theatrical Form': **D2:894**: Barbara Lide, 'Perspectives on a Genre: Strindberg's *Comédies rosses*'; **D2:1247**: Egil Törnqvist, 'Strindberg and Subjective Drama'; **D2:1309**: Margareta Wirmark, 'Strindberg's History Plays: Some Reflections'; **E48:50**: Freddie Rokem, 'The Representation of Death in Strindberg's Chamber Plays'; **E55:4**: Hans-Göran Ekman, '*Abu Casems tofflor*: Strindberg's Worst Play?'; **F1:17**: Kerstin Dahlbäck, 'Strindberg's Autobiographical Space'; **F1:36**: Jan Myrdal, 'August Strindberg and his Tradition in Swedish Literature. Beyond Fiction, Autobiography and the Literature of Established Truth'; **F5:15**: [Ann-Charlotte] Gavel Adams, '*Inferno*: Intended Readers and Genre'; **G1:99**: Göran Printz-Påhlson, '"Passions and Interests": Anthropological Observation in the Short Story'; **H2:58**: James Spens, 'Genre and Aesthetics in Strindberg's "Sårfeber" Poems'; **K7:32**: Margareta Brundin,

'"Kärlekens bok": Life and Fiction in *En blå bok*'; **K7:45**: Magnus Florin, 'Strindberg, Chance Images and *En blå bok*'; **K7:76**: Eva Spens, '*En blå bok* – A Genre of its Own?'; **P1:98**: Harry G. Carlson, 'Strindberg and Visual Imagination'; and **P1:163**: Michelle Facos, 'Strindberg and Painting: 1880-1900'. The volume also contains an Introduction by the editor (pp. 9-13) and his catalogue of Sg's works and their titles in English, arranged chronologically according to genre, pp. 15-18]

[B1:374] — Beardow, Frank, *New Comparison* (Coventry), 15 (1993), 168-170.

[B1:375] — Fahlgren, Margaretha, *Edda* (Oslo), 92 (1992), 197-198.

[B1:376] — Harvey, Anne-Charlotte, *Nordic Theatre Studies* (Copenhagen), 6:1-2 (1993), 81-82.

[B1:377] — Petherick, Karin, *Scandinavica* (Norwich), 31:1 (1992), 105-108.

[B1:378] — Rugg, Linda Haverty, *Scandinavian Studies* (Urbana, Illinois), 65:4 (1993), 564-566.

[B1:379] Robinson, Michael, ed., *Strindberg: The Moscow Papers*, Stockholm: The Strindberg Society, 1998. 224 pp. [The proceedings of the 12th International Sg Conference in Moscow, 1994, on Sg's links with Russia and with symbolism. Contains **B2:128**: Hans-Göran Ekman, 'Strindberg's Senses, Symbols and Synaesthesia'; **B2:330**: Michael Robinson, 'Finding a New Language: Strindberg and Symbolism'; **B3:246**: Nikolaj Kotrelyov, 'Strindberg and Russia'; **B3:323**: Maria Nikolajeva, 'Strindberg Through the Eyes of the Russian Critics'; **C1:842**: Dina Magomedova, 'Blok and Strindberg: Notes on a Theme'; **C1:1310**: Irina Tsimbal, 'Strindberg and Chekhov'; **C2:71**: Birgitta Steene, 'Strindberg, Ingmar Bergman and the Visual Symbol'; **D2:844**: Kela Kvam, 'Strindberg and French Symbolist Theatre'; **D2:957**: Vadim Maximov, 'Strindberg and the French Symbolist Tradition in the Theatre'; **D2:1147**: Wilmar Sauter, 'Strindberg's Words Versus the Actor's Action'; **D2:1166**: Tat'iana Shakh-Azizova, 'Naturalism and Symbolism: The Shadow of Fate in Strindberg's Plays'; **E13:33**: Barbara Lide, 'The Pygmalion Impulse in Strindberg's *Fordringsägare*'; **E26:6**: Jennifer Code, 'Inventing a Form: The Refiguring of Symbols in Strindberg's *Advent*'; **E31:8**: Laurent Bailleux, 'Strindberg's *Gustav Adolf* and French Neo-Classical Drama: Civilization in Question'; **E37:11**: Bertil Nolin, 'Symbolism and the Making of a Fairy-Tale Play: *Svanevit* at the Intimate Theatre'; **E58:7:** Erik Østerud, '*Svarta handsken* as a Modern Morality Play: The 'Greek' Ibsen versus the 'Medieval' Strindberg'; **E59:38**: Margareta Wirmark, 'The Ending of *Stora landsvägen*'; **F5:17**: Lotta Gavel Adams, 'Strindberg's *Inferno* and Rimbaldian Poetics'; **F5:52**: Thomas Bredsdorff, 'Give Us a Sign!" Allegory and Symbol in Strindberg's *Inferno*'; **G1:106**: Barbro Ståhle Sjönell, '"Sådant skräp som ger mig bröd": Strindberg's Short-Stories'; **G12:27**: Boel Westin, 'The Butterfly and the Gold: Symbolist Elements in Strindberg's Fairy Tale, "Blåvinge finner Guldpudran"'; **J:164**: Kerstin Dahlbäck, '"Ryss, ryskt och ryssar" in Strindberg's Correspondence'; **L1:24**: Björn Meidal, 'Strindberg's Russia – Cultural History, Nihilism, Historical Metaphysics and Antimilitarism'; and **N:35**: Freddie Rokem, 'Strindberg and Hebrew: The Poet's Alchemical Dream of Language', together with an Introduction by the editor, pp. 9-11]

[B1:380] Robinson, Michael, *Studies in Strindberg*, Norwich: Norvik Press, 1998. Illus. 244 pp. [A collection of essays on Sg as autobiographer, dramatist, and modernist which seeks to facilitate a re-evaluation of his standing in the English-speaking world.

Contains **B2:329**: 'Finding a New Language: Strindberg's Break with Naturalism'; **B3:365**: 'Leaving Gravesend at Last, or Introducing Strindberg to England'; **D2:1111**: 'History and His-Story'; **E13:46**: 'Naturalism and the Plot in *Creditors*'; **E35:100**: 'Prisoners at Play: Form and Meaning in Strindberg's *Dance of Death* and Beckett's *Endgame*'; **F1:46**: 'Life, Plots and Letters'; **F1:48**: '"P-aris": Notes for an Unwritten Volume of Strindberg's Autobiography'; **F1:58**: 'Translating the Self'; **J:307**: '"Spela den så att Pontoppidan och Fru Nansen få blåskatarrh": Strindberg's Correspondence with Actors and Directors'; **P1:386**: '"New Arts, New Worlds!": Strindberg and Painting'; and **P3:139**: 'August Strindberg and Musical Expressionism in Vienna']

[B1:381] — Beschnitt, Wolfgang, *Skandinavistik* (Kiel), 29:2 (1999), 152-153.

[B1:382] — Blackwell, Marilyn Johns, *TijdSchrift voor Skandinavistiek* (Amsterdam), 20:1 (1999), 170-174. [Critical and condescending]

[B1:383] — Fahlgren, Margaretha, *Samlaren* (Uppsala), 121 (2000), pp. 269-270.

[B1:384] — Gaddy, Kerstin, *Modern Drama* (Toronto), 43:2 (2000), 312-313. [Stresses the interest of the three essays devoted to the plays in illustrating Sg's seminal role in the transition from naturalism to modernism]

[B1:385] — Lide, Barbara, *Scandinavica* (Norwich), 40:1 (2001), 144-149.

[B1:386] — Thompson, Birgitta, *Modern Language Review* (London), 96:2 (2001), 588-589.

See also **A4:48**

[B1:387] Robinson, Michael, and Sven Rossel, eds, *Expressionism and Modernism. New Approaches to August Strindberg*, Wien: Editions Praesens, 1999. 264 pp. [The proceedings of the 13th International Strindberg Conference, held in Linz in 1997. Contains **B2:72**: Friedrich Buchmayr, 'August Strindberg and the Altered Perception of Modernism'; **B2:83**: Harry G. Carlson, 'Theme, Image and Style in August Strindberg's Expressionism'; **B3:252**: Arturo Larcarti, 'August Strindberg in the Periodicals of Austrian Expressionism'; **C1:66**: Paul Austin, 'August Strindberg, Sam Shepard, and the Expressionist Impulse'; **C1:243**: Piotr Bukowski, 'August Strindberg and the Expressionist Aesthetics of Pär Lagerkvist'; **C1:1064**: Hannelore Rodlauer, 'Franz Kafka Reads August Strindberg'; **D2:896**: Barbara Lide, 'Stations of Expressionism: Stora landsvägen from *Till Damaskus* to Contemporary Performance'; **D2:941**: Brigitte Marschall, 'Higher States of Consciousness in August Strindberg's "Inferno Dramas"'; **D2:975**: Christopher Joseph Mitchell, 'Gender and Marriage Constructions Across the "Inferno": August Strindberg's *The Father* and *Dödsdansen I*'; **D2:1227**: Eszter Szalczer, 'August Strindberg's Dramatic Expressionism and the Discourse of the Self'; **D2:1231**: Grażyna Barbara Szewczyk, 'August Strindberg's Influence on the Drama of German Expressionism'; **E35:4**: Lotta Gavel Adams, '*The Dance of Death I*: The Hells of August Strindberg and Lars Norén – From Swedenborgian Vastation to Bourgeois Waste Land'; **E36:19**: Margareta Wirmark, 'The White Ice and the Black Water: Ingmar Bergman Directs August Strindberg's *Kronbruden* at Malmö Stadsteater 1952'; **E38:20**: Barry Jacobs, 'Expressionist Elements in August Strindberg's *Charles the Twelfth*'; **E41:194**: Egil Törnqvist, 'Screening August Strindberg's *A Dream Play*: Meaning and Style'; **E51:130:** Karin Tidström, 'Reception and Translation of August Strindberg's *The Ghost Sonata* in France'; **G10:57**: Agneta Taube, 'The Pattern of Narrative Desire in August Strindberg's *By the Open Sea*'; **G15:50**: Ulf Olsson, 'The Bloodstained Sign:

The Problem of Expressivity in August Strindberg's *Black Banners*'; **P3:87**: Hermann Keckeis, 'August Strindberg and German Opera: Studies in the Transposition of the Genre of Strindberg's Plays in Operatic Dramaturgy – a Textual Analysis'; **P3:138**: Michael Robinson, 'August Strindberg and Musical Expressionism in Vienna'; **P5:70**: Birgitta Steene, 'August Strindberg, Modernism and the Swedish Cinema'; **T:409**: Jan Myrdal, 'An Exemplary Phase Reversal: The Modernity of August Strindberg', and **T:476**: Nina Solomin, 'August Strindberg's Hostility Towards Jews - 1879-1882'; together with a Foreword by Björn Meidal and Kurt Bäckström (pp. 911-912) and an editors' Preface, pp. 13-15]

[B1:388] Rokem, Freddie, *Strindberg's Secret Codes*, Norwich: Norvik Press, 2004. 221 pp. [Collects a number of previously published but thematically linked essays, many of them extensively rewritten to highlight the book's principal concern, which is the enigmatic, mysterious, sometimes contradictory, and always puzzling dimension of Sg's work and its concern with submerged, concealed meaning, whatever the genre or medium. Includes **C1:1071**: 'Slapping Women: Ibsen's Nora, Strindberg's Julie, and Freud's Dora', **D1:661**: '*Deus ex Machina* in the Modern Theatre'; **D2:1118**: 'The Camera and the Aesthetics of Repetition: Strindberg's Use of Space and Scenography in *Miss Julie*, *A Dream Play*, and *Spöksonaten*'; **D2:1120**: 'Strindbergs Optical Unconscious'; **E13:49**: 'Screen-Scenes in *Creditors*'; **E41:152**: 'Strindberg's Dreams and Other Fictions'; **E48:51**: 'The Representation of Death in Strindberg's Chamber Plays'; **E58:10**: '*The Black Glove* at Dramaten, 1988'; and **N:36**: 'Strindberg and the Codes of the Hebrew Language']

[B1:389] Rossholm, Göran, Barbro Ståhle Sjönell, and Boel Westin, eds, *Strindberg and Fiction*, Stockholm Studies in Literary History, Criticism and Theory 1, Stockholm: Almqvist & Wicksell International, 2001. 286 pp. [The Proceedings of the 14th International Strindberg Conference. Contains **B2:138**: Inga-Stina Ewbank, 'Strindberg and the Fiction of History'; **B2:161**: David Gedin, 'In Cover of Reality: The "scandalous" text of the eighties'; **B2:196**: Vreni Hockenjos, 'The World through a Panorama Lens: Strindberg on Vision and Visual Technologies'; **B2:292**: Per Nilsson, 'Names in Strindberg's Fiction'; **B2:379**: Conny Svensson, 'Strindberg on World History'; **D2:1256**: Egil Törnqvist, 'Questions Without Answers? An Aspect of Strindberg's Drama Dialogue'; **E3:5**: Margareta Wirmark, 'Strindberg in Rome'; **E11:133**: Ulf Olsson, 'The Madness of Fiction: Psychiatry and Narrative in Strindberg's *Fadren*'; **E11:167**: Irina Tsimbal, '*Fadren* in Production. Blending Fiction with Reality'; **E35:110**: Lech Sokół, 'Fiction and Reality in *Dödsdansen I*: A Polish Perspective (1917-1998)'; **E41:114**: Christopher Mitchell, 'Fore/shadows of the Postmodern: Strindberg's *Ett drömspel*'; **E41:188**: Eszter Szalczer, 'Growing Castles'; **E49:27**: Karin Marie Svenmo, 'Strindberg on the Phone'; **F5:56**: Piotr Bukowski, 'August Strindberg's *Inferno* and the Absence of the Work'; **F10:64**: Karin Petherick, 'Strindberg's *Ockulta dagboken*'; **G1:111**: Lisa Tereul, 'Defining Strindberg's Prose Fiction'; **G7:40**: Mattias Fyhr, '"Tschandala" Compared to Some Works by Poe'; **G10:18**: Sigrid Ekblad, 'Sailing with Borg: The Making of an Author Concept in Literary Interpretations of *I havsbandet*'; **G12:26**: Eric Svendsen, 'Strindberg in Wonderland. Reflections on *Sagor*'; **J:18**: Elena Balzamo, 'Dichtung und Wahrheit? An analysis of some letters of August Strindberg'; **K7:51**: Sophie Grimal-Robert, '"Guds osynliga tjänare gå omkring oss": Contrastive Pictures of Reality in *En blå bok I-IV*'; **P2:9**: Mats Björkin, 'Telescoping August: Photography and Simultaneity';

R:1484: Eivor Martinus, 'Is not the Truth the Truth?'; and **T:84**: Friedrich Buchmayr, 'The Power of Instinct: Strindberg and the Austrian Racist Lanz-Liebenfels']

[B1:390] — Cavallin, Anna, *Tidskrift för litteraturvetenskap* (Stockholm), 2000:4, pp. 100-104.

[B1:391] Schepens, Piet, *August Strindberg: Leven en Werken*, 2 vols, Vol. 1, Antwerpen: Regenboog, Vol. 2, Gent: Zonnedauw, 1931-33. Illus. 485 pp. and 298 pp. ['August Strindberg: Life and Works'. A Flemish life and works study with reference particularly to German sources. Volume One includes an extensive bibliography, pp. 401-461, with numerous general entries on Scandinavian literature in general and other Scandinavian entries, as well as books and essays on Sg, pp. 420-461. Volume Two includes a table of Sg's life and works, pp. 221-283]

[B1:392] — Backer, Franz de, *Revue belge de philologie et d'histoire* (Brussels), 13:1-2 (1934), 277-280.

[B1:393] Schütze, Peter F., *August Strindberg: mit Selbstzeugnissen und Bilddokumenten*, Dargestellt von Peter Schütze, Reinbek bei Hamburg: Rowohlt Taschenbuch, 1990. Illus. 156 pp. [A popular, biographically disposed introduction to Sg's life and works, drawing directly on his own autobiographical accounts and photographs]

[B1:394] Sergeev, A., and E. Solov'eva, '[Commentaries]', in August Strindberg, *Slovo bezumtsa v svoiu zashchitu*, Moscow: Khudozhestvennaia literatura, 1997. Illus. 560 pp. [The notes and introductions to Russian translations by L. Z. Lungina (*Le Plaidoyer d'un fou*), S. Tarkhanova (*Ensam*), E. Surits (*Spöksonaten*), and V. Tsyrlina (*Erik XIV*), as well as a selection of short stories and fairy tales by S. Fridliand, N. Beliakova, L. Zhdanova, I. Streblova, and L. I. Braude. E.1758]

[B1:395] Smedmark, Carl Reinhold, *Mäster Olof och Röda rummet*, Stockholm: Almqvist & Wiksell, 1952. 391 pp. ['*Master* Olof and *The Red Room*'. A genetic study of Sg's two principal early works which examines the manuscript material, compares the three versions of *Mäster Olof*, and analyses *Röda rummet* (which of the two texts is treated here in greatest detail), relating it to 19th-Century American, Russian, and French prose fiction, as well as to contemporary Scandinavian literature. Smedmark studies the characterisation in both works; examines their links with contemporary political and intellectual revolutionary movements; and relates Sg's personal radicalism with the social and political ideas of the period. He takes issue with the account of *Mäster Olof* in Allan Hagsten's thesis, **B1:151**, assesses the contemporary and subsequent critical reception accorded both works by C. G. Estlander, Martin Lamm, Carl Rupert Nyblom, Nils Åke Sjöstedt, Karl Warburg, and Algot Werin, and discusses the two texts which first established Sg's enduring reputation in Sweden with reference to intertexts by Bjørnson, Georg and Edvard Brandes, Henry Thomas Buckle, Alphonse Daudet, Flaubert, the Goncourt brothers, Ibsen, Kierkegaard, Viktor Rydberg, Émile Zola, Arthur Schopenhauer, J. P. Jacobsen, Hippolyte Taine, and Ivan Turgenev. Smedmark also discusses the relevance of his personal relations with Siri von Essen, Carl Gustaf Wrangel, Rudolf Wall, and A. O. Wallenberg for their writing. Although its positivist approach is now out of step with a great deal of recent Sg criticism, Smedmark's study remains a defining work in post-war Sg scholarship. Doctoral dissertation]

[B1:396] — Ahlström, Stellan, *Afton-Tidningen* (Stockholm), 23 November 1952.

[B1:397] — Åkerhielm, Helge, *Perspektiv* (Stockholm), 4 (1953), p. 286.

[B1:398] — Brandell, Gunnar, *Samlaren* (Uppsala), 33 (1952), pp. 125-130.

[B1:399] — Landquist, John, *Aftonbladet* (Stockholm), 27 May 1952.

[B1:400] — Levander, Hans, *Morgon-Tidningen* (Stockholm), 14 January 1953.

[B1:401] — Lindberger, Örjan, *Nordisk Tidskrift* (Stockholm), 28 (1952), 300-301.

[B1:402] — Rinman, Sven, *Göteborgs Handels- och Sjöfartstidning*, 18 April 1953.

[B1:403] — U . W. [Ulf Wittrock], *Upsala Nya Tidning*, 23 February 1953.

[B1:404] — Wieselgren, Oscar, *Svenska Dagbladet* (Stockholm), 22 January 1953.

See also **A4:1**

[B1:405] [Smedmark, Carl Reinhold], ed. [For the Strindberg Society], *Essays on Strindberg*, Stockholm: Beckmans, 1966. 175 pp. [Contains **B3:233**: Walter Johnson, 'Strindberg and the Swedes: Past and Present'; **B3:296**: Michael Meyer, 'Strindberg in England'; **D2:1305**: Raymond Williams, 'Strindberg and Modern Tragedy'; **E12:254**: Evert Sprinchorn, 'Julie's End'; **E48:52**: Brian Rothwell, 'The Chamber Plays'; **E51:94**: John Northam, 'Strindberg's *Spook Sonata*'; **E50:11**: Göran Lindström, 'Strindberg's Chamber Plays, Opus 2, *After the Fire*'; **E50:12**: Göran Lindström, 'Strindbergs kammarspel Opus 2, *Brända tomten*'; **K3:48**: Elie Poulenard, '*Among French Peasants*'; **K3:49**: Elie Poulenard, '*Bland franska bönder*'; **P5:91**: Rune Waldekranz, 'Strindberg and the Silent Cinema'; and **P5:92**: Rune Waldekranz, 'Strindberg och stumfilmen']

[B1:406] — Anon, *The Times Literary Supplement* (London), 4 April 1968.

[B1:407] — Berendsohn, Walter A[rthur], *Ausblick* (Lübeck), 18:1-2 (1967), p. 30.

[B1:408] — Björck, Staffan, *Dagens Nyheter* (Stockholm), 20 February 1967.

[B1:409] — Gabrieli, Mario, *Scandinavica* (London), 7:1 (1968), 73–75.

[B1:410] — Stenström, Thure, *Svenska Dagbladet* (Stockholm), 12 December 1966.

See also **A4:41, A4:59, A4:68, A4:111**

[B1:411] Söderberg, Hjalmar, 'Litterärt', in *Samlade Verk*, 10 Vols, Stockholm: Albert Bonniers Förlag, 1943, Vol. 10, 'Vers och Varia', pp. 5-34. [Rpr. of **B1:412**]

[B1:412] Söderberg, Hjalmar, 'Strindberg', in *Vers och varia*, Stockholm: Albert Bonniers Förlag, 1921, pp. 124-161. [Reprints reviews of *Till Damaskus*, **E25:170**, *Stora landsvägen*, **E59:29**, and *Sömngångarnätter*, **H3:40**, on publication, as well as personal recollections of Sg in **R:2032**: 'Två kvällar med Strindberg (1915)']

[B1:413] Söderman, Sven, 'August Strindberg', in *Böcker och författare. Kritisker studier (1894-1914)*, Stockholm: Ljus, 1914, pp. 7-39. [A collection of Söderman's literary journalism, for the most part originally published in *Stockholms Dagblad*. Contains book and theatre reviews including **D2:1173** on *Ett drömspel* and *Kronbruden*, **E35:109** on *Dödsdansen*, **E58:13** on *Svarta handsken*, and **E59:30** on *Stora landsvägen*]

[B1:414] Sokół, Lech, *August Strindberg*, Seria Klasycy Literatury XX wieku, Warszawa: Czytelnik, 1981. Illus. [166] pp. [An informed introductory survey of Sg's career as a whole for Polish readers, focusing primarily on the plays but well aware of the importance of his writings in other genres]

[B1:415] — Ciesielski, Zenon, *Roczniki Humanistyczne* KUL (Lublin), 1981, pp. 396-397.

[B1:416] — Janukowicz, Dorota, *Studia Skandinavica* (Gdańsk), 5 (1983), pp. 131-134.

[B1:417] — Sowińska, Beata, *Życie Warszawy* (Warsaw), 1981, No. 257, p. 7.

[B1:418] — Terlecka-Reksnis, Małgorazata, *Perspektywy* (Warsaw), 1981, No. 40, p. 28.

[B1:419] Solov'eva, E., '[Commentaries]', in August Strindberg, *Izbrannye proizvedeniia v dvukh tomakh*, vstupitel'naia stat'ia V[ladimir] P[etrovich] Neustroev, Moscow: Khudozhestvennaia literatura, 1986. 525 pp. [The notes to Volume One of a selected edition of Sg's works including Russian translations of *Röda rummet* by K. Telliatnikova, *Hemsöborna* by F. Zolotarevskaiia, selected short stories, including 'Samvetskval' by A. A. Afinogenova and N. Krymova, and *Fadren* and *Fröken Julie* by E. Surits, together with an introduction by V[ladimir] P[etrovich] Neustroev, pp. 5-26. See also **B1:420**. E.1757]

[B1:420] Solov'eva, E., '[Commentaries]', in August Strindberg, [*The Red Room, Le Plaidoyer d'un fou*, and *Ensam*], Moscow: Pravda, 1989. 636 pp. [The notes to translations by K. I. Teliatnikova, L. Z. Lungina, and S. A. Tarkhanova, with an introduction, 'V. Khudozhestevennyi mir A. Strindberga', (The Artistic World of Strindberg), by V[ladimir] P[etrovich] Neustroev, **B2:289**, pp. 3-20. E.1760]

[B1:421] Sprinchorn, Evert, *Strindberg as Dramatist*, New Haven: Yale University Press, 1982. Illus. XI+332 pp. [Although it focuses primarily on the dramatist, with separate chapters on Sg's brand of naturalism, the dream plays, chamber plays, and the historical dramas, both the specific nature of his autobiographical approach to writing, in which, according to Sprinchorn, he acts out roles and adopts the techniques of an actor, and his scientific method, in which he experiments with different points of view and uses his own life as the raw material of his psychological investigations, are also discussed at length. So, too, are the role of music, often as a structuring device in his later plays, his politics, and the Sg Feud. Sprinchorn discusses *Brända tomten, Brott och brott, Karl XII, En dåres försvarstal, Dödsdansen, Erik XIV, Ett drömspel, Fadren, Fröken Julie, Gustav Vasa, Inferno, Mäster Olof, Oväder, Pelikanen, Spöksonaten, Till Damaskus*, and the *Vivisektioner* of 1887 in detail, and establishes links between works from different periods in different styles via the recurring themes of love, marriage, death, music, myth, psychology, rebirth, religion, sexuality, guilt, suffering, and the role of the unconscious. He also makes frequent comparative reference to Sg's intellectual and artistic relationships with Ibsen, Freud, Jung, Zola, Carl du Prel, Heidenstam, Swedenborg, Maeterlinck, Bernard Shaw, Nietzsche, Shakespeare, Przybyszewski, Darwin, Haeckel, and Jean Genet. A richly suggestive study that remains illuminating even when it overstates its case]

[B1:422] — Ekman, Hans-Göran, *Dagens Nyheter* (Stockholm), 23 March 1984.

[B1:423] — Ekman, Hans-Göran, *Samlaren* (Uppsala), 104 (1983), pp. 121-124.

[B1:424] — Haberman, D., *Rocky Mountain Review* (Salt Lake City), 39:1 (1985), 88-89.

[B1:425] — Leland, Charles, *Nineteenth-Century Theatre* (Amhurst, Maryland), 12:1-2 (1984), 99-101.

[B1:426] — Mattsson, Margareta, *Scandinavian Studies* (Lawrence, Kansas), 56:1 (1984), 83-84.

[B1:427] — Taraba. A. S., *World Literature Today* (Norman, Oklahoma), 57:4 (1983), p. 649.

[B1:428] — Tindemans, C., *Streven* (Amsterdam & Antwerp), 51 (1983-84), p. 192.

See also **A4:38**

[B1:429] Steene, Birgitta, *The Greatest Fire: A Study of August Strindberg*, Carbondale, Ill.: Southern Illinois University Press, 1973. XII+178 pp. [Offers a thematic overview of the major prose works and dramas. Approaches Sg as a conscious artist whose works reveal him to have been engaged in objectifying his personal experiences. A sound introduction for non-Swedish readers]

[B1:430] Steene, Birgitta, *August Strindberg. An Introduction to his Major Works*, Stockholm: Almqvist & Wiksell International, 1982. IX+178 pp. [Revised edition of **B1:429**]

[B1:431] — Ollén, Gunnar, *Sydsvenska Dagbladet* (Malmö), 6 October 1973.

[B1:432] — Seitz, Johann, *Scandinavian Studies* (Lawrence, Kansas), 46:4 (1974), 447-450.

[B1:433] — Vowles, Richard B., *Journal of English and Germanic Philology* (Urbana, Illinois), 72:4 (1973), 585-586.

See also **A4:38, A4:111**

[B1:434] Steene, Birgitta, ed., *Strindberg and History*, Stockholm: Almqvist & Wiksell International, 1992. Illus. 219 pp. [Publishes papers delivered at the 9th International Sg Conference in Seattle, in 1988, many of which had previously appeared in a special issue of *Scandinavian Studies* (Madison), 62:1 (1990) – see **B7:39**. Contains **B2:78**: Harry G. Carlson, 'Strindberg and the Carnival of History'; **B2:318**: Göran Printz-Påhlson, 'Historical Drama and Historical Fiction: The Example of Strindberg'; **C1:384**: Inga-Stina Ewbank, 'Strindberg, Shakespeare and History'; **D2:610**: Hans-Göran Ekman, 'Strindberg's Use of Costume in *Carl XII* and *Kristina*'; **D2:908**: Herbert Lindenberger, 'Experiencing History'; **D2:1112**: Michael Robinson, 'History and His-Story'; **D2:1201**: Barbro Ståhle Sjönell, 'The Plans, Drafts and Manuscripts of the Historical Plays in Strindberg's "Green Bag"'; **E38:14**: Susan Brantly, 'The Formal Tension of Strindberg's *Carl XII*'; **E38:23**: Barbara Lide, 'Strindberg and the Modern Consciousness: *Carl XII*'; **E38:32**: Egil Törnqvist, 'Visual and Verbal Scenery in Strindberg's Historical Plays: The Opening of *Carl XII* as Paradigmatic Example'; **E40:8**: Jennifer Code, 'Kristina, Strindberg's Many-Faced Woman'; **E40:10**: Kerstin Dahlbäck, '*Kristina* and Strindberg's Letters and Diary'; **E40:45**: Margareta Wirmark, 'Strindberg's *Queen Christina*: Eve and Pandora'; **E42:14**: Bertil Nolin, 'Strindberg's *Gustav III* as a Conspiracy Play'; **E42:16**: Göran Söderström, 'Gustav III and Homosexuality. Actor on the Throne'; and **E42:23**: Matthew H. Wikander, 'Historical Vision and Techniques of Dramatic Historiography: Strindberg's *Gustav III* in Light of Shakespeare's *Julius Caesar* and Corneille's *Cinna*'; together with an editor's introduction, 'Strindberg and History', pp. 5-8]

[B1:435] — Alldal, Tomas, 'Historia hos Strindberg', *entré* (Norsborg), 19:4 (1992), 84-85. ['History According to Strindberg']

[B1:436] — Ludvigsen, Christian, *Nordic Theatre Studies* (Copenhagen), 6:1-2 (1993), p. 82.

[B1:437] Stockenström, Göran, *Ismael i öknen: Strindberg som mystiker*, Acta Universitatis Upsaliensis: Historia litterarum, Uppsala, 1972. Illus. 547 pp. ['Ismael in the Desert. Strindberg as Mystic'. A major study of several important post-Inferno works, based on an examination of the striking combination of mystical and modernist ideas that matured in Sg's mind during the Inferno period. Stockenström indicates how these are sometimes anticipated in earlier writings like the Vivisections of 1887, and how he absorbs, transforms, and exploits the concepts of Swedenborg in many of his later plays and prose works. He also considers the impact on Sg's ideas and art of Kierkegaard, Hans Christian Andersen, Viktor Rydberg, Maupassant, Dante, Huysmans, Henry Bulwer-Lytton, Kipling, Linnaeus, Joséphin Péladan, Flaubert, and Balzac, as well as both Byron's *Cain* and Goethe's *Faust*, and examines the origins and development of his religious ideas as well as his preoccupation with myth and folklore and the impulses that he derived from *fin-de-siècle* alchemy and occultism. Much use is also made of the manuscript material in the Sg archive in Kungliga Biblioteket. Stockenström discusses *Inferno*, *Legender*, *Jacob brottas*, *Ockulta dagboken*, *Jardin des Plantes*, *Sylva Sylvarum*, *Till Damaskus I-II*, *Brott och brott*, *Advent*, *Påsk*, *Götiska rummen*, *Svarta fanor*, 'Armageddon', and several of the history plays, in many of which Sg regards the writer's calling as a religious mission to enlighten mankind about the true nature of the reality that is otherwise concealed behind the world of illusions that characterises the madhouse in which we normally live. *Advent* is presented here as a pivotal work, one that anticipates many of the themes and dramaturgical devices of the Chamber Plays of 1907, but numerous links are also established between Sg's later thinking and his analyses of contemporary society in *Röda rummet* and other pre-Inferno works. The absence of an index makes finding one's way around a book that frequently double backs and repeats itself quite infuriating, and the extended summaries which punctuate its argument at regular intervals often introduce new ideas rather than merely recapitulate established ones, but this remains a highly rewarding study, one that illuminates both the works and the mind which created them. Includes a substantial English summary, pp. 451-482. Doctoral Dissertation]

[B1:438] — Anderberg, Rolf, *Göteborgs-Posten*, 12 December 1972.

[B1:439] — Boëthius, Ulf, 'Den stora oredan och det oändliga sammanhanget', *Upsala Nya Tidning*, 24 January 1974. ['The Great Disorder and the Infinite Coherence']

[B1:440] — Delblanc, Sven, 'August Strindberg i Swedenborgs landskap. Göran Stockenströms avhandling om Strindbergs "swedenborgianism"', *Dagens Nyheter* (Stockholm), 8 January 1973. ['August Strindberg in Swedenborg's Landscape. Göran Stockenström's Thesis on Strindberg's "Swedenborgianism"']

[B1:441] — Delblanc, Sven, 'August Strindberg i Swedenborgs landskap. Göran Stockenströms avhandling om Strindbergs "swedenborgianism"', in Lars Ahlbom and Björn Meidal, red., *Strindberg – urtida, samtida, framtida*, **B1:119**, pp. 151-156. [Rpr. of **B1:440**]

[B1:442] — Enquist, Per Olov, *Expressen* (Stockholm), 12 December 1972.

[B1:443] — Ferm, O., *Norrköpings Tidningar-Östergötlands Dagblad*, 18 June 1973.

[B1:444] — Fredén, Gustaf, *Årsbok för kristen humanism* (Uppsala), 35 (1973), pp. 229-231.

[B1:445] — Gustafsson, B., *Barometern* (Kalmar), 29 March 1973.

[B1:446] — Helander, Olle, *Svensk teologisk kvartalsskrift* (Lund), 1974:2, pp. 91-94.

[B1:447] — Henmark, Kai, *Vår lösen* (Sigtuna), 64 (1973), 669-670.

[B1:448] — Johannesson, H.-E., *Horisont* (Vasa), 20:6 (1973), 77-79.

[B1:449] — Johnson, Walter [Gilbert], *Scandinavian Studies* (Lawrence, Kansas), 45:3 (1973), 271-273.

[B1:450] — Jonsson, Inge, *Svenska Dagbladet* (Stockholm), 31 December 1972.

[B1:451] — Landquist, John, *Aftonbladet* (Stockholm), 15 January 1973.

[B1:452] — Lane, Harry, *Modern Drama* (Lawrence, Kansas), 18:4 (1975), 399-401.

[B1:453] — Lindström, Göran, *Sydsvenska Dagbladet* (Malmö), 29 July 1973.

[B1:454] — Lindström, Hans, *Samlaren* (Uppsala). 94 (1973), pp. 187-195.

[**B1:455**] — Jarvis, R., *Books Abroad* (Norman, Oklahoma), 48 (1974), p. 165.

[**B1:456**] — Printz-Påhlson, Göran, *Scandinavica* (London), 12:2 (1973), 145-147.

See also **A4:55**, **A4:147**

[**B1:457**] Stolpe, Sven, *August Strindberg, Svenska folkets litteraturhistoria*, Stockholm: Askild & Kärnekull, 1978. Illus. 384 pp. [A biographically structured overview of Sg's *œuvre* which Stolpe regards from a moral (Christian) perspective and sees it as the product of a repellent personality. He asks if Sg's enormous influence has been for the good? Were his formally brilliant works not irreparably damaged by his unworthy motives and primitive view of mankind, and is the human degradation that pervades them really essential to his creative genius? Idiosyncratic, opinionated, and with an agenda that often obscures, rather than illuminates, the works that Stolpe discusses]

[**B1:458**] — Bergsten, Gunilla, *Upsala Nya Tidning*, 7 March 1979.

[**B1:459**] — Brandell, Gunnar, *Svenska Dagbladet* (Stockholm), 7 December 1978.

[**B1:460**] — Dahlström, B., *Horisont* (Vasa), 27:3 (1980), 97-100.

[**B1:461**] — Forser, Tomas, *Aftonbladet* (Stockholm), 31 December 1978.

[**B1:462**] — Franzén, Lars Olof, *Dagens Nyheter* (Stockholm), 18 December 1978.

[**B1:463**] — Lindström, Göran, *Sydsvenska Dagbladet* (Malmö), 7 December 1978.

[**B1:464**] Svensson, Conny, *Strindberg om världshistorien*, Stockholm: Gidlunds Förlag, 2000. Illus. 285 pp. ['Strindberg and World History'. Describes how, during the early years of the 20th Century, Sg's preoccupation with history shifted from a national to a global perspective. Adopting the uncharacteristic notion of history as a continuous line of development towards a determined goal rather than as a sequence of repetitious circles, Sg formulated this hypothesis in the essay 'Världshistoriens mystik' (1903) and gave it fictional form in *Historiska miniatyrer* (1905). It is these often overlooked stories, in which he maps out the course of history between Moses and the French revolution, and seeks to be both a writer of fiction and a reliable historian, that exemplify the argument of the essay, not the history plays of 1898-1902 which precede it. But the evolutionary order which they follow the essay in presenting becomes increasingly precarious in a further volume, *Nya svenska öden* (1906), where history emerges as chaotic rather than organised, an idea that is subsequently glossed in *En blå bok*. Here, God is no longer the chess player, planning each move on the chess-board of history, but an indifferent absentee. Svensson also comments on the later historical dramas, *Siste riddaren*, *Riksföreståndaren*, *Bjälbo-Jarlen*, and *Näktergalen i Wittenberg*, examines Sg's reflections in *Memorandum till Medlemmarne av Intima Teatern från Regissören* on the history play as a genre, and considers the role which several historical figures, including Socrates, Virgil, St Augustine, Julian the Apostate, Dante, Voltaire, Nero, and Napoleon, assume in his reflections on history, often as a spur to his writing]

[**B1:465**] — Bohn, Ingrid, *Skandinavistik* (Kiel), 32:1 (2002), 76-78.

[**B1:466**] — Lundmark, Lennart, 'Strindberg försökte revolutionera historieskrivningen', *Svenska Dagbladet* (Stockholm), 2 April 2001. ['Strindberg Tried to Revolutionise the Writing of History']

[**B1:467**] — Törnqvist, Egil, *TijdSchrift voor Skandinavistiek* (Amsterdam), 21:2 (2001), 253-257.

[**B1:468**] — Ståhle Sjönell, Barbro, *Samlaren* (Uppsala), 122 (2001), pp. 185-188.

[**B1:469**] Szabo, Charles, *En marge de Strindberg. Pièces détachées*, Paris: Les Génenaux (Imprimerie Artistique de L'Ouest), [1928]. 190 pp. ['In the Margins of Strindberg: Fragments'. An idiosyncratic collection of marginalia to Sg's life and works. Szabo identifies Sg as, amongst much else, the 'reformer of modern chemistry']

[**B1:470**] Taub, Hans, *Strindberg als Traumdichter*, Göteborgs Kungl. Vetenskaps- och Vitterhets-samhälles handlingar, Sjätte följden. Ser. A, Band 2. N:o 3, Göteborg: Elanders boktryckeri, 1945. 123 pp. ['Strindberg as a Writer of Dreams'. Traces Sg's development as a portrayer of dreaming and dreams in literature from *Mäster Olof* and 'Den romantiske klockaren på Rånö' to *Till Damaskus* and *Ett drömspel*. Taub stresses his affinity with, and debt to, Schopenhauer where his conception of the unconscious dream life is concerned, and comments on other works, including *Fadren*, *Sömngångarnätter*, *I havsbandet*, *Inferno*, and *Svarta fanor*. He also considers the role of Swedenborg and Balzac's novels *Séraphita* and *Louis Lambert* in shaping Sg's thinking during the Inferno period]

[**B1:471**] — Reich, Willi, *Erasmus* (Darmstadt), 1 (1947), Sp. 863.

See also **A4:67**

[**B1:472**] Vedel, Valdemar, 'August Strindberg', in *Firsernes Førere. Karakteristiker og Kritiker*, Kjøbenhavn: H. Aschehoug & Co., 1923, pp. 91-108. ['The 1880s. Sketches and Criticisms'. A volume of previously published contributions to Danish journals, including a brief general essay on Sg, **B2:388**, and five theatre reviews: **E12:410**: '*Fröken Julie*'; **E29:64**: '*Gustav Vasa*'; **E34:427**: '*Paaske*'; **E35:1114**: '*Dødedansen*'; and **E42:37**: '*Gustav III*']

[**B1:473**] Wechsel, Kirsten, (ed.), in cooperation with Lill-Ann Körber, *Strindberg and His Media, Proceedings of the 15th International Strindberg Conference*, EKF Wissenschaft, Skandinavistik, Band 1, Leipzig and Berlin: Edition Kirchof & Franke, 2003. Illus. 386 pp. [The proceedings of the 15th International Strindberg Conference, held in Berlin 2001. Contains the following twenty essays, grouped under five main headings: 1. 'Strindberg and Media Studies', 2. 'Media and the Crisis of Identity', 3. 'Strindberg on Stage', 4. 'Visuality', and 5. 'Intermediary/Intertextuality'. The essays are: **B2:55**: Annie Bourguignon, 'Die Poetik der Reportage bei Strindberg'; **B2:305**: Ulf Olsson, 'Telephone. Notes on Commuication Technology and Meaning in Strindberg's Works'; **B9:76**: Anna Cavallin, 'Strindberg's New Women and Some Encounters with the Media'; **C1:245**: Piotr Bukowski, 'Über die Mehrdimensionalität der Goethe-Rezeption in Strindbergs Spätwerk'; **C2:67**: Birgitta Steene, 'Ingmar Bergman Staging Strindberg'; **D2:958**: Eivor Martinus, 'Strindberg Indirect'; **D2:1216**: Marianne Streisand, 'Strindbergs Entwurf einer "Aesthetik der Intimität" und ihre Realiserung bei Max Reinhardt'; **E11:141**: Ulrike Peters, 'Conspired Writing in Strindberg's *The Father*'; **E12:271**: Egil Törnqvist, 'Strindberg on Page and Stage: *Miss Julie* as Paradigmatic Example'; **E13:25**: Annegret Heitmann, 'August Strindberg's *Fordringsägare* and/as Media Studies'; **E15:12**: Henk Van der Liet, 'Two Pariahs. From Short Story to Short Play'; **E48:33**: Joachim Grage, 'Strindbergs "Sista Sonater". Musikalisch-literarische intermedialität in den Kammarspel'; **E51:31**: Jørgen Stender Clausen, 'Strindberg's *The Ghost Sonata*: The Allegorical Role of Multimediality'; **F4:63**: Barbara Lide, '*En dåres försvarstal*. Strindberg's Self-Portrayal and Max Lundqvist's Adaptations'; **K3:42**: Roger Marmus,

'Från kupéfönstret under full fart. Landskapsskildring i rörelse i *Bland franska bönder*'; **P1:462**: Göran Söderström, 'Strindberg och Adolf Paul i Berlin och några mystiferande nyupptäckta strindbergsmålningar'; **P1:366**: Grischka Petri, 'Kunst als Schlüssel zum Himmelrich. Strindbergs Malerei als Medium der Erkenntnis'; **P2:5**: Jan Balbierz, 'Linsen, smältdegeln och ett slags halv verklighet. Om Strindbergs experiment med fotografin 1886-1911'; **P2:33**: Anne-Bitt Gerecke, 'Inszenierte und unterlaufene Autorschaft im Medienwechsel. Textualität, Thealitralität, Photographie bei Strindberg'; and **R:184**: Elena Balzamo, 'Strindberg und sein Verleger'. Preface by Kirsten Wechsel]

[B1:474] Wien, Alfred, *August Strindberg, Mit einem Bildnis des Dichters*, Der moderne Dichter 8, Berlin: Wilhelm Borngräber Verlag, [1913]. [62] pp. ['August Strindberg. With a Portrait of the Writer'. An essay or causerie rather than a critical study, which offers an overview of Sg's career as a writer that is recuperated here in terms of a selective reading of Sg's own autobiographical fictions and interpreted in terms of a pilgrimage in search of belief. Wien examines some of its principal themes, including his attitude to women (for Wien, Sg is 'Der Scharfrichter des Weibes'). He focuses primarily on the plays (especially the post-Inferno dramas rather than *Fadren* and *Fröken Julie*), although he does discuss *Röda rummet*, *Hemsöborna*, and *I havsbandet*]

[B1:475] Wirsén, Carl David af, 'August Strindberg', in *Kritiker*, Stockholm: P. A. Norstedt & Söners Förlag, 1901, pp. 287-392. [Collects the almost uniformly critical reviews of Sg's works by his long-time adversary, who was also the politically and artistically conservative secretary of the Swedish Academy during much of Sg's career. Includes reviews on publication of *Mäster Olof*, pp. 290-300, *Tjänstekvinnans son*, pp. 301-308, *I röda rummet*, pp. 309-315, *Fadren*, pp. 317-319, *Kamraterna*, pp. 326-333, *Giftas II*, pp. 320-325, 'Samvetskval', pp. 372-376, *Tryckt och otryckt II* and *III*, pp. 338-334, 350-359, *Skärkarlsliv*, pp. 334-337, *I havsbandet*, pp. 345-349, *Inferno*, pp. 360-363, *Legender*, pp. 364-368, *Till Damaskus*, pp. 369-371, *Vid högre rätt*, pp. 377-381, *Folkungasagan*, pp. 382-387, and *Gustav Adolf*, pp. 388-392. Their original publication is listed individually elsewhere in this bibliography]

B2. Essays in Books and Journals on General Topics or which Discuss Works in more than a single Genre.

[B2:1] Adams, Ann-Charlotte Gavel, 'Strindberg and Paris 1894-1898: Barbarian, Initiate, and Self', in **B1:170**, *August Strindberg and the Other*, pp. 91-100. [Examines Sg's reception in France and his engagement with French culture during the 1890s, which marks the culmination of his calculated efforts to gain recognition in what, like Walter Benjamin, he regarded as the capital of the 19th Century. Adams is primarily concerned with the series of experimental prose works 'Sensations détraquées' (Deranged Sensations, 1894) 'Le Barbare à Paris' (1895), *Inferno*, and *Jakob brottas*, in which she considers him successful in presenting the modernist self. She also compares *Inferno* with Rimbaud's *Un Saison en Enfer*]

[B2:2] Adolphson, Eva, 'Strindbergs början', in Ulf Olsson, red., **B1:357**, *Strindbergs förvandlingar*, pp. 19-26. ['Strindberg's Beginnings'. Adolphson reflects on Sg's origins as a writer, his modernity, and the subjectivity represented by the solipsistic protagonist of *Till Damaskus*, first encountered writing pensively in the sand]

[B2:3] Ahlberg, Alf, 'Det ondas problem i Strindbergs diktning. Till 10-årsminnet av diktarens bortgång', *Svenska Dagbladet* (Stockholm), 13 May 1922. ['The Problem of Evil in Strindberg's Writings. On the 10th Anniversary of the Writer's Death']

[B2:4] Ahlberg, Alf, 'Det ondas problem i Strindbergs diktning. Till 10-årsminnet av diktarens bortgång', in *Filosofi och dikt. Essayer och meditationer*, Stockholm: Natur och Kultur, 1924, pp. 148-155. [Rpr. of **B2:3**]

[B2:5] Ahlström, Stellan, 'Den moraliska domen över Strindberg', *Samtid och framtid* (Stockholm), 5 (1948), 287-294. ['The Moral Judgement on Strindberg']

[B2:6] Ahlstroem [sic], Stellan, 'Strindberg à Paris. Un aperçu', *Revue d'histoire du théâtre* (Paris), 30:3 (1978), 200-212. ['Strindberg in Paris. An Aperçu'. Surveys Sg's career as a writer, mentioning the majority of his major novels and autobiographical fictions as well as the plays. Stresses his links with France through his interest in Rousseau, Jules Vallés, Victor Hugo, Balzac, Henry Becque, and Voltaire, and concludes by quoting George Bernard Shaw: 'There is no name that strikes [the] European imagination more than Sg's'. Introduces a special issue of the *Revue* which collects papers presented at the 2nd International Sg Conference, held at the Université de Paris-Sorbonne on the theme 'Strindberg à Paris']

[B2:7] Ahnlund, Knut, 'Strindberg och rollerna', *Svenska Dagbladet* (Stockholm), 15 October 1965. ['Strindberg and His Roles']

[B2:8] Åkerhjelm, Helge, 'August Strindberg', *American-Scandinavian Review* (New York), 26 (1938), 312-317. [Claims that Sg is 'the first of our great poets to belong to our own age, to speak our own language, to deal with problems which are still of moment to us. In [him] we honor the first and greatest of our modern authors']

[B2:9] Albert, Henri, 'Auguste Strindberg', *La Revue Blanche* (Paris), 1 December 1894, pp. 481-498. [A relatively well-informed survey of Sg's work to date in one of the leading Symbolist journals, published prior to the French première of *Fadren* at the Théâtre de l'Œuvre. Albert discusses *Röda rummet*, 'Tschandala', *I havsbandet*, and Sg's poetry, as well as several of the plays. He associates Sg with Nietzsche, comments on his individual style, discusses his childhood and early years with reference to *Tjänstekvinnans son*, and questions his portrayal of male and female roles in *En dåres försvarstal* where, had Axel been a real man and not this weeping, female misfit, he would have had no trouble keeping the perverse monsters about him in their place]

[B2:10] Albrecht, Fran, 'Avgust Strindberg', *Slovan* (Ljubljana), 10 (1912), pp. 300-308, 315. [An introductory essay on Sg's work in Slovenian, written in conjunction with Sg's death]

[B2:11] Albrecht, Fran, 'Avgust Strindberg', *Gledališki list NGL* (Ljubljana), 14 (1920-21), 16-19.

[B2:12] Andrejanoff, Victor von, 'Eine Trilogie der Gemeinheit', *Das Zwanzigste Jahrhundert* (München), 5:1 (1894-95), pp. 47-56. ['A Crude Trilogy'. Focuses primarily on the sexual pathology and other features of what Andrejanoff calls the naturalist trilogy *Fadren*, *Fröken Julie*, and *Fordringsägare*, but he also discusses 'Tschandala' and *I havsbandet*, as well as Sg's affinity with both Schopenhauer and Nietzsche in *Die fröhliche Wissenschaft*, *Der Fall Wagner*, and *Götzen-Dämmerung*. Brief reference is made to *Mäster Olof*, *Herr Bengts hustru*, *En dåres försvarstal*, and *Legender*, and numerous comparisons are drawn between Sg and German authors (Goethe, Kleist, and Hebbel), as well as contemporary composers (Wagner and Verdi), with whose works Andrejanoff considers that Sg's modern psychological and pathological form of drama has something in common. A note indicates that the author became aware of *En dåres försvarstal* only after completing the essay]

[**B2:13**] Andrejanoff, Victor von, 'Eine Trilogie der Gemeinheit', in Hans-Peter Bayerdörfer, Hrsg., **B3:85**, *Strindberg auf der deutschen Bühne*, pp. 112-120. ['A Crude Trilogy'. Rpr. of **B2:12**]

[**B2:14**] Anon, 'August Strindberg om realismen', *Skånska Aftonbladet* (Malmö), 17 June 1882. ['August Strindberg on Realism'. Endorses Sg's view of realism in the essay 'Om realism' (1882) as the artistic pursuit of truth, in contrast to the false prophets of idealism]

[**B2:15**] Anon, 'Boknyheter. *Tryckt och otryckt II*', *Budkaflen* (Stockholm), 4 July 1890. [Praises the miscellaneous collection of prose and short, one-act, plays, including *Den starkare*, as evidence of Sg's 'original genius'. Review on publication]

[**B2:16**] Anon, 'Litterärt. A. Strindbergs nya skrifter', *Stockholms Dagblad*, 23 December 1888. [A critical review of *Hemsöborna*, *Skärkarlsliv*, and *Fröken Julie* on publication. Only 'Den romantiske klockaren på Rånö' (The Romantic Sexton on Rånö) in *Skärkarlsliv* produces a positive comment whereas *Fröken Julie* is judged to be decidedly Sg's worst work to date; it is nothing more than one long seduction scene: 'A filthy bundle of rags that one hardly wishes to touch even with a pair of tongs']

[**B2:17**] Anon, 'Litterärt. August Strindberg: *Tryckt och otryckt I*', *Stockholms Dagblad*, 18 May 1890. [A largely unenthusiastic review of this miscellaneous collection of dramas and prose works on publication. *Paria*, *Samum*, and *Fordringsägare* are all described as somewhat strange pieces while the essays on Voltaire and Modern Drama are criticised as too one-sided. So, too, is the attempt to establish the inferiority of women in the essay 'Kvinnans underlägsenhet under mannen' (Woman's Inferiority to Man')]

[**B2:18**] Anon, 'The Plays and Novels of August Strindberg', *Belgravia* (London), 85 (1895), [137]-153. [Augments Justin Huntly McCarthy's first English response to Sg in **B2:264** with a survey of his career to date. Discusses *Herr Bengts hustru*, *Lycko-Pers resa*, *Kamraterna*, *Fadren*, and *Fröken Julie* in some detail, but also comments on *Röda rummet*, *Mäster Olof*, *Gillets hemlighet*, *Giftas*, *I Rom*, *Den Fredlöse*, and 'Les Relations de la France avec la Suède'. 'Few critics will deny that both this ultra-realistic tragedy [*Fröken Julie*] and that of *The Father*...are the work of a man of genius']

[**B2:19**] Anon [Edvard Brandes], '*Tryckt och otryckt II*', *Politiken* (Copenhagen), 3 August 1890. [Reviews Sg's miscellaneous collection of prose and short plays including 'Hjärnornas kamp' (The Battle of the Brains) and *Den starkare* on publication]

[**B2:20**] Antal, Sándor, 'Strindberg', *Hét* (Budapest?), 1910.

[**B2:21**] Banerjee, J., 'August Strindberg (1849-1912)', *The Calcutta Review*, 1 (1921), pp. 53-69; 2 (1921), pp. 116-124, 466-471; 3 (1921), pp. 97-105, 444-451. [The earliest appraisal of Sg's career as a writer to be published in India]

[**B2:22**] Basargin, A. [Pseudonym of A. I. Vvedenskii], 'Avgust Strindberg', 1-3, *Moskovskie vedomosti* (Moscow), 4, 11, and 18 September 1908. [A three-part article. E.775]

[B2:23] Basch, Victor, 'Auguste Strindberg', in *Silhouettes inactuelles*, Paris: Les Écrivains indépendants, n.d., pp. [56]-63.

[B2:24] Baumgartner, Walter, 'Nachwort', 'Anhang', and 'Anmerkungen', in August Strindberg, *Werke in zeitlicher Folge*, Bd 10: *1903-1905*, Hrsg. von Walter Baumgartner, Frankfurt am Main: Insel Verlag, 1987, pp. 713-754, 757-805, 806-864. [The Afterword, Notes, and editorial apparatus to a volume containing new German translations of Sg's works in all genres published between 1903 and 1905]

[B2:25] Belfrage, Sixten, 'Strindberg och kongruensregeln', *Skola och samhälle* (Stockholm), 7 (1926), 52-65. ['Strindberg and the Rule of Congruity'. On Sg's application of the grammatical rules of congruity, or agreement and concord. Discussion of Belfrage's article continues in later issues, pp. 217-221 and 340-341]

[B2:26] Bennich-Björkman, Bo, 'Fåglar och författarroller hos Strindberg', *Samlaren* (Uppsala), 83 (1962), pp. 5-66. ['Birds and Authorial Roles in Strindberg'. A compelling and important analysis of themes and symbols associated with birds which may be related to Sg's predicament as a professional writer and his role as an author during the 1870s and 1880s. Illustrated by reference to a range of earlier works, including *Röda rummet*, *Herr Bengts hustru*, and the short stories 'Odlad frukt' (Cultivated Fruit) in *Svenska öden och äventyr* and 'Återfall' (Relapse) and 'Över molnen' (Beyond the Clouds) in *Utopier i verkligheten*]

[B2:27] Bennich-Björkman, Bo, 'Strindbergs optiska lekar', in Margareta Brundin, *et al.*, red., **B1:88**, *20 x Strindberg*, pp. 57-75. Illus. ['Strindberg's Optical Games'. Charts Sg's abiding interest in different optical phenomena, beginning with the panoramas, kaleidoscopes, and Laterna magica to which he alludes in *Sömngångarnätter*, *Gamla Stockholm*, and the early essay 'Porslinsbilder' (1877). In his later work they assumed the form of life's panorama and are a central feature in *Till Damaskus I*. Indeed, Bennich-Björkman shows how such optical phenomena are a recurring feature of many of the later dramas, including *Advent, Brott och brott*, *Midsommar*, and *Påsk*, where they are linked with the notion of the invisible powers that Sg encounters in *Inferno*, whose task it is to lead him and humanity as a whole back to religion]

[B2:28] Berendsohn, Walter A[rthur], 'August Strindberg', *Julius Weismann Archiv* (Duisburg), 1956, pp. 16-19. [An introductory presentation of Sg's life and work]

[B2:29] Berendsohn, Walter A[rthur], 'August Strindberg – Rebell und Dichter', *Judische Wochenschau* (Buenos Aires), 4 December 1951. ['August Strindberg – Rebel and Writer']

[B2:30] Berendsohn, Walter A[rthur], 'August Strindbergs skapande fantasi', *Värld och vetande* (Göteborg), 6 (1956), 368-376. ['August Strindberg's Creative Imagination']

[B2:31] Berendsohn, Walter A[rthur], '"Mein Feuer is das grösste in Schweden". Gedanken über August Strindbergs schöpferische Phantasie', *Weser-Kurier*, 25 August 1956. ['"My Fire is the Greatest in Sweden". Reflections on August Strindberg's Creative Imagination']

[B2:32] Berendsohn, Walter A[rthur], 'Människokunskap', in **B1:42**, *Strindbergsproblem*, pp. 161-187. ['Knowledge of Humanity'. Berendsohn suggests that it is Sg's knowledge of human behaviour that forms the bedrock of his writing. His insight into the complexities of character and the means whereby he conveys it are exemplified with reference to *Hemsöborna*, 'Den romantiske klockaren på Rånö', *I havsbandet*, *Till Damaskus*, and

Götiska rummen. Berendsohn suggests that his understanding of the mechanisms of the inner life anticipates Freud]

[B2:33] Berendsohn, Walter A[rthur], *Strindbergs Parisschilderungen*, Dortmund Vorträge 49, Dortmund: Kulturamt der Stadt Dortmund, 1962. 19 pp. ['Strindberg's Depictions of Paris'. On the portrayal of Paris in Sg's works, focusing mainly on *Inferno* and *Legender*]

[B2:34] Berg, John, 'August Strindberg. En orientering i hans författarskap', *Studiekamraten* (Tollarp), 30:4-5 (1949), 281-286. ['August Strindberg. An Introduction to His Writings'. An elementary introduction for the general reader]

[B2:35] Berg, John, 'August Strindberg. En orientering i hans författarskap', *Studiekamraten* (Tollarp), 34 (1952), 89-93. [Rpr. of **B2:34**]

[B2:36] Berg, Ruben G:son, 'Strindberg's stilkonst', *Dagens Nyheter* (Stockholm), 21 January 1909. ['Strindberg's Stylistic Art'. Compares Sg with Carl Jonas Love Almqvist and acclaims him as a renewer of the Swedish language who has broadened the power of his means of expression. His prime quality is concentration, but he is impulsive, and the explosive quality of his language finds its best expression in dialogue, in his prose works as well as the dramas. Berg describes his style, characteristic tone, and diction, with reference to *Hemsöborna*, 'Dygdens lön' (The Reward of Virtue) from *Giftas*, 'Pål och Per' in *Svenska öden och äventyr*, and *Inferno*. He also observes that the visionary element in his language recalls E. T. A. Hoffmann (e.g. in *Spöksonaten*) and sometimes the fairy tales of Hans Christian Andersen]

[B2:37] Berg, Ruben G:son, 'August Strindberg', *Ord och Bild* (Stockholm), 21:6 (1912), 289-306. Illus. [An influential assessment of Sg's life and works, published in the immediate aftermath of his death. Berg pays more attention to the pre-Inferno period and his non-dramatic works than to the plays and his later work. He is not uncritical but remains appreciative of *Fröken Julie*, *Kronbruden*, and the 'Hoffmanesque' *Spöksonaten*, and especially of those works (e.g. *Mäster Olof* and *Röda rummet*) which were to remain for many years at the appreciated heart of the Swedish image of Sg. For Berg, Sg 'was the master without a masterpiece....the genius of the fragment' and, 'together with Almqvist, the greatest literary genius we have had to date']

[B2:38] Berg, Ruben G:son, 'August Strindberg', *Valvoja* (Helsinki), 1912:5-6, pp. 317-337. [Finnish version of **B2:37**]

[B2:39] Berg, Ruben G:son, 'August Strindberg', in *Litteraturbilder*, Andra samlingen, Stockholm: P. A. Norstedt & Söners Förlag, 1919, pp. 161-195. [Rpr. of **B2:37**]

[B2:40] Berg, Ruben G:son, 'August Strindberg', *Wetenschappelijke bladen* (Haarlem), 1913:1, pp. 80-93, 236-248. [Dutch version of **B2:37**]

[B2:41] Berman, H., 'The Essence of Strindberg', *Colonnade* (Georgia College), 11 (1916), 58-63.

[B2:42] Bernson, Bernhard, 'Gespräch um Strindberg', *Die weißen Blätter* (Leipzig), 7 (1920), 193-205.

[B2:43] Bérubé, Rénald, 'Un Suédois nommé Strindberg', *Liberté* (Montréal), 91:3 (1974), 26-51. ['A Swede Called Strindberg']

[B2:44] 'Bessie', 'Strindberg och Inferno. Ett litterärt femtioårsminne', *Skånska Dagbladet* (Malmö), 15 March 1941 (Söndags bilaga). ['Strindberg and Inferno. A Literary Memory of Fifty Years'. Presents Sg's Inferno crisis and contemporary literary currents in Paris during the 1890s, with reference to *Inferno, Legender, Advent*, and his return to writing for the theatre with *Till Damaskus I*]

[B2:45] B. H. B. [Bo Bergman], 'Ur bokmarknaden', *Ord och Bild* (Stockholm), 13:11 (1904), 634-636. [Reviews *Ensam* together with *Sagor* and *Götiska rummen*. To judge by the latter, which is dominated throughout by a single voice (the author's own), and which also lacks any vestige of artistic composition, it would seem that art no longer holds much significance for Sg. As a novel, it compares unfavourably with *Röda rummet* and borders upon the pathological, although in *Ensam* there is still much that is both beautiful and profound. Indeed, in their concrete detail, his descriptions of things seen in the streets of Stockholm retain all his old mastery]

[B2:46] Biberi, Ion, 'Strindberg' in *Eseuri literare, filosoficeşi artistice*, Galaţi: Cartea Românească, 1982, pp. 205-216. [Includes a general study of Sg as part of a varied collection of essays on art, literature, and philosophy]

[B2:47] Björkman, Edwin, 'August Strindberg: His Achievements', *Forum* (New York), 47:3 (1912), 274-288. [Offers both a general overview of Sg's works and a more detailed analysis of several key texts (*Fröken Julie, Till Damaskus, Dödsdansen*, and *Ett drömspel*) in which Sg's experimentation with dramatic form is most apparent]

[B2:48] Björkman, Edwin August, 'Strindberg', in *Voices of Tomorrow: Critical Studies of the New Spirit in Literature*, London: Grant Richards Ltd., [1913], pp. 11-20. [Includes material from articles originally published in the New York journal *Forum* and elsewhere. Focuses primarily upon the plays but includes discussion of some of the novels and autobiographical fictions as well. Björkman considers the naturalist period between 1885 and 1894 as in some respects abnormal, 'a deviation from his true line of development', and consequently regrets that, until recently, it is works from that decade which have been most readily available in English. Also published in New York by Mitchell Kennerley. See **B1:368**]

[B2:49] Björkman, Edwin August, 'Strindberg', in *Voices of Tomorrow: Critical Studies of the New Spirit in Literature*, New York: Johnson Rpr., 1970, pp. 11-20. [Facsimile Rpr. of the New York edition of **B2:48**, published by Mitchell Kennerley]

[B2:50] Bld. [J. A. Björklund], 'August Strindberg och hans senaste författarskap', 1-2, *Nya Dagligt Allehanda* (Stockholm), 21 and 23 October 1884. ['August Strindberg and His Latest Writings'. Sg is the most gifted of contemporary Swedish writers, but also the most arrogant and belligerent. Considers *Dikter på prosa och vers, Sömngångarnätter*, and several of the essays in *Likt och olikt*, as well as the newly published Volume One of *Giftas*, which Björklund regards as, without doubt, his most remarkable achievement to date]

[B2:51] Blümner, Rudolf, 'Strindberg', in *Literaturberichte des Verlages Georg Müller*, 1914:1, pp. 13-22. [A biographically inflected study which speculates on Sg's beliefs, his almost 'monomaniacal' obsession with the relationship between men and women, his politics, and his interest in the French novelist and playwright, Joséphin [Sâr] Péladan (1859-1918), Included in a volume issued by the publisher of the German edition of Sg's collected works in order to publicise its own authors]

[B2:52] Blümner, Rudolf, 'Strindberg', *Wissen und Leben* (Zürich), 6:8 (1913). [See **B2:51**]

[B2:53] Boer, R. C., 'Zweedsche dichters van onzen tijd. Aulavoordrachten, gehouden aan de Universiteit van Amsterdam op 3, 10, 17 November 1916. III: Over eenige werken van Strindberg', *Onze Eeuw* (Amsterdam), 17 (1917), 345-379. ['Swedish Writers of Our Time'. The text of a lecture on Sg in a series devoted to contemporary Swedish Writers and delivered at the University of Amsterdam]

[B2:54] Entry cancelled.

[B2:55] Bourguignon, Annie, 'Die Poetik der Reportage bei Strindberg', in Kirsten Wechsel, Hrsg., **B1:473**, *Strindberg and His Media*, pp. 69-93. ['The Poetics of Reportage in Strindberg'. Links the crisis of identity which Sg experienced in so representative a manner in the mid-1880s with the challenge to the concept of the author inherent in modernism, and indicates how, in abandoning poetry (or *skönlitteratur*) in favour of a form of writing that was akin to journalism in e.g. *Bland franska bönder*, he seeks to redefine his position as an author, while at the same time eliding the differences between reportage and fiction. Primarily concerned with *Bland franska bönder* in relation to Sg's existential crisis as depicted in *Tjänstekvinnans son* and other autobiographical writings of the period]

[B2:56] Bourguignon, Annie, 'La Poètique du reportage chez Strindberg', in *Le Reportage d'Ècrivain. Etude d'un phénomène littéraire à partir de textes suédois et d'autres textes scandinaves*, Frankfurt-am-Main: Peter Lang, 2004, pp. 93-117. [French translation of **B2:55**]

[B2:57] Boyer, Régis, 'Déthéâtraliser Strindberg', *Europe* (Paris), No. 858 (October 2000), pp. 3-6. ['Detheatricalise Strindberg'. Introduces a collection of essays on Sg with an appeal that he should be regarded as not merely a dramatist but a formidable writer in numerous genres. Boyer justifies the claim with reference to *Röda rummet*, *Sömngångarnätter*, the letters to Harriet Bosse, *Tjänstekvinnans son*, and the vivisection 'Des arts nouveaux! Du hasard dans la production artistique' (1894)]

[B2:58] Brandell, Gunnar, 'Der moderne Strindberg', *Merkur* (Cologne), 18:1 (1964), 21-33. ['Strindberg the Modern'. Reflections on Sg as a modern, still contemporary writer, published together with a German translation of 'Des arts nouveaux! Du hasard dans la production artistique' (1894)]

[B2:59] Brandell, Gunnar, 'Moderni Strindberg', Translated by Marija Čižmek, *Republika* (Zagreb), 1964:11. ['The Modern Strindberg'. Croatian translation of **B2:58**. R.593]

[B2:60] Brandell, Gunnar, 'Strindberg wciąz aktualny', *Dialog* (Warsaw), 1964:4, pp. 142-147. [Abridged Polish translation of **B2:58**]

[B2:61] Brandes, Georg, 'August Strindberg', *Tilskueren* (Copenhagen), 11:5 (1894), 341-362. [An assessment of Sg's achievement to date by the most influential European literary critic of the period. See **B2:67**]

[B2:62] Brandes, Georg, 'August Strindberg', in *Menschen und Werke*, Frankfurt am Main: Literarische Anstalt, 1894. IV+533 pp. [German translation of **B2:61**]

[B2:63] Brandes, Georg, 'August Strindberg' [1892] and 'Nachschrift' [1899], in *Menschen und Werke*, 3. Aufl., Frankfurt am Main: Rutten & Loening, 1900, pp. 488-521.

[B2:64] Brandes, Georg, 'Avgust Strindberg', in G. Brandes, *Sobranie sochinenii v 12 tomakh*, Vol. 2, Translated and edited by M. V. Luchitskaia, Kiev, 1902, pp. 127-154.

[B2:65] Brandes, Georg, 'Avgust Strindberg', in G. Brandes, *Sobranie sochinenii v 12 tomakh*, Vol. 2, 2nd revised and supplemented edition, translated and edited by M. V. Luchitskaia, Kiev, 1906, pp. 217-268.

[B2:66] Brandes, Georg, 'August Strindberg', in *Samlade Skrifter*, København: Gyldendalske Boghandels Forlag (F. Hegel & Søn), 1900, Vol. 3, pp. 633-661. [Rpr. of **B2:61**]

[B2:67] Brandes, Georg, 'August Strindberg', in Gustaf Fröding, red., **B1:142**, *En bok om Strindberg*, pp. 69-90. [An account of Sg's pre-Inferno writings from *Röda rummet, Mäster Olof*, and *I Rom* to *Hemsöborna*, 'Tschandala', and *I havsbandet*, where Brandes claims that Nietzsche's influence is readily detected. Brandes stresses Sg's frequent, sudden changes in outlook, comments on his important role in contemporary Swedish literature and the ongoing Scandinavian debate over the Woman Question, and discusses *Fadren*, *Giftas*, *Herr Bengts hustru*, and *Utopier i verkligheten*, but not *Fröken Julie*, although he notes it as 'the best' of his most recent plays]

[B2:68] Brandes, Georg, 'August Strindbergs författarskap fram till 1890', 1-4, *Ny Tid* (Göteborg), 15, 17, and 18 May 1912. ['August Strindberg's Writings up to 1890'. Rpr. of **B2:61**, republished in memoriam in four parts]

[B2:69] Brandes, Georg, 'August Strindbergs författarskap fram till 1890', 1-3, *Nya samhället*, 18, 22, and 23 May 1912. [Rpr. of **B2:61**, republished in memoriam in three parts]

[B2:70] Brandes, Georg, 'August Strindberg', *Germanisch-Romanische Monatsschrift* (Heidelberg), 6 (1914), 321-335.

[B2:71] Brandl, Horst, and Jörg Scherzer, 'Nachwort', 'Anhang', and 'Kommentierung', in August Strindberg, *Werke in zeitlicher Folge*, Bd 4: *1886*, Hrsg. von Horst Brandl und Jörg Scherzer, Frankfurt am Main: Insel Verlag, 1984, pp. 759-780, 783-844, 845-888. [The Afterword, Notes, and editorial apparatus for a volume containing new German translations of Sg's works in all genres written and published in 1886]

[B2:72] Buchmayr, Friedrich, 'August Strindberg and the Altered Perception of Modernism', in Michael Robinson and Sven Hakon Rossel, eds, **B1:387**, *Expressionism and Modernism*, pp. 33-45. [A Benjaminian examination of the inward turn that occurs in Sg's prose works of the mid-1880s to the mid-1890s, in which he advances towards a modern mode of perception, one that entails not only a shift in the objects of perception in the external world but the organs and very act of perception itself. Buchmayr exemplifies the process mainly via Sg's account of rail travel in *Bland franska bönder* (1886) and his portrayal of urban experience in the experimental prose sketch 'Sensations détraquées' (Deranged Sensations, 1894)]

[B2:73] Butt, Wolfgang, 'Nachwort', 'Anhang', and 'Kommentierung', in August Strindberg, *Werke in zeitlicher Folge*, Bd 5: *1887-1888*, Hrsg. von Wolfgang Butt, Frankfurt am Main: Insel Verlag, 1984, pp. 819-835, 839-874, 875-890. [The Afterword, Notes, and editorial apparatus to a volume containing new German translations of Sg's works in all genres written and published in 1887-88]

[B2:74] Cargill, Oscar, 'August Strindberg', in *Intellectual America. Ideas on the March*, New York: Cooper Square Publishers, Inc., 1968, pp. 573-582. [Claims that Sg 'had a better reception here [North America] than Ibsen, and is far more important in the development of American thought'. '*Miss Julie*...is undeniably one of the best pieces of theatre of modern times...for all his perversion, Sg was a great liberator'. Cargill focuses mainly on the naturalistic plays, *Giftas*, and *Dödsdansen*, which is dismissed as 'tedious'. See Rpr. in **B1:91**]

[B2:75] Carlson, Harry G[ilbert], 'Landscape as Mediator in Strindberg's Search for the Other', in Poul Houe *et al.*, ed., **B1:170**, *August Strindberg and the Other*, pp. 77-89.

[Argues that Sg's knowledge of the principles of 19th-Century landscape painting underlies the way in which he used natural settings to explore the tensions between the human and the natural world, and the self and the other. Carlson considers Sg's art criticism and his practice as a painter but focuses primarily on descriptions of landscape in literary texts, from 'Samvetskval' (Remorse) in *Utopier i verkligheten* to *Röda rummet*, *Tjänstekvinnans son*, the prose poem 'Solrök' (Heat Haze), and *I havsbandet*]

[B2:76] Carlson, Harry G[ilbert], 'Réflexions sur le processus créatif chez Strindberg: le rôle des références visuelles', Traduit de l'anglais par Pascale Voilley, in Elena Balzamo, ed., **B1:7**, *August Strindberg*, Paris: L'Herne, 2000, pp. 264-270. ['Reflections on Strindberg's Creative Process: The Role of Visual References'. Examines the significance of Sg's visual imagination for his literary works and creative method. Carlson comments on his collaboration with Carl Larsson in *Svenska folket*, the impressionist narrative method underlying the stories 'Samvetskval' (Remorse) and 'Pantomimer från gatan' (Street Pantomimes), and what he suggests is the relevance for the portrayal of Paris and Austria in *Inferno* of Gustave Doré's engravings for Dante's *L'Enfer* (1876)]

[B2:77] Carlson, Harry G[ilbert], 'Strindberg and the Carnival of History', *Scandinavian Studies* (Madison), 62:1 (1990), 39-52. [Discusses Sg's pre-Bakhtin understanding of the carnivalesque nature of history and the overthrow of established hierarchies with reference to works covering almost his entire career: *Historiska miniatyrer*, *Röda rummet*, *Mäster Olof*, *Fröken Julie*, *Erik XIV*, *Kristina*, *Spöksonaten*, and *Till Damaskus*. Carlson claims that 'Sg's use of carnivalesque themes and devices began… as an allegorical weapon in the battle against "official" lies, a tool for revealing Society's Secret, but he transformed its purpose during the last half of his career, making the egalitarianism more ambivalent, and adding a modern dissonance']

[B2:78] Carlson, Harry G[ilbert], 'Strindberg and the Carnival of History', in Birgitta Steene, ed., **B1:434**, *Strindberg and History*, pp. 61-74. Illus. [Rpr. of **B2:77**]

[B2:79] Carlson, Harry G[ilbert], 'Strindberg and the Dream of the Golden Age: The Poetics of History', in Göran Stockenström, ed., **D2:288**, *Strindberg's Dramaturgy*, pp. 27-40. [Examines the influence of particular metaphors on Sg's conception of history and particularly the dynamic tension derived from the myth of the Golden Age, mainly as depicted in Ovid's *Metamorphoses* and Hesiod's *Works and Days*, as well as biblical images of the Fall and the Redemption of mankind. Ovidian themes abound in works from the early 1880s such as *Lycko-Pers resa*, the short story 'De lycksaliges ö' (The Isle of the Blessed) in *Svenska öden och äventyr*, *Svenska folket*, and *Utopier i verkligheten*, where they meld with Rousseau's critique of culture. But these Arcadian visions of an unfissured landscape enshrining goodness and harmony, merge in later works, from *Fröken Julie* to *Ett drömspel*, with a Christian view of the Fall of Man and the Last Judgement, which is discussed here with reference to the essay 'Världshistoriens mystik' and *Historiska miniatyrer*, two texts which reveal 'the scope and brilliance of Sg's understanding of history's drama: its epic structure and its human detail']

[B2:80] Carlson, Harry G[ilbert], 'Strindberg och drömmen om guldåren', Translated by Eva Sjöstrand, *Artes* (Stockholm), 11:4 (1985), 97-110. ['Strindberg and the Dream of the Golden Age'. Swedish version of **B2:79**]

[B2:81] Carlson, Harry G[ilbert], 'Strindberg's Biblical Imagery', in Donald Weaver, ed., **D2:331**, *Strindberg on Stage*, pp. 16-32. [The Bible is fundamental to the way Sg works as an artist, shaping his plays and permeating their language. This is confirmed by a passage from *Ensam* and exemplified here with reference to *Fröken Julie* and *Ett drömspel*]

[B2:82] Carlson, Harry G[ilbert], 'Strindbergova biblijska metaforika', Prijevod s engelskoga Giga Gracan, *Prolog* (Zagreb), Nos 55-56 (1983), pp. 72-80. Illus. ['Strindberg's Biblical Metaphors'. Serbo-Croat translation of **B2:81**]

[B2:83] Carlson, Harry G[ilbert], 'Theme, Image and Style in August Strindberg's Expressionism', in Michael Robinson and Sven Hakon Rossel, eds, **B1:387**, *Expressionism and Modernism*, pp. 53-62. Illus. [Argues that Expressionist tendencies were inherent in the themes that Sg exploited and the stylistic innovations he introduced throughout his career, as much in *Fadren*, which anticipates Oskar Kokoschka's play *Mörder. Hoffnung der Frauen* (1916), and *Fröken Julie* as in the post-Inferno dramas. Carlson observes that Asian art was an important inspirational source for Sg's Expressionism and Robert Lepage's recent staging of *Ett drömspel* is noteworthy for the way in which the former's metamorphic imagination leads to an expressionist theatre of metamorphosis]

[B2:84] Carlsson, Leif, 'August Strindberg', in Lars Ardelius and Gunnar Rydström, red., *Författarnas litteraturhistoria*, Stockholm: Författarförlaget, 1978, pp. 47-54. [Considers Sg under four headings: the social critic (with reference to *Röda rummet* and *Hemsöborna*), the religious polemicist (exemplified by *Inferno*), the portrayer of women (in *Fordringsägare* and *Advent*), and the psychologist. Carlsson questions his reputation as the greatest and most modern of Swedish writers]

[B2:85] Castelli, Ferdinando, S.I., 'August Strindberg. Una stagione all'inferno', *Civiltà cattolica* (Rome), 128:1 (1977), 25-38. ['August Strindberg. A Season in Hell'. Focuses primarily on the autobiographical fictions and the naturalist dramas, arguing that, based as it is on tragic humanism, Sg's work rises to a universal significance and presents itself to us as prophetic insofar as it embodies and expresses a fundamental aspect of man]

[B2:86] Castelli, Ferdinando, S.I., 'August Strindberg. Lampeggiamenti e caos', *Civiltà cattolica* (Rome) 128:1 (1977), 337-351. ['August Strindberg. Lightning and Chaos'. A religiously inflected reading of Sg's post-Inferno outlook as represented here by *Inferno, Legender, Till Damaskus, En blå bok*, and *Ockulta dagboken*, which also takes into account his intellectual relationship with Swedenborg]

[B2:87] Castrén, Gunnar, 'August Strindberg', *Samtiden* (Oslo), 23 (1912), 360-369. [See **B2:160**]

[B2:88] Castrén, Gunnar, 'August Strindberg', in *Studier och kritiker*, Helsingfors: Holger Schildt; Stockholm: Albert Bonniers Förlag, 1918, pp. 42-56. [Rpr. of **B2:160**]

[B2:89] Cecconi, Sergio, 'Strindberg o della solitudine', in Giovanani Cattanei, Ivo Chiesa, and Luigi Squarzina, eds, **E35:24**, *Danza di morte*, Edizioni del Teatro Stabile di Genova 8, 1963. ['Strindberg, or On Loneliness'. Programme essay in conjunction with a production of *Dödsdansen*]

[B2:90] Charlet, Emile, 'Strindberg', *Ontwaking* (Antwerp), 7 (1907), pp. 6-7. [A superficial introduction to Sg as a writer, indicative of the growing interest in his work in Flanders]

[**B2:91**] Charlet, Emile, *Skandinavische Dichterportretten (Zooals ik ze tag)*, Antwerp, 1907, 8 pp. ['Portraits of Scandinavian Writers'. Offprint of **B2:90**]

[**B2:92**] Ghisa, Ioana, 'The Question of the Subject in August Strindberg's "Post-Inferno" Writings', *Transylvanian Review* (Cluj-Napoca: Romanian Cultural Foundation), 12:1 (2003), 128-137. [Interprets Sg's Inferno experiences as a crisis of the subject in its encounter with modernity, of its moral and religious fragmentation, and of its striving for regeneration, all of which Sg represents in three different genres, the diary (*Ockulta dagboken*), autobiographical fiction (*Inferno*), and drama (*Till Damaskus*). Ghisa discusses the role accorded subjectivity in these works, the penitential journey undertaken by the central figure of *Inferno*, and the mythological chameleonism of the protagonist in *Till Damaskus*, who is variously related, among others, to Byron's Cain, Robert le Diable, Napoleon, Merlin, Ishmael, and Job, as well as to the important exemplum of Swedenborg. But whereas the Biblical model entails ultimate conversion, the journey undertaken by the protagonists of *Inferno* and *Till Damaskus* remains one of uncertain identity and unresolved moral torment]

[**B2:93**] Chojecki, Andrzej, 'A Polish Reading of Strindberg', *Studia Scandinavica* (Gdańsk), 11 (1988), pp. 15-28.

[**B2:94**] Ciesielski, Zenon, 'August Strindberg – wielki buntownik', *Program Teatru Wybrzeże* (Gdańsk), 1976, pp. 3-9. ['August Strindberg: The Great Rebel'. Program essay, 16 December 1976]

[**B2:95**] Ciesielski, Zenon, 'Strindberg czyli klopoty z geniuszem', *Punkt* (Gdańsk), 1981:13, pp. 170-173.

[**B2:96**] Cihlar, Milutin, 'August Strindberg', in August Strindberg, *Sin služavke*, Zagreb, 1917, pp. iii-xxviii. [R.487]

[**B2:97**] Cihlar, Milutin, 'August Strindberg', in *Knjiga eseja*, Zagreb, 1936, pp. 71-83. [Rpr. of **B2:96**. R.493]

[**B2:98**] Cihlar, Milutin, 'August Strindberg', in *Eseji*, Zagreb, 1944, pp. 123-146. [Rpr. of **B2:96**. R.496]

[**B2:99**] Cihlar, Milutin, 'Strindberg', in *Članci i kritike*, Zagreb, 1945, pp. 147-157. [Rpr. of **B2:96**. R.497]

[**B2:100**] Cihlar, Milutin, 'Strindberg', in *Članci i kritike*, Zagreb, 1945, pp. 221-224. [Rpr. of **B2:96**. R.498]

[**B2:101**] Codignola, Luciano, 'Strindberg e l'immagine', in *Immagini dal planeta Strindberg – Images from the Strindberg Planet*, Venezia: La Biennale di Venezia, 1980, pp. 19-21. Illus. [Parallel English text, 'Strindberg and the Image', pp. 20-21]

[**B2:102**] Coenen, Frans, 'August Strindberg. Een studie', 1-6, *Groot Nederland* (Amsterdam), 22:1 (1924), pp. 642-656; 22:2 (1924), pp. 303-319, 405-420, 528-546; 23:1 (1925), pp. 93-99, 395-405. [A substantial, biographically organised but, for the period, comparatively well-informed study of Sg's life and work which is nevertheless strongly coloured by the latter's own account of his life in *Tjänstekvinnans son* and elsewhere. Coenen focuses primarily on the plays, some of which, including *Mäster Olof*, *Fröken Julie*, *Fordringsägare*, *Till Damaskus*, *Dödsdansen*, *Gillets hemlighet*, and *Ett drömspel*, are discussed in some detail, and several of the novels are also commented on in passing]

[B2:103] Coenen, Frans, 'August Strindberg. Een studie', in *Verzameld werk*, Amsterdam: G. A. Van Oorschot, 1956, pp. 272-360. [Rpr. of **B2:102**]

[B2:104] Cohn, Alfons Fedor, 'August Strindberg', *Die Neue Zeit* (Stuttgart), 30:2 (1911-12), 285-292.

[B2:105] Coussanges, Jacques de, 'Les dernières œuvres de Strindberg', *La Revue* (Paris), 1909, pp. 104-113. ['Strindberg's most Recent Works']

[B2:106] Curle, Richard, 'More of Strindberg', *The Bookman* (London), 44 (1913), 258-260. [Reviews Volumes One and Two of Edith and Warner Oland's translations of the plays, as well as translations of *Advent* by Claud Field, *Påsk*, by Velmer S. Howard, and *I havsbandet*, by Ellie Schleussner. Curle considers Sg a man of letters rather than a great artist and regards his work as all too personal. Consequently, interest in it will surely cease when interest in the man ceases. In Curle's opinion, *Den starkare* is 'an extraordinarily brilliant piece', *Advent* a 'bundle of nonsense', the ending of *Fadren* 'far-fetched', and *I havsbandet* a failure]

[B2:107] Dahlström, Carl E[noch] W[illiam] L[eonard], 'August Strindberg – 1849-1912. Between Two Eras', *Scandinavian Studies* (Menasha, Wisconsin), 21:1 (1949), 1-18. [An essay written to mark the 1949 centenary of Sg's birth. Dahlström depicts him as an 'artistic colossus having one foot resting uncertainly in the crumbling old and the other seeking support on the yet unstable new'. He maintains that Sg was an intuitional genius who apprehended the uncertain, anxious, directionless condition of man today, but omits any substantial reference to any of the works]

[B2:108] Dahlström, Carl E[noch] W[illiam] L[eonard], 'Origins of Strindberg's Expressionism', *Scandinavian Studies* (Lawrence, Kansas), 34:1 (1962), 36-44. [Sg's expressionism was the product of an age of cultural disintegration produced by the incommensurability of traditional religion and 19th-Century science, and hence of the unresolved clash of two absolute orders. Having nothing outward on which to draw, he had to turn inward, and 'feed upon himself'. Included in the 1968 edition of *Strindberg's Dramatic Expressionism*, **D2:81**]

[B2:109] Daniel-Rops, Henry [Pseudonym of Jules Charles Henri Petiot], 'L'Actualité de Strindberg et le génie du Nord', *Revue de Genève*, 1927:1, pp. 575-595. ['The Topicality of Strindberg and the Genius of the North'. Daniel-Rops attributes the shifts in Sg's point of view to his personal feelings. Thus he 'only became a naturalist and succumbed to a mordant pessimism because he was unhappy. All he needed was deliverance from his money worries, happiness at home, and a few months in Switzerland in order to find a wholly new direction']

[B2:110] Daniel-Rops, Henry [Pseudonym of Jules Charles Henri Petiot], 'L'Actualité de Strindberg et le génie du Nord', in *Carte d'Europe: Strindberg, Conrad, Tchekov, Unamuno, Pirandello, Duhamel, Rilke*, ouvrage orné de sept portraits gravés sur bois par Henri Martin, Paris: Perrin et cie, 1928, pp. 1-51. [Rpr. of **B2:109**]

[B2:111] Daniel-Rops, Henry [Pseudonym of Jules Charles Henri Petiot], 'August Strindberg', *La Revue Hebdomadaire* (Paris), 36:7 (9 July 1927), 159-180. [Abridged version of **B2:109**]

[B2:111a] De Casseres, Benjamin, 'Strindberg', in *Forty Immortals*, New York: J. Lawren, [1926], pp. 240-245.

[B2:112] Delblanc, Sven, 'Den giftiga blomman. Erotiska motiv I Strindbergs ålderdomsdiktning', in *Studier tillägnade Gunnar Tideström den 7 februari 1966*, Litteraturhistoriska institutionen, Uppsala Universitetet, 1965-66, pp. 229-252. ['The Poisonous Flower. Erotic Motifs in the Works of Strindberg's Old Age'. Focuses on a complex of motifs and imagery to do with love, the body, desire, and death in *Till Damaskus*, *Ett drömspel*, and *Spöksonaten* where flowers are associated with woman and love, but extends the discussion to include *Röda rummet*, *Götiska rummen*, and *Ockulta dagboken*. A *Festschrift* published in Stencil]

[B2:113] Delblanc, Sven, 'Den giftiga blomman. Erotiska motiv I Strindbergs ålderdomsdiktning', in Lars Ahlbom and Björn Meidal, red., *Strindberg – urtida, samtida, framtida*, **B1:119**, pp. 35-53. ['The Poisonous Flower. Erotic Motifs in the Works of Strindberg's Old Age'. Rpr. of **B2:112**]

[B2:114] Delblanc, Sven, 'Humanisten Strindberg', *Expressen* (Stockholm), 12 May 1983. ['Strindberg the Humanist'. Delblanc's own Swedish version of a lecture originally delivered in English at the University of Minnesota (see **B2:116**)]

[B2:115] Delblanc, Sven, 'Humanisten Strindberg', in *Strindberg – urtida, samtida, framtida. Texter av Sven Delblanc*, Lars Ahlbom and Björn Meidal, red., Stockholm: Carlssons, 2007, pp. 196-210. [Swedish version of **B2:116** which comprises a translation by Ahlbom of the remainder of the text not published in Swedish by Delblanc in **B2:114**]

[B2:116] Delblanc, Sven, 'Strindberg and Humanism', in Göran Stockenström, ed., **D2:288**, *Strindberg's Dramaturgy*, pp. 3-13. [Suggests that, despite flirting with many other ideologies, Sg remained a beleaguered humanist, advocating human freedom and worth. Thus, in *Fröken Julie*, 'the humanist and the naturalist fight an indecisive battle right to the final curtain', and in his post-Inferno works a religious demand for submission always contests his urge for freedom. See **B2:115**]

[B2:117] Dianova, V[alentina], '[The Philosophy in Strindberg's Life and Creative Activities]', in L[ev] Gitel'man and V[alentina] Dianova, eds, **B1:148**, *Avgust Strindberg i mirovaia kul'tura. Materialy mezhvyzovskoi nauchnoi konferentsii. Stat'i. Soobshcheniia*, pp. 88-97.

[B2:118] Donat, Branimir, 'Opsjednuti pjesnik – Druga scena Augusta Strindberga', *Prolog* (Zagreb), 55-56 (1983), pp. 37-47. Illus. ['Possessed Poet'. Examines Sg's occult ideas and their relevance for the development of his theatre]

[B2:119] Dreyfus, Albert, 'August Strindberg', *Revue franco-allemande. Deutsch-französische Rundschau* (Mais and München), 2 (1900), 70-73, 144-148. [An early overview which reflects on Sg's personality and his affinity with Nietzsche in 'Tschandala' and *I havsbandet*. Dreyfus also comments on *Fadren*, *Fröken Julie*, and several other plays]

[B2:119a] Dreyfus, Albert, 'August Strindberg', in Hans-Peter Bayerdörfer, Hrsg., **B3:85**, *Strindberg auf der deutschen Bühne*, pp. 128-131. [Rpr. of **U5:119**]

[B2:120] Edqvist, Sven-Gustaf, 'Den grönskande ön. Ett motiv hos Strindberg', in Margareta Brundin, *et al.*, red., **B1:88**, *20 x Strindberg*, pp. 225-245. Illus. ['The Greening Island. A Motif in Strindberg'. Traces the origin of a recurring motif in both Sg's writings and paintings, one in which he depicts a sometimes visionary landscape related to his first encounters with the Stockholm archipelago as portrayed in 'Livet i Stockholms skärgård' (Life in Stockholm's Archipelago, 1872) and in *Tjänstekvinnans son*. Edqvist links this motif to his admiration for Jean-Jacques Rousseau and the idea of an isle of the blessed which is associated with the Swedish Romantic poet Per Daniel Amadeus Atterbom (1790-1855) in the dramatic poem *Lycksalighetens ö* (The Isle of the Blessed, 1824-27). Biographically, the motif may also be related to the enduring delight that Sg took in the archipelago, a delight that is articulated in, *inter alia, Svenska folket, Gustav III, Lycko-Pers resa,* several poems in *Dikter på vers och prosa, Sömngångarnätter på vakna dagar, Giftas, Hemsöborna, Ett drömspel, Ordalek och småkonst, Taklagsöl, Sagor, Pelikanen, Toten-Insel,* and *En blå bok*]

[B2:121] Edqvist, Sven-Gustaf, 'Strindberg i Schweiz', *Fenix* (Stockholm), 5:4 (1987), 112-159. Illus. ['Strindberg in Switzerland'. Examines the role that Switzerland played in Sg's life and works (most notably in *Utopier i verkligheten*). Documents the influence of Jean-Jacques Rousseau and the Russian anarchists he met in Geneva, and describes his visit to Jean-Baptiste Godin's phalanstère at Guise. Published in conjunction with the first publication of Sg's 'Ett och annat om Schweiz' ('One or Two Things about Switzerland', pp. 107-111), a brief essay written ca. 1884 and now in the Mörner archive in Örebro Stadsbibliotek]

[B2:122] Edqvist, Sven-Gustaf, 'Strindberg et la Suisse', Translated by Dagmar Almenberg, *Études des lettres. Bulletin de la Faculté des lettres de l'université de Lausanne*, 6 (1963), [157]-191. Illus. ['Strindberg and Switzerland'. A well-documented study, detailing Sg's various sojourns in Switzerland between 1884 and 1886 and his portrayal of the country and the Russian anarchists he encountered there in *Utopier i verkligheten, Tjänstekvinnans son*, and *Kvarstadsresan*. Edqvist also considers the significance which Switzerland had for his thinking about nationality, nature, and democracy in several of the essays in *Likt och olikt*]

[B2:123] Eichenwald, Iu[lij], 'Avgust Strindberg', in Eichenwald, I. *Slova o slovakh*, St Petersburg, 1916, pp. 131-137. ['August Strindberg' in 'Words about Words'. E.878]

[B2:124] Eichenwald, Iulij, *Otdelnyie stranitsy*, Moscow, 1910. [A collection of essays, including remarks on Sg and other Swedish authors]

[B2:124a] Eklund, Torsten, 'August Strindberg', *Studiekamraten* (Tollarp), 11:2 (1929), pp. 1-3.

[B2:125] Eklund, Torsten, 'Sociologiska synpunkter på den unge Strindberg', *Tiden* (Stockholm), 43:9 (1951), 543-550. ['Sociological Observations on the Young Strindberg'. Takes issue with Hagsten's interpretation of Sg's early years in **B1:151**]

[B2:126] Eklund, Torsten, 'Strindberg och diktarkallet', in Gunnar Brandell, red., **B1:82**, *Synpunkter på Strindberg*, Stockholm: Aldus/Bonnier, 1964, pp. 27-49. ['Strindberg and the Writer's Calling'. Reprints an extract from Eklund's thesis, *Tjänstekvinnans son. En psykologisk Strindbergsstudie*, **S:85**, in which he describes Sg's conception of the writer's calling as a truth teller, his early misgivings about the 'primitive' nature of the imagination and art as irresponsible escapism, and the compensatory role which literature and writing played in his life]

[B2:127] Ekman, Hans-Göran, 'Strindberg – en humorist?', *Allt om böcker* (Göteborg), 1985:7-8, pp. 34-36. Illus. ['Strindberg – A Humourist?' Explores the nature of Sg's humour in relation to Gustaf Fröding's essay 'Om humor' (1890) and Swedish comedy in general. Maintains that, 'for Sg, it is a question of "either-or", not, as for the humorist, "both-and"'. Ekman suggests that he never wrote a successful stage comedy although he knew that a serious action taken to an extreme verges upon comedy, as, for example, in *Dödsdansen*. He also discusses *Leka med elden*, *Hemsöborna*, *En dåres försvarstal*, and *Fröken Julie*, if only briefly]

[B2:128] Ekman, Hans-Göran, 'Strindberg's Senses, Symbols and Synaesthesia', in Michael Robinson, ed., **B1:379**, *The Moscow Papers*, pp. 27-36. [On the role of synaesthesia and symbols in Sg's practice as a writer, with reference to *En dåres försvarstal*, *I havsbandet*, *Ockulta dagboken*, *Gamla Stockholm*, *Ett drömspel*, *Oväder*, and *Spöksonaten*. Also relates, Sg's interest in synaesthesia to 19th-Century Symbolism, Rimbaud, and Swedenborg]

[B2:129] Eliasson, Karl-Erik, 'Metaforernas mästare', *Helsingborgs Dagblad*, 18 October 1972. ['The Master of Metaphors'. Discusses Sg's characteristic metaphorical language, with reference to Karl-Åke Kärnell's *Strindbergs bildspråk*, **B1:179**]

[B2:130] Elmquist, Carl Johan, 'August Strindberg', in *Läsefrugter*, København: Carit Andersen, 1961, pp. 51-63.

[B2:131] Elovson, Harald, 'August Strindberg and Emigration to America until ca.1890', *Americana-Norvegica*, Vol. III, Studies in Scandinavian-American Interrelations Dedicated to Einar Haugen, Oslo: Universitetsforlaget, 1971, pp. [129]-152. [On Sg's interest in the question of Swedish emigration to the United States, a country whose development, or so Elovson argues, interested him throughout his life. Elovson traces this interest in a variety of works in several genres, from *Röda rummet*, *Svenska folket*, *Anno 48*, *Fritänkaren*, and *Det nya riket* to the short story 'De lycksaliges ö' in *Svenska öden och äventyr*, *Götiska rummen*, and the essays 'Om det allmänna missnöjet' (On the General Discontent, 1884) and 'Världshistoriens mystik' (The Mysticism of World History, 1903)]

[B2:132] Elovson, Harald, 'August Strindberg and Emigration to the United States 1890-1912', *Americana-Norvegica*, Vol. IV, Studies in Scandinavian-American Interrelations Dedicated to Sigmund Skard, Olso: Universitetsforlaget, 1973, pp. [47]-67. [Continues the discussion of Sg's interest in emigration to the United States in **B2:131**. Documents his encounters with returning emigrants, including Knut Hamsun, his old school friend Gustav Eisen, and Gustaf Uddgren. Elovson discusses *Götiska rummen* in some detail, and comments on *Svarta fanor*, in both of which emigration to North America is a theme. He also identifies 'an emigration theme' in Sg's first published work, *Fritänkaren* (1870), as well as in 'his last important literary work', *Stora landsvägen* (1909)]

[B2:133] Elovson, Harald, 'Den liberala amerikabilden i Sverige', in Lars Åhnebrink, red., *Amerika i Norden*, Stockholm. 1964. XVI+238 pp. ['The Liberal Image of America'. See **B2:131** and **B2:132**]

[B2:134] Essén, Bengt, 'Skärgården i Strindbergs diktning före Inferno-krisen', *Svensk kryssarklubbens årsskrift* (Stockholm), 1945, pp. 47-68. Illus. ['The Archipelago in Strindberg's Writings before the Inferno Crisis'. Discusses the place and significance accorded the Stockholm archipelago in Sg's writings up to *I havsbandet*. Includes references to *Tjänstekvinnans son, Giftas, Skärkarlsliv,* the story 'Silverträsket' (The Silver Marsh, 1898), the poem 'Högsommar' (High Summer), and *Hemsöborna*. Essén treats the latter as his classic portrayal of the archipelago, a novel which embraces all the different tendencies in his writings about the region as a whole]

[B2:135] Estlander, C[arl] G[ustaf], 'August Strindbergs nyare skrifter', *Finsk Tidskrift* (Åbo), 1883:1, pp. 263-269. ['August Strindberg's Most Recent Writings'. An early essay review of *Det nya riket*, *Svenska öden och äventyr*, and *Herr Bengts hustru* by a critic previously favourably disposed to *Röda rummet*. Estlander regrets that so fine a talent as Sg's should be wasted on trivial, transient passions. All too often traces of superb satire are dissipated in trivialities, although his gifts as a dramatist make him one of the most eminent among contemporary Swedish writers. Error in printed pagination; should be pp. 363-369]

[B2:136] Estlander, C[arl] G[ustaf], 'August Strindbergs nyare skrifter', in *Skrifter*, 2:2: Åren 1882-83, Skrifter utgivna av svenska litteratursällskapet i Finland CXLVI, Helsingfors, 1919, pp. 47-74. ['August Strindberg's Most Recent Writings'. Rpr. of **B2:135**]

[B2:137] Eulenberg, Herbert, 'August Strindberg', in *Gestalten und Begebenheiten*, Dresden: Reißner Verlag, 1924, pp. 232-237.

[B2:138] Ewbank, Inga-Stina, 'Strindberg and the Fiction of History', in Göran Rossholm, Barbro Ståhle Sjönell, and Boel Westin, eds, **B1:389**, *Strindberg and Fiction*, pp. 11-22. [Demonstrates how Sg translates historical fact into fiction in both plays and prose narratives, eliding the dichotomy between the two to the point where he makes us see history as fiction. Documented by examples drawn from *Gustav III*, *Karl XII*, and the short stories 'Vid likvakan i Tistedalen' (At the Bier Side in Tistedalen), and 'En kunglig revolution' (A Royal Revolution), all of which demonstrate that 'there is as much power in Sg's narrative as in his dramatic fiction']

[B2:139] Ewbank, Inga-Stina, 'Strindberg, Charles XII and the *History of the World*', in Elizabeth Maslen, ed., *The Timeless and the Temporal. Writings in honour of John Chalker by friends and colleagues*, University of London: Queen Mary and Westfield College, 1993, pp. 306-331. [Considers Sg's life-long preoccupation with history and compares the short story describing Charles XII's death, 'Vid likvakan i Tistedalen' (At the Bier Side in Tistedalen), with the play *Karl XII* to demonstrate how the narrative or dramatic technique he employs is not only partly controlled by the historical subject, but history as written is also controlled by the choice of the narrative or dramatic technique he uses]

[B2:140] Ewbank, Inga-Stina, 'Strindberg: "How Do I Love Thee?"', *Swedish Book Review* (Lampeter), 1986 (Supplement), pp. 8-10. [Argues that the core of Sg's greatness lies in the creative joy that he takes in what can be done with language, exemplified here with reference to *Giftas* and *Taklagsöl*, as well as to the plays which, in performance, manifest the physical and mental power of words. For Sg, language was what no woman could be: both a mother and a mistress, both nurturing and submitting to all his uses, however exalted or outrageous]

[B2:141] Ewbank, Inga-Stina, '"Tragical-Comical-Historical-Pastoral": Strindberg and the Absurdity of Categories', in Michael Robinson, ed., **B1:373**, *Strindberg and Genre*, pp. 35-47. [Celebrates the range and variousness of the Sg corpus, which in such works as *En blå bok* seems to elude classification, not least in the numerous texts where he is reputed to have imitated his own life rather than followed pre-existing literary genres. Yet 'his challenge to "normal" categories goes hand in hand with a profound and often self-conscious interest in genres'. Ewbank discusses a range of plays, autobiographical fictions, essays, and short stories in order to demonstrate how an approach via genre may illuminate Sg's works, even as it helps to define his innovative modernity. She also demonstrates how he sometimes treats the same subject or theme in different genres]

[B2:142] Eyck, P. N. van, 'Buitenlandsche literatur. IV. August Strindberg', *De Nieuwe Gids* (Amsterdam), 25 (1910), 635-646. [Comments on the 'chaos' of Sg's life and work and his eternal search for the meaning of life. Discusses *I havsbandet*, *Inferno*, and the post-Inferno period, and links Sg with Balzac and Swedenborg]

[B2:143] Farinelli, Arturo, *Führende Geister des Nordens. Geist und Poesie der Skandinavier: Björnson – Strindberg – Ibsen*, Stuttgart: Deutsche Verlags-Anstalt, 1940, pp. 71-101. ['Leading Spirits of the North. Spirit and Poetry of the Scandinavian Peoples: Bjørnson, Strindberg, Ibsen'. The title as well as the country and date of publication make this exercise in hagiography something of a curiosity, but Farinelli has a greater awareness of original sources than much other early writing about Sg in German]

[B2:144] Farinelli, Arturo, 'Strindberg', *Nuova Antologia* (Rome), No. 402 (1 March, 1969), 49-66.

[B2:145] F-e [F. A. von Schéele], 'Literatur-bref från en studentkammare', *Barometern* (Kalmar), 28 August 1882. ['Literary Letter from a Student Room'. Discusses Sg's realism, with reference to his essay 'Om realism' (1882), *Svenska folket, Mäster Olof, Gillets hemlighet,* and *Röda rummet*. According to Schéele, the latter owes more to Dickens than to Zola, and, with luck and further studies in cultural history, Sg will become Sweden's foremost dramatist]

[B2:146] F-e [F. A. von Schéele], 'Literatur-bref från en studerkammare', *Östersunds-Posten*, 10 August 1882. ['Literary Letter from a Student Room'. Discusses realism in contemporary Swedish literature and historical writing with reference to *Mäster Olof, Röda rummet, Svenska folket*, and Sg's essay 'Om realism' (1882). Whatever Sg himself maintains, his realism is hardly the same as Zola's]

[B2:147] Fechner-Smarsly, Thomas, 'Von der Suggestion zur Projektion. Die Laterna Magica als Medium und Mittel der Analyse in August Strindbergs *Fräulein Julie* und *Tschandala*', in Walter Baumgartner and Thomas Fechner-Smarsly, Hrsg., **B1:19**, *August Strindberg: Der Dichter und die Medien*, pp. 193-210. ['From Suggestion to Projection. The Magic Lantern as a Medium and Means of Analysis in August Strindberg's *Miss Julie* and *Tschandala*'. Offers a reading of Sg's psychological naturalism which explores its links with notions of suggestion, magnetism, and hypnosis of the kind portrayed by his friend Richard Bergh's painting '*En suggestion*' (1887) and of topical interest in the widely discussed ideas of Jean-Martin Charcot and James Baird. Fechner-Smarsly compares Sg's recourse to the *laterna magica* as a literary trope with its use by several German romantic authors and explores this link with reference to *En blå bok*. He also associates Sg's psychological practice in *Tschandala*, in which the *laterna magica* is a decisive means of mental projection in the battle of the brains around which the story revolves, with Freud's theories of psychological projection and the notion of the talking cure that he was just then developing in the letters he addressed to Wilhelm Fließ at about the same time]

[B2:148] Ferrari, Fulvio, 'August Strindberg. Il mio fuoco è il più grande della Svezia', *Uomini e libri*, No. 105 (September-October 1985), pp. 26-34. ['August Strindberg. My Fire is the Greatest in Sweden'. A soundly informed general essay]

[B2:149] V. F[irsov] [Pseudonym of Baron Forsales], 'Sjvedskii belletrist-otritsatel', *Knizhki 'Nedeli'* (St Petersburg), 1894:3, pp. 159-182. ['Swedish Writer-Nihilist'. An early, relatively well-informed Russian response to Sg. Firsov argues that Georg Brandes is wrong to describe Sg as a naturalist; rather, he 'preaches the gospel of artistic truth' like Gogol in Russia. Firsov considers Sg a poor dramatist, and describes *En dåres försvarstal* as weaker than his previous novels. His best work is *Hemsöborna*, in which his ability to transform life's prose into poetry is most in evidence. *Giftas* is an 'original work, worthy of particular attention' while, according to Firsov, the stories 'Samvetskval' (Remorse) and 'Över molnen' (Beyond the Clouds) in *Utopier i verkligheten* are both artistic masterpieces. E.697]

[B2:150] Florin, Magnus, 'August Strindberg i Stockholmssnäckan', in Magnus Bergh, red., *Staden mellan pärmarna: litterära friluftsessäer i Stockholm*, Stockholm: Albert Bonniers Förlag, 1998, pp. 28-53. Illus. [Florin discusses the importance of Stockholm as a setting in Sg's works, with particular reference to *Gammal Stockholm, Lycko-Pers resa, Tjänstekvinnans son, Oväder, Midsommar, Taklagsöl, En blå bok*, and *Ensam*. He also reflects in Benjaminian fashion on the special significance of Birger Jarl's Passage in Stockholm and the role of the commodity in late 19th-Century European culture, as well as drawing attention to several sites in this urban landscape that are closely associated with Sg's life]

[B2:151] Friedrich, Hans, 'Über Strindberg als Dramatiker und Epiker', *Internationale Literaturberichte* (Leipzig), 4 (1897), pp. 81-83, 101-103. ['On Strindberg as a Dramatist and Novelist']

[B2:152] Fries, Sigurd, 'Strindbergs *men*', in Margareta Brundin, *et al.*, red., **B1:88**, *20 x Strindberg*, pp. 51-56. ['Strindberg's *But*'. A stylistic analysis of Sg's use of the conjunction 'men' in his prose works, exemplified with reference to *Röda rummet, Hemsöborna*, and the short story 'En ovälkommen' (An Unwelcome Guest) from *Svenska öden och äventyr*, and in comparison with both C. J. L. Almqvist and Oscar Levertin]

[B2:153] Fritje [or Friche], V., 'Tragikomediia individualisma', *Obrazovanie* (St Petersburg), 1901:10, pp. 1-17. ['Individualism's Tragi-Comedy'. Fritje discusses Sg's misogyny in *Fadren* and *En dåres försvarstal*, and the contempt he displays for the common people in 'Tschandala' and *I havsbandet*, pp. 5-11. He argues that individualism leads Sg to mysticism, to the detriment of his writing. E.716]

[B2:154] Fritje[or Friche], V., *Khudozhestvennaia literatura i kapitalism*, Moscow: Skirmunt, 1906. 144 pp. ['Literature and Capitalism'. Discusses Sg, pp. 128-131. E.757]

[B2:155] Fritje [or Friche], V., *Ocherki po istorii zapadnoevropeiskoi literatury*, Moscow: Pol'za, 1908. 254 pp. ['Essays on the History of West European Literature'. Includes a discussion of the battle of the sexes as depicted in *En dåres försvarstal, Kamraterna*, and *Fordringsägare*, pp. 194, 241-242. E.771]

[B2:156] Frost, Lucia Dora, 'Strindberg', *Die neue Rundschau* (Berlin), 23:2 (1912), 995-1004.

[B2:157] Gantjeva, Vera, '[Introduction: A Writer For Three Centuries]', in August Strindberg, *Izbrani prozvedeniia v dva toma*, 2 vols, Sofia: Hemus Grup, 2002. [385], 377, pp. [Introduces a two-volume collection of Sg's works in translation, containing 'Den romantiske klockaren på Rånö', *Inferno, Ensam*, and five plays: *Fadren, Fröken Julie, Dödsdansen, Ett drömspel*, and *Spöksonaten*. Volume Two also contains a bibliography of Bulgarian translations from 1898 (*Fadren*) to date, and a production record of the plays in performance in Bulgaria, from *Fadren* in 1902-03 to *Första varningen* in 1999-2000]

[B2:158] Garnert, Jan, 'Hallå Strindberg!', *Strindbergiana* (Stockholm), 21 (2006), pp. 11-30. Illus. [Although usually described as the first modern Swedish novel, Garnert points out that, technologically speaking, *Röda rummet* is pre-modern in that it describes a period before the telephone. But Sg subsequently embraced the new invention and introduced it into several of his novels and plays, including *Taklagsöl, Ensam, Påsk, Oväder*, and *Svarta fanor*, as well as the fairy tales 'Pintorpafruns julafton', and 'Ett halvt ark papper', where it sometimes plays a structural role. Garnert also recognises its relevance to his correspondence with Harriet Bosse and his relationship with Siri von Essen, and presents the role played by the telephone in the life of *fin-de-siècle* Swedish society, particularly among the urban intellectuals in Stockholm with whom Sg was familiar. The article reworks material originally published in Garnert's *Hallå! Om telefonens första tid i Sverige*, Lund, 2005]

[B2:159] G. C. [Gunnar Castrén], 'Strindberg 1897-1899', *Finsk Tidskrift* (Åbo), 48 (1900), 71-77. [An assessment of Sg's life and achievement at fifty in a review essay on *Inferno, Legender, Till Damaskus, Vid högre rätt, Folkungasagan* (judged to be one of his weaker works), *Gustav Vasa*, and *Erik XIV*. In turning away from his earlier bold radicalism, as he does in several of these works, Castrén considers that *Mäster Olof*, the great deed of Sg's youth, can now be seen as his own tragedy. He has himself become an apostate – Prometheus has indeed submitted to Zeus. But this tragedy is not Sg's alone; to some extent, it is that of all his generation. For Sg, the artistic dimension has always taken second place to his desire to be a thinker and reformer; art for art's sake is for him an incomprehensible standpoint, and knowing how to utilise everything that he experiences in what he writes, he has always been a naturalist at heart]

[B2:160] G. C. [Gunnar Castrén], 'August Strindberg', *Nya Argus* (Helsingfors), 5:10 (16 May 1912), pp. 83-86. [Assesses Sg's achievement following his recent death. Castrén suggests that his own image remains the most living impression made by Sg's work. He responded to a profound and irresistible urge to make himself visible at the centre of what he wrote and therefore he was seldom concerned with the purely artistic dimension as such. Hence, one cannot describe his work without portraying him. Castrén also stresses Sg's desire for truth and the tragic element in his destiny, as he tried out all the great ideas of his time and found them wanting. Meanwhile, he foregrounds Sg's acute powers of observation and his ability to formulate what he sees concisely and exactly that is paralleled in Swedish literature only by Linnaeus. See **B2:87**]

[B2:161] Gedin, David, 'In Cover of Reality: The "scandalous" text of the eighties', in Göran Rossholm, Barbro Ståhle Sjönell, and Boel Westin, eds, **B1:389**, *Strindberg and Fiction*, pp. 86-96. [Indicates how Sg's contemporaries identified him directly with the protagonists of his texts while the early 1880s were dominated by a 'tendency' or 'problem-oriented' literature. In fact, the aesthetic Sg adopted as a writer was at odds with today's understanding of a clear distinction between fiction and biographical (or other kinds of) fact, and it strongly offended his own contemporaries. During the 1880s, he developed a form of realism which included scandalous intrusions on a personal level into his own and other people's lives, in which he shifted between fact and fiction, and challenged the literary institution of the period. In so doing, he drew attention to the creative subject and stimulated an important debate about artistic freedom. Gedin exemplifies Sg's practice with reference to *Röda rummet*, *Svenska folket*, *Giftas*, *Det nya riket*, *Dikter på vers och prosa*, and the polemical essay 'Om det allmänna missnöjet' (On the General Discontent, 1884), and grounds his argument in the literary field theories of Pierre Bourdieu]

[B2:162] Geijerstam, Gustaf af, 'August Strindberg', *Ur dagens krönika* (Stockholm), 3 (1883), pp. 74-94. [An important, frequently cited, and generally sympathetic early study which comments on Sg's production up to *Herr Bengts hustru*, with the emphasis on the plays. Geijerstam also discusses *Röda rummet*, *Det nya riket*, and Sg's naturalism in some detail, and applauds the directness of Sg's language. But he is inclined to reductive psychological interpretations, and his failure to be wholly positive about Sg's works is indicative of future divisions between Sg and the other, radically-inclined, Swedish authors of the 1880s]

[B2:163] Geijerstam, Gustaf af, *Ur samtiden. Litteraturstudier*, Stockholm, 1883. 223 pp. [Discusses Sg's works up to *Dikter på vers och prosa*, including *Röda rummet*, *Det nya riket*, *Svenska folket*, and *Mäster Olof*. Geijerstam observes that Sg's satire sometimes intrudes upon the private lives of his subjects in an unacceptable way. Rpr. of **B2:162**]

[B2:164] Geijerstam, Gustaf af, 'August Strindberg', 1-4, *Nationaltidende* (Copenhagen), 25 October, 1, 8, and 15 November 1883. [Rpr. of **B2:162**]

[B2:165] Geijerstam, Gustaf af, 'August Strindberg och genombrottet i den nyare svenska litteraturen', in *Stridsfrågor för dagen. Fem föredrag*, Helsingfors, 1888. 146 pp. ['August Strindberg and the Breakthrough in the most Recent Swedish Literature']

[B2:166] Geijerstam, Gustaf af, 'Om den unga litteraturens ställning', *Revy* (Stockholm), 1886, pp. 1-17. ['On the Situation of the Young Literature']

[B2:167] Geijerstam, Karl af, 'Några ord om August Strindbergs senare litterära arbeten', *Revy i litterära och sociala frågor* (Stockholm), 1885, pp. 77-94. ['A Few Words on August Strindberg's more Recent Literary Works'. Discusses *Sömngångarnätter*, *Likt och olikt*, and *Giftas* which is criticised for a romantic tendency at odds with the literary ideals of the Young Sweden movement. Even in *Sömngångarnätter*, where he goes further than ever before in asking 'what is truth?', Geijerstam suggests that Sg is unable to rid himself of outmoded idealist notions, and cannot fully embrace the conclusions of science]

[B2:168] Geijerstam, Karl af, 'Några ord om August Strindbergs senare litterära arbeten', in *Efterlämnade skrifter*, Stockholm: Beijer, 1899, pp. 223-257. ['A Few Words on August Strindberg's More Recent Literary Works'. Rpr. of **B2:167**]

[B2:169] Geijerstam, Karl af, 'Några ord om August Strindbergs olika utvecklingsskeden', *Varia. Illustrerad månadsskrift* (Stockholm), 1899, pp. 17-24. ['A Few Words on August Strindberg's Different Stages of Development'. Compares Sg's standpoint in his first post-Inferno texts with his earlier writings]

[B2:170] Geijerstam, Karl af, 'Strindberg', in *Efterlemnade skrifter*, Med en inledning af Ellen Key, Stockholm: Beijer, 1899, pp. 279-332. [Collects the recently deceased Geijerstam's articles on Sg]

[B2:171] Gerstinger, Heinz, 'August Strindberg – Prophet des kommenden Jahrhunderts', in *Die andere Welt – August Strindberg in Oberösterreich*, *Literatur im Stifter-Haus*, 4

(1993), pp. 42-54. ['August Strindberg – Prophet of the Coming Century'. A sometimes factually inaccurate survey of Sg's career. Gerstinger refers to numerous works but is primarily concerned with *Till Damaskus* and Sg's experiences in Austria in the 1890s. On the basis of his preoccupations rather than his artistic achievements, he argues that Sg is a precursor of the 20th Century]

[B2:172] Gerstinger, Heinz, 'August Strindberg – det kommande århundradets profet', Översättning av H. O. Thulin, in *Strindberg i Österrike. Från underlandet till Inferno*, En utställning från Adalbert-Stifter-Institut, Linz, Strindbergsmuseet, Stockholm, 1994, pp. [36]-[48]. ['August Strindberg – Prophet of the Coming Century'. Swedish version of **B2:171**]

[B2:173] G-g N [Georg Nordensvan], 'Ströftåg i vår unga litteratur. 3. August Strindberg', *Ny Svensk Tidskrift* (Uppsala), 1883, pp. 263-283. ['Excursions in Our Young Literature'. A largely positive review of Sg's production to date. *Mäster Olof* is the most 'magnificent' of Swedish plays, although the grotesque element in *Röda rummet* somewhat undermines its social pathos and numerous fine descriptions of nature. Nordensvan stresses Sg's originality: he belongs to no school and is certainly not Zola's pupil; but as yet he has produced no unequivocal masterpiece]

[B2:174] Goebel, Heinrich, 'August Strindberg', in H. von Arnim, Hrsg., *Kämpfer. Grosses Menschentum aller Zeiten*, Bd 4, Berlin – Leipzig – Wien – Bern: Franz Schneider Verlag, [1923], pp. 135-167. [Presents Sg's life and work within the framework of a book on 'great men through the ages', who here include August Bebel, Van Gogh, Nietzsche, Tolstoi, Karl Spitteler, Walter Rathenau, and the German imperial explorer, Carl Peters. In this company, Sg emerges as a painfully divided figure, split between his inheritance from his proletarian mother and his middle-class father. Goebel, who was one of Sg's early German translators, discusses his religious beliefs and his relationship to Kierkegaard, but focuses primarily on *Tjänstekvinnans son, Inferno, En dåres försvarstal,* and *I havsbandet*. He also causes confusion by dating the Inferno period to 1885-1896, after which, between 1896 and 1912, he is seen to embody 'the Christian superman'. Although a few other works are mentioned (e.g. *Röda rummet, Karl XII, Götiska rummen, Hemsöborna*, and *Ett drömspel*), the approach throughout is awkwardly biographical]

[B2:175] Götselius, Thomas, 'Helvetet lössläppt: Strindberg skriver', in Ulf Olsson, red., **B1:357**, *Strindbergs förvandlingar*, pp. 95-136. ['Hell Let Loose: Strindberg Writes'. Considers Sg's initiation into language, which for Götselius marks his separation from the mother, and examines the role assumed by the medium of writing in his life as represented by his works, where the pathological subject sometimes merges with the subject of literature. Götselius discusses *Tjänstekvinnans son*, *Inferno*, *Taklagsöl*, *Vivisektioner*, *En blå bok*, and the experimental prose piece, 'Sensations détraquées' (1894), in an analysis of the role of the Sgian writer as vivisector, but he also reflects both on the relevance of Sg's photographic experiments for the different perspectives and ways of seeing with which he experiments in his narrative works, and the gap between perception and knowledge that opens up in his works at the turn-of-the-century]

[B2:176] Götselius, Thomas, 'Die Hölle ist los: Strindberg schreibt', Aus dem Schwedischen von Vreni Hockenjos, in Walter Baumgartner and Thomas Fechner-Smarsly, Hrsg.,

B1:19, *August Strindberg: Der Dichter und die Medien*, pp. 113-132. ['Hell Let Loose: Strindberg Writes'. German version of **B2:175**]

[B2:177] Gregg, Frances M. [Pseudonym of Mrs Louis Wilkinson], and John Cowper Powys, 'Work of August Strindberg', *Forum* (New York), 55:6 (1916), 661-665. ['When to sum up you have said that man is the symbol of consciousness, and women of emotion, you have said all that Sg, with a great deal of tortured misinterpretation of his observation, and much futile bitterness, has indicated in about ten volumes of plays and stories']

[B2:178] Grolman, Adolf von, 'August Strindberg – *Inferno, Ein Traumspiel*', in *Europäische Dichterprofil*, Bd 1, Düsseldorf: Bastion Verlag, 1947, pp. 107-120.

[B2:179] Gurlitt, W., 'August Strindberg', *Weltstimmen* (Stuttgart), 3 (1929), 328-334.

[B2:180] Gurvich, P. B., '[The Subjective and the Objective in Strindberg's Historical Works]', in *Problema lichnosti avtora v khudozhestvennom proizvedenii na materiale zapadnoevropeiskoi literatury: Sbornik nauchnykh trudov*, Vladimir, 1982, pp. 74-92. [E.1773]

[B2:181] Gustafsson, Lars, 'Strindberg as a Forerunner of Scandinavian Modernism', in John M. Weinstock and Robert T. Rovinsky, eds, *The Hero in Scandinavian Literature*, Austin and London: University of Texas Press, 1972, pp. 127-141. [Discusses 'Gatubilder III' (Street Pictures) in *Ordlek och småkonst*, *Svarta handsken*, *Ett drömspel*, *En blå bok*, and the essay 'Sensations détraquées' (Deranged Sensations, 1894) in which Sg anticipates such representative modernist figures as Freud, Gunnar Ekelöf, and Proust. According to Gustafsson, such works have 'become modernism', both formally and in their subject matter, and he criticises orthodox Sgian criticism for misreading the later works as autobiography, as merely the personal drama of August Sg, rather than as a form of innovatory modernist writing: 'what is often perceived as "subjectivity" in Sg's works from *Inferno* onwards is more than a personal peculiarity: it is a compositional principle']

[B2:182] Gustafsson, Lars, 'Tre föreläsningar om estetik. 3: Kreativitet, död och uppståndelse – August Strindberg', in *De andras närvaro*, Stockholm: Natur och Kultur, 1995, pp. 280-287. ['Three Lectures in Aesthetics. 3: Creativity, Death, and Resurrection'. Discusses Sg's experiences in Paris in 1896 and how they influenced his return to writing imaginative literature in *Inferno* and *Till Damaskus*. Translated by Birgitta Dahlgren from a German original]

[B2:183] Haas, Willy, in Stellan Ahlström, Hrsg., *Strindberg im Zeugnis der Zeitgenossen*, pp. xi–xxii. [The introduction to a one-volume German edition of **R:18** and **R:66**. Identifies Sg as a representative figure of his time via comparisons with Otto Weininger, Karl Marx, and John Ruskin, as well as Ibsen, Zola, and Gerhart Hauptmann]

[B2:184] Hansson, Ola, 'August Strindberg', in Ola Hansson, *Lyrik och essäer*, red. Ingvar Holm, Svenska klassiker utgivna av Svenska akademien, Stockholm: Atlantis, 1997, pp. 181-219. [Reprints extracts from several of Hansson's essays on Sg, originally published in German journals in 1889-90 and subsequently republished in his critical study *Den unge Skandinavien*. See **B3:211**]

[B2:185] Hansson, Ola, 'August Strindberg. Kritisk essay', 1-2, *Samtiden* (Oslo), 2:7-8 (1891), pp. 241-251, 289-304. [A substantial early discussion of Sg's 'rich and various production' to date, with comments on each of his works in turn, most substantially on the dramas of the later 1880s. For Hansson, 'he is the poet (*diktare*) of subjectivity' and a 'complex of contradictions' whose work displays a continual battle between the aristocrat and the democrat in him, as well as the artist and the utilitarian. Hansson also insists that Sg is the most strongly Swedish author among his contemporaries]

[B2:186] Hansson, Ola, 'Den svenske Skønliteratur 1887 i Fugleperspektiv', 1-2, *Ny Jord* (Copenhagen), 1 (1888), pp. 291-297, 342-352. ['A Bird's Eye View of Swedish Literature in 1887'. It sometimes seems as if Sg has woven his characters, destinies, conflicts out of his own inner substance, like the spider its net, that the work has grown freely and organically from the depths of the writer's personality. For Hansson, Sg is comparable with Shakespeare as portrayed by Hippolyte Taine in *Histoire de la littérature anglaise* (1863-64). His soul is a kind of microcosm that contains surrounding reality, and is given to metamorphoses that enable him to see with another's eyes, and to think and feel as they do]

[B2:187] Hedberg, Oscar, 'I Strindbergsdiktens värld', *Studiekamraten* (Tollarp), 31 (1949), 19-23. Illus. ['In Strindberg's Literary World']

[B2:188] Heller, Otto, 'August Strindberg – A Study of Eccentricity', in *Prophets of Dissent: Essays on Maeterlinck, Strindberg, Nietzsche and Tolstoy*, New York: Alfred A. Knopf, 1918, pp. 71-105. [Offers a fragmentary overview of Sg's career. Heller comments briefly on his links with Nietzsche, as well as *Röda rummet, Utopier i verkligheten, Inferno, Legender, Fröken Julie, Fadren,* and several other naturalistic plays. 'All that is most dismal and terrifying and therefore most tragical, becomes articulate' in Sg's works. They are propelled by an abysmal pessimism and reflect insuperable prejudices. So, too, are the often ungrounded assumptions informing this essay which questions Sg's fitness as a subject of literary discussion, so reprehensible does Heller consider the man and his work]

[B2:189] Heller, Otto, 'August Strindberg – A Study of Eccentricity', in *Prophets of Dissent: Essays on Maeterlinck, Strindberg, Nietzsche and Tolstoy*, Port Washington, N.Y.: Kennikat Press, Inc., 1968, pp. 71-105. [Facsimile Rpr. of **B2:188**]

[B2:190] Henderson, Archibald, 'August Strindberg: Universalist', *South Atlantic Quarterly* (Durham, North Carolina), 13:1 (1914), [28]-42. [Regards Sg's work as 'the spiritual autobiography of the pre-eminent subjectivist of modern times'. He is a 'congenital dualist' but, despite 'the revelations of his autobiographical novels, his dramas constitute his supreme artistic work'. Henderson relays the anecdote in which Ibsen comments on the fascination that Sg's madness held for him, and comments on the majority of the plays in chronological order, devoting greater space to the naturalistic dramas and *Dödsdansen* than to his other post-Inferno works]

[B2:191] Hergešić, Ivo, 'Strindberg i žena stvorena od čovjeka', in *Strani i domaći*, Zagreb, 1935, pp. 18-20. [R.492]

[B2:192] Hj. Sdg. [Hjalmar Sandberg], 'Litteratur', *Svenska Dagbladet* (Stockholm), 12 June 1891. [A lukewarm review of Sg's miscellaneous collection *Tryckt och otryckt III* on publication]

[B2:193] Hockenjos, Vreni, 'Money, Monney, Monet. Om rörelse, teknologi och perception i Strindbergs "Från Café de l'Ermitage till Marley le Roi och så vidare"', *Tidskrift för litteraturvetenskap* (Stockholm), 33:1 (2004), 4-24. Illus. ['Money, Monney, Monet. On Movement, Technology, and Perception in Strindberg's "From Café de l'Ermitage to

Marley le Roi and onwards'". Hockenjos uses Sg's two-part causerie of 1876 in which he provides one of the first Swedish responses to French impressionism and discusses Manet, Sisley, and Monet (spelled 'Money') as the basis for an examination of both his narrative technique in the essay and what it reveals of his interest in new ways of seeing, modernity, and its new media in general. Hockenjos considers his response to train travel, both here and in *Bland franska bönder*; she also comments on his concern with new perceptions of motion with reference to photography and the work of Edward Muybridge in particular, as well as the stroboscope, and ponders how these technical innovations relate to a fascination with movement that remains a preoccupation in *En blå bok*]

[B2:194] Hockenjos, Vreni, 'Phantom, Schein, Traumbild. Zur visuellen Wahrnehmung bei August Strindberg', in Walter Baumgartner and Thomas Fechner-Smarsly, Hrsg., **B1:19**, *August Strindberg: Der Dichter und die Medien*, pp. 236-252. ['Phantom, Illusion, Dream Image. On Visual Perception in August Strindberg'. Relates Sg's mental crisis in the mid–1890s to a more general crisis in modes of consciousness and ways of seeing which are linked to technological developments (including the emergence of photography and film), as well as to new scientific and philosophical modes of perception. Hockenjos suggests that, as well as experimental prose studies like 'Sensations détraquées' (Deranged Sensations, 1894), Sg's scientific texts, including *Antibarbarus* (1894) and the essays he published in the Parisian occult journal *L'Initiation* in 1896, all document his reponsiveness to a general shift in ways of seeing and are related to the new roles allotted the senses in the innovatory dramaturgy of *Till Damaskus* and *Ett drömspel*. Likewise, she argues that the aesthetic advanced in the vivisection 'Des arts nouveaux! ou Le hasard dans la production artistique' (1894) prefigures the supranaturalistic portrayal of the everyday world in *Inferno* and *Legender*]

[B2:195] Hockenjos, Vreni, 'Time and Place Do Exist: Strindberg and Visual Media', *Performing Arts Journal* (New York), 25:3 (2003), 51-63. Illus. [Stresses the link between Sg's writing and his interest in the visual arts, which may also be associated with his interest in the new technologies of photography and the cinema that rapidly became points of reference in his writing. Hockenjos documents the significance of the Laterna Magica and cinematic projection for Sg's writing with reference to 'Tschandala', *Kronbruden*, *Midsommar*, and *Advent*, where they are related to the genre of the fairy-tale play, as well as to *Till Damaskus* and *Ett drömspel*, in which he experimented with the new technology in his suggestions for their staging. Indeed, with its fluid approach to time and space, the powerfully visual dramaturgy of *Ett drömspel* is akin to the dissolving view practices of lantern performances]

[B2:196] Hockenjos, Vreni, 'The World through a Panorama Lens: Strindberg on Vision and Visual Technologies', in Göran Rossholm, Barbro Ståhle Sjönell, and Boel Westin, eds, **B1:389**, *Strindberg and Fiction*, pp. [169]-182. Illus. [Indicates how the interest which Sg displayed in contemporary visual technologies in e.g. the prose pieces 'Sensations détraquées' (1894) and 'Un regard vers le Ciel' (A Glance into Space, 1896) influenced not only his long-standing preoccupation with the functioning of the eye and modes of perception in general but later literary texts such as *Till Damaskus*, *Ett drömspel*, and *Svarta fanor*. These and other works reflect the specific visual culture of their time, not least the panorama, which enjoyed a new popularity in the 1880s and 1890s, and the cosmorama. They influence the form of *Till Damaskus* where they are both mentioned. Moreover, those qualities in Sg's later plays which are frequently assumed to be cinematic in form can in fact be traced back to the sciopticon, rather than to the emerging techniques of the cinema]

[B2:197] Holm, Erich [Pseudonym of Mathilde Prager], 'August Strindberg', *Moderne Rundschau* (Vienna), 3 (1891), 211-216. [An assessment by one of Sg's earliest German language translators, with whom, between 1885 and 1896, he conducted a sometimes informative correspondence about his works in progress]

[B2:198] Holmberg, Olle, 'Strindbergs skuld', in *Madonnan och järnjungfrun*, Stockholm: Albert Bonniers Förlag, 1927, pp. [201]-220. ['Strindberg's Guilt'. Inculcated in early childhood with a sense of unwarranted but real guilt, Sg carried over the experience of being both afraid and hungry that he describes in the first chapter of *Tjänstekvinnans son* into his adult life. His works (e.g. the stories 'En ovälkommen' and 'En barnsaga', *Till Damaskus*, *Brända tomten*, and *Näktergalen i Wittenberg*) are often haunted by residual, still active, guilt feelings. Holmberg notes a parallel experience in which the burden of guilt is rooted in a real event, but either way, Sg's characters can never work themselves free of the past, and the guilt feelings he imbibed in childhood inform all his major works, from the revolutionary pathos of *Mäster Olof* and *Röda rummet* to *Till Damaskus*, *Dödsdansen*, and *Stora landsvägen*, where his early sense of life's injustice is now complemented by a partly repressed awareness of the guilt which his own mature actions have entailed. Hence the hatred that informs *Dödsdansen* and the regret expressed in *Stora landsvägen* that he could never become the person he once wished to be, are also embodied in the protagonists of *Mäster Olof* and *Röda rummet*]

[B2:199] H. S., 'August Strindbergs senaste arbeten', *Dagens Nyheter* (Stockholm), 22 June 1891. ['August Strindberg's Latest Works'. Reviews Vol. 4, Part 1, of *Svenska öden och äventyr*, with particular praise for 'Vid likvakan i Tistedalen' (At the Bierside in Tistedalen) and *Tryckt och otryckt III*, which makes a valuable contribution to our knowledge of Sg's development. Its high point is the story 'Är det nog?' (Is it Enough?)]

[B2:200] Huneker, James [Gibbons], 'August Strindberg', *The Lamp* (New York), 29:6 (January 1905), 573-582. [Huneker, who had seen and been impressed by a performance of *Fröken Julie* at the Kleinestheater, Berlin, in 1904, discusses several prose works (*Tjänstekvinnans son*, *Inferno*, *Ensam*), as well as the (primarily naturalist) plays with considerable enthusiasm. Reprinted in extended form in *Iconoclasts* (1905), **D1:203**, where the essay enjoyed a wider readership]

[B2:201] Huneker, James [Gibbons], 'Last of the Viking Poets', *Harper's Weekly* (New York), 27 July 1912, pp. 19-20. [Modifies Huneker's earlier opinion of Sg. Huneker now regards him as a classicist who is Greek in his manipulation of the idea of fate and destiny, and whose plays frequently observe the classical unities. 'In my early study I had evolved a Strindberg half monster, half genius. Too much stress was laid upon his morbid side,' whereas, with the help of Edwin Björkman's recent translations of many of the plays, it is now possible to paint a very much more nuanced picture of a 'paradoxical... sensitive and troubled modern genius']

[B2:202] Huneker, James [Gibbons], 'Strindberg', in *Essays*, Selected, with an introduction by Henry L. Mencken, New York: Charles Scribner's Sons, 1929, pp. 28-44. [An influential early general essay in English, which foregrounds the plays over the prose fiction and places the emphasis on Sg's opposition to women's emancipation]

[**B2:203**] Huneker, James [Gibbons], 'Strindberg', in *Essays*, Selected, with an introduction by Henry L. Mencken, New York: AMS Press, 1976, pp. 28-44. [Facsimile Rpr. of **B2:202**]

[**B2:204**] Isaksen, Jógvan, 'Størtsti eldurin í Svøriki: um August Strindberg', in *Í gráum eru allir litir: bókmentagreinir*, Torshavn: Føroya Skúlabókagrunnur, 1988, pp. 78-96. ['The Greatest Fire in Sweden'. A Faroese survey of Sg's life and work]

[**B2:205**] Janssens, Marcel, 'Een apologie van August Strindberg', *Duitser Warande en Belfort* (Antwerp), 1972:1, pp. 48-54. ['An Apology by August Strindberg'. Primarily concerned with *En dåres försvarstal*]

[**B2:206**] Jaarsma, D. Th., 'August Strindberg', *Den gulden winckel* (Amsterdam), 17:12 (15 December 1918), 177-180.

[**B2:207**] Johnsson, Henrik, 'Att skapa någon till sin avbild. Om homunculusmotivet hos Strindberg'; *Tidskrift för litteraturvetenskap* (Stockholm), 33:1 (2004), 90-108. ['To Create Someone in His Own Image. On the Homunculus Motif in Strindberg'. Focusing primarily on *I havsbandet*, where Borg creates his homunculi from nothing, and *Till Damaskus*, where the Unknown seeks to create his version of the Lady from preexisting material, Johnsson examines Sg's occasional use of the humunculus motif, identifying it as one to which he returned throughought his career. It serves to distinguish between art and nature, and functions as both an analogy for technological invention and (first and foremost) a myth of artistic creation. In Sg's case, it derives primarily from his reading of Goethe's *Faust*]

[**B2:208**] Johnsson, Henrik, 'Strindberg och vampyrerna', *Minotauren* (Stockholm), 2003:18, pp. 48-52. ['Strindberg and the Vampires']

[**B2:209**] Jolin, Christopher, 'Strindbergs naturalism', *Borlänge Tidning*, 27 August 1962. ['Strindberg's Naturalism']

[**B2:210**] Jörn, Gunnar, 'Strindberg', in *Svenska diktarporträtt*, Uppsala: Lindblad, 1924, pp. 130-170. Illus.

[**B2:211**] Josephson, Olle, 'Räkna *att* och gå vidare. Om formord in Strindbergs prosa', in Margareta Brundin, *et al.*, red., **B1:88**, *20 x Strindberg*, pp. 40-50. ['Count *To* and Continue. On Form-Words in Strindberg's Prose'. Uses the Gothenburg concordance of Sg's works which is based on the complete texts as printed in *Samlade Verk* and *August Strindbergs brev* to analyse Sg's use of the most common of Swedish words in the form of conjunctions, pronouns, speech act adverbs, and 'att', both in infinitives and when introducing a subordinate clause. Unsurprisingly, the tables and examples which Josephson employs confirm that compression and concretion are prominent features of Sg's style]

[**B2:212**] Kärnell, Karl-Åke, 'På språng i verkligheten', in Folke Olsson, red., **B1:348**, *Strindberg*, pp. 32-39. Illus. ['Headlong into Reality'. Discusses Sg's early journalism and its importance for his development as a writer. It taught him the value of writing 'In vivis', particularly during the 1880s, and became an essential feature of his style in which the use of up-to-date, contemporary language is a prominent feature]

[B2:213] Kärnell, Karl-Åke, 'Strindbergs bildkretsar', in Gunnar Brandell, red., **B1:82**. *Synpunkter på Strindberg*, pp. 182-208. ['Strindberg's Image Clusters'. An abridged version of Chapter 5 in **B1:179**]

[B2:214] Kaufman, R. J., 'Strindberg: The Absence of Irony', *Drama Survey* (Minneapolis), 3:4 (1964), 463-476. [Argues that in Sg, the normal boundaries between thought and act, interior and exterior reality, and past and present are blurred or denied. He wrote compelling but incomplete plays, based on 'a devastated vision of an absurd, divinely abandoned world'. The Sg protagonist says 'I suffer, therefore I am', and in his most characteristic plays from *Kamraterna* and *Fadren* through *Bandet* and *Första varningen* to *Dödsdansen* [sic], he presents a succession of no-exit situations 'in which an economical but perverse deity seems to have matched those who are best qualified to torture each other']

[B2:215] Kaufman, R. J., 'Strindberg: The Absence of Irony', in Otto Reinert, ed., **B1:371**, *Strindberg: A Collection of Critical Essays*, pp. 57-70. [Rpr. of **B2:214**]

[B2:216] Kinnander, Bengt, 'Ordstudier i Strindbergs prosa', *Nysvenska studier* (Uppsala), 19 (1939), 29-67. ['Verbal Studies in Strindberg's Prose'. Studies Sg's language and style in his prose works with examples taken from *I vårbrytningen*, *Röda rummet*, *Svenska öden och äventyr*, *Utopier i verkligheten*, *Tjänstekvinnans son*, *Hemsöborna*, *Skärkarlsliv*, *I havsbandet*, *Fagervik och Skamsund*, and *Svarta fanor*]

[B2:217] Kinnander, Bengt, 'Ordstudier i Strindbergs prosa', in Göran Lindström, red., **B1:291**, *Strindbergs språk och stil*, pp. 46-69. [Lightly revised version of **B2:216**]

[B2:218] Kjær, Nils, 'August Strindberg', in *Bøger og billeder, kritiske forsøg*, Kristiania: Feilberg & Landmark, 1898. 139 pp. [An appreciative discussion of Sg alongside essays on Dürer, Ibsen, Maeterlinck, E. T. A. Hoffmann, Goethe, and Descartes]

[B2:219] Kjær, Nils, 'August Strindberg', in *Svundne somre*, Kristiania: Gyldendal, 1920, pp. 168-173.

[B2:220] Klemensiewiczowa, Józefa, 'Johan August Strindberg', *Sfinks* (Warsaw), 19:5 (1912), 212-222. [An assessment of Sg's life and career, written in memoriam by one of his earliest Polish translators. Emphasises his prose fiction, in which he has remained a realist from first to last, rather than the plays, where he descends to an alien mysticism or a monotonous misogyny]

[B2:221] Kolesnikov, A., '[The Problem of a Subject in Strindberg's Work]', in L[ev] Gitel'man and V[alentina] Dianova, eds, **B1:148**, *Avgust Strindberg i mirovaia kul'tura. Materialy mezhvyzovskoi nauchnoi konferentsii. Stat'i. Soobshcheniia*, pp. 98-108.

[B2:222] Koltonovskaia, E[lena] A., 'Khronika', *Vestnik Evropy* (Moscow), 1912:7, pp. 339-345 [A substantial obituary which concludes that Sg lacks any great artistry and is a weak stylist; it is unlikely he will leave any traces after him, in spite of his indubitably great talent as a storyteller. His best works are *Fadren*, *I havsbandet*, and *Kamraterna* but 'what is most valuable in Sg is his personality, which is in a class apart, novel, vital, unruly, freedom-loving, and restless as the sea'. E.848]

[B2:223] Korolenko, V. G., *Sobranie sochinenii v 10 tomakh*, Vol. 8, Moscow, 1955, pp. 334-338. [Discusses 'Högre ändamål' (Higher Ends) in *Svenska öden och äventyr*, 'Sankt Gotthards saga' (in *Sagor*), and *Spöksonaten*. Previously published in the journal *Russkoe bogatstvo*, 1908:10, pp. 174-178]

[B2:224] Kurdybacha, Łukasz, 'W stulecie urodzin Strindberga', *Twórczość* (Warsaw), 6:3 (1950), 93-99. ['On the Centenary of Strindberg's Birth'. An essay marking the Sg centenary which presents him, sometimes with tendentious pathos, as an important writer who revolted against the capitalist system in Sweden and embraced the proletariat. Sg's life is set against the social and economic background of later 19th-Century and early 20th-Century Sweden, with the stress placed on his origins as a servant's son. Kurdybacha also emphasises his versatility as a writer in numerous genres]

[B2:225] Kurdybacha, Łukasz, 'W stulecie urodzin Strindberga', *Program Teatru Malego* (Warsaw), 23 November 1957. [Rpr. of **B2:224** as a programme essay. See **E51:356**]

[B2:226] K. W-g [Karl Warburg], 'Bokvärlden', *Göteborgs Handels- och Sjöfartstidning*, 7 July 1890. [Reviews the miscellaneous collection *Tryckt och otryckt II* on publication. Some of the brief literary sketches are interesting but the non-literary items lack general interest. The vivisection 'De små' (The Small, 1887) comes off best and, with its impulses from modern psychology, the Nietzschean vivisection 'Hjärnornas kamp' (The Battle of the Brains, 1887) is also of interest, but '*Den starkare*' is 'very weak' – 'merely a curiosity']

[B2:227] Lamm, Martin, 'Strindberg', *Zeitschrift für Ästhetik* (Stuttgart), 20 (1926), 141-155. [A translation of the introduction to **D2:169** (*Strindbergs dramer*). 'When one has portrayed Sg's personality, one has already characterised his writing…his literary production is basically only the reflection of his vital and intense temperament on paper'. His impact, both in Sweden and abroad, may be atributed to this 'astounding immediacy']

[B2:228] Landauer, Gustav, 'Strindberg', *Neue Jugund* (Berlin), 1 (1916-17), 135-136.

[B2:229] Landauer, Gustav, 'Strindberg', in **B1:245**, *Der werdende Mensch*, 1921 edition. [Rpr. of **B2:228**]

[B2:230] Landquist, John, 'August Strindberg', *Bonniers månadshäften* (Stockholm), 1909:1, pp. 9-25. [An acclamation of Sg's career on his 60th birthday. Focuses primarily on the pre-Inferno period, with relatively detailed comments on *Mäster Olof*, *Röda rummet*, *Dikter på vers och prosa*, and his interventions in the Woman Question. Gives priority to the prose works rather than the plays, and deals with his recent works in only the most cursory of fashions]

[B2:231] Landquist, John, 'August Strindberg', in Solveig Landquist, red., **B1:248**, *John Landquist om Strindberg personen och diktaren*, pp. 290-309. [Rpr. of **B2:230**]

[B2:232] Landquist, John, 'Strindberg naturalisten', in *Humanism*, Stockholm: Albert Bonniers Förlag, 1931, pp. 176-191. ['Strindberg the Naturalist'. Part of a longer essay which compares Sg, the naturalist, with Esaias Tegnér (1782-1846), the idealist. Sg not only explores the literary aspects of naturalism but its moral, psychological, and social consequences. 'Naturalism passed like a storm through Sg's life. Or rather, he seized hold of it and made it come alive with all the passion of his being'. Landquist discusses *Röda rummet*, *Giftas*, and the importance of Henry Thomas Buckle's *The History of Civilisation in England* for his early works, as well as both the power games of *Fadren*, 'Tschandala', and *I havsbandet*, on the one hand, and the 'neuropathological' later writings such as *Inferno*, *Advent*, *Till Damaskus*, and *Spöksonaten*, all of which are informed by a dramaturgy of guilt, on the other. See 'Diktaren och livssynen', **C1:734**]

[**B2:233**] Landquist, John, 'Strindberg naturalisten', in Solveig Landquist, red., **B1:248**, *John Landquist om Strindberg personen och diktaren*, pp. 317-327. ['Strindberg the Naturalist'. Rpr. of **B2:232**]

[**B2:234**] Landquist, John, 'Strindbergs filosofi. Nemesis', 1-2, *Svenska Dagladet* (Stockholm), 2 and 3 January 1905. ['Strindberg's Philosophy'. Considers the central problem in Sg's work to concern the question whether existence is governed by chance or purpose. A belief in Nemesis, and consequently the assumption that the world obeys a fundamentally moral order, permeates much of his work, in association with notions of crime and punishment, and guilt and suffering. Landquist links Sg's conception of Nemesis with the ideas of Swedenborg, Linnaeus, Plato, and Marcus Aurelius, and indicates both its philosophical naiveté and literary potential. According to Landquist, 'The nemesis morality is a morality of the nursery', but it is dramatically productive in plays like *Fadren* and several of the other naturalistic plays, as well as in many of the post-Inferno dramas]

[**B2:235**] Landquist, John, 'Strindbergs filosofi. Sangvinisk skepticism', 1-2, *Svenska Dagbladet* (Stockholm), 4 and 5 January 1905. ['Strindberg's Philosophy. Sanguine Scepticism'. A two-part essay on what Landquist regards as Sg's fundamental and, so far as his writing is concerned, productive scepticism, his profound self-consciousness and autobiographical energy. He compares Sg with Rousseau and, more briefly, Goethe, Nietzsche, and Otto Weininger, and refers in passing to several works, including *Fagervik och Skamsund*, *Mäster Olof*, *Röda rummet*, and *Gustav Adolf*]

[**B2:236**] Landquist, John, 'Strindbergs filosofi', in *Filosofiska essayer*, Stockholm: Albert Bonniers Förlag, 1906, pp. 263-301. ['Strindberg's Philosophy'. Reprints substantial extracts from **B2:234** and **B2:235**]

[**B2:237**] Landquist, John, 'Strindberg och suggestionen', in Solveig Landquist, red., **B1:248**, *John Landquist om Strindberg personen och diktaren*, pp. 180-183. ['Strindberg and Suggestion'. In Landquist's reading, it was particularly from the ideas which informed contemporary French psychology that Sg derived the most valuable impulses during the period in the 1880s when he lived abroad. They underlie *Fadren*, *Fordringsägare*, *Fröken Julie*, and 'Tschandala'. Rpr. of Landquist's review of Hans Lindström's *Hjärnornas kamp*, **C1:782**]

[**B2:238**] Landquist, John, 'Strindberg och suggestionspsykologien', in Alf Ahlberg, *et al.*, *Dikten, diktaren och samhället. Aktuella debattinlägg*, Stockholm: Albert Bonniers Förlag, 1935, pp. 73-93. ['Strindberg and Suggestion Psychology'. Identifies the importance of the new, primarily French, schools of psychology represented by Ambroise Liébeault, Hippolyte Bernheim, Charles Richet, Jean-Martin Charcot, and others for the development of Sg's writing in the mid-1880s. Landquist argues that 'No Swedish writer has been as deeply influenced by psychological thinking as Sg', and works like Bernheim's *De la suggestion* (1884) were of crucial importance for his naturalistic dramas, in all of which the battle of the brains, the power of suggestion, and the instability of character are prominent features. Comments on *Fadren*, *Fröken Julie*, *Fordringsägare*, *Paria*, and *Samum* in what was, for the period, a pioneering discussion]

[**B2:239**] Landquist, John, 'Strindberg och suggestionspsykologien', in Solveig Landquist, red., **B1:248**, *John Landquist om Strindberg personen och diktaren*, pp. 328-337. [Rpr. from **B2:238**]

[B2:240] Landquist, John, 'Strindbergs Philosophie', Einzige autorisierte Übersetzung von Marie Franzos, *März* (München) 5:2 (1911), 480-487. ['Strindberg's Philosophy'. An authorised translation of 'Sangvinisk skepticism' in *Filosofiska essayer*, pp. 289-301]

[B2:241] Landquist, Solveig, 'Närgångheter', in *Närgångheter. Åsikter om konst och litteratur*, Stockholm: Natur och Kultur, 1978, pp. 9-42. ['Indiscretions'. Landquist considers the autobiographical tendency in Sg's writing with reference to his correspondence, as well as to *Ockulta dagboken* and his relationship with Harriet Bosse. She also discusses Olle Söderström's portrait of Sg's third marriage in his documentary novel *Röda huset* as well as Per Olov Enquist's portrayal of Sg, Siri von Essen, and Marie David in his play *Tribadernas natt*]

[B2:242] Levertin, Oscar, 'August Strindberg', in *Fyra författarporträtt*, Urval och inledning av Docent Björn Julén, Stockholm: Bokförlaget Prisma, 1962, pp. 41-85. [Includes the sections on Sg from 'Diktare och drömmare' and 'Stockholmsnaturen i svensk dikt', together with reviews on publication of *Sagor*, *Ensam*, and *Götiska rummen*]

[B2:243] Levertin, Oscar, 'August Strindberg', in *Samlade skrifter*, 24 vols, Stockholm: Albert Bonniers Förlag, 1908, Vol. 8, 'Diktare och drömmare', pp. 225-247. [Sometimes lightly revised articles previously published in *Svenska Dagbladet*, including 'En Strindbergsutställning', **P1:300**, and his reviews of *Legender*, **F6:25**, and *Tryckt och otryckt* on publication]

[B2:244] Levertin, Oskar [sic], 'August Strindberg', 1-2, *Die Propyläen* (München), 9 (1911-12), pp. 497-499, 522-525.

[B2:245] Levinson, A. 'Strindberg', *Sovremennyi mir* (St Petersburg), 1910:4, pp. 47-53. [E.815]

[B2:246] Liljekrantz, Birger, 'August Strindberg. Några ord om hans utveckling', *Sånings-mannen* (Stockholm), 1911. ['August Strindberg. A Few Words on His Development'. Asks how Sg's power over the Swedish people is to be explained, and stresses the importance of his truthful self-presentation, as well as his representative role as the embodiment of his times. His development is only apparently confused and aimless; there is in fact a sure and deep context. Liljekrantz focuses primarily on 'Nybyggnad' (New Building) in *Utopier i verkligheten*, but also refers to *Röda rummet, Det nya riket, Herr Bengts hustru, I havsbandet, Giftas, Svanevit*, and *Ordalek och småkonst* in which 'Stadsresan' (The City Journey) shows him at his best. The essay places what is, for the period, an unusual emphasis on Sg's artistry; for Liljekrantz, he is first and foremost an artist who transforms what he has experienced into profound and gripping works of art]

[B2:247] Lindgren, Hellen, 'August Strindberg. Ett utkast med 10 bilder', *Ord och Bild* (Stockholm), 8:9 (1899), 433-455. Illus. ['August Strindberg. A Sketch with 10 Pictures'. An illustrated overview of Sg's work to date, published in conjunction with the 50th anniversary of his birth. Perhaps the most extensive, widely available, such overview published at the time]

[B2:248] Lindgren, Hellen, 'August Strindberg', in *Skalder och tänkare. Litterära essayer*, Stockholm: C. & E. Gernandts Förlag, 1900, pp. 90-108. [Rpr. of **B2:247**]

[B2:249] Lindgren, Hellen, '*Faderns* författare', *Aftonbladet* (Stockholm), 16 January 1888. ['The Author of *The Father*'. Characterises Sg as, at bottom, an unpredictable, quixotic romantic and poet, who plays with ideas and feelings: 'His sufferings and emotions are genuine but at the same time he strikes poses and calculates the effect, and he maintains that his convictions are mature at the very moment he is possessed by the demon called caprice']

[B2:250] Lindgren, Hellen, 'Strindberg – Heidenstam – Hedberg – Pelle Molin. En litterär vårrevy', *Ord och Bild* (Stockholm), 6:5 (1897), 234-240. [Surveys recent publications, including the just published *Tryckt och otryckt IV*, which included *Leka med elden*, *Bandet*, and 'På kyrkogården' (In the Cemetery, 1896), as well as a Swedish edition of 'Tschandala', first published in Denmark]

[B2:251] Lindström, Erik, 'Strindberg', in *Nordisk folkslivsskildring*, Stockholm: P. A. Norstedt & Söners Förlag, 1932, pp. 119-127. [Includes a discussion of *Hemsöborna* in relation to Sg's identification with Rousseau's critique of culture]

[B2:252] Lindström, Göran, 'Inledning', in August Strindberg, *Prosa och lyrik 1882-1905*, Skrifter utgivna av Modersmålslärarnas förening 92, Lund: C. W. K. Gleerup, 1963, 167 pp. [The introduction to a student anthology of Sg's poetry and prose. Also includes recommendations for study plans and further reading]

[B2:252a] Linship, A. '[Strindberg in His Final Works]', *Novyi Zhunal dlia vsekh* (St Petersburg), 1910:20, pp. 78-83. E.816]

[B2:253] Lisovskaya, Polina. '[Vampires. Images in Strindberg's Later Works]', [*Proceedings of the 30th Annual Intercollegial Scientific Conference*], N.15, World Literature Section, Part 1, St Petersburg, 2001, pp. 54-57. [An examination of the vampire theme in *Dödsdansen*, *Spöksonaten*, and elsewhere]

[B2:254] Lohr, Anton, 'August Strindbergs Schriften', *Literarische Warte* (München), 6 (1904-05), 530-543. ['The Writings of August Strindberg']

[B2:255] Loiseau, Georges, 'Auguste Strindberg et son œuvre', in August Strindberg, *Mademoiselle Julie. Samoun*, Paris: A. Savine, 1893, pp. 5-104. ['August Strindberg and His Works'. A presentation of Sg and his writing to date for French readers, accompanying new versions of the plays in translations by Loiseau that sometimes employed Sg's own French drafts and employed information derived in part from Sg himself]

[B2:256] Entry cancelled.

[B2:257] Lukács, Georg, 'August Strindberg', *Huszadik Század* (Budapest), February 1909, pp. 172-175. [A generally positive endorsement of Sg's life and work on the occasion of his 60th birthday, notwithstanding the fact that 'Sg's ultimate fragmentation is our own fragmentation. His life, devoid of purpose, direction, and focus, symbolises our own'. Three years previously, on Ibsen's death, Lukács had offered a far more substantial piece, 'Gondolatok Ibsen Henrikól', in the same journal, 2 (1906), pp. 127-137]

[B2:258] Lukács, Georg, 'August Strindberg: On His Sixtieth Birthday', in Arpad Kadarkay, ed., *The Lukács Reader*, Oxford: Blackwell, 1995, pp. 91-96. [English translation of **B2:257**]

[B2:259] Lukács, György, 'Sezdeset rodendana A. Strindberga', Translated by Sava Babić, *Delo* (Belgrade), 27:8 (1981), pp. 147-151. ['On August Strindberg's Sixtieth Birthday'. Serbo-Croat translation of **B2:257**. R.599]

[B2:260] Lukács, Georg, 'Zum zehnten Todestag August Strindbergs', *Die Röte Fahnen*, 26 June 1922. ['On the Tenth Anniversary of Strindberg's Death']

[B2:261] Lukács, Georg, 'Zum zehnten Todestag August Strindbergs', in Manfred Brauneck, Hrsg., *Die Röte Fahnen. Kritik, Theorie, Feuilleton 1918-1933*, München: Fink, 1973, pp. 157-160. ['On the Tenth Anniversary of Strindberg's Death'. Rpr. of **B2:260**]

[B2:262] Lutz, Köpnick, 'August Strindberg und die Ästhetik der Macht. Rekonstruktion einer Kritikstrategie', *Skandinavistik* (Kiel), 22:2 (1992), [85]-106. ['August Strindberg and the Aesthetic of Power. The Reconstruction of a Critical Strategy'. Analyses critical strategies in the interface between literary and political discourses in Sg's works prior to 1884, focusing especially on *Röda rummet* and *Det nya riket* and the conflict between idealism and realism. Lutz also comments on *Lilla katekes för Underklassen* and *Tjänstekvinnans son*, and employs Ernst Bloch, Walter Benjamin, and Jürgen Habermas as theoretical reference points]

[B2:263] Lynd, Robert, 'The Madness of Strindberg', in *Old and New Masters*, London: T. F. Unwin Ltd.; New York: Charles Scribner's Sons, 1919, pp. 123-129. [The mirror which Sg held up to nature was cracked, giving back broken images. 'His genius was the genius of frank and destructive criticism. His work, an autobiography of raw nerves rather than a revelation of the emotions of men and women, was not a sensational lie but true as the power of truth was in him. It is a genuine document. That is why, badly constructed though his plays may be, some of them have a fair chance of being read [sic] a hundred years hence']

[B2:264] McCarthy, Justin Huntly, 'August Strindberg', *The Fortnightly Review* (London), N.S. 52 (September 1892), 326-334. [The first commentary of any substance on Sg in England, in which he is described as a great personality whose life is a commentary on his work, as well as an exponent of modern pessimism. *Fröken Julie* is related to Victor Hugo's *Cromwell*, but in reaction to the drama of the immediately preceding period he has become the champion of a new movement which nevertheless shares with every sincere dramatist who has ever lived, the aim of being 'true to life'. See Rpr. in **B1:165** and the Swedish version in **D2:924**]

[B2:265] Macy, John, 'Strindberg', in *The Critical Game*, New York: Boni and Liveright, 1922, pp. 135-142. [Macy pays some attention to the novels and autobiographical fictions as well as to the plays, aware that 'Sg's imagination visualized and dramatized everything'. See **B1:368**]

[B2:266] Magris, Claudio, 'Narciso turbato da Cristo', *Corrieri della Serra* (Milan), 19 October 1975. ['Narcissus Perturbed by Christ'. Examines the egocentricity of the Christian imagination as represented by Sg's autobiographical art in *Tjänstekvinnans son* and *En dåres försvarstal*, noting in particular how, in the former, he caresses himself in the third person, always looking within himself rather than casting a glance at events round about him]

[B2:267] Mählqvist, Stefan, and Torsten Pettersson, red., *Tid och evighet. Nedslag i det gångna årtusendets europeiska litteratur*, Uppsala: Litteraturvetenskapiga institutionen, 2000. 168 pp.

[B2:268] Mahrholz, Werner, 'Die Lebensform der Moderne. August Strindberg', *Die Hochschule* (Berlin), 5 (1921-22), 12-28. ['Form of Modern Life. August Strindberg']

[B2:269] Mahrholz, Werner, 'Ein Zwischenspiel: Strindberg und die Lebensform der Moderne', in *Deutsche Dichtung der Gegenwart: Probleme, Ergebniße, Gestalten*, Berlin:

Wegweiser-Verlag, 1926, pp. 351-402. ['An Intermezzo: Strindberg and the Form of Modern Life'. Rpr. of **B2:268**]

[B2:270] Mambrino, Jean 'Auguste Strindberg, ou le crime, le masque et la Croix', *Etudes* (Paris), 327 (November 1967), 499-516. ['August Strindberg, or the Crime, the Masque, and the Cross'. Surveys Sg's main preoccupations with reference, almost exclusively, to the plays, of which the better known naturalistic dramas are not always representative. Discusses *Dödsdansen* in some detail]

[B2:271] Marcus, C[arl] D[avid], 'Ein beitrag zu Strindbergs Weltanschauung', *Literaturberichte des Verlages Georg Müller* (München), 1914:1, pp. 23-26. ['A Contribution to Strindberg's Weltanschauung'. Suggests that Sg's pessimism is a fundamental trait, one that relates him to a specific German tradition. He is a universal spirit and thus close to Goethe, but whereas the latter's scientific studies did not impede his creativity, Sg's entailed an extended hiatus in his career as a writer. Marcus observes how markedly European culture has changed over the years which separate the two men]

[B2:272] Marken, Amy van, 'August Strindberg, de onbekende?', *Elsevier's Maandschrift* (Amsterdam), 1940:2, pp. 29-40. ['August Strindberg, the Unknown?' An introductory article for the general reader]

[B2:273] Marken, Amy van, 'August Strindberg intime', *Litterair paspoort* (Amsterdam), 1949:4, pp. 7-10. Illus.

[B2:274] Markin, V., '[The Rebellious Avgust Strindberg]', *Sever* (Leningrad), 1972:4, pp. 116-121. [E.1058]

[B2:275] Matsevich, A., '[He is Least of All an End, He is Rather a Beginning]', in Avgust Strindberg, *Igra snov: izbrannoe, sostavitel'*, A[leksandra Aleksandrovna] Afinogenova, Moscow: AO "Start", 1994, pp. 532-542. [The Afterword to a Russian edition of Sg's selected works, translated by Aleksandra Afinogenova (*Ett drömspel*, *Dödsdansen*, and several short stories) I. Iakhnina (*Pelikanen, Oväder, Fordringsägare*), L. Lungina (*Le Plaidoyer d'un fou*), and E. Surits (*Fröken Julie*). Also includes a Preface by Lars Kleberg, pp. 3-5. E.1764a; E.1798e]

[B2:276] Meidal, Björn, 'Medalj, lagerkrans och doktorshatt. Drömmen om utmärkelse – ett tema i August Strindbergs liv och diktning', in *Kungliga Vetenskaps-Societetens i Uppsala årsbok*, 1986, pp. 38-51. ['Medal, Wreath, and Doctor's Hat. The Dream of Being Honoured – A Theme in August Strindberg's Life and Work'. The text of a lecture delivered at the Royal Swedish Academy of Sciences, 8 November 1985. Meidal traces Sg's relationship with authority and the motif of official and academic recognition as it appears both in his life and work, referring briefly to *Fritänkaren, Hermione, Tjänstekvinnans son, Kvarstadsresan, Svenska folket, Mäster Olof, Inferno*, the later history plays, *Svarta fanor*, and *En blå bok*]

[B2:277] Meidal, Björn, 'Medalj, lagerkrans och doktorshatt. Drömmen om utmärkelse – ett tema i August Strindbergs liv och diktning', *Strindbergiana* (Stockholm), 8 (1993), pp. 48-64. ['Medal, Wreath, and Doctor's Hat. The Dream of being Honoured – A Theme in August Strindberg's Life and Work'. Rpr. of **B2:276**]

[B2:278] Melberg, Arne, 'Barbaren i Paris', in Ulf Olsson, red., **B1:357**, *Strindbergs förvandlingar*, pp. 73-94. ['The Barbarian in Paris'. Analyses Sg's liminal situation in Paris in the mid-1890s and his exposure to the currents of modernity in an urban milieu that it has become customary to read with the assistance of Baudelaire and Walter Benjamin as a landscape of signs, recuperated via motifs like the *flâneur* and the crowd. Melberg discusses the essay 'Barbaren i Paris' (1895), *Inferno, Legender*, and *Jakob brottas*, as well as Sg's occult and scientific writings in *Jardin des Plantes* and elsewhere. He also compares his response to the urban landscape of Paris with that of Gérard de Nerval, Rilke, Hamsun, and the Danish poet Sophus Claussen (1865-1931), and charts the way in which his engagement with Paris is at the heart of his writing during a decade in which he initially focuses on writing non-fiction in French, before eventually recovering the ability to write fiction again in Swedish with *Till Damaskus*]

[B2:279] Melberg, Arne, 'Om subjektiviteten i historien och historiematerialismen', *Kris* (Stockholm), No. 13-14 (1979), pp. 16-25. ['On Subjectivity in History and Historical Materialism'. Illustrates a discussion of literature as 'an alias for the subjective factor in history' with reference to Jürgen Habermas's *Zur Rekonstruktion des historischen Materialismus, En dåres försvarstal*, and *Röda rummet*]

[B2:280] Melin, Nelly, 'Auguste Strindberg', *Revue de Paris*, 19:20 (15 October 1912), 850-866. [A survey of Sg's life and ideas, focusing primarily on the autobiographical fictions, with brief reference to *Röda rummet* and *I havsbandet*, but to none of the plays. Melin maintains that 'In the whole of Sg's work there is only one hero, himself', yet stresses his marvellous artistry and his rich, audacious, and realistic language, 'which makes of his work, of his autobiography above all, one of the saddest and most pathetic accounts of the human soul']

[B2:281] Menczer, Béla, 'The Royal Drama of Strindberg', *Dublin Review*, 226:1 (1952), 26-34. [Contains impressionistic and anecdotal commentary on a writer whose art Menczer sees as primarily autobiographical. Menczer comments on *Historiska miniatyrer*, several of the history plays, the short story 'Lycksalighetens ö' (The Isle of the Blessed), and *Tjänstekvinnans son*, and maintains that 'Sg was the great tragic poet of the age of Revolutions; he was the dramatist of the modern Apocalypse']

[B2:282] Mikhailovskii, B. V., 'Strindberg', in *Izbrannye stat'i o literature i iskusstve*, Moscow, 1969, pp. 511-546. [An appreciation in Mikhailovskii's 'Selected Essays on Art and Literature'. E.1033]

[B2:283] Moder, Janko, 'Strindbergov problem', *Gledališki list NGL* (Ljubljana), 17 (1943-44), 185-192. ['The Problem of Strindberg']

[B2:284] Molenbroek, P[iet?], 'Strindberg', *De Tijdspiegel* (Amsterdam), 77*:1 (1919), pp. 78-92, 140-149.

[B2:285] M. R. [Jurgis Baltrusaitis], 'Avgust Strindberg', *Pravda* (Moscow), 1904:3, pp. 36-39. [E.724]

[B2:286] Muret, Maurice, 'M. Auguste Strindberg', in *Les Contemporaines étrangers*, Vol. 1, Paris: Fontemoing et Cie., 1911, pp. 120-163. [Includes Sg together with Carducci, Fogazzaro, Vivanti, Lagerlöf, Shaw, Carl Hauptmann, Spitteler, and Schönherr, in a collection of essays on foreign contemporaries. Muret displays a (for the period and outside Scandinavia) fairly extensive knowledge of Sg's work]

[B2:287] Natanson, Wojciech, 'Warto przypomniec Strindberga', *Ilustrowany Kurier Polski* (Bygdgoszcz), 1950, No. 160, p. 5. ['It is Worth Remembering Strindberg'. Presents Sg in terms of the social and economic circumstances governing western capitalism during his career as a writer]

[B2:288] Nataqiyan, Soraya, 'Ákās, Nagāš, Namāyeš-nāmenevis, Šāer va Nevisande-ye bozorg va saršenase sŏedi', in Agust Istrindbirg, *Gfte-gŏ-ye vāge-ha va Honar-hā-ye-kŏčak*, tarjumah-yi Soraya Nateghian, Spånga: Baran, 1999, pp. 5-7. Illus. ['Photographer, Painter, Writer, Poet, and Great and Famous Swedish Writer'. The introduction to Nataqiyan's Persian translation of *Ordalek och småkonst*]

[B2:289] Neustroev, V[ladimir] P[etrovich], 'Khudozhestvennyi mir A. Strindberga', in August Strindberg, *Izbrannye proizvedeniia*, Vol. 1, Moscow: Khudozhestvennaia literatura, 1986, pp. 5-26. ['The Artistic World of Strindberg'. See **B1:419** and **B1:420**]

[B2:290] Nielsen, Erik A., '[Strindberg]', in Johan Rosdhal, red., *Texter vi hader*, København: Dansklærerforeningen, 2002. [Includes a critical analysis of Sg as 'a metaphysical juggler, a charlatan, a demagogue, and braggart']

[B2:291] Nielsen, R. Jahn, *August Strindberg og hans Digtning. En karakteristik udgivet i anledning af digterens 60-Aars Fødselsdag*, København: E. Jespersens Forlag, 1909. 16 pp. [Comments less on Sg's works as literature than on some of the issues they address, e.g. the Woman Question and his association with the principal concerns of the Scandinavian Modern Breakthrough]

[B2:292] Nilsson, Per, 'Names in Strindberg's Fiction', in Göran Rossholm, Barbro Ståhle Sjönell, and Boel Westin, eds, **B1:389**, *Strindberg and Fiction*, pp. 151-156. [An exercise in literary onomastics which demonstrates how Sg displays a lifelong interest in names and a talent for using them in various ways, in his poetry and prose as well as drama. Nilsson exemplifies Sg practice by reference to *Mäster Olof*, *Gillets hemlighet*, *Röda rummet*, *Fadren*, *Fröken Julie*, *Det nya riket*, *Svarta fanor*, *Till Damaskus*, *Svanevit*, and *Stora landsvägen*. He also comments on Sg's interest in Hebrew]

[B2:293] Nilsson, Per, 'Vad betyder ett namn? Strindberg i ett onomastiskt perspektiv', *Strindbergiana* (Stockholm), 14 (1999), pp. 50-78. ['What does a Name Mean? Strindberg in an Onomastic Perspective'. Discusses the various ways in which Sg names his characters, exemplified by his classical practice in *Fadren*, the attempt to endow names with a double function evocative of dreaming and hence to some extent allegorical in *Ett drömspel*, and assigning them a philosophical dimension, as in *Stora landsvägen*]

[B2:294] Nolin, Bertil, 'Det moderna, det faustiska och ondskans triumf. Om Strindberg efter *Inferno*', *Marginal* (Oslo), 4 (1997), pp. 7-16. ['Modernity, the Faustian, and the Triumph of Evil. On Strindberg after *Inferno*'. Traces the Faust motif in *I havsbandet*, *En blå bok*, *Inferno*, *Till Damaskus*, and *Svarta fanor*, the relationship between reality and fiction in such texts, and the materialist world of evil in conflict with knowledge]

[B2:295] Nolin, Bertil, 'Strindberg och Moderniteten. Den faustiske sökaren och det ondas triumf', *Strindbergiana* (Stockholm), 13 (1998), pp. 95-103. ['Strindberg and Modernity. The Faustian Seeker and the Triumph of Evil'. Abridged version of **B2:294**]

[B2:296] Nordensvan, Georg, 'Strindberg. Et utkast', *Ny tidskrift* (Stockholm), 1885, pp. 158-176. ['Strindberg. A Sketch']

[B2:297] Obenauer, K., 'Strindbergs Entwicklung', *Preußische Jahrbücher* (Berlin), 205 (1926), pp. 37-57. ['Strindberg's Development']

[B2:298] Obligado, Pedro Miguel, 'Augusto Strindberg', in *La tristeza de Sancho, y otros ensayos*, Buenos Aires: Cooperativa editorial 'Buenos Aires', 1927. 135 pp.

[B2:299] Oliver, D. E. 'August Strindberg', *Manchester Literary Club Papers*, 41 (1915), 157-185. [Stresses the almost unparalleled 'fecundity' of Sg's mind in an introductory overview of his life and works, many of which are merely listed. A number of his plays 'are masterpieces of beautiful fantasy, penetrating psychology and ennobling thought', and as a dramatist he occupies a place 'in some degree above' both Ibsen and Bjørnson. Oliver discusses only *Fröken Julie* in any detail and draws heavily on Lind-af-Hageby's account of Sg's life and work in **R:1361**]

[B2:300] Olsson, Nils Ludvig, 'Strindberg', in *Skolmästaren. Litterära skuggbilder*, Stockholm: Lindstedt, 1938, pp. 30-36. Illus.

[B2:301] Olsson, Ulf, 'August Strindberg var svensk, eller, Att översätta svenskheten till svenska', *iDialog* (www.idialog.nu), No. 1, 2001. ['August Strindberg was Swedish, Or Translating Swedishness into Swedish']

[B2:302] Olsson, Ulf, 'I varans Inferno. Utkast till en Strindbergsläsning', *Bonniers Litterära Magasin* (Stockholm), 59:1 (1990), 22-28. Illus. ['In the Inferno of the Commodity. Sketch for a Reading of Strindberg'. This reading, primarily of *Inferno*, concludes with a discussion of the commodified world of *fin-de-siècle* Paris during the period described in Sg's autobiographical fiction, as he markets himself in what Olsson's mentor, Walter Benjamin, called 'the capital of the 19th Century'. Olsson, who also considers *Röda rummet*, *Giftas*, 'Sensations détraquées' (Deranged Sensations, 1894), and Sg's authorial role in general, comments on Sg's allegorical method and illuminates his technique with frequent reference to Benjamin's *Passagearbeit*]

[B2:303] Olsson, Ulf, 'Simulakren. Die Geschichte des Wahnsinns bei Strindberg', Aus dem Schwedischen überstezt von Thomas Fechner-Smarsly, in Walter Baumgartner and Thomas Fechner-Smarsly, Hrsg., **B1:19**, *August Strindberg: Der Dichter und die Medien*, pp. 133-155. ['Simulacrum. The History of Madness in Strindberg'. Olsson traces the ways in which Sg employed madness both as a literary trope and as a psychological condition in which he was profoundly interested. Frequently described as mad himself, Sg read widely in contemporary psychology and subjected his own exceptional states of mind to analysis, but Olsson avoids the pitfalls of many other discussions of this topic by his refusal either to reduce Sg by psychoanalysing him, or to regard his works as merely personally revealing documents. He discusses *Fadren, Påsk, Till Damaskus, En blå bok*, and the experimental prose piece 'Sensations détraquées' (1894), as well as several unpublished texts in Sg's *Nachlaß*. He also examines the borderline between madness and fiction which is so often manifest in much of Sg's best work, accomplishing this within an awareness of the context provided by the developing discourse of contemporary psychology and its subsequent critique by Michel Foucault and others]

[B2:304] Olsson, Ulf, 'Stilens sår. Strindbergs ut- och avbrott', *Bonniers Litterära Magasin* (Stockholm), 63:4 (1994), 28-34. Illus. ['Style's Wound. Strindberg's Break and Outbreak'. Discusses Sg's prose, which draws nourishment from Christianity's 'low style', both in the abrupt prose of early novels like *Röda rummet* and *I havsbandet*, and in later works like *Inferno* and *En blå bok*. Olsson augments his analysis of Sg's rhetoric in his published works with reference to manuscript material in 'Gröna säcken']

[B2:305] Olsson, Ulf, 'Telephone. Notes on Communication Technology and Meaning in Strindberg's Works', in Kristen Wechsel, Hrsg., **B1:473**, *Strindberg and His Media*, pp. 35-49. [With reference to *Taklagsöl* and *Oväder*, Olsson examines how Sg's writings may be regarded as an attempt to subvert the disciplinary regime to which new media such as the graphophone and the telephone contributed, both of them conjuring up voices without bodies and speech without the presence of talking subjects. He also refers to *En blå bok*, *Götiska rummen*, *Påsk*, *Stora landsvägen*, and Victoria Benedictsson's play *I telefon*. Throughout Sg's works, he finds that 'society is an organisation marked by violence, oppression, and the representative but hypocritical masquerade of Power', and suggests that in his later writings, power is no longer represented and personified by socially elevated individuals, as is the case in (say) *Det nya riket* or *Röda rummet*, but enacted in more subtle ways, in, for example, the impersonal control exercised via these new technologies]

[B2:306] Pasche, Wolfgang, 'Nachwort', 'Anhang', and 'Anmerkungen', in August Strindberg, *Werke in zeitlicher Folge*, Hrsg. von Wolfgang Pasche, Bde 8:1–2: *1898-1900*, Frankfurt am Main: Insel Verlag, 1992, pp. 1023-1069, 1073-1257, 1259-1401. [The Afterword, Notes, and editorial apparatus to a volume containing new German translations of Sg's works in all genres written and published between 1898 and 1900]

[B2:307] Pellegrini, Alessandro, 'Augusto Strindberg', *Belfagor* (Firenze), 4 (1949), 431-438. [Surveys Sg's changing outlook from *Röda rummet*, *Fadren*, and *Kamraterna* to the Chamber Plays and (mainly) *Till Damaskus*, which the author has translated into Italian. Offers a Catholic reading of what is interpreted as essentially a tragic play]

[B2:308] Pérez Petit, Victor, 'Augusto Strindberg', in *Los modernistas*, Montevideo: Imprenta y Encuadernación de Dornaleche y Reyes, 1903. 333 pp. [The other writers discussed are Gerhart Hauptmann, Tolstoi, Paul Verlaine, Eugenio de Castro, Rubén Dario, Bastilio Yakchakof, Nietzsche, Gabriele D'Annunzio, and Mallarmé]

[B2:309] Pérez Petit, Victor, 'Augusto Strindberg', in *Los modernistas*, Obras completas. Critica, 7, Montevideo: C. Garcia y cía., 1943. 465 pp. [Augumented edition of **B2:308**, with additional essays on Oscar Wilde, Walt Whitman, Enrique Gomez Carrillo, Gustave Kahn, and Maurice Maeterlinck]

[B2:310] Perrelli, Franco, 'Incontrare Strindberg. In cerca dello Strindberg sconosciuto', *STILB*, No. 6 (1981), 21-31. ['Meeting Strindberg. In Search of the Unknown Strindberg']

[B2:311] Picchio, Carlo, 'Prefazione', in August Strindberg, *Romanzi e drammi*, a cura di Carlo Picchio, Firenze-Roma: Casini Editore, 1950. XXXIV+633 pp. [Introduces a volume of Italian translations of *Röda rummet*, *Inferno*, *Fadren*, *Fröken Julie*, *Samum*, and *Ett drömspel*]

[B2:312] 'JotPe' [Pseudonym of Jan Piechocki], 'Dru Przybyszewskiego', *Ziemia Pomorska* (Bydgoszcz), 1949, No. 43. ['Przybyszewski's Friend'. Presents Sg as a regrettable product of an epoch that prevented him from developing consistent and positive ideas about the kind of world he wished to fight for]

[B2:313] Poelhekke, M[artinus] A[ntonius] P. C., *Modernen: Willem Kloos, Paul Verlaine, August Strindberg, Johannes Jørgensen, Frederik van Eeden*, Nijmegen: Malmberg, 1899, pp. 59-80, 261-264. [The first significant presentation of the later Sg in the Netherlands. Mainly concerned with *Till Damaskus* and *Inferno* as representative texts of the symbolist *fin-de-siècle* with its interest in medieval and religious structures of feeling. Poelhekke also mentions his contacts with the Belgian monastery of Maredsous]

[B2:314] Polonskii, G., '[The Roads of August Strindberg]', *Bodroe slovo* (St Petersburg), 21 (November 1909), pp. 38-55. [E.804]

[B2:315] Poritzky, Jakob Elias, 'August Strindberg', in *Dämonische Dichter*, München: Rösl Verlag, 1921, pp. 155-207.

[B2:316] Poritzky, J[akob] E[lias], 'August Strindberg', *Das literarische Echo* (Berlin), 11:9 (1909), Sp. 616-629. [Surveys the scope of Sg's achievement as a writer in light of Emil Schering's collected edition of his works in German, pausing longest over his contribution to the modern theatre. See **F4:89**, where an English version of this essay is used to introduce the first translation into English of *En dåres försvarstal*]

[B2:317] Printz-Påhlson, Göran, 'Historical Drama and Historical Fiction: The Example of Strindberg', *Scandinavian Studies* (Madison), 62:1 (1990), 24-38. [Accepting Georg Lukác's general observations on the distinction between historical drama and historical fiction in *The Historical Novel* as canonical, Printz-Påhlson compares Sg's practice in the twelve major Swedish history plays, as well as in the three volumes of short stories *Svenska öden och äventyr*, *Historiska miniatyrer*, and *Hövdingaminnen*, to which they are sometimes related in terms of subject and point of view. He seeks to identify their generic peculiarities and the extent to which they confirm or diverge from Lukác's premises]

[B2:318] Printz-Påhlson, Göran, 'Historical Drama and Historical Fiction: The Example of Strindberg', in Birgitta Steene, ed., **B1:434**, *Strindberg and History*, pp. 29-43. [Rpr. of **B2:317**]

[B2:319] Printz-Påhlson, Göran, 'Strindberg och "totemismen"', *Konstrevy* (Stockholm), 45:4 (1969), 154-160. Illus. ['Strindberg and "Totemism"'. Printz-Påhlson demonstrates how, for Sg, language is a secret code, one that, especially during the Inferno period and later, is also visible in the phenomena of the natural world. For Sg, language is often employed as an instrument used by man in order to conceal rather than expose the truth, and is thus to be understood in terms of the story of Babel. Such assumptions may be related to German romanticism, as exemplified by Jacob Boehme, Frans Xaver von Baader, and Johan Georg Hamann, as well as Kierkegaard, and they are of a piece with Sg's lifelong anxiety regarding man's continuity with nature, which accounts for his problematic relationship with both Rousseau and Darwin, a relationship that is partly offset by his affinity with the pre-evolutionary thinking of Linnaeus. Printz-Påhlson discusses *En blå bok*, 'Den romantiske klockaren på Rånö', *I havsbandet*, *Tjänstekvinnans son*, the prose fragment 'Armageddon', and Sg's reading of John Locke in several posthumously published texts which were originally intended for inclusion in *En blå bok*. He also uses the anthropology of Claude Levi-Strauss to define a fundamental complex in his thinking, which is defined here as Sg's 'totemism']

[B2:320] Printz-Påhlson, Göran, 'Tankens genvägar. Om Strindbergs antropologi', 1-2, *Bonniers Litterära Magasin* (Stockholm), 38:6 (1969), 430-441, and 38:8 (1969), 594-610. ['The Short-Cuts of Thought: On Strindberg's Anthropology'. One of the most wide-ranging and enthralling of all general contributions to Sg studies, this two-part essay departs from the customary diachronic readings of his career in terms of a chronological series of abrupt transformations of attitude, in favour of a synchronistic approach to his writing by way of an analysis of certain recurrent motifs, patterns, and preoccupations, in order to apprehend a number of fundamental, recurring intellectual drives which Printz-Påhlson describes as the intellectual contents of Sg's conscious or unconscious attitude toward human beings as a generic and social phenomenon. This is what is referred to here as 'Strindberg's anthropology'. Part One thus offers a detailed discussion of Sg's so-called 'primitivism', with reference to his interest in ethnography and primitive religion, and this is complemented with an examination of his familiarity with the ideas of Johan Jakob Bachofen, Edward B. Taylor, Friedrich Engels, Herbert Spencer, and several other contemporary sociologists and anthropologists, which are linked with the protracted dialogue that Sg conducted with Rousseau during the 1880s and after. Printz-Påhlson also examines Sg's conception of both language and religion in general and studies his attempt at self-analysis in *Tjänstekvinnans son* in rational, causal terms. In addition he considers Sg's understanding of marriage, sexuality, and evolution in the form of exogamy and endogamy, on the one hand, and ontogeny and phylogeny on the other, with reference to *Tjänstekvinnans son*, *En dåres försvarstal*, *Fröken Julie*, *Svarta fanor*, and the two collections of *Vivisektioner*. Other works singled out for perceptive commentary include *En blå bok*, *Götiska rummen*, 'De lycksaliges ö' (The Isle of the Blessed) from *Svenska öden och äventyr*, *Fadren*, *Hövdingaminnen*, *Starkodder*, and *Svenska folket*, as well as *Den fredlöse*, *Sömngångarnätter*, and *I havsbandet*, in which nature is again contrasted with culture and the rational is juxtaposed with the primitive and atavistic. Part Two of the essay focuses primarily on Sg's interest in contemporary psychology and the way in which he inscribes the texts of the two stories 'Genvägar' (Short Cuts) and 'Den romantiske klockaren på Rånö' (The Romantic Sexton on Rånö) with the discourse of hysteria and the unconscious. In both of these, Printz-Påhlson illustrates how Sg explores regressive mechanisms in a manner that prefigures Freud, an approach that is scarcely surprising since Printz-Påhlson also confirms that both Freud and Sg shared an interest in the experiments of such contemporary psychologists as Hippolyte Bernheim, Henry Maudsley, and Jean-Martin Charcot]

[B2:321] Printz-Påhlson, Göran, 'The Short-Cuts of Thought: On Strindberg's Anthropology', in Frank Egholm Andersen and John Weinstock, eds, *The Nordic Mind: Current Trends in Scandinavian Literary Criticism*, Lanham, Maryland: University Press of America, 1986, pp. 319-341. [Translation of Part One of **B2:320**]

[B2:322] Rasmussen, Alice, 'Om äppelträden i Strindbergs verk', *Strindbergiana* (Stockholm), 19 (2004), pp. 170-188. Illus. ['On Apple Trees in Strindberg's Works'. Considers the personal, cultural, literary, mythological, and metaphorical significance of such trees in a range of works in several genres, including *Gamla Stockholm*, *Svenska folket*, *Fröken Julie*, *Stora landsvägen*, 'Nemesis Divina', *Han och hon*, *Röda rummet*, *Svenska öden och äventyr*, *Utopier i verkligheten*, *Likt och olikt*, *Giftas*, *Tjänstekvinnans son*, *En dåres försvarstal*, *Inferno*, *Syndabocken*, *Oväder*, *Svarta handsken*, and *Bjälbo-Jarlen*. Two principal motifs are apparent: firstly, man's manipulation of an apple tree represents his violation, or perversion, of nature; secondly, as in *Fröken Julie*, it alludes to the notion of the Garden of Paradise and thus enjoys a mythical dimension. In both cases, Rasmussen confirms that Sg's precise arboricultural knowledge of the apple tree in nature is often apparent in the use he makes of it literature]

[B2:323] Reingol'dt, A., 'Pis'ma o novykh pisateliakh. Pis'mo tret'e: Avg. Strindberg', 1-2, *Sever* (St Petersburg), 1892, Nos 30 (26 July 1892), Sp. 1523-1528, and 35 (30 August 1892), Sp. 1773-1778. ['Letters about New Writers: The Third Letter – August Strindberg'. One of the first discussions of Sg in Russian, in the form of two of four 'Letters on New Authors' by a German critic who also discusses J. P. Jacobsen, Arne Garborg, and Gerhart Hauptmann. Sg is presented as the opposite of Jacobsen, a deeply divided man of iron in whom the aristocrat, contemptuous of the people in 'Tschandala' and *I havsbandet*, contrasts with the democrat, who displays sympathy for the oppressed in *Röda rummet* and *Utopier i verkligheten*. Reingol'dt, who finds that in Sg the romantic is always in conflict with the naturalist, sets his work in its social context, and presents *Giftas* as a response to Ibsen's portrayal of marriage in *A Doll's House*. He also welcomes the innovatory dramaturgy of *Fadren* and *Fordringsägare*, and describes both *Hemsöborna* and *Skärkarlsliv* as realistic masterpieces. E.685]

[B2:324] Reitts, G. V., 'Zhizn' i tvorchestvo A. Strindberga', in *Sbornik, posviashschennyi V. M. Bekhterevu k 40-letiu professorskoi deiatel'nosti*, Leningrad, 1926, pp. 691-710. ['The Life and Works of August Strindberg'. E.930]

[B2:325] Rettinger, M., '*Dwa warsztaty* (organizacja Shawa i Strindberga)', *Krytyka* (Warsaw), 34 (1912), pp. 111-118. ['Two Working Methods'. Discusses structural problems in Sg's plays and the philosophical implications of his work in a comparison with the approach to playwriting of George Bernard Shaw]

[B2:326] Robertson, J[ohn] G[eorge], 'Strindberg's Position in European Literature', in *Essays and Addresses on Literature*, London: George Routledge & Sons, Ltd., 1935, pp. 255-271. [Surveys Sg's career from *Mäster Olof* to *Till Damaskus* and *Stora landsvägen*, focusing exclusively on the plays]

[B2:327] 'Robinson' [Pseudonym of Urban von Feilitzen], 'Strindberg', in *Realister och idealister*, 1 (1885), pp. 53-84.

[B2:328] Robinson, Michael, 'Finding a New Language: Strindberg and Symbolism', *Scandinavica* (Norwich), 33:2 (1994), 201-215. [Examines Sg's relationship with Symbolism. Discusses his individual brand of naturalism as it is defined in the essays 'Om det allmänna missnöje' (On the General Discontent, 1884) and 'Om realism' (On Realism, 1882), and discussed in the story 'Över molnen'(Beyond the Clouds) in *Utopier i verkligheten*. Robinson presents the problems it ultimately posed, which led to the crisis in Sg's career as a creative writer in the mid-1890s, and traces the two paths, via science and painting, by which he found his way back to literature. Few writers have been more haunted by what Mallarmé termed 'the demon of analogy', but his post-Inferno works do not merely suggest and evoke but name quite openly; indeed, as *Dödsdansen*, *Inferno*, *Svarta fanor*, and *Ockulta dagboken* variously demonstrate, Sg never entirely abandons naturalism; rather, encouraged by the example of Swedenborg, he discovered a new significance in the concrete detail of everyday life, one that requires the kind of symbolical interpretation associated with his near contemporary, Freud]

[B2:329] Robinson, Michael, 'Finding a New Language: Strindberg's Break with Naturalism', in *Studies in Strindberg*, **B1:380**, Norwich: Norvik Press, 1998, pp. 132-144. [A lightly revised version of **B2:328**]

[B2:330] Robinson, Michael, 'Towards a New Language: Strindberg and Symbolism', in *Strindberg: The Moscow Papers*, **B1:379**, pp. 15-26. [Rpr. of **B2:328**]

[B2:331] Rochwicz, Jan, 'Strindberga walczył o prawa skrzywdzonych', *Wieczory Teatralne* (Katowice), 1950, 13-14, pp. 41-43.

[B2:332] Rogalski, Aleksander, 'August Strindberg', in *Pod północnym niebem*, Sylwetki pisarzy skandynawskich, Poznań, 1969, pp. 22-42. ['Under Nordic Skies. Silhouettes of Scandinavian Writers'. Discusses Sg's life and work and stresses its character as a 'great confession', a vivisection of his own self obsessively concerned with woman and love]

[B2:333] Röttger, Karl, 'Anmerkungen zu Strindberg', in *Die Flamme. Essais*, München: Müller, 1918, pp. 115-141. ['Observations on Strindberg']

[B2:334] Roy, Matthew M., 'History Revisited and Rewritten: August Strindberg, Magnus Smek, and Heliga Birgitta', in Ann-Charlotte Gavel Adams and Terje L. Leiren, eds, **B1:2**, *Stage and Screen: Studies in Scandinavian Drama and Film. Essays in Honor of Birgitta Steene*, pp. 105-118. [Illustrates how Sg's changing perception of King Eriksson (Magnus Smek) and Heliga Birgitta parallel an event in his own life, thus impacting on his portrayals of them as historical figures. Roy is primarily concerned with *Folkunga-sagan* and its sources in Swedish history, but relates the portrayal of the king to an episode depicted in *Legender* concerning his friend Bengt Lidforss, and associates this with a suggestion by Otto de Joux in *Die Enterbten des Liebesglückes oder Das Dritte Geschlecht* that he (Sg) was inclined to homosexuality. Roy also discusses Sg's portrayal of Magnus and Birgitta in *Svenska folket*, *Det nya riket*, *Hövdingaminnen*, and *Nya svenska öden*]

[B2:335] Roy, Matthew, 'När vetenskapen fallerar. Homosexualitet och religiös moral i Strindbergs verk efter Infernoperioden', Translated by Birgitta Steene, *Strindbergiana* (Stockholm), 18 (2003), pp. 75-[88]. ['When Science Fails. Homosexuality and Religious Morality in Strindberg's Works after the Inferno Period'. Notwithstanding his use of such apparently pejorative references to lesbians and homosexuals as 'tribad' and 'buger', Sg in fact studied the contemporary literature on homosexuality in some depth before portraying homosexuals in a wide range of texts, beginning with *Giftas* and *En dåres försvarstal* in the 1880s. His reading included philosophical, sociological, and medical works by Schopenhauer, Eugène Véron, Charles Letourneau, Théodule Ribot, Seved Ribbing, and Pierre Garnier and, although his views were coloured by contemporary attitudes, he initially treated the subject lightly, and seems not to have feared its association with himself. However, with the new moral standpoint that he assumed during the 1890s, Sg's view of 'perversity' underwent a change, as is evident from 'Les pevers' in the *Vivisektioner* of 1894, and both *Inferno* and *Götiska rummen*, in which homosexuals are portrayed more negatively, in judgmental, religious terms. Nevertheless, Roy maintains that his continuing treatment of the subject kept it alive for the general reader, and his writings can consequently be said to have helped create a public forum in Sweden for the discussion of a previously hermetically closed off subject]

[B2:336] Roy, Matthew, 'Strindbergs förgiftade natur: En textstudie om lika-könad lusta', Translated by Göran Söderström, *lambda nordica* (Stockholm), 8:1 (2002), 45-69. ['Strindberg's Poisoned Nature: A Textual Study of Same-Sex Desire'. Seeks to document what Roy calls Sg's 'careful research' in medical, sociological, and philosophical beliefs and theories regarding homosexuality, which was a persistent preoccupation throughout his career as a writer. In fact it was his writings which made the subject an important scientific and social issue for debate in Sweden. Refers to the same authorities listed under **B2:335**, and is likewise substantially a reworking of material from Roy's thesis, **V:180**]

[B2:337] Ruest, Anselm, 'Strindberg Confessor', *Die Aktion* (Berlin-Charlottenburg), 1:8 (10 April 1911), Sp. 243-247. [Discusses the principal autobiographical fictions, from *Tjänstekvinnans son* to *Ensam*, as well as *I havsbandet*, and *En blå bok*, and considers the extent to which Sg is a confessional writer]

[B2:338] Samuel, H[orace] B[arnett], 'Strindberg and His Plays', *Fortnightly Review* (London), 96 (1 June 1912), pp. 1116-1131. [An overview of Sg's career as a whole, which stresses the way his 'persecution mania expressed itself in his attitude to sex, religion, and society…with all his perversities [and] aberrations, Sg remains the blackest and, in his own particular spheres, the most drastic intelligence in the whole of our European literature'. Discusses *Röda rummet, Giftas, Fadren, Fröken Julie, Fordringsägare, Leka med elden, Svarta fanor*, and *Dödsdansen*, all briefly, and refers to several other novels, plays, and autobiographical fictions, including *Inferno* where 'the aberrations of a disorganised brain are set out with the most unconscious literary art'. Sg can be fully understood only by an appreciation of the new women's movement 'which under the auspices of Ellen Key flourished vigorously in the 80's' (sic)]

[B2:339] Samuel, Horace B[arnett], 'August Strindberg', in *Modernities: Ten Studies*, London: Kegan Paul, Trench, Trübner & Co. Ltd, 1913; New York: E. P. Dutton, 1914, pp. 91-113. [Rpr. of **B2:338**]

[B2:340] Schepens, Piet, 'August Strindberg. Een zweedsch Schrivjer', *De wilde roos* (Brussels), 6:2 (1928), pp. 91-120. ['August Strindberg. A Swedish Writer'. A pamphlet-length study in a series on modern authors. Provides a biographical outline of Sg's life, commenting on several works (*Röda rummet, Fröken Julie, Himmelrikets nycklar, Till Damaskus*, and especially *Fadren* and *Dödsdansen*) in passing. Schepens relates him to both Nietzsche and the Russian critic and novelist Nikolai Chernyshevskii whose *Chto delat'* (What is to be done?, 1864) was greatly admired by Sg during the early 1880s]

[B2:341] Schepens, Piet, 'Inleiding tot Strindberg's naturalistische periode', *De Vlaamsche Gids* (Antwerp), 19 (1930-31), 460-469. ['An Introduction to Strindberg's Naturalistic Period']

[B2:342] Schering, Emil, 'Strindberg und seine letzen Werke', *Die Umschau* (Frankfurt am Main), 3 (1899), 866-899. ['Strindberg and His Recent Works'. Primarily concerned with the occult, post-Inferno Sg, represented most notably by *Inferno* and *Legender*, with their new concern for the life of the soul, and *Till Damaskus*, but Schering also surveys the, then, more familiar author of *Mäster Olof, Röda rummet*, the naturalistic dramas, and *En dåres försvarstal*. He quotes Georg Brandes on Sg and refers to the Sg issue of the journal *Quickborn*, published in Berlin in January 1899 under Schering's editorship. See **B7:34**]

[B2:343] Schering, Emil, 'Strindberg und seine letzen Werke', in Hans-Peter Bayerdörfer, Hrsg., **B3:85**, *Strindberg auf der deutschen Bühne*, pp. 122-127. ['Strindberg and His Recent Works'. Rpr. of **B2:342**]

[B2:344] Schmidt, E., 'Strindberg (Odlomki iz uvoda v knjigo)', *Gledališki list NGL* (Ljubljana), 8:12 (1928-29), 93-94.

[B2:345] Schmidt, Rudolf, 'Skandinavische Litteraturbriefe. III', *Magazin für die Literatur des Auslandes* (Leipzig), 55 (1886), 723-726. [Discusses *Röda rummet, Utopier i verkligheten*, and *Likt och olikt*]

[B2:346] Schneider, Friedrich, 'Strindberg', 1-2, *Über Wassern* (Münster), 1 (1908), pp. 549-558, 594-601. [An overview of Sg's life and works to date]

[B2:347] Schneider, Friedrich, 'August Strindbergs Werke', 1-3, *Über Wassern* (Münster), 2 (1909), pp. 220-225, 269-273, 308-312. [A further overview of Sg's career and works to date, published in conjunction with his 60th birthday]

[B2:348] Schornstein, Waldemar, 'Einiges über Strindberg den Forscher und Dramatiker', *Das Goetheanum* (Dornach), 14 (1935), 146-148. ['Some Comments on Strindberg as a Researcher and Dramatist']

[B2:349] Schur, Ernst, 'Strindberg', *Das Magazin für die Literatur des In- und Auslandes* (Leipzig), 72:2 (1903), Sp. 299-302.

[B2:350] Servaes, Franz, 'August Strindberg', *Die Nation* (Berlin), 9 (1891-92), 414-417.

[B2:351] Sharypkin, D[mitrii] M[ikhailovich], '[August Strindberg and Some Characteristics of Realism in Scandinavian Literature]', *Skandinavskaia filologiia* (Leningrad), Seriia Filologicheskie. nauki 308, Vol. 1, Leningrad,1961, pp. 150-162. [Summary in Swedish. E.985]

[B2:352] Sharpe, Frida Stephenson, 'August Strindberg', *The Critic* (New York), 12 February 1898, pp. 103-105. [One of the earliest North-American notices of Sg as a dramatist. Sharpe observes that with his multiple talents, Sg 'owes allegiance to no school, to no cult, to no time. He is a buccaneer on the high seas of thought and steers to every port in the strangest out of the way places, but skillfully'. *Kamraterna* is described as 'wonderfully clever' and *Fröken Julie* as 'weirdly realistic', and Sharpe also notes the influence which both Schopenhauer and Nietzsche exerted on Sg]

[B2:353] Sharpe, Frida Stephenson, 'August Strindberg', *Valkyrian* (New York), July 1898. [Swedish translation of **B2:352**. Rpr. in *Valkyrian*, February 1908]

[B2:354] Shideler, Ross, 'August Strindberg: Still in the Middle of Battle', *Scandinavian Review* (New York), 2000:3, pp. 75-79. Illus. [An introductory overview]

[B2:355] Sokół, Lech, 'August Strindberg w siedemdziesięciolecie śmierci (1849-1912)', *Teatr* (Warsaw), 1983:2, pp. 3-10. ['Strindberg on the Seventieth Anniversary of His Death']

[B2:356] Sokolov, E., '[The Reserve Fund of Local Apocalypses]', in L[ev] Gitel'man and V[alentina] Dianova, eds, **B1:148**, *Avgust Strindberg i mirovaia kul'tura. Materialy mezhvyzovskoi nauchnoi konferentsii. Stat'i. Soobshcheniia*, pp. 127-140.

[B2:357] Sprengel, David, 'August Strindberg', in *De nya poeterna (80 talet). Dokument och kåserier*, Stockholm: C. & E. Gernandts Förlagsaktiebolag, 1902, pp. 199-230. [Regards Sg as the most important Swedish writer since C. J. L. Almqvist. Sprengel concentrates on the pre-Inferno works of which only *Mäster Olof*, *Röda rummet*, and *Utopier i verkligheten* are discussed in any detail, with brief comments on *Sömngångarnätter*, *Giftas*, *Det nya riket*, *I havsbandet*, and a few others, of which only *Gustav Vasa* was written after 1898. He concludes that 'Sg is a man who lives in words, and no Swedish prose is stronger or more expressive than his']

[B2:358] Sprigge, Elizabeth, 'Strindberg – Towards an Interpretation', *Life and Letters* (London), 52 (1947), 181-191.

[B2:359] Sprinchorn, Evert, 'Strindberg and the Changing World', *Swedish Book Review* (Lampeter), 1986 (Supplement), pp. 10-11, 13. [Argues that, whereas modern sexual politics has made Sg's naturalistic works difficult to assess objectively, in his post-Inferno works he remains 'the most modern of moderns']

[B2:360] Ståhle Sjönell, Barbro, 'Strindberg's Mixing of Genres', in Michael Robinson, ed., **B1:373**, *Strindberg and Genre*, pp. 48-60. [Applies Morten Nøjgaard's terminology, in which literary works are categorised according to four registers – the lyrical, narrative, dramatic, and didactic – in order to chart Sg's often ambivalent relationship with literary genres. Few, if any, of his works adopt one register to the exclusion of at least one other, but there is a greater tendency to mix registers in the works he wrote after the Inferno crisis. Illustrated with brief reference to a wide range of texts]

[B2:361] Ståhle Sjönell, Barbro, 'Strindbergs registerblandning', *Strindbergiana* (Stockholm), 9 (1994), pp. 50-64. ['Strindberg's Mixing of Genres'. Swedish version of **B2:360**]

[B2:362] Stefanov, Konstantin, 'Avgust Strindberg', *Hiperion* (Sofia), 1924, pp. 331-339.

[B2:363] Steiger, Edgar, 'Die Tragödie Strindberg', *März* (München), 3:3 (1909), 459-465. ['Strindberg's Tragedy']

[B2:364] Steiger, Edgar, 'Das Rätsel Strindberg', *Die Glocke* (München), 1 (1915-16), 704-717. ['The Riddle of Strindberg']

[B2:365] Stockenström, Göran, 'The Grain of Sand and The Wild Flower: Strindberg's Representational Dilemma', in Sarah Death and Helena Forsås-Scott, eds, *A Century of Swedish Narrative: Essays in Honour of Karin Petherick*, Norwich: Norvik Press, 1994, pp. 31-50. [Reflects on Sg's recourse to science in the mid-1890s and his subsequent development of new narrative and dramatic modes of representation in order to demonstrate what he describes as 'the infinite order of what seems to be a great chaos' and the complex nature of reality as he now experienced it. *Inferno* and *Legender* open the way for a series of plays in which Sg explains the ways of God to man through stories of individual pilgrimage, but he also explores collective issues and castigates contemporary capitalism for its unrestrained appropriation of human values in e.g. *Götiska rummen* and *Svarta fanor*. Stockenström focuses primarily on *Till Damaskus I*, *Dödsdansen*, *Spöksonaten*, and *Ockulta dagboken*, and seeks to demonstrate how, in the synthesis of *En blå bok*, in which all his later themes are rehearsed, Sg turns away from fiction to discursive practices in order 'to make his readers understand the economy and harmony of his new cosmos, where all things serve as ingredients of the divine plan']

[B2:366] Stoessl, Otto, 'Neues von Strindberg', *Die literarische Echo* (Berlin), 7 (1904-05), Sp. 1625-1627. ['New Work by Strindberg'. Reviews recent German translations of *Ensam*, *Götiska rummen*, and *Dödsdansen*. Remarks of Sg's later dramaturgy: 'The way in which in these plays a schematic, almost linear form of representation depicts the basic features of an individual case is both tragic and deeply moving, even if it can hardly be transferred to the stage']

[B2:367] Stonier, George W., 'Strindberg's Middle Years', in *Gog Magog and Other Critical Essays*, London: J. M. Dent & Son Ltd., 1933, pp. 96-115. [A curiously titled essay since it deals mainly with Sg's experiences in 1894-97, as recorded in *Inferno*. For Stonier there is an affinity here with Van Gogh and these experiences presaged Sg's greatest achievement as a writer, namely the dramatic exploration of unconscious experience and the world of dreams in the later plays, most notably the 'alternately enchanting and terrifying' *Till Damaskus*, *Ett drömspel*, and *Spöksonaten*. Whereas today Ibsen's plays 'have gone shabby', it is increasingly clear that 'there has been no dramatist since [Sg's] death who can compare with him']

[B2:368] Stounbjerg, Per, 'En melankolisk konstellation. Konstruktion av ett mönster i Strindbergs författarskap', in Ulf Olsson, red., **B1:357**, *Strindbergs förvandlingar*, pp. 27-56. ['A Melancholy Constellation. The Construction of a Pattern in Strindberg's Writing'. Although Sg placed experimentation and continual change at the heart of his artistic programme, a number of repeated motifs and patterns do exist. One of these may be associated with melancholy, as defined by Julia Kristeva. Stounbjerg analyses this pattern as one in which pleonastic excesses go hand in hand with hyperbole, and relates it to Sg's recurring sense of a paradise lost and consequently to its significance for his attitude to language and narrative method, making particular reference to *Tjänstekvinnans son*, *Inferno*, *Det nya riket*, *Ensam*, *I havsbandet*, and the Chamber Plays of 1907]

[B2:369] Stounbjerg, Per, 'Strindbergs modbydeligheder', in Christa Lykke Christensen, Knut Ove Eliassen, and Tore Eriksen, red., *Sanseligheder*, Aarhus: Aarhus universitetsforlag, 1993, pp. 217-236. ['Strindberg's Abominations'. Maintains that disgust or loathing is at the heart of Sg's project, which is analysed here in relation to the liminal area between truth and fiction, as well as his need to provoke in a language where 'filth' (*smuds*) is frequently employed as a metaphor and figures as a motif in several works in which the plot often has the dynamic of revulsion. Stounbjerg motivates his argument with reference principally to *Tjänstekvinnans son*, *En dåres försvarstal*, 'Tschandala', *Legender*, *Svarta fanor*, and the Chamber Plays of 1907]

[B2:370] Suesser, Ignacy, 'August Strindberg. Zarys literacki', in A. Strindberg, *Ojciec*, Lvov, 1898, pp. 3-22. ['August Strindberg: A Literary Outline'. The introduction to the 2nd edition of Suesser's pioneering Polish translation of *Fadren* in which he provided the first overview of Sg's life and work to date in Polish. Suesser expresses his sympathy for what he calculates are the four types of women portrayed by Sg *vis-à-vis* Ibsen's more limited range, and praises him for the perception of his psychological analysis in *I havsbandet*, as well as for his unsurpassed artistic mastery in both prose and drama. 'As an artist Sg could meet the sternest requirement. The technique of his novels and plays often differs markedly from the established canons, and gives further proof of his unsurpassed mastery as a writer.... A reader of Sg's works loses his objective judgement, and turns either into a fanatical adversary of the poet, or into his ardent advocate and admirer']

[B2:371] Sundberg, Björn, 'Tecken ristade av Skaparens hand', in Margareta Brundin, *et al.*, red., **B1:88**, *20 x Strindberg*, pp. 174-185. ['Signs Inscribed by the Creator's Hand'. Sundberg identifies a tension in Sg's post-Inferno works between, on the one hand, an apprehension of the world as fragmentary and without meaning in accordance with Sg's experience during the Inferno years, and, on the other, the certainty, or at least hope, that there is a discernable order within apparent disorder, to be deciphered in the traces left by a divine hand in both nature and history. According to Sundberg, one aspect of this dichotomy has correctly been related to Sg's engagement with modernity; the other, is more problematic, especially when it is explored in relation to the later history plays, including *Bjälbo jarlen* and *Siste riddaren*, which Sundberg examines in light of the conception of history articulated by Sg in 'Världshistoriens mystik' and *En blå bok*. Both of these would suggest that, depending on one's angle of vision, it is a question of a 'both-and' rather than an 'either-or': the world is both fragmentary and without apparent meaning, and yet endowed with an infinite coherence]

[B2:372] Svanberg, Victor, 'Strindberg och industrialismens genombrott i Sverige', in Ingvar Andersson, red., *Sverige i dikt och data 1865-1940*, Radiobiblioteket, Stockholm: Radiotjänst, 1941, pp. 34-46. ['Strindberg and the Industrial Revolution in Sweden'. Examines Sg's literary encounter with modernity in *Tjänstekvinnans son* which, for Svanberg, is 'perhaps his finest intellectual achievement', and (primarily) *Röda rummet*. 'His unrest drove him from nervous crisis to nervous crisis in the great cities of Europe', where he bore witness to what it had cost his generation to transform an isolated, homely Sweden into a modern economy. Originally a radio talk, broadcast 28 October 1940]

[**B2:373**] Svanberg, Victor, 'Strindberg och industrialismens genombrott i Sverige', in *Diktaren i samhället. Litteratursociologiska studier*, Stockholm: Wahlström & Widstrand, 1968, pp. 40-48. ['Strindberg and the Industrial Revolution in Sweden'. See **B2:372**]

[**B2:374**] Svanberg, Victor, 'Strindberg och industrialismens genombrott i Sverige', in Birger Bjerre, Gunnar Lokrantz, and Algot Werin, red., *Svenska litteraturstudier*, Lund: C. W. K. Gleerup, 1948, pp. 148-158. ['Strindberg and the Industrial Revolution in Sweden'. Rpr. of **B2:372**]

[**B2:375**] Svanberg, Victor, 'Strindberg och industrialismens genombrott i Sverige', in Sigvard Andrén, *et al.*, red., *Läsebok för grundskolan*, Stockholm: Svenska bokförlaget (Boniers), 1960, pp. 149-158. ['Strindberg and the Industrial Revolution in Sweden'. Rpr. of **B2:372**]

[**B2:376**] Svanberg, Victor, 'Strindberg och industrialismens genombrott i Sverige', in Sune Askaner and Olof Johansson, red., *Diktaren och tiden. litteraturval för fackskolor, fackgymnasier och folkhögskolor*, Lund: C. W. K. Gleerup, 1965, pp. 15-27. Illus. ['Strindberg and the Industrial Revolution in Sweden'. Rpr. of **B2:372**]

[**B2:377**] Svanberg, Nils, 'Ur Strindbergs prosautveckling', *Nysvenska studier* (Uppsala), 15 (1935), 229-249. ['From the Development of Strindberg's Prose'. Examines ways in which Sg's prose style develops from the early collection *Från Fjärdingen och Svartbäcken* to *I havsbandet* in 1890 with additional reference to several stories in *Svenska öden och äventyr* and a comparison with the narrative styles of his near contemporaries Per Hallström, Selma Lagerlöf, and Verner von Heidenstam]

[**B2:378**] Svanberg, Nils, 'Ur Strindbergs prosautveckling', in Göran Lindström, red., **B1:291**, *Strindbergs språk och stil*, pp. 17-35. ['From the Development of Strindberg's Prose'. Rpr. of **B2:377**]

[**B2:379**] Svensson, Conny, 'Strindberg on World History', in Göran Rossholm, Barbro Ståhle Sjönell, and Boel Westin, eds, **B1:389**, *Strindberg and Fiction*, pp. 23-29. [Discusses the collection of short stories *Historiska miniatyrer*, where Sg contravenes many of the conventions of the well-made short story, and the essay 'Världshistoriens mystik' (The Mysticism of World History, 1903), in which he extends his concern with history from a national perspective to the global. Wishing to affirm an underlying order in the sometimes apparently random events of history, an increasing role is assumed by the narrator, or a series of omniscient resoneurs, but in the long run the attempt to prove that behind us lies the best of imaginable world histories becomes an unprofitable strategy for an imaginative writer, and Sg ultimately adopts a new standpoint in *Nya svenska öden* and *En blå bok I-II*, one in which 'chaos manifests itself to be the neighbour of God']

[**B2:380**] Szalczer, Eszter, 'The Modes of the Spirit: Poetic Application of Theosophical Ideas in the Works of August Strindberg', in Berit I. Brown, ed., *Nordic Experiences: Exploration of Scandinavian Cultures*, Contributions to the Study of World Literature 71, Westport, Conn. and London: Greenwood Press, 1997, pp. 39-46. [Documents Sg's familiarity with Theosophy through his acquaintance with its Swedish adept, Carl von Bergen, and his principal correspondent during the Inferno crisis, Torsten Hedlund, as well as his knowledge of Mme Blavatsky and the movement's international dimension. Szalczer also considers both the relevance of Theosophy's conception of a multi-layered reality and its symbolism for his later writings, exemplified here by *I havsbandet*, *Jardin des Plantes*, *Legender*, *Taklagsöl*, *Svarta fanor*, and *Spöksonaten*. See the author's more detailed exposition of Sg's association with Theosophy in **B8:53**]

[B2:381] Szalczer, Eszter, 'Strindberg and the Visual Arts', *Performing Arts Journal* (New York), 25:3 (2003), 42-50. Illus. [Suggests that, paradoxically, Sg's continually shifting image persistently overshadows our perception of his work while during his life he sought, in numerous media, his true image amidst what he conceived of as a multitude of false copies and elusive doubles. Szalczer discusses his interest in various visual media as well as recent stagings of his plays and exhibitions of his paintings and photography in New York and elsewhere]

[B2:382] Szalczer, Eszter, 'Strindberg – vår text', in Anita Persson and Barbara Lide, red., **B1:366**, *Ja, må han leva!*, pp. 13-16. ['Strindberg – Our Text'. Argues for the relevance of Theosophy in Sg's polyphonic intertextuality. Szalczer suggests that Sg's element was controversy and confrontation]

[B2:383] Szewczyk, G[rażyna Barbara], 'Zmartwychwstanie Augusta Strindberga', *Poglądy* (Katowice), 1976:8, pp. 16-18. ['The August Strindberg Revival']

[B2:384] Theodor, Josef, 'Die Tragödie des Hochmuts', *Das literarische Echo* (Berlin), 4 (1901-02), Sp. 602-605. ['The Tragedy of Pride'. Discusses the new, religiously inclined Sg of *Inferno*, *Legender*, and *Till Damaskus*]

[B2:385] Theodor, Josef, 'Der neue Strindberg', *Nord und Süd* (Breslau), 103 (1902), 237-243. ['The New Strindberg'. Comments on the post-Inferno, non-naturalistic Sg]

[B2:386] Törnqvist, Egil, 'Strindberg fornisländare', *TijdSchrift voor Skandinavistiek* (Groningen), 17:2 (1996), 7-19. ['Strindberg the Ancient Islander'. Surveys Sg's interest in early Icelandic literature and its influence on his writing, sometimes mediated by previous literary portrayals of the viking period by Oehlenschläger, Ibsen, and Bjørnson. Törnqvist focuses particularly on *Den fredlöse* and the aborted apprentice piece, *Blotsven*, of which Sg writes in *Tjänstekvinnans son*, but he also discusses the extent of Sg's early reading in Icelandic literature, his student essay on Oehlenschläger's *Hakon Jarl hin Rige* (Earl Hakon the Mighty, 1807), and the attempt in *Den fredlöse* to reproduce something of the laconic style of the Icelandic sagas. According to Törnqvist, Oehlenschläger in *Hakon Jarl*, Ibsen in both *Kongsemnerne* (The Pretenders, 1863) and *Hærmændene paa Helgeland* (The Vikings at Helgeland, 1857), and Bjørnson in *Mellem Slagene* (Between Battles, 1857), have all left their mark on the play's themes and style. He also comments on the early fragment, 'Början av Ån Bogsveigs saga' (The Beginning of Ån Bogsveig's Saga, 1872), Sg's observations on Icelandic in the essay 'Latin eller svenska?' (Latin or Swedish, 1872), and the later stories with Icelandic settings in *Hövdingaminnen*, the dramatic fragment 'Sagan om Stig Storverks son', and the use he made of the Icelandic 'Solsången' (Song of the Sun) in *Spöksonaten*]

[B2:387] Trocki, I. M., 'A. Strindberg', 1-2, *Misao* (Beograd), 1928: 10 and 27, pp. 205-206, 355-360. [R.560]

[B2:388] Vedel, Valdemar, 'August Strindberg (1899. 1912.)', in **B1:472**, *Firsernes Førere. Karakteristiker og Kritiker*, pp. 91-94. [Brings together two commemorative articles in which Vedel maintains that it was through his ability as a creative artist that Sg integrated his turbulent personality, as well as a review of Anna Bloch as Eleonora in *Påsk*, **E34:428**]

[B2:389] Vilas-Boas, Gonçalo, 'August Strindberg: "Um anatomista do falhanço humano"', *Runa revista portuguesa de estudos germanísticos* (Lisbon), 5-6 (1986), 127-142. ['August Strindberg: An Anatomist of Human Failings'. Argues that Sg's works are a projection of the deepest human drives with reference to a broad range of works which include *Mäster Olof*, *Till Damaskus*, *Ett drömspel*, *Inferno*, *Klostret*, *Legender*, *Röda rummet*, *Hemsöborna*, *I havsbandet*, *Giftas*, *Dödsdansen*, *Påsk*, *Stora landsvägen*, the Chamber Plays, *Fröken Julie*, and the other naturalist dramas. German summary]

[B2:390] Vilas-Boas, Gonçalo, 'As vivissecações naturalistas de Strindberg', *Ada'gio* (Evora), No. 17 (December 1996), pp. 22-35. Illus ['Strindberg's Naturalist Vivisections'. Examines Sg's pseudo-scientific role as a psychological naturalist or vivisector, focusing mainly on his authorial stance in *Fordringsägare*, *Den starkare*, *Paria*, *Fröken Julie*, and *Giftas*]

[B2:391] Vinge, Louise, 'De besatta i Lund – om Strindbergs *Legender*, *Påsk* och *Karl XII*', in Helmer Lång, red., *Galningar i Skåne*, Höganäs: Wiken, 1989. Illus. 167 pp. ['The Mad in Lund – Strindberg's *Legends, Easter, and Charles XII*'. Explores Sg's personal links with Lund during the later 1890s, the account which he gives of his sojourns there in *Inferno* and (especially) *Legender*, and his conception of the town as a metaphysical locality given over to the chastising, training, and salvation of the individual soul. To Sg, Lund was 'a place for humiliation and atonement', which he often interpreted in Swedenborgian terms and Vinge demonstrates how these are all aspects of *Påsk* and *Karl XII*, the two plays he later set in Lund, which have much in common with the view of the place he adopted in *Legender*. As in the autobiographical fiction, so in these plays he dramatised his own experiences in terms of other people's fates, unlike *Till Damaskus*, where they are dramatised very much in private terms]

[B2:392] Vinge, Louise, 'De besatta i Lund – om Strindbergs *Legender*, *Påsk* och *Karl XII*', *Strindbergiana* (Stockholm), 9 (1994), pp. 65-79. [Rpr. of **B2:391**]

[B2:393] Vinge, Louise, 'De besatta i Lund – om Strindbergs *Legender*, *Påsk* och *Karl XII*', in *Skånska läsningar*, Malmö: Akademieförlaget Corona AB, 1999, pp. 131-145. [Rpr. of **B2:391**]

[B2:394] Vinge, Louise, 'Mat och makt i *Röda rummet* och *Giftas*', *Meddelanden från Strindbergssällskapet* (Stockholm), 67 (1983), pp. 1-12. ['Food and Power in *The Red Room* and *Getting Married*'. A perceptive examination of the theme and imagery of food in Sg's *œuvre* and how, in *Röda rummet* and *Giftas*, this is related to the manifestation of power, thus anticipating its function in several post-Inferno works, including *Dödsdansen* and the Chamber Plays]

[B2:395] Volboudt, Pierre, 'Strindberg précurseur', *Équivalences et confrontations. XXe siècle*, 25 (1963), 3-9. [Strindberg Our Precursor']

[B2:396] Vowles, Richard B., 'Strindberg and the Symbolic Mill', *Scandinavian Studies* (Lawrence, Kansas), 34:2 (1962), 111-119. [Vowles dates Sg's preoccupation with the symbol of the remorselessly grinding mill from the Inferno period which he derives from the image of God's mills that grind slowly but exceedingly fine. One such mill, which is also derived from the landscape near Klam in Lower Austria that Sg knew from the visits he paid to Frida Uhl's family there, features in Scenes 6 and 12 of

Till Damaskus but, as *Inferno* and *Legender* both make plain, Sg's mill is primarily a mechanism of the mind and a metaphor of conscience, heightened so that its function is both psychopathic and theatrical. In the Swedenborgian terms which he employed at this time, it is related to the action of inspection, examination, or self-scrutiny, and it is as such that it is introduced into *Brott och brott*, *Gustav Adolf*, *Kronbruden*, and *Stora landsvägen*]

[B2:397] Warburg, Karl, 'Litteraturbref från Sverige', *Samtiden* (Oslo), 16 (1905), [105]-118. ['Literary Letter from Sweden'. Comments briefly on the newly published *Ensam*, *Sagor*, *Götiska rummen*, *Gustav III*, and *Ordalek och småkonst*]

[B2:398] Ward, R. H., 'Johan August Strindberg', in Ernest William Martin, ed., *The New Spirit*, London: Denis Dobson Ltd., 1946, pp. 84-102. [Notes the clarity and persistence with which certain themes are woven obsessionally into the texture of Sg's work. These include 'the relative', or the 'relatedness of things', woman, 'self-esteem', the 'superman', and 'persecution'. But what renders Ward's ensuing exploration of Sg's obsessional system and of the general implications of his ultimately religious beliefs for his literary works so inadequate is that it is conducted with virtually no reference to the works themselves]

[B2:399] Wertheimer, Paul, 'Blick auf Strindberg', in *Brüder im Geiste*, Wien und Leipzig, 1923, pp. 198-205.

[B2:400] Wien, Alfred, 'August Strindberg', *Westermanns Jahrbuch der Illustrierten Deutschen Monatshefte* (Braunschweig), 112 (1912), pp. [751]-760. Illus. [A survey of Sg's career, published apropos his recent death]

[B2:401] Young, Vernon, 'Strindberg's Ghosts', *The New Criterion* (New York), 3:7 (1985), 71-79. [A general assessment in a review essay of Olof Lagercrantz's biography, **R:1232**. Young focuses primarily on the plays and rejects what he regards as national characteristics. Thus, 'His best plays are distinguished by their internal consistency and their psychological persuasiveness'. Many of them, however, are 'hard to take', and his 'pious outlook is thoroughly Swedish'. Thus, Sg has no humour, and the morbid intensity of his outlook is antithetical to the non-Swede; overall, he 'commands attention' but 'resists attention'. See **B1:368** and **U1:245**]

[B2:402] Zupan, Vinko, 'Avgust Strindberg', *Ljubljanski zvon* (Ljubljana), 32:7 (1912), 370-375. [An assessment of Sg's achievement prompted by his recent death]

[B2:403] Župančič, Mirko, 'August Strindberg in naturalizem', *Problematika tragedije*, Maribor: ZaloÏba Obzorja, 1987, pp. 107-148. ['August Strindberg and Naturalism'. A study of 19th-Century European literature, including a discussion of Sg as a naturalist tragedian in *Fadren* and *Fröken Julie*]

[B2:404] Z. V. [Z. Vengerova], '[Huneker, J., *Iconoclasts. A Book of Dramatists*]', *Vestnik Evropy* (Moscow), 1906:5, pp. 393-401. [A review of **D1:203**, including a more general discussion of Sg, pp. 397-401. E.759]

B3. Reception Studies

[*The majority of entries in this section concern studies in literary reception, a significant research field particularly where Strindberg studies in Germany and Poland are concerned. It also includes a number of slight but pertinent early pieces, such as Suesser,* **B3:409**, *which* *were among the first to bring Sg's work to the attention of readers in another language area, In this respect, Ola Hansson's role as an intermediary between contemporary Scandinavian literature and its reception in France, Germany, and Russia is also relevant, as are several books or essays which played a significant role for the way in which Sg was initially received in a particular country or language. But the same applies to many of the earliest discussions of his work and personality in Scandinavia as well. Moreover, many accounts of his misogyny or religious views listed in sections* **B8** *and* **B9** *performed a similar role.*

Discussions of Sg's reception in the theatre frequently take a different form and are relevant both to many entries included in sections **D1** *and* **D2** *as well as in numerous items listed under individual plays, where the sheer volume of productions and reviews at different times in various countries is indicative of the ongoing reception of his work. So, too, are many of the entries in the section devoted to miscellaneous material,* **U**, *especially those linked to the various anniversaries of Sg's birth and death*]

[B3:1] Ahé, Karl-Rainer von de, *Rezeption schwedischer Literatur in Deutschland 1933-45*, Hattingen: Verlag Dr Bernd Kretschmer, 1982, pp. 230-235. ['The Reception of Swedish Literature in Germany, 1933-45'. Includes a discussion of Sg's reception in Germany during the Third Reich]

[B3:2] Ahlstedt, Eva, 'L'Accueil critique des *Mariés* en France en 1885 et cent ans plus tard', in Gunnel Engwall, ed., **B1:121**, *Strindberg et la France*, pp. 127-135. ['The Critical Reception of *Getting Married* in France in 1885 and a Century On'. Compares the reception of the two French translations of *Giftas* (by Jules Henry Kramer of Volume One only as *Les Mariés* in 1885 and of both volumes and the two Prefaces by Ahlstedt and Pierre Morizet as *Mariés!* in 1986). This confirms how better prepared present-day French reviewers are to understanding Sg's intentions. The eight reviews of the first translation were generally favourable, even commenting approvingly on the translation itself, and they sometimes included background material on the author, who was seen as neither a feminist nor a misogynist but rather as an author of the 'juste milieu' who was concerned with the subject of marriage and women's emancipation, and argued in favour of the former as woman's natural condition. However, reviewers of the later translation were now aware of Sg's reputation both as a dramatist and a misogynist, and read him accordingly. With two exceptions *Mariés!* elicited a largely positive response, even if the reviewer sometimes sought to rebut Sg's anti-feminism. But whereas his French contemporaries, considered Sg a perfectly 'reasonable' writer, a hundred years later he is grouped among a select set of admirable irrational writers, 'les écrivains admirablement déraisonnables']

[B3:3] Ahlstedt, Eva, 'Strindberg à Paris: l'accueil des *Mariés* (1885-1886)', in Gunnar von Proschwitz, ed., *Influences. Relations culturelles entre la France et la Suède*, Acta Regiae Societatis Scientiarum et Litterarum Gothoburgensis, Humaniora 29, Göteborg: Société Royale des Sciences et des Belles-lettres, 1988, pp. 235-267. ['Strindberg in Paris: The Reception of *Getting Married*'. Ahlstedt explains how, living in voluntary exile during the mid-1880s, Sg sought to secure a reputation in France, partly by writing in French himself and partly through translations like Jules Henri Kramer's version of *Giftas I*. The latter was reviewed at some length in a number of French journals, as well as the Italian *Gazzetta Letteraria Artistica e Scientifica*, 6 June 1885, and these early responses, republished here, indicate how Sg was read in the light of contemporary French writers (especially Zola, Maupassant, and Huysmans), with the reviewers often providing a necessary, but sometimes very partial, overview of his work prior to *Giftas*. Nevertheless, this interest was short-lived and, for the time being at least, he was forced to abandon his hopes of establishing himself as a writer in France]

[B3:4] Ahlström, Stellan, 'Barbaren i Paris', *Ord och Bild* (Stockholm), 56:5 (1947), 257-262. Illus. ['The Barbarian in Paris'. According to Ahlström, Sg experienced the autumn following his arrival in Paris in 1894 as a period of disappointment and miscalculation. French journals were reluctant to publish the essays that he wrote for them in French and he responded by writing 'Le Barbare à Paris' for *Gil Blas* (8 August 1895) in which he traces and identifies with a long tradition of Swedish cultural exchanges with France, dating back to 1542. In fact, French interest in Scandinavia during the 1890s culminated in the staging of *Fadren* at Théâtre de l'Œuvre in December 1894 and the publication of his essay on 'L'Infériorité de la femme' in *La Revue blanche* (1 January 1895). Both *Till Damaskus* and *Brott och brott* record his experience of Paris where he is once again in vogue today, not least through the influence he has had on Sartre's drama *Huis clos*]

[B3:5] Ahlström, Stellan, '*Fadren* i Paris', *Expressen* (Stockholm), 19 July 1954. ['*The Father* in Paris'. Discusses the reception accorded Sg and *Fadren* in the French press following the Parisian première at the Théâtre de l'Œuvre in 1894]

[B3:6] Ahlström, Stellan, 'När Strindberg erövrade Paris', *Göteborg Handels- och Sjöfarts Tidning*, 7 July 1950. ['When Strindberg Conquered Paris']

[B3:7] Ahlström, Stellan, 'Strindberg à la conquête de Paris', *Cahiers naturalistes* (Paris), 3:7 (1957), pp. 315-327. ['Strindberg and the Conquest of Paris'. Reprint of Michèle Cazaux's translation of the compte-rendu of Ahlström's thesis, **B3:13**]

[B3:8] Ahlström, Stellan, 'Strindberg et la critique française de son époque', *Orbis Litterarum* (Copenhagen), 13:3-4 (1958), 133-140. ['Strindberg and the French Critics of His Age'. Documents Sg's reception in the French press between 1888 and 1894, including critical responses to the premières of *Fröken Julie*, *Fadren*, and *Fordringsägare* at the Théâtre Libre and the Théâtre de l'Œuvre, and the controversies provoked by his essays 'L'Infériorité de la femme' in *La Revue Blanche* and 'La barbare à Paris' in *Gil Blas*]

[B3:9] Ahlström, Stellan, 'Strindberg och den belgiska kritiken', *Svensk Litteraturtidskrift* (Stockholm), 25:2 (1962), 82-89. Illus. ['Strindberg and the Belgian Critics'. Charts the progress of Sg's European renown as it passes to Belgium via Germany and France. Lugné-Poe's production of *Fordringsägare* was performed at the Théâtre du Parc in Brussels the day after its Paris première and, though often favourably reviewed, it was received in the light of earlier French reviews, which suggested the play owed as much to Alexandre Dumas *fils* as to Ibsen. While Lugné-Poe was naturally linked with symbolism through his productions of the plays of the Belgian, Maeterlinck, the raw, even brutal power of *Fordringsägare* was acknowledged. Six months later Lugné-Poe returned with his production of *Fadren*, which was also well received. On the whole, Ahlström concludes that the initial impact of these two plays was more favourable in Belgium than in France]

[B3:10] Ahlström, Stellan, 'Strindberg och Italien', *Utlandssvenskarna* (Stockholm), 18:12 (1956), 16-22. ['Strindberg and Italy'. Documents Sg's links with Italy and his reception there]

[B3:11] Ahlström, Stellan, 'Strindberg och Rumänien', *Meddelanden från Strindbergssällskapet* (Stockholm), 53-54 (1974), p. 21. ['Strindberg and Romania'. Reports that Sg's reputation as a dramatist is currently high in Romania where eleven plays have just been published in good translations, made directly from the Swedish by Valeriu Munteanu]

[B3:12] Ahlström, Stellan, 'Strindbergs deutsche Freunde', in Wilhelm Friese, Hrsg., **B3:168**, *Strindberg und die deutschsprachigen Länder*, pp. 45-51. ['Strindberg's German Friends'. Documents Sg's affinity with aspects of German culture, including Beethoven, Goethe, Schiller, and Nietzsche; his association with the Austrian translator Mathilde Präger who published under the pseudonym of Erich Holm and introduced several of his pre-Inferno works to a German readership which included Freud; and his friendship with the doctor and pioneer of local anaesthesia, Carl Ludwig Schleich, the poet, Richard Dehmel (1863-1920), and others in the Ferkel circle in Berlin during the early 1890s]

[B3:13] Ahlström, Stellan, *Strindbergs erövring av Paris. Strindberg och Frankrike 1884-1895*, Acta Universitatis Stockholmiensis 2, Stockholm: Almqvist & Wiksell, 1956. Illus. 371+XVIII pp. ['Strindberg's Conquest of Paris: Strindberg and France, 1884-1895'. Although further material has emerged since Ahlström presented his findings and the book lacks any attempt at literary (or even dramatic) analysis, this remains the standard source of information about Sg's protracted attempt to establish himself as a presence on the Parisian literary and theatrical scene. It traces his endeavours from the publication of *Giftas* in French to the staging of *Fröken Julie* at the Théâtre Libre and of *Fordringsägare* and *Fadren* at the Théâtre de l'Œuvre. But Ahlström also pays attention to the publication in France of Georges Loiseau's revised version of *En dåres försvarstal*, the controversy provoked by publication of the polemical essay 'L'Infériorité de la femme' in *La Revue Blanche*, and Sg's notoriety as a chemist and alchemist as reported in the French dailies. Copious reference is made to comments on Sg in the contemporary French press as well as to the often impassioned discussion occasioned by the passing prominence of Scandinavian writers in France during the 1890s (Ibsen's more entrenched place in the Parisian theatre is a recurring point of comparison). Much use is made of Sg's then largely unpublished letters as well as of other manuscript sources, including the papers of his translator, Georges Loiseau. Many aspects of *fin-de-siècle* French culture which were analysed almost contemporaneously by Gunnar Brandell in *Strindbergs Infernokris*, **B1:55**, are ignored by Ahlström whose emphasis is on Sg's relationship to the Naturalism of Zola and his disciples. Nor does Ahlström offer a detailed study of Sg's own attempts to write directly in French or of Loiseau's later revisions of several of these texts. Nevertheless, the book is rich in circumstantial detail and, wittingly or not, it confirms that, for all his efforts to conquer Paris, it was ironically in Germany some two decades later that Sg finally gained a truly European reputation. Summary in French, translated by Michèle Cazaux, pp. i-xviii. Doctoral dissertation]

[B3:14] — Andersson, H. F., *Samtid och framtid* (Stockholm), 14 (1957), 196-197.

[B3:15] — Bergholz, Harry, *Comparative Literature* (Eugene, Oregon), 10:2 (1958), 167-169. [Ahlström fulfills the highest expectations and illustrates how Sg's 'development ...

was symptomatic and occasionally anticipatory of the general development of Western literature as a whole']

[B3:16] — Bjøl, E., *Information* (Copenhagen), 21 March 1957.

[B3:17] — Björck, Staffan, *Dagens Nyheter* (Stockholm), 18 February 1957.

[B3:18] — Brandell, Gunnar, *Svenska Dagbladet* (Stockholm), 7 January 1957.

[B3:19] — Dahlström, Carl E. W. L., *Scandinavian Studies* (Menasha, Wisconsin), 29:4 (1957), 184-187.

[B3:20] — Ekelund, Erik, *Finsk Tidskrift* (Åbo), 1957, pp. 192-195.

[B3:21] — Elmquist, Carl Johan, *Politiken* (Copenhagen), 13 May 1958.

[B3:22] — Fredén, Gustaf, *Morgonbladet* (Stockholm), 6 May 1957.

[B3:23] — Hallsten, O., *Länstidningen Östersund*, 17 December 1956.

[B3:24] — Harrie, Ivar, *Expressen* (Stockholm), 16 December 1956.

[B3:25] — Jolivet, A[lfred], *Orbis litterarum* (Copenhagen), 12:2 (1957), 107-108. [Judges this to be a valuable addition to our knowledge of Sg's life and work. This scrupulously researched thesis also illuminates the cultural links between France and Sweden during this period]

[B3:26] — Kärnell, Karl-Åke, *Kvällsposten* (Malmö), 29 January 1957.

[B3:27] — Kihlman, H., *Göteborgs-Posten*, 12 February 1957.

[B3:28] — Kirchhoff-Larsen, C., *Børsen* (Copenhagen), 30 June 1957.

[B3:29] — Landquist, John, *Aftonbladet* (Stockholm), 18 December 1956.

[B3:30] — Levander, Hans, *Samlaren* (Uppsala), 37 (1956), pp. 160-165. [An essay review by Ahlström's thesis opponent who confirms that intensive research in French archives has enabled Ahlström to provide a far more detailed account of Sg's attempt to establish himself as a writer in Paris than hitherto. It possesses great documentary value, even if the interpretation placed on the facts presented here is sometimes questionable (for example, in the account of Sg's literary relations with Zola). Nor does this otherwise valuable thesis give a clear picture of Sg's abilities as a writer in French; here, Gravier's discussion in **B4:70** is a worthy complement]

[B3:31] — Levander, Hans, *Morgon-Tidningen* (Stockholm), 16 December 1956.

[B3:32] — Lindström, Hans, *Nya Pressen* (Helsingfors), 31 December 1956.

[B3:33] — Linnér, Sven, *Upsala Nya Tidning*, 19 December 1956.

[B3:34] — Neiiendam, H., *Ekstrabladet* (Copenhagen), 8 June 1957.

[B3:35] — Nils Ludvig [Nils Ludvig Olsson], *Lunds Dagblad*, 9 April 1957.

[B3:36] — Nils Ludvig [Nils Ludvig Olsson], *Studiekamraten* (Tollarp), 39 (1957), 57-59.

[B3:37] — Ollén, Gunnar, *Sydsvenska Dagbladet* (Malmö), 20 December 1956.

[B3:38] — Rinman, Sven, *Göteborgs Handels- och Sjöfartstidning*, 4 April 1957.

[B3:39] Ahlgren, Stig, 'Strindbergsbilden', 1-3, *Arbetet* (Malmö), 2, 9, and 25 September 1939. ['The Image of Strindberg'. A three-part article on Sg's image as it has been represented over the years in the frequently hostile Swedish press]

[B3:40] Ahlgren, Stig, 'Strindbergsbilden', in *Veckopressen och folket och andra stridsartiklar i litterära ämnen*, Stockholm: Tiden, 1940, pp. 164-184. [Rpr. of **B3:39**. Also comments on Sg in the essay 'Veckopressens historia' (The History of the Weekly Press) in the same volume]

[B3:41] Ahlund, Claes, and Bengt Landgren, *Från etableringsfas till konsolidering. Svensk akademisk litteraturundervisning 1890-1946*, Acta Universitatis Uppsaliensis, Historia litterarum 24, Uppsala, 2002. 612 pp. ['From Foundation to Consolidation: The Teaching of Literary History at Swedish Universities, 1890-1946'. Sg's place in the academic canon is a recurring point of reference, as is the teaching and syllabus of many Sg scholars and literary historians, including Karl Warburg, Martin Lamm, Victor Svanberg, Fredrik Böök, Olle Holmberg, and Johan Mortensen, all of whom have been concerned as critics with Sg]

[B3:42] [Ahnfelt, Arvid], 'Continental Literature in 1886: Sweden', *The Athenaeum* (London), No. 3088 (1 January 1887), pp. 7-31. [Sg is discussed by Ahnfelt, pp. 30-31, as part of a general survey. He criticises the second collection of *Giftas* as much inferior to the notorious first volume, which nevertheless displayed great wit and knowledge of life. He also observes that the first two volumes of *Tjänstekvinnans son* contain many examples of Sg's brilliant talent for character drawing. However, he supposes that 'perhaps our most popular writer at present is Alfred Hedenstierna']

[B3:43] Amfreville, P. d', 'L'Ibsen suédois', *Revues des Revues* (Paris), 5 (1892), 261-264. ['The Swedish Ibsen'. This presentation of 'Augustus' [sic] Sg as 'the new star currently lighting up the Scandinavian firmament' is in many respects a summary of Justin Huntly McCarthy's pioneering article in *The Fortnightly Review*, **B2:264**]

[B3:44] Angelov, Bozha, 'Vse okolo Narodnia teatar', *Demokratia* (Sofia), 2:4 (1921), 100-102. ['About the National Theatre once Again'. Defends Sg against those who oppose his introduction to the Bulgarian public in the translation and staging of *Dödsdansen* by the poet Geo Milev in Sofia, in 1920]

[B3:45] Anderberg, Rolf, 'Strindberg i Kina', *Göteborgs-Posten*, 10 June 1981. ['Strindberg in China']

[B3:46] Anderson, Ivar, red., *Svenska Dagbladets historia*, 3 vols, Stockholm: Svenska Dagbladet, 1960-84. ['The History of *Svenska Dagbladet*'. Volume Two includes essays on Oscar Levertin, Ivar Harrie, Fredrik Böök, Erik Hedén, and Victor Svanberg which discuss their response to Sg as man and writer in numerous articles and reviews published in the eminent Swedish daily]

[B3:47] Anon, 'America's Reception of the World's Supreme Woman Hater', *Current Literature* (New York), 51 (June 1912), pp. 698-700. [Includes references to early critics, translators, and translations, as well as to individual plays and productions]

[B3:48] Anon, 'August Strindberg: An Estimate', *The Living Age* (London and New York), No. 276 (22 February 1913), 495-499. [Although this early Anglo-Saxon appreciation of Sg, who is described here as 'the son of a man of family and a woman of none', refers briefly to the 'strange intensity' of some of the plays, the portrait it gives is based mainly on recent translations of the three autobiographical fictions, *En dåres försvarstal*, *Inferno*, and *Legender*, but it also comments on a number of other works (including *Fröken Julie*, *Brott och brott*, and *Den starkare*) in passing. Sg is criticised for his lack of self-mastery as well as for his partial vision: 'the normal mind cannot be the better for being dragged through a minute analysis of such uncleanness, such wretchedness, as are found in the[se] three autobiographical books'. And all of his works 'tell the same story – of a mind raging at life because it is blind to three quarters of life, and cursing the world because it has not learned the rudiments of self-mastery'. 'Till a few months ago scarcely any one in England knew more of Sg than they could learn from floating gossip about a mad Swedish author with no very savoury reputation', and these recent translations prompt the question: 'if this man…had taken plenty of exercise, had known the value of cold water in large quantities for internal and external use, had tuned himself up, body and mind, by the simple self-mastery implied in these things, would not his great brain have produced work with more in it of the beauty that preserves?']

[B3:49] Anon, 'August Strindberg', *New York Times Book Review*, 2 June 1912. [An editorial following Sg's death, which concludes that he will appeal to future generations through his novels rather than his plays]

[B3:50] Anon, 'August Strindberg auf Berliner Bühnen', *Berliner Hefte für geistiges Leben*, 4 (1949), 103-114. ['August Strindberg on the Berlin Stage'. A centennial survey of Sg's changing fortunes in the German theatre]

[B3:51] Anon, 'August Strindberg in America', *New York Times*, 25 October 1931.

[B3:52] Anon, 'August Strindberg i Tyskland', *Dagens Nyheter* (Stockholm), 9 February 1903. ['August Strindberg in Germany'. Points out that most Swedes remain in ignorance of Sg's standing in Germany, where translations of his books are frequently published and his plays are widely performed. Indeed, several works as yet unperformed in Sweden have already been staged there]

[B3:53] Anon, 'August Strindberg på fransk scen', *Dagens Nyheter* (Stockholm), 28 July 1892. ['August Strindberg on the French Stage'. Includes extracts on *Fadren* and *Fröken Julie* from Charles de Casanove's three approving articles about Sg in *Revue d'art dramatique*, **D2:553**, which were written with some input from Sg himself. The author also reports that *Fröken Julie* is shortly to be staged in Paris]

[B3:54] Anon, 'Avgust Strindberg', *Plutarkh XIX Veka* (Moscow?), 1888, pp. 58-59. [A biographical note which constitutes the first notice of Sg and his work in Russian. E.680]

[B3:55] Anon, 'Edward Gosses uttalanden om Sverige', *Vårt Land* (Stockholm), 23 July 1900. ['Edward Gosse's Comments on Sweden'. Reports Gosse's criticism of Sweden in the British press for the unsympathetic treatment it has accorded Sg and his works]

[B3:56] Anon, 'The French stage', *The Times* (London), 15 December 1894. [Reports the success of *Fadren* and *Fordringsägare* at the Théâtre de l'Œuvre in Paris, where the former was accorded 'an enthusiastic reception'. The author asks whether 'the French are growing sick of their own lighter and gayer drama?']

[B3:57] Anon, 'Ibsen in Strindberg v Ljubljani', *Slovenski narod* (Ljubljana), 5 March 1929. ['Ibsen and Strindberg in Ljubljuana']

[B3:58] Anon, 'Konst och litteratur', *Svenska Dagbladet* (Stockholm), 1 October 1889. [Reports that Sg is becoming increasingly noticed abroad, with *Hemsöborna* running as a feuilleton in the Vienna *Neue Freie Presse*, an extract from *Skärkarlsliv* just published in Germany in *Das Magazin für die Litteratur In- und Auslandes*, and general praise being garnered by his naturalist dramas, including acclaim for *Fröken Julie* from Zola in the *Revue d'art dramatique*, which also cites a letter from Sg to Zola]

[B3:59] Anon, 'Literatur och konst', *Stockholms Dagblad*, 31 July 1902. [Sg's latest collection of plays, *Svanevit*, *Kronbruden*, and *Ett drömspel*, has aroused considerable interest in Germany, where Emil Schering is an indefatigable advocate and translator of this 'highly gifted but uneven' writer. Whereas *Svanevit* has been the most favourably received of these plays in Sweden, in Germany it is *Kronbruden* that has garnered special praise]

[B3:60] Anon, 'Om Strindberg – medan han levde', *Konst och kultur* (Stockholm), 5:1 (1949), 16-17. ['On Strindberg – While He Lived'. Summarises contemporary responses to Sg in Sweden during his lifetime in a special issue of *Konst och kultur* commemorating the centenary of Sg's birth]

[B3:61] Anon, 'Rysk furstinna som Fröken Julie. Flera Strindbergspjäser framföras i Frankrike, *Svarta fanor* på scenen', *Svenska Folket* (Stockholm), 19 June 1910. ['Russian Princess as Miss Julie. Several Strindberg Plays Presented in France. *Black Banners* on the Stage'. Reports Lidia Borisovna Iavorskaia's performance as Julie, a role she played in both St Petersburg and Moscow]

[B3:62] Anon, 'Strindberg förbjuden i England', *Öresunds-Posten* (Ängelholm), 21 August 1911. ['Strindberg Forbidden in England'. Reports the continued refusal to license the performance of *Fröken Julie* there]

[B3:63] Anon, 'Strindberg i Amerika', *Arbetet* (Malmö), 2 August 1910. ['Strindberg in [North] America']

[B3:64] Anon, 'Strindberg i Amerika', 1-2, *Öresunds-Posten* (Ängelholm), 2 and 27 September 1912. ['Strindberg in [North] America']

[B3:65] Anon, 'Strindberg i Amerika', *Göteborgs Handels- och Sjöfartstidning*, 21 June 1912. ['Strindberg in America'. Notes the burgeoning interest in Sg in North America in the aftermath of his recent death]

[B3:66] Anon, 'Strindberg i England', *Social-Demokraten* (Stockholm), 14 May 1913. ['Strindberg in England'. On the reception of Sg in England]

[B3:67] Anon [Charles Langbridge Morgan], 'Strindberg in England', *The Times Literary Supplement* (London), 30 January 1930. [A substantial and mainly appreciative consideration of English translations of Sg's works to date, which ponders the reasons behind his continued non-acceptance in England in some detail. Written in conjunction with the publication of *Easter and Other Plays* and *Lucky Peter's Travels and Other Plays* in the Anglo-Swedish Literary Foundation edition of the dramas]

[B3:68] Anon, 'Strindberg introducerad i London', *Stockholms-Tidningen*, 15 December 1906. ['Strindberg Introduced to London'. Reports that *Samum* and *Den starkare* have both just been performed at The New Stage Club in London but the reporter also observes that the censor would not pass *Fröken Julie* for public performance and that there are few English versions of his plays, which have often to be translated from French or German versions]

[B3:69] Anon, 'Strindberg i Tyskland. Hvad en tysk öfversättare tror', *Nya Dagligt Allehanda* (Stockholm), 2 July 1906. ['Strindberg in Germany. What a Translator Thinks'. An interview with Emil Schering, who believes that Sg will soon supplant Ibsen as a major presence in German culture. To that end he is planning to launch a deluge of translations of all his works upon Germany]

[B3:70] Anon, 'Strindberg i Ungern', *Svenska Dagbladet* (Stockholm), 19 May 1912. ['Strindberg in Hungary'. News report on recent productions of several plays in Hungary where *Fordringsägare* had been performed in 1911 and *Kamraterna* in March 1912]

[B3:71] Anon, 'Strindberg och Polen', *Meddelanden från Strindbergssällskapet* (Stockholm), 44 (1970), p. 1. ['Strindberg and Poland'. Introduces an issue containing two articles on the reception of Sg in Poland: **B3:393**, Irena Sławińska and Marion Lewko, 'Strindberg och den polska teatern', and **B3:406**, Zygmunt Stoberski, 'August Strindberg i polska kritikers ögon efter 1945']

[B3:72] Anon, 'Strindbergssuccés i Tyskland', *Stockholms Dagblad*, 17 August 1910. ['Strindberg's Success in Germany'. Reports the successful tour of several German cities by a company of actors led by Albert Steinruck, with *Fröken Julie* among their repertoire]

[B3:73] Anon, 'Svensk litteratur i Ryssland', *Vårt Land* (Stockholm), 15 July 1901. ['Swedish Literature in Russia'. Reports an article in S. Sachenin's recently established Russian journal of historical studies which includes a comment on Sg's history plays by 'Sander']

[B3:74] Anon, 'Teater och musik. August Strindberg i England', *Dagens Nyheter* (Stockholm), 10 November 1892. ['August Strindberg in England'. Reports on Justin Huntly McCarthy's positive article about Sg's plays in *The Fortnightly Review*, **B2:264**]

[B3:75] Anon, 'Våra författare i *Encyclopedia Britannica*', *Stockholms-Tidningen*, 20 December 1902. ['Our Authors in the *Encyclopaedia Britannica*'. Reports that Edward Gosse's entry on Swedish literature in the new edition of *Britannica* displays a wide knowledge of the subject. He maintains that Sg is the foremost Swedish writer of the last twenty years. Summarises Gosse's comments in detail]

[B3:76] Anon, 'Warming Over Strindberg', *The Living Age* (New York), 4 April 1925, pp. 74-75. [Suggests that interest in Sg is waning in England and America due to inadequate translations, the indifference of theatre administrators, and the retention of his letters in the hands of people who are unwilling for them to enter the public domain]

[B3:77] Arbman, Hans, 'Stormare drabbar London. "Jag åker fortfarande på Bergmans klippkort"', *Dagens Nyheter* (Stockholm), 10 January 1995. ['Stormare Hits London. "I'm Still Travelling on [Ingmar] Bergman's Ticket"'. Interviews Peter Stormare about his forthcoming production of *Dödsdansen* at the Almeida Theatre, London, with reflections on Sg's current place in the British theatre]

[B3:78] Ballu, Denis, *Lettres nordiques en traduction française 1720-1995*, Nouvelles du Nord 5, Nantes: L'Elan, 1996. 239 pp. ['Nordic Literature in French Translation, 1720-1995'. Includes bibliographical details of some French studies of Sg, as well as of French translations of his works]

[B3:79] Barnes, Clive, 'Smorgasbord [sic] of Gloom Blooming', *New York Post*, 28 October 2001. [Comments on Ibsen and Sg, both of whom are flourishing on Broadway in the wake of September 11 with new productions of *Hedda Gabler* and *Dödsdansen*]

[B3:80] Baumgartner, Walter, *Triumph des Irrealismus. Rezeption skandinavischer Literatur im ästheticischen Kontext Deutschlands 1860-1910*, Beiträge zur Sprache, Literatur und Kultur der nordischen Länder 10, Neumünster: Karl Wachholz Verlag, 1979. 402 pp. ['The Triumph of Unreality. The Reception of Scandinavian Literature in the Aesthetic Context of Germany, 1860-1910'. Allots Sg a peripheral role in a study which focuses primarily on the German reception of Bjørnstjerne Bjørnson and Arne Garborg]

[B3:81] Baumgartner, Walter, 'Verpaßte Eroberung eines Terrains. Charakter und Funktion des ästhetischen Erwartungshorizonts in der deutschen Rezeption von Strindbergs naturalistischen Dramen um 1890', in Wilhelm Friese, Hrsg., **B3:168**, *Strindberg und die deutschsprachigen Länder*, pp. 195-224. ['The Failed Capture of a Terrain. The Character and Function of the Aesthetic Horizon of Expectation in the German Reception of Strindberg's Naturalistic Plays ca. 1890'. Baumgartner offers a perceptive analysis of Sg's early reception in Germany in the context of both Naturalism and Neo-Romanticism. He focuses on *Fadren*, *Fröken Julie*, and *Fordringsägare*, Sg's naturalism in comparison with that of Flaubert, Ibsen, and Zola, the theatre criticism of Alfred Kerr, and the role of Laura Marholm, Ola Hansson, and Lou Andreas-Salomé as cultural intermediaries between Germany and Scandinavia]

[B3:82] Bauër, Gérard, 'Auguste Strindberg', *Figaro Littéraire* (Paris), 29 January 1949. [Celebrates the centenary of Sg's birth which dates the moment of Sg's definitive arrival in France to Boris's staging of *Dödsdansen* at the Théâtre de l'Œuvre in 1921]

[B3:83] Bayerdörfer, Hans-Peter, '"Gestrig – und ganz modern". Beobachtungen zur Bühnen- und Inszenieringsgeschichte Strindbergs in der Bundesrepublik seit 1960', *Skandinavistik* (Kiel), 11:2 (1981), 127-139. ['"Dated – and Quite Modern". Observations on the Stage and Production History of Strindberg in the Federal Republic of Germany since 1960'. A wide-ranging and well-documented survey of West German productions of Sg's plays post-1960, including Ingmar Bergman's work at the Residenztheater in Munich, the impact on conventional German ideas about Sg of the many stagings of Dürrenmatt's *Play Strindberg*, and performances of several of the plays in new translations by Peter Weiss, which relate his work to Surrealism and the theatre of Arthur Adamov, Samuel Beckett, and Eugene Ionesco. Bayerdörfer sees 1970 and Bergman's production of *Ett drömspel* as a turning point, and believes there is reason to anticipate a Sg renaissance in the 1980s]

[B3:84] Bayerdörfer, Hans-Peter, 'Strindberg, rezensiert. Zur Bedeutung literarischer Klischeebildung für die Bühnenrezeption', in Wilhelm Friese, Hrsg., **B3:168**, *Strindberg und die deutschsprachigen Länder*, pp. 307-334. ['Strindberg Reviewed. On the Significance of Literary Clichés for the Reception of Theatrical Productions'. Focuses mainly on the response to Sg's plays in the German and Austrian press in the decade immediately preceeding the First World War when he had begun to supplant Ibsen in prominence on the German stage and became a seminal influence on the new German drama]

[B2:85] Bayerdörfer, Hans-Peter, Hans Otto Horch and Georg-Michael Schulz, *Strindberg auf der deutschen Bühne. Eine exemplarische Rezeptionsgeschichte der Moderne in Dokumenten (1890 bis 1925)*, Neumünster: Karl Wachholtz Verlag, 1983. 355 pp. ['Strindberg on the German Stage. An Exemplary History of the Reception of the Modern in Documents (1890 to 1925)'. A valuable collection of documents which charts Sg's reception in Germany from the early responses of Otto Rüdiger and Laura Marholm to the mid-1920s, when the great wave of German Sg productions in the first decades of the century had begun to ebb. It includes commentary by Bertolt Brecht, Robert Musil, and Karl Kraus, as well as by such influential drama critics as Alfred Kerr, Bernhard Diebold, and Herbert Ihering. All the documents are annotated, and the collection is prefaced by a scholarly review of Sg's standing in Germany in the light of the, then, present state of Reception theory]

[B3:86] — Jaron, Norbert, *Medienwißenschaft* (Tübingen), 2 (1994), 146-147.

[B3:87] — Menger, C., *Referatedienst zur Literaturwissenschaft* (Berlin), 20 (1988), 135-136.

[B3:88] Benson, Adolph B., and Naboth Hedin, eds, *Swedes in America, 1638-1938*, Published for the Swedish American Tercentenary Association, London: H. Milford, Oxford University Press, 1938, pp. 246-247, 251, 439. [Provides brief data about English translations of Sg's works and observes that, next to Swedenborg, the Swedish author who has exerted the greatest influence abroad is probably Sg]

[B3:89] Benson, Adolph B., and Naboth Hedin, eds, *Swedes in America, 1638-1938*, Published for the Swedish American Tercentenary Association, New York: Haskell House Publishers Ltd., 1969, pp. 246-247, 251, 439. [Facsimile Rpr. of **B3:88**]

[B3:90] Bentley, Eric, 'Strindberg in Europe', *Theatre Arts* (New York), 34:2 (1950), 20-25. Illus. [Surveys Sg's current standing in Europe. France is experiencing a re-enactment of the Strindberg revival which in Germany occurred a generation ago. Bentley includes a brief discussion of Jean Vilar's production of *Dödsdansen*, Roger Blin's staging of *Spöksonaten*, and Sacha Pitoëff's of *Till Damaskus*, but is most enthusiastic about Berthold Viertel's production of *Kronbruden* in Vienna. He wonders if 'European Strindberg' may in the end be 'a more provincial figure than the Swedish Sg?']

[B3:91] Berendsohn, Walter A[rthur], 'Die Wandlung des schwedischen Strindbergbildes', *Argentinisches Tageblatt* (Buenos Aires), 14 February 1954. ['The Transformation of the Swedish Image of Strindberg']

[B3:92] Berendsohn, Walter A[rthur], 'Strindberg heute', *Bühnen der Hansestadt Lübeck*, 1959-60:8, pp. 88-90. ['Strindberg Today']

[B3:93] Berendsohn, Walter A[rthur], 'Strindberg i Tyskland', *Göteborgs Handels- och Sjöfartstidning*, 29 January 1927. ['Strindberg in Germany']

[B3:94] Berendsohn, Walter A[rthur], 'Strindberg och Frankrike', in **B1:42**, *Strindbergsproblem*, pp. 202-227. ['Strindberg and France'. Berendsohn studies the place of France and French culture in Sg's life and work, from his first visit to Paris in 1875 and his early acquaintance with the novels and poetry of Victor Hugo, Alexandre Dumas *père*, and the Impressionists, about whom he was among the first to write in Sweden, to his more extended sojourn in Paris, Normandy, and Grez-sur-Loing during the 1880s, when he wrote *Bland franska bönder*, was commissioned by Mme Juliette Adam to write 'Lettres de Stockholm' for *La Nouvelle revue*, and sought to make his reputation there by writing directly in French. In the 1890s he again sought to establish himself as a writer in France, but while Catholic Paris may have influenced his outlook on religion, Berendsohn argues that he was now less involved in the mainstream of French culture. His correspondence in French with a variety of French speaking contacts was nevertheless considerable, and Balzac and Zola are but two among many French authors whose works he knew well. Berendsohn observes that, while he may not have been open to French culture as a whole, he knew how to utilise his experiences there artistically, and in *Kamraterna*, *Inferno*, *Legender*, and *Brott och brott* his portrayal of Paris is almost as impressive as his many accounts of Stockholm. However, a bibliographical survey of his work in French translation reveals that, compared to his reception in Germany, Sg has made little impact in France outside a relatively small circle of Parisian readers]

[B3:95] Berendsohn, Walter A[rthur], 'Strindberg und Österreich. Anlässlich der Eröffning des Strindbergweges in Klam (Oberösterreich) am 10. September 1950', *Meddel-*

anden från Strindbergssällskapet (Stockholm), 9 (1950), pp. 8-11. ['Strindberg and Austria. On the Occasion of the Opening of the Strindberg Way at Klam (Upper Austria)'. Celebrates the renaming of the path between Klambach and Schlucht as the 'Strindberg-Weg', in honour of the role it plays in the iconography of *Inferno* and *Till Damaskus*. Berendsohn also offers a brief overview of Sg's links with Austria, from his second wife, Frida Uhl, to the racist polemicist Jörgen Lanz-Liebenfelt, and comments on the reception of his plays there, particularly in productions mounted in Vienna by Josef Jarno]

[B3:96] Berendsohn, Walter A[rthur], 'Strindbergsrenässansen i Tyskland', *Meddelanden från Strindbergssällskapet* (Stockholm), 20 (1956), pp. 1-4. ['The Strindberg Renaissance in Germany'. A reawakened interest in Sg in Germany is confirmed not only by the frequent performance of his plays, which establish him as the forerunner of Franz Kafka, Jean-Paul Sartre, Tennessee Williams, and Jean Anouilh, but also through Julius Weismann's settings of *Svanevit*, *Ett drömspel*, and *Spöksonaten* as operas, a new German edition of his works in fresh translations, and the affirmation of his central role in general surveys of the development of modern drama. This renaissance in Sg's reputation can be dated to Oscar Fritz Schuh's production of *Ett drömspel* at the Theater am Kurfürstendamm, Berlin, in 1955]

[B3:97] Berg, Ruben G:son, 'Strindberg och 90-talskritiken', *Svenska Dagbladet* (Stockholm), 17 July 1921. ['Strindberg and the Critics of the 1890s'. Investigates the reasons behind Sg's poor critical reception in Sweden during the 1890s]

[B3:98] Berlogea, Ileana, 'August Strindberg. Omul, scriitorul, dramaturgul şi ce înseamnă el pentru noi', in *Teatrul românesc-teatrul universal: confluențe*, Iaşi: Junimea, 1983, pp. 168-194. ['August Strindberg. The Man, the Dramatist, and What he means to Us', in 'Romanian Theatre-World Theatre: Convergences']

[B3:99] Berlogea, Ileana, 'Strindberg and the Romanian Modern Theatre', in [Carl Reinhold Smedmark], ed., **D2:285**, *Strindberg and Modern Theatre*, pp. 85-100. [As well as surveying Sg's reception in the Romanian theatre from *Fadren* in 1920 and *Fröken Julie* in 1921 to the publication of new translations of the plays by Maria and Petre Banus and Valeriu Munteanu in 1972-73, Berlogea also pays brief attention to early translations of the novels and stories by I. Botez. Although she reveals that no close ties exist between Romanian and Swedish culture, she points out that Sg's plays appealed to Romanian intellectuals in the inter-war years when, often mediated by German Expressionism, they exerted considerable influence on such writers as Ion Marin Sadoveanu whose play, *Molima* (The Epidemics), is a variation on *Pelikanen*. For many years Sg's plays went unperformed, but the renewed interest in Sg of the last decade (1965-1975) may be attributed to a desire to imbue Romanian culture with the values of an authentic humanism. Berlogea quotes several contemporary reviews of productions of *Kristina* and Karlheinz Martin's staging of *Pelikanen*, as well as performances of *Fadren, Fröken Julie*, and *Dödsdansen*]

[B3:100] Bernardini[-Sjöstedt], L[éonie], *La Littérature scandinave*, Paris, 1894. [Includes Sg alongside Carl Michael Bellman, Esaias Tegnér, Viktor Rydberg, Carl Snoilsky, J. P. Jacobsen, Georg Brandes, Herman Bang, Arne Garborg, Alexander Kielland, and Jonas Lie, as well as Bjørnson and Ibsen, in a series of sketches in which modern Scandinavian writers are introduced to French readers. Includes a revised version of Bernardini's essay on *En dåres försvarstal*, **F4:22**]

[B3:101] — F. V., '*La Littérature scandinave*, Paris', *Vestnik Evropy* (St Petersburg), 12 (1894), 886-890. [Comments on Bernardini's presentation of Sg in **B3:100**, pp. 889-890, thus extending her role as a cultural intermediary from France to Russia]

[B3:102] Bethke, Artur, 'Strindberg-Rezeption in der Deutschen Demokratischen Republik', in Sven H. Rossel and Birgitta Steene, eds, *Scandinavian Literature in a Transcultural Context*, Papers from the XVth IASS Conference, Seattle: University of Washington, 1986, pp. 167-170. ['Strindberg's Reception in the German Democratic Republic'. Sg's reception in the DDR has been slow and was established only with the 50th anniversary of his death in 1962 and the publication of a translation of *Röda rummet* in 1963. In the theatre, the 1967 production of *Fröken Julie* at the Volkstheater in Rostock and of *Erik XIV* at the Maksim Gork'ii theatre in 1974 are important landmarks. Bethke notes that the former is now the most frequently performed of Sg's plays in the DDR while one of the most interesting of recent initiatives has been an adaptation of *Ett drömspel* for radio]

[B3:103] Billington, Michael, 'Seduced by Miss Julie', *The Guardian* (London), 29 February 2000. [Anticipates a new production of *Fröken Julie*, which remains Sg's most popular play in Britain, 'partly because it is short, realistic and combines the sex and class wars in a way we can recognise'; it also makes one wish 'our theatre would range more widely over the work of this uncomfortable genius']

[B3:104] Binder, Wolfgang, *Europäisches Drama und amerikanische Kritik. Skandinavische, deutschsprachige und russiche Dramatiker in der nordamerikanischen Kritik, 1890-1914*, Erlanger Beiträge zur Sprach und Kunstwissenschaft 51, Nürnberg: Verlag Hans Carl, 1974, pp. 167-198, 405-409. ['European Drama and American Criticism. Scandinavian, German-Speaking, and Russian Dramatists in North-American Criticism, 1890-1914'. A valuable study of Sg's North American reception, where Binder considers that criticism of European drama is, in the main, more conservative than the critical reaction to the modern novel. Also includes bibliographical material for both Sg's works in translation and critical studies of modern drama. English summary, pp. 488-490]

[B3:105] Bisztray, George, 'Recent Research on the Impact of Scandinavian Literature on Western Europe', *Yearbook of Comparative and General Literature* (Bloomington, Indiana), 34 (1985), pp. [101]-113. [A useful bibliographical survey which maintains that no writer 'has been treated more extensively than Sg' by (primarily West-German) reception research]

[B3:106] Borchsenius, Otto, 'August Strindberg och Danmark', *Sydsvenska Dagbladet* (Malmö), 26 May 1912. ['August Strindberg and Denmark'. Surveys Sg's links with Denmark and his reputation there in light of his recent death]

[B3:107] Björkman, Edwin, 'Strindberg and the Anglo-Saxon Mind', *Harpers Weekly* (New York), 30 August 1913.

[B3:108] Bordeaux, Henri, *Châteaux en Suède*, Paris: Hachette, 1928. 248 pp. ['Castles in Sweden'. Delights in Lucien Maury's extensive Scandinavian library where we can satisfy our curiosity on the spirit of the North, including Sg]

[B3:109] Boterf, Hervé le, *La Vie parisienne sous l'occupation*, 2 vols, Paris: Éditions France-Empire, 1974-75. 435, 371 pp. ['Parisian Life under the Occupation'. Illustrates how Jean

Vilar's productions of *Oväder* and *Dödsdansen* caught the mood of the city under German occupation and hence facilitated Sg's acceptance in France]

[B3:110] Bourdon, Georges, 'Exotisme', *Le Voltaire* (Paris), 15 February 1895. [Extends a positive welcome to Sg and the new Scandinavian drama which had recently criticised by Jules Lemaître in **B3:256** as antithetical to French values]

[B3:111] Boyer, Régis, 'Les Études scandinaves en France', *Scandinavica* (London), 4:2 (1965), 127-144. ['Scandinavian Studies in France'. Surveys the history of Scandinavian studies in France and observes that just now the great man is Sg. The number of translations and performances his plays increase without end. His work is eminently relevant today]

[B3:112] Boyer, Régis, 'Les Études scandinaves en France (1965-1999)', *Etudes Germaniques* (Paris), 54:4 (1999), [519]-580. ['Scandinavian Studies in France (1965-1999)'. See **B3:111**]

[B3:113] Brandell, Gunnar, 'Tredje gången gillt för Strindberg i Paris', *Svenska Dagbladet* (Stockholm), 6 December 1975. ['Third Time Lucky for Strindberg in Paris'. Considers the course of Sg's eventual acceptance as a major writer in France]

[B3:114] Brandenburg, Hans, 'Zur Bilanz der jüngsten literarischen Vergangenheit. Von 1900 bis 1925. A. Strindberg', *Die schöne Literatur* (Leipzig), 27 (1926), 294-299. ['A Resumé of the most Recent Literary History. From 1900 to 1925. A. Strindberg'. Focuses especially on the innovatory form of the Chamber Plays]

[B3:115] Brink, Lars, 'Författaren som idealgestalt. Fyra literaturhistoriska läroböcker för gymnasiet 1880-1945', *Litteratur och samhälle* (Uppsala), 1991:1, 94 pp. ['The Writer as Ideal Figure. Four Textbooks in Literary History for the Secondary School, 1880-1945'. Examines the image of the writer as it is presented in four standard literary textbooks by Karl Warburg, Richard Steffen, Josua Mjöberg, and Hjalmar Alving that have all been widely used in Swedish Secondary Schools. See **B3:116**]

[B3:116] Brink, Lars, *Gymnasiets litterära kanon. Urval och värderingar i läromedel 1910-1945*, Skrifter utgivna av Avdelning för litteratursociologi vid Litteraturvetenskapliga institutionen, Uppsala, 1992. Illus. 335 pp. ['The Literary Canon in the Swedish High School. Selection and Evaluations in School Textbooks, 1910-1945'. Asks if there was a consciously or unconsciously accepted literary canon in Swedish senior high schools in the period 1910-1945. Brink also studies the process of canon formation and the basis on which the selection of authors for inclusion, their evaluation, and the focus of discussion altered in several major textbooks, selected here for their frequent use and prominence in the annual reports of individual high schools. Analyses four such text books and four anthologies in general circulation at five moments – 1910-11, 1920-21, 1930-31, 1940-41, and 1945-46. The four literary histories are Karl Warburg's *Svensk litteraturhistoria i sammandrag* (1880-1907), Richard Steffen's *Svensk litteraturhistoria för den högre elementärundervisningen* (1904-08), Josua Mjöberg's *Svensk litteraturhistoria för den högre undervisningen* (1927-29), and Hjalmar Alving's *Svensk litteraturhistoria I-III* (1929-32, 1935). Brink observes changes in the works that were given most prominence (e.g. by the 1960s *Fröken Julie* and *Ett drömspel* had supplanted *Mäster Olof* as the most widely read of Sg's plays), while writers such as Heidenstam, Tegnér, Geijer, and Runeberg, who generally endorsed prevailing social values and were initially perceived to be of central importance, give way to writers who tend to challenge or attack received opinion, such as Thomas Thorild, C. J. L. Almqvist, and Sg. He also includes data on the reading of an often restricted range of works by Sg in Swedish secondary schools where *Mäster Olof, Röda rummet, Hemsöborna*, and Fredrik Böök's edition of three stories from *Svenska öden och äventyr*, **G7:23**, have enjoyed the widest circulation. Summary in English. Doctoral dissertation]

[B3:117] Brisson, Pierre, 'Strindberg i franska ögon', *Dagens Nyheter* (Stockholm), 9 February 1949. ['Strindberg in French Eyes']

[B3:118] Brown, Nils F:son, 'Strindberg i Amerika', *Sydsvenska Dagbladet* (Malmö), 31 August 1958. ['Strindberg in [North] America']

[B3:119] Brüggemann, Fritz, 'Strindberg-Dämmerung', *Form und Sinn* (Augsburg), 1 (2 June 1925), 331-334. ['The Twilight of Strindberg'. Pro-Ibsen and anti-Sg in tone. The latter is now 'yesterday's man'. 'His doctrines are the doctrines of yesterday']

[B3:120] Brüggemann, Fritz, 'Strindberg-Dämmerung', in Hans-Peter Bayerdörfer, Hrsg., **B2:85**, *Strindberg auf der deutschen Bühne*, pp. 337-338. [Rpr. of **B3:119**]

[B3:121] Bruns, Alken, *Übersetzung als Rezeption. Deutsche Übersetzer skandinavischer Literatur von 1860 bis 1920*, Skandinavistische Studien 8, Neumünster: Karl Wachholtz Verlag, 1977. 211 pp. ['Translation as Reception. German Translators of Scandinavian Literature from 1860 to 1920'. Comments briefly on Sg in a discussion of Marie Herzfeld's literary criticism and her work as a translator and cultural intermediary between Scandinavia and Austria/Germany. See **B1:169**]

[B3:122] Bry, Carl Christian, 'Das Drama des Auslandes. Die deutschen Theater nach dem Kriege 5. Die nordischen Dramatiker – Strindberg', *Die christliche Welt* (Stuttgart), 39 (1925), Sp. 513-515. ['Foreign Drama. The Post-War German Theatre 5. The Nordic Dramatists – Strindberg'. An unsympathetic response to the 'monomaniac' Sg and the place accorded him in post-war German theatre. 'Sg has barely more to say to us than some less-frequently staged German dramatists.... Sg is in fact not just an individual writer, he is an illustrative lesson in literary history; and, particularly in his case, theatre directors, critics, and readers should be at their sharpest when separating the little wheat from the abundance of chaff']

[B3:123] Bučhar, Franjo, 'August Strindberg', *Prosvjeta* (Zagreb), 7:6 (1899), p. 198. [R.507]

[B3:124] Bukowski, Piotr, 'Od *Szće łiwego Piotra* do *Czarnej rêkawiczki*'. O nieznanew w Polsce dramaturgii Augusta Strindberga', *Didaskalia* (Warsaw?), 33:11 (1999), 62-68. Illus. ['From *Lucky Peter's Journey* to *The Black Glove*': On Plays by Strindberg Unknown in Poland'. Seeks to redress the unbalanced impression that Polish theatregoers have of Sg's overall achievement as a dramatist]

[B3:125] Camenius, Lars, 'Strindberg och Kina', *Vestmanlands Läns Tidning* (Västerås), 18 July 1984. ['Strindberg and China']

[B3:126] Carlsson, Anni, 'Forderungen an eines neues Strindberg-Bild. Zur Monographie Albeck Börges' [sic], *Neue Zürcher Zeitung* (Zürich), 18-19 September 1976. ['The Need for a New Image of Strindberg'. Stresses how Børge's study, *Strindberg, Prometheus des Theaters*, **D2:26**, with its stress on the wide-ranging nature of Sg's project, demonstrates the urgent need for a new understanding in Germany of his overall achievement]

[B3:127] Carlsson, Anni, 'Forderungen an ein neues Strindberg-Bild. Zur Monographie Vagn Albeck Börges', in *Ibsen, Strindberg, Hamsun: Essays zur skandinavischen Literatur*, **B1:103**, pp. 39-42. [Rpr. of **B3:126**]

[B3:128] Carlsson, Anni, *Die deutsche Buchkritik von der Reformation bis zur Gegenwart*, Bern und München: Francke Verlag, 1969. [421] pp. ['German Book Criticism from the Reformation to the Present'. Includes thirteen references, mainly focused in a chapter on 'Die neue Wahrheit', pp. [192]-218]

[B3:129] C. D. W. [Carl David af Wirsén], 'Literatur', *Vårt Land* (Stockholm), 30 March 1899. [Notes the publication of *La Vie et l'art des scandinaves*, **B3:176**, where, in spite of the sickly dreariness of his writings, Sg is unfortunately the only Swedish writer that its author, Maurice Gandolphe, seems to know and admire]

[B3:130] Chen Jie, 'Strindberg in China', *China Daily* (Beijing), 26 May 2005. [Reviews Reine Brynolfsson in *Paralysie Generale* in Beijing and the publication of a five-volume collection of Sg's works in Chinese translation as part of a series of events and performances comprising 'Strindberg in China 2005'. Quotes Dürrenmatt, Kafka, and O'Neill in affirming Sg's importance for modern literature and theatre]

[B3:131] Christiansson, T. '*Spöksonaten* inspiration i Kurdistan', *Dagens Nyheter* (Stockholm), 23 October 2001. ['*The Ghost Sonata*: An Inspiration in Kurdistan'. Reports an enthusiasm for Sg in Kurdistan, apropos Dana Marouf's study of the play in **E51:84**]

[B3:132] Ciaravolo, Massimo, *Da Linneo a Gustafsson. 250 anni di letteratura svedese in traduzione italiano*, Milano: Iperborea, 1994. np. ['From Linnaeus to Gustafsson. 250 Years of Swedish Literature in Italian Translation'. Surveys 250 years of translating Swedish literature into Italian and lists translations of Sg's works into Italian between 1893 and 1993]

[B3:133] Ciesielski, Zenon, *Zbliżenia skandynawsko-polskie. Szkice o kontaktach kulturalnych w XIX i XX wieku*, Gdańsk: Morskie, 1972. Illus. 275 pp. [Surveys Scandinavian-Polish cultural relations in the 19th and 20th Centuries, with some reference to Sg]

[B3:134] Claes, Victor, 'De ontdekking van August Strindberg in het Nederlands taalgebied. Een bijdrage tot de studie van de receptie van zijn werk', 1-4, *Koninklijken Zuidnederlandse Maatschappij voor Taal- en Letterkunde en Geschiedenis, Handelingen* 34 (1980), 75-133; 35 (1981), 47-66; 36 (1982), 5-31; 37 (1983), 31-47. ['The Discovery of August Strindberg in the Netherlands' Language Area. A Contribution to the Study of the Reception of His Work'. Four articles which amount to a short monograph and provide the basis for all subsequent research into Sg's early reception in the Netherlands. Claes divides his works into three periods (1869-1978: Romantic-Idealistic; 1879-1896: Realistic-Naturalistic; 1897-1912: Symbolist-Expressionist), and traces their translation history and acceptance in the Dutch and Flemish theatre. He also discusses some general translation issues (e.g. the first Dutch version of *Hemsöborna*) as well as Sg's links with J. T. Grein and the Independent Theatre in London. Part Three is devoted to the reception of Willem Royaards's staging of *Ett drömspel* in Amsterdam, in 1921. Includes a letter from Sg to the Dutch writer Arij Prins (1860-1922) in facsimile]

[B3:135] Claes, Victor, 'Die Strindberg-Rezeption im niederländischen Sprachraum', in Wilhelm Friese, Hrsg., **B3:168**, *Strindberg und die deutschsprachigen Länder*, pp. 369-396. ['The Reception of Strindberg in the Netherlands' Language Area'. Claes divides Sg's reception in the Netherlands into three main periods: (1) an initial encounter with Sg as a naturalist in both prose and drama, including *Röda rummet*, *Giftas*, *Dikter på vers och prosa*, *Fadren*, *Fordringsägare* and *Fröken Julie* (initially on tour to Amsterdam from the Théâtre Libre – *Fröken Julie* was not performed in Dutch until 1912); (2)

the impact of the post-Inferno 'symbolist-expressionist Strindberg' through the productions of Max Reinhardt (e.g. *Dödsdansen* on tour in 1916), Willem Royaards, and Eduard Verkade; and (3) very briefly, Sg as a precursor of the theatre of the absurd. Claes also offers a selective overview of Sg's works in Dutch translation, as well as the critical literature on Sg in Dutch]

[B3:136] Cloesser, Artur, 'Svenska diktare i Tyskland. August Strindberg och Selma Lagerlöf', *Svenska Dagbladet* (Stockholm), 1 May 1905. ['Swedish Writers in Germany. August Strindberg and Selma Lagerlöf']

[B3:137] Commert, Pierre, 'Auguste Strindberg', *Le Temps* (Paris), 13 July 1914. [Observes that a writer so enthusiastically promoted in Germany is unlikely to make headway in France at this moment in history]

[B3:138] Conrad, M[ichael] G[eorg], 'Nordische scheingrößen', *Die Gesellschaft* (München), 15:3 (1899), p. 423. ['Nordic False Eminences'. Dismisses Sg along with Ola Hansson and Laura Marholm as one among many Nordic writers with a 'pseudo' reputation. Discusses *Legender*]

[B3:139] Conrad, Michael Georg, 'Nordische scheingrößen', in Hans-Peter Bayerdörfer, Hrsg., **B3:85**, *Strindberg auf der deutschen Bühne*, pp. 121-122. ['Nordic False Eminences'. Rpr. of **B3:138**]

[B3:140] Dahlström, Carl E. W. L., 'The Parisian Reception of Strindberg's Plays', *Scandinavian Studies* (Menasha, Wisconsin), 19:6 (1947), 195-207. [Partly due to his own careless presentation of the facts, numerous misunderstandings have arisen regarding the early performance and reception of Sg's plays in Paris. None of his plays were performed there before *Fröken Julie* in January 1893, by when Ibsen was already an established presence in the French theatre. Nor was the play very favourably received. *Fordringsägare* fared rather better in 1894, as did *Fadren*, although the enthusiastic reports from Sg and Frida Uhl neeed to be be treated with scepticism. Thus Dahlström concludes that 'For Sg there was no conquering of Paris. Nor was there any breaking of Ibsen's records in the performance of dramas, the publication of dramas, or in the response of audience and dramatic critics']

[B3:141] Daudet, Léon, 'Assez d'étrangers', *Le Figaro* (Paris), 2 February 1896. ['Enough Foreigners'. Among the most vituperative of nationalist attacks on the takeover of French culture by foreign elements, including the infiltration of the theatre by Scandinavians like Ibsen and Sg]

[B3:142] Delius, Rudolf von, 'Deutschland und die Genies der Fremde', *Lese* (Stuttgart), 6:1 (1915), 5-6. ['Germany and Foreign Geniuses'. Expresses scepticism regarding the value to Germany of foreign writers such as Sg in time of war]

[B3:143] Diaz-Plaja, Guillermo, 'Strindberg en España', *El ocio atento*, Madrid: Narcea, 1984, pp. 293-299. ['Strindberg in Spain']

[B3:144] Dobijanka-Witczakowa, Olga, 'Strindberg in Poland', in Leszek Hajdukiewicz, ed., *Charisteria Cracoviensia Universitati Regiae Uppsaliensi quinta sacra saecularia celebranti ab Universitate Iagellonica Cracoviensi oblata*, Universitas Iagellonica Acta Scientiarum Litterarumque DVIII, Schedae Historicae Fascisulus LXI, Translated into English by Marianna Abrahamowicz, Kraków: Nakl. Uniwersytetu Jagiellonskiego, 1979, pp. 137-154. [Surveys Sg's reception in Poland, both in terms of translations and critical commentaries. Initially, Sg 'was chiefly known in Poland as an epic writer'.

Catholic Poland found the stern Protestantism of Scandinavia difficult to accept, and the plays began to gain a hold in the Polish theatre only after the performance of *Samum* in 1905. During the inter-war years it was often the prose works which were most widely translated into Polish, but a marked revival of interest in the plays occurred in the late 1950s and 1960s when several were also produced on television. Sg is now better known as a playwright than a novelist. A useful article, not least for making available some of the research by Marian Lewko published in **B3:263**, **B3:265**, and **B3:266**, in English]

[B3:145] Dobijanka-Witczakowa, Olga, 'Recepcja dramatu skandynawskiego w Polsce', *Komunikaty Instytutu Baltyckiego* (Gdańsk), 1975:3. ['The Reception of Scandinavian Drama in Poland']

[B3:146] 'Dioneo' [I. V. Shklovskii], '[Writers of the End of the Century. Strindberg]', *Odesskie novosti* (Odessa), 16 March 1895, p. 2. [E.700]

[B3:147] Dr. S. [Rainer Schlösser], 'Die unumschränkten Herrscher eines Jahrzehnts: Ausländer und Juden auf deutschen Bühnen', *Völkischer Beobachter* (München), 17 February 1933. ['The Absolute Rulers of the Decade: Foreigners and Jews on the German Stage'. The future 'Reichsdramaturg' presents a National Socialist view of what should be the appropriate repertoire for a truly German theatre. Sg is dismissed along with the theatre of Weimar Germany in general: 'For a nation which had lost its nerve, such *hysterical theatre* was in any case poison!']

[B3:148] Dubech, Lucien, *La Crise du théâtre*, Paris: Librairie de France, 1928. 214 pp. [Attributes the crisis in contemporary French theatre to baleful Jewish and Nordic influences]

[B3:149] Dukes, Ashley, 'Southward Norseman: Ibsen and Strindberg on the Stage of Europe in the Eighteen-Nineties', *Theatre Arts Monthly* (New York), 24:8 (1940), 550-554. [On the reception of Ibsen and Sg in the German and French theatre during the 1890s]

[B3:150] E. K. Stein [J. Ekstein], 'Strindberg-Mode', *Die Wage* (Vienna), 19 (1916), 420-422. ['Strindberg Fashion']

[B3:151] Eklund, Torsten, 'Strindberg e l'Italia', in *Strindberg. Il meglio del teatro per la prima volta*, Torino, 1951, pp. xxxix-xlvi. ['Strindberg and Italy'. Surveys Sg's links with Italy, in a collection of Italian translations of what are reputedly Sg's eighteen best plays]

[B3:152] Eklund, Torsten, 'Strindberg i Paris. Några klipp ur fransk press från 1890-talet', *Meddelanden från Strindbergssällskapet* (Stockholm), 3 (1947), pp. 22-26. ['Strindberg in Paris. Some Cuttings from the French Press in the 1890s'. Documents the French response to the first performances of Sg's plays in Paris in 1893-94, in which he is sometimes mistaken (e.g. by Jules Lemaître and Edmond de Goncourt) for a Danish writer. His misogyny and scientific experiments were also a matter of frequent report, while his articles on these topics in the French press provoked considerable discussion]

[B3:153] Elin Pelin [Pseudonym of Dimitar Ivanov Soyanov], 'Pismoto na Ivan Vazov', *Razvigor* (Sofia), 1:4 (30 January 1921), p. 3. [Criticises Bulgaria's 'national poet', novelist, and short-story writer, Ivan Vazov (1850-1921), for his powerfully argued dislike of *Dödsdansen* in Geo Milev's production in Sofia, in 1920]

[B3:154] E. L-m, 'Strindberg i Amerika', *Dagen* (Stockholm), 24 January 1912. ['Strindberg in America'. Discusses Sg's standing in North America in an article published in conjunction with his 63rd birthday]

[B3:155] Elmfeldt, Johan, *Läsningens röster. Om litteratur, genus och lärarskap*, Stockholm/ Stenag: Brutus Östlings Bokförlag Symposion, 1997. 348 pp. [An empirical study of Swedish secondary school reading based on transcriptions of tape-recorded lessons and group discussions in two classes in a Swedish school, based mainly on Ibsen's *A Doll's House*, Sg's story 'Ett dockhem' (A Doll's House) from *Giftas*, and Zola's novel *Thérèse Raquin* (1867). Where Sg is concerned, this material is supplemented by writing in other genres, such as his correspondence with Siri von Essen, *Fadren*, and *En dåres försvarstal*. English summary]

[B3:156] Elsberga, Solveiga, 'Lettlands tredje våg', *Parnass* (Stockholm), 6:1 (1995), 48-49. Illus. ['Lettland's Third Wave'. Notes that Sg was first translated into Lettish in 1889; his current translator comments on the renewed interest in his plays in Latvia post-1988]

[B3:157] Elsberga, Solveiga, 'Den tredje vågen i Lettland', in Anita Persson and Barbara Lide, red., **B1:366**, *Ja, må han leva!*, pp. 35-37. ['The Third Wave in Latvia'. Identifies three distinct periods in the translation of Sg into Latvian: (1) a few items at the turn of the century, including *Pelikanen*, *Kamraterna*, and *Fadren*; (2) the 1920s and 1930s when *Röda rummet*, *Hemsöborna*, *I havsbandet*, and *En dåres försvarstal* were translated and productions of *Brott och brott*, *Ett drömspel*, *Kronbruden*, *Samum*, and *Erik XIV* were mounted in Riga and Liepaja; and (3) the 1980s when Elsberga translated *Dödsdansen* and *Spöksonaten* herself, and the former was staged by Kärlis Auskaps with Ausma Kantane as Alice and Juris Strenga as Edgar, and the latter by Hans Bertilsson, both of them performed in Riga]

[B3:158] Engström, Ulrika K., 'Strindberg går hem i Kina', *Svenska Dagbladet* (Stockholm), 28 May 2005. ['Strindberg Makes a Splash in China'. Reports on the impact of Sg and his works in the promotion 'Strindberg i Kina 2005' by the Swedish Institute and the Swedish Embassy in China which includes performances of *Fröken Julie*, directed by Meng Jinghui, *Ett drömspel* (Lin Zhaohua), *Brända tomten* (Li Liuyi), *Fadren* (Zhao Lixin), all at the TNT Theatre in Beijing during September and October, and a series of seminars at Beijing University held in conjunction with the Swedish Academy]

[B3:159] Ewbank, Inga-Stina, 'Strindberg and British Culture', *TijdSchrift voor Skandinavistiek* (Amsterdam), 20:1 (1999), 7-28. [Charts British culture's long-standing resistance to Sg, and the reasons why – in spite of some notable recent exceptions – this continues to be the case, focusing on two key years, 1893, when Sg paid a brief visit to England, and 1913, when a generally unsympathetic British perception of Sg crystallised into a form that proved hard enough to withstand many subsequent changes within British culture]

[B3:160] Ewbank, Inga-Stina, 'Strindberg och brittisk kultur', *Strindbergiana* (Stockholm), 14 (1999), pp. 144-158. ['Strindberg and British Culture'. Swedish version of **B3:159**]

[B3:161] Fabre, Emile, 'Europa om August Strindberg', *Dagens Nyheter* (Stockholm), 15 May 1912. ['Europe on August Strindberg'. Surveys the European reaction to Sg and his works in the wake of his recent death]

[B3:162] Falk, Bertil, 'Äntligen erövrar Strindberg London', *Kvällsposten* (Malmö), 3 January 1989. ['Strindberg Conquers London at Last']

[B3:163] Fevre, Henry, 'Le théâtre étranger et M. Strindberg à Paris', *Le Monde moderne* (Paris), 2 (1895), 55-64. ['The Foreign Theatre and Strindberg in Paris']

[B3:164] Fieandt, Einar, 'August Strindberg ja suomalaisuus', *Suomalainenen Suomi* (Helsinki), 1929: 12. ['August Strindberg and Finnishness']

[B3:165] Flakes, Susan, 'Varför amerikansk teater behöver Strindberg', *Dramaten* (Stockholm), 7 (1976-77), No. 62, pp. 27-28. ['Why the American Theatre needs Strindberg']

[B3:166] Fraenkl, Pavel, *Bjørnson og Tsjekkisk Litteratur*, Oslo: Gyldendal Norsk Forlag, 1953. 126 pp. ['Bjørnson and Czech Literature'. Contains some passing references to the reception of Sg in Czech literature and theatre as another representative of the Scandinavian Modern Breakthrough]

[B3:167] Friedell, Egon, 'Die Strindbergmode', *Kölner Zeitung*, 18 October 1922. ['The Fashion for Strindberg']

[B3:168] Friese, Wilhelm, Hrsg., *Strindberg und die deutschsprachigen Länder. Internationale Beiträge zum Tübinger Strindberg-Symposium 1977*, Beiträge zur nordischen Philologie, Hrsg. von der Schweizerischen Gesellschaft, Basel und Stuttgart: Helbing & Lichtenhahn Verlag AG, 1979. 396 pp. ['Strindberg and the German-Speaking Countries. International Contributions to the Tübingen Strindberg Symposium in 1977' (the Third International Strindberg Conference). Contains **A4:31**: Gunnar Brandell, 'Stand und Aufgaben der heutigen Strindbergforschung'; **B3:12**: Stellan Ahlström, 'Strindbergs deutsche Freunde'; **B3:81**: Walter Baumgartner, 'Verpaßte Eroberung eines Terrains. Charakter und Funktion des ästhetischen Erwartungshorizonts in der deutschen Rezeption von Strindbergs naturalistischen Dramen um 1890'; **B3:84**: Hans-Peter Bayerdörfer, 'Strindberg, rezensiert. Zur Bedeutung literarischer Klischeebildung für die Bühnenrezeption'; **B3:135**: Victor Claes, 'Die Strindberg-Rezeption im niederländischen Sprachraum'; **B3:205**: Hilde Haider-Pregler, 'Strindbergs frühe Rezeption auf dem Wiener Theater'; **B3:328**: Otto Oberholzer, 'Wandlungen des Strindbergsbildes in Deutschland'; **B3:336**: Wolfgang Pasche, 'Strindberg auf den deutschen Bühnen 1900 bis 1912'; **B3:479**: Ruprecht Volz, 'Strindbergbilder in der Zeit des deutschen Expressionismus'; **B4:34**: Detlef Brennecke, '*Fröken Julie* auf deutsch. Fünf Übersetzer suchen August Strindberg'; **B4:133**: Fritz Paul, 'Deutsche Strindberg-Ausgaben. Ein Ärgernis?'; **C1:201**: Harald H. Borland, 'Strindberg and Nietzsche'; **C1:922**: Helmut Müssener, 'Deutschland und Österreich in Strindbergs Werken und Briefen'; **D2:842**: Kela Kvam, 'Max Reinhardt und Strindberg. Die Bedeutung der Inszenierungen der "Kammerspiele" und des "Traumspiels" für den deutschen Expressionismus'; **E31:39**: Claes Rosenqvist, 'Strindberg's Thirty Year's War'; **E51:135**: Egil Törnqvist, '*Faust* and *The Ghost Sonata*'; **F1:19**: Maurice Gravier, 'L'Image de l'Allegmagne et de l'Autriche dans les récits autobiographiques de Strindberg'; **T:36**: Oskar Bandle, 'Ideologie und Wirklichkeit. Das Bild der Schweitz in Strindbergs Werken und Briefen']

[B3:169] — [Jessen, Karsten], *Ausblick* (Lübeck), 30 (1979), p. 32.

[B3:170] — Lide, Barbara, *Journal of English and Germanic Philology* (Urbana, Illinois), 81:2 (1982), 308-311.

[B3:171] — Mattsson, Margareta, *Scandinavian Studies* (Lawrence, Kansas), 52:4 (1980), 474-475.

[B3:172] — Rinman, Sven, *Samlaren* (Uppsala), 100 (1979), pp. 311-314.

[B3:173] — Wittrock, Ulf, *Upsala Nya Tidning*, 11 March 1980.

[B3:174] Gabrieli, Mario, 'Echi di Ibsen e di Strindberg in Italia', *Aion-n, Studi Nederlandesi-Studi Nordici. Annali dell'Istituto Universitario Orientali* (Napoli), 7 (1964), 21-39. ['Echoes of Ibsen and Strindberg in Italy']

[B3:175] Galabova, Snezhanka, *et. al.*, *Letopis na narodnia teatar "Ivan Vazov": 1904-1970*, Sofia: Nauka i izkustvo, 1971, p. 579. ['A Chronicle of the National Theatre "Ivan Vazov", 1904-1970'. Comments on the National Theatre's sometimes controversial stagings of Sg's plays, including Geo Milev's production of *Dödsdansen* in 1920]

[B3:176] Gandolphe, Maurice, *La Vie et l'art des scandinaves avec une lettre de Gaston Paris*, Paris: Perrin et cie., 1899. 308 pp. ['The Life and Art of the Scandinavians with a Letter from Gaston Paris'. Sg is the only Swedish author mentioned]

[B3:177] Gantjeva, Vera, 'Bulgarien: Strindbergs timma', in Anita Persson and Barbara Lide, red., **B1:366**, *Ja, må han leva!*, pp. 27-33. ['Bulgaria: Strindberg's Hour'. On the 'Strindberg boom' in Bulgaria since 1989, typified by a performance of *Spöksonaten* at the Theatre Sofia in 1998. 'It was Sg who proved to be the standard-bearer of the important period of transition from artistic and intellectual rigidity under socialism to what was, for many, the confusing and exhausting chaos of the new order.' Sg was previously overshadowed by Ibsen, Hauptmann, Chekhov, and Gorkii, although his work was not entirely unknown and Per Olov Enquist's televisual biography had been screened on Bulgarian television during the 1970s]

[B3:178] Gantjeva, Vera, 'Strindberg i Bulgarien', *Strindbergiana* (Stockholm), 15, Stockholm: Atlantis, 2000, pp. 179-182. ['Strindberg in Bulgaria'. On a symposium in Sofia to celebrate the 150th anniversary of Sg's birth and the opportunity it provided to reassess his position in Bulgaria following the recent transformation of Bulgarian society after 1989. The first Bulgarian performance of *Dödsdansen* in 1920 had been attacked by Bulgaria's leading modern author, Ivan Vazov, and the ensuing scandal determined his standing in Bulgaria for many decades. However, a recent production of the same play directed by Krassimir Spasov has facilitated a reassessment. To date it is J. P. Jacobsen, Ibsen, and Selma Lagerlöf who have been the principal figures in Bulgaria's view of Nordic literature but the symposium enabled contemporary scholars to compare Sg with existentialism, Ivan Turgenev, and the Bulgarian author Elin Pelin, as well as to consider the problems of translating Sg into Bulgarian in connection with the two-volume edition of his Selected Works, shortly to be published in Sofia by HEMUS, **B2:157**]

[B3:179] Garling-Palmér, Signe, 'Vår litteratur inför fransk publik och kritik', *Varia: Illustrerad månadsskrift* (Stockholm), 1906, pp. 451-461. ['Our Literature Face to Face with a French Public and the Critics'. On the reception accorded Swedish literature, including Sg, in France, based partly on conversations with Sg's collaborator during the mid-1890s, Georges Loiseau]

[B3:180] Gassner, John [Waldhorn], 'The Influence of Strindberg in the United States', *World Theatre-Le Théâtre dans le monde* (Brussels), 11:1 (1962), 21-30. Illus. [Pays tribute to the influence of Sg as 'the recognised master of psychological drama' on modern American playwrights, including Eugene O'Neill and Tennessee Williams, who are identified as 'the two most Strindbergian playwrights on the American stage'.

Sg liberated the American theatre from long-standing puritanical constraints in the treatment of sex and 'American gynolatry', and while his psychological expressionism has often been diluted by a theatre that favours sedatives rather than purgatives, he has also acted as a catalyst for those dramatists who, like O'Neill and Williams, sought to move beyond naturalism. Parallel text in French]

[B3:181] Gassner, John [Waldhorn], 'The Influence of Strindberg in the United States', in Hans Itschert, Hrsg., **D1:213**, *Das Amerikanische Drama von den Anfängen bis zur Gegenwart*, Darmstadt: Wissenschaftliche Buchgesellschaft, 1972, pp. 70-76. [Rpr. of **B3:180**]

[B3:182] Gendov, Stefan, 'Nashiat teatar', *Komedia* (Sofia), 1:1 (29 July 1920), p. 4. ['Our Theatre'. On the scandal caused by the first production of *Dödsdansen* in Bulgaria, directed by Geo Milev at the Bulgarian National Theatre in Sofia, in 1920]

[B3:183] Gentikow, Barbara, *Skandinavien als präkapitallistische Idylle. Rezeption gesellschaftskritischer Literatur in deutschen Zeitschriften 1870 bis 1914*, Beiträge zur Sprache, Literatur und Kultur der nordischen Länder 9, Neumünster: Karl Wachholtz Verlag, 1978. 308 pp. ['Scandinavia as a Pre-Capitalist Idyll. The Reception of a Socially Critical Literature in German Periodicals from 1870 to 1914'. Discussion of Sg is restricted to his views on the role of women in relation to Ibsen's Nora and Ellen Key's "Mißbrauchte Frauenkraft", as well as to his place as a forerunner of a modern working-class literature]

[B3:184] George, Manfred, 'Strindberg i USA', *Dagens Nyheter* (Stockholm), 24 January 1949. ['Strindberg in the United States']

[B3:185] [Georg Müller], *Fünfundzwanzig Jahre Georg Müller Verlag (1903-1928)*, München: Georg Müller, 1928, pp. 198-201. [A commemorative volume on the publishing house most closely associated with Sg in Germany through its publication of Emil Schering's German edition of his works]

[B3:186] Gerhardt, Martin, and Walter Hubatsch, *Deutschland und Skandinavien im Wandel der Jahrhunderte*, Bonn: L. Röhrscheid, 1950. VIII+482 pp. ['Germany and Scandinavia at the Turn of the Century']

[B3:187] Ginisty, Paul, 'Chronique', *Le XIXe Siècle* (Paris), 16 January 1893. [Covers similar ground to Ginisty's article in *La République Française*, **B3:188**, but contextualises Sg in terms of the recent French reception of Dostoevskii, Tolstoi, Giovanni Verga, and Ibsen. Ginisty maintains that Sg has always been badly treated in Sweden, where he has enjoyed the support of only a very small circle that includes his ardent admirer, Gustaf af Geijerstam. One of Sg's novels (*En dåres försvarstal*?) should shortly be appearing in French]

[B3:188] Ginisty, Paul, 'La Littérature contemporaine suédoise', *La République Française* (Paris), 16 November 1891. ['Contemporary Swedish literature'. Ginisty identifies two literary schools in Sweden, the 'idealist' and the 'realist'. The latter comprises Anne-Charlotte Edgren-Leffler, who is 'one of the first writers to follow in Sg's footsteps', Victoria Benedictsson, Tor Hedberg, and Verner von Heidenstam. Although Ginisty devotes considerable space to Gustaf af Geijerstam, he acknowledges that Sg is the one Swedish writer of renown in Paris, if only among a select circle, and points out that translations of his other works besides *Giftas* are needed]

[B3:189] Górski, Ryszard, 'Z teatralnych dziejów Augusta Strindberga w Polsce', *Zwierciadła Pólnocy II*, Warszawa, 1992, pp. 55-57. ['On the Theatrical History of August Strindberg in Poland'. Traces Sg's reception in terms of the performance of his plays in the Polish theatre]

[B3:190] Gosse, Edmund, 'Recent Swedish Poetry and Count Snoilsky', *The Contemporary Review* (London), 99 (1911), 463-469. [Although his expressed aim is an exhaustive discussion of contemporary Swedish literature, Gosse names Sg only twice in passing, and then to comment on 'the violent and sinister innovations of Sg and his followers']

[B3:191] Gosse, Edmund, 'Count Snoilsky and Some Recent Swedish Poets', in Edmund Gosse, *Portraits and Sketches*, London: William Heinemann, 1912, pp. 229-240. [Rpr. of **B3:190**]

[B3:192] Götselius, Thomas, 'Paris ger Strindberg ny chans', *Dagens Nyheter* (Stockholm), 8 March 2001. ['Paris Gives Strindberg a New Chance'. Notes the possibility of a new image of Sg in France, made feasible by the publication of a collection of essays, edited by Elena Balzamo for *L'Herne*. See **B1:7**]

[B3:193] Gottschall, Rudolph von, 'Die Ausländerei auf den deutschen Bühnen', *Deutsche Revue* (Berlin), 20:3 (1895), 300-315. ['Foreigners on the German Stage'. Rejects not only naturalism and Sg but the performance of foreign drama in general on the German stage: 'Their heroes are all hysterical']

[B3:194] Grandprey, M. de, 'Strindberg inconnu', *Comœdia* (Paris), 2 April 1922. ['Strindberg Unknown'. Complains that in France Sg is known only as the author of *Fordringsägare, Fröken Julie*, and *Dödsdansen*]

[B3:195] Gravier, Maurice, '"Fortune" de Strindberg sur les scènes de France', *Théâtre/Public* (Gennevilliers), 73:4 (1986), 79-81. ['Strindberg's "Fortunes" in the French Theatre'. Documents Sg's initial reception in the French theatre during the 1890s with the premières of *Fröken Julie, Fadren*, and *Fordringsägare* at the Théâtre Libre and Théâtre de l'Œuvre, the enduring impact of the 1921 production of *Dödsdansen*, and the current state of his post-war reputation, initiated by Roger Blin's production of *Spöksonaten* in 1949. With financial support from the Nobel Prize winner André Gide, the newly-founded Société Strindberg is presiding over the publication of a complete edition of the plays, edited and translated by a consortium of well-known writers, academics, and theatre practitioners. Together with recent French productions of *Ett drömspel* and *Till Damaskus*, this means that Sg is becoming better known in France]

[B3:196] Gravier, Maurice, 'Strindberg et le théâtre danois', *Etudes Germaniques* (Paris), 13:3 (1958), 208-228. ['Strindberg and the Danish Theatre'. Denmark had the honour of staging the premières of *Fadren, Fordringsägare, Paria*, and *Fröken Julie* while several contemporary Danish writers, including Gustav Wied and Edvard Brandes, responded positively to his work. Subsequently, the German 'Strindberg Taumel' of 1913-1918 impacted powerfully on Denmark where his plays were performed in Danish, Swedish, and German. His adherents regarded him as the writer of the new age, but it remained a question of which Sg this was, the naturalist of the 1880s or the mystic of the post-Inferno dramas which seemed, for a number of Danish critics, to threaten the very existence of the theatre. Sg plays a central role in the debate on the theatre of the future and an emerging modern Danish drama, associated in particular with

Svend Borberg. There are comparisons to be made with the theatre of H[enri]-R[ené] Lenormand, Luigi Pirandello, and Pär Lagerkvist, as well as with Frank Wedekind and German Expressionism, aspects of which the Danish theatre has adopted with judicious circumspection]

[B3:197] Grimal, Sophie, 'Strindberg dans la presse française 1894-1902', in Gunnel Engwall, red., **B1:121**, *Strindberg et la France*, pp. 65-67. ['Strindberg in the French Press, 1894-1902'. A bibliography of articles by Sg which appeared in the French press from 1894 to 1902 and which is intended to complement and enlarge upon the lists appended by Brandell to **B1:55**, *Strindbergs Infernokris*, and (for *Vivisections*) the bibliographical material assembled by Engwall in **K5:4**]

[B3:198] Grössel, Hanns, 'Die nördliche Grenze. Zur Rezeption skandinavischer Literatur in Deutschland nach 1945', *Neue Rundschau* (Berlin), 84:1 (1973), 126-133. ['The Northern Border. On the Reception of Scandinavian Literature in Germany Until 1945']

[B3:199] Gruszczyńska, Ewa, 'Literatura szwedzka w Polsce', *Acta Sueco-Polonica* (Uppsala), 1 (1993), pp. 55-68. ['Swedish Literature in Poland']

[B3:200] Gruner, Fritz, 'Einige Bemerkungen zur Rolle und Wirkung der nordeuropäischen Literaturen i China', in Horst Bien, Hrsg., *Die nordischen Literaturen als Gegenstand der Literaturgeschichtsschreibung*, Beiträge zur 13. Studienkonferenz der Internationalen Assoziation für Skandinavische Studien (IASS), 10.-16. August 1980 an der Ernst-Moritz-Arndt-Universität Greifswald, Rostock: VEB Hinstorff Verlag, 1982, pp. 238-240. ['Some Reflections on the Role and Influence of North-European Literature in China'. Includes a brief comment on Sg in the context of the reception of Scandinavian literature in China since 1919]

[B3:201] Günther, Irmgard, *Die Einwirkung des skandinavischen Romans auf den deutschen Naturalismus*, Nordische Studien 14, Greifswald: L. Bamberg, 1934. 158 pp. ['The Influence of the Scandinavian Novel on German Naturalism'. Identifies a mania for Scandinavian literature in Germany towards the end of the 19th Century and discusses the influence of the Scandinavian novel, including several by Sg (primarily *Röda rummet* and *Hemsöborna*), on German naturalism]

[B3:202] Gustafson, Alrik, 'Some Early English and American Strindberg Criticism', in *Scandinavian Studies Presented to George T. Flom by Colleagues and Friends*, Illinois Studies in Language and Literature 29, Urbana, Ill., 1943, pp. 106-124. [In spite of the efforts of a small circle of admirers and one or two exceptions (e.g. Eugene O'Neill and George Bernard Shaw), Sg remains largely unknown in both England and the United States. He was always overshadowed by Ibsen who, unlike Sg, has been frequently translated and performed, his early reputation for challenging subject matter notwithstanding, whereas Sg was dismissed by such an influential intermediary as Edmund Gosse. An investigation of the periodical literature from the first important essay on Sg in English in the *Fortnightly Review* in 1892 (see **B2:264**) to his death in 1912, which marked the beginning of a new period in his reception in England and America, reveals that he was mentioned only seventy-five times and accorded serious discussion on a mere twelve occasions, principally by Justin Huntly McCarthy and Ashley Dukes in England and James Huneker and Edwin Björkman in North America. The latter has written by far the most important articles on Sg in English. A well-balanced and informative essay]

[B3:203] Gustafson, Alrik, 'Strindberg inför samtida engelsk och amerikansk kritik', *Svensk Litteraturtidskrift* (Stockholm), 9:3 (1946), 118-132. ['Some Contemporary English and American Critics of Strindberg'. Swedish version of **B3:202**]

[B3:204] Hagberg, Theodor, 'Strindberg och Japan', *Aftonbladet* (Stockholm), 12 March 1911. ['Strindberg and Japan']

[B3:205] Haider-Pregler, Hilde, 'Strindbergs frühe Rezeption auf dem Wiener Theater', in Wilhelm Friese, Hrsg., **B3:168**, *Strindberg und die deutschsprachigen Länder*, pp. 225-244. ['Strindberg's Early Reception in the Viennese Theatre'. Covers the period between 1893 and the Berlin production of *Fordringsägare* with Rosa Bertens and Rudolf Rittner on tour to Vienna until ca. 1918, as reflected in a representative cross-section of Viennese newspapers, and covering some twenty-five works. The role of Josef Jarno, who was responsible as director, theatre manager, and actor for the premières of fourteen of these productions, including the world première of *Kamraterna*, was central, but the contribution of other theatres is also discussed. So, too, is the impact of touring productions, including Emanuel Reicher in *Fadren* (1897), Gertrud Eysoldt as Fröken Julie (1913), and Max Reinhardt's production of *Pelikanen* (1914). Haider-Pregler also reflects on the enthusiasm which Karl Kraus displayed for Sg in his journal *Die Fackel*]

[B3:206] Hallays, André, 'De l'influence des littératures étrangères', *Revue de Paris*, 15 February 1895, pp. 879-890. ['On the Influence of Foreign Literatures'. Contributes to the wide-ranging debate on the recent influence of Nordic writers on French literature, initiated by Jules Lemaître in **B3:256**. Hallays rejects the latter's thesis with reference to Goethe's concept of 'Weltlitteratur'. Where Sg is concerned, his works demonstrate an admiration for the French naturalists; the relationship between literatures thus cuts both ways]

[B3:207] Halleux, Pierre, 'Présence Suèdois en France', 1-2, *Revue des langues vivantes* (Brussels), 1952, pp. 298-304, 356-364. ['The Swedish Presence in France'. Discusses the critic and translator Lucien Maury as a cultural intermediary between Sweden and France, and comments on his advocacy of Sg]

[B3:208] Hamberg, Lars, 'Strindberg i Finland', *Meddelanden från Strindbergssällskapet* (Stockholm), 20 (1956), pp. 16-20 ['Strindberg in Finland'. Augments Gunnar Ollén's account of Sg's plays in performance in Finland in the first edition of his standard works on *Strindbergs dramatik*, **D2:239**, taking account of radio broadcasts as well as theatre performances]

[B3:209] Hamilton, Clayton, 'Strindberg in America', *The Bookman* (New York), 35:4 (June 1912), 358-365. Illus. [Evaluates Sg, and particularly the plays, in the light of Björkman's recent translations of *Fadren, Fröken Julie, Ett drömspel, Bandet,* and *Dödsdansen*, only to conclude that there is little to Sg apart from the disturbingly negative side these works display; he is therefore unlikely ever to be popular in America: 'We take our life less grimly than this morbid-minded Scandinavian.... For us in America, Sg must remain a sinister dissenter']

[B3:210] Hansen, Uffe, 'Strindberg und die dynamische Psychiatrie der 80er Jahre. Überlegungen zur frühen deutschen Strindbergrezeption', in Klaus Bohnen, Uffe Hansen, and Friedrich Schmöe, Hrsg., *Fin de siècle. Zu naturwissenschaft und Literatur der Jahrhundertwende im deutsch-skandinavischen Kontext*, Kopenhagener Kolloquien zur deutschen Literatur 11 (= TEXT & KONTEXT sonderreihe, Band 20), Kopenhagen: Wilhelm Fink Verlag, 1984, pp. 39-61. ['Strindberg and the Dynamic Psychiatry of the 1880s. Reflections on the Early German Reception of Strindberg'. An illuminating examination of Sg's reception in Germany and Austria by Hermann Bahr, Paul Schlenther, Otto Brahm, and others in relation to his preoccupation with the dynamic psychiatry of Theodule Ribot and the so-called Nancy School of Ambroise Liébeault and Hippolyte Bernheim, whose influence is manifest in the unconscious motivations explored in naturalist texts like *Fadren*, *Fröken Julie*, *Fordringsägare*, *Tjänstekvinnans son*, the 1887 *Vivisektioner*, and *I havsbandet*]

[B3:211] Hansson, Ola, 'August Strindberg', in *Das junge Skandinavien. Vier Essays*, Dresden und Leipzig: E. Piersons Verlag, 1891, pp. 69-133. [Parts of this essay were previously published in *Unsere Zeit*, **B3:218**, *Vossische Zeitung*, **B3:214**, and *Samtiden*, **B2:185**]

[B3:212] Hansson, Ola, 'August Strindberg in der Produktion eines Jahres', 1-2, *Frankfurter Zeitung*, 17 and 18 January 1890. [A two-part article on the prolific nature of Sg's literary production in the course of a single year]

[B3:213] Hansson, Ola, 'August Strindberg', in *Samlade skrifter*, 17 vols, Stockholm: Tidens Förlag, 1921, Vol. 11, 'Det unga Skandinavien', pp. 63-112. [Rpr. of **B3:211** in Swedish in Hansson's Collected Works]

[B3:214] Hansson, Ola, 'August Strindberg', *Vossische Zeitung* (Berlin), 13 April 1890 (Sonntagsbeilage).

[B3:215] Hansson, O[la], 'Literaturnoie dvizienie v Svetsii', *Trud* (St Petersburg), 20:10 (1893), 158-169. ['The Latest Literary Trends in Sweden'. Identical with **B3:219**. Discusses Sg, pp. 162-166. E.686]

[B3:216] Hansson, Ola, 'Le mouvement littéraire en Suède', Traduction de Jean de Néthy, *Revue des Revues* (Paris), 8 (1893), 481-489. ['The Literary Movement in Sweden'. Maintains that little of value is being written in Sweden today. The only exception is Sg who is the greatest modern Swedish writer, with a European reputation, even though his multifaceted work is known only partially both at home and abroad: 'There is an incalculable distance between Sg and the rest']

[B3:217] Hansson, Ola, 'Literaturnoie dvizienie v Svetsii', *Mir Bozhii*, (St Petersburg), No. 3 (1894), 193-196. ['The Latest Literary Trends in Sweden'. Comments on Sg, p. 195. One of several Russian translations of Hansson's critical articles in German, either in whole or in part. E.695]

[B3:218] Hansson, Ola, 'Das junge Schweden. Kritische Studie', *Unsere Zeit. Deutsche Revue der Gegenwart* (Leipzig), 1889:1, pp. 398-420. ['Young Sweden: A Critical Study'. Presents the writers of the Young Sweden group, with whom Sg is associated, to a German readership]

[B3:219] Hansson, Ola, 'Literaturnoie dvizienie v Svetsii', *Vestnik inostrannoi literatury* (St Petersburg), 1893:12, pp. pp. 221-230. [One of the first informed accounts of contemporary Swedish literature to be published in late 19th-Century Russia. Discusses Sg, pp. 224-228. E.686]

[B3:220] Hansson, Ola, 'Skandinavische Litteratur', 1-6, *Das Magazin für die Literatur des In- und Auslandes* (Leipzig), No. 20 (17 May 1890), pp. 305-306; No. 22 (31 May 1890), pp. 337-338; No. 26 (28 June 1890), pp. 404-405; No. 30 (26 July 1890), pp. 457-459; No. 33 (16 August 1890), pp. 513-515; No. 38 (20 September 1890), pp. 593-594. [A series of informed, if polemically biased, discussions of contemporary Scandinavian literature which were instrumental in introducing it, and Sg's work prior to 1890, to a German readership]

[B3:221] Hansson, Ola, 'Den svenske Skønliteratur i Fugleperspektiv', 1-2, *Ny Jord* (Copenhagen), 1 (January-June 1888), pp. 291-297, 342-352. ['A Bird's Eye View of Swedish Literature'. Describes Sg as the foremost living Swedish writer, a true 'modern' who combines intuitive depths of insight and feeling with a sharpness of psychological detail in a wide range of genres]

[B3:222] Harboe, Paul, 'Silhouettes of Some Swedish Writers', *The Bookman* (New York), 24 (October 1906), 143-150. [Comments on Sg's 'multiform individuality'. He is a brilliant pioneer of modern literature, the 'greatest subjectivist of all time', who 'demands to be studied almost, perhaps quite as much, as Henrik Ibsen']

[B3:223] Hartmann, C. Sadakichi, 'Modern Scandinavian Authors: Kielland, Garborg, Strindberg, Ola Hansson', *Poet Lore* (Philadelphia), 3 (1891), 33-38. [Represents the first notice of Sg's work in North America of any significance. Comments on *Röda rummet*, *Giftas*, and *Fadren*]

[B3:224] Heltberg, Bettina, 'Strindberg, teatret og Brandes', *Politiken* (Copenhagen), 21 January 1999. ['Strindberg, the Theatre, and Brandes'. Illustrates how Edvard Brandes's review of the première of *Fadren* in *Politiken*, 15 October 1887, was decisive for Sg's breakthrough on the Danish stage]

[B3:225] Hjorth, Daniel, 'En modern europé', in *Gränslösa*, Stockholm: Bonnier Alba, 1995, pp. 35-50. Illus. ['A Modern European'. Examines Albert Langen's acquaintance with Knut Hamsun and other Scandinavian authors, and his attempts to bring Scandinavian literature to German readers during the 1890s with his Munich based publishing house. Among these authors was Sg who was personally hostile to Langen (1869-1909) following their meeting in Paris in 1894, when he was convinced Langen enjoyed a burgeoning relationship with Frida Uhl]

[B3:226] H. L. [Hans Land], 'Der Fall Strindberg', *Das neue Jahrhundert* (Berlin), 1 (1898-99), 1554-1562. ['The Case of Strindberg'. Among the first published Viennese reponses to Sg]

[B3:227] Idström, Nils, 'Strindberg och miljardärerna', *Blekinge Läns Tidning* (Karlskrona), 31 December 1957. ['Strindberg and the Millionaires'. Comments on the fortunes of Sg's plays in the United States]

[B3:228] Jacobsen, Harry, 'Firsernes litterære Kritik og August Strindberg', in **R:1044**, pp. 9-21. ['Literary Criticism in the 1880s and August Strindberg'. Monitors Sg's reception in the Danish press during the 1880s, when he had close contacts with literary circles in Copenhagen and founded his Scandinavian Experimental Theatre there]

[B3:229] Jacobsen, Harry, 'Strindbergs Verdensry', 1-2, *Tilskueren* (Copenhagen), 41:1 (1924), pp. 338-349, 402-411. ['Strindberg's World Reputation'. Observes that Sg has now supplanted Ibsen in non-Scandinavian eyes as the principal Nordic writer, but Denmark, France, and Germany were already of importance to him during his lifetime. In the face of antipathy in Sweden he sought to make a career as a writer in French, both in the mid-1880s and 1890s, and it was in France that a number of his plays first made an impact outside Scandinavia. Subsequently, his reputation has been highest in Germany where his later works were published in translation at almost the same time as they appeared in Swedish. His plays have been frequently performed there, even during the First World War. When considering Sg's relations with Germany it is worth noting both his correspondence with Nietzsche and the stagnant cultural life of Berlin, where Sg lived briefly in 1893. Enlisting the aid of Ola Hansson and Laura Marholm, he 'manoeuvred with his plays like a Field Marshal with his soldiers', to such good effect that they were taken up and performed by the Freie Bühne and other theatres. His subsequent reception has to be seen in the context of Emil Schering's sometimes faulty translations of his works and the even more questionable studies of psychologising critics like Hermann Esswein and Sigismund Rahmer. The extraordinary upsurge of interest in both the man and his works that followed Sg's death in 1912 also led to a German 'Strindberg Feud' in 1918, in which Otto Kaus's *Strindberg, eine Kritik*, **B3:241**, and Leopold von Wiese's *Strindberg. Ein Beitrag zur Soziologie der Geschlechter*, **B9:257**, played a prominent part. In the aftermath of the war, several other studies have appeared, in which he is treated as an established classic. This contrasts with England, where he has made little headway, and been dismissed by H. G. Wells as 'too gloomy'. J. T. Grein failed to stage his plays at his Independent Theatre and although Bernard Shaw sought to drum up interest in his work, he largely failed. Thus, although a number of translations of both his plays and prose works appeared following his death in 1912, any interest they aroused has now fallen away. Jacobsen notes that the situation in the United States is worse; there, Sg was even cheated out of his royalties for a Swedish language edition of *Svenska folket* that was second only to the Bible on the bookshelves of Swedish-Americans. Sg's standing in Austria, Hungary, Poland, Russia, Finland, Holland, Italy, Spain, Portugal, and Romania is also briefly noted, as is a translation of *Fröken Julie* into Esperanto]

[B3:230] Jamet, Claude, '[Strindberg]', *Germinal* (Paris), 11 August 1944. ['We are ripe, I think, for Sg *in extenso*']

[B3:231] 'John', 'August Strindberg presenteras för London-publiken', *Stockholms Dagblad*, 14 December 1906. ['August Strindberg Presented to a London Audience'. Reports on the reception accorded *Samum* and *Den starkare* at The New Stage Club]

[B3:232] Johnson, Walter [Gilbert], 'Strindberg and the American University Audience', in Carl Reinhold Smedmark, ed., **D2:285**, *Strindberg and Modern Theatre*, pp. 56-72. [Sg's influence on American dramatists like Eugene O'Neill, Tennessee Williams, and Arthur Miller is clear. His impact has otherwise been evident within scholarship and on American university audiences, who know him better now than forty years ago. New translations continue to appear and sell, drama anthologies designed for a college readership almost invariably include a Sg play, the annual bibliographies of scholarly journals demonstrate a burgeoning interest, and his plays are widely performed every season, both on and off campuses. Johnson exemplifies Sg's American reputation with reference to the University of Washington where he teaches and Sg's plays are read on both the Scandinavian and drama programs. The first Sg play ever to be performed there was *Samum* in 1922, followed by *Den starkare* (1932), *Paria* (1933), and *Fadren* (1935). Since then, Sg has become much better known as the facts and figures attached to this article concerning many later productions and their impact on a modern American audience often struck by the contemporary nature of his plays all serve to confirm]

[B3:233] Johnson, Walter [Gilbert], 'Strindberg and the Swedes: Past and Present', in [Carl Reinhold Smedmark], ed., **B1:405**, *Essays on Strindberg*, pp. 75-86. [A foreigner is struck by the critical reception of Sg in his own country, where scholarship has been primarily concerned with the man and only secondarily with his works as literary art or the dramas as theatre. In addition to clarifying his contribution to literature, a re-examination of those of his works which are concerned with Swedish history might also reveal that they represent positive values; they are not barbaric, as these critics often maintain, but highly civilised in practically all their implications. The venom with which his history plays were received in Sweden is startling. No other creator of historical drama has made such painstaking efforts to explain what he believed a historical drama should be and, while the charge that he was not meticulous in his scholarship may be just (as a dramatist he preferred the popular accounts of Swedish history by Anders Fryxell, Arvid Afzelius, and Georg Starbäck), one is nevertheless amazed by the variety and breadth of his reading. Moreover, his refashioning of historical material is necessarily, and in many cases successfully, designed for theatrical effect. He frankly admitted that his portrayal of historical personages was subjective but, as in Shakespeare, whose works meant so much to him, they are realised as credible individuals, immersed in conflicts that are personal as well as historical. What is so amazing in these plays is the virtuosity with which Sg adapts their form to his concept of the central character. Swedish scholars need to stop searching for biographical echoes and examine each work for its own sake, as a work of art, in order to interpret it and judge it without regard merely to Sg's life and personality]

[B3:234] Jolivet, Alfred, 'Strindberg et la France', *Adam* (London), Nos 190-191 (1949), pp. 8-10. ['Strindberg and France'. Comments on Sg's acquaintance with France and its language and his interest in French culture, including Zola, the Goncourts, Maupassant, Balzac, and Joséphin Péladan. Hence his works naturally appeal to a French reader. Nevertheless, 'Sg's work has a universal significance, a greatness that impresses everyone']

[B3:235] Jónsson, Jón Vidar, 'Hvers vegna hefur Strindberg aldrei komist til Islands? I tilefni 150 ára afmaelis August Strindbergs', *Timarit Máls og Menningar* (Reykjavik), 60:4 (1999), 67-88. Illus. ['Why Hasn't Strindberg Ever Arrived in Iceland?' In part an attack on the National Theatre of Iceland, which has only staged two plays by Sg (*Fadren* in 1958 and *Fordringsägare* in 1964), both 'poorly directed' by *Lárus Pálsson*. No mention is made of the staging of *Fröken Julie* by the Akureyri Theatre Company in the 1930s or of more recent fringe and amateur productions. Stagings of *Fadren* and *Dödsdansen* by Reykjavik City Theatre are also not discussed but some attention is paid to the distinct performing traditions of Sg in Sweden (Olof Molander and Alf Sjöberg) and Germany (Max Reinhardt)]

[B3:236] Karásek ze Lvovic, Jiří, 'August Strindberg', in *Umění jako kritika života*, Praha, 1928, pp. 19-21. [An early appreciation of Sg by a Czech poet and essayist who sees in him an apostle of truth, a revolutionary writer from a period of transition who has embraced a new, aristocratic, cultural standpoint where creative work is concerned]

[B3:237] Karlsson, Mats, 'Avtryck i Japan. Strindberg i Akutagawas skrifter', *Strindbergiana* (Stockholm), 11 (1995), pp. 31-50. Illus. ['Imprints on Japan. Strindberg in the Writings of Akutagawa'. Documents Sg's reception in Japan as well as his influence on the Japanese novelist Ryūnosuke Akutagawa (1892-1927) whose short prose narrative 'Haguruma'

(1927) is a paraphrase of *Inferno*. Akutagawa was also impressed by Sg's short story 'På gott och ont' in *Svenska öden och äventyr*, and his library contained twenty-one books by Sg, mostly in English. Karlsson notes that, alhough there was considerable interest in Sg during the Taisho period (1912-26), he is now more or less forgotten and largely unread in Japan. As much a comparative study of Sg's significance for Akutagawa as an overview of Sg's reception in Japan. Karlsson's article considers the relevance of *Inferno* and *Legender* for him as a writer and a man in some detail, and reflects on Sg's relevance for several later Japanese authors]

[B3:238] Kaus, Otto, 'Strindberg-Kult', *Die Aktion* (Berlin), 7 (1917), Nos 47-48, Sp. 631-642. ['Strindberg Cult'. A sharply argued attack on the widespread German 'cult' of Sg by a left-wing critic, subsequently amplified in **B3:241**]

[B3:239] Kaus, Otto, 'Der Strindbergkult', in Hans-Peter Bayerdörfer, Hrsg., **B3:85**, *Strindberg auf der deutschen Bühne*, pp. 258-263. ['The Strindberg Cult'. Rpr. of **B3:238**]

[B3:240] Kaus, Otto, 'Strindberg', *Summa* (Hellerau), 1:4 (1918), 137-148.

[B3:241] Kaus, Otto, *Strindberg. Eine Kritik*, München: R. Piper & Co. Verlag, 1918. 165 pp. [Concentrates on the role Sg has played in German literature and theatre during the war years, and on his place as a representative writer of high capitalism. According to Kaus, his nihilistic dramas have been promoted by a literary and commercial elite which sought to create a literature as inconsequential and irresponsible as itself. This elite enjoys Sg in the theatre while the masses perish on the battlefield. Thus, 'Sg has become the poet (Dichter) of the capitalist high bourgeoisie']

[B3:242] Keel, Aldo, 'Reclam und der Norden. Autoren, Titel, Auflagen 1869-1943', in Dietrich Bode, Hrsg., *Reclam. 125 Jahre Universal Bibliothek 1867-1992. Verlags- und kulturgeschichtlich Aufsätze*, Stuttgart: Reclam, 1992, pp. 132-147. ['Reclam and the Nordic Countries. Authors, Titles, Editions 1869-1943'. A survey of Nordic writers issued in German translation by the publishing house Reclam]

[B3:243] Kejzlar, Radko, 'Strindberg i Tjeckoslovakien', *Meddelanden från Strindbergssällskapet* (Stockholm), 38 (1966), pp. 1-5. ['Strindberg in Czechoslovakia'. Seeks to augment Gunnar Ollén's brief account of Sg's plays in performance in Czechoslovakia in the first edition of his study of Sg's plays in performance, **D2:239**, with an overview of Czech translations of Sg, including the prose works as well as the plays. Kejzlar also lists several important critical studies of his life and work. Many of Sg's plays have been performed in Czechoslovakia, including *Siste riddaren* in 1928 and *Den starkare*, *Fröken Julie*, and *Pelikanen* at the Vinohradské Theatre, when Karel Čapek was dramaturge there. Sg's influence on Czech literature (above all on Czech drama) is undeniable]

[B3:244] Knapp, Gerhard P., '*Strindberg und die deutschsprachigen Länder: Internationale Beiträge zum Tübinger Strindberg-Symposium 1977*. Hrsg. von Wilhelm Friese; *Skandinavische Dramatik in Deutschland. Bjørnstjerne Bjørnson, Henrik Ibsen, August Strindberg auf der deutschen Bühne 1867-1932*. Von Wolfgang Pasche', *Monatshefte*, 73:4 (1981), 471-472. [A descriptive review of both **B3:168** and **B3:338**]

[B3:245] Konforti, Jossif, 'Geo Milev i teatara', *Vecherni novini* (Sofia), No. 4159, 22 January 1965, p. 4. ['Geo Milev and the Theatre'. Reviews the scandal created by the poet and translator Geo Milev's production of *Dödsdansen* in Bulgaria, on the 70th anniversary of Milev's birth. See **B3:44**, **B3:153**, and **B3:182**]

[B3:246] Kotrelyov, Nikolaj, 'Strindberg and Russia', in Michael Robinson, ed., **B1:379**, *The Moscow Papers*, pp. 121-126. [Locates the first references to Sg in Russian periodicals dating back to the late 1880s and confirms that, between 1908 and 1912, two editions of his 'collected' works were published, only for him to vanish almost entirely from sight during the Soviet period, with neither edition actually complete. An examination of the way in which Sg has been perceived in Russia thus facilitates a better understanding of features specific to the formation of Russian culture at the end of the 19th century and during the early 20th Century. Kotrelyov identifies numerous similarities between Sg and the Russian writers of the symbolist period: of particular interest is the role his works played in the amorous and occult triangle formed by Nina Petrovskaya, Andrey Bely, and Valery Bryusov, whose two-part autobiographical novel, *The Fiery Angel* (1907-08), draws upon their collective reading of Sg, as well as upon their three-way emotional entanglement. Bely's novels *The Silver Dove* (1910) and *St Petersburg* (1913) also share something of Sg's vision of the world, but the most important writer to engage deeply with his work was Aleksandr Blok, who described himself as living 'under the sign of Strindberg' during his most creative period, in 1912]

[B3:247] Landa, M. J., *The Jew in Drama*, London: P. S. King & Son Ltd., 1926, p. 290. [Notes Sg's work in the repertoire of London's East End Yiddish theatre: Landa points out that 'Sg, unknown in the West End, was no mere mysterious name to the Yiddish theatre habitués of Whitechapel']

[B3:248] Landgren, Bengt, '"En förvirrad intelligens och ett sjukt känsloliv". Strindberg i svensk akademisk litteraturundervisning 1915-1946', in Margareta Brundin *et al.*, red., *20 x Strindberg*, **B1:88**, pp. 246-261. ['"A Confused Intelligence and an Unhealthy Emotional Life". Strindberg in Swedish Academic Literature Teaching, 1915-1946'. Examines the place accorded Sg and his works in the university training of teachers of Swedish and literature. Landgren considers the role played by Martin Lamm's work at Stockholms högskola, lists many of the topics discussed in postgraduate dissertations, and comments on Gunnar Ollén's thesis on *Strindbergs 1900-talslyrik*. Like Sten-Olof Ullström in **B3:466,** whose work this essay complements, he notes that Lamm fostered work within narrow, uncontroversial boundaries and also seems strangely not to have encouraged further research on one of his own specialisms, modern drama. Landgren also considers the role of Anton Blanck and Victor Svanberg in Uppsala, Sverker Ek and Otto Sylwan in Göteborg, and Albert Nilsson and Fredrik Böök among several others in Lund, and comments on Gunnar Castrén's judgement of Sg in the influential third edition of *Illustrerad svensk literaturhistoria*. He concludes that, in their various ways, Lamm, Böök, and Castrén all queried the relevance of the most experimental Sg of *Spöksonaten* well on into the twentieth century]

[B3:249] Landgren, Bengt, red., *Universitetsämne i brytningstider. Studier i svensk akademisk litteraturundervisning 1947-1995*, Acta Universitatis Upsaliensis Historia litterarum 25, Uppsala: Universitet, 2005. 740 pp. [Surveys the teaching, objectives, content, and outcomes of literary history and poetics (subsequently comparative literature) as a university discipline in Uppsala, Stockholm, Lund, and Göteborg during the period 1947-1995. Includes assessments of the methodology and reception of several prominent doctoral theses on Sg by Carl Reinhold Smedmark (**B1:395**), Gunnar Brandell (**B1:55**), Allan Hagsten (**B1:151**), Nils Norman (**B8:119**), Stellan Ahlström (**B3:13**), Barbro Ståhle Sjönell (**G16:48**), and Torsten Eklund (**S:85**), charts shifts in theoretical direction of relevance to new approaches to Sg's work, and comments on the subjects selected for examination by dissertation at undergraduate and masters level]

[B3:250] Landquist, John, 'Strindberg i Amerika', *Nordisk Tidskrift* (Stockholm), 29 (1916), 216-218. [Reflections on Sg's reputation in the United States, occasioned by Edwin Björkman's welcome translations of the plays in four volumes. Works like *Kronbruden*, *Svanevit*, and *Fordringsägare* ought to be well received there]

[B3:251] Łaniewski, M., 'August Strindberg. Zarys biograficzno-literacki', *Życie* (Kraków), 1890, Nos 11-13. ['August Strindberg. A Biographical and Literary Outline'. The first serious published comment on Sg's life and work to appear in Polish]

[B3:252] Larcarti, Arturo, 'August Strindberg in the Periodicals of Austrian Expressionism', in Michael Robinson and Sven Hakon Rossel, eds, **B1:387**, *Expressionism and Modernism*, pp. 93-99. [Documents the growing interest in Sg's work and personality in Austria during the period 1910-1918, focusing primarily on the Innsbruck journal *Der Brenner*]

[B3:253] Larsen, H. A., 'Strindberg in America', *American-Scandinavian Review* (New York), 1 (1913), 23-24. [A critical review of existing American translations of the plays which ventures a summary overview of Sg's literary and spiritual development. As so often, America here refers merely to the United States]

[B3:254] Lawrence, C. E., 'Top-notes in Letters. The Present Vogue of Strindberg, John Masefield and "Milestones"', *Book Monthly* (London), 10 (1914), p. 391.

[B3:255] Leffler, B., 'Strindberg i Ungern', *Svenska Dagbladet* (Stockholm), 20 May 1912. ['Strindberg in Hungary']

[B3:256] Lemaître, Jules, 'De l'influence récente des littératures du nord', *Revue des Deux Mondes* (Paris), 15 December 1894, pp. 847-872. ['On the Recent Influence of the Literatures of the North'. A widely noticed pronouncement on the influence exerted by Scandinavian, English, and Russian writers on France and French literature during the 1880s and 1890s by a leading French critic of the period, who argues that the Scandinavian writers currently in vogue in Paris are totally lacking in originality and derive all their ideas from France. Sg is mentioned only briefly, as part of a more general and pervasive a phenomena]

[B3:257] Lemaître, Jules, 'De l'influence récente des littératures du nord', in *Les Contemporaines*, Sixième série, Paris: Lecène, Oudin et Cie., 1896, pp. 225-270. ['On the Recent Influence of the Literatures of the North'. Rpr. of **B3:256** in a revised form]

[B3:258] Lengefeld, Cecilia, 'Albert Langen: Verleger als Brückenbauer', *Orbis Litterarum* (Copenhagen), 51 (1996), 118-128. ['Albert Langen: Publisher as Bridge Builder'. Assesses Langen's role in facilitating the spread of Scandinavian literature in Germany during the last decades of the 19th Century and his failure to publish *En dåres försvarstal* there, a book he had nevertheless published in French in France]

[B3:259] Letmark, Peter, 'Ständigt denne Strindberg', *Dagens Nyheter* (Stockholm), 5 December 2005. ['Forever Strindberg'. Reflects on the enduring interest in Sg, several of whose plays, including *Erik XIV*, *Fröken Julie*, and *Pelikanen*, are currently in performance at different theatres in Stockholm]

[B3:260] Letmark, Peter, 'Varför är Strindberg fortfarande så aktuell?', *Dagens Nyheter* (Stockholm), 6 December 2005. ['Why is Strindberg still so Contemporary?' Seeks to answer the question with reference to the opinion of four of those involved in current productions of his plays, Lena Strömdahl, Ingela Olsson, Hannes Meidal, and Lennart Hjulström]

[B3:261] Lengefeld, Cecilia, 'Förlaget Albert Bonniers äventyr i Tyskland 1911-1913', *Litteratur och samhälle* (Uppsala), 32:1 (1997), 5-101. ['The Adventures of the Publishing House Albert Bonnier in Germany, 1911-1913'. Comments on Sg's reception in Germany in the context of the unsuccessful attempt by his principal publisher, Bonniers, to establish a German branch in Leipzig. English summary]

[B3:262] Lewko, Marian, 'Kalendarz wystawień dramatów Strindberg na scnach polskich za lata 1905-1970', *Roczniki Humanistyczne* (Lublin), 19:4 (1971), [65]-71. ['A Calendar of Performances of Strindberg's plays on the Polish Stage During the Period 1905-1970'. Reproduces the list of performances in **B3:266**]

[B3:263] Lewko, Marian, *Obecność Skandynawów w polskiej kulturze teatralnej w latach 1876-1918*, Rozprawa habilitacyjna, Katolicki Uniwersytet Lubelski, Wydzia Nauk Humanistycznych, Lublin: Redakcja Wydawnictw KUL, 1996. 848 pp. [On the reception of Scandinavian theatre in Poland, 1876-1918, a period during which Sg assumes increasing significance]

[B3:264] Lewko, Marian, 'Rezeption der theatralischen Theorie Strindbergs in Polen', in Carl Reinhold Smedmark, ed., **D2:285**, *Strindberg and Modern Theatre*, pp. 151-162. ['The Reception of Strindberg's Theatrical Theories in Poland'. First translated into Polish in the early 1890s, Sg was presented to Polish readers in a series of articles during the same decade. He became a central influence on the theatre in the early years of this century. B. Gorczyński's staging of *Fröken Julie* in Warsaw in 1910 was of particular importance, as was a production of *Spöksonaten* at Witkiewicz's Teatr Formistyczny in 1926. Lewko covers the period 1914-1975 only very briefly]

[B3:265] Lewko, Marian, 'Wczesna recepcja twórczości dramatycznej Augusta Strindberga w krytyce polskiej', *Roczniki Humanistyczne (Annales de lettres et sciences humaines* (Lublin), 23:1 (1975), 157-181. ['The Early Reception of August Strindberg's Dramatic Works by Polish Critics'. Confirms that in Poland Sg was accorded a place alongside Edward Gordon Craig as a theatrical innovator, and that there was a virtual Sg cult among the Young Poland group of writers. Summary in French, pp. 179-181]

[B3:266] Lewko, Marian, and Irena Sławińska, 'Recepcja teatralna Strindberga w okresie Młodej Polski', *Roczniki Humanistyczne (Annales de lettres et sciences humaines)*, (Lublin), 19:4 (1971), 5-64. ['The Theatrical Reception of Strindberg During the Young Poland Period'. Studies Sg's reception in the Polish theatre, focusing mainly on the period 1908-1939, followed, pp. 65-71, by a catalogue of Sg's plays staged in Poland between 1905 and 1970, with details of the theatres and performers in the principal roles. English summary, pp. 73-81]

[B3:267] Lidforss, Bengt, 'Skandinaviska författare i Berlin', *Dagens Nyheter* (Stockholm), 3 March 1894. ['Scandinavian Authors in Berlin'. Reports that Sg is currently the most noticed Scandinavian author in Berlin; his books are in every bookshop window]

[B3:268] Lindeberg, Leo, 'Strindberg i Ryssland', *Nya Argus* (Helsingfors), 45 (1952), 165-168. ['Strindberg in Russia']

[B3:269] Lock, Charles, 'Maurice Browne and the Chicago Little Theatre', *Modern Drama* (Toronto), 31:1 (1988), 106-116. [Notes that Sg was one of several dramatists introduced to an American audience by Browne, whose conception of theatre, presented in *The*

Temple of a Living Art (1913) and *The New Rhythmic Drama* (1914), partly derives from Sg]

[B3:270] Löfman, Nils, 'Strindberg och ryssarna', *Stockholms-Tidningen*, 15 August 1940. ['Strindberg and the Russians']

[B3:271] Low, Lady, 'Swedish Drama in Britain', *Theatre Arts* (London), 24 (1940), 555-556. [Traces the occasional staging of Sg's plays in a national theatre where they 'perplex even the most serious playgoer']

[B3:272] Lulu von Strauss und Torney, 'Nordische Literatur und deutsches Geistesleben', *Schleswig-Holstein Zeitung für Kunst und Literatur* (Altona-Ottensen), 1 (1906-07), 371-380. ['Nordic Literature and German Intellectual Life']

[B3:273] Lunacharskii, Anatoli, 'Velikomuchennik individualizma: Avgust Strindberg', in *Sobranie sochinenii*, Vol. 5, Moskva: Izdatel'stvo Akademii Nauk, 1965, pp. 217-221, 665. [Comments on Sg as a representative writer for bourgeois individualism by the first Soviet Commissar of Education]

[B3:274] Lutz, Volke, 'Strindberg – ein Autor wird entdeckt', *Weimarer Beiträge* (Berlin), 28:2 (1982), 35-49. ['Strindberg – An Author is Discovered'. The Stockholm Sg festival in May 1981 convinced German Marxists that his works have been unduly neglected in the DDR where the current image of him as a 'bourgeois reactionary' is based on inadequate translations and research, and should be revised. Argues Sg's case with reference to Brecht, Martin Andersen Nexø, Maksim Gor'kii, and Thomas Mann, as well as to *Fadren*, *Fröken Julie*, *Till Damaskus*, *Erik XIV*, *Dödsdansen*, and *Ett drömspel* in performances in Sweden and both East and West Germany. Lutz also refers to *Giftas* and to Sg's relevance for the plays of Bertolt Brecht, Friedrich Dürrenmatt, and Peter Weiss]

[B3:275] Luz, J. de, 'Notes du jour', *Le Voltaire* (Paris), 11 January 1893. [Includes responses to a questionnaire about the current vogue for Nordic literature in France from Émile Zola, the administrator of the Théâtre Française, Jules Claretie, and André Antoine]

[B3:276] Magon, Leopold, 'Wegbereiter nordischer Dichtung in Deutschland', in *100 Jahre Reclams Universal-Bibliothek 1867-1967. Beiträge zur Verlagsgeschichte*, Hrsg. H. Marquardt, Leipzig: Reclam, 1967, pp. 204-252, 461-467. ['Forerunners of Nordic Literature in Germany']

[B3:277] Måneskšöld-Öberg, Inger, *Att spegla tiden – eller forma den: Ola Hanssons introduktion av nordisk litteratur i Tyskland 1889-1895*, Skrifter utgivna av litteraturvetenskapliga institutionen vid Göteborgs universitet 12, Göteborg: Litteraturvetenskapliga Institutionen vid Göteborgs universitet, 1984. 243 pp. ['To Reflect the Age – Or Form It: The Introduction of Nordic Literature into Germany by Ola Hansson, 1889-1895'. Analyses Ola Hansson's importance as an intermediary who played a key role in the introduction of Scandinavian literature into Germany between 1889 and 1895, a period when he was also sometimes in close personal and literary contact with Sg, to whom frequent reference is made throughout. German summary]

[B3:278] Marchand, J., 'America's Acquaintance with August Strindberg', *The Bookman* (New York), 38:4 (December 1913), 435-437. [Given the recent upsurge of translations into English, our national consciousness seems to be catching up on Sg, who was discovered by France and Germany as the repellent genius of Swedish poetry some twenty years ago. 'It is August Sg's misfortune that not what he says, but the manner of his saying counts against him....In all the wonderful strength of some of the pictures, types, and characters he has created, there is always that nagging, quarrelsome personal note, that choosing of the unpleasant thing to say, as if in fear that the saying of the pleasant would reveal a weakness']

[B3:279] Marcus, Carl David, 'Was Strindberg von Deutschland empfing', *Die Volksbühne* (Hamburg), 5 (1930-31), pp. 550-553. ['How Strindberg was Received in Germany']

[B3:280] Marken, Amy van, 'Zweeds toneel in Nederland/Swedish Theatre in the Netherlands', in Egil Törnqvist and A. Sonnen, eds, *Niet alleen Strindberg. Zweden op de Planken / Not Only Strindberg. Sweden on Stage*, Catalogue, Holland Festival, 1985, pp. 20-30. Illus. [The history of the performance of Sg's plays in Holland has proceeded in a series of very pronounced waves, unlike the case of Ibsen, whose acceptance was a far more steady process. Initially introduced to Dutch readers in 1882, Marken records that the first translation of note was of *Hemsöborna* in 1890, while the plays were originally encountered in touring French productions by Antoine and Lugné-Poe. *Fadren* received its Dutch language première in 1893 and *Fröken Julie* only in 1912, after which it was not performed again in Dutch until 1960. However, a second wave of interest in Sg was fostered by Max Reinhardt's production of *Dödsdansen* on tour in 1916, which prepared the way for Dutch stagings of *Oväder, Brott och brott, Påsk, Pelikanen*, and *Ett drömspel* (1918-21), as well as *Dödsdansen* in 1927. With one exception, Sg remained unperformed until the 1960s when his plays were seen on television as well as in the theatre. But the 1980s have been 'a real boom period for Sg' in the Netherlands where Dutch television has screened Swedish serialisations of the novels *Röda rummet, Hemsöborna*, and *I havsbandet*]

[B3:281] Märker, Friedrich, 'Strindberg überschätzt?', *Hochland* (München), 13:1 (1915-16), 631-634. ['Strindberg Overrated?' Wonders if the current interest in Sg in Germany does not seriously overvalue him]

[B3:282] Martersteig, Max, 'Das Strindberg-Bild und die Kommenden', *Das deutsche Theater* (Bonn), 1 (1922-23), 69-78. ['The Image of Strindberg and His Succesors'. Reflects on Sg's reception and reputation in Germany]

[B3:283] Martin, Jacqueline, '*Fröken Julie* – en postkolonial utmaning', *Strindbergiana* (Stockholm), 14 (1999), pp. 163-168. ['*Miss Julie* – A Post-Colonial Challenge'. On Sg's reception in Australia, focusing primarily on a production of *Fröken Julie* in which the play is set in the Australian outback in 1888, thus foregrounding the treatment of the indigenous population by European settlers, the divisive education afforded aborginal children by missionary education, and the climate of opinion fostered by 19th-Century evolutionary theory. The play is staged so that when the aboriginal 'Jack' finally hands Julie the razor, her humiliation is complete and white supremacy shattered. A list of Sg's plays produced in Australia between 1988 and 1996 is appended]

[B3:284] Martinoir, F. D., 'August Strindberg en journaux littéraires françaises', *La Quinzaine littéraire* (Paris), 16 January 2001. ['August Strindberg in French Literary Journals']

[B3:285] Martinus, Eivor, 'Strindberg i London 2005', *Strindbergiana* (Stockholm), 21 (2006), pp. 50-59. [A report on the reception accorded Sg in the Brittish press during a year in which a major exhibition of his paintings was mounted at Tate Modern, along with productions of *Påsk, Pelikanen, Leka med elden, Brända tomten*, and *Svarta handsken*, and a controversial adaptation of *Ett drömspel* by Caryl Churchill at the National

Theatre. Martinus finds it unfortunate that these initiatives were greeted with such a lack of understanding and that Sg should have been treated so disrespectfully]

[B3:286] Mathieu, André, *August Strindberg sa modernité, sa reception en France*, 2 vols, Paris: A[ndré] Mathieu, 1990. 303, 386 pp. [A privately published, stencilled thesis which provides the most detailed account of the long-term reception of Sg in France to date. Contains copious bibliographic information, performance dates, and review material. A copy is held in the Royal Library, Stockholm, as well as the Bibliothèque Nordique in Paris]

[B3:287] Mathieu, André, 'August Strindberg – mitt i dödsdansen', Translated by Jens Nordenhök, *Aftonbladet* (Stockholm), 18 May 1987. ['August Strindberg – In the Midst of the Dance of Death'. Discusses the reception accorded *Dödsdansen* on its performance at the Théâtre de l'Œuvre in 1944 during the final days of the German occupation. In Henri Rollan's production, which brought about Sg's breakthrough in France, the play caught the mood of the moment and was applauded by both partisan and collaborationist critics]

[B3:288] Matsui, Shoyo, 'On Strindberg', *Kokumin Shinbun*, 15 May 1912. [Written in conjunction with Sg's death. Argues that 'in today's Japan, which is full of modern girls who blindly admire Ibsen's doll-like Nora, it is necessary to import more Sg and show men's rightful power and authority.' Ibsen's characters resemble marionettes; Sg's figures possess an overwhelming intensity. In Japanese, by a well-known theatre director of the period]

[B3:289] Maury, Lucien, 'Den svenska literaturen i Frankrike', *Göteborgs Handels- och Sjöfartstidning*, 21 November 1921. ['Swedish Literature in France'. Comments on the reception accorded Swedish literature in France]

[B3:290] Maury, Lucien, 'Strindberg et nous', in **B1:303**, *L'Imagination scandinave: études et portraits*, Paris: Perrin et Cie, 1929, pp. 147-153.

[B3:291] Melchinger, Siegfried, 'Die Visionen des Gequälten', in *Die Brücke zur Welt*, (Sonntagsbeilage zur *Stuttgarter Zeitung*), 12 May 1962. ['The Visions of a Tortured Man'. Comments on Sg's position as a proscribed author in Germany during the Nazi period]

[B3:292] Melchinger, Siegfried, 'The German People Face to Face with Strindberg', *World Theatre-Le Théâtre dans le monde* (Bruxelles), 11:1 (1962), 31-44. Illus. [Sg's initial impact on the German theatre with plays like *Fadren*, in which naturalism is linked to the pathological, has to be contextualised in terms of his fellow playwrights Ibsen, Wedekind, Gerhart Hauptmann, and Hugo von Hofmannsthal, as well as the work of Henri Bergson, Ernst Mach, and Freud. Sg introduced a new theatrical language in which what is being said is to be found behind the words; he also discovered his director in Max Reinhardt, who directed *Brott och brott*, 'the play of the dawning century'. But Sg's theatrical project was part of the modernist movement to retheatricalise the theatre associated with Craig, Appia, and Jarry, whose *Ubu Roi* Sg 'must have seen in Paris about 1896' [sic]. Melchinger documents the wave of Sg productions throughout Germany between 1905 and 1922, notes the failure to reinstate his plays in the German theatre after 1945, and sees his re-emergence between 1958 and 1962 as an augury of his future eminence. Parallel French text]

[B3:293] Mencák, Bretislav, 'Tjeckoslovakien och Norden', *Horisont* (Vasa), 14:1 (1967), 4-13. ['Czechoslovakia and the Nordic Countries'. Mentions Sg only briefly]

[B3:294] Merbach, Paul Alfred, 'August Strindberg auf Berliner Bühnen', *Berliner Hefte für geistiges Leben*, 4:2 (1949), 103-114. ['August Strindberg on the Berlin Stage'. An inexactly documented account of Sg's reception in Berlin's theatres up to ca.1920]

[B3:295] Merian, Hans, 'Der Bannherr des schwedischen Realismus', *Die Gesellschaft* (München), 9 (1893), 462-464. ['The Standard-Bearer of Swedish Realism'. Identifies Sg as the greatest living Swedish writer. Apropos the German première of *Fordringsägare* at Berlin's Residenztheater]

[B3:296] Meyer, Michael, 'Strindberg in England', in [Carl Reinhold Smedmark], ed., **B1:405**, *Essays on Strindberg*, pp. 65-74. [Meyer observes that Sg is only now (1966) beginning to receive his due as a dramatist in England, although apart from *Spöksonaten*, this revival of interest embraces only his naturalistic plays. Notwithstanding exceptions like J. B. Fagan's Oxford Players production of *Spöksonaten* (1926) and Robert Loraine's performance as Edgar in *Dödsdansen* in 1928, the reasons for his long neglect may be traced to the haphazard and often under-rehearsed stagings of his plays, usually in out-of-the-way venues, as well as to the fact that the borderline where sanity and insanity merge, which is the location of all Sg's best plays, is a country from which English theatregoers, and particularly English actors, have always shrunk (so much for *Hamlet*! [MR]). Sg has also suffered more than most foreign dramatists in Britain from inadequate translation and there has been no theatre practitioner who could do for Sg in England what was done there for Chekhov by Theodor Komisarjevskii, following the latter's exile from Bolshevik Russia]

[B3:297] Miller, J. Scott, 'Det tidiga mottagandet av Strindberg i Japan', Translated by Eva Liljegran, *Artes* (Stockholm), 11:4 (1985), 77-89. Illus. ['The Early Reception of Strindberg in Japan'. Surveys the reception of Sg's works in Japan during the first two decades of the 20th Century. Sg was introduced there via a translation of Huneker's essay about him in *Iconoclasts*, **D1:203**, and the first Japanese versions of his works were made from the English, French, or German (in Emil Schering's edition). They came in two waves: 1912, when nine of the plays were published, and 1923-25, when five different anthologies of his works appeared. Except in Tokyo, even the conventions of European realism were shocking in performance, and the need to cast women in female roles posed an immediate problem in a theatre from which they had been barred as performers for over two centuries. Traditional female impersonators had neither the experience nor the acting style for such roles. Miller also considers the difficulties of translating Sg into Japanese with examples taken from two translations of *Den starkare* (1911, 1922). Forms of address, aspects of the set (e.g. tables and chairs which played no similar role in Japanese culture), plays on words, unfamiliar customs, and culture-specific references all create particular difficulties]

[B3:298] Minev, Moroslav, 'Pregled na Narodnia teatar: sled devet meseca', *Hiperion* (Sofia), 5-6 (1927), 254-258. ['About the National Theatre: Nine Months Later'. On the controversy provoked by the introduction of Sg's plays to Bulgaria, initiated by a production of *Dödsdansen* at the National Theatre]

[B3:299] Mitchell, P. M., 'Strindberg in Denmark', see Marilyn Johns Blackwell, ed., **C1:142**, *Structures of Influence*, pp. 151-164. [Surveys Sg's role in Danish literary life, beginning with Edvard Brandes, who responded promptly and with enthusiasm to *Röda rummet*, and Hans S. Vodskov, who considered *Gillets hemlighet* 'worthy of a place on every Nordic Christmas table'. Prior to the period Sg spent in Denmark in 1887-1889, his cause was taken up there by the influential critic and editor Otto Borchsenius and included the première of *Fadren* at the Casino theatre. It was while living in Denmark that Sg wrote *Fröken Julie* and sought to establish his Scandinavian Experimental Theatre; he was also involved tangentially and often fractiously in the Danish literary scene, where he knew, among others, Edvard and Georg Brandes, Henrik Pontopiddan, Herman Bang, and Gustav Wied, and contributed to the influential journals *Ny Jord*, *Ude og Hjemme*, and *Illustreret Tidende*. Danish reception of the radical iconoclast of the 1870s was revised in important articles by Georg Brandes and Johannes Jørgensen in the 1890s, and by the time of his death, Sg had become an established figure. During the First World War he enjoyed something of a renaissance on the Danish stage where, in 1915, he was played by Harriet Bosse, Johanne Dywblad, Manda Björling, and Betty Nansen. The plays now given were no longer always the starkly naturalistic pieces, and his reputation as a dramatist in Denmark may be traced in Louis Levy's regular theatre surveys in *Tilskueren*. Max Reinhardt's company performed *Oväder*, *Spöksonaten*, and *Dödsdansen* in 1920, and 1921 saw the publication of the first of Sven Lange's seven-volume Danish edition of Sg's works. But while the 1920s and 1930s were productive years for Danish drama, Sg's fortunes in Denmark were then at a low ebb; not until the late 1950s was his stature fully recognised and his modernity appreciated, with new translations by established writers like Hans Christian Branner and Inger Christensen]

[B3:300] Mittenzwey, Kuno, 'Strindberg und die Welt von 1928', in *Fünfundzwanzig Jahre Georg Müller Verlag München*, München: Georg Müller Verlag, 1928, pp. 49-52. ['Strindberg and the World of 1928'. On Sg as lately the most performed of Scandinavian dramatists in Germany and his links with the Müller Verlag via Emil Schering's German edition]

[B3:301] Mittenzwey, Kuno, 'Strindberg und die Welt von 1928', *Kölner Tagblatt*, 21 January 1929. ['Strindberg and the World of 1928'. Rpr. of **B3:300**]

[B3:302] Mittenzwey, Kuno, 'Strindberg und die Welt von 1929', *Der Kontakt* (Erfurt), 1928-29, pp. 178-180. ['Strindberg and the World of 1929']

[B3:303] Morgan, Margery M., 'Strindberg and the English Theatre', *Modern Drama* (Lawrence, Kansas), 7:3 (1964), 161-173. [Surveys the slow introduction of Sg into the English theatre, from J. T. Grein's aborted notion of staging *Fadren* at the Independent Theatre in 1893 to *Spöksonaten* on BBC Television in 1962. Morgan discusses George Bernard Shaw's endeavours on Sg's behalf (not least in support of a production of *Lycko-Pers resa*) and distinguishes between the two writers as dramatists in some detail. She suggests that the later Shaw was responsive Sg's work: indeed, 'it is to the Swedish dramatist, more than to the late Ibsen, that the British theatre ultimately owes such freedom as it has found from the stranglehold of the well-made play']

[B3:304] Morgan, Margery M., 'Strindberg in England: A Checklist of Productions up to 1947', *Theatre Notebook* (London), 17 (1962), 79-83. [A useful annotated list of 60, mainly professional, stagings of Sg's plays, which affords an overview of his early reception in the English theatre. 'In this country, the original sensation value, and subsequent theatrical success, of *Fadren* and *Fröken Julie* continued to ensure that they should be the two plays most frequently performed'. Accompanied by a comment from Sir St. Vincent Troubridge, p. 144]

[B3:305] m. [Christian Morgenstern], 'Gelegentliches. (Zum Thema Strindberg)', *Das Theater* (Morgenstern), 1 (1903-04), No. 13, pp. 185-186. ['Miscellaneous. (On the Subject of Strindberg)'. Comments on the turn-of-the-century antipathy to Sg in Germany, who is spoken of as 'an ingenious lunatic'. By the translator of *Inferno* into German]

[B3:306] m. [Christian Morgenstern], 'Gelegentliches. (Zum Thema Strindberg)', in Hans-Peter Bayerdörfer, Hrsg., **B3:85**, *Strindberg auf der deutschen Bühne*, pp. 162-163. [Rpr. of **B3:305**]

[B3:307] Mori, Mitsuya, 'Strindberg in the Early History of the Modern Japanese Theatre', in Sven H. Rossel and Birgitta Steene, eds, *Scandinavian Literature in a Transcultural Context*, Papers from the XVth IASS Conference, Seattle: University of Washington, 1986, pp. 171-174. [Reckons that before the end of the 1920s perhaps no country outside Scandinavia and Germany had so many translations of Sg as Japan. During the 1920s two leading publishers began issuing his collected works, but stopped at nine and eight volumes respectively, due to dwindling interest. Indeed, between 1928 and 1946 there were no performances of any of his plays in Japan. Perhaps because it is part of the Japanese mentality to think that the most important thing in life is a readiness to face death at any moment, the first of Sg's plays to be produced in Japan was *Inför döden* in 1912, by a Kabuki company in which the female roles were performed traditionally, by male actors. Of Japanese dramatists, Saneatsu Mushakōji (b.1885) in particular has been influenced by Sg; his play *Aiyoku* (Lust, 1916) bears a marked resemblance to *Fordringsägare*. The article includes a list of Japanese productions of Sg's plays]

[B3:308] Mori, Ogai, 'Tsukikusa jo', in *Ogai zenshu*, Vol. 23, Tokyo: Iwanami shoten, 1973. [Ogai's collected works. Reprints one of the first mentions of Sg in Japan in 1896, in the introduction to a collection of critical essays on art and literature]

[B3:309] Muchina, Tat'iana, *Russko-skandinavskie khudozhestvennye sviazi kontsa XIX–nachala XX veka*, Moskva: Izd. Moskovskogo Universiteta, 1984. Illus. 113 pp. ['Russian-Nordic Artistic Relations at the Turn-of-the-Century']

[B3:310] Mustelin, Olof, 'Estetiska föreningen. Anteckningar om litterära opinioner i Finland 1879-1893', *Skrifter utgivna av Svenska Litteratursällskapet i Finland*, 409 (1965), pp. 79-142. ['The Society of Aesthetics. Notes on Literary Opinions in Finland, 1879-1893'. Summarises the discussion of Sg's early works (primarily *Röda rummet* and *Det nya riket*, the former of which was championed in Finland by the influential Finland-Swedish critic C. G. Estlander), as recorded in the proceedings of the Finnish Society of Aesthetics in 1880-82, pp. 114-117]

[B3:311] Myrdal, Jan, 'En Strindbergspresentation för tyskar', in **B1:323**, *Strindberg och Balzac*, pp. 17-23. ['A Presentation of Strindberg for Germans']

[B3:312] Myrdal, Jan, 'Lika normal som sill och potatis', Översättning Hans O. Sjöström, in **B1:314**, *I de svartare fanors tid. Texter om litteratur, lögn och förbannad dikt*, Skriftställning 18, Stockholm: Hägglunds förlag, 1998, pp. 90-100. ['As Normal as Herring and Potatoes'. The text of a talk first broadcast in English on BBC Radio Three, 4 September 1985. See **B3:316**]

[B3:313] Myrdal, Jan, 'Normal som sill och potatis', *Svenska Dagbladet* (Stockholm), 12 January 1986. ['As Normal as Herring and Potatoes'. See **B3:316**]

[B3:314] Myrdal, Jan, 'Normal som sill och potatis', Translation by Jan Stolpe, in *En annan ordning. Litterärt och Personligt*, pp. 71-80. [Swedish translation of **B3:316**]

[B3:315] Myrdal, Jan, 'One of Ours. As Normal as Herring and Potatoes', *The Listener* (London), 9 January 1986. [Original of **B3:316**, as broadcast on BBC Radio Three, 4 September 1985]

[B3:316] Myrdal, Jan, 'A Swedish Strindberg', *Sweden Now* (Stockholm), 20:5 (1986), pp. 32, 74, 88, 90. [Stresses Sg's essential Swedishness, a quality which neither travels nor translates, in an attempt to redeem him from his international reputation as fostered by an uncomprehending biographer like Michael Meyer (see **R:1533**, **R:1534**, and **R:1535**). His affinities are with refractory writers like Jules Vallès, Dmitrii Pisarev, and Nikolai Chernyshevskii. Novels such as *Svarta fanor* and *Götiska rummen* are as important as international successes like *Fröken Julie* and *Fadren*]

[B3:317] Myrdal, Jan, 'August Strindberg Là ia?', *Tácphâmmoi, Hoi nhà van vietnam*, 1994:7, pp. 27-30. [Presents Sg to a Vietnamese readership]

[B3:318] Nandorf, Tove, 'Strindbergstorm över brittiska öarna', *Dagens Nyheter* (Stockholm), 13 February 2005. ['Strindberg Storm over the Brittish Isles'. Reports the current interest in Sg in the British press apropos the exhibition of his paintings and photographs at Tate Modern and the staging of Caryl Churchill's adaptation of *Ett drömspel* at the National Theatre]

[B3:319] Nathan, George Jean, 'Going Into Theatrical Details', *The Smart Set* (New York), 37:2 (June 1912), 145-152. [Offers an ironic summary of the received image of Sg, in the course of reviewing the American première of *Fadren* at the Berkeley Lyceum Theatre, New York. Sg is (amongst other things) 'a supernormal alienist utilizing himself as his subject, a neurasthenic genius with a pen of moral aconite…a leper in the ballroom who lays hand on the whitest pair of shoulders, a dramatist of the shudder that to him is but a hollow and awful giggle…a sourball, a reporter of hangover psychopathia sexualis…a man who expectorates on the counterpane of the bed chamber, a calm, cool statistician, a sex anarchist, a dramatist of vast wonder']

[B3:320] Németh, Antal, 'Strindberg på ungersk scen 1905-42', *Meddelanden från Strindbergssällskapet* (Stockholm), 61-62 (1979), p. 14. ['Strindberg on the Hungarian Stage, 1905-42'. Lists plays by Sg staged in Hungary between 1905 and 1942, with performance dates and theatres]

[B3:321] Nicholson, Steve, 'Unnecessary Plays: European Drama and the British Censor in the 1920s', *Theatre Research International* (Oxford), 20:1 (1995), 30-36. [Comments on the refusal to license *Fröken Julie* for public performance in Britain in the 1920s, documented with reference to the Lord Chamberlain's papers in which Sg is described as 'a coarse writer', and his 'beastly' play as 'morbid and thoroughly disagreeable'. 'No doctoring can do away with the loathsome atmosphere of this piece', in which the seduction of a working-class male by an upper-class woman who takes the initiative is especially objectionable]

[B3:322] Nicholson, Steve, *The Censorship of British Drama 1900-1968*, 2 vols, 'Volume One 1900-1932', Exeter: University of Exeter Press, 2003, pp. 79-80. [Includes brief details of the rejection of a public performance licence to *Fröken Julie* during this period]

[B3:323] Nikolajeva, Maria, 'Strindberg Through the Eyes of the Russian Critics', Michael Robinson, ed., **B1:379**, *The Moscow Papers*, pp. 113-120. [Nikolajeva points out that it is important to remember that Sg's early reception in Russia concerns merely one among numerous Scandinavian writers to make an impact there during the 1890s and 1900s when Nordic literature was translated into Russian in some abundance. In Sg's case there were sometimes several versions of the same work (e.g. *En dåres försvarstal*, *Fadren*, *Fröken Julie*, and 'Samvetskval' (Remorse) from *Utopier i verkligheten*). The source language for the translation was not always Swedish and much early criticism was devoted to retelling the plot or linking Sg's life with his fictions. His works were also judged in terms of contemporary Russian critical standards which derived from the pronounced utilitarian aesthetics of Vissarion Belinskii and Nikolai Chernyshevskii, and he frequently perplexed readers since he often seemed to contradict himself and change his point of view. Sg's view of women was also often badly received, as was his pessimism and the experimental nature of many of the later plays, particularly *Spöksonaten*. But a typological similarity between many of his works and Russian literature in general led to their enthusiastic reception, not least where his exploration of sacred and profane love in *En dåres försvarstal* was concerned, which echoes the work of writers as diverse as Pushkin, Dostoevskii, Turgenev, and Tolstoi. Likewise, Nikolajeva suggests that the journey on which the protagonist of *I havsbandet* embarks at the end of the novel stands typologically close to the journey as it is generally represented in Russian literature, i.e. one that leads into chaos, or nature, away from a corrupt civilisation]

[B3:324] Nikolajeva, Maria, *När Sverige erövrade Ryssland. En studie i kulturernas samspel*, Stockholm/Stehag: Brutus Östlings Bokförlag Symposion, 1996. 376 pp. ['When Sweden Conquered Russia. A Study in the Interplay of Cultures'. Adopts a semiotic approach to the impact of Swedish literature on Russia ca. 1880-1921, based on Jurij Lotman's theories of cultural interplay and the theoretical models of Roland Posner. Nikolajeva includes repeated references to Sg throughout with two specific sections, pp. 62-66 on the early history of his works in Russian translation, and pp. 123-140, where she selects a range of examples from typical sources to give a representative portrait of his early critical reception in Russia under the heading 'The Nihilist and Woman-Hater: August Strindberg'. This confirms that Sg was initially known in Russia as an historian through his work on the maps of the Caroline prisoners in Siberia during the reign of Peter the Great, and only subsequently as a novelist or dramatist. She also appends a bibliography of Sg's works in Russian translation, pp. 336-350. English summary]

[B3:325] Nilsson, Nils Åke, 'The Reception of Strindberg in Russia: The Introductory Years', *Russian Literature* (The Hague, Paris), 40:3 (1996), 231-254. [Covers the years 1890-1910, including translations into Russian during this period, and beginning with an exchange of letters on *Fröken Julie* between Chekhov and Gor'kii. The latter compared Sg to the legendary Viking, Ragnar Lodbrok, and saw him through the prism of 'Northern Myth' that was very popular in Russia at the turn of the century. During the 1890s Sg's reputation in Russia was based on his stories and novels, and one of his early intermediaries was Sof'ia Kovalevskaia, the prominent, Russian-born Professor of Mathematics in Stockholm. Others included V. Firsov (pseudonym of Baron V. Forsales), who translated several of the major novels, though somewhat cavalierly, the Lithuanian poet Jorgis Baltrusajtis, and the Dane, Peder Hansen (or 'Ganzen'). However, many Russian translations were anonymous and frequently derived from Emil Schering's German versions, whose errors they often compounded, although seemingly not to the detriment of a generally positive response on the part of Russian readers. *Leka med elden*, on the other hand, was translated by one of Lev Tolstoi's sons, L. L. Tolstoi, who knew Swedish. However, the first of Sg's plays to reach the Russian stage was *Brott och brott* in St Petersburg in 1901, with Lidia Iavorskaia as Henrietta, before she went on to perform in both *Fadren* and *Fröken Julie*. Between 1908 and 1911 two incomplete editions of Sg's works appeared in Russia, in twelve and fifteen volumes respectively, while his personality made a profound impact on the Russian symbolists, in particular Aleksandr Blok who declared 1912 to have been for him the 'Year in the Sign of Strindberg'. After 1912, however, interest in Sg suddenly declined and the more experimental post-Inferno dramas went largely unappreciated, even though in 1922 Evgenii Vachtangov followed Meyerhold's staging of *Brott och brott* with his celebrated production of *Erik XIV* at the Moscow Art Theatre, where the play was interpreted as depicting the downfall of feudal society. But after a performance of *Fadren* in 1927, it was almost fifty years before Sg's work was staged again in Russia. His misogyny, pessimism, and mysticism, coupled with the absurdism of *Spöksonaten* and the surrealism of *Ett drömspel*, meant that he could not be accommodated within the ideological framework of Stalinism and the doctrine of Socialist realism. Hence none of his prose works or plays were published in Russia between 1923 and 1964]

[B3:326] Nilsson, Nils Åke, 'Strindberg på rysk scen', *Meddelanden från Strindbergssällskapet* (Stockholm), 20 (1957), pp. 5-16. Illus. ['Strindberg on the Russian Stage'. Surveys Sg's early reception on the Russian stage, including Lidia Iavorskaia as Henriette in *Brott och brott* and Laura in *Fadren*, the first Russian versions of *Fröken Julie*, which sometimes foregrounded the underclass Jean rather than Julie, Meyerhold's staging of *Brott och brott* at Terioki in 1912, Evgenii Vakhtangov's production of *Erik XIV* at the Moscow Arts Theatre in 1922, and the generally positive response to Sg as a cultural personality of both Gor'kii and many of the symbolists]

[B3:327] Nisbet Bain, R[obert], 'Scandinavian Current Belles-Lettres', *Cosmopolis* (London), 11 (1898), 673-683. [Much less positive in its response to Sg than to Verner von Heidenstam and Selma Lagerlöf. For Nisbet Bain, 'Tschandala' and *Inferno* 'mark the last stage of a long-foreseen decadence'. Sg's 'volcanic, self-consuming energy was much too violent for any hope of permanence, and his lurid displays of artistic pyrotechnics have resulted in dust and ashes.' He compares *Inferno* with the conversion literature of Huysmans in *La Route*, and wonders 'whether that great tamer of souls, the Church, will be able to hold this vagabond Berserker for long']

[B3:328] Oberholzer, Otto, 'Wandlungen des Strindbergsbildes in Deutschland', in Wilhelm Friese, Hrsg., **B3:168**, *Strindberg und die deutschsprachigen Länder*, pp. 23-43. ['The Transformation of the Image of Strindberg in Germany'. Discusses Sg's reception in Germany, both in terms of translation and the critical literature to date. Oberholzer traces the shift away from his initial reception as a naturalist and comments on several early German essays devoted to his work by Otto Rüdiger, **B3:371**, Gustaf Steffen, **B3:400**, and Laura Marholm in **B9:171** and **B9:177**, before noting his significance for German Expressionism and the psychological readings of his life and work by Karl Jaspers and numerous others. Oberholzer also notes the impact of recent translations by Peter Weiss and the need for a revised image of Sg in Germany in the light of recent Scandinavian scholarship]

[B3:329] Oberholzer, Otto, *Wandlungen des Strindbergsbildes. Antrittsvorlesung zur Habilitation an der Universität Zürich, 16. Juni 1956*, Winterthur: Verlag Neues Winterthurer Tagblatt, 1956. 24 pp. ['The Transformation of Strindberg's Image'. Covers the changing reception of Sg in German-speaking countries under the headings (1) Das Strindbergbild des Naturalismus; (2) Expressionismus und Psychologie; (3) Anzeichen einer Neuwertung]

[B3:330] Oberholzer, Otto, 'Wandlungen des Strindbergsbildes', [Seperatabzug aus dem] *Neues Winterthurer Tageblatt*, 23 June 1976. [Identical with **B3:329**]

[B3:331] [Ollen, Gunnar?], 'Strindberg i Brasilien', *Meddelanden från Strindbergssällskapet* (Stockholm), 25 (1959), pp. 4-5. Illus. ['Strindberg in Brazil'. Reports on the reception accorded the Brazilian première of *Fröken Julie* in Brazil's fourth city, Salvador, 26 April 1958]

[B3:332] Ollén, Gunnar, 'Dramat erövrar världen', in Folke Olsson, ed., **B1:348**, *Strindberg*, pp. 56-59. Illus. ['The Dramas Conquer the World'. Identifies Sg as one of four dramatists (the others are Brecht, Chekhov, and Ibsen) who are performed regularly throughout the world, on stage, radio, and television. He was so far ahead of his time that he continues to conquer new audiences; among recent productions, Ollén notes *Erik XIV* in Tunisia and *Lycko-Pers resa* in Rio de Janeiro]

[B3:333] Ollén, Gunnar, 'Dramer som erövrat världen', in **B1:347**, *Forskarliv – sex decennier med Strindberg*, red. Catharina Söderberg and Anna Bodin, pp. 82-86. [Rpr. of **B3:332**]

[B3:334] 'Osborne' [Erik Sjöstedt], '[Strindberg]', *Dagens Nyheter* (Stockholm), 20 January 1893. [Reports on Sg's current reputation in France]

[B3:335] Ostrowski, A., 'Literatura skandynawska w Polsce', *Nowe Książki* (Warsaw), 1970, No. 11, pp. 641-644. ['Scandinavian Literature in Poland']

[B3:336] Pasche, Wolfgang, 'Strindberg auf den deutschen Bühnen 1900 bis 1912', in Wilhelm Friese, Hrsg., **B3:168**, *Strindberg und die deutschsprachigen Länder*, pp. 245-264. ['Strindberg on the German Stage, 1900 to 1912'. Although it includes a brief retrospective glance at the reception of the Naturalist dramas between 1890 and 1900, this forms the second of a three-part study of Sg's reception in the German theatre. Focuses on the impact of his works between 1900-1912, including the impression made by Max Reinhardt's early productions and the reception of the historical dramas (notably Sg's 'German play', *Gustav Adolf*), in the light of the new image of Sg that emerged following the first German edition of *Inferno* in 1898]

[B3:337] Pasche, Wolfgang, 'Wer hat Angst vor August Strindberg? Autor- und Dramenrezeption in Deutschland 1890-1980', in Angelika Gundlach, Hrsg., **B1:150**, *Die andere Strindberg. Materialien zu Malerei*, Frankfurt am Mein: Insel Verlag, 1981, pp. 291-332. Illus. ['Whose Afraid of August Strindberg? Reception of the Author and his Dramas in Germany, 1890-1980'. Divides Sg's reception in Germany into five periods: his early reputation as a naturalist writer (1890-1900); the post-Inferno phase in which Sg was often seen as a pathological case (1900-1912); his breakthrough as a precursor of Expressionism in the productions accorded his later plays by Max Reinhardt and the 1915 cycle of eight plays directed by Otto Falckenberg at the Munich Kammerspiele; the barren years (1933-1945); and his resurrection as a classic (1945-1980)]

[B3:338] Pasche, Wolfgang, *Skandinavische Dramatik in Deutschland. Bjørnstjerne Bjørnson, Henrik Ibsen, August Strindberg auf der deutschen Bühne 1867-1932*, Beiträge zur nordischen Philologie 9, Basel und Stuttgart: Helbing und Lichtenhahn Verlag AG, 1979. 310 pp. ['Scandinavian Drama in Germany'. A literary-sociological study of the reception of Scandinavian drama on the German stage which devotes far more space to the 'vergessener Avantgardist', Bjørnson, than to Ibsen or Sg. Sg's plays and their impact on the German theatre are divided into three kinds and periods, naturalist (1890-1900), post-Inferno (1900-1912), and pre-Expressionist (1912-1932), and dispatched in a single chapter, which nevertheless contains some interesting data]

[B3:339] — Greene-Gantzberg, Vivian, *Journal of English and Germanic Philology* (Urbana, Illinois), 81:1 (1982), 99-101.

[B3:340] — Sondrup, Steven P., *Scandinavian Studies* (Lawrence, Kansas), 53:2 (1981), 234-236.

[B3:341] Paul, Fritz, 'Deutschland – Skandinaviens Tor zur Weltliteratur', in Bernd Henningsen, Hrsg., *Wahlverwandtschaft. Skandinavien und Deutschland 1800 bis 1914*, Deutsches Historisches Museum, Berlin: Jovis Verlagsbüro, 1997, pp. 193-202. Illus. ['Germany – Scandinavia's Gateway to World Literature'. See **B3:342**]

[B3:342] Paul, Fritz, 'Tyskland – Skandinaviens port till världslitteraturen', in *Skandinavien und Tyskland*, Utgiven av Bernd Henningsen, *et al.*, Nationalmusei- utställningskatalog 599, Stockholm: Nationalmuseum, 1997, pp. 193-202. Illus. ['Germany – Scandinavia's Gateway to World Literature'. Describes Germany's role as the principal route by which Nordic literature reached a wider international public, mainly through German translations. Includes several bibliographical tables listing Scandinavian literature published in Germany ca. 1870-1915]

[B3:343] Paulson, Arvid, 'The Future of Strindberg in America', *American-Swedish Historical Foundation Yearbook* (Philadelphia), 1966, pp. 16-22.

[B3:344] Pehrson, Lennart, 'Strindberg hyllas i New York', *Dagens Nyheter* (Stockholm), 8 October 2001. ['Strindberg Acclaimed in New York'. Reports a new enthusiasm for Sg in conjunction with the staging of *Dödsdansen* at New York's Broadhurst Theater, with Ian MacKellan as Edgar and Helen Mirren as Alice]

[B3:345] Penzoldt, G., 'Strindberg im deutschen Repertoire', *Die Volksbühne* (Hamburg), 13 (1962-63), 142-143. ['Strindberg in the German Repertoire']

[B3:346] Perrelli, Franco, 'La prima fortuna di Strindberg sulle scene italiane', *Il Castello di Elsinore* (Torino), No. 30 (1997), 5-42. ['The Early Fortunes of Strindberg on the Italian Stage'. An extended version of **B3:347**, based on numerous additional and invaluable references. Perrelli traces Sg's early reception in Italy through the responses of Giuseppe Giacosa, Italo Svevo, and Benedetto Croce, as well as his acceptance by the Italian theatre, providing detailed reference to often unpublished documents and an analysis of the contemporary press. He also considers the determining economic factors of the Italian theatre of the period and the reception of other Scandinavian writers in Italy, including Ibsen and Anne Charlotte Leffler]

[B3:347] Perrelli, Franco, '"Och nu är Italien öppet för barbaren...": Det första mottagandet av Strindberg på de italienska teaterscenerna', Translated by Anna Grönberg, *Strindbergiana* (Stockholm), 14 (1999), pp. 116-134. Illus. ['"And now Italy is Open to the Barbarian...": The Initial Reception of Strindberg on the Italian Stage'. Benedetto

Croce first commented on Sg in 1892, as did Giulio Piccinni, who claimed that Ibsen had modelled Hedda Gabler on Laura in *Fadren*. Interest in Sg developed in the wake of Ibsen's success. The first Italian translations of his plays appeared in 1893 (*Leka med elden* before it even appeared in Sweden). They were mainly done from the German, and the first performance of *Fadren* at the Teatro Valle in 1893 was a disaster. But subsequent productions of *Fadren* with Ermete Zacconi in Trieste and Achille Vitti in Turin, were received more positively. Zacconi continued to play the role with some success until the 1900s, when Italian theatre underwent a stylistic change with the advent of Gabriele D'Annunzio. Moreover, while he neglects to mention them in his autobiography, Perrelli points out that Zacconi also mounted productions of *Fröken Julie* and *Inför döden* in 1898. After Zacconi, however, interest in Sg remained dormant until the 1920s, and as late as the mid-1960s he was rarely read and performed in Italy, a situation that has only recently begun to change]

[B3:348] Phelan, Kappo, 'A Note on Strindberg', *The Commonweal* (New York), 50 (1949), 606-607. [It is shocking that what translations there are of Sg's work have been out of print for many years. The reissue by Scribner's of *Eight Famous Plays* with a biographical introduction by Alan Harris, is to be applauded, although one might wish that place had also been found for *Fordringsägare*, the *Memorandum till Intima Teatern*, and an introduction to *Ett drömspel*]

[B3:349] Poensgen, Wolfgang, *Der deutsche Bühnenspielplan im Ersten Weltkriege*, Schriften der Gesellschaft für Theatergeschichte 45, Berlin: Selbstverlag der Gesellschaft für Theatergeschichte, 1934. [Provides details of the theatre repertoire in Germany during the First World War. Poensgen's statistics confirm that it was not simply the war that accounted for the surge in Sg's popularity there during the early part of the century]

[B3:350] Procházka, Arnošt, '[Some Aspects of Strindberg's Image]', in *Literární studie a silhouety*, Praha, 1912, pp. 30-39. [The first significant treatment of Sg in Czech. Procházka discusses *Röda rummet* in some detail and focuses especially on the social and moral aspects of Sg's work, including his conflict with the Swedish Women's Movement. Originally published in 1895]

[B3:351] Pruner, Francis, 'La première représentation de Strindberg à Paris', *Revue d'histoire du théâtre* (Paris), 30:3 (1978), 273-286. ['The First Strindberg Performance in Paris'. Describes Antoine's production of *Fröken Julie* at the Théâtre Libre, the circumstances surrounding it, and its reception in the French press, with excerpts from contemporary articles and reviews by (among others) Francisque Sarcey, Edmond de Goncourt, Jules Lemaître, and Adolphe Mayer]

[B3:352] Pryce-Jones, Alan, 'Ibsen, Strindberg og engelsk teater', *Vinduet* (Oslo), 9:3 (1955-56), 185-188. ['Ibsen, Strindberg, and English Theatre'. Notes that Sg is rarely performed in England and the English know him as the author of only two plays, *Fadren* and *Fröken Julie*. It is sometimes claimed that Sg offends the English because he lacks a sense of humour, but the latter is not strictly true, even if his humour is somewhat twisted. Indirectly, however, the influence of Sg on the English theatre has been mediated by American dramatists, including Eugene O'Neill and Carson McCullers (in *The Member of a Wedding*), as well as by Sean O'Casey, whose best work possesses an energy that is recognisably Sgian]

[B3:353] 'Qvidam Qvidamsson' [Pseudonym of Nils Peter Svensson], 'Strindbergs Verdensry', *Politiken* (Copenhagen), 30 October 1922. ['Strindberg's Worldwide Reputation']

[B3:354] 'Qvidam Qvidamsson' [Pseudonym of Nils Peter Svensson], 'Strindbergs Verdensry', *Ukens revy* (Oslo), 1922, pp. 1070-1076. ['Strindberg's Worldwide Reputation']

[B3:355] Raha, Kironmoy, *Bengali Theatre*, New Delhi: National Book Trust, India, 1978. Illus. VIII+164 pp. [Notes that Sg has been translated into Bengali and performed in Calcutta]

[B3:356] Ramond, Jean-François de, 'Strindberg actuel et intempestif', in Gunnel Engwall, **B1:121**, *Strindberg et La France*, pp. 11-12. ['Strindberg Timely and Untimely'. On Sg's links with France as an introduction to a collection of essays in French. The improvisatory Sg anticipates Jackson Pollock, John Cage, and Pierre Henry. In some respects, he is also a forerunner of the psychodrama of J.-L. Moreno]

[B3:357] Rangström, Ture, 'Strindberg i världen', *Teatervetenskap* (Stockholm), No. 23 (1981), pp. 6-8. ['Strindberg in the World'. Considers Sg's world-wide reputation from the perspective of the Sg Museum]

[B3:358] R. E. [P. D. Ettinger], '[A. Strindberg in Russia and Germany]', *Kul'tura teatra* (Moscow), 1921:3, p. 59. [Includes a bibliography. E.905]

[B3:359] Reich, Willi, 'Zur Strindberg-Renaissance', *Neue Zürcher Zeitung* (Zürich), 27 January 1957. ['On the Strindberg Renaissance'. Accounts for the renewed interest in Sg in German-speaking countries post-1945, linked in part to Reich's own translations of several of the works]

[B3:360] Reque, A. Dikka, *Trois auteurs dramatiques scandinaves Ibsen, Björnson, Strindberg devant la critique française 1889-1901*, Bibliotèque de la Revue de littérature comparée, Paris: Librairie Ancienne Honoré Champion, 1930. II+227 pp. ['Three Scandinavian Dramatists: The Reception of Ibsen, Bjørnson, and Strindberg by the French Critics, 1889-1901'. Ibsen (understandably) but Bjørnson, too, figure more prominently than Sg in this examination of the early reputation of the three dramatists in France. Reque discusses the reception accorded Sg's plays as performed at the Théâtre Libre and Théâtre de l'Œuvre in the 1890s pp. 16-18 and 146-159. He concludes that the history of Sg's reception in Paris during the 19th Century is brief. None of the three plays performed there in 1893-94 were revived and, apart from a few articles relating to his death in 1912, it was not before 1921 with the staging of *Dödsdansen* by the Théâtre de l'Œuvre, that a new and lively interest in Sg and his work emerged in France]

[B3:361] Reque, A. Dikka, *Trois auteurs dramatiques scandinaves Ibsen, Björnson, Strindberg devant la critique française 1889-1901*, Bibliothèque de la Revue littérature comparée 65, Paris: Slatkine, 1976. [Rpr. of **B3:360**]

[B3:362] Rem, Tore, 'Premature and Belated Modernism? Strindberg and British Censorship', in Mats Jansson, Jakob Lothe, and Hannu Rikonen, eds, *European and Nordic Modernisms*, Norwich: Norvik Press, 2004, pp. 149-161. [A well-documented account of Sg's early reception in England, including his own attempts to promote his works there, with particular reference to Justin Huntly McCarthy, Rebecca West, and the way in which he was perceived by the Lord Chamberlain's Office. Remm's account is revealing as regards what did or did not happen to his work in post-First-World-War Britain and not least the horror which *Fröken Julie* instilled in the censor. Rem's research confirms that it was not until the 1950s that Sg was regarded as a modern classic, and even then only with a degree of ambivalence. This leads him to question the extent to which Sg may really be termed a modernist]

[B3:363] Rg [Roger Gomulicki], 'Strindberg we Włoszech', *Dialog* (Warsaw), 1970:6, pp. 157-159. ['Strindberg in Italy']

[B3:364] Robinson, Michael, 'Aldrig längre än till Gravesend: Strindberg och England', in Björn Meidal and Nils Åke Nilsson, red., **B4:113**, *August Strindberg och hans översättare*, pp. 109-120. Illus. ['No Further than Gravesend'. Studies Sg's failure to gain more than a very limited foothold in England, even in the theatre, and the reasons for the continuing lack of understanding that his work as a whole receives there, in spite of the interest once shown in it by Bernard Shaw and the occasional successful production of one or other of the plays, which lack a stable English performance tradition]

[B3:365] Robinson, Michael, 'Leaving Gravesend at Last, or Introducing Strindberg to England', in **B1:380**, *Studies in Strindberg*, pp. 9-23. [An extended English version of **B3:364**]

[B3:366] Robinson, Michael, 'Sentida genombrott för Strindberg i England', *Parnass* (Stockholm), 6:1 (1995), 46-47. Illus. ['Late Breakthrough for Strindberg in England'. Describes the recent critical recognition accorded Sg in England, following productions of *Påsk*, directed by Katie Mitchell for the Royal Shakespeare Company, and *Dödsdansen*, directed by Peter Stormare at the Almeida Theatre, London]

[B3:367] Roger, G., 'Ce que nous connaissons des littératures scandinaves', *Quinzaine Critique* (Paris), 25 June 1930. ['What We Know of the Scandinavian Literatures'. Surveys the present state of translation from the Scandinavian languages into French, as well as studies of those literatures in France]

[B3:368] Rømhild, Lars Peter, 'Valdemar Vedels svenskere', in Thomas Forser and Sverker Göransson, red., *Kritik och teater. En vänbok till Bertil Nolin*, Skrifter utgivna av Litteraturvetenskapliga institutionen vid Göteborgs universitet 23, Göteborg, 1992, pp. 93-106. ['Valdemar Vedel's Swedes'. Discusses the Danish critic's response to Sg in both contemporary reviews and later overviews, pp. 98-100. See **B1:472**]

[B3:369] Roos, Carl, 'Die nordischen Literaturen in ihrer Bedeutung für die deutsche', in Wolfgang Stammler, Hrsg., *Deutsche Philologie im Aufriß*, Bd 3, Berlin: Erich Schmidt Verlag, 1967. Sp. 3050. ['Nordic Literature and its Significance for the Germans']

[B3:370] Rosengren, Karl Erik, *Sociological Aspects of the Literary System*, Lund Studies in Sociology 4, Lund: Natur och Kultur, 1968, pp. 176-185. [Analyses the Swedish literary institution in the period 1881-1891 which, according to Rosengren's criteria based on the number of citations an author receives in literary reviews, was completely dominated by Sg]

[B3:371] Rüdiger, Otto, 'August Strindberg, ein schwedischer Sensationsschriftsteller', *Preußische Jahrbücher* (Berlin), 56 (1885), pp. 597-627. ['August Strindberg, a Swedish Shocker and Scribbler'. The first article to attract the attention of German readers to Sg. Its presentation of him as a crude sensationalist angered Sg, who sought to respond via a riposte from Gustaf Steffen. See **B3:400**]

[B3:372] Sagehomme, Father G., *Répertoire alphabétique de 16,700 auteurs, 70,000 romans et pièces de théâtre: cotés au point de vue moral*, 10e édition, Paris: Casterman, 1966. 729 pp. [A Catholic list of prescribed and dangerous reading. Classifies *Fordringsägare*,

Dödsdansen, and *Fröken Julie* as morally 'mauvais', and *Fadren*, *Kronbruden*, *Ett drömspel*, and *Svanevit* as 'dangereux à déconseiller']

[B3:373] Samuelson, Sven, 'Strindbergs dramatik i Wien 1899-1923', *Nordisk Tidskrift* (Stockholm), 31:2 (1955), 106-114. ['Strindberg's Dramas in Vienna, 1899-1923'. At the height of Sg's popularity in Vienna, between 1899 and 1923, there were 177 performances of seventeen of his plays, the majority of them at the Theater in der Josefstadt, but he never attained the same eminence with the Viennese public as Ibsen. It was primarily Josef Jarno who staged his plays in a series of Literarischer Abend, playing Maurice in *Brott och brott*, Jean in *Fröken Julie*, and Edgar in *Dödsdansen*. He also mounted a cycle of five plays in 1910. Following a performance of *Erik XIV* at the Volkstheater in 1924, Sg was not performed again in Vienna until the Theater in der Josefstadt staged *Kristina* in 1942. Reviews of the naturalistic plays sometimes saw them as echoes of Ibsen while the post-Inferno dramas were often received with incomprehension. N.B. This article includes several wrongly ascribed dates, including the first sentence, which claims that Sg first wrote to Edvard Brandes in 1877]

[B3:374] Sandberg, Hans, 'Kina. Strindberg och Freud ersätter Mao', *Fönstret* (Stockholm), 1987:2, pp. 4-7. ['China. Strindberg and Freud Replace Mao'. An interview with Sg's Chinese translator, Li Zhiyi, who maintains that Sg and Freud are in the process of replacing Mao in China]

[B3:375] Satō, Toshihiko, 'The Acceptance of Scandinavian Literature in Japan', *Proceedings of the Fifth International Study Conference on Scandinavian Literature held at University College London*, 1964, pp. 82-98. [Abbreviated version of **B3:376**]

[B3:376] Satō, Toshihiko, 'Scandinavian Literature in Japan', *Scandinavica* (London), 4:1 (1965), 16-26. [According to Satō, Sg did not win as large a following in Japan as Ibsen, but his search for truth and his powerful individualism appealed to the modern minds of the Taishō (1912-25) and early Showa periods (1926f.). He also influenced a number of younger Japanese playwrights with regard to dramatic technique]

[B3:377] Sattler, Hanns Walther, 'Schwedische Dichtung und schwedische Kultur in ihrem Einfluß auf das deutsche Theater', *Der Kontakt* (Erfurt), 1929-30, pp. 51-58. ['Swedish Literature and Swedish Culture and their Influence on the German Theatre'. Surveys the impact of Swedish literature on the German theatre in the early decades of the 20th Century]

[B3:378] Saviciunaite, Vida, 'Strindberg i Litauen', *Strindbergiana* (Stockholm), 8 (1993), pp. 15-19. Illus. ['Strindberg in Lithuania'. Outlines Sg's stage history in Lithuania which commences with an amateur prodution of *Fadren* in Russian in 1908. However, the first Lithuanian professional theatre was not founded until 1920 and, save for a (probably) amateur performance of *Fröken Julie* in 1937, it was only in 1973, with Juozas Miltinis's staging of both parts of *Dödsdansen*, that one of Sg's plays was finally accorded a professional performance. *Fröken Julie* was staged there successfully in 1977 by Gytis Padegimas and the same director went on to present *Den starkare* on television in 1977 and *Fordringsägare* on stage in 1981. Since then Padegimas has directed *Till Damaskus I* in 1986 and *Fadren* has also been performed, both in the theatre and on television. Translations into Lithuanian of *Ett drömspel*, *Röda rummet*, *Hemsöborna*, and 'Den romantiske klockaren på Rånö' have also appeared. Translated from the English by Hans-Göran Ekman]

[B3:379] Scheid, Ann, 'The Critical Reception of Strindberg's Dramas in Germany, 1890-1922', in Sven H. Rossel and Birgitta Steene, eds, *Scandinavian Literature in a Transcultural Context*, Papers from the XV IASS Conference, Seattle: University of Washington, 1986, pp. 160-166. [According to Scheid, Sg's reception in Germany can be broken down into three phases, the Naturalist period (1890-1902), the Neo-Romantic, or Max Reinhardt period (1902-1912), and the Expressionist period (1912-1922). During the first phase, there was a mania for Scandinavian literature, particularly in Berlin, and Sg was initially regarded in the light of Ibsen, whose popularity in Germany peaked in 1911. Disciples of naturalism saw *Fadren* as lacking in craftsmanship and overly autobiographical while Otto Brahm interpreted *Fröken Julie* solely in terms of class conflict and others viewed his works as the products of a sick, depraved mind. It was the world première of *Dödsdansen* in Cologne in 1905 that made Sg's name in Germany (the production later toured forty German cities), and his cause was furthered by Emil Schering, both as a translator and an invaluable impressario, and Max Reinhardt with his landmark production of *Dödsdansen* in 1912. This opened the way for the staging of Sg's dream plays in Munich and Frankfurt as well as Berlin, and by 1916 it was evident that Sg had supplanted Ibsen in importance on the German stage. Studies of Sg by Otto Kaus, **B3:239**, Bernhard Diebold, **D1:108**, Arthur Liebert, **B1:264**, and Karl Jaspers, **S:162**, provide a representative spectrum of views of Sg at the height of his reputation in Germany, where he was seen as a 'mächtiger Exponent des Weltgefühls']

[B3:380] Schiller, Harald, 'Carl G. Laurin som teaterkritiker', *Sydsvenska Dagbladet* (Malmö), 1-2, 18 and 21 June 1948. ['Carl G. Laurin as a Theatre Critic'. Assesses the long-serving theatre reviewer of the influential Swedish journal *Ord och Bild*, to which Laurin contributed numerous, sometimes unsympathetic, reviews of Sg's work]

[B3:381] Schiller, Harald, 'Carl G. Laurin som teaterkritiker', in **D1:397**, *Thalia i Malmö och andra essayer*, pp. 207-[215]. [Rpr. of **B3:380**]

[B3:382] Schlyter, Herman, 'Strindberg och Kina', *Skånska Dagbladet* (Malmö), 24 June 1984. ['Strindberg and China']

[B3:383] Schoeller, H. W. A., 'Der 100. Geburtstag Strindbergs in der französischen Presse', *Das Buch* (Baden-Baden), 1:1 (1949), 13-17. ['The Centenary of Strindberg's Birth in the French Press'. Uses the occasion to survey Sg's current reputation in France]

[B3:384] Scwab-Felisch, H., 'Strindberg-Renaissance', *Frankfurter Allgemeine Zeitung*, 28 November 1975.

[B3:385] Sharypkin, D[mitrii] M[ikhailovich], 'Strindberg i G. Ibsen v russkoi literature', in *Skandinavskaia literatura v Rossii*, Leningrad: Akademiia Nauk, 1980, pp. 253-304. ['Strindberg and Ibsen in Russian Literature'. A substantial chapter and bibliography in the standard work on the reception of Scandinavian literature in Russia. Discusses Sg, pp. 253-271]

[B3:386] Sharypkin, D[mitrii] M[ikhailovich], 'Strindberg v Rossii', in *Istoricheskie sviazi Skandinavii i Rossii. IX-XX vek*, Akademiia Nauk SSSR, Leningradskoe otdelenie, Institut istorii SSSR, 1970, pp. 294-313. ['Strindberg in Russia'. An informed survey of Sg's reception in Russia to date. Includes a summary in Swedish, 'Strindberg i Ryssland'. E.1042]

[B3:387] Shepherd-Barr, Kirsten, *Ibsen and Early Modernist Theatre, 1890-1900*, Contributions in Drama and Theatre Studies 78, Westport, Connecticut: Greenwood Press, 1997. XX+200 pp. [Mainly concerned with Ibsen's reception in England and France, but Sg's reception there is also briefly discussed]

[B3:388] Shiokama, Tenpu, 'A Ghostly Fire in the Literary World', *Teikoku Bungaku*, December, 1909. [Among the earliest discussions of Sg and his plays in Japan]

[B3:389] Shi Qin'er, 'August Strindberg in China', in Donald Weaver, ed., **D2:331**, *Strindberg on Stage*, pp. 133-138. [Sg was the first Swedish author to gain some measure of celebrity in China. Two of his stories were published in the journal *The New Youth*, in 1918, and over the next two decades several other works, including three editions of *Giftas*, were published, with the encouragement of both Mao Dun and Lu Xun, who also kept several Japanese translations of Sg in his library. The dissemination of Sg's works in China is linked with the 'Fourth of May Movement' which was concerned with European ideas, including socialism and humanism, and his writings were thus blacklisted and proscribed by the Kuomintang in 1934. He was sometimes criticised as gloomy and eccentric, but he fought against social injustice and, since the founding of the People's Republic, a great deal of attention has been devoted to Sg in China. Translations of *Spöksonaten*, *Mäster Olof*, *Gustav Vasa*, and *Röda rummet* have all been published in recent years]

[B3:390] Shi Qiné [Qin'er], 'Strindberg i Kina', *Kinarapport* (Göteborg), 1981:2, pp. 32-33. ['Strindberg in China']

[B3:391] Shizuka, Yamamuro, 'Scandinavian Literature in Japan', *Japan Quarterly* (Tokyo), 8 (1961), 87-93. [Confirms that the two most widely read and influential Scandinavian writers in Japan are Hans Christian Andersen and Ibsen. Touches on Sg only in passing]

[B3:392] Sjöberg, Leif, '*Fröken Julie* i väst. Om Strindbergs-dramer i Amerika', *Perspektiv* (Stockholm), 13:1 (1962), 25-27. ['*Miss Julie* in the West. Strindberg's Plays in America'. Comments on the fortunes of Sg's plays in the North-American theatre]

[B3:393] Sławińska, Irena, and Marion Lewko, 'Strindberg och den polska teatern', *Meddelanden från Strindbergssällskapet* (Stockholm), 44 (1970), pp. 2-8. ['Strindberg and the Polish Theatre'. The absence of dependable archives and various controversies surrounding Sg's reputation in Poland have made it difficult to establish even the precise early history of his plays on the Polish stage. However, a research project undertaken by Sławińska and one of her students reveals the complex and multifaceted nature of Sg's influence in Poland, not least in terms of the later development of drama. Prior to his death, and following the publication in 1885 and 1886 of some of his prose works, only three of the plays (*Fadren*, *Fröken Julie*, and *Fordringsägare*) had been published in Polish, and, as late as 1962, the situation had barely changed: *Dödsdansen*, *Påsk*, *Advent*, and *Till Damaskus* were known only from stage performances and in typescript. The first play to be performed in Poland was *Samum* in 1905, and it was as a naturalist that Sg initially made an impact, most notably through Karol Adwentowicz's staging of *Fadren*, with which he toured for forty years. Although not all of them have yet been performed in Poland, the major post-Inferno dramas began to arouse interest immediately before, and just after, the First World War. Sometimes the Austrian or Russian censor intervened, sometimes aspirations were thwarted by technical difficulties, but *Advent* was nevertheless staged in 1918 and *Dödsdansen* in 1917, with Adwentowicz as Edgar. It was with *Dödsdansen* that Sg was reintroduced to the Polish stage in 1955, but it is only comparatively recently that his plays have been staged with any frequency. A 1961 production of *Erik XIV* gave rise to lively political as well as theatrical debate, and Sg now enjoys a prominent place in Poland as the precursor of virtually every modern theatrical style and movement, from naturalism to the theatres of cruelty and the absurd]

[B3:394] Söderhjelm, Werner, 'Några anteckningar om Strindberg och Finland', 1-2, *Göteborgs Handels- och Sjöfartstidning*, 1 and 2 August 1912. ['Some Notes on Strindberg and Finland']

[B3:395] Söderhjelm, Werner, 'Några anteckningar om Strindberg och Finland', in *Utklipp om böcker*, Vol. 2, Helsingfors: Söderström, 1918, pp. 13-56. ['Some Notes on Strindberg and Finland'. Rpr. of **B3:394**]

[B3:396] Sokół, Lech, 'Le Strindberg polonais', *Le Théâtre Polonaise* (Warsaw), 1984:8-9, pp. 3-7. ['The Polish Strindberg'. On the reception, dissemination, and staging of Sg's plays in Poland]

[B3:397] Sprinchorn, Evert, 'Winning an Audience for Strindberg', *American Swedish Historical Foundation Yearbook*, Philadelphia: American Swedish Historical Society, 1972, pp. 23-30. [Calls for a less laboured approach to staging Strindberg and a revision of the cliché that he is a mad and gloomy Swede. He might be redeemed in the eyes of contemporary theatre audiences if glamorous actresses were to play leading roles in his dramas opposite handsome actors]

[B3:398] Steene, Birgitta, 'Besatt viking eller uppskattad konstnär: Strindberg och Ingmar Bergman i USA', in Björn Meidal and Nils Åke Nilsson, red., **B4:113**, *August Strindberg och hans översättare*, pp. 87-108. Illus. ['Bedevilled Viking or Appreciated Artist: Strindberg and Ingmar Bergman in the United States'. Steene approaches the reception of Sg and Bergman in North America in three phases: transmission, annexation, and assimilation. She maintains that the transposition of the cultural givens in a text from one culture to another is an essential part of the translation process. It encompasses certain constant features in the image of the transported writer as s/he emerges in the new culture, including popular misconceptions and mythical conceptions which, in Sg's case, are linked to supranational notions of Scandinavia and Scandinavians. In the United States the association of Sg with Eugene O'Neill has diverted attention from those who sought to advance his reputation there, even during his lifetime, although the way in which his later plays were represented established him as a dramatist whose work was mainly appropriate for performance in experimental theatres and the universities. The biography by V. J. McGill, **R:1454**, was also influential in imposing the image of Sg as an atavistic and possessed genius on the American imagination. For the most part, it is the naturalistic dramas with which Sg continues to be represented on North American stages, although he has an indirect presence in the work of the dramatists he has influenced, from Eugene O'Neill and Tennessee Williams to Edward Albee and Sam Shepard]

[B3:399] Steene, Birgitta, 'Strindberg in America: Glimpses from the 1980s', *Swedish Book Review* (Lampeter), 1986 Supplement, pp. 10-13. [Discusses Sg's reception in the United States following recent productions of *Fadren* (New York, 1981), *Fröken Julie* and *Leka* *med elden* (Roundabout Theatre, New York, 1981), and *Spöksonaten* (Yale Repertory Theatre, 1977), as well as two versions of *Ett drömspel* in New York (1981) and Seattle (1982). 'It seems evident that it is Sg as a theatrical innovator, as a pioneering contributor to a drama of vision, fluid structure, and kinetic imagery that the Americans look for and respond to'. They also respond to his ability to elicit laughter]

[B3:400] Steffen, Gustaf F., 'August Strindberg, ein schwedischer Realist', *Die Neue Zeit* (Stuttgart), 6 (1888), 325-335. ['August Strindberg: A Swedish Realist'. A response to Rüddiger in **B3:371**, written at Sg's instigation and in his defence. Published in the journal of the German Social-Democratic party. Steffen points out that Sg is a realist, not a muckraker]

[B3:401] Steffen, Gustaf F., 'August Strindberg, ein schwedischer Realist', in Hans-Peter Bayerdörfer, Hrsg., **B3:85**, *Strindberg auf der deutschen Bühne*, pp. 70-72. [Rpr. of an extract from **B3:400**]

[B3:402] Steffen, Gustaf, 'Iconoclast and Impressionist', *Modern Review* (Chicago?), 2:11 (1893), 265-276. [The earliest informed discussion of Sg and his work in the United States, written by the political scientist who accompanied him on his fact-finding journey through France in 1886, to gather material for *Bland franska bönder*. Steffen stresses the pioneering nature of Sg's work and the fresh impetus it gives to the various forms in which he writes. He also notes the passionate subjectivity of his writing and its 'vehement bias']

[B3:403] Stein, E. K., 'Strindberg-Mode', *Die Wage* (Vienna), 19 (1916). ['The Strindberg Fashion']

[B3:404] Stepins, Laimonis, 'Augustas Strindbergs Latvija', *Karogs* (Riga), 2 (1974) 162-168. [Surveys Sg's reputation in Latvia]

[B3:405] Stieve, Friedrich, 'Die kulturellen Beziehungen zwischen Schweden und Deutschland', *Das neue Deutschland* (Berlin), 4 (1915-16), 94-95. ['Cultural Relations between Sweden and Germany'. Examines contemporary cultural links between Sweden and Germany, including the German reception of Sg, now at a high point]

[B3:406] Stoberski, Zygmunt, 'August Strindberg i polska kritikers ögon efter 1945', Translated by Maria and Magnus Roselius, *Meddelanden från Strindbergssällskapet* (Stockholm), 44 (1970), pp. 9-22. ['August Strindberg in the Eyes of the Polish Critics after 1945'. Documents post-1945 productions of *Fadren*, *Erik XIV* (staged by Teatr Polski in Warsaw in 1961, following a radio broadcast earlier that year), and *Fröken Julie* at the Teatr Mały, Warsaw, in 1957. Includes extended extracts from contemporary reviews and concentrates on how Polish critics now regard the playwright. Stoberski concludes by quoting some more wide-ranging judgements of Sg and his plays by Polish critics in recent articles]

[B3:407] Stokes, John, '"A Woman of Genius": Rebecca West at the Theatre', in Michael R. Booth and Joel H. Caplan, eds, *The Edwardian Theatre*, Cambridge: Cambridge University Press, 1996, pp. 185-200. [Notes West's hostile response to Sg, for example in **B3:482**]

[B3:408] Stritar, Josip, 'Nova pota', *Ljubljanski zvon* (Ljubljana), 14:7 (1894), p. 395.

[B3:409] Suesser, Ignacy, 'August Strindberg, Zarys literacki', *Krytyka* (Warsaw), 1:4 (1896). p. 169. [Introduces Sg in Poland with reference to the, then, more familiar Georg Brandes. By Sg's earliest Polish translator whose versions of *Fadren* and *Fröken Julie*, both made from Ernst Brausewetter's original German translations, appeared in the journal *Przegląd Tygodniowy* in 1890 and 1891 respectively, and in a new edition in 1898. See **B2:370**]

[B3:410] Suesser, Ignacy, 'Młodzi w literaturze skandynawskiej', *Mysli* (Warsaw), 1892, No. 1-6. ['Recent Scandinavian Literature'. A discussion of the reception of Scandinavian literature in Poland by Sg's earliest Polish translator, who comments on Sg's recent works]

[B3:411] Suesser, Ignacy, 'Nowe prace w literaturze skandynawskiej', *Dodatku Miesięcznym do Przeglądu Tygodniowego* (Warsaw), 1892:1, pp. 100-114. ['New Works in Scandinavian Literature']

[B3:412] Sundström, Eskil, 'Strange Case of Swedish Literature', *The London Mercury*, 31 (1935), 355-362. [Defends Sg as a man of his century in a critical review of Swedish literary history, with particular reference to the sometimes derogatory opinions of Edmund Gosse and John George Robertson]

[B3:413] Svanberg, Victor, 'Strindbergskulten', *Spektrum* (Stockholm), 1:1 (1931), 23-34. ['The Strindberg Cult'. An attack on Sg and the 'cult' of his personality, delivered from the political left rather than, as was then more usual, the right. Earlier attacks have been directed against his radicalism, Svanberg argues, 'what I lack in him is a real, properly developed radicalism'. He concludes that 'Sg personifies everything barbaric in the Swedish character'. An influential contribution to the long-standing Swedish debate concerning Sg's real significance which prompted a series of articles in Volume 2 of the Stockholm journal *Fönstret* by Arnold Solvén (No. 37, p. 5), Arvid Petersén (No. 39, p. 3), Leon Fried (No. 42, p. 14), and Vagn Albeck Børge (No. 44, p. 14)]

[B3:414] Svanberg, Victor, 'Strindbergskulten', in *Poesi och politik*, Stockholm: Albert Bonniers Förlag, 1931, pp. 74-87. ['The Strindberg Cult'. Rpr. of **B3:413**]

[B3:415] Svanberg, Victor, 'Strindbergskulten', in Gunnar Brandell, red., **B1:82**, *Synpunkter på Strindberg*, pp. 18-26. ['The Strindberg Cult'. Rpr. of **B3:413**]

[B3:416] Svanberg, Victor, 'The Strindberg Cult', in Otto Reinert, ed., **B1:371**, *Strindberg: A Collection of Essays*, pp. 71-78. [English translation of **B3:413**]

[B3:417] Swan, Arthur, 'Strindberg and American Critics', *New York Dramatic News*, 3 March 1915, p. 5.

[B3:418] Swerling, Anthony, ed., *In Quest of Strindberg: Letters to a Seeker*, Cambridge: Trinity Lane Press, 1972. 229 pp. [Publishes the responses of a cross-section of French and Belgian writers, critics, and theatre practitioners to Swerling's invitation to consider what Sg means to them and the influence he has had on the French theatre. Includes brief and often unhelpful or mischievously misleading contributions by, among many others, Samuel Beckett, Roland Barthes, Jacques Derrida, Claude Levi-Straus, André Maurois, René Clair, and Philippe Soupault]

[B3:419] — Łegeżyński, S., *Gazeta Niedzielna* (Londyn), 1972:20, p. 3.

[B3:420] Swerling, Anthony, *Strindberg's Impact in France 1920-60*, Cambridge: Trinity Lane Press, 1971. Illus. 238 pp. [The position of Sg in pre-1914 France and the nature of his theatre is discussed as a preliminary to a detailed survey of modern French drama. From this it would appear from Swerling's indefatigable preconceptions that Sg's dramas impacted on plays by virtually every dramatist of note who wrote in French between 1920 and 1960, from Lenormand, Vitrac, Salacrou, and Cocteau to

Sartre, Genet, Camus, Beckett, Adamov, Ionesco, and Vauthier. Appendices include an annotated list of major productions of Sg's plays in France, 1920-1960, an account of the furore that accompanied Artaud's production of *Ett drömspel* (1928) and the assault on it by André Breton and his fellow Surrealists, and a survey of some of what Swerling maintains are the omissions, additions, and misrepresentations in seven recent French translations of his plays which thus 'betray a lack of stage sense and little feeling for dialogue'. (See **B4:18** and **B4:143** for two ripostes.) Swerling focuses especially on what he calls 'The Sequestration Cycle' – i.e. those plays which, like *Huis Clos*, *Endgame*, and Vauthier's *Capitaine Bada*, rest in the shadow of *Dödsdansen*. But although he observes that 'in a study of influence one must be wary of odd coincidences and analogies', the book is often concerned with identifying precisely such similarities in the structure, characterisation, and even the diction of just about every French-writing dramatist in the period under review, however incongruous. There is a useful list of reviews of Sg's plays in French performance, grouped chronologically according to production]

[B3:421] — Kärnell, Karl-Åke, *Scandinavica* (London), 11:2 (1972), 144-146. [Reflections on the reception of Sg in France and his influence on the French theatre (most notably the plays of Sartre and Beckett), in the course of a positive review of Swerling's 'meticulous' and 'sensitive' study]

[B3:422] — Knapp, Bettina L., *Romanic Review* (New York), 65:3 (1974), 235-236. ['A most valuable reference work' and 'a judicious and highly readable study']

[B3:423] — Knowles, Dorothy, *French Studies* (Oxford), 29:4 (1975), 489-491. [Swerling gives the impression that every modern French playwright must have had Sg's texts at his elbow when writing, and continually overstates his case. If Sg's influence on the French theatre is ever established, it will not be accomplished by the method employed here. Also reviews *In Quest of Strindberg*, **B3:418**: although beautifully printed on mauve paper, this collection of 182 repetitive responses from writers, directors, and academics about Sg's influence in France has little to offer the reader]

[B3:424] — Landquist, John, 'Vad gjorde Frankrike med Strindberg?', *Aftonbladet* (Stockholm), 22 November 1971. ['What did France do with Strindberg?']

[B3:425] — Legeżyński, S., *Gazeta Niedzielna* (Londyn), 1971:43, p. 4.

[B3:426] — Legeżyński, S., *Dziennik Polski i Dziennik Zołnierza* (Londyn), 1972:4, p. 3.

[B3:427] — Madsen, Børge Gedsø, *Scandinavian Studies* (Lawrence, Kansas), 46:4 (1974), 401-402. [Although the influence of *Dödsdansen* on Sartre's *Huis Clos* (1945) and Anouilh's *La Valse des Toreadors* (1952) is unmistakable, many of Swerling's other instances of Sg's alleged impact on modern French playwrights are unconvincing]

[B3:428] — Picard, Hans Rudolf, *Arcadia* (West Berlin), 9:2 (1974), 212-213.

[B3:429] — Rinman, Sven, *Göteborgs Handels- och Sjöfartstidning*, 10 June 1972. [Also reviews *In Quest of Strindberg*, **B3:418**]

[B3:430] — Scobbie, Irene, *Journal of European Studies* (Chalfont St Giles), 2:2 (1972), 209-210. [While he makes a good case for Sg's influence, particularly on French drama post-1945, Swerling often pushes his evidence too far. His appendix, which criticises several French translations of Sg's works, is out of place here. Also reviews *In Quest of Strindberg*, **B3:418**]

[B3:431] — Stenström, Thure, *Samlaren* (Uppsala), 92 (1971), pp. 248-250. [Swerling's ambitious account of Sg's initial reception and subsequent influence in France produces a wealth of useful detail, like the catalogue of reviews of every major French production of a Sg play, but it cannot conceal the mechanistic and all too ingenious way in which he identifies Sg's presence in every play of note written in France since 1945. The appendix, which criticises several recent French translations of Sg, reveals his mechanical approach to translating]

[B3:432] — Wittrock, Ulf, *Upsala Nya Tidning*, 22 April 1972. [Also reviews *In Quest of Strindberg*, **B3:418**]

See also **A4:8, A4:54**

[B3:433] Stein, Caroline, 'Strindbergsfestivalen i Kina 2005', *Strindbergiana* (Stockholm), 21 (2006), pp. 31-37. Illus. ['The Strindberg Festival in China, 2005'. A report on the theatrical and literary events, including an international Sg conference, which were mounted in Beijing and elsewhere in China in 2005 to coincide with the publication in Chinese of several of Sg's most important works in five volumes]

[B3:434] Törnqvist, Egil, 'De ongespeelde Strindberg', *Vooys: Tijdschrift voor Letteren* (Amsterdam), 19:1 (2001), 48-53. ['The Unperformed Strindberg'. Addresses the very partial nature of the limited repertoire of plays by Sg regularly performed in the Netherlands]

[B3:435] Törnqvist, Egil, 'Ibsen and Strindberg Conquer Paris', in Hub. Hermans, Wessel Krul and Hans van Maanen, eds, *1894 European Theatre in Turmoil: Meaning and Significance of the Theatre a Hundred Years Ago*, Amsterdam: Rodopi, 1996, pp. 83-96. [Briefly surveys the unsuccessful Paris première of *Fröken Julie* in 1893 and the better received *Fordringsägare* and *Fadren* at the Théâtre de l'Œuvre in 1894. Loiseau's revision of Sg's French translation incorporated aspects of Erich Holm's German version and was consequently more verbose than the original. In particular, the relative success of *Fadren* may be attributed to the psychological sensitivity and outstanding directing talent of the Danish author Herman Bang who assisted Lugné-Poe]

[B3:436] Törnqvist, Egil, 'Strindberg i Nederländerna', *Strindbergiana* (Stockholm), 2 (1987), pp. 43-47. ['Strindberg in the Netherlands'. Recent productions of different plays (described here briefly but with insight) suggest that the serious discovery of Sg as a dramatist in the Netherlands is now in progress]

[B3:437] Törnqvist, Egil, 'Strindberg i Nederländerna', *Strindbergiana* (Stockholm), 14 (1999), pp. 136-143. Illus. ['Strindberg in the Netherlands'. Covers the last three decades, including the translation of many of the prose works by Rita Törnqvist Verschuur and Karst Woudstra, and an exhibition of Sg's paintings at the Van Gogh Museum. According to Törnqvist, *Fröken Julie* remains the most frequently performed of the plays in Holland, followed by *Dödsdansen*, *Fadren*, *Ett drömspel*, *Fordringsägare*, *Pelikanen*, and *Spöksonaten*. Indeed, the naturalist Sg continues to dominate, and *Till Damaskus* only reached the Dutch stage in 1982, in a heavily cut version]

[B3:438] Törnqvist, Egil, 'Strindberg: nog steeds niet ontdekt', *Literama* (Amsterdam), December 1981, 315-323. ['Strindberg: Still Undiscovered'. Refers to the very partial awareness of Sg's achievement, even as a dramatist, in the Netherlands]

[B3:439] Trenchovski, Goran, 'The Road to Strindberg', Translated by Katarina Cipusheva, *Shine*, No. 12 (January 2000). [Prefaces a review of *Till Damaskus* as staged by Vojdan Cernodrinski for a tour of the Balkans with a brief survey of Sg's plays in performance in Macedonia, from *Fadren* in several productions (the first in 1924) to *Dödsdansen* (in Skopje, 1940), and *Spöksonaten* (directed by Stojan Stojanski at the Macedonian National Theatre, in 1992)]

[B3:440] Trypúcko, Józef, 'Andrzej Nils Uggla, *Strindberg och den polska teatern 1890-1970. En studie i reception*', *Samlaren* (Uppsala), 100 (1979), pp. 255-259. [Essay review of **B3:444** by its faculty opponent. Among other reservations regarding Uggla's presentation of Sg's impact on the Polish theatre, Trypúcko argues that he is incorrect in claiming that it was almost entirely via stage performances that Sg became generally known in Poland. Initially he was introduced there via translations of the prose works. Seven stories and two novels (*Hemsöborna* and *Inferno*) appeared in Polish between 1885 and 1900; the next eight years saw the publication of a further six stories as well as *Ensam* and parts of *Giftas*. Sg's death brought the publication of further prose works rather than performances of his plays. The latter only began to make an impact after 1908, generally in versions from the German. Uggla's title is consequently misleading, but there are valuable observations about Sg's influence on Stanisław Przybyszewski and the presentation of Sg's plays in performance in Poland is based on painstaking research]

[B3:441] Uggla, Andrzej Nils, 'Polskie widzenie Strindberga', *Acta Sueco-Polonica* (Uppsala), 5 (1996), [151]-166. [Surveys Sg's reception in Poland from the mid-1880s to the 1990s]

[B3:442] Uggla, Andrzej Nils, *Strindberg a teatr polski 1890-1970*, przelozyli Ewa Gruszczyńska, Badania polonistyczne za Granica 4, Warszawa: IBL Wydaw., 2000. Illus. 178 pp. [Polish edition of **B3:444**]

[B3:443] Uggla, Andrzej Nils, 'Strindberg i Polen', *Upsala Nya Tidning*, 23 February 1970. ['Strindberg in Poland']

[B3:444] Uggla, Andrzej Nils, *Strindberg och den polska teatern 1890-1970. En studie i reception*, Skrifter utgivna av Litteraturvetenskapliga Institutionen vid Uppsala universitet 5, Uppsala: AB Lundequistska Bokhandeln, 1977. Illus. 215 pp. ['Strindberg and the Polish Theatre: A Study in Reception, 1890-1970'. Polish critics have often maintained that Sg owed his introduction to the Polish stage to the efforts of Stanisław Przybyszewski but, after the breakdown of their friendship in 1893, the latter never furthered Sg's cause or published him in his Kraców journal, *Życie*. Initially, Polish audiences became familiar with Sg through the actor-manager Karol Adwentowicz who, from 1908, performed the title role in *Fadren* for some forty years with great psychological naturalism, and later added *Fröken Julie* and *Dödsdansen* to his repertoire during the inter-war years. A new perspective on Sg as symbolist and mystic emerged following productions of *Advent* (1918) and *Brott och brott* (1922), and the first Polish production of *Spöksonaten* at Stanisław Witkiewicz's experimental theatre in Zakopane in 1926. Sg's reception in Poland was then disrupted by the Second World War and, although Adwentowicz revived *Fadren* in 1946, the play was now unfavourably received. Uggla finds that during the period of socialist realism there was no place in the Polish theatre for Sg's psychologically complex characters, but from the mid-1950s his reception in Poland may be divided into three periods: 1955-61, 1962-1964, and 1965-1970. Initially, productions of *Fadren* and *Fröken Julie* (the latter on television as well as in the theatre) stressed aspects of contemporary Polish experience as, most notably, did a performance of *Erik XIV* in Warsaw (1961), which illustrated a ruler's struggle with his own political powerlessness. However, interest in Sg increased suddenly and broadened following the 50th anniversary of his death (1962); this was fostered by Zygmunt Łanowski's translation of six plays directly from the Swedish, and the publication in Polish journals of scholarly essays by Martin Lamm, **D2:856**, and Gunnar Brandell, **B2:60**. Sg was subsequently seen to have anticipated many of the trends in modern drama that the Polish theatre was concurrently absorbing: the theatre of the absurd was already implicit in *Spöksonaten* and both Sartre's *Huis clos* and Edward Albee's *Who's Afraid of Virginia Woolf* may be discerned in one of Sg's most frequently performed plays in Poland during the 1960s, *Dödsdansen*. Meanwhile, *Pelikanen* was readily associated with the works of the great Polish absurdist *avant la lettre*, Stanisław Witkiewicz, who replaced Sg's gravity with the grotesque and thus appeared the more modern. Furthermore, it was also Sg's works as a whole which helped promote the renaissance in the reputation of Przybyszewski during the late 1960s. Deprived of his 'authentic context' and introduced into the 'secondary context' of Polish culture, Sg's reception in Poland has therefore developed in a dynamic way, subject to the continually shifting perspectives of a nation that has undergone enormous political change in the period under review. Uggla also supplies short biographical notes on the principal Polish actors, critics, and writers associated with Sg, and a list of premières and their reviewers. Doctoral dissertation]

[B3:445] — Anderberg, Rolf, *Göteborgs-Posten*, 2 November 1979.

[B3:446] — Anon, *Arbetarbladet* (Gävle), 29 July 1977.

[B3:447] — Anon, *Życie Literackie* (Kraków), 20 November 1977.

[B3:448] — Ciesielski, Zenon, *Pamiętnik Teatralny* (Warsaw), 1977:4, pp. 601-604.

[B3:449] — Greń, Zygmunt, *Życie Literackie* (Kraków), 1977:47, p. 9.

[B3:450] — Greń, Zygmunt, 'Strindberg i my, c.d.', *Życie Literackie* (Kraków), 1978:6, p. 16.

[B3:451] — Henneberg, Jens, *Dansk Magasinet* (Copenhagen), 1978:3, p. 16.

[B3:452] — Jałowiczor, K[rystyna], *Głos Szczeciński* (Szezecin), 18 December 1980.

[B3:453] — Lathe, Carla, *Scandinavica* (London), 17:2 (1978), 175-176.

[B3:454] — Lindström, Göran, *Sydsvenska Dagbladet* (Malmö), 8 August 1977.

[B3:455] — Linnér, Sven, *Hufvudstadsbladet* (Helsingfors), 5 June 1977.

[B3:456] — Skuncke, Marie-Christine, *Studia Scandinavica* (Gdańsk), 1979:2, pp. 119-120.

[B3:457] — Sokół, Lech, *Teatr* (Warsaw), 1978:9, pp. 19-20.

[B3:458] — Stykowa, B., *Życie Literacki* (Kraków), 1978:9, p. 13.

[B3:459] — Sokół, Lech, *Le Théâtre en Pologne* (Warsaw), September-October 1977, 34-35.

[B3:460] — Stykowa, B., *Ziemia Łęczycka* (Łęczycka), 1978:9, p. 13.

[B3:461] — Szymanowski, Piotr, 'Uggla, Strindberg i teatr polski', *Dialog* (Warsaw), 23:8 (1978), 159-162.

[B3:462] — Wennergren, Jan, *entré* (Norsborg), 5 (September 1978), p. 32.

[B3:463] — Wittrock, Ulf, *Upsala Nya Tidning*, 25 May 1977.

See also **A4:147**

[B3:464] Uggla, Andrzej Nils, 'Strindberg's Modern Break-Through in Poland', in Nils Åke Nilsson, ed., *Swedish-Polish Literary Contacts*, Kungl. Vitterhets Historie och antikvitets Akademien, Konferenser 3, Stockholm: Almqvist & Wiksell, 1979, pp. 83-89. Illus. [Illustrates how the beginnings of a modern outlook on Sg in Poland which broke with the psychological naturalism associated with the performances of Karol Adwentowicz became apparent as early as the mid-1950s. Following the break with socialist realism, Polish theatre discovered an ethical perspective on contemporary issues in plays like *Fadren* and *Fröken Julie*, and *Erik XIV* was interpreted in terms of modern power politics when it was staged in 1961. Sg also emerged as the precursor of Edward Albee, Eugene O'Neill, Harold Pinter, and Jean-Paul Sartre when his plays were published in new translations by Zygmunt Łanowski and staged by e.g. Jerzy Kreczmar. The latter's production of *Spöksonaten* in 1965 at the Teatr Polski was of decisive importance in creating a new image of Sg. So, too, were several productions of *Dödsdansen* in the late 1960s, which emphasised 'the anguish of the individual caused by his isolation from the surrounding world, something which results in self-destruction'. The psychological aspect of the play was seen to have predicted modern experience and even the older naturalist dramas were now found to have anticipated the existentialism of Heidegger and Sartre, as well as the ideas of Freud, Adler, and Jung. This essay is substantially a translation of part of Uggla's thesis, **B3:444**]

[B3:465] Uggla, Andrzej Nils, 'Uppsalajubileet – en ny impuls för Strindbergsintresse i Polen', *Meddelanden från Strindbergssällskapet* (Stockholm), 59-60 (1978), pp. 68-69. ['The Uppsala Jubilee: A New Impetus for Polish Interest in Strindberg'. Among those honoured during Uppsala University's recent jubilee celebrations was Zygmunt Łanowski whose translations of Sg's plays have been invaluable for the rediscovery of Sg by the Polish theatre ever since they began to appear in 1960. Twelve of the plays in Łanowski's translations have now been published, illuminatingly annotated and with a long introduction by Lech Sokół (see **D2:1176**). The volume also contains an invaluable bibliography of Sg criticism in other languages, which conveys an idea of Sg's international standing and the ongoing scholarship in his life and works in several countries. A proper understanding of Sg's work is thus at last possible in Poland]

[B3:466] Ullström, Sten-Olof, *Likt och olikt. Strindbergsbildens förvandlingar i gymnasiet*, Stockholm/Stehag: Brutus Östlings Bokförlag Symposion, 2002. Illus. 510 pp. ['Alike and Unlike: Changes in the Image of Strindberg in Swedish Senior High School Education.' Traces the frequently rancorous assimilation of Sg into the curriculum of the Swedish gymnasium where the primary objective of native language teaching was often to strengthen the morals and national spirit of young Swedes. The representation of Sg's writings in the core curriculum changed greatly over the period 1880-1960, when a different notion of the writer's function gradually emerged. The image of Sg in student essays reflects both the general and the specifically literary ideologies and repertoires at large in contemporary textbooks, several of which are analysed here in detail, with an emphasis on the developing image of Sg they successively present. The early critiques of Fredrik Böök and Karl Warburg attribute the inconsistency of his works to his unstable psyche and link what is often seen as their offensive nature with flaws in his character. Certain works, e.g. *Röda rummet*, *Mäster Olof*, *Gustav Vasa*, a selection of stories from *Svenska öden och äventyr*, and *Hemsöborna*, are accepted relatively early while many others take a surprisingly long time to find their way into the curriculum, either because of their subject matter (*En dåres försvarstal*, *Fadren*, *Giftas*, and *Fröken Julie*) or their experimental nature (*Ett drömspel*, *Till Damaskus*, *Spöksonaten*). Even the naturalistic plays do not gain general acceptance before the 1940s. Ullström also surveys the critical literature on Sg in Swedish, including the work of John Landquist, Martin Lamm, Victor Svanberg, Oscar Levertin, Henrik Schück, and Sten Linder, and draws a working distinction between the name of the author and his proper name, using the theories of writing and authorship of Mikhail Bakhtin and Michel Foucault, as well as reception theory, in order to analyse the different connotations and more or less stereotypical conceptions that were associated with Sg's name in senior high school teaching. Ullström maintains the importance of August Paul's memoir, **R:1764**, in establishing the public image of Sg in Sweden and notes that after 1960 there has been an increased focus on the works rather than the man and his psychological makeup, even in discussions of the Inferno period. He also analyses the place accorded Sg and the way his image is mediated in textbooks by Hjalmar Alving, **B5:3**, Gudmar Hasselberg, **B5:68** and **B5:69**, Josua Mjöberg, **B5:99**, and others, clarifies the layers of intertextuality they often contain, and traces changes in the repertoire of works by Sg included in the school syllabus. Contains an English summary, translated by Erica Sandlund, pp. 417-428, and the text of five student essays from 1912 to 1960. Doctoral dissertation]

[B3:467] — Bäckstedt, Eva, 'Skolan kapitulerade för Strindbergs mästerskap', *Svenska Dagbladet* (Stockholm), 12 July 2002. ['The School System Capitulated to Strindberg's Mastery']

[B3:468] — Ekblad, Sigrid, *Tidskrift för litteraturvetenskap* (Stockholm), 33:1 (2004), 173-175.

[B3:469] — Stugart, Martin, 'Gymnasisterna fick inte läsa Strindberg', *Dagens Nyheter* (Stockholm), 29 July 2002. ['High School Students weren't Allowed to Read Strindberg']

[B3:470] Ullström, Sten-Olof, 'När Strindberg kom till skolan', *Strindbergiana* (Stockholm), 18 (2003), pp. 171-196. ['When Strindberg Came to School'. Summarises much of the discussion in **B3:466**]

[B3:471] Unger, R., 'Strindberg-Kultus', *Frankfurter Zeitung*, 10 March 1918. [Attacks the cult of Sg as promoted by Arthur Liebert in *August Strindberg. Seine Weltanschauung und seine Kunst*, **B1:264**]

[B3:472] Unglaub, Erich, 'Strindberg in München', in Roger Bauer and Dowe Fokkema, eds, *Proceedings of the XIIth Congress of the International Comparative Literature Association*, 5 vols, München: iudicium verlag, 1990, Vol. 1, pp. 185-200. ['Strindberg in Munich'. Although Sg had only casual links with Munich, Unglaub demonstrates that the subsequent interest in his works by certain of its residents, including Thomas Mann, Max Halbe, and Frank Wedekind, played a significant role in his German reception. Georg Müller Verlag, the publishing house through which Emil Schering issued his German edition of Sg's collected works, was based in Munich and the cycle of eight of his plays spread over six evenings at the Munich Kammerspiele in 1915 was a major cultural event. *Fordringsägare* was also performed there with Max Halbe as Adolf in a performance in a private house in 1895]

[B3:473] [Vasser College], 'Strindberg i Poughkeepsie', *Meddelanden från Strindbergs-sällskapet* (Stockholm), 22 (1958), pp. 15-16. [Assesses Sg's reputation among American college students in the late 1950s. 'For the present college generation living in a time of conformity, the radical, nihilistic Sg provides an exhilarating, albeit disturbing, intellectual experience'. Notes that Vasser College is presenting *To Damascus* to mark International Theatre Month]

[B3:474] Vazov, Ivan, 'Pismo', *Razgivor* (Sofia), 1:3 (23 January 1921), p. 3. ['A Letter'. An attack on *Dödsdansen* and other 'symbolist nonsense' by Bulgaria's foremost modern writer (1850-1921)]

[B3:475] Vendelfelt, Erik, 'Strindberg i högborgerlig kritik', *Värld och vetande* (Göteborg), 12 (1962), 143-147. ['Strindberg in High Bourgeois Criticism'. Assesses the response to Sg of Carl G. Laurin, the long-serving theatre reviewer of the Swedish journal *Ord och Bild*, who was an often unsympathetic critic of Sg's work, particularly of the later plays whose premières he frequently reviewed]

[B3:476] Veselovskii, I., 'K kharakteristike sovremennoi shvedskoi literature', *Obrazovanie* (St Petersburg), 1909:5, pp. 57-77. ['On Modern Swedish Literature'. Comments on the reception of Sg in Russia and his significance for modern Swedish literature, pp. 62, 66-67, 76. E.791]

[B3:477] Veselovskii, I., 'K kharakteristike sovremennoi shvedskoi literature', in *Literary Essays*, Vol. 2, Moscow, 1910, pp. 362-387. [On Sg, pp. 367, 370, 372. Rpr. of **B3:476**. E.791]

[B3:478] V. F. [V. Firsov. Pseudonym of Baron Forsales], 'Sovremennye skandinavskie pisateli', *Russkii vestnik* (Moscow), 1896:11, pp. 257-297. ['Contemporary Scandinavian Writers'. A survey of contemporary Scandinavian literature which gives priority to those authors that Firsov has himself translated. Thus, Anna Wahlenberg takes priority over Sg, who is nevertheless discussed, pp. 274-285. E.702]

[B3:479] Volz, Ruprecht, 'Strindbergbilder in der Zeit des deutschen Expressionismus', in Wilhelm Friese, Hrsg., **B3:168**, *Strindberg und die deutschsprachigen Länder*, pp. 289-306. ['Images of Strindberg in the Age of German Expressionism'. Studies the different perceptions of Sg at large in Germany during the period 1910-1925 rather than any influence he may have exerted on German expressionism itelf. Volz quotes liberally from contemporary sources on the widespread passion for Sg in Germany which is variously described as a 'Strindbergpest', 'Strindberg Epidemie', or 'Strindberg seuche' (Sg plague, epidemic, or infestation), and includes references to critical prose and poems about Sg by M. G. Conrad, Erich Mühsam, Alfred Döblin, Peter Sacher, Siegfried von Vegesack, Kurt Heynicke, Otto Kaus, René Schickele, Wilhelm Worringer, and Bernhard Diebold, in which Sg is variously presented as the poet of the male spirit, a tragic soul, the leader of literary convention, and the unsound destroyer of western drama (Diebold)]

[B3:480] Von Bergen, Louise, *Nordisk teater i Montevideo: Kontextrelaterad reception av Henrik Ibsen och August Strindberg*, Acta Universitatis Stockholmiensis, Stockholm Studies in Literature 51, 2006. Illus. 260 pp. [Studies the impact and place of Scandinavian drama in the Uruguayan theatre during the last century with special reference to productions in Montevideo of two plays by Ibsen and one (*Fordringsägare*) by Sg. Primarily a reception study which also studies the process from the source text to performance, issues of translation and adaptation, and the historical context within which works by the two dramatists were realised at different stages in the development of Uruguayan theatre and society (in Sg's case twenty-one productions in all of

Påsk, *Fröken Julie*, *Dödsdansen*, *Fadren*, *Leka med elden*, *Bandet*, *Oväder*, *Pelikanen*, *Spöksonaten*, *Paria*, and *Fordringsägare*). Summary in Spanish. Doctoral dissertation]

[B3:481] West, Rebecca, 'Cause of Women's Restlessness: Suffragist's Spirited Reply to Male Critics', *Manchester Daily Dispatch*, 23 January 1913. [Maintains that 'there will never be – except among the perverse – any enthusiasm in England for the works of August Strindberg, the foremost European masculinist and hater of women']

[B3:482] West, Rebecca, 'Cause of Women's Restlessness: Suffragist's Spirited Reply to Male Critics', in *The Young Rebecca: Writings of Rebecca West 1911-17*, Selected and Introduced by Jane Marcus, London: Virago Press; Bloomington: Indiana University Press, 1982, pp. 376-380. [Rpr. of **B3:481**]

[B3:483] Westling, Christer, 'Wilhelm Friese (ed.), *Strindberg und die deutschsprachigen Länder*; Wolfgang Pasche, *Skandinavische Dramatik in Deutschland*', *Scandinavica* (Norwich), 20:1 (1981), 103-106. [A detailed, sometimes critical, review of **B3:168** and **B3:338** as studies in the reception of Sg in the German-speaking countries, the former marking the increasing institutionalisation of Sg studies and the latter unbalanced in its detailed treatment of Bjørnson at the expense of both Ibsen and Sg]

[B3:484] Westman, Gösta, *Strindberg i U.S.A.*, Landskrona: Eget förlag/Landskrona Tryckeri Aktiebolag, 1920. 20 pp. [Assesses the almost insurmountable obstacles to Sg's popular acceptance in the United States, a country governed by materialism and with a public that prefers revolvers on stage to Shakespeare, Ibsen, or any other European classic. Westman describes a visit that he paid Sg in Blå Tornet when he was given permission to translate *Utopier i verkligheten*, *Hemsöborna*, and *Svarta fanor* into English but was urged by Sg to give priority to *Inferno* and *Legender*, since there were so many Swedenborgians in North America. He also recalls an early performance of *Fröken Julie* in New York with Elize Hommer as Julie and 'a young, highly gifted character actor with a couple of drops of nigger blood in his veins' as Jean, and records recollections of his conversations about Sg with Maksim Gor'kii and Mark Twain]

[B3:485] Westman, Gösta, 'Strindberg i Amerika', *Afton-Tidningen* (Stockholm), 27 July 1910.

[B3:486] Widsell, Jörgen, 'Strindberg i Kina', *Aftonbladet* (Stockholm), 14 April 1986. ['Strindberg in China'. Discusses Sg's present-day reputation in China]

[B3:487] Wiese [und Kaiserwaldau], Leopold [Max Walter von], *Strindberg und die junge Generation*, Rheinland: Verlag zur Köln, 1921. 16 pp. [The text of lecture delivered in Cologne, 27 May 1921. Contains general reflections Sg's *Weltanschauung*, his profound pessimism, and general state of mind as they impinge on contemporary, post-war Germany. 'His novels and plays lead us through the night of human baseness', but the tragic effect of this experience is to instil a greater will to life in all those who read him']

[B3:488] — Pache, A[lexander], *Die schöne Literatur* (Leipzig), 23 (1922), p. 46.

[B3:489] Wieselgren, Oscar, 'Strindberg i England', *Svensk Tidskrift* (Stockholm), 20 (1930), 219-221.

[B3:490] Wieselgren, Oscar, 'Strindberg och den svenska kritiken', *Svensk Tidskrift* (Stockholm), 36:1 (1949), 46-58. ['Strindberg and the Swedish Critics'. Examines the reception of Sg in Sweden during his lifetime which follows a graph that is typical of the major changes in Swedish society after the publication of *Röda rummet* in 1879. *Mäster Olof* may not have been staged immediately but Sg was generally well received at first by leading figures in the Swedish cultural establishment; it was only with the publication of the satirical *Det nya riket* in 1882 that he broke definitively with the older, liberal generation, many of whom it attacked. It led to his move abroad in 1883 and, though his trial for blasphemy in 1884 reversed a dwindling interest in his works and made him, briefly, the leader of a new literary radical grouping, his continued absence from Sweden distanced him from its cultural life. More particularly, the works he wrote after the Inferno crisis established him as a presence in world, rather than Swedish, literature. When he eventually returned to Sweden, he could not but be aware of this discrepancy. Where he was still, it was as the radical author of the 1880s, and his new works were received with incomprehension or, at best, disappointment. Hardly a single Swedish critic appreciated that he now represented new developments in literature, and the religious dimension of his writing was entirely overlooked. Thus, Sg himself experienced the rift with his erstwhile colleagues as one in which they had remained rooted in the now outmoded standpoint of the 1880s while his experimental dramas were misunderstood by a theatre still dominated by the well-made French play or Meininger-style realism. With the death of Harald Molander (1900), Sg lost the one man who might have realised his new dramaturgy on the Swedish stage. Even the Intimate Theatre did not succeed in this respect, not least because of his own old-fashioned ideas on performance. It was only after his death and the ensuing lapse of interest in his work that these plays were finally done justice, critically by Martin Lamm and on stage by Olof Molander's productions, beginning with the Swedish première of *Advent* in 1926]

[B3:491] Wijsman, Philippine, 'August Strindberg', 1-2, *De Leeswijzer* (Amsterdam), 1 and 15 February 1885. [The first significant discussion of any of Sg's writings in Dutch. Wijsman draws on Gustaf af Geijerstam's essay, **B2:162**, and concentrates on *Mäster Olof*, *Röda rummet*, and *Det nya riket*, with a postscript on the *Giftas* trial]

[B3:492] Williams, Anna, 'Åttitalister och kvinnliga åttitalister. Genus och kanon i litteraturhistoriska översiktsverk', *Litteratur och samhälle* (Uppsala, Univ. Avd. för litteratursociologi,), 31:1, 1996. Illus. 96 pp. ['Men of the 1880s and 1880's Women. Gender and Canon in Literary Histories'. Incorporates Sg in a discussion of the significance of gender in canon formation during the period of the Scandinavian Modern Breakthrough]

[B3:493] Williams, Anna, *Stjärnor utan stjärnbilder. Kvinnor och kanon i litteraturhistoriska översiktsverk under 1900-talet*, Stockholm: Gidlunds Förlag, 1997. 285 pp. ['Stars without Constellations. Women and [the] Canon in General Works of Literary History during the 20th Century'. Examines Swedish literary historiography from a gender perspective by analysing the treatment accorded authors of the 1880s, 1930s, and 1965-1985 in standard histories of Swedish literature, in order to illustrate the process of canon formation. Sg's place in the Swedish canon is discussed pp. 59-64, 66-69, and he also features prominently in the statistical apparatus that accompanies the text and maps the literary field in Sweden during the three periods studied]

[B3:494] Woel, Cai M., 'Kring böcker och människor. August Strindberg i Danmark', *Nordisk Tidskrift* (Stockholm), 25:1 (1949), 31-33. ['Concerning Books and People. Strindberg in Denmark'. Insists that it is Sg's plays, particularly those concerned with married life, on which his reputation is securely based. Several of these were written during the time that Sg spent in Denmark, where he sought to establish his Experimental Theatre, and his contemporary reception there is documented in Harry Jacobsen's study *Strindberg i Firsernes København*, **R:1044**]

[B3:495] Wright, Rochelle, 'From Strindberg to Ekman: Swedish Literature and the American Audience', *Swedish-American Historical Quarterly* (St Peter, Minneapolis), 50:4 (1999), 233-244. [Comments briefly on Sg in the course of a survey of the translation and reception of Swedish literature in the United States]

[B3:496] W. S. [Werner Söderhjelm], 'Några anteckningar om Strindberg och Finland', *Nya Argus* (Helsingfors), 5:15 (1 August 1912), 129-132. ['Some Notes on Strindberg and Finland'. Reviews Sg's reputation in Finland, starting with C. G. Estlander's reviews of *Röda rummet* and *Det nya riket*, **G3:48**, and W. Bolin's review of *Mäster Olof* and other early dramas, **D2:512**. Söderhjelm also discusses Sg's remarks on Finland in 'Nationalitet och svenskhet', *Götiska rummen*, and *Svarta fanor*, and his acquaintance with the Finnish writers and artists Ville Vallgren, Akseli Gallén-Kallela, Albert Edelfelt, and Karl August Tavaststjerna]

[B3:497] Wulle-Wahlberg, Hans, 'Amerika entdeckte Strindberg', *Kulturarbeit* (Stuttgart), 14:4 (1962), 68-69. ['America Discovered Strindberg']

[B3:498] Zech, Paul, 'Strindberg', *Neue Theaterzeitschrift* (Berlin), 27 January 1914. [Considers the passionate German interest in Sg in 1914]

[B3:499] Zhiyi, Li, '[Untitled]', in [Heidi von Born], *Med himlen till tak...och Drottninggatan som golv. Femton balkongtal till Strindberg*, Stockholm: Podium, 1998, pp. 93-96. [The text of a speech delivered at the 1998 Sg festival on Sg's current standing in China]

[B3:500] Ziying, Gao, '"Strindbergs valda verk" på kinesiska', *Strindbergiana* (Stockholm), 1 (1985), pp. 159-162. Illus. ['"Strindberg's Selected Works" in Chinese'. Indicates that there has been a longstanding interest in Sg in China. His books were acquired by Beijing's principal library at the turn of the century in both Swedish and English. During the 1930s, the influential essayist and short-story writer Lu Hsün (1881-1936) sought to introduce his works to China; among other texts *Fröken Julie*, *Moderskärlek*, and a selection from *Giftas* were translated into Chinese while an English edition of *Fadren* with a commentary appeared in Shanghai, only for the reactionary authorities to forbid further publication. Recently, however, Sg has been described in the Chinese press as 'a unique Nordic genius of our time' and since 1980 the People's Literature Publishing House in Beijing has issued *Röda rummet*, *Tjänstekvinnans son*, and a selection of six plays: *Master Olof*, *Fadren*, *Fröken Julie*, *Gustav Vasa*, *Ett drömspel*, and *Spöksonaten*. According to Ziying, three further volumes are planned, and the works issued so far have been enthusiastically received]

See also **A1:51, B4:51, C1:951, D2:128, D2:612, E25:121, E48:48, G5:113, V:2, V:26, V:31, V:42, V:45, V:58, V:64, V:77, V:88, V:122, V:143, V:153, V:164, V:172, V:197, V:222, V:227**

B4. Translation

[*Together with theoretical discussions regarding particular aspects of translation practice applied to versions of Sg's works in different languages and critical evaluations of the work of his translators, this section also includes assessments of Sg's translations of his own and other people's work, as well as of his competence as a writer of French in those texts, including*

En dåres försvarstal *and* Inferno, *that were originally written in that language. Since, for non-Scandinavian readers, access to Sg's works is via translations, many items listed here inevitably impinge closely on material covered in the section on Reception,* **B3**, *and vice versa: which works are translated and when and where is naturally a factor in any discussion of Sg's international reputation. Translation is thus a frequent concern in discussions of non-Swedish editions of his works, including many of the responses to early collections of his plays in English in* **D2**, *and it is likewise sometimes an issue in reviews of individual performances where reviewers (unfortunately only a minority) choose to take account of the text on which a production is based. Indeed, translation is also an issue where the editorial principles adopted in Swedish editions of certain of his works and their translation from French, German, or Danish into Swedish by another author are concerned, as several items listed here demonstrate. While Sg sometimes made French versions of his own Swedish texts (e.g. of* Ett drömspel *and* Fordringsägare*), those works which he wrote in French, like* Inferno, *were always turned into Swedish by another hand – in the case of Inferno by an old student friend, Eugène Fahlstedt*]

[B4:1] Adams, Ann-Charlotte Gavel, 'Om nöjet att översätta Strindberg från franskan: textkritisk och översättningsproblematik i Strindbergs *Legender* inför utgivningen av *Samlade Verk*', in Björn Meidal, red., *Sidor av samma sak? Sex uppsatser om översättning*, Åbo Akademi Litteraturvetenskapliga Institutionen, *Meddelanden* No. 26, Åbo, 1999, pp. 69-80. ['On the Pleasure of Translating Strindberg from the French: Text-Critical and Translation Problems Involved in Editing Strindberg's *Legends* for Publication in *Collected Works*'. Adams discusses issues raised during her work in editing the French text of *Legender* for the National Edition of Sg's *Samlade Verk* and the often contradictory principles involved in providing a parallel Swedish translation for the approximately 80% of the text which he originally wrote in a generally fluent, rhythmic French, using the authorised, but often faulty, 1897 translation into Swedish made at Sg's request by Eugène Fahlstedt, as a starting point]

[B4:2] Ahlstedt, Eva, 'Le Français de Strindberg. Analyse du manuscript autographe de deux nouvelles des *Mariés II*', *Moderna språk* (Stockholm), 84:2 (1990), 132-139. ['Strindberg's French. An Analysis of the Manuscript of Two Short Stories from *Getting Married II*'. Ahlstedt scrutinises the manuscript of two stories from *Giftas II*, 'Le Pain' (Bread) and 'Automne' (Autumn), which Sg wrote in French following his trial for blasphemy in 1884 in an early attempt to establish himself as a writer in France after the proceedings brought against him for blasphemy in *Giftas I* had, in spite of his acquittal, largely closed the Swedish market to his new work. She compares them with the Swedish translation produced by Eugène Fahlstedt at Sg's request for publication in Sweden and concludes that the language of Sg's original French text commands our respect: 'but even so, it is not sufficiently accomplished to serve as a tool for a professional writer']

[B4:3] Ahlström, Stellan, '*En dåres försvarstal* – Det nyupptäckta originalet avviker på många punkter', *Dagens Nyheter* (Stockholm), 15 September 1974. ['*A Madman's Defence* – The Newly Discovered Original Differs in Many Respects'. Presents the recently discovered manuscript of the long-lost, original French text of *En dåres försvarstal* and compares it with existing versions published both before and after Sg's death in French and Swedish. Ahlström remarks on the differences between Sg's French source text and the standard Swedish version published in *Samlade Skrifter*, in a translation by

John Landquist that was based on Georges Loiseau's revision of Sg's French original. This provokes an exchange of views with Solveig Landquist (see **B4:104**). Ahlström also comments on his personal encounters with Loiseau when undertaking research in Paris during the 1950s for his thesis *Strindbergs erövring av Paris. Strindberg och Frankrike 1884-1895* (**B3:13**)]

[B4:4] Ahlström, Stellan, 'Slutreplik om översättningen av *En dåres försvarstal*', *Dagens Nyheter* (Stockholm), 8 October 1974. ['Final Response Regarding the Translation of *A Madman's Defence*'. A response to Solveig Landquist's critical observations in **B4:104**]

[B4:5] Anderman, Gunilla, '*A Dream Play*', in Olive Classe, ed., *Encyclopedia of Literary Translation in English*, 2 vols, London: Fitzroy Dearborn, 2000, Vol. 2, pp. 1350-1351. [Compares ten British and North-American translations of *Ett drömspel*]

[B4:6] Anderman, Gunilla, 'August Strindberg', in *Europe on Stage: Translation and Theatre*, London: Oberon Books, 2004, pp. 160-202. [Takes a chronological approach to the reception of Sg's plays in translation, discussing primarily their transposition into English in Britain and the United States but with some comparisons between their fortunes on English-speaking stages and those elsewhere in Europe. Anderman also considers cultural and language-specific problems frequently encountered in translating Sg in general, with particular focus on *Fadren*, *Fröken Julie*, and *Ett drömspel*]

[B4:7] Anderman, Gunilla, 'Translated Literature. O: Northern European Languages. 11: Strindberg', in Peter France, ed., *The Oxford Guide to Literature in English Translation*, Oxford: Oxford University Press, 2000, pp. 580-581. [A survey of existing English translations. Anderman concludes that 'the price of a fluent English translation is often a watered-down version of his sometimes quirky mode of expression.... What the English-speaking world tends to see as flaws in Sg...may in fact be problems in translation']

[B4:8] Anon, '*Easter* and Other Plays', *The Spectator* (Literary Supplement), 23 March 1929, p. 469. [Discusses the problems involved in translating Sg's plays with reference to the new English versions currently being published under the auspices of the Anglo-Swedish Literary Foundation]

[B4:9] Anon, 'English Adaptation Defended', *The Times* (London), 31 January 1928. [The report of a lecture about Sg by Miss Lizzie Lind af Hageby in which she defends Robert Loraine's English rendering of the Swedish text of *Dödsdansen* as performed by him at the Apollo Theatre, London. Loraine's English version gave 'the very essence of the man and an atmosphere splendidly charged with Sg'. Lind-af-Hageby refutes Sundström's criticisms in **B4:164** with reference to other versions in French and German, as well as English]

[B4:10] Anon, 'Strindberg på ungerska', *Svenska Dagbladet* (Stockholm), 2 November 1912. ['Strindberg in Hungarian']

[B4:11] Anon, 'The Work of the Translator', *The Book Buyer* (New York), March 1913, pp. 34-35. [Comments on Edwin Björkman's translations of several of the plays, quoting a letter from Sg to his English language translator, which gives him permission to 'translate and publish as much as you want of my writings'. Sg also advises Björkman how best to position himself in order to tackle 'a future edition of my collected works (some fifty volumes)' when the time comes to render them in their entirety into English]

[B4:12] Anon, 'Schering, Müller-Verlag und Strindberg', *Der Zwiebelfisch* (München), 10 (1919), 221-222. [A critique of Emil Schering's translations for the German collected edition of Sg's works, published by the Müller Verlag in Munich]

[B4:13] A. S-hjelm [Alma Söderhjelm], 'En litterär fejd', *Nya Argus* (Helsingfors), 8:3 (1915), pp. 23-27. ['A Literary Feud'. Provides a resumé of the debate concerning John Landquist's translation of *Le Plaidoyer d'un fou* involving Fredrik Böök, John Landquist, Anders Österling, and Emanuel Walberg in **B4:30**, **B4:99**, **B4:100**, **B4:129**, and **B4:192**, with extensive quotation]

[B4:14] Banér, Christine, 'Some Observations on Translating August Strindberg's *The Father*', *Proceedings of the Ninth Biennial Conference of the British Association of Scandinavian Studies held at the University of East Anglia, 8-11 April 1991*, Norwich: University of East Anglia, 1992, pp. 37-54. [A comparison of John Osborne's 1989 adaptation of *Fadren* with Michael Meyer's translation from 1964 reveals that, while the latter's knowledge of the source language works well when rendering a character's correct linguistic register and in interpreting the subtext, Osborne's professional understanding of stagecraft makes him the more successful in updating the language and creating a dramatic impact, even though his lack of Swedish sometimes leads him to misinterpret a character's motivation and overlook many of the play's finer linguistic nuances]

[B4:15] Berendsohn, Walter A[rthur], 'Översättningar i Strindbergs *Samlade Skrifter*. Tre berättelser i olika versioner', *Samfundet Örebro stads- och länsbibliotekets vänner, Meddelande* (Örebro), 19 (1951), pp. 7-22. ['Translations in Strindberg's *Collected Works*. Three Stories in Different Versions'. Berendsohn examines the transposition of three texts included in John Landquist's edition of Sg's *Samlade Skrifter* which involved translation into Swedish from another language: 'Blygsamhet och kyla' (Modesty and Coldness), originally written by Sg in French and then translated into Swedish by Eugène Fahlstedt; 'Då myrorna skulle grunda samhälle' (When the Ants Sought to Found a Society), first published in Danish in *Politiken*, 30 August 1886; and the vivisection 'Hallucinationer', also first published in Danish in *Illustreret Tidende*, 19 June 1887]

[B4:16] Bergman, Bo, '*En dåres försvarstal*', *Dagens Nyheter* (Stockholm), 17 November 1914. [Defends John Landquist against Fredrik Böök's criticisms of his translation of *Le Plaidoyer d'un fou* into Swedish in **B4:30**. Bergman considers that Landquist has been successful in capturing the genuine Sgian tone, which is at once powerful, concise, and direct]

[B4:17] Björkman, Edwin August, 'Slaughtering Strindberg', *The Drama* (New York), 3 (August 1911), 175-179. [Criticises several recent English translations of Sg's plays, especially those by Francis J. Ziegler, which derive from German versions and hence entirely fail to convey Sg's original mastery of Swedish, and particularly the way in which he deployed everyday modern idioms to such startling literary effect. According to Björkman, this is a significant failure since Sg made the language of his countrymen and women truly modern by observing and developing the living idiom as it flowed from the lips of his contemporaries. Björkman also seeks to demonstrate the requisites of a successful translation, with examples]

[B4:18] Bjurström, Carl Gustaf, 'Bokstav och ande', *Svensk Litteraturtidskrift* (Stockholm), 36:4 (1973), 3-10. ['Letter and Spirit'. Refutes Anthony Swerling's harsh criticisms of seven French translations of *Fadren*, *Fröken Julie*, *Paria*, *Erik XIV*, *Brända tomten*, *Spöksonaten*, and *Pelikanen* in both **B3:420** and **B4:167**, and demonstrates the 'absurdity' of his all-too literally based strictures as well as his inadequate knowledge of French idioms. Even if he does sometimes identify a translator's occasional lapse, Bjurström considers Swerling's approach to be ultimately 'dishonest']

[B4:19] Bjurström, Carl Gustaf, 'Boris Vian, traducteur de Strindberg', *Obliques Littérature-Théâtre* (Paris), 7-8 (1976), 291-294. ['Boris Vian, Translator of Strindberg'. Comments on the French novelist and playwright Vian (1920-1959) as a translator of Sg for the stage, most notably of *Fröken Julie* in 1952. Based in part on Bjurström's experience of collaborating with Vian]

[B4:20] Bjurström, Carl Gustaf, '*Ett drömspel* av Strinberg [sic!] – eller av Maurice Clavel?', *Meddelanden från Strindbergssällskapet* (Stockholm), 51 (1971), pp. 7-12. ['*A Dream Play* by Strindberg – Or Maurice Clavel?' Maintains that the recent production of *Ett drömspel* at the Comédie Française in Clavel's elaborate reworking of Sg's own French translation is a major theatrical event, irrespective of the fact that Clavel has taken many liberties with the original by the addition of numerous new lines, the reordering of several speeches, and the insertion of an entirely new scene. But how far is the author of an adaptation entitled to intervene? Even if Clavel does sometimes seek to render Sg's text comprehensible to an audience which is not familiar with his work, it is surely wrong to reduce Agnes's role to that of a do-gooder visiting a poor and unfortunate family, or to transform the lyricism of the original into empty phrasemongering. (In fact this was No. 49, of *Meddelanden från Strindbergssällskapet*, not 51 as printed). See the response by Torsten Måtte Schmidt, **E41:477**]

[B4:21] Bjurström, Carl Gustaf, 'L'esprit et la lettre. – Om Anthony Swerlings skrift *Strindberg's Impact in France 1920-1960*', *Babel: International Journal of Translation* (Budapest), 19:3 (1973), 112-116. ['The Spirit and the Letter. – On Anthony Swerling's Publication *Strindberg's Impact in France 1920-1960*'. Bjurström repeats his refutation of Swerling's strictures concerning seven contemporary French translations of Sg in **B4:18** (see also **B3:420** and **B4:167**) and responds with hostility to Swerling's complaints about the general deficiencies of French translations of Sg made in a previously published issue of the translation journal *Babel*, **B4:166**]

[B4:22] Bjurström, Carl Gustaf, 'Strindberg: écrivain français', in August Strindberg, *Œuvre autobiographique*, édition établie et présentée par Carl Gustaf Bjurström, 2 vols, Paris: Mercure de France, 1991, Vol. II, pp. [1198]-1221. ['Strindberg: A French Writer'. Offers an assessment of Sg's linguistic competence as a writer in French with particular reference to *En dåres försvarstal*, *Inferno*, and *Legender*]

[B4:23] Bjurström, Carl Gustaf, 'Strindberg på franska', *Strindbergiana* (Stockholm), 3 (1988), pp. 45-64. ['Strindberg in French'. Charts Sg's attempts to conquer Paris and establish himself as a European writer through the works he originally wrote in French, as well as those, like *Ett drömspel*, which he either translated himself or entrusted to Jules Henri Kramer, Charles de Casanove, Georges Loiseau, and others for translation during his lifetime. According to Bjurström, when Sg writes in French, he often works as a translator, conceiving his sentences in Swedish and writing them in the other language, but although he wrote several prose works directly in French, he never wrote for the theatre in that language. Nevertheless, his plays do not present a translator with any exceptional problems beyond what is customary (i.e. issues of rhythm, accents, idiomatic expressions, archaisms, plays on words, etc.), and there have been numerous attempts to render them into French prior to the edition of the collected plays currently being published in French under Bjurström's general editorship. He notes that a collected edition of Sg's autobiographical writings is also in prospect (see **F1:9**), and that several other prose works, both fiction and non-fiction, have recently been published in France]

[B4:24] Bjurström, Carl Gustaf, 'Strindbergs dramatik i ny fransk översättning', *Meddelanden från Strindbergssällskapet* (Stockholm), 25 (1959), pp. 14-16. ['Strindberg's Plays in a New French Translation'. Reports that the revival of interest in Sg in France thanks to productions of *Fröken Julie* and *Brända tomten* by Frank Sundström at the Théâtre de Babylone, Boris Vian's translation of *Fröken Julie*, and Arthur Adamov's monograph on Sg, **D2:1**, has prompted Editions de l'Arche to commission a new French edition of the plays, with financial support from Sweden. Many of the plays will be translated into French for the first time, and, in order to ensure their stage worthiness, each work will generally entail a collaboration between a recognised translator and a theatre practitioner]

[B4:25] Bjurström, Carl Gustaf, 'Traduire le théâtre de Strindberg', *Théâtre/Public* (Gennevilliers), 73:4 (1986), 75-78. ['Translating Strindberg's Theatrical *Œuvre*'. Comments on Sg's plays in a new generation of translations into French by Arthur Adamov, Boris Vian, Georges Perros, André Mathieu, and Bjurström himself, as well as the problems their translation poses regarding register, forms of address, the subtext, and other such issues]

[B4:26] Blanck, Anton, 'En okänd Strindbergsöversättning från H. C. Andersen', *Samlaren* (Uppsala), N.F. 1 (1920), pp. 167-168. ['An Unknown Strindberg Translation of H. C. Andersen'. Comments on Sg's 'stylistically unremarkable' translation of 'Den store søslange' (The Great Sea Serpent), in Karl Johan Backman's Swedish edition of Hans Christian Andersen's fairy tales, and its resemblance to Sg's own fairy tale, 'Stora grusharpan' (The Great Gravel Harp) in *Sagor*]

[B4:27] Blei, Franz, 'Strindberg – Schering – Péladan', *Das hohe Ufer* (Hannover), 2 (1920), 62-64. [A satirical comment on the authorised German translations by Emil Schering who, in Blei's opinion, has 'decided' rather than 'understood' what Sg writes. Blei also notes Schering's intention to translate the novels and plays of the eccentric French symbolist and Rosicrucian, Joséphin [Sâr] Péladan (1859-1918), in order to provide a context for his translations of Sg's later works. Sg greatly admired Péladan and his works supposedly illuminate Sg's post-Inferno production]

[B4:28] Blume, Herbert, '*Fröken Julie* und *Fräulein Julie*. Modalpartikeln als Übersetzungsproblem in Peter Weiss' deutscher Fassung von Strindbergs Drama', in Dieter Cherubim, Helmut Henne, Helmut Rehbock, Hrsg., *Gespräche zwischen Alltag und Literatur: Beiträge zur germanistischen Gesprächsforschung*, Tübingen: Max Niemeyer Verlag, 1984, pp. 42-63. ['*Miss Julie* and *Fräulein Julie*. Modal Particles as a Translation Problem in Peter Weiss's German Version of Strindberg's Drama'. Blume compares

Weiss's treatment of modal particles in translating Sg with Hans Egon Gerlach's approach in his 1966 translation of *Fröken Julie*. He also considers Weiss's version of *Fröken Julie* in general, and discusses the specific problems posed by so self-consciously naturalistic a drama]

[B4:29] Boehlich, Walter, 'Vom Kreutz des Übersetzens. Zu einer neuen Strindberg-Ausgabe', *Der Monat* (München), 9 (1957), 63-70. ['The Trouble with Translating. On a New Strindberg Edition'. Boehlich offers a critique of Emil Schering as a translator of Sg and enters a plea for a new German edition of his works. Although they represent a stylistic advance on Schering, Boehlich maintains that Willi Reich's versions in the recent nine-volume edition (1955-59) are also inadequate]

[B4:30] Böök, Fredrik, '*En dåres försvarstal*. Textkritiska anmärkningar', *Svenska Dagbladet* (Stockholm), 16 November 1914. ['*A Madman's Defence*. Text-Critical Observations'. A critique of the Swedish text of *Le Plaidoyer d'un fou* in *Samlade Skrifter*. Böök maintains that John Landquist lacks the general linguistic competence to translate from French into Swedish; in fact, it would have been better to publish the text of the French edition, since this would also have prevented the circulation of its dubious contents to the public at large. According to Böök, Landquist has also contrived to occlude and tone down Sg's account of his first marriage and he has further betrayed the original by substituting a culturally acceptable and inappropriate passage from the popular Swedish Gustavian poet, Carl Michael Bellman (1740-95), for the vulgar lyric which the members of the Red Room circle sing in the novel]

[B4:31] Böök, Fredrik '*En dåres försvarstal*', *Svenska Dagbladet* (Stockholm), 26 November 1914. [Continues the polemic with John Landquist begun in **B4:30**, to which Landquist had replied with **B4:100**. Böök now attacks Landquist's feeling for Sg's language and style, and warns those responsible for Sg's *Samlade Skrifter* that, if a reliable translation is not substituted for the version currently in circulation there, he will publically preserve his criticism of Landquist's translation by publishing it in book form]

[B4:32] Böök, Fredrik '*En dåres försvarstal*', *Svenska Dagbladet* (Stockholm), 17 December 1914. [A response to Anders Österling's defence of John Landquist in **B4:129**. See Österling's rejoinder in **B4:129**]

[B4:33] Bouquet, Philippe, 'Boris Vian, traducteur de *Mademoiselle Julie*', in Gunnel Engwall, ed., **B1:121**, *Strindberg et La France*. pp. 121-126. ['Boris Vian, *Miss Julie*'s Translator'. Bouquet points out that Vian's 1952 translation of Sg's drama, which was originally published by the Théâtre de Babylone together with his own play *L'Equarissage pour tous*, is the work of a writer who did not know Swedish and was not a Sgian. It was achieved with frequent reference to an English version and relied heavily on the assistance of the Swedish theatre director Frank Sundström (as well, presumably, of Vian's Swedish-speaking wife, although she goes unmentioned here). A close analysis reveals numerous errors and misunderstandings, as well as a number of inspired French reformulations of Sg's text]

[B4:34] Brennecke, Detlef, '*Fröken Julie* auf deutsch. Fünf Übersetzer suchen August Strindberg', in Wilhelm Friese, Hrsg., **B3:168**, *Strindberg und die deutschsprachigen Länder*, pp. 161-194. ['*Miss Julie* in German. Five Translators in Search of August Strindberg'. Offers a comparison of five German versions of *Fröken Julie* by Ernst Brausewetter, Emil Schering, Willi Reich, Peter Weiss, and Hans Egon Gerlach, which places each translator in his historical context where the state of the language and the practice of translation is concerned. According to Brennecke, Brausewetter omits or dilutes the sexual banter in the text, Schering's literal rendering is strewn with errors, and Reich's version is only a marginal improvement. Weiss, who has had recourse to the original manuscript, as well as to the published text, provides a fresh, uncensored version, while Gerlach, in seeking to render Sg contemporary by omitting anything 'dated', produces an anodyne version, which lacks any sense of period]

[B4:35] Brennecke, Detlef, *Strindberg und Ernst Brausewetter. Ein Beitrag zur Methodik der Übersetzungswissenschaft. Mitt vier bislang unveröffentlichten Briefen August Strindbergs*, Heidelberg: Carl Winter Universitätsverlag, 1979. Illus. 70 pp. ['Strindberg and Ernst Brausewetter. A Contribution to the Theory of Translation and its Methodology. With Four Hitherto Unpublished Letters by August Strindberg'. Reflects on Brausewetter's (1863-1904) work as a translator from the Scandinavian languages, his contacts with Sg, and his German versions of *Fadren* and *Fröken Julie*, with particular reference to the sometimes discrepant understanding of naturalism by the Swedish author in practice and his 'up-to-date' German-based translator where naturalist theory was concerned. The volume includes facsimiles of the extant correspondence between Brausewetter and Sg, together with a letter from Frida Uhl to Brausewetter and a commentary on the printed text of these letters]

[B4:36] — Krömmelbein, Thomas, *Germanistik* (Kiel), 27 (1986), 95-96.

[B4:37] — Swahn, Sigbrit, *Sydsvenska Dagbladet* (Malmö), 20 May 1980.

[B4:38] Brundin, Margareta, 'Vita lamm och svarta får. Om den första svenska översättningen av "Baa, baa, black sheep"', *Strindbergiana* (Stockholm), 3 (1988), pp. 96-105. Illus. ['White Lamb and Black Sheep. On the First Swedish Translation of "Baa, baa, black sheep"'. Presents Sg's translation of the English nursery rhyme, which he produced while working on the first version of *Mäster Olof*, together with Swedish renderings of 'Little Boy Blue', 'There was an Old Woman who Lived in a Shoe', 'Little Bo-Peep has Lost her Sheep', 'Little Jack Horner Sat in a Corner', and 'Hey, Diddle Diddle, the Cat and the Fiddle', all published in 1872 by Bonniers in an illustrated collection entitled *Daddas visor*. Brundin quotes from Sg's correspondence with Karl Otto Bonnier as well as other items in the Bonnier archive, and gives bibliographical details of both the English source material and its dissemination in Swedish]

[B4:39] Bruns, Alken, 'Ernst Brausewetters Dialoge. Zu Entstehungsbedingungen und Funktion der Übersetzung im Prozess der Literaturvermittlung', in *Nicht nur Strindberg. Kulturelle und literarische Beziehungen zwischen Schweden und Deutschland 1870-1933*, Hrsg. von Helmut Müssener, Acta Universitatis Stockholmiensis, Stockholmer Germanistische Forschungen 24, Stockholm: Almqvist & Wicksell International, 1979, pp. 266-278. ['Ernst Brausewetter's Dialogue. On the Development and Role of Translation in the Process of Literary Mediation'. Considers the translator as an intermediary in the process of reception, which is exemplified here by Brausewetter's versions of Sg's naturalistic dramas *Fadren* and *Fröken Julie*; their naturalistic language, with its pretensions to 'normal' speech, confronts German expectations of a 'literary language' as codified by Gustav Freytag in *Die Technik des Dramas* (1863)]

[B4:40] Bruns, Alken, 'Strindbergs *Hemsöborna*. Stilanalyse beim Übersetzen', in *Die literarische Überstezung. Stand und Perspektiven ihrer Erforschung*, Hrsg. von Harald

Kittel, Göttinger Beiträge zur internationalen Überstzungsforschung 2, Berlin: Erich Schmidt, 1988, pp. 209-222. ['Strindberg's *The People of Hemsö*. Stylistic Analysis through Translation'. A stylistic analysis of *Hemsöborna* undertaken through the medium of (German) translation]

[B4:41] Carlson, Harry G[ilbert], 'Problems in Play Translation', *Educational Theatre Journal* (Madison, Wisconsin), 16 (1964), 55-58. [Compares translations of *Fadren* into English by Elizabeth Sprigge and Arvid Paulson. The former is to be preferred on the grounds of 'speakability' and the fact that the dialogue is closer in duration to the original than is the case with Paulson's more prolix version]

[B4:42] Carlson, Harry G[ilbert], 'Reviews of Recent Translations', *Yearbook of Comparative and General Literature* (Bloomington, Indiana), 13 (1964), pp. 76-77. [A positive response to Elizabeth Sprigge's translations of twelve of the plays as well as new versions of the four Chamber Plays of 1907, rendered into English by Evert Sprinchorn and others (see **E48:60**)]

[B4:43] Claes, Viktor, 'De nederländska översättningarna av Strindberg', *Strindbergiana* (Stockholm), 3 (1988), pp. 34-44. ['Dutch Translations of Strindberg'. A mainly bibliographical survey of those works by Sg that have been published in book form in Dutch translation. Claes divides his reception by translation into three distinct periods, 1890-1914, 1918-1939, and 1965-1988, which have yielded two, twelve, and twenty-one volumes respectively. Claes also discusses a recent reworking of *Oväder* for the Dutch stage by the theatre director Ger Thijs]

[B4:44] Ellegård, Alvar, 'Strindbergska eller svenska?', *Dagens Nyheter* (Stockholm), 15 July 1963. ['Strindbergish or Swedish?' Ellegård takes exception to Olle Holmberg's criticism of Tage Aurell's Swedish translation of *Le Plaidoyer d'un fou* in **B4:85**. He maintains that translations should be contemporary and not seek to imitate the time-bound idioms of the original; otherwise they become pastiche. Today's readers should achieve a sense of Sg as he was before he became a classic, which is possible if they read Aurell's version]

[B4:45] Engwall, Gunnel, '"Det knastrar i hjärnan". Strindberg som egen franske översättare', in Björn Meidal and Nils Åke Nilsson, red., **B4:113**, *August Strindberg och hans översättare*, pp. 35-52. Illus. ['"It Crackles in My Brain". Strindberg as His Own French Translator'. Engwall sets out to demonstrate that Sg's knowledge of French culture and language enabled him to translate his own works into French with considerable care and accuracy in the cases of *Fadren*, *Fordringsägare*, and *Ett drömspel*. She considers how he approaches translating their titles, his strategies where references to the Swedish cultural context in the source text and personal names are concerned, as well as what he does with the passages of verse in *Ett drömspel*. How he deals with these issues reveals the extent to which Sg retained much of the force and directness of the original, not least via the changes he made to certain of the characters' names and to local references. Engwall also notes that the specifically Sgian quality of the source texts was often lost in the numerous alterations that were introduced by all those French translators who subsequently edited Sg's own French versions, and she observes that it has also been very variously, and often inadequately, captured in later versions by other translators]

[B4:46] Engwall, Gunnel, '*En dåres försvarstal* i *Samlade Skrifter.* En studie kring John Landquists översättning av August Strindbergs *Le Plaidoyer d'un fou*', in Gunnel Engwall and Regina af Geijerstam, red., *Från språk till språk. Sjutton uppsatser om litterär översättning*, Lund: Studentlitteratur, 1983, pp. 168-196. ['*A Madman's Defence* in *Collected Works.* A Study of John Landquist's Translation and its Background'. In judging Landquist's Swedish translation, which was made from George Loiseau's published French version and elicited widely differing responses on publication, Engwall points out that it is important to understand that Loiseau's revisions to Sg's original manuscript were more wide-ranging than was originally believed, and that Landquist did not have access to Sg's only recently discovered original French text. Consequently, he sought to render a text that only remotely recalled the Sg with which he was familiar, in a manner that was more in keeping with Sg's Swedish style and vocabulary. Several useful diagrams facilitate Engwall's comparison of Landquist's translation with both Sg's original manuscript and Loiseau's quite extensive reworking. She also considers whether he might have made use of other, sometimes pirated, editions of the novel that were published before 1914, and reviews his achievement in the light of the debate that his translation occasioned in the Swedish press on publication (see **B4:30**, **B4:99**, **B4:100**, **B4:129**, and **B4:192**). Engwall examines Erik Staaff's revision of Landquist's translation (1920), which was also based on the assumption that Loiseau's published version differed only marginally from the original. Its aim of bringing the Swedish text into line with 'the French original' was thus compromised from the outset, but it is nevertheless still interesting to see how the two versions compare, both as regards their fidelity to their French source and the ways in which they resolve comparable problems. Staaff's version is the 'more philological' but Landquist produced a translation that gives the illusion of having been written by Sg himself, and thus comes closest to the latter's original text which, of course, he did not know]

[B4:47] Engwall, Gunnel, 'Frenchifying *Fordringsägare*: Strindberg as his own Translator', in Michael Robinson, ed., **B1:373**, *Strindberg and Genre*, pp. 137-147. [A comparison of the original Swedish text of *Fordringsägare* with the manuscript of Sg's own French translation reveals him to have been a faithful translator. He reproduces almost every line of the source text and often retains the same images in French as in Swedish. Where the translation does diverge from the original, it is with the aim of adapting the play to the expectations of a French audience. And this in turn entails some interesting modifications in the relationships between the three characters]

[B4:48] Engwall, Gunnel, '*Le Plaidoyer d'un fou*: Un plaidoyer de Strindberg ou de Loiseau?', *Studier i modern språkvetenskap* (Stockholm), N.S. 6 (1980), 29-54. ['*The Madman's Defence:* Strindberg's Defence or Loiseau's?' A detailed study of Georges Loiseau's role in realising the publication of Sg's autobiographical fiction in French by Albert Langen in 1895. The rediscovery of Sg's French manuscript clarifies the extent of Loiseau's interventions in Sg's original text as well as the use he made of the German version of 1893. Although well-received as a translation, the modern reader with access to Sg's source text can see that Loiseau's version departs significantly from the original, often through ignorance of the Swedish milieu and cultural context. A detailed comparison of Sg's text with Loiseau's modifications demonstrates how the latter text also loses much of the vigour and vitality of Sg's own French version]

[B4:49] Engwall, Gunnel, 'Strindberg, auteur français, traduit en suédois. Le cas du *Plaidoyer d'un fou* et d'*Inferno*', *Studier i modern språkvetenskap* (Stockholm), N.S. 9 (1990), 114-122. ['Strindberg, a French Author Translated into Swedish. The Case of *A Madman's Defence* and *Inferno*'. Engwall returns to the vexed problem of how one should approach Sg as an author who sometimes writes his major works in French which are then revised by a native speaker only to be subsequently translated into Swedish by a third hand, which attempts to recapture the spirit and qualities of Sg's Swedish style. She concentrates on two of his principal autobiographical fictions in Swedish versions of *Le Plaidoyer d'un fou* by John Landquist and Hans Levander and translations of *Inferno* by Eugène Fahlstedt and Lotta Gavel Adams in *Samlade Skrifter* and *Samlade Verk* respectively. Focuses primarily on questions of tense and vocabulary]

[B4:50] Engwall, Gunnel, 'Strindberg et son introducteur français', *Europe* (Paris), No. 858 (October 2000), pp. 120-139. ['Strindberg and his French Presenter'. Version in French of **B4:51**]

[B4:51] Engwall, Gunnel, 'Strindberg och hans franske introduktör', *Kung. Vitterhets Historie och Antikvitets Akademiens Årsbok* (Stockholm), 1999, pp. 85-105. Illus. ['Strindberg and His French Presenter'. Examines Georges Loiseau's role in advancing Sg's interests in Paris during the mid-1890s, their correspondence, personal contacts, and his work as Sg's translator. Engwall discusses Loiseau's reworking of Sg's own translation of *Fordringsägare* for its French première at the Théâtre de l'Oeuvre, as well as of the original French text of *En dåres försvarstal*. The recent (1973) discovery of Sg's manuscript of the latter in French permits an illuminating analysis of Loiseau's revisions and sheds new light on the controversy surrounding its first translation into Swedish for *Samlade Skrifter* by John Landquist, who was severely and, in Engwall's view somewhat unjustly, criticised for his diction and style by Fredrik Böök. Detailed comparison is made here between Sg's original, Loiseau's revision, Landquist's translation, and Böök's suggestions as to how the latter might be improved]

[B4:52] Engwall, Gunnel, 'Strindberg som fransk författare', *Tvärsnitt. Humanistisk och samhällsvetenskaplig forskning* (Uppsala), 1988:2, pp. 35-42. ['Strindberg as a French Author'. Seeks to establish Sg's knowledge of French as exemplified in those works he originally wrote in French or chose to translate himself into that language. These include *En dåres försvarstal, Inferno, Fadren, Fordringsägare, Ett drömspel*, and the *Vivisektioner* of 1894. An examination of *Créanciers* (Creditors) and *Le Plaidoyer d'un fou* (A Madman's Defence) demonstrates that his style when writing in French displays a comparable power and vitality to his works in Swedish, and shares a similar playfulness and bold vocabulary. A more detailed study of *Vivisektioner* confirms how familiar he was with contemporary French literature and culture]

[B4:53] Engwall, Gunnel, 'Strindberg – traducteur français. Exemples extraits de *Créanciers*', *Actes du onzième Congrès des romanistes scandinaves*, Trondheim, 1990, pp. 113-124. ['Strindberg – French Translator. Examples Taken from *Creditors*'. Examines Sg's practice as his own translator, exemplified by his French version of *Fordringsägare*]

[B4:54] Eriksson, Olof, 'Strindbergs franska: en språklig paradox', in Olof Eriksson, red., *Strindberg och det franska språket: föredrag från ett symposium vid Växjö universitet 22-23 maj 2003*, Acta Wexionensia, Humaniora, Växjö: Växjö University Press, 2004, pp. 112-135. ['Strindberg's French: A Linguistic Paradox'. A rigorous linguistic analysis of Sg's language in those autobiographical works originally produced in French, which concludes that his reputation as a bad writer of French is undeserved. Although he is frequently at fault in details and sometimes grammatically, his attention to the broader picture means that he is not far from achieving his declared goal, namely 'un style aussi aérien que Maupassant']

[B4:55] Ewbank, Inga-Stina, 'Introduction', in *Three Chamber Plays by August Strindberg*, Leeds: Alumnus Playtexts in Performance, 1997, pp. 5-9. [Maintains that the translator of these plays needs to be as faithful as possible to Sg's original, even if this entails some awkwardness and apparent infelicities in English style. S/he should try to preserve a sense of his style and use of language, and avoid introducing additional material in order to explain or clarify his sometimes apparently irrational associations, incoherent sentence structure, and unusual dialogue patterns]

[B4:56] Ewbank, Inga-Stina, 'Strindberg in English', *Moderna Språk* (Stockholm), 89:2 (1995), 129-139. [The experience of translating several of Sg's plays for stage productions directed by Peter Hall and Katie Mitchell suggests to Ewbank that translators should not seek to normalise his language in order to produce 'good English'. Many existing English translations are in fact transmutations in which Sg's original has been explained, paraphrased, and generally tidied up. In Sg's hands, Swedish becomes malleable and he shares with Shakespeare a concrete physical perception of language as it is spoken and as it is presented, both in naturalistic plays like *Fordringsägare*, *Fadren*, or *Den starkare*, where the conflict is essentially verbal, and in the advice on performance that he directs to the actors of the Intimate Theatre some twenty years later. Sg's dramatic verbal structures are written for actors to speak and an audience to hear, thus rendering Charles Marowitz's argument in **D2:939** that 'the most dated element in Strindberg's plays is the language' quite ludicrous]

[B4:57] Falk, Bertil, 'Strindberg i Indien', *Studiekamraten* (Tollarp), 66:2 (1984), 8-9. ['Strindberg in India'. Discusses modern Hindi translations of *Fröken Julie* and *Fadren*, designed to facilitate the performance of Sg's plays in the Indian theatre]

[B4:58] F. H. [Fritz Henriksson], 'Strindbergs tyske översättare', *Göteborgs Handels- och Sjöfartstidning*, 7 February 1900. ['Strindberg's German Translator'. Reports that, as Sg's authorised translator, Emil Schering intends to provide German readers with a true picture of an author who has often been misrepresented in the past by translators keen to speculate on his reputation as a woman hater]

[B4:59] Fleisher, Frederic, 'Den misshandlade Strindberg', *Bonniers Litterära Magasin* (Stockholm), 31:5 (1962), 380-384. ['The Mishandled Strindberg'. Argues that the lack of interest in Sg in England and North-America is partly due to poor translations, which often revise the original in significant ways. Fleisher considers Edwin Björkman to have been probably the best of the early translators, but his versions of *Dödsdansen* and *Den starkare* reveal that he, too, committed numerous errors and omitted important material. He therefore considers C. D. Locock's more recent versions to be an improvement on Björkman but, like other English translators, he still adopts an archaic style that does Sg's dialogue a disservice. However, the very latest versions by Elizabeth Sprigge and Arvid Paulson mark a further improvement while Walter Johnson's somewhat pedestrian translations of the history plays have opened up an aspect of Sg's *œuvre* hitherto unknown in England and the United States. Where they have been translated at all, the prose works have suffered even more at the hands of translators who, like Claud Field in his version of *Tjänstekvinnans son*, have omitted significant parts of Sg's text, either with the intention of removing local references or in order to sanitise the frankness of the original]

[B4:60] Fournier, Vincent, 'Le Malentendu et la désillusion. Lettres inédites de Björnson, Strindberg, Snoilsky et de leur traducteur en France', *Etudes Germaniques* (Paris), 40:4 (1985), 439-456. ['Misunderstandings and Disillusionment. Unpublished Letters by Bjørnson, Strindberg, Snoilsky, and their French Translator'. Presents the correspondence of these Scandinavian writers with Maurice Prozor who, Fournier declares, 'was their principal translator and literary agent in France'. Only two of the letters are from Sg, for whom Prozor was, in fact, never a significant intermediary, either as a translator or in facilitating his early reception in France in general]

[B4:61] Freese, Katrin, '"...för man kan översätta på många sätt...". Überlegungen zur Übersetzung von Realienbezeichnungen in August Strindbergs naturalistischem Roman *Hemsöborna*', in Otmar Werner, Hrsg., *Arbeiten zur Skandinavistik 8.* Arbeitstagung der skandinavisten des Deutschen Sprachgebiets, 27.9-3.10.1987 in Freiberg i Br., Texte und Untersuchungen zur Germanistik und Skandinavistik 22, Frankfurt am Main: Peter Lang, 1989, pp. 291-303. ['"Because One can Translate in many Ways". Reflections on the Translation of Factual Terms and Objects in August Strindberg's Naturalist Novel *The People of Hemsö*'. Freese considers issues raised by the translation of factual material and data of the kind in which realist writing often abounds, with particular reference to the detailed geographical references and specific terminological details in *Hemsöborna*]

[B4:62] Freese, Katrin, 'Einige Übersetzungsprobleme in den Dialogen von August Strindbergs Roman *Röda rummet* (Das rote Zimmer)', in *Die literarische Übersetzung. Fallstudien zu ihrer Literaturgeschichte*, Hrsg. von Göttinger Beiträge zur Internationalen Übersetzungsforschung 1, Berlin: Erich Schmidt, 1987, pp. 237-252. ['Some Problems in Translating the Dialogue of August Strindberg's Novel *The Red Room*'. Examines some of the problems raised in translating the dialogue in *Röda rummet* as exemplified by five German versions published to date. Particular reference is paid to the translation of pronouns and forms of address, as well as to the naturalistic use of everyday speech patterns, including slang, which also serve as indices of social difference]

[B4:63] Furuland, Lars, and M. Ørvig, 'En bilderbok ur den borgerliga barnkammaren. Om Ludwig Richter & August Strindbergs: "För våra barn", in Ludwig Richter, *För våra barn. En bok ur den borgerliga barnkammaren*, Facsimile ed., Stockholm: Gidlund, 1980, pp. 43-55. ['A Picture Book from the Bourgeois Nursery. On "For Our Children" by Ludwig Richter and August Strindberg'. Discusses Sg's early involvement in both translating and adapting children's literature from German as well as English (see **B4:38**)]

[B4:64] Gabrieli, Iselin Maria, 'Att översätta H. C. Andersen och A. Strindberg till italienska. Några reflektioner', *Aion-n. Studi nederlandesi – studi nordici*, Annali dell'Istituto Universitario Orientale, Napoli, 29 (1986), pp. 253-275. ['Translating Hans Christian Andersen and August Strindberg into Italian. Some Reflections'. Gabrieli insists that a translation should not replace the sometimes awkward, rough-hewn linguistic riches of the original with an insipid, watered-down version in the target language. He suggests that the Italian translator of *Hemsöborna* might take the naturalistic prose of Giovanni Verga in his novel *I Malavoglia* (1881) as a stylistic example since both writers had much in common, including a passionate concern for telling the truth, a delight in nature, and an interest in the lives and customs of the rural poor. However, every writer creates his own world, and it is essential to reproduce the rhythm and the sound of the original. The kind of lexical and stylistic problems which this entails can best be studied in a series of comparisons between the Swedish text of *Hemsöborna* and the author's own Italian translation, which seeks to capture Sg's characteristic blend of imagination and reality]

[B4:65] Godowska, Marianna, 'Contemporary Polish Translations of Strindberg's Plays', *Le Théâtre Polonaise* (Warsaw), 26:8-9 (1984), p. 13. [Comments on versions of many of the plays translated by Zygmunt Łanowski. Text in French and English]

[B4:66] Gofman, V., '[Translated Literature]', *Vestnik Evropy* (Moscow), 1910:3, pp. 401-410. [Comments on early Russian translations of Sg, often made from German versions rather than the Swedish original, pp. 405-406. E.812]

[B4:67] Gravier, Maurice, 'Strindberg écrivain français', *Revue d'histoire du théâtre* (Paris), 30:3 (1978), 243-265. ['Strindberg as a French Writer'. Studies those works like the *Vivisektioner* of 1894, *En dåres försvarstal, Inferno*, and *Legender* which Sg originally wrote in French, as well as those, like *Ett drömspel*, which he translated himself from Swedish. Gravier discusses Sg's command of French and evaluates his linguistic ability in such texts, most notably *En dåres försvarstal*. The latter he claims should be appreciated as a valid work of literature in its own right rather than merely as a narrative whose sole interest resides in the information it provides about the married life of author of *Kamraterna, Fadren, Fröken Julie*, and *Fordringsägare*]

[B4:68] Gravier, Maurice, 'Strindberg traducteur de lui-même', *Mélanges de philologie romane offerts à M. Karl Michaelsson par ses amis et ses élèves*, Göteborg, 1952, pp. 217-224. ['Strindberg His Own Translator'. Discusses Sg's translations of his own works (most notably *Fadren*) into French]

[B4:69] Gravier, Maurice, 'La Traduction des textes dramatiques', *Études de linguistique appliqué* (Paris), 12 (1973), 39-49. ['The Translation of Dramatic Texts'. On the specific problems involved in translating plays, their dialogue and stage directions, with reference to works by Shakespeare, Ibsen, Molière, and (in Sg's case) *Till Damaskus*]

[B4:70] Gravier, Maurice, 'Traduire Strindberg', in Donald Weaver, ed., **D2:331**, *Strindberg on Stage*, pp. 84-99. ['Translating Strindberg'. Discusses Sg's collaboration with Georges Loiseau on a French version of *Fordringsägare* and his understanding support for Emil Schering in their correspondence, which is a document of major importance for literary historians. Many recent French translations have been assembled from existing versions, sometimes in more than one language, and without reference to the Swedish text; but a translator should remain faithful not only to the letter of the original but also to Sg's 'perspectives spirituelle' at the time of writing. This can be demonstrated by a comparison of the source text of *Ett drömspel* with its various French versions. Moreover, in translating for the stage, the translator needs to work closely with a director, tempering the latter's infidelities to the original but endowing his own literary version with an understanding of its inherent theatricality]

[B4:71] Gregori, Ferdinand, 'Strindbergs Dramen in neuer Verdeutschung', *Die Scene* (Berlin), 10 (1920), p. 112. ['Strindberg's Plays in New German Versions'. Comments on new German translations of several of the plays by Heinrich Goebel]

[B4:72] Grimal, Sophie, 'En författares försvarstal. En omvärdering av Strindbergs franska i *Inferno*', *Strindbergiana* (Stockholm), 11 (1995), pp. 72-81. ['A Writer's Defence. A Revaluation of Strindberg's French in *Inferno*'. According to Grimal, earlier studies of the works which Sg originally wrote in French by Carl Gustaf Bjurström, **B4:22**, and Maurice Gravier, **B4:67**, have criticised him on details of linguistic gender, mood, and syntax. Today, however, more recent critics like Adams in her dissertation *The Generic Ambiguity of August Strindberg's Inferno*, **V:3**, and Gunnel Engwall in **B4:52** and **K5:4**, do not ignore Sg's grammatical errors but display a greater understanding of his style and purpose. The brief analysis here of the French text of *Inferno* is designed to demonstrate the richness, beauty, and originality of Sg's language, as well as the enigmatic discourse in which this text was necessarily written]

[B4:73] Group Report, 'Translating Strindberg' with Supplement: 'Existing Translations of Strindberg's Dramas', in Donald Weaver, ed., **D2:331**, *Strindberg on Stage*, pp. 139-143. [Sg's translator is confronted by the lack of dependable, annotated Swedish editions of many of the plays and the spread of his works abroad has been uneven, with Britain, France, and the United States currently the best served where recent translations of the plays are concerned. Comparison may be made between literal translations, translations produced by a translator working together with a theatre practitioner, or versions that have been developed by a theatre director for a specific production. Of these, the second kind is the most desirable. The ideal, however, would be an Oxford University Press complete edition, along the lines of the editions which they have already devoted to Ibsen and Chekhov]

[B4:74] Gschwantler, Otto, 'Übersetzer aus den skandinavischen Literaturen im Wien der Jahrhundertwende (ca.1880-1920)', *Skandinavisztikai Füzetek / Papers in Scandinavian Studies* (Budapest), 6 (1994), pp. 29-42. ['Translators of Scandinavian Literature in Turn-of-the-Century Vienna'. Where Sg is concerned, the article is relevant for its discussion of early German translations by Marie Herzfeld (1855-1940) and Mathilde Prager (1844-1921, under the pseudonym Erich Holm). With the latter he also enjoyed an extensive correspondence during the 1880s and early 1890s]

[B4:75] Haiduk, Manfred, 'Nachwort', in Peter Weiss, *Der Prozeß (nach Kafka). Strindberg-Übersetzungen: Fräulein Julie, Ein Traumspiel, Der Vater*, Mit einem Nachwort von Manfred Haiduk, Berlin: Henschelverlag Kunst und Gesellschaft, 1979. 246 pp. [The Afterword to Peter Weiss's translations of *Fröken Julie*, *Ett drömspel*, and *Fadren*, which discusses their merits and relates them to Weiss's own work as a dramatist]

[B4:76] Hartmann, Jacob W[ittmer], 'Strindberg in English', *The International* (New York), 7 (1912), pp. 5-6. [Comments on the situation to date]

[B4:77] Hartmann, Jacob W[ittmer], 'Strindberg in 1913', *American-Scandinavian Review* (New York), 2 (1914), 54-55. [Reviews the third volume of translations of the plays by Edwin Björkman, which includes *Dödsdansen* where 'the greatness of the work is in the enormity of its exaggerations', as well as the first English versions of *I havsbandet*, *Röda rummet*, *Tjänstekvinnans son*, *Inferno*, and *En blå bok* (several translated from the German rather than the original Swedish or French and the latter in a selection translated by Claud Field with an introduction by Arthur Babillotte as *Zones of the Spirit*, **K7:25**). Hartmann suggests that in the U.S.A. where women are valued so highly, Sg's value may be that of someone who redresses the balance]

[B4:78] Hartmann, Jacob W[ittmer], 'Strindberg in 1914', *American-Scandinavian Review* (New York), 3 (1915), 214-215. [Surveys recent translations into English]

[B4:79] Hartmann, Jacob W[ittmer], 'Strindberg in 1915', *American-Scandinavian Review* (New York), 4 (1916), 55-56. [Reviews Edwin Björkman's translation of *Mäster Olof*, which omits the cosmic epilogue written for the 1878 version because it had just appeared in an English version by Felix Grendon in *The International* (1911), and Claud Field's translation of *Advent*, which was made from Emil Schering's German version]

[B4:80] Harvey, Anne-Charlotte Hanes, 'Translating Scandinavian Drama – for Whom?', *TijdSchrift voor Skandinavistiek* (Groningen), 19:1 (1998), 25-49. [Describes how the transposition of a play from page to stage magnifies the linguistic and cultural shifts entailed by the original translation of a dramatic text from one language into another. Play translations that convey different kinds of information are required – some published mainly for reading and others designed primarily for performance. In the former case, the target language text is likely to be smooth and readable so as not to come between the reader and the images which the text creates. Such a translation should also be annotated and have a commentary, and thus be intended for a particular kind of reader, the scholar. In the latter case, where the translation is initially read by a dramaturge and/or director, and then mediated to an audience by the actors, the translation needs to be responsive to the punctuation and the musical values of the original, in the form of duration, silences, metre, rhythm, stress patterns, long and short vowel sounds, repetitions, sound motifs, and even specific sounds. A combination of the detail required by a scholarly text with such a concern for performative values would provide the richest possible version, and the issues raised regarding translation by the different demands of these various kinds of text are explored here with reference to existing English editions of both Ibsen and Sg. Where the latter is concerned, Harvey points out that particular attention needs to be paid to his idiosyncratic punctuation, which offers 'a map of the characters' and Sg's inner landscape, and thus affords particular insight into his directorial mind]

[B4:81] Harvey, Anne-Charlotte Hanes, 'Översättaren som Sparf', in Anita Persson and Barbara Lide, red., **B1:366**, *Ja, må han leva!*, pp. 91-97. ['The Translator as Sparrow'. Personal reflections on translating Sg, in the form of a letter addressed to 'Bäste Herr Strindberg' (Dear Mr Strindberg)]

[B4:82] Hatvani, Paul, 'Strindberg in neuer Übersetzung. Elsa [sic] von Hollanders Strindberg-Übersetzungen', *Renaissance* (Vienna), 1:2 (1921), p. 16. ['Strindberg in a New Translation'. Reviews translations of Sg by Else von Hollander and compares them with those by Emil Schering]

[B4:83] H. M. [Hans Meißner], 'Bühnenwerke', *Hamburger Theater-Zeitung*, 2:19 (1920), p. 16. ['Stage Works'. Compares Heinrich Goebel's translations of the plays with those by Emil Schering]

[B4:84] Henry, A. S., 'Strindberg's Plays', *Book News Monthly* (New York), 32:9 (1913), 72-73. [Compares existing translations of similar repertoire by Edwin Björkman and Edith and Warner Oland. Stresses the importance of accuracy in translation, which is essential if the study of dramatic literature is to be advanced]

[B4:85] Hoffmann, Willy, 'Glosse zum Strindberg-Urteil des Reichsgerichts', *Gewerblicher Rechtsschutz und Urheberrecht* (Berlin), 26 (1921), 155-156. [Discusses the 1919 German edition of Sg's novels and plays in four volumes, translated by Else von Hollander]

[B4:86] Holmberg, Olle, 'Aurell, Landquist och Strindberg', *Dagens Nyheter* (Stockholm), 10 July 1963. [Reviews Tage Aurell's Swedish translation of *Le Plaidoyer d'un fou* and compares it with John Landquist's version in *Samlade Skrifter*. Concludes that, as revised by Erik Staaff in 1920, the latter comes closer to Sg's style and language than Aurell's new version]

[B4:87] Hube, J., 'Strindberg auf Deutsch. Probleme der literarischen Übersetzung', *Übersetzungswissenschaft und Sprachmittlerausbildung – Internationalen Konferenz* (Humboldt-Universität), Bd 2, 1988, pp. 232-240. ['Strindberg in German. Problems in Literary Translation']

[B4:88] Ionescu, Gelu, 'Un provocator: August Strindberg', in *Orizontul traducerii*, Bucureşti: Univers, 1981, pp. 98-102. ['A Provocateur: August Strindberg'. A short essay on Sg in Romanian, in a volume entitled 'The Horizon of Translation']

[B4:89] Jacobs, Barry, 'Bland amerikanska läsare och kritiker: Strindberg i översättning', in Björn Meidal and Nils Åke Nilsson, red., **B4:113**, *August Strindberg och hans översättare*, pp. 75-86. Illus. ['Among American Readers and Critics: Strindberg in Translation'. Surveys the early reception of Sg in the United States, based on translations of the plays by Edwin Björkman and others. That both Ibsen and Sg made a powerful impression on readers and audiences abroad indicates to Jacobs that even poor translations succeeded in transposing 'the invariant core' of the source text to the target language. According to Jacobs, literary translation is a special form of interpretation and criticism, and one of its most intractable problems is the difficulty of capturing the mood and rhythm of the source text which is exemplified here in a comparison of ten English versions of *Fadren*. This essay employs many of the same examples from *Fadren* already utilised in **B4:92**]

[B4:90] Jacobs, Barry, 'On Translating Strindberg's *Oväder*', *Scandinavica* (Norwich), 27:1 (1988), 21-29. [Argues that a successful translation must be based on a coherent interpretation of the original, one that accounts for the details in the text. But *Oväder*, which comes closer than the other Chamber Plays of 1907 to realising Sg's musical ideal of dramatic composition, poses special problems. The translator may succeed in finding formal equivalents for nearly everything in the text yet still fail to capture the rhythm and mood of the original. Jacobs points out that reading *Taklagsöl*, the novella which Sg wrote immediately prior to embarking upon *Oväder*, helps clarify certain linguistic issues raised in translating the play, several of which are explored here. But in translating the play text with a view to performance, Jacobs has found working with a theatre practitioner invaluable where finding equivalents for some of the difficulties that arise from the compressed style, elusive subtext, and thematic imagery of the play, are concerned, as well as for encompassing Sg's extraordinary lexical range]

[B4:91] Jacobs, Barry, 'Översättningsproblem i Strindbergs *Fadren*', in *Arbeiten zur Skandinavistik 8*. Hrsg. von Otmar Werner, Arbeitstagung der skandinavisten des Deutschen Sprachgebiets, 27.9-3.10.1987 in Freiberg i. Br., Texte und Untersuchungen zur Germanistik und Skandinavistik 22, Frankfurt am Main: Peter Lang, 1989, pp.

281-290. ['Problems in Translating Strindberg's *The Father*'. Swedish version of **B4:92**, which employs many of the same examples and argumentation]

[B4:92] Jacobs, Barry, 'Strindberg's *Fadren* (The Father) in English Translation', *Yearbook of Comparative and General Literature* (Bloomington, Indiana), 35 (1986), pp. 112-121. [An exemplary comparative study of ten English versions of *Fadren* made between 1899 and 1986. Jacobs identifies a recurring difficulty which is especially pertinent in the translation of dramatic texts, namely how, given the immediacy with which an audience has to grasp them, are the culture-specific details of the original to be conveyed? It is interesting to compare the Swedish original of *Fadren* with Sg's own French translation, in which every name, localised allusion, or Swedish custom that might render the play in any way inaccessible to a Parisian audience have been removed. Swedish forms of address also create problems in English, as do many personal pronouns, names, and shifts between tenses. Moreover, some translators add interpretive stage directions, and pass them off as part of the original text, while others are nonplussed by Sg's often idiosyncratic use of punctuation and regularise it accordingly. Most elusive of all is the tone of the original as exemplified here in a comparison between a short passage in the original and all ten English versions of the same speech. Although none of these translators captures every nuance of the original, Jacobs concludes that it is Walter Johnson, Harry Carlson, and Evert Sprinchorn who between them come closest to providing the most successful currently available English version of *Fadren*]

[B4:93] Jacobs, Barry, 'Translating for the Stage: The Case of Strindberg', *TijdSchrift voor Skandinavistiek* (Groningen), 19:1 (1998), 75-101. [Recounts the experience of translating Sg for the Source Theatre Company of New York, which entailed transposing a version of *Fröken Julie* intended for reading into a text designed for performance. Jacobs also refers to problems in translating several other plays by Sg, including *Moderskärlek* and *Oväder*, and to other translations, into Danish as well as English. He insists that there can be no excuse for literary translators who themselves distort Sg's text in an attempt to clarify the subtext, to redesign the stage set, or to impose their own interpretation onto the original. Besides the particular problems arising from the range and versatility of Sg's language, the most difficult task of all in translating so protean writer as Sg is how to capture his tone which, like the subtext, is ultimately elusive and indeterminate]

[B4:94] Jenner, Suzanne, '*Fröken Julie* i fransk översättning – ett drama i förvandling', in Björn Meidal and Nils Åke Nilsson, red., **B4:113**, *August Strindberg och hans översättare*, pp. 53-60. Illus. ['*Miss Julie* in French Translation: A Drama in Transformation'. Maintains that any translation of a play alters the original, especially as regards its culture specific codes. This and other issues presented by *Fröken Julie*, including the problems inherent in translating linguistic shifters like personal pronouns, Jean's use of French expressions, plays on words, and networks of imagery that operate throughout the text, are exemplified with reference to the existing French translations by Jacques Robnard, Charles de Casanove, and Boris Vian, of whom only the first translated the play directly from the Swedish]

[B4:95] Johannesson, Eric O., 'Strindberg, August. *The Natives of Hemsö*, Translated by Arvid Paulson with an Introduction by Richard Vowles', *Scandinavian Studies* (Lawrence, Kansas), 39:2 (1967), 191-193. [Compares what Johannesson regards as Paulson's new, very prolix, translation, and the unwarranted liberties it takes with the original, with Elspeth Hartley Schubert's 'superior' version of 1959]

[B4:96] Johansson, Ulf R., 'Arvid Paulson Strindbergsöversättare m.m.', *entré* (Norsborg), 2:6 (1975), p. 25. ['Arvid Paulson, Translator of Strindberg and More'. A note on the Swedish-American actor who translated numerous works by Sg]

[B4:97] Josephson, Aksel G. S., 'Strindberg in English', *The Dial* (Chicago), 1 April 1914, pp. 300-303. [A survey of English translations to date. Not only do the English translators of *Giftas* and *Tjänstekvinnans son* by Ellie Schleussner and Claud Field betray a limited knowledge of Swedish, they also cut and adapt the original. However, taken together with Miss Lind-af-Hageby's 'excellent and interesting study', **R:1361**, these and other recent translations of *I havsbandet*, an anthology of Sg's short stories, and the third volume of Edith and Warner Oland's translations of the plays, which 'have succeeded better than others in giving not only a faithful, but a spirited rendering of Sg in something like his own language', it is possible to conclude that 'the time [will] surely come when a knowledge of Sg will be regarded as necessary by anyone who lays claim to a many-sided intellectual equipment']

[B4:98] Koller, Werner, *Grundprobleme der Übersetzungstheorie unter besonderer Berücksichtigung schwedisch-deutscher Übersetzungsfälle*, Stockholmer Germanistische Forschungen 9, Bern & München: Francke Verlag, 1972. 198 pp. [Includes several examples from Sg in a study of fundamental problems of translation theory based on Swedish as the source language with German as the target language]

[B4:99] Landquist, John, 'Är Strindberg en svensk eller en fransk författare? Ett genmäle om skilda översättningsprinciper till prof. Emanuel Walberg av dr John Landquist', in Solveig Landquist, red., **B1:248**, *John Landquist om Strindberg personen och diktaren*, pp. 92-99. ['Is Strindberg a Swedish or a French Writer? A Reply to Prof. Emanuel Walberg Concerning Various Principles of Translation by Dr John Landquist'. Rpr. of **B4:100**]

[B4:100] Landquist, John, 'Är Strindberg en svensk eller en fransk författare? Ett genmäle om skilda översättningsprinciper till prof. Emanuel Walberg av dr John Landquist', *Svenska Dagbladet* (Stockholm), 2 January 1915. ['Is Strindberg a Swedish or a French Writer? A Reply to Prof. Emanuel Walberg Concerning various Principles of Translation by Dr John Landquist'. Landquist defends himself against Walberg's criticism of his translation into Swedish of the first published French edition of *En dåres försvarstal* in **B4:192**. As far as possible he has tried to employ the same vocabulary, style, and tone that Sg used in other works from the mid-1880s, especially *Tjänstekvinnans son*, and to translate the original French as if he had been writing in Swedish. The kind of literal version that his critics desire would have been a monstrosity, not least because it would have entailed transposing Sg's sometimes clumsy French into equally clumsy Swedish. Likewise, Sg's Swedish manuscripts demonstrate the great care with which he sought to avoid tautophonies and pleonasms, and Landquist points out that a similar care has been taken in this translation, which follows Sg in distinguishing between the kind of coarse language appropriate to a work of fiction like *Giftas* and an autobiographical narrative like *Inferno* or *En dåres försvarstal*]

[B4:101] Landquist, John, '*En dåres försvarstal*. Ett genmäle av dr. Landquist och ett svar av docenten Fredrik Böök', *Svenska Dagbladet* (Stockholm), 26 November 1914. ['*A*

Madman's Defence. A Reply by Dr John Landquist and A Response from Docent Fredrik Böök'. Landquist defends his approach to translating *Le Plaidoyer d'un fou* in response to Böök, **B4:30**. A review of all the passages criticised by Böök yields only a single error on the translator's part. To argue that certain words and phrases in the original have been too mildly rendered in Swedish is to ignore what Sg would have written when working in his own language, where he could judge what was appropriate more finely. Every word of the translation has been carefully tried and tested with a knowledge of Sg's style gained from proof-reading 9,000 pages of his collected works. Moreover, the task was unusual in that the source text was not written in its author's own first language and consequently contained numerous passages in which the meaning was infelicitously expressed and had therefore to be teased out by the translator from what he knew of the context – a problem exacerbated by the fact that the original manuscript was missing. Landquist concludes that 'Docent Böök has never understood Sg but with puerile arrogance has continually tried to fight him']

[B4:102] Landquist, John, 'Innan Strindberg blev klassiker. Strindberg och Mathilde Prager', *Litteraturen, Nordens kritiske Revue* (Copenhagen), 3 (1920-21), 193-206. ['Before Strindberg became a Classic. Strindberg and Mathilde Prager'. Documents Sg's links with the Austrian writer and translator (1844-1921, pseudonym Erich Holm) who was, between 1885 and 1895, one of his first German translators and someone with whom he conducted an often illuminating correspondence on his works in progress. Landquist demonstrates how her versions of several pre-Inferno works helped establish his early European reputation]

[B4:103] Landquist, John, 'Die Rechtfertigung eines Irren', *Der Sturm* (Berlin), 6 (1915-16), 10-11. ['The Defence of a Madman'. Criticises Emil Schering's German translation of *En dåres försvarstal*]

[B4:104] Landquist, Solveig, 'Orimliga beskyllningar', *Dagens Nyheter* (Stockholm), 20 September 1974. ['Unreasonable Accusations'. A rejoinder to Stellan Ahlström's disparaging remarks concerning John Landquist's Swedish version of *Le Plaidoyer d'un fou* in **B4:3**]

[B4:105] Larsson, Mats, *Från tjeckiska till svenska: översättningsstrategier för litterärt talspråk*, Stockholm: Insitutionen för nordiska språk, 1992. 190 pp. ['From Czech to Swedish. Translation Strategies for Literary Dialogue'. Makes some reference to Sg's novels and plays in a discussion of how the representation of colloquial spoken language in literature may best be translated from Czech into Swedish]

[B4:106] Lessing, O. E., 'Notes on Some German Translations of Scandinavian Authors', *Scandinavian Studies* (Manasha, Wisconsin), 2 (1914-1915), 107-112. [Points out that Scandinavian authors have been liberally received in Germany, on the basis of an old blood-relationship. The most recent such large-scale enterprise is Emil Schering's edition of Sg's collected works. Indeed, Sg is a writer whose works have held a place of honour in German letters since ca. 1890, all his contradictions and discords notwithstanding. Lessing judges Schering's translations to be far superior to the majority of English and American versions, but in translating the plays his German is not always sufficiently idiomatic]

[B4:107] Lind-af-Hageby, L[izzie], 'Adapted Plays', *The Times* (London), 23 January 1928. [A response to Sundström's remarks in **B4:164**. His objections to Robert Loraine's performance text of *Dödsdansen* in London are 'singularly ungracious…I can find nothing in Mr Loraine's presentation of the play which violates the meaning and intentions of Sg.' The latter's 'own irregularities justify adaptation within the plays'. See also **B4:9**]

[B4:108] Marmus, Roger, 'Réinventer le paysage. La traduction des descriptions de paysages dans *Au bord de la vaste mer*', in Olof Eriksson, red., *Strindberg och det franska språket: Föredrag från ett symposium vid Växjö universitet 22-23 maj 2003*, Acta Wexionensia, Humaniora, Växjö: Växjö University Press, 2004, pp. 141-162. ['Reinventing the Countryside. The Translation of the Descriptions of the Countryside in *By the Open Sea*'. Addresses issues raised by, and offers possible solutions to, the problem of translating a landscape which is particular to a single geographical entity as is the language used to describe it by those who are its familiars, and where the users of the target language are thus unfamiliar with the original setting. Marmus discusses Leopold Littmansson's first French translation of *I havsbandet* ('all things considered, not a bad solution') and the possible revisionary role played by Julien Leclerc and Marcel Réja, examines both general and particular issues, and appends a useful table of passages from the original and Littmansson translation in parallel form]

[B4:109] Martinus, Eivor, 'Strindberg – An Elusive Companion', in Irene Scobbie, ed., *Proceedings of the Eighth Biennial Conference of Teachers of Scandinavian Studies in Great Britain and Northern Ireland*, April 2-7 1989, Edinburgh: University Department of Scandinavian Studies, 1989, pp. 230-248. [A largely anecdotal account of problems encountered when staging Sg in English, based on the experience of translating *Fadren*, *Första varningen*, *Paria*, *Moderskärlek*, and *Oväder*. Martinus contends that Sg's plays need to be made accessible to actors and directors; they are 'elusive and ambiguous', with many 'loose ends' and other obscurities that require some editing by the translator 'in order to make sense at all of the script']

[B4:110] Martinus, Eivor, 'Translating Scandinavian Drama', in David Johnson, ed., *Stages of Translation*, Bath: Absolute Press, 1996, pp. 109-121. [Points out that, whether based on a literal version or not, many contemporary translations from Swedish or Norwegian are often undertaken by people with an inadequate knowledge of the source language. But when translating Sg it is important to recapture the physical force of the original, which is frequently expressed in short, discordant, and yet rhythmic sentences, using what was, for the period, daring imagery, as examples from *Fadren*, *Fröken Julie*, *Paria*, and *Stora landsvägen* demonstrate. Sg had a perfect ear for social accents and each character has his or her own register and vocabulary, while the range of general reference displayed in the plays, from the Bible and Greek and Nordic mythology to the terminology of contemporary science and technology, gives the translator endless problems, not least where the amount of additional explanation that a latter-day audience requires is concerned]

[B4:111] Mattsson, Margareta, 'Strindberg's *Miss Julie* in English: The Value of Literalness in Translation', *Scandinavica* (London), 13:2 (1974), 131-136. [On the value of painstaking literalness, especially in transmitting an author's specific poetic vision in another language. This is demonstrated by a comparison of how individual words and phrases in the source text have been translated in thirteen published English and American versions of *Fröken Julie*. Aside from minor inadvertencies, Mattsson concludes that the most common flaws in the majority of translations of the play stem from an urge to edit, underline, and clarify]

[B4:112] Meidal, Björn, '"En klok råtta måste ha många hål!" Strindberg och översättarna', in Meidal and Nilsson, red., **B4:113**, *August Strindberg och hans översättare*, pp. 11-24. Illus. ['"A Wise Rat needs many Holes!" Strindberg and His Translators'. Documents Sg's strategies in enlisting diverse translators to help establish his reputation abroad and the consequences this had where his precarious income was concerned. His letters reveal how Sg acted as his own impresario, sometimes encouraging translators to adapt his texts to the expectations of non-Swedish audiences and readers, readily granting the translation rights to his works to more than one translator, and often displaying only a quixotic interest in the results]

[B4:113] Meidal, Björn, and Nils Åke Nilsson, red., *August Strindberg och hans översättare: Föredrag vid symposium i Vitterhetsakademien 8 september 1994*, Kungl. Vitterhets Historie och Antikvitets Akademien Konferenser 33, Stockholm: Almqvist & Wiksell International, 1995. Illus. 121 pp. ['August Strindberg and His Translators. Lectures from a Symposium at the Academy of Letters'. The proceedings of a conference in Stockholm devoted to Strindberg, his translators, and his reception in translation, which contains **B3:364**: Michael Robinson, 'Aldrig längre än till Gravesend: Strindberg och England'; **B3:398**: Birgitta Steene, 'Besatt viking eller uppskattad konstnär: Strindberg och Ingmar Bergman i USA'; **B4:45**: Gunnel Engwall, '"Det knastrar i hjärnan". Strindberg som egen franske översättare'; **B4:89**: Barry Jacobs, 'Bland amerikanska läsare och kritiker: Strindberg i översättning'; **B4:94**: Suzanne Jenner, '*Fröken Julie* i fransk översättning – ett drama i förvandling'; **B4:112**: Björn Meidal, '"En klok råtta måste ha många hål!" Strindberg och översättarna'; **B4:122**: Helmut Müssener, '"Det är synd om..." Strindberg och de tyska översättarna'; and **B4:125**: Nils Åke Nilsson, 'Strindbergs ryska översättare']

[B4:114] — Blackwell, Marilyn Johns, *Scandinavian Studies* (Provo), 71:1 (1999), 115-117.

[B4:115] — Petherick, Karin, *Scandinavica* (Norwich), 35:2 (1996), 283-285.

[B4:116] Meyer, Michael, 'On Translating Plays', *Twentieth-Century Studies*, 11 (September 1974), 44-51. [A practitioner's essay based on the experience of translating both Ibsen and Sg. Meyer maintains that when translating drama, tautness of stage dialogue and sensitivity to the subtext are crucial. Where Sg is concerned, a translator needs to have a free hand as regards punctuation since otherwise his repeated exclamation marks suggest melodrama while his liberal use of *points suspensifs* indicates a superabundance of meaningful pauses – neither habit should be reproduced. According to Meyer, a translator must also resist the temptation to sanitise Sg's language and should seek to reproduce the apparent inconsequentiality of Sg's dialogue which, as in *Fröken Julie*, has the internal logic of people speaking under the pressure of great emotion]

[B4:117] Mitrache, Liliana, *Metaphern in literarischen Übersetzungen: eine vergleichende Analyse der sechs deutschen Übersetzungen von Strindbergs Roman Hemsöborna'*, Studia Germanistica Upsaliensis 51, Uppsala: Universitetsbiblioteket, 2006. 222 pp. ['The Metaphor in Literary Translation: A Comparative Analysis of the Six German Translations of Strindberg's Novel *Hemsöborna*']

[B4:118] Moeschlins, Felix, 'Zum Verständnisse Strindbergs und zur Würdigung seines Übersetzers', *Süddeutsche Monatshefte* (München und Leipzig), 10:2 (1913), 390-408. ['Towards an Understanding of Strindberg and an Appreciation of His Translator'.

Discusses Emil Schering's translations of Sg into German, with an appreciation (not always favourable) of their worth]

[B4:119] Moreck, Curt, 'Ausgewählte Romane; Ausgewählte Dramen', *Zeitschrift für Bücherfreunde* (Leipzig), N.F. 13 (1921), 221-222. ['Selected Novels; Selected Plays'. A critique of Else von Hollander's translations in the 1919 German edition of Sg's selected novels and plays in four volumes]

[B4:120] Mori, Mitsuya, 'Japanese Translations of Strindberg', in Donald Weaver, ed., **D2:331**, *Strindberg on Stage*, pp. 144-147. Illus. [Comments briefly on the history of Sg's reception in the Japanese theatre as well as the problems involved in translating European drama into Japanese both generally and in Sg's case in particular, not least where personal pronouns are concerned. Mori's experience of translating both Ibsen and Sg confirms that the latter's dialogue is freer and more spontaneous, with a lyricism that is well suited to Japanese. The rhythm of his sentences can also be translated into Japanese more faithfully than is the case with Ibsen]

[B4:121] Motton, Gregory, 'Introduction', in *Strindberg, The Plays. Volume One: The Father, Miss Julie, The Comrades, Creditors*, London: Oberon Books, 2000, pp. 7-25. [Prefaces a comment on each of the plays in his own translation with a statement about the way that Sg ought to be translated for the English stage and in so doing devotes some aggressively critical observations on versions by Michael Meyer, Kenneth McLeish, Peter Watts, Elizabeth Sprigge, and Eivor Martinus]

[B4:122] Müssener, Helmut, '"Det är synd om..." Strindberg och de tyska översättarna', in Björn Meidal and Nils Åke Nilsson, red., **B4:113**, *August Strindberg och hans översättare*, pp. 25-34. Illus. ['"It is a pity about..." Strindberg and His German Translators'. Virtually all Sg's works have been translated into German, most notably between 1902 and 1930 in 46 volumes by Emil Schering and subsequently in other, more or less complete, editions by Else von Hollander-Lossow, Heinrich Goebel, and Willi Reich. However, the latest attempt at a serious, scholarly edition, the Frankfurt Ausgabe, has just been brought to a premature end. Some thirty-seven translators in all have occupied themselves with turning one or more of Sg's works into German, from Laura Marholm and Mathilde Prager to Peter Weiss, but as yet no systematic comparative study of these translators or their translations exists. While it is all too easy to catalogue basic linguistic and other errors in many of these versions, it is far more interesting to examine the general problems which have come between German-speaking readers, directors, and actors and Sg's original text. These include material which the translator omits for one reason or another, as well as problems concerning the translation of place names, forms of address, stage directions, and other culture-specific aspects. There are also linguistic features that do not admit translation, like the precise use that Sg makes of the three Swedish negatives, 'ej', 'icke', and 'inte' in *Ett drömspel*. A translator like Schering generally works according to the stylistic norms, and within the professional parameters, of his respective period; thus, in German, Sg's works are generally rendered more smoothly and appear more conventional, as well as less drastic, ironic, syntactically complex, vital, and personal, than they are in Swedish]

[B4:123] Nagashima, Yoichi, 'Ogai to Sutorindoberi', in *Mori Ogai no hon'yaku: bungaku: "Sokkyo-shijin" kara "Perikan" made*, Tokyo: Shibundo, Heisei 5 [1993], pp. 86-189. ['Ogai and Strindberg', in *Mori Ogai's Translations from The Improvisator to The Pelican*'. Includes an English summary, 'Beyond Translation. Mori Ogai's Translation or His

Creative (Mis)understanding' in a discussion of Ogai's Japanese translation of Hans Christian Andersen's novel, *Improvisatoren* (The Improvisator, 1835) as well as Sg]

[B4:124] Neuger, Leonard, '*Fröken Julie*: semiotiken vållar problem', *Södertörns högskola – Nyhetsbrev* (Södertörn), 2 (1999), 21-27. ['*Miss Julie*: Semiotics Causes Problems'. Compares how two Polish translations by Zygmunt Łanowski and Grzegorz Kempińsky of the opening scene of *Fröken Julie* prior to Julie's first entrance convey the semiotic range of the original. Neuger focuses primarily on the significance of the relationship between the names, Jean and Julie, Jean's different registers, as he switches between French, Swedish, and Latin, and the significance of the food which Kristin is preparing, both for Jean and Miss Julie's errant dog, Diana]

[B4:125] Nilsson, Nils Åke, 'Strindbergs ryska översättare', in Björn Meidal and Nils Åke Nilsson, red., **B4:113**, *August Strindberg och hans översättare*, pp. 61-74. ['Strindberg's Russian Translators'. The majority of Russian translations of Sg prior to 1917 derive from German versions and, as was the case with *Fröken Julie*, were often given titles that evoked French farce or Viennese operetta. Translators with at least some knowledge of Swedish included V. Firsov [Baron Forsales] who produced versions of several of the novels, including *Hemsöborna*, Lvovitj Tolstoi, the novelist's son, who translated *Leka med elden*, Anna and Petr [Peder] Ganzen, who were responsible for a Russian edition of *Fadren*, the Lithuanian symbolist poet, Jurgis Baltrushaitis, and Beatrice Leontieva, whose translations were authorised by Sg and done for pleasure and without payment. The three extant letters which Leontieva addressed to Sg are reproduced in an appendix]

[B4:126] Ollén, Gunnar, 'De första översättningarna – till franska, danska och tyska – av *Fordringsägare*', *Strindbergiana* (Stockholm), 8 (1993), pp. 20-29. ['The First Translations of *Creditors* into French, Danish, and German'. Compares some of the cuts, additions, and adaptations in Sg's own, relatively free, French version with the Swedish source text, and illustrates the faults and virtues of contemporary translations into Danish (Nathalia Larsen), German (Mathilde Prager), and French (Georges Loiseau), all undertaken with some measure of consultation with Sg]

[B4:127] Ollfors, Anders, 'De tidiga översättningarna av Strindbergs verk till tyska', in Margareta Brundin *et al.*, red., **B1:88**, *20 x Strindberg*, pp. 262-274. Illus. ['Early Translations of Strindberg's Works into German'. A mostly annotated bibliographical catalogue of translations in book form up to, and including, the first of Emil Schering's versions (of *Till Damaskus I-II*) in 1889]

[B4:128] O'Sheel, Shaemas, '*Miss Julie*; *The Stronger*', *New York Times Book Review*, 22 September 1912. [Criticises Edwin Björkman's translations. Compared with the originals, O'Sheel finds them 'sawdust rather than dynamite']

[B4:129] Österling, Anders, 'Det ovederhäftiga vittnesmålet. En replikväxling mellan hr Österling och docenten Böök', *Svenska Dagbladet* (Stockholm), 17 December 1914. ['The Unreliable Testimony. An Exchange between Herr Österling and Docent Böök'. A response to Fredrik Böök's criticism of Landquist's translation of *Le Plaidoyer d'un fou* in **B4:30**. Österling maintains that Landquist captures the tone and vocabulary that Sg used when writing in his own first language]

[B4:130] Österling, Anders, '*En dåres försvarstal*', *Forum* (Stockholm), 28 November 1914, pp. 104-106. [Argues against Fredrik Böök's strictures on John Landquist's Swedish translation of the French original of *En dåres försvarstal* in **B4:30**. Österling maintains that Landquist's translation gives the reader the illusion of reading Sg himself]

[B4:131] Österling, Anders, 'Genmäle', *Forum* (Stockholm), 16 January 1915, pp. 35-36. ['Reply'. Criticises Fredrik Böök for his arrogant conduct in the debate provoked by his critique of John Landquist's translation of *Le Plaidoyer d'un fou*. Österling locates the source of Böök's behaviour in an underlying desire to do damage to Sg the man]

[B4:132] Österling, Anders, 'Strindberg på engelska', *Svenska Dagbladet* (Stockholm), 8 February 1929. ['Strindberg in English'. Reviews the collection *Easter and Other Plays* in the Anglo-Swedish Literary Foundation edition of Sg's dramas]

[B4:133] Paul, Fritz, 'Deutsche Strindberg-Ausgaben. Ein Ärgernis?', in Wilhelm Friese, Hrsg., **B3:168**, *Strindberg und die deutschsprachigen Länder*, pp. 139-160. ['German Strindberg Editions. An Outrage?' A sharply critical review of the current state of Sg translations in German, which Paul divides into three periods. The first, from 1885 to 1900, reflects his early reception in Germany and includes versions of *Leka med elden* and *Bandet* that antedate their publication in Swedish. The second, from 1902 to 1930, coincides with Schering's mechanistic, often carelessly translated and (from a bibliographical point of view) scandalously organised edition of Sg's collected works, and his self-aggrandizing prosecution of his own interests as well as of Sg's German reputation. The third covers the post-1945 versions of Willi Reich, Hans Egon Gerlach, and Peter Weiss. Neither Reich's translations nor even Peter Weiss's versions of *Fröken Julie* and *Ett drömspel* are the answer. In Paul's opinion, Sg still lacks his Schlegel or Tieck]

[B4:134] Paul, Fritz, '"Im Eisschrank sind einige Leichenteile". Soziale Konventionen und Beziehungsdefinitionen im antimimetischen Drama', in Erika Fischer-Lichte, Fritz Paul, Brigitte Schultze, and Horst Turk, Hrsg., *Soziale und theatralische Konventionen als Problem der Dramenübersetzung*, Forum modernes Theater Schriftreihe, Bd 1, Tübingen: Gunter Narr Verlag, 1988, pp. 117-128. ['"There are Body Parts in the Freezer". Social Convention and Definition of Relationships in Anti-Mimetic Drama'. An analysis of the difficulties presented by the translation of personal relationships in non-realist drama with close reference to Scenes 2 and 16 in *Till Damaskus I* as rendered in six German translations by Emil Schering, Else von Hollander, Hans Egon Gerlach, Artur Bethke, and two by Willi Reich. Paul also considers the interpretative implications of their choices for the realisation of the play in performance]

[B4:135] Paul, Fritz, '"Innerlich und äußerlich schrecklich verwickelt". Übersetzer-Inszenierungen in Strindbergs *Gespenstersonate* und *Nach Damaskus II*', in Brigitte Schultze, Erika Fischer-Lichte, Fritz Paul, and Horst Turk, Hrsg., *Literatur und Theater. Traditionen und Konventionen als Problem der Dramenübersetzung*, Forum Modernes Theater Schriftenreihe 4, Tübingen: Gunter Narr Verlag, 1990, pp. 131-159. ['"Inwardly and Outwardly Exceedingly Complicated". Translator-Stagings in Strindberg's *Ghost Sonata* and *Till Damaskus II*'. A finely judged analysis of the ways in which different translators explicate Sg's text with additional stage directions and other insertions, thus directly or indirectly 'setting' or 'staging' the Swedish original and interpreting it in the process of translation. Paul refers to versions of *Spöksonaten* and *Till Damaskus II* by Willi Reich, Emil Schering, Mathilde Mann, Else von Hollander, Heinrich Goebel, Hans Egon Gerlach, and Artur Bethke, and pays particular attention to how they deal with Sg's rhythm, syntax, diction, and punctuation. The kind of innovatory dramaturgy these plays represent and the new form of staging they require are sometimes at odds with the translator's often normative impulse, which tends to iron out their individuality]

[B4:136] Paul, Fritz, 'Realsinn oder poetischer Mehrsinn? Zur Übersetzungs- Problematik "vielstimmiger" Lyrik der Jahrhundertwende am Beispiel von Strindbergs Rollengedicht "Trefaldighetsnatten"', in Brigitte Schultze, Hrsg., *Die literarische Übersetzung. Fallstudien zu ihrer Literaraturgeschichte*, Göttinger Beiträge zur Internationalen Übersetzungsforschung 1, Berlin: Erich Schmidt, 1987, pp. 214-236. ['Realistic Significance or Poetic Polyvalence? On Problems in the Translation of "Multi-Voiced" Poetry from the Turn of the Century, Exemplified by Strindberg's Dramatic Poem "Trinity Sunday Night"'. A valuable essay on translating multi-voiced (dialogic) poetry from the turn-of-the last century as exemplified by Sg's poem 'Trefaldighetsnatten', first published in *Fagervik och Skamsund* (1902). Paul also considers the relationship between monologic and dialogic poetic discourse in modernist poetry in general, with specific reference to German translations of the poem by the 'dilettante' Emil Schering and the 'scholarly' Walter A. Berendsohn. As well as the dialogic nature of 'Trefaldighetsnatten', account is also taken of the culture-specific references in the original, the question of which edition of the source text should be used, and the relationship of this text to *Ett drömspel*]

[B4:137] Paul, Fritz, 'Schwedische Literatur in deutscher Ubersetzung 1700-1975. Ein bibliographisches Projekt', in Helmut Müssener, Hrsg., *Nicht nur Strindberg. Kulturelle und literarische Beziehungen zwischen Schweden und Deutschland 1870-1933*, Acta Universitatis Stockholmiensis, Stockholmer Germanistische Forschungen 24, Stockholm: Almqvist & Wiksell, 1979, pp. 27-51. ['Swedish Literature in German Translation, 1700-1975. A Bibliographic Project'. Presents an ongoing bibliographical study of translation as a mode of reception with reference to Swedish literature, including Sg. See **A1:78**]

[B4:138] Paul, Fritz, '"Strindberg Deutsch" oder die literarische Übersetzung als Gegenstand der Literaturwissenschaft. Ein Bericht aus dem Göttinger Sonderforschungsbereich "Die Literarische Übersetzung"', in Ulrich Groenke, Hrsg., *Arbeiten zur Skandinavistik. 7.* Arbeitstagung der Skandinavisten des Deutsches Sprachgebietes: 4.8-10.8 1985 in Skjeberg: Norwegen, Texte und Untersuchungen zur Germanistik und Skandinavistik 18, Frankfurt am Main: Peter Lang, 1987, pp. 325-337. ['"Strindberg German", or Literary Translation as a Subject for Literary Studies. A Report from the Göttingen Research Group into "Literary Translation"']

[B4:139] Paul, Fritz, 'Strindbergs "Plaidoyer d'un fou". Zur Odyssee eines Texte und seiner Übersetzungen', in Wilfried Floeck, *et al.*, Hrsg., *Formen innerliterarischer Rezeption*, Wolfenbütteler Forschungen 34, Wiesbaden, 1987, pp. 459-479. ['Strindberg's *A Madman's Defence*. On the Odyssey of a Text and its Translations'. Considers the various incarnations of Sg's autobiographical fiction in a succession of revisions or translations of the original French text into German, French, and Swedish which have often influenced one another. However, the recently discovered source text compels a reassessment of all existing translations, and makes a more authoritative version possible]

[B4:140] Paul, Fritz, and Brigitte Schultze, Hrsg., *Probleme von Dramenübersetzung 1960-1988*, Forum Modernes theater. Schriftenreihe, Bd 7, Tübingen: Gunter Narr Verlag, 1991. 106 pp. ['Problems in Translating Drama']

[B4:141] Paulson, Arvid, 'On Translating Strindberg', *Performing Arts Review* (New York), 3:1 (1972), 175-179. [Reflections on translating Sg by one of his most industrious North-American translators, whose work encompasses fiction and poetry, as well as many of the plays]

[B4:142] Perridon, Harry, 'Translating Pronouns of Power and Solidarity: Forms of Address in Strindberg's *Fröken Julie*', in Harry Perridon, ed., *Strindberg, Ibsen & Bergman. Essays on Scandinavian Film and Drama offered to Egil Törnqvist on the Occasion of his 65th Birthday*, Maastricht: Shaker Publishing, 1998, pp. 161-175. [Examines the degrees of intimacy, solidarity, distance, formality, politeness, and condescension in 19th-Century Swedish, and as employed by Sg in *Fröken Julie*, where the translator is faced with the difficult task of finding an alternative way of expressing the solidarity and intimacy connoted by 'du' and the formality and lack of solidarity connoted by 'ni'. Moreover, Sg's subtle use of 19th-Century forms of address also poses problems for modern Swedish actors and directors, who have inherited an address system that has undergone radical changes since the 1880s: 'as the meaning of a large number of words has changed since the days of Sg, the text printed in the new scientific edition of Sg's works...is arguably *not* the same text as the one created by Sg. It is impossible to retain both the wording and the meaning of *Fröken Julie* on stage. The play has to be recreated each time it is staged; it is inevitable that much of the information of the original text is lost in the process, and that new meanings are added']

[B4:143] Petherick, Karin, 'Om svårigheten för en god akademiker att vara stor Strindbergs-översättare. Reflexioner med anledning av Anthony Swerlings artikel Frenchifying Strindberg', *Svensk Litteraturtidskrift* (Stockholm), 36:4 (1973), 11-14. ['On the Difficulty of a Good Academic being a Great Translator of Strindberg'. Deems Anthony Swerling's critique of recent French translations of Sg's plays in **B3:420** to be misguided, not least because he overlooks the fact that drama in translation must facilitate performance. If ever achieved, Swerling's pedantic ideal would lead to a dead perfection, at odds with what Petherick considers are the best of the five principal English translations of *Fröken Julie* by Edwin Björkman, C. D. Locock, Peter Watts, Elizabeth Sprigge, and Michael Meyer. Despite the occasional lexical error, the latter achieves a generally speakable performance text, largely by collaborating closely with a director and the actors. See also **B4:167**]

[B4:144] Rakšányiová, Jana, 'Übersetzen aus kommunikativ-semiotischer Sicht. August Strindberg in slowakischen Übersetzungen', in Otmar Werner, Hrsg., *Arbeiten zur Skandinavistik 8*. Arbeitstagung der skandinavisten des Deutschen Sprachgebiets, 27.9-3.10.1987 in Freiberg i Br., Texte und Untersuchungen zur Germanistik und Skandinavistik 22, Frankfurt am Main, 1989: Peter Lang, pp. 329-336. ['A Communicative-Semiotic Perspective on Translation. August Strindberg in Slovak Translation'. Employs a theoretical approach, based on the model of translation as an act of communication developed by František Miko and Anton Popović, to the principles underlying the three–volume Slovakian edition of Sg's works, to which Rakšányiová herself contributed versions of *Röda rummet*, *Giftas*, *Hemsöborna*, and *Tjänstekvinnans son*. She concludes that 'the creative aspect of a translator's work resides in her critical input, in the fact that the translator becomes the author's partner']

[B4:145] Reusse, Walter, 'Emil Scherings Strindbergübersetzung: Einflüsse des Gymnasialunterrichtes auf die Sprachform', *Skandinavistik* (Kiel), 18:1 (1988), 35-54. ['Emil

Schering's Strindberg Translations: The Influence of High-School Teaching on Linguistic Style'. A detailed critical examination of the influence exerted by a conventional German Grammar School education on Schering's Sg translations in respect of their style, syntax, and diction]

[B4:146] Robinson, Michael, 'Att anglisera *Fröken Julie*', *Strindbergiana* (Stockholm), 14 (1999), pp. 160-162. ['Anglicizing *Miss Julie*'. An abridged version of **B4:150**, translated by Birgitta Steene]

[B4:147] Robinson, Michael, 'August Strindberg', in Olive Classe, ed., *Encyclopedia of Literary Translation in English*, 2 vols, London: Fitzroy Dearborn, 2000, Vol. 2, pp. 1340-1346. [An historical overview of the difficulties of translating Sg into English. All too often in translating Sg's prose there is a levelling down of styles, a simplification of the syntax, and a smoothing over of problematic or offensive passages, while it is usually the same few plays that have been repeatedly translated and therefore staged. Many early translations derive from German versions and frequently omit material, often on prurient grounds. An examination of the English editions of *En dåres försvarstal* reveals that there is sometimes no consensus, even regarding a generally acceptable English title]

[B4:148] Robinson, Michael, '*The Father*', in Olive Classe, ed., *Encyclopedia of Literary Translation in English*, London: Fitzroy Dearborn, 2000, pp. 1346-1347. [Compares seven English-language translations and takes Sg's own French version into account. Concludes that, while Walter Johnson's version is the most accurate of existing versions, those by Michael Meyer, Harry G. Carlson, and Evert Sprinchorn are the most performable]

[B4:149] Robinson, Michael, '*Inferno*', in Olive Classe, ed., *Encyclopedia of Literary Translation in English*, 2 vols, London: Fitzroy Dearborn, 2000, Vol. 2, pp. 1349-1350. [A comparison of three English translations of Sg's autobiographical fiction which recognises that any Swedish version is itself a translation of Sg's French original, initially published in a revised form by Marcel Réja, and including material omitted from the published Swedish text produced by Eugène Fahlstedt. Unlike Claud Field's ludicrously faulty 1912 translation, both the later versions by Sandbach and Sprinchorn are to be commended, not least for their excellent introductions]

[B4:150] Robinson, 'Maid in England: Anglicizing *Miss Julie*', *TijdSchrift voor Skandinavistiek*, (Amsterdam), 20:1 (1999), 29-34. [On the experience of translating and adapting Sg's play from its Swedish setting in 1888 to England in 1945 by way of Patrick Marber's television drama, *After Miss Julie*]

[B4:151] Robinson, Michael, '*Miss Julie*', in Olive Classe, ed., *Encyclopedia of Literary Translation in English*, 2 vols, London: Fitzroy Dearborn, 2000, Vol. 2, pp. 1347-1349. [Compares fifteen English-language versions of Sg's most translated play, several of which are to be criticised for omitting the Preface. Forms of address and even the title, which is variously rendered as 'Miss', 'Lady', or 'Countess' Julie (or 'Julia'), cause problems. More recent versions take advantage of the 1984 text-critical edition in *Samlade Verk* and include, or omit, material not always available to earlier translators]

[B4:152] Rothwell, Brian, 'Strindberg: *The Plays* (Vol. I) Translated by Michael Meyer', *Moderna språk* (Stockholm), 59:1 (1965), 62-65. [Intended as usable translations for the theatre, these versions of seven plays are often careless and contain errors and significant omissions on almost every page. Rothwell points out that Meyer also indulges in some high-handed rewriting of Sg and notes that there is a general lack of settled intention regarding tone throughout. Meanwhile, he observes that the introductions to each of the plays are largely culled without acknowledgement from Gunnar Ollén's *Strindberg's dramatik*, **D2:239**, and that they betray a tendency to simplify; the complex relationship between the man who suffers and the mind which creates these plays is crudely neglected. According to Rothwell, 'Mr. Meyer's work is likely to be much used but the shakiness of its first principles and its high-handed freedom with the text give an insecure basis for Sg studies, and even production, in England']

[B4:153] Rühling, Lutz, 'Fremde Landschaft. Zum Problem der geographischen Eigennamen in den Übersetzungen von Strindbergs naturalistischen Romanen *Röda rummet*, *Hemsöborna* und *I havsbandet*', in *Die literarische Übersetzung als Medium der Fremderfahrung*, Hrsg. von Fred Lönker, Göttinger Beiträge zur Internationalen Übersetzungsforschung 6, Berlin: Erich Schmidt Verlag, 1992, pp. 144-172. ['Foreign Landscapes. On the Problem of the Geographical Proper Nouns in the Translation of Strindberg's Naturalistic Novels *The Red Room*, *The People of Hemsö*, and *By the Open Sea*'. Rühling offers a theoretical discussion of the problems posed in translating the geographically localised and culturally specific place names in Sg's three major 'naturalistic' novels, in which issues of cultural transfer and cultural identity are particularly acute and where such precision is endemic to such realist discourse, with reference to the five published German versions of *Röda rummet*, six of *Hemsöborna*, and six of *I havsbandet*]

[B4:154] Rühling, Lutz, 'Der Übersetzer als Fremder: Zur Interferenz von Aspekten der Fremdartigkeit und ästhetischer Struktur in den Übersetzungen von Strindbergs Roman *Hemsöborna*', *Jahrbuch für internationale Germanistik* (Bad Homburg), 24 (1992), pp. 52-62. ['The Translator as Foreigner. On the Interference of Aspects of Foreignness in the Aesthetic Structure in the Translation of Strindberg's Novel *The People of Hemsö*'. Examines the role of the translator as a stranger to the translated text and considers how the aesthetic structure and exotic elements in the source text influence translation, with reference to six German versions of Sg's novel]

[B4:155] Sandbach, Mary, 'On Translating Strindberg', *Swedish Book Review* (Lampeter), 1985:1, pp. 30-33. [Takes an historical perspective with examples drawn from the author's own practice as a translator of Sg]

[B4:156] Schenck, Linda, 'Some Aspects of Literary Translation: A Study of Strindberg's *Easter* in English', *Svensk Litteraturtidskrift* (Stockholm), 45:4 (1982), 30-50. [Schenck suggests that a study of any discrepancies between the four published English translations of *Påsk* and their Swedish source text will, when conducted in the light of some of the existing literature in English and Swedish on the practice of translating, serve to indicate several more general aspects of literary translation, to which increased attention should be paid. Introductions and a thorough footnote apparatus are to be encouraged as a pendant to such translations while in the development of a "playable" translation, faithfulness to the original in the sense of lexical correctness wherever possible, the retention of linguistically deviant aspects of the author's style, and a literalness that strives to mirror in English the lexical, syntactical, and rhythmic qualities of the original should form a foundation upon which teamwork between translator, director, and the actors can be built. For academic purposes, such a version also offers the most satisfactory second-best to reading the work in the source language]

[B4:157] Schering, Emil, 'Ein Brief', *Die Schaubühne* (Berlin), 2:2 (1906), 43-44. ['A Letter'. Addressed to the theatre critic Siegfried Jacobsohn, in defence of his much criticised translations of Sg]

[B4:158] Schering, Emil, 'Nachwort des Übersetzers', in August Strindberg, *Die Beichte eines Thoren*, Verdeutscht von Emil Schering, München: Georg Müller, 1910, pp. 427-429. ['Afterword from the Translator'. Calls the previous German translation of *En dåres försvarstal* by Wilhelm Kämpf, which had been published in 1893 in a pirated edition, 'a crime against Sg']

[B4:159] Schubert, Elspeth Hartley, '*Hemsöborna* på engelska', *Meddelanden från Strindbergssällskapet* (Stockholm), 24 (1959), pp. 1-2. ['*The People of Hemsö* in English'. Comments on the author's own translation of Sg's novel (1959) and its positive reception in the English press, which saw in it a largely unknown side of his work]

[B4:160] Sjöberg, Leif, '*Five Plays by Strindberg*, Translated by Elizabeth Sprigge; *Three Plays by August Strindberg*, Translated by Peter Watts', *American-Scandinavian Review* (New York), 52:2 (1964), 216–218. [A comparative review of translations by Sprigge and Watts, often of the same plays]

[B4:161] [Söderbergh, Catharina], 'Strindberg på esperanto: *Fraulino Julie* kaj *Paria*', *Nya Meddelanden från Strindbergssällskapet* (Stockholm), No. 18 (November 2002), p. 5. ['Strindberg in Esperanto: *Miss Julie* and *Pariah*'. Reports on a tour of the Baltic in 1935 performing a double-bill of *Fröken Julie* and *Paria* in Esperanto, directed by Sandro Malmquist]

[B4:162] Steene, Birgitta, '"Sommarlovets hägring är inte nödvändigtvis översättarens vision…": Om *Pelikanen*, Kulturspråk och Författarspråk', *Strindbergiana* (Stockholm), 4 (1989), pp. 56-66. ['"The Mirage of Summer Holidays is not Necessarily the Translator's Vision…": On *The Pelican*, Culture-Specific Language and Author's Language'. The culture-specific resonance for Sg's Swedish middle-class contemporaries of his references to summer vacations in the Stockholm archipelago helps to clarify the need for a translator to be aware both of the individual verbal and stylistic registers of the author s/he is translating and the network of codes common to a culture at a specific historical moment, which the author may be challenging as well as take for granted. The opening scene of *Pelikanen* combines specifically Sgian motifs common to his previous Chamber Plays with a more general, but no less historically specific, framework of verbal and cultural codes. A translator is thus presented with almost insuperable problems, not least because – at the remove of some three generations – in realising one system, s/he will, in all likelihood, fail to convey the other. Steene compares two English versions of the opening lines and considers the way in which Sg's once modern dialogue has in some respects atrophied through the now archaic nature of its formulations and forms of address]

[B4:163] Stolt, Birgit, 'Die Relevanz stilistischer Faktoren für die Übersetzung', *Jahrbuch für Internationale Germanistik* (Bad Homburg), 10:2 (1978), 34-54. ['The Relevance of Stylistic Factors in Translation'. A theoretical discussion of stylistics in translation, exemplified by German versions of *Röda rummet* by Emil Schering (1908) and Willi Reich (1955). Stolt also discusses the pasting scene from *Ett drömspel*]

[B4:164] Sundström, Eskil, 'Departure from Originals', *The Times* (London), 21 January 1928. [Criticises the English performing version of *Dödsdansen* by the actor Robert Loraine for the 'artistically disastrous' way in which it both cuts important matter and tries to anglicise a colloquial North-American translation, thus ensuring a change in the spirit of Strindberg's original. This letter by the Secretary to the Swedish Legation in London initiates a correspondence in *The Times* with contributions by Lizzie Lind-af-Hageby, **B4:107**, Loraine himself, W. Farren, T. Beach, and others, with comments on Shakespeare in German, Italian, and French, as well as Sg in English, 23, 31 January, 6, 7, and 9 February. See also **B4:9**]

[B4:165] Swerling, Anthony, *Concerning the Art of Translation. Being Two Letters to an English Review, April-August 1968*, Cambridge: Trinity Lane Press, 1968. 16 pp. [Reprints two letters originally published in *The Times Literary Supplement* in which Swerling is sharply critical of Evert Sprinchorn's 1968 translation of *En dåres försvarstal* which he insists is no more than a revision of Elie Schleusser's error-strewn version from 1912]

[B4:166] Swerling, Anthony, 'Frenchifying Strindberg – A Literary Hoax', *Babel: International Journal of Translation* (Budapest), 18:3 (1972), 3-7. [Identical with **B4:167**]

[B4:167] Swerling, Anthony, 'Frenchifying Strindberg – A Literary Hoax', *Svensk Litteraturtidskrift* (Stockholm), 35:4 (1972), 30-35. [Attacks nine French translations of Sg as lexically and stylistically innacurate, and amounting to 'a series of spurious texts behind whose serious-looking covers lurks folly'. See the rebuttals by Carl Gustaf Bjurström and Karin Petherick in **B4:18** and **B4:143**]

[B4:168] Tallqvist, J. O., 'Strindberg på finska', *Hufvudstadsbladet* (Helsingfors), 23 May 1962. ['Strindberg in Finnish']

[B4:169] Tegelberg, Elisabeth, 'Les verbes d'incise dans *Hemsöborna* et sa traduction française. Étude contrastive', *Studia Neophilologica* (Stockholm), 71:1 (1999), 72-96. ['Interpolated Verbs in *The People of Hemsö* and their Translation into French. A Study in Contrasts'. Examines Sg's use of interpolated verbs in *Hemsöborna* and their place in a translation from Swedish into French, where paraphrase is frequently the favoured method. According to Tegelberg, this can create problems in a text where the style contributes greatly to the characterisation. Her study confirms its original hypothesis that the more one eliminates the "pure" declarative verbs, the more the translation into French of these incidental verbs deviates semantically and stylistically from the Swedish original]

[B4:170] Tegelberg, Elisabeth, 'Översättningarna av *Hemsöborna* till franska – några reflektioner kring svårigheter, strategier och strykningar', in Olof Eriksson, red., *Strindberg och det franska språket: Föredrag från ett symposium vid Växjö universitet 22-23 maj 2003*, Acta Wexionensia, Humaniora, Växjö: Växjö University Press, 2004, pp. 163-204. ['*The People of Hemsö* in French Translation: Some Reflections on the Difficulties, Strategies, and Omissions'. Comments on the now classic Swedish text, its relationship to Naturalism, and its humour and style before comparing the 1909 French translation by Georges Montignac and Jacques Monnier as *Dans les îles* and Jean-Jacques Robert's version, published in 1962 as *Les gens de Hemsö*. The latter displays far greater respect for the original than the former and in an unusually full and detailed account, Tegelberg addresses a series of questions regarding matters of style, rhythm, and tempo, as well as cultural specific terms and the often highly specialised diction of the source text]

[B4:171] Thompson, Laurie, 'Strindberg's Fourth Wife', *Scandinavica* (Norwich), 31:1 (1992), 33-42. [An appreciation of Mary Sandbach and her importance as a translator of Sg: 'her translations will stand as the definitive English versions for some generations to come'. Thompson also considers some specific translation issues raised by *I havsbandet*]

[B4:172] Tidström, Karin, 'De l'avant-garde à l'absurde: l'accueil d'une pièce de chambre de August Strindberg en France et de rôle de la traduction', in Olof Eriksson, red., *Aspekter av litterär översättning*, Rapporter från Växjö universitet, Humaniora, 9, Växjö, [2000], pp. 186-195. ['From the Avant-garde to the Absurd. The Reception of a Chamber Play by August Strindberg in France and the Role Played by the Translation'. Illustrates the significant part played by translation in establishing the terms on which *Spöksonaten* has been received and understood in France in relation to prevailing literary, theatrical, and linguistic conventions]

[B4:173] Tidström, Karin, 'Silence et rythme: deux aspects des pièces de chambre d'August Strindberg en traduction française', in Olof Eriksson, red., *Aspekter av litterär översättning*, Acta Wexionensia Humaniora 11, Växjö: Växjö Univ. Press, 2001, pp. 162-174. ['Silence and Rhythm: Two Aspects of Strindberg's Chamber Plays in French Translation'. Discusses aspects of the musically formed dialogue and structure of the four Chamber Plays of 1907, with examples taken from French and German translations of *Spöksonaten*, and making particular reference to Sg's musical use of silence and verbal rhythm]

[B4:174] Tigerstedt, R., 'En litterär principfråga', *Finsk Tidskrift* (Åbo), 79 (1915), 263-268. ['A Question of Literary Principle'. Provides an overview of the Fredrik Böök-John Landquist controversy concerning the latter's translation of *Le Plaidoyer d'un fou* in *Samlade Skrifter*. See **B4:30**, **B4:99**, **B4:100**, **B4:129**, **B4:192**, and **B4:193**]

[B4:175] Timbers, Jill, 'Interpreting Interpretations: *Fröken Julie*', *Translation Review* (Dallas, Texas), 21-22 (1986), 27-31. [Argues that in translation the subjective interdependence of multiple interpreters of a text in any theatrical performance gains a further layer. An examination of the ways in which tone and characterisation are conveyed in two English translations of *Fröken Julie* by Elizabeth Sprigge and Peter Watts, using Walter Johnson's American-English version as an additional reference point, reveals that, in trying to clarify or improve what may appear vague in the original, translators sometimes succeed and sometimes fail, but always produce different effects from one another. Sprigge's Jean appears more self-confident than Watts's and her Julie is bold and assured while the latter's 'quaver[s] a bit in confusion'. Of the two, Watts best captures the fragmented quality of casual conversation but omits the important Preface while Sprigge unjustifiably inserts her own views via additional stage directions. The essay as a whole suggests that its author is not familiar enough with the Swedish source text to reach these (or any other) conclusions regarding the play's translation]

[B4:176] Törnqvist, Egil, 'Ett dramatiskt dilemma', *Svensk Litteraturtidskrift* (Stockholm), 41:2 (1978), 18-29. ['A Dramatic Dilemma'. In contrast to prose fiction and poetry, Törnqvist points out that dramatic texts are designed for performance as well as to be read; a text may exist in two versions, even in its source language. A translator sometimes feels obliged to insert additional stage directions as Elizabeth Sprigge does in her versions of *Ett drömspel* and *Påsk*. Törnqvist focuses mainly on Ibsen's *The Wild Duck* but also discusses *Fröken Julie* and *Spöksonaten* in order to illuminate the difficulties of translating culture-specific references in a dramatic source text in translation]

[B4:177] Törnqvist, Egil, 'A "Play"-within-the-Play: The Opening of Strindberg's *The Father*', *Nordic Theatre Studies* (Copenhagen), 6:1-2 (1994), 59-67. [Asks what is the function of the first two scenes of *Fadren* concerning the orderly, Nöjd: how does the information provided in this subplot relate to the ensuing main action; how are the signifiers of the source text conveyed in translation; and to what extent are they retained in productions of the play, whether in Swedish or another language? These questions are explored by way of a close textual analysis which demonstrates how the setting and seemingly down-to-earth but carefully patterned early exchanges establish the central action of the play as a whole, and present its British and American translators with numerous difficulties, not least because many of its signifiers are culture-specific. A comparison of Swedish, German, British, and Flemish versions of *Fadren* for television and film reveals further departures from the source text. They differ from each other in their directorial choices regarding the setting, costume, dialogue, gestures, grouping, by-play, and tone of voice, as well as in their visual pointing in terms of cutting and camera angles. Even when performed in Swedish, the language spoken on stage departs from the original text in significant ways. However, no performance omits the Nöjd episode, which confirms how integral it is to a drama in which the title draws attention, not so much to an individual father as to the paternal species]

[B4:178] Törnqvist, Egil, 'Att översätta för scenen. Strindbergs *Fröken Julie*', in Otmar Werner, Hrsg., *Arbeiten zur Skandinavistik 8*. Arbeitstagung der skandinavisten des Deutschen Sprachgebiets, 27.9-3.10.1987 in Freiberg i Br., Texte und Untersuchungen zur Germanistik und Skandinavistik 22, Frankfurt am Main, 1989, pp. 317-328. ['Translating for the Stage. Strindberg's *Miss Julie*'. Unlike most translators, the translator of drama is not only confronted by two languages but two kinds of recipient (both the reader and the spectator), and the audio-visual dimension of plays as performance texts has been neglected in translation theory. For historical and other reasons there are in fact four different published texts of *Fröken Julie* in Swedish, and which version a translator or director chooses is therefore a relevant issue. Moreover, consciously or unconsciously, any performance, even in the source language, will depart in some respects from the text used, altering it phonetically or grammatically, if only slightly. Most of the twenty-odd published English translations of *Fröken Julie* are based on the corrupt text in *Samlade Skrifter*, but analysis of an exchange between Jean and Kristin near the start of the play, which was altered by Sg in the original manuscript and only restored in Sweden in 1984 as part of *Samlade Verk*, enables Törnqvist to examine the characteristic vicissitudes of a dramatic text as it emerges in different translations into Dutch, English, French, and German, as well as on stage in Swedish. Another passage about Julie's bitch, Diana, which contains the central conflict of the play *in nuce*, enables Törnqvist to gauge how successful the different translators have been in understanding and conveying the play's interlocking verbal network in details of lexis, style, and the use of pronouns, in a text where linguistic simplicity is more apparent than real. Törnqvist's analysis confirms that in order to achieve a version which may be performed as well as read, the translator of a dramatic text like *Fröken Julie* must have a developed theatrical imagination, as well as an acute ear for its verbal subtext]

[B4:179] Törnqvist, Egil, 'Att översätta Strindberg. *Spöksonaten* på engelska', *Svensk Litteraturtidskrift* (Stockholm), 39:2 (1976), 4-31. ['Translating Strindberg. *The Ghost Sonata* in English'. Although it covers only eight, rather than nine, English translations of *Spöksonaten*, this is largely a Swedish version of **B4:181**. Törnqvist also comments on the Swerling-Bjurström controversy debated in **B4:18** and **B4:167**, coming down solidly in support of Bjurström]

[B4:180] Törnqvist, Egil, 'Grönsiskan och påskliljan. Två översättningsproblem', *Strindbergiana* (Stockholm), 20 (2005), pp. 117-128. ['The Siskin and the Daffodil. Two Translation Problems'. [Discusses alternative ways (one more familiar, the other more specific) of translating the species of Julie's pet bird in *Fröken Julie* and the flower carried by Eleonora in *Påsk* to illustrate what is inevitably lost and won in any act of translation where the choice comes down to what is given preference, the spirit or the letter. Thus the title of this essay could also have been translated as 'The Greenfinch and the Easter Lily']

[B4:181] Törnqvist, Egil, 'Strindbergs *Spöksonaten* in het Engels', in *Vertalen vertolkt: Vertalen over vertalen*, Amsterdam: Nederlands Genootschap van Vertalers, 1976, pp. 71-79. ['Strindberg's *Ghost Sonata* in English'. Presents substantially the same material as **B4:183**]

[B4:182] Törnqvist, Egil, 'Translating for the Stage: Strindberg's *Fröken Julie* in English', in Sven H. Rossel and Birgitta Steene, eds, *Scandinavian Literature in a Transcultural Context*, Papers from the XVth IASS Conference, University of Washington, 12-18 August 1984, Seattle: University of Washington, 1986, pp. 230-234. [Employs many of the same examples utilised in **B4:178** in order to analyse variations in tempo, pitch, and accentuation in six generally available English translations of *Fröken Julie*. Törnqvist concludes that the simplicity of Sg's text is more apparent than real, and that the translator for the stage has to struggle with problems of a special kind, e.g. actability and the need for rapid comprehension on the part of an audience, which explains why a 'good' translator is not necessarily a 'good' translator for the stage]

[B4:183] Törnqvist, Egil, 'Translating Strindbergian Drama: *Spöksonaten* in English', in Törnqvist, **D2:310**, *Strindbergian Drama*, pp. 220-241. [Contends that successful play translations need to remain faithful to the original text while being at once idiomatic, speakable, and easy to grasp, since a theatre audience has little time to dwell on a word or phrase. An examination of nine English translations of *Spöksonaten* in the light of these general criteria highlights a series of issues that confront any translator of Sg. Apart from specific lexical problems that would tax even the most linguistically aware of translators, these include the question of which edition to use and how to deal with inadvertencies in the source text, the felt need for additional stage directions, the difficulty of conveying aspects of Swedish culture foreign to English readers and whether to include or delete local and historical references, as well as differences in stage conventions, and the temptation the translator often feels to clarify and thereby diminish what is sometimes imprecise in the original. The title itself, and the names of the characters, also create difficulties, as do the play's many literary and biblical allusions. One of the hardest tasks in translating *Spöksonaten* is finding the right stylistic level, particularly in a play where the style varies considerably. This extends to Sg's idiosyncratic use of punctuation marks and the question whether or not they should be reproduced verbatim in translation since, even though unidiomatic in English, they evidently function as directorial signs]

[B4:184] Törnqvist, Egil, 'Translating Strindbergian Imagery for the Stage', *TijdSchrift voor Skandinavistiek* (Groningen), 19:1 (1998), 7-23. [Törnqvist suggests that problems related to the translation of imagery in drama have been generally neglected by theorists and, since no major modern playwright has made such frequent use of verbal imagery as Sg, this is of particular concern where the translation of his plays is concerned. It is made yet more complex by his ambition to write prose dialogue that resembles everyday speech. Consequently, he frequently gives new life to conventional metaphors and makes common words metaphorically pregnant as, for example, in *Fröken Julie*, where the text is patterned by the Swedish for 'dirt' and 'dirty' (or conceivably 'filth' and 'filthy'), as well as by references to a 'fall' or 'falling'. A translator is often tempted to vary these words in the target language. In *Ett drömspel* and *Påsk* a character's name sometimes has a metaphoric quality that is thematically related to the plot, and in the Chamber Plays of 1907, the metaphorical dimension is at once so precise and complex that its retention in the target language risks confusing an audience with little time for reflection. Even a contemporary Swedish audience may find the imagery of the source text difficult, and certain concepts embedded in an image, like 'sommarlovet' (summer holidays) in *Pelikanen*, mark the limits of what a translator for the stage can achieve]

[B4:185] Uggla, Andrez Nils, 'Strindberg a współczesność', *Przegląd Humanistyczny* (Warsaw), 1979:11-12, pp. 41-52. ['Strindberg Today'. Comments on the current situation regarding the translation of Sg's works into Polish in light of the Swedish four-volume project *Strindberg i offentligheten*, **A1:51**, edited by Björn Meidal]

[B4:186] Uttenthal, Benedikte, 'Translation and Drama', in Susan Khin Zaw *et al.*, eds, *The Beginnings of Modern Drama*, Milton Keynes: The Open University Press, 1977, pp. 69-83. [Uses Michael Meyer's English version of *Fröken Julie* to exemplify some of the general issues which confront readers of drama in translation]

[B4:187] Vendelfelt, Erik, '*Hemsöborna* på danska', *Meddelanden från Strindbergssällskapet* (Stockholm), 34 (1964), pp. 19-23. ['*The People of Hemsö* in Danish'. Finds that the more translations of *Hemsöborna* one reads, the more convinced one becomes that it is untranslatable. A recent (1962) Danish version, which is in fact a revision of an earlier translation by Sven Lange, has its good points, but close analysis demonstrates that the particular charm of the original, namely Sg's inimitable temperament conveyed in a language that is at once vital and realistic, is largely lost in translation]

[B4:188] Vendelfelt, Erik, '*Hemsöborna* på franska', *Meddelanden från Strindbergssällskapet* (Stockholm), 37 (1965), pp. 18-19. ['*The People of Hemsö* in French'. Although one must admire the labours of the translator, Jean-Jacques Robert, who has solved many problems of detail and inserted a number of the passages omitted from the first Swedish edition, this second French translation contains numerous errors, many of which might have been avoided had a scholarly Swedish text been available. Nevertheless, French readers now have access to what is, for them, an unjustly neglected masterpiece]

[B4:189] Vendelfelt, Erik, '*Hemsöborna* på tyska', *Meddelanden från Strindbergssällskapet* (Stockholm), 24 (1959), pp. 3-8. ['*The People of Hemsö* in German'. Points out that the recent (1957) German edition is a reprint of Else von Hollander's 1923 translation. Hers was already the fourth German version of the novel and, although quite sound, it was made from the first, bowdlerised Swedish edition. In not at least revising it, the opportunity of providing German readers with a translation worthy of the original has been lost. All the published German versions have made the novel more conventional than it is in Swedish, especially where the use of dialect is concerned. While Hollander's version provides German readers with a fair impression of Sg's text, they can gain little idea of how singularly fresh, sparkling, and powerful his prose really is]

[B4:190] Viertel, Berthold, 'Eine deutsche Ausgabe Péladans', *Die Fackel* (Vienna), No. 315-316 (26 January 1911), pp. 37-41. ['A German Edition of Péladan'. Comments critically on the pretensions that inform Emil Schering's translation of Sg's collected works. As for the translation itself, 'In his [Schering's] mouth, Sg's battle cry assumes the coarse tone of a military barracks']

[B4:191] Vowles, Richard B., 'Reviews of Recent Translations', *Yearbook of Comparative and General Literature* (Bloomington, Indiana), 10 (1961), pp. 83-85. [Compares translations of six of Sg's plays by Elizabeth Sprigge with seven plays translated by Arvid Paulson. 'At best Miss Sprigge is crisp and concrete: at worst she is somewhat terse and elliptical. At best Mr. Paulson is fluent and at ease; at worst he leans toward the verbose and the conventional.... There are fewer ambiguities in Sprigge']

[B4:192] Walberg, Emanuel, 'Förvanskningen av *En dåres försvarstal*', *Svenska Dagbladet* (Stockholm), 12 December 1914. ['The Mutilation of *A Madman's Defence*'. Attacks John Landquist's Swedish version of *Le Plaidoyer d'un fou* in *Samlade Skrifter*. The principles on which it is based are erroneous and Landquist's philological qualifications inadequate. Moreover, he has tried to ameliorate the personal aggression behind the way in which the narrator's wife is portrayed in the original, thus presenting Sg in an advantageous light. Walberg highlights a number of linguistic errors other than those listed by Böök in **B4:30**]

[B4:193] Walberg, Emanuel, 'Strindberg är Strindberg både på franska och svenska. Anvisningar om de riktiga översättningsprinciperna till dr. John Landquist av Prof. Emanuel Walberg', *Svenska Dagbladet* (Stockholm), 2 January 1915. ['Strindberg is Strindberg in both French and Swedish. Advice to Dr. John Landquist on the Proper Principles of Translation from Prof. Emanuel Walberg'. Maintains that a good translator ought to combine fidelity to the original's content and tone with a certain freedom and fluency, but he does not have the right to misrepresent the source text, either by altering the meaning or modifying its manner of expression. Like the other contributions to this debate (see **B4:30**, **B4:99**, **B4:100**, **B4:129**, and **B4:192**), Walberg is unaware that Landquist's translation is based on a modified French text which departs, at times significantly, from Sg's original]

[B4:194] Warme, Lars G., 'Translations as Distorting Mirrors: Strindberg Redivivus', *Canadian Review of Comparative Literature* (Toronto), 7 (1980), 183-195. [Charts the vicissitudes of *En dåres försvarstal*, which was originally written in French while Sg was living in Germany and Denmark, and first published in German. Only then did it appear in Swedish, in a pirated edition and, with revisions to Sg's original French by Georges Loiseau, in France, in a version that formed the basis for John Landquist's Swedish translation in *Samlade Skrifter*. Since then it has been translated into English three times as *The Confessions of a Fool*, *A Madman's Defence*, and *A Madman's*

Manifesto. Of these English versions, the first was made from the German and includes a number of expurgations, prettifications, and euphemisms; the second is a revision of the first with the omissions largely restored; and the third (by Anthony Swerling) is an exemplary rendering into English of the 1895 French edition, on the mistaken assumption that the latter remains close to Sg's text. However, the recent discovery in Oslo of Sg's original manuscript reveals numerous stylistic changes and a number of passages, especially of a sexual nature, which Loiseau toned down when revising Sg's original. It is therefore hardly surprising that the English-speaking world has never quite caught up with Sg]

[B4:195] Westman, Margareta, 'När Strindberg översatte H. C. Andersen', in *Från språk till språk. Sjutton uppsatser om litterär översättning*, utg. av Gunnel Engwall and Regina af Geijerstam, Lund: Studentlitteratur, 1983, pp. 151-167. ['When Strindberg Translated H. C. Andersen'. Considers Sg's Swedish versions of several of Hans Christian Andersen's fairy-tales]

[B4:196] Wetzig, Karl-Ludwig, 'Diskrete Bewegungen des kleinen Fingers. Nebentext im Zusammenspiel des Systems theatralischer Zeichen', in Harald Kittel and Horst Turk, Hrsg., *Geschichte, System, literarische Übersetzung Histories, Systems, Literary Translations*, Göttinger Beiträge zur Internationalen Übersetzungsforschung 5, Berlin: Erich Schmidt, 1992, pp. 142-165. ['Discrete Movements of the Little Finger. The *Nebentext* in the Ensemble of the System of Theatrical Signs'. Wetzig adopts a semiotic approach which applies the theories of Niklas Luhman to Sg's *Den starkare* and its intertextual relationship with Per Olov Enquist's play, *Tribadernas natt*]

[B4:197] Wetzig, Karl-Ludwig, '"Kom och pröva!" Beziehungsordnungen als Übersetzungsproblem in Peter Weiss' Strindberg-Übersetzungen', in Otmar Werner, Hrsg., *Arbeiten zur Skandinavistik 8*. Arbeitstagung der skandinavisten des Deutschen Sprachgebiets, 27.9-3.10.1987 in Freiberg i Br., Texte und Untersuchungen zur Germanistik und Skandinavistik 22, Frankfurt am Main: Peter Lang, 1989, pp. 304-316. ['"Come and Try!" Categories of Relationship as a Translation Problem in Peter Weiss's Translations of Strindberg'. Documents the research of a working group of German Scandinavianists into the specific problems of translating drama, which often entails the dramatisation of social convention. This issue can be usefully explored via a study of Peter Weiss's translations of *Fadren* and *Fröken Julie*, where the relationship between mistress and servants makes it particularly acute]

[B4:198] Wetzig, Karl-Ludwig, 'Komteß Julie. Soziale Konventionen als Übersetzungsproblem pragmatischer Kontexte in Strindbergs naturalistischen Trauerspiel', in Erika Fischer-Lichte, Fritz Paul, Brigitte Schultze and Horst Turk, Hrsg., *Soziale und theatralische Konventionen als Problem der Dramenübersetzung*, Forum modernes Theater Schriftreihe, Bd 1, Tübingen: Gunter Narr Verlag, 1988, pp. 95-115. ['*Countess Julie*. Social Conventions as a Problem in Translating the Pragmatic Context of Strindberg's Naturalistic Tragedy'. A theoretical analysis of problems raised in translating *Fröken Julie*, where aspects of social class and shared convention are embedded in forms of address, personal pronouns, and other linguistic elements. This is made even more complex by the different versions of the source text from which the eight German translations referred to here have been made. These problems are compounded by the fact that Julie and Jean play games with social conventions in a play that itself challenges prevailing social proprieties that are enshrined in language. Moreover, earlier translators did not have their successors' awareness of how such a play was to become a central strand in 20th-Century drama]

[B4:199] Wonderley, A. Wayne, 'August Strindberg, *World Historical Plays*', *Germanic Review* (New York), 47:4 (1972), 305-306. [Reviews Arvid Paulson's versions of four plays not previously translated into English. Wonderley concludes that, although they are sometimes marred by stiffness and infelicitous phraseology, the plays are well translated]

[B4:200] Zc [Zenon Ciesielski], 'Strindberg w Polsce', *Dialog* (Warsaw), 1970:6, pp. 155 -157. ['Strindberg in Polish'. Reflects on the reception of Sg in Poland via the medium of translation, including Zygmunt Łanowski's recent versions of the dramas]

[B4:201] Zettersten, K. V., *Henrik Ibsen, En Folkefiende och August Strindberg, Fadren på arabiska*, Uppsala: Almqvist & Wiksells Boktryckeri, 1949. 14 pp. ['Ibsen's *An Enemy of the People* and Strindberg's *The Father* in Arabic']

See also **B3:420, D2:948, D2:956, E12:86, K4:10, U1:89, V:118, V:147**

B5. General Histories of Swedish, Scandinavian, and European Literature; Textbooks; and Selected Works of Reference

[*As well as a number of frequently reprinted general literary histories which were instrumental in establishing Sg's reputation in Sweden, and not always for the best, this section also contains several works in which an account of Swedish literature and Sg's place in it was conveyed to a non-Swedish readership in translation and a number of Swedish school textbooks, which performed a similar function for generations of young Swedes. Many of these works appeared in many editions, either reprinted verbatim or in a sometimes significantly revised form. This latter process is discussed by Sten-Olof Ullström in* **B3:466**, Likt och olikt. Strindbergsbildens förvandlingar i gymnasiet, *where Sg's assimilation into the Swedish secondary school curriculum and the changes made over many years to the account of Sg and his works as it was presented to schoolchildren in several of the most widely read textbooks is charted in detail. A limited number of encyclopaedic reference works are also noted here especially where, as in the case of Russia, such treatments have played a culturally significant role*]

[B5:1] Aarseth, Asbjørn, 'August Strindberg (1849-1912)', in *Norsk litteratur i tusen år*, Oslo: Landslaget for norskundervisning, 1994, p. 323. ['A Thousand Years of Norwegian Literature'. A textbook which includes a short assessment of the relevance of Sg for Norwegian literature]

[B5:2] Algulin, Ingemar, *A History of Swedish Literature*, Translated by John Weinstock, Revised by Judith Black, Stockholm: Swedish Institute, 1989. 286 pp. [Discusses Sg pp. 115-132. Algulin suggests that Sg only received true recognition in the middle of the 20th Century when his post-Inferno works struck a chord with the prevailing sense of absurdity. 'Only then did his literary status grow in Sweden, until he rose to the position of a brilliant and indisputable literary saint']

[B5:3] Alving, Hjalmar, *Svensk litteraturhistoria*, 3 vols, Stockholm: Albert Bonniers Förlag, 1929-32, Vol. 3, 'Adertonhundratalet', 1932. 208 pp. [The most widely used Swedish secondary-school textbook for the teaching of literature during the period in the decade prior to World War Two. Alving frequently interprets Sg's works in terms of their author's personality, including what he takes for granted was his mental instability]

[B5:4] Alving, Hjalmar, *Svensk litteraturhistoria jämte översikt av den isländska litteraturen*, Andra, genomsedda och förkortade upplagan, Stockholm: Svenska bokförlaget, Albert Bonniers Förlag, 1935, pp. 409-422. ['A History of Swedish Literature together with a Survey of the Literature of Iceland']

[B5:5] Alving, Hjalmar, and Gudmar Hasselberg, *Svensk litteraturhistoria, jämte en översikt av svenskspråkets historia av Gösta Bergman*, 5:e upplagan, utgiven under medverkan av Carl Reinhold Smedmark, Stockholm: Svensk Bokförlaget, Bonniers, 1963. 482 pp. ['A History of Swedish Literature together with a Survey of the History of the Swedish Language by Gösta Bergman'. Sg is discussed pp. 236-253. From the third edition of 1949 onwards, this influential textbook gives new and serious consideration to the naturalistic dramas: *Fadren* is now described as possessing 'some of the harrowing effects of the classical tragedies of fate' while *Fröken Julie* is characterised as 'the foremost masterpiece among naturalist plays'. But the post-Inferno works are still not given their due]

[B5:6] Andreæ, David, 'Åttiotalet. August Strindberg', in *Den svenska historien*, Del. 9, 'Industri och folkrörelser, 1866-1920, Stockholm: Albert Bonniers Förlag, 1968. Illus. 371 pp. ['The 1880s. August Strindberg'. A chapter in Volume 9 of a history of Sweden which is devoted to 'Industry and Popular Movements, 1866-1920']

[B5:7] Anttila, Aarne, *Johdatus uuden ajan kirjallisuuden valtavirtauksiin ja lähteitä nüden valaisemiseksi*, Porvoo [Finland]: WSOY, 1926. 503 pp. ['An Introduction to the Latest Trends in Contemporary Literature']

[B5:8] Appelberg, Bertel, *Svensk litteraturhistoria för lärdomsskolor*, Helsingfors: Söderström, 1921. XV+157 pp. ['A History of Swedish Literature for Teacher-Training Colleges']

[B5:9] Ardelius, Lars, and Gunnar Rydström, red., *Författarnas litteraturhistoria*, Den andra boken, Stockholm: Författarförlaget, 1978. 464 pp. ['The Writers' History of Literature'. A history of Swedish literature which comprises essays on previous writers by contemporary Swedish authors. Includes four personal essays on different aspects of Sg's work by Leif Carlsson, **B2:84**, Theodor Kallifatides, **C1:635**, Ebbe Linde, **D2:901**, and Maria Bergom-Larsson, **F4:21**, as well as a poem by Barbro Lindgren based on a motif in *Ockulta dagboken*]

[B5:10] Bach, Giovanni, 'Swedish Literature: Impressionism and Naturalism', Translated and enlarged by Frederika Blankner, Litt. D., in *The History of the Scandinavian Literatures. A Survey of the Literatures of Norway, Sweden, Denmark, Iceland and Finland, From their Origins to the Present Day, Including Scandinavian-American Authors, and Selected Bibliographies*, Based in part on the work of Giovanni Bach with additional sections by Richard Beck, Adolph B. Benson, Axel Johan Uppvall, and Others, Compiled, Translated in Part, and Edited by Frederika Blankner, New York: Dial Press, 1938, pp. 120-132.

[B5:11] Bach, Giovanni, 'Swedish Literature: Impressionism and Naturalism', Translated and enlarged by Frederika Blankner, Litt. D., in *The History of the Scandinavian Literatures. A Survey of the Literatures of Norway, Sweden, Denmark, Iceland and Finland, From their Origins to the Present Day, Including Scandinavian-American Authors, and Selected Bibliographies*, Based in part on the work of Giovanni Bach with additional sections by Richard Beck, Adolph B. Benson, Axel Johan Uppvall, and others, Compiled, Translated in Part, and Edited by Frederika Blankner, Port Washington, N.Y.: Kennikat Press, Inc., 1968, pp. 120-132. [Facsimile Rpr. of **B5:10**]

[B5:12] Bandle, Oskar, Hans-Peter Neumann, and Egon Wilhelm, Hrsg., *Studien zur dänischen und schwedischen Literatur des 19.Jahrhunderts*, Basel und Stuttgart: Helbing & Lichtenhahn, 1976. Illus. 255 pp. ['Studies in Danish and Swedish Literature of the 19th Century']

[B5:13] Benson, Adolph B., 'Swedish Literature: Its Tendencies and Principal Writers', in *World Literatures*, Pittsburgh: University of Pittsburgh Press, 1956, pp. 269-289.

[B5:14] Berg, John, and Wilhelm Tham, 'August Strindberg', in *Från Eddan till Ekelöf. Översikt av vår litteratur- och språkhistoria*, 6 uppl., Stockholm, 160 pp. ['From the Edda to Ekelöf. An Historical Survey of Our Literature and Language'. Includes a section on Sg, pp. 88-99. One of the most widely read of Swedish secondary school textbooks. First edition 1945; 16th edition 1967]

[B5:15] Bergsten, Staffan, 'Den nordiska litteraturen', in F. J. Billeskov Jansen, red., *Litteraturens världshistoria*, Vol. 10, *Sekelskiftet. Första världskriget*, Stockholm: Norstedts, 1973, pp. 291-303. ['Nordic Literature' in 'The Literature of the World, a History'. Discusses Sg, pp. 294-297]

[B5:16] Bermel, Albert, 'August Strindberg', in Jacques Barzun, ed., *European Writers*, Vol. 7, New York: Scribner, 1985, pp. 1731-1751.

[B5:17] Bien, Horst, Hrsg., *Nordeuropäische Literaturen*, Mitarb. Artur Bethke, Meyers Taschenlexikon, Leipzig: Bibliographisches Inst., 1978. 344 pp. ['The Literature of Northern Europe']

[B5:18] Blanck, Anton, *Vår svenska litteraturens historia. En första vägledning*, Stockholm: Almqvist & Wiksells skolböcker, 1949. 123 pp. ['The History of Our Swedish Literature. A First Handbook']

[B5:19] Bogoslovskii, V[ladimir] N[ikolaevich], and Z[oia] T[ikhonovna] Grazhdanskaia, 'A. Strindberg', in *Zarubezhnaia literatura XX veka, I, 1871-1917*, Moscow: Prosveshchenie, 1979, pp. 170-173.

[B5:20] Bolckmans, Alex, *Scandinavische Letterkunde*, Aula pocket 711, Utrecht and Antwerp: Aula, Het Spectrum, 1984. 368 pp. ['Scandinavian Literature'. An introductory survey in Dutch which includes a section on Sg as a novelist as well as dramatist]

[B5:21] Böök, [Martin] Fredrik [Christofferson], 'August Strindberg', in *Sveriges moderna litteratur*, Stockholm: P. A. Norstedt & Söners Förlag, 1921, pp. 86-127, 332-346. [Surveys Sg's place in Swedish literature, dividing his career for treatment conventionally into pre- and post-Inferno works. A widely disseminated study of 'Sweden's Modern Literature' by a critic not ideologically disposed to Sg and often downright hostile (e.g. during the Strindberg Feud), but on this occasion sometimes perceptive and with a (for the period) useful bibliography (**A1:10**)]

[B5:22] Böök, [Martin] Fredrik [Christofferson], 'August Strindberg', in *Svenska litteraturens historia*, rev. upplagan, 3 Del, Stockholm: P. A. Norstedt & Söners Förlag, 1929, Vol. 3, pp. 98-137, 327-340. [Revised edition of **B5:21**]

[B5:23] Böök, Martin Fredrik Christofferson, *Kurze Übersicht über die schwedische Literatur*, Brieflicher Sprach- und Sprech-Unterricht für das Selbststudium der schwedischen Sprache, Berlin, 1906. 20 pp. ['A Short Survey of Swedish Literature'. Summarises Sg's literary career, pp. 13-14]

[B5:24] Boor, Helmut A. W. de, *Schwedische Literatur*, Breslau: Jedermans Bücherei, 1924. Illus. 116 pp. ['Swedish Literature'. An elementary introduction for German readers]

[B5:25] Borelius, Hilma, *Die nordischen Literaturen*, Übersetzung aus dem Schwedischen Gerhard Klose, Potsdam: Akademische Verl.-Ges. Athenaion, 1931. 170 pp. ['Nordic Literature'. An introductory history for German readers]

[B5:26] Boyer, Régis, *Histoire des littératures scandinaves*, Paris: Fayard, 1996. 561 pp. ['A History of Scandinavian Literature'. Now the standard account of the subject in French with a section on Sg that situates him in relation to Scandinavian literature in general during the 1880s and 1890s]

[B5:26a] Boyer, Régis, 'Johann August Strindberg', in *Les grands écrivains du monde*, Paris: Nathan, 1977, pp. 320-327.

[B5:27] Bradbury, Malcolm, and James [Walter] McFarlane, eds, *Modernism 1890-1930*, Harmondsworth: Penguin Books, 1976. [684] pp. [Sg's contribution to the emergence of modernism is noted throughout and his central role in the creation of modernism in the theatre with *Till Damaskus*, *Ett drömspel*, and the Chamber Plays of 1907 is discussed by James McFarlane in some detail as part of a chapter on 'Intimate Theatre: Maeterlinck to Strindberg', pp. 523-526]

[B5:28] Brandell, Gunnar, 'August Strindberg', in Gunnar Brandell and Jan Stenkvist, *Svensk litteratur 1870-1970*, 3 vols, Del. 1: 'Från 1870 till första världskriget', Stockholm: Aldus, 1974, pp. 50-109. Illus. [Builds upon Brandell's earlier accounts of Sg and Swedish literature in the 1880s and 1890s in **B5:30** and **B5:31**]

[B5:29] Brandell, Gunnar, 'Die skandinavische Literaturen 1870-1900', in *Jahrhundertende-Jahrhundertwende*, 2 Bde, Hrsg. von Helmut Kreutzer, Bd 1, Wiesbaden: Akademische Verlagsanstalt Athenaion, 1976, pp. 103-152. ['Scandinavian Literature 1870-1900'. German translation of **B5:28**]

[B5:30] Brandell, Gunnar, 'Åttiotalet', in E[ugène] N[apoleon] Tigerstedt, red., *Ny illustrerad svensk litteraturhistoria*, 2 uppl., Del. IV, Stockholm: Natur och Kultur, 1967, pp. 144-194. ['The 1880s'. An account of the work of the pre-Inferno Sg in its historical context by an eminent Sg scholar in a standard history of Swedish literature]

[B5:31] Brandell, Gunnar, 'Nittiotalet på längre sikt. Strindberg', in E[ugène] N[apoleon] Tigerstedt, red., *Ny illustrerad svensk litteraturhistoria*, Del. IV, Stockholm: Natur och Kultur, 1967, pp. 225-226. ['The 1890s in a Longer View – Strindberg'. Devotes part of a chapter on Oscar Levertin and Swedish literature in the 1890s to Sg]

[B5:32] Bredsdorff, Elias, Brita Mortensen, and Ronald Poperwell, *An Introduction to Scandinavian Literature from the Earliest Time to Our Day*, Copenhagen: Ejnar Munksgaard; Cambridge: Cambridge University Press, 1951, pp. 181-186, 194-198.

[B5:33] Breitholtz, Lennart, red., *Epoker och diktare 2. Allmän och svensk litteraturhistoria*, Stockholm: Almqvist & Wiksell, 1972. 673 pp. ['Periods and Writers. 2. A History of General and Swedish Literature'. Discusses Sg, pp. 240-250]

[B5:34] Brodow, Bengt, Börje Bergström, and Ingrid Nettervik, *Dikten och vi. Litteraturhistoria för gymnasieskolans 3- och 4-åriga linjer*, Malmö: LiberLäromedel. 1987. 452 pp. [Secondary school textbook]

[B5:35] Brøndsted, Mogens, red., *Nordens litteratur*, 2 Del, København: Gyldendalske Boghandel, 1972. [593] pp. [Includes numerous occasional references with an overview of Sg's career by Gunnar Svanfeldt, pp. 76-89]

[B5:36] Bull, Francis, 'August Strindberg', in *Verdenslitteraturens historie*, 2 utg., Oslo: Gyldendal, 1947, pp. 498-502. Illus. ['The History of World Literature']

[B5:37] Buße, Carl, *Geschichte der Weltliteratur*, Bd 2, Bielefeld-Leipzig: Velhagen & Klasing, 1913. 77+24 pp. plates. ['A History of World Literature'. Among the earliest such histories to include any discussion of Sg]

[B5:38] Butt, Wolfgang, 'Der moderne Durchbruch und die Zeit bis zur Jahrhundertwende', in Fritz Paul, Hrsg., *Grundzüge der neueren skandinavischen Literaturen*, Darmstadt: Wissenschaftliche Buchgesellschaft, 1982, pp. 147-214. ['The Modern Breakthrough and the Period up to the Turn of the Century'. Considers Sg together with Georg Brandes and Ibsen in the context of the Scandinavian Modern Breakthrough. Focuses on both the pre- and post-Inferno Sg, pp. 194-200 and pp. 210-214 respectively]

[B5:39] Castrén, Gunnar, 'Strindberg', in *Den nya tiden*, in Henrik Schück and Karl Warberg, red., *Illustrerad svensk litteraturhistoria*, 7 vols, Tredje fullständigt omarbetade upplagan, Stockholm: Rabén & Sjögren, 1932, Del. 7, pp. 96-154. Illus. ['The New Age'. Surveys the whole of Sg's career in a widely disseminated standard history of Swedish literature]

[B5:40] Ciesielski, Zenon, *Historia literatury szwedzkiej*, Wrocław: Zaklad narodowy im Ossolinskich, 1990. Illus. 340 pp. ['A History of Swedish literature'. Discusses Sg, pp. 120-172]

[B5:41] Ciesielski, Zenon, and Ryszard K. Nitschke, 'Literatura szwedzka', in *Dzieje literatur europejskich*, Vol. 2, edited by Władysława Floryana, Warszawa, 1983, pp. 227-314. [A chapter on 'Swedish Literature' which includes some discussion of Sg, in a two-volume general history of European literature]

[B5:42] Conrad, Michael Georg, *Von Zola bis Hauptmann*, Leipzig & Berlin: Hermann Seemann, 1902. 153 pp. ['From Zola to Hauptmann']

[B5:43] Dahl, Torsten, *Realism och naturalism*, Del. 5 in E[ugène] N[apoleon] Tigerstedt, *Bonniers allmänna litteraturhistoria*, Stockholm: Albert Bonniers Förlag, 1962. Illus. 252 pp. ['Realism and Naturalism'. Includes discussion of Sg's writings during the 1870s and 1880s]

[B5:44] Delblanc, Sven, 'Från förklaringsberget till barrikaden – Strindbergs senare författarskap', in Lars Lönnroth and Sven Delblanc, red., *Den svenska litteraturen*, 7 vols, Del. 4: 'Den storsvensk generationen: 1890-1920', Stockholm: Bonniers, 1989, pp. 33-68. Illus. ['From the Mount of Affirmation to the Barricades – Strindberg's Later Works'. Reprinted in Sven Delblanc, *Strindberg – urtida, samtida, framtida*, red. Lars Ahlbom and Björn Meidal, Stockholm: Carlssons, 2007, pp. 252-288, together with other short pieces on Sg from Vols 3 and 4]

[B5:45] Delblanc, Sven, 'Från förklaringsberget till barrikaden – Strindbergs senare författarskap', in Lars Lönnroth and Sven Delblanc, red., *Den svenska litteraturen*, Del. 2, Stockholm: Bonniers, 1999, pp. 325-360. Illus. ['From the Mount of Affirmation to the Barricades – Strindberg's Later Works'. Revised edition of **B5:44** in three rather than seven volumes]

[B5:46] Drake, William A., *Contemporary European Writers*, London: George G. Harrap & Company, Ltd., 1929, pp. 79, 90.

[B5:47] Erslev, Anna, *Fremmed Digtning – til Brug for Skole og Hjem*, København: Høst & Søns Forlag, 1894. 127 pp. ['Foreign Literature – For Use in School and the Home'. Includes perhaps the earliest comment on Sg in a non-Swedish literary history]

[B5:48] Ewbank, Inga-Stina, 'August Strindberg', in Irene Scobbie, ed., *Aspects of Modern Swedish Literature*, Norwich: Norvik Press, 1988, pp. 18-52. [See **B5:49**]

[B5:49] Ewbank, Inga-Stina, 'August Strindberg', in Irene Scobbie, ed., *Aspects of Modern Swedish Literature*, 2nd revised and augmented edition, Norwich: Norvik Press, 1999, pp. 31-73. [The most knowledgeable and informative brief introduction to Sg's work in several genres currently available in English. Demonstrates that Sg is more robust, more versatile, and more of a conscious artist than the received image of the neurotic genius indicates, is particularly illuminating about the relationship between the verbal and the visual dimensions of his post-Inferno theatre, and restores several passages inadvertently omitted from the essay included in the 1988 edition (**B5:49**). Ewbank suggests the importance of developing strategies for approaching the works rather than the man and explores what she calls the 'anatomy' and 'physiology' of a representative range of Sgian texts while seeking to define his multiple vision and some of the principal features encompassed by the adjective 'Sgian'. She focuses especially on *Tjänstekvinnans son, Fadren, Fröken Julie, Fordringsägare, Den starkare, Inferno, Ett drömspel,* and *Spöksonaten,* but comments perceptively on numerous other works in passing]

[B5:50] Elovson, Harald, 'August Strindberg och åttiotalet', in Ewert Wrangel, red., *Svenska folket genom tiderna*, Del. 9, 'Vid 1800-talets mitt', Malmö: Allhem, 1939, pp. 283-304. ['August Strindberg and the 1880s']

[B5:51] Fehrman, Carl, 'Die schwedische Literatur nach 1900', *Schweizerische Monatshefte* (Zürich), 45 (1965-66), 447-460. ['Swedish Literature Since 1900'. Provides an overview of Swedish literature since 1900, which embraces Sg's post-Inferno works in general]

[B5:52] Fritje [or Friche], V. M., *Ocherk razvitiia zapadnoevropeiskoi literatury*, Moscow: Gos. Izd-vo, 1922. 267 pp. [An early Soviet literary history of the development of West-European literature. Discusses Sg, pp. 232-233. E.906]

[B5:53] Fritje, V. M., *Ocherk razvitiia zapadnoevropeiskoi literatury*, 3rd ed., Khar'kov: Proletarii, 1927. 242 pp. ['*A History of the Development of West European Literature*'. Comments on Sg, p. 204. E.933]

[B5:54] Fritje, V. M., 'Strindberg', in *Entsiklopedicheskii Slovar'. Granat.* (Moscow), 7th ed., Vol. 41:5 (1927), pp. 26-27. [E.934]

[B5:55] Gabetti, Giuseppi, 'H. Ibsen e Aug. Strindberg', in Donato Donati and Filippo Carli, eds, *L'Europa nel secolo XIX*, Vol. 2, Padova: Milano, 1927, pp. 290-318. [Discusses Sg together with Ibsen in a cultural history of Europe in the 19th Century]

[B5:56] Gabrieli, Mario, *Storia delle letterature della Scandinavia*, Milano: Nuova Accademia Editrice, 1958. 289 pp. ['A History of Scandinavian Literature']

[B5:57] Gabrieli, Mario, *Le letterature della Scandinavia: Danese, Norvegese, Svedese, Islandese*, Le Letterature del Mondo 17, Nuova ed. aggiornata, Firenze: Sansoni; Milano: Nuova Accademia, 1969. 430 pp. [Retitled edition of **B5:56**]

[B5:58] Gaskell, Philip, *Landmarks in European Literature*, Edinburgh: Edinburgh University Press, 1999. XII+251 pp. [Includes a poorly researched presentation of Sg and *Fröken Julie*, pp. 149-154]

[B5:59] Gertsfel'd, M., *Skandinavskaia literatura i ee sovremennye tendentsii*, Edited by I. A. Shliapkin, St Petersburg: Voennaia Tipografiia, 1899. 85 pp. ['Scandinavian Literature and its Modern Tendencies'. Surveys trends in contemporary Scandinavian literature. Discusses Sg, pp. 52-55]

[B5:60] Gorbunov, A. M., 'Johan August Strindberg', in *Panorama vekov: Zarubezhnaia khudozhestvennaia proza ot vozniknoveniia do XX veka*, Lenin State Library, SSSR, Moscow, 1991, pp. 482-484.

[B5:61] Grazhdanskaiia, Z[oia] T[ikhonovna], 'Literatura Danii, Shvetsii, Norvegii', in *Istoriia zarubezhnoi literatury XX veka 1871-1917*, ed., V[ladimir] N[ikolaevich] Bogoslovskii, and Z[oia] T[ikhonovna], Grazhdanskaiia, Moscow: Prosveshchenie, 1979, pp. 208-210. [Presents Sg as the foremost representative of Swedish critical realism and a spokesman for progressive ideas; he is both an anti-monarchist and an atheist. Behind the portrait of the daily lives of the artists and writers in *Röda rummet* one sees the great tragedy that is their dependence on capitalism. After a period of apostasy, in which he embraced misogyny, Nietzscheanism, mysticism, symbolism, and allegory, Grazhdanskaiia points out that he found the strength to overcome decadent influences and return to the ideals of democracy in his last years. E.1786]

[B5:62] Gustafson, Alrik, *Dějiny švédské literatury*, Ze švédského originálu…přeložil a bibliografi sesatvil Libor Štukavec, Brno: Masarykova univerzita, 1998. 481+32 pp. ['A History of Swedish Literature'. A Czech translation of **B5:63**. Includes a bibliography of Sg's works in Czech translation]

[B5:63] Gustafson, Alrik, *A History of Swedish Literature*, Published for the American-Scandinavian Foundation by the University of Minnesota Press. London: Oxford University Press, Minneapolis: University of Minnesota Press, 1961, pp. 243-275, 602-609. [Reviews Sg's career as a writer in the context of a chapter entitled 'Strindberg and the Realistic Breakthrough'. Also includes a lightly annotated bibliography]

[B5:64] Gustafson, Alrik, *Den svenska litteraturens historia*, Översättning av Nils Holmberg; Redigerad av Nils P. Sundgren, 2 Del, Stockholm: Albert Bonniers Förlag, 1963. 320; 347 pp. [A lightly adapted edition of **B5:63** for Swedish readers]

[B5:65] Gustafson, Alrik, *August Strindberg*, Stockholm: Swedish Institute, 1961. 19 pp. [An offprint of the chapter on Sg in **B5:63**]

[B5:66] Hägg, Göran, 'Från Röda rummet till Blå Tornet. Strindberg och författarrollerna', in *Den svenska litteraturhistorien*, Stockholm: Wahlström & Widstrand, 1996, pp. 311-327. ['From the Red Room to the Blue Tower. Strindberg and the Writer's Roles']

[B5:67] Hansen, Peder, 'Shvedskaia literatura', in *Entsiklopedicheskii slovar*, Vol. 77, St Petersburg: Brockhaus & Efron, 1903. ['Swedish Literature'. Presents Sg in the course of an encyclopaedia entry on Swedish literature by a (Danish) translator of Scandinavian writing into Russian (whose surname is sometimes given as 'Ganzen')]

[B5:68] Hasselberg, Gudmar, red., *Svensk nittonhundratalslitteratur. En översikt av vår moderna diktning*, Skrifter utgivna av Modersmålslärarnas förening, Lund: Gleerup, 1941. 83 pp. ['Swedish Nineteenth-Century Literature. A Survey of Our Modern Literature']

[B5:69] Hasselberg, Gudmar, Carl Reinhold Smedmark, and Rune Waldecrantz, *Litteraturhistoria för gymnasiet*, Stockholm: Svenska Bokförlaget, Bonniers, 1967. 520 pp. [A high school textbook, updating **B5:3** by the now deceased Alving (†1958). Makes frequent reference to Sg but especially pp. 232-234, 252-262, 309-317]

[B5:70] Helén, Gunnar, and Ingrid Helén, *Svenska författare från Strindberg till Sara Lidman*, Grundskolans sista och gymnasiets första årskurs, Stockholm: Läromedelsförlaget, 1969. Illus. 313 pp. ['Swedish Writers from Strindberg to Sara Lidman'. Designed for use in Swedish secondary schools]

[B5:71] Henriques, Alf, *Svensk Literatur, 1900-1940*, København: Athenæum, 1942. 258 pp. ['Swedish Literature, 1900-1940'. Includes an evaluation of the Chamber Plays and several other of Sg's later works written between 1900 and 1912]

[B5:72] Henriques, Alf, *Svensk litteratur efter 1900*, Översättning av Herbert Friedlander, Stockholm: Forum, 1945. 309 pp. [Swedish edition of **B5:71**]

[B5:73] Hertel, Hans, red., *Litteraturens historia*, Vol. 5: 1830-1914, Stockholm: Norstedts, 1989, pp. 240-242, 259-263, 308-309, and Index. [Originally published in Copenhagen by the Gyldendalske Boghandel Nordisk Forlag, 1988]

[B5:74] Herzfeld, Marie, *Die skandinavische Literatur und ihre Tendenzen*, Berlin und Leipzig: Schuster & Loeffler, 1898. VIII+225 pp. ['Scandinavian Literature and its Trends'. A study of Scandinavian writing in the 1880s and 1890s by one of the period's foremost cultural mediators and translators]

[B5:75] Hillman, Rolf, *et al.*, *Vår litteratur och dess historia. Läro- och läsebok för gymnasiet*, Del. 4: 'Från Strindberg till våra dagar', Stockholm: Albert Bonniers Förlag, 1945. Illus. 380 pp. ['Our Literature and Its History. A Manual and Reader for the Senior High School', Part 4, 'Strindberg to Our Time'. Discusses Sg both in a separate chapter, which stresses the openly personal nature of his writing, and under the heading 'Åttiotalet' (The 1880s), which contextualises his work alongside that of Gustaf af Geijerstam, Ernst Ahlgren, Å. U. Bååth, and Ola Hansson. The treatment of Sg places unusual emphasis on the political radicalism of *Svenska folket* and *Svenska öden och äventyr*, as well as on its relevance to *Mäster Olof* and *Röda rummet*]

[B5:76] Hillman, Rolf, *et al.*, *Vårt språk och litteratur*, 4 Vols, Stockholm: Albert Bonniers Förlag, 1955-59. Illus. 374, 382, 366, 207 pp. ['Our Language and Literature'. Revised edition of **B5:75**]

[B5:77] Holm, Ingvar, *Från Baudelaire till första världskriget*, Vol. 6 in E[ugène] N[apoleon] Tigerstedt, *Bonniers allmänna litteraturhistoria*, Stockholm: Albert Bonniers Förlag, 1964. Illus. 265 pp. ['From Baudelaire to the First World War'. A history of world literature with some reference to Sg and his links with developments in European writing at the end of the 19th Century, primarily in France and Germany]

[B5:78] Holm, Ingvar, *La Littérature suédoise*, Stockholm: Institut Suédois, 1957. 240 pp. ['Swedish Literature']

[B5:79] Holmberg, Bengt, and Mauritz Persson, *Från Strindberg till Harry Martinson. Studieuppgifter till modern svensk prosalitteratur*, Skrifter utgivna av Modersmålslärarnas förening 63, Stockholm, 1944. 46 pp. [A secondary-school textbook with suggestions for the study of extracts drawn from literature in prose from Strindberg to Harry Martinson in the 1930s]

[B5:80] Jansson, Sven-Erik, *August Strindberg*, Svensklärarserien 183, Stockholm: Skriptor, 1981. 46 pp. [An introductory guide to Sg's life and works for use in schools]

[B5:81] Johnson, Walter, 'Strindberg, Johan August', in Virpi Zuck, Editor-in-Chief, *Dictionary of Scandinavian Literature*, New York: Greenwood Press, 1990, pp. 583-588. [A substantial dictionary entry by an eminent Sg scholar who concludes that Sg's 'importance for world literature lies in his autobiographical works and in his contributions to drama and theatre']

[B5:82] Kallio, O. A., *Yleisen kirjallisuuden historian pääpiirteet*, Kansanvalistus-seuran historiallisia lukukirjoja 2, Kupio: Kansanvalistus-seura, 1905. 311 pp. ['The Principal Features of Contemporary Literature'. Includes Sg in a Finnish survey of turn-of-the-century European literature]

[B5:83] Klemensiewiczowa, Józefa, *Literatura Skandynawii*, Kraków: S. S. Kryzanowski, 1914. III+[160] pp. ['The Literature of Scandinavia'. Includes a sharply critical account of the plays by one of Sg's first Polish translators, who was more in tune with his prose fiction. She denies any major importance to the plays, and is especially unsympathetic where the post-Inferno dramas are concerned. Moreover, in their harping upon misogyny, she finds the earlier works monotonous and the history plays lacking in any real insight into the past]

[B5:84] Kotas, Walther Hjalmar, 'Strindberg', in *Die skandinavische Literatur der Gegenwart seit 1870*, Wiesbaden: Im Dioskuren Verlag, 1925, pp. 138-158. [An overview of Sg's career as a writer in several genres as part of a study of Scandinavian literature since 1870. Kotas concludes that, 'He was too great for his time, for his country, for Europe']

[B5:85] Larsen, Hanna Astrup, *Scandinavian Literature*, Reading with a Purpose Series 54, Chicago: American Library Association, pp. 28-29. [Concludes that 'Sg's works not only reveal the inner and outer crises in his own turbulent life, but also reflect the spirit of his age, its revolt, its restless seeking after truth, its moral indignation, its iconoclasm, and its disillusion, leading to the inevitable reaction…mystical religion']

[B5:86] Lewisohn, Ludwig, 'August Strindberg', in *The Columbia University Course in Literature*, Vol. 10, New York: Columbia University Press, 1928, pp. 167-170. [Maintains that, together with *Giftas* and *En dåres försvarstal*, Sg's most solid contribution to literature was made during his naturalistic period. Lewisohn suggests that the fourteen plays from *Fadren* to *Bandet* are more memorable than his later dream fantasies]

[B5:87] Leyen, Friedrich von der, *Deutsche Dichtung in neuer Zeit*, Jena: Diedrich Verlag, 1922. 374 pp. [A survey of recent German literature which includes an assessment of Sg's impact on the expressionist generation of writers for whom he represented 'the summit of ambition and the patent of nobility on the German stage']

[B5:88] Linder, Erik Hjalmar, *Fyra decennier av 1900-talet*, Tredje bearbetade och utökade upplagan, Stockholm: Natur och Kultur, 1958. Illus. 880 pp. ['Four Decades of the 20th Century'. The impact which Sg and his works exerted on succeeding generations of Swedish writers is noted throughout. Linder also surveys the Strindberg Feud of 1910-12, pp. 26-29]

[B5:89] Linder, Erik Hjalmar, *Fem decennier av 1900-talet*, 4. omarbetade och utökade upplagan, 2 Del, Stockholm: Natur och Kultur, 1965-66. Illus. 1186 pp. ['Five Decades of the 20th Century'. Revised edition of **B5:88**]

[B5:90] Lindström, Hans, 'August Strindberg', in *Litteraturhistoria*, Stockholm: Natur och Kultur, 1966, pp. 214-229. [A standard high-school textbook, written by a major Sg scholar]

[B5:91] Lunacharskii, A[natoli] V., 'A. Strindberg', in [*A History of the Highlights in West European Literature*], Vol. 2, Moscow, 1924, pp. 200-202. [An assessment of Sg in an early Soviet literary history by the first Soviet commissar of education and the arts. E.925]

[B5:92] Lunacharskii, A[natoli] V., 'A. Strindberg', in *Sobranie sochinenii*, Vol. 4, Moscow, 1964, pp. 345-346. [Rpr. of **B5:91** in Lunacharskii's collected works. E.925]

[B5:93] Mahrholz, Werner, 'Die Lebensform der Moderne: August Strindberg', in *Deutsche Literatur der Gegenwart*, Berlin: Wegweiser-Verlag G.m.b.h., 1925, pp. 351-402. ['The Life Form of Modernity: August Strindberg'. Mahrholz concludes that Sg has both lived through and portrayed the modern European form of mental and spiritual life, which is nihilism, with astounding force and consequence]

[B5:94] Mahrholz, Werner, 'Die Lebensform der Moderne: August Strindberg', in *Deutsche Literatur der Gegenwart. Probleme – Ergebnisse – Gestalten*, Durchgesehen und erweitert von Max Wieser, Berlin: Sieben-Stäbe-Verlag, 1930, pp. 319-358. ['The Life Form of Modernity: August Strindberg'. Revised edition of **B5:93**]

[B5:95] Märker, Friedrich, *Zur Literatur der Gegenwart*, München: Langen, 1921, pp. 63-66. ['On Contemporary Literature'. Comments unsympathetically on the unwarranted place accorded Sg in modern literature]

[B5:96] Maury, Lucien, *Littérature suédois*: *Panorama de la littérature suédoise contemporaine*, Paris: Le Sagittaire, 1940, pp. 65-81, 155-163. ['Swedish Literature: A Panorama of Contemporary Swedish Literature'. One of Sg's most sympathetic French critics and translators, who devotes two chapters to Sg]

[B5:97] Meijer, Bernhard, 'Strindberg, Johan August, skald, kulturhistoriker', in *Svenskt literatur-lexikon*, Stockholm: Jos. Seligmann & C:Is Förlag, 1886, pp. 409-410. ['Strindberg, Johan August, Writer and Cultural Historian'. Perhaps the first entries on Sg in a literary handbook, contributed by one of his colleagues in the literary world of 1880's Stockholm]

[B5:98] Mikhailovskii, B., 'Strindberg', *Literaturnaia entsiklopediia*, Vol. 11, Moscow, 1932, pp. 85-91. [Entry in a Soviet literary encyclopaedia. E.939]

[B5:99] Mjöberg, Josua, *Svensk litteraturhistoria för den högre undervisningen*, Lund: C. W. K. Gleerups Förlag, 1927. 237 pp. ['Swedish Literature for the Higher Level'. One of the most widely read and influential 20th-Century Swedish school textbooks which concludes that 'Only part of Sg's extensive production can be highly regarded from an artistic point of view. The majority of his dramas, particularly the later ones, fall away in the later acts.…The flaws in his work derive from a flaw in his personality. He is a creature of moods and lacks human self-control. He is the child of a hurried, fumbling, and restless age, and this is closely reflected in his work.' Mjöberg's view of Sg's achievements, both regarding the naturalist and the post-Inferno dramas, is updated in revised editions, including a 2nd enlarged edition, 1929, a 9th enlarged edition, 1949, a 10th revised and enlarged edition, 1956, and a 12th revised and enlarged edition, 1963]

[B5:100] Mortensen, Johan Martin, 'August Strindberg', in *Sveriges Nationallitteratur 1500-1900*, Del 17, Stockholm: Albert Bonniers Förlag, 1910, pp. 5-16. [Introduces a selection of Sg's works in a series devoted to (and hence defining) the 'national literature of Sweden']

[B5:101] Mortensen, Johan Martin, *Från Röda rummet till sekelskiftet. Strömningar i svensk litteratur under adertonhundraåttio- och nittio-talen*, 2 del., Stockholm: Albert Bonniers Förlag, 1918-19, Del. 1, pp. 49-159; Del. 2, pp. 253-304. ['From *The Red Room* to the Turn of the Century. Currents in Swedish Literature During the 1880s and 1990s'. A relatively sympathetic treatment of Sg's authorship both before and immediately after the Inferno crisis by a critic with whom he was on good terms during his residence in Lund in 1887-1888]

[B5:102] Natev, Atanas, 'Trivialna literatura s ideini pretenzii', in *Literaturni idei na XX vek Individ i kultura*, Sofia: Nauka i izkustvo, 1985, pp. 41-49. [Sg is discussed under the heading 'Trivial Literature with Pretensions to Ideas' in a Bulgarian study of *Literary Ideas of the 20th Century: The Individual and Culture*]

[B5:103] Naumann, Hans, *Die deutsche Dichtung der Gegenwart. Vom Naturalismus bis zum Expressionismus*, 4., durchges. erweiterte Auflage, Stuttgart, 1930. 402 pp. ['Contemporary German Literature. From Naturalism to Expressionism'. Records Sg's role in respect of contemporary Germany literature between ca. 1880 and 1925. Comprises Volume Six of *Epochen der deutschen Literatur: Geschichtliche Darstellungen*]

[B5:104] Neustroev, V[ladimir] P[etrovich], 'August Strindberg', in Andreev, L. G., and Samarin, R. M., eds, *Istoriia zarubezhnoi literatury kontsa XIX – nachala XX veka*, Moscow: Moscow University Press, 1968, pp. 284-296. [E.1026]

[B5:105] Neustroev, V[ladimir] P[etrovich], 'August Strindberg', in Andreev, L. G., and Samarin, R. M., eds, *Istoriia zarubezhnoi literatury kontsa XIX – nachala XX veka*, Moscow: Izdatel'stvo Moskovskogo universiteta, 1978, pp. 175-184. [2nd, revised edition of **B5:104**. E.1026]

[B5:106] Neustroev, V[ladimir] P[etrovich], *Literaturnye ocherki i portrety*, Moscow: Izdatel'stvo Moskovskogo universiteta, 1983. Illus. 262 pp.

[B5:107] Neustroev, V[ladimir] P[etrovich], *Skandinavskaia literatura 1870-1970*, Moscow: Vysshaia shkola, 1980. [Includes Sg in a general entry on 'Scandinavian Literature, 1870-1970']

[B5:108] Neustroev, V[ladimir] P[etrovich], 'Strindberg', in *Kratkaia literaturnaia entsiklopediia*, Vol. 7, Moscow, 1972, pp. 218-222.

[B5:109] Neustroev, V[ladimir] P[etrovich], 'Strindberg', in *Bol'shaia sovetskaia entsiklopediia*, Vol. 24, Moscow, 1976, pp. 570-571. E.1091. Previous editions, 1946, Vol. 53, p. 42, E.958; 1956, 2nd ed., Vol. 41, pp. 112-113. E.964]

[B5:110] Niewiarowska, Ewa, 'Das dichterische Schaffen von August Strindberg', in Bernard Piotrowski and Boleslaw Mrozewicz, Hrsg., *Die Literatur des modernen Durchbruchs in Skandinavien*, Poznan: Uniwersytet im. Adama Mickiewicza w Poznaniu, 1989, pp.

73-79. ['The Literary Works of August Strindberg'. A short chapter in a study of the literature of the Scandinavian Modern Breakthrough as a whole]

[B5:111] Nordberg, Olof, and Ulf Wittrock, 'August Strindberg', in *Dikt och data. Litteraturhistoria för gymnasiet*, Lund: C. W. K. Gleerups, 1969, 215-231. [A chapter on Sg in a literary history designed for use in Swedish secondary schools]

[B5:112] Oberholzer, Otto, 'Die skandinavische Literatur 1900-1918', in *Jahrhundertwende-Jahrhundertwende*, 2 Bde, Hrsg. von Hans Hinterhäuser, Wiesbaden: Akademische Verlagsanstalt Athenaion, 1976, Bd 2, pp. 307-326. ['Scandinavian Literature, 1900-1918']

[B5:113] Olsson, Bernt, and Ingemar Algulin, *Litteraturens historia i Sverige*, Stockholm: Norstedts Förlag, 1987. Illus. 605 pp. ['The History of Swedish Literature'. Includes numerous references to Sg throughout, but divides specific discussion of his writing into three periods: the 1880s (pp. 313-324), the early 1890s (pp. 332-334, in conjunction with Ola Hansson), and the post-Inferno period (pp. 357-364)]

[B5:114] Olsson, Bernt, and Ingemar Algulin, *Litteraturens historia i Sverige*, 4. uppdaterade och utökade upplagan, Stockholm: Norstedts Förlag, 1995. Illus. 619 pp. ['The History of Swedish Literature'. Revised and augmented edition of **B5:113**]

[B5:115] Priestly, J. B., *Literature and Western Man*, London: Heinemann, 1960, pp. 232-235.

[B5:116] Priestly, J. B., *Literature and Western Man*, New York: Harper, 1960, pp. 289-292. [North-American edition of **B5:115**]

[B5:117] Rinman, Sven, 'Strindberg', in E[ugène] N[apoleon] Tigerstedt, red., *Ny illustrerad svensk litteraturhistoria*, Del 4: 'Åttiotal Nittiotal', Andra bearbetade upplagan, Stockholm: Natur och Kultur, 1967, pp. 30-143, 415-425. [An admirable survey, which remains the best short introduction in Swedish to Sg's achievements as a writer. Rinman stresses his accomplishments in numerous genres and draws attention to the conscious artistry which underlies his work, rather than to its biographical basis. Also includes a helpful bibliography, see **A1:84**]

[B5:118] Robinson, Michael, 'August Strindberg', in James Vinson, ed., *Major World Writers*, London and New York: St Martin's Press, 1985, pp. 78-83. [Emphasises the variousness of Sg's project and his achievement in several genres and media]

[B5:119] Rørdam, Valdemar, *Svensk Literatur: En folkelig vejledning*, København: Gyldendalske Boghandel, Nordisk Forlag, 1911. 148 pp. ['Swedish Literature. A Popular Guide']

[B5:120] Rose, E. W., and J. Isaacs, *Contemporary Movements in European Literature*, London: George Routledge and Sons, 1928, pp. 68-74.

[B5:121] Rossel, Sven Hakon, *A History of Scandinavian Literature 1870-1980*, Translated by Anne C. Ulmer, Minneapolis: University of Minnesota Press, 1982, pp. 45-58. [Presents Sg as a novelist as well as a dramatist, but argues that it was nevertheless in his plays that he accomplished his most significant work, creating the modern visionary, irrational, and experimental theatre for which he is best known. It is there that he remains the boldest and most poetic experimenter of all modern playwrights]

[B5:122] Rossel, Sven Hakon, *Skandinavische Literatur*, Stuttgart-Berlin-Köln-Mainz: Verlag W. Kohlhammer, 1973, pp. 48-60. [See **B5:121**]

[B5:123] Saintsbury, George, *The Later Nineteenth Century*, Periods of European Literature 12, Edinburgh and London: William Blackwood and Sons, 1907, pp. 326-327. [A survey by one of the most established British critics of the period who finds that Sg 'is, it seems, a Naturalist-misoygnist, a Nietzschean after a sort, a convert to all the madder 'isms which have pullulated during the period, and a rover through all the fields of literature']

[B5:124] Saxtorph, Vilhelm, 'August Strindberg', in Ejnar Skovrup, Udg., *Hovedtræk af nordisk digtning i nytiden*, 2 Del, København: Aschehoug, 1921, Del 2, pp. 599-612. [Summarises Sg's achievements as a writer in a two-volume survey of 'The Main Characteristics of Contemporary Nordic Literature']

[B5:125] Shiller, F., 'Strindberg', in *Istoriia zapadnoevropeiskoi literatury novogo vremeni*, Vol. 2, Moscow, 1936, pp. 354-359. ['A History of Modern West-European Literature'. 2nd edition 1937, pp. 398-404. E.942]

[B5:126] Schmidt, Adalbert, *Literaturgeschichte Wege und Wandlungen moderne Dichtung*, Tweite, erweiterte Auflage, Salzburg/Stuttgart: Verlag 'Das Bergland-Buch', 1959, pp. 116-117.

[B5:127] Schoolfield, George C., 'Die schwedische Literatur', in Gero von Wilpert and Ivar Ivask, Hrsg., *Moderne Weltliteratur: die Gegenwartsliteraturen Europas und Amerikas*, Stuttgart: Kröner Verlag, 1972, pp. 486-524. ['Swedish Literature'. A survey of modern Swedish writing in a volume devoted to 'Modern World Literature: The Contemporary Literature of Europe and America']

[B5:128] Schück, [Johan] Henrik [Emil], *Histoire de la littérature suédoise*, Traduite du suédois sur 8e manuscrit de l'auteur avec un avant-propos par Lucien Maury, Paris: Éditions Ernest Leroux, 1923. XXIII+348 pp. ['A History of Swedish Literature']

[B5:129] Schück, Henrik, *Sveriges litteratur intill 1900,* Vol. 2, Stockholm: Hugo Gebers Förlag, 1935. 311 pp. ['Swedish Literature Prior to 1900'. Includes a chapter on Sg which attempts a balanced summary of his achievement, but nevertheless displays a divided response to both the man and his work. Schück focuses mainly on *Mäster Olof, Röda rummet, Giftas,* and *Fröken Julie*, and his is one of the first Swedish literary histories to emphasise the epoch-making and dramaturgically innovative character of the naturalistic plays. Written with an eye to previous, largely hostile, Swedish judgements by Victor Svanberg (**B3:413**), Fredrik Böök (**B5:21**). and Oscar Levertin]

[B5:130] Schück, Henrik, *Sveriges litteratur intill 1900,* Stockholm: Hugo Gebers Förlag, 1952, pp. 529-555. [Revised edition of **B5:129**, updated by Örjan Lindberger]

[B5:131] Schück, Henrik, and Karl Warburg, *Huvuddragen av Sveriges litteratur. Del III*, Stockholm: Geber, 1918. IX+312 pp. ['The Main Outlines of Swedish Literature'. Includes a short chapter on Sg by Warburg, one of his fellow students at Uppsala, who notes the widespread German interest in the later plays, especially *Påsk, Kronbruden, Dödsdansen*, and *Ett drömspel*, whereas in Sweden it is his earlier works that have been more widely admired. Even so, for Warburg 'the 'sharp psychological observations and truly dramatic dialogue [of *Fröken Julie*] cannot compensate for the repugnant improbability of this so-called naturalistic drama's description of reality']

[B5:132] Shweitzer, F., 'Skandinavskoe tvorchestvo noveishego vremeni', in Gorn, F. V., ed., *Istoriia skandinavskoi literatury. S. prilozheniem etuida F. Shveitsera*, Moscow, 1894, pp. 315-407. ['Contemporary Scandinavian Literature' in 'A History of Scandinavian Literature'. Discusses Sg, pp. 390, 392-396. E.692]

[B5:133] Sharypkin, D[mitrii] M[ikhailovich], 'Literatura XIX-XX veka', in Alexander Kan, ed., *Shvedskaia istoriia*, Moscow: Nauka, 1974, pp. 617-635. [Comments on Sg in the course of an informed survey of trends in Swedish literature during the 19th and 20th centuries. On Sg, pp. 621-623, 625-627. E.1072]

[B5:134] Skoglund, Svante, *Texter & tankar. Litteraturen från antiken till 1900*, Malmö: Gleerup, 1996. Illus. 254 pp. [A survey of world literature, from ancient Greece to 1900. Observes that while Sg, 'the public hooligan who became a national monument', may be the greatest of Swedish writers, this does not mean one has to worship him, or even to like his books]

[B5:135] Söderblom, Inga, and Sven Gustaf Edqvist, *Litteraturhistoria*, Stockholm: Biblioteksförlaget, 1985, pp. 326-[334]. Illus.

[B5:136] Soergel, Albert, 'August Strindberg', in *Dichtung und Dichter der Zeit. Eine Schilderung der deutschen Literatur der letzten Jahrzehnte*, Neue Folge, 'Im Banne der Expressionismus', Leipzig: R. Voigtländer, 1925, pp. 176-204. [Assesses Sg's influence on recent German literature through *Till Damaskus* and other post-Inferno plays. 1st edition 1911 and in print for much of the century]

[B5:137] Soergel, Albert, and Curt Hohoff, 'Die fremden Vorbilder. [2] Skandinavien. Ibsen und Strindberg', in Soergel und Hohoff, Hrsg., *Dichtung und Dichter der Zeit. Vom Naturalismus bis zur Gegenwart*, Bd 1, Neubearb., Düsseldorf: Bagel, 1961, pp. 79-106. ['Foreign Models. [2] Scandinavia. Ibsen and Strindberg. From Naturalism to the Present'. Revised edition of **B5:136**. Takes account of the influence exerted by Sg and Ibsen on recent and contemporary German literature]

[B5:138] Steene, Birgitta, 'August Strindberg', in Stanley Hochman, ed., *McGraw-Hill Encyclopedia of World Drama: An International Reference Work in 5 Volumes*, 2nd edition, Vol. 4, New York: McGraw-Hill, [1984], pp. 557-577.

[B5:139] Steene, Birgitta, 'Liberalism, Realism, and the Modern Breakthrough', in Lars G. Warme, ed., *A History of Swedish Literature*, Lincoln and London: University of Nebraska Press, 1996, pp. 204-272. [Disusses Sg as a representative writer of the Scandinavian Modern Breakthrough and under the headings 'Prose Fiction', 'Strindberg and Autobiography', and 'Strindberg and the "Skerries Novels"', pp. 245-251, where the focus is primarily on his prose works. Steene considers the plays of the 1870s and 1880s, pp. 253-257, as well as his transition to modernism in conjunction with the Inferno crisis, pp. 257-272. The account of this later period focuses principally on the dramatic works (including the history plays), and the polemical novels *Götiska rummen* and *Svarta fanor*]

[B5:140] Steffen, Richard, *Svensk litteraturhistoria för den högre elementärundervisningen*, Stockholm: P. A. Norstedt & Söners Förlag, 1904, pp. 225-226. ['A History of Swedish Literature for the Upper Secondary School'. Steffen presents Sg as the most interesting representative of the naturalist school, highlights the importance of *Mäster Olof* in his development, and mentions only *Folkungasagan* add *Gustav Vasa* by name of his post-Inferno works. As a dramatist, he accepts that Sg occupies pride of place in Swedish literature and few have possessed his ability to convey the special qualities of the

Swedish landscape, but Steffen maintains that, even so, his works abound in disfiguring and ruthless outbursts, which are directed against every conceivable target]

[B5:141] Steffen, Richard, *Svensk litteraturhistoria för den högre elementärundervisningen*, 10:e upl., reviderad och framförd till nuverande tid, Stockholm: Svensk Bokförlaget, 1944. 300 pp. [The 10th, revised and enlarged edition of **B5:140**. An influential secondary-school textbook, continuously in print since its first edition in 1904]

[B5:142] Steffen, Richard, *Svensk litteraturhistoria. Förkortad upplaga för realskola och högre flickskolor*, Stockholm, 1904. [An abridged version of the first edition of **B5:140** designed for junior secondary schools and high schools for girls]

[B5:143] Stern, Adolf, 'August Strindberg', in *Studien zur Literatur der Gegenwart*, Dresden und Leipzig: Koch Verlag, 1904, pp. 365-387. ['Studies in Contemporary Literature']

[B5:144] Stern, Adolf, 'August Strindberg', in *Studien zur Literatur der Gegenwart*, 3. verm. und neue bearb. Auflage, Dresden und Leipzig: Koch Verlag, 1905. VIII+ 504 pp. [Revised and enlarged edition of **B5:143**]

[B5:145] Stolpe, Sven, 'August Strindberg', in *40 svenska författare*, Stockholm: Askild & Kärnkull, 1980, pp. [94]-103. Illus.

[B5:146] Stounbjerg, Per, 'Strindberg (1849-1912)', in Annick Benoit-Dusausoy and Guy Fontaine, eds, *A History of European Literature*, London: Routledge, 2000, pp. 520-523. [A short essay by an established Sg scholar in a standard reference work]

[B5:147] Stounbjerg, P[er], 'Strindberg, Johan August', in *Den store danske encyklopædi*, Vol. 18, København: Gyldendal, 2000, pp. 191-192. [An authoritative encyclopædia entry by the leading Danish Sg scholar of his generation]

[B5:148] Strömberg, Kjell, *Modern svensk litteratur*, Stockholm: Natur och Kultur, 1932. 239 pp. ['Modern Swedish Literature'. Focuses specifically on Sg, pp. 12-19 and 22-26, in discussions of Swedish literature in the 1880s and 1890s respectively]

[B5:149] Sundén, D[aniel] A[nton], *Svensk litteraturhistoria i sammandrag jämte öfversikt af diktkonsten och dess arter*, Tredje omarbetade upplagan, Stockholm: J. Beckmans Förlag, 1897, p. 158. ['A Concise History of Swedish Literature together with a Survey of the Art of Poetry and its Forms'. Includes one of the first mentions of Sg in an official Swedish literary history; he was not included in the edition of 1881]

[B5:150] Svanfeldt, Gunnar, '1860-1890', in Mogens Brøndsted, red., *Nordens Litteratur: Efter 1860*, København: Gyldendalske Boghandel, Nordisk Forlag, 1972, pp. 76-89. [Surveys Sg's pre-Inferno writings in a contribution to a general history of Scandinavian literature]

[B5:151] Tideström, Gunnar, *Dikt och bild. Epoker och strömningar. Glimtar av samspelet mellan konst, litteratur och liv*, Lund: C.W.K Gleerups Bokförlag, 1965. Illus. 384 pp. [Includes twelve references to Sg]

[B5:152] Tigerstedt, E[ugène] N[apoleon], *Svensk litteraturhistoria*, Tredje reviderade upplagan, Stockholm: Natur och Kultur, 1969, pp. 392-405. ['A History of Swedish Literature'. Observes that 'Everyone who now writes Swedish is, with or without wishing to be, August Sg's pupil'. First edition 1960]

[B5:153] Tjäder, Per Arne, 'Strindberg och genombrottstiden 1849-1893', in Lars Lönnroth and Sven Delblanc, red., *Den svenska litteraturen*, 7 Del., Vol. 3: 'Den liberala genombrotten: 1830-1890', Stockholm: Bonniers, 1988, pp. 220-248. Illus. ['Strindberg and the Time of the [Modern] Breakthrough, 1849-1893']

[B5:154] Tjäder, Per Arne, 'Strindberg och genombrottstiden 1849-1893', in Lars Lönnroth and Sven Delblanc, red., *Den svenska litteraturen*, Del 2, Stockholm: Bonniers, 1999, pp. 220-248. Illus. [Revised edition of **B5:153** in three volumes]

[B5:155] Topsøe-Jensen, H[elge] G., *Den skandinaviske Litteratur fra 1870 til vore Dage*, København: P. Haase & Søns Forlag, 1928, pp. 89-90. ['Scandinavian Literature from 1870 to Our Time'. Is concerned with Sg's work rather than his life; concludes that, 'compared with Sg, the other Swedish writers of the period seem small indeed']

[B5:156] Topsöe-Jensen, Helge G., *Scandinavian Literature from Brandes to Our Day*, Translated from the Danish by Isaac Anderson, New York: The American-Scandinavian Foundation and W. W. Norton & Company, Inc., 1929, pp. 105-117. [English edition of **B5:155**]

[B5:157] Topsöe-Jensen, Helge G., *Scandinavian Literature from Brandes to Our Day*, Translated from the Danish by Isaac Anderson, New York: Kraus Reprint Co., New York, 1971. [Rpr. of **B5:156**]

[B5:158] Uecker, Heiko, 'August Strindberg', in *Die Klassiker der skandinavischen Literatur, Vom 18. Jahrhundert bis zur Gegenwart*, Düsseldorf: ECON Taschenbuch Verlag, 1990, pp. 219-223. [The entry on Sg in a German reference work on the last two centuries of Scandinavian literature]

[B5:159] Vengerova, Z., 'Strindberg', in *Entsiklopediia* 'Brockhaus i Efron', Moscow, Vol. 62 (1900), pp. 800-801. [The entry on Sg in an early pre-Soviet reference work. E.709]

[B5:160] Vinge, Louise, red., *Skånes litteraturhistoria*, medarbetare Per Erik Ljung, 2 vols, Malmö: Corona, 1997, Vol. 1, 'Fram till 1940-talet'. Illus. 284 pp. ['A Literary History of Skåne'. An important regional literary history which identifies numerous links between Sg and his contemporary Scanian writers and critics, including Bengt Lidforss and Ola Hansson]

[B5:161] Warburg, Karl, 'De senaste årtiondena', in *Svensk litteraturhistoria i sammandrag. För skolor och sjelfstudium*, 5:e omarb. upplagan, Stockholm: P. A. Norstedt & Söners Förlag, 1899. Illus. 203 pp. ['The Most Recent Decades'. One of the earliest accounts of Sg's works ever to be included in a standard Swedish textbook by a writer who had known him at university in Uppsala and been the object of his personal satire in *Det nya riket*. Warburg was likewise highly partial]

[B5:162] Warburg, Karl, *Svensk litteraturhistoria i sammandrag. Lärobok för skolor och självstudium*, 10:e omarb. upplagan ombesörjd av Gösta Montelin, Stockholm: P. A. Norstedt & Söners Förlag, 1927. 180 pp. ['A Concise History of Swedish Literature. A Textbook for Schools and Private Study'. Revised edition of **B5:161**]

[B5:163] Warburg, Karl, 'August Strindberg', in Henrik Schück and Karl Warburg, *Illustrerad Svensk Litteraturhistoria*, Vol. 4.2: 'Sveriges litteratur under realismens och efterhumanismens samt naturalismens tid', Stockholm: Hugo Geber, 1916. 680 pp. ['Swedish Literature in the Age of Realism, Post-Humanism, and Naturalism'. Includes an influential, if not always sympathetic, discussion of Sg's achievement as a writer by a respected critic who had been a fellow student at Uppsala and a butt of Sg's satire in *Det nya riket*. Warburg seeks to endow his treatment with a form of authority by quoting from his early correspondence with Sg, and the general availability of this multi-volume history by several leading scholars bestowed considerable prestige on this account during the first six decades of the 20th Century]

[B5:164] Waschnitius, Viktor, 'Das Schrifttum der nordischen Länder in neuerer Zeit', in Hans Friedrich Blunck, Hrsg., *Die nordische Welt. Geschichte, Wesen und Bedeutung der nordischen Völker*, Berlin, 1937, pp. 532-547. ['The Literature of the Nordic Countries in Recent Times'. Considers Scandinavian literature since 1870, pp. 541-547]

B6. Conference Reports

[*The greater part of this section lists reports on the series of International Strindberg Conferences, initiated in Stockholm in 1973 and held subsequently at different venues, usually on a biennial basis. It also lists reports on a number of other, more occasional, symposia devoted to Sg and his work*]

[B6:1] Alekseeva, K., '[Watching Strindberg]', *Ekran i stsena* (Moscow), 1994:26, p. 3 [A report in Russian on the 12th International Sg Conference, held in Moscow in June 1994 with the theme 'Strindberg and Symbolism'. Proceedings published in **B1:379**, Michael Robinson, ed., *The Moscow Papers*. E.1798a]

[B6:2] Andriasova, T., '[The End and the Beginning of Strindberg]', *Moskovskie novosti* (Moscow), 1994:2, p. 4. [A report on the 12th International Sg Conference, held in Moscow in June 1994 with the theme 'Strindberg and Symbolism'. Proceedings publis -hed in **B1:379**, Michael Robinson, ed., *The Moscow Papers*. Andriasova also comments on Sg's reception in Russia. E.1798b]

[B6:3] Bergstrom, Gunnel, 'Also in the Symposium', in **D2:99**, Claes Englund and Gunnel Bergström, eds, *Strindberg, O'Neill and the Modern Theatre*, pp. 71-77. [Provides an overview of contributions and panel discussions not published in the proceedings as edited by Englund and Bergström]

[B6:4] Bilke, Jörg Bernhard, 'Strindbergs Wirkung auf das Theater. Herbsttagung der Stockholmer "Strindberg-Gesellschaft" im "Blauen Turm"', *Skandinavistik* (Kiel), 4:1 (1974), 64-65. ['Strindberg's Influence on the Theatre. Autumn Conference of the Stockholm Strindberg Society'. A report on a symposium devoted to Sg and the modern theatre, held at the Strindberg Museum, Stockholm, 2-6 September 1973. Proceedings published in **D2:285**, Carl Reinhold Smedmark, ed., *Strindberg and Modern Theatre*]

[B6:5] Ciesielski, Zenon, 'Dramaty Strindberga w świetle nowych koncepcji metodologicznych – sympozjum', *Dialog* (Warsaw), 1980:1, pp. 168-169. ['Strindberg's Dramas in the Light of Recent Conceptual Methods – Symposium'. A report on the 4th International Sg Conference, held in Zürich in 1979 with the theme 'Strindbergs Dramen im Lichte neuerer Methoden-diskussionen'. Proceedings published in **D2:8**, Oskar Bandle, Walter Baumgartner, and Jürg Glauser, Hrsg., *Strindbergs Dramen im Lichte neuerer Methodendiskussionen*]

[B6:6] Ciesielski, Zenon, 'Le Théâtre dans le contexte européen. Symposium international "Strindberg" de Varsovie', *Le Théâtre Polonaise* (Warsaw), 1985:5-7, pp. 42-46. ['The Theatre in a European Context. International Strindberg Conference in Warsaw'. A report on the 7th International Strindberg Conference with the theme 'Dramat Strindbergowski w kontekscie europejskim' (Strindbergian Drama in a European Context), held in Warsaw, 1-6 October 1984]

[B6:7] Ciesielski, Zenon, 'Międzynarodowe Sympozjum Strindbergowskie w Warszawie', *Dialog* (Warsaw), 1985:2, pp. 170-172. ['International Strindberg Conference in Warsaw'. A report on the 7th International Strindberg Conference with the theme 'Dramat Strindbergowski w kontekscie europejskim' (Strindbergian Drama in a European Context), held in Warsaw, 1-6 October 1984]

[B6:8] Codignola, Luciano, 'Strindberg symposium', *Sipario* (Milan), No. 330 (November 1973), p. 48. [A report on the first International Sg Conference, held in Stockholm under the auspices of the Strindberg Society. Proceedings published in **D2:285**, Carl Reinhold Smedmark, ed., *Strindberg and Modern Theatre*]

[B6:9] Edberg, Ulla-Britt, 'Strindberg ute i världen', *Svenska Dagbladet* (Stockholm), 14 September 1973. ['Strindberg at Large in the World'. A report about the first international Symposium, convened in Stockholm. Proceedings published in **D2:285**, Carl Reinhold Smedmark, ed., *Strindberg and Modern Theatre*]

[B6:10] Friese, Wilhelm, '500 Jahre Universität Tübingen 1477-1977. Symposion des Fachbereichs Neuphilologie "Strindberg und die deutschsprachigen Länder"', *Skandinavistik* (Kiel), 8:1 (1978), 64-66. ['500 Years of the University of Tübingen, 1477-1977. Conference of the Faculty of Modern Languages on "Strindberg and the German-Speaking Countries"'. Presents the 3rd International Strindberg Conference. Proceedings published in **B3:166**, Wilhelm Friese, Hrsg., *Strindberg und die deutschsprachigen Länder. Internationale Beiträge zum Tübinger Strindberg-Symposium 1977*]

[B6:11] Janukowicz, Dorota, 'Sympozjum Strindbergowskie', *Zeszyty Naukowe – Studia Scandinavica* (Gdańsk), 9 (1985), 91-92. ['Strindberg Symposium'. A report on the International Strindberg Conference with the theme 'Dramat Strindbergowski w kontekscie europejskim' (Strindbergian Drama in a European Context), held in Warsaw, 1-6 October 1984. Lists the titles of the papers given in Polish]

[B6:12] Kärnell, Karl-Åke, 'Strindbergsmanifestation i Italien', *Meddelanden från Strindbergssällskapet* (Stockholm), 67 (1983), pp. 35-36. ['Strindberg Event in Italy'. A report on a conference in Bari with the theme 'Strindberg nella cultura moderna' (Strindberg and Modern Culture). Proceedings published in **B1:365**, Franco Perrelli, ed., *Omaggio a Strindberg. Strindberg nella cultura moderna*]

[B6:13] [Katowice], *Szwedzki dramat i film u progu XXI wieku*, Katowice: Katowickie Towarzystwo Polsko-Szwedzkie, 1999. 62 pp. ['Swedish Drama and Film in the Twentieth Century'. Contains details of a conference in Katowice devoted to Swedish drama and cinema in general but focusing mainly on Sg and Ingmar Bergman]

[B6:14] Kotrelev, N[ikolai], '[They Used to Love Strindberg in Russia. Will They Love Him Again?]', *Kommersant* (Moscow), 1 June 1994, p. 13. [A report on the 12th International Sg Conference, held in Moscow in June 1994 with the theme 'Strindberg and Symbolism'. Proceedings published in **B1:379**, Michael Robinson, ed., *The Moscow Papers*. Kotrelev also places Sg in the context of Russian literature and appends a copy of the programme for the 'Strindberg Days' in Moscow in June 1994. E.1798f]

[B6:15] Kvam, Kela, 'Strindberg-Konferencen i København', *Strindbergiana* (Stockholm), 8 (1993), pp. 9-14. ['Strindberg Conference in Copenhagen. A report on the 11th International Conference devoted to Sg's later dramas. Proceedings published in **D2:158**, Kela Kvam, ed., *Strindberg's Post-Inferno Plays*]

[B6:16] Lachinger, Johann, '13. Internazionale Strindberg-Konferenz', *Ausblick* (Lübeck), 4:1 (1998), 30-31. Illus. [A report on the 13th International Sg Conference, held in Linz with the theme 'Strindberg and Expressionism'. Proceedings published in **B1:387**, Michael Robinson and Sven Hakon Rossel, eds, *Expressionism and Modernism: New Approaches to August Strindberg*]

[B6:17] Levinskaia, E., '[Only Strindberg Knows Everything]', *Moskovskii Nabliudatel'* (Moscow), 1994:9-10, pp. 31-36. [A report on the 12th International Sg Conference, held in Moscow in June 1994 with the theme 'Strindberg and Symbolism'. Proceedings published in **B1:379**, Michael Robinson, ed., *The Moscow Papers*]

[B6:18] Lewko, Marian, 'Strindberg – O'Neill – współczesny teatr. Sztokholmskie obrady pod egidą Fundacji Nobla', *Zeszyty Naukowe* KUL (Lublin), No. 42 (1988), pp. 55-61. ['Strindberg – O'Neill – Contemporary Theatre'. Gives details of the papers delivered at the Nobel Symposium devoted to the dramas of Sg and Eugene O'Neill, held at the Royal Dramatic Theatre, Stockholm, 24-27 May. Proceedings published in **D2:99**, Claes Englund and Gunnel Bergström, eds, *Strindberg, O'Neill and the Modern Theatre*]

[B6:19] Myrdal, Jan, 'Strindbergiana', *Folket i Bild* (Stockholm), 14:10 (1985), p. 27. [Reports on a symposium devoted to Sg at the University of Turin]

[B6:20] Myrdal, Jan, 'Strindbergiana', in *En annan ordning. Litterärt och Personligt*, Stockholm: Norstedts, 1988, pp. 65-70. [Rpr. of **B6:19**]

[B6:21] Nolin, Bertil, 'Strindberg i Ryssland', *Göteborgs-Posten*, 22 July 1994. ['Strindberg in Russia'. A report on the 12th International Conference, held in Moscow, with the theme 'Strindberg and Symbolism'. Proceedings published in **B1:379**, Michael Robinson, ed., *The Moscow Papers*]

[B6:22] Panov, A., '[A Ghost Play or Words Sonata: Belated Epilogue to the "Strindberg Days" in Moscow]', *Nezavisimaia gazeta* (Moscow), 1 July 1994, p. 7. [Reflections on the Sg conference and theatre programme mounted in Moscow during June 1994. Proceedings published in **B1:379**, Michael Robinson, ed., *The Moscow Papers*. E.1798h]

[B6:23] pa. [Pawel Chynowski], 'Dramat Strindbergowski w kontekscie europejskim', *Życie Warszawy* (Warsaw), 1984, No. 235, p. 7. ['Strindberg's Dramas in a European Context'. A report on the 7th International Strindberg Conference with theme 'Dramat Strindbergowski w kontekscie europejskim' (Strindbergian Drama in a European Context), held in Warsaw, 1-6 October 1984]

[B6:24] Robinson, Michael, 'Strindbergssymposium i England', *Strindbergiana* (Stockholm), 6 (1991), pp. 9-16. Illus. ['Strindberg Conference in England'. A report on the 10th International Sg Conference, held at the University of East Anglia, Norwich, with the theme 'Strindberg and Genre'. Proceedings published in **B1:373**, Michael Robinson, ed., *Strindberg and Genre*]

[B6:25] [Sekreteraren], 'Strindberg and Modern Theatre', *Meddelanden från Strindbergssällskapet* (Stockholm), 53-54 (1974), pp. 10-11. [A report on the 1st International Sg Conference, convened in Stockholm. Proceedings published in **D2:285**, Carl Reinhold Smedmark, ed., *Strindberg and Modern Theatre*]

[B6:26] 'Sekreteraren' [Carl Reinhold Smedmark], 'Strindberg och Paris', *Meddelanden från Strindbergssällskapet* (Stockholm), 56 (1976), p. 18. ['Strindberg and Paris'. A report on the 2nd International Sg Conference, held at the Université de Paris-Sorbonne with the theme 'Strindberg à Paris'. Proceedings published in a special issue of *Revue d'histoire du théâtre*, **B7:35**]

[B6:27] 'Sekreteraren' [Carl Reinhold Smedmark], 'Strindbergssymposium i Minneapolis', *Meddelanden från Strindbergssällskapet* (Stockholm), 68 (1984), pp. 24-25. ['Strindberg Conference in Minneapolis'. A report on the 6th International Sg Conference, held in Minneapolis with the theme 'Strindberg's Dramaturgy'. Proceedings published in **D2:288**, Göran Stockenström, ed., *Strindberg's Dramaturgy*]

[B6:28] 'Sekreteraren' [Carl Reinhold Smedmark], 'Strindbergssymposium i Stockholm', *Meddelanden från Strindbergssällskapet* (Stockholm), 66 (1982), pp. 17-18. ['Strindberg Conference in Stockholm'. A report on the 5th International Sg Conference, held in Stockholm in 1981 with the theme 'Strindberg and the Modern Stage'. Proceedings published in **D2:331**, Donald K. Weaver, ed., *Strindberg on Stage*]

[B6:29] 'Sekreteraren'[Carl Reinhold Smedmark], 'Strindbergssymposium i Tübingen', *Meddelanden från Strindbergssällskapet* (Stockholm), 59-60 (1978), pp. 70-71. ['Strindberg Conference in Tübingen'. A report on the 3rd International Sg conference, held in Tübingen with the theme 'Strindberg and the German-Speaking Countries'. Proceedings published in **B3:166**, Wilhelm Friese, Hrsg., *Strindberg und die deutschsprachigen Länder. Internationale Beiträge zum Tübinger Strindberg-Symposium 1977*]

[B6:30] [Sekreteraren], 'Strindbergssymposium i Zürich', *Meddelanden från Strindbergssällskapet* (Stockholm), 63-64 (1980), pp 28-29. ['Strindberg Conference in Zürich'. A report on the 4th International Sg Conference, held in Zürich with the theme 'Strindbergs Dramen im Lichte neuerer Methoden-diskussionen'. Proceedings published in **D2:8**, Oskar Bandle, Walter Baumgartner, and Jürg Glauser, Hrsg., *Strindbergs Dramen im Lichte neuerer Methodendiskussionen*]

[B6:31] Shakh-Azizova, Tat'iana, '[Under the Sign of Strindberg]', *Ekran i stsena* (Moscow), 1994:37-38 (6-13 October), pp. 10-11. [A report on the 12th International Sg Conference, held in Moscow in June 1994 with the theme 'Strindberg and Symbolism'. Proceedings published in **B1:379**, Michael Robinson, ed., *The Moscow Papers*]

[B6:32] Sinko, Tadeusz, 'Skandynawia – Polska – Europa. Spotkanie Strindbergowskie w Warszawie', *Teatr* (Warsaw), 1984:12, pp. 8-9. ['Scandinavia – Poland – Europe. Strindbergian Meeting in Warsaw'. A report on the 7th International Strindberg Conference with theme 'Dramat Strindbergowski w kontekscie europejskim' (Strindbergian Drama in a European Context), held in Warsaw, 1-6 October 1984]

[B6:33] Snopek, Jerzy, 'Polsko-szwedzkie kolokwium Strindbergowskie', *Acta Sueco-Polonica* (Uppsala), 5 (1996), [137]-138. ['Polish-Swedish Strindberg Colloquium'. A report on a colloquium, held in Warsaw 12-13 June 1996, to plan a ten-volume edition of Sg's works in Polish. See **B7:1**]

[B6:34] Sokół, Lech, 'Sympozjum polsko-szwedzkie', *Pamiętnik Teatralny* (Warsaw), 1977:4, pp. 2-7. [Reports on a Polish-Swedish symposium]

[B6:35] Steene, Birgitta, 'Kring Strindbergskonferensen i Berlin', *Strindbergiana* (Stockholm), 17 (2002), pp. 107-[112]. ['On the Strindberg Conference in Berlin'. A report on the 15th International Sg Conference, 2001, held in Berlin with the theme 'Strindberg and His Media'. Proceedings published in **B1:473**, Kirsten Wechsel, Hrsg., *Strindberg and His Media*]

[B6:36] Steene, Birgitta, 'Med Strindberg i Österrike. En rapport kring den 13:e internationella Strindbergskonferensen i Linz', *Strindbergiana* (Stockholm), 13 (1998), pp. 21-36. Illus. ['With Strindberg in Austria. A Report on the 13th International Strindberg Conference in Linz'. Reports on a conference with the theme 'Strindberg and Expressionism'. Proceedings published in **B1:387**, Michael Robinson and Sven Hakon Rossel, eds, *Expressionism and Modernism: New Approaches to August Strindberg*]

[B6:37] Steene, Birgitta, 'Strindbergssymposium i Seattle', *Strindbergiana* (Stockholm), 4 (1989), pp. 67-72. ['Strindberg Conference in Seattle'. A report on the 9th International Sg Conference, held at the University of Washington, Seattle, in April 1988 with the theme 'Strindberg and History'. Proceedings published in **B7:39** and **B1:434**]

[B6:38] Törnqvist, Egil, 'Strindbergssymposium i Amsterdam', *Strindbergiana* (Stockholm), 3 (1988), pp. 12-14. ['Strindberg Conference in Amsterdam'. A report on the 8th International Sg Conference, held at the University of Amsterdam in May 1986 with the theme 'Transposing Strindberg's Drama']

[B6:39] Uggla, Andrzej Nils, 'Strindbergssymposium i Warszawa', *Strindbergiana* (Stockholm), 1 (1985), pp. 163-165. ['Strindberg Conference in Warsaw'. A report on the 7th International Sg Conference, held in Warsaw with the theme 'Dramat Strindbergowski w kontekscie europejskim' (Strindbergian Drama in a European Context)]

[B6:40] Uggla, Andrzej Nils, 'Strindbergssymposium i Warszawa', *Upsala Nya Tidning*, 20 November 1984. ['Strindberg Conference in Warsaw'. See **B6:39**]

[B6:41] Westin, Boel, Göran Rossholm, and Barbro Ståhle Sjönell, 'Strindberg and Fiction. Den 14:e Internationella Strindbergskonferensen i Stockholm 1999', *Strindbergiana* (Stockholm), 15 (2000), pp. 183-185. Illus. [A report on the 14th International Sg Conference, held in Stockholm with the theme 'Strindberg and Fiction'. Proceedings published in **B1:389**, Göran Rossholm, Barbro Ståhle Sjönell, and Boel Westin, eds, *Strindberg and Fiction*]

[B6:42] Wirmark, Margareta, 'Strindberg i Amerika', *Upsala Nya Tidning*, 11 June 1983. ['Strindberg in America'. A report on the 6th International Sg Conference, held in Minneapolis in 1983 with the theme 'Strindberg's Dramaturgy'. Proceedings published in Göran Stockenström, ed., *Strindberg's Dramaturgy*, **D2:288**]

B7. Special Issues of Academic, Theatre, and Literary Journals

[This section provides details of journals and yearbooks that have devoted one or more special issues to Strindberg and his works, including the annual Strindbergiana, published from 1985 to date, but not its less substantial predecessor, Meddelanden från Strindbergssällskapet, *which enjoyed only a comparatively limited circulation among members of the Strindberg Society (see* **A1:37**). *Articles from the latter have been listed in the appropriate section elsewhere in the bibliography. English translations of the titles of those essays listed here, or further details of those which are identified only by their reference number, are to be found together with other annotation at the reference given]*

[B7:1] *Acta Sueco-Polonica* (Uppsala), No. 5 (1996). [Includes **A1:100**, **A3:34**, **A3:60**, **A3:82**, **A3:132**, **A3:150**, **B3:441**, and **B6:33**, with an introduction by Elżbieta Sarnowska-

Temeriusz, pp. 139-140. Contains the papers from a colloquium devoted to establishing the format and editorial principles for a Polish edition of Sg's works in ten volumes]

[B7:2] *Adam* (London), 17, Nos 190-191 (Jan-Feb 1949). [An issue published in conjunction with the centenary of Sg's birth. Contains **B3:234** as well as **C1:236**, Max Brod on Sg and Kafka; **E59:32**: Elizabeth Sprigge, 'Strindberg's Last Play'; **R:1100**: Alfred Jolivet, 'Strindberg et la France'; **R:1811**: on Sg's acquaintance with the theatre director J. T. Grein; **R:2098**: Marika Stiernstedt on meeting Sg in Paris; and **T:287**: John Landquist on Sg's sympathy for the Communards. It also reprints brief tributes culled from various unspecified sources by Roger Martin du Gard, André Gide, Georges Duhamel, Thornton Wilder, Jules Romains, H.-R. Lenormand, André Gide, Jean Cocteau, Albert Camus, Johan Bojer, Arnold Zweig, George Bernard Shaw (for whom Sg 'is among the greatest of the great'), and Thomas Mann, who recalls that: 'The brilliant speculations of the *Blue Books*...left behind in me a ferment which has worked on me irrepressibly ever since. It is quite possible that in...my *Dr Faustus*, this memory subconsciously played its part'. The issue also contains translations from *Historiska miniatyrer* and Sg's correspondence with both Nietzsche and Georg Brandes (the latter in extract), as well as excerpts from his memoranda to members of the Intimate Theatre on acting, *King Lear*, and *Hamlet*]

[B7:3] *Adam* (London), 47, Nos 455-467 (1985). [Contains a number of short comparative and biographical items including **C1:299**, **C3:4**, **R:476**, **R:587**, and **R:1235**, as well as several shorter prose pieces, stories, and essays in translation, and a substantial selection from Sg's correspondence in annotated translation, **J:305**]

[B7:4] *Alla världens berättare* (Stockholm), 'Hur de mötte Strindberg', 1949:1. ['How They Encountered Strindberg'. An issue marking the centenary of Sg's birth with comments on their first encounter with Sg by Swedish writers from different generations and various literary schools, including Stig Dagerman, Eyvind Johnson, and Gustav Hedenvind-Eriksson]

[B7:5] *Das Programm. Blätter der Münchener Kammerspiele*, 1915:1. [Published in conjunction with the staging of eight of Sg's plays as a so-called cycle at the Munich Kammerspiele in 1915. Includes **D2:829**: 'Klabund', 'Eine Fahne des Triumphs...']

[B7:6] *Bonniers månadshäften* (Stockholm), 1909:1. [An issue marking Sg's 60th birthday. Includes **B2:230**: John Landquist, 'August Strindberg'; **D2:535**: August Brunius, 'Något om Strindbergs dramatiska personligheter'; and **R:2122**: a Swedish translation of Georg Brøchner's questionnaire detailing Sg's personal likes and dislikes, together with several illustrations]

[B7:7] *Bonniers månadshäften* (Stockholm), 1912:6. [An issue published in memoriam. Contains **B8:160**: Nathan Söderblom, 'Till frågan om Strindberg och religionen'; **H1:26**: John Landquist, 'Strindbergs lyrik'; and **T:185**: Erik Hedén, 'Strindberg och nutidens sociala strider', together with the prose piece, 'Upp till solen!' (1890), a selection from *Kvarstadsresan* (The Sequestration Journey), and several illustrations]

[B7:8] *Bonniers Litterära Magasin* (Stockholm), 18:1 (1949). [An issue commemorating the centenary of Sg's birth. Includes **J:285**: Olof Molander, 'Kring några brev från August Strindberg', and **P1:254**: Gotthard Johansson, 'Strindberg och konsten']

[B7:9] *Bonniers Litterära Magasin* (Stockholm), 38:6 (1969). [Includes **A4:42**: Sven Delblanc, 'Om Strindbergsstudier'; **B2:320**: Göran Printz-Påhlson, 'Tankens genvägar. Om Strindbergs antropologi, 1'; **B9:89**: Asta Ekenvall, 'Strindberg och kvinnans fysiologi'; **E5:11**: Kenth-Åke Andersson, *et al.*, 'Reform och revolution. En tolkning av *Mäster Olof* och en studie i dess litteraturhistoriska behandling'; **F5:95**: Jan Hafström, 'Bilder till Strindbergs *Inferno*'; **H1:42**: Nils Åke Sjöstedt, 'Strindberg och lyriken'; **T:424**: Jan Myrdal, 'Om Svanbergsproblemet i Strindbergsdiskussionen'; and **T:502**: Victor Svanberg, 'Strindberg i skjortärmarna']

[B7:9a] *Bonniers Litterära Magasin* (Stockholm), 38:8 (1969). [Continues **B7:9** with **B2:320**: Göran Printz-Påhlson, 'Tankens genvägar. Om Strindbergs antropologi, 2'; **E5:26**: Tobias Berggren, '"Tror du det var farligt, Olof, Gud välsigne dig för det!"'; **T:504**: Victor Svanberg, 'Strindberg moralen. Till Jan Myrdal', which complete the collection in the following issue, 38:8 (1969), and **U1:335**: Lars Gustafsson, 'Strindbergsnummer i bakspegeln']

See also **U1:483 and U1:620**

[B7:10] *Bulletin of the American Institute of Swedish Arts, Literature and Science* (Minneapolis), 4:2 (1949). [An issue marking the centenary of Sg's birth. Includes miscellaneous celebratory articles by Walter A. Berendsohn, Torsten Eklund, and Gunnar Ollén, as well as Bertil Nydahl on *Stora landsvägen*, pp. 19-21 (**E59:19**), and the program of events in a celebratory American 'Strindberg Week, pp. 15-18]

[B7:11] *Classiconorroena* (Perugia), No. 13 (January-June) 1999. [Contains the proceedings of a symposium on 'Strindberg e la tradizione classica' (Strindberg and the Classical Tradition), held in Perugia, 11 May 1998. Includes two essays, **E2:3** and **E2:4**, on *Hermione* and **D2:1051**, Renzo Pavese, 'August Strindberg e la tragedia classica', as well as Serena Innamorati, 'August Strindberg nelle biblioteche dell'Umbria']

[B7:12] *Das neue Magazin für Litteratur* (Leipzig), 73:16 (1904). [Includes extracts from Sg's correspondence and translations of his comments on Balzac, Goethe, and Schiller in *Ensam*, on Kierkegaard, and the letter which Zola addressed to Sg about *Fadren*, as well as René Schickele (see **C1:1110**) 'Strindberg'; **R:1383**: Theodor Lindblom, 'Monsieur Strindberg und Madame Charlotte'; **R:1506**: Paul Meijer-Granqvist, 'Die Familie Strindberg'; and a translation of Gustaf Fröding's 'Strindbergs Lyrik']

[B7:13] *Dikt och konst* (Stockholm), 27 (1949). [An issue published in commemoration of the centenary of Sg's birth]

[B7:14] *entré* (Norsborg), 8:3 (1981). [Includes five short articles on contemporary Swedish productions or adaptations of *Ett drömspel* (see **E41:72**, **E41:75**, **E41:203**, and **E41:687**), plus an appeal for the reopening of Sg's old Intimate Theatre]

[B7:15] *Europe* (Paris), No. 858 (October 2000). [Contains **A4:29**: Régis Boyer, 'Repères bibliographiques'; **A3:46**: Lars Dahlbäck, 'Strindberg au complet'; **B2:57**: Régis Boyer, 'Déthéâtraliser Strindberg'; **B4:50**: Gunnel Engwall, 'Strindberg et son introducteur français'; **C1:307**: Sven Delblanc, 'Strindberg et Weininger'; **D2:608**: Hans-Göran Ekman, 'La Magie des vêtements'; **D2:933**: Jean-MarieMaillefer, 'Un précurseur du théâtre de l'absurde'; **E11:35**: Régis Boyer, '*Père*, un grand parcours initiatique'; **E41:6**: Elena Balzamo, '*Le Songe*, modes d'emploi'; **G1:125**: Boel Westin, 'Conte et écriture'; **H1:17**: Olivier Gouchet, 'Les poèmes de Strindberg'; **J:144**: Kerstin Dahlbäck, 'August Strindberg épistolier'; **M:88**: Sophie Grimal, 'L'Intuition du tout et l'objectivité expérimentale: La pensée scientifique d'August Strindberg'; **M:183**: Guy Vogelweith, 'Strindberg et les lendemains de l'évolution'; **P1:445**: Göran Söderström, 'La peinture de Strindberg'; and **T:38**: Jean-François Battail, 'De l'exil aux prix Nobel du peuple: L'étrange parcours d'un intellectuel hors normes'; **T:258**: Martin Kylhammar, 'Critique de la civilisation'; and **T:429**: Jan Myrdal, 'Qui est Strindberg?'; as well as Olivier Grouchet, 'Les poèmes de Strindberg', and a selection of extracts from *En blå bok* in French translation]

[B7:16] *Expressen* (Stockholm), 3 March 1985. [Strindberg Supplement. Contains several short illustrated pieces and brief articles, including **R:1964**]

[B7:17] *Fram* (Stockholm), August 1910. [An issue of the radical socialist paper, published in conjunction with the Strindberg Feud]

[B7:18] *Il Dramma* (Rome), 46:3 (March) 1970. [An issue published in conjunction with Michael Meschke's staging of *Ett drömspel* at the Teatro Stabile di Torino. Includes contributions by Vagn Børge, **D2:516**, Michael Meschke, **E41:108**, and Giorgio Zampa, **E41:207**, and a translation of Antonin Artaud's programme note, **E41:3**]

[B7:19] *Il Dramma* (Rome), 1978:6-7. [An issue dedicated to Sg in conjunction with Mario Missiroli's production of *Till Damaskus* at the Teatro Stabile di Torino. Includes articles by Odoardo Bertani, **E25:16**, 'Un sogno, un'autobiografia e qualcosa di piu', and Luciano Codignola, **E25:31**, 'Mimesi e tempo in *Verso Damasco*', as well as **E25:61**, Enrico Job, 'Il tempo reso in immagini', and an interview with Missiroli, **E25:94**, 'L'Inquietudine del buio']

[B7:20] *Julius Weismann Archiv* (Duisburg), 1956. Hrsg. Wilhelm Falcke. [Contains **P3:18**: Ernst Brugger, 'Aus einem Gespräch mit Julius Weismann zur Entstehung der *Gespenstersonate*'; **P3:44**: Hans Hebberling, 'Die Musik im Schaffen August Strindbergs'; **P3:94**: Karl Laux, 'Oper als Märchenspiel – Gedanken zu *enweiß*'; **P3:113**: Otto C. A. Zur Nedden, '"Das Evangelium der Hoffnung". Von August Strindberg zu Julius Weismann'; **P3:141**: Saladin Schmitt, 'Zu Julius Weismanns Oper *Traumspiel*', and **U1:99**, Walter A. Berendsohn, 'August Strindberg']

[B7:21] *Konst och kultur* (Stockholm), 5:1 (1949). [An issue marking the centenary of Sg's birth. Includes **R:2096**: Marika Stiernstedt, 'Möte med Strindberg', pp. 2-4; **T:534**: Per-Olov Zettström, 'Fredskämpen', pp. 5-10, 18-19, 27; and **P1:325:** Egil Malmsten, 'Målaren', pp. 11-13, 27, as well as **B3:60**: 'Om Strindberg – medan han levde', which reprints comments on Sg by his Swedish contemporaries Sven Hedin, Fredrik Böök, Verner von Heidenstam, and Per Hallström]

[B7:22] *lambda nordica* (Stockholm), 8:1 (2002). [Includes **B2:336**: Matthew Roy, 'Strindbergs förgiftade natur: En textstudie om lika-könad lusta'; **F4:65**: Ann-Sofie Lönngren, 'Illusionen av en kvinna. En queerteoretisk analys av det homosexuella tabut i *En dåres försvarstal*'; and **R:2039**: Göran Söderström, 'Strindberg och homosexualiteten. En biografisk studie']

[B7:23] *Literaturberichte des Verlages Georg Müller* (München), 1914:1. [The journal of the publishing house responsible for Emil Schering's German edition of Sg's collected works. Contains **B2:51**: Rudolf Blümner, 'Strindberg', pp. 13-22; comments on Sg by Thomas Mann, p. 10, Gerhart Hauptmann, pp. 9-10, and Maximilian Harden, p. 10; Sg's correspondence with Schering about *Svanevit*, pp. 3-8; a comment by Oskar A. M. Schmitz on 'Ibsen und Strindberg', pp. 11-12; **B2:271**: Carl David Marcus, 'Ein Beitrag zu Strindbergs Weltanschauung', pp. 23-26; and a personal note by the actress Irene Triesch, 'Warum Ich Strindberg vorlese' (Why I Read Strindberg), pp. 27-28]

[**B7:24**] *Marginal* (Oslo), No. 4 (1997). [Contains **B2:294**: Bertil Nolin, 'Det moderna, det faustiska och ondskans triumf. Om Strindberg efter *Inferno*'; **E25:117**: Björn Sandmark, 'Sönderfallets fenomenologi. Om *Till Damaskus* (1898-1904)'; **E35:42**: Merete Pryds Helle, 'En sten af ord. Om *Dödsdansen* (1901)'; **E41:186**: Ole Robert Sunde, 'Vet du hva jeg ser i speilet her? Om *Ett drömspel* (1902)'; **E51:29**: Ivan Cicmanec, 'Det skapte og det virkelige. Om *Spöksonaten* (1907)'; **E53:10**: Gro Dahle, 'En underlig fugle. Om *Pelikanen* (1907)'; **F5:78**, Freddy Fjellheim, 'Fortellerens tvisynte selvtukt i leseren om *Inferno* (1897)'; **F9:35**: Stig Sæterbakken, 'Å være er å ikke være: om *Ensam* (1903)'; **G15:71**: Per Stounbjerg, 'Klosterporten og køkkenvinduet. Om *Svarta fanor* (1907)'; **G16:32**: Peer Hultberg, 'Rejsegilde for en indre skranke: om *Taklagsöl* (1907)'; and **K7:40**: Helena Eriksson, 'Crex, crex: om *En blå bok* (1907-1912)']

[**B7:25**] *Modern Drama* (Lawrence, Kansas), 5:3 (1962). [Issue commemorating the 50th anniversary of Sg's death. Includes **A1:14**: Jackson R. Bryer, 'Strindberg 1951-62: A Bibliography'; **A4:142**: Richard B. Vowles, 'A Cook's Tour of Strindberg Scholarship'; **C1:1370**: Kenneth S. White, 'Visions of a Transfigured Humanity: Strindberg and Lenormand'; **D2:506**: Haskell M. Block, 'Strindberg and the Symbolist Drama'; and **R:99**: Hans Alin, 'August Strindberg: Reminiscences of a Protégé'; as well as essays on *Fordringsägare*, **E13:27**, *Bandet*, **E24:7**, *Till Damaskus*, **E25:118** and **E25:142**, *Ett drömspel*, **E41:174**, *Toten-Insel*, **E52:8**, *Inferno*, **F5:136**, and **G1:9**: Harold H. Borland, 'The Dramatic Quality of Strindberg's Novels']

[**B7:26**] *Nordic Theatre Studies* (Copenhagen), 6:1-2 (1993). [Contains **A2:30**: Margareta Brundin, 'The Royal Library's Strindberg Collections'; **A3:39**: Lars Dahlbäck, 'The National Edition of Strindberg's Collected Works'; **B4:177**: Egil Törnqvist, 'A "Play"-within-the-Play: The Opening of Strindberg's *The Father*'; **C2:69**: Birgitta Steene, 'Ingmar Bergman's First Meeting with Thalia'; **D2:1012**: Bertil Nolin, 'Towards a Concept of an Intimate Theatre'; **E12:95**: Edward S Franchuk, 'Symbolism in *Miss Julie*'; **E12:244**: Willmar Sauter, Jacqueline Martin, and Knut Ove Arntzen, 'Reflections on *Miss Julie*. The New Scandinavian Experimental Theatre's *Miss Julie* in Copenhagen, 1992'; **E48:63**: Birgitta Steene, 'The House as Setting and Metaphor in Strindberg's Chamber Plays'; **E58:9**: Freddie Rokem, '*The Black Glove*: Wilhelm Carlsson's Production at Dramaten, 1988'; **P3:95**: Inga Lewenhaupt, '*A Dream Play* on the Opera Stage'; **P4:46**: Erik Näslund, '*Miss Julie* – The Ballet, 1950-1'; and **P5:93**: Rune Waldekrantz, 'Strindberg and the Silent Cinema']

[**B7:27**] *Norskrift: Tidskrift for nordisk språk og literatur* (Oslo), No. 107 (2004). [On the theme 'Ibsen og Strindbergs dramatik', including **E11:48**: Mads B. Claudi, 'Stridens gudinne – den religiøse maktovertagelsen i *Fadren*'; **E35:5**: Maria Alnæs, 'Isolasjon og fangenskap i Strindbergs *Dödsdansen*'; and **D2:1002**: Anna Karolina Netland, 'Virkelighet og illusjon i August Strindbergs *Till Damaskus I* og *Spöksonaten*']

[**B7:28**] *Obliques. Littérature – Théâtre* (Paris), 1:1, 1972. [Contains numerous short articles, including **B4:19**: Carl Gustaf Bjurström, 'Boris Vian, traducteur de Strindberg'; **B9:214**: Jean Roudaut, 'L'éroccultisme'; **C1:942**: Jacques Naville, 'Accueils'; **C1:1060**: Marthe Robert, 'Strindberg et Weininger'; **C1:1336**: Guy Vogelweith, 'Strindberg et Freud'; **C1:1327**: Guy Vogelweith, 'Le Désir d'être bonne'; **D2:687**: Maurice Gravier, 'Harriet Bosse et la théâtre mystique'; **E12:255**: Evert Sprinchorn, 'La Fin de Julie'; **E41:19**: Carl Gustaf Bjurström, '*Le Songe*'; **E41:131**: 'La Bataille du *Songe*'; **E41:201**: Roger Vitrac, 'Les Mystères du rêve'; **E48:54**: Brian Rothwell, 'Les Pièces de chambre'; as well as

R:283: Carl Gustaf Bjurström, 'Biographies', and **R:908**: Sverker Hallen [sic]), 'Qui donc poursuivait Strindberg? (Un cryptogramme menaçant)'. The issue also includes numerous illustrations and translations of Sg's correspondence with Nietzsche and the fairy tale 'Ett halvt ark papper' (Half a Sheet of Paper), as well as his frequently republished and translated interview with the Danish journalist Georg Brøchner, **R:2120**]

See **U1:454** and **U1:466**.

[B7:29] *Parnass* (Stockholm), 6:1 (1995). [Includes a collection of short popular articles on Sg's life and reputation. See **B3:156**, **B3:366**, **B9:92**, **C2:72**, **G15:63**, **P2:85**, **P3:57**, **R:1307**, **R:1433**, **R:1550**, **R:1844**, and **R:1860**]

[B7:30] *Parnass* (Stockholm), 10:1 (1999). [Includes **J:273**: Björn Meidal, 'Brev, brev och ännu flera brev', **P3:52**: Per-Anders Hellqvist, 'Den gammalmodige avantgardisten'; **P5:71**: Birgitta Steene, 'Att filma Strindberg'; **R:1005**: Bure Holmbäck, 'Strindberg, teknologerna och ryssen'; **T:521**: Egil Törnqvist, 'Strindberg som europé', and **U1:540**]

[B7:31] *Pinhole Journal* (San Lorenzo, New Mexico), 4:1 (1988). [Contains **P2:70** and **P2:78**, as well as a translation by Jan-Erik Lundström of Sg's essay 'Om Ljusverkan vid Fotografering' (On the Action of Light in Photography). Copiously illustrated with prints of Sg's photographs]

[B7:32] *Przegląd Humanistyczny* (Warsaw), 1979. [Includes **B4:185**: Andrzej N. Uggla, 'Strindberg a współczesność'; **C2:16**: Zenon Ciesielski, 'Bergman i Strindberg'; and **T:73**: Gunnar Brandell, 'Strindberg a Kommuna Paryska']

[B7:33] *Prolog* (Zagreb), 55-56 (1983). [Includes an important bibliography of publications about Sg in Serbia and Croatia, **A1:86**: Mirko Rumac, 'Bibliografija: prijevoda Strindbergovih djela, prikaza izvedaba njegovih drama napisa of A. Strindbergu na hrvatskom odnosno srpskom jezivnom podrucj'; **B2:82**: Harry G. Carlson, 'Strindbergova biblijska metaforika'; **B2:118**: Branimir Donat, 'Opsjednuti pjesnik – Druga scena Augusta Strindberga'; **D2:940**: Charles Marowitz, 'Pristupati Strindbergu zaobilazeći ga'; **D2:1092**: Ture Rangström, 'Intima teatern'; **D2:1175**: Göran Söderström, 'Strindbergove ideje o scenografiji'; **E11:103**: Miroslav Krleža, 'Otac Augusta Strindberga'; **E27:41**: Evert Sprinchorn, 'Glazbena struktura drame Ima zlocina i zlocina'; **P1:484**: Göran Söderström, 'Strindbergovo slikarstvo'; **R:478**: Harry G. Carlson, 'Strindberg – biografska skica'; **R:1248**: Olof Lagercrantz, 'August Strindberg (IX. poglavlje)'; and **R:1883**: Mirko Rumac, 'Biograf i pjesnik: Lagercrantz i Strindberg. Zamierke i pohvale jednoj izvrsnoj knjzi'; together with an introduction, 'Uvodni fragmenti', by Giga Gracan, pp. 7-10]

[B7:34] *Quickborn* (Berlin), January 1899. [Contains contributions by, as well as on, Sg and Edvard Munch, solicited, where Sg was concerned, with stubborn diplomacy by Emil Schering]

[B7:35] *Revue d'histoire du théâtre* (Paris), 30:3 (1978). [Contains the Actes du colloque of the 3rd International Sg Conference, 'Strindberg à Paris', held at the Université de Paris-Sorbonne in 1975. Contains **B2:6**: Stellan Ahlstroem [sic], 'Strindberg à Paris. Un aperçu'; **B3:351**: Francis Pruner, 'La première représentation de Strindberg à Paris'; **B4:67**: Maurice Gravier, 'Strindberg écrivain français'; **C1:81**: Oskar Bandle, 'Strindberg et les Norvégiens à Paris'; **C1:211**: Régis Boyer, 'Strindberg et Villiers de l'Isle-Adam'; **D2:533**: Pierre Brunel, 'Strindberg et Artaud'; **D2:1110**: Jacques Robichez, 'Strindberg et Lugné-Poe'; **D2:1308**: Göran Wiren, 'Strindberg et Jean Vilar'; **E27:43**: Richard W. [sic], Vowles, 'Une nouvelle lecture "de *Crime et Crime*", la plus parisienne des pièces de Strindberg'; **E59:35**: Pierre della Torre, 'Deux représentations de *La Grande Route*'; **M:182**: Guy Vogelweith, 'Strindberg et l'ésotérisme parisien'; **P1:449**: Göran Söderström, 'Strindberg et les cercles d'art parisiens'; **J:318**: Göran Roscholm [sic], 'Les Lettres de Strindberg à Albert Savine'; and **T:72**: Gunnar Brandell, '"Ils voulaient brûler Paris": Strindberg et la Commune'; together with an introduction by Maurice Gravier, p. 199]

[**B7:36**] *Ridå* (Stockholm), No. 1 (1909). [Marks Sg's fiftieth birthday with a collection of reminiscences by Swedish critics and theatre workers together with a poem, 'Till August Strindberg!', by Olof Bruno]

[**B7:37**] *Scandinavica* (Norwich), 38:1 (1999). [An issue commemorating the 150th anniversary of Sg's birth. Includes **A4:119**: Michael Robinson, 'Sesquicentennial Strindberg: An Anglo-Swedish Editorial Note'; **D2:1255**: Egil Törnqvist, 'Unreliable Narration in Strindbergian Drama'; **F5:167**: Per Stounbjerg, 'A Modernist Hell: On August Strindberg's *Inferno*'; and **G3:120**: Ulf Olsson, 'The Blue Void: Dialogicity, Narration and the Future in Strindberg's *Röda rummet*']

[**B7:38**] *Scandinavian Review* (New York), 64:3 (1978). [Includes **B9:232**: Birgitta Steene, 'The Ambiguous Feminist'; **C2:35**: Marilyn Johns, 'Kindred Spirits: Strindberg and Bergman'; **C4:13**: Per Olov Enquist, 'Notes for a Play about Strindberg'; **D2:1323**: Leif Zern, 'The Devil Being Exorcised; and **P1:99**: Harry G. Carlson, 'The Unknown Painter of Myth'; together with a brief introduction, 'Several Unknown Strindbergs', by Harry G. Carlson, pp. 5-6, a presentation of the Strindberg Museum, 'Strindberg Alive in the Blue Tower', by Raymond Jarvi and Harry G. Carlson, and a translation of the short story, 'Hercules']

[**B7:39**] *Scandinavian Studies* (Madison), 62:1 (1990). [Contains many of the papers presented at the 9th International Sg Conference on the subject of 'Strindberg and History', held at the University of Washington in 1988. See **B2:77**: Harry G. Carlson, 'Strindberg and the Carnival of History'; **B2:317**: Göran Printz-Påhlson, 'Historical Drama and Historical Fiction: The Example of Strindberg': **D2:907**: Herbert Lindenberger, 'Experiencing History'; **D2:1113**: Michael Robinson, 'History and His-Story'; **D2:1202**: Barbro Ståhle Sjönell, 'The Plans, Drafts and Manuscripts of the Historical Plays in Strindberg's "Green Bag"'; **E38:13**: Susan Brantly, 'The Formal Tension of Strindberg's *Carl XII*'; **E38:22**: Barbara Lide, 'Strindberg and the Modern Consciousness: *Carl XII*'; **E38:31**: Egil Törnqvist, 'Visual and Verbal Scenery in Strindberg's Historical Plays: The Opening of *Carl XII* as Paradigmatic Example'; **E40:9**: Kerstin Dahlbäck, '*Kristina* and Strindberg's Letters and Diary'; **E40:44**: Margareta Wirmark, 'Strindberg's *Queen Christina*: Eve and Pandora'; and **E42:22**: Matthew H. Wikander, 'Historical Vision and Techniques of Dramatic Historiography: Strindberg's *Gustav III* in Light of Shakespeare's *Julius Caesar* and Corneille's *Cinna*'; together with an introduction by the editor, Birgitta Steene, pp. 1-4, and a bibliography charting Sg's interest in history and the history plays, **A1:91**. For subsequent publication of this material in book form with additional essays, see Birgitta Steene, ed., *Strindberg and History*, **B1:434**]

[**B7:40**] *Die Scene* (Berlin), 11:2-3 (1921). [Contributions by the editor, F. Gregori, 'Zum Thema Strindberg', pp. 19-20, and 'Aus der Strindberg-literatur', pp. 59-63, and articles and comments listed separately by Bernhard Diebold, **D2:589** and **D2:591**, Berthold Held, **D2:740**, Franz Horch, **D2:761**, Karl Loewenberg, **D2:913**, A. Neuweiler, **D2:1003**,

Robert Pirk, **D2:1065**, Friedrich Sebrecht, **D2:1159**, Friedrich Kayßler, **E25:69**, Edgar Gross, **E10:11**: 'Dramaturgische Glossen zu Strindbergs *Kameraden*', Erwin Piscator, **E51:98** on *Spöksonaten*, and Renato Mordo, '*Der Scheiterhaufen*', **E53:364**]

[B7:41] *Strindberg-Blätter* (Piersons Verlag, Dresden), Nos 1-3, 1901. [Edited by Emil Schering. No. 1 includes translations of Tor Hedberg's reviews of the premières of *Till Damaskus* and *Folkungasagan*; No. 2 includes translations of the principal reviews of the première of *Påsk* in Stockholm with Harriet Bosse as Eleonora and a performance of the same play in Frankfurt; No. 3 includes **D2:1287**: Richard Wendriner, 'Die neue Strindberg'; **E34:62**: Josef Theodor, 'Ein Drama der Passion', on *Påsk*; and translations of reviews of *Erik XIV* in performance in Stockholm]

[B7:42] *Strindbergiana* (Stockholm), Första samlingen, Stockholm: Atlantis, 1985. [167] pp. [Contains **A2:29**: Margareta Brundin, 'Kungliga Bibliotekets Strindbergssamlingar'; **A2:33**: Monika Carlheim-Gyllensköld, 'Ordning eller oordning i Strindbergs bibliotek. Vilhelm Carlheim-Gyllenskölds insats'; **A4:113**: Sven Rinman, 'Femton års Strindbergs-forskning'; **B3:500**: Gao Ziying, '"Strindbergs valda verk" på kinesiska'; **B6:39**: Andrzej Nils Uggla, 'Strindbergssymposium i Warszawa'; **C1:336**: Vivi [Blom-] Edström, 'Selma Lagerlöf och Strindberg'; **G5:97**: Jan Myrdal, 'På tal om *Giftas*'; **P1:373**: Alice Rasmussen, 'Ett opublicerat porträtt av Gustav Vigeland'; **P1:444**: Göran Söderström, 'En återfunnen Strindbergsmålning från Berlintiden'; **R:1406**: Hans Lindström, '"Utan böcker hungrar jag…"'; and a 'Förord' by [Karl-Åke Kärnell], pp. 5-6]

[B7:43] — Behring, Bertil, *Kvällsposten* (Malmö), 11 July 1987.

[B7:44] — Brandell, Gunnar, *Svenska Dagbladet* (Stockholm), 24 July 1985.

[B7:45] — Granberg, Nils, *Aftonbladet* (Stockholm), 3 July 1985.

[B7:46] — Lundh, Tryggve, *Folket* (Eskilstuna), 31 July 1985.

[B7:47] — Nilsson, Björn, *Expressen* (Stockholm), 26 June 1985.

[B7:48] — Ollén, Gunnar, *Sydsvenska Dagbladet* (Malmö), 18 July 1985.

[B7:49] — Svenson, Lars, *Helsingborgs Dagblad*, 8 October 1985.

[B7:50] — Tjäder, Per Arne, *Göteborgs-Posten*, 17 August Strindberg 1985.

[B7:51] — Warmland, K., *Nya Wermlands Tidningen* (Karlstad), 7 September 1985.

[B7:52] — Wittrock, Ulf, *Upsala Nya Tidning*, 12 July 1987.

[B7:53] — Wizelius, I., *Dagens Nyheter* (Stockholm), 16 August 1985.

[B7:54] *Strindbergiana* (Stockholm), Andra samlingen, Stockholm: Atlantis, 1987. [162] pp. [Contains **B3:436**: Egil Törnqvist, 'Strindberg i Nederländerna'; **D3:128**: Michael Meyer, 'Strindberg Productions in Great Britain 1984-86'; **D3:176**: Gunnar Ollén, 'Strindbergspremiärer 1984-85-86'; **D3:227**: Ruprecht Volz, 'Strindberg-Premieren in Deutschland 1984-85'; **E41:12**: Tamás Bécsy, '*A Dream Play*: Is it a Drama Indeed?'; **E53:31**: Per Arne Tjäder, 'Mågen som försvann. En dramatisk detalj i Strindbergs *Pelikanen*'; **F5:153**: Mary Sandbach, 'Introduktion till *Inferno*'; **G16:47**: Franco Perrelli, '*Taklagsöl*: Strindberg's Last Tape'; and **P1:483**: Göran Söderström, 'Strindbergs Gauguinföretal']

[B7:55] — Fischer, W., *Västerbottens-Kuriren* (Umeå), 10 March 1987.

[B7:56] — Granberg, Nils, *Aftonbladet* (Stockholm), 25 March 1987.

[B7:57] — Lundstedt, Göran, *Sydsvenska Dagbladet* (Malmö), 7 April 1987.

[B7:58] — Olsson, T., *Västerbottens-Kuriren* (Umeå), 1 April 1987.

[**B7:59**] — Rinman, Sven, *Upsala Nya Tidning*, 2 May 1987.

[**B7:60**] — Svenson, Lars, *Helsingborgs Dagblad*, 25 March 1987.

[**B7:61**] — Warmland, K., *Nya Wermlands Tidningen* (Karlstad), 25 March 1987.

[**B7:62**] *Strindbergiana* (Stockholm), Tredje samlingen, Stockholm: Atlantis, 1988. [142] pp. [Contains **B6:38**: Egil Törnqvist, 'Strindbergssymposium i Amsterdam'; **B4:23**: Carl Gustaf Bjurström, 'Strindberg på franska'; **B4:38**: Margareta Brundin, 'Vita lamm och svarta får. Om den första svenska översättningen av "Baa, baa, black sheep"'; **B4:43**: Viktor Claes, 'De nederländska översättningarna av Strindberg'; **C1:1326**: Karl Vennberg, 'August Strindberg'; **D2:1250**: Egil Törnqvist, 'Strindbergs bitext'; **D3:177**: Gunnar Ollén, 'Strindbergspremiärer 1986-87'; **E13:47**: Michael Robinson, 'Naturalism och intrig i *Fordringsägare*'; **E25:86**: Roland Lysell, '"Varför tala när orden icke täcka tanken?" - Strindberg post strukturalismen'; **G1:46**: Karl-Åke Kärnell, 'Strindbergs ungdomsprosa i svensk stiltradition'; **R:874**: J[ack] T. Grein, 'Ett möte med Strindberg'; and a 'Förord' by [Hans-Göran Ekman], pp. 7-8]

[**B7:63**] — Ekerwald, Carl-Göran, *Dagens Nyheter* (Stockholm), 23 April 1989.

[**B7:64**] — Gustafsson, Lars, *Nerikes Allehanda* (Örebro), 30 May 1989.

[**B7:65**] — Hultsberg, Peter, *Barometern* (Kalmar), 25 May 1989.

[**B7:66**] — Levander, Hans, *Svenska Dagbladet* (Stockholm), 14 July 1989.

[**B7:67**] — Lundstedt, Göran, *Sydsvenska Dagbladet* (Malmö), 5 May 1989.

[**B7:68**] — Sommar, Carl Olof, *Östgöta Correspondenten* (Linköping), 12 May 1989.

[**B7:69**] — Steinick, K., *Göteborgs-Tidningen*, 26 May 1989.

[**B7:70**] — Wittrock, Ulf, *Upsala Nya Tidning*, 7 June 1989.

[**B7:71**] *Strindbergiana* (Stockholm), Fjärde samlingen, Stockholm: Atlantis, 1989. [182] pp. [Contains **A4:117**: Sven Rinman, 'Tre års Strindbergsforskning'; **A4:131**: Göran Stockenström, 'Strindberg i Amerika 1988'; **B4:162**: Birgitta Steene, '"Sommarlovets hägring är inte nödvändigtvis översättarens vision...": Om *Pelikanen*, Kulturspråk och Författarspråk'; **B6:37**: Birgitta Steene, 'Strindbergssymposium i Seattle'; **C1:803**: Magnus Ljungren, 'Aleksandr Blok och Strindbergs ansikte'; **D3:108**: Lars Löfgren, 'Strindberg på Dramaten 1988'; **E12:82**: Hans-Göran Ekman, 'Klädernas magi i *Fröken Julie*'; **E12:242**: Freddie Rokem, 'Länge leve hundraåringarna'; **E12:269**: Egil Törnqvist, 'Slutet i *Fröken Julie*'; **M:166**: Barbro Ståhle Sjönell, 'Ur Gröna säcken. Strindbergs "människoherbarium" och vetenskapliga "depôt"'; **M:192**: Arne Wyller, 'August Strindberg och astronomien'; **R:538**: Maj Dahlbäck, 'Änglamakerskan - en myt i Strindbergs fantasi'; and a 'Förord' by [Hans-Göran Ekman], pp. 7-8]

[**B7:72**] — Andrée, L., *Förr och nu* (Stockholm), 1989:4, pp. 61-62.

[**B7:73**] *Strindbergiana* (Stockholm), Femte samlingen, Stockholm: Atlantis, 1990. [175] pp. [Contains **C1:800**: Per Erik Ljung, 'August Strindberg, Vilhelm Ekelund och "uppsvenskarna"'; **C1:1193**: Carl Olov Sommar, 'Ekelöf och Strindberg'; **D2:729**: Anne-Charlotte Hanes Harvey, 'Strindbergs scenografi'; **E11:144**: Freddie Rokem, 'Strindbergs *Fadren* på Habima-teatern i Tel Aviv'; **E41:178**: Barbro Ståhle Sjönell, '*Ett drömspel* på Nationaltheatret i Oslo. Samtal med föreställningens regissör och scenograf'; **E48:47**: Birgitta Ottosson-Pinna, 'Strindbergs levande hus'; **J:161**: Kerstin Dahlbäck, 'Kärlekens språk. Några anteckningar kring brevväxlingen mellan August Strindberg och Harriet Bosse 1900-1901'; **M:117**: George B. Kauffman, 'August Strindbergs kemiska och alkemiska studier'; and **P1:182**: Catherine C. Fraser, 'Allén och *Ensam* - en jämförelse'.

Also contains miscellaneous articles on the Sg Museum by Anita Persson (**U1:641**) pp. 9-12, and **U1:600**, Gunilla Norming, pp. 13-15, and a 'Förord' by [Hans-Göran Ekman], pp. 7-8]

[**B7:74**] — Granberg, Nils, *Aftonbladet* (Stockholm), 28 March 1990.

[**B7:75**] — Levander, Hans, *Svenska Dagbladet* (Stockholm), 15 May 1990.

[**B7:76**] — Lundstedt, Göran, *Sydsvenska Dagbladet* (Malmö), 10 May 1990.

[**B7:77**] — Nurmi, Kurt, *Arbetet* (Malmö), 26 April 1990.

[**B7:78**] *Strindbergiana* (Stockholm), Sjätte samlingen, Stockholm: Atlantis, 1991. [175] pp. [Contains **B6:24**: Michael Robinson, 'Strindbergssymposium i England'; **D3:17**: Richard Bark, 'Strindbergsuppsättningar i Skandinavien 1987-1990'; **D3:192**: Freddie Rokem, 'Mörka ljusstrålar. Strindberg på scenen 1987-1988'; **E25:129**: Göran Söderström, 'En *Till Damaskus*-scenografi ur Strindbergsmuseets samlingar'; **E38:35**: Margareta Wirmark, '"Skaffa mig en spindel att leka med!" Strindbergs drama *Carl XII* som förabsurdistisk text'; **K7:48**: Thomas Gilek, 'Strindbergs tankevärld i *En blå bok*'; **P5:95**: Gösta Werner, 'Strindberg som förebådare av ett nytt medium: filmen'; and **R:5**: Åke Åberg, 'Den unge Strindberg och folkbildningsrörelsen'. Also contains a comment on receiving the Sg Prize by Mary Sandbach (**U1:695**) and a 'Förord' by [Hans-Göran Ekman], pp. 5-6]

[**B7:79**] — Berman, Nils, *Norrköpings Tidningar-Östergötlands Dagblad*, 25 June 1991.

[**B7:80**] — Granberg, Nils, *Aftonbladet* (Stockholm), 25 June 1991.

[**B7:81**] *Strindbergiana* (Stockholm), Sjunde samlingen, Stockholm: Atlantis, 1992. [176] pp. [Contains **C1:1125**: Anita Segerberg, 'Strindberg och Christina Stead. Om Strindbergs inflytande i Australien'; **G12:18**: Ulf Olsson, 'Snäckornas sagor. Anmärkningar till Strindbergs passagearbeten'; **L4:22**: Magnus Röhl, 'Vid Strindbergs källor. Till frågan om materialet bakom tre lärdomshistoriska studier'; **P1:168**: Douglas Feuk, 'Omfale / Omfalos. Kring några målningar av Strindberg från hösten 1901'; **R:298**: Jean Bolinder, 'Strindberg var mannen som gjorde himmelen blå! Den döende August Strindberg och Stockholmpressen'; **R:2038**: Göran Söderström, 'Strindberg och hans finska kontakter'; **T:262**: Nils-Erik Landell, 'Tal vid invigningen av utställningen "Det går framåt - ja framåt, åt helvete" på Strindbergsmuseet den 16 November 1990'; and a 'Förord' by [Hans-Göran Ekman], pp. 7-8]

[**B7:82**] — Florin, Magnus, *Expressen* (Stockholm), 4 July 1992.

[**B7:83**] — Granberg, Nils, *Aftonbladet* (Stockholm), 3 September 1992.

[**B7:84**] — Sommar, Carl Olof, *Östgöta Correspondenten* (Linköping), 1 July 1992.

[**B7:85**] — Syréhn, Gunnar, *Vestmanlands Läns Tidning* (Västerås), 10 June 1992.

[**B7:86**] — Tjäder, Per Arne, *Göteborgs-Posten*, 14 July 1992.

[**B7:87**] *Strindbergiana* (Stockholm), Åttonde samlingen, Stockholm: Atlantis, 1993. [182] pp. [Contains **A3:48**: Lars Dahlbäck, 'Strindbergs ordvärld i Nationalupplagan'; **B2:277**: Björn Meidal, 'Medalj, lagerkrans och doktorshatt. Drömmen om utmärkelse – ett tema i August Strindbergs liv och diktning'; **B3:378**: Vida Saviciunaite, 'Strindberg i Litauen'; **B4:126**: Gunnar Ollén, 'De första översättningarna – till franska, danska och tyska – av *Fordringsägare*'; **B6:15**: Kela Kvam, 'Strindberg-Konferencen i København'; **E41:9**: Richard Bark, 'Människans fångenskap i materien och upphävandet av tid och rum. *Ett drömspel* på Orionteatern 1990'; **F5:16**: Lotta Gavel Adams, 'Strindberg som Ockultismens Zola'; **F10:62**: Karin Petherick, '"Hvad betyder det?" Ett ledmotiv i *Ockulta Dagboken*'; **K7:33**: Margareta Brundin, '"Kärlekens bok" - Liv - dikt i *En ny Blå bok*'; **K7:77**: Eva Spens, '*En blå bok* - ett stenbrott?'; **P1:372**: Alice Rasmussen, 'Carl Larssons och Albert Engströms Strindbergsporträtt'; **R:2060**: Carl Olov Sommar, 'Strindberg - sina vänners vän'; and a 'Förord' by [Hans-Göran Ekman], pp. 7-8]

[B7:88] — Holmqvist, Ivo, *Jönköpings-Posten*, 18 August Strindberg 1993.

[B7:89] — Lindberg, Börje, *Arbetet* (Malmö), 10 April 1993.

[B7:90] — Lindvåg, Alf, *Smålandsposten* (Växjö), 1 June 1993.

[B7:91] — Lundberg, Bengt, *Östgöta Correspondenten* (Linköping), 23 April 1993.

[B7:92] — Lundstedt, Göran, *Sydsvenska Dagbladet* (Malmö), 23 June 1993.

[B7:93] — Säll, Arne, *Sundsvalls Tidning*, 12 May 1993.

[B7:94] — Schmidt, Henrik, *Idag* (Stockholm), 17 May 1993.

[B7:95] — Sundberg, Björn, *Expressen* (Stockholm), 26 April 1993.

[B7:96] — Wittrock, Ulf, *Upsala Nya Tidning*, 26 January 1994.

[B7:97] *Strindbergiana* (Stockholm), Nionde samlingen, Stockholm: Atlantis, 1994. [185] pp. [Contains **A2:72**: Göran Söderström, 'Strindbergsällskapets och Strindbergmuseets pressklippsamling'; **B2:361**: Barbro Ståhle Sjönell, 'Strindbergs registerblandning'; **B2:392**: Louise Vinge, 'De besatta i Lund - om Strindbergs *Legender*, *Påsk* och *Karl XII*'; **D3:18**: Richard Bark, 'Strindbergsuppsättningar 1990-1993'; **D3:42**: Magnus Florin, 'Strindberg Dramaten 93'; **E13:54**: Gunnar Syréhn, '"Hämnd är en så naturlig känsla". Ett motiv i Strindbergs *Fordringsägare*'; **E41:48**: Maria Fridh, '*Ett drömspel* i Ryssland'; **E53:16**: Karl-Ivar Hildeman, 'Strindberg, hans släktingar och *Pelikanen*'; **R:584**: Birgitta Delbrand, '"Fick jag något att hushålla med; så blefve jag hushållsaktig". Bonniers förlag och utgivningen av Strindbergs *Samlade skrifter*'; **R:1842**: Ture Rangström, 'Den förälskade turnéledaren. På resa i Sverige med Strindbergs Intima teatern'; and a 'Förord' by [Richard Bark], pp. 7-8]

[B7:98] — Andersson, Ulf, *Hallandsposten* (Halmstad), 13 May 1994.

[B7:99] — Granberg, Nils, *Aftonbladet* (Stockholm), 12 May 1994.

[B7:100] — Lindvåg, Alf, *Smålandsposten* (Växjö), 31 may 1994.

[B7:101] — Lundstedt, Göran, *Sydsvenska Dagbladet* (Malmö), 27 May 1994.

[B7:102] — Waern, Carina, *Dagens Nyheter* (Stockholm), 1 July 1994.

[B7:103] — Wittrock, Ulf, *Samlaren* (Uppsala), 115 (1994), p. 155.

[B7:104] *Strindbergiana* (Stockholm), Tionde samlingen, Stockholm: Atlantis, 1995. [182] pp. [Contains **C1:163**: Aleksandr Blok, 'Till August Strindbergs minne'; **C1:1367**: Boel Westin, '"Hexmästaren". Strindberg, Andersen och sagotraditionen'; **E14:2**: Lotta Gavel Adams, 'Maktkamp och kvinnokamp. August Strindbergs *Den starkare* och Dorrit Willumsens *Den stærkeste II. En dialog över nio decennier*'; **F5:140**: Ulf Olsson, 'Tecknets anarkism. En kommentar till Strindbergs *Inferno*'; **F5:154**: Mona Sandqvist, '*Inferno* som alkemistroman'; **P3:121**: Stig Norrman, '"Jag ser din musik". Om musiken i August Strindbergs berättarkonst'; **P3:127**: Märta Ramsten, '"Håll upp att röra i gammal urmusik". Några anteckningar om Strindberg och folkmusiken'; **R:585**: Birgitta Delbrand, '"Fick jag något att hushålla med; så blefve jag hushållsaktig". Bonniers förlag och utgivningen av Strindbergs *Samlade skrifter*'; and **R:1726**: Anders Ollfors, 'Strindbergs dedikationer än en gång'. Also contains an account of the early years of the Sg Society by Gunnar Ollén, pp. 9-16, recollections of fifty years of the Society by Carl Olof Johansson, pp. 17-46, and a 'Förord' by [Boel Westin], pp. 7-8]

[B7:105] — Bladh, Curt, *Sundsvalls Tidning*, 3 June 1995.

[B7:106] — Lindvåg, Alf, *Smålandsposten* (Växjö), 24 July 1995.

[B7:107] — Lundstedt, Göran, *Sydsvenska Dagbladet* (Malmö), 10 July 1995.

[B7:108] — Tjäder, Per Arne, *Göteborgs-Posten*, 16 May 1995.

[B7:109] — Wittrock, Ulf, *Upsala Nya Tidning*, 30 July 1995.

[B7:110] *Strindbergiana* (Stockholm), Elfte samlingen, Stockholm: Atlantis, 1996. 182 pp. [Contains **B3:237**: Mats Karlsson, 'Avtryck i Japan. Strindberg i Akutagawas skrifter'; **B4:72**: Sophie Grimal, 'En författares försvarstal'. En omvärdering av Strindbergs franska i *Inferno*'; **E14:11**: Anna Lyngfelt, 'Strindbergs *Den starkare*, ett moderniserat proverb'; **E25:58**: Ola Holmgren, '"Att måla fan på scenväggen för att sedan stryka över och gå vidare." Symbolisering och avsymbolisering i *Till Damaskus I*'; **E26:16**: Jan Esper Olsson, 'Trolleri, grotesk och idyll. Strindbergs val av uttrycksmedel i botgörar-dramat *Advent*'; **E41:154**: Göran Rossholm, 'Öra och mun. Perspektiv i Strindbergs *Ett drömspel*'; **L2:10**: Anders Ollfors, 'Några bibliografiska notiser kring Strindbergs *Gamla Stockholm*'; **P3:81**: Erik Höök, 'Musik i färg': **R:2355**: Kåa Wennberg, 'Strindbergs dotter berättar från svunna tider'; **T:478**: Nina Solomin, 'Strindbergs judefientlighet fram till 1882'; and a 'Förord' by [Boel Westin], pp. 7-8]

[B7:111] — Bladh, Curt, *Sundsvalls Tidning*, 20 April 1996.

[B7:112] — Lindvåg, Alf, *Smålandsposten* (Växjö), 26 July 1996.

[B7:113] — Lundstedt, Göran, *Sydsvenska Dagbladet* (Malmö), 18 June 1996.

[B7:114] — Nurmi, Kurt, *Hallandsposten* (Halmstad), 3 July 1996.

[B7:115] — Uisk, Ahto, *Arbetaren* (Stockholm), 75:30 (1996), p. 7.

[B7:116] — Wittrock, Ulf, *Upsala Nya Tidning*, 10 August 1996.

[B7:117] *Strindbergiana* (Stockholm), Tolfte samlingen, Stockholm: Atlantis, 1997. [182] pp. [Contains **D2:1116**: Freddie Rokem, 'Det filmiska som visuell struktur och metafor i Strindbergs teater'; **D3:19**: Richard Bark, 'Strindbergsuppsättningar 1993-1996'; **P5:11**: Mats Björkin, 'En Strindbergspjäs blir film. *Synd*: "fritt efter August Strindbergs *Brott och brott*"'; **P5:32**: Marika, V. Lagercrantz, 'Anna Hofmann Uddgren. Varietéaktris, cirkusdirektris och Strindbergs första regissör på vita duken'; **P5:34**: Bengt Lagerkvist, 'Strindberg och jag'; **P5:69**: Birgitta Steene, 'Asta Nielsen och Strindberg. Ett möte i stumfilmens tecken'; **P5:72**: Birgitta Steene and Elizabeth de Noma, 'Filmatiseringar och TV-produktioner av August Strindbergs verk'; **P5:80**: Egil Törnqvist, 'Strindberg och den intima teatern. *Pelikanen* som TV-drama'; and a 'Förord' by [Birgitta Steene], pp. 7-8]

[B7:118] — Hedling, Erik, *Svenska Dagbladet* (Stockholm), 24 June 1997.

[B7:119] — Jönsson, Ulf, *Gefle Dagblad* (Gävle), 12 May 1997.

[B7:120] — Lindvåg, Alf, *Smålandsposten* (Växjö), 26 May 1997.

[B7:121] — Lundstedt, Göran, *Sydsvenska Dagbladet* (Malmö), 22 April 1997.

[B7:122] — Ringby, Per, *Samlaren* (Uppsala), 118 (1997), pp. 299-300.

[B7:123] — Rune, Alf, *Nerikes Allehanda* (Örebro), 7 April 1997.

[B7:124] — Tjäder, Per Arne, *Göteborgs-Posten*, 25 March 1997.

[B7:125] — Waern, Carina, *Dagens Nyheter* (Stockholm), 29 July 1997.

[B7:126] *Strindbergiana* (Stockholm), Trettonde samlingen, Stockholm: Atlantis, 1998. [160] pp. [Contains **B2:295**: Bertil Nolin, 'Strindberg och Moderniteten. Den faustiske sökaren och det ondas triumf'; **B6:36**: Birgitta Steene, 'Med Strindberg i Österrike. En rapport kring den 13:e internationella Strindbergskonferensen i Linz'; **C1:1264**: Eszter Szalczer, 'Strindberg och Georg Ljungström. En teosofisk bekantskap'; **D2:424**: John Austin, '"En reform? Falck har verkat!" Intima teaterns betydelse i Stockholms teaterliv'; **D2:898**: Barbara Lide, 'Strindberg på scenen i dag. Postmoderna parodier'; **E37:10**: Björn Meidal, 'Strindbergscensur 1908. Anna Branting recenserar *Svanevit* på Intima teatern'; **G16:58**: Björn Sundberg, '"Silverträsket" och *Taklagsöl* – två prosastycken från sekelskiftet'; **P2:39**: Per Hemmingsson, 'Strindbergs "blixtkamera"'; **P2:65**: Agneta Lalander, 'Strindbergs Gersau-kamera återfunnen'; **R:10**: [Ann-Charlotte] Gavel Adams, 'Strindbergs Paris. Promenader i 6:e arrondissementet'; and **S:231**: Ulf Olsson, 'Den andra rösten. Strindbergs galenskap och litteraturhistorien'; together with 'Strindberg och Gustaf Falkvinge', a causerie by Heidi von Born, pp. 10-13. a translation of Hugo F. Königsgarten's Sgian take on *Romeo and Juliet*, and a 'Förord' by Birgitta Steene, pp. 7-8]

[B7:127] *Strindbergiana* (Stockholm), Fjortonde samlingen, Stockholm: Atlantis, 1999. [192] pp. [Contains **B2:293**: Per Nilsson, 'Vad betyder ett namn? Strindberg i ett onomastiskt perspektiv'; **B3:159**: Inga-Stina Ewbank, 'Strindberg och brittisk kultur'; **B3:283**: Jacqueline Martin, '*Fröken Julie* – en postkolonial utmaning'; **B3:347**: Franco Perrelli, '"Och nu är Italien öppet för barbaren...": Det första mottagandet av Strindberg på de italienska teaterscenerna'; **B3:437**: Egil Törnqvist, 'Strindberg i Nederländerna'; **B4:146**: Michael Robinson, 'Att anglisera *Fröken Julie*'; **C1:283**: Balachandran Chullikkad, 'I Stockholm i början av en höst'; **C1:1197**: Villy Sørensen, 'Mitt förhållande till Strindberg'; **C2:66**: Birgitta Steene, 'Ingmar Bergman möter August Strindberg'; **D2:1307**: Winge, Stein, 'Strindberg – en förförare i helvetet'; **E51:88**: Hannes Meidal, 'Gubben Hummel – Hamms anfader?: Samuel Becketts *Slutspel* i ljuset av August Strindbergs *Spöksonaten*'; **F1:39**: Jan Myrdal, 'Om August Strindbergs jagromaner och fallet Frida'; and **P3:29**: Gunnar Edander, 'Att tonsätta Strindberg. En hyllning'. The volume also contains a personal tribute to 'Ågust' from the actor Erland Josephson, (**U1:406**) pp. 11-12, a poem, 'Dimman som driver i själens håla', by Kazuko Shiraishi, pp. 39-42, a tribute in respect of the 150th anniversary of Sg's birth by Per Arne Tjäder, 'Strindberg: den förste som var sådan han verkligen var', pp. 43-45, an article, 'Strindberg som hobby', by Torsten Husén (**U1:382**), and a 'Förord' by [Birgitta Steene], pp. 7-8]

[B7:128] — Jönsson, Ulf, *Gefle Dagblad* (Gävle), 29 April 1999.

[B7:129] — Lundstedt, Göran, *Sydsvenska Dagbladet* (Malmö), 1 June 1999.

[B7:130] *Strindbergiana* (Stockholm), Femtonde samlingen, Stockholm: Atlantis, 2000. [191] pp. [Contains **B3:178**: Vera Gantjeva, 'Strindberg i Bulgarien'; **B6:41**: Boel Westin, Göran Rossholm, and Barbro Ståhle Sjönell, 'Strindberg and Fiction. Den 14:e Internationella Strindbergskonferensen i Stockholm 1999'; **E25:19**: Marilyn Johns Blackwell, 'Syn och subjektivitet i *Till Damaskus I*'; **E41:128**: Birgitta Nilsdotter, '*Ett drömspel*: några reflexioner kring modersgestalten'; **E52:5**: Karen Knape, '*Toten-Insel*: Ett dramatist "experiment"'; **G6:20**: Anna Cavallin, 'Från magnolia till körsbärsträd. Strindbergs novell "Nybyggnad" och den Nya kvinnan'; **R:533**: [Edward] Gordon Craig, 'Ett besök hos August Strindberg'; **R:1895**: Lizzie Sarah Saks, 'Berättelsen som Strindberg aldrig skrev. Om Karin Smirnoff och hennes syskon som vuxna'; **R:2085**:

[Birgitta Steene], 'Strindberg och finngubbarne. Teckning av Carolus Lindberg'; and **T:77**: Ove Bring, 'Strindberg och folkrätten'. The volume also contains 'Årets Strindbergsmejl', a report on Swedish Radio's broadcasts of Sg's letters by Håkan Sandblad, pp. 17-34, a Monologue for Sg by Per Lange, pp. 35-42, and a 'Förord' by [Birgitta Steene], pp. 7-8]

[B7:131] *Strindbergiana* (Stockholm), Sextonde samlingen, Stockholm: Atlantis, 2001. [182] pp. [Contains **D2:963**: Björn Meidal, 'Punk- och plockepinn-teater? Thorsten Flincks uppsättningar av *Fadren* och *Paria*'; **D2:1285**: Margreth Weivers, 'Ett möte med Anna Flygare – aktris vid Intima teatern'; **D2:1322**: Leif Zern, 'Därför skulle diktaren inte ha någon grav'; **E51:139**: Egil Törnqvist, 'Ingmar Bergmans fjärde *Spöksonaten*'; **G7:26**: Sebastian Casinge, 'Zigenar- och tattarschabloner i August Strindbergs *Tschandala*'; **M:155**: Alice Rasmussen, 'Polygonum Strindbergii'; **R:190**: Richard Bark, 'När Strindberg och Ibsen inte träffades i Lund'; **R:446**: Margareta Brundin, 'Eleonora Strindberg: *Till mina Gossar*. Ett nyförvärvat manuskript i Kungl. biblioteket'; **R:1714**: Gunnar Ollén, 'Strindbergska författarhemligheter: Kärleksdrama och dubbelmord'; and **R:1731**: Anders Ollfors, 'Strindbergs dedikationer en sista (?) gång'. The volume also contains an article by the actor Keve Hjelm on his first encounter with Sg's works, **U1:364**, pp. 32-31, Ture Rangström on the need to reopen the Intimate Theatre, **U1:668**, pp. 54-61, a fiction about Sg by the Dutch author Maarten Asscher, pp. 123-137, an anecdote by Richard Bark about Sg's failure to meet Ibsen in 1898, pp. 138-139, and a 'Förord' by Birgitta Steene, pp. 7-8]

[B7:132] *Strindbergiana* (Stockholm), Sjuttonde samlingen, Stockholm: Atlantis, 2002. [168] pp. [Contains **B6:35**: Birgitta Steene, 'Kring Strindbergskonferensen i Berlin'; **D2:973**: Gudrun Milekic, 'Television och film som strukturer i *Vasasagans* dramaturgi'; **D2:1251**: Egil Törnqvist, 'Strindbergs dramatik i Sveriges Radio 1925-2000'; **D3:20**: Richard Bark, 'Svenska Strindbergsuppsättningar 1996-2001'; **E35:145**: Karst Woudstra, 'Blåskägg, jungfrun och brodern. *Dödsdansen* pa Hessisches Staatstheater'; **E41:106**: Federica Mazzocchi, 'Drömmar vid Piccolo Teatro. Luca Ronconi och Strindbergs dramaturgi'; **E41:153**: Freddie Rokem, 'En Strindbergsdröm inscenerad'; **E49:2**: Massimo Ciaravalo, 'Giorgio Strehlers *Temporale* (*Oväder*)'; **E49:11**: Anne-Charlotte Hanes Harvey, 'Att resa baklänges. Scenisk funktion och progression i *Oväder*'; **E49:24**: Giorgio Strehler, 'Den borgerliga familjens tragiska futtighet'; **P5:22**: Magnus Florin, '*Brott och brott* och *Påsk*. Ingmar Bergman regisserar Strindberg för Radioteatern'; **P5:79**: Egil Törnqvist, '"Själens finaste rörelser". Strindberg som TV-dramatiker'; and **P5:102**: Clas Zilliacus, 'Historiedramerna i finlandssvensk radio'; together with a 'Förord' by [Egil Törnqvist], pp. 7-8]

[B7:133] *Strindbergiana* (Stockholm), Artonde samlingen, Stockholm: Atlantis, 2003. [198] pp. [Contains **B2:335**: Matthew Roy, 'När vetenskapen fallerar. Homosexualitet och religiös moral i Strindbergs verk efter Infernoperioden'; **B3:470**: Sten-Olof Ullström, 'När Strindberg kom till skolan'; **C1:828**: Lars O. Lundgren, '"Min ungdoms stora bloss". Hjalmar Söderberg om August Strindberg'; **D2:1091**: Ture Rangström, 'Strindbergs Intima teater. En ny teater med en gammal historia'; **E51:64**: Henrik Johnsson, 'Strindbergs hyacintflicka och Rappaccinis dotter'; **G8:88**: Ewa Mrozek-Sadowska, 'Det krympta rummet. Om *Hemsöbornas* transponering från roman till scenkomedi'; **P2:58**: Vreni Hockenjos, '"För övrigt tar jag ögonblicksbilder". Strindberg i en fotohistorisk kontext'; **P3:170**: Inger Wikström, 'Att göra opera av Strindberg'; **R:845**:

David Gedin, 'Fähundarna på Alhambra. Heidenstams skildring av sitt och Strindbergs sista möte'; and **R:2037**: Göran Söderström, '"Mästaren" och "husslaven". Om förhållandet Strindberg – Adolf Paul'; together with a 'Förord' by Birgitta Steene]

[B7:134] *Strindbergiana* (Stockholm), Nittonde samlingen, Stockholm: Atlantis, 2004. [191] pp. [Contains **B2:322**: Alice Rasmussen, 'Om äppelträden i Strindbergs verk'; **C1:1244**: Emilia Ström, 'Strindberg och Witkiewicz – likt och olikt'; **D2:1228**: Eszter Szalczer, Främmande röster. Besatthet och exorcism i Strindbergs dramatik'; **E11:131**: Lotten Nimar, August Strindbergs drama *Fadren*. En retorisk argumentationsanalys'; **E11:148**: Hanif Sabzevari, 'Vad har Ludvig med den sak att göra? Om passiva bifigurer i August Strindbergs *Fadren*'; **E12:125**: Tomas Högberg, 'Strindbergs *Fröken Julie* och Rousseaus *Julie eller Den nya Héloïse*. En komparativ analys'; **E12:183**: Bodil Lindqvist, '"Och allt detta för en grönsiskas skull!" Om namnens betydelse i *Fröken Julie*'; **E34:51**: Katja Sandqvist, '"Familjen" Heyst. En familjesystemteoretisk läsning av Strindbergs drama *Påsk*'; **E41:197**: Egil Törnqvist, '"Tid och rum existera icke". Tidsproblematiken i Strindbergs *Ett drömspel*'; **F9:19**: Germund Larsson, 'Ensamhetens berättarjag. Hjalmar Söderbergs *Hjärtats oro* och August Strindbergs *Ensam*'; **G3:162**: Anna Westerståhl Stenport, '*Röda rummet* som nationsbygge'; **P1:556**: Kåa Wennberg, 'Är det icke månne herr Strindberg? Om en målning av Nils Kreuger'; together with a poem, 'Författare' (Writer) by Anders Fügelstad and a 'Förord' by Birgitta Steene, pp. 7–8]

[B7:135] *Strindbergiana* (Stockholm), Tjugonde samlingen, Stockholm: Atlantis, 2005. [182] pp. [Contains **A1:37**: Carl Olof Johansson, 'Register över Strindbergssällskapets publikationer 1945-2005; **B4:180**: Egil Törnqvist, 'Grönsiskan och påskliljan. Två översättningsproblem'; **C1:354**: Hans-Göran Ekman, 'Kabeljo och ölsupa. Om Strindberg och Karen Blixen'; **D2:1204**: Per Stam, '"Alltså Teater", svarade Strindberg'; **D3:21**: Richard Bark, 'Svenska Strindbergsuppsättningar 2001-2004'; **E12:204**: Teresa Murjas, 'Strindberg i England: Fallet *Fröken Julie*'; **E51:101**: Alice Rasmussen, 'På spaning efter Askalonlöken. Kommentar till märklig flora i Strindbergs texter'; **E53:2**: Björn Apelkvist, 'Från *Pelikanen* till *Underjordens leende*. Om Strindberg, Norén och den destruktiva modersmaktens problem'; **N:8**: Jan Balbierz, 'Strindberg bland hieroglyfer'; **P1:362**: Anita Persson, '"Det började med ordet 'drömspel'"'; and **P2:96**: Astrid Söderbergh Widding, '"Bakvänt var det". Anteckningar kring en bok om Strindberg och medierna'; and a 'Förord' by Birgitta Steene, pp. 7-10]

[B7:136] *Strindbergiana* (Stockholm), Tjugoförsta samlingen, Stockholm: Atlantis, 2006. [191] pp. [Contains **B2:158**: Jan Garnert, 'Hallå Strindberg!'; **B3:285**: Eivor Martinus, 'Strindberg i London 2005'; **B3:433**: Caroline Stein, 'Strindbergsfestivalen i Kina 2005'; **C1:960**: Anna Nordlund, 'Geniet och sagoberätterskan. August Strindberg och Selma Lagerlöf i den svenska litteraturhistorien'; **F2:22**: Karin Aspenberg, 'Strindberg och Intet. En fenomenologisk kommentar till *Tjänstekvinnans son*'; **G3:56**: David Gedin, '"...och de krossade hjertan, som man knäcker sönder ägg!" – litteratörerna i och kring *Röda rummet*'; **G3:116**: Jens Viggo Nielsen, '"Platon hade redan sagt det...". Om Strindberg's förhållande till Platon och Sokrates i *Röda rummet*'; **J:303**: Alice Rasmussen, 'Strindbergs brevväxling med Bengt Lidforss 1891-1894. Några kommentarer till hur den i breven nämnda floran återspeglas i Strindbergs texter'; **P3:46**: Florian Heesch, 'Strindbergsmusik. Ett dussin vårsånger och en förteckning'; **T:79**: Ove Bring, 'Strindberg, folkrätten och unionsupplösningen', and a 'Förord' by Per Stam, pp. 7-9]

[B7:137] *Studiekamraten* (Tollarp), 1922:10. [Issue commemorating the 10th anniversary of Sg's death]

[B7:138] *Studiekamraten* (Tollarp), 1949:1-2. [Issue commemorating the centenary of Sg's birth]

[B7:139] *Swedish Book Review* (Lampeter), Supplement 1986. [Contains several short articles including **B2:140**, **B2:359**, **B3:399**, **D2:675**, **D3:119**, **D3:209**, and **R:1279**, as well as translations from *Skärkarlsliv* and *Ockulta dagboken*, and three miscellaneous pieces by Jan Myrdal, 'Who is Strindberg?', 'Michael Meyer', 'Strindberg and his Disciples', and a personal note by the translator Mary Sandbach, 'What Strindberg Means to Me', **U1:696**]

[B7:140] *Teatervetenskap* (Stockholm), No. 23 (1981). [Includes several short articles: **B3:357**: Ture Rangström, 'Strindberg i världen'; **D2:680**: Inga Grabe, 'Röster från Strindbergs teater'; **D2:769**: Curt Isaksson, 'Strindberg gör entré'; **D2:1014**: Marianne Norlin, 'Strindbergs-föreställningar i Stockholm 1870-1912'; **D2:1015**: Marianne Norlin, 'Sven Erik Skawonius 1908-1981'; and **E30:32**: Acke Oldenburg, '*Erik* XIV – Dramaten 1977']

[B7:141] *Teatr* (Warsaw), 1983:2. [Includes translations of an interview with Sg in *Bonniers månadshäften* (See **B7:6** and **R:2122**) and the 'Erinran' to *Ett drömspel*, an article by Andrej Nils Uggla, and several photographs documenting Polish productions of the plays between 19661 and 1982]

[B7:142] *Thalia* (Stockholm), 3:3 (20 January 1912). [Includes **D2:986**: Johan Mortensen, 'August Strindberg'; **D2:683**: Emil Grandinson, 'En regissör om August Strindberg'; **D2:779**: Siegfried Jacobsohn, 'Strindberg i Tyskland'; **D3:214**: Erik Thyselius, 'Från några Strindbergsföreställningar'; together with several shorter articles and illustrations of recent Swedish productions]

[B7:143] *Théâtre en Europe* (Paris), 5 (1985). [Includes **C1:989**: Eugene O'Neill, 'Strindberg et notre théâtre'; **D1:523**: Carl Gustaf Bjurström, 'De la difficulté du dialogue: quelques auteurs dramatiques suédois de Strindberg à Norén'; **D2:1063**: 'Strindberg, le temps et l'espace'; **D2:1145**: Jean-Pierre Sarrazac, 'Strindberg, la scène'; **D2:1270**: Guy Vogelweith, 'Le Théâtre Intime de Strindberg: un dramaturge en attente du 7e art'; **D3:216**: Renzo Tian, 'De *La Contessa* au *Sogno*'; **E41:8**: Richard Bark, '*La Songe*, de Harriet Bosse à Ingmar Bergman'; and **E49:4**: Luciano Codignola, '*Orage*: la double écriture scénique de Strehler'. The issue is richly illustrated with numerous photographs of productions of Sg's plays by Strehler, Ingmar Bergman, and others]

[B7:144] *Théâtre/Public* (Gennevilliers), No. 73 (1983). Dossier présenté par les Ateliers de Formation et de Recherche de la Comédie de Caen sous la direction de Jean-Pierre Sarrazac. [Contains **B3:195**: Maurice Gravier, '"Fortune" de Strindberg sur les scènes de France'; **B4:25**: Carl Gustaf Bjurström, 'Traduire le théâtre de Strindberg', **C1:322**: Bernard Dort, 'Strindberg nourricier. A propos d'Adamov et du "nouveau théâtre"'; **C1:1161**: Terje Sinding, 'Strindberg, Ibsen – tours et détours de la subjectivité'; **D2:425**: Jacqueline Autrusseau-Adamov, 'De la femme à la scène. Portrait du dramaturge en personnage bisexuel'; **D2:1150**: Jean-Pierre Sarrazac, 'Dramaturgie de l'autoportrait'; **D3:23**: Daniel Besnehard, 'Guirlande'; **D3:24**: Daniel Besnehard and Tristan Valès, 'Strindberg aux Ateliers de Formation et de Recherche'; **E13:56**: Charles Tordjman, 'Représenter le chaos'; **E25:91**: Alain de Mijolla, 'Réflexions d'un psychanalyste autour du *Chemin de Damas*'; **E25:143**: Guy Vogelweith, 'En reprenant *Le chemin de Damas*'; **E35:18**: Michel Bouquet, 'Entretien avec Michel Bouquet'; **E35:125**: Michel Vinaver, 'Sur les deux cent douze premières répliques de *La Danse de mort*''; **E49:25**: Giorgio Strehler, 'Mesquinerie tragique de la famille bourgeoise'; **E51:139**: Egil Törnqvist, 'Ingmar Bergman met en scène: *La Sonate des spectres*'; **E52:7**: Hans-Peter Litscher, '*L'île des morts*: L'ailleurs n'es pas compris dans le prix de billet'; and **E52:21**: Terje Sinding, 'Impressions de *L'île des morts*'; as well as a translation of Sg's discussion of *Othello* in the 4th of his memoranda to the Intimate Theatre]

[**B7:145**] *Tidskrift för litteraturvetenskap* (Lund), 23:2 (1994). [Contains **A4:105**: Ulf Olsson, 'Korrekta texter, korrekt forskning och bristen på förnyelse – ett samtal om Strindberg och litteraturvetenskapen'; **B9:110**: Margaretha Fahlgren, 'Mannen, försoningen och kvinnan'; **K7:35**: Johan Dahlbäck, 'Strindberg och bokens slut'; **K7:44**: Magnus Florin, 'Pratet och tystnaden'; **K7:68**: Gunnar Ollén, 'Personangreppen i *En blå bok I*'; and **K7:70**: Thomas Olsson, '"Religiös intuition och vetenskaplig". Litterär tematik i *En blå bok*'; with an introduction, 'En blå *TFL*', by the editor, Ulf Olsson, pp. [3]-5]

[**B7:146**] *Tidskrift för litteraturvetenskap* (Lund), 33:1 (2004). [Includes **B2:193**: Vreni Hockenjos, 'Money, Monney, Monet. Om rörelse, teknologi och perception i Strindbergs "Från Café de l'Ermitage till Marley le Roi och så vidare"'; **B2:207**: Henrik Johnsson, 'Att skapa någon till sin avbild. Om homunculusmotivet hos Strindberg'; **E15:8**: Göran Rossholm, 'Katthjärnans lek med råtthjärnan – aspekt och perspektiv i *Paria*'; **E27:28**: Ann-Sofie Lönngren, 'Att gjutas i en annan form – en queerteoretisk analys av homosociala begär i Strindberg's drama *Brott och brott*'; **E59:10**: Ola Holmgren, 'Skapelsens skrift och författarens text i August Strindbergs *Stora landsvägen*'; and a brief introduction, 'Ännu en Strindbergsbok' (Yet another Strindberg Book), by Göran Rossholm]

[**B7:147**] *TijdSchrift voor Skandinavistiek* (Groningen), 19:1 (1998). [Includes **B4:80**: Anne-Charlotte Hanes Harvey, 'Translating Scandinavian Drama – for Whom?'; **B4:93**: Barry Jacobs, 'Translating for the Stage: The Case of Strindberg'; **B4:184**: Egil Törnqvist, 'Translating Strindbergian Imagery for the Stage'; and **D2:624**: Johannes F. Evelein, 'Drama Turning Inward: Strindberg's Station Play and its Expressionist Continuum']

[**B7:148**] *TijdSchrift voor Skandinavistiek* (Amsterdam), 20:1 (1999). [Publishes papers from a conference on the theme of 'The Artist and Cultural Identity' with reference to Sg, Alf Sjöberg and Ingmar Bergman. Includes **B3:159**: Inga-Stina Ewbank, 'Strindberg and British Culture'; **B4:150**: Michael Robinson, 'Maid in England: Anglicizing *Miss Julie*'; **C2:30**: Vreni Hockenjos, 'Strindberg through Bergman: A Case of Mutation'; **C2:41**: Paisley Livingston, 'Self-Reflexivity in Strindberg and Bergman'; **C2:84**: Egil Törnqvist, 'Strindberg, Bergman and the Silent Character'; and **E51:160**: Margareta Wirmark, 'Strindberg versus Bergman: The End of *Spöksonaten*']

[**B7:149**] *Vecko-Journalen* (Stockholm), 21 January 1912. [An issue of a popular journal commemorating Sg's 63rd birthday. Includes brief articles by Harald Johnsson and 'Troil', the text of the fairy tale 'Pintorpa fruns julafton', a facsimile of a list of dates in Sg's hand which chart significant events in his life, and several illustrations]

[**B7:150**] *World Theatre-Le théâtre dans le monde* (Bruxelles), 11:1 (1962). [An issue commemorating the 50th anniversary of Sg's death. Contains **B3:180**: John Gassner, 'The Influence of Strindberg in the United States'; **B3:292**, Siegfried Melchinger, 'The

German People Face to Face with Strindberg'; **C1:475**: Maurice Gravier, 'Strindberg and French Drama'; **D2:759**: Claes Hoogland, 'How to Produce Strindberg?'; **D2:1024**: Gunnar Ollén, 'Strindberg 1962'; and **D2:1303**: Raymond Williams, 'Strindberg and the New Drama in England'. Text in both French and English]

B8. Religion

[*In addition to specific discussions of Sg's religious beliefs, this section includes several items in which his life and work is interpreted in religious terms, including those that Sg himself provided for his readers when reading and structuring his experience in the form of a Calvary or a journey to Damascus, or when he used the terminology of Theosophy, Anthroposophy, or Buddhism, rather than the language he had inherited from Christianity, in order to recuperate the details of his life in what seemed to him a meaningful form. Similar issues are discussed in many general studies of his work, of course, particularly those, like Gunnar Brandell,* **B1:55**, *or Göran Stockenström,* **B1:437**, *which focus on the Inferno crisis and the works most immediately related to it, including* Inferno *and* Till Damaskus, *but the same is true of many other studies, both of early plays like* Fritänkaren *and* Mäster Olof *and later works in different genres, including* Ett drömspel, Spöksonaten, Svarta fanor, *and* En blå bok]

[B8:1] Andrén, Erik, 'Strindbergs gudstro', *Växjöbladet*, 24 December 1982. ['Strindberg's Belief in God']

[B8:2] Anon, 'Ett och annat om hvartannat. Affällingen Strindberg', *Svenska Morgonbladet* (Stockholm), 16 November 1904. ['One Thing and Another, Turn and Turn About. Strindberg the Apostate'. Compares Sg's pre-Inferno works with the religious tone of his later writings. Although his earlier novels enjoy the greater acclaim, the author believes his later works are to be preferred as morally superior to their harmful predecessors]

[B8:3] Anon, 'August Strindberg om "religion och teologi"', *Stockholms Dagblad*, 4 August 1910. ['August Strindberg on "Religion and Theology"'. Discusses Sg's views concerning religion apropos the Strindberg Feud]

[B8:4] Anon, 'Strid om religion och teologi', *Nyaste Kristianstadsbladet*, 3 August 1910. ['Conflict over Religion and Theology'. Interprets the ongoing Sg Feud as fundamentally a religious conflict]

[B8:5] Anon, 'Strindberg o religiji', *Čas* (Belgrade & Ljubljana), 5:9 (1911), 426-427. ['Strindberg on Religion'. R.199]

[B8:6] Anon, 'Strindberg om religion och teologi', *Barometern* (Kalmar), 6 August 1910. ['Strindberg on Religion and Theology']

[B8:7] Bahr, Hermann, 'Strindberg i katolicizam', *Život* (Split), 7:4 (1926), 234-237. ['Strindberg and Catholicism'. Translation of an article originally published in German. R.558]

[B8:8] Baldus, Alexander, 'August Strindberg', *Allgemeine Rundschau* (München), 23 (1926), 649-651. [Discusses Sg's rediscovery of Christianity during his later years]

[B8:9] Beisswänger, Gustav, 'Strindberg', *Christliches Kunstblatt für Kirche, Schule und Haus* (Stuttgart), 1-3, 60 (1918), pp. 7-12, 57-64, 72-77. [A Christian interpretation of Sg's life and work]

[B8:10] Benzow, Kristofer, 'Strindberg och Kierkegaard', in *Idealitet och religiositet. Studier kring det moderna religionsproblemet*, Lund: C. W. K. Gleerups Förlag, 1921, pp. 48-66. [An essay that is more concerned with Sg's religious beliefs and their relationship with Kierkegaard's religious thinking than a comparative study of the influence which Kierkegaard exerted on his literary works. Benzow traces the development of Sg's faith and his links with religion from early childhood on, as well as his exposure to Pietism in adolescence and the impression made on him by a theologian in whose categories of the aesthetic, the ethic, and the religious, and the notion of life as a series of stages, the young Sg found his own life's problem rendered both more profound and more intense. Benzow discusses *Tjänstekvinnans son*, Sg's student essay on Oehlenschläger's drama *Hakon Jarl* from 1871, and the importance which Georg Brandes's *Hovedstrømninger i det Nittende Aarhundredes Literatur* (Main Currents in Nineteenth-Century Literature, 1872-1890) and his monograph on Kierkegaard had for his understanding of the latter. Already fundamental to Sg's thinking in *Mäster Olof*, Kierkegaard would remain of importance to him even in the later 1880s, for example in both *I havsbandet* and the story 'Min sommarpräst' (My Summer Priest) in *Skärkarlsliv*, which were written during a period when he had seemingly abandoned Christianity. However, according to Benzow, Sg 'had Christianity in his blood in spite of all his freethinking', and his point of departure is that of Kierkegaard in *Begrebet Angst* (The Concept of Dread, 1844) and the concept of the poet of anguish and guilt. However, in later works like *Påsk*, he realises that good may come of suffering and toys with a novel humility, even if he also suffers from a new kind of hubris, the pride of one who knows that he is called – a pride to which Kierkegaard was also no stranger]

[B8:11] Bjurman, G., 'Strindbergs nye troesbekendelse', *Politiken* (Copenhagen), 21 September 1907. ['Strindberg's New Creed']

[B8:12] Blom, Ture, 'Strindbergs ställning till religionen', *Ariel* (Tollarp), 11 (1931), 204-211. ['Strindberg's Attitude to Religion']

[B8:13] Bourguignon, Annie, 'Religion et identité dans *Maître Olof* et *La grand'route*, August Strindberg', in Philippe Alexandre, ed., *Religions, nations, identités*, Nancy : Presses Universitaires de Nancy, 2004, pp. 217-231. ['Religion and Identity in *Master Olof* and *The Great Highway*']

[B8:14] Braun, Robert, 'Gottlos mit Strindberg? Der "erste moderne Mensch" widerrief seine Lästerungen', *Rheinischer Merkur* (Coblenz), 20:17 (1965), p. 17. ['Godless with Strindberg? The "First Modern Man" Retracts his Blasphemy'. Reflects on Sg's reconciliation with Christianity in his later years]

[B8:15] Braun, Robert, 'Möte med friheten', *Credo: Katolsk Tidskrift* (Uppsala), 48 (1967), 110-118. ['Encounter with Freedom'. Examines anti-Christian sentiments in Swedish authors, with particular reference to Sg and Olof Lagercrantz]

[B8:16] Braun, Robert, 'Strindberg och den katolska kyrkan', *Credo: Katolsk Tidskrift* (Uppsala), 30 (1949), 100-107. ['Strindberg and the Catholic Church'. Considers the feelings that Sg entertained for Catholicism, for which he often expresses a contradictory amalgam of secret longing and dread, especially during the Inferno crisis. His attitude is reminiscent of agoraphobia and may be related to the fact that, like other writers of the period, he had abandoned himself to the cult of personality and the cultivation of his own self, and was consequently at odds with what the Christian self should be. This struggle is evident in *Till Damaskus*, written after Sg has begun to display a greater intellectual appreciation of the Church as early as *I havsbandet*, and it is this problematic that he grapples with during the Inferno period, finally overcoming his cult of the personality in his last years, during which the debate over Catholicism continues in *En blå bok*]

[B8:17] Cavallin, Paul, *Ur Inferno till Damaskus. En omvändelsehistoria*, Acta Regiæ Societatis Scientiarum et Litterarum Gothoburgensis, Humaniora 38, Göteborg: Kungl. Vetenskaps- och Vitterhets Samhället, 1998. 47 pp. ['Out of Inferno to Damascus. A Tale of Conversion'. Contains an account of the philosopher Paul Cavallin's (1868-1901) contacts with Sg in Lund in the late 1890s, as well as of his own conversion following a period of mutual religious turmoil during which Sg urged him to bear witness in print]

[B8:18] Cedergren, Mickaëlle, *L'écriture biblique de Strindberg : étude textuelle des citations bibliques dans Inferno, Legendes, et Jacob lutte*, Institutionen för franska, italienska och klassiska språk, Stockholms universitet, Edsbruk: Akademitryck, 2005. VII+219 pp. ['Strindberg's Biblical écriture: A Textual Study of the Biblical Quotations in *Inferno, Legends,* and *Jacob Wrestles*'. See **V:40**]

[B8:18a] Connor, Herbert, 'Jesus och Buddha', *Växjöbladet*, 30 March 1955. ['Jesus and Buddha'. Reflects on Strindberg's evidently profound interest in both Christianity and Buddhism]

[B8:19] Cronqvist, Th., 'Strindberg och religionen', *Blekinge Läns Tidning* (Karlskrona), 7 August 1971. ['Strindberg and Religion']

[B8:20] Cvitanović, Gabro, 'Strindberg i katoličanstvo', *Nova revija* (Dubrovnik), 2:1 (1923), 85-88. ['Strindberg and Catholicism'. A discussion of Sg's relationship with Catholicism based primarily on a reading of *Inferno* and *Legender*, both of which are treated unproblematically as reliable autobiographical sources. R.552]

[B8:21] Dopychai, Gregor, 'Die Seinsgemäßheit der Religion. Aufgezeigt am Lebenswege Strindbergs', *Die Kirche in der Welt* (Münster), 6 (1953), 139-144. ['The Due Existence of Religion. Illustrated by the Course of Strindberg's Life']

[B8:22] Eklund, Dan, 'Strindberg, Teosofin och Swedenborg', *Online Teosofiska Kompaniet Malmö*, 2002. http: //www.teosofiskakompaniet.net/Strindberg.htm. ['Strindberg, Theosophy, and Swedenborg'. Maintains the importance which Theosophy, Madam Blavatsky, and Swedenborg held for the post-Inferno Sg, focusing primarily on *Spöksonaten* and *Toten-Insel*. In what was originally a so-called 'B-uppsats' presented at the Institute for Cultural Knowledge at the University of Lund, Eklund also discusses *En blå bok* and the significance which Arnold Böcklin's painting *Toten-Insel* held for Sg]

[B8:23] Engelstad, Carl Fr., 'Lidelsens skole – en Strindbergstudie', *Kirke og kultur* (Oslo), 46 (1939), 348-360. ['The School of Suffering: A Strindberg Study'. Offers a Christian reading of Sg's life and work and the attainment of knowledge through suffering]

[B8:24] Fibiger, A., 'Ave Crux', *Plovfuren* (Marburg), 6 (1916), 617-619. [Discusses Sg's relationship with Christianity with reference to the inscription he selected for the cross that marked his grave]

[B8:25] Fischer, Hans, 'August Strindberg und die Hinzu Rom-Bewegung', 1-2, *Die Christliche Welt* (Marburg), 14 (19 and 26 April 1900), Sp. 376-381, 399-402. ['August Strindberg and his Turn towards Rome'. Discusses the development of Sg's religious beliefs in *Inferno* and his rejection of naturalism. Fischer points out that the pirated 1893 Berlin edition of *En dåres försvarstal* gained him the reputation of a pornographer and was thus a contributing factor in the feelings of guilt that assailed him during the Inferno period]

[B8:26] Fischer, Max, *August Strindberg. Ein Beitrag zur Kenntnis der religiösen Psyche unserer Zeit*, Religiöse Geister. Texte und Studien. Bändchen 6, Mainz: Matthias Grünewald Verlag, 1921. 40 pp. ['August Strindberg. A Contribution to an Understanding of the Religious Psyche of Our Time'. Fischer maintains that Sg has made a major contribution to the renewal of religious literature and discusses his relationship with Theosophy and Occultism as well as Catholicism. *Till Damaskus, Ett drömspel, Brott och brott,* and *Näktergalen i Wittenberg* provide the main sources of supporting evidence. Fischer also comments on Sg's views on women]

[B8:27] — Piper, Otto, *Die Christliche Welt* (Marburg), 37 (1923), Sp. 790-791.

[B8:28] — Sprengler, Joseph, *Das literarische Echo* (Berlin), 24 (1921-22), Sp. 507.

[B8:29] Fischer, Paul, 'Strindbergs Weg nach Damaskus', *Die Christliche Welt* (Marburg), 41 (1927), Sp. 378-386. ['Strindberg's Road to Damascus'. Offers a Christian reading of *Till Damaskus* in terms of personal conversion]

[B8:30] Fritsche, Herbert, 'August Strindbergs Erweckung durch Emanuel Swedenborg', in *Swedenborg als Wegweiser in den Problemen des Daseins. Eine Schriftenreihe 1-4*, Leipzig, 1940-42. ['August Strindberg's Awakening through Emanuel Swedenborg'. Discusses the latter's role in the revival of Sg's religious belief during the Inferno crisis in No. II, pp. 29-52, but many of Fritsche's self-confident assertions about both Sg and Swedenborg are vitiated by his ignorance of the relevant primary material on this topic in Sg's literary remains and elsewhere, or even by his ignorance concerning precisely which of Swedenborg's works Sg knew]

[B8:31] Fritsche, Herbert, 'August Strindbergs Erweckung durch Emanuel Swedenborg', *Offene Tore* (Zürich): 13:2 (1969), pp. 1-22, 71-72. ['August Strindberg's Awakening through Emanuel Swedenborg'. Rpr. of **B8:30**]

[B8:32] Fuchs, J. F., 'Nordische Gottsucher. August Strindberg', *Lebe mit der Kirche* (Klosterneuburg bei Wien), 11 (1938-39), 39-45. ['Nordic Seekers after God. August Strindberg']

[B8:33] Goranov, Krastjo, 'Avgust Strindberg – velikomachenik i predtecha', *ABV*, 14 (3 April 1979), p. 3. ['August Strindberg – A Martyr and a Prophet']

[B8:34] Grevenius, Herbert, 'Var Strindberg kristen?', *Dramaten* (Stockholm), No. 34 (1973-74), 18-19. ['Was Strindberg a Christian?' Reflections on the nature of Sg's religious belief in conjunction with Ingmar Bergman's production of *Till Damaskus I* and *II* at Dramaten]

[B8:35] Gruchy, Alfred de, 'Auguste Strindberg', *Revue chrétienne* (Paris), 61 (1914), 296-298. [A Christian misreading of Sg's life which concludes, piously but erroneously, that 'at the end of his final long and painful illness, his family was reunited around his bed. He took the Bible on his bedside table, pressed it to his breast, and said: "My life is at an end. Here is the only truth!". Those were his last words']

[B8:36] Gunne, Birger, *Strindberg och kristendomen*, Stockholm: Studieförbundet Medborgarskolans rekvisionsbyrå, [1951]. 48 pp. ['Strindberg and Christianity'. A study guide and outline syllabus divided into ten short sections, each of which introduces a different aspect of Sg's faith and his relationship with religion for consideration. Gunne also suggests appropriate readings from his works under each heading, as well as questions to stimulate further discussion]

[B8:37] Håkanson, Nils, 'Två predikanter', *Nya Wermlands Tidningen* (Karlstad), 14 April 2000. ['Two Preachers'. On the role of religion in the life and work of Sg and hs fellow Swedish writer, Tage Aurell (1895-1976)]

[B8:38] Hans, Wilhelm, 'Strindberg auf dem Weg zu Christus und Buddha', *Der Kreis* (Hamburg), 2:2 (1925), 7-18. ['Strindberg on the Road to Christ and Buddha'. A biographical reading of Sg's religious development primarily in terms of his literary works, but linking him with Goethe, Nietzsche, Kierkegaard, Swedenborg, Maeterlinck, Ibsen's *Brand*, and the *fin-de-siècle* French author and occultist, Joséphin [Sâr] Péladan (1859-1918)]

[B8:39] Hans, Wilhelm, 'Strindbergs Religiosität', *Zeitschrift für deutsche Bildung* (Frankfurt am Main), 3 (1927), 357-381. ['Strindberg's Religious Sentiments']

[B8:40] Hans, Wilhelm, 'Strindbergs Weg nach Damaskus', *Euphorion. Zeitschrift für Literaturgeschichte* (Stuttgart), 28 (1927), 253-273. ['Strindberg's Road to Damascus'. A substantial discussion of Sg's rediscovery of Christianity in the later 1890s as documented in *Inferno* and *Legender*, and with reference to his earlier faith and works, including *Mäster Olof*, *Röda rummet*, *Gillets hemlighet*, and *Giftas*, his later attitudes to religion, and the impact of both Eduard von Hartmann's philosophical pessimism and Nietzsche's more radical philosophy in the 1870s and 1880s respectively]

[B8:41] Hans, Wilhelm, 'Strindbergs Weg nach Damaskus', *Zeitschrift für deutsche Bildung* (Frankfurt am Main), 3 (1927), 357-381. ['Strindberg's Road to Damascus']

[B8:42] Helander, Olle, 'Blev Strindberg kristen?', *Svenska Dagbladet* (Stockholm), 9 July 1951. ['Did Strindberg Become a Christian?' Helander reflects on the extent to which Sg really was (re-)converted to Christianity following his Inferno crisis and elicits a response from Jakob Kulling (9 July)]

[B8:43] Helander, Olle, 'Människan Strindberg', *Svensk kyrkotidning* (Stockholm), 1982, pp. 430-431. ['Strindberg the Man']

[B8:44] Helander, Olle, 'Strindberg på väg in i kristendom', *Svensk teologisk kvartalskrift* (Lund), 39 (1963), 53-56. ['Strindberg's Road to Christianity'. Traces Sg's path to an acceptance of Christianity. Maintains that in later life, Sg revolted against his own early rebellion and began to worship what he had previously attacked. His later religious outlook needs to be seen in the context of the traditions in which he grew up, e.g. Rosenian revivalism, and its roots are to be found in their dogmas concerning atonement and justification by faith. Sg rejected official Christianity and, having also rejected Nietzsche, he found temporary guidance in Swedenborg, in whose account of Hell he recognised his own experiences. But the latter provided no answer to the question of guilt, which tormented Sg profoundly, whereas his readings in the *Kabala* did. Gradually, however, he found his way to a belief based on dogma and in *En blå bok* he eventually comes closer to Rosenius than to Swedenborg, having moved away from individualism towards human communion]

[B8:45] Herwig, Franz, 'Das religiöse Gefühl in der zeitgenössischen Dichtung', 1–3, *Der Gral* (Trier), 16 (1921-22), pp. 194-201, 244-248, 360-363. ['The Religious Sense in Contemporary Literature'. Discusses Sg in the first of three articles surveying the contemporary scene, pp. 194-197]

[B8:46] Hjelm, Carl Gustaf, 'August Strindberg', in *C. G. Hjelms bästa*, 3 vols, Örebro: Evangelii press, 1980, Vol. 3, pp. 99-121. [Includes extracts from **B8:47**]

[B8:47] Hjelm, C[arl] G[ustaf], *August Strindbergs och Sven Lidmans väg till korset. Två monumentalgestalter i svensk omvändelsehistoria*, Örebro: Evangeliipress, 1944. 88 pp. ['August Strindberg's and Sven Lidman's Way to the Cross. Two Monumental Figures in the History of Religious Conversion in Sweden'. Details the exemplary aspects of Sg's religious conversion from a non-conformist perspective. Hjelm traces his progress from childhood belief to arrogant atheism, remorse, and the spiritual conflict of the Inferno crisis, before terminating in the humility of faith recovered in old age, a progress which is both dramatically individual in its personal nature and exemplary in its universal significance]

[B8:48] Hjelm, Carl Gustaf, *August Strindbergs och Sven Lidmans väg till korset. Två monumentalgestalter i svensk omvändelsehistoria*, Tredje upplagan, Örebro: Evangelii-press, 1971. [92] pp. [Third edition of **B8:47**]

[B8:49] Hjelm, Carl Gustaf, *August Strindbergs väg till korset: en monumentalgestalt i svensk omvändelsehistoria*, Örebro: Evangeliipress, 1985. 41 pp. ['August Strindberg's Road to the Cross: A Monumental Figure in the History of Swedish Conversion'. Previously published as part of **B8:47**]

[B8:50] Hülphers, E[rnst] W[alter], 'Strindberg och "makterna"', *Göteborgs Handels- och Sjöfartstidning*, 10 September 1927. ['Strindberg and "The Powers"'. Presents Sg's almost occult conviction that a man's life is subject to the corrective intervention of the unseen 'powers', demonstrating this with reference to *Inferno*, as well as to other works from the late 1890s and after]

[B8:51] Hülphers, E[rnst] W[alter], 'Strindberg und "Die Mächte"', *Theosophie* (Leipzig), 16 (1928), 67-70. ['Strindberg and "The Powers"'. German version of **B8:50**]

[B8:52] Kihlström, B[engt] I[ngmar], 'Vad Strindbergs psalmbok berättar', *Svenska Dagbladet* (Stockholm), 20 January 1946. ['What Strindberg's Hymnal has to Tell Us']

[B8:53] Kiss, Eszter [Szalczer], 'Strindberg och teosofin', 1-5, *Teosofiska Rörelsen* (Malmö), 54 (November-December 1988), pp. 144-149; 55 (January-February 1989), pp. 20-24; 56 (March-April 1989), pp. 41-49; 57 (May-June 1989), pp. 66-75; 58 (July-August 1989), pp. 96-99. Illus. ['Strindberg and Theosophy'. Examines Sg's familiarity with the precepts and images of Theosophy and traces both the impression it made on his writings and its implications for his later religious ideas. Kiss discusses several natural-scientific texts from the mid-1890s, including 'Solrosen' (The Sunflower), 'Stenarnes suckan' (The Sighing of the Stones), 'En blick mot rymden' (A Glance into Space), and *Antibarbarus*, notes his close link during this period with the Theosophist, Torsten Hedlund, from Göteborg, and the French alchemist, François Jollivet-Castelot, and documents his knowledge of Annie Besant and Helena Blavatsky, as well as Jakob Böhme. She refers mainly to *Inferno*, *Legender*, *Jardin des Plantes*, *Ett drömspel*, *En blå bok*, and *Taklagsöl*, and demonstrates how the latter is composed throughout with theosophical motifs in mind. Indeed, Kiss indicates the way in which numerous terms and images that Sg employed from the Inferno period onwards (e.g. Karma, reincarnation, a world of illusions, astral body, and astral life) derive from Theosophy.

In fact, she maintains that theosophical ideas and symbolism permeate several of Sg's major works, including *Till Damaskus*, *Advent*, *Påsk*, *Spöksonaten*, and *Stora landsvägen*]

[B8:54] Klein, Erich, 'Strindbergs letzte Meinungen', *Das heilige Feuer* (Paderborn), 10 (1922-23), 251-253. ['Strindberg's Last Standpoint']

[B8:55] Klein, Paul, 'Strindberg und der Katholizismus', *Stimmen der Zeit* (Freiburg), 104 (1923), 149-150. ['Strindberg and Catholicism']

[B8:56] Koepke, Ewald, *August Strindberg. Durch den Abgrund zur Individuation*, Hamburg: Hamburger Kulturverlag G.m.b.H., [1970]. 60 pp. ['August Strindberg: Through the Abyss of Individuation'. Offers a psycho-religious, Christian, and loosely Swedenborgian reading of Sg's life which refers to some of the autobiographical fictions, *Till Damaskus*, and *Ockulta dagboken*, as if they can be read unproblematically as reliable personal documents. Koepke also considers Sg's hostility to women and (very briefly) his interest in Nietzsche. 2nd edition Stuttgart, 1978]

[B8:57] Krause, Sabine, 'Die Religion des späten Strindberg im Spiegel von *Ensam* und Briefen aus der Zeit zwischen 1898 und 1904', *Ausblick* (Lübeck), 35:3-4 (1985), 15-21. ['The Religion of the Late Strindberg in the Light of *Ensam* and his Letters from the Period between 1899 and 1904'. Collates the numerous references to religion in both Sg's extensive correspondence and in *Ensam* in order to clarify his links with different strands of Christianity. Krause also considers the nature of his belief in God, his conception of guilt and atonement, and his notions of death and resurrection. She also comments on his attitude to Buddhism and Hinduism, as well as to the occult, mysticism, and Theosophy]

[B8:58] Krause, Sabine, 'Die Religion des späten Strindberg im Spiegel von *Ensam* und Briefen aus der Zeit zwischen 1898 und 1904', *Text & Kontext* (København & München), 13:2 (1985), 288-314. ['The Religion of the Late Strindberg in the Light of *Ensam* and his Letters from the Period between 1899 and 1904'. Rpr. of **B8:57**]

[B8:59] Krück von Poturzyn, M[aria] J[osepha], 'Auf dem Wege nach Damaskus. Zum 100 Geburtstag von August Strindberg am 22. Januar 1949', *Die Christengemeinschaft* (Stuttgart), 21 (1949), 23-25. ['On the Road to Damascus. For the 100th Anniversary of Strindberg's Birth, 22 January 1949'. Marks the centenary of Sg's birth with a religiously inflected account of his life as a painful progress towards a Saul-like conversion on the way to Damascus, following a period of disbelief and an interest in several anti-religious currents of contemporary thought]

[B8:60] Kulling, Jacob, *Att spjärna mot udden. En studie om Kristusgestaltens betydelse i Strindbergs religiösa utveckling*, Stockholm: Svenska Kyrkans Diakonistyrelses Bokförlag, 1950. 117 pp. ['To Kick against the Pricks. A Study of the Importance of the Figure of Christ in Strindberg's Religious Development'. Kulling examines the role allotted to Christ in Sg's thinking and religious beliefs with frequent reference to the account of his early evangelical-Lutheran belief in *Tjänstekvinnans son* and *Religiös renaissance*, and a range of comments on religion in 'Dygdens lön' (The Reward of Virtue) from *Giftas*, 'Utveckling' (Development) in *Svenska öden och äventyr*, *Sömngångarnätter*, 'Den romantiske klockaren på Rånö' (The Romantic Sexton on Rånö), *I havsbandet*, *Till Damaskus*, *Advent*, *Syndabocken*, and several other post-Inferno works. No attempt is made to distinguish between the words that may be ascribed to Sg and those which derive from his characters. Kulling comments briefly on Sg's almost pathological animosity towards religion during the 1880s and maintains that his final conversion represents a return to the belief of his forefathers. Indeed, he argues that Sg never entirely lost touch with the faith which he acquired in his childhood, and consequently is hardly concerned with *Inferno* or *Legender*. He insists that Christ, either in person or through a surrogate like Magnus Eriksson in *Folkungasagan*, was the only way Sg had of assuaging his guilt feelings by placing the emphasis on belief, as in childhood, rather than in deeds, as in the hubris of his early adulthood]

[B8:61] — Fredén, Gustaf, *Svenska Morgonbladet* (Stockholm), 23 February 1951.

[B8:62] — Fredén, Gustaf, *Årsbok för kristen humanism* (Uppsala), 13 (1951), p. 149.

[B8:63] — Hallsten, Olof, *Folklig kultur* (Stockholm), 16 (1951), 159-160.

[B8:64] — Levander, Hans, *Morgon-Tidningen* (Stockholm), 14 February 1951.

[B8:65] — Linnér, Sven, *Vår lösen* (Sigtuna), 42 (1951), 93-99.

[B8:66] — Norberg, Ivar, *Vår kyrka* (Stockholm), 90:29 (1951), 9-10.

[B8:67] — Stolpe, Sven, *Credo: Katolsk Tidskrift* (Uppsala), 32 (1951), 141-143.

[B8:68] — Wittrock, Ulf, *Upsala Nya Tidning*, 20 January 1951.

See also **A4:89**

[B8:69] Kulling, Jacob, 'Infernokrisens innebörd', *Credo: Katolsk Tidskrift* (Uppsala), 32 (1951), 107-120. ['The Meaning of the Inferno Crisis'. A religious interpretation of Sg's Inferno crisis, prompted by Gunnar Brandell's *Strindbergs Infernokris*, **B1:55**, which provokes a response from Brandell (pp. 163-167) and a rejoinder by Kulling (pp. 167-172)]

[B8:70] Lamm, Martin, *Strindberg och makterna*, Olaus Petriföreläsningar vid Uppsala Universitet, Uppsala: Svenska Kyrkans Diakonistyrelses Bokförlag, 1936. 163 pp. ['Strindberg and the Powers'. The text of four lectures on Sg's 'primitive' religious ideas and his conversion at the time of the Inferno crisis, which has its roots in his religious experiences from childhood on. Lamm discusses his early religiosity as described in *Tjänstekvinnans son* and as it was subsequently quickened or questioned by his reading of Viktor Rydberg, Kierkegaard, Ernest Renan, Theodore Parker, and others, including the Swedish non-conformist pastor, Carl Olof Rosenius (1816-1868). He investigates Sg's conception of Nemesis and mysticism, as articulated in the *Vivisektioner* of 1887, and notes its possible debt to Linnaeus's posthumous collection of observations, *Nemesis Divina*. He examines Sg's frame of mind immediately before and during the crisis, as documented by his letters and *Ockulta dagboken* and takes cognisance of his lively response to various strands of *fin-de-siècle* occultism,. These include Theosophy and Martinism, and the impact on Sg of Swedenborg, Albert de Rochas, 'Papus' [Gérard Encausse], and several activists in the occult sub-culture of the period to whom he often alludes both in his letters and scientific essays from the 1890s, and in *Inferno*, *Legender*, and *Ockulta dagboken*. Lamm also considers how the *Weltanschauung* that emerges from this period, with its stress on the active moral intervention of Nemesis and the world as an abode of necessary suffering governed by a God whose behaviour often seems to resemble that of the capricious 'powers' which he encountered during the Inferno crisis, manifests itself in a series of later works, including *Ett drömspel*, *Påsk*, *Gustav Adolf*, *Erik XIV*, *Svarta fanor*, and *Ensam*]

[**B8:71**] — A. Ö. [Anders Österling], *Stockholms-Tidningen*, 24 April 1936.

[**B8:72**] — B. B-m [Birger Bæckström], *Göteborgs Handels- och Sjöfartstidning*, 2 May 1936.

[**B8:73**] — Edfelt, Johannes, *Bonniers Litterära Magasin* (Stockholm), 5:7 (1936), 571-573.

[**B8:74**] — Erdmann, Nils, *Nya Dagligt Allehanda* (Stockholm), 29 April 1936.

[**B8:75**] — Es An [Elis Andersson], *Göteborgs-Posten*, 2 May 1936.

[**B8:76**] — G. A. [Gunnar Axberger], *Nordisk Tidskrift* (Stockholm), N. S. 12 (1936), p. 565.

[**B8:77**] — Håkansson, Hans Erik, *Litt. kritik*, 2 (1936), pp. 2, 6.

[**B8:78**] — Källström, Harald, *Janus* (Oslo), 3 (1936), pp. 65-67, 76.

[**B8:79**] — Källström, Harald, 'Strindberg och makterna', in *Människan först. Essayer*, Stockholm: P. A. Norstedt & Söners Förlag, 1937, pp. 151-160. [Rpr. of **B8:78**]

[**B8:80**] — Landquist, John, *Aftonbladet* (Stockholm), 16 May 1936.

[**B8:81**] — m [E. Hörnström], *Vår lösen* (Sigtuna), 28 (1937), 70-71.

[**B8:82**] — R. K. [Rafael (Kaarlo) Koskimies], *Valvoja-Aika*, (Helsinki), 14 (1936), 280-281.

[**B8:83**] — Schiller, Harald, *Sydsvenska Dagbladet* (Malmö), 13 May 1936.

[**B8:84**] — Selander, Sten, *Svenska Dagbladet* (Stockholm), 23 April 1936.

[**B8:85**] — Sjöberg, Ragnar, *Nya Argus* (Helsingfors), 29 (1936), p. 160-161.

[**B8:86**] — T. F-t [Torsten Fogelqvist], *Dagens Nyheter* (Stockholm), 4 May 1936.

[**B8:87**] — Vedel, Valdemar, *Dagens Nyheder* (Copenhagen), 5 June 1936.

See also **A4:46**

[**B8:87a**] Lamm, Martin, *Strindberg og magterna*, oversat fra svensk af Erik Henriques Bing, Copenhagen: Tågeliden, 2006. 100 pp. [Danish translation of **B8:70**]

[**B8:88**] Lannér, R., 'Några drag ur August Strindbergs religiösa utveckling', *Kyrklig Tidskrift* (Uppsala), 18 (1912), 410-439. ['Some Aspects of Strindberg's Religious Development'. Examines Sg's Evangelical childhood belief as well as the Inferno crisis and his subsequent eclectic faith]

[**B8:89**] Leibbrand, Werner, 'Strindbergs religiöse Metamorphosen', *Hochland* (München), 41 (1948-49), 123-137. ['Strindberg's Religious Metamorphosis'. Leibbrand examines how Sg's religious conversion is portrayed in the works of the Inferno period, concentrating mainly on *Inferno* and *Legender*]

[**B8:90**] Leufstedt, G[ustaf] J[oakim], *Jesus Kristus och August Strindberg. Tanker och åsigter*, Stockholm, 1884. 20 pp. ['Jesus Christ and August Strindberg. Thoughts and Views']

[**B8:91**] Lindahl, Per-Erik, 'Kulturkrock i maten. Den nya svenskarna', in *Från Braut-Anund till Vilhelm Ekelund*, Vinsløv: Kairos, 1999, pp. 101-105. ['Cultural Collision in Food. The New Swedes'. Presents two letters concerning religion, addressed to Sg by Eric Hermelin (1860-1944)]

[**B8:92**] Lindblad, Boris, 'Den unge Strindberg och religionen', *Stjärnljus* (Stockholm), 1942, pp. 16-18. ['The Young Strindberg and Religion'. Discusses Sg's early religious outlook, up to and including *Mäster Olof*]

[**B8:93**] Lindblom, Joh., 'Strindberg och teologin', *Sydsvenska Dagbladet* (Malmö), 2 June 1962. ['Strindberg and Theology']

[B8:94] Lindberg, H., 'Strindberg i hans förhållande till nutidens andliga problem', 1-2, *Axevalla. Tidning for Axevalla folkhögskoleförbund* (Axvall), 6:1 (1929), pp. 2-4; 6:2 (1929), pp. 2-3. ['Strindberg and His Relationship to Today's Spiritual Problems']

[B8:95] Lindberg, H., 'Strindberg i hans förhållande till nutidens andliga problem', *J.U.F. -bladet* (Stockholm), 10 (1930), 184-186. ['Strindberg and his Relationship to Today's Spiritual Problems']

[B8:96] Lindeberg, Giovanni, 'Strindberg och religion', *Religion och kultur* (Solna), 20 (1949), 84-93. ['Strindberg and Religion']

[B8:97] Lindeberg, Giovanni, 'En blick på Strindbergs religiösa utveckling', *Unga tankar* (Stockholm), 17 (1922), 56-58. ['A Glance at Strindberg's Religious Development'. Surveys the history of Sg's beliefs with reference mainly to *Mäster Olof*. The article is heavily indebted to the views of Nathan Söderblom in **B8:158** and **B8:160**, as well as Erik Hedén's biographical study, **R:942**]

[B8:98] Lindeberg, Giovanni, 'En blick på Strindbergs religiösa utveckling', in *Svenska diktarsilhuetter*, Stockholm: Oskar Eklunds Bokförlag, 1923, pp. 23-31. ['A Glance at Strindberg's Religious Development'. Rpr. of **B8:97**]

[B8:99] Linder, Eric Hjalmar, 'Från Strindberg till Lars Ahlin. Om den religiösa frågan i svensk diktning', in *Guds pennfäktare och andra essayer*, Stockholm: Natur & Kultur, 1955, pp. 87-104. ['From Strindberg to Lars Ahlin. On the Religious Question in Swedish Literature']

[B8:100] Linnér, Sven, 'Strindbergs Jacobskamp', *Vår lösen* (Sigtuna), 42 (1951), 86-100. ['Strindberg's Jacob's Struggle'. Examines Sg's religious conflicts at the time of the Inferno crisis. These were associated in his own mind with the Biblical account of Jacob's wrestling with the angel and became a central motif in *Inferno* as well as in the third of his autobiographical fictions from the Inferno years, *Jakob brottas*]

[B8:101] Ludvig, Nils [Nils Ludvig Olsson], 'Nemesis Divina', *Göteborgs-Posten*, 27 June 1967. [Probes Sg's deeply-rooted conception of Nemesis Divina, possibly derived in part from Linnaeus's posthumously published collection of observations on that theme but discusses it here mainly with reference to his correspondence post-1890 with the Lund lawyer and amateur musicologist, Nils Andersson]

[B8:102] Ludvig, Nils [Nils Ludvig Olsson], 'Nemesis Divina', in **B1:295**, *På vandring i Skåne*, pp. 46-53. [Rpr. of **B8:101**]

[B8:103] Lundmark, Knut, 'Strindberg och religionen', *Religion och kultur* (Solna), 14 (1943), 7-22. ['Strindberg and Religion'. Stresses the profoundly personal nature of Sg's religion, from his adolescent Pietism to the syncretic, self-fashioned faith which he evolved following the Inferno crisis, a faith that is far closer to the Old rather than the New Testament. According to Lundmark, Sg was hardly a true Christian even if, in his final years, he displayed certain affinities with nonconformism, but he often resembles an Old Testament prophet. Moreover, his religious development is logical and consequential, and by no means precludes his early political radicalism, as many admirers of his earlier works have assumed. Rpr. in **B1:296**, pp. 243-262]

[B8:104] Lux, Joseph August, 'Brief an eine Dame über den Dichter und Mystiker August Strindberg', *Kunst- und Kulturrat* (Salzburg), 1 (1919-20), pp. 21-23, 54-55, 80-82, 116-118, 145-147, 182-184. ['Letter to a Lady on the Writer and Mystic August Strindberg'.

Includes a discussion of Sg's metaphysics, his inner personality, and religious beliefs, as well as his attitude to women]

[B8:105] Mahrholz, Werner, 'Strindbergs Religiosität', *Die Propyläen* (München), 1919, pp. 193, 203. ['Strindberg's Religiosity']

[B8:106] Mahrholz, Werner, 'Über Strindbergs Religiosität', *Deutsche Monatshefte* (Leipzig), 18:9 (1918). ['On Strindberg's Religiosity']

[B8:107] Mahrholz, Werner, 'Über Strindbergs Religiosität', *Die Rheinlande* (Düsseldorf), 27 (1917), 225-228. ['On Strindberg's Religiosity']

[B8:108] Mahrholz, Werner, 'Strindberg und der Nihilismus', *Der unsichtbare Tempel* (München), 1 (1916), 25-38. ['Strindberg and Nihilism']

[B8:109] Mahrholz, Werner, 'Strindberg und der Nihilismus', *Das literarische Echo* (Berlin), 19 (1916), Sp. 299. ['Strindberg and Nihilism'. An extract from **B8:108**]

[B8:110] Mändl, Hans, 'Carl Larsson, August Strindberg und der Reinkarnationsgedanke', *Das Goetheanum* (Dornach), 45 (1966), pp. 11-13, 20-21. ['Carl Larsson, August Strindberg and the Idea of Reincarnation']

[B8:111] Mändl, Hans, 'Strindberg und die Karma-Idee', *Das Goetheanum* (Dornach), 45 (1966), 26-27. ['Strindberg and the Idea of Karma']

[B8:112] Mereschkowskii, Dimitri, 'Prophetentum und Provokation', in *Auf dem Weg nach Emmaus*, München, 1919, pp. 153-160. ['Prophecy and Provocation']

[B8:113] Möhlig, Karl, 'Strindberg und sein Weltbild', *Der Gral* (Trier), 21 (1926-27), 224-231. ['Strindberg and his World View']

[B8:114] Möhlig, Karl, 'Strindbergs geistiger Entwicklungsgang bis zu seiner Annäherung an den Katholizismus. Ein Beitrag zur Strindbergforschung', *Die Bücherwelt* (Bonn), 22 (1925), pp. 3-11, 57-65. ['Strindberg's Spiritual Development Prior to his Encounter with Catholicism. A Contribution to Strindberg Research']

[B8:115] Möhlig, Karl, *Strindbergs Weltanschauung. I: Strindberg und der Katholizismus*, Mit einem Titelbild, Elberfeld: Bergland-Verlag, 1923. XV+320 pp. ['Strindberg's *Weltanschauung*. I: Strindberg and Catholicism'. Möhlig offers a wide-ranging examination of Sg's association with Catholicism, taking into account what is considered to be his fundamentally religious psyche, the general relationship of Swedish Protestantism to Catholicism, and his thinking on a number of metaphysical and religious issues, including the role of Christ, the Papacy, the Bible, Prayer, the Clergy, the Sacraments, and the doctrines of Hell and Grace. He concludes with a summary of the syncretic set of beliefs that Sg adopted following the Inferno crisis and places roughly equal authority on works of presumed autobiography, like *Inferno* and *Tjänstekvinnans son*, and manifest fiction, like *Till Damaskus*]

[B8:116] — Muckermann, Friedrich, 'Dichtung und Leben', *Der Gral* (Trier), 17 (1922-23), 313-314. ['Poetry and Life']

See also **A4:52, A4:65**

[B8:117] Muckermann, Friedrich, 'Strindberg, Sphinx und Weihnachtskind', *Der Gral* (Trier), 18 (1923-24), 115-117. ['Strindberg, Sphinx, and Christmas Child']

[B8:118] N. Hb-g, 'Strindbergs religiositet. En psykologisk studie', *Skånska Dagbladet* (Malmö), 21 May 1912. ['Strindberg's Religiosity. A Psychological Study']

[B8:119] Norman, Nils, *Den unge Strindberg och väckelserörelsen*, Malmö: Gleerups, 1953. 362 pp. ['The Young Strindberg and the Revivalist Movement'. On Sg's youthful involvement with the evangelical, revivalist movement in 1860s Sweden, his relationship to his pietistic mother, and his religiously inflected, adolescent friendship with his more mature neighbour, Edla Hejkorn, as well as the influence of his confirmation teacher, Gustav Gottfrid Flyborg. Norman provides a detailed account of Sg's early religious beliefs and inclinations, and the importance which the idea of apostasy, so prominent in *Mäster Olof*, held for him in both his life and work. He successfully argues the importance of religion in Sg's emotional and mental world, and recognises that the role of guilt, suffering, penance, and punishment was more fundamental during his early years than Martin Lamm in **B1:205a/205b** or Allan Hagsten in **B1:151** have indicated. Norman discusses the relevance of these ideas for *Fritänkaren*, *Den fredlöse* and *Mäster Olof*, and relates them to Sg's reading of Ibsen's *Brand*, Byron's *Manfred*, Kierkegaard (especially in *Enten-Eller*), Oehlenschläger, and Viktor Rydberg, as well as the repressive German educationalist, Carl Kapff, the American theologian Theodore Parker (1810-1860), and the Swedish non-conformist pastor, Carl Olof Rosenius (1816-1868). Doctoral thesis. No bibliography]

[B8:120] — Ahlenius, Holger, 'Unga snillen', *Bonniers Litterära Magasin* (Stockholm), 22:8 (1953), 547-548. ['The Young Genius']

[B8:121] — Brandell, Gunnar, *Svenska Dagbladet* (Stockholm), 11 June 1953.

[B8:122] — Dahlbäck, O., *Jönköpings-Posten*, 3 February 1954.

[B8:123] — Fredén, Gustaf, *Svenska Morgonbladet* (Stockholm), 22 August 1953.

[B8:124] — G. B[erggren], *Biblioteksbladet* (Stockholm), 38 (1953), p. 538.

[B8:125] — Grönberg, A., *Dala-Demokraten* (Falun), 4 February 1954.

[B8:126] — Hagsten, Allan, *Samlaren* (Uppsala), 34 (1953), pp. 113-121.

[B8:127] — Landquist, John, *Aftonbladet* (Stockholm), 20 May 1953.

See also **A4:68**

[B8:128] — Landquist, John, 'Varför tålde Strindberg inte Bellman?' *Aftonbladet* (Stockholm), 20 May 1953. ['Why Couldn't Strindberg Stand Bellman?'. Discusses Sg's lifelong antipathy for the Swedish Gustavian poet, Carl Michael Bellman (1740-1795), while endorsing Norman's criticism of Martin Lamm for not taking Sg's relationship with Christianity seriously enough in **B8:70** and **B1:205a/B1:205b**. Landquist also comments on *Mäster Olof*, *Fritänkaren*, *Det nya riket*, and *Tjänstekvinnans son*]

[B8:129] — Landquist, John, 'Varför tålde Strindberg inte Bellman?' in Solveig Landquist, red., **B1:248**, *John Landquist om Strindberg personen och diktaren*, Stockholm: Legenda, 1984, pp. 184-187. ['Why Couldn't Strindberg Tolerate Bellman?' Rpr. of **B8:128**]

[B8:130] — Lindberger, Örjan, *Dagens Nyheter* (Stockholm), 2 July 1953.

[B8:131] — Linder, Erik Hjalmar, *Årsbok för kristen humanism* (Uppsala), 10 (1954), pp. 163-165.

[B8:132] — Linder, Erik Hjalmar, *Stockholms-Tidningen*, 5 June 1953.

[B8:133] — Lindqvist, Sven, *Arbetaren* (Stockholm), 24 September 1953.

[B8:134] — Nils Ludvig [Nils Ludvig Olsson], *Ystads Allehanda*, 28 July 1962.

[B8:135] — Rinman, Sven, *Göteborgs Handels- och Sjöfartstidning*, 29 July 1953.

[B8:136] — St[olpe], S[ven], *Credo: Katolsk Tidskrift* (Uppsala), 34 (1953), 141-142.

[B8:137] — Wittrock, Ulf, *Upsala Nya Tidning*, 11 August 1953.

[B8:138] Oljelund, Ivan, 'Job-Strindberg', *Social-Demokraten* (Stockholm), 13 May 1922. [Examines Sg's self-identification with Job apropos the 10th anniversary of his death]

[B8:139] Oljelund, Ivan, 'Strindbergs religiositet', *Frihet* (Stockholm), 1922:6, pp. 6-7. ['Strindberg's Religiosity'. Reflections by a Swedish working-class author]

[B8:140] Overmans S. J., Jakob, 'Mit Strindberg nach Damaskus', *Stimmen der Zeit* (Freiburg), 96 (1919), 75-84. ['With Strindberg to Damascus'. A Catholic reading of Sg's religious experiences, focusing particularly on his inclination to convert to Catholicism in *Inferno*]

[B8:141] Prilipp, Beda, 'Strindberg als Mystiker', *März* (München), 6:4 (1912), 9-15. [Strindberg as a Mystic']

[B8:142] 'Qvidam Qvidamsson' [Pseudonym of Nils Peter Svensson], 'Mystikern Strindberg', *Politiken* (Copenhagen), 20 October 1918. ['Strindberg the Mystic']

[B8:143] Röttger, Karl, 'Strindberg und die Krise des modernen Menschen', *Die Christliche Welt* (Marburg), 38 (1924), Sp. 642-651. ['Strindberg and the Crisis of Modern Man']

[B8:144] Rydsjö, Daniel, 'Två stjärnor. (En episod i Strindbergs religiösa utveckling)', *Kristendom och vår tid* (Lund), 26:9-10 (1931), 273-277. ['Two Stars. (An Episode in Strindberg's Religious Development)'. Examines Sg's differences with Nietzsche and his engagement with Nietzschean ideas in *I havsbandet* (1890), in comparison with Viktor Rydberg criticism of Nietzsche in his poems 'Livslust och livsleda' (Delight in Life and Deep Depression) and 'Betlehems stjärna' (The Star of Bethlehem) in *Vapensmeden* (The Weapon Smith, 1891). The latter offers a direct, Christian response to the Pagan, or classical, image of Hercules' star as it is evoked at the close of Sg's novel]

[B8:145] Salewski, Wilhelm, 'Das Strindbergsschicksal. Eine Adventsgeschichte', *Die Christengemeinschaft*, (Stuttgart), 4:9 (1927), 262-270. ['Strindberg's Destiny. An Advent Story'. An anthroposophical reading of Sg's life and work]

[B8:146] Salewski, W[ilhelm], 'Auf dem Wege nach Damaskus. Zum 100. Geburtstag von August Strindberg am 22 Januar 1949', *Die Christengemeinschaft* (Stuttgart), 21 (1949), 25-26. ['On the Road to Damascus. For the 100th Anniversary of Strindberg's Birth, 22 January 1949'. Reflections on Sg's rediscovery of his faith during the Inferno crisis, in commemoration of the centenary of his birth]

[B8:147] Salewski, W[ilhelm], 'Auf dem Wege nach Damaskus', *Die Christengemeinschaft* (Stuttgart), 34 (1962), 150-152. ['On the Road to Damascus'. Seeks to account for Sg's rediscovery of his faith and its significance for his spiritual well-being]

[B8:148] Salewski, W[ilhelm], 'August Strindbergs Ringen um den Menschen', 1-3, *Das Goetheanum* (Dornach), 6 (1927), pp. 324-326, 331-333, 341-342. ['August Strindberg's Struggle for Mankind'. An anthroposophical interpretation of Sg's destiny which Salewski considers was that of a Priest of Isis, i.e. someone endowed with cosmic wisdom]

[B8:149] Salewski, Wilhelm, 'Strindbergs livsöde', *Antroposofisk tidskrift* (Stockholm), 7 (1930), 193-205. ['Strindberg's Destiny'. Attempts an anthroposophical reading of Sg's destiny based mainly upon data culled from *Till Damaskus*, *Legender*, and *Jakob brottas*, which are read as credible accounts of Sg's life and experiences, not works of literature. Swedish version of **B8:148**]

[B8:150] Sandén, Kurt, 'Strindberg och korset', *Smålandsposten* (Växjö), 31 March 1958. ['Strindberg and the Cross']

[B8:151] Sanner, B. Fr., 'Strindbergs väg ur atheism. En litterär studie till Strindbergs religiösa utveckling', *Religion och kultur* (Solna), 6 (1935), 79-112. ['Strindberg's Path from Atheism. A Literary Study of Strindberg's Religious Development'. Traces Sg's religious development with reference to his works, including both the plays and his prose fiction]

[B8:152] Schelzig, Alfred, 'August Strindbergs religiöser Weg', *Eckart* (Berlin), 22 (1952-53), 263-267. ['August Strindberg's Religious Path']

[B8:153] Schönebeck, Erich, *Strindberg als Erzieher*, Entschiedene Schulreform, heft 3, Berlin: Oldenburg & Co. Verlag, [1923]. [70] pp. ['Strindberg as Educator'. Primarily concerned with Sg the God seeker, or the seeker after enlightenment, who sought answers to the spiritual questions that troubled him in Nietzscheanism and Socialism as well as in several religions. Schönebeck comments on his early pietism, his attitude to women, and the Faustian thirst for knowledge which is manifest in his abiding interest in science. But he bases his biographical observations on Sg's own autobiographical fictions, without treating them as such, and makes only superficial comments on a number of his works, including *Tjänstekvinnans son, Till Damaskus, Götiska rummen,* and *I havsbandet*]

[B8:154] — Schulhof, H[edwig], *Internationale Zeitschrift für Individualpsychologie* (Vienna), 2:4 (1923-24), 32-33.

[B8:155] Selling, Magnus, 'Strindberg och religionen. En studie', *Kristendomen och vår tid* (Lund), 24:5-6 (1929), 145-156. ['Strindberg and Religion. A Study'. Argues that Sg is everywhere visible in his works which may consequently be taken as evidence in an assessment of his religious beliefs. God, for Sg, is primarily the Old Testament Jehovah, who may be related to Nietzsche's contemporary image of strength, the superman, but his manic depressive personality means that Sg oscillates between elation and dejection, pride and despondency, and consequently he cannot embrace Nietzsche's ideal but must complement it with a fear of hubris. Religion for Sg is associated with persecution mania. He is not a mystic (see his rejection of Theosophy in *Inferno*), and his stress on religious freedom is in fact an argument against the Catholicism, with which he sometimes appears to flirt. Selling refers frequently to *En blå bok* as well as to *Inferno* and *Legender*, notes his admiration for the French novelist, dramatist, and mystic Joséphin [Sâr] Péladan (1859-1918)], and comments on some of the events in Paris during the 1890s that turned Sg back towards religion, but he does not discuss his childhood faith, earlier beliefs, or atheism]

[B8:156] Sjöholm, Öyvind, 'Med Strindbergs psalmbok i hand', *Ärkestiftet* (Uppsala), 1982-83, pp. 102-111. ['With Strindberg's Hymnal in Hand']

[B8:157] Söderblom, Nathan, 'Skuld och försoning', in Gunnar Brandell, red., **B1:82**, *Synpunkter på Strindberg*, pp. 9-17. ['Guilt and Atonement'. Rpr. of **B8:160**]

[B8:158] Söderblom, Nathan, 'Strindberg och makterna', *Stockholms Dagblad*, 22 January 1909. ['Strindberg and the Powers'. Maintains that Sg can never settle comfortably into a single point of view but stresses the 'primitive' element in his belief in Nemesis and what he called 'makterna' (the powers), a pattern of belief which in his case was nevertheless united with an elevated, creative intelligence, and a fine and sensitive soul. According to Söderblom, who knew Sg in Paris during the 1890s before he (Söderblom) became Archbishop of Sweden, no one has depicted the experiences of someone who has gone astray and fallen into the hands of these powers better than Sg. He also argues that every line Sg wrote was autobiographical and that among self-portraitists, Sg distinguishes himself by his unwavering desire to see clearly even in the most burdensome circumstances. In this he is superior to Kierkegaard. Sg therefore writes with his own heart's blood, and those who come off worst when he portrays them are always in some respect the authors of their own misfortune. It is Söderblom's view that his much maligned novel, *Svarta fanor*, will last as long as Sg's other monumental works, *Röda rummet* and *Tjänstekvinnans son*]

[B8:159] Söderblom, Nathan, 'Strindberg und die "Mächte"', *Die Gegenwart* (Berlin), 88 (1916), 3-6. ['Strindberg and the "Powers"'. German translation of **B8:158**]

[B8:160] Söderblom, Nathan, 'Till frågan om Strindberg och religionen', *Bonniers månadshäften* (Stockholm), 1912:6, pp. 435-441. Illus. ['On the Question of Strindberg and Religion'. A series of sympathetic and perceptive reflections on Sg's 'fundamentally Christian' religious temper which form the text of the address delivered at Sg's funeral by the eminent Swedish theologian and archbishop, who had known him in Paris during the 1890s and was familiar with his literary works. Söderblom both questions and confirms the 'primitive' dimension of Sg's religion, comments on the nature of his faith as evidenced by his hymnal and the other theological writings that were found on his bedside table at his death, and affirms that even when he denied them during the 1880s, God and religion were always central to his experience. According to Söderblom, even Sg's attacks on Sven Hedin, Ellen Key, and others in the recent literary and political feud derive from his religious beliefs]

[B8:161] Söderblom, Nathan, 'Till frågan om Strindberg och religionen', *Svenskars fromhet*, 2 vols, Med förord av Anna Söderblom, Stockholm, 1933, Vol. 2, pp. 287-306. ['On the Question of Strindberg and Religion'. Rpr. of **B8:158** and **B8:160**]

[B8:162] Söderblom, Nathan, *Tal och skrifter. Uppsatser och föredrag*, 5 vols, Malmö: Världslitteraturen, 1930. [Includes a Rpr. of **B8:160** and other comments on Sg]

[B8:163] Sprengler, Joseph, 'Strindbergs religiöse Tragik', *Literarischer Handweiser* (Freiburg), 60 (1924), 193-196. ['Strindberg's Religious Tragedy'. Discusses Ludwig Marcuse's *Strindberg: Das Leben einer tragischen Seele*, **R:1465**, and Karl Möhlig's *Strindbergs Weltanschauung*, **B8:115**]

[B8:164] Steiger, Edgar, 'Nach Damascus?', *Die Glocke* (München), 2:1 (1916), 461-467. ['To Damascus?']

[B8:165] Stolpe, Sven, 'Strindbergs religionen än en gång', *Göteborgs-Posten*, 23 April 1950. ['Strindberg's Religion Revisited']

[B8:166] Sundström, Erland, 'Strindberg och gudstron', 1-2, *Dagen* (Stockholm), 17 and 18 April 1985. ['Strindberg and the Belief in God']

[B8:167] S. W—l [Sven Wetterdal], 'Strindbergs väg till Damaskus', *Svenska Tidningsutgivare föreningen* (Stockholm), 17 February 1956. ['Strindberg's Road to Damascus']

[B8:168] Vegel, Jon, 'August Strindberg', *Kirke og kultur* (Oslo), 54 (1949), 24-37. [Reflects on Sg's life and work from a Christian perspective in conjunction with the centenary of his birth]

[B8:169] Waack, Karl, 'Strindberg als Mystiker. Eine Studie', *Psychische Studien* (Leipzig), 44 (1917), pp. 308-312, 364-369. ['Strindberg as a Mystic. A Study']

[B8:170] Waschnitius, Viktor, Der religiöse Gehalt in der neueren nordischen Dichtung', *Deutsch -Nordische Zeitschrift* (Breslau), 2 (1929), 133-148. ['The Religious Element in Recent Nordic Literature'. Examines the place accorded religion in Scandinavian literature during the preceding half century. Touches only briefly on Sg, p. 146]

[B8:171] Wolfram, E[lise], 'Der Mensch August Strindberg im Spiegel seiner Werke und das Problem seines Lebens als Zeitproblem', in *Das Reich* (München), 4 (1919), 177-196. ['Strindberg the Man Reflected in his Works, and the Problem of his Life as the Problem of the Age'. Primarily concerned with the religious mind set of Sg's 'tragic being' as it is delineated in *Till Damaskus, Ett drömspel, Kronbruden, Brott och brott*, and *Dödsdansen*, which depict both Sg's struggle with the corrective, chastising force that he called 'the powers' and chronicle his search for a new, moral way of life]

[B8:172] Wolfram, Elise, 'Der Mensch August Strindberg im Spiegel seiner Werke und das Problem seines Lebens als Zeitproblem', in *Das Übersinnliche in Kunst und Mythus*, Konstantz, 1919, pp. 118-137. ['Strindberg the Man Reflected in his Works, and the Problem of his Life as the Problem of the Age'. Rpr. of **B8:171**]

[B8:173] Wolfram, Elise, 'Mennesket August Strindberg og hans livsproblem som tidsproblem', *Janus* (Oslo), 4 (1936), pp. 632-649. ['Strindberg the Man and the Problem of his Life as a Problem of the Age'. Norwegian version of **B8:171**]

[B8:174] Zinkernagel, Franz, 'Strindberg und das religiöse Problem', 1-2, *Die Christliche Welt* (Marburg), 35 (1921), Sp. 74-78, 98-105. ['Strindberg and the Problem of Religion']

See also **A4:89, B1:8, B1:55, B1:134, B1:296, B1:364, B1:437, B2:86, B2:335, B2:380, C1:116, C1:286, C1:543, C1:569, C1:697, C1:729, C1:743, C1:945, C1:1282, D2:203, D2:271, D2:734, D2:805, E25:93, E41:145, F1:14, F1:41, F1:70, F5:107, R:1146, R:1466, R:1606, R:1679, R:2378, S:182, V:28, V:40, V:53, V:112, V:165**

B9. The Woman Question

[*Although Sg's portrayal of women and his views on marriage and gender relationships are frequently discussed at length in many general studies of his work and accounts of his life, as well as in discussions of individual novels, stories, and plays (particularly* Giftas *and the naturalist dramas), this section brings together much of the vast literature regarding his attitudes to women, as they are expressed in the essays he devoted to the topic and those literary works in which he (mis)represents them. This was one of the principal ways in which Sg impacted most immediately upon his contemporaries, and some of their, often equally polemical, responses feature here. But the topic is also relevant to many comparative studies of the literature and writers of the Scandinavian Modern Breakthrough listed in section* **C1**, *and his reputation as a woman-hater and anti-Ibsenite misogynist frequently coloured his early reception outside Sweden in significant ways. Likewise, Strindberg's reputation for misogyny was also noted in many of the obituaries and other comments on his life and work that appeared in the months immediately following his death in 1912*]

[B9:1] Abramovich, I. Ia, *Zhenschchina i mir muzhskoi kul'tury. Mirovoe tvorchestvo i polovaia liubov'*, Moscow: Svobodnyi Put', 1913. 113 pp. [Discusses Sg, pp. 16-19, 21, 56-59, and 89 in a study of woman and the world of male culture: world art and sexual love. E.869]

[B9:2]: Adams, Ann-Charlotte Gavel, 'Vetenskap och manlighet', in Anna Cavallin and Anna Westerståhl Stenport, red., **B9:78**, *Det gäckande könet: Strindberg och genusteori*, pp. 69-79. ['Science and Masculinity'. Compares Sg, the author of numerous scientifically ambitious texts during the 1990s, not only with Faust but also the protagonist of Mary Shelley's *Frankenstein* in a study which illustrates the identification of scientism with masculinity in *Fadren*, *I havsbandet*, and *Inferno*. The failure of the dream of scientific conquest depicted in *Inferno* presages a manner of reconciliation with the (eternal) feminine in *Legender* and other later works]

[B9:3] Ahlström, Stellan, 'De mötes i sitt kvinnohat', *Vecko-Journalen* (Stockholm), 1948, No. 23, pp. 24, 28-29. ['They are at One in their Hatred of Women'. Comments on Sg's friendship with the painter Paul Gauguin and the consanguinity they enjoyed, not least in their opinions concerning women]

[B9:4] Ajalbert, Jean, 'L'Ennemi des Femmes', *Gil Blas* (Paris), 15 January 1895. ['The Enemy of Women'. Prompted by the newly published translation of Sg's essay 'L'Infériorité de la femme' (The Inferiority of Women) in *La Revue Blanche*, 7 January 1895]

[B9:5] Aleksijević, Vlastoje D., 'Feminizam Avgusta Strindberga', *Život i rad* (Novi Sad), 27:8 (1938), 289-291. ['August Strindberg's Feminism'. R.574]

[B9:6] Andreas-Salomé, Lou, *Strindberg & de vrouw*, ingeleid en vertaald door Rody Chamuleau, Geschriften van het Lou Salomé Genootschap 11, Oosterbeek: Bosbespers, 1985. 25 pp. ['Strindberg and Woman'. Dutch translation of **B9:7** with a short introduction by the translator, Chamuleau]

[B9:7] Andreas-Salomé, Lou, 'Zum Bilde Strindbergs', *Das literarische Echo* (Berlin), 17 (1915), Sp. 645-653. [Presents a rather more nuanced view of Sg's works than earlier comments on his work and personality by the same author, who regards him as a latent homosexual]

[B9:8] Anon, 'The Anti-Feminist Genius of August Strindberg', *Current Literature* (New York), 50 (March 1911), pp. 316-317.

[B9:9] Anon, 'Les défenseurs de la femme. Sur un article de M. Strindberg', *Gil Blas* (Paris), 1 February 1895. ['The Defenders of Woman. On an Article by M[onsieur] Strindberg'. Publishes the responses to a questionnaire prompted by the recently published French translation of Sg's essay 'L'Infériorité de la femme' (On the Inferiority of Women) with contributions from several eminent French authors including Alexandre Dumas *fils*, Joris-Karl Huysmans, Alphonse Daudet, and Maurice Barrès, all of whom speak up on behalf of woman, and sometimes account for their admiration for them by taking exception to Sg's hostility on national grounds]

[B9:10] Anon, 'Der Frauenfeind', *Laibacher Zeitung* (Ljubljana), 9 December 1886, Sp. 2322. ['The Enemy of Women'. Among the earliest presentations of Sg to a Slovenian readership]

[B9:11] Anon, 'A Literary Woman Hater', *Literature* (New York), 19 (2 September 1899), p. 278.

[B9:12] †, 'Matriarkatet', *Politiken* (Copenhagen), 8 March 1887. ['The Matriarchy'. An anonymous intervention in an ongoing discussion in Denmark on the status of women, to which Sg frequently contributed during the period he spent there in 1887-89]

[B9:13] Anon, '[On Strindberg's Essay "Woman's Inferiority to Man"]', *Knizhki 'Nedeli'* (St Petersburg) 1893:4 (April), pp. 238-253. [Discusses Sg's views on women, pp. 243-248. E.688]

[B9:14] Anon, 'The Swedish Ibsen', *Current Literature* (New York), 39 (1905), 437-438. [Suggests that, as a misogynist, Sg surpasses both Schopenhauer and Nietzsche. His idea of woman is exemplified by *Kristina*, which the author considers a faithful portrait of Sg's third wife, Harriet Bosse]

[B9:15] Anon, 'Warum wurde Strindberg Frauenfeind', *Neue Wiener Journal* (Vienna), 1918, Sp. 8882. ['Why Strindberg became a Misogynist']

[B9:16] Apelkvist, Björn, 'Mamma först och främst. Om Strindbergs kvinnnosyn', *Horisont* (Vasa), 51:1 (2004), 35-41. Illus. ['Mummy First of All: On Strindberg's View of Women'. Apelkvist reflects on Sg's fixation with the mother's role as woman's primary business, with reference to *Giftas* as a counter-blast to Ibsen's *A Doll's House*, *En dåres försvarstal*, *Fadren*, and (principally) the one-acter *Moderskärlek*. He suggests that this fixation is responsible for his demonisation of any woman who deviates from the mother's role as the breeding ground of the species, and argues for the decisive influence of the dramatisation of Zola's *Thérèse Raquin* and its psychological perspective for the development of Sg's naturalism. Apelkvist reads *Moderskärlek* as a profoundly ironic play in which, as in *Oedipus*, the principal theme is the exposure of the truth; it is a miniature detective story about women's emancipation in which the daughter, Hélène, ultimately sees through her mother's irresponsible falsehood. Together with her sister, Lisen, Hélène and her mother exemplify the complexity with which Sg as dramatist could endow his female figures]

[B9:17] Arnér, Sivar, 'En tanke om Strindbergs kvinnohat', *Bonniers Litterära Magasin* (Stockholm), 25:9 (1956), 731-732. ['A View on Strindberg's Misogyny'. Observes that there is surprisingly little misogyny in *Giftas*; the theories advanced in the Foreword and the misogyny of Sg's other essays on the Woman Question are replaced by the sympathetic realities of fiction]

[B9:18] Asenijeff, Elsa, 'Strindberg tout court und Fräulein Dr. Ella Mensch', *Das neue Magazin für Literatur* (Leipzig), 73:2 (1904), 810-812. [A response to Mensch's comments in **B9:188**]

[B9:19] Bade, Patrick, *Femme Fatale: Images of Evil and Fascinating Women*, London: Ash & Grant, 1979, pp. 23-27. Illus. [Argues that, together with Ibsen and Munch, Sg depicts 'the conflict of the sexes and the destructive power of women in a modern bourgeois domestic setting.' Bade's study offers a reductive biographical reading in which Sg is portrayed as an extreme example of 'the almost schizophrenic attitude of many 19th-Century men towards women']

[B9:20] Baillon, Jacques, 'Monter un auteur "misogyne"', *l'Avant-Scène*, Théâtre (Paris), No. 670 (15 May 1980), pp. 5-6. Illus. ['To become a "Misogynous" Writer'. A comment on Sg's misogyny by the director of a production of *Fordringsägare* at the Petit-Odéon, Paris, performed in a translation by Jacques Robnard]

[B9:21] Balzamo, Elena, 'De bon usage de la misogynie', in **B9:245**, *August Strindberg et les femmes*, Paris: Centre culturel suédois, 2000, pp. 25-34. ['Making Good Use of Misogyny'. Maintains with reference to numerous literary and non-literary texts, including *Fadren, Pelikanen*, and *Giftas*, that Sg's misogyny was both more various and a great deal more subtle than is generally appreciated. It was also deployed quite inconsistently and for a variety of ends, particularly where his fictional works are concerned. Indeed, Balzamo argues that *Giftas* is one of only five wholly misogynist texts in his *œuvre*, and is thus clearly at odds in its tenor with many other works such as *Påsk* or *Ett drömspel*. In fact, Sg's anti-feminism is one of the elements which helps to establish order and prevent the Sgian edifice from collapsing; it therefore has a vital literary function, which is its supreme justification, if one were needed]

[B9:22] Baüer, Henri, 'Strindberg et de l'infériorité', 1-2, '*L'Écho de Paris*, 2 and 4 February 1895. ['Strindberg and On the Inferiority'. Defends Sg against criticism of 'L'Infériorité de la femme' (On the Inferiority of Women) in *La Revue Blanche*, 7 January 1895. By the dedicatee of the first French edition of *En dåres försvarstal*]

[B9:23] Beck, Steen, 'Moderne maend', *Nord Nytt* (Lyndby), 71-72 (1988), pp. 157-177, 191-192. ['Modern Men'. Compares the representation of woman in the work of Goethe, Kierkegaard, and the painter Gustav Klimt, as well as Sg. Summary in English]

[B9:24] Berendsohn, Walter A[rthur], 'August Strindberg och kvinnorna', *Värld och vetande* (Göteborg), 5 (1965), 199-208. ['August Strindberg and Women'. Surveys Sg's attitude to the women in his life and how they (principally Siri von Essen, Frida Uhl, Harriet Bosse, and his mother) are represented in his works]

[B9:25] Berendsohn, Walter A[rthur], 'August Strindberg og Kvinderne', *Vor Viden* (Copenhagen), 1965-66:8, pp. 498-512. ['August Strindberg and Women'. Danish version of **B9:24**]

[B9:26] Berendsohn, Walter A[rthur], 'August Strindberg und die Frauen', 1-2, *Lübeckische Blätter*, 125 (1965), pp. 132-135, 147-150. ['August Strindberg and Women'. German version of **B9:24**]

[B9:27] Berendsohn, Walter A[rthur], 'August Strindberg und die Frauen', *Mitteilungsblatt des Irgun Olej Mercas Europa*, 1965. ['August Strindberg and Women'. A further German version of **B9:24**]

[B9:28] Berendsohn, Walter A[rthur], *August Strindberg und die Frauen*, Dortmunder Vorträge 85, Dortmund: Kulturamt der Stadt Dortmund, 1968. 22 pp. ['August Strindberg and Women'. An expanded version in German of **B9:24**]

[B9:29] Bigeon, Maurice, 'Auguste Strindberg et les femmes émancipées', in *Les Révoltés Scandinaves*, Paris, 1894, pp. [167]-205. ['August Strindberg and Emancipated Women'. An account of Sg's position on the Woman Question, partly inspired by Sg himself. Prompted by Sg, Bigeon argues that the latter may have fallen foul of Amazonian fury and been forced into exile from Sweden, but he notes that the opposing army of emancipationists has not been without its defeats as well. Thus, 'Fru Benediksen' [sic] has committed suicide while 'Fru Ahlgren' [sic] has been subdued by an Italian nobleman. Bigeon discusses *Fadren*, *Fröken Julie*, and *Fordringsägare*, and relates the contemporary Scandinavian debate about women and marriage to current French perceptions of woman as articulated by Baudelaire and Jules Michelet. He also introduces an extended extract from Sg's long short story 'Samvetskval' (Remorse) from *Utopier i verkligheten* to a French readership]

[B9:30] Boëthius, Ulf, *Strindberg och kvinnofrågan till och med Giftas I*, Stockholm: Prisma, 1969. Illus. 528 pp. ['Strindberg and the Woman Question: Up to and Including *Getting Married*'. Boëthius charts the evolution of Sg's ideas about women and their sexual and social roles from his sympathetic portrayal of their emancipatory desires in several early works to the clearly apparent hostility in the first volume of *Giftas*. He demonstrates how Sg's notions changed in response to his personal situation and documents the debate about the nature and status of women both in contemporary Sweden and within a Scandinavian context that was dominated during the 1870s and 1880s by the writings of Ibsen, Bjørnson, and Georg Brandes. Boëthius discusses *Mäster Olof*, *Röda rummet*, *Herr Bengts hustru*, and *Svenska folket* in some detail, as well as *Fritänkaren*, *Den fredlöse*, *Det sjunkande Hellas*, *Gillets hemlighet*, *Lycko-Pers resa*, and the early journalism; he also considers the impact on Sg's thinking both of his relationship with Siri von Essen and the ideas of Eduard von Hartmann, Kierkegaard, Schopenhauer, Rousseau, Max Nordau, and Nils Herman Quiding. He charts his response to contributions to the ongoing Swedish debate about woman's status by Ellen Anckarsvärd, Knut Wicksell, Sophie Leijonhufvud-Adlersparre, and several other Swedish writers, publicists, and activists of the period, including Anne-Charlotte Edgren, Sophie Agrell, Carl David af Wirsén, Pehr Staaff, and Hjalmar Branting. Boëthius also provides a summary in French, 'Strindberg et le débat sur l'emancipation de la femme, jusqu'a "*Les Mariés I*"', pp. 403-418, and his widely distributed study is notable as the first Swedish doctoral dissertation to be published directly in popular paperback format]

[B9:31] — Andrén, Sigvard, *Vestmanlands Läns Tidning* (Västerås), 18 October 1969.

[B9:32] — Beyer, Nils, *Arbetet* (Malmö), 19 October 1969.

[B9:33] — Ekenvall, Asta, *Göteborgs Handels- och Sjöfartstidning*, 12 November 1969.

[B9:34] — Johnson, Walter [Gilbert], *Scandinavian Studies* (Lawrence, Kansas), 44:4 (1972), 571-572.

[B9:35] — Kärnell, Karl-Åke, *Kvällsposten* (Malmö), 4 November 1969.

[B9:36] — Landquist, John, 'Den glada 80-tal', *Aftonbladet* (Stockholm), 18 October 1969.

[B9:37] — Qvist, G., *Dagens Nyheter* (Stockholm), 26 November 1969.

[B9:38] — Svanberg, B., *Tidsignal* (Stockholm), 5:5 (1969), pp. 10, 12.

[B9:39] — Svanberg, Victor, *Svenska Dagbladet* (Stockholm), 8 March 1970.

[B9:40] — Tarschys, Karin, *Samlaren* (Uppsala), 91 (1970), pp. 156-165.

[B9:41] — Westman Berg, Karin, *Hertha* (Stockholm), 57:2 (1970), 22-24.

[B9:42] — Westman Berg, Karin, *Upsala Nya Tidning*, 26 November 1969.

[B9:43] — Wieselgren, Greta, *Nordisk Tidskrift* (Stockholm), 46:3 (1970), 147-149.

[B9:44] — Ydén, L., *Tidsignal* (Stockholm), 5:48 (1969), p. 12.

See **A4:54**

[B9:45] Boëthius, Ulf, 'Strindberg och den emanciperade kvinnan', *Hertha* (Stockholm), 48:1 (1968), 6-8. ['Strindberg and the Emancipated Woman']

[B9:46] Boëthius, Ulf, 'Den unge Strindbergs kvinnohat', *Dagens Nyheter* (Stockholm), 25 January 1964. ['The Young Strindberg's Misogyny']

[B9:47] Børge, Vagn, *Kvinden i Strindbergs liv og digtning*, København: Levin & Munksgaard; Lund: C. W. K. Gleerups Förlag, 1936. Illus. 427 pp. ['Woman in Strindberg's Life and Writing'. Offers an account of Sg's early development and the female characters of *Mäster Olof* and his first plays which is followed by a discussion of his portrayal of women in a selection of works that are related throughout to the women with whom he shared his life or those that he supposedly had in mind when writing them. Thus

En dåres försvarstal, *Fadren*, *Fröken Julie*, and the correspondence assembled in *Han och hon* illuminate his marriage to Siri von Essen, the 'inferno' of his relationship with Frida Uhl informs the discussion of *Till Damaskus*, *Erik XIV*, *Dödsdansen*, and some other works, while his marriage to Harriet Bosse is viewed in terms of *Kristina*, *Svanevit*, and *Ett drömspel*. Comparisons are made between Sg's outlook on marriage and Tolstoi's, and his attitudes to women and gender relationships are linked with those of Otto Weininger in *Geschlecht und Charakter* (1903). General assumptions regarding both Sg's personality and his private opinions are readily 'documented' with ready reference to his literary works]

[B9:48] — Aas, L., *Urd* (Oslo), 1938, pp. 29-31.

[B9:49] — Ahlenius, Holger, *Bonniers Litterära Magasin* (Stockholm), 5:8 (1936), 651-652.

[B9:50] — Andersson, Ragnar, *Social-Demokraten* (Stockholm), 27 October 1936.

[B9:51] — B. B-m [Birger Bæckström], *Göteborgs Handels- och Sjöfartstidning*, 10 July 1936.

[B9:52] — Berendsohn, Walter A[rthur], 'Liv og Digtning', *Forum* (Stockholm), July 1936, pp. 16-18.

[B9:53] — Berggren, Kerstin, *Hertha* (Stockholm), 23 (1936), pp. 210-211, 215.

[B9:54] — Berggren Axberger, Kerstin, *Studiekamraten* (Tollarp), 19 (1937), pp. 38-39.

[B9:55] — Bryde, R., *Viborg Stifts Folkebladet*, 1936.

[B9:56] — Enckell, Olof, *Hufvudstadsbladet* (Helsingfors), 26 July 1936.

[B9:57] — Engelstad, Carl Fr[ederik], *Aftenpostens kronikk* (Oslo), 11 January 1937.

[B9:58] — Erdmann, Nils, *Nya Dagligt Allehanda* (Stockholm), 1 July 1936.

[B9:59] — K. L. M. [Nils Kjellström], *Arbetet* (Malmö), 31 August 1936.

[B9:60] — O. Hg [Olle Holmberg], *Dagens Nyheter* (Stockholm), 18 September 1936.

[B9:61] — Oppel, Horst, *Deutsche Literaturzeitung* (Berlin), 57 (1936), Sp. 1665-1667.

[B9:62] — Thomsen, Ejnar, *Aarhus Stiftstidning*, 8 June 1936.

[B9:63] — Thomsen, Ejnar, *Strejftog* (Copenhagen), 8 June 1936.

[B9:64] — Vedel, Valdemar, *Dagens Nyheder* (Copenhagen), 5 June 1936.

[B9:65] — Wieselgren, Oscar, *Svenska Dagbladet* (Stockholm), 19 September 1936.

[B9:65a] Borgström, Eva, 'Emancipation och perversion: Strindberg och den besvärgliga (homo)-sexualiteten', *ResPublica* (Stockholm), 62-63 (2004). ['Emancipation and Perversion: Strindberg and Troublesome (Homo)-Sexuality'. Considers Sg's depiction of both male and female homosexuality in the light of the contemporary movement towards the emancipation of women. Works from different phases of his career associate emancipation with perversity and the late novel, *Svarta fanor*, depicts marriage as a form of 'double homosexuality' and necrophilia]

[B9:66] Boukay, Maurice, 'Auguste Strindberg', *L'Echo de la semaine* (Paris), 2 February 1895. [On the furore which Sg's article 'L'Infériorité de la femme' (The Inferiority of Women) in *La Revue Blanche*, 7 January 1895, has occasioned in Paris]

[B9:67] Brandell, Gunnar, 'Ibsen, Strindberg and the Emancipation Movement in 19th-Century Scandinavia', in [Roberto Alonge], ed., **D2:7**, *Alle origini della drammaturgia moderna Ibsen, Strindberg, Pirandello*, Atti del Convegno Internazionale Torino, 18/20 aprile 1985, Centro regionale universitario per il Teatro del Piemonte, Genova: Costa & Nolan, 1987, pp. 24-32. [Concentrates on *A Doll's House* and *Fadren* in a discussion of the preoccupation with the emancipation of women in much Scandinavian realist drama. Contextualises this concern historically and ideologically, and presents *Fadren* and its depiction of women and marriage as a counter play to Ibsen's earlier drama. Nevertheless, both dramatists may be seen moving away from some of the conventions of realist drama in order to present their themes more effectively on stage]

[B9:68] Branting, Hjalmar, 'Strindberg och qvinnofrågan', *Ur dagens krönika* (Stockholm), 5 (1885), pp. 302-322. ['Strindberg and the Woman Question'. A significant contemporary response to Sg's contribution to the ongoing Swedish debate on the Woman Question. Branting praises him for his willingness to attack political humbug and social hypocrisy, but is critical of his recent stance on women in *Giftas*, and of his social thought in general. This is inspired by Rousseau and his hostility to culture, and may have some relevance to his view of women, given the dominant role played by upper-class women in the movement for female emancipation. But Branting regards Sg's thinking as otherwise divorced from contemporary social reality and hence wholly unrealistic, unlike the writings of John Stuart Mill or, indeed, Ibsen, against whom he conducts a savage polemic in *Giftas* and elsewhere]

[B9:69] Branting, Hjalmar, 'Strindberg och kvinnofrågan', in *Tal och skrifter*, 11 vols, Stockholm: Tidens Förlag, 1927, Vol. 2, pp. 256-285. ['Strindberg and the Woman Question'. Rpr. of **B9:68**]

[B9:70] Bruggen, [Kees] van, 'Strindberg', *Algemeen Handelsblad* (Amsterdam), 10 January 1912. [A feuilleton on Sg the misogynist]

[B9:71] Brunnström, J.-O., 'Strindberg, Munch och kvinnorna', *Blekinge Läns Tidning* (Karlskrona), 9 March 1985. ['Strindberg, [Edvard] Munch, and Women']

[B9:72] Budtz, Palle, 'Strindberg, Marx och kvinnorna', *Aftonbladet* (Stockholm), 19 January 1968. ['Strindberg, [Karl] Marx, and Women']

[B9:73] C., 'Kvinnofrågan efter allra nyaste upptäckter', *Ur dagens krönika* (Stockholm), 10 (1890), pp. 478-480. ['The Woman Question According to the very Latest Discoveries'. Remarks on Sg's old-fashioned view of women in the essay 'Kvinnans underlägsenhet under mannen' (Woman's Inferiority to Man) and suggests that Elna Tenow's response in **B9:244** to Sg's calumnies demonstrates precisely the logic that Sg claims women do not possess]

[B9:74] Carlsson, Erik, 'Ett brev i kvinnofrågan', *Bokvännen* (Stockholm), 29:6 (1974), 113-118. ['A Letter on the Woman Question'. Discusses Elna Tenow's open letter, **B9:244**, which challenges Sg about his insistence concerning woman's inferiority to man]

[B9:75] Carsten-Montén, Karin, ed., *Han tror på Strindberg, hon tror på kvinnan: Om det moderna genombrottet i nordisk litteratur*, Hrsg. von Karin Carsten Montén unter redaktioneller Mitarbeit von Ralf Schröder und Sabine Tiedke, nørrona Sonderband 1, Kiel: Nørrona, 1988. 104 pp. ['He Believes in Strindberg, She Believes in Woman'. Contains five essays on the literature of the Scandinavian Modern Breakthrough and its concern with gender politics, two of which focus on the way in which women are portrayed by Ibsen, Georg Brandes, and Victoria Benedictsson; but while Sg never becomes the specific focus of attention in either, he remains a point of reference throughout the volume]

[B9:76] Cavallin, Anna, 'Strindberg's New Women and Some Encounters with the Media', in Kirsten Wechsel, Hrsg., **B1:473**, *Strindberg and His Media*, pp. 95-106. [Links the crisis of identity which Cavallin maintains is a preocupation in much of Sg's writing with contemporary discourses on gender. She asks how the discourse of the New Woman is represented in 'Mot betalning' (For Payment) and 'Slitningar' (Torn Apart) from *Giftas* and 'Nybyggnad' (New Building) in *Utopier i verkligheten*, and explores what happens to the women in his texts when they are confronted by the publicity that is an integral component of the modern media. Since the latter is controlled by men, not women, it consequently determines how the image of the New Woman is received, in whatever guise she is conveyed]

[B9:77] Cavallin, Anna, 'Den fängslade kroppen. Äktenskap som disciplinär institution', in Anna Cavallin and Anna Westerståhl Stenport, red., **B9:78**, *Det gäckande könet: Strindberg och genusteori*, pp. 169-194. ['The Imprisoning Body. Marriage as a Disciplinary Institution'. Examines the way in which various 19th-Century discourses associated with the body and sexuality manifest themselves in two stories from *Giftas*, 'Ett dockhem' (A Doll's House) and 'Tvekamp' (Duel). The body which Sg writes in these stories is intersected by economic as well as erotic discourses, and is seeking to escape the regulatory prison of the discourses imposed on it in marriage in which the partners suffer the inescapable imposition of contemporary gender roles]

[B9:78] Cavallin, Anna, and Anna Westerståhl Stenport, red., *Det gäckande könet: Strindberg och genusteori*, Stockholm/Stehag: Brutus Östlings Bokförlag Symposium, 2006. 300 pp. [Contains **B9:254**: Anna Westerståhl Stenport, 'Från kvinnohat till maskulinitetskris'; **B9:2**: Ann-Charlotte Gavel Adams, 'Vetenskap och manlighet'; **B9:77**: Anna Cavallin, 'Den fängslade kroppen. Äktenskap som disciplinär institution'; **B9:189**: Christopher Joseph Mitchell, 'Radikalfeministen Strindberg'; **B9:216**: Eszter Salczer, 'Strindbergs fäder och döttrar och de Andras röster'; **E11:33**: Marilyn Johns Blackwell, 'Empirism, optik och perspektiv på genus i *Fadern*'; **E13:13**: Hedwig Fraunhoffer, 'Kön och sexuella normer i *Fordringsägare*'; **E13:34**: Ann-Sofie Lönngren, 'Att skapa i "de tre dimensionerna". En performativ analysis av *Fordringsägare*'; **E41:177:** Kristina Hagström Ståhl, 'Att känna min syn försvagad av ett öga: Sätt at se *Ett drömspel*'; **F4:85**: Ulrike Peters Nichols, 'Den manliga sfinxens lidanden. *En dåres försvarstal* som en berättelse utan melankoli'; **F4:100**: Stefanie von Schnurbein, 'Maskulinitetens kris och *En dåres försvarstal*'; **F6:6**: Maxime Abolgassemi, 'Makterna, dubbelgångare och homosexualitet i *Legender*'; **F9:12**: Margaretha Fahlgren, '*Ensam* – det manliga jaget, staden och kvinnan'; **G15:19**: Eva Borgström, 'Perversitetens hydra. En queerläsning av *Svarta fanor*']

[B9:79] Clemenceau, Georges, 'La Question de la femme', *La Justice* (Paris), 5 March 1895. ['The Woman Question'. A contribution to the debate provoked by Sg's essay 'L'Infériorité de la femme' (The Inferiority of Women) in *La Revue Blanche*, 7 January 1895. Clemenceau examines Sg's argument and concludes that it is not only women who might be called capricious and illogical]

[B9:80] 'Colomba' [Henry Fouquier], 'Strindberg', *L'Écho de Paris*, 15 January 1895. [Ridicules Sg's views on women in 'L'Infériorité de la femme' (The Inferiority of Women) in *La Revue Blanche*, 7 January 1895. Maintains that France's homegrown misogynists are more original, and display a sharper clarity of expression]

[B9:81] Dahlbäck, Lars, 'En Strindbergsartikel i *Politiken*', *Meddelanden från Strindbergssällskapet* (Stockholm), 27 (1960), pp. 4-8. ['An Article by Strindberg in *Politiken*'. Introduces a Danish article of Sg's on the woman question from 1887, addressed 'Till

"V"', i.e. the editor of the Copenhagen daily *Politiken*, Viggo Hørup, and hitherto unpublished in Swedish]

[B9:82] Dickson, Walter, 'En ny äktenskapsepok', *Afton-Tidningen* (Stockholm), 13 January 1946. ['A New Epoch in Marriage'. Considers the ideas concerning the nature and basis of marriage discussed in the 1870s and 1880s in *Giftas* and elsewhere]

[B9:83] Dosenheimer, Elise, 'Strindberg und die Frau', *Illustrierte Zeitung* (Leipzig), 156 (10 February 1921), p. 104. ['Strindberg and Woman']

[B9:84] Dottin-Orsini, Mireille, *Cette femme qu'ils disent fatale. Textes et images de la misogynie fin-de-siècle*, Paris: Bernard Grasset, 1993. 373 pp. ['This Woman they call Fatale. Texts and Images of Fin-de-Siècle Misogyny'. An unindexed comparative study of the representation of women in late 19th-Century literature and painting. Includes references to *Fadren*, *Fröken Julie*, 'De l'infériorité de la femme', and Sg's commentary on Munch's paintings, 'L'Exposition Edvard Munch', first published in *La Revue Blanche*, 7 January 1895]

[B9:85] E. B. [Elena Balzamo], 'Strindberg et les femmes', in Elena Balzamo, ed., **B1:7**, *August Strindberg*, pp. 428-429. ['Strindberg and Women'. A brief note on the often hostile representations of women in Sg's novels, the both positive and negative female figures in his plays, and his theoretical essays on the Woman Question]

[B9:86] Ekenvall, Asta, *Manligt och kvinnligt. Idéhistoriska studier*, Kvinnohistoriskt arkiv 5, Göteborg: Akademieförlaget-Gumperts, 1966, pp. 156-157, 175-178, 187-188. ['Male and Female. Studies in the History of Ideas'. Places Sg's ideas on the physiology of women in 'Kvinnans underlägsenhet under mannen' (Woman's Inferiority to Man') in their historical context in terms of contemporary social and scientific thought. Summary in English]

[B9:87] Ekenvall, Asta, 'Myten om det manliga och det kvinnliga. Om Strindbergs "kvinnohat"', *Dramaten* (Stockholm), 6 (1975-76), No. 49, pp. 15-16. ['The Myth about Masculinity and Femininity. On Strindberg's "Misogyny"'. Examines late 19th-Century notions of gender and their relevance for the way in which Sg portrays women in both his naturalistic plays and *Giftas*]

[B9:88] Ekenvall, Asta, 'Strindberg, kvinnan och alstringen', *Meddelanden från Strindbergssällskapet* (Stockholm), 26 (1960), pp. 11-16. ['Strindberg, Woman, and Procreation'. Relates Sg's notions concerning woman and procreation, as well as the imagery of sexual and spiritual potency that permeates his writing in e.g. *Svarta fanor* and *En blå bok* to 19th-Century biology, alchemy, Plato's *Timaeus*, and the *Oresteia*]

[B9:89] Ekenvall, Asta, 'Strindberg och kvinnans fysiologi', *Bonniers Litterära Magasin* (Stockholm), 38:6 (1969), 457-464. ['Strindberg and Woman's Physiology'. Relates Sg's ideas about the physiology of women in 'Kvinnans underlägsenhet under mannen' (Woman's Inferiority to Man) and several of his other theoretical texts to their historical context, which includes not only the contemporary social, biological, and medical theories of Charles Darwin, Paul Topinard, and Cesare Lombroso, but a range of received ideas derived from Aristotle and elsewhere. Ekenvall suggests that Sg affords incomparable insight into the psychology of misogyny]

[B9:90] 'En Kvinde', 'Strindberg om Kvindens Dovenskab', *Social-Demokraten* (Copenhagen), 23 November 1886. ['Strindberg and Woman's Idleness', by 'A Woman'. Refutes Sg's polemical claim that cultivated middle-class women are lazy and parasitical]

[B9:91] Esselde [Sophie Adlersparre], 'Reaktionen mot det af qvinnofrågan framkallade äktenskapsidealet', *Dagny* (Stockholm), 1887. ['The Reaction against the Ideal of Marriage Promoted by the Woman Question'. Includes critical comments on Sg and *Giftas* by the woman to whom Sg ascribed responsibility for the charge for blasphemy, brought against him in 1884]

[B9:92] Fahlgren, Margaretha, 'Att kontrollera kvinnan', *Parnass* (Stockholm), 6:1 (1995), 50-53. Illus. ['To Control Woman'. Examines the patriarchal premises which underpin Sg's writings from the mid-1880s onwards when, as in both *Fröken Julie* and *En dåres försvarstal*, he seeks to control the threat to masculinity that is apparently posed by the emotional and physical drives of modern women, which he considers are implicit in her demand for social and sexual liberation. Fahlgren observes that such works often recall the burgeoning contemporary medical discourse on 'hysterical' women as developed by Jean-Martin Charcot at the Hôpital Salpêtrière in Paris. She also points out that some post-Inferno works, like *Påsk* and *Spöksonaten*, accord women a rather more positive, liminal role even though they are still defined by their relation to man. But in such cases, it is they who endow him with significance]

[B9:93] Fahlgren, Margaretha, '"Jag har alltid tillbett kvinnorna, dessa förtjusande tokor" – kvinnan i Strindbergs författarskap', in **B1:346**, *Strindberg i världen*, pp. 57-72. ['"I have always Worshipped Women, These Charming Idiots": Woman in Strindberg's Writings'. Studies the patriarchal premises underlying such works from the mid 1880s as *Fadren* and *En dåres försvarstal*, in which Sg seeks to control the threat which women's physical and emotional drives, and their demand for social and sexual liberation pose for masculinity. Fahlgren points out that the contemporary women's movement had traumatic consequences for men like Sg who feared not least for their sexuality, and he consequently sought to maintain a greater polarity between the genders; thus, he was led to question certain aspects of modernity, as in the vivisection 'Det moderna?' (The Modern?, 1894). Although she is given a more elevated position in a post-Inferno work like *Ett drömspel*, woman in Sg's texts nevertheless remains without an independent role or identity apart from what she derives from the man with whom she is inevitably coupled. According to Fahlgren, all his attempts to depict the relationship between men and women are underpinned by a profound melancholy, as defined by Julia Kristeva. Fahlgren also discusses the representation of women in *Kristina*, *Dödsdansen*, and *En blå bok*]

[B9:94] Fahlgren, Margaretha, '"Jag har alltid tillbett kvinnorna, dessa förtjusande tokor" – kvinnan i Strindbergs författarskap', in Stefan Mählqvist and Torsten Pettersson, red., *Tid och evighet. Nedslag i det gångna årtusendets europeiska litteratur*, Uppsala: Litteraturvetenskapliga institutionen, Uppsala universitet, 2000, pp. 125-144. ['"I Have always Worshipped Women, These Charming Idiots": Woman in Strindberg's Writings'. Rpr. of **B9:93**]

[B9:95] Fahlgren, Margaretha, *Kvinnans ekvation. Kön, makt och rationalitet i Strindbergs författarskap*, Stockholm: Carlssons Bokförlag, 1994. Illus. 292 pp. ['Woman's Equation. Gender, Power, and Rationality in the Works of Strindberg'. Employs a Kristevan psychoanalytical approach in order to examine the crisis in patriarchal society which obtained during Sg's lifetime and the patriarchal structures of thought and feeling that inform the way in which women are defined in his essays and represented in his literary works. Fahlgren discusses *En dåres försvarstal*, *Fadren*, *Fröken Julie*, *I* *havsbandet*, *Himmelrikets nycklar*, *Kristina*, *Svarta fanor*, *Pelikanen*, *Påsk*, 'Jubal utan jag' (Jubal Without a Self) from *Sagor*, *Ett drömspel*, and *Spöksonaten*, as well as the essay 'Kvinnans underlägsenhet under mannen' (Woman's Inferiority to Man). She situates Sg's ideas briefly in relation to contemporary scientific and social discourses on women's sexuality, as well as to received ideas regarding their mental and emotional life, and the nature of the family. She also demonstrates how the hostile view of women which he adopted during the 1880s is subsequently supplanted by a sometimes more conciliatory, religiously inflected view of women in his post-Inferno works. Here, the role he reserves for women becomes one in which they not only endow man with meaning but also reconcile him with life. Nevertheless, throughout his work, woman is always defined in relation to man and to masculinity, and Sg signally fails to discover a solution to the gender equation for which he had searched since the early 1880s]

[B9:96] — Borgström, Eva, *Tvärtanten* (Göteborg), 1995:3, pp. 22-24.

[B9:97] — Dalenstam, Ulrika, *Helsingborgs Dagblad*, 8 October 1994.

[B9:98] — Enander, Crister, *Folket i Bild* (Stockholm), 1995:1, pp. 36-37.

[B9:99] — Franzén, Carin, *Tidskrift för litteraturvetenskap* (Stockholm), 23:2 (1994), 66-68.

[B9:100] — Gustafsson, Margareta, *Smålandsposten* (Halmstad), 2 August 1994.

[B9:101] — Hirdwall, Jacob, *Göteborgs-Posten*, 22 November 1994.

[B9:102] — Levin, Hjördis, *Kvinnobulletinen* (Stockholm), 25:2 (1995), p. 51.

[B9:103] — Monié, Karin, 'Strindbergs kvinnoförakt en olösbar ekvation', *LO-tidningen* (Stockholm), 73:31 (1994), p. 14. ['Strindberg's Contempt for Women an Insoluble Equation']

[B9:104] — Ohlson, Per-Ove, *Borås Tidning*, 8 November 1994.

[B9:105] — Öhman, Anders, *Kvinnovetenskaplig tidskrift* (Stockholm), 16:4 (1995), 79-81.

[B9:106] — Schnurbein, S[tefanie] von, *Skandinavistik* (Kiel), 26:1 (1996), 57-59.

[B9:107] — Sjöblad, Christina, *Svenska Dagbladet* (Stockholm), 6 October 1994.

[B9:108] — Sundberg, Björn, *Samlaren* (Uppsala), 116 (1995), pp. 257-258. [See **B9:111**]

[B9:109] — Wittrock, Ulf, *Upsala Nya Tidning*, 20 September 1994.

[B9:110] Fahlgren, Margaretha, 'Mannen, försoningen och kvinnan', *Tidskrift för litteraturvetenskap* (Stockholm), 23:2 (1994), 41-48. ['Man, Reconciliation, and Woman'. Discusses Sg's later, post-Inferno conception of woman as the source of man's redemption, through whom he might be reconciled to life, as it is articulated in *En blå bok*, *Påsk*, and *Spöksonaten*]

[B9:111] Fahlgren, Margaretha, 'Replik', *Samlaren* (Uppsala), 116 (1995), p. 165. ['Reply'. A response to Björn Sundberg's review of **B9:95** in **B9:108**]

[B9:112] Fantl, Grete, 'Strindberg und das Eheproblem', *Die neue Generation. Zeitschrift für Mutterschutz und Sexualreform* (Berlin), 16 (1920), 355-357. ['Strindberg and the Problem of Marriage']

[B9:113] F. B., 'Mit drei Frauen unglücklich verheiratet. August Strindberg, der Dichter zwischen zei Welten. "Bei 40 Jahren findet man das Rätsel unlösbar!"', *Reclams Universum* (Stuttgart), 52 (1935-36), p. 575. ['Unhappily Married to Three Women. August Strindberg, the Writer between Two Worlds. "At the Age of 40 one finds no Solution to the Enigma!"'. The enigma here still puzzling Sg being woman]

[B9:114] Fertonani, Roberto, 'Per Strindberg la donna era come il diavolo', *Paese Sera* (Rome), 4 February 1979. ['For Strindberg Woman is Like the Devil'. Discusses Sg's representations of modern women with their emotional and sexual drives and demand for independence in *Fadren, Fröken Julie*, and *Fordringsägare*]

[B9:115] Figes, Eva, *Patriarchal Attitudes: Women in Society*, London: Faber and Faber, 1970. 191 pp. [Includes six brief references to Sg]

[B9:116] Fraisse, Geneviève, 'La misogynie de Strindberg, entre politique et métaphysique', in Georges Labica, ed., *Les Nouveaux espaces politiques*, Paris: Harmattan, 1995, pp. 73-85. ['Strindberg's Misogyny: Between Politics and Metaphysics'. Examines the psychological and ideological roots of Sg's misogyny with reference to *Tjänstekvinnans son, En dåres försvarstal, Giftas, Inferno,* and *Ockulta dagboken*. Also seeks to uncover its political significance. Fraisse compares Sg's misogyny with that of Proudhon and Schopenhauer and examines his polemics with the Swedish social thinker, Ellen Key. Originally written apropos a production of *Pelikanen* at the Théâtre du Volcan, Le Havre, in 1993]

[B9:117] Fraisse, Geneviève, 'La misogynie de Strindberg entre politique et métaphysique', in *La controverse des sexes*, Paris: Presses Universitaires de France, 2001, pp. 152-167. ['Strindberg's Misogyny: Between Politics and Metaphysics'. See **B9:116**]

[B9:118] Fraisse, Geneviève, 'Sous le regard misogyne de Strindberg, la figure de Nora', in Cécile Dauphin and Arlette Farge, eds, *De la violence et des femme*, Paris: Éditions Albin Michel, 1997, pp. 187-200. ['Beneath the Misogynist Gaze of Strindberg: The Figure of Nora'. Illustrates Sg's misogyny, which Fraisse regards as a response to the demand for women's emancipation and exemplified by the protagonist of Ibsen's *A Doll's House*, who is revisioned by Sg in one of the stories in *Giftas*. Fraisse also examines his views on women in *Tjänstekvinnans son* and *En dåres försvarstal*, his concern over the contemporary lack of clear boundaries between the genders, and what appears to have been his increasing reconciliation with woman in later life, under the influence of both Swedenborg and Harriet Bosse]

[B9:119] Fraisse, Geneviève, 'Strindbergs kvinnohat, mellan politisk och metafysik', in Ulf Olsson, red., **B1:357**, *Strindbergs förvandlingar*, Översättning Carin Franzén, Stockholm-Stehag: Brutus Östlings Bokförlag Symposion, 1999, pp. 57-72. ['Strindberg's Misogyny: Between Politics and Metaphysics'. Swedish version of **B9:116**]

[B9:120] Frederiksen, Kristine, 'Strindberg-Kvindesagen', *Kvinden og Samfundet* (Copenhagen), March 1885. ['Strindberg–Feminism']

[B9:121] Freksa, Friedrich, 'Strindberg und der Frauen', *Dramaturgische Blätter* (Metz), 1915:3, pp. 57-60. ['Strindberg and Woman']

[B9:122] Galich, L. [Pseudonym of L. E. Gabrilovich], '[A Slave's Revolt]', *Rech* (Moscow), 8 April 1907, p. 2. [On Sg and the question of equal rights for women. E.768]

[B9:123] Gerner, Cornelia, *Die "Madonna" in Edvard Munchs Werk. Frauenbilder und Frauenbild im ausgehenden 19. Jahrhundert*, Artes et litterae septentrionales 9, Morsbach: Reinhardt, 1993. Illus. 360 pp. ['The "Madonna" in Edward Munch's Work. Pictures of Women and the Image of Woman at the End of the 19th Century'. Discusses the representation of women in Munch's paintings and lithographs from th 1890s. Gerner compares their depiction by Munch with several female figures in the plays of his Scandinavian contemporararies, Ibsen and Sg, pp. 165-169. She also includes a separate section entitled '"Femmes fatales" und "Emanzipierte" bei Strindberg', pp. 176-181, in which she notes an affinity between his portrayal of women and Munch's images; in both cases the emancipated woman emerges as a figure whose sexuality is threatening, if not fatal]

[B9:124] Ghil, René, 'Strindberg et la femme', *La Patrie* (Paris), 12 February 1895. ['Strindberg and Woman'. The only article in the French press to support Sg unequivocally over the opinions on women expressed in the essay 'L'Infériorité de la femme' (On the Inferiority of Women), published in *La Revue Blanche*, 7 January 1895. Ghil praises Sg's logic and embraces him as an ally in the battle against these 'mentally weak creatures', who are advised to return from their misguided forays into public life and the workplace to the homes where they rightly belong]

[B9:125] Gizycki, Lily von, *Die neue Frau in der Dichtung*, Stuttgart, 1896. 40 pp. ['The New Woman in Literature'. Comments on Sg's representation of women in his literary works, especially the naturalistic dramas of the 1880s, including *Fadren* and *Fröken Julie*]

[B9:126] Gizycki, Lily von, 'Streifzüge durch die moderne Litteratur I', *Ethische Kultur* (Berlin), 1 (1893), 214-216. ['A Survey of Modern Literature, I'. Focuses on Sg's representation of women]

[B9:127] Glas. Peter, 'Efterord', in August Strindberg, *"Jag har alltid tillbett kvinnorna, dessa förtjusande brottsliga tokor": valda noveller, brev och andra texter*, urval och efterord av Peter Glas, Lund: Bakhåll, 2005. 126 pp. [The Afterword to Glas's selection of texts by Sg on women with a title, 'I have always worshipped women, these Charming, Criminal Idiots', drawn from one of Sg's own characteristic statements]

[B9:128] Gödecke, Anna, 'Felfinnaren – feltagaren: reflektioner med anledning af Strindbergs kvinnohat', 1-3, *Brand* (Stockholm), 1905:1, pp. 9-10; 1905:2, pp. 5-7; 1905:3, pp. 6-7. ['The Fault Finder – The Fault Taker: Reflections in Respect of Strindberg's Misogyny']

[B9:129] Gordon, Robert, 'Rewriting the Sex War in *The Father*, *Miss Julie*, and *Fordringsägare*: Strindberg, Authorship and Authority', in Katherine H. Burkman and Judith Roof, *Staging the Rage: The Web of Misogyny in Modern Drama*, Madison, N.J.: Fairleigh Dickinson University Press, 1998, pp. 139-157. [According to Gordon, *Fadren*, in which Sg struggles against his own identification with the feminine he so despised, seeks to naturalise the patriarchal association of male with masculine and female with feminine. Thus the play emerges as the first text thoroughly to problematise the relationship of male to female in modern Western theatre. For, building on ideas developed in *Giftas*, Sg's almost paranoid misogyny allowed him to introduce aspects of gender and sexuality into the theatre in novel ways. *Fröken Julie* is possibly the first 19th-Century play by a male writer to have conceived the woman's role in a sexual relationship as a suitable subject for drama, her point of view being as fully explored as the man's. In *Fordringsägare*, meanwhile, he invented a dramatic form that expressed a new ideology of personal relationships according to which sex is conceived as an aspect of the general will to power in human nature, irrespective of any gender difference, and even though in practice it is always inscribed within a history of gender-defined power positions]

[B9:130] Großmann, Stefan, 'Der Frauenhasser. Strindberg-Zitat', *Blätter des Deutschen Theaters* (Berlin), 3 (1913-14), 747-748. ['The Woman Hater: Quotations from Strindberg']

[B9:131] Grubiński, Wacław, 'Strindberg i kobiety', *Świat* (Warsaw), 1909:11, p. 8. ['Strindberg and Women'. Attributes Sg's hatred of women to the fact that he once loved them all too passionately, as well as to an unrequited desire to experience true love]

[B9:132] Günther, Herbert, 'Strindberg und die Frauen', in *Das unzerstörbare Erbe. Dichter der Weltliteratur. Fünfzehn Essays*, München: Gesellschaft der Bibliophilen, 1973, pp. 103-107. ['Strindberg and Women'. A series of naïve reflections on Sg's attitude to women, with reference to Siri von Essen, Frida Uhl, Laura in *Fadren*, *Kristina*, and *Dödsdansen*. Concludes that his search for woman was really a search for God]

[B9:133] Hans, Wilhelm, 'Strindbergs Frauenhaß', *Nordische Rundschau* (Reval), 4 (1931), 69-74. ['Strindberg's Misogyny'. Looks at Sg's portrayal of women throughout his career, not just at the naturalist period. Hans suggests that 'Sg's "hatred" of women is nothing but a reaction against the irresistible attraction which they had for him, and from which he vainly tried to liberate himself']

[B9:134] Hansson, Laura M[ohr] [i.e. Laura Marholm (Pseudonym of Laura Mohr)], 'The Women-Haters Tolstoy and Strindberg', in *We Women and Our Authors. A Rendering from the Second Edition of the German Work* by Hermione Ramsden, London: John Lane, 1899, pp. 146-178. [English version of **B9:182**]

[B9:135] Hård, Calle, 'Kvinnorna var hans livs tragedi', *Expressen* (Stockholm), 3 March 1985, pp. 10-13. Illus. ['Women were his Life's Tragedy'. Maintains that Sg's susceptibility to women was his tragedy. He might have claimed to hate them, but he could not resist them]

[B9:136] Haslund, Fredrik Juel, 'Det seksuelle gjennembrudd i 1880- og 1890-årene', in Harald Bache-Wiig and Astrid Sæther, red., *100-år etter – om det litterære livet i Norge i 1890-åra*, Oslo: Aschehoug, 1993, pp. 142-151. ['The Sexual Breakthrough in the 1880s and 1890s'. Contextualises Sg in relationship to two periods of intense concern with gender roles, firstly through the publication of *Giftas* in 1884 as part of the ongoing debate in Scandinavia regarding marriage and sexuality which embraced Bjørnstjerne Bjørnson, Ibsen, Hans Jaeger, Arne Garborg, Amalie Skram, Sigbjørn Obstfelder, and several other writers of the Scandinavian Modern Breakthrough, and again in the 1890s as a member of the Ferkel Circle in Berlin, together with Stanisław Przybyszewski, Dagny Juel, Ola Hansson, and Gunnar Heiberg]

[B9:137] Heinitz, W., 'Strindbergs Stellung zur Frau', *Zeitung für Literatur* (Hamburg), No. 20 (1917). ['Strindberg's Attitude towards Women']

[B9:138] Herzfeld, Marie, 'Die Emanzipation des Mannes', *Moderne Rundschau* (Vienna), 4 (1891), 10-14. ['Male Emancipation'. Discusses Sg's portrayal of the relationship between the sexes, mainly with reference to the naturalistic dramas]

[B9:139] Herzfeld, Marie, 'Die Emanzipation des Mannes', in *Menschen und Bücher*, **B1:169**, pp. 116-129. ['Male Emancipation'. Rpr. of **B9:138**]

[B9:140] Hortenbach, Jenny C., *Freiheitsstreben und Destruktivität. Frauen in den Dramen August Strindbergs und Gerhart Hauptmanns*, Germanistische Schriftenreihe der norwegischen Universitäten und Hochschulen 2, Oslo: Universitetsforlaget, 1965. 212 pp. ['A Striving for Freedom and Destructiveness. Women in the Plays of August

Strindberg and Gerhart Hauptmann'. Hortenbach compares female figures, their striving for independence, and their vampire-like tendencies, in nine plays by Sg (*Mäster Olof, Herr Bengts hustru, Marodörer – Kamraterna, Fadren, Fröken Julie, Fordringsägare, Brott och brott, Dödsdansen*, and *Pelikanen*) and six by Hauptmann (*Vor Sonnenaufgang, Einsame Menschen, Fuhrmann Henschel, Gabriel Schillings Flucht, Kaiser Karls Geisel*, and *Winterballade*). She groups the principal female figures in these plays under three headings, as feminine, idealistic women who desire to be good wives and mothers (Kristina in *Mäster Olof* and Margit in *Herr Bengts hustru*), women who are incapable of love and consequently seek emancipation (Bertha Alberg in *Kamraterna*, Laura in *Fadren*, and both Miss Julie and her mother), and the female vampires (Tekla in *Fordringsägare*, Henriette in *Brott och brott*, Alice in *Dödsdansen*, and Elise in *Pelikanen*). Where Hauptmann's characters are concerned, they seem to Hortenbach to derive closely from their Sgian predecessors. See **V:97**]

[B9:141] — Berendsohn, Walter A[rthur], *Orbis Litterarum* (Copenhagen), 23:4 (1968), 327-328.

[B9:142] — Berendsohn, Walter A[rthur], *Erasmus* (Darmstadt), 19:19-20 (1967), Sp. 601-602.

[B9:143] — Boëthius, Ulf, *Upsala Nya Tidning*, 14 March 1967.

[B9:144] — [Jessen, Heinrich], *Ausblick* (Lübeck), 20 (1969), p. 76.

[B9:145] — Lide, Barbara, *Modern Language Notes* (Baltimore), 85:5 (1970), 761-763.

[B9:146] — Madsen, Børge Gedsø, *Scandinavian Studies* (Lawrence, Kansas), 39:2 (1967), 190-191.

[B9:147] — Robinson, A. R., *German Life and Letters* (Oxford), 21:2 (1968), 142-143.

[B9:148] Howlett, Marc-Vincent, 'Tekla au miroir des femmes', in Elena Balzamo, ed., **B1:7**, *August Strindberg*, pp. 407-427. ['Tekla before the Mirror of Women'. Discusses Sg's often misogynistic representation of women in *Fordringsägare*, with reference also to *Giftas, Fadren, En dåres försvarstal*, and *Fröken Julie*]

[B9:149] Indahl, Ragni, 'Feminisme som prosjekt og som objekt', *Arr: idéhistorisk tidskrift* (Oslo), 8:4 (1996), 56-65. ['Feminism as Project and as Object'. Discusses feminism with reference to Sg and two Norwegian authors, Bjørnstjerne Bjørnson and Arnulf Øverland]

[B9:150] Karvelis, Ugné, 'Les Femmes dans les œuvres de Strindberg', in **B9:245,** *August Strindberg et les femmes*, Paris: Centre culturel suédois, 2000, pp. 8-14. ['Women in the Works of Strindberg'. A non-specialist response to Sg's portrayal of women with brief reference to *Fadren, Pelikanen* (in which the father has been eliminated altogether), *Fröken Julie*, and *Giftas*, two works in which women have been reduced merely to their reproductive function. Karvelis considers what underpinned Sg's opinions in his upbringing and contemporary society, and considers whether it may also have influenced his choice of partners, first by annulling his humble past in marrying Siri von Essen and subsequently fulfilling the logic of the notion of incest articulated in *Fadren* by successive marriages to two women both much younger than himself]

[B9:151] Key, Ellen, *Lifslinjer*, 3 vols, Stockholm: Albert Bonniers Förlag, 1903-06. [Compares Sg's misogyny with the attitudes to women of Otto Weininger and Nietzsche in Volume Two]

[B9:152] Key, Ellen, 'Moderne Liebe', *Die Zukunft* (Berlin), 46 (1904), 291-296. ['Modern Love']

[B9:153] Key, E[llen], '[Modern Love]', *Vestnik znaniia* (St Petersburg), 1904:6, pp. 33-60. [Russian translation of **B12:152** with Key's comments on Sg, p. 59]

[B9:154] Key, Ellen, 'Om reaktionen mot qvinnofrågan', *Revy i litterära och sociala frågor* (Stockholm), 1886, pp. 67ff. ['On the Reaction against the Woman Question'. Discusses *Giftas* and shares some of Sg's opinions, such as his rejection of the idea that the twisted upbringing boys are given should be made a pattern for girls. Sg is also right to warn against the introduction of women into an already overcrowded labour-market. Key is likewise afraid that a sexual relationship between the sexes based on eroticism would be superseded by 'friendship between work-mates']

[B9:155] Key, Ellen, 'Hyllning till August Strindbergs 50-årsdag', *Svenska Dagbladet* (Stockholm), 22 January 1899. ['A Tribute on August Strindberg's 50th Birthday'. Describes Sg as 'today's genius in the abuse of women', a man whose strange portrayal of women and the erotic life in *Giftas* has failed to impress women. Since he has never been a liberator for them, it is by virtue of those qualities which he denies to women, the application of impartial thought, that they recognise his great genius]

[B9:156] Kiberd, Declan, 'Strindberg's Villains: The New Woman as Predator', in *Men and Feminism in Modern Literature*, London: Macmillan, 1985, pp. 34-60. [Discusses Sg's response to the new woman in *Fadren*, *Fröken Julie*, *Kamraterna*, and *Bandet*. Kiberd maintains that Sg was 'the first modern writer to make androgyny *the* central issue in his accounts of sexual relations']

[B9:157] Krebs, Johanne, 'August Strindberg og Kvinden', 1-2, *Morgenbladet* (Copenhagen), 9 and 10 February 1887. ['August Strindberg and Woman']

[B9:158] Kullenberg, Annette, 'Annette Kullenberg träffar August Strindberg: kvinnohatare? Jag?', *Vi* (Stockholm), 63:41 (1976), 11-13. ['Annette Kullenberg Meets August Strindberg: A Misogynist? Me?' A fictional interview between a modern feminist journalist and Sg concerning his standpoint on women]

[B9:159] Kvam, Kela, 'Strindberg and the Roles of the Sexes', in Donald Weaver, ed., **D2:331**, *Strindberg on Stage*, pp. 112-127. [Kvam points out that during Sg's lifetime familiar gender roles came increasingly to be acknowledged as precisely that – something that is reflected in both his life and work. She discusses *Fadren*, which dramatises the impossibility of the traditional male role, and *En dåres försvarstal*, which documents the failure to establish new possibilities, with other, briefer, references to *Giftas*, *Herr Bengts hustru*, *Dödsdansen*, and Per Olov Enquist's documentary drama *Tribadernas natt* which depicts Sg's relationship with Siri von Essen in 1888]

[B9:160] Kvam, Kela, 'Strindberg och kønsroller', in Hans Bekker-Nielsen, Hans Anton Koefoed, and Johan de Mylius, red., *Nordisk Litteraturhistoria – en bog til Brøndsted*, Odense: Odense Universitetsforlag, 1978, pp. 248-262. ['Strindberg and Gender Roles'. Compares Sg's notions about the appropriate gender roles for men and women with Per Olov Enquist's portrait of Sg in the documentary drama *Tribadernas natt*]

[B9:161] K. W-g [Karl Warburg], 'Bokvärlden', *Göteborgs Handels- och Sjöfartstidning*, 19 May 1890. [Discusses Elna Tenow's response to Sg's essay, 'Kvinnans underordnade ställning', in **B9:244**]

[B9:162] Lacour, Léopold, 'Auguste Strindberg', *Gil Blas* (Paris), 25 July 1895. [A sharply critical response to Sg's view of women in the essay 'Misogynie et gynolatrie', published in *Gil Blas* the previous day]

[B9:163] Landquist, John, 'Strindberg och kvinnorna', *Bonniers månadshäften* (Stockholm), 1912:1, pp. 38-54. ['Strindberg and Women'. Suggests that Sg's standpoint on the Woman Question up to and including *Giftas I* is comparatively open-minded and radical, and suggests that it is really only in the interval before the publication of *Giftas II* that the great change in his attitude to women occurs. This was prompted by his 1884 trial for blasphemy in *Giftas*, which he attributed in large part to the hostility towards him of the Swedish women's movement, and his experiences while staying with Siri von Essen at the artists' colony at Grez-sur-Loing. Hereafter, however telling his portrayal of women might on occasion be, the critique he subsequently subjects them to is illogical, as is his complaint that women are parasitic when one of the principal demands of the feminists he so excoriated was the right of women to work. Landquist examines these contradictions and Sg's frequently perceptive representation of women, marriage, sexuality, and gender roles in a wide range of texts in several genres, including *Fadren*, *En dåres försvarstal*, *Mäster Olof*, *Giftas*, *Svenska folket*, *Kvarstadsresan*, *Tjänstekvinnans son*, *Fordringsägare*, *Brott och brott*, *Dödsdansen*, *Götiska rummen*, *Taklagsöl*, and 'Trefaldighetsnatten' (Trinity Sunday Night, a poem in hexameters)]

[B9:164] Landquist, John, 'Strindberg och kvinnorna', in Solveig Landquist, red., **B1:248**, *John Landquist om Strindberg personen och diktaren*, pp. 260-285. ['Strindberg and Women'. Rpr. of **B9:163**]

[B9:165] Landquist, John, 'Strindberg und die Frauen', 1-2, Autorisierte Übertragung aus dem Schwedischen von Marie Franzos, *Die Frau* (Berlin), 21 (1914), pp. 273-280, 361-368. ['Strindberg and Women'. German translation of **B9:163**]

[B9:166] Lantier, Eugène, 'L'Ennemi des femmes', *Le Temps* (Paris), 25 January 1895. ['The Enemy of Women'. A critical response to Sg's essay 'L'Infériorité de la femme' (The Inferiority of Women) in *La Revue Blanche*, 7 January 1895, which also makes sceptical fun of Sg's chemical and alchemical experiments]

[B9:167] Lide, Barbara, 'Kvinnan var din fiende…och modern var inte heller din vän', Översättning Kerstin Trowbridge, in Anita Persson and Barbara Lide, red., **B1:366**, *Ja, må han leva!*, pp. 153-161. ['Woman was your Enemy…And the Mother wasn't your Friend Either'. Lide adopts the terminology of Jung and Erich Neumann to discuss the figure of the 'bad mother' in *Fadren*, *Kamraterna*, *Pelikanen*, *Mäster Olof*, and *Moderskärlek*, a woman who loves too much or too little, and wreaks havoc in her children's lives. She also contrasts her with the far rarer figure of the 'good mother', represented in Sg's plays by Margaretha in *Gillets hemlighet* and Jeanne in *Brott och brott*]

[B9:168] Lindberg, Augusta, 'Strindberg och kvinnan', *Dagens Nyheter* (Stockholm), 22 January 1909. '[Strindberg and Woman'. Argues that Sg has never hated woman, only certain women, and in his writing he has presented 'us' with a whole gallery of them, both wicked and good. By an eminent Swedish actress with the experience of performing in several of his plays]

[B9:169] Lindén, Claudia, *Om kärlek. Litteratur, sexualitet och politik hos Ellen Key*, Stockholm/Stehag: Brutus Östlings Bokförlag Symposion, 2002. 410 pp. ['On Love, Literature, Sexuality, and Politics in Ellen Key'. Associates Sg and his notion of the New

Woman as a lesbian vampire with the general patriarchal response to Key's theories represented by Vitalis Norström and Carl David af Wirsén in discussing 'Strindberg och den monstruösa lesbianism', pp. 178-183, with particular reference to *En dåres försvarstal* and *Svarta fanor*. The accusations of indecency and his malicious portrait of Key as Hanna Paj in *Svarta fanor* link the threat posed by the New Woman with lesbianism and reduce the woman writer and agitator to a sexualised body which could thus be judged and rejected. English summary, 'On Love, Literature, Sexuality, and Politics in Ellen Key', pp. 309-316]

[B9:170] Lindström, Göran, 'Kvinnan hos Strindberg och Ibsen', *Dramaten* (Stockholm), No. 27 (1973), 3-6. Illus. ['Woman in Strindberg and Ibsen']

[B9:170a] Lönngren, Ann-Sofie, *Att röra en värld – en queerfeministisk analysis av erotiska trianglar i sex verk av August Strindberg*, Uppsala, 2007. [304] pp. ['To Touch a World: A Queer-Feminist Analysis of Erotic Triangles in Six Works by August Strindberg'. Analyses erotic triangles composed of two men and one woman in *En dåres försvarstal, Leka med elden, Brott och brott, Fordringsägare, Dödsdansen I*, and *Till Damaskus I-III*. Utilising a theoretical framework provided by Judith Butler and Eve Sedgwick's concept of male homosocial desire, the action of 'sex' and erotic desire in these texts is interpreted as constructed by performative means. Lönngren focuses especially on the dynamic relationship between the male rivals in each triangle. She detects an essential likeness where Sg's presentation of these triangles over time is concerned and establishes how, from a heteronormative standpoint, the male characters are frequently 'feminized' and the female 'masculinized'. In so doing, she frequently casts an oblique, new light on accepted readings of these texts. English summary, pp. 239-245]

[B9:170b] Lönngren, Ann-Sofie, '"Break the Narrative" – literaturvetenskap i förvandling. Om icke heteronormativa litteraturtolkningar: exemplet Strindberg', *Vandring och förvandling: förflyttning – förändring – framtid*, Humanistdagarna vid Uppsala universitet, 2004, Uppsala, 2006.

[B9:171] Marholm, Laura [Pseudonym of Laura Mohr], 'August Strindberg', *Nord und Süd* (Breslau), 66 (July 1893), 23-50. [Includes a brief account of the author's personal acquaintance with Sg, as well as an overview of his life and work. Marholm comments on *Röda rummet, Giftas, Utopier i verkligheten*, 'Tschandala', and *Tjänstekvinnans son*, and (less critically than in her later essays) on his representation of women and marriage in *Herr Bengts hustru, Kamraterna, Fadren, Fordringsägare*, and *Fröken Julie*. She also observes that Sg is now at a turning point in his career]

[B9:172] Marholm, Laura [Pseudonym of Laura Mohr], 'August Strindberg', in Gustaf Fröding, red., **B1:142**, *En bok om Strindberg*, pp. 173-211. [Abridged version of **B9:171**]

[B9:173] Marholm, Laura [Pseudonym of Laura Mohr], *Das Buch der Frauen: Zeitpsychologische Porträts*, Paris: Langen, n.d. [1895], 204 pp. [Includes the chapter 'Die Frauenhasser Tolstoj och Strindberg', based in part on Marholm's essay 'Der Lauratypus', **B9:175**, and published here by Albert Langen, a good friend of both Frida Uhl and Frank Wedekind and hence disliked by Sg]

[B9:174] Marholm, Leopold [Pseudonym of Laura Mohr], 'Ein Dichter des Weiberhasses', *Die Gegenwart* (Berlin), 33 (1888), pp. 4-6. ['A Misogynist Writer']

[B9:175] Marholm, Laura [Pseudonym of Laura Mohr], 'Die Fraue in der skandinavischen Dichtung: Strindbergs Lauratypus', *Freie Bühne für modernes Leben*, 1 (1890), 364-368.

['Woman in Scandinavian Literature'. Strindberg's 'Laura-type'. Marholm exemplifies her discussion mainly by reference to the heroine of Sg's *Fadren*, which was shortly to be premièred by the Freie Bühne, but notes that the type is also to be encountered in his other naturalistic plays *Kamraterna*, *Fordringsägare*, and *Fröken Julie*: 'Sg is a sensualist without a trace of feminism; this has determined the special quality of his *œuvre*'. See Marholm's companion pieces on 'Die Frau in der skandinavischen Dichtung: Der Noratypus', *Freie Bühne für modernes Leben*, 1 (1890), pp. 168-171, on Ibsen's *A Doll's House*, and 'Der Svavatypus', pp. 261-265, on the plays of Bjørnstjerne Bjørnson]

[B9:176] Marholm, Laura [Pseudonym of Laura Mohr], 'Die Frauen in der skandinavischen Dichtung. Strindbergs Lauratypus', in Hans-Peter Bayerdörfer, Hrsg., **B3:85**, *Strindberg auf der deutschen Bühne*, pp. 81-86. ['Woman in Scandinavian Literature. Strindberg's 'Laura-type'. See **B9:175**]

[B9:177] Marholm, Laura [Pseudonym of Laura Mohr], 'I. Noratypen. II. Svavatypen. III. Strindbergs Lauratype', IV. Begge sider af medaljen', *Samtiden* (Oslo), 1:9-10 (1890), pp. 353-367, 396-401. [Discusses Sg, pp. 362-367 and 400]

[B9:178] Marholm, Laura [Pseudonym of Laura Mohr], 'Om kvindesagen. Strindbergs Lauratype', in Øyvind Pharo, red., *Fin de Siècle: Tidsskriftet Samtiden i 1890-årene*, Oslo: Aschehoug, 1990, pp. 76-85. ['On Feminism. Strindberg's Laura Type'. Norwegian version of **B9:175**]

[B9:179] Marholm, Laura [Pseudonym of Laura Mohr], 'Symptomatische Stücke', *Freie Bühne für modernes Leben* (Berlin), 3 (1892), 427-432. ['Symptomatic Plays']

[B9:180] Marholm Hansson, Laura [Pseudonym of Laura Mohr], *Vi kvinder og vore digtere*, Autoriseret oversættelse ved docent Olaf Broch, Kristiania: H. Aschehoug & Co., 1896. 184 pp. ['We Women and Our Writers'. Norwegian edition of **B9:182**]

[B9:181] Marholm, Laura [Pseudonym of Laura Mohr], 'Die Weiberhasser Tolstoi und Strindberg, II. Strindberg', in *Wir Frauen und unsere Dichter*, Wien und Leipzig: Wiener-Mode, 1895, pp. 165-198. ['The Women Haters Tolstoy and Strindberg'. Includes Marholm's proposition that Sg's collected works are really only biographical contributions to the solution of the mystery of his ego]

[B9:182] Marholm, Laura [Pseudonym of Laura Mohr], 'Die Weiberhasser Tolstoi und Strindberg', II. Strindberg, in *Wir Frauen und unsere Dichter*, 2. umgearb. und wesentlich vermehrte Ausgabe, Berlin: Carl Dunker, 1896, pp. 199-243. ['The Women Haters Tolstoy and Strindberg'. An enlarged edition of **B9:181**. Marholm defines Sg according to contemporary categories of physiology, race, and criminal anthropology as a 'Mischtypus', i.e. a hybrid combination of 'finno-lapp' and 'Mongolian' blood, which thus explains his misogynist views on women]

[B9:183] Marno, Heinrich, 'Betrachtungen über Strindberg', *Der Brenner* (Innsbruck), 3 (1912-13), 352-361. ['Reflections on Strindberg'. Focuses on Sg's depiction of the battle of the sexes as a conflict between cerebral man and the simple nature of intellectually challenged woman. Concerned as much with Sg's character as with his art]

[B9:184] Martinus, Eivor, 'Strindberg och kvinnorna', in Anita Persson and Barbara Lide, red., **B1:366**, *Ja, må han leva!*, pp. 143-150. ['Strindberg and Women'. Disusses the role of Siri von Essen, Frida Uhl, Harriet Bosse, and Fanny Falkner in Sg's life and his attitude to women in general. Offers a summary of Martinus's general argument concerning Sg's relationship to women in **R:1480**]

[B9:185] Masters, Robert E. L., and Eduard Lea, eds, *The Anti-Sex: The Belief in the Natural Inferiority of Women. Studies in Male Frustration and Sexual Conflict*, New York: Julian Press, 1964. 492 pp. [Includes an extract from *En dåres försvarstal*, pp. 315-327]

[B9:186] Mathieu, André, 'Misogyne, avec excuses', *Le Magazin littéraire* (Paris), No. 224 (1985), p. 33. ['Misogynist, with Excuses'. Seeks to refute the notion that Sg hated women. Mathieu wonders if Sg's alleged misogyny is 'nothing other than the "modest" reaction of a lover disappointed at not being able to be woman's equal?']

[B9:187] Mauritzson, Jules, 'August Strindberg and the Woman Question', *Scandinavian Studies and Notes* (Menasha, Wisconsin) 1 (1912-13), 207-213. [Maintains that prior to *Giftas*, Sg's female characters are drawn with a touch that is warmly sympathetic, at times verging on romantic adoration, but even in *Giftas* and the works he wrote on the recoil from his experiences in 1884, it is not woman as such that he rails against but the idle, emancipated woman, whom he considers a degenerate type. Mauritzson defends Sg primarily on the grounds of what he considers were his private experiences, based on the way that the latter are depicted in various of his works, and consequently makes no attempt to deal with any of these works as literature]

[B9:188] Mensch, Ella, 'Sollen die frauen Strindberg lesen?', 1-2, *Frauen-Rundschau* (Wien und Leipzig), 5 (1904), Hefte 47; 6 (1905), pp. 91-94. ['Should Women Read Strindberg?']

[B9:189] Mitchell, Christopher Joseph, 'Radikalfeministen Strindberg', in Anna Cavallin and Anna Westerståhl Stenport, red., **B9:78**, *Det gäckande könet: Strindberg och genusteori*, pp. 217-232. ['Strindberg the Radical Feminist'. Translated by Sonia Wichman. Reads *Fadren* and *Fröken Julie* and their problematising of conventional women's roles as an anticipation of feminist thinking during the 1960s and 1970s, represented here by Mary Daly and Adrienne Rich. Thus Laura in *Fadren* is diametrically opposed to the 'normal' emotional woman while Julie is exceptional in her capacity to take the sexual initiative and to command]

[B9:190] Moberg, Eva X., 'Mannen hatade verkligen kvinnor', *Aftonbladet* (Stockholm), 22 January 1999. ['The Man really did Hate Women'. By the convenor of the Anti-Strindberg Society]

[B9:191] Monié, Karin, 'Kvinnosyn i dikt och verklighet', in Folke Olsson, red., **B1:348**, *Strindberg*, pp. 14-21. Illus. ['His Views on Women in Literature and Reality'. Situates the opinions which Sg expressed about women in *Mäster Olof*, *Giftas*, and *Svenska folket* in their contemporary context, which included both the eminent Stockholm based, Russian mathematician, Sof'ia Kovalevskaia, and Ellen Key, whom he lampooned in *Svarta fanor* as Hanna Paj]

[B9:192] Mortensen, Anna Berg, 'Strindberg och kvinnofrågan', *Studentföreningen Verdandis tidningsartiklar* (Uppsala), No. 259 (1912). ['Strindberg and the Woman Question'. Rpr. of **B9:193**]

[B9:193] Mortensen, Anna Berg, 'Strindberg och kvinnofrågan', *Upsala Nya Tidning*, 17 October 1912. ['Strindberg and the Woman Question']

[B9:194] M. P. 'Strindberg i kobiety', *Przegląd Poznański* (Poznań), 1895, No. 32, p. 378. ['Strindberg and Women']

[B9:195] M. S. [Maurice Spronck], 'La Question des Femmes', *Journal des Débats* (Paris), 7 January 1895. ['The Woman Question'. Comments on Sg's essay 'L'Infériorité de la femme' (The Inferiority of Women) in *La Revue Blanche*, 7 January 1895]

[B9:196] Myrdal, Jan, 'Apropå Strindbergs kvinnor', *Folket i Bild/Kulturfront* (Stockholm), 14:9 (1985), p. 27. ['Apropos Strindberg's Women'. Maintains that what is often regarded as Sg's neurotic attitude to women, penis size, and paternity is perfectly Swedish and quite normal behaviour]

[B9:197] Myrdal, Jan, 'Apropå Strindbergs kvinnor', in *En annan ordning. Litterärt och Personligt*, Stockholm: Norstedts, 1988, pp. 61-64. ['Apropos Strindberg's Women'. Rpr. of **B9:196**]

[B9:198] Myrdal, Jan, 'Strindberg et les femmes – une dichotomie', in **B9:245**, *August Strindberg et les femmes*, Paris: Centre culturel suédois, 2000, pp. 35-42. ['Strindberg and Women: A Dichotomy'. Myrdal maintains Sg's profound Swedishness and discusses his outlook on women which, he insists, was both deeply personal and rooted in his relationships with his three wives, all of whom he treated in a more enlightened fashion than was the custom with many of his radical contemporaries, such as Hjalmar Branting. It was this existential position that he developed theoretically in many of his works. Myrdal quotes at length from *Svenska folket* and refers in passing to *En dåres försvarstal* and *Fadren*]

[B9:199] Myrdal, Jan, 'En passionerad make som slogs för kvinnans rätt och tog hand om barn och hushåll', *Aftonbladet* (Stockholm), 23 October 1999. ['A Passionate Husband who Fought for Women's Rights and took Care of his Children and the Housekeeping'. Offers an alternative view of Sg's relationships with women]

[B9:200] Néthy, Jean de, 'La Question de la Femme dans la récente littérature scandinave', *L'Ermitage* (Paris), 2 (1892), pp. 1-9. ['The Woman Question in Recent Scandinavian Literature'. An article based largely on Ola Hansson's discussion of the issue in *Das junge Skandinavien*, **B3:211**]

[B9:201] Obermayer, F., 'Strindberg, l'ennemi des femmes', *Le Figaro* (Paris), 21 June 1894. ['Strindberg, the Enemy of Women'. Introduces Sg to French readers primarily as a misogynist]

[B9:202] Ogilvie, Dorothea, 'Von Ibsens Nora zu Shaws Candida. Ein Stück Entwicklung der Frauenfrage', *Die Christengemeinschaft* (Stuttgart), 7 (1930-31), 7-11. ['From Ibsen's Nora to Shaw's Candida. A Stage in the Development of the Woman Question'. Surveys the Woman Question as portrayed in drama from Ibsen to Shaw. Sg discussed, pp. 9-11]

[B9:203] *Politiken* (Copenhagen) [Viggo Hørup?], 'Kvinnosaken enligt evolutionsteorien', 24 September 1888. ['Feminism According to Evolutionary Theory'. An editorial contribution to an ongoing discussion in the Danish press concerning the nature of women, which specifically comments on Sg's portrayal of woman as an inferior, undeveloped creature, as formulated in his essay 'Kvinnans underlägsenhet under mannen' (Woman's Inferiority to Man)]

[B9:204] Polonskii, Gr[igori], 'Puti Avgusta Strindberga', *Bodroe slovo* (St Petersburg), 1909:21, pp. 38-55. ['The Roads of August Strindberg'. Considers that, even if Sg is the father of contemporary misogynistic literature, he is far from being a doctrinaire misogynist. What he hates is woman as she has lured and tormented him throughout his life, not woman herself. Polonskii criticises *Röda rummet*, which he finds boring, and *Utopier i verkligheten*, which is abstract and resembles a textbook in political economy rather than a work of art. E.804]

[B9:205] Prévost, Marcel, 'Théorie de l'inferiorité', *Gil Blas* (Paris), 2 February 1995. ['Theory of Inferiority'. A humorous response to the French version of Sg's essay on woman's inferiority to man in *La Revue Blanche*, 7 January 1895]

[B9:206] Prokop, Ulrike, 'Elemente der Moderne. Bilder des Weiblichen bei Strindberg und Wedekind', in Elke Austermühl, Alfred Kessler, Hartmut Vinçon, Hrsg., *Kein Funke mehr, kein Stern aus früh'rer Welt. Frank Wedekind: Texte, Interviews, Studien*, Darmstadt: Georg Büchner Buchhandlung, 1989, pp. 187-214. ['Elements of Modernity. Images of the Feminine in Strindberg and Wedekind'. Prokop compares Sg's image of woman and the feminine in *Fadren*, *Fröken Julie*, and *Fordringsägare* with Wedekind's in the Lulu plays, which she regards as a key document of modernity]

[B9:207] Pu Shunquing, 'Yibusheing yu Sitelinbao zhi funüguan', *Funü zazhi* (Beijing), 13:9 (September 1927), 19-24. ['Ibsen and Strindberg's Views on Women'. A comparative study which suggests that Sg's opinions about women may be attributed to his own misfortunes in life; whereas Ibsen is more sympathetic to the liberation of women, Sg's negative view is a projection of his personal sufferings]

[B9:208] Rasmussen, Agnete, *Dansk kvindesamfund og Sædelighedsfejden 1887*, Aarhus: GMT, 1972. 89 pp. [Deals with the participation of Sg, Georg Brandes, and Bjørnstjerne Bjørnson in the wide-ranging debate on sexual morality and marriage that was a major preoccupation in Scandinavia during the 1880s, pp. 22-37]

[B9:209] Robert, Marthe, *Le Puits de Babel*, Paris: Bernard Grasset, 1987, pp. 238-240. [Contemplates a comparison of Ibsen with Sg in order to demonstrate how their expressed opinions of feminism sometimes contradict the men revealed by their works. For Robert, a work like *Fröken Julie* indicates Sg's astonishing capacity for identification with women which results in extremely complex female portraits, whereas Ibsen's women are flat and lacking in colour]

[B9:210] Rohmder, Käthe, 'Strindberg und die Frauen', *Bühne und Welt* (Hamburg), 18:8 (1916), 365-367. ['Strindberg and Woman']

[B9:211] Rosen, Kristina, 'Margartha Fahlgren om Strindberg. Könsproblematiken central', *Upsala Nya Tidning*, 11 May 1894. ['Margartha Fahlgren on Strindberg. The Problem of Gender is Central'. An interview with Fahlgren about her study of Sg, **B9:95**]

[B9:212] Röttger, Karl, 'Strindbergs "Frauenhass"', *Die Brücke* (GroßLichterfelde West), 3 (1913), 129-133. ['Strindberg's Misogyny']

[B9:213] Röttger, Karl, 'Strindbergs "Frauenhass"', *Illustrierte Zeiting* (Leipzig), 152 (1919), No. 3952, p. 319. ['Strindberg's "Misogyny"']

[B9:214] Roudaut, Jean, 'L'éroccultisme', *Obliques. Littérature-Théâtre* (Paris), 1 (1972), 57-61. [Considers love as portrayed in Sg's works as always a battle for possession in which man fights an unequal conflict with woman, who has the nocturnal powers of a vampire. Refers to *Dödsdansen*, *Inferno*, *En dåres försvarstal*, *Ockulta dagboken*, *Brott och brott*, *Ensam*, and Sg's relationship with Harriet Bosse. His theatrical relationship with her is the public manifestation of their nocturnal eroticism, at once secret and fictional, and Roudaut links it with his incestuous feelings for his sister, Anna. Marginalia accompanying the essay link eroticism with occultism, both in the form of

Jean-Martin Charcot's hypnotic experiments at the Hôpital Salpetrière, the speculations of the French occultists Émile Vial and Albert de Rochas, and Swedenborg's theories of telepathic relationship]

[B9:215] Rubin, Birgitta, '"Det är mannen som lägger ägget". Strindbergs kvinnosyn givet ämne för feministiska forskare', *Dagens Nyheter* (Stockholm), 15 March 1995. ['"It is the Man who Lays the Egg". Strindberg's View of Women a Natural Subject for Feminist Researchers'. An interview with the Sg scholars Margaretha Fahlgren and Margareta Wirmark about Sg and contemporary feminist criticism which takes its title from one of his cherished notions concerning human reproductive behaviour]

[B9:216] Salczer, Eszter, 'Strindbergs fäder och döttrar och de Andras röster', in Anna Cavallin and Anna Westerståhl Stenport, red., **B9:78**, *Det gäckande könet: Strindberg och genusteori*, pp. 103-123. ['Strindberg's Fathers and Daughters and the Voices of the Others'. Translated by Anna Cavallin. Examines the relevance of Sg's inescapably masculine author's role for his portrayal of daughters in (especially) *Fadren* and *Ett drömspel*. Presents some of the ideas developed further in **B9:217**]

[B9:217] Salczer, Eszter, *Writing Daughters: August Strindberg's Other Voices*, Norwich: Norvik Press, 2008.

[B9:218] Sandstrøm, Bjarne, 'Kvindesagen og det moderne gennembrud', *Kritik* (Copenhagen), No. 38 (1976), pp. 5-32. ['Feminism and the Modern Breakthrough'. Places Sg centrally, alongside Georg Brandes and Ibsen, in a discussion of the Woman Question as part of an analysis of the ideological field of the literature of the Scandinavian Modern Breakthrough. Sandstrøm considers the challenge which *Giftas* and its treatment of sexuality posed to conventional views of every kind, radical as well as conservative. Concerned as it was with the conflict between nature and culture, he argues that Sg's anti-feminism is not pathological but the desperate outcry of a man who feels excluded by the ideology of emancipation. He also analyses *Fadren* as a counterweight to the portrayal of gender relationships in Ibsen's plays *A Doll's House*, *The Wild Duck*, and *Rosmersholm*, and concludes that its protagonist experiences the Oedipal conflict of the new emancipatory order as one in which a wife is at once a man's mother and his lover. Sandstrøm compares the situation depicted in *Fadren* with the stories 'Dygdens lön' (The Reward of Virtue), 'Barnet' (The Child), and 'Tvekamp' (Duel) in *Giftas I* and *II*. The play anticipates several of Freud's perceptions concerning gender relationships and, in Sandstrøm's view, it thus reflects the cultural crisis of the later 19th Century when a long established patriarchal order is dissolving, vital sexual energies are being released, and there is a regression towards what he terms a 'motherly' order]

[B9:219] Sch[ickele], R[ené], 'Sollen die Frauen Strindberg lesen?', *Das neue Magazin für Literatur* (Leipzig), 73:2 (1904), 777-778. ['Should Women Read Strindberg?' A response to Mensch, **B9:188**]

[B9:220] Schleich, Carl Ludwig, 'Strindbergs Frauenerlebnis', *Vossische Zeitung* (Berlin), 15 January 1916. ['Strindberg's Experience of Women']

[B9:221] Schmahl, Jeanne E., 'Le prejugé des sexes', *La Nouvelle Revue* (Paris), 1 March 1895, pp. 125-135. ['Sexual Prejudice'. Attacks the misogynist prejudices expressed in Sg's essay 'L'Infériorité de la femme' (The Inferiority of Women) in *La Revue Blanche*, and refutes his comments on the inferior physiology of the female brain]

[B9:222] Schoch, Hilde, 'Die Darstellung der Frau in der modernen Literatur', *Die Frau* (Berlin), 32 (1924-25), 33-39. ['The Representation of Women in Modern Literature'. Comments on Sg, p. 36]

[B9:223] Schultz, Julius, 'Anti-Strindberg', *Das Magazin für die Literatur des In- und Auslandes* (Leipzig), 62 (1893), 129-130. [A critique of Sg's views in the essay 'Kvinnans underlägsenhet under mannen' (Woman's Inferiority to Man)]

[B9:224] Schulze, Theodor, 'Strindberg und die Frauen. Zum 70. Geburtstage des Dichters', *Deutsche Internierten-Zeitung* (Bern), No. 109 (1919), 20-22. ['Strindberg and Women. On the Author's 70th Birthday'. Commemorates the 70th anniversary of Sg's birth with reflections on his attitude to women]

[B9:225] Scott-Jones, Marilyn, 'Laura Marholm and the Question of Female Nature', in Susan L. Cocalis and Kay Goodman, eds, *Beyond the Eternal Feminine: Critical Essays on Women and German Literature*, Stuttgart: Verlag Hans-Dieter Heinz, 1982, pp. 203-223. [Touches only briefly on Sg but serves to contextualise him and his views on women in *fin-de-siècle* Berlin, together with Marholm herself, her partner, Ola Hanson, the poet Richard Dehmel, and others among the city's artistic bohemia]

[B9:226] Servæs, Franz, 'Strindberg und das Weib', *Die Gegenwart* (Berlin), 43 (1893), 166-169. ['Strindberg and Woman'. Discusses Sg's representations of women, focusing in particular on the figure of Tekla in *Fordringsägare*]

[B9:227] Silvia Bennet [Pseudonym of Olivia Sandstrøm], 'Kvindfolket', *Politiken* (Copenhagen), 22 February 1887. ['Women'. Contests Sg's articles about women in the Danish press]

[B9:228] Sinclair, Upton, 'La peur de la femme chez Strindberg et Nietzsche', *L'Age Nouveau* (Paris), 1951, pp. 7-12. ['Fear of Women in Strindberg and Nietzsche']

[B9:229] Silvia Bennet [Olivia Sandstrøm], 'Strindberg og Kvindespørgsmaalet', *Illustreret Tidende* (Copenhagen), 27 February 1887. ['Strindberg and the Woman Question']

[B9:230] Ss [P. Sveistrup], 'August Strindberg i Kamp med Vejrmøller', *Kvinden og Samfundet* (Copenhagen), 1887. ['August Strindberg Tilting at Windmills'. A contribution to the lively debate on the nature and role of women in Denmark during the later 1880s, which was partly fomented by Sg's plays, short stories, essays, and pronouncements]

[B9:231] Stafseng, Ola, 'Vad är det för fel på Ellen Key? August Strindberg skrämdes av hennes hjärna', *Dagens Nyheter* (Stockholm), 30 January 2003. ['What's the Matter with Ellen Key. August Strindberg was Frightened by Her Brain'. Apropos Claudia Lindén's thesis, **B9:169**]

[B9:232] Steene, Birgitta, 'The Ambiguous Feminist', *Scandinavian Review* (New York), 64:3 (1976), 27-31. Illus. [Discusses Sg's conflict-ridden view of women as variously mothers, madonnas, child-bearers, and parasites]

[B9:233] Stéenhoff, Frida, 'Strindberg och kvinnorna', *Social-Demokraten* (Stockholm), 13 May 1922. ['Strindberg and Women']

[B9:234] Sterner, Jan, 'Kvinnor, kärlek och erotik i Strindbergs liv', *Gefle Dagblad* (Gävle), 20 August Strindberg 1999. ['Women, Love, and Eroticism in Strindberg's Life']

[B9:235] [Stümcke, Heinrich], 'Strindberg und die Frauen', *Archiv für Frauenkunde und Eugenetik* (Berlin), 5 (1919), 331-334. ['Strindberg and Women'. A discussion of Sg's sexual pathology with reference to Stümcke's comments in **B9:237**]

[B9:236] Stümcke, Heinrich, 'Strindberg und die Frauen', *Baden-Badener Bühnenblätter*, 2 (1922), 69-71. ['Strindberg and Women']

[B9:237] Stümcke, Heinrich, 'Strindberg und die Frauen', *Zeitschrift für Sexualwissenschaft* (Bonn), 6 (1919), 367-375. ['Strindberg and Women']

[B9:238] Svanberg, Birgitta, and Ulla Torpe, *Manligt och kvinnligt i litteraturen, Antologi och analyser för gymnasiekolan och folkbildningen*, Stockholm: Biblioteksförlaget, 1991, pp. 44-57. Illus. [Juxtaposes *Tjänstekvinnans son* with Selma Lagerlöf's novel *Liljecronas hem* (1911) under the heading 'Barnens vrede' (The Child's Anger). Mistakes Sg's date of birth]

[B9:239] Svanberg, Victor, 'Kvinnans natur och Strindbergs', *Svenska Dagbladet* (Stockholm), 5 April 1970. ['Woman's Nature and Strindberg's'. Comments critically on Sg's distorting view of women]

[B9:240] Tallgren, Anna-Maria, 'Nainen Strindbergin draamarunoudessa', in *Elämyksiä. Esseitä, arvosteluja, pakinoita 1910-1949*, Helsinki: Suomalaisen kirjallisuuden seura, 1990, pp. 79-102. [Rpr. of **B9:241**]

[B9:241] Tallgren, Anna-Maria, 'Nainen Strindbergin draamarunoudessa', *Valvoja* (Helsinki), 1916, pp. 551-568. ['Woman in Strindberg's Dramas'. Focuses primarily on *Fröken Julie*, *Fordringsägare*, and other plays of the late-1880s]

[B9:242] Taube, Agneta, 'August Strindberg och den moderna kvinnan', in Harald Bache-Wiig and Astrid Sæther, eds, *100-år etter – om det litterære livet i Norge i 1890-åra*, Oslo: Aschehoug, 1993, pp. 155-[171]. ['August Strindberg and the Modern Woman'. Examines the image of the modern women in Sg's works during the 1880s and argues that his general views on women, at least as they are represented in *Giftas*, *Fadren*, *En dåres försvarstal*, and *Fordringsägare*, are more complex than they have been assumed to be. In these texts there is an irony which can be interpreted as an expression of man's ambivalence regarding the new woman and her changed status and roles in society and the family. These works reveal Sg's illusions about women and his ability to meet a figure he feared as an equal although, as in *Fordringsägare*, he can also take a critical view of the past, and consequently of patriarchy, since here he suggests that man's notion of woman is founded upon an illusion that is created by man himself. This is most apparent in *En dåres försvarstal*, which Taube characterises as one of the most remarkable love stories ever written]

[B9:243] Taylor, Paul, 'Strindberg and the Zuni Curse', *The Independent* (London), 11 January 1996.

[B9:244] Tenow, Elna, *Öppet bref till August Strindberg. Om kvinnans underordnade ställning*, Stockholm: G. Walfrid Wilhelmsson, 1890. 64 pp. ['Open Letter to August Strindberg. On Woman's Inferior Position'. A pamphlet which strongly refutes Sg's assertion that women are inferior to men and the general tenor of both his literary and non-fictional treatment of women]

[B9:245] Unesco, *August Strindberg et les femmes. Séminaire organisé sous les auspices de l' UNESCO à l'occasion du Centre culturel suédois*, Paris: Centre culturel suédois, 2000. Illus. ['Strindberg and Women'. Contains the proceedings of a colloquium comprising **B9:21**: Elena Balzamo, 'De bon usage de la misogynie'; **B9:150**: Ugné Karvelis, 'Les Femmes dans les œuvres de Strindberg'; **B9:198**: Jan Myrdal, 'Strindberg et les femmes – une dichotomie'; **F5:91**: Sophie Grimal, 'Portraits des femmes dans *Inferno*'; and **J:1**:

Kristina Adolphson, 'Lettres de Strindberg à Harriet Bosse', as well as an introductory statement, 'August Strindberg et les femmes', by Ingemar Lindahl, pp. 5-7]

[B9:246] V. [Viggo Hørup], 'Er der et Kvindespørgsmaal?', *Politiken* (Copenhagen), 4 February 1887. ['Is there a Woman Question?'. A contribution by the editor of the Danish newspaper *Politiken* to an ongoing discussion in the Danish press about the nature of woman, which was partly fuelled by Sg's opinions in *Giftas* and elsewhere]

[B9:247] V. [Viggo Hørup], 'Gifte og ugifte. En Replik til Hr. Strindberg', *Politiken* (Copenhagen), 3 March 1887. ['Married and Unmarried. A Reply to Herr Strindberg'. A critique of Sg's current position on the Woman Question post *Giftas*]

[B9:248] V. F. [V. F. Firsov. Pseudonym of Baron Forsales], 'Vrag zhenshchin', 1-4, *Vestnik inostrannoi literatury* (St Petersburg), 1899, Nos 1, 2, 3, and 4 January 1899, pp. 83-122; February 1899, pp. 99-122; March 1899, pp. 105-131; April 1899, pp. 139-159. ['Woman's Enemy'. A tendentious introduction of Sg to Russian readers with the stress on his misogyny. Includes extracts from *Tjänstekvinnans son*, *En dåres försvarstal*, *I havsbandet*, *Hemsöborna*, *Skärkarlsliv*, and several short stories, translated by Firsov. Like many contemporary and later critics, Firsov treats the autobiographical fictions as reliable documentary sources. E.708]

[B9:249] Vinberg, Ola, *August Strindberg och hans kvinnohat*, Stockholm: A.-B. Chelius & C:o, 1929. 111 pp. ['August Strindberg and his Misogyny'. A largely biographical discussion which questions the extent to which Sg could really be accused of misogyny in a discourse that is itself redolent with questionable assumptions concerning Finnish women and Frida Uhl's Jewish [sic] background. According to Vinberg, Sg the misogynist is a cliché, and he argues that he had in fact a weakness for women, made some bad marriage choices, and might have found peace and contentment with a series of moderately intelligent mistresses and/or good cooks]

[B9:250] — Kj. S-g [Kjell Strömberg], *Stockholms-Tidningen*, 5 May 1929.

[B9:251] Weinstock, John, 'Strindberg and Women's Lib', *Germanic Notes* (Lexington, Kentucky), 2 (1971), 58-62. [Comments briefly and superficially on *Den fredlöse*, *Mäster Olof*, *Herr Bengts hustru*, and *Giftas*, and contrasts Sg's views with Ibsen's in *A Doll's House*. Weinstock concludes that 'the principle difference between Sg and the feminists was his strong feeling for the wife and mother role, other than that it is clear that Sg was in favor of women's lib, or in any case women']

[B9:252] West, Rebecca, 'Strindberg: the English Gentleman', 1-2, *The Freewoman* (London), 15 and 22 August 1912. [A critical response by a notable English feminist to translations of *En dåres försvarstal*, *Fadren*, and *Bandet*. West insists that Sg 'could not write'. Moreover, in her Ibsenite opinion, his attitude to women, marriage, and the family resembles that of 'an English gentleman']

[B9:253] West, Rebecca, 'Strindberg: The English Gentleman 1-2', in *The Young Rebecca. Writings of Rebecca West 1911-1917*, ed. Jane Marcus, London: Virago, 1983, pp. 53-60. [Rpr. of **B9:252**]

[B9:254] Westerståhl Stenport, Anna, 'Från kvinnohat till maskulinitetskris', in Anna Cavallin and Anna Westerståhl Stenport, red., **B9:78**, *Det gäckande könet: Strindberg och genusteori*, pp. 7-15. ['From Misogyny to Masculinity's Crisis'. Introduces a collection of essays which argues that the range of Sg's construction of gender in his literary works is seriously underestimated, and places this in relation both to his own time and to the 21st Century]

[B9:255] Westman Berg, Karin, '"Kvinnohjärnan liknar idioternas". Strindbergs kvinnouppfattning', *Expressen* (Stockholm), 15 April 1976. ['Women's Brains Resemble an Idiot's. Strindberg's Conception of Women'. Westman Berg takes one of Sg's own polemical statements as the title and starting point for her discussion]

[B9:256] Widéen, L. M., 'Strindberg, makten och det imaginära sexuallivet', *Gefle Dagblad* (Gävle), 2 July 1986. ['Strindberg, Power, and the Imaginary Sexual Life']

[B9:257] Wiese [und Kaiserwaldau], Leopold [Max Walter von], *Strindberg. Ein Beitrag zur Soziologie der Geschlechter*, München und Leipzig: Verlag von Duncker & Humblot, 1918. VI+143 pp. ['Strindberg. A Contribution to the Sociology of the Sexes'. What Wiese terms Sg's 'sociology of the sexes' is discussed pp. 6-34 as the pretext for a series of reflections on anti-feminism, the nature of women, politics, and race. He also relates Sg's views to a, then, fashionable distinction between 'Der Weg Asiens' and 'Der Weg Europas'. Indeed, his study is characteristic of much pseudo-Spenglerian discourse of the era, in which Sg was only one of several figures enlisted to explain the European waste land at the end of the First World War. Symptomatic of its period, the book has therefore no value whatsoever as literary criticism. 2nd edition, 1920]

[B9:258] — Andreas-Salomé, Lou, *Das literarische Echo* (Berlin), 21 (1918-19), Sp. 692-693.

[B9:259] — Anon, *Die Frau* (Berlin), 28 (1920-21), 158-159.

[B9:260] — Brunnemann, Anna, *Die Frauenfrage* (Berlin), 21 (1919), p. 63.

[B9:261] — D., *Deutsche Revue* (Stuttgart), 45:1 (1920), p. 94.

[B9:262] — Dege, Marie, *Deutsche Literaturzeitung* (Berlin), 41 (1920), 748-750.

[B9:263] — F. [Johann Frerking], *Das hohe Ufer* (Hannover), 1 (1919), p. 27.

[B9:264] — Flaskamp, Christoph, *Literarischer Handweiser* (Freiburg), 56 (1920), 132-133.

[B9:265] — Mahrholz, Werner, *Preußische Jahrbücher* (Berlin), 177 (1919), pp. 215-216.

[B9:266] — Raab, Rudolf, *Literarisches Zentralblatt für Deutschland* (Leipzig), 72 (1921), 215-216.

See also **A4:63, A4:64, A4:129**

[B9:267] Wittner, Doris, 'Strindberg und die Frauen', *Roland* (Berlin), 22: 21, (1924), pp. 15-18. ['Strindberg and Women']

[B9:268] Worringer, Wilhelm, 'Geschlechterkampf', *Zeit-Echo. Ein Kriegs-Tagebuch der Künstler* (München), 1:2 (1914), 20-22. ['The Battle of the Sexes'. For Worringer, Sg's work exemplifies the eternal conflict between man and woman that is currently reflected in Germany's present war situation]

[B9:269] Wulffen, Erich, 'Das nordische Drama', in *Sexualspiegel von Kunst und Verbrechen*, Dresden, 1928, pp. 169-198. ['Scandinavian Drama'. Examines the representation of women in the plays of (mainly) Ibsen and Sg, forcing in Sg's case primarily on the dramas of the 1880s]

See also **B1:8, B1:104, B1:134, B1:474, B2:332, B3:183, C1:67, C1:107, C1:172, C1:212, C1:232, C1:307, C1:402, C1:406, C1:565, C1:728, C1:750, C1:868, C1:870, C1:871, C1:995, C1:1021, C1:1070, C1:1179, C1:1180, C1:1201, C1:1202, C1:1228, C1:1229, C1:1230, C1:1287, C1:1345, D1:428, D1:494, D2:128, D2:332, D2:365, D2:576, D2:616, D2:751, D2:975, E9:11, E11:141,**

E11:143, E12:48, E12:55, E12:87. E12:110, E14:2, E17:3a, F4:98, F4:99, F5:91, G5 on *Giftas* passim, G6:20, P1:74, R:1480, V:6, V:7, V:49, V:66, V:86, V:92, V:93, V:132, V:137, V:149, V:151, V:155, V:162, V:167, V:180, V:181, V:187, V:196, V:241, V:246, V:246, V:251

C1. Comparative Studies

[*As well as books and essays which compare Sg's works with those of other writers in the manner generally associated with comparative literary criticism, this section contains critical articles, reviews, and statements about Sg by major authors, including Aleksandr Blok, Knut Hamsun, Franz Kafka, Maksim Gor'kii, and Thomas Mann, which sometimes reveal more about their authors than they do about Sg. It also lists books and articles which study Sg in the context of those literary movements such as Naturalism and Symbolism with which he was involved, as well as studies which seek to place him in terms of the development of Scandinavian literature, such as Gunnar Ahlström's* Det moderna genombrottet i Nordens litteratur, *or relate him to a major theme or topos, like Charles Dédéyan's* Le Thème de Faust dans la littérature européenne. *But comparisons between Sg and other writers regarding specific novels or plays (e.g. the relevance of Alphonse Daudet or Zola for* Röda rummet*) are listed in the section devoted to the work in question.*

Some comparisons or studies in influence like those which relate Sg to the plays of Ibsen or O'Neill are recurring topics in Strindberg studies. Others, e.g. the coupling of Sg with Dürrenmatt apropos the latter's adaptation of Dödsdansen, Play Strindberg, *are the prolific preoccupation of a short period only. (Indeed, it could be argued that it was Dürrenmatt's play rather than Sg's own texts which served briefly to mediate his image to a speculative public in performances from New York to Moscow just as, six years later, Per Olov Enquist's biographical drama on Sg's relationship with Siri von Essen,* Tribadernas natt, *represented him to audiences that were often unfamiliar with his own works, let alone the life which Enquist's play purported to dramatise. The widespread discussion which these plays provoked motivates the grouping of a selection of this material in two sub-sections (***C:3** *and* **C:4***) at the end of what is, all the same, an extensive list of comparative material. The length and range of this section as a whole is hardly surprising, however, since it reflects from the work of an author who read widely and willingly acknowledged the inspiration that his writing often derived from his study of other authors.*

Finally, the majority of items concerned with the frequently explored affinity between Sg and Ingmar Bergman are also listed here rather than in **D2** *and* **P5***, since they are generally concerned as much with Sg's influence on Bergman the film director as with Bergman's work as a theatre director. Hence, they too are grouped in a separate Section,* **C:2**]

[**C1:1**] Adamov, Arthur, 'Strindberg le comptable', *Les Lettres Nouvelles* (Paris), March 1955, pp. 347-366. ['Strindberg the Book-Keeper'. Excerpted from Adamov's study of Sg's theatre, **D2:1**]

[**C1:2**] Adamov, Arthur, 'Sur Strindberg', in *Ici et maintenant*, Paris: Gallimard, 1964, pp. 189-192. ['On Strindberg'. An extract from **D2:1** (pp. 47-52)]

[**C1:3**] Adams, Ann-Charlotte Gavel, 'Strindberg et Huysmans: un cas de plagiat?', in Gunnel Engwall, red., **B1:121**, *Strindberg et La France*, pp. 39-51. Illus. ['Strindberg and Huysmans: A Case of Plagiarism?'. Compares Joris-Karl Huysmans's conversion novels *Là-bas* (1891) and *En Route* (1895) with *Inferno* and *Legender*, and examines the accusation of plagiarism levelled against Sg by V. Hugo Wickström who maintained in a review of *Inferno*, **F5:170**, that Sg had drawn heavily on *En Route*. An analysis of their accounts of religious conversion as well as their mutual interest in both the occult and artistic 'supra-naturalism' demonstrates that, for all their temperamental consanguinity and striking similarity, any resemblance actually conceals fundamental differences. Sg was surely familiar with Huysmans's narratives, but certainly no plagiarist]

[C1:4] Adrup, Karl Anders, 'Författarnas författare: Henrik Ibsen alltid steget före Strindberg', *Röster i Radio och TV* (Stockholm), 25 (1989), 76-77. ['The Writer's Writer: Henrik Ibsen, always one Step ahead of Strindberg']

[C1:5] Agthe, Kai, '"Der Nomade setzt seine Wanderung fort": Ola Hansson als Nietzsche-Vermittler und Publizist zwischen Brandes und Strindberg', in *Widersprüche. Zur frühen Nietzsche-Rezeption*, Hrsg. im Auftrag der Stiftung Weimarer Klassik von Andreas Schirmer und Rüdiger Schmidt, Weimar: Verlag Hermann Böhlaus Nachfolger, 2000, pp. 52-64. ['"The Nomad continues his Wanderings": Ola Hansson as Nietzsche's Middle Man and Publicist Between Georg Brandes and Strindberg'. Outlines Hansson's role as an intermediary in familiarising both Sg and Brandes with Nietzsche and his works. Also documents Hansson's relationship with Sg, Max Dauthendey, and other artists and writers associated with the Berlin suburb of Friedrichshagen in 1892-93]

[C1:6] Ahlberg, Alf, 'Julstjärnan och Herkulesstjärnan', *Dagens Nyheter* (Stockholm), 19 December 1937. ['The Star of Bethlehem and the Star of Hercules'. Discusses Sg's interest in Nietzsche and the *Übermensch* with reference primarily to *I havsbandet*, and contrasts the image of the star of Hercules at the close of that novel with the Star of Bethlehem in the work of Viktor Rydberg's novel *Vapensmeden* (The Weapon Smith, 1891)]

[C1:7] Ahlberg, Alf, 'Julstjärnan och Herkulesstjärnan', *Svenska Dagbladet* (Stockholm), 8 January 1971. ['The Star of Bethlehem and the Star of Hercules'. See **C1:6**]

[C1:8] Ahlberg, Alf, 'Strindberg och Heidenstam', *Dala-Demokraten* (Falun), 26 June 1959. [Discusses the personal and literary links between Sg and Verner von Heidenstam (1859-1940)]

[C1:9] Ahlberg, Alf, 'Strindberg och Ibsen', *Kjölen* (Korsnäs), 4 (1944), pp. 7-9. ['Strindberg and Ibsen']

[C1:10] Ahlenius, Holger, *Georg Brandes i svensk litteratur till och med 1890. Hans ställning och inflytande*, Stockholm: Albert Bonniers Förlag, 1932. 418 pp. ['Georg Brandes in Swedish Literature up to and Including 1890. His Place and Influence'. A pioneering thesis which includes a discussion of Sg's literary links with Brandes and examines the latter's influence on his opinions regarding a socially committed literature during the 1870s and 1880s, pp. 201-221, 251-260, 298-301, 307-313, 327-331, 327-374. Doctoral dissertation]

[C1:11] Ahlenius, Holger, *Oscar Levertin. En studie i hans tankevärld*, Stockholm: Albert Bonniers Förlag, 1934. 217 pp. ['Oscar Levertin. A Study of His Ideas'. Includes a discussion of Levertin's often severely critical treatment of Sg's post-Inferno works which he frequently reviewed on publication in *Svenska Dagbladet*, pp. 87-94]

[C1:12] Ahlstedt, Eva, and Pierre Morizet, 'Strindberg et Zola', *Les Cahiers Naturalistes* (Paris), 35 (1989), No. 63, pp. 27-38. [Documents Sg's knowledge of Zola's works and charts his shifting relationship with naturalism via his letters and literary works, from *Röda rummet* to *En blå bok*. The authors suggest that Sg's prose fiction was barely influenced by Zola's novels, but he was interested in *Le Naturalisme au théâtre* and 'all' [sic] the plays that he wrote between 1887 and 1902 were strongly influenced by the doctrine of naturalism, even though he never adhered entirely to the movement as a whole, and still less to Zolaism *per se*]

[C1:13] Ahlström, Gunnar, *Det moderna genombrottet i Nordens litteratur*, Stockholm: Kooperativa Förbundets Bokförlag, 1947. 511 pp. ['The Modern Breakthrough in Nordic Literature'. A definitive and enduring study of the literature of the Modern Breakthrough, which is contextualised here in social, political, economic, literary, religious, and philosophical terms. Sg's works (most particularly *Röda rummet*, *Det nya riket*, *Dikter på vers och prosa*, *Giftas*, *Sömngångarnätter*, *Tjänstekvinnans son*, and the essays in *Likt och olikt*) are used frequently to illustrate themes, trends, and tendencies in Scandinavian literature during the 1870s and 1880s, as well as for what they convey of the society in which it was produced. They are also frequently compared with the writings of Ibsen, Georg Brandes, Bjørnstjerne Bjørnson, Alexander Kielland, Gustaf af Geijerstam, Victoria Benedictsson, Karl Gjellerup, J. P. Jacobsen, and others]

[C1:14] Ahlström, Stellan, 'Huysmans *En Route* och *Inferno*', *Svenska Dagbladet* (Stockholm), 29 November 1956. ['Huysmans's *En Route* and *Inferno*'. Compares Sg's autobiographical fiction with J.-K. Huysmans's novel of 1895 which documents his conversion to Catholicism in fictional form. Ahlström repudiates the charge of plagiarism sometimes levelled against Sg for having imitated *En Route* in *Inferno*, made initially by V. Hugo Wickström in his early review of *Inferno* in **F5:170**]

[C1:15] Ahlström, Stellan, 'Lawrence Durrell och Strindberg', *Svenska Dagbladet* (Stockholm), 28 September 1964. [Comments on the significance of Sg in *Inferno* for Durrell's writing, most particularly in the Alexandrian Quartet. See a later version of the same material in English in **F5:18**]

[C1:16] Ahlström, Stellan, 'Strindberg och Edouard Rod', *Sydsvenska Dagbladet* (Malmö), 12 March 1959. [Discusses Sg's contacts with, and admiration for, the Swiss-French author (1857-1910) and editor of the *Revue Contemporaine* in Paris, with whom he corresponded briefly in the mid-1880s]

[C1:17] Ahlström, Stellan, 'Zola och Strindberg', *Svenska Dagbladet* (Stockholm), 9 April 1954. [Examines Sg's links with Zola, both personal but primarily literary]

[C1:18] Ahnlund, Knut, 'August Strindberg och Gustaf Wied', in *Diktarliv i Norden. Litterära essäer*, Uppsala: Brombergs, 1981, pp. 224-247. Illus. ['August Strindberg and Gustaf Wied'. Provides a more detailed but otherwise similar account of Wied's personal and literary relationship with Sg to **C1:19**]

[C1:19] Ahnlund, Knut, 'August Strindberg och Gustav Wied', *Meddelanden från Strindbergssällskapet* (Stockholm), 35 (1964), pp. 10-17. [Documents Sg's acquaintance with the Danish novelist and playwright (1858-1914) whose drama, *En Hjemkomst* (A Homecoming), was strongly indebted to *Fadren*. In 1888-89 Sg considered it as possible repertoire for his Scandinavian Experimental Theatre where Wied also appeared an actor in *Fordringsägare*. As the partner of Nathalia Larsen, who translated *Fröken Julie* into Danish and appeared opposite Wied as Tekla in *Fordringsägare*, he was also deeply embroiled in that venture's colourful sexual politics. Wied's own most innovatory dramas were written after Sg had left Denmark, but he remained under his influence, not least for the merciless way that he emulated Sg in his fictional exploitation of material taken directly from life]

[C1:20] Akutagawa, Ryūnosuke, 'Ano koro no jibun no koto (bekko)', *Akutagawa, Ryūnosuke Zenshu*, vol. 2, Tokyo: Iwanami shoten, 1977, pp. 458-459. ['I Myself at that Time'. A prose text in which the Japanese novelist (1892-1927) comments on his response to Sg's works]

[C1:21] Akutagawa, Ryunosuke, 'Chokodo zakki; Kokuhaku', *Akutagawa, Ryunosuke Zenshu*, vol. 6, Tokyo: Iwanami shoten, 1978, pp. 203-204. ['Confessions'. Includes comments by the Japanese novelist Ryunosuke Akutagawa (1892-1927) on Sg as an autobiographical artist]

[C1:22] Albert, Henri, 'Nietzsche et Strindberg', *Mercure de France* (Paris), 16 April 1913, pp. 725-737. [A presentation of the Nietzsche-Sg correspondence in French translation with a commentary that is more sympathetically inclined to Nietzsche than to Sg]

[C1:23] Albert-Lasard, Lou, *Wege mitt Rilke*, Frankfurt am Main: S. Fischer Verlag, 1952, pp. 71-72. [Notes Rilke's positive response to 'the sinister thrill' of *Spöksonaten*, as directed by Otto Falckenberg in Munich, in 1915. Confirms that 'Sg exerted a great influence on Rilke']

[C1:24] Alonge, Roberto, 'Solitudine dei maschi e mitologemi femminili in Ibsen, Strindberg, Pirandello', in Roberto Alonge, ed., **D2:7**, *Alle origini della drammaturgia moderna Ibsen, Strindberg, Pirandello*, pp. 11-23. ['Male Loneliness and Feminine Myths in Ibsen, Strindberg, and Pirandello'. A study of ideas concerning masculine solitude and early modernist myths about women in the work of three modern dramatists. Primarily concerned with Ibsen's *A Doll's House, The Master Builder, John Gabriel Borkman*, and *When We Dead Awaken*, which are compared with Pirandello's plays *Diana e la Tuda, Trovarsi, Giganti della montagna, Giuoco delle parti*, and *Enrico IV*, but Alonge also discusses *Fadren* and demonstrates how Sg's military protagonist exemplifies no longer sustainable notions of male virility and consequently regresses to childhood, where his suffering is resolved by death]

[C1:25] Ambjörnsson, Ronny, 'Hemma på jorden', *Ord och Bild* (Stockholm), 92:1, 1984, pp. 75-87. Illus. ['At Home on Earth'. Discusses ideas of nature, sexuality, and morality in Swedish literature and art during the 1890s, with particular reference to Sg in *I havsbandet* and to Ellen Key, approached by Ambjörnsson as two post-Darwinian writers who were both influenced by Nietzsche]

[C1:26] Ambjörnsson, Ronny, 'Nordiskt ljus', in *Tokstollen och andra idéhistorier*, Stockholm: Carlssons, 1995, pp. 88-110. ['Nordic Light'. Rpr. of **C1:25**]

[C1:27] Anderson, Carl L., *Poe in Northlight: The Scandinavian Response to His Life and Work*, Durham, North Carolina: Duke University Press, 1973, pp. 52-53, 103-141. [Reflects on Sg's interest in Edgar Allan Poe during the later 1880s, an interest largely inspired by Ola Hansson, whose short story, 'Paria', Sg adapted for the stage in the spirit of Poe. The latter's work fused with his interest in the kind of extreme states of mind currently being explored by Théodule Ribot, Henry Maudsley, Cesare Lombroso, and Max Nordau, whose writings and psychological ideas Sg variously admired during the 1880s. Anderson discusses *Samum*, the vivisections 'Hjärnornas kamp' (The Battle of the Brains) and Själamord' (Soul Murder), from 1887, and the novellas 'Tschandala' (1888) and 'Genvägar' (Short Cuts, 1887), as well as *Paria, Fordringsägare*, and *I havsbandet*. His account illustrates how the tensions in Sg's relationship with Hansson are reflected in his enthusiasm for Poe. A stimulating discussion which is as relevant to documenting Sg's association with Hansson as it is to his literary encounter with Poe]

[C1:28] Anderson, Carl L., 'Strindberg's Translations of American Humour', in Harald Næss and Sigmund Skard, eds, *Americana Norvegica III. Studies in Scandinavian-American Interrelations dedicated to Einar Haugen*, Oslo: Universitetsforlaget, 1971, pp. 153-194. [A valuable study of the two collections of stories and sketches by Artemus Ward, Mark Twain, Charles Dudley Warner, Bret Harte, Thomas Bailey Aldrich, and James M. Bailey, which were published in Swedish translation under Sg's name but actually produced in 1878-79 in close collaboration with Siri von Essen. Contains detailed bibliographical data about the original stories and the Swedish series in which they were reissued; compares several passages in translation with the original; and assesses their impact on the development of Sg's prose style. Anderson stresses that, as with everything he laid his hands on, Twain's humour 'was assimilated, diffused, transformed, and converted to Sg's own uses'. In fact, it contributed to the satirical style of *Röda rummet* and is again in evidence in *Götiska rummen*]

[C1:29] Andersen Nexø, Martin, 'August Strindberg', *Social-Demokraten* (Stockholm), 15 May 1912. [Offers an appreciation of Sg following his recent death, together with a frequently reprinted and translated account of a visit he paid to Sg in Blå Tornet in 1911]

[C1:30] Andersen Nexø, Martin, 'August Strindberg', *La littérature populaire* (Paris), 2:2 (1921). [French version of **C1:29**]

[C1:31] Andersen Nexø, Martin, 'August Strindberg', *März* (München), 6:2 (1912), 281-287. [German version of **C1:29**]

[C1:32] Andersen Nexø, Martin, 'Ein Besuch bei August Strindberg', Übertragung von Hermann Kiy, *Das Inselschiff* (Leipzig), 1:3 (February 1920), pp. 143-150. ['A Visit to Strindberg'. German version of **C1:29**]

[C1:33] Andersen Nexø, Martin, 'August Strindberg', *Westdeutsche illustrierte Zeitung* (Essen), 30 January 1926. [German version of **C1:29**]

[C1:34] Andersen Nexø, Martin, 'August Strindberg', *Julblommar* (Stockholm), 1932, pp. 7-9. [Swedish version of **C1:29**]

[C1:35] Andersen Nexø, Martin, 'August Strindberg', in *Kultur och barbari*, Taler og artikler I udvalg ved Børge Houmann, Band 3, København: Forlaget Tiden, 1955, pp. 39-45. [Rpr. of **C1:29**]

[C1:36] Andersen Nexø, Martin, 'August Strindberg', in *Kultur und Barbarei, Gesammelte Werke in Einzelausgaben*, Bd III, Berlin: Dietz, 1957, pp. 46-54.

[C1:37] Andersen Nexö, Martin, 'August Strindberg', in *Gesammelte Werke in Einzelausgaben*, Bd III, Reden und Artikel, Berlin, 1957, p. 46.

[C1:38] Andersen Nexø, Martin, 'Odwiedziny u Strindberga', *Wieczory Teatralne* (Katowice), 1950, No. 13-14, pp. 41-43. ['A Call on Strindberg'. Polish version of **C1:29**]

[C1:39] Andersen Nexø, Martin, 'Strindberg, de eenzame', *De Amsterdammer*, 23 June 1912. ['Strindberg the Solitary'. Dutch version of **C1:29**]

[C1:40] Andersen Nexø, Martin, '[A Visit to Strindberg: Private Recollections]', *Krasnyi zhurnal dlia vsekh* (St Petersburg), 1923:1-2, pp. 63-64. [Russian translation of **C1:29**. E.914b]

[C1:41] Andersson, Ragnar, 'Victor Rydberg och August Strindberg', *Social-Demokraten* (Stockholm), 8 November 1935. [Reflects on the personal rather than the literary relationship between Sg and the most eminent Swedish poet and man of letters of the preceding generation (1828-1895)]

[C1:42] Andreichin, Ivan, 'Strindberg, Maeterlinck', *Misyl* (Sofia?), 9 (1899), 386-398. [Identifies affinities between the theatres of Sg and Maeterlinck, and considers their role in the development of modern drama]

[C1:43] Anon, '[From Abroad]', *Teatral'noe obozrenie* (Moscow), 1921:3, pp. 13-14. [Comments on Sg's correspondence with Nietzsche, recently published by Karl Strecker in Munich in **C1:1236**. E.897]

[C1:44] Anon, '[From Foreign Reviews]', *Knizhki 'Nedeli'* (St Petersburg), August 1896, pp. 261-270. [Reports remarks by the Swedish author Verner von Heidenstam (1859-1940) on Sg and his writing, pp. 268-270. E.701]

[C1:45] Anon, 'Litteratur', 1-2, *Svenska Dagbladet* (Stockholm), 28 February and 1 March, 1911. [Discusses Sg's links with the Swedish poet Gustaf Fröding (1860-1911) with reference to what has recently been confirmed is a spurious correspondence]

[C1:46] Anon, 'Möten med Swedenborg', *Nya kyrkans tidning* (Stockholm), 95:5-6 (1970), 54-56. ['Encounters with Swedenborg'. Notes the importance of Swedenborg for the work of the Swedish authors Tage Aurell (1895-1976) and Vilhelm Eklund (1880-1949) as well as Sg]

[C1:47] Anon, 'Nietzsches brev till Strindberg', *Dagens Nyheter* (Stockholm), 2* July 1911. ['Nietzsche's Letters to Strindberg']

[C1:48] Anon, 'Playwright of Many Interests', *The Times* (London), 19 August 1964. [A substantial interview with Peter Weiss prior to Peter Brook's staging of the *Marat/Sade* in London. Quotes him on Sg: 'I am interested in the technique of Sg's late plays...but I find his usual problems not of so much interest. I don't care who is the father of the child']

[C1:49] Anon, 'Strindberg och Brandes', *Hallandsposten* (Halmstad), 7 July 1914. [Comments on Sg's relationship with Georg Brandes]

[C1:50] Anon, 'The Swedish Ibsen', *Current Literature* (New York), October 1905, pp. 437-348. [Compares Sg with Ibsen. Also maintains that, as a misogynist, Sg goes beyond both Schopenhauer and Nietzsche, and that, in *Kristina*, he presents his conception of woman in terms of 'a literal portrait of Harriet Bosse']

[C1:51] Anz, Heinrich, '"Hiobs Gemeinde": Überlegungen zur Poetologie des Dichters bei S. Kierkegaard, H. Ibsen, A. Strindberg und K. Blixen', *Text & Kontext* (Copenhagen /München), 21:1 (1998), 7-25. ['"Job's Parish". Reflections on the Poetology of the Writer in S. Kierkegaard, H. Ibsen, A. Strindberg, and K. Blixen'. Compares Sg's use of the topos of Job's suffering and Old Testament typology in *Inferno* with Ibsen's *Love's Comedy* (1862), Karen Blixen's collection *Vinter-Eventyr* (Winter Tales, 1942), and Kierkegaard's *Gjentagelsen* (Repetition, 1843)]

[C1:52] Arestad, Sverre, 'Ibsen, Strindberg and Naturalist Tragedy', *Theater Annual* (Albany, New York), 24 (1969), 6-13. [Includes comments on *Fadren* and *Fröken Julie*]

[C1:53] Arnaoutovitch, Alexandre, *Henry Becque*, 3 vols, Paris: Presses Universitaires de France, 1927. [Comments briefly on Sg's personal and literary relations with Becque in Volume One]

[C1:54] Arntzen, Even, 'Hamsun og Strindberg', in Nils M. Knutsen, red., *Hamsun og Norden: ni foredrag fra Hamsun-dagene på Hamarøy 1992*, Hamsun-selskapets skriftserie 5, Hamarøy, 1992, pp. 13-32. ['Hamsun and Strindberg'. Charts the personal and literary relationship between the two writers]

[C1:55] Arons, Wendy, 'From *Miss Sara Sampson* to *Miss Julie*: Naturalist Configurations of the Fallen Woman', *Text and Presentation The Journal of the Comparative Drama Conference*, 22 (2001), 147-157. [Offers a comparative study of the fallen woman in drama from Gotthold Ephraim Lessing's play of 1755 to *Fröken Julie* in 1888]

[C1:56] Arvidsson, Rolf, 'Per Hellström och August Strindberg. Några anteckningar till relationen', in Erik Carlquist, red., *Humanismen som salt & styrka. Bilder och betraktelser tillägnade Harry Järv*, Stockholm: Atlantis, 1987, pp. 47-62. ['Per Hellström and August Strindberg. Some Notes on Their Relationship'. Traces the Swedish novelist's initially positive response to Sg as man and writer in *Ett drömspel* and *Till Damaskus III*, and his increasing hostility following Sg's savage attacks in *Götiska rummen*, *Svarta fanor*, and *Stora landsvägen* on their mutual friend, the novelist and editor Gustaf af Geijerstam (1858-1909). Draws on Hellström's correspondence with Geijerstam]

[C1:57] Arvidsson, Rolf, *Den unge Per Hellström. Lyriskt åttiotal*, Lund: Gleerups, 1969. 464 pp. ['The Young Per Hellström. Poetic Eighties'. Compares Hallström's upbringing with Sg's childhood as narrated in *Tjänstekvinnans son*, pp. 208-210. Includes nineteen other references to Sg]

[C1:58] Aslaksen, Kamilla, 'Oppdragelse eller katharisis. Noen kommentarer omkring Strindbergs *Fröken Julie* og Ibsens *Hedda Gabler*', *Norskrift* (Oslo), 74 (1992), 14-32. ['Upbringing or Catharsis. Some Comments on Strindberg's *Miss Julie* and Ibsen's *Hedda Gabler*'. Relates both plays to the ongoing debate in Scandinavia during the 1880s concerning sexuality and the role of women, to which Sg and Ibsen had already made significant contributions with *Giftas* and *A Doll's House*. Aslaksen analyses the dialogue and settings of both plays as metaphorical rather than mimetic, compares tensions and parallels between their plots and central characters, and examines their respective final scenes, in order to illuminate their relationship to Greek tragedy]

[C1:59] Asmundsson, Doris R., 'Georg Brandes's Relationships with Ibsen and Strindberg', *Scandinavian Review* (New York), 74:1 (1986), 85-91. [Comments on Brandes's contacts with Sg and his role in introducing the latter to Nietzsche and his writings]

[C1:60] Aspelin, Kurt, 'Schiller i Sverige. Randanteckningar till den litterära utvecklingen från Leopold till Strindberg', *Clarté* (Stockholm), 28:3 (1955), 12-18. ['Schiller in Sweden. Notes on the Development of Literature from Leopold to Strindberg'. Includes reflections on the influence of Schiller's history plays upon Sg, through whose work Schiller as a dramatist truly entered Swedish literature. According to Aspelin, *Mäster Olof* derives a great deal from Schiller's desire for freedom and his tragic passion for determining right action, while later plays, such as *Gustav Vasa* and *Erik XIV*, are the culmination of a process of development in the Swedish theatre which has its origins in Schiller's concern with the theatrical portrayal of a nation's destiny in drama]

[C1:61] Aspelin, Kurt, 'Schiller i Sverige. Randanteckningar till den litterära utvecklingen från Leopold till Strindberg', in *Spår. Studier kring litteratur, samhälle och idéer*, Stockholm: Bokförlaget Pan/Norstedts, 1974, pp. 48-63. ['Schiller in Sweden. Notes on the Development of Literature from Leopold to Strindberg'. Rpr. of **C1:60**]

[C1:62] Aster, Ernst von, *Ibsen und Strindberg. Menschenschilderung und Weltanschauung*, Philosophische Reihe 4, München: Rösl & Cie, 1923. 129 pp. ['Ibsen and Strindberg. Characterisation and World View'. Compares the philosophies of Ibsen and Sg and the ways in which they portray their characters. Focuses in detail on Sg, pp. 103-129. Also discusses the two dramatists' relationship to Nietzsche]

[C1:63] Axberger, Gunnar, 'En romantisk klockare och ett svärmisk bodbiträde. Om Birger Sjöberg och Strindberg', *Samlaren* (Uppsala), 36 (1955), pp. 38-52. ['A Romantic Sexton and a Dreamy Shop Assistant'. Sjöberg's (1885-1925) admiration for Sg is apparent in several unpublished notes related to the poems in *Fridas bok* (1922) while his novel, *Kvartetten som sprängdes* (1924), was certainly influenced by *Röda rummet*. Axberger focuses mainly on 'Den romantiske klockaren på Rånö' (The Romantic Sexton on Rånö) from *Skärkarlsliv* and especially the affinity between its daydreaming hero and the young Sjöberg, whose early poems reflect its influence on him]

[C1:64] Axberger, Gunnar, 'En romantisk klockare och ett svärmisk bodbiträde. Om Birger Sjöberg och Strindberg', in Eva Haettner Olafsson and Lars Helge Tunving, red., *Efterlämnat*, Vänersborg: Birger Sjöbergs-sällskapet, 1989, pp. 107-129. ['A Romantic Sexton and a Dreamy Shop Assistant'. Rpr. **C1:63**]

[C1:65] Aulhorn, Edith, 'Strindbergisches bei Ibsen', *Der Zwinger* (Dresden), 4 (1920), 532-535. ['Strindbergian Elements in Ibsen']

[C1:66] Austin, Paul, 'August Strindberg, Sam Shepard, and the Expressionist Impulse', in Michael Robinson and Sven Hakan Rossel, eds, **B1:387**, *Expressionism and Modernism*, pp. 25-32. [Explores parallels between Sg and Shepard, both of whom wrote plays informed by a masculine identity, built on musical structures, and based on their own recalled and mythologized experiences. Their Janus-like expressionist dramaturgy was also similarly performed in the most prominent experimental theatres of their respective times]

[C1:67] Ayers, Herlinde Nitsch, *Selbstverwirklichung / Selbstverneinung: Rollenkonflikte im Werk von Hebbel, Ibsen und Strindberg*, Studies on Themes and Motifs in Literature 15, New York: Peter Lang, 1995. 177 pp. ['Self-Realisation / Self-Negation: Role Conflicts in the Work of Hebbel, Ibsen, and Strindberg'. Focuses mainly on *Fadren, Fröken Julie*, and *Dödsdansen* in a discussion of gender and familial roles in two chapters devoted to 'Die Frau als Eigenthum' and 'Strindbergs Laura in *der Vater*']

[C1:68] — Eddy, Beverley Driver, *Seminar* (Toronto), 33 (1997), 172-174.

[C1:69] — Finney, Gail, *German Quarterly* (Philadelphia), 70:3 (1997), 302-303.

[C1:70] — Kramarz-Bein, Susanne, *Skandinavistik* (Kiel), 27:1 (1997), 60-61.

[C1:71] Bæhrendt, Nils Erik, *Alexander Kiellands litterära genombrott*, Uddevalla: Forum, n.d. [404] pp. ['Alexander Kielland's Literary Breakthrough'. Includes thirteen references to Sg but has no detailed account of their correspondence or of the period in the early 1880s when he and Kielland made common cause in the literature of the Scandinavian Modern Breakthrough]

[C1:72] Babillotte, Arthur, 'Das Dämonische in August Strindberg', *Xenien-Almanach* (Leipzig), 3:1 (1910), 193-201. ['The Daemonic in August Strindberg'. Suggests that, where Ibsen was the Saviour and Healer, Sg 'points the way to the promised land as John the Baptist for the Messiah. His strange, lonely ideas are as magnificently sublime and terrifying as the midnight sun']

[C1:73] Baguley, David, *Naturalist Fiction: The Entropic Vision*, Cambridge: Cambridge University Press, 1990, pp. 102-103. [Comments on *Fröken Julie* which is discussed together with Zola's *L'Assommoir* (1877) and Paul Bonnetain's novel *Carlot s'amuse* (1883) in a chapter devoted to a discussion of 'The Tragic Model' of naturalism]

[C1:74] Bahr, Hermann, 'Die Krisis des Naturalismus', in *Zur Überwindung des Naturalismus: Theoretische Schriften 1887-1904*, Hrsg. von Gotthard Wunberg, Stuttgart: W. Kohlhammer Verlag, 1968, pp. 48-53. ['The Crisis of Naturalism'. Observes that, along with Ola Hansson and Arne Garborg, it is Sg who best exemplifies the psychological trend within late naturalism in Scandinavia]

[C1:75] Bal'mont, K[onstantin] D[mitrievich], 'Elementarnye slova o simvolicheskoi poezii', in Bal'mont, [*Mountain Heights*], Moscow, 1904, pp. 75-79. ['Elementary Words on Symbolist Poetry'. Mentions Sg, p. 79. E.723]

[C1:76] Balzamo, Elena, 'A l'ombre de Strindberg: l'univers romanesque de Hjalmar Söderberg (1869-1941) et ses lois', *Le Texte et l'idée*, 1991:6, pp. 117-136. ['In the Shadow of Strindberg: The Fictional Universe of Hjalmar Söderberg (1869-1941)'. Demonstrates how, in terms of form, style, and theme, Söderberg wrote his major novels, *Martin Bircks ungdom* (1901), *Doktor Glas* (1905), and *Den allvarsamma leken* (1912), in Sg's shadow. Documents the significance of Sg for Söderberg's work as a novelist in terms of theme and form]

[C1:77] Balzamo, Elena, 'Almqvist et Strindberg face et face à la justice', in Philippe Bouquet and Pascale Voilley, eds, *Droit et littérature dans le contexte Suédois*, Paris: Flies France, 1999, pp. 83-105. ['Almqvist and Strindberg Face to Face With Justice'. Observes that both Sg and the Swedish poet and novelist Carl Johan Love Almqvist (1793-1866) were preoccupied with notions of right, justice, law, and jurisprudence. Thus, Balzamo suggests that in the essay 'Om det allmänna missnöjet, dess orsaker och botemedel' (On the General Discontent, Its Causes and Remedies, 1884), Sg conducts a dialogue with his dead predecessor in 'Ur Europeiska missnöjets grunder' (On the Causes of Europe's Discontent, 1838). Moreover, quite apart from their mutual interest in Swedenborg, Almqvist assumed a new relevance for Sg in the 1890s, not least when Sg felt compelled to respond to Ellen Key and her polemical concern with elevating Almqvist at his expense as Sweden's most modern author in **C1:657**. Balzamo highlights the significance of Almqvist's essay on the treatment of criminals in *Hermès* (1822), his interest in criminal psychology as exemplified in his 'poetic fugue' *Amorina* (1822), and the idea of therapeutic justice; she also considers (although more briefly) Sg's critique of justice as a repressive social institution in several early works, including *Röda rummet, Det nya riket, Svenska folket*, and *Svenska öden och äventyr*. Balzamo comments on his attitude to crime and punishment in *Bandet, Inferno, Brott och brott, Ett drömspel, Svarta fanor, Syndabocken*, and *En blå bok*, where his concept of justice becomes progressively less negative. Whereas, for Almqvist, the divine presence was grounds for uncertainty regarding the boundary between good and evil, for Sg the return of God following *Inferno* in 1897 allowed him to entertain the notion of an innate sense of immanent justice and hence of repudiating the forms of justice established by human institutions as being at once inadequate and inefficient]

[C1:78] Balzamo, Elena, 'Le Joli Métier', *Orbis Litterarum* (Copenhagen), 45 (1990), 154-168. ['The Pleasant Profession'. Compares the figure of the journalist in four Swedish novels: Sg's *Röda rummet*, Hjalmar Söderberg's *Den allvarsamma leken* (1912), Birger Sjöberg's *Kvartetten som sprängdes* (1924), and Ulf Lundell's *Hjärtats ljust* (1983)]

[C1:79] Balzamo, Elena, 'Récit d'enfance: mythe ou réalité? Esquisse d'une typologie littéraire', *Germanica* (Paris), 15 (1994), 173-192. ['Narrative of Childhood: Myth or Reality? Outline of a Literary Typology'. Compares Sg's account of his childhood in *Tjänstekvinnans son* with similar accounts by Jean-Jacques Rousseau, Hans Christian Andersen, Olof Lagercrantz, and Ingmar Bergman, in order to establish a generic typology]

[C1:80] Balzamo, Elena, 'Regards obliques: Auguste Strindberg vu par Hjalmar Söderberg', *Germanica* (Paris), 10 (1992), 121-133. ['Oblique Views. August Strindberg as Seen by Hjalmar Söderberg'. Examines Söderberg's ambivalent attitude to Sg, including his admiration for the earlier, more socially and politically challenging works, and his recoil in particular from the religious elements in the post-Inferno writings. Summary in German, pp. 220-221]

[C1:81] Bandle, Oskar, 'Strindberg et les Norvégiens à Paris', *Revue d'histoire du théâtre* (Paris), 30:3 (1978), 224-242. ['Strindberg and the Norwegians in Paris'. Places Sg's friendship with Bjørnstjerne Bjørnson and Jonas Lie in Paris in 1883-84 in context and comments on their writings. In Sg's case this includes *Det nya riket*, *Sömngångarnätter*, *Giftas*, and *Tjänstekvinnans son*, in Lie's novel *Familjen paa Gilje* (1883), and in Bjørnson's plays *En Hanske* (1883) and *Over Ævne* (1883)]

[C1:82] Barnes, T. R., 'Yeats, Synge, Ibsen and Strindberg', *Scrutiny* (Cambridge), 5:3 (1936), 257-262. [Identifies similarities between Sg's ideas about theatre in the Preface to *Fröken Julie* and Yeats's theatre theories: both sought simplicity, a small stage, a small theatre, a fit audience, and no fake realism, but there all similarity between his drama and the 'antiseptic, delocalized [and] universal' drama of Sg ends. Refers only to Sg's 'naturalistic' plays which have some permanence since he bases his conflicts on persons rather than social theories]

[C1:83] Bartol, Vladimir, 'Zakrinkani trubadur: Ob Weiningerjevi knjigi Spol in značaj', *Modra ptica* (Ljubljana?), 7:6 (1935-36), p. 184. ['Disguised Troubadour'. Comments on Sg in the course of a discussion of Otto Weininger's views on women in *Geschlecht und Charakter* (1903)]

[C1:84] Barzel, Hilel, 'Bein Strindberg ve-Shakspeer', *Bama* (Jerusalem), No. 50 (1971), pp. 67-69. [Discusses Strindberg's admiration for, and debt to, Shakespeare in *Fadren*]

[C1:85] Barzel, Hilel, 'Bein Strindberg ve-Shakspeer', in *Drama shel mazavim kizonim. Milhama ve-shoa*, Jerusalem, 1995, (1971), pp. 67-69. [Rpr. of **C1:84**]

[C1:86] Baumgartner, Walter, 'Drömtekniken i Strindbergs och Kafkas verk', *Svensk Litteraturtidskrift* (Stockholm), 31:3 (1968), 18-26. ['The Dream Technique in the Works of Strindberg and Kafka'. A stylistic analysis which demonstrates that Kafka's writing is hermetically enclosed within itself whereas in his 'dream technique', Sg seeks only to imitate the form of dreams. In *Ett drömspel*, the synthesising activity of the conscious mind remains in evidence in the arrangement of the material, which is dynamic and capable of development. Baumgartner concludes that the notion that Kafka was influenced by Sg is absurd; he was far too subtle and acute in his own perceptions to be seduced by Sg's dream depictions]

[C1:87] Baumgartner, Walter, 'Kafka und Strindberg', *Nerthus, Nordisch-deutsche Beiträge*, Düsseldorf-Köln: Eugen Diedrichs Verlag, 2 (1969), pp. 9-51. [An extended version of **C1:86** which documents Kafka's knowledge of Sg, explores their contrasting dream styles in detail, and compares their prose styles and personalities. Where Kafka was given to resignation, Sg demanded compensation]

[C1:88] Baumgartner, Walter, 'Kafkas Strindbergslektüre', *Scandinavica* (London), 6:2 (1967), 95-107. ['Kafka's Reading of Strindberg'. Explores Kafka's characteristically one-sided familiarity with Sg's writings, which entailed ignoring the plays in favour of the prose works, most notably *Giftas*, *I havsbandet*, *Götiska rummen*, *Inferno*, *Legender*, *Ensam*, and 'Karantänmästarens andra berättelse' (translated by Emil Schering as *Entzweit*). In the latter, the themes which may have caught his attention are Sg's views on women and marriage in relation to his own 'Künstlerproblematik']

[C1:89] Bauzyte, Galina, 'Salygiskumas XXa. Vakuru dramoje (Augustas Strindbergas ir Judzinas O'Nilas)', *Literatura* (Vilnius), 14:3 (1972), 93-111. [A comparative study of Sg as a playwright with Eugene O'Neill]

[C1:90] Beckmann, Heinz, 'Ein Hauch von Lebenslüge', in **D1:39**, *Nach dem Spiel. Theaterkritiken 1950-1962*, München – Wien: Albert Langen-Georg Müller, 1963, pp. 209-212. ['A Touch of the Life Lie'. Compares Eugene O'Neill and his notion of the life lie in e.g. *The Iceman Cometh* with Sg]

[C1:91] Beer, Taco H. de, '[*Joseph*]', *De Portefeuille* (Arnhem), 10 November 1894. p. 255. [Identifies a common tendency to mysticism in four contemporary naturalist works: Edmond de Goncourt's novel *La Fille Elisa*, *Fröken Julie*, *Ghosts*, and *Fadren*. This is one of the earliest references in Dutch to any of Sg's works, in the course of a discussion of Étienne-Nicolas Méhul's opera, *Joseph* (1807)]

[C1:92] Behrens, Carl, 'Holger Drachmann og August Strindberg', *Nationaltidende* (Copenhagen), 13 October 1917. [Examines the personal and literary links between Sg and the Danish poet and novelist Holger Drachmann (1846-1908)]

[C1:93] Beissner, Friedrich, *Der Erzähler Franz Kafka*, Stuttgart: W. Kohlhammer Verlag, 1972, pp. 24-25. [Comments on the significance of *I havsbandet* for the development of Kafka's narrative style]

[C1:94] Bellquist, John Eric, 'Mythic Consciousness: Cassirer's Theories and Strindberg's Practice', *Mosaic* (Winnipeg), 20:2 (1987), 71-81. [Defines Sg as a mythopeic author who thinks mythically, a 'naive' writer whose belief in spiritual powers corresponds with 'primitive man's religious conceptions'. Bellquist seeks to demonstrate the extent to which his works and development reflect the kind of mythic consciousness described by Cassirer in *The Philosophy of Symbolic Forms* with reference to a range of works from *Röda rummet*, *Tjänstekvinnans son*, the prose poem 'Solrök' (Heat Haze), and *Inferno* to *Fadren*, *Fröken Julie*, and *I havsbandet*, all three of which Bellquist considers have affinities with symbolism]

[C1:95] Benedictsson, Victoria, *Stora boken och Dagboken*, Utgiven och kommenterad av Christina Sjöblad, 3 vols, Lund: Cavefors and Liberforlag, 1978-1985. [The edited text of Benedictsson's diary, personal notebook, and correspondence which includes thirty-seven separate references to Sg]

[C1:96] Benedikt, Ernst, 'Grillparzer und Strindberg: Eine vergleichende Characterstudie', *Jahrbuch der Grillparzer-Gesellschaft* (Vienna), Dritte Folge 6 (1967), pp. 139-59.

['Grillparzer and Strindberg: A Comparative Study'. Compares the personalities and beliefs of Sg and the Austrian dramatist Franz Grillparzer (1791-1872). Benedikt traces affinities in both their lives and works, their charged relationships with their respective fathers and with women, their attitude to religion, and (though relatively briefly) their playwriting]

[C1:97] Benstock, Bernard, '*Exiles*: "Paradox Lust" and "Lost Paladays"', *ELH* (Baltimore), 36:4 (1969), 739-756. [Confined where Sg is concerned to a single observation, namely that Joyce's play, *Exiles*, 'owes its central trauma to Sg (whom Joyce did not regard highly, probably out of loyalty to Ibsen); the doubt which perpetually rankles the central character in *The Father* is the doubt which obsesses Richard...And yet, if *Exiles* is Strindberg, it is also highly diluted, Strindberg without the hysteria']

[C1:98] Benzow, Kristofer, 'Sören Kierkegaard och nordisk diktning', *Årsbok för kristen humanism* (Uppsala), 1949, pp. 35-39. ['Sören Kierkegaard and Nordic Literature'. Includes Sg among the principal Scandinavian writers on whom Kierkegaard has made a significant impact. Maintains that Sg was never able to forget his youthful master, who haunted him and his imagination throughout his life]

[C1:99] Berendsohn, Walter, A[rthur], 'August Strindberg und Franz Kafka', *Deutsche Vierteljahrsschrift für Litteraturwissenschaft und Geistesgeschichte* (Stuttgart), 35:4 (1961), 630-633. [A critical response to Tramer's study of the psychic structures of the two writers in **C1:1304**]

[C1:100] Berendsohn, Walter A[rthur], 'Blå böckerna och *Doktor Faustus*', *Dagens Nyheter* (Stockholm), 15 March 1948. ['The Blue Books and *Doctor Faustus*'. Explains the relevance of Sg's genre-bending *En blå bok* for Thomas Mann's conception of his novel *Doktor Faustus* and its narrative technique]

[C1:101] Berendsohn, Walter A[rthur], 'Franz Kafka liest Strindberg', *Neue literarische Welt* (Heidelberg), 3:4 (25 February 1952), p. 7. ['Franz Kafka Reads Strindberg'. On Kafka's knowledge of Sg's work as documented in his diaries and correspondence]

[C1:102] Berendsohn, Walter, A[rthur], 'Goethe och Strindberg', *Samlaren* (Uppsala), 30 (1949), pp. 118-128. ['Goethe and Strindberg'. Documents Sg's familiarity to Goethe and his works with reference to the former's writings and correspondence where Goethe is frequently cited. Demonstrates that before the Inferno crisis it was *Götz von Berlichingen* (an important pretext for *Mäster Olof*), *Die Leiden des jungen Werther*, and *Faust* that mainly interested Sg; after it, he remains concerned with *Götz* and *Faust* but his interest now extends to *Egmont*, *Clavigo*, *Stella*, *Tasso*, *Hermann und Dorothea*, *Wahlverwandtschaften*, *Aus meinem Leben*, the *West-östlicher Divan*, and *Wilhelm Meister*. *Faust* is an important model, or intertext, for several of the plays, including those with a journey framework, such as *Lycko-Pers resa*, *Till Damaskus*, *Ett drömspel*, *Stora landsvägen*, and *Himmelrikets nycklar*, in the last of which the silver wedding of Romeo and Juliet is inspired by the golden wedding of Oberon and Titania in *Faust I*. Berendsohn also discusses Sg's comments on *Faust* in *Memorandum till Medlemmarne av Intima Teatern från Regissören* and various observations about Goethe in *Tjänstekvinnans son*, *Ensam*, and *En blå bok*]

[C1:103] Berendsohn, Walter A[rthur], 'Kafka och Strindberg', *Dagens Nyheter* (Stockholm), 28 November 1951.

[C1:104] Berendsohn, Walter, A[rthur], 'Knut Hamsun über Strindberg', *Vossische Zeitung* (Berlin), 4 August 1929. ['Knut Hamsun on Strindberg'. Examines Hamsun's opinion of Sg and his literary works]

[C1:105] Berendsohn, Walter A[rthur], 'Strindberg och Nietzsche', *Samfundet Örebro Stads- och länsbibliotekets vänner, Meddelande* (Örebro), 16 (1948), pp. 9-37. [An authoritative account of Sg's personal links with Nietzsche, his familiarity with certain of the latter's writings, and Nietzsche's relevance for aspects of the style and themes of his work during the later 1880s. Berendsohn also includes the verbatim text of the Strindberg-Nietzsche correspondence, thus correcting the faulty transcripts made available by Strecker in **C1:1236**]

[C1:106] Berendsohn, Walter A[rthur], *Der lebendige Heine im germanischen Norden*, Mit einem einleitenden Beitrag von Johannes V. Jensen, Kopenhagen: Schønberg, 1935. Illus. 159 pp. ['The Living Heine in Germanic Scandinavia'. Discusses Heine's significance for Sg as one among many Scandinavian authors whom he influenced, pp. 84-86]

[C1:107] Berendsohn, Walter A[rthur], 'Strindbergs krans på Weiningers grav', *Ord och Bild* (Stockholm), 58:1 (1949), 23-28. Illus. ['Strindberg's Wreath on Weininger's Grave'. Publishes Sg's exchange of letters with Otto Weininger (1880-1903), as well as with several other addressees, including Karl Kraus. Berendsohn also compares Sg's views on women with the theories advanced by Weininger in *Geschlecht und Charakter* (1903) and considers his comments on the latter in *En blå bok*]

[C1:108] Berendsohn, Walter A[rthur], 'Tyska röster vid 100-årsjubileet', *Meddelanden från Strindbergssällskapet* (Stockholm), 7 (1949), pp. 2-4, 10. ['German Voices at the Centenary'. Introduces and reprints comments about Sg made in conjunction with the centenary of his birth by Heinrich Mann, Arnold Zweig, Alfred Neumann, Ludwig Marcuse, and Ferdinand Bruckner]

[C1:109] Berenguer, Angel, 'Galdós y el teatro, in Manuel Losada-Goya and Kurt Reichenberger, ed., *De Baudelaire a Lorca: Acercamiento a la modernidad literaria, 1-111*, Kassel: Reichenberger, 1995, pp. 165-189. ['Galdós and the Theatre'. Discusses the relationship of the Spanish novelist Benito Pérez Galdós (1843-1920) to the vaudeville tradition, as well as to Ibsen and Strindberg]

[C1:110] Berg, Leo, *Der Übermensch in der modernen Litteratur. Ein Kapitel zur Geistesgeschichte des 19. Jahrhunderts*, Paris: Albert Langen, 1897. 281 pp. ['The Superman in Modern Literature. A Chapter in the History of 19th-Century Ideas'. Maintains that only Maeterlinck surpasses Sg in dramatic power and suggests that the dramatic force and psychology of the latter's 'sex-trilogy', *Fadren*, *Fröken Julie*, and *Fordringsägare*, is probably unique in contemporary literature. Berg also discusses the novella 'Tschandala' (1888) and *I havsbandet* as literary representations of the superman ideal]

[C1:111] Berg, L[eo], *Sverkhchelovek v sovremennoi literature*, Translated by L. Gorbunova, Moscow: Kushnerev, 1905. 258 pp. ['The Superman in Modern Literature'. Russian translation of **C1:110**. Includes a discussion of Sg in relation to Nietzsche and the concept of the superman, focusing primarily on 'Tschandala' and *I havsbandet*, pp. 119-143. E.741]

[C1:112] Berg, R[uben] G:son, 'Fröding och Strindberg', *Aftonbladet* (Stockholm), 27 February 1911. [Comments on an article in *Stockholms Dagblad* concerning Sg's personal relationship with the Swedish poet Gustaf Fröding (1860-1911), based on their correspondence]

[C1:113] Berggren, Kersti, 'Midsommar – en junirapsodi', *Borås Tidning*, 17 June 1962. ['Midsummer – A June Rhapsody'. Compares the representation of midsummer in Swedish literature by Erik Axel Karlfeldt, Johan Ludvig Runeberg, Esaias Tegnér, and Sg (most notably in *Fröken Julie*)]

[C1:114] Bergholz, Harry, 'Strindberg's Anthologies of American Humorists, Bibliographically Identified', *Scandinavian Studies* (Lawrence, Kansas), 43: 4 (1971), 335-343. [Compared with the material in Andersson's article, **C1:28**, Bergholz's essay offers only a brief bibliographical examination of the texts included in Sg's two-volume collection of translations of sketches and short stories by Artemus Ward, Charles Dudley Warner, Mark Twain, Bret Harte, Thomas Bailey Aldrich, and James M. Bailey]

[C1:115] Bergman, Gösta M., *Pär Lagerkvists dramatik*, Stockholm: P. A. Norstedt & Söners Förlag, 1928. 171 pp. [Demonstrates the role that Sg's post-Inferno works played in Lagerkvist's development as a dramatist, influencing both the essay 'Modern Theatre' (see **D1:604**) and his early, expressionist plays. Without Sg, these plays would hardly have existed, any more than those of the German expressionists, although Lagerkvist displays greater insight into the dramaturgy of *Ett drömspel* and *Till Damaskus* than did his German contemporaries]

[C1:116] Bergquist, Lars, 'Solve et coagula: om Swedenborg, Strindberg, subjektiviteten och sanningen', *Parnass* (Stockholm), 1994:4, pp. 32-36. ['Solve et coagula: On Swedenborg, Strindberg, Subjectivity, and Truth'. Compares and contrasts the scientific and religious investigations of Swedenborg and Sg under the heading 'Subjectivity and Truth', and considers the former's influence on the latter in his post-Inferno works]

[C1:117] Bergquist, Lars, 'Subjektivitet och sanning: Swedenborg och Strindberg', in *Biblioteket i lusthuset: tio uppsatser om Swedenborg*, Stockholm: Natur och Kultur, 1996, pp. 202-224. ['Subjectivity and Truth: Swedenborg and Strindberg'. Considers the influence of Swedenborg on Sg's later scientific as well as religious thinking. Bergquist focuses on the concepts of '*vastatio*' and '*devastatio*', the recognisable affinities in the two writer's ideas on dreaming, marriage, and love, their concern with the relationship between truth and experience, and the making visible of a concealed world behind the façade of what is normally visible, all of which Bergquist recognises in *En blå bok*, *Ett drömspel*, and elsewhere]

[C1:118] Bergquist, Lars, 'Subjectivity and Truth', in Stephen McNeilly, ed., *In Search of the Absolute – Essays on Swedenborg and Literature*, London: Swedenborg Society, 2004, pp. 61-69. [English version of **C1:117**]

[C1:119] Bergsøe, Clara, 'August Strindberg og Jonas Lie', *Framåt* (Göteborg), 1887, pp. 114-117. [Comments on Sg's familiarity with the Norwegian novelist (1833-1908) with whom he had been acquainted in Paris in 1883-84 and again in 1886]

[C1:120] Bethke, Artur, 'Periodisierung als methodologisches Problem der Literaturgeschichtsschreibung', in Horst Bien, Hrsg., *Die nordischen Literaturen als Gegenstand der Literaturgeschichtsschreibung*, Beiträge zur 13. Studienkonferenz der Internationalen Assoziation für Skandinavische Studien (IASS), 10.-16. August 1980 an der Ernst-

Moritz-Arndt-Universität Greifswald, Rostock: VEB Hinstorff Verlag, 1982, pp. 127-139. ['Periodisation as a Methodological Problem in the Writing of Literary History'. Exemplifies the problems of periodisation in literary history with reference to realism in Sweden and consequently the role of *Röda rummet* and the place of *Fadren*]

[C1:121] Betz, Frederick, 'Strindberg or Stauffer?: A Note on Thomas Mann's Misquotation of Fontane', *Germanic Notes* (Lexington, Kentucky), 10 (1979), 36-39. [Comments on Mann's error in attributing a reference by Fontane to Stauffer rather than to Sg, noting in his essay 'Der alte Fontane' (The Elderly Fontane) the latter's opinion that Sg represented the great embodiement of modernity]

[C1:122] Beyer, Harald, 'Nietzsche's betydning før nordisk åndsliv i 1890-årerne', *Nordisk Tidskrift* (Stockholm), 36:3 (1960), 121-134. ['Nietzsche's Importance for Nordic Intellectual Life in the 1890s'. Discusses Nietzsche's immediate impact on Sg, pp. 129-131. Although powerful, the impression that Nietzsche made on him was only a brief intoxication, discernible in the major naturalistic plays and (particularly) *I havsbandet*. If Nietzsche appeared to validate Sg in what he called his 'galenskap att opponera mot allt' (mad desire to oppose everything), the latter turned away from him in his post-Inferno works]

[C1:123] Beyer, Harald, 'Nietzsche og Norden', *Universitetet i Bergen Årbok*, Historisk-antikvarisk rekke 1, 2 vols, 1958, pp. [7]-204, and 1959, pp. [7]-351. ['Nietzsche and Scandinavia'. A broad and detailed study of Nietzsche's impact in Scandinavia, in which Sg is a recurring point of reference and the subject of detailed discussion in Volume Two, pp. 49-65. Beyer comments on several works in which Sg anticipates Nietzsche, including the vivisection 'De små' (The Small) and the long short story 'Genvägar' (Short Cuts, 1887), before his influence is apparent in the Preface to *Fröken Julie*, *I havsbandet*, *Götiska rummen*, and *En blå bok*. Summary in German]

[C1:124] Beyer, William, 'The State of the Theatre: The Strindberg Heritage', *School and Society* (Lancaster, Philadelphia), 71 (1950), 23-28. [Notes the relevance of Sg for the plays of Lillian Hellman (1905-1984)]

[C1:125] Billington, Michael, 'The Troll in the Drawing Room', *The Guardian* (London), 15 February 2003 (Saturday Review). [Presents Ibsen and Sg as 'the two indispensable props of modern drama']

[C1:126] Björck, Albert, *Emanuel Swedenborg, August Strindberg och det ondas problem. Ett föredrag*, Populär vetenskapliga afhandlingar 13, Stockholm: Albert Bonniers Förlag, 1898. [44] pp. ['Emanuel Swedenborg, August Strindberg, and the Problem of Evil. A Lecture'. Primarily concerned with the relevance of Swedenborg and his *Arcana Cœlestia* for Sg in *Inferno*, where his example helps focus the discussion of the problem of evil and suffering, a long-standing preoccupation of Sg's, dating back to *Mäster Olof*, which is discussed pp. 6-10, 14-15, 21-27. Björck also considers Swedenborg's relationship to literature and occult chemistry, and the religiously sanctioned roles variously ascribed to men and women]

[C1:127] — Lilliefors, M., 'Emanuel Swedenborg, August Strindberg and the Problem of Evil', *New-Church Review* (Boston, Mass.), 5 (1898), 477-478.

[C1:128] Björck, Staffan, 'Slottet och värdshuset', *Dagens Nyheter* (Stockholm), 31 July 1954. ['The Castle and the Inn'. Examines Sg's association with Verner von Heidenstam (1859-1940) in Switzerland during 1886, when Heidenstam resided at Brunegg Castle and Sg was briefly ensconced at the local inn. Björck recognises the relevance of their encounter for the development of Swedish literature as well as for the immediate work of both men. Immediately in Sg's case in *Tjänstekvinnans son*]

[C1:129] Björck, Staffan, 'Wir weben – ich weissle', *Svensk Litteraturtidskrift* (Stockholm), 30:3 (1967), 143-144. ['We are Weaving – I Know full Well'. Identifies a link between the refrain 'Ich weissle, ich weissle' in Max Frisch's play *Andorra* (1961) and similar songs in the work of the Swedish proletarian authors Henrik Menander, K. J. Gabrielsson, and Leon Larsson. Björck points out that Sg parodies the song in *Himmelrikets nycklar* and *Ett drömspel*, and connects it with a possible source in Heine]

[C1:130] Björck, Staffan, 'Hjärtat: brandplats och båtmotor. Kring en poetisk metafor', *Ord och Bild* (Stockholm), 70 (1961), 180-188. Illus. ['The Heart: Fire Scene and Boat Engine. On a Poetic Metaphor'. Studies the motif of a sacrificed heart in Maksim Gor'kii, Jean-Jacques Rousseau, Staffan Larsson, Johan Ludvig Runeberg, Pär Lagerkvist, Erik Axel Karlfeldt, Verner von Heidenstam, and Birger Sjöberg, as well as in Sg where it occurs in the poem 'Vid avenue de Neuilly' which introduces the *Sömngångarnätter* sequence]

[C1:131] Björck, Staffan, 'Litterära explosioner. Ett motiv – tre tidsskeden', *Studiekamraten* (Tollarp), 28 (1946), 292-294. ['Literary Explosions. One Motif – Three Epochs']

[C1:132] Bjørneboe, Jens, 'Strindberg – den fruktbare', *Aftenposten* (Oslo), 4 April 1963. ['Strindberg the Fertile'. An eloquent defence of Sg by a major modern Norwegian writer (1920-1976). See **C1:134**]

[C1:133] Bjørneboe, Jens, 'Strindberg – den fruktbare', in *Bøker og mennesker*, Oslo: Gyldendalske Norsk Forlag, 1979, pp. 189-194. ['Strindberg the Fertile'. Rpr. of **C1:132**]

[C1:134] Bjørneboe, Jens, 'Strindberg the Fertile', Translated by Esther Greenleaf Müre, *Jens Bjørneboe in English*, Online Archive, http://home.att.net/~ emurer/ texts/ strindberg.htm [Translation of **C1:133**. Maintains that 'On a purely theatrical plane Sg has become an inspiration, whereas Ibsen has become a burden, an immovable gravestone which preserves that form of theater which Ibsen mastered and therefore wished to keep unchanged. In dramatic world literature Sg has many descendants, Ibsen none…the shoots of the future are to be found precisely in his least noticed, least performed, and most criticized plays']

[C1:135] Björnson, Björnstjerne, 'August Strindberg', *Tiden* (Stockholm), 14 February 1884.

[C1:136] Björnson, Björnstjerne, 'Strindberg', *Tiden* (Stockholm), 20 October 1884.

[C1:137] Bjurman, Gunnar, *Edgar Allan Poe. En litteraturhistorisk studie*, Lund: Gleerupska Universitets Bokhandeln, 1916, pp. 442-444. [Part of a pioneering Swedish doctoral thesis on Poe which argues that he stimulated Sg's interest in the obscure and mystical aspects of existence, above all in the psychological realm since he was fascinated by psychic phenomena that tend toward horror, compulsive thinking, and madness. The long short story 'Tschandala' (1888) and two of Sg's one-acters, *Samum* and *Paria*, are obvious instances of the importance of Poe for the development of Sg's writing in the later 1880s. Published in 250 numbered copies]

[C1:138] B. L. [Bengt Lidforss], 'Viktor Rydberg som filosof', *Arbetet* (Malmö), 13 August 1900. ['Viktor Rydberg as a Philosopher'. Reviews the posthumous publication of Rydberg's lectures in philosophy, and maintains that, while he may have written a score of fine poems, Rydberg (1828-1895) should not be mentioned in the same breath as Sg]

[C1:139] B. L. [Bengt Lidforss], 'Viktor Rydbergs vapendragare', *Arbetet* (Malmö), 6 September 1900. ['Viktor Rydberg's Partisan'. An attack on *Aftonbladet* and *Lunds Dagblad*, both of which had taken exception to Lidforss' statement in **C1:138**, that Sg is the only Swedish writer who measures up to the other great writers of Europe]

[C1:140] Black, Stephen A., *Eugene O'Neill: Beyond Mourning and Tragedy*, New Haven and London: Yale University Press, 1999. Illus. XXIV+534 pp. [A major biography of O'Neill containing numerous references to the importance that Sg held for both his life and work]

[C1:141] Blackburn, Clara, 'Continental Influences on Eugene O'Neill's Expressionist Drama', *American Literature* (Durham, North Carolina), 13:2 (1941), 109-133. [Observes that Sg and O'Neill were temperamentally alike in their subjectivism and shared a predilection for mysticism. It was Sg who first turned O'Neill towards expressionism, influencing him in his use of verbal and dramatic rhythm and musical effects. Thus *The Emperor Jones* closely resembles *Till Damaskus I*, certain scenes in *The Hairy Ape* recall *Ett drömspel*, *Strange Interlude* emulates *Dödsdansen* in its portrayal of the war of the sexes, and the characterisation of *The Great God Brown* applies Sg's remarks on character in the prefatory note to *Ett drömspel*]

[C1:142] Blackwell, Marilyn Johns, ed., *Structures of Influence: A Comparative Approach to August Strindberg*, Chapel Hill: The University of North Carolina Press, 1981. XIV+306 pp. [A *Festschrift* for Walter Johnson with a wide-ranging series of comparative essays. See **A1:90**: Birgitta Steene, 'August Strindberg in America, 1963-1979. A Bibliographical Assessment'; **B3:299**: P. M. Mitchell, 'Strindberg in Denmark'; **C1:225**: Gunnar Brandell, 'Questions without Answers: On Strindberg's and Ibsen's Dialogue'; **C1:562**: Karl-Ivar Hildeman, 'Strindberg and Karlfeldt'; **C1:768**: Örjan Lindberger, 'Some Notes on Strindberg and Péladan'; **C1:930**: Harald Næss: 'Strindberg and Hamsun'; **C1:1119**: George C. Schoolfield, 'Strindberg and Diktonius: A Second Chapter'; **C1:1127**: Henning K. Sehmsdorf, 'Strindberg's *Ett drömspel* and Peder W. Cappelen's *Sverre. Berget og Ordet*: Two Dreams of Love'; **C1:1149**: Ross Shideler, 'Strindberg: The Man and the Myth as Seen in the Mirror of Per Olov Enquist'; **C1:1168**: Carl Reinhold Smedmark, 'Edvard Brandes and August Strindberg. Encounter Between Critic and Artist'; **C1:1223**: Göran Stockenström, 'The Symbiosis of "Spirits" in *Inferno*: Strindberg and Swedenborg'; **C1:1296**: Egil Törnqvist, 'Strindberg and O'Neill'; **C1:1394**: Rochelle Wright, 'Strindberg's *Ett drömspel* and Hofmannsthal's *Die Frau ohne Schatten*'; **C2:32**: Marilyn, Johns [Blackwell], 'The Chamber Plays and the Trilogy: A Revaluation of the Case of Strindberg and Bergman'; **C3:8**: Gerhard P., Knapp, 'From *lilla helvetet* to the Boxing Ring: Strindberg and Dürrenmatt'; **P1:142**: Reidar Dittmann, 'Art and Passion: The Relationship Between Strindberg and Munch'; and **P3:84**: Raymond Järvi, 'Strindberg at the Opera']

[C1:143] — Paul, Fritz, *Journal of English and German Philology* (Urbana, Illinois), 82:2 (1983), 306-307.

[C1:144] — Reinert, Otto, *Yearbook of Comparative and General Literature* (Bloomington, Indiana), 31 (1982), pp. 155-156.

[C1:145] — Robinson, Michael, *Scandinavica* (Norwich), 21:2 (1982), 197-198.

See also **A4:11**

[C1:146] Blanchart, Paul, *Le Théâtre de H.-R. Lenormand: Apocalypse d'une société*, Documents sur le théâtre contemporain 1, Masques, éditeur, *Revue Internationale d'Art Dramatique*, Paris: Masques, 1947. 248 pp. [A monograph on the theatre of Henri-René Lenormand (1882-1951) which notes the impact of Sg's later plays on his pessimistic vision and dramaturgy of the unconscious]

[C1:147] Blanck, Anton, 'Sverige och den franska litteraturen', in *Bellman vid skiljovägen och andra studier*, Stockholm: Gebers, 1941, pp. 60-108. ['Sweden and French Literature']

[C1:148] Blanck, Anton, *La Suède et la littérature française des origines à nos jours*, trad. Lucien Maury, Paris: Stock, 1947. 97 pp. ['Sweden and French Literature from its Origins to the Present Day']

[C1:149] Blixen, Samuel, *Estudio compendiado de la literatura contemporáea*, Montevideo, 1894. [A survey of contemporary literature with two pages on Sg. Blixen presents him as at once the most powerful and unbalanced talent of the age. His main fault is his espousal of so many different theories with such passion so, ultimately, the ideas in his head become a tumultuous life and death struggle of contradictory elements]

[C1:150] Block, Haskell M., 'Expressionism in Modern American Drama', in Werner P. Friedrich, ed., *Proceedings of the Second Congress of the International Literature Association*, Vol. 2, Chapel Hill, N.C.: University of North Carolina Press, 1959, pp. 528-541. [Observes that 'It is in large part through the powerful genius of Sg that Expressionism made its impact on the American theatre']

[C1:151] Block, Haskell M., 'Symbolist Drama: Villiers de l'Isle-Adam, Strindberg and Yeats', *New York Literary Forum*, 4 (1980), 43-48. [Block is primarily concerned with Villiers's play *Axel* but also discusses *Till Damaskus* and *Spöksonaten* as mystical dramas in accordance with the *fin-de-siècle* pattern of spiritual initiation, and *Karl XII* as typical of symbolist drama for the way in which the supernatural and the occult are present not as spectacular effects but as the revelation of sacred truth. He notes that, in Sg's plays, occultism provides the groundwork of a new dramatic art, and is inseparable from his expressionism]

[C1:152] Blok, A[leksandr Aleksandrovich], '[Autobiography]', in *Russkaia literatura XX veka*, Vol. 2, Moscow, 1915, pp. 312-319. [On Sg p. 318. E.871. Reprinted in Vol. 7 of the eight-volume edition of Blok, A., *Sobranie sochinenii v 8 tomakh*, 1963, pp. 7-16]

[C1:153] Blok, A[leksandr Aleksandrovich], [Diary of A. Blok], Vol. 1, Leningrad, 1928, pp. 78, 127. [Rpr. in P. N. Medvedev, ed., Blok, A., *Sobranie sochinenii v 8 tomakh*, Vol. 7, Moscow and Leningrad: Literatura, 1963, pp 124-125, 169. E.936]

[C1:154] Blok, A[leksandr Aleksandrovich], 'Ot Ibsena k Strindbergu', *Trudy i dni* (St Petersburg), 1912:2, pp. 8-14. ['From Ibsen to Strindberg'. In spite of the title, Blok barely discusses Sg at all. E.834]

[C1:155] Blok, A[leksandr Aleksandrovich], 'Ibsen i Strindberg. Nabrosok', in Blok, A., *Sobranie sochinenii*, Vol. 9, Leningrad, 1936, pp. 142-143. [Rpr. of **C1:154**. E.941]

[C1:156] Blok, A[leksandr Aleksandrovich], 'Ot Ibsena k Strindbergu', in Blok, A., *Sobranie sochinenii*, Vol. 5, Moscow and Leningrad: Literatura, 1963, pp. 455-462. [Rpr. of **C1:154**. E.834]

[C1:157] Blok, A[leksandr Aleksandrovich], 'Ot Ibsena k Strindbergu', and 'Pamiati Avgusta Strindberga', in Parfenova, A. T., ed., *Zapad na vostoke: Russkie pisateli XX veka o* *zapnadnoevropeiskoi literatury: Khrestomatiia*, Moscow, 1992, pp. 59-61, 69-79. ['From Ibsen to Strindberg' and 'In Memoriam August Strindberg'. Rpr. of **C1:154** and **C1:160** in a source book of readings of Russian 20th-Century Writers on West-European Literature. E.1792]

[**C1:158**] Blok, Aleksand[e]r [Aleksandrovich], 'Om August Strindberg. Ur två porträttskisser', Översättning Kurt and Tamara Johansson, *Ord och Bild* (Stockholm), 71:5 (1962), 415-417. ['On August Strindberg. From Two Portrait Sketches']

[**C1:159**] Blok, Aleksandr Aleksandrovich, 'Pamiati Avgusta Strindberga', in Blok, A., *Sobranie sochinenii*, Vol. 5, Moscow and Leningrad: Literatura, 1963, pp. 463-469. ['In Memory of August Strindberg'. Rpr. of **C1:160**. E.835]

[**C1:160**] Blok, A[leksandr Aleksandrovich], 'Pamiati Avgusta Strindberga', *Sovremennik* (St Petersburg), 1912:5, pp. 377-381. ['In Memory of August Strindberg'. An emotional obituary which records Blok's positive response to a portrait of Sg, his work, and Russia's need for such a man, who is portrayed here as a true democrat and the harbinger of the future ('He is least of all an end, more a beginning'). Sg, whose legacy is for all mankind, is someone that Blok wished to call 'comrade'. E.835]

[**C1:161**] Blok, Aleksandr Aleksandrovich, 'Pamiati Avgusta Strindberga', in *O literature*, Moscow: Khudozhestvennaia literatura, 1989, pp. 271-[276]. ['In Memory of August Strindberg'. Rpr. of **C1:160**]

[**C1:162**] Blok, A[leksandr Aleksandrovich], *Pis'ma, 1898-1921*, Vol. 8, Moscow-Leningrad: Goslitizdat, 1963. ['Letters'. Volume 8 of Blok's collected works containing his correspondence with Vladimir Piast about the latter's journey to Stockholm in 1912 and Sg's funeral, pp. 389-390, and the staging of *Brott och brott* by Meyerhold in Terioki with Blok's wife as Henriette, pp. 398-399]

[**C1:163**] Blok, Aleksandr, 'Till August Strindbergs minne', Översättning Lars Kleberg, *Strindbergiana* (Stockholm), 10 (1995), pp. 199-204. ['In Memory of August Strindberg'. Swedish translation of **C1:160**]

[**C1:164**] Blume, Herbert, 'Schmelzkopf, Tegnér, Strindberg und andere. Oder: Skandinavische Nationalromantik als Filter poetischer Wahrnehmung', in Lennart Elmevik und Kurt Erich Schondorf, Hrsg., *Niederdeutsch in Skandinavien*, Akkten des 3. nordischen Symposions, Berlin: Schmidt, 1992, pp. 212-230. ['Schmelzkopf, Tegnér, Strindberg, and Others. Or Scandinavian National Romanticism as a Filter for Poetic Perception'. Identifies the sources of Edvard Schmelzkopf's 'Balder und Hoder', 'Islant in den Titen', and 'An Stockholm' in works by Esaias Tegnér and Sg]

[**C1:165**] B-nr [Otto Groothoff], 'När Strindberg härjade med blåpennan i *Faust*', *Göteborgs Handels- och Sjöfartstidning*, 2 July 1949. ['When Strindberg Ran Riot with a Blue Pencil in *Faust*'. Comments on Sg's marginalia during a reading of Goethe's *Faust* in the translation by Viktor Rydberg, a version to which he took violent exception]

[**C1:166**] Böckmann, Paul, 'Wandlungen der Dramenform im Expressionismus', in *Untersuchungen zur Literatur als Geschichte*, Festschrift für Benno von Weise, Berlin, 1973, pp. 445-464. ['The Transformation of Dramatic Form in Expressionism'. Examines Sg's seminal influence on German expressionist drama and assesses the transformation which the movement wrought on dramatic form. Primarily concerned with *Ett drömspel*]

[**C1:167**] Bockstahler, O. L., 'Strindberg and Nietzsche', *Modern Language Journal* (Madison, Wisconsin), 16 (1931), 442-444. [Examines Sg's intellectual links with Nietzsche. Relies heavily on Karl Strecker's questionable presentation of their correspondence in **C1:1236**]

[**C1:168**] Boer, R. C., 'Een oorlogsheld in de literatuur', 1-2, *Onze Eeuw* (Haarlem), 18 (1918), pp. 185-202, 323-341. ['A War Hero in Literature'. Compares literary portraits of the Swedish monarch Charles XII by Esaias Tegnér, Verner von Heidenstam, and Sg. Considers the latter's drama *Karl XII* to be a pamphlet against power-seekers rather than merely a personal attack on the king]

[**C1:169**] Bogard, Travis, *Contour in Time: The Plays of Eugene O'Neill*, New York: Oxford University Press, 1972, pp. 76-78 and Index. [Suggests that O'Neill's play *Before Breakfast* is closely imitative of *Den starkare* but 'a paltry affair' compared to its original. Acknowledges the influence of Sg on *Welded* and other plays throughout, with specific reference to *Lycko-Pers resa*, *Fadren*, *Himmelrikets nycklar*, *Till Damaskus*, *Ett drömspel*, *Dödsdansen*, and *Stora landsvägen*]

[**C1:170**] Bohnen, Klaus, 'Skandinavische "Moderne" und die österreichische Literature. Zu einem "Literaturgespräch" an der Jahrhundertwende', in Herbert Zeman, Hrsg., *Die österreichische Literatur. Ihr Profil von der Jahrhundertwende bis zur Gegenwart. 1880-1980*, Teil 1, Graz: Akademische Druck- und Verlagsanstalt, 1989, pp. 317-341. ['Scandinavian "Modernity" and Austrian Literature. On a "Literary Exchange" at the Turn-of-the-Century'. Studies the influence of the writers of the Scandinavian Modern Breakthrough, including Sg, on *fin-de-siècle* Austrian literature]

[**C1:171**] Bolckmans, Alex, 'Der Naturalismus in Skandinavien', *Nordeuropa* (Greifswald), 13 (1980), 127-138. ['Naturalism in Scandinavia']

[**C1:172**] Boniecki, Edward, 'Stanisław Przybyzsweski's Berlin Essays on Artists and Art', in Piotr Paszkiewicz, ed., *Totenmesse: Modernism in the Culture of Northern and Central Europe*, Warsaw: Institute of Art/Polish Academy of Sciences, 1996, pp. 51-60. [Discusses Przybyzsweski's essays on Chopin, Munch, Nietzsche, Mombert, Vigelund, Ola Hansson, and Franciszek Flaum, all written during the period in Berlin during the 1890s when he was closely associated with Sg. Boniecki compares their opinions on women and comments briefly on Przybyzsweski's provocative view of Sg as 'the only essentially creative woman [sic] of genius']

[**C1:173**] Bonn, Friedrich, 'Strindberg und Faust', *Bühnen-Genossenschaft* (Hamburg), 14 (1962), 165-166. ['Strindberg and Faust'. Concentrates on the Faust theme in Sg's works, focusing primarily on his historical drama about Luther, *Näktergalen i Wittenberg*]

[**C1:174**] Bonneau, Sophie Glikman, *L'univers poétique d'Alexandre Blok*, Paris: M. Lavergne imprimeur, 1946. 375 pp. [See **C1:175**]

[**C1:175**] Bonneau, Sophie Glikman, *L'univers poétique d'Alexandre Blok*, Bibliothéque russe de l'Institut d'études slaves, 20, Paris: Institut d'études l'université de Paris, 1946. 519 pp. [Includes several comments on Blok's intense, if short-lived, admiration for Sg. Doctoral disseration]

[**C1:176**] Böök, [Martin] Fredrik [Christofferson], 'Brandes eller Brand?', *Svensk Litteraturtidskrift* (Stockholm), 5:4 (1942), 186-191. ['Brandes or Brand?' Compares conflicting currents in Scandinavian literature at the end of the 1880s, represented by Georg Brandes and his outgoing internationalism, on the one hand, and the inward-looking religious hero of Ibsen's *Brand*, on the other. Also contrasts Sg as a writer with the Swedish poet and novelist Verner von Heidenstam (1859-1940)]

[C1:177] Böök, [Martin] Fredrik [Christofferson], 'Snoilsky och åttiotalet', *Ord och Bild* (Stockholm), 30:1 (1921), 17-32. ['Snoilsky and the 1880s'. Examines the relevance of the Signature poet, Count Carl Snoilsky (1841-1903), and especially his collection *Dikter* (Poems, 1883) for the socially committed literature of the 1880s, including Sg's *Dikter på vers och prosa* and *Sömngångarnätter*, both composed with Snoilsky sometimes in mind]

[C1:178] Böök, [Martin] Fredrik [Christofferson], 'Strindberg och Heidenstam i Schweiz', 1: 'Attraktionen'; 2: 'Repulsionen', *Svenska Dagbladet* (Stockholm), 3 and 4 February 1921. ['Strindberg and Heidenstam in Switzerland. 1. Attraction. 2. Repulsion'. Examines the initially warm relationship between Sg and Heidenstam (1859-1940), who admired the former's boldness, love of contradiction, and independence. Their acquaintance in Switzerland in 1886 is depicted in *Tjänstekvinnans son* and Heidenstam's *Den ombytlige* as well as in his volume of reminiscences *Från Col di Tenda till Blocksberg* (1888) in which he displays an outlook not incompatible with Sg's in 'Återfall' (Relapse) from *Utopier i verkligheten*. But Heidenstam also countered Sg's standpoint in other works. Thus his novel *Hans Alienus* (1892) is a critique of *Sömngångarnätter* and the espousal of aristocratic values at the expense of democracy expressed in the poetic manifesto *Renässans* (1889) is likewise undertaken very much with Sg as an opponent in mind]

[C1:179] Böök, [Martin] Fredrik [Christofferson], 'Strindberg och Heidenstam i Schweiz', in *Från åttiotalet*, Stockholm: P. A. Norstedt & Söners Förlag, 1926, pp. 249-277. ['Strindberg and Heidenstam in Switzerland'. Rpr. of **C1:178**]

[C1:180] Böök, [Martin] Fredrik [Christofferson], *Verner von Heidenstam*, 2 vols, Stockholm: Albert Bonniers Förlag, 1945-46. [392] pp. 381 pp. [A life-and-letters study which includes discussion of Heidenstam's personal and literary relationship with Sg. Volume One covers their personal and intellectual association in Switzerland in 1886, pp. 83-101, and their break in the early 1890s, pp. 205-209; Volume Two covers the Strindberg Feud in which Böök was himself a partisan member of the grouping most opposed to Sg]

[C1:181] Børge, Vagn, *August Strindberg og H. C. Andersen*, København: Levin & Munksgaards Forlag, 1931. 146 pp. [Discusses the fairy tales which Sg wrote before the Inferno crisis as well as the better known *Sagor*, which Børge relates to the Andersenian tradition of story-telling. Børge also reviews his links with Hans Christian Andersen in general, establishes the basis of the latter's acknowledged influence on Sg, and compares their personalities]

[C1:182] — Ahlenius, Holger, *Fronten* (Stockholm), 1:3 (1931), p. 10.

[C1:183] — Björkman, Carl, *Nya Dagligt Allehanda* (Stockholm), 21 March 1931.

[C1:184] — Blanck, Anton, *Göteborgs Handels- och Sjöfartstidning*, 2 July 1931.

[C1:185] — C. A. B. [C. A. Bolander], *Dagens Nyheter* (Stockholm), 9 March 1931.

[C1:186] — Gandrup, C., *Social-Demokraten* (Copenhagen), 15 March 1931.

[C1:187] — Rinman, Sven, *Studiekamraten* (Tollarp), 13 (1931), 245-246.

[C1:188] — Rubow, Paul V., *Politiken* (Copenhagen), 16 March 1931.

[C1:189] — Schiller, Harald, 'Strindberg och sagokungen', *Sydsvenska Dagbladet* (Malmö), 9 March 1931. ['Strindberg and the Fairy-Tale King']

[C1:190] Börge [Børge], Vagn, *Der unbekannte Strindberg. Studie in nordischer Märchendichtung*, Aus dem Dänischen übertragen von Emil Schering, Mit einem Vorwort von Friedrich von der Leyen, Kopenhagen: Levin & Munksgaard; Marburg: N. G. Elwert'sche, 1935. 155 pp. ['The Unknown Strindberg. Studies in the Nordic Fairy-Tale'. German edition of **C1:181** which includes an additional chapter on *Ett drömspel*]

[C1:191] — Büscher, Alfred, *Nordische Rundschau* (Braunschweig), 9 (1936-38), 85-86.

[C1:192] — Reichardt, Konstantin, *Deutsche Literaturzeitung* (Berlin), 57 (1936), 285-287.

[C1:193] Børge, Vagn, 'Strindberg den mest moderne af alle Dramatikere', *Ekstrabladet* (Copenhagen), 29 March 1938. ['Strindberg the most Modern of Dramatists'. Comments on Eugene O'Neill's evaluation of Sg as the most modern of dramatists in **C1:987**]

[C1:194] Børge, Vagn, 'Strindberg und Shakespeare', *Shakespeare-Jahrbuch* (Leipzig), 73 (1937), pp. 142-149. ['Strindberg and Shakespeare'. Examines Sg's profound interest in, and debt to, Shakespeare]

[C1:195] Borglund, Tore, and E. R. Gummerus, 'Efter 65 år kunde stora brevgåtan bli knäckt. Strindberg gav Dan mod att skriva', *Kvällsposten* (Malmö), 19 February 1972. ['After 65 Years the great Letter Riddle could be Solved. Strindberg gave Dan the Courage to Write'. Confirms the relevance of Sg as an inspiration for the Swedish proletarian author Dan Andersson (1888-1920)]

[C1:196] Borland, Harald H., *Nietzsche's Influence on Swedish Literature with Special Reference to Strindberg, Ola Hansson, Heidenstam and Fröding*, Göteborg: Wettergren and Kerber, 1957, pp. 17-46. [Examines Sg's links with Nietzsche, both direct and indirect. Documents which of Nietzsche's works Sg knew and where the impact of this knowledge may be discerned in his writing, including the vivisection 'Hjärnornas kamp' (The Battle of the Brains), the naturalistic dramas, including *Fröken Julie*, 'Tschandala', the Voltaire essay of 1890, and *I havsbandet*, where it merges with ideas derived from the 19th-Century French psychologist Théodule Ribot and Max Nordau's *Paradoxer* (1885). Borland concludes that 'the encounter was primarily of psychological importance' for Sg who 'found in Nietzsche's attacks on conventional social and ethical values justification for his own violent attitude'. Doctoral dissertation]

[C1:197] — Engblom, Carl J., *Scandinavian Studies* (Lawrence, Kansas), 30:1 (1958), 42-44.

[C1:198] — Johnson, Walter [Gilbert], *Modern Language Quarterly* (London), 19 (1959), 355-356.

[C1:199] — Rinman, Sven, *Göteborgs Handels- och Sjöfartstidning*, 31 May 1957.

[C1:200] — Schoolfield, George C., *Modern Language Notes* (Baltimore), 80:1 (1965), 141-144.

[C1:201] Borland, Harald H., 'Strindberg and Nietzsche', in Wilhelm Friese, Hrsg., **B3:168**, *Strindberg und die deutschsprachigen Länder*, pp. 53-69. [Largely confirms the conclusions of Borland's earlier study, **C1:196**]

[C1:202] Born, Eric von, 'Swedenborg och Strindberg', 1 and 2, *Nya kyrkans tidning* (Stockholm), 89 (1964), pp. 59-64, 79-81.

[C1:203] Born, Eric von, 'Swedenborg och Strindberg', 3 and 4, *Nya kyrkans tidning* (Stockholm), 90 (1965), pp. 52-59, 81-88.

[C1:204] Born, Eric von, 'Swedenborg och Strindberg', 5: 'Andra delen av *En blå bok*', *Nya kyrkans tidning* (Stockholm), 91:1-2 (1966), pp. 5-14.

[C1:205] Born, Eric von, 'Swedenborg och Strindberg', 6i and 6ii: 'Tredje bandet av *En blå bok*', *Nya kyrkans tidning* (Stockholm), 91:5-6 (1966), pp. 42-48; 91:7-8 (1966), pp. 53-57.

[C1:206] Born, Jürgen, *et al.*, *Kafkas Bibliotek. Ein beschreibendes Verzeichnis*, Frankfurt am Main: S. Fischer Verlag, 1990, pp. 46-49. ['Kafka's Library. A Descriptive Index'. Includes an annotated list of the books by Sg in Franz Kafka's library]

[C1:207] Boulton, Agnes, *Part of a Long Story*, Garden City: Doubleday, 1958, pp. 76-77. [Eugene O'Neill's second wife recalls that 'Gene was very impressed by Sg's anguished personal life as it was shown in his novels (*The Son of a Servant* and others, all autobiographical)...These novels Gene kept by him for many years, reading them even more frequently than the plays. I don't know – but I imagine he had the same feeling of identification with the great tortured Swede up to the time of his own death']

[C1:208] Bourguignon, Annie, 'Peter Weiss und Strindberg', in *Der Schriftsteller Peter Weiss und Schweden*, Saabrücker Beiträge zur Literaturwissenschaft 54, St. Ingbert: Röhrig Universitätsverlag, 1997, pp. 47-93. [Discusses Weiss's abiding interest in Sg; compares their lives in exile; documents Weiss's knowledge of Sg's works; examines his translations of several of the plays, including *Fröken Julie* and *Ett drömspel*; and compares both authors' views on the role of the writer. For Weiss, Sg anticipates Surrealism and provides a model for a revolt against established literary norms. Bourguignon comments specifically on *Till Damaskus*, *Svarta fanor*, *Ett drömspel*, *Inferno*, *Fröken Julie*, *Röda rummet*, and *Tjänstekvinnans son*, and identifies Sgian quotations, formulations, and themes, including Jacob's struggle with the angel, in Weiss's autobiographical books *Abschied von den Eltern* (1961) and *Fluchtpunkt* (1962), as well as *Ästhetik des Widerstands* and his play *Hölderlin* (1971)]

[C1:209] Boyer, Régis, 'Elisabeth – Laura – Nora', in Alex Bolckmans, ed., *Literature and Reality: Creatio versus Mimesis. Problems of Realism in Modern Nordic Literature*, Proceedings of the 11th Study Conference of the International Association for Scandinavian Studies, Ghent: Scandinavian Institute, University of Ghent, 1977, pp. 181-194. [Identifies affinities between the heroines of Villiers de l'Isle Adam's play *La Révolte* (1869), Sg's *Fadren*, and Ibsen's *A Doll's House*]

[C1:210] Boyer, Régis, 'Genombrott Scandinave: XVIIIe siècle français', in Bertil Nolin and Peter Forsgren, red., *The Modern Breakthrough in Scandinavian Literature*, Skrifter utgivna av Litteraturvetenskapliga institutionen vid Göteborgs universitet 17, Göteborg, 1988, pp. 23-31. ['The Scandinavian Breakthrough: The French 18th Century'. Identifies a similarity between the ideas and writings of the Scandinavian Modern Breakthrough and the French Enlightenment of the 18th Century, ca. 1720-1780, both of which foreground the importance of critical reason and *joie de vivre* in a world that is open to new ideas. Sg exemplifies this tendency for Boyer, not least because of the affinity that he felt in the 1880s with the ideas of Jean-Jacques Rousseau]

[C1:211] Boyer, Régis, 'Strindberg et Villiers de l'Isle-Adam', *Revue d'histoire du théâtre* (Paris), 30:3 (1978), 291-306. [Documents Sg's knowledge of Villiers's work and identifies common traits and themes, especially in their writing about women. Claims that among several other works, *Till Damaskus*, *Ett drömspel*, *Stora landsvägen*, *Herr Bengts hustru*, *Pelikanen*, and *Karl XII* contain echoes of Villiers's novels and plays, including *L'Eve Future*, *Axel*, *La Révolte*, *L'Amour suprême*, and *Contes cruels*. Moreover, their heroes are often interchangeable. As writers, they are both the spiritual descendants of Edgar Allan Poe; like Jacob they have struggled with the Angel, and both of them share an interest in androgyny and a common misogyny]

[C1:212] Bradbrook, M[uriel] C[lara], 'In Dreams begin Responsibilities', in *Women and Literature, 1779-1982*, The Collected Papers of Muriel Bradbrook, Vol. 2, Brighton: Harvester Press; New York: Barnes & Noble Books, 1982, pp. 93-109. [A deft account of Sg's contribution to the development of modern drama and its representation of women in comparison with Ibsen, Chekhov, Synge, and Pirandello. Refers to *Fadren*, *Den starkare*, *Fröken Julie*, *Spöksonaten*, *Påsk*, *Stora landsvägen*, and *Kronbruden*]

[C1:213] Braem, Helmut M., *Eugene O'Neill*, Velber bei Hannover: Friedrich Verlag, 1965. 149 pp. [The influence of Sg on O'Neill's plays, e.g. of *Ett drömspel* on *More Stately Mansions*, is noted throughout]

[C1:214] Brandell, Gunnar, 'Ett halvsekels dramatik', in *Svensk litteratur 1900-1950*, Stockholm: Bokförlaget Aldus/Bonniers, Andra omarbetade och utvidgade upplagan, 1967, pp. 382-396. ['Drama over Half a Century'. Discusses the plays of Hjalmar Söderberg, Hjalmar Bergman, and Pär Lagerkvist in relation to their major predecessor, Sg, and asserts the radical theatricality of both *Ett drömspel* and the Chamber Plays of 1907. First edition 1958]

[C1:215] Brandell, Gunnar, 'Fragen ohne Antworten. Zum Dialog von Strindberg - und Ibsen', in Oskar Bandle, Hrsg., **D2:8**, *Strindbergs Dramen im Lichte neuerer Methodendiskussionen*, pp. 29-43. ['Questions without Answers. On Dialogue in Strindberg and Ibsen'. Analyses the dialogue in Sg's plays, where information is often replaced by mystification and insistent questions, in a stylistic comparison with the practice of Ibsen and (more briefly) Chekhov. Brandell argues that one of Sg's greatest resources as a dramatist was his use of 'haphazard' dialogue, which is directed by the associations governing the responses of both the onstage interlocutors; its numerous abrupt changes or gliding transitions between short segments of dialogue is 'unparalleled' in the work of other dramatists. He focuses primarily on *Spöksonaten* and *Ghosts* but also exemplifies this technique with reference to *Fadren* and *Dödsdansen*]

[C1:216] Brandell, Gunnar, 'Frågor utan svar. Något om Strindbergs dialog – och Ibsens', in *Nordiskt drama – studier och belysningar*, Uppsala: Svensk litteratursällskapet, 1993, pp. 64-74. ['Questions without Answers. Dialogue in Strindberg and Ibsen'. Swedish version of **C1:222**]

[C1:217] Brandell, Gunnar, *Freud: A Man of his Century*, Translated by Iain White, Hassocks, Sussex: Harvester Press/New Jersey: Humanities Press, 1979. XI+110 pp. [Revised English edition of **C1:222**]

[C1:218] Brandell, Gunnar, *Freud, enfant de son siècle*, Préface de Maurice Gravier, Paris: Lettres modernes, 1967. 113 pp. [Revised French edition of **C1:222**]

[C1:219] Brandell, Gunnar, *Freud og hans tid*, på dansk ved Aage Jørgensen, København: Gyldendal, 1963. 98 pp. [Revised Danish edition of **C1:222**]

[C1:220] Brandell, Gunnar, *Freud och hans tid*, Stockholm: Bokförlaget Aldus-Bonniers, 1970. [106] pp. [Revised edition of **C1:222**]

[C1:221] Brandell, Gunnar, *Freud – Kind seiner Zeit*, Übers. aus dem Schwedischen von Detlef Bennecke, München: Kindler Verlag, 1976. 84 pp. [Revised German edition of **C1:222**]

[C1:222] Brandell, Gunnar, 'Freud och sekelslutet', in *Vid seklets källor*, Stockholm: Albert Bonniers Förlag, 1961, pp. 37-138. ['Freud and the Fin de Siècle'. Places Freud in the context of his contemporaries among mainly naturalist novelists and dramatists with whom, as Brandell demonstrates, he had a great deal in common, and to whom he was often deeply indebted for the development of his ideas. Brandell is more concerned with Ibsen in e.g. *The Lady from the Sea* than with Sg, but he comments on the latter's treatment of hysteria in 'Genvägar' (Short Cuts, 1887)]

[C1:223] Brandell, Gunnar, 'Om gycklares och diktares liv. Tal på Övralid den 6 juli 1988', *Strindbergiana* (Stockholm), 5 (1990), pp. 116-122. ['On the Lives of Jesters and Poets. A lecture, delivered at the Heidenstam Museum, 6 July 1988'. Assesses Sg's relationship with Verner von Heidenstam (1859-1940), both personal and literary]

[C1:224] Brandell, Gunnar, 'Pytania bez odpowiedzi. dialog Strindberga i Ibsena', Thum. A[ndrzej] N[ils] Uggla, *Teatr* (Warsaw), 1982:2, pp. 8-10. ['Questions without Answers: On Dialogue in Strindberg and Ibsen'. Polish translation of **C1:215** by Andrzej Uggla]

[C1:225] Brandell, Gunnar, 'Questions without Answers: On Strindberg's and Ibsen's Dialogue', Translated by Marilyn Johns Blackwell, in Marilyn Johns Blackwell, ed., **C1:142**, *Structures of Influence*, pp. 79-91. [English version of **C1:215**]

[C1:226] Brandes, Georg, 'Brandes on Strindberg', *The Bookman* (New York), 40 (1914), 241-242. [For Brandes in this anecdotal account, Sg's complex nature was visible in his appearance, which combined the forehead of Jupiter and the mouth and chin of a Stockholm street urchin. 'The upper part of his face was that of a mental aristocrat – the lower belonged to the "Servant-Girl's Son", as he called himself in his autobiography']

[C1:227] Brandes, Georg, and Edvard Brandes, *Brevveksling med nordiske forfattare og videnskabsmænd*, Udgivet af Morten Borup under medvirkning af Francis Bull og John Landquist, 8 vols, København: Gyldendalske Boghandel Nordisk Forlag, 1939-42. ['Correspondence with Nordic Writers and Scholars'. Includes not only Sg's correspondence with Georg and Edvard Brandes in Volume Six, together with an introduction by John Landquist on his relationship with the brothers, pp. ix-xxvii, but numerous references to him and his works in many of the other correspondences collected here. These volumes remain a prime source for research into Scandinavian literature in the period 1862-1923. Volume Six was also published in Stockholm by Albert Bonniers Förlag, as *Brevväxling med svenska och finska författare och vetenskapsmän* (1939)]

[C1:228] Brandl, Horst, *Persönlichkeitsidealismus und Willenkult. Aspekte der Nietzsche-Rezeption in Schweden*, Heidelberg: Winter Verlag, 1977. 223 pp. [Includes some discussion of Sg's response to Nietzsche's ideas in a study of the latter's reception in Sweden in terms of idealism of the personality and the cult of the will]

[C1:229] Braun, Robert, 'Strindberg und Nietzsche', *Rheinischer Merkur* (Koblenz), 16 (1961), No. 36, pp. 8-9. ['Strindberg and Nietzsche']

[C1:230] Brecht, Bertolt, *Schriften zum Theater*, 7 Bde, Frankfurt am Main: Suhrkamp, 1963-64, Bd 3, p. 189. ['During the phase of retrogressive development, as shown in the mystic plays of Maeterlinck and Sg, the old V-effect reappears – the inexplicable aspect of things is set to triumph – their indominability. These experiments come very close to the chasm of the ludicrous']

[C1:231] Brecht, Bertolt, '[From a Work Diary]', in *Brekht o literature*, Moscow, 1977, pp. 341-398. [Includes comments on Sg's historical dramas, pp. 368-369, and his theory of one-act drama, p. 390]

[C1:232] Bredsdorff, Elias, *Den store nordiske Krig om Seksualmoralen. En dokumentariske fremstilling af sædlighedsdebatten i nordisk litteratur i 1880'erne*, København: Gyldendal, 1973, pp. 81-99, 154-159, 194-198, 234-243. ['The Great Nordic War over Sexual Morality. A Documentary Presentation of the Moral Debate in Nordic Literature during the 1880s'. Includes an examination of Sg's role in a discussion of the wide-ranging debate about sexual morality which flourished throughout Scandinavia during the 1880s and occupied a central place in much of the literature of the period. Bredsdorff discusses his relationship, both personal and intellectual, with Edvard and Georg Brandes, as well as his disputes with Bjørnstjerne Bjørnson and Ibsen about the nature of women and marriage. He also reflects on the significance of the attack on *Giftas* and Sg's other 'immoral' writings by John Personne in **G5:102**]

[C1:233] Bredsdorff, Thomas, 'Three Post-Inferno Strindberg Plays which Strindberg did not Write: Bergman's *Wild Strawberries* and *Persona* and Enquist's *The Night of the Tribades*', in Kela Kvam, ed., **D2:158**, *Strindberg's Post-Inferno Plays*, pp. 196-203. [Explores the relationship between *Wild Strawberries* and *Ett drömspel*, which Bredsdorff finds less conventional than Bergman's derivative film. In *Persona*, however, which is indebted to *Den starkare*, he takes advantage of Sg's dramatic achievements and transforms them into a modern idiom. Bredsdorff notes that *Den starkare* is also of relevance to Per Olov Enquist's documentary drama *Tribadernas natt*, with its conventional 19th-Century dramaturgy]

[C1:234] Bredsdorff, Thomas, 'Per Olov Enquists många masker', Översättning av Jan Stolpe, *Tulipak*, Dramaten Spelblad (Stockholm), 1993-94, pp. 18-23. ['Per Olov Enquist's Many Masks'. Comments on the relevance of Sg for Enquist's playwriting, including (but not only) *Tribadernas natt*]

[C1:235] Broch, Hermann, 'Philistrosität, Realismus, Idealismus der Kunst', *Der Brenner* (Innsbruck), 3 (1912-13), 399-415. [Identifies mysticism as the central characteristic of Sg's works, in the course of an essay on realism and idealism in art]

[C1:236] Brod, Max, 'Strindberg and Kafka', *Adam* (London), Nos 190-191 (1949), p. 12. [Recalls that Kafka admired the realistic and satirical power with which Sg depicted his age in such novels as *I havsbandet* and *Götiska rummen*; the autobiographical novels also 'had a powerful influence on him, and for a time he read nothing else']

[C1:237] Brod, Max, *Über Franz Kafka*, Frankfurt am Main: Fischer Taschenbuch Verlag, 1974. 407 pp. [Includes the suggestion that Sg's influence on Kafka's symbolist style has been insufficiently researched]

[C1:238] Brooke, Rupert, 'The Plays of August Strindberg', *Cambridge Magazine*, 11 October 1913, 13-15. [A generally positive early English response to 'this tragic and prodigiously fertile madman' apropos the publication of three volumes of the plays in translations by Edwin Björkman. Brooke maintains that 'Sg saw people, in their general nature…as they really are, and not as the rationally moved, explanatory puppets of other drama'. This is refreshing 'after the petulant hermaphrodites Ibsen crowded the theatre with', and 'that denial of sex called feminism, with its resulting shallowness of women and degradation of man']

[C1:239] Brunius, Teddy, 'Återvändning av litterära verk – Bellman och Strindberg', *Upsala Nya Tidning*, 5 February 1986. ['The Recycling of Literary Works – Bellman and Strindberg'. Considers the sometimes quite opportunistic way in which writers frequently adapt and rework their writing with reference to Sg and the Swedish Gustavian poet Carl Michael Bellman (1740-95)]

[C1:240] Bruno, Birgitta, 'Präster i litteraturen', in *Från ådalar och fjäll* (Härnösand), 48 (1961), pp. 67-74. ['Priests in Literature'. Compares the depiction of clergymen in literary works by Frans G. Bengtsson, Anna Maria Lenngren, Olle Hedberg, Birger Sjöberg, and Sg (Pastor Nordström in *Hemsöborna*)]

[C1:241] Brynhildsvoll, Knut, 'Henrik Ibsens *Kærlighedens komedie* og August Strindbergs *Röda rummet*: to intertekster i Stanisław Przybyszewskis romantrilogi *Homo sapiens*?', *Studia Scandinavica*, Særudgave i anledning af 25. års jubilæet, Gdańsk: Uniwersytet Gdański, 1996, pp. [31]-43. ['Henrik Ibsen's *Love's Comedy* and August Strindberg's *The Red Room*: Two Intertexts in Stanisław Przybyszewski's trilogy of novels *Homo sapiens*?' Explores the possible relevance of *Röda rummet* and Ibsen's *Love's Comedy* for Przybyszewski's trilogy from the 1890s, a work in which Przybyszewski provides a thinly veiled portrait of Sg]

[C1:242] Bühler, Charlotte, 'Strindberg und Ibsen', *Die neueren Sprachen* (Marburg), 31 (1923), 146-153. ['Strindberg and Ibsen'. Stresses Sg's importance for German expressionism]

[C1:243] Bukowski, Piotr, 'August Strindberg and the Expressionist Aesthetics of Pär Lagerkvist', in Michael Robinson and Sven Hakon Rossel, eds, **B1:387**, *Expressionism and Modernism*, pp. 47-52. [Discusses Sg's importance as a reformer of dramatic form and precursor of expressionism in the theatre apropos Lagerkvist's seminal essay, 'Modern Theatre', **D1:604**. According to Bukowski, Sg was led to a new poetic experience of reality by the dissociation of the self he experienced during the Inferno period]

[C1:244] Bukowski, Piotr, 'The Prophet's Authority on Trial. The Image of Emanuel Swedenborg's Word in August Strindberg's *Inferno* and *Legender*', *Universita Jagellońica, Acte Scientiarum Litterarumque*, Kraków, 2003, pp. 7-18.

[C1:245] Bukowski, Piotr, 'Über die Mehrdimensionalität der Goethe-Rezeption in Strindbergs Spätwerk', in Kirsten Wechsel, Hrsg., **B1:473**, *Strindberg and His Media*, pp. 325-340. [Discusses Sg's admiration for Goethe in *En blå bok* and elsewhere in his later works where he was an epistemic and personal authority enlisted by Sg in order to legitimate his alchemistic discourse]

[C1:246] Bull, Francis, 'Alexander Kielland og August Strindberg', in *Møter med mennesker: artikler og taler i utvalg*, Oslo: Gyldendal, 1987, pp. 218-229. [Rpr. of **C1:249**]

[C1:247] Bull, Francis, 'Bjørnson og Sverige', in *Bjørnson-Studier*, Kristiania: Mallingske Bogtrykeri, 1911, pp. 171-281. ['Bjørnson and Sweden'. Documents Bjørnstjerne Bjørnson's contacts, both literary and personal, with Swedish writers, including Sg]

[C1:248] Bull, Francis, 'Kielland og Strindberg', in *Omkring Alexander L. Kielland*, Oslo: Gyldendal Norsk Forlag, 1949, pp. 110-[130]. [Rpr. of **C1:249**]

[C1:249] Bull, Francis, 'Kielland og Strindberg', *Samtiden* (Oslo), 58 (1949), 96-108. [Charts Sg's personal and literary links with the Norwegian novelist Alexander Kielland during the 1880s, quoting from their correspondence and comparing Kielland's *Arbeidsfolk*

(1881) with *Röda rummet* (1879) and his novel *Else* (1894) with Sg's stories 'Genvägar' (Short Cuts, 1887) and 'En häxa' (A Witch, 1890)]

[C1:250] Bulman, Joan, *Strindberg and Shakespeare: Shakespeare's Influence on Strindberg's Historical Drama*, London: Jonathan Cape, 1933. 221 pp. [An enduring study which demonstrates how Sg rejuvenated conventional 19th-Century historical drama via the example of Shakespeare, whom he read in Karl August Hagberg's translations and on whose *Henry IV*, as analysed by Georg Brandes, he modelled *Mäster Olof*. Bulman also considers those historical plays which have little if anything in common with Shakespeare (*Lycko-Pers resa*, *Gillets hemlighet*, and *Herr Bengts hustru*), and discusses the post-Inferno cycle of plays based on Swedish history in detail, drawing particular attention to aspects of characterisation, scenic structure, and diction]

[C1:251] — B. B-m [Birger Bæckström], *Göteborgs Handels- och Sjöfartstidning*, 1 June 1933.

[C1:252] — Mortensen, Johan, *Sydsvenska Dagbladet* (Malmö), 12 March 1933.

[C1:253] — Österling, Anders, *Svenska Dagbladet* (Stockholm), 11 February 1933.

[C1:254] Busch, C. Trent, and Orton A. Jones, 'Immortality Enough: The Influence of Strindberg on the Expressionism of Eugene O'Neill', *Southern Speech Journal* (Tuscaloosa, Alabama), 33:2 (1967), 129-139. [Argues that the plays by O'Neill which bear Sg's imprint the most strongly as regards style and expressionistic devices are *The Emperor Jones*, *The Hairy Ape*, and *The Great God Brown*]

[C1:255] Cain, Geoffrey, 'The Truth-Seekers: Ibsen, Strindberg, and Kierkegaard', in Leon Nikulin, red., *Litteratur & Magt. Nordisk-Baltisk Litterært Symposium: Föredrag-samling*, Viby, Jutland: Diapazon, 2000. 175 pp.

[C1:256] Calendoli, Giovanni, 'La drammaturgia di Federici fra Strindberg e Betti', in Giovanni Antonucci, ed., *Mario Fedrici*, Quaderni dell'Instituto di Studi Pirandelliani 6, Rome: Bulzoni, 1983, pp. 11-27. [Examines the influence of Sg and Ugo Betti on the dramaturgy of Mario Federici in his plays *Marta la madre*, *Nessumo sali a bordo*, and *Un garofano roos*]

[C1:257] Cardullo, Bert, 'Autumn Interiors, Or the Ladies' Eve: Woody Allen's Ingmar Bergman Complex', *Antioch Review* (Ann Arbor, Michigan), 58:4 (2000), 428-440. [Documents Allen's interest in Sg as mediated by Bergman. Mentions *Fadren*, *Den starkare*, and *Spöksonaten*]

[C1:258] Entry cancelled.

[C1:259] Carlson, Harry G., 'Strindberg's Naturalism: Nature Malign and Benign and the Triumph of the Imagination', in Bertil Nolin and Peter Forsgren, eds, *The Modern Breakthrough in Scandinavian Literature*, Skrifter utgivna av Litteraturvetenskapliga institutionen vid Göteborgs universitet 17, Göteborg, 1988, pp. 249-255. [Compares nature as a presence which exerts a powerful influence over both character and the action in *Fröken Julie* with the portrayal of nature in one of Sg's favourite novels, Zola's *La faute de l'abbé Mouret* (1875). Carlson focuses on the evocation of an Edenic landscape in both works]

[C1:260] Carlson, Marvin, 'Ibsen, Strindberg, and Telegony', *P.M.L.A.* (New York), 100:5 (1985), 774-782. [Examines the impact of ideas about heredity and the notion of the enduring significance of impressions received at the moment of conception (telegony, or 'offspring at a distance') in works by Ibsen (*Lady from the Sea*, *Ghosts*, and *John*

Gabriel Borkman) and Sg (*Fadren*, *Till Damaskus*, and *En dåres försvarstal*). In Sg's later works there is a constant tension between 'real' and presumed fathers, and he often depicts heredity as working more powerfully on a psychic than a physical level. Carlson relates Sg's ideas to his reading in contemporary science, including the theories of Darwin and Théodule Ribot, in whose *L'Hérédité psychologique* (1882) he encountered the most frequently cited 19th-Century example of telegony, that of Lord Morton's mare, which is alluded to in *Fadren*. He also demonstrates how both Ibsen and Sg found in telegony the potential for revealing hidden familial relationships, thus enabling classical notions of fate or destiny to be modernised and given a moral dimension, imbued with ambiguity and the play of alternative possibilities]

[C1:261] Carlsson, Anni, 'Der Sohn der Magd und der Dovre-Alte. Strindberg und Ibsen', *Neue Zürcher Zeitung* (Zürich), 1 September 1974. ['The Son of a Servant and the Old Man of Dovre. Strindberg and Ibsen'. Compares Sg, self-personified as the Son of a Servant, with the image of Ibsen as 'Dovre-Gubben' (The Old Man of the Mountain), from *Peer Gynt*, and charts the changes in Sg's attitude to Ibsen, which moves from early respect to enduring antipathy in the *Giftas* period onwards]

[C1:262] Carlsson, Anni, 'Der Sohn der Magd und der Dovre-Alte', in **B1:103**, *Ibsen – Strindberg – Hamsun. Essays zur skandinavischen Literatur*, pp. 29-36. [Rpr. of **C1:261**]

[C1:263] Carlsson, Anni, 'Die Tragödie Gustaf af Geijerstams', in **B1:103**, *Ibsen – Strindberg – Hamsun. Essays zur skandinavischen Literatur*, pp. 45-60. ['The Tragedy of Gustaf af Geijerstam'. Considers Sg's personal and professional relationship with the Swedish man of letters Gustaf af Geijerstam (1858-1909), ranging from their sometimes common purpose in furthering a socially committed literature during the 1880s to the merciless satirical portrait which Sg drew of his fellow writer in *Svarta fanor*]

[C1:264] Carr, Philip, 'Carrying on the Strindberg Tradition', *New York Times*, 28 April 1929. [Identifies Sg's *Fordringsägare* as the source of A.-P. Antoine's play *L'Ennemie*]

[C1:265] Castrén, Gunnar, *Norden i den franska litteraturen*, Helsingfors: Waseniuska bokhandeln i distribution, 1910. 270 pp. ['Scandinavia in French Literature']

[C1:266] Caufman-Blumenfeld, Odette, 'August Strindberg' and 'August Strindberg şi teatrul american', in *Teatrul european-teatrul american: influenţe*, Iaşi: Editura Universităţii "Alexandru Ioan Cuza", 1998, pp. 91-94, 94-127. ['August Strindberg' and 'August Strindberg and the American Theatre'. Accords Sg considerable space in a Romanian study of the links between European and American drama]

[C1:267] Cazaux, Michèle, 'Zola en Suède', *Revue de littérature comparée* (Paris), 27 (1953), 428-437. ['Zola in Sweden'. Broaches the 'vast and complex' subject of Zola's impact on Swedish literature with reference, in Sg's case, to *Röda rummet*, *Giftas*, *Fadren*, *Fröken Julie*, and *Fordringsägare*]

[C1:268] Cederschiöld, W., 'Två landskap och två män. En detaljstudie över Strindberg och Ola Hansson', *Göteborgs Handels- och Sjöfartstidning*, 13 June 1928. ['Two Landscapes and Two Men'. Compares the rural background of the Swedish poet and novelist Ola Hansson (1860-1925) in the agricultural province of Skåne with Sg, whose writing is rooted in Stockholm and its archipelago]

[C1:269] Chapiro, J., 'Gerhart Hauptmann über grosse Künstler. Gespräch über Wedekind, Strindberg und Tolstoi', *Neue freie Presse* (Vienna), 25 December 1926 (Supplement).

['Gerhart Hauptmann on Great Artists. Conversations about Wedekind, Strindberg, and Tolstoi'. Reports Hauptmann's opinions about Sg and other writers]

[C1:270] Chekhov, Anton, *Polnoe sobranie sochinenii*, Bd 8, Moscow: Nauka, 1980. [Includes Chekhov's several comments on Sg and *Fröken Julie*, mainly in the course of his correspondence with Maksim Gor'kii and others]

[C1:271] Chekhov, Anton, *Polnoe sobranie sochinenii i pis'em A. P. Chekhova*, ed. S. D. Balukhaty *et al.*, Vol. 18, Moscow: Goslitizda, 1949. 672 pp. [Contains references to Sg and *Fröken Julie* in his correspondence with Gor'kii, 9 May 1899, and to E. M. Sharova, 9 and 15 May, pp. 145, 146, 155. Gor'kii's response with comments, p. 488. E.961]

[C1:272] Chmelarz-Moswitzer, Martina, *Mimesis und Auflösung der Form. Bildende Künstler und bildende Kunst in den Werken der skandinavischen Autoren Herman Bang, Henrik Ibsen und August Strindberg*, Wiener Studien zur Skandinavistik 13, Wien: Edition Praesens, 2005. 425 pp. [A substantial examination of the depiction and role of the pictorial artist in the work of the three Scandinavian authors with further reference to their treatment of the conflict between bohemia and the bourgeoisie. In Sg's case this entails a substantial chapter on *Röda rummet* and comparative studies of *I havsbandet* with Ibsen's *John Gabriel Borkman* and *Röda rummet* with Bang's *Det graa Hus (*1901) and *De Uden Fædreland* (1906)]

[C1:273] Chevrel, Yves, 'L'armure et le quenouille: l'homme mystifié', in Ann-Deborah Lévy-Bertherat, ed., *Le Père déposséde. Délire et théâtralité*, Cahiers de Littérature Générale, Recherche et Concours 3, Nantes: Éditions Opéra, 1995. ['The Armour and the Distaff: Man Mystified'. Treats the theme of the lost father and madness in Seneca's *Hercules furens*, Shakespeare's *King Lear*, and Sg's *Fadren*]

[C1:274] — Vieuille, Marie-Françoise, *Revue de littérature comparée* (Paris), 70:1 (1996), 107-108.

[C1:275] Chevrel, Yves, 'Le modernisme et l'héritage du naturalisme', *Neohelicon* (Budapest), 29:1 (2002), 45-55. ['Modernism and the Heritage of Naturalism'. Discusses Sg and the interface between modernism and naturalism together with the writings of Italo Svevo (1861-1928), Arno Holz (1863-1929), and Johannes Schlaf (1862-1941)]

[C1:276] Chevrel, Yves, 'Naturalisme et modernité', in Christian Berg, Frank Durieux, and Geert Lernout, eds, *The Turn of the Century: Modernism and Modernity in Literature and the Arts*, Berlin: Walter de Gruyter, 1995, pp. 101-118. ['Naturalism and Modernity'. Discusses *Fröken Julie* together with *Papa Hamlet* (1889) by Arno Holz and Johannes Schlaf as an instance of naturalism as an element of modernity in the process of constructing itself. Chevrel argues that in such works the anonymous collective character of the hero is as 'naturalist' as the écriture itself, while the themes come close to those of modernism]

[C1:277] Chevrel, Yves, 'Le naturalisme peut-il être considéré comme un movement moderniste?', *Revue de Littérature Comparée* (Paris), 66:4 (1992), 387-395. ['Can Naturalism be Considered a Modernist Movement?' Discusses the question with reference to works by Zola, Arno Holz, Johannes Schlaf, Stephen Crane, and Sg (refers briefly to *Fadren* and *Fröken Julie*)]

[C1:278] Chirkov, N[ikolai] M[aksimovich], 'Avgust Strindberg i russkaia literatura', Uchenye zapiski/Moskovskii oblastnoi pedagogicheskii institut, Vol. 45, 1956, pp. 243-

276. ['August Strindberg and Russian Literature', in Papers of the Moscow Regional Pedagogical Institute. E.965]

[C1:279] Chirkov, N[ikolai] M[aksimovich], 'Henrik Ibsen i August Strindberg', *Skandinavskoe sobranie* (Tallin), 11 (1966), 197-223. ['Henrik Ibsen and August Strindberg'. E.1019]

[C1:280] Chojecki, Andrzej, 'A Polish Reading of Strindberg', *Studia Scandinavica* (Gdańsk), 11 (1988), 15-28. [Discusses Sg in conjunction with Adam Mickiewicz]

[C1:281] Chothia, Jean, *Forging a Language: A Study in the Plays of Eugene O'Neill*, Cambridge: Cambridge University Press, 1979, pp. 199-206. [Includes a list of books and authors read by O'Neill and, in tabular form, a catalogue of those works by Sg and others which are sometimes seen to have influenced the plays on which O'Neill was concurrently working. Sg (particularly where *Fadren*, *Fröken Julie*, *Den starkare*, *Ett drömspel*, and *Dödsdansen* are concerned) is a point of reference throughout]

[C1:282] Christiani, Dounia Bunis, 'Strindberg's Growing Castle', in *Scandinavian Elements of Finnegans Wake*, Evanston: Northwestern University Press, 1965, pp. 76-83. [Relates Joyce's technique in the *Wake* to Sg's prefatory note to *Ett drömspel* and its phallic castle to the Eddic Yggdrasil, as it appears to Earwicker. Christiani notes that Sg also features in the *Wake* together with his third wife as 'Harriet and stringbag' (p. 221, line 30). Also compares *Exiles* with *Fröken Julie*]

[C1:283] Chullikkad, Balachandran, 'I Stockholm i början av en höst', *Strindbergiana* (Stockholm), 14 (1999), pp. 79-81. ['In Stockholm at the Beginning of Autumn'. A poem depicting an Indian writer's encounter with Sweden in 1997 as mediated by reading Strindberg]

[C1:284] Clark, Barrett H[arper], *Eugene O'Neill: The Man and His Plays*, New York: Dover Publications, 1936, pp. 178-179. [Stresses Sg's influence, which Clark considers is all too close in *Strange Interlude* where the female beast of prey, Nina, could be Sg's invention]

[C1:285] Clarke, Margaret, 'Strindberg and Samuel de Constant: The Source of *The Father* and Strindbergian Sociology', *Revue de littérature comparée* (Paris), 42:4 (1968), 583-596. [Identifies Constant's epistolary novel *Mariage sentimental ou le Mariage comme il y en a quelques-uns* (1783) as the source of *Fadren*, both on internal evidence, in a comparison of its plot with that of Sg's play, and because of the opportunity that Sg would have had of reading it while employed at Stockholm's Royal Library. Clarke links 'Otur' (Bad Luck) in *Giftas* with Letter V in Constant's novel and stresses its significance for Sg's views regarding women and the peasantry. She also claims that the Swiss novelist is the missing link between Rousseau and Nietzsche in the development of Sg's thinking]

[C1:286] Claussen, Christian, 'Digteromvendelserne ved aarhundredskiftet. Typiske personligheter i den nordiske literatur', *Edda* (Oslo), 10 (1918), 296-318. ['Writers' Conversions at the Turn of the Century. Typical Figures in Nordic Literature'. Notes the turn away from naturalism made by Joris-Karl Huysmans, François Coppée, Édouard Rod, Paul Bourget, Jules Lemaître, Ferdinand Brunetière, and Maurice Barrés, and identifies several elements in the naturalist world view that might ultimately induce a feeling of emptiness, thus prompting those who espoused it to turn towards religion. Claussen analyses Johannes Jørgensen, Sg, and Arne Garborg as the three most striking examples of *fin-de-siècle* religious conversion in Denmark, Sweden, and Norway respectively. Sg's restless and seeking spirit exemplifies the spirit of the age, and his life, with its numerous changes of direction and point of view, best reflects this widespread process]

[C1:287] Clausen, Jørgen Stender, 'Fin de Siècle', in *En Dag i Ekbátana. Sophus Claussen (1835-1931) og Fin de Siècle*, Konference, Firenze den 19. februar 1999, *Studi Nordici* V, Pisa-Roma: Istituti editoriali e poligrafici internationali, (1998 [sic]), pp. 53-70. [Discusses the move away from naturalism in late 19th-Century Scandinavian literature, with detailed reference to *Röda rummet* and Sg's dreamplay style exemplified by both *Till Damaskus* and *Spöksonaten*. Clausen stresses an affinity between the latter and traditional rites of carnival, as well as with texts by the Danish poet Sophus Claussen (1865-1931) and the novelists Henrik Pontoppidan ((1857-1943) and Martin Andersen Nexø (1869-1954)]

[C1:288] Clausen, Jørgen Stender, 'Fin de Siècle', traduzione di Alessandro Frambini, in *En Dag i Ekbátana. Sophus Claussen (1835-1931) og Fin de Siècle*, Konference, Firenze den 19. februar 1999, *Studi Nordici V*, Pisa-Roma: Istituti editoriali e poligrafici internationali, (1998 [sic]), pp. 71-89. [Italian version of **C1:287**]

[C1:289] Cocteau, Jean, '*Le Diable au corps*', *Le Carrefour* (Paris), 9 July 1947. ['We wonder at Sg because he did not know how to sell himself. He comes from nowhere. He was surrounded by a void, stickle-backed, studded with harsh light. He should be approached with caution. One cannot grasp hold of him, only learn from him. There are no secrets to be seen'. In an article on Cocteau's film *Le Diable au corps*]

[C1:290] Codignola, Luciano, 'Two Ideas of Dramatic Structure: Strindberg's Last Period and Pirandello's Third Period, a Confrontation', in [Carl Reinhold Smedmark], ed., **D2:287**, *Strindberg and Modern Theatre*, pp. 30-42. [Compares Sg's dramaturgy with Pirandello's in order to establish the ways in which they both enlarged the idea of naturalism. Also seeks to demonstrate how, following on from Zola's doctrine, it was necessary to introduce a new experience, that of the artist himself, into a text like *Till Damaskus*, which thus becomes modernist in both form and style]

[C1:291] Cohn, Alfons Fedor, 'Hauptmann und Strindberg', *Die Glocke* (München), 28 November 1921. [Compares the range of styles and forms in Gerhart Hauptmann's dramaturgy with Sg's]

[C1:292] Cohn, Helge, 'Strindberg hatade Ibsen – Dyngherrens störste profet', *Nya Wermlands Tidningen*, 13 September 1972. ['Strindberg Hated Ibsen – The Lord of Dung's Greatest Prophet'. Comments on Sg's antipathy for Ibsen as documented principally by the soubriquet with which he endowed him in *En blå bok*]

[C1:293] Colum, Mary, 'The Confessions of James Joyce', *Freeman's Journal* (London), 5 (1922), 450-452. [Associates *Ulysses* with the confessional mode of Sg and Rousseau]

[C1:294] Colum, Mary, 'Mary Colum, Review, *Freeman*', in Robert H. Deming, ed., *James Joyce: The Critical Heritage*, London: Routledge and Kegan Paul, 1972, I, pp. 231-232. [Rpr. of **C1:295**]

[C1:295] Cornell, Peter, *Den hemliga källan. Om initiationsmönster i konst, litteratur och politik*, Hedemora: Gidlunds Bokförlag, 1981, pp. 112-116. ['The Secret Source. On Patterns of Initiation in Art, Literature, and Politics'. Discusses Sg's links with *fin-de-siècle* occultism and the ideas of the Austrian racist ideologue Jörgen Lanz-Liebenfels

(1874-1954) in a wide-ranging discussion of occult undercurrents and esoteric doctrines endemic to the emergence of modernism]

[C1:296] Croce, Benedetto, 'Prefazione', in Anne Charlotte Leffler, *Come si fa il bene*, tr. di Salvatore di Giacomo, Napoli: Pierro Editore, 1892. [Alludes to Sg in the introduction to an Italian translation of Leffler's play *Huru man gör godt* (How One Does Good, 1885)]

[C1:297] Czarnocka, Anna, 'Nietzsche, Przybyszewski and the Berlin *Bohême* from the Circle of the Kneipe *"Zum Schwarzen Ferkel"*, in Piotr Paszkiewicz, ed., *Totenmesse: Modernism in the Culture of Northern and Central Europe*, Warsaw: Institute of Art / Polish Academy of Sciences, 1996, pp. 41-50. [Identifies the bohemian circle associated with the Berlin tavern that Sg christened 'Zum Schwarzen Ferkel' as a significant event in the emergence of modernism, one that, according to Czarnocka, draws its vital inspiration from Nietzsche and the Polish novelist Stanisław Przybyszewski (1868-1927) rather than Sg]

[C1:298] D'Abdank, C., 'Strindberg and Björnson', *Theatre* (New York), 20 (1914), pp. 27-28, 42.

[C1:299] Dagerman, Stig, 'How I Met Strindberg', *Adam* (London), Nos 455-467, (1985), p. 70. [Concerns Dagerman's first encounter with Sg's books, not Sg the man]

[C1:300] Dahlbäck, Bengt, 'Beaumarchais – Gustav III – Strindberg', in Erik Carlquist, red., *Humanismen som salt & styrka. Bilder och betraktelser tillägnade Harry Järv*, Stockholm: Atlantis, 1987, pp. 150-156. Illus. [Explores possible historical and literary links between Sg's *Gustav III* and Beaumarchais's *Le Mariage de Figaro*, as well as between Beaumarchais's play and *Fröken Julie*, in both of which a servant engages in sexual conflict with an aristocrat. Dahlbäck also compares the Preface which Sg appended to *Fröken Julie* with Beaumarchais's 'Essai sur le genre dramatique sérieux']

[C1:301] Dahlström, Carl E[noch] W[illiam] L[eonard], 'Theomachy: Zola, Strindberg, Andreyev', *Scandinavian Studies* (Menasha, Wisconsin), 17:4 (1942), 121-132. [Compares Zola's novels *La Faute de l'Abbé Mouret* (which Sg greatly admired) and *La Terre*, Andreyev's *Zhizn' Chelovieka*, and Sg's *Till Damaskus* in which, as in *Inferno* and the miracle play in the Postludium to the verse edition of *Mäster Olof*, a character emulates *inter alia* Jacob wrestling with the angel, Saul, Prometheus, Milton's Satan, and Julian the Apostate in challenging the supernatural powers. Dahlström concludes that 'There is little doubt Sg knew Zola's works and profited by them. There is a strong suspicion that Andreyev, in turn, fed on Sg']

[C1:302] Dashwood, J. R., 'Pirandello and Dream Theatre', in J. R. Dashwood and J. E. Everson, eds, *Writers and Performers in Italian Drama from the Time of Dante to Pirandello*, Essays in Honour of G. H. McWilliam, Studies in Theatre Arts 1, Lewiston-Queenston-Lampeter: Edward Mellen Press, 1991, pp. 145-164. [Suggests that Pirandello may well have found some of the techniques he uses when inventing dreams for the theatre in Sg's work, notably *Ett drömspel*, which Dashwood compares with *Sogno (ma forse no)*. He also compares the work of both dramatists with Freud's *Interpretation of Dreams*]

[C1:303] Davies, H. Neville, 'Repetition and Renewal in T. S. Eliot's "Marina": A Scandinavian Perspective', *Scandinavica* (Norwich), 21:2 (1982), 167-178. [Traces similarities in imagery and theme between Eliot's poem and Sg, who is one among several Scandinavian associations in Eliot's work, pp. 172-175]

[C1:304] Dawber, Thomas C., 'Strindberg and O'Neill', *Players Magazine* (DeKalb, Illinois), 45:4 (1970), 183-185.

[C1:305] Dédéyan, Charles, *Le Thème de Faust dans la littérature européenne*, 6 vols, Vol. IV:2, Paris: Lettres Modernes, 1967, pp. 405-412. ['The Faust Theme in European Literature'. Analyses *Till Damaskus* as a modern Faust drama in the course of a study of the Faust motif in European literature]

[C1:306] Degler, Janusz, 'Strindberg, Witkacy i inni', *Program Teatru Polskiego* (Wrocław), 21 March 1970, pp. 10-13. [Programme essay which discusses Sg's affinities with the Polish dramatist Stanisław Witkiewicz]

[C1:307] Delblanc, Sven, 'Strindberg et Weininger', Traduit du suédois par Régis Boyer, *Europe* (Paris), No. 858 (October 2000), pp. 205-206. ['Strindberg and Weininger'. Compares Sg's portraits of woman as mother in *Pelikanen*, *Ett drömspel*, and *Götiska rummen* with Otto Weininger's theories concerning the maternal woman in *Geschlecht und Charakter* (1903)]

[C1:308] Dervin, Daniel, 'George Eliot and the Paradox of Maturity: August Strindberg and the Pathology of Creativity', in *Creativity and Culture: A Psychoanalytic Study of the Creative Process in the Arts, Sciences, and Culture*, Rutherford-Madison-Teaneck: Fairleigh Dickinson University Press; London: Associated University Presses, 1990, pp. 115-134. [Presents a psychoanalytical reading of *Middlemarch* in conjunction with Sg's 'paranoid' *Spöksonaten*. Eliot's characters escape their narcissism to reproduce their antiselves, which are the morbid projections of their inner malaise; in Sg, on the other hand, until the deliverance of death, the pattern is circular and depicts a species trapped in a web that expands to the limits of the world]

[C1:309] Deryng, Xavier, 'Les variations Popoffsky (Strindberg – Reja – Biegas)', *Bibliotheca Artibus et Historiae* (Vienna), No. 37, 1998, pp. 103-123, Illus. ['The Popoffsky Variations (Strindberg – Reja – Biegas)'. Examines links between the Polish artist Bolesław Biegas, active in Paris in 1902, and two other Poles associated with Sg's Inferno crisis, Stanisław Przybyszewski and Władisław Ślewiński, his links with the French poet and psychiatrist, Marcel Réja (pseudonym of Paul Meunier, 1873-1957), the Symbolist journals *La Plume* and *La Revue Blanche*, and Sg's portrayal of his telepathic experiences in *Inferno*]

[C1:310] Detering, Heinrich, '"Das Ich wird zum Wortspiel": Ibsen, Strindberg, Nietzsche und das Drama der Abstraktion', in *Widersprüche. Zur frühen Nietzsche-Rezeption*, Hrsg. im Auftrag der Stiftung Weimarer Klassik von Andreas Schirmer und Rüdiger Schmidt, Weimar: Verlag Hermann Böhlaus Nachfolger, 2000, pp. 79-101. ['"The Ego becomes a Play on Words": Nietzsche, Ibsen, Strindberg and the Drama of Abstraction'. Includes two sections, 'Sprachrohr und Stiefel: Macht als Diskurs in Strindbergs *Fröken Julie*' (Speaking Tube and Boots: Power as a Form of Discourse in Strindberg's *Miss Julie*), pp. 87-92, and '"Ergebnis": Nietzsche und Strindberg', pp. 92-98, together with an analysis of the power struggle in Ibsen's *A Doll's House* in Nietzschean terms. See **C1: :311**]

[C1:311] Detering, Heinrich, '"Das Ich wird zum Wortspiel": Nietzsche, Ibsen, Strindberg und das Drama der Abstraktion', *Hofmannsthal-Jahrbuch zur europäischen Moderne*

(Freiburg), 6 (1999), pp. 239-256. ['"The Ego becomes a Play on Words": Nietzsche, Ibsen, Strindberg and the Drama of Abstraction'. Undertakes a subtle comparison of Nietzschean elements in the plays of Ibsen and Sg, focusing on *A Doll's House* and *Fröken Julie*. Detering analyses the latter in terms of the way in which discourse embodies power relationships, with reference both to Foucault and Sg's correspondence with Nietzsche and Georg Brandes]

[C1:312] Detering, Heinrich, '"Es geschieht": Nietzsche, Ibsen, Strindberg und das Drama der Abstraktion', in Maria Deppermann, *et al.*, Hrsg., *Ibsen im europäischen Spannungsfeld zwischen Naturalismus und Symbolismus*, Kongreßakten der 8. Internationalen Ibsen-Konferenz, Gossensaß, 23-28.6.1997, Frankfurt am Main: Peter Lang, 1998, pp. 235-255. ['"It Really Happens": Nietzsche, Ibsen, Strindberg and the drama of Abstraction'. Primarily concerned with *Fröken Julie*, which is compared with *A Doll's House* in the light of the theory of drama advanced in Nietzsche's *The Birth of Tragedy* (1872)]

[C1:313] Dickson, Walter, 'Gunnar Björling och Strindberg', *Blekinge Läns Tidning* (Karlskrona), 12 June 1968. [Couples Sg with the Finland-Swedish modernist poet (1887-1960)]

[C1:314] Dietrich,* 'Strindberg und O'Neill', *Hamburger Jahrbuch*, 1950, pp. 76-85.

[C1:315] Diktonius, Elmer, 'Tavaststjerna och den nya dikten', *Arbetarbladet* (Helsingfors), 1923, No. 32. ['Tavaststjerna and the New Literature'. Comments on the Finland-Swedish author Karl August Tavaststjerna's (1860-1898) admiration for Sg's realism in *Röda rummet* by one of the leading figures in Finnish modernism]

[C1:316] Döblin, Alfred, 'Brod: *Die Fälscher*', *Prager Tagblatt* (Prague), 1 March 1922. [Reviews Max Brod's play *Die Fälscher* (1920) with reference to several of Sg's post-Inferno dramas]

[C1:317] Döblin, Alfred, 'Brod: *Die Fälscher*', in **D1:113,** *Ein Kerl muß eine Meinung haben. Berichte und Kritiken 1921-1924*, pp. 60-61. [Rpr. of **C1:316**]

[C1:318] Döblin, Alfred, '*Gabriel Schillings Flucht in die Öffentlichkeit*', *Der Sturm* (Berlin), 3 (1912-13), p. 207. [Accuses Gerhart Hauptmann of plagiarising Sg and his drama *Kamraterna* in his play from 1906, which depicts a painter torn between his mistress and his wife]

[C1:319] Döblin, Alfred, '*Die Seele vor dem Arzt und dem Philosophen. Schriften zur Psychoanalyse*', *Vossische Zeitung* (Berlin), 28 November 1926. ['The Soul Examined by the Doctor and the Philosopher. Writings on Psychoanalysis'. Discusses Sg together with Flaubert, Wedekind, and Freud in an article on recent psychoanalytical literature]

[C1:320] Döblin, Alfred, 'Unterwelt – Oberwelt', *Das goldene Tor* (Lahr), 2:6 (1947), p. 488. ['Underworld – Overworld'. Discusses Wedekind, Villon, Freud, Sg, and Tolstoi]

[C1:321] Dolgopolov, L. K., *Poemy Bloka i russkaia poema kontsa XIX-nachala XX vekov*, Moscow-Leningrad: Nauka, 1964. 189 pp. ['Long Poems in the Works of Blok and in Russian Literature at the Beginning of the 19th and the End of the 20th Centuries'. Includes a comparison of *Inferno* with Aleksandr Blok's poem 'Retribution'. E.998]

[C1:322] Dort, Bernard, 'Strindberg nourricier. A propos d'Adamov et du "nouveau théâtre"', *Théâtre/Public* (Gennevilliers), 73 (1986), 55-59. Illus. ['Strindberg the Source. Apropos Adamov and the "New Theatre"'. Identifies the post-Inferno Sg as the vital inseminator of the French theatre of the 1950s, represented here by Adamov in *La parodie* (which was inspired by *Ett drömspel*) and *Professeur Taranne* (which is indebted to Act 3 of *Till Damaskus II*). According to Dort, Sg's theatre exemplifies the logic of dreams and the dramaturgy of the self as analysed by Peter Szondi in *Theorie des modernen Dramas* (**D1:450**), but the Sg who inspires the contemporary French theatre is no longer the naturalist of Antoine, the symbolist of Lugné-Poe, or the German expressionist, but a new force, mediated by Antonin Artaud]

[C1:323] Dostalová, Zdenka, 'K pojeti naturalismu ve strukture dramatu: L. N. Tolstoj-A. Strindberg', *Rossica Olomucensia* (Olomouc, Czech Republic), 20 (1981), 88-95. ['On the Poetics of Naturalism and Dramatic Structure'. Compares Tolstoi's approach to naturalism with Sg's]

[C1:324] Dottin-Orsini, Mireille, *Cette femme qu'ils disent fatale. Textes et images de la misogynie fin-de-siècle*, Paris: Bernard Grasset, 1993, pp. 300-304. ['This Woman Called Fatal. Texts and Images of *Fin-de-Siècle* Misogyny'. Contextualises Sg's conception of woman as vampire in relation to other late 19th-Century writers and philosophers]

[C1:325] Douglas, Dennis, 'Influence and Individuality: The Indebtedness of Patrick White's *The Ham Funeral* and *The Season at Sarsaparilla* to Strindberg and the German Expressionist Movement', in Leon Cantrell, ed., *Bards, Bohemians, and Bookmen: Essays in Australian Literature*, St. Lucia: University of Queensland Press, 1976, pp. 266-280. [Identifies a link between White's use of stage settings to embody dramatically functional concepts in his two published plays, which have usually been linked with symbolism rather than expressionism, and Sg's use of symbolic settings in *Spöksonaten* and *Ett drömspel*]

[C1:326] Drews, Wolfgang, 'Strindberg und die Erben', *Bühne und Parkett* (Berlin), 20:2 (1974), p. 19. ['Strindberg and his Heirs'. Comments on Sg's relevance for contemporary German dramatists]

[C1:327] Dubois, Margareta, *Algot Ruhe – kulturförmedlare och europeisk visionär*, Lund: Lund University Press, 1989, pp. 151-186. Illus. ['Algot Ruhe – Cultural Intermediary and European Visionary'. Includes a discussion of Sg's influence on the Swedish writer Algot Ruhe (1867-1943), to whom he was known as 'the Master'. Dubois documents their personal contacts, as well as Ruhe's sometimes critical judgements on *Inferno*, *Legender*, and *Karl XII*. Summary in French]

[C1:328] Dumoulié, Camille, 'Formes théâtrales du délire: La folie du pouvoir', *Littératures* (Toulouse), 31 (1994), 117-128. ['Theatrical Forms of Madness. The Madness of Power'. Discusses the dramatic portrayal of hubris, madness, and its relationship to power in Seneca's *Hercules Furens*, Shakespeare's *King Lear*, and Sg's *Fadren*]

[C1:329] Dumoulié, Camille, 'Fureurs. Trois pères furieux', *Nouvelle Revue Française* (Paris), No. 512 (September 1995), 83-102. ['Beside Themselves. Three Enraged Fathers'. Discusses the protagonists of Shakespeare's *King Lear*, Seneca's *Hercules Furens*, and *Fadren* with their common 'Hysterico passio', in light of Jean Starobinski's concept of the 'fureur', who is the actor *par excellence* as touched by hubris]

[C1:330] Durbach, Errol, 'Ibsenian Uterus, Strindbergian Seed: Ingmar Bergman's *Hedda Gabler*', *Essays in Theatre* (Guelph, Ontario), 12:1 (1993), 41-49. [Examines Sg's claim that *Fröken Julie* was Ibsen's inspiration when he conceived the character of Hedda and analyses how Bergman is influenced by Sg in his production of *A Doll's House* as well as his staging of *Hedda Gabler*. The latter is characterised by Sgian aesthetics, converts realism into expressionism and tragedy into hysteria, and virtually translates Hedda into Julie]

[C1:331] Eaton, Walter Prichard, 'O'Neill – "New Risen Attic Stream"', *American Scholar* (Williamsburg), 6:3 (1937), 304-312. [Maintains that O'Neill's debt to Sg is greater even than to Aeschylus or Euripides, not least in *Mourning Becomes Electra*]

[C1:332] Eaton, Winifred Kittredge, *Contrasts in the Representation of Death by Sophocles, Webster and Strindberg*, Jacobean Drama Studies 17, Salzburg: Institut für englische Sprache und Literatur, Universität Salzburg, 1975, pp. 160-226. [Suggests that Sg regarded death not merely as the end of life but as an element pervading the whole of existence. He thus initiated a new era of stage production in response to an unfamiliar way of regarding human experience. Eaton discusses *Fadren*, *Fröken Julie*, *Fordringsägare*, *Till Damaskus*, *Gustav Vasa*, *Erik XIV*, *Ett drömspel*, and *Spöksonaten* in a prolix chapter on 'Death as a Continuing Element of Existence in Strindberg's Plays', which is based entirely on a reading of his works and previous criticism in translation. She also comments on Sg's response to Nietzsche, Shakespeare, Kierkegaard, and Ibsen]

[C1:333] Ebanoidze, Igor', '"Rech' ne o knigakh, a o zhizni…": Perepiska Fridrikha Nitsshe s Gotfridom Kellerom, Georgom Brandesom i Avgustom Strindbergom', edited and translated by Igor' Ebanoidze, *Novyi Mir: Literaturno-Khudozhestvennyi i Obshchestvenno-Politicheskii Zhurnal*, (Moscow), No. 888 (April 1999), 130-162. [Translation of Nietzsche's correspondence with Gottfried Keller, Georg Brandes, and Sg, together with an introduction and notes by Ebanoidze]

[C1:334] Edström, Mauritz, *Äran, kärleken, klassen. En bok om Ivar Lo-Johanssons författarskap*, [Malmö]: Forum, 1976. [265] pp. ['Honour, Love, Class. A Book about the Works of Ivar Lo-Johansson'. A biographical and critical study of the Swedish proletarian author (1901-1990), linking him with Sg in twelve separate references]

[C1:335] Edström, Vivi Blom-, 'Vävsymboliken hos Rydberg, Selma Lagerlöf och Strindberg', in *Göteborgsstudier i litteraturhistoria tillägnade Sverker Ek*, Göteborg: Wettergren & Kerber, 1954, pp. 269-282. ['The Web as Symbol in Rydberg, Selma Lagerlöf, and Strindberg'. Discusses *Brända tomten* and *Brott och brott* in a comparison of the use made of the traditional symbol of the web of life in the work of three Swedish writers. In Sg's later works (notably the Chamber Plays of 1907), it is used to project the frequently recurring motif of the way in which everyone is mysteriously interlinked with everyone else]

[C1:336] Edström, Vivi [Blom-], 'Selma Lagerlöf och Strindberg', *Strindbergiana* (Stockholm), 1 (1985), pp. 109-144. Illus. ['Selma Lagerlöf and Strindberg', Edström seeks to rectify misconceptions arising from the way in which what might be regarded as the two major Swedish authors of the turn-of-the-century have usually been compared and contrasted to each other's disadvantage. She compares their intentions as writers and their conceptions of the writer's role, documents their views of one another, discusses *Hemsöborna* and *Jerusalem* under the heading 'realism and romanticism', and compares *Körkarlen* with *Ett drömspel*. They need not be seen only as rivals and each other's antithesis, either temperamentally or as representatives of the 1880s (Sg) and 1890s (Lagerlöf)]

[C1:337] Eggum, Arne, 'Literary Reflections in Munch's Frieze of Life', in Piotr Paszkiewicz, ed., *Totenmesse: Modernism in the Culture of Northern and Central Europe*, Warsaw:

Institute of Art/Polish Academy of Sciences, 1996, pp. 65-78. Illus. [Eggum discusses Munch's association with Sg in Berlin in 1893-94, but suggests that it was Stanisław Przybyszewski's notion of sexuality as the prime, but blind, force in nature that was the major influence on his paintings during this period]

[C1:338] Egri, Péter, 'Epic Retardation and Diversion: Hemingway, Strindberg and O'Neill', *Neohelicon* (Budapest), 14:1 (1987), 9-20. [Rpr. of **C1:339**]

[C1:339] Egri, Péter, 'Epic Retardation and Diversion: Hemingway, Strindberg and O'Neill', *Zeitschrift für Anglistik und Amerikanistik* (Leipzig), 33:4 (1985), 324-330. [See **C1:340**]

[C1:340] Egri, Péter, 'The Fusion of the Epic and Dramatic: Hemingway, Strindberg and O'Neill', *Eugene O'Neill Newsletter* (Boston, Mass.), 10:1 (1986), 16-22. [Examines structural affinities between *Dödsdansen* and works by Ernest Hemingway (*A Farewell to Arms* and *For Whom the Bell Tolls*) and Eugene O'Neill (*Strange Interlude*)]

[C1:341] Eisen, Kurt, *The Inner Strength of Opposites: O'Neill's Novelistic Drama and the Melodramatic Imagination*, Athens (Georgia) and London: The University of Georgia Press, 1994. XI+241 pp. [Compares Sg with Eugene O'Neill and charts a development in dramatic form away from notions of character as a fixed subject towards a novelistic conception that nonetheless perpetuates the psychological dynamic of melodrama. Through its use of transferable masks, Eisen asserts that *The Great God Brown* strives for the kind of shifting divisions and reintegrations of character that Sg describes in his preface to *Ett drömspel*. Moreover, several of O'Neill's later plays feature a character whose position can be compared with that of Sg's dreamer, a dramatic central consciousness whose relationship to the action and dialogue is much as Peter Szondi describes it in *Theorie des modernen Dramas*, **D1:450**. Eisen also associates both Sg and O'Neill with a series of melodramatic works preoccupied with the figure of Napoleon]

[C1:342] Ek, Sverker R., *Verklighet och vision. En studie i Hjalmar Bergmans romankonst*, Stockholm: Albert Bonniers Förlag, 1964, pp. 299-309. ['Reality and Vision. A Study in Hjalmar Bergman's Art of the Novel'. Considers Sg's influence on both Pär Lagerkvist and Bergman with reference in the latter's case to his novel *En döds memoarer* (1918)]

[C1:343] Ekelund, Erik, *Ola Hanssons ungdomsdiktning*, Helsingfors: Holger Schildts Förlag, [1930]. 284 pp. [Discusses Hansson's literary relationship with Sg, including their mutual interest in Edgar Allan Poe and Nietzsche, in the course of a study of Hansson's early writings. Ekelund considers Sg's adaptation of Hansson's short story 'Paria' as a one-act play, their alignment with the psychological naturalism that emerged in the later 1880s in the work of Paul Bourget and others, and their conflict with Verner von Heidenstam and his critique of naturalism in the literary manifestoes *Renässans* (1889) and *Pepitas bröllop* (1890)]

[C1:344] Ekelund, Erik, *Tavaststjerna och hans diktning*, Helsingfors: Svenska litteratursällskapet i Finland; København: Ejnar Munksgaard Forlag, 1950. VIII+321. ['Tavaststjerna and his Work'. Discusses the Finland-Swedish author Karl August Tavaststjerna's (1860-1898) personal contacts with Sg in Skåne, Weimar, and Berlin during 1892-93, and documents Sg's influence on his individualism and the realism of his novels and short stories]

[C1:345] Ekelund, Vilhelm, *Antikt ideal*, Malmö: Aktiebolaget Framtiden, 1909. 180 pp. [Associates Sg variously with Goethe, Nietzsche, Dostoevskii, and Friedrich Hölderlin]

[C1:346] Ekelund, Vilhelm, *Båge och lyra*, Malmö: Aktiebolaget Framtiden, 1912. 82 pp. [Ekelund ranks Sg together with Ibsen, Kierkegaard, and Heinrich von Kleist as a 'hypochondriac' writer]

[C1:347] Ekelund, Vilhelm, *Veri similia*, 2 vols, Stockholm: Albert Bonniers Förlag, 1915-16. [Associates Sg with Dostoevskii as two writers who penetrate the painful aspects of experience more profoundly than others]

[C1:348] Eklund, Torsten, 'Afrodite och Sliparen. Några betraktelser över ett diktmotiv', *Studiekamraten* (Tollarp), 13 (1931), 72-74. ['Aphrodite and the Knife Grinder. Some Reflections on a Poetic Motif'. Compares Carl Snoilsky's poem 'Afrodite och Sliparen' (Aphrodite and the Knife Grinder') in the collection *Dikter* (1883) with Sg's poetic rejoinder on a similar theme in *Sömngångarnätter* (1884)]

[C1:349] Eklund, Torsten, 'Strindberg – det moderna genombrottets man i svensk litteratur', *Studiekamraten* (Tollarp), 19 (1937), 123-125. Illus. ['Strindberg – The Man of the Modern Breakthrough in Swedish Literature'. Presents Sg as the foremost Swedish writer of the Scandinavian Modern Breakthrough]

[C1:350] Eklund, Torsten, 'Strindberg – det moderna genombrottets man i svensk litteratur', *Studiekamraten* (Tollarp), 34:3 (1952), 94-96. ['Strindberg – The Man of the Modern Breakthrough in Swedish Literature'. Rpr. of **C1:349**]

[C1:351] Eklund, Torsten, 'Strindberg och åttiotalets unga Sverige', *Tiden* (Stockholm), 18 (1926), 289-298. ['Strindberg and Young Sweden in the 1880s'. Examines Sg's relationship with the writers and publicists of the Young Sweden group and charts their growing differences in the social and literary debates of the period, particularly after Sg's trial for blasphemy over *Giftas* in 1884]

[C1:352] [Eklund, Torsten], 'Fyra nobelpristagare uttalar sig i Strindbergssällskapets juileumsenkät', *Meddelanden från Strindbergssällskapet* (Stockholm), 6 (1949), pp. 1-5. ['Four Nobel Prize Winners Express an Opinion in the Strindberg Society's Anniversary Questionnaire'. Publishes reponses by Albert Camus, Max Brod, Roger Martin du Gard, Thomas Mann, Jean Schlumberger, André Gide, and Hermann Hesse to a questionnaire about Sg's continuing significance, circulated in conjunction with the centenary of his birth]

[C1:353] Ekman, Hans-Göran, 'Humor, dubbelmoral och Strindbergs kritik av Bellman', in Margareta Brundin, *et al.*, red., **B1:88**, *20 x Strindberg*, pp. 105-116. ['Humour, Double-Moral, and Strindberg's Criticism of Bellman'. Identifies a recurring patterned sequence of dialogue in Sg's plays in which one character questions the seriousness of what is being said and the extent to which the ongoing conversation is a playful game. This is exemplified here with reference to *Fröken Julie, Fadren, Kristina, Marodörer, Gustav III, Mäster Olof, Erik XIV, Fordringsägare, Leka med elden*, and *Midsommar*, and provides Ekman with an opportunity to demonstrate how Sg's work, which is not without comedy as well as satire and irony, is nevertheless hostile to humour, where this is defined as a combination of jest and seriousness. This serves in turn both to explain the antipathy with which he regarded the Swedish Gustavian poet Carl Michael Bellman (1740-95), whom he attacks in *Det nya riket*, and the critique of

Hemsöborna as a comic work without sympathy for those it portrays by the Swedish poet Gustaf Fröding, whose essay 'Om humor' appeared in 1890]

[C1:354] Ekman, Hans-Göran, 'Kabeljo och ölsupa. Om Strindberg och Karen Blixen', *Strindbergiana* (Stockholm), 20 (2005), pp. 63-72. [Finds associations and parallels between Sg's works and those of Blixen, most notably in the Chamber Plays and *Babettes Gæstebud* (1958)]

[C1:355] Ekman, Kerstin, 'Hundra år av hädelse. Om Strindbergs, Söderbergs och Rushdies plats i historien', *Expressen* (Stockholm). 26 October 1994. ['One Hundred Years of Blasphemy. On Strindberg's, Söderberg's, and Rushdie's Place in History'. Considers three instances of literary blasphemy brought to trial (in Sg's case for *Giftas*), written apropos the fatwa on Salman Rushdie]

[C1:356] Ek-Nilsson, Katarina, 'Titanen och sagodrottningen: kulturella representationer av August Strindberg och Selma Lagerlöf', in Inga-Lill Aronson and Birgitta Meurling, red., *Det bekönade museet: genusperspektiv i museologi och museiverksamhet*, Uppsala: Institutionen för ABM vid Uppsala Universitet, 2005, pp. 53-95. ['The Titan and the Fairy-Tale Queen: Cultural Representations of August Strindberg and Selma Lagerlöf'. Adopts a perspective derived from gender studies to compare the representation of the two writers in the respective museums dedicated to their lives and work in Stockholm and Mårbacka]

[C1:357] Ekström, Arthur, 'Då Strindberg slog Shakespeare på fingrarna', *Studiekamraten* (Tollarp), 58 (1976), 71-72. ['When Strindberg Rapped Shakespeare over the Knuckles']

[C1:358] Elbek, Jørgen, 'Halvfemserne i Norden', *Dansk Udsyn* (Kolding), 70 (1990), 67-82. ['The Nineties in Scandinavia'. Includes Sg in a discussion of the *fin-de-siècle* writings of Sg, Sophus Clausson, and Knut Hamsun, and their relationship with Symbolism as a successor to Naturalism in the 1890s]

[C1:359] Elbek, Jørgen, 'Halvfemserne i Norden', in *På sporet efter enhørningen*, Aarhus: Huset, 1993, pp. 9-22. ['The Nineties in Scandinavia'. Rpr. of **C1:358**]

[C1:360] Elbek, Jørgen, 'The Nordic Nineties', in Faith Ingwersen and Mary Kay Norseng, eds, *Fin(s) de Siècle in Scandinavian Perspective: Studies in Honor* of Harald S. Næss, Columbia, South Carolina: Camden House, 1993, pp. 55-68. [Aspects of *fin-de-siècle* Scandinavian literature with reference to Sophus Claussen, Knut Hamsun, Symbolism, and Sg]

[C1:361] Elgeskog, Justus, 'Två svenska diktens hövdingar. Viktor Rydberg. August Strindberg', in *Några folkhögskoleföreläsningar*, Stockholm: N.T.O:s Förlag, 1923, pp. [87]-123. ['Two Lords of Swedish Letters. Viktor Rydberg and August Strindberg'. Offers a somewhat sanctimonious biographical reading of Sg's literary career, pp. 109-123, juxtaposed with an account of Viktor Rydberg's. Sg is a spirit of the mightiest measure. Nevertheless, Rydberg's path inwards towards profundity and unity is the way we should follow, not Sg's, which is rather a warning to us and coming generations to preserve our souls from evil. Designed for use in Swedish Folk High Schools]

[C1:362] [Eliot, T. S.], 'Strindbergs inflytande på T. S. Eliot betydande. Intressant brev i *Svenska Dagbladets* rundfråga från Nobelpristagaren', *Svenska Dagbladet* (Stockholm), 20 January 1949. ['Strindberg's Influence on T. S. Eliot Considerable. Interesting Letter in response to *Svenska Dagbladet*'s Questionnaire from the Noble Prize Winner'. The notion that Sg's influence on Eliot is confirmed by the latter's letter in response to a questionnaire marking the centenary of Sg's birth]

[C1:363] [Eliot, T. S.], 'August Strindberg', *The Times* (London), 2 February 1949. [Reports Eliot's appreciative statement about Sg's enduring significance, uttered at a luncheon of the Anglo-Swedish Society, held to commemorate the centenary of his birth]

[C1:364] Elizarova, M. E., *Tvorchestvo Chekhova i problemy realizma v kontse XIX veka*, Moscow: Goslitizdat, 1958. 200 pp. [Deals with Sg in the context of *fin-de-siècle* decadence, p. 126, in a study of 'Chekhov and the Problem of Realism at the End of the Nineteenth Century. E.972]

[C1:365] Ellehauge, Martin, *The Position of Bernard Shaw in European Drama and Philosophy*, Copenhagen: Levin & Munksgaard, 1931. 390 pp. [Relates Shaw briefly to Sg as a dramatist, with reference to *Fröken Julie*, *Gustav Adolf*, and *Mäster Olof*]

[C1:366] Ellehauge, Martin, *The Position of Bernard Shaw in European Drama and Philosophy*, New York: Haskell House, 1966. 390 pp. [Facsimile Rpr. of **C1:365**]

[C1:367] Elliot, Beverly, and Tom Markus, 'Through the Piercing Eyes of Edvard Munch. Ibsen and Strindberg on Stage', *Journal of Dramatic Theory and Criticism* (Lawrence, Kansas), 5:2 (1991), 153-165. Illus. [Concentrates primarily on *Ghosts* and *Fadren* as realised in stage designs by Munch, where the stress is less on the naturalistic and more on the evocation of mood, or expressionism]

[C1:368] Elovson, Harald, 'Bengt Lidforss och litteraturen', *Arbetet* (Malmö), 17 August 1947. ['Bengt Lidforss and Literature']

[C1:369] Elovson, Harald, 'Studier i brytningarna i nordisk litteratur omkring 1890', *Edda* (Oslo), 36 (1936), 369-449. ['Studies in the Turmoil in Nordic Literature around 1890'. Examines the conflicts in Scandinavian literature ca. 1890 when Verner von Heidenstam and Arne Garborg broke with naturalism and largely abandoned the socially committed realism of the 1880s. Elovson touches briefly on Sg's poem 'Lokes smädelser' (Loki's Blasphemies, 1883), *Tjänstekvinnans son*, and the essay 'Om modernt drama och modern teater' (On Modern Drama and the Modern Theatre), as well as on his naturalistic works for the theatre in a discussion of Heidenstam's personal contacts and literary conflicts with the older writer. According to Elovson, the former's attempt at a definition of new literary values in the manifestoes *Renässans* (Renaissance, 1889) and *Pepitas Bröllop* (Pepita's Wedding, 1890) entails a break with the realism of the 1880s, then immediately associated with Sg, whether or not he was mentioned by name]

[C1:370] Engberg, Magnus, 'Den ensamma giftsvampen', in *Vid kanten av tidvattnet. Tre författare - tre öar*, Linköping: Ytforum, 1992. Illus. 108 pp. ['The Solitary Poisonous Mushroom'. Discusses Sg's links with the island of Kymmendö and the Stockholm archipelago in a popular study of three Swedish authors (Sg, Verner von Heidenstam, and Hjalmar Söderberg), and their association with three different Swedish islands. Discusses Sg pp. 11-32]

[C1:371] Engelstad, Carl F., *Drømmen om mennesket. Litterære essays*, Oslo: Aschehoug, 1982, pp. 90-109. [Includes a comparison of Ibsen and Sg]

[C1:372] Engwall, Gunnel, 'Strindberg segrar i litterärt maraton', *Forskning och framsteg* (Stockholm), 25:4 (1990), 38-43. ['Strindberg Victorious in Literary Marathon'. Explores the literary and intellectual relationship between Sg and Émile Zola. Engwall also includes reflections on Sg's works in French, his relationship with symbolism as well as naturalism and realism, the Dreyfus Affaire, and the ongoing publication of the new edition of his *Samlade Verk*]

[C1:373] Engwall, Gunnel, 'Strindberg: Sveriges Zola?', Föreläsning vid Stockholms universitets installations- och promotionshögtidlighet, 6.10.1989, 8 pp. ['Is Strindberg Sweden's Zola?' An inaugural lecture which charts the shifts in Sg's opinion of Zola, both as a man and a writer, as his opinions changed throughout his career. Engwall documents his attempt to interest Zola in French editions of *Giftas* and *Fadren*, and the possibility that Zola may have exerted an influence on the style and subject matter of *Röda rummet*]

[C1:374] Erdmann, Nils, 'Den moderne svenske Literaturs Folketyper, Folkeliv og Folkelivskildrere', 1-2, *Tilskueren* (Copenhagen), 6:9-10 (1889), pp. 830-842, 918-932. ['The Common People, their Lives and Portrayers in Modern Swedish Literature'. Discusses the portrayal of rural life in *Hemsöborna* and *Skärkarlsliv* briefly in Part 2, alongside a fuller treatment of works from the 1880s on similar themes by Gustaf af Geijerstam, Ernst Ahlgren (pseudonym of Victoria Benedictsson), and other Swedish writers of the period]

[C1:375] Esenbaeva, R. M., '[The Influence of Ibsenism and Strindberg's Ideas on the French Theatre]', in *Gertsenovskie chteniia. Filologischeskie nauki*, Vol. 24, Leningrad: Filologicheskie Nauki, 1971, pp. 125-126. [E.1052]

[C1:376] Etzler, Allan, 'Strindberg och Tegnér', *Svensk Litteraturtidskrift* (Stockholm), 30:1 (1967), 14-23. [Chart's Sg's view of the poetry and personality of the Swedish poet Esaias Tegnér (1782-1846), from his early journalism to *Tal till svenska nationen*. Also compares a passage in the fourth of Sg's *Sömngångarnätter* with Tegnér's 'Sång till solen' (Song to the Sun)]

[C1:377] Eustachiewicz, Lesław, *Miedzy wspólczesnoscia, a historia*, Warszawa: Pax, 1973. 342 pp. [Notes the impact of Sg's work on the theatre of Stanisław Witkiewicz]

[C1:378] Ewbank, Inga-Stina, 'German Poets in Strindberg's Theatre: The Repertoire that Never Was', in Dorothy James, *et al.*, *Patterns of Change: German Drama and the European Tradition*, Bern: Peter Lang, 1990, pp. 151-163. Illus. [Points out that, while Sg was a major influence on German expressionist drama, he was himself influenced by numerous German playwrights and thought highly of many of their works. Indeed, he envisaged several works by Hebbel (*Gyges und sin Ring*, *Judith*, *Agnes Bernauer*, *Genoveva*, *Maria Magdalena*), Grabbe (*Don Juan und Faust*, *Napoleon*, *Aschendbrödel*), Immerman (*Merlin*), and Wagner (*Tristan und Isolde*, but without the music) as possible repertoire for his Intimate Theatre. Indeed, these plays help clarify Sg's relationship to German drama and suggest that there is a lineal development in the modern theatre which runs from the period of the German *Sturm und Drang* via naturalism and the dramas of Frank Wedekind to Brecht and the Theatre of the Absurd, a development in which Sg is a crucial link in the chain]

[C1:379] Ewbank, Inga-Stina, '"Hjemland…fødeland": Ibsen, Strindberg och landsflykt', in *Ibsen-Strindberg seminar pa Voksenåsen 15-17 september 1997*, Oslo: Voksenåsen, 1997, pp. 41-53. ['Homeland – Fatherland: Ibsen, Strindberg and Exile'. Swedish version of **C1:380**]

[C1:380] Ewbank, Inga-Stina, 'Ibsen, Strindberg and Exile', in Ann-Charlotte Gavel Adams and Terje L. Leiren, eds, **B1:2**, *Stage and Screen: Studies in Scandinavian Drama and Film. Essays in Honor of Birgitta Steene*, pp. 9-30. [Compares and contrasts the experience of real and existential exile in the lives and works of Ibsen and Sg, and discusses Sg's decision to write in French, *Sömngångarnätter*, *Till Damaskus*, the Chamber Plays of 1907, and *Stora landsvägen*. Ewbank concludes that the essential modernity of both writers resides in their discovery of the Freudian unconscious whereby any notion of unity is divided and we are all our own foreigners]

[C1:381] Ewbank, Inga-Stina, '*Richard III* (c.1591), *Gustav III* (1902), and the Drama of Nationalism', in Vincent Newey and Ann Thompson, eds, *Literature and Nationalism*, Savage, MD.: Barnes & Noble, 1991, pp. 98-110. [Both Richard and Gustav are self-conscious actors and playwright plotters whose control is ultimately seen to be illusory. Like Shakespeare, Sg turned national history into a sequence of plays, and learnt a great deal from his predecessor. He read *Richard III* anew in writing *Gustav III*, responding in particular to Shakespeare's language, which concentrates on the gap between words and their meaning, intentions and their fulfilment. Shakespeare taught Sg to dramatise not a nationalist myth but the 'ugly story' of a nation whose king is firstly an actor]

[C1:382] Ewbank, Inga-Stina, 'Shakespeare and Strindberg: Influence as Insemination', in John Batchelor, Tom Cain, and Claire Lamont, eds, *Shakespearean Continuities. Essays in Honour of E. A. J. Honigmann*, Basingstoke and London: Macmillan, 1997, pp. 335-347. [Points out that Sg's interest in Shakespeare was lifelong and is evident in the dramaturgy of *Fadren* as well as in the history plays. Ewbank discusses Sg's knowledge of Shakespeare criticism, his account of Shakespeare in *En blå bok* as the exemplary writer *par excellence*, and the treatment accorded his plays in the various memoranda he addressed to the members of the Intimate Theatre. Sg learnt much about characterisation and dramatic structure from Shakespeare and, most especially and helpfully in the post-Inferno period, it was in part through Shakespeare that Sg gained a new insight into theatre practice. The 'Shakespeare-Bühne' which was introduced in Munich in 1889 by Jocza Savits and Karl Lautenschläger suggested the kind of stage space that would liberate drama from the proscenium arch and hence provide an appropriate setting for the dematerialised form of the more experimental plays that he was then writing, such as *Ett drömspel* and the Chamber Plays]

[C1:383] Ewbank, Inga-Stina, 'Shakespeare, Shaw, Strindberg – and Kenneth Muir', in *KM 80: A Birthday Album for Kenneth Muir*, Liverpool: Liverpool University Press, 1987, pp. 44-46. [Identifies affinities between the three dramatists]

[C1:384] Ewbank, Inga-Stina, 'Strindberg, Shakespeare and History', in Birgitta Steene, ed., **B1:434**, *Strindberg and History*, pp. 75-92. Illus. [Examines Sg's abiding and varied interest in history and the influence of Shakespeare on his history plays. Although both *Memorandum till Medlemmarne av Intima Teatern från Regissören* and the essay 'Världshistoriens mystik' suggest that the pattern of history is abstract and neat, the plays, like Shakespeare's, confirm that it is implacable and ghostly, undeniable and elusive. Shakespeare is integral to Sg's thinking about drama and theatre; he is not merely a dramatic model but, as *En blå bok* makes clear, becomes 'a kind of language through which he thinks', acquiring from him and the example of e.g. *Richard III*, an insight into how to wed dramatic word to action and both to a sense of history. Ewbank discusses *Karl XII, Gustav Adolf*, and *Kristina*, where the most Shakespearean quality is 'the sense of language as at once immensely powerful and immensely impotent']

[C1:385] Ewbank, Inga-Stina, '*The Tempest* and After', *Shakespeare Survey* (Cambridge), 43 (1991), pp. 109-119. [Discusses Sg's characteristically self-identificatory reading of *The Tempest* in his fourth memoranda to members of the Intimate Theatre and *En blå bok*, alongside other readings of the same play by Ibsen, Georg Brandes, and Isak Dinesen]

[C1:386] Falk, Doris V., *Eugene O'Neill and the Tragic Tension: An Interpretive Study of the Plays*, 2nd edn, New York: Gordian Press, 1982, pp. 153-154. [Compares O'Neill's *Days Without End* with *Till Damaskus* as two struggles over religious faith in dramatic form]

[C1:387] F. V. [Fredrik Vetterlund], 'Lagerkvist, *Modern teater*', *Aftonbladet* (Stockholm), 20 October 1918. [Reviews Pär Lagerkvist's early one-act plays and his essay on the modern theatre, **D1:604**. Observes that Lagerkvist needs urgently to liberate himself from the intimate influence of Sg]

[C1:388] Fechter, Paul, 'Strindberg, Schiller, Kotzebue und andere', *Deutsche Zukunft* (Berlin), 5:39 (1937), pp. 7-9. ['Strindberg, Schiller, Kotzebue, and Others']

[C1:389] Fedin, Konstantin, *Sobranie sochinenii v dvukh tomakh*, Vol. 4, Moscow, 1960, p. 11. [Mentions Sg together with Bjørnstjerne Bjørnson as one of the writers, along with Dostoevskii, who impressed him in his youth]

[C1:390] Fehrman, Carl, 'Levertins kritiska principer', in *Poesi och parodi*, Stockholm: P. A. Norstedt & Söners Förlag, 1957, 323 pp. ['Levertin's Critical Principles'. Comments on the controversial critique of Sg's post-Inferno works by the influential Swedish poet and critic, Oscar Levertin (1862-1906), in the course of a discussion of the principles underlying his critical standpoint in general]

[C1:391] Fehrman, Carl, '"Min ungdoms skald, Oehlenschläger". Om Strindbergs relation till den danske diktaren', in Svend Christiansen and Povl Ingerslev-Jensen, red., *Til Adam Oehlenschläger 1779-1979. Otte afhandlinger*, Teatervidenskabelige studier 7, København: C. A. Reitzel, 1979, pp. 11-20. ['"The Poet of My Youth, Oehlenschläger". On Strindberg's Relationship to the Danish Writer'. Considers Sg's literary links with the Danish Romantic poet and dramatist, Adam Oehlenschläger (1779-1850), whom he once described as 'the poet of my youth', having written an essay on his play, *Hakon Jarl hin Rige* (Earl Hakon the Mighty, 1807), while a student at Uppsala. Fehrman notes that Oehlenschläger's influence is apparent in several of Sg's earliest plays, particularly those like *Den fredlöse*, in which he depicts the Nordic past]

[C1:392] Fehrman, Carl, 'Originalitet och påverkan. Notiser om en litteraturhistorisk 1900- tals debatt', in Karl Erik Gustafsson, *et al.*, red., *I ordets smedja*, Festskrift till Per Ryden, Stockholm: Carlssons, 2002, pp. 192-210. ['Originality and Influence. Notes on a Literary Historical Debate From the 1900s'. Discusses the literary differences between Sg and Verner von Heidenstam, and Fredrik Böök's critical opinion of them both in e.g. *Sveriges modern litteratur* (1921), **B5:21**]

[C1:393] Fialek, Marek, 'August Strindberg und Stanisław Przybyszewski: zwei "Kometen" am Berliner Himmel des ausgehenden 19. Jahrhunderts', *Studia Germanica Posnaniensia* (Poznan), 27 (2002). ['August Strindberg and Stanisław Przybyszewski: Two "Comets" in the Berlin Sky at the End of the 19th Century']

[C1:394] Fichte, Hubert, 'Ich erlaube mir die Revolte: Ein skandalöser Dichter – Gesprach mit Jean Genet', *Die Zeit* (Hamburg), 20 February 1976 (overseas edition), 17-18. ['I Allow Myself Revolt: A Scandalous Writer – Conversation With Jean Genet'. Records Genet's view that with Brecht one always knows precisely what is coming next, with Sg one never does. Nothing Sg says can be said other than in a poetic way]

[C1:395] Fish, Charles, 'Beginnings: O'Neill's "The Web"', *Princeton University Library Chronicle*, 27:1 (1965), 3-20. [Discusses Sg's influence on the first play that Eugene O'Neill claims to have written]

[C1:396] Flakes, Susan, 'Månen, de icke dumma och den skuldmedvetna publiken', *Dramaten* (Stockholm), 7 (1976-77), No. 61, pp. 26-28. ['The Moon, the not Stupid, and the Guilt Conscious Audience'. Reflections on *Paria* and Eugene O'Neill's play *Moon for the Misbegotten*]

[C1:397] Flaxman, Seymour L[awrence], 'The Debt of Williams and Miller to Ibsen and Strindberg', *Comparative Literature Studies* (Urbana, Illinois), Special Advance Issue, (1963), pp. 51-60. [Traces Sgian themes and techniques in several plays by Tennessee Williams, including *A Streetcar Named Desire*, *Camino Real*, *The Glass Menagerie*, and *Summer and Smoke*, whereas Arthur Miller is identified more closely with Ibsen. However, in neither dramatist is there anything like the suggestive, ambiguous, unfinished dialogue traded by the characters of Ibsen and Sg]

[C1:398] Fleisher, Frederic, 'Strindberg and O'Neill', *Symposium* (Syracuse University, New York), 10:1 (1956), 84-94. [Surveys O'Neill's debt to Sg in *Before Breakfast* (which is indebted to *Den starkare*), *The Emperor Jones* (*Till Damaskus*), *The Hairy Ape* (*Ett drömspel*), and *Beyond the Horizon*, *Welded*, *The First Man*, *All God's Children Got Wings*, and *Strange Interlude* (all of which recall *Fadren*). Fleisher concludes that 'Sg's influence on O'Neill appears strongest in those works produced during the first part of the 1920s']

[C1:399] Fleisher, Frederic, 'Strindberg and O'Neill', in Hans Itschert, Hrsg., **D1:213**, *Das Amerikanische Drama von den Anfängen bis zur Gegenwart*, Darmstadt: Wissenschaftliche Buchgesellschaft, 1972, pp. [118]-128. [Rpr. of **C1:398**]

[C1:400] Florin, Magnus, 'Textställen', *Ord och Bild* (Stockholm), 92:1 (1984), pp. 3-15. Illus. [Includes Sg along with Shakespeare, C. J. L. Almqvist, Rousseau, Stendhal, Nerval, Calvino and Borges in a discussion of a western canon of authors for whom sign systems in the natural world play an important role in their writing]

[C1:401] Fogelqvist, Torsten, 'Andersen och Strindberg', in *Typer och tänkesätt*, Stockholm: Albert Bonniers Förlag, 1927, pp. 288-303. [Identifies affinities in narrative style and mood between Sg and Hans Christian Andersen from as early as the collection of stories *Från Fjärdingen och Svartbäcken* when Sg had already translated some of his Danish predecessor's stories and tales. In fact, he had experimented with the latter's motifs as early as the prose piece 'För konsten' (For Art, 1872). Both writers had an eye for living, everyday, picturesque detail, and a sure sense of narrative rhythm, and Sg's close familiarity with Andersen was important for the development of his prose style. Hence, these early stories of Sg deserve greater respect than they have hitherto received]

[C1:402] Forsås-Scott, Helena, 'August Strindberg, the New Woman and Elin Wägner', *Women: A Cultural Review* (Oxford), 10:1 (1999), 78-86. [Indicates how the concept of gender and the conflict of identity which it entails in comparatively early works like *En dåres försvarstal* (1887) and *Fröken Julie* (1888) remains relevant to a late text such as *Taklagsöl* (1907), which 'graphically depicts patriarchy in a state of terminal disintegration'. Forsås-Scott suggests that Sg's representation of woman is countered by Wägner in her portrait of the New Woman in *Pennskaftet* (1910), and by her radicalisation of the enquiry into identity that is also Sg's preoccupation]

[C1:403] Forsås-Scott, Helena, 'Gasmaskmadonnan. Om Elin Wägner', in Elisabeth Møller Jensen, red., *Nordisk kvinolitteraturhistoria*, Band III, Höganäs: Wiken, 1996, pp. 174-178. ['The Gas Mask Madonna. On Elin Wägner'. Maintains that Elin Wägner's portrait of the new woman in her novel *Pennskaftet* (1910) engages in a dialogue with Sg in *Taklagsöl* (1907)]

[C1:404] Forssell, Lars, *LF. Loggbok: artiklar om litteratur och kultur 1944-91*, Stockholm: Hägglund, 1996, pp. 132-136. [Reprints several comments by the Swedish poet and dramatist on Sg]

[C1:405] Forssell, Lars, 'Om Strindberg', in *Vänner*, Höganäs: Wiken, 1991, pp. 312-325. ['About Strindberg'. Intersperses comments and reflections on Sg with fictional elements. For Forssell (b.1928), Sg is 'the unsurpassed journalist' in his plays as well as the prose works]

[C1:406] Forsström, Axel, *Ellen Key*, Lund: C. W. K. Gleerup, 1940. Illus 203 pp. [Includes an anecdotal account of Key's mixed feelings for Sg the man and her hatred of the author of *Svarta fanor* where she is portrayed with satirical venom as the meddling harpy, Hanna Paj, pp. 30-36. Rpr. of **C1:407**]

[C1:407] Forsström, Axel, 'Minnen från Strand', *Svensk Litteraturtidskrift* (Stockholm), 1:9 (1946), 1-23. ['Memories from Strand'. See **C1:406**]

[C1:408] Fournier, Vincent, 'Le discours français sur la Scandinavie entre 1882 et 1914 ou l'utopie ambiguë. Essai d'analyse', *Revue de littérature comparée* (Paris), 49:3 (1975), 373-395. ['French Discourse on Scandinavia between 1882 and 1914, Or the Ambiguous Utopia. An Analytical Essay'. Comments briefly on Sg's image in France at the end of the 19th Century in an essay on the French image of Scandinavia in general]

[C1:409] Fournier, Vincent, 'La "Percée moderne" au Danemark, en Suède et en Norvège: Notes et réflexions', *Revue de littérature comparée* (Paris), 62:2 (1988), 165-181. ['The "Modern Breakthrough" in Denmark, Sweden, and Norway. Notes and Reflections'. Touches briefly on *Röda rummet*, *Giftas*, the stories 'Tschandala' and 'De lycksaliges ö' (The Isle of the Blessed) from *Svenska öden och äventyr*, and *I havsbandet* in a wide-ranging discussion of the literature of the Scandinavian Modern Breakthrough]

[C1:410] Fraenkel, Pavel, 'Tore Ørjasæters dramatik', *Samtiden* (Oslo), 75 (1966), 155-164. ['Tore Ørjasæter's Dramas'. Touches briefly on the significance of Sg for the plays of the Norwegian dramatist (1886-1968)]

[C1:411] Fredén, Gustaf, 'Balzac dans la littérature suédoise', in *Hommage à Balzac*, Paris: Mercure de France, 1950, pp. 239-265. ['Balzac in Swedish Literature'. Argues the importance of Balzac's *Illusions perdues* (1837-42) and *L'Envers de l'histoire contemporaine* (1842-8) as pre-texts for *Röda rummet*, and the significance of his Swedenborgian novel *Séraphita* (1834-5) for both *Påsk* and *Ett drömspel*, particularly in the depiction of Eleonora and Agnes respectively. Fredén compares similarities in their vision of modern society as well as the stress they both place on the mysterious power of money, Balzac in the *Comédie humaine* in general and, in Sg's case, in *Svarta fanor*]

[C1:412] Frenz, Horst, *Eugene O'Neill*, Translated by Helen Sebba, New York: Frederick Ungar Publishing Co., 1971, pp. 76-78, 101-102. [Indicates how the dramatic monologue *Before Breakfast* recalls Sg's one-act play *Den starkare* and the visions of the Emperor Jones may have been inspired by *Till Damaskus*. Frenz suggests that there are also traces of Sg in *All God's Chillun Got Wings*, *Welded*, and *Strange Interlude*. But he notes that O'Neill was much more deeply affected by Sg the man as he appears in his autobiographical writings than he was by Sg the playwright]

[C1:413] Fridell, Folke, 'August Strindberg', *Folket i Bild* (Stockholm), 3:3 (1974), pp. 24, 27. [A personal note on his relationship to Sg as writer by the Swedish proletarian author (1904-1985)]

[C1:414] Fridell, Folke, 'Mitt möte med August Strindberg', in *Våra författare. Sexton radikala berättare ur svensk folklig tradition*, Stockholm: Kulturfront Förlag, 1974, pp. 202-209. ['My Encounter with August Strindberg'. An account of Fridell's early response to reading Sg. Rpr. of **C1:413**]

[C1:415] Friedell, Egon, *A Cultural History of the Modern Age*, Translated by Charles Francis Atkinson, 3 vols, New York: Alfred A. Knopf, Inc., 1932, Vol. 3, pp. 378-382. [English translation of **C1:416**]

[C1:416] Friedell, Egon, *Kulturgeschichte der Neuzeit*, Vol. 3, München: C. H. Beck'sche Verlagsbuchhandlung, 1931. XII+594 pp. [Stresses the pathological aspect of Sg's temperament and his mythological method of observation. The atmosphere in which his characters live is that of an oppressive, paralysing, stifling spiritual eclipse, although in the works of his old age, his steel-hard hatred which, in its supreme moments, has the force and splendour of an act of nature, dwindles to a feeble detestation]

[C1:417] Friedlander, F., 'Strindberg and the Crisis of Modern Civilisation. Epilegomena to His Centenary (Jan. 22, 1949)', *The Australian Quarterly* (Sydney), 22:3 (1950), 85-89. [Regards Sg as symptomatic of his historical moment and gestures vaguely in the direction of affinities with Nietzsche, Marx, Spengler, Dostoevskii, and Artzybaschev, in what remains a poorly informed and ultimately forlorn attempt to contextualise him]

[C1:418] Fritsche, Herbert, *August Strindberg, Gustav Meyrink, Kurt Aram. Drei magische Dichter und Deuter*, Prag-Smichov: V. Neubert & Söhne, 1935. Illus. 35 pp. [Includes the essay 'August Strindberg (22. 1. 1849–14. 5. 1912)', pp. 7-16, in which Sg is defined as a magical (*magischer*) writer and mystic]

[C1:419] Fröberg, Gudmund, red., *Verner von Heidenstam och August Strindberg: Brev 1884-1890*, Med en inledning av Magnus von Platen, Kommentarer av Gudmund Fröberg Stockholm: Wahlström & Widstrand, 1999. [261] pp. [An introduction, pp. 5-15, surveys Sg's personal relationship with Heidenstam (1859-1940). The contextualising commentary, which is concerned with the persons and events alluded to in the letters rather than with literary issues, complements Torsten Eklund's notes on this correspondence in *August Strindbergs brev*]

[C1:420] Frykman, Erik, 'Byron i svensk litteratur', *Samlaren* (Uppsala), 98 (1977), pp. 58-86. ['Byron in Swedish Literature'. Traces impulses from Byron in 19th-Century Swedish literature, and notes that towards the end of the century his direct influence was mediated by Georg Brandes's treatment of the English poet in *Hovedstrømninger i det 19de Aarhundredes Litteratur*. Surprisingly, Sg rarely mentions Byron, although he comments positively on *Manfred* which, in Frykman's opinion, has something in common with *Stora landsvägen*]

[C1:421] Fuchs, Elinor, 'The Apocalyptic Ibsen: *When We Dead Awaken*', *Twentieth Century Literature* (Hempstead, N.Y.) 46:4 (2000), 396-404. [Speculates on the possibility of a link between Ibsen's last play, and *Ett drömspel*, pp. 402-403]

[C1:422] Fuchs, Robert, 'Skandinavische Autoren im Berliner Kulturleben der Jahrhundertwende', in Bernd Henningsen, Hrsg., *Wahlverwandtschaft. Skandinavien und Deutschland 1800 bis 1914*, Deutsches Historisches Museum, Berlin: Jovis, 1997, pp. 340-343. ['Scandinavian Writers in the Cultural Life of Berlin at the Turn-of-the-Century'. See **C1:423**]

[C1:423] Fuchs, Robert, 'Skandinaviska författare i Berlins kulturliv vid sekelskiftet', in *Skandinavien och Tyskland 1800-1914. Möten och vänskapsband*, Utgiven av Bernd Henningsen, *et al.*, Nationalmusei utställningskatalog 599, Stockholm: Nationalmuseum; Berlin: Jovis, 1997, pp. 340-343. Illus. ['Scandinavian Writers in the Cultural Life of Berlin at the Turn-of-the-Century'. Documents Berlin's artistic bohemia and the literary grouping associated with the suburb of Friedrichshagen as centres of artistic experiment and voluntary exile by writers and artists from Denmark, Finland, Norway, and Sweden, including, relatively briefly, Sg in 1892-93. Just as Berlin was a gateway through which Scandinavian writers entered into contact with a larger European readership, so these writers made a significant contribution to the emergence of modernism in Germany]

[C1:424] Furuland, Lars, 'Från Strindberg till arbetarförfattarna', *Förr och nu* (Stockholm), 1977:2, pp. 4-20. Illus. ['From Strindberg to the Working-Class Writers'. Indicates how Sg's socially concerned works of the 1880s, with their insight into class conflict, made a considerable impact on the generation of Swedish proletarian writers that emerged early in the next century. Also discusses the Sg Feud of the 1900s and the dissemination of his ideas and books by politicians and publicists such as Hjalmar Branting and Axel Danielsson, and the libraries maintained by the Swedish Social Democrats. Furuland concludes that it is easy to overlook how revolutionary Sg's impact was at the time]

[C1:425] Furuland, Lars, *Statarna i litteraturen. En studie i svensk dikt och samhällsdebatt*, Stockholm: Tidens Förlag, 1962, pp. 207-210, 250-260. Illus. [Considers Sg's reflections on French rural life in *Bland franska bönder* and the ensuing dispute over the agrarian question with his friend Hjalmar Branting, the leading Swedish Marxist of the period. Furuland also discusses Sg's Rousseau-inspired attitude to the portrait of the peasantry in *Likt och olikt, Röda rummet, Fröken Julie, Fritänkaren, Giftas, Götiska rummen,* the pamphlet 'Folkstaten', and *Tjänstekvinnans son*, the last of which was of particular importance for the later generation of self-educated writers who emerged from the Swedish rural poor, including Ivar Lo-Johansson (1901-1990) and Jan Fridegård (1897-1968), both of whom made common cause with Sg's radicalism and his merciless critique of society in terms of an 'over' and 'under' class. Nevertheless, although Sg had some first-hand experience of the peasantry from the periods he spent in the Stockholm archipelago and on the estate at Hammersta where he worked briefly as a tutor during his youth, in his writing it is always romanticised]

[C1:426] Furuland, Lars, 'Strindberg, Ivar Lo och statarna', in Margareta Brundin, *et al.*, red., **B1:88**, *20 x Strindberg*, pp. 117-122. ['Strindberg, Ivar Lo, and the Tied Labourers'. Argues that Sg's depiction of class difference in *Tjänstekvinnans son* became a central paradigm in Swedish literature and was of particular importance for the next generation of self-educated working-class authors, including Ivar Lo-Johansson (1901-1990). Sg had personal links with the estate of Hammersta where Lo-Johansson's father was a tied-worker, or *statare*, and this is the subject of one of the finest of Lo-Johansson's short stories, 'Informatorn på Hammersta' (The Tutor at Hammersta). Furuland also comments on the agrarian socialism that Sg promoted in the mid 1880s and summarises his depiction of the rural poor in *Fröken Julie, Fritänkaren,* and *Giftas,* as well as his reflections on how to improve the life of the peasantry in *Bland franska bönder, Tjänstekvinnans son*, the late pamphlet 'Folkstaten', and a posthumously published essay in *Budkaflen*, in 1912]

[C1:427] Furuland, Lars, 'Strindberg på Hammersta', *Perspektiv* (Stockholm), 1962:2, 93ff. ['Strindberg at Hammersta'. A study of Ivar Lo-Johansson's fictional account of the period that Sg spent as a tutor on the estate of Hammersta in Södermanland, in the short story 'Informatorn på Hammersta' (The Tutor at Hammersta') in the collection *Jordproletärerna* (Proletarians of the Soil, 1941)]

[C1:428] Gamper, Herbert, 'Horváths Auseinandersetzung mit Strindberg. Sein erstes Stück *Mord in der Mohrengasse*', in Traugott Krischke, Hrsg., *Horváths Stücke*, Surhkamp Taschenbuch 2092, Frankfurt am Main: Surhrkamp, 1988, pp. 65-54. ['Horvath's Debate with Strindberg. His First Play, *Mord in der Mohrengasse*'. Gamper claims that Sg's post-Inferno plays are central to the 'Episierung' of modern drama, and their specific influence on Horváth is examined here with reference mainly to the latter's first play and *Advent*, but also to *Ett drömspel* and *Till Damaskus*]

[C1:429] Gantjeva, Vera, 'Za Avgust Strindberg', in *Sinjo + Zhalto = Zeleno. Obshto-evropeiski koordinati v razvitieto na shvedskata literatura*, Sofia: University Press St Kliment Ohridski, 1992, pp. 194-213. ['About August Strindberg' in '*Blue + Yellow = Green. General European Co-ordinates in the Development of Swedish Literature*']

[C1:430] Garborg, Arne, 'Etterskrift', in *Artiklar og essay II*, Oslo: H. Aschehoug & Co. (W. Nygaard), 1980, p. 146. [Rpr. of **C1:431**]

[C1:431] Garborg, Arne, 'Etterskrift', in *Straumdrag. Literære Utgreidningar fraa Aatti- og Nittiaari*, Kristiania: H. Aschehoug & Co., 1920, p. 75. ['Afterword'. Defines Sg as 'the 19th century in person…He was the Faust of our time']

[C1:432] Garborg, Arne, 'Das Liebesproblem bei Strindberg', *Blätter des Deutschen Theaters* (Berlin), 3 (1913-14), 750-752. ['The Problem of Love in Strindberg']

[C1:433] Garborg, Arne, 'Strindberg-Indtryck', in Gustaf Fröding, red., **B1:142**, *En bok om Strindberg* pp. 115-133. ['Impressions of Strindberg'. Presents Sg as an independent 'anti-mystic' whose work explores different intellectual standpoints. Garborg discusses *I havsbandet* at some length, considers 'Tschandala' to be 'perhaps his most admirable book', and comments on the penetrating psychology of *Fadren, Fordringsägare*, and *Kamraterna*, his Schopenhauerian view of women, and his newly assumed aristocratic radicalism]

[C1:434] Garborg, Arne, 'Strindberg-Indtryck', *Vinduet* (Oslo), 3 (1949), 67-77. Illus. [Rpr. of **C1:433**]

[C1:435] Gardner, Charles, *Vision and Vesture: A Study of William Blake in Modern Thought*, London: J. M. Dent & Sons Limited, 1916, pp. vii-viii and 118-121. [Links Sg with both Swedenborg and Kierkegaard]

[C1:436] Gedin, David, *Fältets herrar. Framväxten av en modern författarroll. Artonhundra-åttitalet*, Stockholm•Stehag: Brutus Östlings Bokförlag Symposion, 2004. [525] pp. ['Masters of the Field. The Growth of a Modern Authorial Role. The 1880s'. Applies Pierre Bourdieu's theory of the autonomous literary field in (mainly) *Le Règles de l'art* (1992)) to Swedish literature during the 1880s when the radical critique of bourgeois life undertaken by the generation of writers of whom Sg was the most prominent, coincided with the development in Sweden of the identity and role of a recognisably modern writer. Gedin describes how, having briefly courted established society in an attempt to launch himself as a writer on traditional lines, Sg forged his identity as an 'uncontrolled' figure, someone repeatedly in conflict with a social order that he both attacked and disturbed by his continually shifting standpoint. In so doing, he may have lost his intellectual credibility, but gained a far greater freedom to write as he desired, and for a much larger audience than would otherwise have been possible. At the same time, his writing undermined the values of conventional decency by breaking the wall which bourgeois society had erected between the private and the public spheres, not least by writing openly what were regarded as facts about his private life. Gedin's study quotes freely from Sg throughout and discusses his literary relationships with e.g. Verner von Heidenstam, Gustaf af Geijerstam, and Carl David af Wirsén. Among other works, he refers to *Mäster Olof*, *Röda rummet*, *Det nya rikt*, *Gamla Stockholm*, *Svenska folket*, *Giftas*, *Dikter på vers och prosa*, *Sömngångarnätter*, and the essays of *Likt och olikt*. He also assesses press reactions to Sg's trial for blasphemy and places him within the context of the wider Scandinavian debate concerning marriage and sexual morality. But as well as contemporary reviews, Gedin considers Sg's reception by later literary historians. English summary, pp. 385-396. Doctoral dissertation]

[C1:437] — Pedersen, Arne Toftegaard, *Tidskrift för litteraturvetenskap* (Stockholm), 33:1 (2004), 149-152.

[C1:438] Geissler, Rolf, Hrsg., *Zur Interpretation des modernen Dramas: Brecht, Dürrenmatt, Frisch*, Unter mitarb. von Therese Poser und Wilhelm Ziskoven, 6. durchges. Auflage, Frankfurt am Main: Verlag Moritz Diesterweg, 1970. 140 pp.

[C1:439] Gelb, Arthur and Barbara, *O'Neill*, London: Jonathan Cape, 1962. Illus. 970 pp. [Makes Sg a frequent point of reference in this standard account of Eugene O'Neill's life and works]

[C1:440] Gerould, Daniel, *Witkacy: Stanisław Ignacy Witkiewicz as an Imaginative Writer*, Seattle and London: University of Washington Press, 1981. 362 pp. [Acknowledges Witkiewicz's debt to Sg with reference to *Dödsdansen*, *Fadren*, and *Spöksonaten*, which had a decisive influence on the former's play *Matka* (The Mother, 1924). For Witkiewicz, Sg was 'the turning point in modern drama']

[C1:441] Gerould, Daniel, *Stanisław Ignacy Witkiewicz jako pisarz*, Translated by I. Sieradzki, Warszawa: Panstwowy Instytut Wydawniczy, 1981. 470 pp. [Polish edition of **C1:440**]

[C1:442] Ghelderode, Michel de, *Les Entretiens d'Ostende*, recueillis par Roger Iglésis et Alain Trutat, Paris: L'Arche, 1956. 206 pp. [A collection of interviews with Ghelderode in which he observes: 'I owe something to August Strindberg, which has never been observed of me before, and yet I experienced him like a lightning-bolt']

[C1:443] Ghelderode, Michel de, *Les Entretiens d'Ostende*, recueillis par Roger Iglésis et Alain Trutat, Toulouse: L'Éther vague/P. Thierry, 1992. 196 pp. [Rpr. of **C1:442**]

[C1:444] Gilleman, Luc, *John Osborne Vituperative Artist: A Reading of His Life and Work*, London: Routledge, 2002, pp. 170-172. [Considers Osborne's adaptation of *Fadren* for the National Theatre, London, which confirms that Sg was 'a playwright with whom he closely identified'. Gilleman displays even less understanding of Sg than Osborne did]

[C1:445] Gilman, Richard, 'Ibsen and Strindberg', in *The Confusion of Realms*, London: Weidenfeld and Nicolson, 1970, pp. 172-218. [A substantial discussion of Ibsen as the initiator of modern theatre and a briefer account of Sg as 'both a conscious and unconscious explicator of pathology's ways' in *Fadren* and *Fröken Julie*. In *Till Damaskus* he broke 'wholly through the bounds of drama as they had existed until then'. See Rpr. in **B1:368**]

[C1:446] Glienke, Bernhard, 'Kunstens København – Om Storbyperceptionens Æstetik i Det moderne Gennembrud og i *Pelle Erobreren*', *Nordica* (Odense), 11 (1994), 97-110. ['Art's Copenhagen – On the Aesthetic of the Great City in the Modern Breakthrough and in *Pelle the Conqueror*'. Discusses the representation of the modern city and of urban life in the literature of the Scandinavian Modern Breakthrough, with reference primarily to Herman Bang's *Stuk* (1887), Knut Hamsun's *Sult* (1890), Martin Andersen-Nexø's *Pelle Erobreren* (1906-10), and (very briefly) *Röda rummet* (1879)]

[C1:447] Glienke, Bernhard, 'Metropolis und nordische Moderne: zur frühen Großstadtdarstellung in der Skandinavischen Litteraturen', in *Metropolis und nordische Moderne: Großstadtthematik als Herausforderung literarischer Innovationen in Skandinavien seit 1830*, Beiarbeitet von Annika Krummacher, Klaus Müller-Wille, Frithjof Strauß, und Antje Wischmann, Beiträge zur Skandinavistik 15, Frankfurt am Main: Peter Lang, 1999, pp. 11-26. ['Metropolis and Nordic Modernity: On Early Representations of the Great City in Scandinavian Literature'. Includes *Röda rummet* in a discussion of several early Scandinavian urban novels]

[C1:448] Gloßmann, Erik, 'Die Apollobrüder am Musenhof. Ein Versuch über Künstler und Überlebenskunstler' – Ola Hansson, August Strindberg und der "Friedrichshagener Dichterkreis", 1892/93', in Walter Baumgartner and Thomas Fechner-Smarsly, Hrsg., **B1:19**, *August Strindberg: Der Dichter und die Medien*, pp. 23-44. [Documents the links between Hansson and Sg and the early modernist circle of writers and artists associated with the Berlin suburb of Friedrichshagan in the early 1890s, including Max Halbe, Bruno Wille, and several other figures associated with the Berlin Freie Bühne. Gloßmann also discusses their contacts with the Berlin-based Polish author Stanisław Przybyszewski (1868-1927)]

[C1:449] Glicksberg, Charles I., *The Self in Modern Literature*, University Park, Pennsylvania: The Pennsylvania State University Press, 1963, pp. 27-35. [Observes that 'Sg's expressionist dramas highlight the dark obsessions of the unconscious, the irrationality of the inner self'. He is the forerunner of the theatre of the absurd and anticipates many modern developments in the literary delineation of the 'lost self'. Glicksberg focuses almost exclusively on the 'profoundly religious' *Till Damaskus*]

[C1:450] Glicksberg, Charles I., *Tragic Vision in Twentieth-Century Literature*, Carbondale: Southern Illinois University Press, 1963, pp. 85-96. [Comments in passing on Sg in a chapter entited 'Psychoanalysis and the Tragic Vision']

[C1:451] Godin, Stig-Lennart, *Klassmedvetandet i tidig svensk arbetarlitteratur*, Litteratur Teater Film, Nya Serien 11, Lund: Lund University Press, 1994. 261 pp. ['Class-Consciousness in Early Swedish Workers' Literature'. Comments on aspects of Sg's work which anticipate the class-conscious literature produced by Swedish working-class writers of the next generation]

[C1:452] Goldberg, Michael, 'Dickens and the Early Modern Theatre', in Carol Hanbery MacKay, ed., *Dramatic Dickens*, New York: St Martin's Press, 1989, pp. 168-183. [Recalls that, like Shaw and Ibsen, Sg readily acknowledged a debt to Dickens. This is apparent in the plays where Sg's dramatic technique has many affinities with Dickens's surrealism, as well as, more obviously, in both *Röda rummet* and *Det nya riket*]

[C1:453] Goldschmit, Rudolf K., 'Ibsen und Strindberg', *Rheinische Thalia* (Mannheim und Leipzig), 1:6 (1921), 104-107.

[C1:454] Golik, N., '[The Tragedy of Human Existence: Kierkegaard – Strindberg]', in L[ev] Gitel'man and V[alentina] Dianova, eds, **B1:148**, *Avgust Strindberg i mirovaia kul'tura. Materialy mezhvyzovskoi nauchnoi konferentsii. Stat'i. Soobshcheniia*, pp. 117-126]

[C1:455] Golovina, S. A, and N. F. Kornitskaia, *Gor'kovskie chteniia*, Moscow, 1962, pp. 120-122. [A volume documenting Gor'kii's reading. Comments on his opinion of Sg and his attendance at a performance of *Till Damaskus* in Helsinki]

[C1:456] Goodman, Randolph, 'Playwriting with a Third Eye: Fun and Games with Albee, Ibsen and Strindberg', *Columbia University Forum* (New York), 10:1 (1967), 18-22. [Maintains that Edward Albee's *Who's Afraid of Virginia Woolf?* was really modelled on *Hedda Gabler*, but that Ibsen's drama was itself inspired by Sg's life and work]

[C1:457] Goodman, Randolph, 'Hava Nesaheka – Ezel Albi, Ibsen ve-Strindberg', *Bama* (Jerusalem), No. 36 (1968), pp. 10-14. [Hebrew version of **C1:456**]

[C1:458] Gordin, A. M., and Vladimir Nikolaevich Orlov, *Aleksandr Blok v portretakh, illiustratsiiakh i dokumentakh*, Leningrad: Prosveshchenie, 1973. Illus. 381 pp. [On Blok's well-documented admiration for Sg, p. 381]

[C1:459] Gor'kii, M[aksim], 'Razrushenie lichnosti', in *Ocherki filosofii kollektivizma*, Vol. 1, St Petersburg, 1909, pp. 353-403. ['The Disintegration of Personality', in '*Essays on the Philosophy of Collectivism*'. Comments on Sg, p. 374. E.788]

[C1:460] Gor'kii, M[aksim], 'Avgust Strindberg', *Rossiia* (Moscow), 11 May 1912. [A telegram apropos Sg's impending death, maintaining that 'No one has ever made a greater impression on me as Sg. In all of European literature, August Sg is the one who has been closest to me, the writer who has stimulated my thoughts and feelings the strongest. Every one of his books has awakened a desire to dispute with him, to contradict him, and with every book my feelings of love and worship have grown deeper and stronger']

[C1:461] Gorki, Maksim, 'August Strindberg', *Dagens Nyheter* (Stockholm), 15 May 1912. [A translation of Gor'kii's response to a questionnaire in which he maintains that 'Sg was the man closest to me in European literature, the writer who has most troubled my heart and mind'. Mentions *I havsbandet* and 'The Viking' (possibly a reference to one of the early stories in *Hövdingaminnen*)]

[C1:462] Gor'kii, Maksim, 'Avgust Strindberg', *Russkoe Slovo* (Moscow), 11 May 1912, pp. [Russian version of **C1:461. E.842**]

[C1:463] Gorki, Maxim, 'August Strindberg', *Nya Samhället* (Stockholm), 22 May 1912. [Rpr. of **C1:461**]

[C1:464] Gorkii, Maxim, 'August Strindberg', *Ost und West* (East Berlin), 3:1 (1949), 24-25. [German translation of **C1:461**]

[C1:465] Gor'kii, M[aksim], 'Razrushenie lichnosti', in Gor'kii, M., *Sobranie sochinenii*, Vol. 24, Moscow, 1953, pp. 26-79. [Rpr. of **C1:459**. Comments on Sg, p. 49. E.788]

[C1:466] Gorky, M[aksim], 'The Disintegration of Personality', in *On Literature: Selected Articles*, Moscow: Foreign Languages Publishing House, nd., pp. 71-137. [English translation of **C1:459**. Comments on Sg, p.99]

[C1:467] Gor'kii, M[aksim], 'Avgust Strindberg', in *Izbrannye literaturno-kriticheskie stat'i*, Moscow: Gos. izd-vo Khudozh. lit-ra, 1941, pp. 272-273. [Rpr. of **C1:461.** E.842]

[C1:468] Gor'kii, M[aksim], 'Avgust Strindberg', in Gor'kii, M., *Materialy i issledovanniia*, Vol. 6, pod redaktsiei V. A. Desnitskogo, Moscow and Leningrad: Izd-vo Akademii nauk SSSR, 1934, p. 89-90. [Rpr. of **C1:461**. E.842]

[C1:469] Gor'kii, M[aksim], *Pis'ma. Telegrammy. Nadpisi*, in Gor'kii, M., *Polnoe sobranie sochinenii v 30 tomakh*, Vol. 28, Moscow: Goslitizdat, 1954. 599 pp. [Includes Gor'kii's comments on Sg and *Fröken Julie* in a letter to Chekhov, pp. 77-79. Of *Fröken Julie*, he remarks: 'He's bold, that Swede! I've never seen the thralls' aristocratic tendencies presented so clearly…I was struck by the idea of the play and the power of its author provoked jealousy and amazement in me, pity for myself and many sorrowful thoughts about our own literature'. E.962]

[C1:470] Gor'kii, M[aksim], *Pis'ma. Telegrammy. Nadpisi*, in Gor'kii, M., *Polnoe sobranie sochinenii v 30 tomakh*, Vol. 29, Moscow: Goslitizdat, 1955. 672 pp. [Includes Gor'kii's comments on Sg's death in a letter of May 1912 to Leonid Andreev, p. 242. E.963]

[C1:471] Grabowski, Simon, 'Unreality in Plays of Ibsen, Strindberg and Hamsun', *Mosaic* (Manitoba), 4:2 (1970), 63-76. [Considers the departure from realistic everyday experience in *The Lady from the Sea* and other plays by Ibsen, Hamsun (*Ved Rikets Port*), and *Ett drömspel* which, for Grabowski, represents a journey from cosmic reality to material earth-dream. The dreamer is 'a supra-personal, supra-objective eye with a claim to total awareness']

[C1:472] Grabowski, Simon, 'Unreality in Plays of Ibsen, Strindberg and Hamsun', in Janet Witalec, ed., **D2:348**, *Drama Criticism*, pp. 276-279. [Rpr. of **C1:471**]

[C1:473] Gravier, Maurice, 'Skandinaviske forfattere i eksil', *Edda* (Oslo), 57 (1957), 301-316. ['Scandinavian Writers in Exile'. Discusses the cases of the Swedish Signature poet Carl Snoilsky and Ibsen as well as Sg. The periods which the latter spent abroad during the 1880s are discussed, pp. 312-315]

[C1:474] Gravier, Maurice, 'Strindberg et H.-R. Lenormand', *Maske und Kothurn* (Vienna), 10:4 (1964), 603-610. [Discusses the impact of *Dödsdansen* and Sg's post-Inferno dramaturgy in *Till Damaskus* on the plays of Henri-René Lenormand (1882-1951), most notably *L'Homme et ses fantômes* (1924). Gravier suggests that an attentive reading of Sg's *Vivisektioner* and plays such as *Samum*, which depict the power of suggestion and the battle of the brains, would contribute to a better understanding of other plays, such as *L'Amour magicien* (1926)]

[C1:475] Gravier, Maurice, 'Strindberg and French Drama' / 'Strindberg et les Dramaturges français', *World Theatre-Le théâtre dans le monde* (Bruxelles), 11:1 (1962), 45-60. [Points out that Sg's abiding influence on 20th-Century French drama is apparent in the plays of Lenormand, Adamov, Pellerin, Sartre, and Cocteau. Text in both English and French]

[C1:476] Gravier, Maurice, 'Strindberg et Ionesco', in Carl Reinhold Smedmark, ed., **D2:285**, *Strindberg and Modern Theatre*, pp. 9-29. [Considers how Sg and Ionesco find ways of making their private experience relevant to their readers and spectators, and compares Sg's dramaturgy in *Till Damaskus* with Ionesco's *La Soif et la faim* (1966), concentrating on themes they have in common, even though one was written pre-Freud and the other after]

[C1:477] Gravier, Maurice, 'Strindberg et Kafka', *Etudes Germaniques* (Paris), 8:2-3 (1953), 118-140. [Compares Sg with Kafka and notes a number of affinities, not least that they both present themselves as strangers in an environment with which they have lost immediate contact, as is the case in Sg's *Inferno*. Gravier also documents Kafka's reading of Sg with reference to his diary and to Max Brod's biography, and compares *Till Damaskus* with the oneiric dimension of both *Der Prozeß* and *Das Schloss*. However, he notes that, instead of being drawn to Sg's dream method, it was the realist and satirist of *I havsbandet*, *Svarta fanor*, and *Inferno* who particularly fascinated Kafka]

[C1:478] Gravier, Maurice, 'Strindberg et Maeterlinck', *Revue d'histoire du théâtre* (Paris), 40:1 (1988), 71-100. [A comparative study of Sg's links with Maeterlinck in which Gravier documents Sg's familiarity with French naturalism as well as symbolism, his *fin-de-siècle* passion for Maeterlinck's plays, and the influence they exerted on his post-Inferno attempt to create a drama which placed the inner life, or soul, upon the stage. He comments on *Påsk*, *Advent*, and *Ett drömspel*, and discusses *Svanevit* and the Chamber Plays of 1907 in some detail, comparing *Spöksonaten* and the theme of 'unmasking' with Maeterlinck's *Intérieur*, and acknowledging the impact on Sg of the essays in *Le Trésor des Humbles*]

[C1:479] Gravier, Maurice, 'Strindberg et Wedekind', *Etudes Germaniques* (Paris), 3:2-3 (1948), 309-318. [Compares Sg's post-Inferno dramaturgy in e.g. *Till Damaskus* with Wedekind's Lulu plays and *König Nicolo*. Gravier also relates Wedekind's *Frühlings Erwachen* (1891) to the debate about marriage and sexual freedom which Ibsen had initiated in *A Doll's House*, and to which Sg had also contributed with the story 'Dygdens lön' (The Reward of Virtue) in *Giftas I*. Part of Gravier's study of Sg and German expressionism, **D2:128**]

[C1:480] Gravier, Maurice, 'Le Tragique dans les drames modernes d'Ibsen et de Strindberg', in Gérard Antoine and Jean Jacquot, eds, *Le théâtre tragique*, Collection "Les choeur des muses", Paris: Editions du centre national de la recherche scientifique, 1962, pp. 383-391. ['Tragedy in the Modern Dramas of Ibsen and Strindberg']

[C1:481] Gregor, Hans, 'Ekdal oder Edgar? "*Holzfällen*" im Spannungsfeld zwischen Ibsen und Strindberg', in *Thomas Bernhard: Traditionen und Trabanten*, Hrsg. von Joachim Hoel, Würzburg: Könighausen und Neumann, 1999, pp. 143-150. ['Ekdal or Edgar? "Tree-Felling" in the Combat Zone between Ibsen and Strindberg.' Explores distinctions between Ibsen and Sg, focusing on *The Wild Duck* (Hjalmar Ekdal) and *Dödsdansen* (Edgar)]

[C1:482] Gretlund, Jan Nordby, Elisabeth Herion-Sarafidis, and Hans H. Skei, 'Poe in Scandinavia', in Lois Davis Vines, ed., *Poe Abroad: Influence, Reputation, Affinities*, Iowa City: University of Iowa Press, 1999, pp. 3-37. [Acknowledges Sg's role in establishing Edgar Allan Poe's reputation in Sweden]

[C1:483] Grigor'ev, A. L., '[Gor'kii on the Literature of the West]', *Uchenye zapiski. Leningradskii gosudarstvennyi pegagogicheskii institut im. A. Gertsena*, Vol. 15, Leningrad, 1938, pp. 5-46. [Discusses Gor'kii's largely positive opinion of Sg, pp. 31-32. E.945]

[C1:484] Griolet, Patrick, 'Fenomenul capitalei literare. August Strindberg et Paris ou Le troisième cercle', *Revista de istorie si teorie literara* (Bucharest), 33:2 (1985), 99-103. [See **C1:485**]

[C1:485] Griolet, Patrick, 'August Strindberg et Paris ou Le troisième cercle', in *Paris et le phénomène des capitales littéraires: carrefour ou dialogue des cultures 2*. Actes du premier congrès international du Centre de recherche en littérature comparée, 22-26 mai 1984, Paris: Presses de l'universitaire de Paris-Sorbonne, 1986, pp. 771-780. ['August Strindberg and Paris, Or the Third Circle'. Discusses the sometimes infernal role which Paris played as a setting in both Sg's life and work]

[C1:486] Gruszczyńska, Ewa, 'Czy Strindberg czytal Sienkiewicza?', in Elżbieta Szwejkowska-Olsson and Michal Bron Jr., *En festskrift tillägnad Andrzej Nils Uggla*, Uppsala Multiethnic Papers 43, Uppsala: Centurm för multiethnisk forskning, 2000, pp. 177-186. ['Did Strindberg Read Sienkiewicz?'. Although they represent quite distinct literary tendencies and have very different aims as writers, Gruszczyńska notes that Sg and Sienkiewicz nevertheless have several features in common. Most notably, Sg's fairy tale 'Sjusovaren' (The Lie-Abed) in *Sagor* resembles Sienkiewicz's 'Lux in tenebris lucet' (1891), first published in Sweden in 1895, and widely disseminated there through publication in the daily press as well as in book form]

[C1:487] Günther, Irmgard, *Die Einwirkung des skandinavischen Romans auf den deutschen Naturalismus*, Nordische Studien 14, Greifswald, 1934. 158 pp. ['The Influence of the Scandinavian Novel on German Naturalism'. Discusses Sg in conjunction with Frank Wedekind (1864-1918)]

[C1:488] Gustafson, Alrik, *Six Scandinavian Novelists*, Minneapolis: University of Minnesota Press for The American-Scandinavian Foundation, 1940, pp. 123-129. [Considers Sg's personal and literary relations with Verner von Heidenstam during the period ca.1886-1892 and the implications for their literary work, pp. 123-129. Includes 24 other references to Sg]

[C1:489] Gustafsson, Lars, 'Strindberg – P. O. Enquist', *Forum* (Warsaw), 1986:13, p. 21.

[C1:490] Gyllensten, Lars, 'Opening Address', in Claes Englund and Gunnel Bergström, eds, **D2:99**, *Strindberg, O'Neill and the Modern Theatre*, pp. 8-14. [Comments on Dramaten's association with both dramatists and stresses Sg's 'scurrilous aspects', his lack of humour, and the amount of 'sheer drivel' in his writing, which is often inspired by the 'fertile mud of second- or third-rate occultist thinkers, shady psychologists, and now rightly forgotten sociologists and scientific fantasts, visionaries and charlatans… [as well as by] Swedenborg and Nietzsche, misinterpreted and coarsely comprehended'. What largely redeems him in Gyllensten's eyes is his language, but even so, Sg should be kept at a distance, and only taken in small doses]

[C1:491] Gyllensten, Lars, 'Strindberg – geni och charlatan', in *Så var det sagt*, Stockholm: Albert Bonniers Förlag, 1992, pp. 39-45. ['Strindberg – Genius and Charlatan'. Displays the antipathy which the Swedish novelist and academician ordinarily feels for Sg. The latter survives only because of the vitality of his language and his protean nature]

[C1:492] Gyllensten, Lars, 'Vadå Strindberg?', in [Heidi von Born], red., **U1:148**, *Balkongtal under Strindbergsfestivalen 1995*, pp. 9-12. ['What's with Strindberg!?' Text as in **C1:491**]

[C1:493] Gyllensten, Lars, 'Vadå Strindberg!?', in [Heidi von Born], red., **U1:149**, *Med himlen till tak...och Drottninggatan som golv. Femton balkongtal till Strindberg*, pp. 13-17. ['What's with Strindberg!?' Reflections on Sg by the novelist and Secretary of the Swedish Academy (b.1921) who makes no apology for his dislike of Sg but seeks to ascertain why the latter should continue to exert so powerful an attraction even today, when so many of his ideas have become quaint and redundant]

[C1:494] Haag, Ansgar, and Ursula Kreissig, Hrsg., *August Strindberg – Arthur Schnitzler, Ehe statt Liebe?!: ein Begleitheft zur Aufführung von August Strindberg's Schauspiel "Mit dem Feuer spielen" und Arthur Schnitzler's Einakter "Die Stunde des Erkennens*, Bonn: Theater der Stadt Bonn, [1980]. Illus. 80 pp. [Compares *Leka med elden* with Schnitzler's one-acter *Ehe statt Liebe?!* about marriage and love, prompted by their coupling in a double-bill]

[C1:495] Haaland, Arild, 'Nietzsche i Norden. Streiftog omkring en tenkers innflytelse', *Edda* (Oslo), 66:3 (1966), 204-216. ['Nietzsche in Scandinavia. A Rapid Survey of a Thinker's Influence'. Surveys Nietzsche's impact in Scandinavia, with mention of his relevance for Sg]

[C1:496] Hagberg, Knut, 'Linné och Strindberg', *Svenska Dagbladet* (Stockholm), 31 March 1945. ['Linnaeus and Strindberg'. Accounts for Sg's interest in Carl von Linnaeus both as a natural historian and for their similar notions regarding the everyday workings of Nemesis. Prompts a response by Frank Heller (M. G. Serner), 4 April 1945]

[C1:497] Hägg, Göran, '*Övertalning och underhållning. Den svenska essäistiken 1890-1930*, Stockholm: Wahlström & Widstrand, 1978, 320 pp. [A doctoral thesis on the essay as a genre in Sweden during the period 1890-1930, with occasional comments on Sg who features as the subject of essays by many of the authors studied, including Oscar Levertin, Erik Hedén, Fredrik Böök, and Bengt Lidforss. English summary, pp. 307-314]

[C1:498] Halfmann, Ulrich, *"Unreal Realism". O'Neills dramatisches Werk in Spiegel seiner szenischen Kunst*, Bern, München: Francke Verlag, [1969]. 191 pp. [Draws several comparisons between the form of Eugene O'Neill's dramaturgy and Sg's]

[C1:499] Hallengren, Anders, 'Kärleken, hatet och spegelvärlden: Swedenborg, Strindberg, Linné', in *Tingens tydning: Swedenborg studier*, Stockholm: Åsak, 1997, pp. 32-45. ['Love, Hate, and the Mirrored World. Swedenborg, Strindberg, and Linnaeus']

[C1:500] Hallengren, Anders, 'Magna Tartarias Hemlighet', *Värdarnas möte*, 3 (1992), 104-122. ['Magna Tartaria's Secret'. Preliminary Swedish version of Chapter 2, 'The Secret of Magna Tartaria', in **C1:502**]

[C1:501] Hallengren, Anders, 'The Secret of Great Tartary', *Arcana* (Bryn Athyn, Philadelphia), 1:1 (1995), 35-54. [An earlier version of Chapter 2, 'The Secret of Magna Tartaria', in **C1:502**]

[C1:502] Hallengren, Anders, *Gallery of Mirrors: Reflections of Swedenborgian Thought*, Foreword by Inge Jonsson, Swedenborg Studies 7, West Chester, Pennsylvania: Swedenborg Foundation Publishers, 1999, pp. 17-20, 24-27. [Studies the widespread impact of Swedenborgian thought and the influence of his writings on Schoenberg, Whitman, and Emerson as well as Sg. Hallengren stresses the significant role that Swedenborg played in Sg's Inferno crisis and the latter's speculations on Greater Tartary in *Kulturhistoriska Studier* (1881), when he edited and published material dealing with the Carolinian prisoners from Charles XII's war with Russia, one of whom was Swedenborg's cousin, Peter Schönström. He also comments on Sg's polemics about Tartary and the geography of Russia with the eminent Swedish explorer, Sven Hedin, during the Strindberg Feud]

[C1:503] Hamsun, Knut, 'August Strindberg', *America* (Chicago), 20 December 1888. [One of the first North-American comments on Sg, which proclaims that 'The mere fact that this man has lived, is a literary phenomenon and a historical event. He has but one predecessor – Rousseau; he has no party, he stands alone', thus drawing attention to the conflict between nature and culture in Sg's early work. Hamsun discusses *Sömngångarnätter* and, writing in English, remarks of Sg: 'He is an ingenious mind who receives suggestions, suspicions on the first hand. He is an observer, of the finest any age has ever produced. The manner in which he knows is just the manner in which he feels; he is the man of strong convictions – his heart is warmer than his head is cold. Sg is a complex nature, coarse and tough as a butcher, delicate and tender as a child, as a woman – a heart and brain being']

[C1:504] Hamsun, Knut, 'August Strindberg', 1-2, *Dagbladet* (Oslo), 10 and 11 December 1889. [A sympathetic early appreciation of Sg's work which stresses his debt to Eduard von Hartmann's *Philosophie des Unbewußten* (1869), the psychological acuity of *Fordringsägare*, the conception of character outlined in the Preface to *Fröken Julie*, and his views on women in the essay 'Kvinnosaken enligt evolutionsteorien' (Feminism According to Evolutionary Theory)]

[C1:505] Hamsun, Knut, *Etwas über Strindberg. Essays*, Deutsch von Jutta and Theodor Knust, Langen-Müllers kleine Geschenkbücher 80, München: Langen-Georg Müller, 1958. [63] pp. [Contains 'Etwas über Strindberg' (1894), pp. 7-50; 'Gläubiger', pp. 50-59; 'Aufruf' (Hamsun's appeal with others in Paris for financial assistance for Sg, 1895), pp. 59-60; and 'Hamsuns Gruß zu Strindbergs letzten Geburtstag am 22. 1. 1912', pp. 60-63]

[C1:506] — Eyssen, Jürgen, *Bücherei und Bildung* (Bremen), 11 (1959), Teil B, p. 225.

[C1:507] Hamsun, Knut, 'Hamsun om Strindberg', *Politiken* (Copenhagen), 9 June 2001. [Reprinted from 'Lidt om August Strindberg', **C1:509**]

[C1:508] Hamsun, Knut, *Knut Hamsuns brev Brev 1879-1895*, Utgitt av Harald S. Næss, Oslo: Gyldendal Norsk Forlag, 1994. [511] pp. [Volume One of Hamsun's collected letters covering the period when he knew, and wrote frequently about, Sg. Thus '*Miss Julie* is a remarkable work – a hundred times better and more ingenious than Ibsen's *The Lady from the Sea*....He is so fantastically productive that he turns even Balzac into a dwarf']

[C1:509] Hamsun, Knut, 'Lidt om Strindberg', in *Artiklar*, i utvalg ved Francis Bull, Oslo: Gyldendal Norsk Forlag, 1939, pp. 14-45. ['Briefly about Strindberg'. Rpr. of Hamsun's essay in Gustaf Fröding, red., **B1:142**. See **C1:512**]

[C1:510] Hamsun, Knut, 'Lidt om Strindberg', in *Artiklar 1889-1928*, i utvalg ved Francis Bull, Oslo: Gyldendal Norsk Forlag, 1965, pp. 14-32. ['Briefly About Strindberg'. New edition of **C1:509**]

[C1:511] Hamsun, Knut, 'Lidt om Strindberg', in Helge Nordahl, red., *Utvalgte Essayister*, Oslo: Grøndahl Dreyer, 1997, pp. 125-[143]. [Rpr. of **C1:509**]

[C1:512] Hamsun, Knut, 'Et Overblik. Skrevet for mange Aar siden', in Gustaf Fröding, red., **B1:142**, *En bok om Strindberg*, pp. 7-33. ['An Overview. Written many Years Ago'. Hamsun's contribution to this pioneering collection of essays on Sg which makes use of earlier, largely appreciative material]

[C1:513] [Hamsun, Knut], 'Referat av foredrag om Strindberg i Gjøvik', *Samhold* (Gjøvik), 11 May 1886. ['Report of a Lecture on Strindberg in Gjøvik'. Summarises Hamsun's lecture on Sg, delivered at Gjøvik in Northern Norway. Also reported in the Oslo newspaper *Dagbladet*, 13-14 May 1886]

[C1:514] Hamsun, Knut, 'Die Strindberg-Frauen', *Blätter des Deutschen Theaters* (Berlin), 3 (1913-14), 700-702. ['Strindberg's Women'. Discusses Sg's female characters and his view of women in the naturalist dramas of the 1880s]

[C1:515] Hamsun, Knut, 'Till August Strindberg på Fødselsdagen', *Afton-Tidningen* (Stockholm), 22 January 1912. ['To August Strindberg on His Birthday'. Commemorates Sg's 63rd birthday]

[C1:516] Hamsun, Knut, 'Ved Strindbergs død', *Dagbladet* (Oslo), 20 May 1912. ['On Strindberg's Death'. Hamsun's obituary for Sg]

[C1:517] Hamsun, Knut, 'Ved Strindbergs død', *Nationaltidende* (Copenhagen), 19 May 1912. [Danish version of Hamsun's obituary for Sg, **C1:516**]

[C1:518] Hamsun, Thore, 'Strindberg – Hamsun – og Spångberg', *Aftenposten* (Oslo), 13 November 1962. [On Hamsun's contribution to Valfrid Spångberg's newspaper *Afton-Tidningen* in 1909, in respect of Sg's 60th birthday]

[C1:519] Hanson, Thelma, *Karl Kraus och Strindberg*. Acta Regiae Societatis Scientiarum et Litterarum Gothoburgensis. Humaniora 36, Göteborg: Kungl. Vetenskaps- och Vitterhets-Samhället, 1996. Illus. 86 pp. [Documents Kraus's interest in Sg, including his public readings of Sg's works, as well as the place accorded him in Kraus's journal *Die Fackel*, their common ground with the German philosopher Otto Weininger (1880-1903), and a controversy with Emil Schering over a German Strindberg Prize. German summary, pp. 76-82]

[C1:520] Hansson, Ola, 'Arnold Böcklin', in *Samlade Skrifter*, 17 vols, Stockholm: Tidens Förlag, 1921, Vol. 10, 'Tolkare och siare', pp. 321-336. [Hansson's Collected Works with the first publication of **C1:522** in Swedish]

[C1:521] Hansson, Ola, 'Arnold Böcklin', in *Seher und Deuter*, Berlin: Rosenbaum und Hart, 1894. VIII+168 pp. [German edition of **C1:522**]

[C1:522] Hansson, Ola, 'Arnold Böcklin', in *Tolke og Seere. Kritiske Essays*, Kristiania: H. Aschehoug & Co.s Forlag, 1893, pp. 202-218. [Introduces Sg into a discussion of Böcklin's painting. Sg's mind is an orgy of ideas, a restless masquerade of thoughts, a battlefield of ideas. His life is one of conflict and contradiction, and his unpredictable changes are indicative of a fundamental disorientation and chaos]

[C1:523] Hansson, Ola, 'Ibsen, Strindberg och Tyskland', in *Efterlämnade skrifter*, 5 vols, Utgivna av Hjalmar Gullberg, under medverkan av Axel Herrlin och Albert Nilsson, Vol. 4, Hälsingborg, 1931, pp. 65-69. [Swedish version of **C1:524**]

[C1:524] Hansson, Ola, 'Ibsen, Strindberg und Deutschland', *Das Magazin für die Literatur des In- und Auslandes* (Leipzig), 59 (4 October 1890), No. 40, p. 628. ['Ibsen, Strindberg, and Germany'. Written in conjunction with the German première of *Fadren* at the Freie Bühne in Berlin. Distinguishes between the modern Scandinavian woman depicted in the plays of Ibsen and Sg and her more homely German counterparts. However, according to Hansson, Ibsen and Sg are not to be confused with one another: 'With Sg everything is intuition and image; with Ibsen everything is reflection and thought. Ibsen is nothing but simplified correlations, Sg is nothing but fertile chaos. Ibsen's writing is more "structure" whereas Sg's is more "life"']

[C1:525] Hansson, Ola, 'Ibsen, Strindberg und Deutschland', in Hans-Peter Bayerdörfer, Hrsg., **B3:85**, *Strindberg auf der deutschen Bühne*, pp. 87-89. [Rpr. of **C1:524**]

[C1:526] Hansson, Ola, 'Die Literaturentwicklung in Skandinavien', *Der Kunstwart* (München), 4:2 (1891), 177-179. ['Literary Developments in Scandinavia']

[C1:527] Hansson, Ola, 'Les livres des plus sains de l'époque', *Revue des Revues* (Paris), May 1893, pp. 363-367. ['The Soundest Books of the Age'. Among contemporary Nordic writers, Hansson praises Sg and the Finnish authors Juhani Aho and Karl August Tavaststjerna at the expense of Bjørnstjerne Bjørnson and Ibsen]

[C1:528] Hansson, Ola, 'Nietzscheanismus in Skandinavien', *Neue Freie Presse* (Vienna), 18 October 1889. ['Nietzscheanism in Scandinavia'. Proclaims Sg the first proselyte of Nietzsche's ideas in Scandinavia, after being introduced to them by Georg Brandes]

[C1:529] Harding, Gunnar, 'Strindberg, Munch, and Przybyszewski', *Artes. An International Reader of Literature, Art and Music* (Stockholm), 4 (1997), pp. 31-32. [Presents the colourful artistic and personal association between the three men in Berlin during the early 1890s. Yearbook of the Swedish journal *Artes* with contributions in English]

[C1:530] Harrie, Ivar, 'John Osborne i Strindbergs helvete', *Expressen* (Stockholm), 28 May 1965. ['John Osborne in Strindberg's Hell']

[C1:531] Hartman, Murray, '*Desire under the Elms* in the Light of Strindberg's Influence', *American Literature* (Durham, North Carolina), 33:3 (1961-62), 360-369. [Identifies the influence of Sg on Eugene O'Neill's play]

[C1:532] Hartman, Murray, 'Strindberg and O'Neill', *Educational Theatre Journal* (Columbia, Montana), 18:3 (1966), 216-231. [Identifies several common patterns in the lives of Sg and Eugene O'Neill. These include an Oedipal obsession, misogyny, and rebellion against middle-class complacency. Hartman notes that both playwrights also experimented constantly with dramatic technique]

[C1:533] Hauptmann, Gerhart, 'Über Strindberg', *Die Lese* (Stuttgart), 3 (1912), p. 5. ['On Strindberg'. Proclaims Sg to be one of the remarkable personalities of the epoch, someone to whom many in Germany are indebted]

[C1:534] Hauptmann, Gerhart, 'Strindberg', in *Das gesammelte Werk*, Bd 17, Berlin, 1942, pp. 308-309. [Rpr. of **C1:533**]

[C1:535] Hauptmann, Gerhart, 'Strindberg', in *Das gesammelte Werk*, Hrsg. Hans-Egon Hass, Bd 6, Frankfurt am Main und Berlin: Propyläen Verlag, 1963, pp. 916-917. [Rpr. of **C1:533**]

[C1:536] Hayward, Ira N., 'Strindberg's Influence on Eugene O'Neill', *Poet Lore* (Philadelphia), 39 (1928), 596-604. [Compares the two dramatists in terms of language, characterisation, and dramatic technique]

[C1:537] Hedberg, Oscar, 'To nordiske Nietzsche-lærlinge', *Extrabladet* (Copenhagen), 30 August 1947. ['Two Nordic Apprentices of Nietzsche'. Identifies Sg and Ola Hansson as among the foremost of Nietzsche's disciples in Scandinavia]

[C1:538] Hedén, Erik, 'Wagners *Siegfried* och Strindbergs *Lycko-Per*', *Social-Demokraten* (Stockholm), 8 November 1912. [Compares the heroes, themes, and structure of Sg's play with the third opera in Wagner's Ring cycle. Prompts a response by Rune Zetterlund, 12 November, and a reply from Hedén, 15 November]

[C1:539] Heggestad, Eva, *Fången och fri. 1880-talets svenska kvinnliga författare om hemmet, yrkeslivet och konstnärskapet*, Skrifter utgivna av Avdelningen för littertursociologi vid Litteraturvetenskapliga institutionen i Uppsala 27, Uppsala, 1991. 264 pp. [Sg is an occasional and briefly noted point of comparison in the course of a discussion of the circumstances of his contemporary Swedish women writers in relation to their literary representations of the home, the world of work, and artistic life]

[C1:540] Hegner, J[acob], 'Strindberg contra Ibsen', *Das Magazin für die Literatur des In- und Auslandes* (Leipzig), 72:2 (1903), 117-120. ['Strindberg versus Ibsen'. Maintains that 'Ibsen is the prototype of the sort of person who was alive about two decades ago, and who has not merely an historical existence. But there you have Sg the "artist". He puts Ibsen the "social critic" in the shade. And I wish to tell you in confidence that Sg is the man of the day after tomorrow']

[C1:541] Hegner, J[acob], 'Strindberg contra Ibsen', in Hans-Peter Bayerdörfer, Hrsg., **B3:85**, *Strindberg auf der deutschen Bühne*, pp. 156-161. [Rpr. of **C1:540**]

[C1:542] Heilborn, Ernst, 'Nietzsche und Strindberg', *Das zwanzigste Jahrhundert* (Berlin), 5 (1894-95), p. 468. [An early note linking Sg with Nietzsche]

[C1:543] Helander, Olle, '"För stolt att se en annan sona". Om försoningsmotivet i svensk skönlitteratur med särskild hänsyn till Strindberg', *Svensk Teologisk Kvartalskrift* (Lund), 60 (1984), 27-33. ['"Too Proud to See another Atone". On the Atonement Motif in Swedish Literature with Particular Reference to Strindberg']

[C1:544] Helander, Olle, 'Strindberg och Lagerkvist', *Kristendomslärarnes föreningens årsbok*, 11 (1967), pp. 94-97. [Discusses the work of Sg and Pär Lagerkvist from a Christian perspective]

[C1:545] Helander, Olle, 'Strindberg och Lagerkvist', *Sydsvenska Dagbladet* (Malmö), 30 November 1961. [See **C1:544**]

[C1:546] Helén, Gunnar, *Birger Sjöbergs Kriser och kransar i stilhistorisk belysning*, Nordiska texter och undersökningar 16, Stockholm: Gebers, 1946. 329 pp. [Demonstrates that Sg influenced the development of Sjöberg's style in his innovatory collection of poems, *Kriser och kransar* (1926)]

[C1:547] Heller, Otto, 'Strindberg and Ibsen', *American Review of Reviews* (New York), 46 (1912), p. 251. [Compares Sg and Ibsen as dramatists]

[C1:548] Helmecke, Carl Albert, *Buckle's Influence on Strindberg*, Philadelphia: Pennsylvania University Press, 1924. 52 pp. [A pioneering academic thesis concerning the influence which the philosophy of history embodied in Henry Thomas Buckle's *History of Civilisation in England* (1857-61) exerted on Sg's early historical relativism in *Mäster Olof* (he read Buckle in the Swedish translation of 1871). Helmecke also indicates how Buckle acted as a spur to Sg's political radicalism during the 1870s and 1880s]

[C1:549] Helsztynski, Stanisław, 'Stan[isław] Przybyszewski and Scandinavia', *Baltic and Scandinavian Countries* (Gdynia), 3:1 (1937), 121-125. [Documents Przybyszewski's links with Sweden through Sg and Ola Hansson, with Norway through Edvard Munch, Dagny Juel, and Gunnar Heiberg, and with Denmark through Holger Drachmann]

[C1:550] Hennig, Gerda, *Traumwelten im Spiegel der Dichtung: Jean Paul, Dostojewski, Nerval, Strindberg*, Frankfurt am Main: R. G. Fischer, 1995. pp. 89-141. [The discussion of Sg in this study of dreams and their representation in literature focuses almost entirely on *Ett drömspel*]

[C1:551] Henningsson, Per, 'Nathan Söderblom, Strindberg och nittiotalisterna', *Studiekamraten*, (Tollarp), 33 (1951), 99-101. ['Nathan Söderblom, Strindberg, and the Writers of the 1990s'. On the eminent Swedish archbishop and theologian and his relationship with both Sg and the writers of the 1890s, including Verner von Heidenstam and Oscar Levertin]

[C1:552] Hentzel, Roland, and Gunnar Brandell, 'Strindberg och Péladan', *Svenska Dagbladet* (Stockholm), 10 March 1951. [Documents Sg's considerable admiration for the novels and plays of the eccentric French symbolist and Rosicrucian, Joséphin [Sâr] Péladan (1859-1918), and suggests the relevance of the latter for the development of his post-Inferno dramaturgy in *Till Damaskus* and *Ett drömspel*]

[C1:553] Hepe, Gertrud, 'Strindberg und unser Altmeister Goethe. Eine kurze Betrachtung zu dem Problem des "Gewissens"', *Die Hochwacht* (Berlin), 11:3 (1921), 214-215. ['Strindberg and Our Old Master, Goethe. A Brief Consideration of the Problem of "Conscience"'. Compares the ways in which Sg and Goethe deal with the problem of conscience in their literary works]

[C1:554] Herrlin, Axel, 'Det omedvetnas filosof och Lundensiskt tankeliv', in *Under Lundagårds kronor. Minnen upptecknade av gamle studenter*, Ny Samling, Lund, 1921. 620 pp. ['On the Philosophy of the Unconscious and Intellectual Life in Lund'. A study of 19th-Century conceptions of the unconscious by one of Sg's companions in Lund in the late 1890s who features in *Legender* and became a professional philosopher. Includes reflections on Sg's early interest in Eduard von Hartmann's *Philosophie des Unbewußten*, 1869]

[C1:555] Hesse, Hermann, 'Strindberg', *Neue Zürcher Zeitung* (Zürich), 2 July 1947.

[C1:556] Hesse, Hermann, 'August Strindberg 1849-1912', *Neue Zürcher Zeitung* (Zürich), 22 January 1912. [A comment in respect of Sg's 63rd birthday]

[C1:557] Hesse, Hermann, 'August Strindberg 1849-1912', in *Hermann Hesse. Schriften zur Literatur*, Hrsg. von Volker Michels, Zweiter band, Frankfurt am Main: Suhrkamp Verlag, 1972, pp. 359-360. [Rpr. of **C1:556**]

[C1:558] Hesse, Hermann, 'August Strindberg In Memoriam', in **B1:368**, Dennis Poupard, ed., '(Johan) August Strindberg', in *Twentieth-Century Literary Criticism*, Vol. 21, 356-358.

[C1:559] Hesse, Hermann, 'In memoriam Strindberg', *Deutsche Zeitung* und *Wirtschafts-Zeitung* (Köln, Stuttgart), 19 March 1949. [See **C1:561**]

[C1:560] Hesse, Hermann, 'In memoriam Strindberg', in *Hermann Hesse. Schriften zur Literatur*, Hrsg. von Volker Michels, Zweiter band, Frankfurt am Main: Suhrkamp Verlag, 1972, pp. 361-362. [Rpr. of **C1:559**]

[C1:561] Hesse, Hermann, 'August Strindberg', in *My Belief: Essays on Life and Art*, Edited with an Introduction by Theodore Ziolkowski, Translated by Denver Lindley, New York: Farrar, Straus & Giroux, 1974, pp. 314-316. [An English version of **C1:559**. Hesse recognises in Sg one of 'that small group of martyr poets, those lonely seers who only critically recognized and intellectually explored the ambiguous, pathological, and perilous quality of their epoch, the apparently happy time of the long European peace and of liberalism and confidence in progress, but suffered it biologically, in their own bodies, these men to whom the still-unconscious problems of the times had become personal, physical and psychological distress and illness']

[C1:562] Hildeman, Karl-Ivar, 'Strindberg and Karlfeldt', in Marilyn Johns Blackwell, ed., **C1:142**, *Structures of Influence*, pp. 38-48. [Documents Sg's acquaintance with the Swedish poet Erik Axel Karlfeldt (1864-1931) and charts the latter's position during the Strindberg Feud of 1910-12 when his natural affiliation was with Verner von Heidenstam and the writers of the 1890s. Hildeman notes that 'There is little evidence that Sg's lyric works were of any importance to Karlfeldt'; nor were his novels and plays, although *Folkungasagan* may have contributed to Karlfeldt's image of the middle ages in his last great poem, 'Vallfärd' (Pilgrimage, 1930)]

[C1:563] Hildeman, Karl-Ivar, 'Karlfeldt och Strindberg', in Jöran Moberg, red., *Vägvisare för Karlfeldt. Nio uppsatser om bakgrunden till Karlfeldts diktning*, Karlfeldt-samfundets skriftserie 22, Falun, 1990, pp. 137-155. [Swedish version of **C1:562**]

[C1:564] Hilleström, Gustaf, 'Strindbergskt kammarspel och Shakespeare-komedi', *Studie-kamraten* (Tollarp), 28 (1946), 28-31. ['Strindbergian Chamber Play and Shakespearian Comedy']

[C1:565] Hilliker, Rebecca, 'Strindberg and Munch: The Powerlessness of the Individual Before the Great Forces of Love and Death', in Karelisa H. Hartigan, ed., *From the Bard to Broadway*, The University of Florida Department of Classics Comparative Drama Conference Papers, Vol. VII, Lanham, Maryland: University Press of America, 1987, pp. 107-124. Illus. [Comments on Sg's acquaintance with Munch in Berlin during the 1890s and their mutual misogyny. This is an error-strewn essay which claims that Sg adopted Munch's vampire imagery while the latter learnt how to literalise his canvases from Sg. Hilliker discusses *Fadren* in some detail and *Dödsdansen*, *Till Damaskus I*, and *Spöksonaten* more briefly, linking them with Munch's paintings *The Kiss* and *Vampire*. She reaches the unexceptional conclusion that death and love are mutually dependent motifs in the work of both men]

[C1:566] Hirn, Yrjö, 'Människohat och gästebud', *Samtid och framtid* (Stockholm), 6 (1949), 339-346. ['Misanthropy and Banquets'. Compares accounts of hate-filled mealtimes and food in the works of Sg and Pär Lagerkvist, in Sg's case most notably in *Svarta fanor*]

[C1:567] Hirn, Yrjö, 'Människohat och gästebud', in *Den förgyllda balustraden och andra uppsatser från åren 1949-1952*, Stockholm: Wahlström & Widstrand, 1953, pp. 124-135.

['Misanthropy and Banquets'. Rpr. of **C1:566**. The collection also includes a causerie, 'Det ätligt sköna', pp. 136-147, which includes comments on the crab-eating school-teacher in *Giftas*, pp. 144-145. Also published in a Finnish edition, Helsingfors: Holger Schildts Förlag, 1952]

[C1:568] Hjern, Olle, 'Swedenborg i Paris', *Nya Kyrkans Tidning* (Stockholm), 88 (1963), 119-126. ['Swedenborg in Paris'. Discusses Sg's 'discovery' of Swedenborg during his Inferno crisis in Paris, in 1896]

[C1:569] Höckert, Robert, 'Viktor Rydberg och August Strindberg', *Svenska Dagbladet* (Stockholm), 20 October 1936. [Discusses Sg's hostile comments on Rydberg in the post-Inferno period with reference to *Inferno*, *Legender*, *Götiska rummen*, and *Religiös renässans*, where Sg assumes the role of the spokesman of faith against unbelief, and unjustifiably casts Rydberg in the latter role since, throughout his life,. Rydberg was religiously inclined]

[C1:570] Hochbaum, Ingo F. W., 'Strindberg och den tyska expressionismen', *Sydsvenska Dagbladet* (Malmö), 10 November 1953. ['Strindberg and German Expressionism']

[C1:571] Hoffmansthal, Hugo von, *Prosa IV*, in *Gesammelte Werke*, Frankfurt am Main: S. Fischer Verlag, 1972, p. 200. ['What holds Sg's plays together is...not the narrative tale, but rather their atmosphere between reality and dream']

[C1:572] Holm, A., 'Strindbergs Forhold til Bjørnson', *Dansk Aand* (Copenhagen), 1912. ['Strindberg's Relationship with Bjørnson']

[C1:573] Holm, Ingvar, *Ola Hansson. En studie i åttitalsromantik*, Lund: C. W. K. Gleerup, 1957. 508 pp. ['Ola Hansson. A Study in 1880s' Romanticism'. Sg's personal and literary relationship with Hansson during the later 1880s is a repeated source of reference throughout. Holm considers Hansson's response to Sg's early writings, the latter's dramatisation of Hansson's short story in *Paria*, and their mutual interest in the ideas of Edgar Allan Poe, Cesare Lombroso, and Friedrich Nietzsche, as well as their awareness of trends in contemporary French psychology. Holm also comments on Hansson's role as Sg's prophet and apostle on the continent between 1889 and 1992, especially in Germany]

[C1:574] Holm, Ingvar, 'På Schloss Brunegg', in Verner von Heidenstam, *Fragment och aforismer*, Stockholm: Bonniers, 1959, pp. 109-131. ['At Castle Brunegg'. Provides details of the personal association between Sg and Heidenstam (1859-1940) in Switzerland in 1886, and considers the implications of their personal relationship for their writing]

[C1:575] Holm, Ingvar, 'Strindberg et l'expressionnisme. Notes sur l'art dramatique du naturalisme et de l'expressionnisme', in Denis Bablet and Jean Jacquot, eds, **D1:33**, *L'Expressionnisme dans le théâtre européen*, 1971, pp. 39-63. Illus. ['Strindberg and Expressionism. Notes on the Drama of Naturalism and Expressionism'. A detailed analysis of the style of Sg's later plays and their importance for the German expressionists, who created a Sg in their own image. Sg's dramaturgy could scarcely have had the impact it did in Germany during the first decades of the 20th Century had the theatre there not been prepared to accept it]

[C1:576] Holm, Ingwar [sic], 'Strindberg i ekspresjonizm', in Denis Bablet and Jean Jacquot, eds, *Exspresjonism w teatrze europejskim*, przeł. E[lżbieta] Radziwiłłowa, Warszawa: Panstwowy Instytut Wydawniczy, 1983, pp. 29-64. ['Strindberg and Expressionism'. Polish version of **C1:575**]

[C1:577] Holmbäck, Bure, '*Hjalmar Söderberg. Ett författarliv*, Stockholm: Bonniers, 1988. Illus. 631+[4] pp. ['Hjalmar Söderberg. A Writer's Life'. A life and works biography of Söderberg (1869-1941) which comments briefly on his literary relationship with Sg, pp. 60-62. Includes thirty-two other references to Sg]

[C1:578] Holmberg, Hans, 'Møde med absintdrikkeren', in *Kunstens veje over Sundet. Om svensk-danske Kulturmøder*, København: Reitzel, 1993, pp. 31-35. Illus. ['Encounter with the Absinthe Drinkers'. A study of Manet's celebrated painting with reference to writers who have written about absinthe, one of whom is Sg]

[C1:579] Holmberg, N., 'Nietzscheanismen hos Strindberg. Från *Fritänkaren* till *I havsbandet*', *Orfeus* (Stockholm), 1925, pp. 189-196. ['Nietzscheanism in Strindberg. From *The Freethinker* to *By the Open Sea*'. Confirms that Sg's 'Nietzscheanism' was already formed before Georg Brandes introduced him to Nietzsche and the latter's works with reference to *Lycko-Pers resa, Gillets hemlighet, Den fredlöse, Mäster Olof*, the poem 'Lokes smädelser' (Loki's Blasphemies, 1883), *Herr Bengts hustru*, and the short story 'De lycksaliges ö' (The Isle of the Blessed) in *Svenska öden och äventyr*, as well as to other works in which he demonstrates his contempt for the compact majority. On the whole, Holmberg suggests that Nietzsche only confirmed for Sg what he had already established for himself]

[C1:580] Holmberg, Olle, 'Ibsen och Sverige. En sammanfattning', *Samtiden* (Oslo), 41:1 (1930), 41-52. ['Ibsen and Sweden. An Outline'. Examines Ibsen's impact on Swedish literature during the 1880s and 1890s, including Sg's hostile response to *A Doll's House* in *Giftas* and the influence of *Peer Gynt* on *Gillets hemlighet*]

[C1:581] Holmberg, Olle, 'Strindberg och Leopold', *Dagens Nyheter* (Stockholm), 3 August 1964. [Discusses Sg together with the Swedish Gustavian poet Carl Gustaf af Leopold (1756-1829)]

[C1:582] Holmberg, Olle, 'Viktor Rydberg och August Strindberg. Några beröringspunkter', *Samlaren* (Uppsala), 16 (1935), pp. 1-56. [This remains the major account of Sg's response, both positive and negative, to the Swedish poet and man of letters Viktor Rydberg (1828-1895), both as a writer and cultural personality. Holmberg demonstrates that Sg's earliest plays, from *Fritänkaren* to *Mäster Olof*, reveal a debt to Rydberg's novel *Den siste Atenaren* (The Last Athenian, 1859), as well as the influence of his theological study *Bibelns lära om Kristus* (The Bible's Teaching Concerning Christ, 1862) which was composed in the tradition of Ernest Renan and David Strauss. According to Holmberg, 'One can hardly say that in some respects Sg wanted to make of Master Olof a portrait of Rydberg, but had Rydberg not existed *Mäster Olof* would not have done so either'. Sg acknowledges Rydberg's impact in *Tjänstekvinnans son*, while Holmberg regards the older writer's philosophical dialogue 'Prometeus och Ahasverus' as an intertext for his poem 'Lokes smädelser' (Loki's Blasphemies, 1883); and suggests that Rydberg is likewise of relevance to *Giftas*. But he also documents the impact of Sg's works on Rydberg, the idealist who always regarded Sg as the personification of literary realism. He discusses Sg's essay 'Om realism' (1882) and his aggressive satire in *Det nya riket*, which Rydberg disliked, surveys Rydberg's role in the events surrounding Sg's trial for blasphemy in 1884, and considers the two men's brief personal acquaintance. Sg's later, often critical, comments on Rydberg in *Lettres de Stockholm*, *Legender*, *Svarta fanor*, *Götiska rummen*, *En blå bok*, and *Tal till Svenska nationen* are noted, and Holmberg also considers Rydberg's treatment of Sg in his correspondence and elsewhere, including the poem 'Livslust och livsleda' (Delight in Life and Deep Depression, 1891) and the novel *Vapensmeden* (The Weapon Smith, 1891), in which the figure of Lars may be considered, in certain respects, an unflattering portrait of Sg]

[C1:583] Holmgren, Ola, *Kärlek och ära. En studie i Ivar Lo-Johanssons Måna-romaner*, Stockholm: LiberFörlag, 1978. 254 pp. [A study of Lo-Johansson's novels about Måna, including nine references to Sg]

[C1:584] Entry cancelled.

[C1:585] Larsson, Lars Olof, 'Symbolismus im Skandinavien', in Roger Bauer, *et al.*, Hrsg., *Fin de Siècle: Zu Kunst und Literatur der Jahrhundertwende*, Studien zur Philosophie und Literatur des neunzehnten Jahrhunderts 35, Frankfurt am Main: Vittorio Klostermann, 1977, pp. 442-463. ['Symbolism in Scandinavia'. Alludes to the vampire motif in *Dödsdansen*, in a discussion that focuses primarily on Oscar Wilde and Frank Wedekind]

[C1:586] Høst, Else, 'Strindberg, Ibsen og Lampl', *Morgenbladet* (Oslo), 15 September 1962. [A response to Lampl's article, **C1:730**. See Lampl's rejoinder, **C1:732**]

[C1:587] Houken, Aage, 'Thomas Mann og Norden', *Nordisk Tidskrift* (Stockholm), 45:5 (1969), 213-229. ['Thomas Mann and Scandinavia'. Includes the German text of Mann's article, written to commemorate the centenary of Sg's birth in 1949]

[C1:588] Huppert, Hugo, 'Strindberg und wir', *Österreichisches Tagebuch* (Vienna), 4:2 (1949), 13-14. ['Strindberg and Us'. Compares Goethe's last words, 'Mehr Licht!' (More Light), with Sg's chosen epitaph, 'O crux! Ave spes unica!' (Oh Cross! Our Only Hope!)]

[C1:589] Hurwicz, Elias, 'Strindberg und Przybyszewski', *Der Freihafen* (Hamburg), 10:6 (1927-1928), 10-13. [Traces Sg's literary and personal links with the Berlin-based Polish writer Stanisław Przybyszewski (1868-1927)]

[C1:590] Husén, Torsten, 'Strindberg, Geijerstam och förbryteriet', *Svensk Litteraturtidskrift* (Stockholm), 3:4 (1940), 187-196. ['Strindberg, Geijerstam, and Crime'. Compares criminal motifs in works from the 1880s by Ola Hansson and Victoria Benedictsson, as well as Sg (*Skärkarlsliv*, *Paria*, and 'Tschandala') and Gustaf af Geijerstam (the stories 'Förbrytare' (Criminal) and 'Fadermord' (Parricide)). Husén links them with the contemporary psychological case studies of the French psychologists Théodule Ribot and Hippolyte Bernheim, and – most particularly – the physiognomic criminology of Cesare Lombroso]

[C1:591] H. V. [Hans S. Vodskov], 'Carl Snoilsky og August Strindberg', *Illustrerad Tidende* (Copenhagen), 1 January 1882. ['Carl Snoilsky and August Strindberg'. A comparison between Sg and the Signature poet and aristocrat (1841-1903) which, in Sg's case, focuses mainly on *Dikter på vers och prosa* and *Gillets hemlighet*, and what Vodskov considers is their relationship to Snoilsky's socially concerned poetry of the early 1880s. Vodskov also comments on several earlier works, including *Röda rummet*]

[C1:592] Ingdahl, Kazimiera, 'Przybysewskas ambivalens inför Strindberg', *Svenska Dagbladet* (Stockholm), 25 January 2001. ['Przybyszewska's Ambivalent Attitude towards Strindberg'. Observes that, like her father, Stanisława Przybyszewska (1901-1935) had a complicated relationship with Sg, with whom she conducted a lifelong inner dialogue. For Przybyszewska, Sg represented blind subjectivity and a slavish subordination to sexuality. With their lack of objectivity such artistically imperfect works as *Fadren* and *Tjänstekvinnans son* can be rewarding for a psychologist, who approaches their problematic documentary nature with a scientific apparatus, but although often critical, Przybyszewska discerns in his many portrayals of marriage a form of Gnostic struggle that endows Sg's personal and contingent family dramas with a universal and timeless actuality]

[C1:593] Ingdahl, Kazimiera, 'Stanisława Przybyszewska and August Strindberg', in Maria Janion and Nils Åke Nilsson, eds, *Polish-Swedish Literary Contacts. A Symposium in Warsaw, September 22-26 1986*, Kungl. Vitterhets Historie och Antikvitets Akademien Konferenser 19, Stockholm: Almqvist & Wicksell International, 1988, pp. 93-104. Illus. [Confirms that the Polish writer and daughter of his sometime friend, Stanisław Przybyszewski, had little regard for the aesthetic value of Sg's works, since his narrative form conflicted sharply with her own demands for objectivity, yet his approach to human nature and existence undeniably nourished and reinforced the basis of her aesthetics. Ingdahl discusses Przybyszewska's unpublished essay 'Vita nuova' about *Fadren* and *Tjänstekvinnans son*, her understanding of marriage in relation to *Mäster Olof* and *Giftas*, and her concept of the superman in comparison with Sg's portrayal of Axel Borg in *I havsbandet*]

[C1:594] Ingdahl, Kazimiera, 'Stanisława Przybysewska i August Strindberg', in Maria Janion, ed., *Zwierciadla pólnocy. Zwiazki i paralele literatur polskiej i skandynawskiej*, Warszawa: Instytut Badan Literackich PAN, 1991, pp. 130-141. [Polish version of **C1:593**]

[C1:595] Ionesco, Eugene, 'Mes critiques et moi', *Notes et contre-notes*, Paris: Gallimard, 1962, pp. 22-28. ['My Critics and I'. Includes the flippant observation: 'It was proved to me that I was influenced by Sg. This obliged me to read the Scandinavian dramatist and I realised that it was in fact true'. Originally published in *Arts*, 22-28 February 1956]

[C1:596] Ionesco, Eugene, 'My Critics and I', in *Notes and Counternotes*, Translated from the French by Donald Watson, London: John Calder, 1964, pp. 86-89. [English version of **C1:595**]

[C1:597] Ivanov, V[iacheslav] I., 'Blok i Strindberg', *Literaturnoe nasledstvo*, 92:5 (1993), 412-417. ['Aleksandr Blok and Strindberg']

[C1:598] Ivanov, V[iacheslav] I., 'Strindberg si Blok', *Revista de istorie si literara* (Bucharest), 37 (1989), 213-218. [Examines Aleksandr Blok's admiration for Sg]

[C1:599] Ivanov, V[iacheslav] I., 'Strindberg si Blok 2', *Revista de istorie si literara* (Bucharest), 38-39 (1989-90), 289-296. [Discusses the importance of Sg for Aleksandr Blok during a period of the latter's life and work prior to 1914]

[C1:600] Jacobsen, Harry, *Aarene der gik tabt. Den miskendte Herman Bang*, København: H. Hagerup, 1961. [232] pp. [The third volume of Jacobsen's biography of Bang touches only briefly on his involvement with the staging of *Fordringsägare* in Paris by Lugné-Poe, but contains plentiful information on the Scandinavian presence in Paris and the performance of plays by Ibsen and Sg at the Théâtre de l'Œuvre during the 1890s]

[C1:601] Jacobsen, Harry, 'Inspiration genierne immelem', *Berlingske Aftenvis* (Copenhagen), 14 April 1969. ['Inspiration among Geniuses'. Accounts for Sg and Nietzsche's mutual admiration and their impact upon one another]

[C1:602] Jacobson, Christer, *På väg mot tiotalet. Två studier. Några principfrågor i svensk litteraturkritik 1900-1910. Viljeproblemet i svensk litteratur*, Uppsala: Almqvist & Wicksell, 1961. 414 pp. [A study of Swedish literary criticism in the first decade of the 20th Century when Sg frequently preoccupied the literary journalism of Oscar Levertin, Bo Bergman, Fredrik Böök, John Landquist, Bengt Lidforss, and Erik Hedén. French summary]

[C1:603] Jalkanen, Hugo, *Esseitä ja arvosteluja*, Hämeenlinna, 1919, pp. 163-166. [Includes a comparison of Sg with Nietzsche]

[C1:604] Janicka-Swiderska, Irena, 'The Function of Dance in Modern Drama. A. Strindberg, S. Wyspiański, W. B. Yeats', *Bulletin de la Societé des sciences et des lettres de Lodz*, 37:11 (1987), pp. 1-16. [Analyses the role of dance in the early modernist theatre when it was used as a stage, or verbal, symbol incorporated into the vision of a play and employed to intensify its meaning. Janicka-Swiderska compares both *Fröken Julie* and *Dödsdansen* with Yeats's play *At the Hawk's Well* (1916) and Stanisław Wyspiański's drama *Wesele* (The Wedding, 1901)]

[C1:605] Janicka-Swiderska, Irena, *The Function of Dance in Modern Drama. A. Strindberg, S. Wyspiański, W. B. Yeats*. Lodz, 1987, 16 pp. [Offprint of **C1:604**]

[C1:606] Janukowicz, Dorota, 'Dramaty Augusta Strindberga i Stanisława Wyspiańskiego na tle Mallarmeńskiego i Verlainowskiego symbolizmu', *Studia Scandinavica* (Gdańsk), 13 (1991), 25-39. ['The Dramas of August Strindberg and Stanisław Wyspiański in the Light of Mallarmé's and Verlaine's Symbolism']

[C1:607] Janukowicz, Dorota, 'Kilka uwag o Strindbergu, Wyspiański i Maeterlincku', in Marii Janion, ed., *Zwierciadła pólnocy. Zwiazki i paralele literatur polskiej i skandynawskiej*, Warszawa: Instytut Badan Literackich PAN, 1991, pp. 120-129. [Polish version of **C1:610**]

[C1:608] Janukowicz, Dorota, 'Niektóre aspekty czasorprzestrzeni w 'Grze snów" Augusta Strindberga i "Weselu" Stanisława Wyspiańskiego', *Studia Scandinavica* (Gdańsk), 4 (1982), 19-32. ['Some Aspects of Time-Space in August Strindberg's *Ett drömspel* and Stanisław Wyspański's *Wesele* (The Wedding, 1901)'. English summary]

[C1:609] Janukowicz, Dorota, 'Some Aspects of the Typological Comparative Study of *Ett drömspel* by August Strindberg and *Wesele* by Stanisław Wyspiański', *Studia Maritima* (Wrocław), 5 (1985), 154-160. [English version of **C1:608**]

[C1:610] Janukowicz, Dorota, 'Some Notes on Strindberg, Wyspiański and Maeterlinck', in Maria Janion and Nils Åke Nilsson, eds, *Polish-Swedish Literary Contacts. A Symposium in Warsaw, September 22-26 1986*, Kungl. Vitterhets Historie och Antikvitets Akademien, Konferenser 19, Stockholm: Almqvist & Wicksell International, 1988, pp. 73-80. [Documents the extent of Sg's and Wyspiański's familiarity with the work of Maeterlinck, and assesses his influence on their writing. Janukowicz refers to the vivisection 'L'Origine d'un style' (1894), *Påsk*, *Folkungasagan*, *Dödsdansen*, *Karl XII*, *Oväder*, and especially *Till Damaskus*, in which 'we can assume that Sg...searched for gold in his own slag heap by means of Maeterlinck's art']

[C1:611] 'Jacques Bonhomme' [A. F. Hellborg], 'Liten winterkrönika', *Norrköpings Tidningar*, 25 November 1882. ['Little Winter Chronicle'. A brief comparison of Sg with the Swedish writer Thomas Thorild (1759-1808)]

[C1:612] Jaarsma, D. Th., 'Schrijvers van over de grenzen. August Strindberg', *Den gulden winckel* (Amsterdam), 15 December 1918, pp. 177-180. ['Writers from Beyond the Frontier: August Strindberg'. Discusses Swedenborgian aspects of Sg's later work]

[C1:613] Jarvi, Raymond, 'Hjalmar Söderberg on August Strindberg: The Perspective of a Theater Critic and the Influence of a Dramatist', *Scandinavian Studies* (Provo), 68:3 (1996), 343-355. [Examines the younger Swedish novelist's (1869-1941) reviews of *Mäster Olof*, *Till Damaskus*, and *Stora landsvägen* in order to measure his response to Sg and his works. Jarvi argues that any influence which the post-Inferno Sg may have exerted on the anti-religious Söderberg as a the writer was minimal. He found *Till Damaskus* and *Stora landsvägen* antipathetic and made fun of them, always reserving his admiration for the works of the younger, socially radical Sg he had encountered in his youth]

[C1:614] Jeffares, A. Norman, ed., *Yeats the European*, Princess Grace Irish Library 3, Gerrards Cross: Colin Smythe, 1989. XV+340 pp. [Includes several brief references to Yeats's acquaintance with Sg and his works]

[C1:615] Jefferson, M., 'Fin of Another Siècle', *New York Times Book Review*, 27 August 2001. [Discusses Strindberg together with Bernard Shaw, Oscar Wilde, and Chekhov from the perspective of a later *fin de siècle*]

[C1:616] Jensen, Niels L., 'Realism in Scandinavian Fiction', in David Daiches and Anthony Thorlby, eds, *The Modern World II, Realities*, London: Aldus Books, 1972, pp. 319-328. [Notes of Sg in a general discussion of the prose fiction of the Scandinavian Modern Breakthrough that *Röda rummet* and *Det nya riket* take the attack on the rottenness of modern industrial society to extremes; in both of them, grotesque caricature transcends (and even obliterates) their critical purpose]

[C1:617] Jern, Knut, 'Strindberg och Merodach-Péladan', *Flamman* (Stockholm), 1917:8-9. ['Strindberg and Merodach-Péladan'. Examines Sg's considerable interest in the French symbolist and Rosicrucian novelist and playwright, Joséphin [Sâr] Péladan (1859-1918)]

[C1:618] Jevtić, Borivoje, 'Niče i Strindberg', *Srpska riječ* (Sarajevo), 1913, No. 279, p. 8. ['Nietzsche and Strindberg'. R.544]

[C1:619] Joergense [sic], Johannes, 'J. K. Huysmans', *Cas* (Ljubjana), 3:3 (1909), p. 141. [A Slovenian translation of comments by the Danish Catholic convert and poet Jørgensen (1866-1956) on similarities in the religious conversions of Huysmans and Sg during the 1890s. See **F5:110**]

[C1:620] Johanson, Kjell E., 'Folkbildare och nykterhetsivrare', in Siv Hackzell, red., *Ny syn på Ellen Key. 32 texter av 23 författare*, Nacka: Bembo Book, 2000, pp. 80-95. ['Popular Educator and Advocate of Temperance'. Discusses the place of *Röda rummet* in Key's political development, her complex relationship to Sg the man, and his scurrilous portrait of her as Hanna Paj in *Svarta fanor*. In retrospect their conflict seems unnecessary since, with their mutual stress on the role of woman as mother and their opposition to a society characterised by class divisions, they actually had much in common]

[C1:621] Johnsson, Melker, *En åttiotalist. Gustaf af Geijerstam 1858-1895*, Göteborg: Elanders Boktryckeri Aktiebolaget, 1934. IX+393 pp. [Remains the most authoritative study of Geijerstam's life (1858-1909) and authorship to date. Consequently it discusses both his complex personal relationship with Sg and charts their often interwoven careers as writers and cultural personalities in e.g. the autobiographical novels *Erik Grane* (1885) and *Tjänstekvinnans son* (1886)]

[C1:622] Jolivet, Alfred, 'Le rousseauisme d'August Strindberg', *Revue de littérature comparée* (Paris), 13:4 (1933), 606-622. ['August Strindberg's Rousseaueanism'. Discusses the importance which Rousseau's ideas on morality and social order had for Sg during the 1870s and 1880s. His presence is most relevant in *Röda rummet*, *Det nya riket*, *Svenska folket*, *Svenska öden och äventyr* (e.g. the stories 'Paul och Per' and 'De lycksaliges ö' (The Isle of the Blessed)), and *Utopier i verkligheten*, as well as in his views on art and society articulated in 'Om det allmänna missnöjet' (On the General Discontent, 1884), the *Lilla katekes för underklassen* (Little Catechism for the Underclass, 1884), *Bland franska bönder*, and elsewhere. Sometimes in tandem with the ideas of other social thinkers, including Nils Herman Quiding, Max Nordau, or Nikolai Cherneshevskii in his novel *What is to be Done?* (1864), Jolivet claims that Rousseau's critique of culture encouraged Sg in his attack on the social lie during the 1880s and his scepticism regarding evolutionary theory and the idea of progress. But in his view, all these figures were eventually superseded in Sg's awareness by Nietzsche]

[C1:623] Jolivet, Alfred, 'Balzac et Strindberg', *Revue de littérature comparée* (Paris), 24:2 (1950), 293-298. [Although *Röda rummet* has an evident affinity with *Le Père Goriot* and *Illusions perdues*, Jolivet notes that Sg does not refer to Balzac before *Inferno*, when he stresses the importance of *Séraphita* (1834-5) as an intermediary between himself and Swedenborg. He also assumes that Sg must have read Balzac's other Swedenborgian novel, *Louis Lambert* (1832-5), around this time, and identifies Balzacian features in both *Ensam* and *Syndabocken*]

[C1:624] Jolivet, Alfred, 'Strindberg et Jeremias Gotthelf', *Études Germaniques* (Paris), 3:2-3 (1948), 305-308. [Compares *Hemsöborna* with Gotthelf's rural novel with a Swiss setting, *Uli der Knecht* (1841), to which it is clearly indebted]

[C1:625] Jolivet, Alfred, 'Strindberg et Nietzsche', *Revue de littérature comparée* (Paris), 19:3 (1939), 390-406. [Concludes that Nietzsche's influence on Sg's plays and fiction is questionable, however marked it may be in the essays and prefaces of the later 1880s. Jolivet suggests that what Sg finds in the writers he enthuses over is less new inspiration than evidence for, and a defence of, his own ideas]

[C1:626] Jong, E. de, *Herman Heijermans en de vernieuwing van het Europese drama*, Studia litteraria rheno-traiectina 9, Groningen, 1967, pp. 63-67. ['Herman Heijermans and the Renewal of European Drama'. Comments on Heijermans's (1864-1924) professional familiarity with Sg's works. English summary]

[C1:627] Jonsson, Inge, *Emanuel Swedenborg*, Translated from the Swedish by Catherine Djurklou, New York: Twayne Publishers Inc., 1971, pp. 192-195. [Documents Sg's knowledge of Swedenborg's works and the latter's significance for his post-Inferno writing. According to Jonsson, 'It is clear that the complex, sombre sense of life portrayed in Sg's later dramas with such extraordinary power had profound roots in the works of Swedenborg']

[C1:628] Jonsson, Stefan, 'Society Degree Zero: Christ, Communism, and the Madness of Crowds', *Representations* (Berkeley), No. 75 (2001), pp. 1-32. Illus. [Compares the scene in *Ensam* in which the narrator associates his confrontation with the urban underclass that he both identifies with and abhors, with the face of madness in the crowd scenes painted by James Ensor. It represents a 'modernist primal scene' in which 'the lone individual confronts a society of threatening masses. To protect his fragile sense of self, Sg's alter ego shuts himself up in solitude. But this existential vacuum offers him no recognition; there is no external Other to help him establish the boundaries of his person. Psychic forces tear his identity in contrary directions, dissolving his individuality. His consciousness can master these forces, but only by projecting them onto the external reality. The struggle the writer fights against his own demons is transformed into a war against society']

[C1:629] Jørgensen, Bo Hakon, 'Strindberg, tegnene og århundredskiftet', *Kritik* (Copenhagen), 39 (1976), 32-51. ['Strindberg, Signs, and the Turn of the Century'. Demonstrates how Sg's preoccupation with seemingly arbitrary, even aleatory signs and their significance for the story he relates in *Inferno* becomes a compositional principal in *Till Damaskus*. Jørgensen places Sg's concerns in their *fin-de-siècle* context with reference to the Danish writers Sophus Claussen, Johannes V. Jensen, and Einar Elkær]

[C1:630] Josephson, Ragnar, 'Skalderna och staden', in *Fri vandring*, Stockholm: Albert Bonniers Förlag, 1937, 151-182. ['The Poets and the City'. Comments on 'Esplanadsystemet', *Röda rummet, Svarta fanor, Midsommar, Ensam*, and 'Pantomimer från gatan' (Street Pantomimes) in a general discussion of the portrayal of Stockholm in literature, with reference also to works by August Blanche, Oscar Levertin, Tor Hedberg, Hjalmar Söderberg, Carl Snoilsky, Carl Michael Bellman, and Bo Bergman]

[C1:631] 'JotPe' [Pseudonym of Jan Piechocki], 'Druh Przybyszewskiego', *Ziemia Pomorska* (Bydgoszcz), 1949, No. 43. [Discusses Sg's links with the Polish novelist and playwright Stanisław Przybyszewski (1868-1927)]

[C1:632] Kafka, Franz, *Briefe an Felice und andere Korrespondenz aus der Verlobungszeit*, Hrsg. von Erich Heller und Jürgen Born, Frankfurt am Main: S. Fischer, 1967. Illus. 782 pp. [Helps clarify the extent of Kafka's familiarity with Sg's works, which played a significant role in his relationship with Felice Bauer]

[C1:633] Kafka, Franz, *Letters to Felice*, Edited by Erich Heller and Jurgen Born, Translated by James Stern and Elisabeth Duckworth, London: Secker & Warburg, 1974, pp. XXV+592. [English edition of **C1:632**]

[C1:634] Kagan-Moore, Patrick, 'Dramatic Time and the Production Process. Reading for Rhythm in *Miss Julie* and *The Duchess of Malfi*', in Karelisa Hartigan, ed., *Text and Presentation*, The University of Florida Department of Classics Comparative Drama Conference Papers 8, Lanham, Maryland: University Press of America, 1988, pp. 103-116.

[C1:635] Kallifatides, Theodor, 'Strindberg som humorist', in Lars Ardelius and Gunnar Rydström, red., *Författarnas litteraturhistoria*, Stockholm: Författarförlaget, 1978, pp. 78-83. ['Strindberg as Humourist'. Compares Sg with Mark Twain, although the satire he directs against a sick society in e.g. *Det nya riket* lacks a comparable sympathy for its subject]

[C1:636] Kalson, Albert E., and Lisa M. Schwerdt, 'Eternal Recurrence and the Shaping of O'Neill's Dramatic Structures', *Comparative Drama* (Kalamazoo, Michigan), 24 (1990-91), 133-150. [Outlines Eugene O'Neill's general debt to Sg and stresses structural similarities between both *Till Damaskus* and *Brott och brott* and *The Emperor Jones*, as well as *Beyond the Horizon* and *Long Day's Journey into Night*, all of which share 'a cyclical pattern of a forward progression followed by a movement backward, a pattern evident in dramatic structure and underscored by scenic arrangement'. The essay also discusses the cyclical structure of *Ett drömspel*, compares it with O'Neill's plays *The Fountain*, *All God's Chillun Got Wings*, and *Lazarus Laughed*, and notes affinities between *Fadren* and *Spöksonaten* and several other plays by O'Neill. According to Kalson and Schwerdt, both writers were indebted to Nietzsche's concept of 'eternal recurrence', but 'Sg's repetitive closures, despite an overall pessimism in his works, are more positive than O'Neill's', which remain trapped in a Nietzschean framework]

[C1:637] Kalson, Albert E., and Lisa M. Schwerdt, 'Eternal Recurrence and the Shaping of O'Neill's Dramatic Structures', in Haiping Liu and Lowell Swortzell, eds, *Eugene O'Neill in China: An International Centenary Celebration*, Contributions in Drama and Theatre Studies 44, New York/Westport, Connecticut/London: Greenwood Press, 1992, pp. [71]-88. [Rpr. of **C1:636**]

[C1:638] Kamras, Hugo, *Den unge Heidenstam: Personlighet och idéutveckling*, Stockholm: Hugo Gebers Förlag, 1942, 422 pp. ['The Young Heidenstam. Personality and Intellectual Development'. Makes frequent reference to Verner von Heidenstam's personal and literary relationship with Sg during the 1880s, detailing their association in Switzerland in 1886 and Heidenstam's break with the realism closely associated with Sg in his literary manifestos *Renässans* (1889) and *Pepitas Bröllop* (1890)]

[C1:639] Karahka, Urpu-Liisa, *Jaget och ismerna. Studier i Pär Lagerkvists estetiska teori och lyriska praktik t.o.m. 1916*, Stockholm: Bo Cavefors Bokförlag, 1978. 360 pp. [Includes evidence that Sg was an influence on, and literary model for, the young Lagerkvist, noting the latter's response to the Sg Feud and the poems he wrote on Sg's death]

[C1:640] Karahka, Urpu-Liisa, 'Pär Lagerkvist och Strindberg – Några kommentarer', *Meddelanden från Strindbergssällskapet* (Stockholm), 55 (1975), pp. 13-23. ['Pär Lagerkvist and Strindberg: Some Observations'. Documents Lagerkvist's early reading of Sg, which included *Hemsöborna*, *Röda rummet*, *Utopier i verkligheten*, and *Giftas*, and quotes numerous, often unpublished, youthful remarks by Lagerkvist on both the man and the writer, as well as several poems written in conjunction with Sg's death. Sometimes surprisingly critical of Sg, the young Lagerkvist gradually engages more closely with his dramatic works until, with the expressionism of his later dramas, he becomes an exemplary writer for Lagerkvist's own theatre, and a significant influence on his early plays]

[C1:641] Karkhu, E. G., *Istoriia literatury Finliandii*, Leningrad: Nauka, 1979, p. 249. [Comments on Zachris Topelius's opinion of Sg in a Russian history of Finnish literature. E.1104]

[C1:642] Karlzén, John, 'John Karlzéns "Möte med Strindberg"', *Studiekamraten* (Tollarp), 56:2 (1974), p. 29. ['John Karlzén's "Encounter with Strindberg"']

[C1:643] Kärnell, Karl-Åke, 'Vilhelm Ekelund om August Strindberg', *Meddelanden från Strindbergssällskapet* (Stockholm), 35 (1964), pp. 17-26. ['Vilhelm Ekelund on August Strindberg'. Documents Ekelund's knowledge of Sg's works, including *Tjänstekvinnans son* and his poetry, as well as the many shifts in his response, both sympathetic and critical, to a writer he variously compared to Goethe, Nietzsche, Rousseau, Hölderlin, and Dostoevskii]

[C1:644] Kassius, Gabriella, 'Strötankar kring två "spöksonater"', *Samtid och framtid* (Stockholm), 14 (1957), 41-43. ['Scattered Thoughts on Two "Ghost Sonatas"'. Examines the affinities between *Spöksonaten* and Eugene O'Neill's *Long Day's Journey into Night*]

[C1:645] Kaus, Otto, 'Dostojewski und Strindberg', *Neue Blätter für sozialistische Literatur* (Berlin), 1:3 (1920), pp. 1-3. [Primarily concerned with the impact of Sg on the German theatre rather than in drawing a comparison between Sg and Dostoevskii]

[C1:646] Kayser, Rudolf, 'Hauptmann und Strindberg', *Blätter des Deutschen Theaters* (Berlin), 7 (1920-21), 4-5. [Compares Sg as a dramatist with Gerhart Hauptmann]

[C1:647] Kehn, Wolfgang, *Von Dante zu Hölderlin. Traditionswahl und Engagement im Werk von Peter Weiss*, Böhlau Forum Litterarum 1, Köln Wien: Böhlau-Verlag, 1975. 130 pp. [A study of the intertextual dimension of Weiss's work. Discusses the significance that Sg held for him under the heading 'Der Traum vom richtig totaler Freiheit' (The Dream of a Real, Complete Freedom), pp. 31-34, and in conjunction with Weiss's plays based on the lives of Leon Trotskii and Friedrich Hölderlin]

[C1:648] Keldysch, V., 'Concerning the Problem of Transition Phenomena in Literature at the Beginning of the 20th Century', in Bela Kopczi and Gyorgy M. Vajda, eds, *Actes du VIIIe Congres de l'Association Internationale de Litterature Comparée / Proceedings of the 8th Congress of The International Comparative Literature Association*, Stuttgart: Bieber, 1980, pp. 633-639. [Considers the place of Andreyev, Pirandello, and Sg in the transition from naturalism to modernism]

[C1:649] Kennedy, J. Gerald, *Imagining Paris: Exile, Writing, and American Identity*, New Haven: Yale University Press, 1993, pp. 32-33. [Considers Paris as Sg portrays it in *Inferno* in a chapter entitled 'Place, Self and Writing: Towards a Poetic Exile' where Henry Miller's autobiographical fiction *Tropic of Cancer* is also discussed]

[C1:650] Kerr, Alfred, '*Geschichten aus dem Wiener Wald*', *Berliner Tageblatt*, 3 November 1931. [A review of Ödön von Horváth's play, *Tales from the Vienna Woods*, which stresses its affinity with Sg]

[C1:651] Kerr, Alfred, 'Strindberg und Ibsen', in *Die Welt im Drama*, 5 Bde, Bd 3, *Die Sucher und die Seligen*, Berlin: S. Fischer Verlag, 1917, pp. 35-43. ['Strindberg and Ibsen'. Compares Ibsen with Sg, to the former's advantage. Contrasts *When We Dead Awaken* with *Spöksonaten* where 'there is no requiem in isolated climaxes but moment by moment astonishment'. Kerr repeats many of the distinctions advanced in **C1:654** and concludes that: 'Ibsen was a master who extended our knowledge of human beings (not only our knowledge of some special individuals), and who bore the character of the eternal within him. In the final analysis, Sg is simply a great mouthpiece for those who have fallen short']

[C1:652] Kerr, Alfred, 'Strindberg und Ibsen', in *Die Welt im Drama*, Hrsg. von Gerhard F. Hering, Köln und Berlin: Kiepenheur & Witsch, 1954, pp. 260-266. [Rpr. of **C1:651**]

[C1:653] Kerr, Alfred, 'Strindberg und Ibsen', in *Die Welt im Drama*, Hrsg. von Gerhard F. Hering, 2. Aufl., Köln und Berlin: Kiepenheuer & Witsch, 1964, pp. 58-64. [Rpr. of **C1:651**]

[C1:654] Kerr, Alfred, 'Totenrede', in *Die Welt im Drama*, 5 Bde, Bd 5, Berlin: S. Fischer Verlag, 1917, pp. 18-22. ['Memorial Address'. Delivered in honour of Otto Brahm, 22 December 1912. Ibsen is 'the dramatist of human destinies whereas Sg is only the dramatist of monomania. Ibsen shows us the power of morality, Sg merely the power of hatred. Ibsen creates human beings, Sg only individual features. Ibsen gives us the flesh and blood surrounding the skeleton, Sg usually depicts only a skeleton, and a very odd skeleton at that']

[C1:655] Kesting, Marianne, 'Welttheater des Ichs. Strindberg – Artaud – Ionesco', in Peter Csobádi, Hrsg., *Welttheater, Mysterienspiel, rituelle Theater: "Vom Himmel durch die Welt zur Hölle"*, Gesammelte Vorträge des Salzburger Symposions 1991, Anif: Müller-Speiser, 1992, pp. 41-52.

[C1:656] Keustermans, Lisette, '*Homunculus* som konstnärsroman. Delblanc i dialog med Strindberg', *Tidskrift för litteraturvetenskap* (Lund), 16:4 (1987), 102-109. ['*Homunculus* as an Artist Novel. Delblanc in Dialogue with Strindberg'. Compares Sven Delblanc's early novel from 1965 with *I havsbandet*, in response to his remark that the central characters of both books are culture heroes of the kind analysed by Frazer in *The Golden Bough*, individuals who are punished for seeking to aid mankind]

[C1:657] Key, Ellen, 'Sveriges modernaste diktare. Carl Jonas Ludvig Almqvist', 1-3, *Ord och Bild* (Stockholm), 3: 8, 9, 10 (1894), pp. 418-427, 472-480, 523-528. ['Sweden's most Modern Writer. Carl Jonas Love Almqvist'. Key's celebrated series of articles in which she contributed significantly to the revival of Almqvist's (1793-1866) literary reputation in Sweden, while also affirming his precedence over Sg as the most modern of Swedish writers, thereby incurring the latter's enduring wrath]

[C1:658] Key, Ellen, *Sveriges modernaste diktare. Carl Jonas Ludvig Almqvist*, Stockholm: Wahlström & Widstrand, 1897. 53 pp. [Rpr. of **C1:657**. Facsimile edition published by Recolid, Stockholm, 1992]

[C1:659] Entry cancelled.

[C1:660] K. H. [Knut Hamsun], 'Klokkeren på Rånö og andre Skjærgaardshistorier', *Dagbladet* (Oslo), 26 January 1890. ['The Sexton on Rånö and other Tales of the Archipelago'. Reviews the Danish editions of *Skärkarlsliv* and *Bland franska bönder*. Dismisses the long short story 'Den romantiske klockaren på Rånö' in *Skärkarlsliv* as a slovenly piece of work, a mere sketch, without artistry or psychology, whereas *Bland franska bönder* contains a wealth of observations, and is 'so penetrating and skillfully worked out that it surpasses all Sg's other dissertations']

[C1:661] Kielland, Alexander L., *Brev I 1869-1883*, Utvalg, innledning og kommentar ved Johs. Lunde, Oslo: Gyldendal Norsk Forlag, 1978, 330 pp. [The first volume of Kielland's collected letters, which covers the period when he corresponded with Sg at a time when both writers found common cause in furthering the aims of the Scandinavian Modern Breakthrough]

[C1:662] Kienzl, Hermann, 'Der Briefwechsel zwischen Nietzsche und Strindberg', *Der Türmer* (Stuttgart), 15:2 (1912-13), 235-239. ['The Correspondence between Nietzsche and Strindberg'. Presents Sg's exchange of letters with Nietzsche, first published by Karl Strecker in **C1:1232**]

[C1:663] Kihlman, Erik [Lorenzo], *Karl August Tavaststjernas diktning*, Helsingfors: [Mercators tryckeri], 1926. 368 pp. [An important monograph on the works of the Finland-Swedish author (1860-1898) which includes some details concerning the personal and literary impact that Sg had on him]

[C1:664] Kim, Jean-Jacques, 'Adamov et Strindberg', *Combat* (Paris), 8 August 1955. [Considers the relevance of Sg for the dramas of Arthur Adamov in light of the latter's study of Sg's theatre, **D2:1**]

[C1:665] Kim, Mija, 'Hyeondae yeongmi heulgok e jun Strindberg eul yeonghyang', *Articles and Essays* (Seoul), 17 (1984), 57-76. ['Strindberg's Influence on Modern English and American Drama'. An essay in a collection published by Hankuk University of Foreign Studies, Seoul]

[C1:666] Kindermann, Heinz, *Hermann Bahr. Ein leben für das europäischer Theater*, Mit einer Hermann-Bahr-Bibliographie von Kurt Thomasberger, Graz-Köln: Verlag Hermann Böhlaus, 1954. 379 pp. [That there are only three references to Sg throughout this study of Bahr's wide-ranging interest in the European theatre underlines his comparative lack of interest in Sg's plays, especially given his otherwise passionate engagement with the drama and theatre of his age]

[C1:667] Kirkeby, A., Strindberg og Bjørnson', *Politiken* (Copenhagen), 4 November 1917.

[C1:668] Kiss [Szalczer], Eszter, *Világkép és drámai forma összefüggése Ibsen és Strindberg müveiben*, Budapest: Magyar Szinházi Intézet, 1987. 115 pp. ['World View and Dramatic Form in the Works of Ibsen and Strindberg']

[C1:669] Kjærgaard, Helge, 'Ibsens *Djukkehjem* og August Strindberg', *Jyllandsposten* (Viby), 19 July 1954. ['Ibsen's *A Doll's House* and August Strindberg'. Traces Sg's response to Ibsen's play in both *Giftas* and *Herr Bengts hustru*]

[C1:670] Kjellén, Alf, *Bakom den officiella fasaden. En studie över Carl David af Wirséns personlighet*, Stockholm: Almqvist & Wiksell International, 1979. 193 pp. ['Behind the Public Façade. A Study of Carl David af Wirsén'. A monograph on the idealist poet, literary critic, and secretary of the Swedish Academy, Carl David af Wirsén (1842-1912), whose ideological antipathy and aesthetic differences with Sg were a feature of both men's professional lives. Kjellén makes frequent reference to Wirsén's generally hostile attitude towards Sg, as well as to their long-lasting mutual dislike]

[C1:671] Kjellén, Alf, *Flanören och hans storstadsvärld. Synpunkter på ett litterärt motiv*, Stockholm Studies in the History of Literature 28, Stockholm: Almqvist & Wicksell International, 1985. Illus. 303 pp. ['The Flâneur and his Metropolitan World: Aspects of a Literary Theme'. Notes how Sg's autobiographical fiction, *Ensam*, displays an evident kinship with the so-called 'flaneur' school of writing by several Stockholm novelists of the younger generation, including Henning Berger (1872-1924) and Hjalmar Söderberg (1869-1941). However, Sg's narrative is distinguished from their work by its author's (and the narrator's) pronounced religious commitment]

[C1:672] 'Klabund' [Pseudonym for Alfred Henschke], 'Eine Fahne des Triumphs...', *Programm* (München), 1915:1, pp. 10-11. ['A Flag of Triumph'. Argues that 'Ibsen may come and go, but Sg will endure']

[C1:673] Klim, George, *Stanisław Przybyszewski. Leben, Werk und Weltanschauung im Rahmen der deutschen Literatur der Jahrhundertwende*, Reihe Literatur- und Medienwissenschaften 6; Kölner Arbeiten zur Jahrhundertwende 2, Paderborn: Igel-Verlag, 1992. Illus. 376 pp. [Examines Sg's personal and literary contacts with the Polish novelist and playwright during the 1890s]

[C1:674] Knipovich, Y., 'Franz Kafka', in Knipovich, *Sila pravdy*, Moscow, 1965, pp. 321-355. [Compares Sg with both Kafka and Maksim Gor'kii, pp. 135-137. E.1006]

[C1:675] Kolbe, Gunlög, 'Marie Sophie Schwartz, August Strindberg och det moderna genombrottet', *Personhistorisk tidskrift* (Stockholm), 100:1 (2004), 24-35. Illus. [Marie Sophie Schwartz, August Strindberg and the Modern Breakthrough'. Compares Sg with the novelist and dramatist Schwartz (1819-1894) in a discussion of the literature of the Scandinavian Modern Breakthrough]

[C1:676] Komiya, Toyotaka, *Higeki to Kigeki* (Tokyo), 1947. 223 pp. [Includes lectures on Goethe and Antique Comedy as well as on Sg]

[C1:677] Konrad, Linn B., 'Ariadne and the Labyrinth of the Creative Mind', in Karelisa V. Hartigan, ed., *From the Bard to Broadway*, Lanham, Maryland: University of Florida Press, 1987, pp. 147-156. [Explores the Ariadne theme in Ibsen's *The Master Builder*, Maeterlinck's *Ariane et Barbe-Bleue*, and *Ett drömspel*]

[C1:678] Koponen, Jari, *Mielikuvituksen mestarit: 13 unohdettua fantasia*, Jyväskylä: Atena, 2000. 240 pp. [Includes essays on Alfred Jarry, Stanisław Witkiewicz, Raymond Roussel, and Villiers de l'Isle Adam, as well as Sg]

[C1:679] Kordt, Walter, 'Strindberg-Wedekind. Eine dramatische Prinzipienfrage', *Das Deutsche Theater* (Berlin), 2 (1923-24), 60-69. ['Strindberg and Wedekind. A Matter of Dramatic Principles'. Claims that Sg and Wedekind are 'totally different in spirit'; it is only the indolence of contemporary taste that couples them with one another]

[C1:680] Koren, Evald, 'Govekar, Zola in *V krvi*', *Slavistična revija* (Ljubljana), 21:3 (1973), 281-319.

[C1:681] Kos, Janko, *Primerjalna zgodovina slovenske literature*, Ljubljana, 1987.

[C1:682] Koskenniemi, Veikko Autero, *Goethe-studier och andra litteraturhistoriska essäer*, Med förord av Magnus von Platen, Urval av Edwin Linkomies, Till svenska av Ole Torvalds, Stockholm: Natur och Kultur, 1963. 251 pp. [Discusses Sg in conjunction with the Swedish poet and essayist Vilhelm Ekelund (1880-1949)]

[C1:683] Koskenniemi, V[eikko] A[utero], 'Strindberg-Heidenstam-Hans Larsson', *Aika* (Helsinki), 1911, pp. 673-676.

[C1:684] Koskimies, Rafael (Kaarlo), *Der nordische Faust: Adam Homo, Peer Gynt, Hans Alienus*, Annales Academiae scientiarum Fennicae, Ser. B, 142:1, Helsingissä: Suomalainen tiedeakatemia, 1965. 106 pp. [Traces the existence of the Faust theme in Nordic literature, focusing mainly on works by Oehlenschläger, Ibsen, and Verner von Heidenstam, but also commenting on *Mäster Olof* and *I havsbandet*]

[C1:685] Kovalenko, G., 'A. Strindberg i E. Olbi', in L[ev] Gitel'man and V[alentina] Dianova, eds, **B1:148**, *Avgust Strindberg i mirovaia kul'tura. Materialy mezhvyzovskoi nauchnoi konferentsii. Stat'i. Soobshcheniia*, pp. 70-77. [Compares *Dödsdansen* with Edward Albee's *Who's Afraid of Virginia Woolf*]

[C1:686] Kralj, Lado, 'Kje stoji mesto Goga?', in Slavko Grum, ed., *Goga, čaudovito mesto - Dogodek v mestu Gogi, proza, pisma*, Ljubljana, 1987, pp. 189-241.

[C1:687] Kratch, D. V., '[Eugene O'Neill]', in *Istoriia literatury Krach*, Vol. 3, Moscow, 1979, pp. 357-370. [Comments on Sg's significance for Eugene O'Neill in a literary history of the United States, pp. 358, 363. E.1105]

[C1:688] Kraus, Karl, 'August Strindberg †', *Die Fackel* (Vienna), 14 (1912-1913), Nos 351-353, pp. 1-3. [The original publication of Kraus's frequently reprinted obituary of Sg with its reflections on his achievement as both man and writer]

[**C1:689**] Kraus, Karl, 'August Strindberg †', in *Untergang der Welt durch schwarze Magie*, Wien-Leipzig: Verlag "Die Fackel", 1922, pp. 277-279. [Rpr. of **C1:688**]

[**C1:690**] Kraus, Karl, 'August Strindberg †', in Hans-Peter Bayerdörfer, Hrsg., **B3:85**, *Strindberg auf der deutschen Bühne*, pp. 204-206. [Rpr. of **C1:688**]

[**C1:691**] Kraus, Karl, 'August Strindberg', in Eliane Kaufholz, ed., *Karl Kraus*, Paris: Editions de L'Herne, 1975, pp. 65-66. [French translation of **C1:688**]

[**C1:692**] Kraus, Karl, 'August Strindberg', in *I denna stora tid. Texter ur Die Fackel*, Urval och översättning av Lars Bjurman, Stockholm: Brutus Österlings Bokförlag Symposion, pp. 130-131. [Swedish translation of **C1:688**]

[**C1:693**] K[raus], K[arl], 'Strindberg und Wien', *Die Fackel* (Vienna), 15 (1913-14), Nos 391-392, pp. 4-5. ['Strindberg and Vienna'. Sums up Sg's relationship with Vienna as 'Der Teufel und der Apfelstrudel']

[**C1:694**] Kraus, K[arl], 'Strindberg und Wien', in Hans-Peter Bayerdörfer, Hrsg., **B3:85**, *Strindberg auf der deutschen Bühne*, pp. 218-220. [Rpr. of **C1:693**]

[**C1:695**] K[raus], K[arl], 'Über Strindberg, Rahmer und das *Neue Wiener Journal*', *Die Fackel* (Vienna), 9 (1907-08), Nos 239-240, pp. 33-34. ['On Strindberg, Rahmer, and the *Neue Wiener Journal*']

[**C1:696**] K[raus], K[arl], 'Vorbemerkung zum Abruch von "Mann und Weib"', *Die Fackel* (Vienna), 11 (1909-10), Nos 281-282, pp. 18-19. ['A Prologue to the Breakup of "Man and Woman"']

[**C1:697**] Kreutzer, Gert, 'Strindberg, Linné und die Nemesis Divina', in Wolfgang Butt and Bernhard Glienke, Hrsg., *Der nahe Norden. Otto Oberholzer zum 65. Gerburtstag: eine Festschrift*, Frankfurt am Main: Peter Lang, 1985, pp. [23]-35. ['Strindberg, Linnaeus, and Nemesis Divina'. Aware of Sg's considerable admiration for Linnaeus, Kreutzer compares his conception of divine justice, or Nemesis, through which a form of moral order, or structuring pattern of crime and punishment, was introduced into the otherwise chaotic world of *Inferno* without any form of visible justice, with Linnaeus's notes on the same topic, posthumously published as *Nemesis Divina*]

[**C1:698**] Kristensen, Tom, 'August Strindberg', *Politiken* (Copenhagen), 14 May 1937.

[**C1:699**] Kristensen, Tom, 'Problemet: Strindberg', *Politiken* (Copenhagen), 22 January 1939. [Reflections on Sg as a precursor of the post-1918 period, his pietistic Christianity, and problematical subjectivity, by the eminent Danish modernist novelist (1893-1974), who compares him with D. H. Lawrence and James Joyce]

[**C1:700**] Kristensen, Tom, 'Problemet: Strindberg', in *Kritiker eller Anmelder*, København: Gydendals Uglebøger, 1966, pp. 99-105. [Rpr. of **C1:699**]

[**C1:701**] Kristensen, Tom, 'Problemet: Strindberg', in *Til dags dato. Artikler og kroniker*, Udvalgt af Carl-Bergstrøm-Nielsen, København: Gyldendal, 1953, pp. 227-232. [Rpr. of **C1:699**]

[**C1:702**] Kristensen, Tom, 'Strindberg og det yngre Danmark', *Dagens Nyheter* (Stockholm), 23 January 1949. ['Strindberg and the Younger Danish Writers'. Written by the Danish novelist and critic (1893-1974) in conjunction with the centenary of Sg's birth]

[**C1:703**] Kristensen, Tom, 'Strindberg og det yngre Danmark', in *Til dags dato Artikler og kroniker*, Udvalgt af Carl Bergstrøm-Nielsen, København: Gyldendal, 1953, pp. 233-235. ['Strindberg and the Younger Danish Writers'. Rpr. of **C1:702**]

[C1:704] Krogvig, Anders, 'Strindberg og Bjørnstjerne Bjørnson', in *Bøker og mennesker*, Kristiania: H. Aschehoug & Co., 1919, pp. 150-174. [Accepts without reservation Sg's own highly charged account of his relationship with Bjørnson in *Tjänstekvinnans son*]

[C1:705] Krysztofiak, Maria, 'Karl Kraus und die skandinavische Moderne', in Annegret Heitmann und Karin Hoff, eds, *Ästhetik der skandinavischen Moderne*, Beiträge zur Skandinavistik 14, Frankfurt am Main: Peter Lang, 1998, pp. 327-342. ['Karl Kraus and Scandinavian Modernism'. Surveys the translation and presentation of Scandinavian writers in Kraus's journal *Die Fackel*, including Sg, who was greatly admired, and often published, by Kraus]

[C1:706] Küchler, Walther, *Arthur Rimbaud: Bildnis eines Dichters*, Heidelberg: L. Schneider, 1948. 253 pp. [Includes a passing comparison of *Inferno* with Rimbaud's *Une saison en enfer* as two modernist urban hells, p. 153]

[C1:707] Kudahl, Inger Jakobsen, 'Parasitiske talehandlinger: Lader Austins talehandlingsteoretiske begreber sig også anvende i forbindelse med analyser af fiktive tekster?', *Danske Studier* (Copenhagen), 2000, pp. 26-53. ['Parasitic Speech Acts. Is it also Possible to Employ Austin's Speech-Act Theory in the Analysis of Fictional Texts?'. Explores the application of J. L. Austin's Speech-Act Theory in dramatic texts via an analysis of segments of dialogue from *Fröken Julie* (pp. 43-46) and *Waiting for Godot*]

[C1:708] Kuntz, Hélène, 'De la catastrophe finale à la catastrophe inaugurale: Corneille, Strindberg, Beckett', *Littératures Classiques* (Paris), 48 (2003), 183-192. [Compares the treatment of terminal catastrophe in classical drama (Corneille), focusing on two plays in which the catastrophe has occurred before the action commences, Samuel Beckett's *Endgame* and Sg's *Brända tomten*. The second of these implements a retrospective logic through the inquiring figure of the Stranger as he uncovers the family drama which the house fire has already laid bare before the play begins. But in comparison with classic dramaturgy, this method of construction after the event poses questions regarding the theatrical effectiveness of the play]

[C1:709] Kutik, Ilja, *Långa linjer: Hans Vikstens korrespondenser*, Översättning Hans Björkegren, *Ord och Bild* (Stockholm), 102:1 (1993), 71-75. Illus. [Discusses Viksten's use of correspondences in his art, with reference to Sg, Baudelaire, and Ovid]

[C1:710] Kutscher, Artur, *Wedekind. Leben und Werk*, bearbeitet und Hrsg. von Karl Ude, München: List Verlag, 1964. [380] pp. [Revised edition of **C1:711**]

[C1:711] Kutscher, Artur, *Frank Wedekind. Sein Leben und seine Werke*, 2 vols, München: G. Müller Verlag, 1922-27. 422, 264 pp. [Documents Wedekind's encounters with Sg in 1886 and 1894, his knowledge of Sg's works, their impact on his own writing, and the consequences of his affair with Frida Uhl during the 1890s]

[C1:712] Kvalsvik, Bjørn, 'Holberg og Strindberg – en komparativ analyse', *Eigenproduksjon* (Oslo), 10 (1980), 16-35. ['Holberg and Strindberg: A Comparative Analysis'. Compares Sg and Ludvig Holberg as dramatists]

[C1:713] Kvastad, Nils Björn, 'Hamsun om Strindberg', *Ystads Allehanda*, 30 November 1963. ['Hamsun on Strindberg'. Assesses Knut Hamsun's opinion of Sg as man and writer]

[C1:714] Kvastad, Nils Björn, 'Hamsun om Strindberg', *Östersunds-Posten*, 4 March 1965. ['Hamsun on Strindberg'. Identical with **C1:713**]

[C1:715] Kylhammar, Martin, *Maskin och idyll. Teknik och pastorala ideal hos Strindberg och Heidenstam*, Stockholm: Liber Förlag, 1985. Illus. 253 pp. ['Machine and Idyll. Technology and Pastoral Ideal in Strindberg and Heidenstam'. Although Sg and Verner von Heidenstam (1859-1940) both claimed to be the standard-bearers of the new age and yet also seemed to be antithetical to one another, Kylhammar observes that they reacted similarly to the birth of modern society, repudiating both its urban base and the emphasis it placed on technology, industry, science, and capital. They were both critics of civilisation, investing emotionally and intellectually in an alternative pastoral model, Heidenstam through his orientalism and Sg by embracing the ideal of a peasant society *à la* Rousseau, an ideal that he entertained for much of the 1880s. Kylhammar discusses the essay 'Om det allmänna missnöjet' (On the General Discontent, 1884), *Det nya riket*, *Bland franska bönder*, *Lycko-Pers resa*, the story 'Nybyggnad' (New Building) in *Utopier i verkligheten*, *Sömngångarnätter*, 'De lycksaliges ö' (The Isle of the Blessed) in *Svenska öden och äventyr*, and *I havsbandet*, as well as Sg's scientific speculations in the mid-1890s and several later, less anti-technological reflections in *Götiska rummen*, *En blå bok*, *Svarta fanor*, and *Ordalek och småkonst*]

[C1:716] — Hägg, Göran, '90-talets rädsla för maskintekniken', *Aftonbladet* (Stockholm), 15 February 1986. ['Fear of Industrial Technology in the 1890s']

[C1:717] — Janson, R. H., *Technology and Culture* (Detroit), 28:4 (1987), 857-858.

[C1:718] — Robinson, Michael, *Scandinavica* (Norwich), 27:2 (1988), 191-193.

See also **A4:50**

[C1:719] Kylhammar, Martin, 'Slaget om det moderna. Civilasionskritikerna August Strindberg och Vitalis Norström', in Annika Alzén and Johan Hedrén, red., *Kulturarvets natur*, Stockholm/Stehag: Brutus Östlings bokförlaget Symposion, 1998, pp. 229-260. ['The Battle Over the Modern. August Strindberg and Vitalis Norström as Critics of Civilisation'. Compares Sg's analyses of technology, modernity, science, progress, and history, with those of the contemporary Swedish philospher, Norström, and examines the intellectual context in Sweden within which this debate about modernity was conducted during the latter part of the 19th Century]

[C1:720] Laan, Thomas F. van, 'Ibsen and Strindberg: Interactions in the 1880s', *Annals of Scholarship* (New York), 9:3 (1992), 239-255. [Traces the influence which Ibsen and Sg exerted on one another during the 1880s, between the publication of *A Doll's House* and Sg's rejoinder in Volume One of *Giftas*. Laan also compares *Rosmersholm* with Sg's analysis of Ibsen's play in the vivisection 'Själamord' (Soul Murder, 1887) and *Fröken Julie* with *Hedda Gabler*; he suggests that the more explicitly autobiographical tenor of Ibsen's work in the 1890s may derive from his reading of Sg]

[C1:721] Lagercrantz, Olof, 'August Strindberg och Viktor Rydberg', *Svenska Dagbladet* (Stockholm), 22 January 1999. [Focuses on Sg's personal rather than literary relationship with the Swedish poet and novelist (1828-1895)]

[C1:722] Lagerlöf, Karl Erik, 'Mellan tro och misstro', in *Samtal med 60-talister*, Stockholm: Albert Bonniers Förlag, pp. 108-117. ['Between Belief and Doubt'. A conversation with the Swedish author Per Olov Enquist, who identifies the implicit and explicit Sgian aspects of his second novel, *Färdvägen* (1963): 'The basic idea is from Sg's *Till Damaskus*. The decisive scene in my book corresponds to the asylum scene...the decisive experience in the middle of it, the extreme attempt to challenge God to make himself known – I borrow the external contours of it from an episode in Sg's life']

[C1:723] Lagerkvist, Pär, 'Gerhard Gran, *Henrik Ibsen. Liv og verket*', *Svenska Dagbladet* (Stockholm), 14 February 1919. [Contrasts Ibsen with Sg to the latter's advantage as 'the creator of the modern theatre']

[C1:724] Lagerkvist, Pär, *Ordkonst och bildkonst. Om modärn skönlitteraturs dekadans, om den modärna konstens vitalitet*, Med ett förord av August Brunius, Stockholm: Lagerström, 1913. 61 pp.

[C1:725] Lagerkvist, Pär, 'Strindberg och Ibsen på dansk scen', *Svenska Dagbladet* (Stockholm), 26 May 1918. ['Strindberg and Ibsen on the Danish Stage'. Lagerkvist contrasts the two dramatists to Sg's advantage in line with his subsequent treatment of their work in his widely disseminated manifesto 'Modern Teater. Synpunkter och angrepp'. See **D1:604**]

[C1:726] Lagerroth, Ulla-Britta, 'Pär Lagerkvist och scenkonsten. Kring otryckta och tryckta ungdomsverk', in Rolf Arvidsson, Bernt Olsson, and Louise Vinge, red., *Diktaren och hans formvärld. Lundastudier i litteraturvetenskap tillägnade Staffan Björck och Carl Fehrman*, Malmö: Allhems Förlag, 1975, pp. 133-155. ['Pär Lagerkvist and Dramatic Art. On Unpublished and Published Works of His Youth'. Considers Lagerkvist's early unpublished dramatic writings, the one-acters *Den svåra stunden* and *Himlens hemlighet*, and his essay 'Modern teater. Synpunkter och angrepp' (**D1:604**) in which Sg is a defining presence]

[C1:727] Lagerstedt, Sven, *Drömmaren från Norrlandsgatan. En studie i Henning Bergers liv och författarskap*, Monografier utgivna av Stockholms Kommunalförvaltning, Stockholm: Almqvist & Wicksells Boktryckeri Aktiebolag, 1963, pp. 202-208. Illus. ['The Dreamer from Norrlandsgatan. A Study in Henning Berger's Life and Works'. Compares the descriptions of Stockholm in Sg's *Ensam* with the depiction of the city in numerous novels by Berger (1872-1924). Lagerstedt also notes Berger's admiration for Sg as man and writer]

[C1:728] Lagerström, Mona, *Dramatisk teknik och könsideologi. Anne-Charlotte Lefflers tidiga kärleks- och äktenskapsdramatik*, Skrifter utgivna av Litteraturvetenskapliga institutionen vid Göteborgs universitet 36, Göteborg, 1999. 262 pp. ['Dramatic Technique and Sexual Ideology. Anne-Charlotte Leffler's Early Plays of Love and Marriage'. Maintains that in her early bourgeois plays concerned with love and matrimony, Leffler adopts the German form of the well-made-play, as defined by Sg's professor in aesthetics at Uppsala, Carl Rupert Nyblom. Her subject matter thus invites comparison with Sg, to whom frequent reference is made in passing. English summary]

[C1:729] Lambert, Carole J[ane], *The Empty Cross. Medieval Hopes, Modern Futility in the Theater of Maurice Maeterlinck, Paul Claudel, August Strindberg and Georg Kaiser*, New York & London: Garland Publishing, 1990. Illus. VI+345 pp. [Explores medieval themes and symbols in four dramatists whose work Lambert reads as indebted to the symbolism of Baudelaire and Mallarmé, and which consequently provided an alternative to the prevailing positivism, Darwinism, historicism, and naturalism of the 1890s and beyond. Lambert discusses *Inferno*, *Legender*, *Stora landsvägen*, and (mainly) *Till Damaskus*, and suggests that in the latter Sg's interest in contemporary psychology turns inward under the influence of Maeterlinck and becomes an ultra-subjective analysis of the soul, conducted in medieval terminology in the form of a redemptive pilgrimage from one station to another]

[C1:730] Lampl, Hans Erich, 'Festina Lente! Omkring anti-romanen *Sult* og forholdet mellom Hamsun og Strindberg', *Aftenposten* (Oslo), 10 October 1966. ['Festina Lente! On the Anti-Novel *Hunger* and the Relationship between Hamsun and Strindberg'. Discusses Hamsun's early novel *Hunger* (1890) and his relationship with Sg, with whose *Inferno* it has an affinity as a first-person account describing extreme states of mind in an urban milieu. See Martin Nag, **C1:931**]

[C1:731] Lampl, Hans Erich, 'Hans Henny Jahn. Rebell med personlig ansvar', *Vinduet* (Oslo), 17:3 (1963), 215-224. ['Hans Henny Jahn. Rebel with Personal Responsibility'. Identifies a deep affinity between the Norwegian writer Jahn and Sg]

[C1:732] Lampl, Hans Erich, 'Hansken tas opp. Et svar på ti punkter til fru Høst', *Morgenbladet* (Oslo), 21 September 1962. ['The Gauntlet Picked Up. A Reply on Ten Points to Fru Høst'. A rejoinder to Høst's article, **C1:586**]

[C1:733] Lampl, Hans Erich, 'Ibsen og Strindberg. Forholdet mellom antipodene', *Samtiden* (Oslo), 73 (1964), 101-117. ['Ibsen and Strindberg. The Relationship between the Antipodes'. Discusses Sg's relatively positive early response to the Ibsen of *Brand* as displayed in *Fritänkaren*, *Mäster Olof*, and *Gillets hemlighet*, where Margaretha recalls both Solveig and Agnes, and his increasingly polemical stance after *A Doll's House* in *Herr Bengts hustru* and *Giftas*. In the naturalistic dramas *Kamraterna*, *Fadren*, *Fröken Julie*, and *Fordringsägare*, Lampl finds that he enters into a dialogue with Ibsen in *Rosmersholm* and *Hedda Gabler*. He also documents Ibsen's response to Sg and his works. See the ensuing correspondence between Lampl and Else Høst, **C1:586** and **C1:732**]

[C1:734] Landquist, John, 'Diktaren och livssynen', *Stockholms-Tidningen*, 13 September 1922. ['The Writer and his View of Life'. Contrasts the idealism of the Swedish romantic poet, Esaias Tegnér (1782-1846), with Sg's naturalism]

[C1:735] Landquist, John, 'Das künstlerische Symbol. III. Persönlichkeit als Symbole. Strindbergs *Der Vater* und Goethes *Werther*. Zweifache Symbolik in Hinblick auf den Schaffenden und auf den Empfänger', *Imago* (Leipzig), 6 (1920), 312-316. ['The Artistic Symbol. III. Personality as Symbol. Strindberg's *The Father* and Goethe's *Werther*'. A psychological study of literary symbolism]

[C1:736] Landsberg, Hans, 'Strindberg und Nietzsche', *Neue Revue* (Berlin), 3 (1909), 176-177.

[C1:737] Lång, Helmer, 'Albert Engström och Strindberg – myt och verklighet', *Värld och vetande* (Göteborg), 16:2 (1966), 37-45. ['Albert Engström and Strindberg: Myth and Reality'. Focuses on Sg's personal and literary association with the Swedish artist, writer, and humorist, Albert Engström (1869-1940), who was initially critical of Sg but grew to be strongly influenced by him. Engström considered *Hemsöborna* Sg's best work and derived much from *Skärkarlsliv*, *Från Fjärdingen och Svartbäcken*, and, above all, the early prose sketches 'Sandhamn i storm' (Sandhamn in Storm) and 'Huruledes jag fann Sehlstedt' (How I Found Sehlstedt) in developing his own narrative style. Lång points out that Engström admired *En blå bok* and was on friendly terms with Sg between 1900 and 1912, although it is hard to distinguish true from false in Engström's retrospective accounts of their encounters, in which he always places himself at the centre of events]

[C1:738] Lång, Helmer, 'Rimbaud och sekelskiftets Sverige', *Samlaren* (Uppsala), 35 (1954), pp. [113]-132. ['Rimbaud and Turn-of-the-Century Sweden'. Considers the possibility that Sg was familiar with Rimbaud's *Une saison en enfer* (1873) and compares the way in which both writers depicted contemporary urban life as a modern hell. Both Rimbaud's poems and Sg's *Inferno* are played out in the mind and entail a disorder of the senses, which Lång considers may extend to a stylistic debt to Rimbaud on Sg's part]

[C1:739] Lange, Sven, 'August Strindberg', in *Meninger om Litteratur*, København: Gyldendal, 1929, pp. 209-211. [An appreciation by one of Sg's Danish translators]

[C1:740] Lapisardi, Frederick S., 'The Same Enemies: Notes on Certain Similarities between Yeats and Strindberg', *Modern Drama* (Lawrence, Kansas), 12:2 (1969), 146-154. [Considers the two writer's mutual interest in the occult, theosophy, Maeterlinck, Edward Gordon Craig, and impressionism. Lapisardi suggests that Sg's comments on asymmetrical staging in the Preface to *Fröken Julie* may have inspired Yeats in *Four Plays for Dancers* and observes that, as dramatists, they both gave primacy to the spoken word, preferring the short, well-constructed play to longer forms. They often employed leitmotivs (for example, everything tends to repeat itself in Yeats's *Purgatory*, *The Dreaming of the Bones*, and *The Words upon the Window-Pane* as it does in many of Sg's later plays) and stressed the musical dimension of theatre]

[C1:741] Larsson, Börje, 'Två män som vågat trotsa etablissemanget', *Statsanställd* (Stockholm), 1988: 1, pp. 18-19. ['Two Men who Dared Defy the Establishment'. Compares Sg and the Swedish proletarian novelist Ivar Lo-Johansson (1901-1990) as two authors who used their writing to challenge the established social and political order]

[C1:742] Larue, Anne, *Délire et tragèdie: Sénèque: Hercule furieux, Shakespeare: Le roi Lear, Strindberg: Père*, Mont-de-Marsan: Editions Interuniversitaires, 1995. Illus. 303 pp. [A study of mental illness in literature and its links with tragedy and hysteria in plays by Seneca (*Hercules Furens*), Shakespeare (*King Lear*), and Sg (*Fadren*)]

[C1:743] Lavrin, Janko, 'Huysmans and Strindberg', in *Studies in European Literature*, London: Constable and Co., Ltd., 1929, pp. 118-134. [Describes how both Sg and J.-K. Huysmans reacted against naturalism and 'were strongly introspective…it was through their exaggerated introspection…that they came into contact with the irrational contradictions, puzzles and mysteries of the modern psyche'. Lavrin compares *Inferno* and *Legender* with Joris-Karl Huysman's novels *Là Bas* (1891) and *En Route* (1895)]

[C1:744] Lavrin, Janko, 'Huysmans and Strindberg', in *Studies in European Literature*, New York: Ray Long and Richard R. Smith, Inc., 1930, pp. 118-134. [North-American edition of **C1:743**]

[C1:745] Lavrin, Janko, 'Huysmans and Strindberg', in *Studies in European Literature*, Port Washington, N.Y.; London: Kennikat Press, 1970, pp. 118-134. [Facsimile Rpr. of **C1:743**]

[C1:746] Lavrin, Janko, 'Huysmans in Strindberg', *Ljubljanski zvon* (Ljubljana), 1928:12, pp. 734-741. [Presents substantially the same text as the chapter on Huysmans and Sg in **C1:743**]

[C1:747] Laxness, Halldór, *Úngur eg var*, Reykjavík: Helgafell, 1976. 243 pp. [Laxness's autobiography which includes an account of his teenage admiration for Sg, whose *Inferno* almost convinced him that he was not mad enough to become a writer]

[C1:748] Lazurskii, V., 'Dnevnik', in *L. N. Tolstoi v vospominaniiakh sovremennikov*, Moscow: Izdatel'stvo Akademii nauk, 1960, Vol. II. [Records Leo Tolstoi's appreciation of Sg's pacifism in the story 'Samvetskval' (Remorse) from *Utopier i verkligheten*]

[C1:749] Lecercle, François, 'Vers une dramaturgie de l'intériorité: Le Délire et son spectateur', *Revue de littératures Française et Comparée* (Paris), 3 (1994), 209-14. ['For a Dramaturgy of Inwardness. Madness and Its Spectator'. Compares the representation of madness in drama, applying a psychoanalytical approach to *King Lear*, *Fadren*, and Seneca's *Hercules Furens*]

[C1:750] Leeney, Cathy, 'The New Woman in a New Ireland? *Grania* after Naturalism', *The Irish University Review: A Journal of Irish Studies* (Dublin), 34:1 (2004), 157-170. [Includes a comparison of *Fordringsägare* and *Fröken Julie*, two plays in which Sg explores a triangular relationship, with Lady Gregory's dramas *Grania* (1912) and *Kincora* (1905). 'Reading [the former] in relation with *Miss Julie* and *Creditors* reveals how radical Gregory's creation is, and yet how constrained her heroine is by mythic association, and by the iconography of Celtic fatefulness']

[C1:751] Lenas, Sverker, 'Den köttiga litteraturen', *Allt om böcker* (Stockholm), 1998:6, pp. 24-27. Illus. ['Literature with Flesh'. Comments on Sg in a discussion of food in literature devoted primarily to Rabelais and Calvino]

[C1:752] Lenormand, H[enri]-R[ené], *Les Confessions d'un auteur dramatique*, 2 vols, Paris: Editions Albin Michel, 1949-53, Vol. 1, pp. 251-256. ['The Confessions of a Dramatist'. Lenormand describes the impact which Max Reinhardt's productions of *Dödsdansen* and *Spöksonaten* made on him while he was convalescing in Switzerland during the First World War. He comments on *Tjänstekvinnans son* as well as what he considers the confessional dramas (e.g. *Till Damaskus*), and praises both Sg's subjectivity and the 'ambivalence' of his characters, which is a quality that he seeks to emulate in his own plays. Lenormand (1882-1951) was astonished by the affinity between Sg and Freud, whose writings he encountered at about the same time. Although he applauded the 'moral tortures and cruelties of malignant love' in the naturalistic plays, it was the subjective dramatist of the post-Inferno plays whom Lenormand most admired]

[C1:753] Lenormand, H[enri]-R[ené], 'Möte med Strindberg', *Svenska Dagbladet* (Stockholm), 17 January 1949. ['Encounter with Strindberg'. Recalls the initial impact which Sg's plays made on him. Published in conjunction with the centenary of Sg's birth]

[C1:754] Leopold, Lennart, *Skönhetsdyrkare och socialdemokrat. Studier in Bengt Lidforss litteraturkritiska gärning*, Hedemora: Gidlund, 2001. Illus. 547 pp. ['Worshipper of Beauty and Social-Democrat. Studies in Bengt Lidforss's Literary Critical Achievement'. Makes regular reference to Sg throughout, both as a writer and an occasional friend of Lidforss during the 1890s. Leopold focuses primarily on Lidforss's activity as a publicist and political essayist, most particularly in a detailed discussion of his role in the Sg Feud, to which he contributed *August Strindberg och den litterära nittittalsreklamen*, **T:299**, and an attack on the recently deceased Oscar Levertin, pp. 425-489. Includes a German summary, pp. 495-502, and a schematic diagram of the literary field in Sweden at the time of the Strindberg Feud]

[C1:755] Le Rider, Jacques, *Le Cas Otto Weininger*, Paris: Presses Universitaires de France, 1982. 255 pp. [See **C1:756**]

[C1:756] Le Rider, Jacques, *Der Fall Otto Weininger. Wurzeln des Antifeminismus und Antisemitismus*, übersetzung von Dieter Hornig, Wien-München: Löcker, 1984. [293] pp. [Revised and enlarged edition of **C1:755**. Reflects on the mutual admiration between Sg and Weininger which was based on their common antipathy to women, pp. 51-52, 57, 77, and 154-155]

[C1:757] Le Rider, Jacques, und Norbert Leser, *Otto Weininger. Werk und Wirkung*, Wien: Österreichischer Bundesverlag, 1984. 215 pp. [Sg is a recurring point of reference throughout a study of Weininger's work and his ideas on sex and gender]

[C1:758] Letsovich, V., '[Strindberg in the Misogynist Tradition of European Culture]', in L[ev] Gitel'man and V[alentina] Dianova, eds, **B1:148**, *Avgust Strindberg i mirovaia kul'tura. Materialy mezhvyzovskoi nauchnoi konferentsii. Stat'i. Soobshcheniia*, pp. 109-116.

[C1:759] Levander, Hans, '*Séraphita*: le roman de Balzac et son importance pour Strindberg', in Gunnel Engwall, red., **B1:121**, *Strindberg et La France*, pp. 53-64. ['Balzac's Novel *Séraphita* and its Importance for Strindberg'. Presents Balzac's novel *Séraphita* (1834-5) as a source of Swedenborgian ideas during Sg's Inferno crisis, with reference mainly to *Inferno* and *Legender*. As well as inspiring the creation of Eleonora in *Påsk*, Levander suggests that the eponymous heroine of *Séraphita* may also be relevant to the depiction of both Gerda in *Pelikanen* and the Young Lady in *Spöksonaten*, while *Le Père Goriot* is a likely intertext for *Röda rummet*]

[C1:760] Levy, Louis, 'Densamme, Holbergs Lucretia og Strindbergs Alice', *Tilskueren* (Copenhagen), 37:2 (1920), 372-377. ['The Same, Holberg's Lucretia and Strindberg's Alice'. Compares the character of Alice in *Dödsdansen* with Ludvig Holberg's Lucretia in his comedy *Den Vægelsindede* (The Weather-Cock, 1723), apropos performances of both plays at Copenhagen's Dagmar Theatre with Bodil Ipsen as Alice and Fru Bloch as Holberg's heroine]

[C1:761] Lide, Barbara, 'Strindberg and Molière – Parallels, Influence, Image', in Roger Johnson Jr., Edith S. Neumann, and Guy T. Trail, eds, *Molière and the Commonwealth of Letters: Patrimony and Posterity*, Jackson, Miss.: University of Mississippi Press, 1975, pp. 259-268. [Although Sg made some disparaging remarks about Molière, it is arguable that he admired the theatrical economy with which a character like Tartuffe is vivisected. A comparison reveals similarities between the Gustav-Tekla scene in *Fordringsägare* and the Elmire-Tartuffe scene, while the delayed entrance of the protagonist in *Tartuffe* may have influenced the construction of *Gustav Vasa*. Lide also notes that the account of Molière's staging techniques in H. A. Ring's *Teaterns historia* (1898) suggested to Sg how he might stage his plays at the Intimate Theatre with decorative economy]

[C1:762] Lidén, Arne, 'Strindberg', in *Den norska strömningen i svensk litteratur under 1800-talet*, Uppsala: Almqvist & Wicksell boktryckeri A.B., 1926, pp. 226-291. [Traces the influence of contemporary Norwegian writers, including Ibsen and Kielland, on Sg's works up to, and including, *Lycko-Pers resa*]

[C1:763] Liedgren, Emil, 'Åttiotalsrealismen och vår tid', in *Kyrka och dikt. Några uppsatser*, Stockholm, 1917, pp. 55-71. ['Eighties Realism and Our Time']

[C1:764] Liedgren, Emil, 'Det realistiska genombrottet i vår litteratur', in *Kyrka och dikt. Några uppsatser*, Stockholm, 1917, pp. 28-54. ['The Realistic Breakthrough in Our Literature'. Includes Sg in a discussion of Swedish writing in the 1880s and after]

[C1:765] Liljegren, S. B., 'Randanmärkningar till temat Shakespeare-Strindberg', in *Festskrift till Anders Karitz*, Skrifter utgivna av Föreningen för filosofi och specialvetenskap 1, Uppsala and Stockholm: Almqvist & Wicksell, 1946, pp. 136-138. ['Marginalia on the Theme Shakespeare-Strindberg']

[C1:766] Lindahl, Ivar, 'Zarathustra och hans apa', *Lantarbetaren* (Stockholm), 39:2 (1954), 12-13. ['Zarathustra and His Ape'. Discusses Sg, Nietzsche, and the Scanian socialist, Axel Danielsson]

[C1:767] Lindberg, Per, '*Strindberg and Shakespeare*', *Bonniers Litterära Magasin* (Stockholm), 2:6 (1933), 42-47. [Reflections prompted by Joan Bulman's monograph, **C1:250**, by the eminent Swedish theatre director, who had written an academic study of *Mäster Olof*, **E5:65**, as well as staged the play]

[C1:768] Lindberger, Örjan, 'Some Notes on Strindberg and Péladan', in Marilyn Johns Blackwell, ed., **C1:142**, *Structures of Influence*, pp. 245-255. [Documents Sg's admiration for the French symbolist and Rosicrucian novelist and dramatist, Joséphin Péladan (1859-1918), with reference to *Ockulta dagboken*, his correspondence, and *Götiska rummen*. Lindberger points out that Péladan's conception of the adrogyne in his novel *Le Prince de Byzance* (1896) also combines sexual with spiritual love, and is pertinent to *Påsk*, *Till Damaskus III*, *Kristina*, and *Ett drömspel*, all of which were written with Harriet Bosse in mind. Meanwhile, he suggests that the fluid dialogue and lyric intensity of Péladan's plays may likewise have been of significance for the development of Sg's later dramaturgy]

[C1:769] Lindberger, Örjan, 'Strindberg, Bosse och Péladan', *Artes* (Stockholm), 11:4 (1985), 90-96. Illus. [Swedish version of **C1:768**]

[C1:770] Lindberger, Örjan, 'Strindberg var ett kinkigt problem för Rydberg', *Aftonbladet* (Stockholm), 11 July 1935. ['Strindberg was a Tricky Problem for Rydberg'. Comments on the difficulties Viktor Rydberg experienced in relating to Sg, both as a person and a writer. Lindberger also compares *Mäster Olof* with Axel Krook's novel *Tro och otro* to which he suggests it is indebted]

[C1:771] Linde, Ebbe, 'Drömstilen hos Strindberg och Kafka', *Bonniers Litterära Magasin* (Stockholm), 15:9 (1946), 760-765. ['The Dream Style in Strindberg and Kafka'. Points out that, whereas Sg's dream plays depict a clearly ordered, artistically composed world, rich in colour, plastic, expressive, and effective in a way seldom encountered in dreams, the frighteningly indefinite and indeterminate nature of Kafka's world suggests it was contrived out of real dream materials. In Sg the idea of dream is a working hypothesis, but in Kafka it is as if one subconscious is speaking directly to another, which makes the symbolic content of his works more readily accessible]

[C1:772] Lindeberg, Leo, 'De ryske diktarna och Strindberg', *Dagens Nyheter* (Stockholm), 7 February 1955. ['The Russian Writers and Strindberg']

[C1:773] Linder, Sten, *Ernst Ahlgren i hennes romaner*, Stockholm: Albert Bonniers Förlag, 1930. 429 pp. ['Ernst Ahlgren in her Novels'. Sg is a frequent point of reference and comparison in discussions of Ahlgren's (pseudonym of Victoria Benedictsson) novels *Pengar* and *Fru Marianne*, focusing especially on the status of women and marriage, self-realisation, 'livsglädje' (joy of life), and the polarity between a rural working environment and urban cultivation. Linder discusses *Likt och olikt*, *Tjänstekvinnans son*, *Röda rummet*, and *Kamrater*, and suggests that 'Mot betalning' (For Payment) in *Giftas* is a source text for *Hedda Gabler*]

[C1:774] Linder, Sten, 'Ibsen och Strindberg. En litteraturpsykologisk parallell', *Samlaren* (Uppsala), 13 (1932), pp. 52-105. ['Ibsen and Strindberg. A Literary Psychological Parallel'. Draws a detailed comparison of the two dramatists' careers, works, and personalities. Whereas Ibsen strives for unity, Sg's experiments foster multiplicity. Ibsen seeks perfection within bounds, and his work is relatively even in quality; Sg's is richly various but he is an extremely uneven writer. Linder also discusses Sg's generally positive early response to Ibsen (the heroes of *Röda rummet* and *Mäster Olof* are more or less copies of Brand and his first dramatic masterpiece, in which a reformer's beliefs bring him into conflict with his family and society, follows the pattern of Ibsen's verse drama). He then charts his increasingly fierce dialogue with the Ibsen of *A Doll's House* in *Herr Bengts hustru*, *Kamraterna*, and *Giftas*]

[C1:775] Linder, Sten, 'Ibsen och Strindberg. En litteraturpsykologisk parallell', in *Ibsen, Strindberg och andra. Litteraturhistoriska essayer*, Stockholm: Albert Bonniers Förlag, 1936 pp. 11-96. Illus. ['Ibsen and Strindberg. A Literary-Psychological Parallel'. Substantially the same as **C1:774**]

[C1:776] Linder, Sten, 'Strindberg och Levertin', *Svensk Litteraturtidskrift* (Stockholm), 2:3 (1939), 97-103. [Discusses the antipathy which Sg expressed for the Swedish critic Oscar Levertin in *En blå bok* and maintains that the latter's short story 'I elfte timmen' (At the Eleventh Hour) is a relevant intertext for Sg's 'Samvetskval' (Remorse) in *Utopier i verkligheten*]

[C1:777] Lindhé, May, *Anna Branting. Ett literärt författarskap i skuggan av förvärvsarbete och politik*, Uppsala: Centrum för kvinnolitteraturforskning, 1998. 81 pp. [Studies Anna Branting's achievement as a writer, including the theatre criticism which she wrote under the pseudonym 'René', and where she frequently found fault with Sg's post-Inferno plays]

[C1:778] Lindqvist, Sigvard, *Symbolism i det svenska 1890-talets litteratur*, Jönköping: Wettern, 1985. 149 pp. ['Symbolism in Swedish Literature in the 1890s']

[C1:779] Lindström, Erik, *Nordisk folklivsskildring*, Stockholm: P. A. Norstedt & Söners Förlag, 1932. 250 pp. [Includes *Hemsöborna*, *Skärkarlsliv*, and 'En ovälkommen' (An Unwelcome Guest) in a discussion of the portrayal of the ordinary people in the literature of the 1880s, pp. 119-127. Comments on the concept of primitivism in *Skärkarlsliv* and the essays of *Likt och olikt* as well as the image of natural man vis-à-vis cultivated man in Sg's writings during this period. For Lindström, *Hemsöborna* is typical of this phase of Sg's career in its positivistic approach, and it displays more surface glitter than substance. Real social problems are air-brushed out even though the novel is based on considerable first-hand study and has meant much for later literary accounts of rural life. By *I havsbandet* in 1890, however, the people of the archipelago are being judged on scientific rather than moral grounds, and they appear dull, backward, and ignoble]

[C1:780] Lindström, Göran, 'Fadren i dockhemmet. Något om Strindberg og Ibsens Nora', *Samtiden* (Oslo), 66:4 (1957), 239-255. ['The Father in the Doll's House. On Strindberg's Nora and Ibsen's'. Sg's *Kamraterna* is a direct parody of *A Doll's House*, a play which is of relevance to numerous works in which Sg opposed Ibsen's view of 'Nora-woman' and marriage. Lindström also discusses *Herr Bengts hustru*, 'Ett dockhem' (A Doll's House) in *Giftas*, and *Fadren*, where the Captain's doubts about his daughter's paternity and a young girl over whom the adults fight recall *The Wild Duck*]

[C1:781] Lindström, Gösta, 'Strindberg och "dekadentpoeten" Emil Kléen', *Bokvännen* (Stockholm), 93:4 (1988), 74-78. ['Strindberg and "The Decadent Poet" Emil Kléen'. Presents Sg's friendship with the young Scanian poet and journalist (1868-98) for whose posthumous collection of poems he wrote an introduction]

[C1:782] Lindström, Hans, *Hjärnornas kamp. Psykologiska idéer och motiv i Strindbergs åttiotalsdiktning*, Uppsala: Appelbergs Boktryckeri AB, 1952. [330] pp. ['The Battle of the Brains. Psychological Ideas and Motifs in Strindberg's Writing in the 1880s'. Describes how, in the mid-1880s, Sg turns away from the socially engaged literature which had made him the leading Swedish exponent of Naturalism and its most prominent representative in the literature of the Scandinavian Modern Breakthrough. Prompted in part by the prolonged self-scrutiny that *Tjänstekvinnans son* entailed, he now became deeply concerned with psychological ideas. Comparisons with Ola Hansson, Herman Bang, J. P. Jacobsen, Gustaf af Geijerstam, and Victoria Benedictsson indicate that this shift was in keeping with developments elsewhere in Scandinavia, as well as with the pretensions to a scientific literature entertained by French writers such as Guy de Maupassant, the Goncourt brothers, Flaubert, Alphonse Daudet, Paul Bourget, Édouard Rod, and Emile Zola, all of whom were responding in various ways to the contemporary psychological investigations of Claude Bernard, Jean-Martin Charcot, Hippolyte Taine, Hippolyte Bernheim, Théodule Ribot, Henry Maudsley, and Cesare Lombroso. Together with Max Nordau and, in due course, Nietzsche, such psychological studies now became Sg's principal reading matter and stimulated both his deeply rooted inclination to self-analysis and his interest in the unconscious and heightened, or exceptional, states of mind. This includes not least the kind of psychological mysticism associated with such marginal figures as Mesmer, Carl du Prel, and Carl von Bergen, as well as the philosophers Eduard von Hartmann and Schopenhauer, in both of whom he had a longstanding interest. Precisely how these ideas influenced the subjects and form of Sg's writing during the latter half of the 1880s is demonstrated with reference to 'En häxa' (A Witch), 'Genvägar' (Short Cuts, 1887), *Fordringsägare*, 'Tschandala', *Paria*, *Skärkarlsliv*, *Fröken Julie*, *Samum*, *I havsbandet*, and the *Vivisektioner* of 1887, most notably 'Hjärnornas kamp' (The Battle of the Brains). Lindström also compares these works with his naturalistic approach to characterisation in *Giftas* and *Utopier i verkligheten*. This enduring study documents the intellectual ferment of the 1880s in both Scandinavia and Europe and establishes the common concerns of literature and science during one of Sg's most creative periods, while Lindström also discusses his interest in the psychopathology of crime and the theories of moral and physiological degeneration associated with Cesare Lombroso and others. He also comments on Sg's enthusiasm for Edgar Allan Poe, compares him with numerous Scandinavian and European writers of the period, among them Dostoevskii, and indicates how the preoccupations of the Sgian vivisector of the 1880s frequently prefigure those of the Inferno period. Doctoral dissertation]

[C1:783] — Ahlenius, Holger, *Bonniers Litterära Magasin* (Stockholm), 22 (1953), 224-225.

[C1:784] — Ahlström, Stellan, *Afton-Tidningen* (Stockholm), 20 May 1952.

[C1:785] — Beck, R., *Books Abroad* (Norman, Oklahoma), 28 (1954), p. 496.

[C1:786] — Björck, Staffan, 'Strindbergs psykologi', *Dagens Nyheter* (Stockholm), 9 June 1952. ['Strindberg's Psychology']

[C1:787] — Dahlström, Carl E. W. L., *Scandinavian Studies* (Menasha, Wisconsin), 25:2 (1953), 75-77.

[C1:788] — Hallsten, Olof, *Metallarbetaren* (Stockholm), 63:31-2 (1952), pp. 8-9.

[C1:789] — Landquist, John, 'Strindberg och suggestionen', *Aftonbladet* (Stockholm), 27 May 1952. ['Strindberg and Suggestion']

[C1:790] — Landquist, John, 'Strindberg och suggestionen', in Solveig Landquist, **B1:248**, *John Landquist om Strindberg*, pp. 180-183. [Rpr. of **C1:789**]

[C1:791] — Norberg, Elsa, *Samlaren* (Uppsala), 33 (1952), pp. 115-123. [Essay review by Lindström's faculty opponent, who argues that W. Wundt's *Grundzüge der physiologischen Psychologie* influenced Sg's early art criticism and made him receptive to the theories of Théodule Ribot and other French psychologists during the later 1880s]

[C1:792] — Rinman, Sven, 'Åttiotalets ockultism och Strindberg', *Göteborgs Handels- och Sjöfartstidning*, 9 May 1953. ['Strindberg and Occultism in the 1880s']

[C1:793] — Svanberg, Victor, 'Strindberg förvandlas', *Stockholms-Tidningen*, 8 June 1952. ['Strindberg Transformed']

[C1:794] — Wallquist, Ö., *Arbetaren* (Stockholm), 30 January 1953.

See also **A4:1, A4:68, B2:237**

[C1:795] Lindström, Hans, 'Strindberg och kriminalpsykologien', in Gunnar Brandell, red., **B1:82**, *Synpunkter på Strindberg*, pp. 135-150. ['Strindberg and Criminal Psychology'. Excerpted from the discussion in **C1:782** of Sg's interest in psychopathology, degeneration, and criminality in which Lindström stresses his links during the late-1880s with the crime fiction of Edgar Allan Poe, Émile Gaboriau, and Ola Hansson, and the theories on criminology of, among others, Cesare Lombroso and Nietzsche]

[C1:796] Lingard, Lorelei, 'The Daughter's Double Bind: The Single-Parent Family as Cultural Analogue in Two Turn-of-the-Century Dramas', *Modern Drama* (Toronto), 40:1 (1997), 123-138. [Compares *Fröken Julie* with *Hedda Gabler* as two among many late 19th-Century plays in which the single-parent family symbolises dysfunction and reflects a functional flaw in society as a whole. The harsh closure of both plays indicates a need for change in prevailing social codes, not only so that women survive and emerge as a stronger and better species, but also so that human relationships as a whole evolve and flourish]

[C1:797] Lingard, Lorelei, 'The Daughter's Double Bind: The Single-Parent Family as Cultural Analogue in Two Turn-of-the-Century Dramas', in Janet Witalec, ed., **D2:348**, *Drama Criticism*, Volume 18, pp. 256-262. [Rpr. of **C1:796**]

[C1:798] Linzer, Martin, *Trilogie der Leidenschaft.* Medea *von Euripides,* Stella *von Goethe,* Totentanz *von Strindberg in Inszenierungen des Deutschen Theaters*, Regie Alexander Lang, Bühnenbild und Kostüme Volker Pfüller, fotogr. von Christian Brachwitz. Eingeleitet und Hrsg. von Martin Linzer. Mit einem Essay 'Über Theaterfotografie' von Ilse Galfert, Berlin: Henschelverlag Kunst und Gesellschaft, 1988. Illus. 189 pp. ['Trilogy of Passion. Euripides's *Medea*, Goethe's *Stella*, and Strindberg's *The Dance* *of Death* Produced in the German Theatre'. A richly illustrated study of three theatre productions by Alexander Lang]

[C1:799] Liotta, Giuseppe, 'Strindberg e Zola (ovvero la questione del naturalismo)', in Franco Perrelli, ed., **B1:365**, *Omaggio a Strindberg*, pp. 31-38. ['Strindberg and Zola (Concerning the Question of Naturalism)'. Compares Sg's developing understanding of literary naturalism with Zola's established template for the movement in *Le Naturalisme au théâtre* and the Preface to *Thérèse Raquin*. Liotta documents his recorded opinions of Zola and assesses his achievement as a naturalist, focusing on the plays of the 1880s from *Fadren* on, rather than the novels]

[C1:800] Ljung, Per Erik, 'August Strindberg, Vilhelm Ekelund och "uppsvenskarna"', *Strindbergiana* (Stockholm), 5 (1990), pp. 123-143. ['August Strindberg, Vilhelm Ekelund and the "Northern Swedes"'. Documents Sg's significant place in Ekelund's thought and writings. But whereas there are at least seventy references to Sg in Ekelund's (1880-1949) works, Sg does not appear to have concerned himself at all with either Ekelund or his work]

[C1:801] Ljung, Per Erik, *Vilhelm Ekelund och den problematiska författarrollen*, Lund: LiberLäromedlet, 1980. 287 pp. [Compares the Swedish poet and essayist Ekelund (1880-1949) with Sg in a study of the problematical role of the writer in modern Sweden]

[C1:802] Ljungdorff, V., 'E. T. A. Hoffmann och Sverige', 1-2, *Edda* (Oslo), 18 (1918), pp. 96-140, 249-295. [Includes Sg only briefly (pp. 289-292) in a survey of Hoffmann's significance for Swedish literature. Refers to the story 'Den romantiske klockaren på Rånö' (The Romantic Sexton on Rånö) in *Skärkarlsliv*, 'För konsten' (For Art) in *I Vårbrytningen*, 'Pantomimer på gatan' (Street Pantomimes), *Svarta fanor*, *Till Damaskus*, and *Spöksonaten*]

[C1:803] Ljungren, Magnus, 'Aleksandr Blok och Strindbergs ansikte', *Strindbergiana* (Stockholm), 4 (1989), pp. 100-126. Illus. ['Aleksandr Blok and Strindberg's Face'. A usefully documented account of the importance which Sg (and especially his face) held for Blok during a difficult period of his life in 1911-12, when he read *Ensam*, *Röda rummet*, and *I havsbandet*, and even considered visiting Sg in Stockholm. Blok recognises his own situation in *Tjänstekvinnans son*, *En dåres försvarstal*, and *Inferno*, which he discusses with (among others) Andrey Bely. Ljungren comments on the poetic sequence *Pljaski smerti* (Dances of Death) and Blok's essay on Sg, as well as his links with Meyerhold, who staged *Brott och brott* with Blok's wife as Jean. He also discusses Nikolai Kulbin, whose portrait of Sg exerted an almost occult influence over Blok. Ljungren documents the contact which Blok made with Sg's eldest daughter, Karin, and her Russian husband, Wladimir Smirnoff, via his friend Vladimir Piast, who visited Stockholm on his behalf towards the end of Sg's life]

[C1:804] Ljungquist, Sarah, *Den litterära utopin och dystopin Sverige 1734-1940*, Hedemora: Gidlunds Förlag, 2001. Illus. 319 pp. ['Literary Utopia and Dystopia in Sweden, 1734-1940'. Mentions Sg only in passing. Ljungquist considers neither 'Nybyggnad' (New Building) nor 'De lyksaliges ö' (The Isle of the Blessed), although one of Sg's political mentors of the early 1880s, Nils Herman Quiding, is discussed in some detail]

[C1:805] Löfman, Nils, 'Strindberg – Anacreon', *Modersmålslärarnas förening årskrift* (Lund), 1949, pp. 214-218. [Points out that both the elderly Sg's interest in the middle ages, which is reflected in the typography of the first edition of *En blå bok*, and his emotional involvement with the young Fanny Falkner, are evoked by the pseudonym 'Anacreon Monachus', with which he twice signed his correspondence with Albert Engström. The hermit-like Anacreon confronted by Amor resembles the ageing, sick, and pious Sg, tormented by his erotic feelings for Falkner]

[C1:806] Loliée, Frederic, *A Short History of Comparative Literature, from the Earliest Times to the Present Day*, London: Hodder and Stoughton, 1907, p. 304. [One of the earliest mentions of Sg in an English literary history]

[C1:807] Lotass, Lotta, '"Bortom alla horisonter är öar" – Stig Dagermans *Upptäcksresanden* mot bakgrund av August Strindbergs kartografi och Sven Hedin', *Samlaren* (Uppsala), 122 (2001), pp. 62-73. ['"Beyond every Horizon there are Islands": Stig Dagerman's *The Explorer* in Light of August Strindberg's Cartography and Sven Hedin'. With its partly veiled attack on Sven Hedin, Lotass suggests that the play *Upptäcksresanden* (The Explorer) by the Swedish author Stig Dagerman (1923-54) draws on the criticism that Sg had directed against the well-known Swedish traveller and explorer during the Strindberg Feud]

[C1:808] Lott, Robert E., 'Scandinavian Reminiscences in Antonio Buero Vallejo's Theater', *Romance Notes* (Chapel Hill, North Carolina), 7 (1966), 113-116. [Identifies Miss Y in *Den starkare* as an obvious precedent for the role of Anita in Vallejo's play *Las cartas boca abajo*. Sg is often evoked in his frequent treatment of family bickerings and hatred. Like Lorca, Vallejo was able to adapt Sg's war between the sexes in *Fadren* and *Ett drömspel* to Spanish themes and situations]

[C1:809] Loving, Pierre, 'Eugene O'Neill', *The Bookman* (New York), 53 (August 1921), 511-520. [An early journalistic account of O'Neill, in whose work the influence of Sg can be detected]

[C1:810] Lüger, Bernt, 'Prins, Netscher en Strindberg', *Bzzlletin* [Sic] (Amsterdam), 14, No. 129 (1929), 67-70. [Considers Sg's impact on the Dutch writers Arij Prins (1860-1922) and Frans Netscher (1864-1923)]

[C1:811] Lumsden, James A., 'Sartre and Strindberg', *The Times Literary Supplement* (London), 23 November, 1946, p. 577. [A letter. Draws specific comparisons between Sartre's play *Huis Clos* (1945) and *Brott och brott* as claustrophobic dramas in which the setting is hell]

[C1:812] Lucas, F[rank] L[awrence], *The Drama of Ibsen and Strindberg*, London: Cassell, 1962. Illus. 484 pp. [Less a proper comparison, more a worthless diatribe of prejudice and misreading, which praises Ibsen at Sg's expense and directs at the latter the kind of mindless vituperation originally reserved by English critics of the late-19th Century for the Norwegian dramatist. Lucas regards most of Sg's work as 'not only bad, but evil', and he laments that 'even in England' *Dödsdansen* 'has sometimes been thought by academic minds worth setting in University examinations'. For Lucas, who does not have the excuse of not being able to read Sg or the critical literature about him in the original Swedish, the latter is 'one of those writers who have tended to debase the world's moral currency'. Fortunately, the evil he did his contemporaries is now over 'except in so far as he can still corrupt the unbalanced reader'. Maintaining that Sg is 'like a poisoned rat in a hole', a 'cad', and the author of 'odious, diseased and corrupting' plays, such as 'the clever, cruel, and nasty…ballet of three clockwork toads' that is *Fordringsägare*, Lucas's loosely-written and subjective study, with its sinister suggestion that the characters of Tennessee Williams, like Sg's, should be removed to an extermination camp, confirms its author as just as unbalanced and neurotic as he makes his subject out to be]

[C1:813] — Anon, 'Sardonic English Critic Makes a Scandinavian Journey', *The Times* (London), 17 May 1962.

[C1:814] — Anon, 'F. L. Lucas, *Ibsen and Strindberg*', *The Times Literary Supplement* (London), 18 May 1962. [Prompts a letter, 25 May]

[C1:815] — Brandell, Gunnar, *Svenska Dagbladet* (Stockholm), 4 June 1962.

[C1:816] — Bredsdorff, Elias, *Scandinavica* (London), 1:2 (1962), 140-143.

[C1:817] — Clay, James H., *Quarterly Journal of Speech* (Annandale, Virginia), 49:2 (1963), 201-202.

[C1:818] — Deer, Irving, *Educational Theatre Journal* (Washington, D.C.), 18:3 (1966), 216-217.

[C1:819] — Fenger, Henning, *Kvällsposten* (Malmö), 9 June 1962.

[C1:820] — Garnett, David, 'Ibsen after the Ibsenites', *The Observer* (London), 20 May 1962. ['After Ibsen, Strindberg is a cold potato....Mr Lucas, though he does not like Sg, is scrupulously fair to him, and one could not have a better factual account of the monster']

[C1:821] — Kejzlar, Radko, 'Strindberg och den moderna teatern: Några anmärkningar med anledning av Mr. Lucas' bok', *Meddelanden från Strindbergssällskapet* (Stockholm), 40-41 (1968), pp. 16-23. ['Strindberg and the Modern Theatre: Some Notes in Respect of Mr. Lucas's Book'. Kejzlar argues that Lucas fails to observe the basic responsibilities of a literary critic; his own prejudices lead him into misrepresenting the literary works he is judging, and examples taken from *Dödsdansen* and *Spöksonaten* demonstrate his comprehensive misrepresentation of Sg's achievement]

[C1:822] — Landquist, John, 'Smädeskrift mot Strindberg', *Aftonbladet* (Stockholm), 13 July 1963. ['A Libel against Strindberg']

[C1:823] — Rinman, Sven, *Göteborgs Handels- och Sjöfartstidning*, 2 October 1962.

[C1:824] — Scobbie, Irene, *Modern Drama* (Lawrence, Kansas), 5:3 (1962), p. 379.

[C1:825] Lundegård, Erik, 'När Strindberg kommenterade *Pengar*', *Bokvännen* (Stockholm), 24 (1969), 171-174. ['When Strindberg Commented on *Money*'. Documents the dialogue that Sg conducted with his Swedish contemporary, Victoria Benedictsson, in his marginalia to a copy of her novel *Pengar* (1885)]

[C1:826] Lundgren, Lars O., *Liv, jag förstår dig inte. Hjalmar Söderbergs Doktor Glas*, Stockholm: Carlssons, 1987, pp. 90-94. ['Life, I don't Understand You. Hjalmar Söderberg's *Doktor Glas*'. Discusses the story 'Dygdens lön' (The Reward of Virtue) from *Giftas* and *Ensam* in examining Sg's influence on Söderberg's novel, *Doktor Glas* (1905)]

[C1:827] Lundgren, Lars O., '"Min ungdoms stora bloss"', *Parnass* (Stockholm), 1994:1, pp. 20-23. Illus. ['The Greatest Flame of My Youth. Hjalmar Söderberg on August Strindberg'. Discusses the enthusiastic response of the Swedish novelist Hjalmar Söderberg (1869-1941) to Sg's pre-Inferno works]

[C1:828] Lundgren, Lars O., '"Min ungdoms stora bloss". Hjalmar Söderberg om August Strindberg', *Strindbergiana* (Stockholm), 18 (2003), pp. 141-170. Illus. ['"The Greatest Flame of my Youth". Hjalmar Söderberg on August Strindberg'. Documents Söderberg's admiration for the early Sg, whose *Fröken Julie* was the subject of his first (unpublished) article for *Dagens Nyheter*. Lundgren also accounts for his lack of sympathy with the religiously inflected post-Inferno works. He points out that, although Söderberg was never close to Sg personally, he wrote about him and his works in several articles, as well as in his novel *Den allvarsamma leken* (1912) and the polemical prose works *Hjärtats oro* (1909) and *Jesus Barabbas* (1928). A fuller version of **C1:827**]

[C1:829] Lundgren, Lars O., '"Den visaste i antiken". Strindberg om Sokrates', in *Den svenske Sokrates. Sokratesbilden från Rydelius till Gyllensten*, Svenska Humanistiska Förbundet, Lund, Hilding Hansson i distr., 1980, pp. 109-132. ['"The Wisest in Antiquity". Strindberg on Socrates'. A general study of the image of Socrates in Swedish literature which documents Sg's youthful reading in Latin and Greek and his familiarity with Axel Krook's novel *Tro och otro* (Belief and Unbelief), in which Socrates is depicted as a freethinker, as well as his opinion of Socrates throughout the different phases of his life. Lundgren discusses *Fritänkaren*, *Röda rummet*, 'Latin eller svenska', *Sömngångarnätter*, *Giftas*, the essay on Voltaire, *En blå bok*, 'Världshistoriens mystik' (The Mysticism of World History), *Historiska miniatyrer*, and the trilogy of world-historical plays, including *Hellas* (or *Sokrates*, 1903). He concludes that Socrates remained throughout Sg's life one of the most important figures of antiquity, an interest originally encouraged by his early reading of Kierkegaard and the Danish romantic poet and dramatist Adam Oehlenschläger. Lundgren also comments on Sg's knowledge of classical literature and languages in general]

[C1:830] Lundgren, Lars O., '"Den visaste i antiken!": Strindberg om Sokrates', *Radix* (Stockholm), 3:3-4 (1980), 275-302. Illus. ['"The Wisest in Antiquity". Strindberg on Socrates'. An edited and augmented version of the chapter on Sg and Socrates in **C1:829**]

[C1:831] Lundevall, Karl-Erik, 'Författarinkomster i slutet av 1800-talet', *Ekonomisk revy* (Stockholm), 1951:1, pp. 24-35. ['Writers' Incomes at the End of the 19th Century'. Studies the earnings of professional writers in Scandinavia at the end of the 19th Century. Discusses Sg, pp. 28-29]

[C1:832] Lundevall, Karl-Erik, *Från åttital till nittital. Om åttitalslitteraturen och Heidenstams debut och program*, Stockholm: Almqvist & Wiksell, 1953. 411 pp. ['From the Eighties to the Nineties. On the Literature of the 1880s and Heidenstam's Debut and Literary Programme'. Places Sg within the context of the realism which dominated Swedish literature during the 1880s. Lundevall defines the nature of this realism and charts the emergence of a new style, associated with Verner von Heidenstam (1859-1940), which opposed its documentary, scientific tendencies. However, he demonstrates that, in the 1880s, Sg's writing already contains examples of the lyricism which made Heidenstam's reputation, even though he responded critically to the latter's literary initiative in *I havsbandet*. English summary. Doctoral dissertation]

[C1:833] — Landquist, John, 'Strindberg som kansliråd', *Aftonbladet* (Stockholm), 25 March 1953. ['Strindberg as a Civil Servant']

[C1:834] Lundegård, Axel [Wilhelm], 'Det vittra decimalsystemet', *Afton-Tidning* (Stockholm), 9 June 1910. ['The Literary Decimal System'. A polemical article on what, for Lundegård in 1910, was the still relevant conflict between the literature written in Sweden during the 1880s, and associated primarily with Sg, and the literature of the 1890s, in the transition to which Verner von Heidenstam and Oscar Levertin are the foreground figures. Lundegård writes as the author of the autobiographical novel *Röde prinsen* (The Red Prince, 1889), in which this conflict is vividly portrayed, and from a perspective that had once made him the one-time colleague of both Sg and Victoria Benedictsson. In his opinion, the major fault line in Swedish literature occurs at the end of the 1870s, not in 1890 with Heidenstam and Levertin's manifesto *Pepitas bröllop*. Indeed, Lundegård maintains that during the 1880s Sg created a literature that was characterised not only by realism but by all the imagination and fantasy that Heidenstam and the writers of the next generation in Sweden made the prerequisites of their new literature]

[C1:835] Lundström, Gösta, 'Strindberg och "dekadentpoeten" Emil Kléen', *Bokvännen* (Stockholm), 43:4 (1988), 74-78. ['Strindberg and "The Decadent Poet" Emil Kléen'. Discusses Sg's personal and inspirational relationship with the much younger Scanian poet in Lund during the late 1890s and comments on the Preface which he wrote for a posthumous edition of Kléen's poems]

[C1:836] Lutteman, Sven, 'Hjalmar Söderberg som teaterkritiker', *Studiekamraten* (Tollarp), 57:9-10 (1975), 159-162. ['Hjalmar Söderberg as a Theatre Critic'. Notes Söderberg's critical response to Sg's post-Inferno dramas, notably *Till Damaskus*]

[C1:837] Luyat-Moore, Anne, 'Conrad's Feminine Grotesques', *The Conradian* (Hull), 2:1 (1986), 4-15. [Identifies common ground between Joseph Conrad's ridiculing of feminism in *Chance* and Sg's *Kamraterna*]

[C1:838] Luyat-Moore, Anne, 'The Swedish Connection to *Victory* and *Chance*', *Conradiana* (Lubbock, Texas), 18:3 (1986), 219-223. [Links Elis Heyst in *Påsk* with the Heyst of Joseph Conrad's novel *Victory*. Luyat-Moore also finds echoes of the Fyne subplot and the DeBarral main plot in *Chance* in Sg's play *Kamraterna*. She suggests, too, that Axel Ahlberg in the latter was another model for Heyst who, as 'Axel Heyst', is a composite of both these Sgian characters]

[C1:839] Lyday, Leon F., 'Whence Wolff's Canary? A Conjecture on Commonality', *Latin American Theatre Review* (Lawrence, Kansas), 16:2 (1983), 23-29. [Compares Egon Wolff's play *Flores de papel* with *Fröken Julie*]

[C1:840] Mack, Fritz, 'Von Strindberg bis Unruh', *Der Zwinger* (Dresden), 4 (1920), 621-624. ['From Strindberg to Unruh'. Examines the influence of Sg on the German expressionist dramatist, Fritz von Unruh (1885–1970)]

[C1:841] Mack, Fritz, 'Weib und Liebe im Drama der Jüngsten', *Illustrierte Zeitung* (Leipzig), 156 (1921), No. 4040, p. 58. ['Woman and Love in the Latest Drama'. Comments on the influence exerted by Sg upon recent German expressionist drama]

[C1:842] Magomedova, Dina, 'Blok and Strindberg: Notes on a Theme', in Michael Robinson, ed., **B1:379**, *The Moscow Papers*, pp. 133-140. [Clarifies Blok's ardent response to Sg's works in the light of recent Russian scholarship. Magomedova also draws parallels between events in Blok's life and Sg's autobiographical sequence *Tjänstekvinnans son*,

En dåres försvarstal, and *Inferno*, and points out the relevance of a hitherto overlooked set of notes by Blok on Sg]

[C1:843] Magris, Claudio, *Utopi och klarsyn. Modernismens sagor, förhoppningar och illusioner*, Översättning Barbro Andersson, Stockholm: Forum, 2001. 305 pp. [Includes comments on Sg's notion of Nemesis Divina which is compared with that of Linnaeus, and notes Theodor Fontane's revulsion at the revelatory personal discourse of *En dåres försvarstal*]

[C1:844] Mahal, Günther, *Naturalismus*, 2 Aufl., München: Fink Verlag, 1975. 260 pp. [Includes Sg briefly in a discussion of naturalism as a literary movement]

[C1:845] Makovitskii, D., *Iasnaia Poliana*, 2 Vols, Moscow: Zadruga, 1923, Vol. 2, p. 5. [Records Leo Tolstoi's comments on Sg. E.913]

[C1:846] Maksimov, D., *Poeziia i proza Aleksandra Bloka*, Leningrad: Sovetskii pisatel', 1975. 526 pp. [Comments on Sg's relevance for Blok in a study of his poetry and prose, pp. 438, 443-444. E.1084]

[C1:847] Malkin, Jeanette R., *Verbal Violence in Contemporary Drama: From Handke to Shepard*, Cambridge: Cambridge University Press, 1992, pp. 184-190. [*Fordringsägare*, *Bandet*, *Dödsdansen*, and *Fadren* define the cultural tradition behind Edward Albee's *Who's Afraid of Virginia Woolf*, but the shifting chain of incidents at the heart of Sg's theatre is transformed by Albee into strictly verbal moves. Sg's language reveals while Albee's enacts, and though he shares Sg's intensity and moral seriousness, as well as his surface realism and certain recurrent themes, Albee breaks out of the psychological Sgian model and travesties his seriousness]

[C1:848] Malmberg, Carl-Johan, 'Betrakta och gå vidare', *Kris* (Stockholm), 1988: 36-37, pp. 76-83. Illus. ['Look and Pass On'. Discusses Sg together with Dante, Adorno, Yeats, and Vilhelm Ekelund, illustrated with paintings by J. M. W. Turner]

[C1:849] Malmberg, Carl-Johan, 'En garde, Strindberg! Duellen som inspirationskälla', *Bonniers Litterära Magasin* (Stockholm), 62:4 (1993), 4-9. Illus. ['En garde, Strindberg! The Duel as a Source of Inspiration'. Discusses conflict as a source of artistic creation with reference to Sg and the Swedish painter Carl Larsson, as well as Gustav Mahler and Hans von Bülow]

[C1:850] Manheim, Michael, 'Eugene O'Neil and the Founders of Modern Drama', in Marc Maufort, ed., *Eugene O'Neill and the Emergence of American Drama*, Amsterdam: Rodopi, 1989, pp. 47-57. [Discusses O'Neill's relationship with the theatres of Ibsen and Chekhov, as well as Sg and postmodernism. Includes an analysis of the contradictory feelings which underlie the dialogue between Julie and Jean in *Fröken Julie*]

[C1:851] Mann, Thomas, 'August Strindberg', *Ost und West* (Berlin), 3:1 (1949), 24-25.

[C1:852] Mann, Thomas, 'August Strindberg', *Dagens Nyheter* (Stockholm), 16 May 1912. [A formal comment on Sg's significance as a European writer, made in conjunction with his recent death]

[C1:853] Mann, Thomas, 'August Strindberg', in *Altes und Neues: kleine Prosa aus fünf Jahrzehnten*, Frankfurt am Main: S. Fischer Verlag, 1953, pp. 233-236. [Rpr. of **C1:856**]

[C1:854] Mann, Thomas, 'August Strindberg', in *Altes und Neues: kleine Prosa aus fünf Jahrzehnten*, Berlin [East], 1956, pp. 233-236. [Rpr. of **C1:856**]

[C1:855] Mann, T[homas], 'Avgust Strindberg', Translated F. Zaibel, [*Collected Works*], Vol. 10, Moscow, 1961, pp. 438-441. [Russian translation of **C1:856**. E.983]

[C1:856] Mann, Thomas, 'Hyllning till August Strindberg', *Svenska Dagbladet* (Stockholm), 27 December 1948. ['Homage to August Strindberg'. Acknowledges the early impact that Sg's provocative work made on him. According to Mann, the universal nature of Sg's genius demands comparison with Goethe]

[C1:857] Mann, Tomasz, 'August Strindberg', Translated by Wanda Jedlicka, *Dialog* (Warsaw), 1961:2, pp. 101-102. [Polish translation of **C1:856**]

[C1:858] Mann, Thomas, 'August Strindberg' in *Eseja*, Wybór P. Hertza, redakeja M. Zurowskiego, Warszawa, 1964, pp. 443-444. [Polish translation of **C1:856**]

[C1:859] Mann, Thomas, 'August Strindberg', *Bühnen der Hansestadt Lübeck*, 1959-60, p. 85. [Rpr. of **C1:856**]

[C1:860] Mann, Thomas, 'Über August Strindberg I', in *Nachträge*, *Gesammelte Werke in dreizehn Bänden*, Frankfurt am Main: S. Fischer Verlag GmbH., 1974, pp. 817-818. ['On August Strindberg I'. Rpr. of Mann's response, dated 'München 10. Mai', to a questionnaire entitled 'Europa om August Strindberg', first published in *Dagens Nyheter*, 16 May 1912, **C1:852**, and again, without the concluding sentence, in *Frankfurter Zeitung*, 19 May 1912]

[C1:861] Mann, Thomas, 'Über August Strindberg II', in *Nachträge*, *Gesammelte Werke in dreizehn Bänden*, Frankfurt am Main: S. Fischer Verlag GmbH., 1974, pp. 869-870. ['On August Strindberg II'. Originally published in an issue of *Svensk litteraturtidskrift*, **C1:1255**, in response to a questionnaire marking the centenary of Sg's birth]

[C1:862] Mansson, Th., 'Rydberg och Strindberg. Några nya upplysningar till förhållandet mellan dem', *Aftonbladet* (Stockholm), 5 October 1945. ['Rydberg and Strindberg. Some New Information on their Relationship'. Examines the personal rather than the literary relationship between Sg and the Swedish poet and novelist Viktor Rydberg (1828-1895)]

[C1:863] Maraković, Ljubomir, 'Ekspresionizam u Hrvatskoj', *Cas* (Ljubljana), 17:5 (1923), pp. 289, 300.

[C1:864] Marcus, Carl David, 'Ibsen och Strindbergs dramer', 1-2, *Svenska Dagbladet* (Stockholm), 11 and 13 August 1921. ['Ibsen and Strindberg's Plays'. Compares and contrasts their plays in terms of 'open' and 'closed' dramatic form. In many respects, the Chamber Plays of 1907, in which the present is caught in the long reach of the past, resemble the Ibsen of *Ghosts* and *John Gabriel Borkman* most strongly, although in *Spöksonaten* Sg continues to take the open form that he adopts in *Till Damaskus* and *Ett drömspel* in the direction of poetry and music. Ibsen abandoned historical drama whereas it continues to offer Sg new perspectives, and many of the post-Inferno plays have an affinity with *Peer Gynt* and *Brand*. However, as musical variations on a theme, they are closer to Bach and Beethoven. Marcus also comments on their use of dialogue as well as their portrayal of women, and compares their protagonists, many of whom, with their revolutionary pathos and sense of calling, have a common source in the works of Kierkegaard. Reference is also made to *Fadren*, *Mäster Olof*, *Dödsdansen*, *Fordringsägare*, *Gustav Adolf*, *Brott och brott*, *Påsk*, *Fröken Julie*, and the vivisection 'Själamord' (Soul Murder, 1887), and Marcus notes the links between both dramatists and Nietzsche. Their heroes are afflicted with a sick conscience and the problem of guilt is at the heart of Sg's best plays. A rarely noted but relevant early essay]

[C1:865] Marcus, Carl David, 'Gerhart Hauptmann och det nordiska dramat', *Nordisk Tidskrift* (Stockholm), 8 (1932), 359-371 ['Gerhart Hauptmann and Scandinavian Drama'. Marcus focuses mainly on Hauptmann's debt to Ibsen but considers the possibility that, while *Gabriel Schillings Flucht* (1906) may owe something to *Fordringsägare*, both *Ett drömspel* and *Gustav Adolf* can also be indebted in turn to Hauptmann]

[C1:866] Marcus, Carl David, 'Nietzsche, Brandes und Strindberg', *Deutsches-nordisches Jahrbuch* (Jena), 1928, pp. 14-26. ['Nietzsche, Brandes, and Strindberg'. Examines Nietzsche's influence on Sg as it was mediated, in part at least, by Georg Brandes]

[C1:867] Marcus, Carl David, 'Ett ord om Ibsen och Strindbergs dramer', in *Nordiska essayer*, Helsingfors: Söderström & C:o Förlagsaktiebolaget, 1923, pp. 174-190. ['A Word about the Plays of Ibsen and Strindberg'. Rpr. of **C1:864**]

[C1:868] Marcus, Carl David, 'Strindberg och Wedekind', *Stockholms Dagblad*, 17 September 1923. [Compares Sg's characters with those of Frank Wedekind since both dramatists depict men and women as creatures entangled in the chains of sexuality. Marcus also explores the latter's possible debt to Sg]

[C1:869] Marcus, Carl David, 'Thomas Mann und das Nordische', *Deutsch-Nordisches Jahrbuch* (Jena), 1930, pp. 88-103. ['Thomas Mann and Scandinavia'. Comments briefly on Sg as one among several Scandinavian figures associated with Mann and his works]

[C1:870] Marcuse, Ludwig, 'Theologie des Eros. Strindberg und Wedekind', *Blätter des deutschen Theaters* (Berlin), 94 (1923), 1-5. ['The Theology of Eros. Strindberg and Wedekind'. Compares the two dramatists' attitudes to women and love]

[C1:871] Marowitz, Charles, 'Ibsen, Strindberg and the Sex War', *Contemporary Review* (London), 236 (1980), 147-149.

[C1:872] Marrone, Nicola, 'Strindberg/Moor', in Franco Perrelli, ed., **B1:365**, *Omaggio a Strindberg*, pp. 147-149. [Links Sg with Schiller's Karl Moor in *Die Räuber*, in which he once appeared, and Verdi's early opera *Il Masnedieri*, which is based on Schiller's play]

[C1:873] Marsicovétere y Durán, Miguel, *3 maestros*, Biblioteca Minima, Guatemala, C. A.: Editorial Minima, 1937. 32 pp. [Compares three 'master' dramatists: Racine, Georges Courteline, and Sg]

[C1:874] Masát, András, 'Die Insel und das Paradies. Zu Utopie und Utopieverlust bei Strindberg und Gauguin', in Walter Baumgartner and Thomas Fechner-Smarsly, Hrsg., **B1:19**, *August Strindberg: Der Dichter und die Medien*, pp. 58-82. ['The Island and Paradise. On Utopia and Utopia Lost in Strindberg and Gauguin'. Presents Sg's correspondence with the painter Paul Gauguin and their association in Paris in 1893-94. Masát comments on Sg's essays 'Des arts nouveaux! ou Le hasard dans la production artistique' (1894) and 'Qu'est-ce que le "moderne"?' (1894), and compares his vision of utopia in 'De lycksaliges ö' (The Isle of the Blessed) in *Svenska öden och äventyr* with Gauguin's painting 'Eiaha ohipa' (1896). According to Masát, they have common antecedents in Ludwig Tieck's *Alla-Moddin* (1790-91) and Adam Oehlenschläger's *Die Inseln im Südmeer* (1826), and draw inspiration from Rousseau's *Discours sur l'origine et les fondements de l'inégalité parmi les hommes* (1775). He also notes how Sg's writing resembles Gauguin's painting in the tension it displays between modernity and culture on the one hand, and nature and a critique of civilisation on the other]

[C1:875] Masinton, Charles, G., 'Strindberg and Hamsun', *Ohio Review* (Athens, Ohio), 14:1 (1972), 100-105.

[C1:876] Matthias, Klaus, *Thomas Mann und Skandinavien mit 2 Aufsätzen von Thomas Mann und 4 Faksimile-Seiten*, Lübeck: Verlag Max Schmidt-Römhild. 48 pp.+4 pp. facsimiles. ['Thomas Mann and Scandinavia with two Essays by Thomas Mann and Four Pages in Facsimile'. Provides bibliographical and other documentation concerning Mann's familiarity with Scandinavian literature and its significance for his work (Sg is discussed pp. 17-23). Matthias also publishes Mann's Nobel acceptance speech as well as the text of a lecture delivered in Copenhagen]

[C1:877] Mathieu, André, 'Strindberg, encore et toujours d'avant-garde malgré ses 150 ans', *Le Jardin d'Essai* (Paris), No. 15 (October-December 1999), pp. 15-18. ['Strindberg, still and forever Avant-Garde inspite of his 150 Years'. On Sg's enduring modernity, with reference to his autobiographical fictions and his relevance for the modern theatre, as well as the impact of his work on numerous later writers and dramatists, including Kafka, Adamov, and Beckett]

[C1:878] Matsson, Ragnar, 'Strindberg, Ekelund och ensamheten', *Studiekamraten* (Tollarp), 34 (1952), 102-105. ['Strindberg, Ekelund, and Solitude'. Compares the theme of solitude in works by Sg (most notably *Ensam*) and the Swedish poet and essayist Vilhelm Ekelund (1880-1949)]

[C1:879] Mazzarella, Merete, 'Förord', in Karl August Tavaststjerna, *Barndomsvänner*, Helsingfors: Schildts, 1988, pp. 5-9. [Confirms Tavaststjerna's admiration for the realism of *Röda rummet* and his intention of writing a Finland-Swedish counterpart to Sg's novel]

[C1:880] Maufort, Marc, 'The Playwright as Lord of Touraine: O'Neill and French Civilization', *English Studies* (Amersfoort, Holland), 71:6 (1990), 501-508. [An account of Eugene O'Neill's stay in the Loire Valley in 1929-31 and his reading of Sg]

[C1:881] Maury, Lucien, *Les Scandinaves et nous. Essai d'explication des relations littéraires franco-scandinaves*, Paris: Didot, 1948. 30 pp. [An essay on Franco-Scandinavian literary relations]

[C1:882] Mazor, Yair, 'August Strindberg and S. Y. Agnon: Swedish Cantons in the Regions of Modern Hebrew Literature', *Scandinavica* (Norwich), 24:1 (1985), 35-55. [Explores similarities between Sg's naturalistic plays (principally *Fröken Julie*) and the stories and novels of Samuel Joseph Agnon (1888-1970), who shared Sg's interest in the battle of the sexes and included several of his motifs, scenes, plot devices, characters, and methods of characterisation in his long novel *Shirah*. Largely identical with Chapter 5 in **C1:883**]

[C1:883] Mazor, Yair, *The Triple Cord: Agnon, Hamsun, Strindberg. Where Scandinavian and Hebrew Literature Meet*, Tel Aviv: Papyrus, 1987. 250 pp. [A poorly proofread as well as awkwardly written study of the influence exerted by Sg and (more especially) Knut Hamsun on the prose fiction of Samuel Joseph Agnon (1888-1970), who is indebted in his novel *Shirah* to the erotic motif of the shoe in *Fröken Julie* and, in *The Book of Deeds*, to the dreamlike qualities in many of Sg's works. In Mazor's reading, several of Agnon's novels and stories have numerous themes in common with Sg and, although mainly influenced by the naturalistic plays, he was also attracted to post-

Inferno works including *Ett drömspel* and *Spöksonaten*, as well as the autobiographical fictions of the 1880s]

[C1:884] Meidal, Björn, 'Författaren som detektiv. August Strindberg och Edgar Allan Poe. Några beröringspunkter', in Pär Hellström and Tore Wretö, red., *Läskonst, skrivkonst, diktkonst. Aderton betraktelser över dikt och diktande*, Festskrift till Thure Stenström 12/4 1987, Vänersborg: Askelin & Hägglund, 1987, pp. 147-160. ['The Author as Detective. August Strindberg and Edgar Allan Poe. Some Common Ground'. Meidal points out that, just as Sg wrote *Röda rummet* before he read Zola, so he completed 'Tschandala' before becoming acquainted with Poe, Nevertheless, Poe continues to have a discernible impact on his work in post-Inferno texts like *Ett drömspel* and *Spöksonaten*, as well as in those plays and stories he produced in the late-1880s, including *Samum* and *Paria*]

[C1:885] Meidal, Björn, 'Lotten Brenner, Indra's Daughter, Ugly Edith and Esther Borg: A Study of Hjalmar Bergman's novel *Lotten Brenners ferier*', in Sarah Death and Helena Forsås-Scott, eds, *A Century of Swedish Narrative*, Norwich: Norvik Press, 1994, pp. 119-135. [Primarily a reading of Bergman's neglected novel from 1928 in which Meidal identifies *Ett drömspel* and *Götiska rummen* as two of its significant intertexts]

[C1:886] Meidal, Björn, 'Ola Hansson and August Strindberg', in Lois Davis Vines, ed., *Poe Abroad: Influence, Reputation, Affinities*, Iowa City: University of Iowa Press, 1999, pp. 183-188. [Briefly records the impact of Poe on Hansson and Sg in the late 1880s. He was briefly Sg's literary ideal, sustaining his conception of 'the battle of the brains' and playing a central role as a symbolist guide. Poe is of possible importance for Sg's dreamplay technique and was paid lasting tribute in *Dödsdansen*, where the setting recalls the House of Usher and two of the characters are named Edgar and Allan]

[C1:887] Meidal, Björn, 'Odalmannen och vikingen. Bonden i svensk litteratur', in Bo Larsson, red., *Bonden i dikt och verklighet*, Skrifter om skogs- och lantbrukshistoria 4, Stockholm: Nordiska museet, 1993, pp. 5-21. Illus. ['Odal Man and the Viking. The Peasant in Swedish Literature'. Discusses the figure of the sedentary peasant – or 'free-farmer' – in Swedish literature with particular reference to Erik Gustaf Geijer's celebrated poem 'Odalmannen' (1811) and contrasts it with his complementary portrait of the Viking free booter in 'Vikingen' (1811), as well as with Sophie von Knorring's novel *Torparen och hans omgifning*, Gustaf af Geijerstam's short stories of the 1880s, and Sg's *Bland franska bönder* and *Hemsöborna*. Meidal points out that Sg is indebted for his concept of the peasant to Rousseau and polemicised widely against the industrial socialism of his friend Hjalmar Branting who considered the independent smallholder a relic of the past. He also suggests that Geijer's, sometimes opposing, protagonists, i.e. the mobile Viking and the sedentary peasant farmer, may be embodied in the characterisation of *Hemsöborna* in Carlson's encounter with the people of Hemsö]

[C1:888] Melberg, Arne, 'Modernist Time/Realist Time', in Danuta Fjellestad and Elizabeth Kella, *Realism and its Discontents*, Karlskrona: Blekinge Institute of Technology, 2003, pp. 155-167. [Includes Sg together with Proust, Musil, and Joyce in a comparative study of the treatment of time in literary realism and modernist prose fiction]

[C1:889] Melberg, Arne, 'Rilkes Malte – ännu en skandinav i Paris?', in *Läsa långsamt. Essäer om litteratur och läsning*, Eslöv: Brutus Österlings Bokförlag Symposion, 1999, pp. 109-125. ['Rilke's Malte. Yet another Scandinavian in Paris?' Rpr. of **C1:890**]

[C1:890] Melberg, Arne, 'Rilkes Malte: Ännu en skandinav i Paris?', *Working Paper* No. 57 (98), Centre for Cultural Research, University of Aarhus. ['Rilke's Malte. Yet another Scandinavian in Paris?' Links Rilke's account of Malte Laurids Brigge's life in Paris with previous accounts of largely solitary Scandinavian writers at large in the metropolis by Sophus Claussen, Sigbjørn Obstfelder, and Sg in both *Inferno* and *Legender*, with which Rilke was in some cases familiar. All of them aspire in some respect to the prose poetry into which Baudelaire had originally transposed the city in *Le Spleen de Paris*. Also published electronically: URL: www.hum.aau.dk/ckulturf /pages/ publications/ am/rilkes–malte.htm]

[C1:891] Meyer, Michael, 'Ibsen versus Strindberg', *Essays by Diverse Hands* (London), N.S. 42 (1982), pp. 1-14. [Contrasts Ibsen and Sg as the pioneers of modern drama, to the disadvantage of the latter, who, Meyer claims, 'wrote more rubbish than any other great writer'. Summarises their opinions of one another]

[C1:892] Mikhailovskii, B. V., 'Gor'kii i Skandinavskaia literatura', *Nauchnye doklady vysshei shkoly. Filologischeskie nauki*, 1960:2, pp. 90-98. ['Gor'kii and Scandinavian Literature'. Notes Maksim Gor'kii's admiration for Sg, pp. 90, 95-96. E.980]

[C1:893] Milochevitch, Nicolas, *Nietzsche et Strindberg: Psychologie de la connaissance*, Traduit du serbe par Zorica Hadji-Vidoïkovitch avec l'aide de Svetlana Nikchitch, Lausanne: L'Age d'homme, 1997. [331] pp. [Milochevitch is primarily concerned with Nietzsche but he also provides a psycho-biographical study of 'Le cas Strindberg' and an analysis of *Fröken Julie* and *Fadren*, pp. 217-285. This is conducted largely in terms of the sociology of knowledge but governed by the precepts of the new discipline of the psychology of knowledge, which these case studies are intended to define. He also discusses *En dåres försvarstal* in conjunction with *Fröken Julie*, and makes some comparisons between Sg's project and Nietzsche's, though with little evidence of any detailed primary knowledge of Sg's works]

[C1:894] Mints, Z[ara] G., 'Stikhotvorenie Al. Bloka' "Zhenshchina"', *Poeziia Aleksandra Bloka i fol'klorno-literaturnye traditsii*, Omsk, 1984, pp. 65-77. [Stresses the importance of Sg for Aleksandr Blok's incarnation trilogy in a study of traditional elements in his poetry. The latter's conception of the eternal feminine in his poem 'A Woman' is also indebted to Sg]

[C1:895] Mints, Z[ara] G., ed., in A. A. Blok, *Literaturnoe nasledstvo. Aleksandr Blok. Novye materialy i issledovaniia*, Moscow, 1981. [Blok's opinion of Sg as recorded in his correspondence with V[ladimir] A[lekseevich], Piast, pp. 74-92. E.1772]

[C1:896] Mirbeau, Octave, 'Knut Hamsun', *Le Journal* (Paris), 19 March 1895. [Introduces Hamsun and his first novel, *Sult* (Hunger), to a French readership via reference to Sg]

[C1:897] Misiak, Tomasz, 'Dramat a myslenie mityczne', *Dialog: Miesiecznik Posiecony Dramaturgii Wspolczesnej: Teatralnej, Filmowej, Radiowej, Telewizyj* (Warsaw), 26:3 (1981), 94-99. [An anthropological approach to genres in which *Ett drömspel* is compared with the absurdist plays of the Polish dramatist, Tadeusz Rozewicz (b.1921)]

[C1:898] Mjöberg, Jöran, *Drömmen om sagatiden*, Vol. 2, 'De senaste hundra åren – idealbildning och avidealisering', Stockholm: Natur och Kultur, 1968, pp. 138-142. ['The Dream of the Age of the Sagas. The Last Hundred Years'. Within the framework of what remains the standard work on the representation of the Viking period in later works of Scandinavian literature, Mjöberg discusses the stories which Sg devoted to the Viking period in *Nya svenska öden*, two of which convey a disgust with the Nordic past without previous parallel in literature. Mjöberg concludes that Sg's originality lies in his direct style and the way in which the cruel and grim events he depicts fill the reader with revulsion]

[C1:899] M. N., 'Das Sterben bei Ibsen und Strindberg', *Das Goetheanum* (Dornach), 40 (1961), 214-215. ['Death in Ibsen and Strindberg'. Compares the portrayal of death in *Peer Gynt* and *Ett drömspel*]

[C1:900] Moberg, Verne, 'In de voetstappen van Strindberg: een interview met Per Olov Enquist/In the Footsteps of Strindberg: An Interview with Per Olov Enquist', in Egil Törnqvist and A. Sonnen, eds, *Niet alleen Strindberg. Zweden op de Planken / Not Only Strindberg. Sweden on Stage*, Catalogue, Holland Festival, 1985, pp. 32-36. Illus. [An interview with Enquist on his view of Sg as man and writer. Dual Dutch-English text]

[C1:901] Moberg, Verne, 'Walking in Strindberg's Footsteps', *Sweden Now* (Stockholm), 18 (1984), 36-38. [See **C1:900**]

[C1:902] Moberg, Vilhelm, 'Böckerna i mitt liv', in *Berättelser ur min levnad*, Stockholm: Albert Bonniers Förlag, 1968, pp. 241-261. ['The Books in My Life'. The eminent Swedish novelist and dramatist (1898-1973) includes *Hemsöborna*, which he read by chance in 1913, among the books that made the greatest impact on his life and work. Moberg also expresses his admiration for the satirical vigour of *Det nya riket*]

[C1:903] Moerk, Ernst L., 'From War-Hero to Villain: Reversal of the Symbolic Value of War and a Warrior King', *Journal of Peace Research* (London), 35:4 (1998), 453-469. [Traces the changing image of Charles XII in Sweden as mediated via Swedish literature, exemplified here in works by Esaias Tegnér, Erik Gustaf Geijer, Verner von Heidenstam, and Sg]

[C1:904] Möhlig, Karl, 'Dante und Strindberg', in *Städtebilder und Kulturprobleme aus Italien. Betrachtungen über Erlebtes und Erschautes*, Elberfeld: Bergland Verlag, 1924, pp. 219-232.

[C1:905] Monneyron, Frédéric, 'Strindberg et Proust: deux écritures de la jalousie au tournant du siècle', *Revue de littérature comparée* (Paris), 67:4 (1993), 473-491. ['Strindberg and Proust: Two Discourses on Jealousy at the Turn of the Century'. Traces parallels in the ways both writers portray jealousy, exemplified by *Le Plaidoyer d'un fou* and *Un amour du Swann*]

[C1:906] Moorhouse, Frank, '[Untitled]', Översättning Heidi von Born, in [Born], red., **U1:149**, *Med himlen till tak...och Drottninggatan som golv. Femton balkongtal till Strindberg*, pp. 61-67. [Reflections by the Australian author on what Sg has meant to him. The text of a speech delivered at the Stockholm Sg Festival]

[C1:907] Morgenstern, Christian, 'Christian Morgenstern über Strindberg', *Die Kommenden* (Freiburg), 3:3 (1949), p. 7. ['Christian Morgenstern on Strindberg'. Reflections on Sg by the German poet and translator of *Inferno*]

[C1:908] Morgenstern, Christian, 'Strindberg', *Freiburger Theaterblätter*, 1929-30, pp. 286-287.

[C1:909] Morgenstern, Christian, 'Strindberg – ein genialer Sonderling?', *Das neue Forum* (Darmstadt), 1 (1921-22), 165-166. ['Strindberg – An Eccentric Genius?' See **C1:910**]

[C1:910] Morgenstern, Christian, 'Zum Thema Strindberg', *Der Bücherwurm* (Dachau bei München), 5 (1919–20), p. 50. ['On the Theme of Strindberg'. Reflections on Sg by the German poet and translator of *Inferno*]

[C1:911] Morgenstern, Christian, 'Zum Thema Strindberg', *Schwäbische Thalia* (Stuttgart), 8 (1926-27), 257-258. [Rpr. of **C1:910**]

[C1:912] Morimoto, Osamu, 'Akutagawa, Ryūnosuke ni okeru Strindberg', *Ritsumeikan bungaku*, 149 (1957). [Traces Sg's introduction to Japan and his influence on the Japanese novelist Ryūnosuke Akutagawa (1892-1927)]

[C1:913] Moricheva, M. D., '[A. Strindberg on Lev Tolstoi]', *Skandinavskii sbornik* (Tallinn), 14 (1969), 302-311. [Documents Sg's respect for Tolstoi and comments on the latter's admiration for Sg's story 'Samvetskval' (Remorse) from *Utopier i verkligheten*. Summary in Swedish]

[C1:914] 'Möten med Strindberg', Uttalanden av John Karlzén, Stig Sjödin, Ivan Oljelund, Johannes Edfelt, Vilgot Sjöman, *Studiekamraten* (Tollarp), 34:3-4 (1952), 97-100. ['Encounters with Strindberg'. Comments on Sg by five contemporary Swedish writers on the 40th anniversary of his death]

[C1:915] Motyleva, T., *Voina i mir za rubezhom*, Moscow: Sovetskii pisatel', 1978. 437 pp. ['War and Peace Abroad'. A monograph on the reception of *War and Peace* outside Russia in which Motyleva comments on Sg's appreciative remarks about Tolstoi's novel in his correspondence with Albert Bonnier during 1886, pp. 234-235. E.1101]

[C1:916] Mühsam, Erich, 'Strindberg', *Kain. Zeitschrift für Menschlichkeit* (München), 2 (1912-13), 33-34. [Reflections on Sg by the German anarchist poet, dramatist, and satirist (1878-1934)]

[C1:917] Müller-Freienfels, Richard, 'Die Literatur und 1915', *Das literarische Echo* (Berlin), 19 (1916-17), Sp. 1103-1112. [Comments on Sg's influence on German expressionism during the war years]

[C1:918] Müller-Loreck, Leonie, *Die erzählende Dichtung Lou Andreas-Salomés. Ihr Zusammenhang mit der Literatur um 1900*, Stuttgarter Arbeiten zur Germanistik 16, Stuttgart: Akademischer Verlag Hans-Dieter Heinz, 1976. [248] pp. [Comments on Andreas-Salomé's knowledge of Sg as a man and a writer, with the emphasis on his naturalistic plays as performed at the Berlin Freie Bühne]

[C1:919] Mummert, Otto, 'Zwei Dichter über die spiritualistische Philosophie', *Psychologische Studien* (Leipzig), 25 (1898), 628-635.* ['Two Writers on Spiritualist Philosophy'. Compares the responses to spiritualism of Sg and Tolstoi]

[C1:920] Munkhammar, Birgit, 'Ett brev till framtiden', *Dagens Nyheter* (Stockholm), 15 October 2000. ['A Letter to the Future'. Indicates the influence exerted by Sg in *Till Damaskus* and Knut Hamsun in *Svult* (Hunger) on Eyvind Johnson's novel *Stad i ljus* (City in Light, 1928)]

[C1:921] Munkhammar, Birgit, *Hemligskrivaren. En essä om Eyvind Johnson*, Stockholm: Albert Bonniers Förlag, 2000, pp. 64-68. [Discusses the influence of *Till Damaskus* on Johnson's novel *Stad i ljus* (1928). Munkhammar relates the predicament of Sg's protagonist Den Okände (The Unknown) to Johnson's personal situation as an impecunious author in Paris in 1927]

[C1:922] Müssener, Helmut, 'Deutschland und Österreich in Strindbergs Werken und Briefen', in Wilhelm Friese, Hrsg., **B3:168**, *Strindberg und die deutschsprachigen Länder*, pp. 117-138. ['Germany and Austria in Strindberg's Works and Letters'. Reviews the representation and significance of Germany and Austria for Sg, and the impression made on him by German thinkers and contemporaries, from Bismarck to Max Nordau. Müssener assesses what Germany meant to Sg, and how much he actually knew of it at first hand. He considers his response to its literature, including Mme de Staël, Goethe, Schiller, Heine, and the German romantics, as well as the rural novels of the German-Swiss writer Jeremias Gotthelf. Ola Hansson's role as a cultural intermediary between Germany and Sweden, and Sg's familiarity with the contemporary literary scene, which included the work of Gerhart Hauptmann and Hermann Sudermann, are also discussed. But according to Müssener, for Sg Germany really meant the writings of Luther, Kant, Schopenhauer, Nietzsche, Ferdinand Lassalle, Eduard von Hartmann, and August Bebel. Moreover, as *Gustav Adolf* and *Historiska miniatyrer* indicate, he was well aware how the history of Sweden was inextricably linked with that of Germany. Thus, it was fundamentally the land of poets and thinkers which Sg sought and found in Germany, drawing eclectically on the work of a wide range of authors as and when it suited him]

[**C1:923**] Myrdal, Jan, *August Strindberg and Ole Edvart Roelvaag* [sic], *or, The Literary Importance of Being Nordic: Five Texts*, Skinnskatterberg: Print on Demand, 1997. 38 pp. {http://www.marebalticum.se} [Sg and the emigrant Norwegian novelist Rølvaag (1876-1931) illustrate Myrdal's thesis that Nordic writers should remain Nordic; what is written in one language remains indigenous to the experience it alone expresses. Includes versions of 'August Strindberg and His Tradition', **F1:37**, 'As Normal as Herring and Potatoes' (see **B3:312**), 'The Occultation of August Strindberg', and '*The Father*', the text of a lecture delivered at the National Theatre, London, 26 October 1988]

[**C1:924**] Myrdal, Jan, 'Jules Vallès', *Folket i Bild* (Stockholm), 1975:5. [Considers the importance of Vallès (1832-1885) as a 'refractory' writer, whose sequence of autobiographical novels about Jacques Vingtras (1879-86) helped inspire Sg's narrative method and standpoint in *Tjänstekvinnans son*]

[**C1:925**] Myrdal, Jan, 'Jules Vallès', in **B1:323**, *Strindberg and Balzac*, pp. 58-62. [Rpr. of **C1:924**]

[**C1:926**] Myrdal, Jan, 'Strindberg och James Montgomery Bailey', *Förr och nu* (Stockholm), 1983:4, pp. 11-13. [Argues that Bailey and the other American humorists that Sg translated together with Siri von Essen and the opera singer Algot Lange in the later 1870s were among his formative influences; their style and narrative perspective is apparent alongside that of Dickens in *Röda rummet*]

[**C1:927**] Myrdal, Jan, 'Strindberg och James Montgomery Bailey', in *En annan ordning. Litterärt & Personligt*, Stockholm: Norstedts, 1988, pp. 100-103. [Rpr. of **C1:926**]

[**C1:928**] Næss, Harald S., 'Georg Brandes and 19th-Century Scandinavian Realism', *Neohelicon* (Budapest), 15:2 (1989), 113-134. [Discusses Brandes's role in introducing realism into Scandinavian literature with reference to *Röda rummet*, *Giftas*, *Fadren*, and *Fröken Julie*. Næss points out that, even in the later phase of his career, Sg remained a realist in his use of language, and everything he represented was something that he had lived through and accurately recorded]

[C1:929] Næss, Harald S., *Knut Hamsun og Amerika*, Oslo: Gyldendal Norsk Forlag, 1969. 282 pp. [Includes seventeen references to Sg, one, on Hamsun's early article on Sg in English in the Wisconsin journal *Amerika* (**C1:503**) of substance]

[C1:930] Næss, Harald S., 'Strindberg and Hamsun', in Marilyn Johns Blackwell, ed., **C1:142**, *Structures of Influence*, pp. 121-136. [Stresses Knut Hamsun's early admiration for Sg and his work, to which he was temperamentally attracted. Næss documents his lectures and articles on Sg and their later falling out. Nevertheless, Hamsun was strongly influenced by Sg, e.g. in the important essay 'Fra det ubevidste Sjæleliv' (From the Unconscious Life of the Soul, 1890). However, it was as a mediator of Rousseau's ideas that he exerted a major influence on Hamsun]

[C1:931] Nag, Martin, 'Hamsun og Strindberg', *Morgenbladet* (Oslo), 12 February 1965. [Maintains that Knut Hamsun's early comments on Sg as a reactionary radical and a perceptive psychologist illuminate his own writing in his earliest novels *Sult* (1890) and *Mysterier* (1892). See Lampl's response in **C1:730**]

[C1:932] Nag, Martin, *Ibsen i russisk åndsliv*, Oslo: Gyldendal Norsk Forlag, 1967, pp. 137-140. ['Ibsen in Russian Intellectual Life'. Comments on Alexandr Blok's response to Sg as well as to Ibsen]

[C1:933] Nag, Martin, *Hamsun i russisk åndsliv*, Oslo: Gyldendal Norsk Forlag, 1969. ['Hamsun in Russian Intellectual Life'. Includes eight references to Sg]

[C1:934] Nagashima, Yoichi, 'Iwano Homei, Akutagawa, and Strindberg', in Bjarke Frellesvig, and Christian Morimoto Hermansen, eds, *Florilegium Japonicum: Studies Presented to Olof G. Lidin on the Occasion of his 70th Birthday*, København: Akademisk Forlag, 1996, pp. 197-203. [On the relevance of *En dåres försvarstal* for *Aru ahoo no isshoo* (A Fool's Life) by the Japanese author, Ryūnosuke Akutagawa (1892-1927), who read Sg's fiction as a 'sincere confession, not as the narration of Axel – [its] hero'. Nagashima also presents Iwano Homei's (1873-1920) theory of fiction]

[C1:935] Nathan, George Jean, *The Magic Mirror: Selected Writings on the Theatre*, Edited, Together with an introduction by Thomas Quinn Curtiss, New York: Alfred A. Knopf, 1960, pp. 229-230. [Includes the same material as in *Materia Critica*, **C1:936**]

[C1:936] Nathan, George Jean, 'O'Neill', in *Materia Critica*, New York: Alfred A. Knopf, 1924, pp. 122-123. [A comparison of Eugene O'Neill's plays *Welded* and *The First Man* with *Fadren* illustrates that, whereas Sg intensifies a theme from within, 'O'Neill intensifies his theme from without. He piles psychological and physical situation upon situation until the structure topples over with a burlesque clatter. Sg magnified the psyche of his characters. O'Neill magnifies their action']

[C1:937] Nathan, George Jean, 'O'Neill', in *Materia Critica*, New Introduction by Charles Angoff, Rutherford Madison Teaneck: Fairleigh Dickinson University Press, 1971, pp. 122-123. [Rpr. of **C1:936**]

[C1:938] Nathan, George Jean, 'The Theatre', *The American Mercury* (New York), 63 (1946), p. 717. [Observes that Eugene O'Neill's play *Strange Interlude* is 'touched by the Sg philosophy']

[C1:939] Nathan, George Jean, '*Welded*', in Alan Downer, *American Drama and its Critics*, Chicago: University of Chicago Press, 1965, pp. 81-83. [A reprint of Nathan's original review in *The American Mercury*, May 1924, which sees in O'Neill's play an analysis of love after the manner of Sg's *Dödsdansen*. According to Nathan, 'O'Neill has tried on Sg's whiskers with the same unfortunate result as in... *The First Man*']

[C1:940] Naumann, Karin, *Utopien von Freiheit: Die Schweiz im Spiegel schwedischer Literatur*, Beiträge zur nordischen Philologie 23, Basel und Frankfurt am Main: Helbing & Lichtenhahn Verlag AG, 1994, pp. 84-104. Illus. ['Freedom's Utopia. Switzerland Reflected in Swedish Literature'. Surveys Sg's response to Switzerland in *Tjänstekvinnans son*, *Utopier i verkligheten*, and *En dåres försvarstal*. In the mid-1880s, it seemed to him an idyllic, democratic haven, in sharp contrast to Sweden, where his recent books, including *Det nya riket*, *Svenska folket*, and *Giftas*, had met with hostility. Its associations with Rousseau, whom he greatly admired at this time, was another attraction. Naumann also notes the relevance of Jeremias Gotthelf's rural novels *Uli der Knecht* (1841) and *Uli der Pächter* (1848) for *Hemsöborna*, and surveys Sg's relationship with Verner von Heidenstam (1859-1940) at Schloss Brunegg in 1886]

[C1:941] Naumann-Magnusson, Karin, 'Freiheit und Alpenglühen – Schwedische Literatur im Schweizer Exil', in *Studien zur dänischen und schwedischen Literatur des 19. Jahrhunderts*, Beiträge zur nordischen Philologie 4, Basel: Helbing & Lichtenhahn Verlag AG, 1976, pp. 207-239 ['Freedom and Alp Worship – Swedish Literature in Swiss Exile'. Discusses Sg pp. 208-215, along with Verner von Heidenstam, Ola Hansson, Oscar Levertin, Eyvind Johnson, and Edith Södergran, apropos the role and image of Switzerland in these writers' lives and work]

[C1:942] Naville, Jacques, 'Accueils', *Obliques. Littérature Théâtre* (Paris), 1:1 (1972), 80-81. [Records André Gide's admiration for Sg]

[C1:943] Nedergaard, Leif, 'Georg Brandes' Forhold till Ibsen, Björnson og Strindberg Belyst gennem deres indbyrdes Brevveksling', *Nordisk Tidskrift* (Stockholm), 36:1 (1960), 1-17. ['Georg Brandes's Relationship with Ibsen, Bjørnson, and Strindberg Illuminated by their Reciprocal Correspondence'. Considers what Brandes meant to Ibsen, Bjørnson, and Sg and they to him in the light of their often extensive correspondence which, in Sg's case, was confined to the pre-Inferno period and primarily the 1880s]

[C1:944] Nedergaard-Hansen, Leif, 'Georg Brandes' Forhold till Ibsen, Björnson og Strindberg Belyst gennem deres indbyrdes Brevveksling', in *Kritiske Studier*, Redøvre: ROLV, 1984, pp. 197-213. ['Georg Brandes's Relationship with Ibsen, Bjørnson, and Strindberg Illuminated by their Reciprocal Correspondence'. Rpr. of **C1:943**]

[C1:945] Nekrasova, I., '[A. Strindberg i P. Claudel]', i in L[ev] Gitel'man and V[alentina] Dianova, eds, **B1:148**, *Avgust Strindberg i mirovaia kul'tura. Materialy mezhvyzovskoi nauchnoi konferentsii. Stat'i. Soobshcheniia*, pp. 63-70. ['A[ugust] Strindberg and P[aul] Claudel'. Compares the religious beliefs of the two dramatists via a study of religious motifs in *Till Damaskus* and Claudel's play *Partage de midi* (1906)]

[C1:946] Neustroev, V. N., '[Russian Classical and Soviet Literature in the Scandinavian Countries]', in *Uchennye zapiski/Voennyi institut inostrannykh iazykov*, Vol. 5, 1948, pp. 82-94. [Comments (p. 86) on Sg's admiration for the Russian radical critic and novelist N[ikolai] G. Chernyshevskii (1828-1889), most specifically his novel *What is to be Done?* (1864) which, for a period during the 1880s around the time of *Giftas* (1884), became a catchword for Sg. In the Publications of the Military Institute of Modern Languages. E.960]

[C1:947] *New York Times* (editorial), 'Eugene O'Neill's Teacher', 12 December 1936. [A report of O'Neill's Nobel Prize acceptance speech, which credits Sg with inspiring him to become a dramatist]

[C1:948] Niemi, Irmeli, 'Demoner och drömmar. Maria Jotuni och August Strindberg', in Michel Ekman and Roger Holmström, *Kunskapens hugsvavelse. Litteraturvetenskapliga studier tillägnade Clas Zilliacus*, Åbo: Åbo Akademis förlag, 2003, pp. 44-52. ['Demons and Dreams. Maria Jotuni and August Strindberg'. Documents the literary links between Sg and Jotuni (pseudonym of Maria Tarkiainen, 1880-1943), as well as others in the circle around the Finnish publishing house *Agricola*. Niemi notes that it was Sg's representation of marriage and gender relationships which most interested Jotuni, notably apropos her novel *Huojuva talo* (1963). One of Jotuni's short stories, in which only a woman's side of a conversation with her lover is recorded, may well have been influenced by *Den starkare*, and the same play may also be of relevance to the situation depicted in her comedy *Kultainen vasikka* (1918)]

[C1:949] Nils Ludvig [Nils Ludvig Olsson], *Kring en diktare. Markens melodi, prosastycken och vers*, Lund: C. W. K. Gleerup, 1937. Illus. 127 pp. ['About a Poet. The Earth's Melody, Prose Pieces and Poems'. A study of the Scanian poet, Emil Kléen (1868-1898), including comments on his personal, as well as literary, relationship with Sg, whom he knew in Lund in the late-1890s, and who wrote the introduction to a posthumous collection of Kléen's poems]

[C1:950] Nilsson, N., 'Strindberg, Olle Hedberg och övermänniskan', *Bokvännen* (Stockholm), 1952, pp. 210-211. ['Strindberg, Olle Hedberg, and the Superman'. Discusses the significance of the idea of the Nietzschean superman for Sg in *I havsbandet*, as well as for the Swedish novelist Hedberg (1899-1974)]

[C1:951] Nilsson, Nils Åke, 'Strindberg, Gorky and Blok', *Scando-Slavica* (Copenhagen), 4 (1958), 23-42. [A well-documented essay on the interest accorded Sg's personality in Russia during the early years of the 20th Century, the dissemination of his works there in two separate editions, as well as performances of his plays. Nilsson documents the strong impression which Sg made on both Maksim Gor'kii, who saw him as a modern descendant of the Norsemen and likened him to the Viking hero, Ragnar Lodbrok, and Aleksandr Blok, who particularly admired his autobiographical novels, responded positively to his misogyny, and saw in him the man of the future]

[C1:952] Nilsson, N[ils] Å[ke], 'Strindberg, Gor'kii i Blok', *IV Mezhdunarodnyi s'ezd slavistov*, Vol. 1, Moscow, 1962, pp. 413-414. [Comments on the importance of Sg for both Maksim Gor'kii and Alexandr Blok. Presents substantially the material presented in **C1:951**, but in Russian. See the responses to Nilsson's paper by G. V. Shatkov, pp. 428-429, M[artin] Nag, p. 429, and I. E. Zhuravskaia, p. 430. Published in the proceedings of the 4th International Congress of Slavists. E.988]

[C1:953] N. K. [N. P. Karelin], '[Scandinavian Literature and its Trends]', *Russkaia mysl'* (Moscow), 7 (1899), 135-149. [A discussion translated into Russian from the German by Karelin. Includes comments on Sg, p. 144. E.707]

[C1:954] N-m [J. Nordström], 'Strindberg och Stiernhielm', *Aftonbladet* (Stockholm), 2 September 1917. [Rpr. of **C1:955**]

[C1:955] N-m [J. Nordström], 'Strindberg och Stiernhielm', *Göteborgs Handels- och Sjöfartstidning*, 25 August 1917. [Compares Sg with the Swedish poet Georg Stiernhielm (1598-

1672) and comments on their mastery of the hexameter, in Sg's case in such poems as 'Stadsresan' (The City Journey)]

[C1:956] Nolin, Bertil, *Den gode européen. Studier i Georg Brandes' idéutveckling 1871-1893 med speciell hänsyn till hans förhållande till tysk, engelsk, slavisk och fransk litteratur*, Stockholm: Svenska bokförlaget/Norstedts, 1965. 474 pp. ['The Good European. Studies in Georg Brandes's Intellectual Development 1871-1893 with Special Reference to His Relationship to German, English, Slavic, and French Literature'. Nolin notes Brandes's relevance for Sg's development as a writer only briefly and in passing. Doctoral dissertation]

[C1:957] Nolin, Bertil, 'Den moderna genombrottet. En konturteckning', *Göteborgs-Posten*, 3 August 1986. ['The Modern Breathrough. An Outline']

[C1:958] Nordberg, Carl-Eric, *Ett horn av skapelsen – Emile Zola och hans värld*, Stockholm: Bokförlaget Prisma, 1988. 572 pp. ['A Corner of Creation: Émile Zola and his World'. A life-and-letters biography of Zola which includes twenty-one references to Sg]

[C1:959] Nordberg, Carl-Eric, 'Tjänstekvinnans son och pojken från Jante', *Svenska Dagbladet* (Stockholm), 4 March 1968. ['The Son of a Servant and the Boy from Jante'. Explores personal and literary affinities between Sg and the Norwegian novelist Aksel Sandemose (1899-1965)]

[C1:960] Nordlund, Anna, 'Geniet och sagoberätterskan. August Strindberg och Selma Lagerlöf i den svenska litteraturhistorien', *Strindbergiana* (Stockholm), 21 (2006), pp. 132-153. ['The Genius and the Storyteller. August Strindberg and Selma Lagerlöf in Swedish Literary History'. Compares the treatment of Sg and Lagerlöf in major Swedish literary histories both as regards the space accorded each author and the different criteria used in evaluating their work, which is frequently coloured by gender prejudice. Nordlund considers their critical reception in terms of originality, their relationship to literary tradition, and the significance attributed to their relevance for later authors. It emerges that both writers are approached from a fundamentally biographical perspective but in discussing Lagerlöf the emphasis is on her reliance on traditional, localised cultural forms and narrative traditions while with Sg there is a great dependence on a comparative approach, which places him in terms of the history of ideas. Thus the emphasis where Lagerlöf is concerned is on her indebtedness to those who have influenced her while in Sg's case he is generally presented as the forerunner who influenced both his own and later times]

[C1:961] Norlinder, Eva, *Sekelskiftets svenska konstsaga och sagodiktaren Helena Nyblom*, Stockholm: Bonniers Junior Förlag AB, 1991. 281 pp. [Includes eleven references to Sg and *Sagor*, in a study of Nyblom (1843-1926) and the turn-of-the-century Swedish fairy tale]

[C1:962] Norman, Nils, 'Strindberg och Dante', *Svensk Litteraturtidskrift* (Stockholm), 27:3 (1964), 103-115. [Discusses Sg's use of Dantean motifs during the Inferno period in both *Sylva Sylvarum* and *Inferno*, where Swedenborg is allotted a role which resembles that of Virgil in the *Divine Comedy*. Norman notes that Sg had read Dante as early as 1871 and, as well as the links which he forged in *Inferno* between Dante's vision of hell and Viktor Rydberg's account of a Nordic inferno in *Undersökningar i germanisk mytologi* (Studies in Teutonic Mythology, 1886-89), he also shows how Sg recognised the iconography of Dante's *Divine Comedy* in the landscape near Frida Uhl's family home at Dornach in Austria, and utilised it in the infernal imagery of both *Till Damaskus* and *Inferno*. He also comments on Sg's use of Ovid as a counter to contemporary Darwinian science]

[C1:963] Norman, Nils, 'Strindberg och Napoleon', *Svensk Litteraturtidskrift* (Stockholm), 22:4 (1959), 151-170. [An invaluable essay which explores Sg's associational manner of thinking and writing through a study of the way in which he found correlations for many aspects of his own life with that of Napoleon, and explored these parallels in his private correspondence, as well as in the literary works from the Inferno period. At the time, he associated Frida Uhl and her family with Napoleon's second wife, the Austrian Marie Louise, and Norman illustrates how Sg elaborated a complex pattern of, sometimes occult, relationships, in which his own destiny was enmeshed with that of the French emperor, thus allowing him partly to assuage his feelings of guilt towards Siri von Essen and his abandoned first family. Norman discusses his friendship with Ossian Ekbohrn, the Napoleonic customs' inspector on the island of Sandhamn in the Stockholm archipelago and its bearing on the vivisection 'Nemesis divina' (1887) and *I havsbandet*. He considers the roles which Sg played in his exchange of letters with Nietzsche, and the relevance for his thinking of Hippolyte Taine's portrait of Napoleon in *Les Origines de la France contemporaine* (1875-93) and Chateaubriand's anti-Napoleonic stance in *Mémoires d'outre-tombe* (1849-50). Norman also comments on 'Den romantiske klockaren på Rånö' (The Romantic Sexton on Rånö) and Sg's response to Ovid's *Metamorphoses*, which contributed significantly to the complex network of imagery and allusion that permeates *Jardin des Plantes*, *Till Damaskus I*, and other works of the Inferno period]

[C1:964] Normann, I. C., '*Faderen* og *Rosmersholm*', *Edda* (Oslo), 52 (1952), 166-172. ['*The Father* and *Rosmersholm*'. Establishes a link between the two plays via the vivisection 'Själamord' (Soul Murder, 1887) in which Sg analyses Rebekka West's psychic murder of Rosmer's wife in Ibsen's play, and compares it with Iago leading Othello on to murder Desdemona]

[C1:965] Northam, John, 'Waiting for Prospero', in Marie Axton and Raymond Williams, eds, *English Drama: Forms and Development. Essays in Honour of Muriel Clara Bradbrook*, Cambridge: Cambridge University Press, 1977, pp. 188-202. [Introduces *Spöksonaten* into a comparison of *The Tempest* with *Waiting for Godot*. Northam considers Sg's play the photographic negative of Shakespeare's picture of life, although his comments on *The Tempest* in both *Memorandum till Medlemmarne av Intima Teatern från Regissören* and *En blå bok* indicate thematic parallels between the two works. Hence it is possible to match the constellation of characters formed by Miranda, Ferdinand, Prospero, and Ariel in *The Tempest* with the Young Lady, Student, Hummel, and Milkmaid in *Spöksonaten*. But Sg's play depicts an altogether bleaker universe than Shakespeare's: it is little wonder, then, that where *The Tempest* ends with a return from isolation on the island to life in society, *Spöksonaten* concludes with a departure from society to the island of the dead]

[C1:966] Nylander, Lars, *Den långa vägen hem. Lars Noréns författarskap från poesi till dramatik*, Stockholm: Albert Bonniers Förlag, 1997. 372 pp. ['The Long Way Home. Lars Norén's Writings from Poetry to Drama'. Compares Norén with Sg in e.g. *Fadren* as two dramatists for whom personal experience and fiction are closely intertwined, pp. 8-9. Includes seven further incidental references to Sg]

[C1:967] Nylander, Lars, and Jørgen Lorentzen, 'Manlighetens och kvinnlighetens öde i textens lustgård', in Helga Kress, Hrsg., *Litteratur og kjønn i Norden. Foredrag på den XX. studiekonferanse i International Association for Scandinavian Studies (IASS)*, Reykjavík: Háskólaútgáfan Universitets forlag, 1996, pp. [319] -333. ['Masculinity's and Femininity's Fate in the Textual Paradise'. Discusses male and female roles in *Fadren* together with Gunnar Ekelöf's collection of poetry *Strountes* (1955) and (mainly) Knut Hamsun's novel *Mysterier* (1892)]

[C1:968] Nyman, Alf, 'Arthur Schopenhauer och Ultima Thule. Ett filosofiskt hundraårsminne', *Nordisk Tidskrift* (Stockholm), 16 (1940), 481-502. ['Arthur Schopenhauer and Ultima Thule. A Philosophical Centennial Memory'. Examines Schopenhauer's influence on several Scandinavian writers, including Per Daniel Amadeus Atterbom, Viktor Rydberg, Karl Gjellerup, and Sigurd Agrell, as well as Sg, whose debt to his philosophy in the story 'Samvetskval' (Remorse) from *Utopier i verkligheten* is discussed, pp. 497-499]

[C1:969] Obraztsova, A., *Dramaturgischeskii metod Bernarda Shou*, Moscow: Nauka, 1965. 315 pp. [Presents Sg as one the founders of intellectual drama, p. 65, in a study of the dramatic method of George Bernard Shaw. E.1008]

[C1:970] Obrestad, Tor, 'Gudlause heltar og ein ny moral', *Forfattaren* (Oslo), 29:3-4 (1999), 20-25. ['Godless Heroes and a New Morality'. A discussion of several writers of the Scandinavian Modern Breakthrough in which Sg is linked with Georg Brandes, Alexander Kielland, and Arne Garborg]

[C1:971] Ocvirk, Anton, 'Stilni premiki v Cankarjevem zgodnjem pripovedništvu v simbolizem', *Sodobnost* (Ljubljana), 18:2 (1970), 105-130. [Includes a comparison of the Slovenian novelist, dramatist, and poet, Ivan Cankar (1875-1918), with Sg]

[C1:972] Ofrat, Gideon, 'Ha-Alma Yulia ve-Halom Leil KaQuitz', *Bikkoret u-Parshanut*, 11-12 (1978), 269-284. [Compares the dramatic portrayal of two radically different nights of theatrical enchantment in *Fröken Julie* with Shakespeare's *A Midsummer Night's Dream*. In Hebrew with an English summary, pp. xviii-xx]

[C1:973] Öhman, Anders, *Apologier. En linje i den svenska romanen från August Strindberg till Agnes von Krusenstjerna*, Stockholm-Stehag: Brutus Östlings Bokförlag Symposion, 2001. 232 pp. ['Apologies. A Line in the Swedish Novel from August Strindberg to Agnes von Krusentjerna'. Includes *En dåres försvarstal* in a discussion of autobiographical fictions from the 1880s (the others are Victoria Benedictsson's *Pengar* and Bernhard Meijer's *Excelsior!*), pp. 33-78. Such works take the form of aggressively self-defensive apologias in which the author adopts a rhetorical strategy that legitimises her/his right to reveal and confess intimate private details and, in so doing, establishes a major genre in Swedish literature, one that also includes Ivar Lo-Johansson's *Måna är död*, K. G. Ossiannilsson's *Barbarskogen*, and Agnes von Krusentjerna's *Fattigadel*]

[C1:974] — Jansson, Bo G., *Samlaren* (Uppsala), 123 (2002), pp. 434-437.

[C1:975] — Pedersen, Arne Toftegaard, 'Den retoriska ursäkten', *Hufvudstadsbladet* (Helsingfors), 27 December 2001. ['The Rhetorical Apology']

[C1:976] Oliva Herrer, Maria de la, 'La huella de Strindberg en el teatro documental alemán', in Francisco Manuel Mariño, ed., *España u Alemania: Interrelaciones literarias*, Madrid: Iberoamericana/Frankfurt am Main: Verveurt, 2001, pp. 163-169.

['The Impact of Strindberg on German Documentary Theatre'. Particularly concerned with the influence of Sg on Peter Weiss in the *Marat/Sade* and elsewhere]

[C1:976a] Ollfors, Anders, *August Strindberg och den grekisk-romerska antiken*, Studies in Mediterranean Archeology and Literature, Sävedalen: Per Alströms förlag, 2007. Illus. 371 pp. ['August Strindberg and Greco-Roman Classicism'. A systematic survey and commentary in seven chapters on Sg's knowledge of the Classical world and literatures and their place in his writing, not least the way in which he often finds correlations for his own experience in certain figures from classical mythology, with whom he identifies]

[C1:977] Ollfors, Anders, 'Strindberg och latinet', *Bokvännen* (Stockholm), 29:10 (1974), 193-196. ['Strindberg and Latin'. Sg was critical of his classical education, which he considered out-of-date, and there are relatively few traces of antique culture and literature in his work. Analyses a parody of Livy and Tacitus in *Från Fjärdingen och Svartbäcken*]

[C1:978] Ollfors, Anders, 'Strindberg och latinet', in *Hjalmar Söderberg och antiken och andra essayer*, Studies in Mediterranean Archaeology 38, Göteborg: P. Åström, 1986, pp. 27-33. Illus. ['Strindberg and Latin'. Revised and enlarged version of **C1:977**]

[C1:979] Ollfors, Anders, 'Strindberg och latinet', *Medusa* (Stockholm), 1984:3, pp. 2-7. ['Strindberg and Latin'. On Sg's knowledge of classical languages and literatures]

[C1:980] Olrik, Hilde, 'La Théorie de l'impregnation', *Nineteenth-Century French Studies* (Fredonia, N.Y.), 15:1-2 (1986-87), 128-140. ['The Theory of Impregnation'. Alludes briefly to *Fordringsägare* in a study of various pseudo-scientific 19th-Century notions concerning the ways in which women could be spiritually as well as physically impregnated by men. Otherwise Olrik is concerned primarily with Jules Michelet, Zola, and Villiers de l'Isle Adam]

[C1:981] Olsson, Henry, 'Strindberg, Brandes och "lidelsens poesi"', in *Vinlövsranka och hagtornskrans. En bok om Fröding*, Stockholm: P. A. Norstedt & Söners Förlag, 1970, pp. 215-235. ['Strindberg, Brandes, and "The Poetry of Suffering"'. Discusses Sg's literary and personal relationship with the Swedish poet Gustaf Fröding (1860-1911) and comments on the latter's essay on Sg's poetry in **B1:142**, where he approaches Sg in terms of a poetry that is conceived as passion, which Olsson considers Fröding has derived from Georg Brandes's *Hovedstrømninger i det Nittende Aarhundredes Literatur* (1872-1890)]

[C1:982] Olsson, Henry, 'Två Jakobsbrottare stämmer möte', in *Vinlövsranka och hagtornskrans. En bok om Fröding*, Stockholm: P. A. Norstedt & Söners Förlag, 1970, pp. 236-257. ['Two Jacob's Wrestlers Arrange to Meet'. Considers Sg's personal and professional links with the Swedish poet Gustaf Fröding (1860-1911), the latter's editorship of *En bok om Strindberg*, **B1:142**, and their fortunes as sometimes proscribed authors, both of whom underwent serious intellectual and spiritual crises. Olsson discusses Sg's reading of Fröding's controversial collection of poetry *Stänk och flikar* (1896) and the latter's response to *Inferno*, as well as Sg's reflections on Fröding and the role which his late world view led him to ascribe to him and his misfortunes in both *Legender* and *Götiska rummen*, where he is depicted as another wrestler with God]

[C1:983] Olsson, Tomas, 'Brandes och Strindbergs läroår', in Tomas Forser and Sverker Göransson, red., *Kritik och teater. En vänbok till Bertil Nolin*, Skrifter utgivna av

Literaturvetenskapliga institutionen vid Göteborgs universitet 23, Göteborg, 1992, pp. 55-80. ['Brandes and Strindberg's Apprenticeship'. Queries received views of 19th-Century Swedish literature in terms of a conflict between idealism and realism in the course of a re-examination of Georg Brandes's influence on the early Sg, up to and including *Mäster Olof*. Olsson discusses Brandes's views on Kierkegaard, Oehlenschläger, Shakespeare, the theatre, and realism, and argues that it is those works which he wrote prior to *Hovedstrømninger i det Nittende Aarhundredes Literatur* (1872-1890) that meant the most to Sg. Olsson also considers Sg's intellectual relationship with the idealist critic Carl Rupert Nyblom (1832-1907), who had been his professor in aethetics at Uppsala]

[C1:984] Olsson, Ulf, 'Ibsen som Strindbergs livmoder. Några reflexioner kring förbindelsen mellan två författarskap', in *Ibsen-Strindberg seminar på Voksenåsen 15-17 september 1997*, Oslo: Voksenåsen, 1997, pp. 54-66. ['Ibsen as Strindberg's Uterus. Some Reflections on the Relationship between the Two Writers and their Work'. Examines elements of mutual influence and parody in *Giftas*, *A Doll's House*, and *Hedda Gabler*]

[C1:985] O'Neill, Eugene, 'Strindberg and Our Theatre', *New York Times*, 6 January 1924. [Rpr. of **C1:987**]

[C1:986] O'Neill, Eugene, 'Strindberg and Our Theatre', in Helen Deutsch and Stella Hanau, *The Provincetown: A Story of the Theatre*, New York: Farrar & Rinehart, Inc., 1931, pp. 191-193. [Rpr. of **C1:987**. See also **B1:368**]

[C1:987] O'Neill, Eugene, 'Strindberg and Our Theatre', *Provincetown Playbill*, 1 (1923-24), p. 1. [For O'Neill in a much-quoted statement, Sg is 'the precursor of all modernity in our present theater, just as Ibsen, a lesser man...was the father of the modernity of twenty years or so ago....Sg still remains among the most modern of moderns, the great interpreter in the theater of the characteristic spiritual conflicts which constitute the drama – the blood of our lives to-day']

[C1:988] O'Neill, Eugene, '[Strindberg and Our Theatre]', in [*American Writers about Literature*], Moscow, 1974, pp. 71-72. [Russian translation of **C1:987**. E.1070]

[C1:989] O'Neill, Eugene, 'Strindberg et notre théâtre', Traduit par Jacqueline Autrusseau, *Théâtre en Europe* (Paris), 5:1 (1985), p. 13. [French translation of **C1:987**]

[C1:990] O'Neill, Eugene, 'Strindberg und das neue Drama', in Horst Frenz, Hrsg., *Amerikanische Dramaturgie*, Reinbeck bei Hamburg: Rowohlt Verlag, 1962, pp. 82-83. ['Strindberg and the New Drama'. German translation of **C1:987**]

[C1:991] Oppel, Horst, 'Die Nachwirkung Kierkegaards in der nordischen Dichtung', *Nordische Rundschau* (Braunschweig), 9 (1936-38), 145-157. ['The Influence of Kierkegaard on Scandinavian Literature'. Discusses Kierkegaard's importance for Sg, pp. 155-157]

[C1:992] Ørjasæter, Tore, 'Ungdomsinntrykk av Strindberg', *Vinduet* (Oslo), 3 (1949), 78-80. ['Youthful Impressions of Strindberg'. Stresses the importance of plays like *Spöksonaten* for modern drama, including Ørjasæter's own. Ørjasæter (1886-1968) declares Sg more modern today than ever]

[C1:993] Orlov, V[ladimir] N[ikolaevich], *Aleksandr Blok: ocherk tvorchestva*, Moscow: Gos. izd-vo khudozhestvennoi literatury, 1956. 260 pp. [Discusses Blok's interest in Sg, p. 187]

[C1:994] Orlov, V[ladimir] N[ikolaevich], in *Zapisnye knizhki Aleksandra Bloka, 1901-1920*, Moscow: Khudozhestvennaia literatura, 1965, p. 395. [A note on Blok's correspondence concerning Sg, 16 March 1918. E.1004]

[C1:995] Orsini, François, 'Strindberg, Wedekind, Rosso di San Secondo: il mito della donna fatale – origine, significato', in *Visione e architepiti: il mito nell'arte sperimentale e di avanguardia del primo novecento*, A cura di F. Bartoli, Trento: Università degli Studi di Trento, 1996, pp. 427-450. ['The Origins and Significance of the Myth of the *femme fatale* in Wedekind, Strindberg, and Rosso di San Secondo']

[C1:996] Ortensi, U., 'Letterati contemporanei: Augusto Strindberg', *Emporium* (Bergamo), No. 102 (June 1903), p. 445. ['Contemporary Writers: August Strindberg'. Identifies Laura in *Fadren* as the precursor of *Hedda Gabler*]

[C1:997] Österlund, Bodil, and Marianne Gröndal, *Nora. Ett dockhem genom åren*, Malmö: Liber, 1984. Illus. 168 pp. ['Nora. *A Doll's House* over the Years'. Comments on Sg's response to *A Doll's House* in a study of the reception accorded Ibsen's play]

[C1:998] Othman, Hans, 'Dostoevskij och Strindberg', *Horisont* (Vasa), 35:5 (1988), 68-84. [Establishes a number of psychological similarities and literary parallels between Sg and Dostoevskii]

[C1:999] Øverland, Arnulf, 'Strindberg på avstand', in *I beundring og forargelse*, Oslo: H. Aschehoug & Co., 1954, pp. 63-74. ['Strindberg at a Distance'. Rpr. of **C1:1000**]

[C1:1000] Överland, Arnulf, 'Strindberg på avstand', *Svensk Litteraturtidskrift* (Stockholm), 12:1 (1949), 63-71. ['Strindberg at a Distance'. Reflections on Sg and his centenary by the Norwegian novelist (1890-1960)]

[C1:1001] Øyslebø, Olaf, 'Referat av foredrag om Strindberg i Gjøvik', *Edda* (Oslo), 63 (1963), 143-156. ['Report of a Lecture on Strindberg in Gjøvik'. An account of Hamsun's lecture tour of Norway in 1886 with extensive quotation from contemporary news reports, including his comments on Sg]

[C1:1002] Palm, Anders, 'Strindbergs huvud och Baudelaires ögon. Porträttdikten som estetiskt problem och lyrisk praxis', in Bernt Olsson, Jan Olsson, Hans Lund, red., *I musernas sällskap. Konstarter och deras relationer. En vänbok till Ulla-Britta Lagerroth 19.10.1992*, Höganäs: Wiken, 1992, pp. 157-185. Illus. ['Strindberg's Head and Baudelaire's Eyes. The Portrait Poem as Aesthetic Problem and Lyrical Praxis'. Examines the genre of the 'portrait poem' with reference to Roland Barthes's study of photography, *La Chambre claire* (1980), and to Baudelaire, but Palm also explores the way in which a figure may be evoked in language through the formation of a visual figure by means of a comparison between Hjalmar Gullberg's poem 'Till Christian Krohgs Strindbergs-porträtt' and Krohg's original painting. He comments briefly on Sg's photographic self-portraits, partly inspired, as Baudelaire also was, by Nadar's development of the new visual technology]

[C1:1003] Palmblad, Harry V. E., 'Shakspere and Strindberg', 1-2, *Germanic Review* (New York), 3:1 (1928), 71-79, and 3:2 (1928), 168-177. [Documents the importance of Shakespeare for Sg's history plays with reference to *Memorandum till Medlemmarne av Intima Teatern*, *Gustav Adolf*, *Karl XII*, *Gustav III*, *Kristina*, *Gustav Vasa*, *Näktergalen i Wittenberg*, and *Mäster Olof*. Palmblad compares their characterisation as well as the ways in which both dramatists enlarge the action of their dramas and employ parallelism. He maintains that Sg never imitates Shakespeare slavishly, but varies his methods to suit his own purpose, or else uses them for new ends, most frequently in the direction of a greater realism. 'Where Shakspere's (sic) method seems due to his instinctive feeling for the artistically fitting or to his source material, Sg's is evidently conscious and at times expressive of certain philosophical doctrines']

[C1:1004] Palme, Sven Ulric, 'Madame de Staël utlöste fejd Strindberg – Selma Lagerlöf', *Göteborgs-Posten*, 18 July 1971. ['Madame de Staël Initiated the Feud between Strindberg and Selma Lagerlöf']

[C1:1005] Palola, Eino, 'Brandesin veljekset ja August Strindberg', *Valvoja-Aika* (Helsinki), 18 (1940), 211-227. ['The Brothers Brandes and August Strindberg'. On Sg's relationship with both Edvard and Georg Brandes, mainly in terms of their activity as writers of the Scandinavian Modern Breakthrough in the 1870s and 1880s]

[C1:1006] Pannenborg, Willem August, *Satirische schrijvers: karakter en temperament*, Assen: Van Gorcum, 1953. 86 pp. [See **C1:1007**]

[C1:1007] Pannenborg, Willem August, *Ecrivains satiriques, caractère et tempérament*, Paris: Presses Universitaires de France, 1955. XII+95 pp. [Discusses Sg as a satirist together with Beaumarchais, Gogol, Victor Hugo, Machiavelli, Voltaire, and others in a study of the character and temperament of satirical authors]

[C1:1008] Pantléon, Thomas, *Volkstümliche Tendenzen in der schwedischen Literatur 1880-1900: Soziologische, Ideengeschichtliche, literarische Hintergründe*, Beiträge zur Skandinavistik 1, Frankfurt am Main Bern New York: Verlag Peter Lang, 1984. 249 pp. [A mainly sociological reading of the predilection for 'folkish', or popular and (usually provincial or rural) traditional elements in late 19th-Century Swedish literature, which is contextualised in terms of contemporary social developments and scientific thinking (Darwin, Haeckel, and Taine), industrialisation, and the changing role of the peasantry. In Sg's case, Pantléon focuses on his debt to Rousseau, with reference to *Likt och olikt*, *Hemsöborna*, *Det nya riket*, and *Röda rummet*, pp. 204-210]

[C1:1009] Parm, *? von, 'Strindberg, Lord Byron und Lessing, eine vergleichende Studie', *Die Astrologie* (Berlin), 19 (July-August 1937), 82-96. ['Strindberg, Byron, and Lessing: A Comparative Study']

[C1:1010] Parrington, Vernon L., *Beginnings of Critical Realism in America*, New York: Harcourt, Brace and Company, 1930, pp. 299, 324-325.

[C1:1011] Paul, Fritz, 'Die Bohème als kreatives Milieu. Strindberg und Munch im Berlin der neunziger Jahre', *Georgia Augusta* (Göttingen), 33 (1980), 13-28. ['Bohemia as a Creative Milieu. Strindberg and Munch in Berlin in the 1890s'. Documents the participation of Sg and Edvard Munch in the bohemian circle which gathered at the Berlin tavern that Sg christened 'Zum schwarzen Ferkel' in the mid-1890s, and assesses the role of artistic Bohemia in the emergence of modernism]

[C1:1012] Paul, Fritz, 'Die Bohème als subkultureller "Salon". Strindberg, Munch und Przybyszewski im Berliner Künstlerkreis des Schwarzen Ferkels', in Roberto Simanowski, Horst Turk, und Thomas Schmidt, Hrsg., *Europa – ein Salon? Beiträge zur Internationalität des literarischen Salons*, Europäische Literaturen und internationale Prozesse 6, Göttingen: Wallstein-Verlag, 1999, pp. 305-327. ['Bohemia as a Sub-Cultural "Salon". Strindberg, Munch, and Przybyszewski in the Berlin Artistic Circle of the Black Piglet'. Paul examines the formation of an urban, artistic Bohemia as a modernist cultural phenomena with reference to the predominantly Scandinavian and German-speaking circle which foregathered in the early 1890s at the Berlin tavern that Sg christened 'Zum schwarzen Ferkel']

[C1:1013] Paul, Fritz, 'Die Bohème als subkultureller "Salon". Strindberg, Munch und Przybyszewski im Berliner Künstlerkreis des Schwarzen Ferkels', in Fritz Paul, **B1:361**, *Kleine Schriften zur Nordischen Philologie*, Hrsg. von Joachim Grage, Heinrich Detering, Wilhelm Heizmann, und Lutz Rühling, 350 pp. ['Bohemia as a Sub-Cultural "Salon". Strindberg, Munch, and Przybyszewski in the Berlin Artistic Circle of the Black Piglet'. Rpr. of **C1:1012**]

[C1:1014] Paul, Fritz, 'Die Legende von der Femme Fatale. Lou Andreas-Salomé in ihren Beziehungen zu skandinavischen Schriftstellern und zur skandinavischen Literatur', in Wolfgang Butt and Bernhard Glienke, Hrsg., *Der nahe Norden. Otto Oberholzer zum 65. Gerburtstag: eine Festschrift*, Frankfurt am Main: Peter Lang, 1985, pp. [215]-234. ['The Legend of the Femme Fatale. Lou Andreas-Salomé's Contacts with Scandinavian Authors and on Scandinavian Literature'. Paul comments briefly on Andreas-Salomé's acquaintance with the Friedrichshagen Circle with which Sg was briefly associated in 1892, and documents both her familiarity with his naturalistic plays as they were premièred at the Berlin Freie Bühne in the early 1890s, and her interest in Sg's psychological make-up]

[C1:1015] Paul, Fritz, 'Motiv: Eifersucht! Strindberg, Munch und Przybyszewski in der Berliner Bohème des Fin de siècle', in Ulrike Jekutsch und Walter Kroll, Hrsg., *Slavische Literaturen im Dialog*, Festschrift für Reinhard Lauer zum 65. Geburtstag, Wiesbaden, 2000, pp. 495-519. ['Motif: Jealousy! Strindberg, Munch, and Przybyszewski in the Bohemia of *fin-de-siècle* Berlin'. Explores the biographical and artistic aspects of a theme that is common to the writings and paintings of Sg, Edvard Munch, and Stanisław Przybyszewski. Just as they were jealous of one another in their relationships with the Norwegian bohemian Dagny Juel, so the motif of jealousy passes between their paintings and literary works during the 1890s, and all of them often write or paint with the characters, as well as the works, of the other two men in mind]

[C1:1016] Pedersen, Arne Toftegaard, *Det marginaliserede gennembrud. Tre moderne svensksprogede romaner fra 1880ernes Finland*, Åbo Akademis Förlag: Åbo Akademi University Press, 2002. 333 pp. ['The Marginalised Breakthrough. Three Modern Swedish Language Novels from 1880's Finland'. Refers frequently to Sg in a study of three Finland-Swedish novels of the 1880s by Alexandra Gripenberg, Ina Lange, and Karl August Tavaststjerna. Pedersen comments on the impact of *Röda rummet*, *Giftas*, *Det nya riket*, *Tjänstekvinnans son*, *Mäster Olof*, and Sg's naturalistic dramas in Finland, and their significance for the development of a new literary realism, as well as the debate over the Woman Question. Doctoral dissertation. German summary]

[C1:1017] Pérez Petit, Victor, *Los modernistas*, 2 vols, Montevideo: Biblioteca Artigas, 1963. [Originally published in 1903, Pérez Petit's discussion of Sg presents his misogyny in a positive light. He considers *Fadren* and *En dåres försvarstal* in some detail and mentions *Fröken Julie*, *Kamraterna*, and *Fordringsägare*]

[C1:1018] Perrelli, Franco, 'A Note on Strindberg and Euripides', *North-West Passage* (Turin), No. 1 (2004), pp. 69-78. [Documents Sg's interest in Euripides, and in Greek tragedy more generally, with reference to *Teaterns historia* (1898) by Herman A. Ring. Perrelli speculates on the relevance that Euripides's view of women, the idea of fate, and the conflict between man and the gods may have for *Pelikanen*, *Taklagsöl*, and *En blå bok*]

[C1:1019] Perrelli, Franco, 'Concordanze con Nietzsche', *Primafila*, November 1997, pp. 18-19. ['Affinities with Nietzsche']

[C1:1020] Perrelli, Franco, 'Eine Zimelie: der Briefwechsel zwischen August Strindberg und Friedrich Nietzsche', Hrsg. Sandro Barbera, Paolo D'Iorio, Justus H. Ulbricht, *Friedrich Nietzsche – Rezeption und Kultus*, Pisa: Ed. ETS, 2004, pp. 163-183. ['A Simile: The Exchange of Letters between August Strindberg and Friedrich Nietzsche']

[C1:1021] Perrelli, Franco, 'Strindberg e Weininger', in Franco Perrelli, ed., **B1:365**, *Omaggio a Strindberg*, pp. 59-70. ['Strindberg and Weininger'. Documents the personal and theoretical links which united Sg and the Austrian philosopher Otto Weininger (1880-1903). The article is accompanied by Italian translations of Sg's letters to Emil Schering, Karl Kraus, Artur Geber, and the Swedish man of letters, Algot Ruhe, in which Weininger's ideas concerning sexuality are discussed, as well as his correspondence with Weininger himself]

[C1:1022] Perrelli, Franco, 'The Strange Case of Dr Ibsen and Mr Strindberg', *North-West Passage* (Turin), No. 2 (2005), pp. 147-156. [Traces the significance of Ibsen and his work for Sg's creative space and the way in which several of his works (most notably *Giftas*, *Kvarstadsresan*, and *Fadren*) were designed to 'overturn' Ibsen, to supplant him or, in the case of *Fadren* in relation to *Hedda Gabler*, to 'kill him off']

[C1:1023] Perrelli, Franco, *Strindberg e Nietzsche. Un problema di storia del nichilismo*, Bari: Adriatica editrice, 1984. [200] pp. ['Strindberg and Nietzsche. A Problem in the History of Nihilism'. Perrelli questions the received image of Sg as a mad misogynist. Rather, his mind was shaped by the merging of a radical, liberal current associated with Georg Brandes, Henry Thomas Buckle, and Alexis de Tocqueville, and by a romantic current related to mysticism, which is associated with the ideas of Kierkegaard, Schopenhauer, and Eduard von Hartmann. Moreover, the aristocratic radicalism towards which Sg was moving in the late 1880s made him receptive to Nietzsche's ideas; but whereas Nietzsche sought to go beyond nihilism, Sg remained within the crisis analysed by the former, and in *Till Damaskus* and *I havsbandet* he anticipates the 'underman' of the Absurd rather than the superman of his sometime correspondent. Perrelli analyses Nietzsche's modest influence on Sg's plays as well as the two prose narratives 'Tschandala' and *I havsbandet*, and concludes with an overview of Sg's later opinion of Nietzsche as articulated after 1891 in his letters and *En blå bok*. Even the late Christian and socialist Sg provides further evidence of the spiritual and existential ground that he and Nietzsche explored. Indeed, Perrelli suggests that, in some respects, *En blå bok* may be considered the apex of Sg's nihilism]

[C1:1024] — Borio, Gianmario, *Skandinavistik* (Kiel), 15:1 (1985), 66-67.

[C1:1025] — Tiozzo, E., *Dagens Nyheter* (Stockholm), 2 December 1984.

[C1:1026] Perrelli, Franco, 'Strindberg: l'expérience du surhomme', Traduit de l'Italien par Michel Balzamo, in Elena Balzamo, ed., **B1:7**, *August Strindberg*, pp. 135-146. ['Strindberg: The Experience of the Superman'. Discusses Sg's direct and indirect relationship with Nietzsche, his familiarity with the latter's works, which he anticipated in the vivisections and plays of the 1880s, and Nietzschean motifs in his later novels and plays, including both *I havsbandet* and 'Tschandala'. Summarises much of the argument in **C1:1023**]

[C1:1027] Perrelli, Franco, 'Una lettera di Giacosa a Strindberg', in Roberto Alonge, ed., *Materiali per Giacosa*, Genova-Milano: Costa & Nolan, 1998, pp. 334-339. ['A Letter From Giacosa to Strindberg'. Introduces a letter to Sg from the Italian dramatist Giuseppi Giacosa (1847-1906)]

[C1:1028] Peterson, August, *Birger Sjöberg den okände*, Stockholm: Natur och Kultur, 1944, 427 pp. ['Birger Sjöberg the Unknown'. Documents Sjöberg's admiration for Sg and speculates on the possible influence of *Röda rummet* on his novel *Kvartetten som sprängdes* (1924)]

[C1:1029] Petrić, V[ladimir], 'Strindberg protiv Ibsena', *Knjizevnost* (Belgrade), 19:10 (1954), 300-314. ['Strindberg versus Ibsen'. Essentially a comparison of *Fröken Julie* with *A Doll's House*. R.584]

[C1:1030] Petty, John Carson, 'The Stranger's Return: Strindberg, Kierkegaard, and Nietzsche', *Orbis Litterarum* (Copenhagen), 46:1 (1991), 15-26. [Compares the symmetrical structural pattern of *Till Damaskus I*, which exemplifies the theme of the Stranger's return, with ideas of recurrence and repetition in Kierkegaard's *Gjentagelsen* (Repetition, 1843) and Nietzsche's *Also Sprach Zarathustra* (1883), which also contribute to the 'typification' of the *dramatis personae* in the play]

[C1:1031] Piast, V[ladimir Alekseevich], '[August Strindberg. Instead of an Obituary]', *Novaia zhizn'* (St Petersburg), 1912:5, pp. 203-212. [An alternative obituary in the form of reflections on Sg's final years and a comparison with Tolstoi's last days. Piast also includes an account of the journey he made to Stockholm, partly at Alexandr Blok's behest, when he met Sg's eldest daughter, Karin Smirnoff, and saw *Fröken Julie* at the Intimate Theatre. E.864]

[C1:1032] Piast, Vladimir Alekseevich, 'Vospominaniia o Bloke', in *Aleksandr Blok v vospominaniiakh sovremennikov v dvukh tomakh*, 1, Moscow, 1980. Illus. 549 pp. ['Recollections of Blok'. Discusses Blok's admiration for Sg during the period of his close friendship with Piast in 1911-1912]

[C1:1033] Piast, Vl[adimir Alekseevich], *Vospominaniia o Bloke, Pis'ma A. Bloka*, Moscow and Leningrad: Atenei, 1923. 105 pp. [Gives details of Aleksandr Blok's acquaintance with Sg's works and his correspondence with Piast about Sg, pp. 91-92. Republished in Blok's *Sobranie sochinenii*, Vol. 8, Moscow and Leningrad: Literatura, 1963, p. 339. E.914]

[C1:1034] Pimenova, E., '[Bjørnson's Views on Strindberg and Ibsen]', *Studia* (Moscow), 1912:22, p. 16. [Apropos the publication of some of Bjørnson's letters in Berlin. E.859]

[C1:1035] Pirjeveć, Dušan, *Ivan Cankar in evropska literatura*, V Ljubljani, Cankarjeva zal., 1964. Illus. 489 pp. ['Ivan Cankar and European Literature'. Comments briefly on Sg's relevance for the work of the Slovenian novelist, dramatist, and poet (1875-1918)]

[C1:1036] Pochljobkin, W. W., 'The Development of Scandinavian Studies in Russia up to 1917', *Scandinavica* (London), 1:2 (1962), 89-113. [Notes the influence of Sg on both Maksim Gor'kii and Alexandr Blok, pp. 91-92]

[C1:1037] Poort, Herman, 'Letterkundig overzicht: IX. Ibsen-Strindberg-Wedekind', *De opbouw* (Utrecht), 4 (1921-22), 518-532. [Discusses Sg together with Ibsen and Wedekind]

[C1:1038] Poppenberg, Felix, 'Zwischen den Dramen', *Der Türmer* (Stuttgart), 5 (1903), 456-464. ['Between Plays'. Compares *Brott och brott* with Bjørnstjerne Bjørnson's play *Paul Lange og Tora Parsberg* (1893)]

[C1:1039] Pos, W[illy] Ph[ilip], *De toneelkunstenaar August Defresne: Toneelschrijver, regisseur toneelleider*, Amsterdam: Moussault, 1971. Illus. 271 pp. ['The Theatre Artist August Defresne: Playwright, Director, Company Leader'. A monograph on the Dutch dramatist and director who played a significant role as an intermediary for the reception of Sg's works in Holland]

[C1:1040] Poulenard, Elie, *Strindberg et Rousseau*, Paris: Presses Universitaires de France, 1959. [188] pp. [A well-documented examination of Sg's claim to have been a disciple of Rousseau during the 1880s. Poulenard considers his agrarian socialism in *Bland franska bönder* and elsewhere, his critique of culture and material luxury, and his subjectivism. He discusses *Det nya riket, Svenska öden och äventyr*, and the essays 'Om realism' (On Realism, 1882) and 'Om det allmänna missnöjet' (On the General Discontent, 1884), and compares aspects of Sg's project with the ideas of C. J. L. Almqvist, Tolstoi, and Zola. He also relates Sg's Rousseauism to his interest in contemporary thinkers, including Herbert Spencer, Max Nordau, Henry George, and Charles Darwin, and charts his interest in the ideas of Rousseau from *Röda rummet* in 1879 to his encounter with Nietzsche's philosophy in 1888]

[C1:1041] — Ahlström, Stellan, *Sydsvenska Dagbladet* (Malmö), 15 December 1959.

[C1:1042] — Dahlström, Carl E. W. L., *Scandinavian Studies* (Lawrence, Kansas), 32:3 (1960), 170-171.

[C1:1043] — Edqvist, Sven-Gustaf, *Arbetet* (Malmö), 3 January 1960.

See also **A4:61**

[C1:1044] Poulenard, Elie, 'Verner von Heidenstam et Auguste Strindberg', *Etudes Germaniques* (Paris), 15:4 (1960), 338-352. [Compares and contrasts Sg with Heidenstam (1859-1940), and charts the profound impact which each writer had on the other from their first contacts in the mid-1880s to the Strindberg Feud in 1910-12]

[C1:1045] Printz-Påhlson, Göran, 'Realism as Negation', in Alex Bolckmans, ed., *Literature and Reality: Creatio versus Mimesis. Problems of Realism in Modern Nordic Literature*, Proceedings of the 11th Study Conference of the International Association for Scandinavian Studies, Ghent: Scandinavian Institute, University of Ghent, 1977, pp. 133-147. [Identifies Sg as a prime example of the anxiety of influence and comments on his opinion of the Swedish romantic novelist and poet C. J. L. Almqvist (1793-1866), as he articulates it in the essay 'Om realism' (1892) and *Tal till svenska nationen*]

[C1:1046] Prunier, Francis, 'Au-delà de l'Ibsénisme. Un Nietzschéen: Strindberg', *La Revue des lettres modernes* (Paris), 30 (1958), 413-424. ['After Ibsenism. A Nietzschean: Strindberg'. Suggests that, as a tragedian, Sg is a late-comer and influenced in his naturalism by Zola, Ibsen, and the Goncourt brothers, as well as by numerous thinkers and psychologists, from Edouard von Hartmann in *Philosophie des Unbewußten* to the experimental psychology of Jean-Martin Charcot and Hippolyte Bernheim. Moreover, while Jolivet claims in **C1:625** that Sg's work does not display the impact of Nietzsche before 'Tschandala' and *I havsbandet*, a study of *Fröken Julie* (especially its Preface), suggests that it was thanks to him that Sg had already rediscovered 'the spirit of Greek tragedy']

[C1:1047] Radoff, Sarah F., 'The Intellectualist in Strindberg and Turgeniev', *Texas Review* (Dallas), 7:3 (1922), 215-235.*

[C1:1048] Raleigh, John H., 'Strindberg and O'Neill as Historical Dramatists', in Marc Maufort, ed., *Eugene O'Neill and the Emergence of American Drama*, Amsterdam: Rodopi, 1989, pp. 59-75.

[C1:1049] Raleigh, John Henry, 'Strindberg in Andrew Jackson's America: O'Neill's *More Stately Mansions*', *Clio* (Fort Wayne, Indiana), 13:1 (1983), 1-15. [In fact Raleigh compares *More Stately Mansions* with several of O'Neill's other plays, but only very briefly with Sg]

[C1:1050] Ramsden, G., '[Scandinavian Mystics]', Translated by L. Umanets, *Russkaia mysl'* (Moscow), 7 (1903), 117-136. [On Sg as an exemplary figure in the inward, mystical turn taken by Scandinavian literature at the *fin de siècle*, p. 133. E.721]

[C1:1051] Rasch, Wolfdietrich, 'Edvard Munch und das literarische Berlin der neuenziger Jahre', in Henning Bock and Günther Busch, Hrsg., *Edvard Munch. Probleme – Forschungen – Thesen*, München: Prestel, 1973, pp. 14-24. ['Edvard Munch and Literary Berlin in the 1890s'. Surveys Munch's association with literary circles in Berlin during the 1890s, including the tavern 'Zum schwarzen Ferkel', which he frequented together with Sg]

[C1:1052] Rawińskiego, Marian, *Miedzy misterium a farsa. Polska dramaturgia miedzywoienne w kontekscie europejskim*, Lublin, 1986. [A comparative study of Polish and European drama which links the work of Stanisław Ignacy Witkiewicz with Sg, Edgar Allan Poe, and Antonin Artaud, in the course of a general discussion of the modern grotesque]

[C1:1053] Reding, Yngve J:son, 'Strindberg och Snoilsky', *Sundsvalls Tidning*, 2 September 1959. [Compares Sg with the Swedish Signature poet Count Carl Snoilsky (1841-1903)]

[C1:1054] Reilly, John H., 'August Strindberg, Dramaturge', in *Arthur Adamov*, New York: Twayne Publishers, Inc., 1974, pp. 80-82. [Suggests that Adamov is as much the subject of his study of Sg (**D2:1**) as is its ostensible subject, Sg, whose *Ett drömspel* prompted Adamov to write for the theatre. Both authors write autobiographical drama, using the stage as an arena for the expression of personal obsessions, and the real subject of Sg's plays is the relationship between dream and reality, something with which the author of *Professor Taranne* readily identified]

[C1:1055] Rem, Tore, 'Strindberg som Kiellands litterære agent', in *Bokhistorie*, Oslo: Gyldendal, 2003. 255 pp. ['Strindberg as [Alexander] Kielland's Literary Agent'. Discusses Sg's personal and practical links with the Norwegian novelist during the early 1880s when he sometimes sought to intervene in placing Kielland's works with Swedish publishers and theatres]

[C1:1056] R. H. [Richard Hejll], 'Kierkegaard och Sverige', *Den Enskilde* (Ramlösabrunn), 4:3-4 (1948), 104-105. ['Kierkegaard and Sweden'. Claims that, of all Swedish writers, Sg is the most influenced by Kierkegaard, although he never succeeded in understanding him]

[C1:1057] Richardson, Brian, 'Words made Flesh: Imagery as Causality in the Drama', in Karelisa V. Hartigan, ed., *Within the Dramatic Spectrum*, The University of Florida Department of Classics Comparative Drama Conference Papers 6, Lanham, Maryland:

University Press of America, 1986, pp. 160-167. [Compares the language of gender, will, and entrapment in Aeschylus's *Agamemnon* with the dialogue and action of *Fadren* in a discussion of dramatic imagery, both verbal and scenic, that also considers *Othello* and Sophocles's *Oedipus the King*]

[C1:1058] Rilke, Rainer Maria, *Briefe aus den Jahren 1914 bis 1921*, Hrsg. von Ruth Sieber-Rilke und Carl Sieber, Leipzig: Insel-Verlag, 1937. 421 pp. [Includes several references to Sg from the period when Rilke was particularly impressed by the Chamber Plays]

[C1:1059] Rinman, Sven, 'Strindberg och Runeberg. Föredrag vid Runebergsällskapets i Åbo fest den 5 februari 1959', *Finsk Tidskrift* (Åbo), 1959:3, pp. 102-115. ['Strindberg and Runeberg. Lecture at the Meeting of the Runeberg Society in Åbo, 5 February 1959'. Notes references to the Finland-Swedish writer Johan Ludvig Runeberg (1804-1877) in Sg's works, discussing Runeberg's tragedy *Kungarne på Salamis* (1863) and linking his poem 'Den gamle trädgårdsmästarens brev' (The Old Gardener's Letter) with Sg's play *Fritänkaren*. Rinman notes that Zacharias Topelius's story, 'Fritänkaren', in *Fältskärns berättelser* (1854-66) may also be of relevance here]

[C1:1060] Robert, Marthe, 'Strindberg et Weininger', *Obliques. Littérature Théâtre* (Paris), 1:1 (1972), p. 72. [A translation of two of Sg's letters concerning the Austrian philosopher Otto Weininger (1880-1903), together with a note on his significance for Sg]

[C1:1061] Robida, Adolf, 'Moderne slovenske enodejanke in dialogi', *Čas* (Ljubljana), 5:6 (1911), 255-267. ['Dialogue in the Modern Slovenian One-Act Play']

[C1:1062] Robida, Adolf, 'Naturalistične in realistične moderne slovenske drame', 1-2, *Čas* (Ljubljana), 5:3 (1911), p. 128; 5:4-5 (1911), pp. 178-179. ['Naturalism and Realism in Modern Slovenian Drama'. Includes comments on the importance of Sg's naturalistic plays for the development of dramatic naturalism in Slovenia]

[C1:1063] Robinson, James A., *Eugene O'Neill and Oriental Thought: A Divided Vision*, Carbondale & Edwardsville: Southern Illinois University Press, 1982, pp. 62-68, 120-121.

[C1:1064] Rodlauer, Hannelore, 'Franz Kafka Reads August Strindberg', Translated by Olivia Bittmann, in Michael Robinson and Sven Hakon Rossel, eds, **B1:387** *Expressionism and Modernism*, pp. 161-174. [Documents Kafka's familiarity with Sg's works and the dialogue which he conducted with his predecessor via his correspondence with Felice and Erna Bauer, who sent him several of Sg's books in German translation, including *I havsbandet*, *Götiska rummen*, *Ensam*, and 'Karantänmästarens andra berättelser'. Rodlauer also discusses Karl Kraus's view of Sg and the latter's influence on Kafka's *Die Verwandlung* (Metamorphosis, 1912)]

[C1:1065] Rogalski, Aleksander, *Próba konfrontacji. Przeglądy i syudia z zakresu literatury rosyjskiej, skandynawskiej, wloskiej i amerykanskiej* Warszawa: PAX, 1965. 324 pp. [Includes a comparison of Sg with Dostoyevskii in a study of Russian, Scandinavian, Polish, and North-American literature]

[C1:1066] Rogowski, Christian, 'Seduced Seducers. Strindberg as Intertext in Robert Musil's Comedy *Vinzenz und die Freundin bedeutender Männer*', *Deutsche Vierteljahrsschrift für Literaturwissenschaft und Geistesgeschichte* (Stuttgart), 64:3 (1990), 549-559. [Insists that in *Vinzenz und die Freundin bedeutender Männer*' (1924). Musil's farcical dramaturgy of surprise engages in a comprehensive dramaturgical debate with the realist poetics of drama in *Fröken Julie*. By way of several structural and textual resonances,

Musil questions the political and psychological assumptions that contribute to a demonisation of social and sexual roles in Sg. Musil's comedy is not only a parody of Sg's play but of theatrical conventions *per se*, and for which the latter is a representative example. Hence his rejection of Sg's naturalistic poetics and the philosophical assumptions about the nature of human relationships which provide the basis of naturalism]

[C1:1067] Röhl, Magnus, 'Inte bara Strindberg. Om nordisk litteratur och om Strindberg i en kosmopolitisk 1800-talskulturtidskrift', in Margareta Brundin, *et al.*, red., **B1:88**, *20 x Strindberg*, pp. 138-149. ['Not Only Strindberg. On Nordic Literature and on Strindberg in a Cosmopolitan 19th-Century Journal'. Focuses primarily on the brief but very early international presentations of Sg and his work by Robert Nisbet Bain (see **B3:327**) and Oskar Gustaf von Heidenstam in *Cosmopolis. Revue Internationale*, a journal edited by Fernand Ortmans and published monthly in 1896-1898 in Paris, London, and Berlin]

[C1:1068] Roininen, Aimo, 'Ulkomainen kirjallisuus', in *Kirja liikkeessä: kirjallisuus instituutiona vanhassa työväenliikkeessä (1895-1918)*, Suomalaisen kirjallisuuden seuran toimituksia 600, Helsingissä, 1993, pp. 248-256. ['Foreign Literature'. Examines Sg's influence on Finnish working-class literature in a study of writing as an institution in the early Finnish labour movement]

[C1:1069] Rokem, Freddie, 'Det hysteriska genombrottet', in Bertil Nolin and Peter Forsgren, eds, *The Modern Breakthrough in Scandinavian Literature*, Skrifter utgivna av Litteraturvetenskapliga institutionen vid Göteborgs universitet 17, Göteborg, 1988, pp. 137-144. ['The Hysterical Breakthrough'. Compares representations of hysteria in Ibsen's *Lille Eyolf* and Freud's case study of *"Dora"*, as well as both *Fröken Julie* and *Fadren*]

[C1:1070] Rokem, Freddie, 'Slapping Women: Ibsen's Nora, Strindberg's Julie, and Freud's Dora', in Lori Hope Lefkovitz, ed., *Textual Bodies: Changing Boundaries of Literary Representation*, Albany, N.Y.: State University of New York Press, 1997, pp. 221-243. [Identifies affinities between *A Doll's House*, *Fröken Julie*, and Freud's *Fragment of an Analysis of a Case of Hysteria* (1905), and traces similarities in the psyches as well as in the behaviour of the heroines of all these male-authored texts. According to Rokem, these women represent both a period-specific male view of the feminine and an almost paradigmatic example of the way in which men not only create fictional female characters but also watch them in the theatre, with a gaze that has been institutionalised. Moreover, by focusing on the slaps to the face which are administered and endured in all three of these texts, it is possible to analyse and illuminate the nature of this gaze, as well as of each work in relation to its fellows. Rokem also explores what he detects is a kinship between the textual systems of psychoanalysis and drama]

[C1:1071] Rokem, Freddie, 'Slapping Women: Ibsen's Nora, Strindberg's Julie, and Freud's Dora', in **B1:388**, *Strindberg's Secret Codes*, pp. 143-165. [A lightly revised version of **C1:1070**]

[C1:1072] Roloff, Volker, '*Luces de Bohemia* als Stationendrama', in Harald Wentzlaff-Eggebert and Sylvia Gonzalvo, eds, *Ramón del Valle-Inclán (1866-1936)*, Akten des Bamberger Kolloquiums von 6-8 November 1986, Beihefte zur Iberoromania 5, 1988, Tübingen: Niemeyer, pp. 125-138. ['*Luces de Bohemia* as a Station Drama'. Compares Valle-Inclán's play with *Till Damaskus* and *Stora landsvägen* in terms of their cyclical structure and protagonists. Like Sg's plays, *Luces de Bohemia* (1924) may be defined as a Station Drama]

[C1:1073] Romains, Jules, 'Le Centenaire d'Auguste Strindberg', *Les Nouvelles Littéraires* (Paris), 27 January 1949. ['The Centenary of August Strindberg'. Marks the centenary of Sg's birth with reflections on the image of him currently in circulation in Western Europe]

[C1:1074] Romains, Jules, 'Strindberg och vi', *Svenska Dagbladet* (Stockholm), 4 January 1949. ['Strindberg and Us'. Swedish version of **C1:1073**]

[C1:1075] Romains, Jules, 'Strindberg pour des yeux d'occident', in *Saints de notre calendrier*, Paris: Flammarion, 1952, pp. 133-139. ['Strindberg in Western Eyes'. Rpr. of **C1:1073**]

[C1:1076] Romberg, Bertil, 'Strindberg och Almqvist', in Rolf Arvidsson, Bernt Olsson, and Louise Vinge, red., *Diktaren och hans formvärld. Lundastudier i litteraturvetenskap tillägnade Staffan Björck och Carl Fehrman*, Malmö: Allhems Förlag, 1975, pp. 21-40. [Romberg identifies striking literary and temperamental similarities between Sg and the Swedish poet, novelist, and pamphleteer C. J. L. Almqvist (1793-1866), discusses how the received image of Almqvist was perceived by Sg and his contemporaries, and traces Sg's often hostile reaction to his forerunner, both in his letters and works. Sg sometimes appears to be consciously avoiding a writer with whose rich imagination and radical ideas he had much in common. Romberg also discusses Almqvist's role as a counterweight to Sg in *fin-de-siècle* Swedish cultural debate, driven largely by Ellen Key with an essay in which she dubs him Sweden's most modern writer, **C1:657**]

[C1:1077] Romefors, Bill, *Expressionisten Elmer Diktonius: En studie i hans lyrik 1921-1930*, Helsingfors: Svenska Litteratursällskapet i Finland, 1979, pp. 117-120. ['Elmer Diktonius the Expressionist: A Study of His Poetry, 1921-1930'. Identifies a strong temperamental as well as literary affinity between Sg and the Finnish modernist poet (1896-1961)]

[C1:1078] Roos, Carl, 'Die nordischen Litteraturen in ihrer Bedeutung für die deutsche', in Wolfgang Stammler, Hrsg., *Deutsche Philologie im Ausriß*, Bd 3, 2.Ausgabe, Berlin: Erich Schmidt Verlag, 1962, Sp. 373-406. ['The Importance of Nordic Literature for German Literature']

[C1:1079] Rops, Daniel, 'L'actualité de Strindberg et le génie du nord', *Revue de Genève*, May 1927, pp. 575-595. ['The Current Relevance of Strindberg and the Genius of the North']

[C1:1080] Rosefeldt, Paul, 'Questioning the Father's Authority: Henrik Ibsen's *A Doll's House*, Henrik Ibsen's *Ghosts*, August Strindberg's *Miss Julie*, August Strindberg's *The Pelican*', in *The Absent Father in Modern Drama*, American University Studies, Series III, Comparative Literature, Vol. 54, New York: Peter Lang, 1995, pp. 25-38. [Compares two plays by each dramatist, which are given psychological and sociological depth by their use of the absent father, through whom paternity, legitimacy, heredity, and family life in general are problematised. Also discusses *Fadren*]

[C1:1081] Rost, Nico, 'Strindberg en Nietzsche', *Nieuwe Rotterdamsche courant*, 23 September 1922. ['Strindberg and Nietzsche']

[C1:1082] Roters, Eberhard, 'August Strindberg', in Gesine Asmus, Hrsg., *Berlin um 1900*, Ausstellung der Berlinischen Galerie in Verbindung mit der Akademie der Kunste zu den Berliner Festwochen 1984, Berlin: Nicolaie Verlag, 1984, pp. 348-349. Illus.

[Identifies Sg as a significant presence in Berlin in 1892-93 (not 1891 as stated) in the richly-illustrated catalogue for an exhibition documenting *fin-de-siècle* Berlin]

[C1:1083] Rottem, Øystein, '"Humbug det også, bare humbug…" – Nietzsche, Hamsun og Den Store Illusjon', *Bogens Verden* (Copenhagen), 1995:2. On line: http://www.kb. dk/guests/natl/db/bv-95/2-95/rottem.htm ['"Humbug, that Too, Just Humbug": Nietzsche, Hamsun, and the Great Illusion'. Demonstrates that Sg was instrumental in alerting Knut Hamsun to the work of Nietzsche who, alongside Dostoevskii and Sg himself, exerted a powerful impression on the younger writer]

[C1:1084] Ruest, Anselm, 'Von Swedenborg zu Strindberg', *Die Aktion* (Berlin-Charlottenburg), 2:4 (22 January 1912), Sp. 104-108. ['From Swedenborg to Strindberg']

[C1:1085] Ryan, Steven T., 'The Terroristic Universe of *The Narrow House*', *Southern Quarterly* (Hattiesburg, Virginia), 28:4 (1990), 35-44. [Discusses the treatment of family life in Evelyn Scott's novel *The Narrow House* (1921) which, in Ryan's opinion, successfully merges the naturalism of Ibsen and the expressionism of Sg, as represented by its pretexts, *Ghosts* and *Dödsdansen I*]

[C1:1086] Rydén, Per, *Domedagar. Svensk litteraturkritik efter 1880*, Skrifter utgivna av Avd. för pressforskning [14], Lund: PRESS & LITTERATUR, 1987. 584 pp. [Discusses the role of the literary critic and the increasing professionalisation of criticism in the Swedish press after 1880 with reference to the work of Carl David af Wirsén, Oscar Levertin, Fredrik Böök, Klara Johanson, Anders Österling, John Landquist, Sten Selander, *et al.* Includes numerous occasional references to Sg and a detailed discussion of Wirsén's hostile response to the innovatory dramaturgy of *Till Damaskus*]

[C1:1087] Rydén, Per, *En kritikers väg. Studier i Oscar Levertins litteraturkritik 1883-1896*, Lund: C. W. K. Gleerup Bokförlag, 1974, pp. 31-36, 43-46, 75-84, 168-170, 193-195. [Discusses Levertin's generally positive opinion of Sg's pre-Inferno works, his influence on Levertin as a writer, and the latter's subsequent divergence from the literary ideals of the 1880s as represented by the early Sg, of whose later works he was, for the most part, highly critical]

[C1:1088] Rydén, Per, *En kritikers värderingar. Studier i Oscar Levertins litteraturkritik 1897-1906*, Skrifter utgivna av Avd. för pressforskning 9, Lund: Liberläromedel; C. W. K. Gleerup Bokförlag, 1977. 373 pp. [Includes a discussion of Levertin's mainly critical response to Sg's post-Inferno works in a series of high-profile reviews in the Stockholm daily, *Svenska Dagbladet*]

[C1:1089] Rydén, Per, 'Strindberg och Levertin', in Rolf Arvidsson, Bernt Olsson, and Louise Vinge, red., *Diktaren och hans formvärld. Lundastudier i litteraturvetenskap tillägnade Staffan Björck och Carl Fehrman*, Malmö: Allhems Förlag, 1975, pp. 41-59. [Identifies three stages in Oscar Levertin's personal relationship with Sg, from mutual respect in the 1880s, their growing enmity after the publication of Levertin's and Heidenstam's manifesto, *Pepitas Bröllop* (1890), and Sg's scurrilous attack on the recently dead Levertin as 'his worst enemy' in *En blå bok*. Rydén also considers their literary influence, one on the other, as well as Levertin's frequently pre-judged reviews of many of Sg's later works, in which his preference for the pre-Inferno author is often apparent]

[C1:1090] Rydsjö, D., 'Ibsen and Strindberg', *Bokstugan* (Chicago), 12 (1928), 129-132.

[C1:1091] Saarenheimo, Mikko, *1880-luvun suomalainen realismi: kirjallinen tutkimus*, Porvoo: WSOY, 1924. 212 pp. ['Finnish Realism in the 1880s: A Literary Study'. A thesis on Finnish literary realism in the 1880s, for which Sg in *Röda rummet* was a important example]

[C1:1092] Saarenheimo, Mikko, *1880-luvun suomalainen realismi*, Turku: Kirja-Aurora, 2000. VIII+212 pp. ['Finnish Realism in the 1880s'. Rpr. of **C1:1091**]

[C1:1093] Sabaté Planes, Dolors, 'Locos y marionetas: Estudio comparativo de las tipologías expresionista y esperpéntica', *Exemplaria: Revista de Literatura Comparada* (Huelva), 3 (1999), 191-200. ['Madmen and Marionettes: A Comparative Study of the Forms of Expressionism and the Absurd'. Compares Ramón María del Valle-Inclán's play *Luces de Bohemia* (1924) and his 'Comedias bárbaras' (1907-1922) with *Till Damaskus I*]

[C1:1094] Salvesen, Hugh, 'The Disappointed Idealist: August Strindberg in Karl Kraus' Periodical *Die Fackel*', *New German Studies* (Hull), 9:3 (1981), 157-179. [Considers Sg as a figure of general contemporary interest in Vienna as well as the particular significance he held for Kraus. Documents the important place accorded him in Kraus's journal *Die Fackel* where he was, for a time, one of the most prominent contributors, often in extracts from his work edited by Emil Schering. Salvesen also discusses the constellation formed by Sg, Kraus, and Otto Weininger, and their mutually sustaining opinions about women and sexuality]

[C1:1095] Samuelsson, Rune, 'Tre Strix. Strindberg, Engström och tidskriften', *Årsbok Albert Engström* (Stockholm), 18 (1999), pp. 11-18. ['Three Strix. Strindberg, Engström, and the Journal'. An account of Engström's relationship with Sg whom he sometimes referred to affectionately as 'Strix', the name he also gave the humorous journal in which he published his drawings and sketches]

[C1:1096] Sanborn, Torunn Ystaas, 'Strindberg og Nora, om "Det vidunderlige"', *Vinduet* (Oslo), 31:2 (1977), 83-88. ['Strindberg and Nora, On the "Miraculous"'. Discusses Sg's story 'Ett dockhem' in *Giftas* as a critical reading of Ibsen's *A Doll's House*, focusing on Nora's recurring phrase of ultimately disappointed expectation, 'Det vidunderlige' (the miraculous)]

[C1:1097] Sandbach, Mary, 'August Strindberg and John Stuart Mill', *Scandinavica* (Norwich), 25:1 (1986), 33-48. [Argues that, although they were temperamentally and intellectually so different, Mill was important to Sg who knew, and was impressed by, some of his work, including *On Liberty* and *The Subjection of Women*. He refers to Mill in *Giftas* as well as several of his essays on the woman question, and Sandbach claims that Sg also had Mill clearly in mind when writing both *I havsbandet* and *En blå bok*]

[C1:1098] Sarrazac, Jean-Pierre, 'Adamov devant Strindberg: la dramaturgie de l'aveu', in Gunnel Engwall, red., **B1:121**, *Strindberg et La France*, pp. 83-96. ['Adamov on Strindberg: The Dramaturgy of Confession'. Confirms that Sg was a constant inspiration to, and influence on, Adamov in plays as seemingly dissimilar as *Le Professeur Taranne*, *Paolo Paoli*, and *Si l'été revenait*. Sarrazac also considers Adamov's writings about Sg and his response to productions (or planned productions) of his plays by Artaud and Roger Blin]

[C1:1099] Sartre, Jean-Paul, 'Strindberg, vår "fordringsägare"', *Dagens Nyheter* (Stockholm), 28 January 1949. ['Strindberg, Our "Creditor"'. 'All those who nowadays believe that man is no more than his life have something to learn and profit from Sg's drama. ...

What is the husband in *Dödsdansen* other than what he has made of his wife and what his wife has made of him? What are they both except the frightful and ambiguous link which shackles them to each other in love and hate – and what is that link except the twenty (sic) years of life in a mutual prison']

[C1:1100] Sayers, William, 'A Schoolmaster's June Day Walk Round the City: Joyce and Strindberg's Albert Blom', *Studia Neophilologica* (Stockholm), 61:2 (1989), 183-192. [Documents Joyce's knowledge of *Tjänstekvinnans son*, *En dåres försvarstal*, and several of the plays, two of which (*Dödsdansen* and *Spöksonaten*) he saw in Zürich. He seems also to have known *Giftas* and the account of Albert Blom's walk from one part of Stockholm to another in 'Måste' (Needs Must) may well have contributed to his account of Bloom's day in *Ulysses*, since the latter contains numerous echoes of the former, all identified here. In all probability, Joyce may have been encouraged by the interpenetration of biography and fiction in Sg's works to forge other such links between his own life and his writing]

[C1:1101] Sayers, William, 'Aweghost Stringbag in *Finnegans Wake*', *James Joyce Quarterly* (Tulsa, Oklahoma), 27:1 (1989-90), 859-862. [Sayers points out that, although Joyce had no great regard for Sg, he knew several of his works and included him and his marriage to Harriet Bosse in the *Wake*, along with references to his scientific experiments as recounted in *Inferno*. He also carried over some of Sg's compositional techniques and the practice of cross-referencing of biographical and fictional material, which he knew from *En dåres försvarstal*, *Tjänstekvinnans son*, and *Giftas*]

[C1:1102] Schäfer, Theo, 'Wedekind und Strindberg', *Der Stadt-Anzeiger* (Mannheim), 26 (1928), No. 33.

[C1:1103] Schajowicz, Ludwig, 'Strindberg y el expresionismo', in *Los nuevos sofistas. La subversión cultural de Nietzsche a Beckett*, Rio Pedras: Universitaria, 1979, pp. 173-204. ['Strindberg and Expressionism']

[C1:1104] Scheffeuer, Herman, 'A Correspondence Between Nietzsche and Strindberg', *North American Review* (Boston, Mass.), No. 198 (August 1913), pp. 197-205. [Presents the brief 'pyrotechnic interchange of letters' between Sg, 'the wild, eccentric genius of the North', and 'the hapless philosopher', Nietzsche. The text of the letters is given in English translation]

[C1:1105] Schepens, Piet, 'Nietzsche en Strindberg', *De Vlaamsche gids* (Brussels), 18 (1929-30), 75-79. ['Nietzsche and Strindberg']

[C1:1106] Schickele, René, 'August Strindberg', 1-2, *Die Aktion* (Berlin), 2:4 (22 January 1912), Sp. 103-104, 656-657. [Regards Sg as the prototype of 'der unglücklich Glücklichen'. Declares that 'Sg is our password']

[C1:1107] Schickele, René, 'August Strindberg', in Hans-Peter Bayerdörfer, Hrsg., **B3:85**, *Strindberg auf der deutschen Bühne*, pp. 199-201. [Rpr. of part one of Schickele's essay in *Die Aktion*, **C1:1106**]

[C1:1108] Schickele, René, 'August Strindberg', in Benno von Wiese. Hrsg., *Deutsche Dramaturgie vom Naturalismus bis zur Gegenwart*, Tübingen: Max Niemeyer Verlag, 1970, pp. 38-39. [Rpr. of part two of Schickele's essay in *Die Aktion*, **C1:1106**]

[C1:1109] Schickele, René, 'August Strindberg', *Slavko Vesna* (Bjelovar), 1:2 (1912), 30-31. [Serbo-Croat version of **C1:1106**. R.531]

[**C1:1110**] Schickele, René, 'Strindberg', *Das neue Magazin für Literatur* (Leipzig), 73:16 (1904), 477-478.

[**C1:1111**] Schimanski, Folke, 'Nietzsche im Norden', in *Widersprüche. Zur frühen Nietzsche-Rezeption*, Hrsg. im Auftrag der Stiftung Weimarer Klassik von Andreas Schirmer und Rüdiger Schmidt, Weimar: Verlag Hermann Böhlaus Nachfolger, 2000, pp. 35-51. ['Nietzsche in Scandinavia'. Surveys Nietzsche's impact on Scandinavian writers, from Ibsen to Edith Södergran. Discusses his relevance for Sg, pp. 37-38]

[**C1:1112**] Schleich, Carl Ludwig, 'Goethe und Strindberg. Eine Betrachtung', *Berliner Tageblatt*, 30 May 1918. ['Goethe and Strindberg. A Reflection'. Compares Sg with Goethe as multifaceted writers, both of whom had an interest in the natural sciences]

[**C1:1113**] Schleich, Carl Ludwig, 'Goethe und Strindberg. Eine Betrachtung', *Deutsch-Nordisches Jahrubuch für Kulturaustausch und Volkskunde* (Jena), 1921, pp. 29-33. ['Goethe and Strindberg. A Reflection'. Rpr. of **C1:1112**]

[**C1:1114**] Schluchter, Manfred, *Stanisław Przybyszewski und seine deutschsprachigen Prosawerke 1892-1899*, Stuttgart: Photo-Offsetdruck P. Illg., 1969. 117 pp. [Stanisław Przybyszewski and his German Prose Works, 1892-1899'. Deals with the tense relationship that developed between the Polish novelist and dramatist (1868-1927) and Sg in Berlin in 1893, and considers how the latter is represented in Przybyszewski's fictional trilogy, *Homo Sapiens*]

[**C1:1115**] Schön, Folke, 'Folkets sångmö. Nittiotalisterna och folkkulturen', *Fatuburen* (Stockholm), 1991, pp. 19-43. Illus. ['The People's Muse. Writers of the 1890s and Popular Culture'. Comments briefly on Sg alongside Selma Lagerlöf, Vernar von Heidenstam, Gustaf Fröding, and Erik Axel Karlfeldt, in a discussion of Swedish writers of the 1890s and the influence exerted by folklore and peasant culture on their work. Schön suggests that the rural literature with which the 1890s is particularly associated, and to which so many of these writers contributed, is framed by *Hemsöborna* in 1887 and *Kronbruden* in 1901]

[**C1:1116**] Schönström, Rikard, 'Diktarnas försvarstal. Strindberg, Per Olov Enqvist och förförelsens ängel', in Helga Kress, Hrsg., *Litteratur og kjønn i Norden. Foredrag på den XX. studiekonferanse i International Association for Scandinavian Studies (IASS)*, Reykjavík: Háskólaútgáfan Universitets forlag, 1996, pp. [257]-270. ['The Writers' Apology. Strindberg, Per Olov Enquist, and the Angel of Seduction'. Considers the background to *Fröken Julie*, the personal guilt which the play partly conceals but also expresses concerning Sg's relationships with the under-age Martha Hansen, her brother Ludvig (who Schönström identifies as undoubtedly the model for Jean), and Siri von Essen. Also examines Enquist's reading of the play in *Kartritarna*, **E12:84**, and comments on motifs it shares with 'Genvägar' (Short Cuts), '*Fadren*, 'Tschandala', and *I havsbandet*]

[**C1:1117**] Schoolfield, George C., 'Scandinavian-German Literary Relations', *Yearbook of Comparative and General Literature* (Bloomington, Indiana), 15 (1966), pp. 19-35. [Comments briefly on Sg's 'manifold effects on German literature' in a largely bibliographical overview of German-Scandinavian literary relations]

[**C1:1118**] Schoolfield, George C., 'Rilke and Strindberg: A Doxochronology', *Modern Austrian Literature* (Binghamton, N.Y.), 15:3-4 (1982), 145-168. [Clarifies the extent of Rilke's familiarity with Sg's life and works, initially gleaned from intermediaries like

Laura Marholm, Lou Andreas-Salomé, and Ellen Key. Schoolfield surmises possible links between Sg's writings and some of Rilke's (e.g. *Inferno* and *Malte Laurids Brigge*). Rilke became better acquainted with Sg's works in 1911, when he responded warmly to the Chamber Plays of 1907, got to know the autobiographical fictions, and eulogised Sg in his correspondence, but 1915 was his true '*annus Strindbergensis*', when he saw and rated *Spöksonaten* and *Dödsdansen* highly in performance. Later productions of *Advent* and *Ett drömspel* impressed him less, and he was disappointed by Carl Ludwig Schleich's volume of recollections, **R:1929**, as well as by Sg's daughter with Frida Uhl, whom he met in October 1915]

[C1:1119] Schoolfield, George C., 'Strindberg and Diktonius: A Second Chapter', in Marilyn Johns Blackwell, ed., **C1:142**, *Structures of Influence*, pp. 183-199. [On Sg's place in the life and work of the major Finland-Swedish modernist poet (1896-1961) who 'learned a great deal' from Sg's poetry. Identifies and analyses Sg's presence in a sequence of three poems entitled 'Kuokkala', in *Jordisk ömhet* (Earthly Tenderness, 1938). Schoolfield also comments briefly on *I havsbandet*]

[C1:1120] Schottmann, Hans, 'Ahasver in Schweden', in José Cajot, Ludger Kremer, und Hermann Niebaum, Hrsg., *Lingua theodisca: Beiträge zur Sprach- und Literaturwissenschaft. Jan Goossens zum 65. Geburtstag*, Niederlande Studien 16, Münster, 1995, pp. [1043]-1051. ['Ahasuerus in Sweden'. On the Ahasuerus motif in the work of Viktor Rydberg, Gustaf Fröding, Per Hallström, Pär Lagerkvist, and Sg]

[C1:1121] Schultz, H. Stefan, 'Thomas Mann's *Betrachtungen eines Unpolitischen*: Some Observations', *Modern Language Notes* (Baltimore), 90:3 (1975), 431-447. [Discusses Mann's use of quotation, exemplified by references to *Fagervik och Skamsund* and *Svarta fanor* in his *Betrachtungen*]

[C1:1122] Scobbie, Irene, 'Strindberg and Lagerkvist', *Modern Drama* (Lawrence, Kansas), 7:2 (1964), 126-134. [Compares *Till Damaskus* with Lagerkvist's play *Sista människan* (The Last Man). Both plays have abstract characters and a protagonist who has a supernatural force as his antagonist. They also implement a dramaturgy in which mood predominates over analysis]

[C1:1123] Sebald, W[infried] G[eorg] [Max], 'Mord an den Vatern: Bemerkungen zu einigen Dramen der spätbürgerlichen Zeit', *Neophilologus* (Groningen), 60 (1976), 432-441. ['The Father's Murder. Observations on some Dramas of the Late Bourgeois Era'. Studies the theme of parricide in plays by Sg (*Fadren*), Ibsen (*Ghosts*), and J. M. Synge (*The Playboy of the Western World*)]

[C1:1124] See, Klaus von, 'Hamsun – ein Zeitgenosse Strindbergs', *Staatstheater Darmstadt*, 11 (1978), 6-8. ['Hamsun – A Contemporary of Strindberg']

[C1:1125] Segerberg, Anita, 'Strindberg och Christina Stead. Om Strindbergs inflytande i Australien', *Strindbergiana* (Stockholm), 7 (1992), pp. 28-44. Illus. ['Strindberg and Christina Stead. On Strindberg's Influence in Australia'. Traces literary echoes and Sgian resonances in Stead's work, most notably in her novel *The Man Who Loved Children* (1940), which she sometimes referred to as 'A *Strindberg* Family Robinson'. Segerberg also documents her admiration for *Spöksonaten* which features in *Seven Poor Men of Sidney* (1934) and may be linked with her novel *The Beauties and Furies* (1936)]

[C1:1126] Segrestin, Marthe, 'Shakespeare, modèle ou miroir, le cas d'Ibsen et de Strindberg', *Littératures Classiques* (Paris), 48 (2003), 161-171. [Examines the influence of Shakespeare on both Ibsen and Strindberg. Documents the latter's knowledge of Shakespeare and suggests that the metaphor of life as a dream in *The Tempest* and the notion that 'Life's but a walking shadow' in *Macbeth* are relevant to the development of Sg's post-Inferno dramaturgy in *Till Damaskus* and *Ett drömspel*, and that Shakespeare not only indicated the reversability of everything that Sg explores in *Till Damaskus* and elsewhere, but also played an intertextual role in *Fadren* and *Dödsdansen*]

[C1:1127] Sehmsdorf, Henning K., 'Strindberg's *Ett drömspel* and Peder W. Cappelen's *Sverre. Berget og Ordet*: Two Dreams of Love', in Marilyn Johns Blackwell, ed., **C1:142**, *Structures of Influence*, pp. 137-150. [Discusses Sg's influence on the Norwegian dramatist who has acknowledged his importance for his own development, and particularly the relevance of *Ett drömspel* for his drama *Sverre. The Mountain and the Word* (1977) which, like Sg's play, is polyphonic in structure, steeped in mythological imagery, and focuses on the theme of love]

[C1:1128] Shakh-Azizova, T[at'iana] K., *Chekhov i zapadnoevropeiskaia drama ego vremeni*, Moscow: Nauka, 1966. 151 pp. ['Chekhov and West-European Drama of his Time'. An important Russian contribution to the history of drama with references to Sg, pp. 7, 11, 13, 16, 23, 47, 51, 98, 104, 140. E.1017]

[C1:1129] Sharypkin, D[mitrii] M[ikhailovich], 'Blok i Strindberg', *Izvestiia Leningradskogo universiteta*, 18:1 (1963), 82-91. ['Blok and Strindberg'. Documents Alexandr Blok's admiration for Sg as a cultural personality as well as the latter's significance for Blok's writing. E.989]

[C1:1130] Sharypkin, D[mitrii Mikhailovich], 'Chekhov i Strindberg', *Russkaia literatura* (Leningrad), 1966, pp. 162-166. [Compares Chekhov with Sg and documents to what extent the former was familiar with the latter's works, mainly with reference to his correspondence with Maksim Gor'kii. E.1021]

[C1:1131] Sharypkin, D[mitrii] M[ikhailovich], '"Pamiati Avgusta Strindberga" Aleksandra Bloka', in *Blokovskii sbornik*, Vol. 1, Tartu, 1964, pp. 552-556. [Discusses the original version of Blok's essay 'Pamjati Avgusta Strindberga' (In Memoriam August Strindberg). E.999]

[C1:1132] Sharypkin, D[mitrii] M[ikhailovich], '[August Strindberg's Creative Development; Strindberg and Russian Writers]', in Sharypkin, *Russkaia literatura v skandinavskikh stranakh*, Leningrad: Nauka, 1975, pp. 142-213. [Traces Sg's contacts with Russian culture at different stages of his career, including his enthusiasm for Nikolai Chernyshevskii's novel *What is to be Done?* (1864) during the 1880s, in the course of a general study of the reception and influence of Russian literature in Scandinavia. E.1085]

[C1:1133] Shatkov, G. V. '[M. Gor'kii and Scandinavian Writers]', in *Gor'kii i skandinavskie pisateli*, Moscow, 1961, pp. 82-107. [Discusses the significance which Sg's writing had for Maksim Gor'kii, pp. 95-97. E.986]

[C1:1134] [Shaw, George Bernard], 'G.B.S. the Mystic', *Tomorrow* (London), 8 (August 1949), 29-35. [Quotes from an interview which Shaw gave to Paul Green: 'Sg was a great genius… one of the greatest. But his sense of the miraculous was so overpowering that he failed as an artist to give adequate place to the ordinary world of common sense']

[C1:1135] Shaw, George Bernard, 'The Greatest of the Great', *Adam* (London), 17 (January-February 1949), p. 1. [English version of **C1:1138**]

[C1:1136] Shaw, [George] B[ernard], *O dramaturgii i teatre*, Moscow: Izdatel'stvo Inostrannaia Literatura, 1963. 640 pp. [Includes comments on Dickens and Sg, pp. 60-61, Shakespeare and Sg, p. 458, and Sg's plays, p. 493, in a translation of Shaw on theatre and drama. E.995]

[C1:1137] Shaw, George Bernard, 'Strindberg', *Dagens Nyheter* (Stockholm), 15 May 1912. [A statement by Shaw written just prior to Sg's death]

[C1:1138] Shaw, George Bernard, 'Världsnamn inom litteraturen om Strindbergs verk och inflytande', *Svenska Dagbladet* (Stockholm), 24 December 1948. ['Renowned Names on Strindberg's Work and Influence'. Includes Shaw's contribution to a questionnaire on the importance of Sg]

[C1:1139] Sheaffer, Louis, *O'Neill: Son and Artist*, London: Paul Elek, 1974. Illus. XVIII+750 pp. [Sg's influence on Eugene O'Neill and O'Neill's views on Sg are referred to throughout this standard life-and-letters biography]

[C1:1140] Sheaffer, Louis, *O'Neill: Son and Playwright*, London: J. M. Dent & Sons Ltd, 1969, pp. 252-254, 420. [Comments on the influence of Sg on O'Neill, for whom he was 'the second god in his literary pantheon' after Nietzsche. To O'Neill, Sg was 'not only a daring innovator who had gone beyond Ibsen in broadening the dimensions of the drama but a kindred spirit, a man who expressed his own sombre view of life'. According to Shaeffer, to read Sg's plays was like reading pages from his own family history but 'perhaps the most important thing he took from Sg was the courage to explore his own character']

[C1:1141] Shideler, Ross, 'The Absent Authority: From Darwin to Nora and Julie', in Roger Bauer and Douwe Fokkema, eds, *Space and Boundaries, Proceedings of the XIIth Congress of the International Comparative Literature Association*, München, 1988, 5 vols, München: iudicium verlag, Vol. 3, pp. 185-190. [Examines the significance of the absence of a divine father implicit in *On the Origin of Species* for Ibsen in *A Doll's House* and *Hedda Gabler* and Sg in *Fadren* and *Fröken Julie*. Shideler observes that in both of the latter, the breakdown of male-oriented society implicit in Darwin is apparent]

[C1:1142] Shideler, Ross, 'Darwinism, Naturalism, and Strindberg', in Bertil Nolin and Peter Forsgren, eds, *The Modern Breakthrough in Scandinavian Literature 1870-1905*, Skrifter utgivna av Litteraturvetenskapliga institutionen vid Göteborgs universitet 17, Göteborg: Göteborgs Universitet, 1988, pp. 145-151. [Mainly concerned with *Fadren* and the Preface to *Fröken Julie*, but Shideler also includes a number of general observations on the implications of Darwinism for the 19th-Century naturalist writer, taking Gillian Beer's *Darwin's Plots* (1983) as an important critical reference point]

[C1:1143] Shideler, Ross, 'The Family Prison in Ibsen and Strindberg', in *New Visions of Creation: Feminist Innovations in Literary Theory*, International Comparative Literature Association 13, Tokyo 1991, Tokyo: ICLA, 1995, pp. 105-111. [See **C1:1148**]

[C1:1144] Shideler, Ross, *Questioning the Father: From Darwin to Zola, Ibsen, Strindberg, and Hardy*, Stanford, California: Stanford University Press, 1999. Illus. 240 pp. [Analyses a crisis in the 19th-Century patriarchal family within the intellectual and cultural context defined by Darwin's theory of evolution and the challenge it presents to the notion of a divine father, and to patriarchal structures of social order and feeling in general. The bourgeois male's resistance to the loss of the father's privileged role is exemplified in *Tjänstekvinnans son*, *Fadren*, *Pelikanen*, *Dödsdansen*, *Oväder*, and *Fordringsägare*, but Sg's work is also situated in relation to the debate on the role of women and sexual mores pursued in the literature of the Scandinavian Modern Breakthrough, as well as to texts by Zola and Thomas Hardy. Shideler also places Sg's ideas in the context of contemporary social and scientific thought]

[C1:1145] — Blackwell, Marilyn Johns, *Journal of English and Germanic Philology* (Urbana, Illinois), 100:4 (2001), 607-609.

[C1:1146] — Lorentzen, Jorgen, *Men and Masculinities* (Stony Brook), 5:4 (2003), 403-404.

[C1:1147] — White, Nicholas, *Journal of European Studies* (London), 20:4 (2000), 416-419.

[C1:1148] Shideler, Ross, 'The Patriarchal Prison in *Hedda Gabler* and *Dödsdansen*', in Faith Ingwersen and Mary Kay Norseng, eds, *Fin(s) de Siècle in Scandinavian Perspective. Studies in Honor of Harald S. Næss*, Columbia: Camden House, 1993, pp. 78-90. [Both these plays present what is a familiar struggle for the 20th Century – the battleground of the family in which a woman seeks to escape the prison of patriarchy and adapt to new roles in the light of both the contemporary Woman's Movement and Darwinian thinking, both of which challenge the patriarchal authority that is ironically restored at the end of each play]

[C1:1149] Shideler, Ross, 'Strindberg: The Man and the Myth as Seen in the Mirror of Per Olov Enquist', in Marilyn Johns Blackwell, ed., **C1:142**, *Structures of Influence*, pp. 65-78. [Establishes Sg's significance for Enquist before the documentary drama *Tribadernas natt*. Notes the presence of Sgian techniques and themes in *Färdvägen* and *Sekonden* before considering why he chose Sg as the subject for a play which uses literary, historical, political, and personal devices that had been previously employed by Sg, in order to wage an intellectual and ideological battle in the latter's manner]

[C1:1150] Shipley, Joseph T., *The Quest for Literature: A Survey of Literary Criticism and the Theories of Literary Forms*, New York: R. R. Smith, Inc., pp. 69-76, 95, 125, 138, 143, 148.

[C1:1151] Shonami, Gidon, 'Melodrama be-attifa shel tragedi-a (Iyun Hashva'ati)', *Bama* (Jerusalem), 34-35 (1975), 15-24. ['Melodrama Wearing the Mantle of Tragedy'. Compares *Fröken Julie* and *Hedda Gabler*, reading them as two 19th-Century dramas that are ultimately more closely related to melodrama than tragedy]

[C1:1152] Sichert, Margit, 'Die Moderne, das Unbewußte und der Traum: O'Neill's *The Emperor Jones*', *Amerikastudien/American Studies* (Heidelberg), 34:4 (1989), 403-412. ['The Modern, the Unconscious, and the Dream. O'Neill's *The Emperor Jones*'. Assesses the influence of Sg on O'Neill's play in respect of modernity, the unconscious, and dreaming. English summary]

[C1:1153] Siebenmorgen, Franz Rolf, 'Die vergessene Generation. Strindberg und der deutsche Expressionismus', *Theater und Zeit* (Wuppertal), 1 (1954), 173-174. ['The Forgotten Generation. Strindberg and German Expressionism']

[C1:1154] Sillanpää, Frans Eemil, 'August Strindberg', in *Kootut teokset, 8: Poika eli elämäänsä: taata nuistelee*, Helsingissä: Otava, 1991, pp. 319-325. [Reflections on Sg by the Finnish novelist (1888-1964) and Nobel Prize winner]

[C1:1155] 'Sil'vio', 'Bjørnson i Strindberg', *Ezhegodnik imperatorskikh teatrov* (St Petersburg), 3 (1910), pp. 46-60. ['Bjørnson and Strindberg'. Argues that the difference between these writers is largely generational: Bjørnson fights against the wrongs of the world on behalf of the historically wronged Norwegian people; Sg's protest is on a more individual plane – he is in revolt against the wrongs committed against him in the course of his own life. E.810]

[C1:1156] Sjöberg, Alf, 'The Secondary Role: The Vision of Master and Servant in *Anthony and Cleopatra*', in Gunnar Sorelius, ed., *Shakespeare and Scandinavia: A Collection of Nordic Studies*, Newark: University of Delaware Press, 2002, pp. 31-43. [Compares Sg's visions in Inferno with Shakespeare's standpoint in *Anthony and Cleopatra*, pp. 34-35. The volume also includes a translation of Sg's comments on *Julius Caesar* and the nature of historical drama from *Memorandum till Medlemmarne av Intima Teatern från Regissören*, pp. 19-30]

[C1:1157] Sjöberg, Alf, 'Strindberg och Moliére', in **D1:416**, *Teater som besvärjelse. Artiklar från fem decennier*, Red. av Sverker R. Ek, Ulla Åberg, Elsa Sjöberg, and Katarina Sjöberg, Dramatens skriftserie nr 4, Stockholm: P. A. Norstedt & Söners Förlag, 1982, pp. 141-155. Illus. [Includes a comparison of Molière's comedy *L'école des femmes* (1662) with *Fröken Julie*]

[C1:1158] Sjöberg, Leif, 'Tre citat i en Ekelöf dikt', *Horisont* (Vasa), 15:4 (1968), 71-74. ['Three Quotations in a Poem by Ekelöf'. Studies Sg and Rimbaud as intertextual presences in Gunnar Ekelöf's poem 'Absentia Animi' (1945). The Sg text alluded to is 'Indiansommar' from *Dikter i vers och prosa* (1883)]

[C1:1159] Sjöberg, Leif, 'Two Quotations in Ekelöf's "Absentia Animi"', *Germanic Review* (New York), 64:1 (1969), 45-60. [English version of **C1:1158**]

[C1:1160] Sjödén, K. E., 'På parkett i Paris: Strindberg och Ibsen', *Perspektiv* (Stockholm), 15 (1964), 165-167. ['In the Stalls in Paris: Strindberg and Ibsen']

[C1:1161] Sinding, Terje, 'Strindberg, Ibsen – tours et détours de la subjectivité', *Théâtre /Public* (Gennevilliers), 73 (1983), 17-19. Illus. ['Strindberg, Ibsen – The Twists and Turns of Subjectivity'. Considers the subjective nature of the later drama of Ibsen and Sg, with their interest in the inner life of the mind, or soul. Sinding compares Ibsen's approach in *When We Dead Awaken* with Sg's in *Till Damaskus*]

[C1:1162] S. J. [Siegfried Jacobsohn], 'Strindberg und Ibsen', *Die Schaubühne* (Berlin), 2:1 (1906), 604-608.

[C1:1163] Sjöstedt, Nils Åke, 'August Strindberg', in *Søren Kierkegaard och svensk litteratur. Från Fredrika Bremer till Hjalmar Söderberg*, Göteborg: Wettergren & Kerber, 1950, pp. 146-291. [Provides a detailed examination of Kierkegaard's relevance for Sg's works, their temperamental affinities, and common themes and preoccupations. Sjöstedt documents Sg's early reading of Kierkegaard and his lifelong adherence to certain key notions that were derived from the latter – for example of life as a sequence of stages that proved so significant for Sg's post-Inferno dramaturgy, or the notion that it should be lived by experimenting with standpoints, which played a central role both in his life and in the frequent shifts of direction in his writing, and his concern with point of view in narrative. The moral imperative in Kierkegaard's concept of the writer's calling and his role as a truth-teller colours Sg's work and his understanding of the artist's task from *Röda rummet* to the Chamber Plays of 1907 and *Tal till svenska nationen*, while the idea of repetition, which Kierkegaard analysed so probingly in *Gjentagelsen* (1843), is central to the form of *Till Damaskus*. This remains the most complete and suggestive published examination of a central topic in Sg studies and includes sometimes detailed discussion of individual works, including *Den Fredlöse*, *Mäster Olof*, *Röda rummet*, *Svenska öden och äventyr*, *Gillets hemlighet*, *Herr Bengts hustru*, *Sömngångarnätter*, *Tjänstekvinnans son*, *Skärkarlsliv*, *Till Damaskus*, *Ett drömspel*, and *Götiska rummen*]

[C1:1164] Sjöstrand, Martin, *Bonden i svensk litteratur*, Stockholm: LT:s Förlag, 1949, pp. 57-61. ['The Peasant in Swedish Literature'. Discusses Sg's Rousseau-inspired image of the peasant in the essays of *Likt och olikt* and his fictional portrayal of rustic life in *Svenska öden och äventyr* and *Hemsöborna*]

[C1:1165] Skloot, Robert, 'Warpaths and Boulevards: Sam Shepard on the Road of American Non-Realism', *Assaph: Studies in Theatre* (Tel-Aviv), C:3 (1986), pp. 207-214. [Considers how Shepard breaks free of the grip which Ibsen's realistic dramas of family life and their narratives of a search for truth that is knowable and finally revealed have exerted on American playwrights; he comes closer to Sg's irrational, expressionist form of drama, in which truth is unknowable and the ghosts from the past are intractable]

[C1:1166] Sławińska, Irena, 'August Strindberg i wczesny ekspresjonizm polski', *Biuletyn Lubelskiego Towarzystwa Naukowego Humanistyka* (Lublin), 1976:1, pp. 63-69. ['August Strindberg and Polish Expressionism'. Examines Sg's literary relations as an expressionist and symbolist with both his one-time friend, Stanisław Przybyszewski (1868-1927), in Berlin, and the dramatist and painter Stanisław Wyspiański (1869-1907)]

[C1:1167] Sławińska, Irena, 'Strindberg and Early Expressionism in Poland', in [Carl Reinhold Smedmark], ed., **D2:285**, *Strindberg and Modern Theatre*, pp. 73-84. [Compares Sg with Tadeusz Miciński (1873-1918), as well as Stanisław Wyspiański and Stanisław Przybyszewski, each of whom knew his work well. Although initially a personal friend, Przybyszewski was later estranged from Sg, yet both his prose fiction and dramatic works display many affinities with Sg's writings. This is especially so in the two plays *Große Glück* (1897) and *Das Goldene Vliess* (1901), which were published with two others as *Totentanz der Liebe* (Love's Dance of Death). But Przybyszewski's concept of man as entirely dominated by the power of sex reduced his characters to marionettes, and they consequently lacked the complexities with which Sg endowed his figures. Meanwhile, Wyspiański's visionary drama *Wesele* (The Wedding, 1901) has much in common with Sg's post-Inferno plays, not least for the way in which it juxtaposes the naturalistic and the visionary, and its concern with extra-verbal means of expression. Miciński, meanwhile, followed Sg's development in moving from naturalism to symbolism around 1900]

[C1:1168] Smedmark, Carl Reinhold, 'Edvard Brandes and August Strindberg. Encounter Between Critic and Artist', Translated by Horace Engdahl, in Marilyn Johns Blackwell, ed., **C1:142**, *Structures of Influence*, pp. 165-182. [Charts the personal and intellectual association between Edvard Brandes and Sg, their lively correspondence during the 1880s, and Brandes's response to Sg's work which was initially positive where *Röda rummet* was concerned, but subsequently critical, not least when confronted by *Fadren*, *Fröken Julie*, and *Fordringsägare*. His later lack of enthusiasm was often coloured by the two men's differences regarding the Woman Question although, following the cooling in their relationship, Brandes continued to fight on Sg's behalf in his reviews of *Hemsöborna* and *Skärkarlsliv*. However, he failed to appreciate the novelty of Sg's dramatic writings, especially where their innovative psychology or construction were concerned]

[C1:1169] Söderhjelm, Werner, *Oscar Levertin. En minnesteckning*, Förre delen: 'Levnad', Stockholm: Albert Bonniers Förlag, 1914. 502 pp. [A biographical study which includes an account of Levertin's early links with Sg, both personal and literary]

[C1:1170] Söderhjelm, Werner, *Oscar Levertin. En minnesteckning*, Senare delen: 'Författarskap', Stockholm: Albert Bonniers Förlag, 1917, pp. 322-343. [Surveys Levertin's hostility towards Sg's post-Inferno works, which he reviewed harshly in *Svenska Dagbladet*, thus contributing to the polemics surrounding Sg in the lead up to the Sg Feud of 1910-12, by which time Levertin was dead. Temperamentally the two writers had little in common]

[C1:1171] Söderhjelm, Werner, *Karl August Tavaststjerna. En lefnadsteckning*, Skrifter utgifna af Svenska Litteratursällskapet i Finland 46, Helsingfors, 1900. 324 pp. [The standard account of Tavaststjerna's life and work. Includes material concerning his personal acquaintance with Sg during the early 1890s and the impression which the latter's writings made on him]

[C1:1172] Söderhjelm, Werner, *Karl August Tavaststjerna. En lefnadsteckning*, 2. genomsedda upplagan, Helsingfors: V. Hoving, 1913. Illus. 375 pp. [Revised edition of **C1:1171**]

[C1:1173] Sokel, Walter H., *The Writer in Extremis: Expressionism in Twentieth-Century German Literature*, Stanford, California: Stanford University Press, 1959, pp. 34-39. [Compares the beggar portrayed by Flaubert in *Madame Bovary* with the Beggar in *Till Damaskus I* in order to distinguish Expressionism from Realism. With its focus on dream states, its subjectivity, and a tendency to make its characters aesthetic attributes and the literal embodiments of leitmotivs, Sokel regards *Till Damaskus* as the first fully expressionist drama. The expressionist character is not a fixed personality but the crystallisation of psychic forces, something that Sg was the first to develop on stage]

[C1:1174] Sokół, Lech, 'August Strindberg and Stanisław Ignacy Witkiewicz. A Parallel', in Nils Åke Nilsson, ed., *Swedish-Polish Literary Contacts. A Symposium in Warsaw, September 22-26 1986*, Kungl. Vitterhets Historie och antikvitets Akademien, Konferenser 3, Stockholm: Almqvist & Wiksell, 1979, pp. 73-82. [Traces the influence of Sg's dramatic theory and practice on Witkiewicz and discusses the 'striking' but 'complex' relationship between their plays. Sokół identifies common motifs and comparable plots such as the ghosts, vampires, and mummies which feature in the plays of both writers and confirm the profound spiritual affinity between them, one that may be traced both to a direct influence of Sg on Witkiewicz or to their common response to earlier sources, e.g. to Edgar Allen Poe. In brief, Witkiewicz inherited and portrayed the world that Sg depicted and criticised]

[C1:1175] Sokół, Lech, 'Dialektyka płci: Swedenborg, Balzac, Strindberg i Witkiewicz', *Studia Scandinavica* (Gdańsk), 10 (1988), 75-87. ['The Dialectics of Sex: Swedenborg, Balzac, Strindberg, and Witkiewicz'. English summary]

[C1:1176] Sokół, Lech, 'The Drama of Initiation: Villiers de l'Isle-Adam, Strindberg and S. I. Witkiewicz', in Donald Weaver, ed., **D2:331**, *Strindberg on Stage*, pp. 100-111. [Discusses Villiers and Sg as spiritual brothers who follow a similar evolution as artists. The former 'impregnates' the latter while Witkiewicz knew the work of both men well. Sokół thus links numerous plays by Witkiewicz with both Villiers's *Axel* and Sg's *Till Damaskus*, as well as *Ett drömspel*, and *Spöksonaten*, all of which share a concern with initiation that is at the heart of Villiers's play]

[C1:1177] Sokół, Lech, 'The Drama of Initiation: Villiers de l'Isle-Adam, Strindberg and S. I. Witkiewicz', Translated by Grzegorz Sinko, *Literary Studies in Poland*, 11 (1983), pp. 95-105. [See **C1:1176**]

[C1:1178] Sokół, Lech, *Groteska w teatrze Stanisława Ignacego Witkiewicza*, Studia i Materiały do Dziejów Teatru Polskiego, Tom 4, Wrockław: Zakład Narodowy imienia Ossolińskich-wydawnictwo Polskiej Akademii Nauk, 1973, pp. 106-110, 117-122. [Discusses Sg's importance for Witkiewicz's 'grotesque' theatre with reference to *Fadren, Fröken Julie, Samum, Dödsdansen, Pelikanen*, and *Spöksonaten*, concentrating in particular on the relevance of the grotesque elements in *Spöksonaten* for his play *Matka* (The Mother, 1924). Summary in French, pp. 211-213]

[C1:1179] Sokół, Lech, 'Hermaphroditic and Androgynous Characters in Strindberg and Witkiewicz', in Maria Janion and Nils Åke Nilsson, eds, *Polish-Swedish Literary Contacts*, Kungl. Vitterhets Historie och Antikvitets Akademien Konferenser 19, Stockholm: Almqvist & Wicksell International, 1988, pp. 63-72. [Discusses Sg's portrayal of hermaphrodites in *En dåres försvarstal*, *Giftas*, *Kamraterna*, *Fadren*, and *Påsk*, and comments on the influence they may have exerted on Witkiewicz's portrayal of women in his drama *Maciej Korbowa* and elsewhere. Nevertheless, the two dramatists differ in their notion of androgyny, and Witkiewicz subjected any borrowings he made from Sg to the laws of his own cosmos]

[C1:1180] Sokół, Lech, 'Metafizyka płci. Strindberg, Weininger i Witkacy', *Pamiętnik literacki* (Wrocław), 76:4 (1985), 3-15. ['The Metaphysics of Sex: Strindberg, Weininger, and Witkiewicz'. Suggests that Sg recognised in Weininger (1880-1903) the thinker who presented in discursive language those ideas that he had himself expressed in literary form. Weininger, meanwhile, used *Fadren* and *Fordringsägare* to define the nature of woman and, although it sometimes assumed parodic form, the man-woman relationship was also fundamental to the novels and plays of Witkiewicz, who knew the work of both men well]

[C1:1181] Sokół, Lech, 'The Metaphysics of Sex: Strindberg, Weininger and S. I. Witkiewicz', *Theatre Research International* (Oxford), 12:1 (1987), 39-51. [English version of **C1:1180**]

[C1:1182] Sokół, Lech, 'Postacie hermafrodytyczne i androgyniczne u Strindberga i Witacego', in Marii Janion, Nils Åke Nilsson, and Anny Sobolewskiej, eds, *Zwierciadła Pólnocy. Związki i paralele literatur polskiej i skandynawskiej*, Warszawa: Instytut Badan Literackich PAN, 1991, pp. 142-161. ['Hermaphroditic and Androgynous Characters in Strindberg and Witkiewicz'. New version of **C1:1179**]

[C1:1183] Sokół, Lech, 'S. I. Witkiewicz und Strindberg', *Die Welt der Slaven* (München), 22:2 (1978), 391-400. [Confirms the importance of *Spöksonaten* for Witkiewicz's development as a dramatist in whose twenty-three extant dramas the ghost motif appears seventeen times, reaching its apogee in *In a Small Country House* (1923) and *Matka* (The Mother, 1924), a play in which the vampire motif is also prominent]

[C1:1184] Sokół, Lech, 'Strindberg and Stanisław Ignacy Witkiewicz', *Swedish-Polish Literary Contacts* (Stockholm), No. 79 (1984), pp. 73-82.

[C1:1185] Sokół, Lech, 'Strindberg and Witkacy', *Le Théâtre Polonaise* (Warsaw), 20:6-7 (1978), pp. 16-20, 21-24. Illus. [Text in both French and English]

[C1:1186] Sokół, Lech, 'Strindberg i Witkacy. Paralela', *Spotkanie z Witkacym*, Jelenia Góra, 1979. ['Strindberg and Witkacy. Parallels'. Explores thematic and dramaturgical parallels between the plays of Sg and Stanisław Witkiewicz]

[C1:1187] Sokół, Lech, 'Witkacy w świetle Strindberga', *Teatr* (Warsaw), 1981:19-20, pp. 12-13. [Apropos the staging of Witkiewicz's play *Kurka Wodna* (The Water Hen) at Dramaten]

[C1:1188] Sokół, Lech, *Witkacy i Strindberg. Studium porównawcze*, Czesc I i II, Warszawa: Instytut Sztuki PAN, 1990, 215, 625 pp.

[C1:1189] Sokół, Lech, *Witkacy i Strindberg: dalecy i bliscy*, Wrocław: Wiedza o Kulturze, 1995. [449] pp. [A detailed analysis of Witkiewicz's debt to Sg and their affinities as writers and thinkers. Sokół focuses on their view of women, the metaphysics of sex, their interest in hermaphroditism as an index of decadence, and both men's break with naturalism in the theatre. The volume includes a summary in English: 'Witkacy and Strindberg: Distant and Close', and reworks some material previously published in **C1:1175**, **C1:1180**, and elsewhere. Of the plays, *Fröken Julie*, *Brott och brott*, *Dödsdansen*, *Till Damaskus*, *Ett drömspel*, and *Spöksonaten* are discussed in some detail]

[C1:1190] — Godlewska, Joanna, 'Witkacy i Strindberg', *Teatr* (Warsaw), 1995:12, p. 48. ['Witkiewicz and Strindberg']

[C1:1191] Sölvén, Arnold, 'Strindberg och Weininger', *Social-Demokraten* (Stockholm), 13 June 1921. [Comments on Sg's links with the Austrian thinker Otto Weininger (1880-1903) through affinities in their attitude to women]

[C1:1192] Sölvén, Arnold, *Strindberg och Weininger*, Göteborg: Framåt, 1921. 4 pp.* [Off-print of **C1:1191**]

[C1:1193] Sommar, Carl Olov, 'Ekelöf och Strindberg', *Strindbergiana* (Stockholm), 5 (1990), pp. 144-159. Illus. [Surveys Sg's place in Ekelöf's life and *œuvre*, as well as his response to *Ett drömspel*. Discusses Ekelöf's poems 'Blommorna sover i fönstret', 'Absentia animi', *En Mölna elegi* (1960), and 'Röster under jorden' (1951)]

[C1:1194] Sommar, Carl Olov, 'Ekelöf och Strindberg', in *Strindberg, Ekelöf och andra*, Stockholm: Sällskapet Bokvännerna, 1995, pp. 66-82. [Rpr. of **C1:1193**]

[C1:1195] Sommar, Carl Olov, 'Nittitalisternas värld – Sverige eller Europa?', in *Strindberg, Ekelöf och andra*, Stockholm: Bokvännens bibliotek, 1995, pp. 9-23. ['The World of the 1890's Generation – Sweden or Europe?' On the choice confronting Swedish writers in the 1890s between Sweden and nationalism, on the one hand, and Europe and internationalism, on the other. In the main, Sg assumed an international profile vis-à-vis the provincial regionalism of the next generation of Swedish writers, such as Karl Erik Karlfeldt and Selma Lagerlöf]

[C1:1196] Sommer, Bodil, 'Tre poetiska manifest i svensk litteratur', in Asmund Lien, red., *Modernism i skandinavisk literatur som historisk fenomen og teoretisk problem*, Trondheim: University of Trondheim, 1991, pp. 129-133. ['Three Poetic Manifestoes in Swedish literature'. On three Swedish poems about the writers' poetic intentions: Sg's 'Sångare', in *Dikter på vers och prosa*, Pär Lagerkvist's 'Ångest', in *Ångest* (Anguish, 1916) and Artur Lundkvist's 'Vi måste lära de nya melodierna' (We must Learn the new Songs) in *Svart stad* (Black City, 1930)]

[C1:1197] Sørensen, Villy, 'Mitt förhållande till Strindberg', Translated by Birgitta Steene, *Strindbergiana* (Stockholm), 14 (1999), pp. 46-49. ['My Relationship with Strindberg'. Reflections on the author's attitude to Sg by the Danish essayist and writer (b.1929)]

[C1:1198] Spector, Robert Donald, *Pär Lagerkvist*, Twayne World Authors Series, New York: Twayne Publishers, 1973, pp. 153-159. [Describes how Lagerkvist completed Sg's break with naturalistic drama and demonstrates how the latter's role in his development is apparent in 'Modern Theatre', **D1:604**. Lagerkvist's early plays are heavily indebted to *Till Damaskus* and *Spöksonaten*]

[C1:1199] Spengler, Oswald, *Der Untergang des Abendlandes. Umrisse einer Morphologie der Weltgeschichte*, 3 vols, Wien: Braunmüller, 1919-1923.

[C1:1200] Spengler, Oswald, *The Decline of the West*, Authorised Translation with Notes by Charles F. Atkinson, 2 vols, London: Allen & Unwin; New York: Alfred F. Knopf, 1926, Vol. I, pp. 24, 33, 35, 346, 352, 374. [English translation of **C1:1199**]

[C1:1201] Sprinchorn, Evert, 'Ibsen, Strindberg, and the New Woman', in Michael Bertin, ed., *The Play and its Critics: Essays for Eric Bentley*, Lanham, Maryland: University Press of America, 1956, pp. 45-66. [Discusses Sg's early response to Ibsen's *Brand* as well as the dialogue he conducted with *A Doll's House* in *Giftas*, *Kamraterna*, and *Fröken Julie*. Sprinchorn also considers *Hedda Gabler*, where Ibsen 'out-Sg's Sg in displaying the negative force of the unmotherly woman who can find no outlet for her energies and intellect', something Sg had previously depicted 'Mot betalning' (For Payment) in *Giftas*]

[C1:1202] Sprinchorn, Evert, 'Shaw and Strindberg', in John A. Bertolini, ed., *Shaw and Other Playwrights*, The Annual of Bernard Shaw Studies 13, University Park, Pennsylvania: Pennsylvania State University Press, 1993, pp. 9-24. Illus. [Sprinchorn retells Shaw's colourful account of his personal contacts with Sg and his attempts to interest the English theatre in Sg's plays. He compares Shaw's account of sexual conflict and his portrayal of women in *Candida* and *Man and Superman* with *Fadren* (the two last 'are unrealistic dramas, the one a debate and the other a nightmare, because their authors are more concerned with getting at what underlies the sexual conflict than with depicting believable, flesh-and-blood individuals'), and describes how both writers went on to transform their earlier world views in their later works, often in bitter dispute with their contemporaries, especially where their mutual anti-militarism was concerned]

[C1:1203] Sprinchorn, Evert, 'Strindberg Among the Prophets', in Paul Houe, *et al.*, ed., **B1:170**, *August Strindberg and the Other*, pp. 1-14. [Contextualises the intellectual and artistic revolution initiated by Sg's experimental science and dramaturgy during the 1890s. His work is characterised by a wide variety of artistic techniques and 'future historians may well see Sg as the Euripides of the new millennium, inaugurated when he tried to smash the atom using mortar and pestle'. Sprinchorn compares Sg's experimentalism with that of Ibsen, Thomas Mann, Robert Musil, and (especially) T. S. Eliot, whose definition of the mythical method is foreshadowed by Sg's practice in *Till Damaskus*. Eliot's *The Waste Land* (1922) also bears the imprint of *Spöksonaten* while Musil and Sg both used 'essay-ism' in their prose fiction to explore the middle ground between philosophy and literature, science and art, and the rational and the intuitive]

[C1:1204] Sprinchorn, Evert, 'Strindberg and Samuel Butler', *Meddelanden från Strindbergssällskapet* (Stockholm), 57-58 (1977), pp. 27-30. [Suggests that Butler's utopian novel *Erewhon* (1872) is a source for the way in which Fingal's Cave is depicted in *Ett drömspel*; Sg may well have been drawn to Butler by their mutual abhorrence of Darwinism]

[C1:1205] Sprinchorn, Evert, 'Strindberg and the Superman', in Göran Stockenström, ed., **D2:288**, *Strindberg's Dramaturgy*, pp. 14-26. [Although Sg's career intersected with Nietzsche's, whose impact on his works is evident in *Fröken Julie*, 'Tschandala', and *I havsbandet*, the nature of any direct influence is ambiguous. Sg differed from Nietzsche as to the nature of the coming superman and saw his insanity as proof of the fatuity of his ideas; thus he drew very different conclusions regarding the nature of the historical and cultural forces they were both responding to. Sg realised that the irrational and mystical side of existence has to intrude into the rational world of science and the logic of *I havsbandet* demonstrates that the moral ideal of the future must be a combination of the mystical or religious with the scientific or rational. He therefore deserves to be taken more seriously as a man of ideas]

[C1:1206] Sprinchorn, Evert, 'Strindberg and Georg Brandes', in Hans Hertel and Sven Møller Kristensen, eds, *The Activist Critic: A Symposium on the Political Ideas, Literary Methods and International Reception of Georg Brandes*, *Orbis Litterarum* (Copenhagen), 5 (1980, Supplement), pp. 109-126. [Discusses Brandes's influence on Sg, their personal relationship, Brandes's role in drawing Sg's attention to Nietzsche, and their subsequent divergence. Brandes regarded Sg's later works as a retreat into superstition, timidity, and mediocrity]

[C1:1207] S. S. [Sven Stolpe], 'Strindberg och Shakespeare', *Samtid och Framtid* (Stockholm), 7 (1950), 372-375.

[C1:1208] Ståhle, Carl Ivar, 'Tre soluppgångar', *Studier i nordisk filologi* (Helsingfors), 58 (1971), 270-279. ['Three Sunrises'. A comparative study of sunrises as depicted in Swedish poetry by Georg Stiernhielm (1598-1672), Gustaf Philip Creutz (1731-85), and Sg in his poem in hexameters, 'Stadsresan' (The City Journey), in the collection *Ordalek och småkonst*]

[C1:1209] Ståhle Sjönell, Barbro, 'Strindberg om Ibsen', *Nordisk Tidskrift* (Stockholm), 63:4 (1987), 495-510. Illus. ['Strindberg on Ibsen'. Documents the changes in Sg's view of Ibsen and his works from youth to age, and accounts for the often highly personal motives behind them]

[C1:1210] Stamenković, Vl., 'Dostojevski i Strindberg', *Književna novine* (Belgrade), 1961, 10. III. ['Dostoevskii and Strindberg'. R.588]

[C1:1211] Startman, Hans, 'Poe, Strindberg och Woolrich', *Jury* (Bromma), 5:1 (1976), 9-11.

[C1:1212] Steene, Birgitta, 'Maria Gripe's *Agnes Cecilia* as an Adult Children's Book', *Scandinavian Newsletter* (Groningen), 8 (1994-95), 2-4. [As well as *Agnes Cecilia*, Steene discusses accounts of childhood by other Swedish writers, including Astrid Lindgren and Sg in *Tjänstekvinnans son*]

[C1:1213] Steffen, Albert, 'Über Swedenborg, Goethe, Strindberg', *Das Goetheanum* (Dornach), 1 (1921-22), 319-320. ['On Swedenborg, Goethe, and Strindberg']

[C1:1214] Stenberg, Peter A., 'Servants of Two Masters: Strindberg and Hofmannsthal', *Modern Language Review* (London), 70:4 (1975), 820-829. [Essays an unconvincing comparison of Sg with Hugo von Hofmannsthal as two political rebels. Stenberg discusses Sg's *Lilla katekes för underklassen* (Little Catechesis for the Under Class, 1884) and compares *Fröken Julie* with Hofmannsthal's late comedy *Der Unbestechliche* (1923) on no firmer grounds than that in both plays servants have a key role and hence would seem to articulate their authors' political views]

[C1:1215] Stenberg, Peter, 'Strindberg and Grillparzer: Contrasting Approaches to the War of the Sexes', *Canadian Review of Comparative Literature* (Toronto), 1:1 (1974), 65-75. [Focuses on *Fadren*, which is dealt with here as a modern version of Clytemnestra's murder of Agamemnon, and Grillparzer's retelling of the Hero and Leander legend in *Des Meeres und der Liebe Wellen* (1831). Despite their formal differences, Stenberg proposes that the two plays are thematically similar. Thus, while one hides securely behind older theatrical traditions and the other initiates the development which leads to the transformation of those same traditions, both writers depict man as vulnerable to the rising power of woman, and portray patriarchy under threat from matriarchy]

[C1:1216] Stensgård, Erling, *Strindberg og Fru Marie Grubbe. Et fund fra firserne m.m.*, Aarhus: Phønix-Trykkeriet, 1960, 31 pp. ['Strindberg and *Fru Marie Grubbe.* A Find from the Eighties and other Matters'. Documents Sg's plans for a dramatisation of J. P. Jacobsen's historical novel from 1876 which describes a woman's misalliance with a servant with reference to an exchange of letters between Sg and Edvard Brandes in 1881-82, and to Brandes's correspondence with Jacobsen (1847-1885). How the transposition from novel into play was to be achieved can be seen in a copy of the novel now deposited in the Royal Library, Stockholm, in which Sg has divided up the text into acts and scenes. Stensgård also discusses subsequent dramatisations of Jacobsen's novel by Sven Lange and Beatrice Bonnesen, as well as Ebbe Hamerik's operatic setting with a libretto by Fredrik Nygaard]

[C1:1217] — Rinman, Sven, 'En Strindbergsepisod', *Göteborgs Handels- och Sjöfartstidning*, 3 June 1960. '['A Strindberg Episode']

[C1:1218] Stenström, Thure, *Den ensamme. En motivstudie i det moderna genombrottets litteratur*, Stockholm: Natur & Kultur, 1961, pp. 151-170, 240-253, 315-325. ['The Solitary. A Motif Study in the Literature of the Modern Breakthrough'. Considers what Stenström identifies as one of the central motifs in the literature of the Scandinavian Modern Breakthrough, which entails a fluctuating conflict between romantic individualism, on the one hand, and the more objective demands of naturalism, on the other. Where Sg is concerned, Stenström concentrates mainly on *Mäster Olof*, *Röda rummet*, the prose poem 'Solrök' (Heat Haze), *Utopier i verkligheten*, *Tjänstekvinnans son*, and *I havsbandet*, but touches on several other titles in pursuit of this main theme. Summary in French, pp. 366-375. Doctoral dissertation]

[C1:1219] — Wittrock, Ulf, *Samlaren* (Uppsala), 81 (1960), pp. 230-233.

[C1:1220] Stenström, Thure, 'Strindberg och Heidenstam i Visby', *Gotlands Folkblad* (Visby), 23 May 1954. ['Strindberg and Heidenstam in Visby']

[C1:1221] Stern, Martin, 'Funktion des Traums in der neueren Dichtung – am Beispiel Strindbergs, Trakls und Kafkas', *Universitas* (Stuttgart), 39 (1984), 279-291. ['The Function of Dreams in Recent Literature: The Example of Strindberg, Trakl, and Kafka'. Compares the role of dreams in the work of Sg, Kafka, and Georg Trakl. Heavily dependent on previous German interpretations of Sg's works, which are represented here primarily by *Ett drömspel*]

[C1:1222] Stockenström, Göran, '"The Great Chaos and the Infinite Order": The Spiritual Journeys of Swedenborg and Strindberg', in Erland J. Brock, ed., *Swedenborg and His Influence*, Bryn Athyn: Academy of the New Church Press, 1988, pp. 47-78. [Suggests that Sg and Swedenborg both encountered situations similar to that of Saul on the road to Damascus and found in the latter a paradigm for their own experience, although a comparison reveals distinct differences as well as general similarities between the two which are glossed here by (1) a collation of their lives; (2) an analysis of their mutual interest in science and dreams, documented by Sg's *Ockulta dagboken* and Swedenborg's Dream Journal of 1743-44; and (3) a discussion of Sg's encounter with Swedenborg's works in the mid-1890s, and their subsequent defining impact on his life and writing. For Stockenström, the innovations of his later dramaturgy represent the vision of the world he went on to construct after Sg's encounter with the man he adopted as his guiding spirit]

[C1:1223] Stockenström, Göran, 'The Symbiosis of "Spirits" in *Inferno*: Strindberg and Swedenborg', in Marilyn Johns Blackwell, ed., **C1:142**, *Structures of Influence*, pp. 3-37. [A detailed, well-documented discussion of Sg's debt to Swedenborg, focusing primarily on his discovery of the latter's works and the account he gives of his conception of hell, guilt, and punishment in *Inferno*. The essay also considers the implications of Swedenborg's theories for the experimental dramaturgy of *Ett drömspel* and *Till Damaskus* and the form and purpose of *En blå bok*. Stockenström confirms that Sg knew some of Swedenborg's work as early as the mid-1870s and charts the significance of its rediscovery during the 1890s, partly mediated by Balzac's *Séraphita* (1834-35). However, he points out that Sg's devotion to Swedenborg was always narrowly subjective; he prized him as the dreamer and seer who knew best how to decipher the riddles of existence in a manner that sometimes recalled the contemporary symbolist movement, and thus provided him with a productive method of translating his experience into his writing, and of structuring his later plays by means of repetition and a dramatic reversal that was associated less with classical models than with Swedenborg's concept of 'vastation']

[C1:1224] Stodelle, Ernestine, 'Strindberg, Ibsen, the Greeks', *National Review* (New York), 9:8 (1960), p. 123.

[C1:1225] Stolz, H., 'Strindberg hüben – Grillparzer drüben', *Rheinisch-Westfalen Zeitung* (Düsseldorf), 7 May 1917. ['Strindberg over Here – Grillparzer over There']

[C1:1226] Storå, Siv, *Lyriker med förhinder. Studier i Olof Lagercrantz' tidiga författarskap*, Åbo: Åbo Akademis Förlag – Åbo Academy Press, 1990. VIII+521 pp. ['Lyricist with Obstacles. Studies in Olof Lagercrantz's Early Authorship'. Discusses Sg's influence on the young Lagercrantz (1911-2002) and the latter's unpublished dissertation, **V:126**, on 'Strindberg's Satirical and Polemical Works from *Röda rummet* to His Departure for the Continent in 1883', considering the implications this had for Lagercrantz's conception of the writer's role and several of his own future standpoints. English summary]

[C1:1227] Stössinger, Felix, 'Mode und Werturteil', *März* (München), 10:3 (1916), 106-109. ['Fashion and Contemporary Judgements'. Concludes that Sg is a more profound genius than Ibsen; it is not, however, a question of Sg *or* Ibsen, but of Sg *and* Ibsen]

[C1:1228] Stounbjerg, Per, 'Kvindens teatralske indtog i det moderne: myter om kvinden som skuespillerinde hos Rousseau, Almqvist, Strindberg, Zola m. fl.', *Kritik* (Copenhagen), 28 (1995), 44-53. ['Woman's Theatrical Entry into Modernity: Myths of Woman as Actress in Rousseau, Almqvist, Strindberg, Zola, *et al*'. Examines the literary and philosophical myth (e.g. in Nietzsche) which essentialises women as actresses and discusses its psychoanalytical interpretation in the notion of masquerade by Joan Riviere. Stounbjerg includes *En dåres försvarstal* in a discussion of the deeply rooted conception of woman as a changeable and public figure, in which Rousseau, to whom Sg is variously indebted, also plays a central role]

[C1:1229] Stounbjerg, Per, 'Kvindens teatralske indtog i det moderne: myter om kvinden som skuespillerinde hos Rousseau, Almqvist, Strindberg, Zola m.fl.', in Helga Kress, Hrsg., *Litteratur og kjønn i Norden. Foredrag på den XX. studiekonferanse i International Association for Scandinavian Studies (IASS)*, Reykjavík: Háskólaútgáfan, 1996, pp.15-27. ['Woman's Theatrical Entry into Modernity: Myths of Woman as Actress in Rousseau, Almqvist, Strindberg, Zola, *et al*'. See **C1:1228**]

[C1:1230] Stounbjerg, Per, 'Offentlige kvinder: Lulu, Kristina og den moderne myte om skuespillerinden', in Irene Iversen og Anne Birgitte Rønning, eds, *Modernismens kjønn*, Oslo: Pax, 1996, pp. 25-41. ['Public Women: Lulu, Kristina, and the Modern Myth of the Actress'. Studies the idea of the public woman and the modern myth of the actress embodied in Wedekind's Lulu and Sg's Queen Christina, which concludes with a dramatisation of the Pandora myth that is also associated with the heroine of Wedekind's *Erdgeist* and *Die Büchse der Pandora*. Stounbjerg compares and contrasts the two figures and relates them to prevailing notions of woman as a performer in the developing discourse of modernity]

[C1:1231] Strecker, Karl, 'Aus Nietzsches Briefwechsel mit Strindberg', *Das literarische Echo* (Berlin), 15 (1912-13), Sp. 873-876. ['From Nietzsche's Correspondence with Strindberg'. Introduces excerpts from Nietzsche's exchange of letters with Sg]

[C1:1232] Strecker, Karl, 'Nietzsches Briefwechsel mit Strindberg', *Frankfurter Zeitung*, 1913, Nos 40 and 42. ['Nietzsche's Correspondence with Strindberg'. Presents Sg's brief but intense correspondence with Nietzsche during 1888, together with a sometimes faulty text of the letters themselves which Strecker was making publically available for the first time]

[C1:1233] Strecker, Karl, 'En brevväxling mellan Nietzsche och Strindberg', 1-2, *Aftonbladet* (Stockholm), 8 and 10 February 1913. ['A Correspondence between Nietzsche and Strindberg'. Translation of Strecker's articles in *Frankfurter Zeitung*]

[C1:1234] Strecker, Karl, 'Nietzsches Briefwechsel mit Strindberg', *Tägliche Rundschau* (Berlin), Unterhaltungsbeilage, Nos 33 and 35, 9-11 February 1913. [See **C1:1232**]

[C1:1235] Strecker, Karl, 'Lettres inédites de Nietzsche et Strindberg', *La Revue* (Paris), 1913, pp. 310-326. ['Unpublished Letters of Nietzsche and Strindberg'. On Sg's correspondence with Nietzsche, including a sometimes faulty text of their letters translated into French. French translation of **C1:1232**]

[C1:1236] Strecker, Karl, *Nietzsche und Strindberg. Mit ihrem Briefwechsel*, München: Georg Müller, 1921. [155] pp. ['Nietzsche and Strindberg. With Their Correspondence'. The text of Sg's brief correspondence with Nietzsche that Strecker makes public here contains numerous errors while his discussion of their personal relationship gave rise to many misconceptions that were to colour later opinions on the subject for many years, especially in Germany]

[C1:1237] — Anon [Alec Randall], 'Nietzsche Revalued', *The Times Literary Supplement* (London), 19 March 1925. [Comments on Strecker's edition in a round-up of recent Nietzsche criticism]

[C1:1238] — Fischer, Heinrich, *Die Weltbühne* (Berlin), 19:2 (1923), 579-580.

[C1:1239] — Kihlman, Erik, *Nya Argus* (Helsingfors), 14 (1921), 124-125.

[C1:1240] — Laufklötter, Heinrich, *Die Neue Zeit* (Stuttgart), 40:1 (1921-22), p. 311.

[C1:1241] — Lindblad, Göran, *Svenska Dagbladet* (Stockholm), 28 September 1921.

[C1:1242] — Rabenius, Olof, *Stockholms Dagblad*, 1 November 1921.

[C1:1243] — R. B. [Rolf Berg], *Hellweg* (Essen), 1 (1921), p. 180.

[C1:1244] Ström, Emilia, 'Strindberg och Witkiewicz - likt och olikt', *Strindbergiana* (Stockholm), 19 (2004), pp. 20-29. Illus. ['Strindberg and Witkiewicz - Alike and Unlike'. Compares the visual art of two writers who were also painters and photographers: considers their mutual interest in self-portraiture, their role as forerunners of both expressionism and spontanism, and their powerfully visual imaginations. Ström suggests that, as well as employing the imagination to probe established notions of reality, both men also played philosophical games, using their own personalities as the principal role. She also discusses Władysław Ślewiński's portrait of Sg (ca. 1895) and claims for Ślewiński (1854-1918) a crucial role in forging a link between Sg and Witkiewicz]

[C1:1245] Strömberg, Kjell, 'Pär Lagerkvist', *Forum* (Stockholm), 1918:5. [Discusses Lagerkvist's early one-act plays and the essay on 'Modern Theatre', **D1:604**. The plays are an attempt to go beyond the dramaturgy of Sg's Chamber Plays and achieve 'an entirely new form of play, to create an expressionist theatre whose frame is the modern mind itself, here at the moment of extinction']

[C1:1246] Stromberg, Lars, 'Jules Vallès vu par quelques contemporaines suedois', *Revue d'études Vallèsiennes* (Saint-Étienne), 12 (1991), 75-81. ['Jules Vallès in the Eyes of some Swedish Contemporaries'. Examines the influence of Vallès (1832-1885) upon Sg and Gustaf af Geijerstam in their autobiographical fictions *Tjänstekvinnans son* and *Erik Grane*, both of which found inspiration in Vallès's novel sequence, *Jacques Vingtras* (1879-86), in which he offers an account of his life in the third person]

[C1:1247] Strugatskii, A., '[Introduction]', in R. Akutagawa, *Novelly, Esse, Miniatiury*, Translated by N. Fel'dman, Edited and Revised by V. Grivnin, Moscow, 1985, pp. 65-73, 545-562. [The introduction to a Russian edition of selected works by the Japanese author Ryūnosuke Akutagawa (1892-1927) which reflects on his interest in Sg, the use of imagery deriving from Sg in some of his works, and particularly on Sg's attitude to death, as that of someone longing for death but incapable of effecting it. E.1778]

[C1:1248] Strunk, Volker, 'Taking Care of Strindberg', in *Harold Pinter. Towards a Poetics of His Plays*, American University Studies Series, IV, English Language and Literature 44, New York: Peter Lang, 1989, pp. 98-112. [Argues very unconvincingly that Pinter's play *The Caretaker* (1959) is heavily indebted to Sg while also maintaining that the kaleidoscopic proliferation of meaning in their plays and their mutual use of indeterminate referential techniques, wherein the audience remains uncertain of the precise truth content of what a character says, create a 'mad' dramaturgy. Strunk maintains that 'the one historical person…who would have had no difficulty to [sic] appreciate the play's paranoid perspective is none other than August Sg', in whose *Till Damaskus* and *Spöksonaten* he identifies many 'curious parallels' with *The Caretaker*. He also argues that the affinity between Pinter's play and the material of Sg's life as it is represented in *Inferno*, *Legender*, and *Jakob brottas* is so evident that it is reasonable to regard Davies, the tramp around whom Pinter's play revolves, as 'clearly patterned after Sg the man'. The younger brother, Aston, also displays 'certain Sgian characteristics']

[C1:1249] Sundberg, Björn, *Sanningen, myterna och intressenas spel. En studie i Hjalmar Söderbergs författarskap från och med Hjärtats oro*, Skrifter utgivna av Litteraturvetenskapliga institutionen vid Uppsala universtitet 15, Uppsala: Lundequistska bokhandel (distr.), 1981. Illus. 208 pp. ['Truth, Myths, and the Play of Interests. A Study in the Works of Hjalmar Söderberg from *Hjärtats oro* Onward'. Comments on Söderberg's critical response to Sg's post-Inferno works. German and English summaries]

[C1:1250] Suomi, Vilho, *Nuori Volter Kilpi: vuosisadan vaihteen romantikko*, Helsingissä: Otava, 1952. 327 pp. [Comments on Sg's relevance for the work of the Finnish novelist and essayist Volter Kilpi (originally Ericsson, 1874-1939)]

[C1:1251] Svanberg, Birgitta, 'Birgitta i litteraturen', in Eva Nyström Tagesson, red., *Europabilden av Birgitta*, Östergötlands länsmuseums utställningskatalog 83, 2003, pp. 56-83. Illus. [On the image of the Swedish visionary (1303–73) and her representation in literature, including *Folkungasagan*]

[C1:1252] Svanberg, Victor, 'Godtycklig censur', *Stockholms-Tidning*, 10 November 1963. ['Arbitrary Censorship'. Refers to to Gustav Fröding and Selma Lagerlöf, as well as to Sg]

[C1:1253] Svedfelt, Torsten, 'Alexander Kielland och det svenska åttiotalet', *Edda* (Oslo), 31 (1931), 287-312. ['Alexander Kielland and the Swedish 1880s'. Surveys Kielland's influence on Swedish literature during the 1880s. Svedfelt describes *Röda rummet* as a Swedish pendant to Kielland's novel *Arbeidsfolk* (1881) and demonstrates that Sg initially displayed great sympathy and understanding for the latter's work, about which he corresponded with its author]

[C1:1254] Svedlund, Karl-Erik, 'Brandes, Strindberg, Wagner – var de profeter?', *Dagen* (Stockholm), 8 October 1964. ['[Georg] Brandes, Strindberg, Wagner – Were They Prophets?']

[C1:1255] *Svensk Litteraturtidskrift* (Stockholm), 'Strindberg och världen. En internationell rundfråga', 12:1 (1949), 1-63. ['Strindberg and the World. An International Questionnaire'. Publishes the responses of numerous writers, critics, and theatre workers, including Jean Cocteau, Johannes Jørgensen, Thomas Mann, Jules Romains, Thornton Wilder, and Tarjei Vesaas, who give their opinion of Sg and his significance in response to a questionnaire circulated in conjunction with the centenary of his birth. See also Øverland, **C1:1000**]

[C1:1256] Svensson, Barbro, 'Ett intrigspel på Parnassen', 1-2, *Svenska Dagbladet* (Stockholm), 8 and 10 October 1970. ['An Intrigue on Parnassus'. Explores Sg's literary and personal relations with the Swedish novelist Gustaf af Geijerstam (1858-1909) who also acted as his editor at Gernandts immediately after the Inferno crisis, only to became the object of his savage satire in *Svarta fanor*. Prompts a comment by Nils Beyer, 19 October]

[C1:1257] Svensson, Nils, 'Frödings korta poetiska sommar', *Barometern* (Kalmar), 21 September 1991. ['Fröding's Short Poetic Summer'. Comments briefly on Gustaf Fröding's editorship of *En bok om Strindberg*, **B1:142**]

[C1:1258] Svensson-Graner, Carl, 'Hagars son och graalsökaren', *Norrköpings Tidningar*, 10 August 1954. ['Hagar's Son and the Seeker after Graal'. Compares Sg with the Swedish poet Gustaf Fröding (1860-1911) in terms of their respective literary self-images]

[C1:1259] Svevo, Italo [Pseudonym of Ettore Schmitz], *Opera Omnia: Epistolario*, Milano: Dall'Oglio, 1966, p. 103. [Svevo's collected correspondence which documents the interest of the eminent novelist from Trieste (1861-1928) in Sg]

[C1:1260] Swahn, Sigbrit, 'De befruktade intrycken. En studie om Strindbergs läsning av Huysmans roman *A rebours*', *Artes* (Stockholm), 12:1 (1986), 100-111. Illus. ['The Fertilised Impressions. A Study of Strindbergs Reading of Huysmans' Novel *A rebours*'. Examines the importance of *A rebours* (1884) for Sg's redefinition of his complex relationship with Zola and orthodox naturalism. A detailed analysis demonstrates its role as an important intertext for *I havsbandet*, the novel in which Sg negotiates his passage from naturalism towards a new kind of post-naturalistic literature]

[C1:1261] Sybel-Petersen, Adelheid von, 'Strindberg und Albert Steffen', 1-3, *Das Goetheanum* (Dornach), 8 (1929), pp. 137-140, 145-148, 163-167. [Comments on Sg's significance for the editor of the Rudolf Steiner organ, *Das Goetheanum*]

[C1:1262] Sylvan, Maj, *Anne Charlotte Leffler. En kvinna finner sin väg*, Stockholm: Biblioteksförlaget, 1984. 252 pp. ['Anne Charlotte Leffler. A Woman Discovers Her Way'. The standard modern study of Leffler as a writer which includes brief comparisons of her situation as a woman author with Sg's during the 1880s]

[C1:1263] Syréhn, Gunnar, *Osäkerhetens teater. Studier i Lars Forssells dramatik*, Skrifter utgivna av Litteraturvetenskapliga institutionen vid Uppsala universitet 8, Uppsala: Lundequistska bokhandel i distr., 1979. 220 pp. ['The Theatre of Uncertainty. Studies in the Plays of Lars Forssell'. A detailed study of Forssell's plays which argues that, in his dreamplay technique, Sg employs numerous metatheatrical features, or roles within a role. Consequently, the work of those dramatists who have learnt from him displays an evident link between the desire to instil uncertainty in an audience and the application of metatheatrical techniques. English summary]

[C1:1264] Szalczer, Eszter, 'Strindberg och Georg Ljungström. En teosofisk bekantskap', *Strindbergiana* (Stockholm), 13 (1998), pp. 37-48. ['Strindberg and Georg Ljungström. A Theosophical Acquaintance'. Argues the importance of the Swedish theosophist Ljungström (1861-1930) for Sg's thinking following his return to Stockholm in 1899. Like the abstract painters Vassily Kandinsky and Piet Mondrian, as well as W. B. Yeats, Sg was inspired by occult ideas, and read widely, if erratically, in the literature of Theosophy, including Ljungström's contributions to *Teosofiska småskrifter*. According to Szalczer, traces of this reading are to be discerned in *Spöksonaten*, *En blå bok*, and the prose fragment 'Armageddon']

[C1:1265] Taube, Agneta, 'Kvinnlighet och manligt blick i Strindbergs och Ibsens 90-talsdiktning', in *Ibsen-Strindberg seminar pa Voksenåsen 15-17 september 1997*, Oslo: Voksenåsen, 1997, pp. 115-134. ['Female and Male Gaze in Works from the 1890s by Strindberg and Ibsen'. Focuses principally on *I havsbandet* and *The Lady of the Sea*]

[C1:1266] Taub, Hans, 'Strindberg och Pär Lagerkvist', *Göteborgs Handels- och Sjöfarts-tidning*, 26 April 1953.

[C1:1267] Taub, Hans, 'Strindberg und Schopenhauer', *Frankfurter Zeitung*, 21 August 1917. [Considers Schopenhauer's influence on Sg which is apparent in his interest in Eastern religions and the notion of the world as one beset by illusions. Taub also comments on the importance which both writers attribute to dreams]

[C1:1268] Taub, Hans, 'Strindberg und Schopenhauer', *Jahrbuch der Schopenhauergesell-schaft* (Kiel), 7 (1918), 250-252. [See **C1:1269**]

[C1:1269] Taub, Hans, 'Schopenhauer und Strindberg', 1-2, *Schopenhauer-Jahrbuch* (Kiel), 37 (1956), pp. 42-54, 38 (1957), p. 159. [Documents Sg's abiding interest in Schopenhauer and details the latter's relevance for several of his works from *Röda rummet* in 1879 to *I havsbandet*, the essay 'Un regard vers le ciel' (1896), *Till Damaskus*, and *Påsk*, as well as for how he depicts the world as a site of dream and illusion in *Ett drömspel*]

[C1:1270] Taylor, A. Carey, 'Balzac et les romanciers scandinaves', *Revue de littérature comparée* (Paris), 38:2 (1964), 202-237. ['Balzac and the Scandinavian Novelists'. Discusses Balzac's influence on the Scandinavian novel, noting in Sg's case the frequently argued importance of *Illusions perdues* (1837-42) and *L' Envers de l'histoire contemporaine* (1842-8) for *Röda rummet*, which Taylor questions. Sg is quite correct in pointing out in *Ensam* that he only discovered Balzac much later, when he read the latter's Swedenborgian novels *Séraphita* and *Louis Lambert*, which left a powerful imprint on *Inferno*, *Till Damaskus*, *Påsk*, and *Ett drömspel*. Taylor observes that Balzac is also a significant presence in *Ensam*, *Svarta fanor*, and *Taklagsöl*, as well as, most potently, in Sg's last novel *Syndabocken*, which resembles one of his *Études de la vie de province*]

[C1:1271] Taylor, Marion A., 'A Note on Strindberg's *The Dance of Death* and Edward Albee's *Who's Afraid of Virginia Woolf?*', *Papers on English Language and Literature*, (Southern Illinois University, Carbondale), 2 (1966), 187-188. [Compares briefly how the two dramatists represent marital-sexual conflict]

[C1:1272] Taylor, Marion A., 'Edward Albee and Strindberg: Some Parallels between *The Dance of Death* and *Who's Afraid of Virginia Woolf?*', *Papers on English Language and Literature* (Southern Illinois University, Carbondale), 1:1 (1965), 59-71. [Identifies a close resemblance between the two plays, drawing mechanistic parallels between Albee's plays and C. D. Locock's 1929 translation of *Dödsdansen*, as if its verbal similarities with the later text are necessarily present in Sg's Swedish original. According to Taylor, dancing represents the most powerful weapon deployed in both plays to further the marital conflict which they present, affording as it does a theatrical device which facilitates the stage presentation of a complex fusion of love and hate]

[C1:1273] Templeton, Joan, 'Fallen Women and Upright Wives: "Woman's Place" in Early Modern Tragedy', in Margaret R. Higonnet and Joan Templeton, eds, *Feminist Explorations of Literary Space*, Amherst: University of Massachusetts Press, 1994, pp. 60-71. [Includes *Fröken Julie* in a discussion that also encompasses Hebbel's *Maria Magdalena* (1844) and Ibsen's *Ghosts*. Argues that '*Julie* is essentially non-tragic both because its protagonist's suicide seems more contrived than inevitable and because her death signifies that justice has been served. Julie redeems herself through the ultimate reinscription of patriarchy's sexual ethos: she removes herself as an offense']

[C1:1274] Templeton, Joan, 'Sean O'Casey and Expressionism', *Modern Drama* (Lawrence, Kansas), 14:1 (1971), 47-62. [Includes a brief comparison of O'Casey's play *Within the Gates* (1934) with *Ett drömspel*]

[C1:1275] Templeton, Joan, 'Women's Sphere and the Creation of Modern Tragedy: Hebbel's *Maria Magdalena*, Ibsen's *Ghosts*, and Strindberg's *Miss Julie*', in Roger Bauer and Dowe Fokkema, eds, *Proceedings of the XIIth Congress of the International Comparative Literature Association*, 5 vols, München: iudicium verlag, 1988, Vol. 3, pp. 487-493. [See **C1:1273**]

[C1:1276] Tennant, P. F. D., 'Strindberg and Holberg', *The Cambridge Review*, 59 (21 January 1938), p. 192. [Discusses *Leka med elden*, described here as 'only a trivial incident in Sg's dramatic production', and Ludvig Holberg's play *Count Ulysses of Ithaca* as examples of Scandinavian comedies]

[C1:1277] T. F-t [Torsten Fogelkvist], 'Andersen och Strindberg. Apropå en minnesdag', 1-2, *Dagens Nyheter* (Stockholm), 4 and 7 August 1925. ['Andersen and Strindberg. Apropos a Commemoration'. Links Sg with Hans Christian Andersen, whom the former both admired and translated]

[C1:1278] Thesen, Rolv, 'Litt om Strindberg och Norge', *Vinduet* (Oslo), 3 (1949), 63-66. ['A Little on Strindberg and Norway'. Surveys several Norwegian authors who have responded to Sg, from Ibsen and Alexander Kielland to Knut Hamsun, Tore Ørjasæter (in *Christophoros*, 1948), and Arne Garborg, who Thesen considers contributed 'perhaps the most important' essay to *En bok om Strindberg*, **B1:142**, in 1894]

[C1:1279] Thiede, Carsten Peter, 'Meer und Wasser in drei Dramen Rilkes, Strindbergs und d'Annunzios', *Blätter der Rilke-Gesellschaft* (Saas-Fee), 6 (1979), 7-13. ['Sea and Water in Three Plays by Rilke, Strindberg, and D'Annunzio'. Compares the symbolic role given to sea and water in Rilke's poem *Weiße Fürstin* (1909), D'Annunzio's play *La città morta* (1898), and *Till Damaskus*, concluding that 'all three seem to have one thing in common: water as that element in which the daemonic and *tristesse*, but also hope – hope against hope - are symbolised'] '

[C1:1280] Thente, Jonas, 'Fulla nyckelknippor skramlar mest', *90tal* (Stockholm), 8:2 (1997), 26-29. ['Full Key-Rings Jangle the Most'. A study of the *roman à clef* in Sweden, exemplified by Sg's *Svarta fanor*, Carina Rydberg's *Den högsta kasten*, and Kerstin Ekman's *Gör mig levande igen*. Comments on the reactions such novels can provoke in the media]

[C1:1281] Thompson, Birgitta, 'Three Sisters: Benedictsson's Selma and Marianne, and Strindberg's Miss Julie', *Swedish Book Review* (Lampeter), 1992:1-2, pp. 24-29. [Links Miss Julie with the heroines of Victoria Benedictsson's novels *Pengar* (1885) and *Fru Marianne* (1887). Thompson suggests that reading the former contributed considerably to Sg's portrait of the 'characterless' Julie]

[C1:1282] Thompson, Paul, 'The Search for Faith and Fixing Points: Strindberg, Obstfelder and the Age of Post-Naturalism', *Scandinavica* (Norwich), 28:1 (1989), 55-73. [Studies the philosophical and literary reaction against 19th-Century scientific materialism as articulated by William James in his Gifford lectures and *The Varieties of Religious Experience* (1902), as well as in the emerging thought of C. G. Jung. In literature, this movement entailed a turning away from naturalism in search of a new religious faith, something that is common to both Sg and Sigbjørn Obstfelder (1866-1900). In Sg's case, which is readily documented by *I havsbandet*, *Inferno*, *Legender*, and *Jakob brottas*, as well as his scientific essays of the 1890s, Thompson sees these explorations as part of a continuing naturalist-occultist scientific enterprise, which was later refuted by 20th-Century physics. Excerpted from Thompson's doctoral thesis, **V218**]

[C1:1283] Timms, Edward, *Karl Kraus: Apocalyptic Satirist. Culture and Catastrophe in Habsburg Vienna*, New Haven and London: Yale University Press, 1986, pp. 69-71. [Comments briefly on the evident links between Kraus, Otto Weininger, and Sg, and their common preoccupation with gender roles and feminine sexuality]

[C1:1284] Timms, Edward, *Karl Kraus. Satiriker der Apokalypse*, Aus dem Englischen von Max Looser und Michael Strand, Wien: Deuticke, 1995. Illus. 559 pp. [German edition of **C1:1283**]

[C1:1285] Tiusanen, Timo, *O'Neill's Scenic Images*, Princeton, New Jersey: Princeton University Press, 1968. 388 pp. [Sg's significant influence on Eugene O'Neill's *The Emperor Jones*, *Welded*, *The Hairy Ape* and several other plays is noted throughout]

[C1:1286] Tolstoi, L[ev], '[Letters from Sweden]', *Sankt Peterburgskie vedomosti*, No. 26 (27 January 1900), p. 2. [N.B. *not* the novelist but Tolstoi's Swedish-reading son, who comments on Sg in a discussion of contemporary Swedish literature. E.711]

[C1:1287] Tomazin, Katarina, 'Strindberg, antifeminizem in slovenska literatura', *Primerjalna Književnost* (Ljubljana), 20:1 (1997), 21-42. ['Strindberg, Anti-Feminism and Slovenian Literature'. Demonstrates how Sg's literary project, and especially his antifeminism, influenced several Slovenian writers around the turn of the century and again in the 1920s, when German expressionist drama created a new interest in Slovenia in Sg's naturalist and symbolist texts]

[C1:1288] Törnqvist, Egil, *A Drama of Souls: Studies in O'Neill's Super-naturalistic Technique*, New Haven and London: Yale University Press, 1969. 284 pp. [Traces the influence of the 'super-naturalism' of Sg's post-Inferno plays on the development of O'Neill's dramaturgy. Previously published as a doctoral dissertation by Almqvist & Wiksell, 1968]

[C1:1289] Törnqvist, Egil, 'Delad livssyn: Ibsen, Strindberg och deras regissörer', in Carl Reinhold Bråkenhielm and Torsten Petersson, red., *Modernitetens ansikten: Livsåskådningar i nordisk 1900-talslitteratur*, Nora: Nya Doxa, 2001, pp. 361-372. ['Shared View of Life: Ibsen, Strindberg, and their Directors']

[C1:1290] Törnqvist, Egil, *Et dukkehjem och det moderna dramat*, Lørdagsforum høst 1993: Ibsen i fokus, Oslo, 1997. 16 pp. ['*A Doll's House* and Modern Drama'. Sg's *Herr Bengts hustru* is only one of numerous plays by many dramatists, including Bernard Shaw, J. M. Synge, Eugene O'Neill, David Roylston, Helge Krog, and Ingmar Bergman, to have been written under the influence of Ibsen's play]

[C1:1291] Törnqvist, Egil, *Eugene O'Neill: A Playwright's Theatre*, Jefferson, North Carolina: McFarland & Company, Inc., Publishers, 2004, pp. 67-83. [Identifies numerous intertextual associations as well as structural and thematic affinities between several of O'Neill's major dramas and Sg's theatre. Törnqvist concludes that in his restless experimentation with dramatic form, O'Neill is the latter's true inheritor, and observes how, in Sg's work, O'Neill could recognise much of his own personal situation]

[C1:1292] Törnqvist, Egil, '*Fröken Julie* och O'Neill', *Meddelanden från Strindbergssällskapet* (Stockholm), 42-43 (1969), pp. 5-16. [Documents Eugene O'Neill's debt to Sg in general prior to tracing the influence of *Fröken Julie* on several of his plays, including *Recklessness*, *Bound East for Cardiff*, *Diff'rent*, *Before Breakfast*, *The Emperor Jones*, and especially *Mourning Becomes Electra*. Törnqvist highlights similarities in their concept of fate, dramatic techniques, characterisation, and use of symbolism]

[**C1:1293**] Törnqvist, Egil, '*Miss Julie* and O'Neill', *Modern Drama* (Lawrence, Kansas), 19:4 (1976), 351-364. [English version of **C1:1292**]

[**C1:1294**] Törnqvist, Egil, 'O'Neill's Philosophical and Literary Paragons', in Michael Manheim, ed., *The Cambridge Companion to Eugene O'Neill*, Cambridge: Cambridge University Press, 1998, pp. 18-32. [Discusses O'Neill's admiration for Sg as both man and dramatist, pp. 26-30]

[**C1:1295**] Törnqvist, Egil, 'Playwright on Playwright: Per Olov Enquist's Strindberg and Lars Norén's O'Neill', in Poul Houe and Sven Hakon Rossel, eds, *Documentarism in Scandinavian Literature*, Amsterdam: Rodopi, 1997, pp. 155-164. [Discusses the 'semi-documentary' genre in general and compares two plays by Swedish playwrights based on the lives of major dramatists from the tradition in which they themselves write, each of which is linked with one of their subject's plays (*Tribadernas natt* by Enquist with *Den starkare* and *Och ge oss skuggorna* by Norén with *Long Day's Journey into Night*)]

[**C1:1296**] Törnqvist, Egil, 'Strindberg and O'Neill', see Marilyn Johns Blackwell, ed., **C1:142**, *Structures of Influence*, pp. 277-292. [An informed account of Sg's influence on O'Neill, both thematically and dramaturgically, in *The Hairy Ape* (which derives from *Ett drömspel*), *Days Without End* (*Till Damaskus I*), *Morning Becomes Electra* and *The Emperor Jones* (both *Fröken Julie*). Törnqvist documents O'Neill's knowledge of Sg's work and confirms him as Sg's disciple in his response to Sg's ability to deal with modern psychological problems in a dramatically convincing and arresting way. Includes material previously published in **C1:1292**]

[**C1:1297**] Törnqvist, Egil, 'Strindberg, O'Neill and their Impact on the Dramatists of Today', in Claes Englund and Gunnel Bergström, eds, **D2:99**, *Strindberg, O'Neill and the Modern Theatre*, pp. 15-24. [Surveys Sg's significance for the development of modern drama, and argues that those for whom he proved 'inimitably influential' include Genet, Dürrenmatt, Tennessee Williams, Edward Albee, and Pinter. However, Törnqvist suggests that, like O'Neill, Sg may mean even more today as a myth than his actual plays do, given their rarity value in performance outside Sweden]

[**C1:1298**] Törnqvist, Egil, 'Strindberg, O'Neill, Norén: A Swedish-American Triangle', *The Eugene O'Neill Review* (Boston, Mass.), 15:1 (1991), 65-78. Illus. [Acknowledges that Sg's importance for O'Neill is well-documented and agrees that there are numerous similarities between their plays (e.g. *Mourning Becomes Electra* and *Fröken Julie* or *Den starkare* and both *Before Breakfast* and *Hughie*). Meanwhile, where Norén is concerned, his family trilogy *Natten är dagens mor*, *Kaos är granne med Gud*, and *Stillheten*, is in many respects a direct descendant from the work both writers, in particular the O'Neill of *Long Day's Journey into Night*. But if the relationship between husband and wife in Norén's later dramatisation of O'Neill's life, *Och ge oss skuggorna*, recalls Sg's *Fadren*, it would seem that O'Neill seems to have meant even more to him than Sg]

[C1:1299] Torp, Thaddeus L., 'Introduction', in Henrik Ibsen, *Ghosts: A Family Drama in Three Acts* and August Strindberg, *Miss Julia: A Naturalistic Tragedy*, Translated and edited by Thaddeus L. Torp, Arlington Heights, Illinois: H. Davidson, 1992. XXI+116 pp.

[C1:1300] Torp, Thaddeus L., 'Introduction', in August Strindberg, *Ghost Sonata*, and Henrik Ibsen, *When We Dead Awaken: A Dramatic Epilogue in Three Acts*, Translated and Edited by Thaddeus L. Torp, Arlington Heights, Illinois: AHM Pub. Corp., 1977. XV+91 pp.

[C1:1301] Torsslow, Stig, *Edvard Bäckström och hans dramatiska diktning*, Göteborg, 1947, pp. 318-331. ['Edvard Bäckström and His Dramatic Works'. Discusses Sg's personal and professional relationship with the Signature poet and dramatist (1841-1886) with whose work and career Sg and his early writings were sometimes compared. Torsslow establishes the different trajectories in their careers as professional writers]

[C1:1302] Torsslow, Stig, *Eugene O'Neill*, Studentföreningen Verdandis småskrifter 397, Stockholm: Albert Bonniers Förlag, 1937. 97 pp. [Notes the relevance of Sg's theatre for several of O'Neill's earlier plays]

[C1:1303] T. R. [Gustaf Theodor Rabenius], 'Strindberg kontra Ibsen', *Göteborgs Handels- och Sjöfartstidning*, 25 October 1884. ['Strindberg versus Ibsen'. Maintains that Ibsen creates individuals while Sg generalises]

[C1:1304] Tramer, Friedrich, 'August Strindberg und Franz Kafka', *Deutsche Vierteljahrsschrift für Litteraturwissenschaft und Geistesgeschichte* (Stuttgart), 34:2 (1960), 249-256. [Details Kafka's knowledge of Sg's prose works and considers their possible influence on his writings, notably the significance of *Röda rummet* and its exposure of aimless, ineffectual bureaucracy for *Das Schloss* and *Der Prozeß*. Tramer also identifies similarities in the personal sensibilities and psychic structures of the two writers; in both cases, he concludes that these are rooted in their Oedipal situations. Contains little on Sg, however]

[C1:1305] Trayser, Hans, 'Strindbergs Einfluß auf die mögliche Nachkommenschaft', *Bühnen der Hansestadt Lübeck*, 1959-60, pp. 92-96. ['Strindberg's Influence on His Potential Successors']

[C1:1306] Treib, Manfred, *August Strindberg und Edward Albee: eine vergleichende Analyse moderner Ehedramen (Mit einem Exkurs über Friedrich Dürrenmatts Play Strindberg)*, Europäische Hochschulschriften: Reihe 18, Vergleichende Literaturwißenschaften 23, Bern und Frankfurt am Main: Peter Lang, 1980. 186 pp. ['August Strindberg and Edward Albee. A Comparative Analysis of Modern Marriage Dramas (With a Digression on Friedrich Dürrenmatt's *Play Strindberg*)'. Treib focuses primarily on *Dödsdansen* and Albee's *Who's Afraid of Virginia Woolf* as modern dramas of marriage, with the former treated as a self-evident precursor of the latter. He also considers Dürrenmatt's adaptation of *Dödsdansen*]

[C1:1307] Tripathi, Vanashree, 'Self-Appropriation, Fabulation and Play of Meaning in Ibsen, Chekhov, Strindberg and Albee', *Aligarh Critical Miscellany* (Aligarh, India), 9:1 (1996), 85-96. [A psychoanalytic approach to the treatment of the fantastic and the role of polysemy in dramas by the named authors]

[C1:1308] Trotzig, Birgitta, 'En förvandlingskonstnär', in Ulf Olsson, red., **B1:357**, *Strindbergs förvandlingar*, pp. 13-17. ['An Artist of Transformations'. Sg exemplifies the way art transforms the world into signs, in a process of continual metamorphosis, a process clearly demonstrated in *Inferno* and *Legender*, where the essential role of the unconscious is most apparent. A personal essay by one of Sweden's most eminent modern novelists]

[C1:1309] Tsaneva, Milena, 'Vazov i Strindberg', *Literaturen forum* (Sofia?), 9:16 (1999), pp. 1, 6. ['Vazov and Strindberg'. On Bulgaria's 'national poet', novelist, short-story writer, and dramatist, Ivan Vazov (1850-1921), and his antipathy for Strindberg]

[C1:1310] Tsimbal, Irina, 'Strindberg and Chekhov', in Michael Robinson, ed., **B1:379**, *The Moscow Papers*, pp. 127-132. [Explores a series of possible associations between Sg and Chekhov, and affirms their affinities rather than, as is generally assumed in Russia, their difference. Tsimbal documents Chekhov's knowledge of Sg's works and suggests there is a link between *Fröken Julie* and *The Cherry Orchard*, where Jean is a forerunner of both Lopakhin and Iasha. The fatal end of a family and a house is common to both plays, and their underlying affinity has been foregrounded in several recent productions, which have stressed the notion of a misalliance between Ranevskaia and Lopakhin or Iasha]

[C1:1311] Turkka, Jouko, 'A Line Strindberg – Salama?', in Donald Weaver, ed., *Strindberg on Stage*, **D2:331**, pp. 128-132. [Claims that Finnish literature has taken its understanding of the role of the professional author from Sg and that, of all Finnish writers, the Noble Prize winner Frans Sillanpää (1888-1964) is the one most deeply indebted to him. Even though he learned to write from Sg and has been accused of sharing his misogyny, negativism, criminality, and subjectivity, the contemporary Finnish novelist Hannu Salama (b.1936) has little in common with Sg. Turkka comments briefly on the hostility with which both Zacharias Topelius (1818-1898) and Minna Canth (1844-1897) regarded Sg, and his importance for the Finnish working-class movement]

[C1:1312] Uggla, Andrzej Nils, 'Przybyszewski and Strindberg', Translated by Magda Iwinska, in Piotr Paszkiewicz, ed., *Totenmesse: Modernism in the Culture of Northern and Central Europe*, Warsaw: Institute of Art, Polish Academy of Sciences, 1996, pp. 201-2110. [Examines the relationship between Sg and the Polish novelist and dramatist Stanisław Przybyszewski (1868-1927) during the early 1890s, their personal conflicts, the role that Przybyszewski played in promoting Sg in Poland before the First World War, and what lies behind the recent revival of both their works on the Polish stage]

[C1:1313] Uggla, Andrzej Nils, 'Przybyszewski i Strindberg – dwaj przyjaciele i antagonisci', in *Zbliżenia. Szkice z literatury szwedzkiej i polskiej*, Katowice, 1998, pp. 33-46. ['Przybyszewski and Strindberg – Two Friends and Enemies'. An account of their brief friendship in Berlin in 1892 and subsequent emnity, expressed in their derogatory portraits of one another in their literary works, including *Inferno*]

[C1:1314] Uggla, Andrzej Nils, 'Przybyszewski och Strindberg. Konflikter och utbyte', *Meddelanden från Strindbergssällskapet* (Stockholm), 53-54 (1974), pp. 12-20. ['Przybyszewski and Strindberg: Conflicts and Exchanges'. Charts Sg's personal relationship with the Polish author Stanisław Przybyszewski (1868-1927), compares the latter's essay 'O dramacie i scenie' with the Preface to *Fröken Julie*, and reflects on the influence which Sg exerted on Przybyszewski as a dramatist]

[C1:1315] Uggla, Andrzej Nils, 'S. I. Witkiewicz och August Strindberg', *Svenska Dagbladet* (Stockholm), 26 July 1976. [Assesses Sg's relevance for the plays of the Polish writer Stanisław Ignacy Witkiewicz]

[C1:1316] Uggla, Andrzej Nils, 'Stanisław Przybyszewski – Strindberg och andra skandinaver', *Studia Scandinavica* (Gdańsk), 1:1 (1978), 27-53. ['Stanisław Przybyszewski – Strindberg and Other Scandinavians'. Examines Przybyszewski's personal and literary relationships with Sg and the other Scandinavian writers and artists whom he knew in Berlin during the 1890s, including the Norwegian dramatist, Gunnar Heiberg (1857-1929), and the Norwegian pianist and writer Dagny Juel (1867-1901), whom he married]

[C1:1317] Uggla, Andrzej Nils, 'Witkiewicz – Strindbergs efterföljare', *Dramaten* (Stockholm), No. 17 (1980-81), 13-15. Illus. ['Witkiewicz – Strindberg's Imitator']

[C1:1318] Uhlin, Eric, *Dan Andersson före Svarta ballader. Liv och diktning fram till 1916*, Stockholm: Tidens Förlag, 1950. 625 pp. ['Dan Andersson before *Black Ballads*. His Life and Works to 1916'. Includes reflections on Sg as a precursor of Andersson and other Swedish proletarian writers in the early years of the 20th Century]

[C1:1319] Unglaub, Erich, 'Strindberg, Weininger und Karl Kraus: Eine Überprüfung', *Recherches Germaniques* (Strasbourg), 18 (1988), 121-150. ['Strindberg, Weininger, and Karl Kraus: A Study'. A detailed survey of the relationship between Sg, Otto Weininger, and Kraus, citing relevant passages in *En blå bok*, their correspondence, and the text of other letters to Arthur Geber and Algot Ruhe, in which Sg mentions Weininger. Unglaub also lists Sg's contributions to *Die Fackel*, translated and edited by Emil Schering, quoting from the latter's correspondence with Kraus and Kraus's obituary of Sg]

[C1:1320] Urbanska, Agata, 'Cherchez la femme!', *Dialog* (Warsaw), 41:4 (1996), 181-189. ['Find the Woman!' Apropos Sokół, **C1:1178**, focusing on his treatment of gender and sex in Sg and Stanisław Witkiewicz]

[C1:1321] Uscatescu, George, *Ontologia culturii*, Bucureşti: Editura stiintifica si enciclopedica, 1987. 435 pp. [Studies in aesthetics which includes discussion of Peter Weiss and Sg]

[C1:1322] Uri, Sikko Pieter, *Leven en werken van Arij Prins. Een bijdrage tot de studie van de beweging van Tachtig*, (Proefschrift), Delft: N.V. Technische Boekhandel, 1935. pp. 53-54. ['Life and Works of Arij Prins. A Contribution to the Study of the Movement of the 1880s'. Notes Prins's (1860-1922) response to Sg's naturalism and quotes from his correspondence about *Giftas* with his fellow Dutch writer, Frans Netscher]

[C1:1323] Vaittinen, Pirjo, *Pohjoismainen ja suomalainen realismi*, Oulu: Oulu yliopisto, 1988. 142 pp. ['Nordic and Finnish Realism'. Compares Finnish realism with literary realism elsewhere in Scandinavia, with several references to Sg]

[C1:1324] Valdén, Nils Gösta, 'Keller, Strindberg och uppbyggelsen', *Svensk Litteraturtidskrift* (Stockholm), 33:3 (1970), 44-45. [Identifies similarities between a passage from Gottfried Keller's novel *Der grüne Heinrich* (1846-55) and the final, defiant lines of Sg's poem 'Esplanadsystemet' (1873)]

[C1:1325] Vengrov, N., *Tvorcheskoe razvitie Aleksandra Bloka*, Moscow: Izd-vo Akademii Nauk SSSR, 1963. 415 pp. [Discusses Blok's opinion of Sg, pp 281-284. E.994]

[C1:1326] Vennberg, Karl, 'August Strindberg', *Strindbergiana* (Stockholm), 3 (1988), pp. 9-11. [A personal response to Sg by the Swedish poet (1910–1995), who comments on the multiplicity of ends to which Sg and his works can be used]

[C1:1327] Veveris-Pehrsson, Dzidra, 'Zigenaren utanför oss', *Lundagård* (Lund), 44:19 (1963), 420-421. ['The Gypsy Without'. Discusses the figure of the gypsy in Swedish literature with reference to works by C. J. L. Almqvist (1793-1866), August Blanche (1811-1868), Ivar Lo-Johansson (1901-1990), Viktor Rydberg (1828-1895), and Sg who is represented here by 'Tschandala']

[C1:1328] Vickery, John B., 'The Scapegoat in Literature: Some Kinds and Uses', in Marjorie W. McCune, Tucker Orbison, and Philip M. Withim, eds, *The Binding of Proteus: Perspectives in Myth and the Literary Process*, Lewis, Philadelphia: Bucknell University Press, 1980, pp. 264-278. [A Jungian survey of the scapegoat theme in Western literature, with reference to Euripides, Hawthorne, Faulkner, D. H. Lawrence, Ibsen, Melville, and Sg in *Syndabocken*]

[C1:1329] Vilgfors, Siv, 'Tre prästgestalter i svensk diktning', *Gymnasisten* (Lund), 20 (1946), 92-95. ['Three Priests in Swedish Literature'. Compares Sg's Pastor Nordström in *Hemsöborna* with clergymen in Selma Lagerlöf's *Gösta Berlings saga* (1891) and C. J. L. Almqvist's *Kapellet* (1838)]

[C1:1330] Viksten, Albert, in *Mitt möte med boken. Tjugo svenska författare berättar om sig själva och om böcker*, red. Ivar Öhman, Stockholm: Folket i Bild, 1943. Illus. 214 pp. [Viksten describes his first encounter with *Röda rummet* and how Sg's rebelliousness encouraged him, as a proletarian, to start writing]

[C1:1331] Vilhjalmsson, Thor, 'Den som diktar sitt eget liv, innebärande andras med, om tillfälle ges', in [Heidi von Born], red., **U1:149**, *Med himlen till tak...och Drottninggatan som golv. Femton balkongtal till Strindberg*, pp. 83-88. ['He who Composes his own Life, Meaning other Lives too, if the Opportunity Arises'. The text of a public declaration of the Icelandic author's appreciation of Sg's work]

[C1:1332] Virmaux. Alain, *Antonin Artaud et le théâtre*, Paris: Union Générale d'Éditions, Seghers, 1977. 436 pp. [Includes a chapter on Artaud's theoretical and practical links with Sg, including his production of *Ett drömspel*]

[C1:1333] Vodskov, Hans, 'Carl Snoilsky og August Strindberg', in *Litteraturkritik i udvalg*, 2 vols, København: Reitzels, 1992, Vol. I, pp. 281-291. ['Carl Snoilsky and August Strindberg'. Rpr. of **C1:591**]

[C1:1334] Vodskov, Hans, 'Carl Snoilsky og August Strindberg', in *Spredte Studier*, Københaven: Gyldendalske Boghandels Forlag, 1884, pp. 137-154. ['Carl Snoilsky and August Strindberg'. Rpr. of **C1:591**]

[C1:1335] Vogelweith, Guy, 'Naissance d'un expressionnisme', *Obliques. Littérature Théâtre* (Paris), 9 (1981), 15-23. Illus. ['The Birth of an Expressionism'. Presents Edvard Munch, Vincent Van Gogh, and Sg as significant precursors of expressionism. Describes how the latter moves from the naturalism of *Fadren* to expressionism as part of an ever more finely attuned descent into the unconscious that becomes apparent in the experiences of the protagonist of *Till Damaskus I*]

[C1:1336] Vogelweith, Guy, 'Strindberg et Freud', *Obliques: Littérature-Théâtre* (Paris), 1:1 (1972), 32-39. [Compares the parallel paths of Freud and Sg, both of whom were fascinated by the psychological theories and experiments of Jean-Martin Charcot and

Hippolyte Bernheim. Vogelweith indicates how, quite unbeknown to one another, they conducted similar analytical experiments on themselves during the 1880s and 1890s, in the course of which they uncovered the psychological mechanisms underlying guilt, repression, and the Oedipus complex. He discusses *Legender*, *Holländaren*, *Ett drömspel*, and (particularly) *Till Damaskus*, where the palindromic structure of the play facilitates the uncovering of the terrifying reality of dreams in a comparable manner to the processes uncovered in the course of Freud's theoretical work]

[C1:1337] Vogelweith, Guy, 'Le Désir d'être bonne', *Obliques. Littérature Théâtre* (Paris), No. 2 (1972), 7-10. [Compares the structure and thematic organisation of *Fröken Julie* with Jean Genet's play *Les bonnes*]

[C1:1338] *Voksenåsen* [Gerd Aarsland Rosander?], red., *Ibsen-Strindberg: Seminar på Voksenåsen 15-17. september 1995. Rapport*, Oslo: Svenskhemmet Voksenåsen, 1997. 140 pp. [Contains the proceedings of a colloquium on the two dramatists held in Oslo. Includes **C1:951**: Ulf Olsson, 'Ibsen som Strindbergs livmoder. Några reflexioner kring förbindelsen mellan två författarskap'; **C1:379**: Inga-Stina Ewbank, '"Hjemland... fødeland": Ibsen, Strindberg och landsflykt'; **C1:984**: Ulf Olsson, 'Ibsen som Strindbergs livmoder. Några reflexioner kring förbindelsen mellan två författarskap'; **C1:1265**: Agneta Taube, 'Kvinnlighet och manligt blick i Strindbergs och Ibsens 90-talsdiktning'; **D2:1222**: Björn Sundberg, 'Strindberg på jakt efter guds hand i historien'; and **F6:32**: Per Stounbjerg, 'Modernisme maskeret som middelalder. Om August Strindbergs *Legender*']

[C1:1339] Vowles, Richard B., 'Expressionism in Scandinavia', in **C1:1360**, Ulrich Weisstein, ed., *Expressionism as an International Literary Phenomenon*, pp. 221-224. [Concludes that 'Sg can probably be called the first Expressionist, independent of whether he is more important as an originator, synthesiser or transmitter'. Vowles discusses Sg's influence on Pär Lagerkvist as well as on German drama and the German theatre in general]

[C1:1340] Vowles, Richard B., 'Tennessee Williams and August Strindberg', *Modern Drama* (Lawrence, Kansas), 1:3 (1958), 166-171. [Vowles looks at a number of general similarities between Williams and Sg that might confirm the latter's influence on the American dramatist, but he focuses mainly on the presumed importance of *Fröken Julie* for *A Streetcar Named Desire* (1947) and affinities between both *Stora landsvägen* and *Himmelrikets nycklar* and Williams's *Camino Real* (1953)]

[C1:1341] Vowles, Richard B., 'Tennessee Williams and August Strindberg', *Svenska Dagbladet* (Stockholm), 11 April 1956. [Examines Williams's debt to Sg as a dramatist, notably in *A Streetcar Named Desire* which owes much to *Fröken Julie*]

[C1:1342] Vrieze, F. S. de, 'Het occulte als motief in de Zweedse literatuur', *Handelingen van het eenendertigste Nederlands Filogencongress: Gehouden te Groningen op woensdag 1, donderdag 2 en vrijdag 3 april 1970*, Groningen: Wolters-Noordhoff, 1971, pp. 219-221. ['The Occult as a Motif in Swedish Literature'. Examines occult elements and motifs in Swedish literature, with reference mainly to Sg and Selma Lagerlöf]

[C1:1343] Vutova, Svetlana, 'Stradanieto prez prizmata na otchuzhdavaneto: Strindberg i Beckett', *Teatyr* (Sofia), 47:1 (1993), 77-80. ['Suffering through the Prism of Alienation: Strindberg and Beckett']

[C1:1344] Wachler, Ernst, 'Nietzsche und Strindberg als Antipoden', *Telos. Der Volkswart* (Prague), 18 (1942), p. 102. ['Nietzsche and Strindberg as Opposites']

[C1:1345] Wagner, Nike, *Geist und Geschlecht. Karl Kraus und die Erotik der Wiener Moderne*, Frankfurt am Main: Suhrkamp, 1982. 288+28 pp. plates. ['Spirit and Sex. Karl Kraus and the Eroticism of Modern Vienna'. Discusses Kraus's relationship with both Otto Wieninger in *Geschlecht und Charakter* (1903) and Sg's naturalistic plays]

[C1:1346] Walden, Herwarth, 'Wichtige Leute. Die Dichter über Strindberg', *Der Sturm* (Berlin), 6 (1915-16), p. 95. ['Important People. Writers on Strindberg'. Publishes comments on the recently deceased Sg by Maximilian Harden, Thomas Mann, and Gerhart Hauptmann]

[C1:1347] Walter, Jürgen, 'Wolfgang Borchert und August Strindberg', *Moderna Språk* (Stockholm), 61:3 (1967), 263-274. [Compares Borchert's play *Draussen vor der Tür* as a Station Drama with *Till Damaskus* and *Ett drömspel*, referring to Peter Szondi's remarks in *Theorie des modernen Dramas*, **D1:450**, on how, with Sg, the central 'Dramen-Ich' becomes 'ein episches Ich', as the great theatre of the world of the Baroque gives way to the drama of modern subjectivity, in which the effect is lyrical rather than dramatic]

[C1:1348] Wardle, Irving, 'A Strindberg of Our Own', *The Times* (London), 2 March 1968. [Maintains that D. H. Lawrence's plays make him 'British drama's closest relative to Sg.... There is a curious biographical parallel between the two writers: both haunted by the fact that their parents came from opposing classes and both acquiring their wives by aristocratic adultery. As artists they were both afflicted by messianic delusions which, for a time, they kept in check by submitting to the discipline of strict naturalism']

[C1:1349] Weininger, Otto, *Geschlecht und Charakter: Eine prinzippielle Untersuching*, Wien-Leipzig: W. Braumüller, 1903. XXIII+599 pp. [The first edition of Weininger's resonating study which was written with Sg's portrayal of gender relationships as one of its principal reference points]

[C1:1350] Weininger, Otto, *Geschlecht und Charakter: Eine prinzipielle Untersuchung, im Anhang Weingingers Tagebuch, Briefe August Strindbergs sowie Beiträge aus heutiger Sicht von Annegret Stopczyk*, München: Matthes & Seitz, 1980. Illus. XXIII+667 pp. [Rpr. of the first edition together with Weininger's diary and his correspondence with Sg as an addenda]

[C1:1351] Weininger, Otto, *Geslacht en karakter: een principeel onderzoek*, Vertald door Tinke Davids, Amsterdam: De Arbeiderspers, 1984. 569 pp. [Dutch translation of **C1:1349**, including Sg's correspondence with Weininger and a commentary on their relationship]

[C1:1352] Weininger, Otto, *Eros und Psyche. Studien und Briefe 1899-1902*, Hrsg. Hannelore Rodlauer, Wien: Verlag der Österreichischen Akademie der Wissenschaften, 1990. Illus. 223 pp.

[C1:1353] Weinstein, Arnold, 'Heaven and Hell: The Parameters of Self in Borges and Strindberg', *The Fiction of Relationship*, Princeton, New Jersey: Princeton University Press, 1988, pp. 197-243. [Counterpoints Sg's portrayal of relationships as a threat to the self in *Inferno* with Jorge Luis Borge's celebration of a boundless web of relationships that transforms 'one's murky brief life into a luminous part of something longer and larger than individual experience'. Weinstein also comments on *Ett drömspel*, 'Gatubilder III' (Street Pictures III), and *Spöksonaten*, but for him it is *Inferno* 'that most provocatively and succinctly makes the prophetic link between energy and writing, between power and language']

[C1:1354] Weiss, Peter, *Die Ästhetik des Widerstands*, Vol. 3, Frankfurt am Main: Suhrkamp Verlag, 1984, pp. 154-156. [Includes the reflections on Sg of the narrator of Weiss's 'novel' during a walk through Stockholm]

[C1:1355] Weiss, Peter, 'En frisk människa i ett sjukt samhälle', *Expressen* (Stockholm), 8 March 1986. ['A Healthy Man in a Sick Society'. Argues that, unlike the society with which he so often came into conflict, Sg was healthy]

[C1:1356] Weiss, Peter, 'Gegen die Gesetze der Normalität', *Akzente. Zeitschrift für Dichtung* (München), 9 (1962), 322-330. ['Against the Laws of Normality'. Offers a deeply personal portrait of Sg in which the Preface to *Fröken Julie* is regarded as among the epoch-making texts of dramatic theory and just as revolutionary in its time as the later manifestos of Artaud: 'I believe that today we are on the threshold of a new understanding of Sg, for we are the first generation able to grasp the scope of his vision.' *Spöksonaten*, in which the fantastic dominates and the characters give expression to a world of madness, is especially relevant for our own period, and anticipates the theatre of Beckett, Adamov, and Ionesco]

[C1:1357] Weiss, Peter, 'Gegen die Gesetze der Normalität', in *Rapporte*, Vol. 1, Frankfurt am Main: Suhrkamp, 1968, pp. 72-82. [Rpr. of **C1:1356**]

[C1:1358] Weiss, Peter, 'Gegen die Gesetze der Normalität', in *Aufsätze / Journale / Arbeitspunkte. Schriften zu Kunst und Literatur*, Berlin: Henschel Verlag, 1979. 187 pp. [Rpr. of **C1:1356**]

[C1:1359] Weiss, Peter, 'Naprzeciw zasadom normalności. Szkic ze zbioru *Rapporte*', *Dialog* (Warsaw), 1982:8, pp. 103-107. [Polish version of **C1:1356**]

[C1:1360] Weisstein, Ulrich, ed., *Expressionism as an International Literary Phenomenon*, Paris: Didier / Budapest: Akadémie Kiadó, 1973. [Includes **C1:1339**: Richard B. Vowles, 'Expressionism in Scandinavia'; **D1:560**: H. F. Garten, 'Foreign Influences on German Expressionist Drama'; and Henry A. Lea, 'Expressionist Literature and Music', pp. 141-160]

[C1:1361] Wenger, C. N., and C[arl] E. W. L. Dahlström, 'Aesthetics of the Modern Awakening in Scandinavia: Ibsen and Strindberg', *Scandinavian Studies* (Menasha, Wisconsin), 15:1 (1938), 58-65. [Whereas Ibsen's dramaturgy is characterised by an organic unity that now appears somewhat conventional, the extreme subjectivity of Sg's expressionism, which embodied the conflicts Ibsen observed, has become increasingly contemporary. Prompts a letter by A. E. Zucker in 1938, p. 172, and a rejoinder by Wenger in *Scandinavian Studies*, 16:1 (1939), p. 41]

[C1:1362] Werin, Algot, *Den svenske Faust och andra essayer*, Lund: C. W. K. Gleerup, 1950, pp. 5-42. ['The Swedish Faust and other Essays'. Includes Sg in a discussion of the Faust figure in Swedish literature, pp. 24-37. Faust provides a prototype for many of the post-Inferno dramas, but Axel Borg in *I havsbandet* is already a modern Faust, both spiritually cultivated and versed in natural science, and since he bears an unmistakable kinship with Sg himself, the latter 'may with every right be called "the Swedish Faust"'. Sg had the boundless ambition for knowledge of a renaissance man, but also his superstition]

[**C1:1363**] Werin, Algot, '"Kulturens offerväsen". Litet om 1870-talets pessimism', in Alf Nyman, red., *Festskrift tillägnad Hans Larsson den 18 februari 1927. Studier och uppsatser överräckta på sextiofemårsdagen av kolleger och lärjungar*, Stockholm: Albert Bonniers Förlag, 1927, pp. 339-354. ['"Culture's Sacrificial Being". A Comment on the Pessimism of the 1870s'. Includes Sg among those most closely associated with a philosophical outlook and attitude to life which was grounded in realism and frequently associated in Sweden during the 1870s with pessimism and a critique of culture]

[**C1:1364**] Werin, Algot, 'Naturalism och romantik', *Ord och Bild* (Stockholm), 41:3 (1932), 169-175. ['Naturalism and Romanticism'. Reviews Sten Linder, **C1:773**, *Ernst Ahlgren i hennes romaner*, and Vagn Børge, **C1:181**, *August Strindberg og H. C. Andersen*]

[**C1:1365**] Werin, Algot, 'Thomas Mann om Strindberg', *Svensk Litteraturtidskrift* (Stockholm), 38:4 (1975), 24-29. ['Thomas Mann on Strindberg'. Argues that Mann was not influenced by Sg but appreciated his grotesque humour]

[**C1:1366**] Werin, Algot, *Vilhelm Ekelund*, 2 vols, Stockholm: C. W. K. Gleerup, 1960-61. Vol. 1, 1880-1908, 439 pp.; Vol. 2, 1908-1925, 433 pp. [The standard life-and-letters study of the Swedish poet, essayist, and aphorist which includes numerous references to Sg. Werin argues that Ekelund (1880-1949) was drawn more closely to Sg than to any of his Swedish contemporaries once he became acquainted with his Inferno writings. Illustrates Eklund's growing appreciation of a writer whom he variously associated with Goethe, Nietzsche, and (particularly) Dostoevskii]

[**C1:1367**] Westin, Boel, '"Hexmästaren". Strindberg, Andersen och sagotraditionen', *Strindbergiana* (Stockholm), 10 (1995), pp. 183-197. Illus. ['"The Wizard". Strindberg, Andersen, and Fairy-Tale Tradition'. Challenges Vagn Børge's view of Sg as an unsuccessful writer of fairy tales in **C1:181** and demonstrates that Hans Christian Andersen is only one among many intertexts, including several other examples from the fairy-tale tradition, in both *Sagor* and *Svanevit*. A fixation on the part of many critics with Andersen has obscured Sg's familiarity (or affinity) with a wide range of Swedish and other sources, from A. I. Arwidsson's *Svenska fornsånger* and R. Dybeck's *Runa* to a French tradition that includes Charles Perrault and Edouard de Laboulaye]

[**C1:1368**] Wettenhovi-Aspa, Sigurd, 'August Strindberg – Arthur Schopenhauer', *Nya Dagligt Allehanda* (Stockholm), 24 December 1927. [Swedish version of an excerpt from **R:2368**]

[**C1:1369**] White, Kenneth S., 'Toward a New Interpretation of Lenormand's Theatrical Ethos', *Modern Drama* (Lawrence, Kansas), 2:4 (1960), 334-348. [Examines the spiritual aspect of Henri-René Lenormand's plays and argues that he was more influenced by Sg than by Freud. His 'dramatic universe was perhaps closer to Sg's than to that of any other playwright', and he remained enthralled by Sg's dramas throughout his life. White quotes extensively from a previously unpublished typescript by Lenormand (1882-1951) on Sg]

[**C1:1370**] White, Kenneth S., 'Visions of a Transfigured Humanity: Strindberg and Lenormand', *Modern Drama* (Lawrence, Kansas), 5:3 (1962), 323-330. [Compares *Påsk* with Henri-René Lenormand's drama *La Maison des Remparts* and stresses the evident temperamental affinity between two playwrights who both believed that life was a nightmare illuminated now and then 'by lightening flashes of regained purity']

[C1:1371] Widell, Arne, *Ola Hansson i Tyskland. En studie i hans liv och diktning åren 1890-1893*, Skrifter utgivna av Litteraturvetenskapliga Institutionen vid Uppsala universitet 9, Uppsala: AB Lundequistska Bokhandeln, 1979. 202 pp. [Examines Hansson's personal and literary contacts with Sg in the bohemian milieu and intellectual life of Berlin during the early 1890s. This included the influence they exerted on one another's writing and a mutual interest in both contemporary psychology and psychopathology, as well as in Edgar Allan Poe, the Woman Question, Nietzsche, and the mystical philosophy of Carl du Prel. Summary in German]

[C1:1372] Widén, Albin, 'Christliche und nordische Weltanschauung im Spiegel der nordischen Dichtung', *Buchbesprechung* (Leipzig), 2 (1938), 363-369. ['Christian and Nordic World Views as Mirrored in Nordic Literature'. Discusses Sg, pp. 367-368]

[C1:1373] Wieczorkowski, Aleksander, 'Naturalistyczne jasnowidzenie', *Współczesność* (Warsaw), 1962:14, p. 5.

[C1:1374] Wieselgren, Oscar, 'Strindbergs Inferno och Hopes bar', *Svenska Dagbladet* (Stockholm), 6 December 1947. [Identifies Sgian elements in Eugene O'Neill's play *The Iceman Cometh* in which the setting, Harry Hope's Bar, may be related to *Inferno*]

[C1:1375] Wikander, Matthew H., 'Reinventing the History Play', in Christopher Innes, ed., *The Cambridge Companion to George Bernard Shaw*, Cambridge: Cambridge University Press, 1998, pp. 195-217. [Comments briefly on Sg and Shaw as writers of history plays. Wikander points out that they both derived from Henry Thomas Buckle a view of history as an evolutionary struggle of ideas in conflict]

[C1:1376] Wikmark, Gunnar, 'Doktor Selma och stygge August', *Upsala Nya Tidning*, 3 June 1985. ['Doctor Selma [Lagerlöf] and Horrid August']

[C1:1377] Wilson, Colin, 'Shaw and Strindberg', *The Shavian* (Ashford, Middlesex), 1:15 (1959), 22-24. [Insists that Sg was self-obsessed and anticipated the overly personal literature of the 20th Century, thus becoming rapidly and hopelessly out-of-date, while Shaw was his necessary antithesis, and possessed a Goethean detatchment]

[C1:1378] Wilson, Colin, *The Strength to Dream: Literature and the Imagination*, London: Victor Gollancz Ltd; Boston: Houghton Mifflin Company, 1962, pp. 37-43. [Discusses Sg together with W. B. Yeats, Oscar Wilde, and H. P. Lovecraft in a chapter on 'The Assault on Rationality'. Sg allowed rejection to drive him into insanity; he distrusts life and dislikes society while his 'realistic' brain had to manufacture evidence to enable him finally to accept a 'supernatural' view]

[C1:1379] Wilson, Edwin, ed., *Shaw on Shakespeare*, Harmondsworth: Penguin, 1961. 298 pp. [Quotes Shaw on Sg as 'the only genuinely Shakespearean modern dramatist']

[C1:1380] Winther, Sophus Keith, 'Strindberg and O'Neill: A Study in Influence', *Scandinavian Studies* (Larence, Kansas), 31:3 (1959), 103-120. [Rather than try and establish the usual link between the early O'Neill and Sg via passages adopted by the former from the latter almost verbatim, Winther is more concerned with the nature of an influence that continued throughout O'Neill's life, arguing that he turned more to the autobiographical works than the plays, 'for it was Sg's conception of life that influenced [him] in his mature work, and not specific scenes from the plays'. Nevertheless, similarities, both textual and formal, are identified along with common themes and affinities that both dramatists shared with Schopenhauer and Nietzsche. O'Neill learned self-analysis from *Inferno* and *Röda rummet* rather than from, as is so often claimed, Freud. Thus Winther suggests that *Long Day's Journey into Night* owes much to *Tjänstekvinnans son* and both *The Iceman Cometh* and *Lazarus Laughed* are indebted to *Röda rummet*]

[C1:1381] Wirmark, Margareta, *Spelhuset. En monografi över Hjalmar Bergmans Drama*, Stockholm: Rabén & Sjögren, 1971, pp. 129-147. ['*The Gaming House.* A Monograph on Hjalmar Bergman's Drama'. Describes how Sg's post-Inferno plays are the most important dramaturgical influence on Bergman's geometrically structured play which, like *Spöksonaten*, also uses dumb show and employs a house as an organising symbol. Bergman shares Sg's view of language, emulating him in the richness of his associations, abrupt turns, radical abbreviations, and persistent repetition. Wirmark argues that, like Pär Lagerkvist, Bergman extends the Sgian tradition in the Swedish theatre and, together with *En skugga* (A Shadow) and *Herr Sleeman kommer* (Herr Sleeman is Coming), *Spelhuset* occupies as central a place in Bergman's work as the Chamber Plays do in Sg's. English summary, pp. 208-213]

[C1:1382] Wittrock, Ulf, 'Ellen Key och Strindberg', *Dagens Nyheter* (Stockholm), 31 January 1948. [Documents Key's intellectual relationship with Sg and her understandably critical response to his savage portrayal of her as Hanna Paj in *Svarta fanor*]

[C1:1383] Wittrock, Ulf, 'Ellen Key och nittiotalets kulturdebatt', *Samlaren* (Uppsala), 88 (1967), pp. 7-55. ['Ellen Key and 1890's Cultural Debate'. Discusses Key's role in the dethronement of the naturalist Sg by the writers of the 1890s with her controversial 1894 essay on C. J. L. Almqvist (1793-1866), elevating him as 'Sweden's most modern writer' at Sg's expense (**C1:657**). Wittrock also notes Sg's general antipathy for Almqvist]

[C1:1384] Wittrock, Ulf, 'Ellen Key, Almqvist och sekelskiftets idédebatt', in Ulla-Britta Lagerroth and Bertil Romberg, red., *Perspektiv på Almqvist*, Stockholm: Rabén & Sjögren, 1973, pp. 24-28. ['Ellen Key, Almqvist, and Turn-of-the-Century Intellectual Debate'. Rpr. of **C1:1383**]

[C1:1385] Wittrock, Ulf, 'Jugundstilforskningen, expressionismen och Richard Dehmel', *Samlaren* (Uppsala), 92 (1971), pp. 164-175. Illus. ['Jugund Style, Expressionism, and Richard Dehmel'. Includes comments on the *art nouveau* elements in *Pelikanen* and *Ett drömspel*, and the interest which Sg and Dehmel (1863-1920), who knew one another in Berlin in 1893, shared in the natural sciences]

[C1:1386] Wittrock, Ulf, *Marika Stiernstedt*, Stockholm: Albert Bonniers Förlag, 1959. 478 pp. [A life-and-letters study of the Swedish writer (1875-1954) which recognises her slender personal and literary links with Sg]

[C1:1387] Wittrock, Ulf, 'Strindberg och sekelskiftets symbolism', *Ord och Bild* (Stockholm), 71:5 (1962), 409-414. Illus. ['Strindberg and Turn-of-the Century Symbolism'. Uses several recent books by Gunnar Brandell, **B1:55**, Karl-Åke Kärnell, **B1:179**, and F. L. Lucas, **C1:812**, to reflect on Sg's relationship to *fin-de-siècle* symbolism and Ellen Key's reclamation of C. J. L. Almqvist with her essay **C1:657**]

[C1:1388] Wizelius, Ingemar, 'Ludvig Nordström och Strindbergsarvet', *Dagens Nyheter* (Stockholm), 10 August 1959. ['Ludvig Nordström and Strindberg's Heritage'. Maintains that it was the expressionist and mystic Sg who preoccupied the generation of Swedish writers numbering Hjalmar Bergman, Vilhelm Ekelund, Martin Koch, and Pär Lagerkvist, as well as Nordström (1882-1942)]

[C1:1389] Wright, H[erbert] G[ladstone], 'Rupert Brooke och Strindberg', *Forum* (Stockholm), 6 (1919), 164-166. [Argues that Brooke was one of the most ardent of Sg's admirers in England, particularly of the later dramas, which he knew in German translation. Quotes prolifically from Brooke's 1913 appreciation of Sg, **C1:238**]

[C1:1390] Wright, H[erbert] G[ladstone], 'Strindberg and England', in *Anglo-Scandinavian Literary Relations*, Bangor: Jarvis & Foster, Printers, 1919, pp. 110-156. [An impressively informed study of Sg's knowledge of England and his indebtedness to English thought, both in literature and science. Wright documents Sg's reading of English journals and his knowledge of English history as represented in the historical plays and stories. His survey includes an account of Sg's short visit to England in 1893 and its importance for his later writing, but focuses primarily on his familiarity with numerous English authors, both literary and non-literary. These include Byron, Buckle, Dickens, Darwin, Mill, Spencer, Grenville-Murray, Lubbock, Owen, Marryat, Scott, and especially Shakespeare, and Wright considers their place in his work. The essay includes a version of the article on Rupert Brooke and Sg, **C1:1389**]

[C1:1391] Wright, H[erbert] G[ladstone], 'Strindberg och England', *Forum* (Stockholm), 6 (1919), 222-224. [See **C1:1390**]

[C1:1392] Wright, H[erbert] G[ladstone], 'Strindberg och några engelska författare. I. Hans intryck från Byron, Buckle, Dickens and Darwin', *Afton-Tidningen* (Stockholm), 28 April 1920. ['Strindberg and some English Writers. I. The Impression made on Him by Byron, Buckle, Dickens, and Darwin'. See **C1:1390**]

[C1:1393] Wright, H[erbert] G[ladstone], 'Strindberg och några engelska författare. II. Strindberg och Shakespeare', *Afton-Tidningen* (Stockholm), 2 May 1920. ['Strindberg and some English Writers. II. Strindberg and Shakespeare'. See **C1:1390**]

[C1:1394] Wright, Rochelle, 'Strindberg's *Ett drömspel* and Hofmannsthal's *Die Frau ohne Schatten*', in Marilyn Johns Blackwell, ed., **C1:142**, *Structures of Influence*, pp. 211-225. ['Strindberg's *A Dream Play* and [Hugo von] Hofmannsthal's *The Woman without a Shadow*'. Explores similarities between the two works. In both of them the central theme is the quest for what is essentially human; they are structurally similar, draw their inspiration in part from Eastern tradition, have allegorical and symbolic characters, and employ the associational logic of dreams and fairy tale. Their protagonists both descend from a higher realm in order to experience earthly life and form a judgement on it. Sg envisaged the thematically composed *Ett drömspel* as performed with music, thus removing its most obvious difference with *Die Frau*. Nevertheless, 'the parallels in overall framework, dramatic structure, characterization, and theme…do not demonstrate direct influence so much as an affinity between the two authors and similarities in their approaches to writing for the stage']

[C1:1395] Wulff, Johannes, 'Norges Strindberg', in Niels Berger Wamberg, red., *Sandemoses Ansigter*, København: Schonberg/Oslo: Aschehoug, 1969, pp. 135-143. ['Norway's Strindberg'. An appreciation of the Norwegian novelist Axel Sandamose (1899-1965), sometimes called 'Norway's Strindberg']

[C1:1396] Iatsimirskii, A. I., *Noveishaia pol'skaia literatura*, Vol. 2, St Petersburg: Ponova, 1908, p. 258. [Modern Polish Literature. Discusses Sg's literary and personal links with Stanisław Przybyszewski. E.772]

[C1:1397] Iur'ev, A[ndrei Alekseevich], 'G. Ibsen i A. Strindberg', in L[ev] Gitel'man and V[alentina] Dianova, eds, **B1:148**, *Avgust Strindberg i mirovaia kul'tura. Materialy mezhvyzovskoi nauchnoi konferentsii. Stat'i. Soobshcheniia*, pp. 51-62. ['Henrik Ibsen and August Strindberg']

[C1:1398] Zadravec, Franc, 'Dramatika Slavka Gruma', *Slavistična revija* (Ljubljana), 16 (1968), 413-469. [On the plays of Slavko Grum]

[C1:1399] Zadravec, Franc, 'Ivan Cankar kot naturalist in realist v teoriji in praksi', in *Obdobje realizma v slovenskem jeziku, knjizevnosti in kulturi*, Ljubljana, 1982, pp. 73-100. ['Ivan Cankar as a Naturalist and Realist in Theory and Practice'. Comments on the relationship of the Slovenian novelist (1875-1918), dramatist, and poet to European naturalism and realism]

[C1:1400] Zadravec, Franc, 'Slovenska ekspresionistična literatura', in *Obdobje ekspresionizma v slovenskem jeziku, kniiževnosti in kulturi*, Ljubljana, 1984, pp. 9-39. ['Slovenian Expressionist Literature']

[C1:1401] Zaharieva, Bourjana, 'Strindberg i amerikanskata drama', *Problemi na izkustvoto* (Sofia), 3 (1990), 33-39. ['Strindberg and American Drama'. Traces Sg's relevance for the plays of Tennessee Williams and Edward Albee]

[C1:1402] Zimmermann, Willi, 'Strindberg, der Schwede, und Holberg, der Däne', *Volksbühnenwarte* (Berlin), 21:7 (1940), 3-4. ['Strindberg, the Swede, and [Ludvig] Holberg, the Dane']

[C1:1403] Zlobin, G., 'Privety i poritsaniia Shona O'Keisi', in O'Keisi, *Za teatral'nym zanavesom*, Moscow, 1971, pp. 3-15. [Introduces a collection of texts by Sean O'Casey with comments on the latter's debt as a dramatist to Sg, p. 12. E.1048]

See also **B1:55, B1:104, B1:395, B1:421, B1:437, B2:1, B2:79, B2:120, B2:128, B2:193, B2:194, B2:294, B2:302, B2:319, B2:320, B3:237, B3:246, B3:323, B3:324, B4:64, B8:144, B9:2, B9:140, B9:218, D1:27, D1:44, D1:65, D1:111, D1:405, D1:487, D1:494, D1:556, D1:561, D1:567, D1:569, D1:575, D1:583, D1:596, D1:598, D1:664, D1:668, D1:692, D1:708, D2:206, D2:506, D2:543, D2:612, D2:627, D2:708, D2:775, D2:819, D2:844, D2:958, D2:1908, D2:1041, D2:1043, D2:1047, D2:1166, D2:1194, D2:1206, E4:3, E5:8, E5:60, E8:28, E11:43, E11:65, E11:78, E11:93, E11:115, E12:28, E12:79, E12:105, E12:125, E12:137, E12:208, E25:47, E25:142, E31:27, E35:104, E51:62, E51:64, E51:77, E51:135, E51:137, E53:2, E53:11, F1:34, F1:37, F2:64, F4:78, F4:85, F5:53a, F5:166, F5:168, F5:172, F9:19, G1:26, G1:54, G1:99, G3:110, G3:116, G3:126, G3:127, G3:139, G3:141, G3:142, G10:9, G10:41, G14:12, G16:39, H4:53, P1:142, P1:143, P1:240, P1:295, P1:356, P1:358, P2:35, P3:39, P3:132, P3:139, P3:143, P3:144, P3:165, V:10, V:22, V:28, V:38, V:45, V:46, V:49, V:50, V:52, V:55, V:60, V:63, V:69, V:71, V:83, V:90, V:92, V:103, V:104, V:112, V:113, V:114, V:116, V:125, V:127, V:133, V:137, V:138, V:142, V:144, V:155, V:171, V:179, V:184, V:189, V:191, V:192, V:193, V:194, V:200, V:205, V:207, V:208, V:209, V:211, V:214, V:215, V:218, V:231, V:235, V:238, V:242, V:243, V:245, V:251**

C2. Strindberg and Ingmar Bergman

[*N.B. Bergman's comments on specific plays and reviews of the productions he has directed of many of Strindberg's dramas for radio, television, and the stage are listed in the section on the relevant play. Likewise, general discussion of directorial approaches to the plays which take account of his work as a director are listed under Section* **D2**]

[C2:1] Abraham, Henry H. L., 'A Successor to Strindberg: Alienation in Ingmar Bergman', *The Commonweal* (New York), 29 (1964), p. 291. [Describes the characters of Bergman's films as the gloomy descendants of the neurotics in Sg's plays]

[C2:2] Ahlgren, Stig, 'Riset bakom spegeln', *Vecko-Journalen* (Stockholm), 24 November 1961. ['The Cane behind the Mirror'. Maintains that *Påsk* is an important influence on Ingmar Bergman's film *Through a Glass Darkly*, which echoes and reverses several elements in Sg's play]

[C2:3] Almer, Johan, 'Klistrande och livskatastrof: Ingmar Bergman och den svenska äktenskapskrisens urscen', in Barbro Ryder Liljegren, red., *Kriser och förnyelser*, Göteborg: Humanistiska facultätsnämnden, Universitetet, 1998, pp. 39-46. ['Pasting and Life's Catastrophe. Ingmar Bergman and the Ur-Scene of Swedish Marital Crisis'. Argues that all the marital crises in Bergman's film manuscripts have their origin in the scene between Agnes and the Lawyer in *Ett drömspel* during which their maid continues to paste over the cracks round the windows]

[C2:4] Aristarco, Guido, 'Fonti culturali di Bergman: da Kierkegaard a Strindberg', in [Roberto Alonge], ed., **D2:7**, *Alle origini della drammaturgia moderna: Ibsen, Strindberg, Pirandello*, pp. 226-232. ['Bergman's Cultural Sources: From Kierkegaard to Strindberg'. Identifies Kierkegaard and Sg as prominent among cultural influences on the films of Ingmar Bergman]

[C2:5] Assayas, Olivier, and Stig Björkman, *Tre dagar med Strindberg*, *Filmkonst* (Göteborg), No. 13 (1993), 143 pp. [A series of conversations with Bergman in which he recalls that 'the first time I came in content with Sg, I was twelve. It was a tremendous experience, and I believe that in my first plays I simply copied Sg. I tried to write like him, dialogues, scenes, everything. Strindberg was my idol, without comparison. His vitality, his anger, I felt it inside me']

[C2:6] Bergman, Ingmar, *Laterna magica*, Stockholm: Norstedts, 1987. Illus. 337 pp. [Bergman's autobiography in which Sg is a recurring reference point. It includes an account of the difficulties encountered in achieving an adequate staging of *Ett drömspel*, pp. 47-51]

[C2:7] Bergman, Ingmar, *The Magic Lantern: An Autobiography*, Translated by Joan Tate, London: Hamish Hamilton, 1988. Illus. 312 pp. [English edition of **C2:6**]

[C2:8] Bergman, Ingmar, [*Articles, Criticism, Scripts, Interviews*], Moscow: Iskusstvo, 1969, pp. 247, 261. [Includes Russian translations of Bergman's comments on *Hemsöborna* and Sg's innovations as a dramatist]

[C2:9] Billquist, Fritiof, *Ingmar Bergman. Teatermannen och filmskaparen*, Stockholm: Natur och Kultur, 1960. Illus. 279 pp. [Surveys Bergman's career as a film director and man of the theatre to date, with Sg as one of his principal preoccupations]

[C2:10] Björkman, Stig, Torsten Manns, and Jonas Sima, eds, *Bergman on Bergman*, Translated by Paul Britten Austin, London: Secker & Warburg/New York: Simon & Schuster, 1973. Illus. 288 pp. [According to Bergman, Sg 'has followed me all my life…[he] expressed things which I'd experienced and which I couldn't find words for']

[C2:11] Björkman, Stig, Torsten Manns and Jonas Sima, red., *Bergman om Bergman*, Stockholm: P. A. Norstedt & Söners Förlag, 1970. Illus. 307 pp. [Swedish edition of **C2:10**]

[C2:12] Entry cancelled.

[C2:13] Blokker, A., '*Het Uur van de Wolf*, *Vrij Nederland* (Amsterdam), 29 June 1969. ['The Hour of the Wolf'. Compares Bergman's film *Vargtimmen* with *Inferno*]

[C2:14] Bono, Francesco, 'Ingmar Bergman in the Eyes of Italian Theatre Critics', *Nordic Theatre Studies* (Copenhagen), 11 (1998), 105-113. [Includes discussion of the reception of Bergman's 1970 production of *Ett drömspel* at the Venice Biennale]

[C2:15] Chicco, Elisabetta, 'Cinema e teatro nell 'opera di Bergman', *Cinema nuovo* (Milano), 17 (March-April 1968), 96-108. ['Film and Theatre in the Works of Bergman'. Traces a relationship between Ingmar Bergman's films and various theatre traditions: (1) medieval stations-of-the-cross drama and Sg's post-Inferno dramaturgy in *The Seventh Seal* and *Wild Strawberries*; (2) Aristotelian dramatic structure in *Thirst*; and (3) the form of the Sgian Chamber Play in Bergman's film trilogy]

[C2:16] Ciesielski, Zenon, 'Bergman i Strindberg', *Przegląd Humanistyczny* (Warsaw), 1979:11-12, pp. 33-40. ['Bergman and Strindberg'. A Polish study of Ingmar Bergman's relationship with Sg]

[C2:17] Cohen, Hubert I., *Ingmar Bergman: The Art of Confession*, New York: Twayne, 1993. Illus. 507 pp. [Stresses Sg's importance for Bergman's confessional art throughout, with specific comparisons between one or other of the films and *Tjänstekvinnans son*, *Inferno*, *Lycko-Pers resa*, *Till Damaskus*, *Folkungasagan*, *Advent*, *Dödsdansen*, *Ett drömspel*, *Spöksonaten*, and *Stora landsvägen*]

[C2:18] Cohen-Stratyner, Barbara, 'Ingmar Bergman and the Theatre', *Nordic Theatre Studies* (Copenhagen), 11 (1998), 98-104.

[C2:19] Corbucci, G., 'Un omaggio a Strindberg nell' ultimo Bergman', *Cinema Nuovo* (Milano), No. 289 (June 1984), pp. 10-11. Illus. ['A Homage to Strindberg in Bergman's Last Film'. Reads *Fanny and Alexander*, originally understood erroneously to have been Bergman's final contribution to the cinema, as a tribute to Sg]

[C2:20] Cowie, Peter, *Ingmar Bergman: A Critical Biography*, New York: Charles Scribner's Sons, 1982. Illus. 397 pp.

[C2:21] Cowie, Peter, *Ingmar Bergman: A Critical Biography*, New York: Limelight Editions, 1992, pp. 41-46. [Identifies Sg as an integral part of Bergman's 'cultural heritage' in an updated edition of **C2:20**]

[C2:22] Cowie, Peter, *Ingmar Bergman. Biographie critique*, Traduit de l'anglais par Mimi et Isabelle Perrin, Paris: Seghers, 1986. Illus. 411 pp. [French edition of **C2:20**]

[C2:23] DePaul, Brother C. F. X., 'Bergman and Strindberg: Two Philosophies of Suffering', *College English* (Urbana, Illinois), 26:8 (1965), 620-630. [A superficial analysis of Bergman's filmic world with reference to such 'Sgian' themes as suffering, atonement, and estrangement]

[C2:24] Farbshtein, A. A., '[Ingmar Bergman as a Philosopher and a Moralist]', *Skandinavskii sbornik* (Talinn), 13 (1968), 141-154. [Comments on the significance of Sg for Bergman, pp. 141, 146. E.1028]

[C2:25] Fletcher, John, 'Bergman and Strindberg', *Journal of Modern Literature* (Philadelphia), 3:2 (1973), 173-190. [Establishes common ground between Sg and Bergman, especially in their intermingling of dream and reality and the past with the present, as well as their obsession with religious questions. Comments briefly on *Fordringsägare*, *Dödsdansen*, *Spöksonaten*, *Ett drömspel*, and *Fröken Julie* in relation to several of

Bergman's films and concludes that, in transmuting several of Sg's recurring themes, Bergman is the greater artist]

[C2:26] Garibova, O., '[Performing Strindberg]', *Teatr* (Moscow), 1976:11, pp. 1129-1131. [Discusses Ingmar Bergman's productions of *Ett drömspel*, *Till Damaskus*, and *Spöksonaten*]

[C2:27] Hagen, Eric, 'Bergman at B. A. M.: A Perspective of Stage Space', *Theatre Topics* (Baltimore), 2:1 (1992), 77-85. [Discusses Bergman's productions of *Long Day's Journey into Night*, *A Doll's House*, and *Fröken Julie* on tour to New York]

[C2:28] Haverty [Rugg], Linda, 'Strindbergman: The Problem of Filming Autobiography in Bergman's *Fanny and Alexander*', *Literature/Film Quarterly* (Salisbury, MD), 16:3 (1988), 174-180. Illus. [On film as a medium for autobiography and the association between the figure of Ishmael in Bergman's film and its relevance for Sg's autobiographical fiction, *Tjänstekvinnans son*. Haverty also comments on *Ett drömspel* and *Spöksonaten*]

[C2:29] Hayes, Jarrod, 'The Seduction of Alexander. Behind the Postmodern door: Ingmar Bergman and Baudrillard's *De la seduction*', *Film Quarterly* (Salisbury, MD), 25:1 (1997), 40-47. [Identifies the mysterious door in *Ett drömspel* with the series of doors that Bergman exploits to such effect in *Fanny and Alexander*. In both cases they may be related to the mysterious, the mask, and the image]

[C2:30] Hockenjos, Vreni, 'Strindberg through Bergman: A Case of Mutation', *TijdSchrift voor Skandinavistiek* (Amsterdam), 20:1 (1999), 45-60. [Surveys Sg's abiding presence in much of Ingmar Bergman's work in the cinema, compares *Ett drömspel* with *Persona*, and discusses his productions of the play for both television and the theatre. Hockenjos concludes that Bergman actively shapes and elaborates the Sgian material for his own purposes, using it as a point of departure to stretch and expand the devices of a different medium]

[C2:31] Holden, David F., 'Three Literary Sources for *Through a Glass Darkly*', *Literature Film Quarterly* (Salisbury, Maryland), 2:1 (1974), 22-29. [Identifies *Påsk* as one of three literary works which exerted a considerable influence on Ingmar Bergman's film (the others are Charlotte Gilman's story 'The Yellow Wallpaper' and Chekhov's *The Seagull*)]

[C2:32] Johns [Blackwell], Marilyn, 'The Chamber Plays and the Trilogy: A Revaluation of the Case of Strindberg and Bergman', in Marilyn Johns Blackwell, ed., **C1:142**, *Structures of Influence*, pp. 49-64. [Explores affinities between Sg's Chamber Plays and the film trilogy *Through a Glass Darkly*, *Winter Night*, and *The Silence*, which represent a major shift in Bergman's aesthetics, one founded on the innovations that Sg introduced into his dramaturgy in 1907. Bergman's appropriation of certain themes and techniques from his literary mentor and their transposition into a new medium which also aspires to the condition of chamber music thus facilitates a comparison between the two media]

[C2:33] Johns [Blackwell], Marilyn, 'Dream Reality in August Strindberg's *A Dreamplay* and Ingmar Bergman's *Wild Strawberries*', *Proceedings of the Pacific North West Council on Foreign Languages*, 27:1 (1976), 122-125. [On the logic and distortion of the dream state as it affects the depersonalisation of character and the organic scene structure in both film and play. Identifies four scenes in the film that are derivative of the play]

[C2:34] Johns [Blackwell], Marilyn, 'Journey into Autumn: *Oväder* and *Smultronstället*', *Scandinavian Studies* (Lawrence, Kansas), 50:3 (1978), 292-303. [Compares Sg's play with Bergman's film *Wild Strawberries* in terms of the main character (an elderly gentleman), the theme, characterisation, and narrative technique]

[C2:35] Johns [Blackwell], Marilyn, 'Kindred Spirits: Strindberg and Bergman', *Scandinavian Review* (New York), 64:3 (1976), p. 16. [A note regarding Sg's temperamental affinity with Ingmar Bergman. Rpr. in **B1:165**]

[C2:36] Kael, Pauline, 'För släkt och vänner. Om Ingmar Bergmans *Fanny och Alexander*', översättning Leif Janzon, *Ord och Bild* (Stockholm), 94:2 (1985), 76-84. Illus. ['For Relations and Friends. On Ingmar Bergman's *Fanny and Alexander*'. Reads Bergman's valedictory film *Fanny and Alexander* as a cinematic autobiography, strongly influenced by both *Ett drömspel* and *Hamlet*]

[C2:37] Kinder, Marsha, 'The Dialectic of Dreams and Theater in the Films of Ingmar Bergman', *Dreamworks* (New York), 5:3-4 (1988), 179-192. [Traces many of the sources of Bergman's inspiration to Sg, most notably in *Ett drömspel*, 'which provides the deep structure for Bergman's exploration of the dialectic between theater and dreams'. A brief analysis of *The Devil's Wanton, Sawdust and Tinsel, Wild Strawberries, The Ritual, From the Life of the Marionettes*, and *Fanny and Alexander* identifies techniques and motifs which they share with *Ett drömspel* while, in his film trilogy of 1961-63, Bergman draws on the Chamber Plays and *Den starkare*]

[C2:38] Koskinen, Maaret, *Ingmar Bergman: "Allting föreställer, ingenting är". Filmen och teatern – en tvärestetisk studie*, Nora: Nya Doxa, 2001. Illus. 238 pp. [A study of Bergman's cinema which includes brief comments on the influence of Sg's dreamplay style on Bergman, pp. 38-39, 171-174]

[C2:39] Koskinen, Maaret, *Spel och speglingar. En studie i Ingmar Bergmans filmiska estetik*, Stockholm: University of Stockholm, 1993. Illus. 278 pp. [A study of Bergman's cinematic aesthetic which includes references to its affinity with Sg's late dramaturgy. English summary]

[C2:40] Landquist, John, 'Så stora smultron finns inte…', *Aftonbladet* (Stockholm), 25 February 1957. ['Such big Strawberries don't Exist…'. [Criticises Ingmar Bergman's film *The Seventh Seal* as derivative of the medieval features of Sg's *Till Damaskus* and *Folkungasagan*. Prompts a comment by Marianne Höök in *Svenska Dagbladet*, 28 February]

[C2:41] Livingston, Paisley, 'Self-Reflexivity in Strindberg and Bergman', *TijdSchrift voor Skandinavistiek* (Amsterdam), 20:1 (1999), 34-43. [Maintains that the kind of self-reflexivity which Roland Barthes sees as the essence of artistic modernity in his essay 'Littérature et métalangage', but this does not entirely account for the mimetic reflexivity which, in Ingmar Bergman's works, has an essentially ethical character and motivation that is reminiscent of Sg in *Fordringsägare*]

[C2:42] Livingston, Paisley, *Ingmar Bergman and the Rituals of Art*, New York: Cornell University Press, 1982. 291 pp. [Argues that Berman's *Sommarnattens leende* is based on *Leka med elden*, associates the vampire motif in *Persona* with *Dödsdansen* and Sg's comments on the artist as vampire in *Klostret*, examines Bergman's understanding of effective dramaturgy in relation to Sg's, and identifies their mutual interest in suggestion]

[C2:43] Mieß, Werner, 'Bergmans Strindberg', *Theater heute* (Hannover), 7:2 (1966), 50-51.

[C2:44] Mosley, Philip, *Ingmar Bergman: The Cinema as Mistress*, London: Marion Boyars, 1982. [Discusses Bergman's debt to Sg, pp. 19-33]

[C2:45] Oldrini, Guido, 'L'esperanza letteraria "nazionale" in Sjöberg et Bergman', *Civilta dell'imagine*, 1 (1966), n.p. [Discusses Sg's influence on Alf Sjöberg as well as Bergman]

[C2:46] Oliver, Roger W., 'Bergman's Trilogy: Tradition and Innovation', *Performing Arts Journal* (New York), 14:1 (1992), 75-86. Illus. [Discusses Bergman's stagings of three key naturalist theatre texts, in all of which heredity and history are determining factors: *Long Day's Journey into Night*, *A Doll's House*, and *Fröken Julie*]

[C2:47] Pal'tsev, N., '[Foreword]', in Ingmar Bergman, [Scenes from a Marriage], Moscow, 1979, pp. 5-19. [Discusses Sg and Bergman, pp. 8-9. E.1107]

[C2:48] [Partyga, Ewa], 'Ibsen, Strindberg i Bergman', *Dialog* (Warsaw), 35:11 (1990), 147-148. [Examines Ingmar Bergman's debt to Ibsen and Sg]

[C2:49] Peña, Jaime Barrios, 'Strindberg-Bergman. *Sueño*', in *Strindberg, Bergman y Norén. La Tragedia de la restitución*, Bromma/Stockholm: Fénix, n.d., pp. 73-118, Illus. [Discusses Ingmar Bergman treatment of Sg's post-Inferno dramaturgy, focusing in particular on his stagings of *Ett drömspel*]

[C2:50] Samuels, Charles Thomas, 'Ingmar Bergman: An Interview', in Stuart M. Kaminsky, *Ingmar Bergman: Essays in Criticism*, London: Oxford University Press, 1975, pp. 98-132. ['If you live in a Sg tradition, you are breathing Sg air. After all, I have been seeing Sg at the theater since I was ten years old, so it is difficult to say, what belongs to him and what to me']

[C2:51] Schuh, Oscar Fritz, 'Vom *Traumspiel* zum *Schweigen*. Ein Gespräch über August Strindberg und Ingmar Bergman', *Eckart Jahrbuch* (Berlin), 1964-65, pp. 81-88. ['From *A Dreamplay* to *The Silence*. A Dialogue about August Strindberg and Ingmar Bergman']

[C2:52] Simon, John, *Ingmar Bergman Directs*, New York: Harcourt Brace Jovanovich, Inc., 1972. Illus. 315 pp. [Compares Bergman's treatment of silence in *Persona* with Sg's silent figure, Mlle Y, in *Den starkare*, concluding: 'silence is, in the final reckoning, vampirism, a vacuum into which the other person, the speaker's, lifeblood ebbs as surely as if it were being sucked']

[C2:53] Sjöman, Vilgot, *L136: Dagbok med Ingmar Bergman*, Stockholm: P. A. Norstedt & Söners Förlag, 1963. Illus. 240 pp. ['Diary with Ingmar Bergman'. An account of working with Bergman in diary form. Quotes Bergman: 'As much as I love the first two acts (of *Spöksonaten*), as much do I detest the last one; but it is my damned duty as a director to shape it with exactly the same objectivity']

[C2:54] Skawonius, Betty, 'Varför just Strindberg – Bergman?', *Dagens Nyheter* (Stockholm), 11 March 1970. ['Why Strindberg Precisely – Bergman?' Related to Bergman's 1970 staging of *Ett drömspel* at Dramaten]

[C2:55] Sontag, Susan, '*Persona*', *Sight and Sound* (London), 36:4 (1967), pp. 186-191, 212. [Includes a comparison of Bergman's treatment of silence in *Persona* with Sg's silent figure, Mlle Y, in *Den starkare*: 'the one who talks, who spills her soul, turns out to be weaker than the one who keeps silent.... Language is presented as an instrument of fraud and cruelty']

[C2:56] Sontag, Susan, 'Bergman's *Persona*', in *Styles of Radical Will*, New York: Farrar, Straus & Giroux; London: Secker & Warburg, 1969, pp. 123-145. [Rpr. of **C2:55**]

[C2:57] Sontag, Susan, '*Persona*: The Film in Depth', in Stuart M. Kaminsky, ed., *Ingmar Bergman: Essays in Criticism*, London: Oxford University Press, 1975, pp. 253-269. [Rpr. of **C2:55**]

[C2:58] Sprinchorn, Evert, '*Fanny and Alexander* and Strindberg and Ibsen and…', in Michael Perridon, ed., *Strindberg, Ibsen & Strindberg. Essays on Scandinavian Film and Drama*, Maastricht: Shaker Publishing, 1998, pp. 177-178. [Identifies the relationship between dream and reality as one of the central themes in Bergman's film and compares it with *Ett drömspel*]

[C2:59] Stańczuk, Dariusz, 'Strindberg a Bergman', *Didaskalia* (Warsaw), 33:11 (1999), 70-73. [A note in Polish on Ingmar Bergman's links with Sg]

[C2:60] Steene, Birgitta, 'Fire Rekindled: Strindberg and Bergman', in Michael Perridon, ed., *Strindberg, Ibsen & Strindberg. Essays on Scandinavian Film and Drama*, Maastricht: Shaker Publishing, 1998, pp. 189-204.

[C2:61] Steene, Birgitta, ed., *Focus on "The Seventh Seal"*, Englewood Cliffs, N.J.: Prentice-Hall, 1972. VII+182 pp. [Includes six references to Sg's relevance for Ingmar Bergman's film]

[C2:62] Steene, Birgitta, *Ingmar Bergman*, New York: Twayne Publishers Inc., 1968, pp. 19-24. [Discusses the significance of Sg's work for Bergman as a film-maker and writer. Elsewhere sees *The Seventh Seal* as indebted to Sg's 'cinematic' play *Folkungasagan*]

[C2:63] Steene, Birgitta, *Ingmar Bergman: A Guide to References and Resources*, Boston: Mass.: G. K. Hall & Co., 1982. 342 pp. [Documents Bergman's career as a film director and identifies numerous points of contact with Sg. Includes details of theatre programmes and interviews in which Bergman discusses Sg, as well as a filmography and annotated catalogue of the secondary literature on Bergman]

[C2:64] Steene, Birgitta, *Ingmar Bergman: A Reference Guide*, Amsterdam University Press, 2005. 1150 pp. [A valuable annotated bibliographical guide to Bergman's achievement as author, film-maker, and theatre director with details, including cast lists and technical support for all his productions of Sg's plays and information regarding their press reception]

[C2:65] Steene, Birgitta, 'Ingmar Bergman möter Strindberg', *Upsala Nya Tidning*, 23 February 2000. ['Ingmar Bergman Encounters Strindberg']

[C2:66] Steene, Birgitta, 'Ingmar Bergman möter August Strindberg', *Strindbergiana* (Stockholm), 14 (1999), pp. 13-33. Illus. ['Ingmar Bergman Encounters August Strindberg'. Assesses Sg's influence on Bergman as the director of *Ett drömspel*, as a creative example, and as a personality]

[C2:67] Steene, Birgitta, 'Ingmar Bergman Staging Strindberg', in Kirsten Wechsel, Hrsg., **B1:473**, *Strindberg and His Media*, pp. 173-186. [Surveys Bergman's work with Sg as a theatre director, his relationship with his predecessor in Sweden, Olof Molander, and the reception accorded his productions by the Swedish critics.

[C2:68] Steene, Birgitta, 'Ingmar Bergmans *Bilder* och den självbiografiska genre', *Finsk Tidskrift* (Åbo), 1991:5, pp. 274-286. [Discusses Bergman's book *Bilder* as an autobiography, with several comparative references to Sg's contributions to the genre in *Tjänstekvinnans son* and elsewhere]

[C2:69] Steene, Birgitta, 'Ingmar Bergman's First Meeting with Thalia', *Nordic Theatre Studies* (Copenhagen), 11 (1998), 12-33. Illus. [Surveys Bergman's early amateur experience of the theatre at the Christian settlement of Mäster Olofsgården in Stockholm where, in 1939-40, he directed *Lycko-Pers resa*, *Advent*, *Svarta handsken*, and *Svanevit*. Steene assesses the importance of these productions for the development of his directorial style and quotes several responses to his work there, including one from Brecht, then passing through Stockholm]

[C2:70] Steene, Birgitta, 'Ingmar Bergmans första möte med Thalia', *Upsala Nya Tidning*, 14 July 1998. ['Ingmar Bergman's First Meeting with Thalia'. Includes material published in greater detail in **C2:69**]

[C2:71] Steene, Birgitta, 'Strindberg, Ingmar Bergman and the Visual Symbol', in Michael Robinson, ed., *The Moscow Papers*, **B1:379**, pp. 85-92. [Documents Bergman's early admiration for Sg as reflected in his student productions, and Sg's multi-levelled influence on his films and in the theatre, where his work emphasises representational symbolism over dramatic verisimilitude. Steene compares *Ett drömspel* with *Summer Interlude* and discusses Begman's debt to Sg in general]

[C2:72] Steene, Birgitta, '"Strindbergs språk brände sig in i mitt kött"', *Parnass* (Stockholm), 6:1 (1995), 40-44. Illus. ['"Strindberg's Language Burned its Way into My Flesh'. Describes the powerful initial impression which Sg's language made on Ingmar Bergman]

[C2:73] Syréhn, Gunnar, '*Den starkare* och *Persona* – några jämförelsepunkter', *Fenix* (Stockholm), 13:4 (1997), 114-123. ['*The Stronger* and *Persona* – Some Points of Comparison'. Compares Sg's play, in which one of the two characters (an actress) remains silent throughout, with Ingmar Bergman's film, where one of two sisters (also an actress) remains mute]

[C2:74] Timm, Mikael, 'Bergman – gränslandets filmare', in *Ögats glädje: Texter om film*, Stockholm: Carlssons, 1994, pp. 40-167. ['Bergman – Filmmaker of the Borderland'. Includes occasional references only]

[C2:75] Törnqvist, Egil, 'August StrindBERG?man', *Skrien* (Amsterdam), No. 132-133 (1983), pp. 31-34. [On the temperamental and artistic affinity between Ingmar Bergman and Sg]

[C2:76] Törnqvist, Egil, *Bergman's Muses: Æsthetic Versatility in Film, Theatre, Television and Radio*, Jefferson, North Carolina, and London: McFarland & Company, Inc., Publishers, 2003. VI+265 pp. [Although only one chapter of this wide-ranging study of Bergman's work in several media makes reference to Sg by name in its title, he is referred to repeatedly throughout. In his examination of Bergman as a director of radio drama in 'From Drama Text to Radio Play: Aural Strindberg' (pp. 36-45), Törnqvist studies his productions of *Första varningen, Leka med elden,* and *Oväder* for Sveriges Radio, and analyses Bergman's numerous subtle alterations to Sg's original texts, in the interests of communicating with a mass audience in a new medium. Elsewhere those plays which receive more than a single reference are *Till Damaskus, Påsk, Erik XIV, Fordringsägare*, and *Den starkare*, as well as (especially) *Ett drömspel* and *Spöksonaten*]

[C2:77] Törnqvist, Egil, 'Den lilla världen och den stora: Kring Ingmar Bergmans *Fanny och Alexander*', *Chaplin* (Stockholm), 25:6 (1983), 253-259. ['The Little World and the

Great: On Ingmar Bergman's *Fanny and Alexander*'. An account of Bergman's autobiographical film and the links he establishes in it between himself and Sg]

[C2:78] Törnqvist, Egil, *Filmdiktaren Ingmar Bergman*, Värnamo: Bokförlaget Arena, 1993, pp. 12-16, 95-96. [Illustrates how Sg's plays, many of which Bergman has directed, are of considerable importance for the issues explored by his work in the cinema, and the manner in which his films are made. Difficulties in interpersonal communication, scenes of unmasking, vampirism, and a powerful subjectivity which plunges the spectator into the diffuse borderline between dream and reality, are common to the work of both men. With his Chamber Plays, Sg renewed drama. By applying Sg's ideas to film, Bergman has renewed the art of the film. Törnqvist identifies a structural affinity between *Höstsonaten* (1978) and the Chamber Plays, notably *Pelikanen*]

[C2:79] Törnqvist, Egil, '"I min fantasi!" Subjektivt gestaltande hos Ingmar Bergman', in Margareta Wirmark, red., *Ingmar Bergman: Film och teater i växelverkan*, Stockholm: Carlssons, 1996, pp. 79-99. Illus. ['"In My Imagination!" Subjective Creation in Ingmar Bergman'. Discusses subjectivity and point of view in dramatic structure, character, and the role of the spectator in Bergman's theatre work and films with reference to *Fröken Julie, Till Damaskus, Ett drömspel*, and *Spöksonaten*]

[C2:80] Törnqvist, Egil, 'Ingmar Bergmans dolda iakttagare', *Nordica* (Odense), 15 (1999), 139-159. ['Ingmar Bergman's Concealed Observer'. In the course of a more detailed examination of the role played by episodes of eavesdropping in Bergman's cinema, Törnqvist includes a brief discussion of screen scenes in *Fordringsägare, Erik XIV, Första varningen, Till Damaskus,* and *Spöksonaten*, in all of which the stage action is momentarily witnessed by a concealed observer]

[C2:81] Törnqvist, Egil, 'Kammarspel på tre sätt', in Jan Stenkvist, red., *Från Snoilsky till Sonnevi. Litteraturvetenskapliga studier tillägnade Gunnar Brandell*, Stockholm: Natur och Kultur, 1976, pp. 76-94. ['Chamber Play in Three Ways'. Discusses the influence that Sg has exerted on the films of Ingmar Bergman, together with the latter's 1973 staging of *Spöksonaten*]

[C2:82] Törnqvist, Egil, 'A Life in the Theatre: Intertextuality in Ingmar Bergman's *Efter Repetitionen*', *Scandinavian Studies* (Provo), 73:1 (2001), [25]-42. [Establishes the theatrical references in Bergman's autobiographical teleplay, first screened on Swedish television in 1984, in which he alludes pointedly to dramas by Euripides (*The Bacchae*) and Sg (*Första varningen, Dödsdansen, Oväder, Ett drömspel*, and *Spöksonaten*)]

[C2:83] Törnqvist, Egil, 'Long Day's Journey into Night: Bergman's TV-Version of *Oväder* Compared to *Smultronstället*', in Kela Kvam, ed., **D2:158**, *Strindberg's Post-Inferno Plays*, pp. 186-195. Illus. [Compares Bergman's film *Wild Strawberries* (1958), in which Victor Sjöström has the principal role, with his production of *Oväder* (1960), a play in which Sjöström had previously appeared in 1955. Close analysis confirms that *Smultronstället* and Bergman's teleplay of *Oväder* are twin creations, both visually and thematically]

[C2:84] Törnqvist, Egil, 'Strindberg, Bergman and the Silent Character', *TijdSchrift voor Skandinavistiek* (Amsterdam), 20:1 (1999), 61-72. [Compares the use of silent characters in two of Sg's plays (Mlle Y in *Den starkare* and the Milkmaid in *Spöksonaten*) and two of Ingmar Bergman's films (the Girl in *The Seventh Seal* and Elisabeth in *Persona*). Within drama, Sg anticipates what Bergman does in film with silent characters, in what is normally an audiovisual medium]

[C2:85] Tsimbal, Irina, '[A Portrait in the Mirror. Strindberg and Bergman]', *Shou* (St Petersburg), 13 (1996), 55-58.

[C2:86] Uggla, Andrzej Nils, 'Strindberg w teatrze Bergmana', *Dialog* (Warsaw) 23:8 (1978), 153-158. ['Strindberg in Bergman's Theatre'. Stresses Sg's relevance for the plays and screenplays of Ingmar Bergman, as well as for his work in the theatre]

[C2:87] Uritz, Francisco J., and Marina Torres de Uriz, 'Ingmar Bergman por los caminos de Strindberg y de la creación teatral', *Espacio de critica e investigación teatral* (Argentina), 2:3 (1987), 15-30. ['Ingmar Bergman on Strindberg's Methods and Creating Theatre'. An interview with Bergman about his relationship with Sg and the staging of his plays which also discusses Sg as portrayed in the biographical studies by Olof Lagercrantz, **R:1171**, and Martin Lamm, **B1:205a/B1:205b**, the directing styles of Max Reinhardt and Olof Molander, and Bergman's interest in the dramas of Lorca and Valle-Inclán. Published in conjunction with Dramaten's tour to Madrid with *Fröken Julie*, but Bergman also comments on *Spöksonaten*, *Pelikanen*, and other plays. Previously published in *El Publico* (Madrid)]

[C2:88] Verdone, Mario, 'Religione e personalità nell 'opera di Ingmar Bergman', *Studi cinematografici e televisivi* (Rome), 1:2 (1968), 25-44. ['Religion and Personality in the Works of Ingmar Bergman'. Traces literary and religious influences on Bergman from Ibsen, Kierkegaard, Kaj Munk, and Carl Dreyer, as well as Sg]

[C2:89] Widegren, Björn, 'Vad skulle mitt liv varit utan Strindberg', *Gefle Dagblad* (Gävle), 21 January 1986. ['What would my Life have been without Strindberg?'. An interview with Bergman apropos a performance of his 1985 production of *Fröken Julie* on tour to Gefle Stadsteater, in which he declares his fidelity to Sg's text]

[C2:90] Wirmark, Margareta, *Smultronstället och dödens ekipage*, Stockholm: Carlssons, 1998, pp. 36-46. ['*Wild Strawberries* and Death's Carriage'. A monograph on Ingmar Bergman's film *Smultronstället* which argues that it is a dream play and has affinities with several works by Sg, including *Pelikanen*, *Spöksonaten*, and *Till Damaskus*. Also discusses Bergman's staging of *Kronbruden* in Malmö in 1952, pp. 37-41]

[C2:91] Young, Vernon, *Cinema Borealis: Ingmar Bergman and the Swedish Ethos*, New York: David Lewis, 1971. 331 pp. [An unsympathetic reading of Bergman's films in terms of a social and cultural background where 'the shadow of Sg looms [large] on the wall of Bergman's cave'. The latter's film *A Passion*, for example, is 'permeated with the gospel according to St. August', particularly as it is formulated in *Spöksonaten*]

[C2:92] Zern, Leif, *Se Bergman*, Stockholm: Norstedts, 1993. Illus. 204 pp. [Takes issue with Paisley Livingston's thesis in **C2:42** that Ingmar Bergman's film *Sommarnattens leende* draws heavily on *Leka med elden*]

See also **D1:294, D1:297, D1:417, D1:418, D1:454, D1:679, E41:65, P5:70, V:10, V:114, V:152, V:166, V:247**

C3. *Friedrich Dürrenmatt's* Play Strindberg

[C3:1] Boyd, Ursel D., 'Friedrich Dürenmatt und sein Drama *Play Strindberg*', *Germanic Notes* (Lexington, Kentucky), 3:3 (1972), 18-21. ['Friedrich Dürenmatt and his Drama, *Play Strindberg*'. Discusses Dürenmatt's version of *Dödsdansen* in terms of theatrical motifs, plot structure, and *mise-en-scène*]

[C3:2] Brater, Enoch, '*Play Strindberg* and the Theater of Adaptation', *Comparative Drama* (Kalamazoo, Michigan), 16:1 (1982), 12-25. [Analyses the process of adaptation in Friedrich Dürrenmatt's reworking of *Dödsdansen* as *Play Strindberg*, where he 'rides roughshod over his fellow playwright'. Brater compares Dürrenmatt's dialogue with Beckett's and Pinter's and concludes that, 'what you don't get in this truncated language makes you remember all the more the tragicomic eloquence of Sg's haunting lines']

[C3:3] Brater, Enoch, '*Play Strindberg* and the Theater of Adaptation', in Moshe Lazar, ed., *Play Dürrenmatt*, Malibu: Undena Publications, 1983, pp. 125-137. [Rpr. of **C3:2**]

[C3:4] Chamberlain, Leslie, 'Dürrenmatt's *Play Strindberg*', *Adam* (London), 47 (1985), Nos 455-467, pp. 110-112. [Comments on Friedrich Dürrenmatt's adaptation of *Dödsdansen*, apropos a performance at the Kellertheater, Leipzig]

[C3:5] Dürrenmatt, Friedrich, 'Entretien avec Raymond Spira', *Théâtre Populaire* (Paris), No. 31 (1958). ['Interview with Raymond Spira'. Observes that 'Sg had moments which went further, which were purer than Beckett and Adamov. Like Kafka's weakness: purity at any price...but that only leads to repetition. Modern theatre comes from Sg: the second act of *The Ghost Sonata* has never been surpassed']

[C3:6] Freitag, Annette, and Jack Metzger, 'Dürrenmatt macht Strindberg à la Godard', *Neue Presse*, 3 February 1969. ['Dürenmatt makes Strindberg *à la* Godard'. An interview with Dürrenmatt apropos *Play Strindberg*, in advance of its impending première. Suggests there is an affinity between his adaptation of *Dödsdansen* and the films of Jean-Luc Godard]

[C3:7] Jenny, Urs, *Dürrenmatt: A Study of His Plays*, London: Eyre Methuen Ltd, 1973, pp. 146-148. [In *Play Strindberg* Dürrenmatt has rewritten, rather than adapted, *Dödsdansen* in order to stress the elements of game-playing and the grotesque: 'Sg's wide-ranging dialogue, often laden with the pathos of the confessional, has been rigorously reduced to spare, hard-hitting, cut-and-thrust exchanges; all the sorrow and self-pity has been expunged from the characters...whatever plot there is in Sg has been distorted by the addition of different motivation into something grotesque']

[C3:8] Knapp, Gerhard P., 'From *lilla helvetet* to the Boxing Ring: Strindberg and Dürrenmatt', in Marilyn Johns Blackwell, ed., **C1:142**, *Structures of Influence*, pp. 226-244. [Observes that, for Sg, the suffering of his protagonists is a tragic necessity. But in adapting *Dödsdansen* as *Play Strindberg* according to a notion of comedy as a means of provoking an audience into questioning the order of the world depicted on stage, Dürrenmatt leaves the spectator with a strictly rational, double-edged alternative: either to resist and learn from the implications of his tragi-comic model, or to accept it as a confirmation of inevitable reality]

[C3:9] Otten, N., '[New Dürrenmatt]', *Teatr* (Moscow), 1972:3, pp. 164-174. [On the European success of Dürrenmatt's *Play Strindberg*. E.1060]

[C3:10] Pavlova, N., '[New Trends in the Work of Dürrenmatt]', *Inostrannaia literatura* (Moscow), 1973:3, pp. 88-90. [On *Play Strindberg*. See **C3:12**. E.1065]

[C3:11] Pritzker, Markus, 'Strindberg und Dürrenmatt', in Oskar Bandle, *et al.*, Hrsg., *Studien zur danischen und schwedischen Literatur des 19. Jahrhunderts*, Basel and Stuttgart: Helbing & Lichtenhahn, 1976, pp. 241-255. [Argues that Dürrenmatt's reduction of *Dödsdansen* in *Play Strindberg* transforms a play concerned with existential issues into a mere anti-bourgeois tract]

[C3:12] Rondeli, L., '[Is it Necessary to Defend Dürrenmatt?]', *Ogonek* (Moscow), 1974:6, pp. 28-29. [Response to N. Pavlova's article **C3:10**. E.1081]

[C3:13] Rubinstein, Hilde, 'Der Schaukampf des Friedrich Dürrenmatt', *Frankfurter Hefte*, 25:3 (1970), 202-206. ['Friedrich Dürrenmatt's Match'. On *Play Strindberg*]

[C3:14] Rumler-Gross, Hanna, *Thema und Variation. Eine Analyse der Shakespeare- und Strindberg-Bearbeitungen Durrenmatts unter Berucksichtigung seiner Komödienkonzeption*, Kölner germanistische Studien 20, Köln und Wien: Böhlau Verlag, 1985. IX+285 pp. [Includes a discussion of *Play Strindberg* in detail, pp. 217-240, with particular reference to Dürrenmatt's notion of comedy]

[C3:15] Sammern-Frankenegg, Fritz, 'Exit Strindberg. Zur Eliminierung Strindbergs in Friedrich Dürrenmatts *Play Strindberg*', *Studia Neophilologica* (Stockholm), 63:1 (1991), 89-93. ['Exit Strindberg. On the Elimination of Strindberg in Friedrich Dürrenmatt's *Play Strindberg*'. Maintains that Dürrenmatt's version of *Dödsdansen* strips the original of all its vital Sgian qualities]

[C3:16] Schmidt, Aurel, 'Friedrich Dürrenmatt', *National-Zeitung* (Basel), 6 February 1969. [An interview with Dürrenmatt, who claims that *Dödsdansen* is a 'third-class' drama and *passé* as theatre]

[C3:17] Sharp, Sister Corona, 'Dürrenmatt's *Play Strindberg*', *Modern Drama* (Lawrence, Kansas), 13:3 (1970), 276-283. [Concludes that, whereas Sg explores the motivations behind marital warfare, Dürrenmatt studies the battle tactics themselves]

[C3:18] Sharp, Sister Corona, 'Dürrenmatt and the Spirit of Play', *University of Toronto Quarterly*, 39 (1969-70), 63-76. [Analyses the element of game playing in Dürrenmatt's *Play Strindberg*]

[C3:19] Sharp, Sister Corona, 'Strindberg and Dürrenmatt: The Dynamics of Play', *Modern Language Quarterly* (London), 38:3 (1977), 292-303. [Considers Dürrenmatt's claim to have diverged almost completely from *Dödsdansen* in writing *Play Strindberg* to be an exaggeration. Sg's play is more comic than tragic: the Captain is modelled on the *alazon* of Greek comedy and Dürrenmatt merely picks up on the element of game playing that is already present in *Dödsdansen* and retains its comic structure and comedic effects both in the action and the dialogue, even though he rejects its Aristotelian imitation of an action and its naturalist residues, and pares down the dialogue to a minimum. The substance of the original is replaced with the idea of a sporting contest, thus reducing the conflict at the heart of the play to a boxing match – i.e. a pure form of play in which skill alone counts]

[C3:20] Shonami, Gidon, 'Direnmat be-ikvot Strindberg', *Bama* (Jerusalem), No. 52 (1972), pp. 80-87. [A comparative study of *Play Strindberg* and *Dödsdansen*]

[C3:21] Slawińska, Irena, 'Strindberg i teatr współczesny', *Dialog* (Warsaw), 1974:1, pp. 169-171. [On Sg the dramatist vis-à-vis Dürrenmatt's reworking of *Dödsdansen* in *Play Strindberg*]

[C3:22] Tiusanen, Timo, *Dürrenmatt. A Study in Plays, Prose, Theory*, Princeton: Princeton University Press, 1977, pp. 322-335. [Includes a revised version of **C3:23**]

[C3:23] Tiusanen, Timo, '"Strindmatt or Dürrenberg?" Dürrenmatt's *Play Strindberg*', in [Carl Reinhold Smedmark], ed., **D2:285**, *Strindberg and Modern Theatre*, pp. 43-55. [A comparative study of *Play Strindberg* and *Dödsdansen* which argues that the former is inferior to its Sgian original, from which Dürrenmatt has cut away 'the texture of life'.

Not only has he stripped it of much that he considered merely literary or metaphysical; he has also divested it of the greater part of its theatricality]

[C3:24] Whitton, Kenneth S[tuart], *Dürrenmatt: Reinterpretation in Restrospect*, New York/ Oxford/Munich: Oswald Wolff Books, 1880, pp. 136-138. [Links *Leka med elden* biographically with Dürrenmatt's heart attack in 1969 and suggests that *Play Strindberg* essays a new theatrical style which excises the literary and rhetorical elements from Sg's original dialogue]

Première, Stadstheater, Basel, 1969. Dir. Dürrenmatt; Edgar: Horst Christian Bockmann; Alice: Regine Lutz; Kurt: Laus Höring.

[C3:25] Ammann, H. J., 'Theaterarbeit. Zur Enstehung von *Play Strindberg*, arrangiert von Friedrich Dürrenmatt', *Neue Zürcher Zeitung* (Zürich), 15 June 1969.

[C3:26] Anon, 'Dürrenmatt Turns to Strindberg', *The Times* (London), 25 May 1969.

[C3:27] Anon, 'Friedrich Dürrenmatt, *Play Strindberg*. August Strindbergs *Totentanz* arrangiert von Friedrich Dürrenmatt', *Volksbühnenspiegel* (West Berlin), 15:4-5 (1969), 23-24. [A round up of reviews of the Basel première]

[C3:28] Beckmann, Heinz, 'Dürrenmatt spielt Strindberg', *Zeitwende* (München), 40 (1969), 354-355. ['Dürrenmatt Plays Strindberg']

[C3:29] Beckmann, Heinz, 'Plüsch oder Play. Aufforderung zum Zweikampf zwischen Dürrenmatt und Strindberg', *Rheinischer Merkur* (Koblenz), 28 February 1969. ['Plush or Play. A Challenge to Single Combat between Strindberg and Dürrenmatt']

[C3:30] Benesch, Gerda, 'Basler Theater: Dürrenmatt contra Strindberg. Problematische *Totentanz*-Neufassung', *Die Bühne* (Vienna), No. 126, (1969), p. 18.

[C3:31] Brock-Sulzer, Elisabeth, 'Strindberg im Ei. Dürrenmatts gelungene Operation Totenzanz', *Christ und Welt* (Stuttgart), 22:8 (1969), p. 10.

[C3:32] Buschkiel, Jürgen, 'Ehe im Boxing. Friedrich Dürrenmatts *Play Strindberg* in Basel uraufgeführte', *Die Welt* (Hamburg), 11 February 1969. ['Marriage as Boxing. The Première of Friedrich Dürrenmatt's *Play Strindberg* in Basel']

[C3:33] Colberg, K., 'Im seelischen Boxring. Uraufführung von Dürrenmatts *Play Strindberg* in Basel', *Die Presse* (Vienna), 12 February 1969. ['In The Soul's Boxing Ring. The Première of Friedrich Dürrenmatt's *Play Strindberg*']

[C3:34] Hensel, Georg, 'Tränen trägt man nich mehr. Beobachtungen in der Spielzeit 1968-69', *Jahresring* (Stuttgart), 1969-70, pp. 333-345.

[C3:35] Jacobi, Johannes, 'Wie Dürrenmatt den Strindberg änderte. Zu einer Première in Basel', *Die Zeit* (Hamburg), 24:7 (1969), p. 15.

[C3:36] Jaensch, Wilfrid, 'Strindberg, Marx und Dürrenmatt. Zur Basler *Totentanz*-Inszenierung', *Polemos* (Basel), 1969:10, pp. 37-40.

[C3:37] Jaggard, W., '*Play Strindberg*', *Göteborgs-Tidningen*, 29 March 1969.

[C3:38] Jenny, Urs, 'Dürrenmatts Zimmerschlacht. *Play Strindberg* – in Basel uraufgeführt', *Süddeutsche Zeitung* (München), 10 February 1969.

[C3:39] Leber, Hugo, 'Spiel im Ring. August Strindbergs Totentanz – arrangiert von Friedrich Dürrenmatt, in der Komödie Basel', *Publik*, 14 February 1969.

[C3:40] Leber, Hugo, 'Strindberg-Playground für Friedrich Dürrenmatt', *Die Weltwoche* (Zürich), 14 February 1969.

[C3:41] Leiser, Erwin, '*Play Strindberg*', *Expressen* (Stockholm), 24 March 1969.

[C3:42] Melchinger, Siegfried, 'Was hat der bitterböse Friedrich mit Strindberg nur Gemacht. *Play Strindberg* in Basel', *Theater heute* (Hannover), 10:3 (1969), 36-39. ['What on Earth has Furious Friedrich done to Strindberg. *Play Strindberg* in Basel'. Insists that humour is a characteristic conspicuously lacking in Sg's plays. Nevertheless, *Dödsdansen* is a work of theatrical genius while *Play Strindberg* is more a brilliant persiflage]

[C3:43] Michaelis, R., '*Play Strindberg* verspielt', *Theater heute* (Hannover), 11:7 (1970), p. 22.

[C3:44] Rüedi, Peter, '*Play Strindberg*', *Zürcher Woche* (Zürich), 14 February 1969. [Maintains that Dürrenmatt sacrifices the complexity of the original]

[C3:45] Rühle, Günther, 'Strindberg – schlagkräftig. Dürrenmatts *Play Strindberg*. Uraufführung in Basel', *Frankfurter Allgemeine Zeitung*, 11 February 1969.

[C3:46] Rumler, Fritz, 'Mit Strindberg in den Boxring', *Der Spiegel* (Hannover), 3 February 1969. ['With Strindberg in the Boxing-Ring']

[C3:47] Schäble, Gunter, 'Play Strindberg in Basel. 12 Runden Zimmerschlacht. Dürrenmatts Totentanz-Bearbeitung', *Stuttgarter Zeitung*, 10 February 1969.

[C3:48] Schwengeler, Arnold H., '*Play Strindberg* oder: Abgenagter Dichter. Dürrenmatt "arrangierte" den *Totentanz* in Basel', *Theater-Rundschau* (Bonn), 15:3 (1969), p. 2.

[C3:49] Tank, Kurt Lothar, 'Turandot und die Totentanz-Komödie. In Zürich und Basel: Brecht-Nachlaß Der Kongreß der Weißwäscher und ein Anti-Strindberg von Dürrenmatt', *Deutsches Allgemeines Sonntagsblatt* (Hamburg), (1969), No. 22, p. 27.

[C3:50] Zampa, Giorgio, 'Il match Strindberg-Dürrenmatt – e in appendice 'Il crak' Roversi-Trionfo', *Il Dramma* (Rome), 1969:8.

Teatr Współczesny, Warsaw, 19 March 1970, Polish première. Dir. Andrzej Wajda.

[C3:51] Bereznitskii, I.A., and B. Rostotskii, '[Encounters in Warsaw]', *Teatr* (Moscow), 1971:8, pp. 151-162. [Comments on similarities between *Play Strindberg* and Edward Albee as well as *Dödsdansen*. E.1053]

[C3:52] El. Zmij [Elżbieta Zmudzka], '*Play Strindberg*', *Teatr* (Warsaw), 1970, Nr. 29

[C3:53] Grodzicki, August, 'Dwoje bokserów i s´dzia', *Życie Warszawy* (Warsaw), 1970, No. 72. ['Two Boxers and an Umpire']

[C3:54] Jakubowska, Jadwiga, 'Zabawa w dramat', *Zołnierz Polski* (Warsaw), 1970, No. 35. ['Playing with Drama']

[C3:55] 'Jaszcz' [Jan Alfred Szczepański], 'Nienawiśç uszminkowana', *Trybuna Ludu* (Warsaw), 1970, No. 85. ['Hate in Make-Up']

[C3:56] Koening, Jerzy, 'Teatr w dwunastu rundach', *Express Wieczorny* (Warsaw), 1970, No. 82. ['Theatre in Twelve Rounds']

[C3:57] Kydryński, Juliusz, 'Wajda kaze Łomnickuemu umieraç przez 12 sekund', *Twórczośç* (Warsaw), 1970, No. 1307. ['Wajda Let Łomnicki Die for 12 Seconds']

[C3:58] Marciewicz, Andrzej, 'Podwójny knock-out', *Trybuna Mazowiecka* (Warsaw), 1970, No. 194. ['A Double Knock-Out']

[C3:59] Polanica, S[tefan], [Pseudonym of Stanisław Edward Bury], 'Play Strindberg', *Słowo Powszechne* (Warsaw), 1970, No. 72.

[C3:60] Szydłowski, Roman, 'Dürrenmatt, Strindberg i Brecht', *Życie Literackie* (Kraków), 1970, No. 19.

[C3:61] Zagórski, Jerzy, 'Bolesna drwina i obojetny ból', *Kurier Polski* (Warsaw), 1970, No. 70. ['A Painful Scorn and an Indifferent Pain']

Some other productions:

[C3:62] Badischen Landesbühne, *Die Play-Akte: Berichte, Zeugnisse, Gutlachten des Prozesses Strindberg-Dürrenmatt*, Programmbuch der Badischen Landesbühne Bruchsal zu *Play Strindberg* von Friedrich Dürrenmatt, Bruchsal: Badischen Landesbühne, 1987. 57 pp. [The programme-book accompanying a revival of *Play Strindberg*]

[C3:63] Barnes, Clive, '*Play Strindberg*', *New York Times*, 4 June 1971. [Forum Theatre, Lincoln Centre, New York]

[C3:64] Esslin, Martin, '*Play Strindberg*', *Plays and Players* (London), 20:11 (1973), pp. 52-53. [Hampstead Theatre Club. Edgar: Freddie Jones; Alice: Yvonne Mitchell; Kurt: Patrick Allen]

[C3:65] Gro. [Eberhard Groenewold], '*Play Strindberg* in den Kammerspielen', *Lübeckische Blätter*, 129 (1969), 255-256. [Dir. Lothar Trautmann, Lübeck]

[C3:66] Grut, Mario, '*Play Strindberg*', *Aftonbladet* (Stockholm), 26 September 1969. [Swedish première. Stockholm Stadsteater]

[C3:67] Hobi, Hans B., 'Makelloses Skelett': *Play Strindberg*', *Schweitzerische Theaterzeitung* (Elgg), 1970:3, p. 44. [Dir. Ernst Brukbar]

[C3:68] Holm, Hans Axel, '*Play Strindberg*', *Dagens Nyheter* (Stockholm), 26 September 1969. [Swedish première. Stockholm's Stadsteater]

[C3:69] Kerr, Walter, '*Play Strindberg*', *New York Times*, 13 June 1971. [Forum Theatre, Lincoln Centre, New York]

[C3:70] Khimiashvili, I., '[From Humanism's Point of View]', *Vechernii Tbilisi*, 22 January 1977. [M. I. Ermolova Theatre on tour in Tbilisi. E.1100b]

[C3:71] Kirpichnikova, N., '[Affirmation of Character]', *Vechernii Leningrad*, 26 March 1977. [V. F. Komissarzhevskaia Theatre, Leningrad. E.1097a]

[C3:72] Kliuevskaia, K., '[The Verdict on Egoism]', *Leningradskaia pravda*, 10 March 1977. [V. F. Komissarzhevskaia Theatre, Leningrad. E.1098]

[C3:73] Kolesnikova, R., '[*Play Strindberg*]', *Krasnoe Znamia*, 27 July 1976. [M. I. Ermolova Theatre on tour in Tomsk]

[C3:74] Kragh-Jacobsen, Svend, 'Stor komisk massakre', in *Teateraftener. Anmeldelser fra fire årtier*, [København: Nyt Nordisk Forlag Arnold Busck A/S, 1980, pp. 172-173. ['Big Comic Massacre'. Danish première]

[C3:75] Kuzicheva, A., 'The Stance of Theatre', *Moskovskaia Pravda*, 13 November 1974. [M. I. Ermolova Theatre, Moscow. E.1088]

[C3:76] Lewy, Hermann, 'Teuer bezahlte Erkenntnis. Dürrenmatts *Play Strindberg* im Düsseldorfer Schauspielhaus', *Allgemeine unabhängige jüdische Wochenzeitung*, 24:14 (1969), p. 5. [Schauspielhaus Düsseldorf. Dir. Karlheinz Stroux]

[C3:77] Lossmann, Hans, 'Wiener Premieren', *Die Bühne* (Vienna), 1971, No. 148, pp. 4-10. Illus. [Austrian première, Akademietheater, Vienna]

[C3:78] McMillan, Joyce, '*The Dance of Death*', *The Guardian* (London), 29 April 1993. [Glasgow. Dürrenmatt takes a big, complex play about sexual politics and transforms it into a slight, short squib against the bourgeois institution of marriage]

[C3:79] Novikov, V., 'Arkhangel'sk', *Pravda severa*, 10 September 1977. [M. I. Ermolova Theatre on tour in Archangel. E.1100a]

[C3:80] Pietzsch, Ingeborg, '*Play Strindberg*', *Theater der Zeit* (East Berlin), 30:10 (1975), 13-14. [The Intimate Theatre, Rostock]

[C3:81] Potemkin, V., '[Theatre Tears off Masks]', *Vechernii Leningrad*, 12 February 1975. [M. I. Ermolova Theatre, Moscow. E.1086a]

[C3:82] Reiter, Helga, 'Stirb mal, dann nehmen wir dich ernst', *Neue Literatur* (Bucharest), 22:3 (1971), 112-114. ['Just Die, then we can take you seriously'. Munich Kammerspiele, on tour to Bucharest]

[C3:83] Ross, Werner, 'Zimmerschlachten', *Merkur* (Baden-Baden), 23:10 (1969), p. 969.

[C3:84] Schmidt, Aurel, 'Ein Stück Theaterarbeit', *National-Zeitung* (Basel), 15 October 1969.

[C3:85] Schödel, Helmut, 'Zeitlupe: *Play Strindberg* in Memmingen', *Theater heute* (Hannover), 17:3 (1976), p. 52.

[C3:86] Svobodin, A., '[A Play About a Play]', *Komsomol'skaia pravda* (Moscow), 20 March 1975. [M. I. Ermolova Theatre in Moscow. E.1088]

[C3:87] *Svobodné slovo* (Prague), '*Play Strindberg*', 1988, No. 131, p. 13. [Czech Television. Dir. Petr Koliha; Transl. Bohumil Černik]

[C3:88] Traun, François, '*Play Strindberg*', *Schweitzerische Theaterzeitung* (Elgg), 1971:4, p. 35. [Dir. Walter Weideli]

[C3:89] Tumanov, A., '[Twelve Rounds of Egoism]', *Kuzbass* (Kemerovo), 2 July 1976. [M. I. Ermolova Theatre of Moscow on tour. E.1093b]

[C3:90] Vielhaber, Gerd, 'Düsseldorfer Streiflichter', *Die Bühne* (Vienna), 1969, No. 132, p. 23. [Schauspielhaus Düsseldorf. Dir. Karlheinz Stroux]

[C3:91] Wardle, Irving, 'Mechanical Figures in 12-Round Fight', *The Times* (London), 14 January 1972. [British première in Newcastle. Edgar: Freddie Jones; Alice: Yvonne Mitchell; Kurt: Gerald Flood. Insists that 'there are far more laughs' in the Laurence Olivier production of *Dödsdansen* than in Dürrenmatt's comic by-product]

[C3:92] Zatonskii, D., '[Shakespeare, Strindberg, Dürrenmatt and Modern Art]', *Inostrannaia literatura* (Moscow), 1974:8, pp. 211-219. [E.1075]

[C3:93] Zatonskii, D., 'Shakespeare, Strindberg, Dürrenmatt', in *V nashe vremia*, Moscow, 1979, pp. 83-105. [Rpr. of **C3:92**. E.1075]

See also **C1:1036, V:54, V:100, V:146, V:184**

C4. Per Olov Enquist, *Tribadernas natt*

[C4:1] Anderman, Gunilla, '*The Night of the Tribades*: Fact and Fiction in Grez-sur-Loing', in Poul Houe and Sven Hakon Rossel, eds, *Documentarism in Scandinavian Literature*, Amsterdam: Rodopi, 1997, pp. 148-154. [Compares three versions of events in Sg's life during his stay at the artist colony of Grez-sur-Loing with 'the truth' as it is supposedly presented in Enquist's play]

[C4:2] Baeckström, Tord, '*Tribadernas natt*', *Göteborgs Handels- och Sjöfartstidning*, 30 April 1976. [Concludes that Enquist's aim seems to be to ridicule Sg, though it is done with a great deal of talent]

[C4:3] Blackwell, Marilyn Johns, 'Ideology and Specularity in P. O. Enquist's *Tribadernas natt*', *Scandinavian Studies* (Provo), 67:2 (1995), 196-215. [In depicting Sg and Siri von Essen during rehearsals for the première of *Den starkare* in 1889, Enquist's drama re-reads and problematises the text of Sg's play, and deconstructs an elaborate and extensive series of commingled myths of Sg as both the national literary hero and Enquist's literary father, as well as myths of textual autonomy, patriarchal omnipotence, and gender as identity]

[C4:4] Bolin, Asta, 'Verkligheten vinner alltid', *Dramaten* (Stockholm), No. 55 (1975-76), pp. 19-21. ['Reality always Wins'. Programme essay published in conjunction with the Swedish première]

[C4:5] Bredsdorff, Thomas, *Den svarta hålen. Om tillkomsten av ett språk i P. O. Enquists författarskap*, Översättning av Jan Stolpe, Stockholm: Norstedts, 1991. [263] pp. [Swedish edition of **C4:6**]

[C4:6] Bredsdorff, Thomas, *De sorte huller. Om tllblivelsen af et sprog i P. O. Enquists forfatterskab*, København: Gyldendal, 1991. 233 pp. [A thematic study of Enquist's work as a whole which reads *Tribadernas natt* as a literary analysis of Sg's *Den starkare* in dramatic form. Discusses the play together with his other dramas, *Til Fædra* and *Fra regnormernes liv*, pp. 134-160]

[C4:7] Bredsdorff, Thomas, 'The Rhetoric of the Documentary. Per Olov Enquist and Scandinavian Documentary Literature', *The Nordic Roundtable Papers*, 12, University of Minnesota: The Center for Nordic Studies, 1993. [Includes some comment on Enquist's documentary practice in *Tribadernas natt*]

[C4:8] Cohn, Helge, 'Falsk vittnesbörd om Strindberg!', *Arbetaren* (Stockholm), 55:23 (1976), p. 5. ['False Witness About Strindberg!']

[C4:9] Ekbom, Torsten, 'Fallet Strindberg', *Dramaten* (Stockholm), 6 (1975-76), No. 52, pp. 2-5. ['The Strindberg Case'. Claims that if Sg had really behaved as he does in Enquist's play, he would never have written a single line. Like the professional writer he was, Sg saved all his mental energy for his writing. Essay published in conjunction with the première at Dramaten]

[C4:10] Ekenwall, Asta, 'En August Strindbergs like?', *Göteborgs-Posten*, 10 March 1977. ['August Strindberg's Image?' Questions Enquist's practice in *Tribadernas Natt* of blurring the distinction between his own words and quotations from Sg]

[C4:11] Enander, Crister, 'Pjäser som lämpar sig utmärkt väl som läsning. Per Olov Enquists dramer korsbefruktar varandra oavbrutet', *Svenska Dagbladet* (Stockholm), 22 March 1992. ['Plays well Suited for Reading. Per Olov Enquist's Dramas continually Cross-Pollinate one Another']

[C4:12] Enquist, Per Olov, '9 byggstenar till *Tribadernas natt*', *Dramaten* (Stockholm), No. 47 (1975-76), pp. 6-11. ['9 Building Blocks for *The Night of the Tribades*'. Provides a background to the drama and comments on its underlying purpose]

[C4:13] Enquist, Per Olov, 'Notes for a Play About Strindberg', *Scandinavian Review* (New York), 64:3 (1976), 11-15. Illus. [On the background to *Tribadernas natt* and the contemporary relevance of Sg's situation to California in 1973, where and when Enquist partly wrote the play]

[C4:14] Enquist, Per Olov, 'Strindberg inte ensam på scenen', *Göteborgs-Posten*, 3 April 1977. ['Strindberg is not Alone on Stage'. Responds to comments on his portrait of Sg in *Tribadernas natt* by Asta Ekenwall, **C4:10**, and Margareta Zetterström, **C4:33**. 'I have used both Sg himself and his myth. With the help of that myth, in the mirror of myth and history, we can see the back of our own heads']

[C4:15] Lagercrantz, Olof, 'Scenens Strindberg och verklighetens', *Dagens Nyheter* (Stockholm), 19 November 1975. ['Strindberg on Stage and in Reality'. Identifies discrepancies between Enquist's portrayal of Sg in *Tribadernas natt* and his biographical original. Further comment 29 November]

[C4:16] Lagercrantz, Olof, 'Scenens Strindberg och verklighetens', in *Från Aeneas till Ahlin. Kritik 1951-1975*, urval Bengt Hallgren, Stockholm: Wahlström & Widstrand, 1978, pp. 307-311. [Rpr. of **C4:15**]

[C4:17] Muradian, K., '[*Tribadernas natt: ett skådespel fran 1889*]', *Sovremennaia khudozhestvennaia literature za rubezhom* (Moscow), 1977:6, pp. 152-153. [E.1099]

[C4:18] Reslová, Marie, 'Téma Strindberg', *Lidové noviny* (Praha), 19 December 1996, p. 11. [On the Czech translation of *Tribadernas natt* by František Fröhlich]

[C4:19] Rock, Freddie, 'Strindberg in Our Time', *Dagens Nyheter* (Stockholm), 28 October 1975.

[C4:20] Rokem, Freddie, '*Tribadernas natt* och Strindbergs privata liv', *Dramaten* (Stockholm), March 1976. ['*The Night of the Tribades* and Strindberg's Private Life'. Programme essay accompanying the première at Dramaten]

[C4:21] Rosenquist, Christina, 'Enquist och ondskan', *Dramaten* (Stockholm), 1993:2, pp. 22-27. ['Enquist and Evil']

[C4:22] Segala, Anna Maria, 'Tra testo apparente e testo latente: le didascalie nella *Notte delle Tribadi* (1) di Per Olov Enquist', in Merete Kjøller Ritzu, ed., **D1:375**, *La Didascalia nella letteratura teatrale scandinava: Testo drammatico e sintesi scenica*, pp. 183-196. ['Between Apparent Text and Latent Text: Stage Directions in *The Night of the Tribades*'. Studies the metadrammatic aspects of Enquist's drama and its complex layering of biographical truth with dramatic fiction, which invites comparison with Luigi Pirandello's *Sei personaggi in cerca d'autore*]

[C4:23] Shideler, Ross, *Per Olov Enquist. A Critical Study*, Contributions to the Study of World Literature 5, Westport, Connecticut/London: Greenwood Press, 1984, pp. 112-118.

[C4:24] Sokół, Lech, 'Strindberg i sztuka Enquista', *Dialog: Miesiecznik Posiecony Dramaturgii Współczesnej: Teatralnej, Filmowej, Radiowej, Telewizyj* (Warsaw), 21:2 (1976), 87-91. ['The Strindberg in Enquist's Play']

[C4:25] Sporrong, Tony, and Karl-Axel Lindholm, 'Två reaktioner på *Tribadernas natt*', *Dramaten* (Stockholm), No. 53 (1975-76), pp. 24, 26-27. ['Two Reactions to *The Night of the Tribades*', published in conjunction with the play's première]

[C4:26] Syréhn, Gunnar, *Mellan sanningen och lögnen. Studier i Per Olov Enquists dramatik*, Stockholm: Almqvist & Wicksell International, 2001. Illus. 235 pp. ['Between Truth and Lie. Studies in the Dramas of Per Olov Enquist'. An important study of Enquist as a dramatist which includes a lengthy analysis of *Tribadernas natt*. The latter is not a drama documentary but a metadrama which is as concerned with exploring the theatricality of everyday life and of the theatre itself as it is with reproducing Sg's biography. Moreover, the play within the play, i.e. Sg's *Den starkare*, is itself metadramatic, and the actress playing Marie David, who is here depicted playing Mme X, is deconstructing its author, Sg, even as she is seen deconstructing her husband in the play. Syréhn discusses the play's première at Dramaten, the Swedish television production, and the Danish première at Det kongelige Teater, Copenhagen]

[C4:27] Syréhn, Gunnar, 'The Phenomenon of "Otherness" in P. O. Enquist's View of Strindberg in *The Night of the Tribades*', Translated by Mark Boseley, in Poul Houe, *et al.*, ed., **B1:170**, *August Strindberg and the Other*, pp. 167-176. [According to Syréhn, Enquist 'wants us to perceive his Sg as being for the most part unconscious of the forces within him'. *Den starkare* is about Sg, and as he wished the relationship between Siri von Essen and Marie David might have been. He also examines how the play moves between the documentary and the literary in a way that renders the Sg depicted in the play both familiar and other to the reader/spectator. Thus, Enquist also emphasises the problematic relationship which links the creative writer to other people, not least because of the way in which he frequently inscribes them in his texts]

[C4:28] Törnqvist, Egil, 'Scenens Strindberg och verklighetens: Per Olov Enquists *Tribadernas natt* (1975) som dokumentärt drama', in Alex Bolckmans, ed., *Literature and Reality: Creatio versus Mimesis: Problems of Realism in Modern Nordic Literature*, Proceedings of the 11th Study Conference of the International Association for Scandinavian Studies, Ghent: Scandinavian Institute, University of Ghent, 1977, pp. 195-211. ['Strindberg on Stage and in Reality: Per Olov Enquist's *The Night of the Tribades* (1975) as Documentary Drama'. Examines the documentary dimension of Enquist's play about Sg and his marriage to Siri von Essen, set during rehearsals for the première of *Den starkare*. Enquist's reading of Sg's play and the events he records in his own drama is interpretative and frequently inventive in relation to what is reliably recorded. Törnqvist also considers the lively debate about its portrait of Sg in the Swedish press, questioning in particular Olof Lagercrantz's hostile response in **C4:15**, and affirms the significant contemporaneity of Enquist's play]

[C4:29] Törnqvist, Egil, 'Translating Docudrama: Per Olov Enquist's *Tribadernas natt* in English and French', *Tijdschrift voor Skandinavistiek* (Groningen), 19:1 (1998), 128-148.

[C4:30] Uggla, Andrzej Nils, 'Strindberg po *Noc Trybad*', *Dialog* (Warsaw), 24:9 (1979), 154-157. ['Strindberg in *The Night of the Tribades*'. Reports on the debate about Sg's 'true' personality to which Enquist's *Tribadernas natt* has given rise in Sweden]

[C4:31] Uggla, Andrzej, 'Vitt äktenskap – *Tribadernas natt*. Trådar som knyts samman', *Dramaten* (Stockholm), No. 59 (1976-77), pp. 13-14, 21. ['White Marriage – Night of the Tribades. Threads which are Tied Together'. Programme essay apropos its première at Dramaten]

[C4:32] Zern, Leif, 'Sanningen om oss själva', *Dagens Nyheter* (Stockholm), 28 October 1975. ['The Truth about Ourselves'. Points out that Enquist uses Sg as a pretext for an ideological discussion that escapes its 19th-Century historical framework and opens out towards our own time. 'Behind the man we see the society which has formed him, and which continues to form us both historically and ideologically']

[C4:33] Zetterström, Margareta, 'Enquist sviker Strindberg', *Göteborgs-Posten*, 23 March 1977. ['Enquist Fails Strindberg'. Maintains that the play fails to present Sg as 'above all else the scornful radical who challenged the established authorities of his generation with unique critical accuracy and satirical bite. He is the great man of the Modern Breakthrough.' Responds to Asta Ekenwall in **C4:10**]

Dramaten, Stockholm, 27 September 1975. Première.

[C4:34] Behring, Bertil, *Kvällsposten* (Malmö), 28 September 1975.

[C4:35] Brotherus, Greta, *Hufvudstadsbladet* (Helsingfors), 1 October 1975.

[C4:36] Brunius, Teddy, *Upsala Nya Tidning*, 29 September 1975.

[C4:37] Donnér, Jarl W., *Sydsvenska Dagbladet* (Malmö), 10 December 1975.

[C4:38] Fagerström, Allan, *Aftonbladet* (Stockholm), 28 September 1975. ['As far as I can see, Enquist is out to make Sg look ridiculous. And he does that with a vengeance']

[C4:39] Frendel, Yvonne, *Arbetarbladet* (Gävle), 2 October 1975.

[C4:40] Hammarén, Carl, *Nerikes Allehanda* (Örebro), 29 September 1975.

[C4:41] Holmberg, Diana, *Helsingborgs Dagblad*, 5 October 1975.

[C4:42] Janzon, Åke, *Svenska Dagbladet* (Stockholm), 28 September 1975.

[C4:43] Lundin, Bo, *Göteborgs-Tidningen*, 28 September 1975.

[C4:44] Ollén, Gunnar, *Sydsvenska Dagbladet* (Malmö), 5 November 1975.

[C4:45] Örnberg, Sune, *Göteborgs-Posten*, 28 September 1975.

[C4:46] Schein, Harry, *Expressen* (Stockholm), 28 September 1975.

[C4:47] Sjögren, Henrik, *Arbetet* (Malmö), 28 September 1975.

[C4:48] Strömstedt, Bo, *Expressen* (Stockholm), 30 September 1975.

[C4:49] Törnqvist, Lars, *Stockholms-Tidningen*, 28 September 1975.

[C4:50] Zern, Leif, *Dagens Nyheter* (Stockholm), 28 September 1975.

Malmö Stadsteater, 1975.

[C4:51] Donnér, Jarl W., *Sydsvenska Dagbladet* (Malmö), 18 October 1975.

[C4:52] Håkanson, Jan, *Hallandsposten* (Halmstad), 30 October 1975.

[C4:53] Halldén, Ruth, *Dagens Nyheter* (Stockholm), 20 October 1975.

[C4:54] Holmberg, Diana, *Helsingborgs Dagblad*, 18 October 1975.

[C4:55] Palmqvist, Bertil, *Arbetet* (Malmö), 18 October 1975.

[C4:56] Sjögren, Henrik, *Expressen* (Stockholm), 18 October 1975.

[C4:57] Svenninger, Bengt, *Norrköpings-Tidningar*, 4 November 1975.

[C4:58] Wahlund, Per Erik, *Svenska Dagbladet* (Stockholm), 19 October 1975.

[C4:59] Wahlund, Per Erik, 'Dagmarteatrets kulisser', in **D1:474**, *Sortirepliker*, pp. 96-98. [Rpr. of **C4:58**]

Other

[C4:60] Anon, *El Día* (Montevideo), 9 January 1979. [Uruguayan première, Teatro Circular, Montevideo, 5 January 1979. Dir. Mario Morgan; Strindberg: Luis Cerminara; Siri: Gloria Demassis]

[C4:61] Chaillet, Ned, 'Tainted Memories', *The Times* (London), 17 May 1978. [Hampstead. Siri: Susan Hampshire; Strindberg: Peter Woodthorpe; Marie: Georgina Hale; Transl. Gunilla Anderman. Also 18 May]

[C4:62] Hanson, Hans Ingvar, 'Strindberg blir koleriker i scener med vacklande närvaro', *Svenska Dagbladet* (Stockholm), 21 September 2000. ['Strindberg becomes a Choleric in Scenes with Fluctuating Presence'. Göteborg Folkteatern]

[C4:63] Uggla, Andrzej Nils, 'Strindberg behöver inte vara så dyster', *Upsala Nya Tidning*, 15 November 1979. ['Strindberg doesn't Need to be so Miserable'. Teatr Powszechny, on tour to Sweden from Warsaw]

[C4:64] Viale, Luis, *Mundocolor* (Montevideo), 10 February 1979. [Uruguayan première, Teatro Circular, Montevideo, 5 January 1979. Dir. Mario Morgan; Strindberg: Luis Cerminara; Siri: Gloria Demassis]

See also **B9:156**

D1. Drama General: A

A. General Studies of Nineteenth and Twentieth Century Drama and the Modern Theatre

[This section is devoted to histories of the theatre and studies of modern drama in which Strindberg features, either at length, in a particular chapter, or more diffusely as a defining presence. Occasionally, he is accorded only brief mention but, in the case of many of the first published of these items, this is itself significant for an appreciation of his initial recognition. Indeed, the lack, or brevity, of serious comment is itself often eloquent, and likewise, the date and focus of any discussion may also be revealing.

The section also includes collections of republished theatre reviews which sometimes bring together numerous individual items that are listed elsewhere in the bibliography under the respective play or plays discussed, and lists the autobiographies or biographies of actors whose careers were closely associated with Sg's work, like Karol Adwentowicz, as well as studies of directors like Max Reinhardt and Olof Molander, who likewise devoted a significant part their career to staging his plays. Many of the discussions below regarding Sg's impact on the modern theatre also assess his influence on later dramatists and thus cover ground which might have been listed in Section ***C1****, but the element of theatre history or dramatic theory involved justifies their inclusion here. Nevertheless, many related studies which compare Sg with e.g. Albee, Dürrenmatt, Ibsen, Lenormand, or O'Neill, are to be found among the comparative studies in* ***C1****]*

(i) Books

[D1:1] Aarseth, Asbjørn, *Den Nationale Scene 1901-31*, Oslo: Gyldendal Norsk Forlag, 1969. Illus. 499 pp. ['The National Stage, 1901-31'. Gives brief details of plays by Sg staged at Norway's oldest extant theatre, in Bergen. This includes performances of *Påsk*, *Bandet*, *Fadren*, and *Dödsdansen*. The volume also records the repertoire of the, then homeless, Intimate Theatre, on tour to Norway in 1914 with *Fadren*, *Fröken Julie*, *Fordringsägare*, and *Dödsdansen*]

[D1:2] Abell, Kjeld, *Teaterstreif i paaskevejr*, København: Thaning & Appel, 1948. 111 pp. [Includes an account of Max Reinhardt's production of *Spöksonaten* with Paul Wegener as Hummel and Gertrud Eysoldt as the Mummy, which afforded Abell an insight into the possibilities of a modernist theatre, one that impacts on all the senses]

[D1:3] Abell, Kjeld, *Teaterstreif i paaskevejr*, København: Gyldendal, 1962. 71 pp. [Rpr. of **D1:2**]

[D1:4] Abbott, Anthony S., *The Vital Lie. Reality and Illusion in Modern Drama*, Tuscaloosa: University of Alabama Press, 1989, pp. 22-33. [Abbott suggests that, like Hegel, Sg sees life in triadic terms, but he is unfortunately misunderstood by those unable to discern a link between the naturalist plays and his later dramas. Plays like *Fadren* are based on the sustaining illusion of the happy family, which Sg both nurtured and struggled to outgrow throughout his life, thus creating one of the central themes of modern drama – the notion that love is a state of war in which each party, like a vampire, sustains his or her own life by feeding upon the other. But many aspects of the early plays are carried over into *Till Damaskus* and *Brott och brott* where an attempt is made to integrate the male-female conflict with religious themes. However, for Abbott, *Påsk* and *Ett drömspel* best illustrate the imperfect resolution of the ageing Sg's struggle to reconcile himself with woman through love]

[D1:5] Ackerman Jr., Alan L., 'Visualizing Hamlet's Ghost: The Spirit of Modern Subjectivity', *Theatre Journal* (Baltimore), 53:1 (2001), 119-144. [A phenomenological approach to the problem of how human interiority may be expressed on stage, which compares the nature of perception in *Hamlet* with Ibsen's *Ghosts*, *Spöksonaten*, and Sg's essay 'Un regard vers le Ciel' (1896). Ackerman argues that a widespread re-imagining of the subject in the early 19th Century is fundamental to what is now seen as 'modern' drama]

[D1:6] Abirached, Robert, *La Crise du personnage dans le théâtre moderne*, Paris: Bernard Grasset, 1978, pp. 204-212. ['The Crisis of Character in the Modern Theatre'. Abirached considers characterisation, or its absence, in Sg's theatre under the heading 'Des ombres dans la nuit' (Shadows in the Night). To this end he discusses the major naturalist plays which are directly linked to the post-Inferno dramas and suggests that, from '*Creditors* to *To Damascus*, Sg develops the same quest to see through reality, by means of an oneiric realism which goes against discursive analysis and scorns the false illuminations of psychology'. In Abirached's view, Sg's dramaturgy, which has an affinity with Nietzsche's philosophy, anticipates Freud as well as expressionism]

[D1:7] Adler, Gusti, *Max Reinhardt: Sein Leben*, Salzburg: Festungs Verlag, 1964. 305 pp. ['Max Reinhardt: His Life'. Briefly chronicles Reinhardt's Sg productions during, and immediately after the First World War]

[D1:8] Adler, Stella, *Stella Adler on Ibsen, Strindberg and Chekhov*, Edited and with a Preface by Barry Paris, New York: Alfred A. Knopf, 1999, pp. 119-173. [Lectures by a disciple of Stanislavski on plays that 'have been instrumental in the development of the modern theatre'. Adler maintains that Sg responds to monumental changes in society; he seems more contemporary than Ibsen or Chekhov, and 'deals with the drama of man, not individual dramas'. He is 'the first Freudian playwright', a psychological dramatist of exceptional situations and the most influential playwright of his time. Subjects include 'Ibsen versus Strindberg', 'Strindberg and Women', and 'Strindberg's Characters', in the last of which the complexity and intensity of his figures are stressed. *Fadren* and *Fröken Julie* are both analysed in order to demonstrate how actors should approach them while Adler points out that, in both gender and class terms, Julie and Jean resemble Blanche DuBois and Stanley Kowalski in Tennessee Williams's drama *A Streetcar Named Desire*, characters who do not really know what they feel about things because they 'feel double']

[D1:9] Admoni, V. G., *Istoriia zapadnoevropeiskogo teatra*, Vol. 5, Moscow, 1970, pp. 400-418. [An assessment of Sg's place in the history of the European theatre and its theory. E.1040]

[D1:10] Adwentowicz, Karol, *Wspominki*, Warszawa: Panstwowy Instytut Wydawniczy, 1960. 215 pp. ['Recollections'. The memoirs of the actor whose performances in *Fadren* and *Dödsdansen* helped establish Sg's reputation in the Polish theatre. Includes nine references to Sg and recalls that early audiences often responded to *Fadren* with fainting fits, hysteria, and spasmodic convulsions: 'These pathological consequences were so infectious that the police finally insisted that an attendant should be on hand with water and other remedies']

[D1:11] Ahlenius, Holger, *Fem år med Thalia. Från Stockholms teatrar 1948-1953*, Stockholm: Albert Bonniers Förlag, 1954. 285 pp. ['Five Years with Thalia. From Stockholm's Theatres, 1948-1953'. Collects reviews originally published in *Ord och Bild* of, among many, Olof Molander's staging of *Stora landsvägen* and Alf Sjöberg's productions of *Den starkare* and *Fröken Julie, Leka med elden*, and *Lycko-Pers resa* (all 1949), pp. 37-44; as well as *Brott och brott* and *Dödsdansen*, pp. 57-59; *Paria* with Lars Hanson and Anders Henrikson at Dramaten, pp. 71-73; and a dramatisation of *Taklagsöl* by Toivo Paulo, pp. 113-114. Also includes reviews of Alf Sjöberg's productions of *Erik XIV*, pp. 133-138, and *Mäster Olof*, pp. 178–181; *Fadren*, directed by Bengt Ekerot, pp. 258–261; and Gösta Folke's staging of *Gustav III*, pp. 271–272. See **D3:1**]

[D1:12] Albright, Hardie, *Acting: The Creative Process*, Belmont, Calif.: Dickenson Publishing Company, 1967. XI+287 pp.

[D1:13] Alonge, Roberto, and Guido Davico Bonino, *Storia del teatro moderno e contemporaneo*, 3 vols, Torino: G. Einaudi, 2000-2001. Illus. ['A History of the Modern and Contemporary Theatre']

[D1:14] Alonge, Roberto, *Teatro e spettacolo nel secondo Ottocento*, Biblioteca universale Laterza 249, Roma-Bari: Editori Laterza, 1994. [XII]+[268] pp. ['Theatre and Performance in the Later 19th Century'. Includes numerous brief references to Sg and discusses *Fadren, Fröken Julie*, and *Fordringsägare* with several works in Ibsen's realist cycle in a section entitled 'Uno spettro s'aggira per l'Europa: la donna' (A Spectre is Haunting Europe: Woman'), pp. 105-111]

[D1:15] Amico, Silvio d', *Storia del teatro drammatico*, Ed. ridotta. a cura di Alessandro D'Amico, con un aggiornamento di Paul Radice, Biblioteca di cultura 230, 2 vols, Roma: Bulzoni Editore, 1982. ['History of the Dramatic Theatre'. Original edition in 4 volumes, Illus., 1940-1950]

[D1:16] Amsinck, Hanne, *Sceneinstruktøren Herman Bang og det franske symbolistiske teater*, Studier fra sprog- og oldtidsforskning 282, København: Gads Forlag, 1972. Illus. 123+9 pp. plates. ['The Stage Director Herman Bang and French Symbolist Theatre'. Discusses Bang's contribution to productions of plays by Ibsen, Bjørnson, and Sg in Paris at the Théâtre de l'Œuvre, where the Danish novelist acted as an adviser and assistant director for the Scandinavian dramas staged by Lugné-Poe. Amsinck comments on the French première of *Fordringsägare* there in 1894, pp. 96-99]

[D1:17] Andersson Elis, *Tjugofem säsonger. Pjäser och föreställningar på Lorensbergsteatern och Göteborgs Stadsteater 1926-1951*, Göteborg: Erik Hoglunds Förlag, 1957. Illus. 368 pp. + *Register och tillägg*, 11 pp., 1957. ['Twenty-Five Seasons. Plays and Performances at the Lorensberg Theatre and Gothenburg City Theatre, 1926-1951'. A survey of twenty-five theatrical seasons in Göteborg, based mainly on reviews originally contributed to *Göteborgs-Posten*, but extensively rewritten here. Includes brief discussions of productions of *Näktergalen i Wittenberg* (1927), *Gustav III* (1930), *Gustav Adolf*, (1932), *Gustav Vasa* (1934), *Lycko-Pers resa* (1934), *Dödsdansen* (1938), *Till Damaskus III* (1938), *Fröken Julie* (1940), *Mäster Olof* (1944), *Spöksonaten* (1946), *Ett drömspel* (1947), *Brott och brott* (1949), *Fordringsägare* (1949), and *Oväder* (1951)]

[D1:18] Andrews, Charlton, *The Drama To-day*, Philadelphia: J. B. Lippincott Company, 1913, pp. 169, 174-176. [Presents Sg as 'the Swedish Schopenhauer...who satirises humanity and wages relentless war against restraint']

[D1:19] Anikst, Aleksandr Abramovich, *Teoriia dramy na Zapade vo vtoroi polovine XIX veka*, Moscow: Nauka, 1988. 310 pp. [Considers Sg pp. 223-237 in the course of a discussion of the theory of drama in relation to Polish drama during the 19th Century]

[D1:20] Arnold, Paul, *Frontières du théâtre*, Paris: Éditions du Pavois, 1946. 282 pp. ['Frontiers of Theatre'. Devotes two chapters pp. 190-246 to the post-Inferno plays. Arnold focuses primarily on *Till Damaskus*, *Advent*, *Brott och brott*, *Påsk*, and *Ett drömspel* and recognises both the importance of Swedenborg for Sg's dramaturgy in these increasingly dematerialised, mystical dramas, and their resemblance to the structures of depth psychology. Sg has explored the same 'protuberances of the soul' as Maeterlinck, and the inward turn of his later plays anticipates the theatre of Paul Claudel. Arnold identifies Sg as one of the greatest of dramatists, alongside Aeschylus, Shakespeare, and Racine]

[D1:21] Arnold, Robert F[ranz], *Das moderne Drama*, 2nd ed., Strassburg: K. J. Trubner, 1912, pp. 121-123. ['Modern Drama'. A standard history of drama. Comments briefly on Sg, with reference mainly to the naturalistic dramas. First edition 1908]

[D1:22] Arpe, Verner, *Das schwedische Theater. Von den Gauklern bis zum Happening*, Scandinavian University Books, Stockholm: Svenska Bokförlaget, 1969. Illus. [426] pp. ['The Swedish Theatre: From the Strolling Player to the Happening'. A history of the Swedish theatre and of drama in performance in Sweden. Discusses early productions of *Mäster Olof*, pp. 185-187, 208-209, the work of the Intimate Theatre, pp. 217-219, 226-236, and the repertoire of the Lorensberg Theatre in Göteborg, pp. 243-245, with twenty-three other references to Sg]

[D1:23] Aslan, Odette, *Roger Blin and Twentieth-Century Playwrights*, Translated by Ruby Cohn, Cambridge: Cambridge University Press, 1988. Illus. XIII+178 pp. [Comments briefly on Blin's post-1945 productions of *Ett drömspel* and *Spöksonaten*, in which he 'captured the uneasy atmosphere that bathes Sg's work; he suggested subterranean currents, halftones, and scarcely perceptible vibrations']

[D1:24] A. Sp[aini], 'Strindberg', in *Enciclopedia dello spettacolo*, Fondata da Silvio D'Amico, Vol. 9, Roma: Casa Editrice le maschere, 1962, Sp. 492-500. [A detailed entry on Sg's contribution to the development of the modern theatre and drama in one of the most authoritative international encyclopaedias of the theatre]

[D1:25] Atkinson, Brooks, *Broadway*, London: Cassel, 1971. 484 pp. [An influential newspaper critic's account of theatre on Broadway between 1900 and 1970, with eight references to Sg]

[D1:26] Atkinson, Brooks, *Broadway*, Revised edition, New York: Macmillan, 1974. Illus. IX+564 pp. [See **D1:25**]

[D1:27] Aylen, Leo, *Greek Tragedy and the Modern World*, London: Methuen, 1964, pp. 230-231, 242-247. [Discusses *Fröken Julie*, which 'structurally...has many affinities with Greek tragedy', and is the only one of Sg's plays 'generally relevant to this inquiry'. It hints at the essential tragic rhythm and has 'something analagous to the effect of Greek tragedy']

[D1:28] Bab, Julius, 'Die Lebenden' and 'Expressionismus', in *Das deutsche Drama*, Hrsg. von Robert Franz Arnold, München: Beck, 1925. X+868 pp. [In his comments on

'Contemporaries', pp. 658-659, and 'Expressionism', pp. 783-811, Bab remarks on Sg's relevance for both naturalism and expressionism in the German theatre]

[D1:29] Bab, Julius, *Schauspieler und Schauspielkunst*, Berlin: Oesterheld, 1928. 304 pp. ['The Actor and the Art of Acting'. Includes some brief comments on acting in Sg]

[D1:30] Bab, Julius, *Das Theater der Gegenwart. Geschichter der dramatischen Bühne seit 1870*, Illustrierte theatergeschichtliche Monographien 1, Leipzig: Verlagsbuchhandlung von J. J. Weber, 1928, pp. 77-78. ['The Modern Theatre. A History of the Stage Since 1870'. Bab suggests that during its brief existence between 1907 and 1910, Sg's Intimate Theatre was in all probability the only notable avant-garde theatre in Scandinavia. He also includes scattered references to productions of Sg's plays by Otto Brahm, Max Reinhardt, and others, including a telling account of Gertrud Eysoldt as Mlle Y in *Den starkare*]

[D1:31] Bab, Julius, *Teatr współczesny*, Przełozyl Edmund Misiolek, Warszawa: Panstwowy Instytut Wydawniczy, 1959. 355 pp. [Polish translation of **D1:30**]

[D1:32] Bablet, Denis, 'Ekspresjonizm na scenie', in A. and K. Chonski, eds, *Ekspresjonizm w teatrze europejskim*, Warszawa: Panstwowy Instytut Wydawniczy, 1983. 342 pp. ['Expressionism on Stage'. Polish translation of one of Bablet's contributions to **D1:33** with some reference to Sg]

[D1:33] Bablet, Denis, and Jean Jacquot, eds, *L'Expressionnisme dans le théâtre européen*, Colloque organisé par le Centre d'Etudes Germaniques de l'Université de Strasbourg et l'Equipe de Recherches Théâtrales et Musicologiques du C.N.R.S. (Strasbourg, 27 nov.-1er déc. 1968), Paris: Editions du Centre National de la Recherche Scientifique, 1971. 407 pp. Illus. 407 pp. [A major, copiously illustrated study of expressionist theatre with multiple references to Sg. See specifically **C1:575**: Ingvar Holm, 'Strindberg et l'expressionnisme. Notes sur l'art dramatique du naturalisme et de l'expressionnisme'; **D1:567**: Maurice Gravier, 'L'expressionnisme dramatique en France entre les deux guerres'; and **D1:577**: Pierre Halleux, 'Le domaine Scandinavie']

[D1:34] Bahr, Hermann, *Glossen zum Wiener Theater (1903-1906)*, Berlin: S. Fischer Verlag, 1907. 487 pp. ['A Commentary on the Viennese Theatre, 1903-1906'. Includes five occasional references to Sg]

[D1:35] Barr, Richard L., *Rooms with a View: The Stages of Community in the Modern Theater*, Ann Arbor: University of Michigan Press, 1998, pp. 73-114. [Argues that, since theatrical performance combines social and aesthetic concerns, Sg's achievement is difficult to assess, infected as it is by his infamous social opinions. Focuses instead on his ideas about hypnotism and his general interest in psychology with reference to several of the prose works, including the vivisection 'Hjärnornas kamp' (The Battle of the Brains), *Giftas*, and *Memorandum till Medlemmarne av Intima Teatern*, as well as *Fordringsägare, Fröken Julie, Den starkare, Paria*, and *Fadren*. Following the ideas of Foucault in *Discipline and Punish*, Barr maintains that knowledge in Sg's plays is never disinterested and, as in the life they depict, the theatrical battle of the brains reveals communal existence to be a conceptual struggle in which individuals contest rival ways of knowing themselves and their common world. Sg thus anticipates Freud in *Group Psychology and the Analysis of the Ego* (1921)]

[D1:36] Barry, Jackson G., *Dramatic Structure: The Shaping of Experience*, Berkeley: University of California Press, 1970, p. 127. [Notes an affinity between the form and style of Sg's post-Inferno plays and chamber music]

[D1:37] Bauer, Anton, *Das Theater in der Josefstadt zu Wien*, Wien-München, 1957. Illus. 226 pp. ['Vienna's Josefstadt Theatre'. Discusses the career of Josef Jarno who, as director and actor, was responsible for the premières of fourteen of Sg's plays in Austria, including *Fordringsägare*, *Fröken Julie*, *Till Damaskus*, *Kristina*, *Ett drömspel*, *Påsk*, *Brott och brott*, *Kronbruden*, *Oväder*, and *Kamraterna*, many of them at Vienna's Theater in der Josefstadt]

[D1:38] Bauer, Anton, and Gustav Kropatschek, *200 Jahre Theater in der Josefstadt: 1788-1988*, Wien: Schroll Verlag, 1988. Illus. 320 pp. [Covers two centuries in the history of the Viennese theatre where Josef Jarno staged the Austrian premières of several of Sg's plays. See **D1:37**]

[D1:39] Beckmann, Heinz, *Nach dem Spiel. Theaterkritiken 1950-1962*, München - Wien: Albert Langen-Georg Müller, 1963. 398 pp. ['After the Play. Theatre Criticism 1950-1962'. Theatre reviews, including **E49:165** (*Oväder*), **E51:626** (*Spöksonaten*), and **C1:90** on Sg and Eugene O'Neill]

[D1:40] Beigbeder, Marc, *La Théâtre en France depuis la Libération*, Paris: Bordas, 1959. Illus. 258 pp. ['The Theatre in France since the Liberation'. Makes frequent reference to Sg, pp 36-37 in conjunction with Artaud; pp. 67-68 as an innovator with contemporary relevance to French drama in 1959; and pp. 139 and 180-181 on Sg and Boris Vian and Charles Dullin respectively. Beigbeder also lists significant productions, most notably those by Roger Blin of *Pelikanen* and *Spöksonaten*, and Jean Vilar of *Dödsdansen*]

[D1:41] Beijer, Agne, *Dramatik och teater*, Lund: Studentlitteratur, 1966. Illus. [75] pp. [Rpr. of **D1:42**]

[D1:42] Beijer, Agne, 'Svensk dramatik och teater', in *Vor tids kunst og digtning i Skandinavien*, red. Frithiof Brandt, *et al.*, 3 vols, København: Martins Førlag, 1948, Vol. 1 pp. [157]-212. Illus. ['Swedish Drama and Theatre'. Contains numerous references to Sg and his relevance for the development of drama and the theatre during the 20th Century, as well as a brief but illuminating account of the revolutionary aspects of his post-Inferno dramaturgy, pp. 7-20, which prefaces an account of contemporary Swedish drama. Beijer's short but perceptive comments amount to one of the earliest, truly comprehending, general appreciation of Sg's non-naturalistic theatre in Swedish]

[D1:43] Beijer, Agne, *Teaterrecensioner 1925-1949 jämte en översikt av teater och drama i Sverige under seklets första hälft*, Skrifter utgivna av Föreningen Drottningholmsteaterns Vänner 10, Stockholm, 1954. XVI+ 562 pp. ['Theatre Reviews 1925-1949 Together with a Survey of Theatre and Drama in Sweden during the First Half of the Century'. Includes **E25:276** and **E25:296**, on *Till Damaskus*, **E28:46**, *Folkungasagan*, **E29:173**, *Gustav Vasa*, **E35:945**, *Dödsdansen*, **E38:60**, *Karl XII*, **E40:89**, *Kristina*, **E41:352**, *Ett drömspel*, and **E59:49**, *Stora landsvägen*. The Introduction to this important collection of theatre reviews comprises a reprint of **D1:42** with its invaluable presentation of Sg's post-Inferno dramaturgy]

[D1:44] Bennett, Benjamin, *Modern Drama and German Classicism: Renaissance from Lessing to Brecht*, Ithaca and London: Cornell University Press, 1979, pp. 247-254. [Argues that modern European drama developed out of German drama and theory from Lessing to Nietzsche. According to Bennett, 'The most important example of Nietzsche's influence in modern drama is Sg, whose influence upon later drama, and especially upon the development of dramatic form, is difficult to overestimate.' His early reading of plays like Schiller's *Die Räuber* and Goethe's *Götz von Berlichingen* as well as of Schopenhauer and Kierkegaard predisposed Sg to the idea of drama as a painful confrontation with the human condition at its worst, thus placing him firmly in the German dramatic tradition. However, the Nietzschean component of joy only blossoms in the great works of the last period with their essentially musical form. Here, in spite of Sg's turn to Swedenborg, it is still correct to speak of a Nietzschean rather than a Swedenborgian affirmativeness. For Bennett, this is confirmed by a detailed comparison of *Fadren* with *Dödsdansen* where the basic musicality of the latter distinguishes it from the psychologically rational nature of the former]

[D1:45] Bennett, Benjamin, *Theatre as Problem: Modern Drama and Its Place in Literature*, Ithaca & London: Cornell University Press, 1990. 272 pp. [Includes several references to Sg as well as a reworking of **D1:44** in a chapter entitled 'Strindberg and Ibsen: Cubism, Communication Ethics, and the Theater of Readers', pp. 17-54. Focuses primarily on *Till Damaskus* and *Stora landsvägen* but also comments on *Fordringsägare*, *Påsk*, *Dödsdansen*, *Ett drömspel*, *Fadren*, *Spöksonaten*, and *Fröken Julie*]

[D1:46] Benoist-Hanappier, Louis, *Le drame naturaliste en Allemagne*, Bibliothèque de la Fondation Thiers 7, Paris: Félix Alcan, 1905. 389 pp. ['Naturalist Drama in Germany'. Comments on Sg's significance for Gerhart Hauptmann and German naturalism, pp. 318-321]

[D1:47] Bentley, Eric, *The Modern Theatre: A Study of Dramatists and the Drama*, London: Robert Hale Limited, 1948, pp. 135-153, 156-157, 238-239, 266-270. [For Bentley, Sg embodies the transition in drama from the 19th to the 20th Century but nevertheless remains largely unknown to English readers. He has the gift of ruthless introspection, and understanding Sg begins with his autobiographies, which confirm him to be an existential writer like both Kierkegaard and Nietzsche. He is 'almost a synopsis of the century's beliefs, illusions and attitudes', looking backwards to the Romantics and forwards to Freud and Modernism. He surpasses Zola in the naturalist dramaturgy of *Fröken Julie* and *Fordringsägare*, and discovers fluid form in the later dream plays, of which *Spöksonaten* is perhaps the most interesting. However, maybe 'the Sg we come to respect is neither the dazzling lunatic of the naturalistic "tragedies" nor the melodramatic mystic of the dream plays [but]...the less unequivocal, more ironic Sg of his comedies', such as *Brott och brott*. Bentley also includes the text in translation of Sg's exchange of letters with Zola about *Fadren*. English edition of **D1:48**]

[D1:48] Bentley, Eric, *The Playwright as Thinker: A Study of Drama in Modern Times*, New York: Reynal and Hitchcock, 1946, pp. 193-215. [See **D1:47**]

[D1:49] Bentley, Eric, *The Playwright as Thinker: A Study of Drama in Modern Times*, New York: Meridian Books, 1955, pp. 158-180, 183-185, 269-270, 273-274, 297-300. [Rpr. of **D1:48**]

[D1:50] Bergeaud, Jean, *Je choisies mon théâtre. Encyclopédie du théâtre contemporaine*, Preface by Louis Barjon, Paris: Ed. Odilis, 1956. 720 pp. ['I Choose My Theatre. Encyclopaedia of the Contemporary Theatre'. Includes references to *Fadren*, *Fröken*

Julie, Fordringsägare, Dödsdansen, Till Damaskus, Spöksonaten, and Pelikanen as Sg's 'most prominent' plays (i.e. not *Ett drömspel*)]

[D1:51] Berger, Ludwig, *Wir sind vom gleichen Stoff aus dem die Träume sind: Summe eines Lebens*, Tübingen: Rainer Wunderlich Verlag, 1953. [404] pp. ['We are such Stuff as Dreams are made Of: The Sum of a Life'. Berger's autobiography which comments briefly on his production of *Advent* at the Deutsches Theater, Berlin, in 1919]

[D1:52] Bergman, Gösta, M., *Den moderna teaterns genombrott 1890-1925*, Stockholm: Albert Bonniers Förlag, 1966, pp. 271-312. Illus. ['The Breakthrough of the Modern Theatre, 1890-1925'. Considers Sg's place in the development of a modernist theatre. Bergman discusses the Stockholm premières of *Till Damaskus I* (1900) and *Ett drömspel* (1907), identifies affinities between Sg's later theatre and the scenic ideas of Edward Gordon Craig, and documents his knowledge of contemporary developments in the European theatre, including the theories of Georg Fuchs and Jocza Savits's 'Shakespearebühne' in Munich. Bergman also discusses the founding of the Intimate Theatre, its repertoire and performance style, and reflects on Sg's ideas concerning the staging of his plays, both by employing modern technology such as backlit gauzes and projections, or by resurrecting older, pre-naturalist forms, including the use of simultaneous sets and 'periakter']

[D1:53] Berstl, Julius, Hrsg., *25 Jahre Berliner theater und Victor Barnowsky*, Berlin: Gustav Kiepenhauer Verlag, 1930. Illus. 103 pp. [Apart from some observations by Emil Schering, pp. 59-60, Berstl makes only a few, very disparate, comments on Barnowsky's Sg productions, including the German première of *Till Damaskus I* in 1914]

[D1:54] Bethléhem, Abbé L., *Les Pièces de théâtre*, Paris: Ed. de la Revue des Lectures, 1924. 470 pp. [Maintains that Sg's entire *œuvre* 'is nothing less than a series of pamphlets directed against religion, monarchy, science, etc.... In sum, he is one of the most execrated and execrable men and writers of our age'. Bethléhem condemns *Fordringsägare, Fröken Julie, Fadren*, and *Dödsdansen* by name from a Catholic perspective]

[D1:55] Beyer, Nils, *Skådespelare*, Stockholm: Kooperativa Förbundets Bokförlag, 1945. 164 pp. ['Actors'. Surveys the theatre work of numerous, mainly Swedish, actors, with eleven references to Sg]

[D1:56] Beyer, Nils, *Teaterkvällar: 1940-1953*, Stockholm: LTs Förlag, 1953. 261 pp. ['Evenings in the Theatre, 1940-1953'. Theatre reviews, including **E27:255**, on *Brott och brott*, **E35:949**, *Dödsdansen*, and **E51:267**, *Spöksonaten*]

[D1:57] Björkstén, Ingmar, *Det förtätade livet. Teaterkritik 1980-1990*, Stockholm: Carlssons, 1995. 377 pp. ['Concentrated Life. Theatre Criticism 1980-1990'. A collection of theatre reviews, including **E5:321** and **E5:334**, on *Mäster Olof*, **E11:787** and **E11:830**, *Fadren*, **E12:890**, **E12:905**, and **E12:1007**, *Fröken Julie*, **E25:452**, *Till Damaskus*, **E26:98**, *Advent*, **E34:300**, *Påsk*, **E35:694**, *Dödsdansen*, **E36:127**, *Kronbruden*, **E38:127**, *Karl XII*, **E40:145**, *Kristina*, **E41:770**, *Ett drömspel*, **E42:136**, *Gustav III*, **E58:31**, *Svarta handsken*, and **E59:70**, *Stora landsvägen*]

[D1:58] Blei, Franz, *Über Wedekind, Sternheim und das Theater. Fünfzehn Kapitel von Franz Blei*, Leipzig: Kurt Wolff Verlag, 1915. ['On Wedekind, Sternheim, and the Theatre'. Discusses Sg, pp. 24-27]

[D1:59] Blin, Roger, *Roger Blin: Souvenirs et propos recueilles par Lynda Bellity Peskine*, Paris: Gallimard, 1986. 330 pp. ['Recollections and Observations Recorded by Lynda Bellity

Peskine'. A collection of conversations with Blin which includes some discussion of his productions of *Spöksonaten* at the Gaîté-Montparnasse in 1949 and *Ett drömspel* in Zürich, pp. 268-279. Blin also comments on Arthur Adamov's admiration for Sg]

[D1:60] Block, Haskell M., and Robert G. Shedd, eds, *Masters of Modern Drama*, New York: Random House, 1962, pp. 92-93, 112. [Includes short discussions of *Fröken Julie* and *Spöksonaten*. 1st edition 1940]

[D1:61] Bødtker, Sigurd, *S. B. Kristiania-premierer gjennem 30 aar: Sigurd Bødtkers teater-artikler*, 3 Vols, utvalget besørget av Einar Skavlan og Anton Rønneberg, Vol. 3, Kristiania: H. Aschehoug & Co. (W. Nygaard), 1923-29. Illus. 286, 312, 202 pp. ['30 Years of Kristiania Premieres. Sigurd Bødtker's Articles on the Theatre'. Collects many of Bødtker's influential reviews of performances in Oslo, including **E5:372**, on *Mäster Olof*, **E27:256**, *Brott och brott*, **E35:952**, *Dödsdansen*, **E49:183**, *Oväder*, and **E53:329**, *Pelikanen*]

[D1:62] Bonazza, Blaze Odell, and Emil Roy, eds, 'A Structural Approach to Drama', in *Studies in Drama*, 2nd ed., New York: Harper & Row, 1968, pp. 1-7. [Introduces a textbook anthology of twelve plays, including *Fröken Julie*]

[D1:63] Borgal, Clément, *Metteurs en scène: Jacques Copeau, Louis Jouvet, Charles Dullin, Gaston Baty, Georges Pitoëff*, Paris: Éditions Fernand Lanore, 1963. Illus. 222 pp. [Merely notes the productions of *Fröken Julie* by Gaston Baty and Georges Pitoëff]

[D1:64] Boeser, Knut, and Renata Vatkóva, *Max Reinhardt in Berlin*, Sonderausgabe für die Mitglieder der Theatergemeinde e.V.Berlin, Berlin: Edition Hentrich im Verlag Frölich & Kaufmann, 1984. Illus. 354 pp. [Includes twenty-six references to Sg and his place in Max Reinhardt's career as a director]

[D1:65] Bradbrook, M[uriel] C[lara], *English Dramatic Form*, London: Chatto & Windus, 1964, pp. 144-149. [Comments perceptively on Sg's dramaturgy in a discussion of British drama in its contemporary context. Bradbrook identifies similarities between both *Kronbruden* and *Ett drömspel* and the plays of W. B. Yeats, and comments on *Fröken Julie*, *Spöksonaten*, *Till Damaskus*, *Fadren*, and *Dödsdansen*. The latter embrace a violence to which audiences have only recently become attuned]

[D1:66] Brandenburg, Hans, *Das neue Theater. Erlebnisse / Forschungen / Forderungen*, Leipzig: H. Haessel Verlag, 1926. 588 pp. [Discusses Sg together with Bernard Shaw and Frank Wedekind, pp. 384-391]

[D1:67] Brandes, Edvard, *Edv. Brandes om Teater: Anmeldelser og Erindringer fra henved 50 Aar*, Udvalgt af Harald Engberg, Copenhagen: Politikens Forlag, 1947, pp. 43-52. ['Edvard Brandes on Theatre: Reviews and Recollections from almost 50 Years'. Includes influential reviews of *Fröken Julie* and *Fordringsägare* on publication, and of Sg's Scandinavian Experimental Theatre in 1888-89. See **D2:524**, *Fröken Julie* and *Fordringsägare*, and **E13:75**, *Fordringsägare*. Published in a limited edition of 800 copies]

[D1:68] Brandes, Edvard, *Litterære Tendenser. Artikler og Anmeldelser i Udvalg ved Carl Bergstrøm-Nielsen*, København: Gyldendals Uglebøger, 1968. 268 pp. ['Literary Trends: Articles and Reviews, Selected by Carl Bergstrøm-Nielsen'. Includes **E11:38**, on *Fadren*, **E34:6**, *Påsk*, and **G8:21**, *Hemsöborna*, among a selection of Brandes's book and theatre reviews]

[D1:69] Braulich, Heinrich, *Max Reinhardt. Theater zwischen Traum und Wirklichkeit*, Berlin: Henschelverlag, 1969, pp. 40-44, 68-77. ['Max Reinhardt. Theatre between

Dream and Reality'. An historical rather than analytical account of Sg's place in Max Reinhardt's career as a director, focusing on the link between Reinhardt's Kammerspiele and Sg's Intimate Theatre as well as on Reinhardt's productions of *Brott och brott*, *Dödsdansen*, *Spöksonaten*, and *Pelikanen*. Braulich suggests that in these grim last plays, Reinhardt uncovered a note of compassion and reconciliation that had been hitherto overlooked]

[D1:70] Brisson, Pierre, *Au hasard des soirées*, Paris: N. R. F. Gallimard, 1935. [460] pp. ['Chance Encounters in the Evening'. Discusses Sg, pp. 171-179. Includes a short review of Poul Reumert's 1928 staging of *Dödsdansen* (**E35:20** and **E35:300**) and defends Sg against the accusation of morbidity and decadence made by Gabriel Boissy in the journal *Comœdia* (see **E35:299**)]

[D1:71] Brisson, Pierre, *Propos de théâtre*, 2. éd., Paris: N. R. F. Gallimard, 1957. 238 pp. [A survey of post-Second-World-War French theatre. Includes a chapter entitled 'La Place de Strindberg', pp. 121-129, in which Brisson discusses Sg as an innovator in dramatic form and compares his naturalist dramas with those of Henry Becque]

[D1:72] Brockett, Oscar G., and Robert Findlay, *Century of Innovation: A History of European and American Theatre and Drama Since 1870*, Englewood Cliffs, New Jersey: Prentice Hall, Inc., 1973, pp. 77-81, 155-160. Illus. [Refers frequently to Sg with separate sections on the major naturalistic and post-Inferno plays. 'Although his works have never held a truly secure place in theatrical repertories, they have commanded deep and continuing respect from readers and above all from other writers'. A frequently reprinted college textbook]

[D1:73] Brunius, Niklas, Göra O. Eriksson, and Rolf Rembe, *Swedish Theatre*, Translated by Keith Bradfield, Stockholm: The Swedish Institute for Cultural Relations with Foreign Countries, nd. Illus. 109 pp. [Maintains that 20th-Century Swedish playwrights up to and including the post-Second-World-War generation have suffered from 'the curse of Sg', in whose shadow they remain. Provides an outline of the directorial contributions of Olof Molander, Per Lindberg, Alf Sjöberg, and Ingmar Bergman, often in connection with Sg's plays. Includes an extensive bibliography of Swedish drama in translation]

[D1:74] Brustein, Robert [Sandford], *De Ibsen a Genet: La rebelión en el teatro*, Traducción de Jorge L. Garcia Venturini, Buenos Aires: Editorial Troquel, 1970. 444 pp. [Translation of **D1:75** into Spanish]

[D1:75] Brustein, Robert [Sandford], *The Theatre of Revolt: An Approach to the Modern Drama*, Boston: Little, Brown & Company, 1962, pp. 85-134. [According to Brustein, Sg's plays are at once deeply personal and strangely representative: 'More than any other dramatist who ever lived, Sg writes *himself*, and the self he continually exposes is that of alienated modern man, crawling between heaven and earth, desperately trying to pluck some absolutes from a forsaken universe.' Although he is less the polar opposite of Ibsen than is commonly maintained, Sg's rebellion is that of a self-involved Romantic who anticipates Pirandello in assuming that the world beyond his imagination has no fixed form or truth. It is impossible to analyse his work without reference to his sometimes paranoid life. The roots of his art are clearly sexual and pathological and result in a dualism that pervades all his work, which is dominated by the conflict between male and female principles. His career falls into two well-defined periods, separated by the Inferno crisis. In *Fadren* and *Fröken Julie*, which are the finest products of his first phase, works conceived in a naturalistic style are contradicted in execution by a number of non-naturalistic elements in which Sg betrays an affinity with Nietzsche rather than Zola, and where his self-analysis anticipates Freud. Following his profound spiritual crisis in the mid-1890s, Sg's conception of theme, subject matter, character, and form underwent a significant change, and in plays like *Brott och brott*, *Påsk*, *Svanevit*, and *Ett drömspel* he was more willing to regard the struggle between the sexes from the woman's point of view. Many of his later plays are designed as acts of penance, in which he tries to expiate his sense of guilt, while the compact form and psychological detail of the naturalist plays is replaced by 'a flowing, formless, fluid series of episodes – so feminine in their feeling of flux – in which Strindberg imaginatively uses lights, music, visual symbols, and atmospheric effects to cut through the materiality of life to the spiritual truths beneath.' Even in the later history plays we are never far from the author's unconscious mind, but while *Ett drömspel* is probably the most typical and powerful work of this second period, many of them also display a Swiftian disgust at the physical grossness of eating and excreting. Except for his most disordered years, he was usually able to convert pathology into penetrating, powerful, and profound drama. This transformation was perhaps his most impressive achievement, for his art was in a constant state of flux, always yielding to impulses from his unconscious. An influential essay, out of all proportion to its real importance, because of its numerous reprints and frequent inclusion in anthologies]

[D1:76] Brustein, Robert [Sandford], *The Theatre of Revolt: An Approach to the Modern Drama*, London: Methuen, 1965, pp. 87-134. [First British edition of **D1:75**]

[D1:77] Brustein, Robert [Sandford], *Who Needs Theatre?*, New York: Atlantic Monthly Press, 1987. XIV+320 pp.

[D1:78] Busse, Bruno, *Das Drama*, Bd IV, 'Vom Realismus bis zur Gegenwart', Zweite Auflage, bearbeitet von Oberstudiendir. Dr. Ludwig und Prof. Dr. Glaser, Aus Natur und Geisteswelt, Sammlung wissenschaftlich-gemeinverständlicher Darstellungen 290, Leipzig und Berlin: Verlag und Druck von B. G. Teubner, 1922, pp. 75-85. ['From Realism to the Present'. Offers a brief overview, under the general heading 'Nordischer Naturalismus' (Scandinavian Naturalism), of the plays of the dramatist who, Busse claims, has recently supplanted Ibsen to become the greatly admired model of the younger German expressionist playwrights]

[D1:79] Büttner, Ludwig, Hrsg., *Das europäische Drama von Ibsen bis Zuckmayer*, Unter Mitarb. von Hermann Glaser, Frankfurt am Main, Berlin, Bonn: Diesterweg, [1960]. 208 pp. ['European Drama from Ibsen to Zuckmayer']

[D1:80] Capablanca, Enrique, 'Prologo', in *Teatro realista escandinavo: Ibsen, Bjornson, Strindberg*, Habana: Instituto Cubano del Libro, 1972. XX+380 pp. [Introduces a volume of plays by Ibsen, Bjørnson, and Sg in Spanish translation]

[D1:81] Chandler, Frank W[adleigh], 'Strindberg – Father of Naturalism and Expressionism', in *Modern Continental Playwrights*, Plays and Playwrights Series, New York and London: Harper & Brothers, 1931, pp. 21-38. [Next to Ibsen and Hauptmann, Chandler finds Sg 'the most striking figure in the pantheon of European drama at the close of the 19th Century. More of a genius than either, he was less understandable; unbalanced, eccentric, intense, he went his lonely way with little care for tradition or schools.' He fell under the spell of both Nietzsche and Swedenborg, and his autobiographical fictions laid bare his personal life with a frankness unknown since Rousseau. However, although he composed voluminously in various genres, the bulk of his work that will survive is dramatic. His concise, technically adroit, naturalistic plays of the later 1880s reveal a morbid antipathy to woman, engendered in part by his personal experience of marriage, while his symbolist dramas prepare the way for expressionism. But he is also an innovator in the field of imaginative romance where *Ett drömspel* anticipates the monodrama of Evreinov. The most distinctive of his romantic plays are *Kronbruden* and *Spöksonaten*, which Chandler regards as the finest example of what he calls Sg's free imaginative treatment of reality]

[D1:82] Chandler, Frank W[adleigh], *Aspects of Modern Drama*, New York: The Macmillan Co., 1914. VIII+494 pp. [Discusses Sg under the heading 'The Tyranny of Love', in which the focus is primarily on the naturalistic dramas of the 1880s, including *Fadren*, *Fröken Julie*, and *Fordringsägare*. New edition 1922]

[D1:83] Chiarini, Paulo, *Il teatro tedesco expressionista*, Documenti di teatro 3, Bologna: Capelli, 1929. Illus. 139 pp. ['German Expressionist Theatre'. Touches briefly on Sg's significance for the emergence of theatrical expressionism]

[D1:84] Cima, Gay Gibson, *Performing Women: Female Characters, Male Playwrights, and the Modern Stage*, Ithaca, N.Y.: Cornell University Press, 1994, pp. 60-90. Illus. [An important study of the demands made on actresses in modern drama, including a chapter entitled 'Strindberg and the Transformational Actor'. Cima maintains that in his dream plays Sg sought a 'dematerial' actor, who would reflect his concept of the waking dream. But he failed to create a unified performance style, and the authority bestowed on Harriet Bosse by a role written for her and about her, meant that her performance as Indra's Daughter locked later performers into a damaging stereotype, which distorted the Hindu myth that permeates *Ett drömspel*, through which Sg projected his misogyny. In fact, 'through his unique structural method Sg urges female actors, and their directors and audiences, to explore the liminal zone between illusion and reality instead of examining a particular representation of reality, as Ibsen does with his retrospective method.' The Sg actor has to portray the nature of a waking dream, and advances in film and theatre technology now enable directors and actors to realise his vision. Likewise, the diverse performance codes that his writing fosters operate in ways that could not have been contemplated at the time the play was written. In his various memoranda to the members of the Intimate Theatre, Sg sometimes promoted the concept of the naïve actor, one who instinctively senses the demands of the script, whereas these later plays demand new techniques that break with the psychological realism of a literary acting style]

[D1:85] Clark, Barrett H[arper], *A Study of the Modern Drama. A Handbook for the Study and Appreciation of the Best Plays, European, English, and American, of the Last Half Century*, New York & London: D. Appleton and Company, 1925, pp. 33-41. [Includes some brief remarks on *Fadren*, *Den starkare*, and *Brott och brott*, together with bibliographical material relating to translations of Sg's plays and early critical commentaries in English]

[D1:86] Clark, Barrett H[arper], *A Study of the Modern Drama. A Handbook for the Study and Appreciation of the Best Plays, European, English, and American, of the Last Half Century*, New York & London: Appleton-Century and Company, 1938. XV+534 pp. [Revised edition of **D1:85**]

[D1:87] Clark, Barrett H[arper], *The Continental Drama of To-Day: Outlines for Its Study, Suggestions, Questions, Biographies, and Bibliographies for Use in Connection with the Study of the more Important Plays*, New York: Henry Holt and Company, 1914, pp. 77-84. [Focuses almost exclusively on *Fadren* and *Brott och brott*, and concludes that Sg's 'greatest power lies in the portrayal of character and the conflict of human minds']

[D1:88] Clausen, Sven, *Skuespillets Teknik: En nordisk Handbog i Dramaturgi*, København: Morten A. Korch, 1949. 195 pp. ['The Technique of Playwriting. A Nordic Handbook in Dramaturgy'. Uses *Fadren*, *Fröken Julie*, and *Dödsdansen* to exemplify different aspects of dramatic technique. For Clausen, these are the plays that represent Sg's lasting contribution to drama, whereas his experimental, post-Inferno plays threaten the very destruction of the theatre]

[D1:89] Clurman, Harold, 'August Strindberg', in *Lies Like Truth: Theatre Reviews and Essays*, New York: The Macmillan Company, 1958, pp. 126-129, 340-341. [Includes reviews of North-American productions of *Fadren* and *Fröken Julie*, **E12:549**]

[D1:90] Codignola, Luciano, *Due momenti della crisi del naturalismo teatrale: J. A. Strindberg, G. B. Shaw*. Dispense del corso del prof. L. Codignola, Urbino: Libreria moderna universitaria, 1971. 173 pp. ['Two Moments in the Crisis of Naturalism in the Theatre. J[ohan] A[ugust] Strindberg, George Bernard Shaw']

[D1:91] Cohn, Ruby, *From Desire to Godot: Pocket Theater of Postwar Paris*, Berkeley: University of California Press, 1987. XIV+204 pp. [Notes Arthur Adamov's admiration for Sg, pp. 100-101, Roger Blin's pre-Beckett production of *Spöksonaten*, and *Fröken Julie* at Jean-Marie Serreau's Théâtre de Babylone, with Eléonore Hirt as Julie]

[D1:92] Collijn, Gustaf, *Intiman: Historien om en teater*, Stockholm: Wahlström & Widstrand, 1943. Illus. 253 pp. [The history of the New Intimate Theatre in Stockholm by its manager. Discusses the première of *Gustav III*, with Lars Hanson in the title role, pp. 149-167. Also comments briefly on Lars Hanson and Einar Fröberg in *Paria*, pp. 88-89, Doris Nelson in *Leka med elden*, p. 89, and Mauritz Stiller's production of *Oväder* in Stockholm in 1915, pp. 97-98]

[D1:93] Cortina, Jose Ramon, *Ensayos sobre el teatro moderno*, Madrid: Editorial Gredos, 1973, pp. 38-51. ['Essays on the Modern Theatre']

[D1:94] Cowell, Raymond, *Twelve Modern Dramatists*, The Commonwealth and International Library, Oxford and New York: The Pergamon Press, 1967, pp. 27-29. [Introduces an extract from *Fröken Julie* in a textbook on modern drama]

[D1:95] Crumbach, Franz Herbert, *Die Struktur des Epischen Theaters. Dramaturgie der Kontraste*, Schriftenreihe der Pädagogischen Hochschule Braunschweig 8, Braunschweig: Waisenhaus – Buchdruckerei und Verlag, 1960. 373 pp. ['The Structure of Epic Theatre. Dramaturgy of Contrasts'. Discusses *Ett drömspel* under the heading 'Welttragödie', pp. 100-108]

[D1:96] Csató, Edward, *Polski teatr współczesny pierwszej połowy XX wieku*, Warszawa: 'Polonia', 1967. 194 pp. [A history of Polish theatre during the first half of the 20th Century. Csató illustrates how, during the 1950s and 1960s, performances of Sg's plays both on Polish television and in the theatre stressed their links with contemporary controversies and perplexities. He also discusses Jerzy Kreczmar's revelatory staging of

Spöksonaten at Warsaw's Teatr Polski (1965), with Barbara Ludwiżanka as the Mummy and Bronisław Pawlik as Hummel]

[D1:97] Csató, Edward, *The Polish Theatre*, Warsaw: Polonia Publishing House, 1963, p. 101. [Comments briefly on Karol Adwentowicz's 'magnificent' acting as the Captain in *Fadren* and Edgar in *Dödsdansen*]

[D1:98] Czempiński, J., opr., *Teatry polskie w Warszawie*, Warszawa, 1917. ['Polish Theatre in Warsaw'. Includes comments on early performances of *Fadren* and *Dödsdansen*]

[D1:99] Davies, Hugh Sykes, *Realism in the Drama*, Cambridge: Cambridge University Press, 1934, pp. 109-112. [Comments on *Fadren* and *Fröken Julie*, in which Sg 'attains a kind of realism which is found nowhere else', and *Spöksonaten*, in which he 'was evolving a method of symbolical representation which is the very reverse of realism', all in the course of a general discussion of 19th-Century dramatic realism, pp. 88-118]

[D1:100] Deák, Frantisek, *Symbolist Theater: The Formation of an Avant-Garde*, Baltimore: John Hopkins University Press, 1993, pp. 210-214. [Claims that the French premières of *Fordringsägare* and *Fadren* at the Théâtre de l'Œuvre were in fact directed by Herman Bang rather than Lugné-Poe. Sg's 'use of myths, fairy tales, and the hidden psychological motivation connected to the fragments of myths and fairy tales make him relevant to symbolist drama']

[D1:101] Delius, Annette, *Intimes Theater: Untersuchungen zur Programmatik und Dramaturgie einer bevorzugten Theaterform der Jahrhundertwende*, Hochschilschriften Literaturwissenschaft 19, Kronberg/TS: Scriptor Verlag, 1976. 162 pp. ['Intimate Theatre. A Study of the Theories and Dramaturgy of a Favoured Turn-of-the-Century Form of Theatre'. Examines the theatrical practice and dramatic genre of intimate theatre, called by Georg Lukács an 'in principle paradoxical institution'. Delius focuses mainly on the one-act plays which Sg wrote between 1888 and 1892, pp. 22-51, and his theories regarding an intimate theatre articulated in the Preface to *Fröken Julie* and elsewhere. She notes the essentially psychological nature of this form of drama and examines the intimate theatres of Mallarmé and Maeterlinck in France and Max Halbe, Hugo von Hofmannsthal, and Arthur Schnitzler in Germany and Austria before considering Sg's programme for both the Intimate Theatre which he founded in Stockholm with August Falck in 1907 and the Chamber Plays that he composed directly for it. Of these, only *Spöksonaten* and its relationship with chamber music is discussed here in any detail (pp.132-149)]

[D1:102] Denkler, Horst, *Drama des Expressionismus. Programm, Spieltext, Theater*, München: Fink Verlag, 1967. 260 pp. [Includes numerous references, primarily to *Till Damaskus* and *Ett drömspel*, and comments on Sg's move towards a monologue-driven drama, pp. 53-55]

[D1:103] Deutsch, Helen, and Stella Hanau, *The Provincetown: A Story of the Theatre*, New York: Russell & Russell, 1931. Illus. XVI+313 pp. [Documents the Provincetown staging of *Spöksonaten* and Eugene O'Neill's early encounters with Sg's plays in performance]

[D1:104] Dickinson, Thomas Herbert, *An Outline of Contemporary Drama*, Boston and New York: Houghton Mifflin Company, 1927, pp. 179-193. [Sg used naturalistic methods to uncover a deeper reality. 'If by naturalism we mean balance, impassivity, and a consistent external view of life, Sg was not a naturalist…He was not interested in the composition of external values but in distilling their essence…Charges of insanity neither explain nor destroy his genius' although his method 'carried him beyond the sympathies of any but the strongest mind in his audience']

[D1:105] Dickinson, Thomas H[erbert], *Playwrights of the New American New Theater*, New York: The Macmillan Company, 1925, pp. 99-102, 104-105. [Discusses Eugene O'Neill's tribute to Sg as the most modern of Moderns and the Provincetown Playhouse production of *Spöksonaten*]

[D1:106] Dickinson, Thomas H[erbert], *Theatre in A Changing Europe*, by Thomas H. Dickinson in collaboration with 16 European and American Authorities on the Theater of the Continent, London and New York: Putnam, [1938]. 492 pp. [Relates Sg to the French, Yugoslavian, Czech, Romanian, Bulgarian, and German-language theatres. The Danish director Johannes Poulsen observes that nearly all the great dramatic poets, including Sg, have been theatre managers]

[D1:107] Diebold, Bernhard, *Anarchie im Drama. Kritik und Darstellung der modernen Dramatik*, Frankfurt, Frankfurter Verlags-Anstalt, 1921. 479 pp. [See **D1:108**]

[D1:108] Diebold, Bernhard, *Anarchie im Drama. Kritik und Darstellung der modernen Dramatik*, Vierte, neu erweiterte Auflage, Berlin – Wilmersdorf: Verlag Heinrich Keller, 1928. Illus. [470] pp. [A central text in the German theatre's understanding of Sg, who is discussed pp. 147-232, both on his own account and as a precursor of the modern German theatre. Includes (1) 'Der Psycholog' (notably *Dödsdansen*); (2) 'Der Monologißt von *Damaskus*', in which attention is also paid to *Advent*, *Brott och brott*, and *Påsk*; (3) 'Det Theatraliter Strindberg', with the stress on *Ett drömspel* and the Chamber Plays; and (4) 'Der komplex Strindberg', which discusses psychopathological readings of Sg as 'Der Nervenspieler'. In his later plays, Diebold considers that Sg sometimes resorts to trickery and once he leaves behind the sexual conflict of the naturalistic plays, there is a tendency to monologue where effective drama requires dialogue. Hence, he has need of a director like Max Reinhardt to conceal his weaknesses. Nevertheless, Diebold finds Sg 'the greatest theatrical figure of a nervous age'; his influence on the German theatre has been profound, and *Till Damaskus*, with its lyrical soliloquist hero, is 'die Mutterzelle des expressionistischen Dramas']

[D1:109] Diebold, Bernhard, *Anarchie im Drama. Kritik und Darstellung der modernen Dramatik*, neu erweiterte Auflage mit einer Einführung von Klaus Kilian, Classics in Germanic Literatures and Philosophy, 4., New York & London: Johnson Reprint Corporation, 1972. XXIX+[470] pp. [Rpr. of **D1:108** with an introduction which places Diebold's influential analysis of the development of modern drama in context]

[D1:110] Dieckmann, Friedrich, *Streifzüge. Aufsätze und Kritiken*, Berlin: Aufbau-Verlag, 1977. Illus. 363 pp. ['Surveys, Essays and Reviews', including **E12:76**, *Fröken Julie*]

[D1:111] Dietrich, Margret, 'Die Ergründung der Seele und des psychischen Lebens. Wanderer durch das Inferno: Strindberg und seine Nachfolge', in *Das moderne Drama: Strömungen – Gestalten – Motive*, Zweite, überarbeitete und erweiterte Auflage, Stuttgart: Alfred Kröner Verlag, 1963, pp. 133-151. ['The Discovery of the Soul and of the Psychological Life. Wanderers through Inferno: Strindberg and his Successors'. In the introspective, theme-centred dramaturgy of his later plays, Sg anticipates the dramas of Paul Claudel, Eugene O'Neill, and Luigi Pirandello, as well as Tennessee Williams's *Camino Real* and German Expressionism. Dietrich also recognises the significance of the history plays as dramatic character studies related both to Shakespeare and

Goethe's *Götz von Berlichingen*, the revolutionary psychological naturalism of *Fröken Julie*, and the battle of the sexes portrayed in *Fadren*, *Fordringsägare*, *Kamraterna*, and *Dödsdansen*]

[D1:112] Dietrich, Margret, *Das moderne Drama: Strömungen – Gestalten – Motive*, 3. überarbeitete und erweiterte Auflage, Stuttgart: Alfred Kröner Verlag, 1974, pp. 142-166. ['Modern Drama: Trends – Characters – Motifs'. 1st edition 1961]

[D1:113] Döblin, Alfred, *Ein Kerl muß eine Meinung haben. Berichte und Kritiken 1921-1924*, Olten und Freiburg im Breisgau: Walter-Verlag, 1976. 286 pp. [Theatre reviews, including **E11:458**, *Fadren*, **E12:484**, *Fröken Julie*, **E27:166**, *Brott och brott*, **E34:147**, *Påsk*, **E35:962**, *Dödsdansen*, **E40:73**, *Kristina*, **E41:274**, *Ett drömspel*, and **C1:317**, 'Brod: *Die Fälscher*', as well as several comments on Sg in relation to the drama and theatre of the period]

[D1:114] Döblin, Alfred, *Ein Kerl muß eine Meining haben. Berichte und Kritiken 1921-1924*, Olten: Walter-Verlag, 1976. 286 pp. [See **D1:113**]

[D1:115] Döblin, Alfred, *Ein Kerl muß eine Meining haben. Berichte und Kritiken 1921-1924*, München: dtv, 1976. 286 pp. [See **D1:113**]

[D1:116] Downer, Alan S., *The Art of the Play*, New York: Henry Holt and Company, 1955, pp. 321-326. [Discusses *Spöksonaten* under the heading 'Non-Representational Drama']

[D1:117] *Dramat i scena krajów skandynawskich*. Praca zbiorowa pod redakcja Pracowni Historii Powszechnej PIS, Łódź, 1957. 111 pp. ['The Theatre and Drama of the Scandinavian Countries'. Group Project under the Direction of the Institution for Theatre History in Kraków. Discusses Sg, pp. 65-76]

[D1:118] Driver, Tom F., *Romantic Quest and Modern Query: A History of the Modern Theatre*, New York: Delacorte Press, 1970, pp. 193-216. [Relates *Fadren* to Nietzsche and Ibsen as well as to Sg's misogyny and introduces a rapid survey of Sg's career as a dramatist which is unusual for recognising the importance of the history plays, even if 'he failed…to attain anything remotely comparable to Shakespeare's universality'. Driver interweaves brief biographical material with comments on several of the plays (*Brott och brott*, *Dödsdansen*, and *Spöksonaten*, which is preferred here to *Ett drömspel*), in an attempt to establish Sg's status as 'the patron of all those in the theater who engage knowingly in "the struggle of the modern"']

[D1:119] Drury, Francis K. W., *Viewpoints in Modern Drama: An Arrangement of Plays According to their Essential Interest*, Chicago: American Library Association, 1925. 119 pp. [A largely bibliographical listing with brief comments on the 'psychological' *Fadren*, 'uncanny' *Simoon*, 'striking' *Den starkare*, and 'delightful' *Svanevit*]

[D1:120] Dubech, Lucien, *Histoire générale illustrée du théâtre*, Avec la collaboration de Jazues de Montbrial et de Madeleine Horn-Monval, 5 vols, Paris: Librairie de France, 1931-34. Illus. ['General Illustrated History of the Theatre'. Includes a hostile account of both Ibsen and Sg in Volume Five. Dismisses the latter as a pessimist and an anarchist]

[D1:121] Dukes, Ashley, *Drama*, London: Williams & Norgate, 1926, pp. 109-110. [Maintains that Sg's 'modern plays are strongly coloured by prejudice.…His historical plays alone ensure him the foremost place among Swedish dramatists']

[D1:122] Dukes, Ashley, *Drama*, London: Thornton Butterworth, 1936. 256 pp. [Revised edition of **D1:121**]

[D1:123] Dukes, Ashley, *Modern Dramatists*, London: Frank Palmer, 1912, pp. 49-64. [Like the best of the modern theatre, Sg cannot be confined within the limitations of any school, naturalist, symbolist, realist, or romantic. He 'presents, not the determinist puppets of the modern realist drama but gods and fighting men with wills.…Of all living dramatists he aims highest, and his failings are the failure of the craftsman unable to set so prodigious a scheme convincingly upon the stage…I need only add one word which sums up the man and his work: Nietzsche admired him greatly']

[D1:124] Dukes, Ashley, *The Youngest Drama: Studies of Fifty Dramatists*, London: Ernest Benn and Chicago: C. H. Sergel and Company, 1923, pp. 47-49.

[D1:125] Durrière, Germaine, *Jules Lemaître et le théâtre*, Paris: Boivin et Cie., 1934. III+320 pp. ['Jules Lemaître and the Theatre'. A study of the influential French theatre critic, which comments on his largely negative response to Scandinavian drama during the 1890s, including the French premières of *Fröken Julie* and *Fadren*]

[D1:126] Dussane, Béatrix, *J'étais dans la salle*, Paris: Mercure de France, 1963. 224 pp. [Theatre reviews. Notes that just as Ibsen had been the great foreign influence on French theatre at the end of the 19th Century and Pirandello played that role during the 1930s, it is Sg 'who has been passionately adopted in recent times' (p. 35). Also comments briefly on Lars Hanson in *Fadren* at the Théâtre Sarah-Bernhardt]

[D1:127] Dussane, Béatrix, *Notes de théâtre (1940-1950)*, Paris: Lardanchet, 1951. 286 pp. [Refers only twice to Sg, including the similarity in form between Sartre's *Huis clos* and *Dödsdansen*]

[D1:128] Dyfverman, Henrik, *Dramats teknik. Vägledning för författaren, teatermannen och publiken*, Stockholm: Natur och Kultur, 1949. 288 pp. ['Dramatic Technique. A Guide for the Author, Theatre Practitioner, and Audience'. Illustrates aspects of dramatic technique and playwriting with frequent reference both to *Fröken Julie* and the naturalistic plays, pp. 61-64, and the post-Inferno plays, pp. 66-69]

[D1:129] Dyfverman, Henrik, *Dramats teknik. Vägledning för författaren, teatermannen och publiken*, 2:a omarb. uppl., Stockholm: Natur och Kultur, 1962. 253 pp. [Revised edition of **D1:128**]

[D1:130] Egri, Péter, 'Törésvonalak', in *Törésvonalak, drámai irányok az európai századfordulón (1871-1917)*, Budapest: Gondolat, 1983, pp. 173-265.

[D1:131] Ek, Sverker R., red., *Teater i Stockholm 1910-1970*, Med bidrag av Lennart Forslund, Birgitta Jansson, Dag Nordmark, Per Ringby, and Claes Rosenqvist, 4 vols, Acta Universitatis Umensis, Umeå: Almqvist & Wicksell International, 1982. Illus. 436, 227, 367, 393 pp. ['Theatre in Stockholm, 1910-1970'. Studies the structure, composition, and repertoire of sixty years of theatre in Stockholm. Volume One is divided into two parts, the first of which includes a substantial study of the Swedish première of *Gustav Vasa* by Claes Rosenqvist (see **E31:38**). Volume Four is the Index]

[D1:132] Ek, Sverker R., Per Ringby, Claes Rosenqvist, and Eva Vikström, red., *Teater i Göteborg 1910-1975*, 3 vols, Stockholm: Almqvist & Wicksell, 1978. Illus. 552, 259, 261 pp. [Studies the structure and repertoire of sixty years of theatre in Göteborg. Volume Three is the Index. Volume One includes a short discussion of Sg's place in the repertoire of the Lorensbergsteater during the 1920s, pp. 331-336]

[D1:133] Ek, Sverker R., *Spelplatsens magi. Alf Sjöbergs regikonst 1930-1957*, Värnamo: Gidlunds 1988. Illus. [390] pp. ['The Magic of the Performing Space. Alf Sjöberg's

Art of Directing, 1830-1957'. A major study of Sjöberg's career as a theatre director in which, alongside Shakespeare, Sg emerges as the most prominent among the dramatists whose plays he has directed. The volume includes a brief discussion of his 'unsuccessful' production of *Oväder* in 1933 with Harriet Bosse as Gerda and Carl Browallius as the Gentleman, which was inspired, at least in part, by Sg's then only newly published correspondence with Bosse, pp. 73-76. The production foundered on the clash between Bosse's older, declamatory acting style and the more subdued ensemble style of the other actors. Ek's study is especially valuable for its detailed discussion of Sjöberg's production of *Fröken Julie* at Dramaten in 1949 with Inga Tidblad as Julie and Ulf Palme as Jean, approached here under the heading 'Spel för manlig och kvinnlig stämma' (Play for a Male and a Female Voice), pp. 304-320]

[D1:134] Eklund, Hans, *Från Humlan till Intiman. Stockholms privatteatrar*, Med bidrag av Barbro Stribolt och Bengt Wittström, Lund: Bokförlaget Signum, 1990. Illus. [249] pp. [A richly illustrated survey of the history and repertoire of the non-subsidised theatre in Stockholm during the 19th and 20th centuries, with frequent reference to Sg. Catalogues the repertoires of four such private theatres in an appendix]

[D1:135] Elster, Kristian, *Teater, 1929-1939*, Artikler i utvalg ved Anton Rønneberg, Oslo: H. Aschehoug & Co (W. Nygaard), 1941. 342 pp. [Theatre reviews, including **E11:965**, *Fadren*, and **E25:499**, *Till Damaskus*]

[D1:136] Emmel, Felix, *Das ekstatische Theater*, Prien: Kampmann & Schnabel Verlag, 1924, pp. 215-220. ['The Ecstatic Theatre'. Focuses primarily on the impact of *Ett drömspel* as directed by Max Reinhardt: Ernst Toller's *Masse Mensch* (1920) would be inconceivable without Sg's expressionist art. Emmel advocates the replacement of psychological action with a performance style based on 'ecstasy of the blood']

[D1:137] *En bok om Per Lindberg*, Stockholm: Wahlström & Widstrand, 1944. Illus. 326 pp. ['A Book About Per Lindberg'. Touches only briefly on Lindberg's Sg productions but comments on his monograph on *Mäster Olof*, **E5:64**, in Johannes Edfelt's essay, 'Skriftställaren Per Lindberg', pp. 247-251]

[D1:138] Engel, P. G., and Leif Janzon, *Sju decennier. Svensk teater under 1900-talet*, Stockholm: Forum, 1980. Illus. 212 pp. ['Seven Decades. Swedish Theatre during the 20th Century'. Sg's influence on the Swedish theatre, including the work of the Intimate Theatre and Olof Molander's productions of the post-Inferno dramas is discussed, pp. 17-19, 24-25, 28-31, 40-43, 80-81, 98-99]

[D1:139] Epstein, Max, *Max Reinhardt. Zur Theatergeschichte der letzten fünfzig Jahre*, Leipzig-Berlin: Winckelmann söhne, 1919. Illus. 318 pp. [An account of Max Reinhardt's work in the theatre between 1904 and 1919, with comments on several of his Sg productions]

[D1:140] Ericson, Uno Myggan, *Karin Kavli. Från Kassandra till Farmor*, Stockholm: Albert Bonniers Förlag, 1984. Illus. 334 pp. ['Karin Kavli. From Cassandra to Grandma'. A biographical study of the Swedish actress. Comments on her principal Sg roles as Miss Julie, Tekla in *Fordringsägare*, Henriette in *Brott och brott*, Kersti in *Kronbruden*, Alice in *Dödsdansen*, and Queen Kristina]

[D1:141] Esslin, Martin, *The Theatre of the Absurd*, London: Eyre & Spottiswoode Ltd., 1962. 344 pp. [See **D1:142**]

[D1:142] Esslin, Martin, *The Theatre of the Absurd*, Revised and Enlarged Edition, Harmondsworth: Penguin Books, 1968, pp. 342-343. [For Esslin, *Till Damaskus*, *Ett drömspel*, and *Spöksonaten* 'are masterly transcriptions of dreams and obsessions, and direct sources of the Theatre of the Absurd' as it is characterised in this defining study. 'In these plays the shift from the objective reality of the world outside surface appearance to the subjective reality of inner states of consciousness – a shift that marks the watershed between the traditional and the modern, the representational and the Expressionist projection of mental realities – is finally and triumphantly accomplished']

[D1:143] Eustachiewicz, Lesław, *Dramat europejski w latach 1887-1918*, Warszawa: Wydawniczy Nauk, 1993. 462 pp. ['European Drama in the Period 1887-1918'. Accords a substantial place to Sg's role in the emergence of modern drama. Includes a bibliography, pp. 419-427]

[D1:144] Eustachiewicz, Lesław, *Dramaturgia Młodej Polski. Próba monografii dramatu z lat 1890-1918*, Warszawa: Panstwowe Wydawniczy Nauk, 1982. 455 pp. [Studies the plays and dramaturgy of the Young Poland group and includes an assessment of the impact of Sg on Stanisław Przybyszewski and others in the movement]

[D1:145] Falckenberg, Otto, *Mein Leben. Mein Theater*, Nach Gesprächen und Dokumenten aufgezeichnet von Wolfgang Petzet, München, Wien, Leipzig: Zinnen-Verlag, 1944. Illus. 502 pp. ['My Life. My Theatre'. A theatrical autobiography assembled from conversations with Falckenberg by Wolfgang Petzet. Includes material on Falckenberg's important productions of Sg's plays in Munich, beginning with *Kronbruden* in 1914 and including the so-called Strindberg-Zyklus, in which eight of his plays were performed over six evenings at the Kammerspiele in 1915. Falckenberg also discusses his productions of *Till Damaskus II and III* with Friedrich Kayßler as The Unknown in 1916 and *Svanevit* in revolutionary Bavaria, in 1918]

[D1:146] Faludi, I., 'Shvedskii teatr', *Zhizn' iskusstva* (Leningrad), 1925:1, pp. 4-5. [On Sg and the present state of Swedish theatre. E.929]

[D1:147] Fechter, Paul, *Das europäische Drama. Geist und Kultur im Spiegel des Theaters*, Bd II, Mannheim: Bibliografisches Institut AG., 1957, pp. 133-154. Illus. ['European Drama. Mind and Culture as Reflected in the Theatre'. Includes a chronological overview of Sg's career as a dramatist under the heading 'Vom Naturalismus zum Expressionismus' (From Naturalism to Expressionism)]

[D1:148] Feeney, William J., *Drama in Hardwicke Street: A History of the Irish Theatre Company*, Rutherford, New Jersey: Fairleigh Dickinson University Press, 1984. 319 pp. [A documentary history of the philosophy and repertoire of the Irish Theatre established in Hardwicke Street, Dublin, and covering the period 1914-1920. Feeney discusses its decision to stage both *Paria* (which he describes as 'less a drama than a dialogue on criminality') and *Påsk* in 1919 and 1916 respectively, while also quoting generously from their reception in the Irish press]

[D1:149] Fischer-Lichte, Erika, *Geschichte des Dramas: Epochen der Identität auf dem Theater von der Antike bis zur Gegenwart*, Bd 2, 'Von der Romantik bis zur Gegenwart', Tübingen: Francke Verlag, 1990. VI+306 pp. ['A History of Drama']

[D1:150] Fischer-Lichte, Erika, *History of European Drama and Theatre*, London: Routledge, 2001. 416 pp. [Discusses *Fadren* and *Dödsdansen* under the heading 'The Battle of the Sexes', pp. 252-257, and *Till Damaskus* in a section on 'The Search for the Self', pp. 271-277. English edition of **D1:149**]

[D1:151] Flanagan, Hallie, *Shifting Scenes of the Modern European Theatre*, London: George G. Harrap & Company Ltd, 1929. Illus. 280 pp. [Includes some brief comments on Sg by Harriet Bosse, pp. 59-61. Flanagan also comments first-hand on Vakhtangov's production of *Erik XIV*. See **E30:105**]

[D1:152] Flanagan, Hallie, *Shifting Scenes of the Modern European Theatre*, New York: Blom, 1982. Illus. 280 pp. [Rpr. of **D1:151**]

[D1:153] Fønss, Olaf, *Fra Dagmarteatrets Glansperiode: Erindringer*, København: Chr. Erichsen, 1949. Illus. 334 pp. ['From the Golden Age of the Dagmar Theatre: Recollections'. A history of the Copenhagen theatre which was occasionally associated with productions of Sg's plays, including the world première of *Fadren*]

[D1:154] Fontana, Oskar Maurus, *Das große Welttheater. Theaterkritiken 1909-1967*, Hrsg. Kollegium Wiener Dramaturgie, Auswahl: Dr. Paul Wimmer, Amalthea, 1976. 392 pp. ['The Great Theatre of the World. Theatre Criticism 1909-1967'. Includes reviews of *Brott och brott*, **E27:266**, *Kristina*, **E40:179** and **E40:181**, and *Svarta handsken*, **E58:50**]

[D1:155] Franz, Rudolf, *Kritiken und Gedanken über das Drama. Eine Einführung in das Theater der Gegenwart*, München: G. Birk & Co., 1915, pp. 101-107. ['Critical Essays and Reflections on the Drama. An Introduction to the Contemporary Theatre'. Offers a brief Marxist comment on Sg as a dramatist with reference to *Fröken Julie*, *Dödsdansen*, and *Pelikanen*, and compares him in passing to Paul Bourget and Clemens Brentano as an analyst of late-bourgeois cultural formations]

[D1:156] Freedley, George, and John A. Reeves, *A History of the Theatre*, New York: Crown Publishers, 1941. Illus. XIV+688. [An ill-informed, partial, and very dated account of Sg as a dramatist who, it is claimed, will probably be far surpassed by 'his greatest disciple', Eugene O'Neill, pp. 385-388]

[D1:157] Freedley, George, and John A. Reeves, *A History of the Theatre*, Third newly revised ed., New York: Crown Publishers, 1968. Illus. XVI+1008. [See **D1:156**]

[D1:158] Freedman, Morris, *The Moral Impulse: The Drama from Ibsen to the Present*, Carbondale, Illinois: University of Southern Illinois Press, 1967, pp. 19-30. [Includes a Rpr. of **D2:641**, 'Strindberg's Positive Nihilism']

[D1:159] Frerking, Johann, *Augenblicke des Theater: Aus vier Jahrzeiten hannoverscher Bühnengeschichte*, Hrsg. und mit einem Nachwort versehen von Henning Rischbieter, Velber bei Hannover: Friedrich Verlag, 1963. 268 pp. ['Moments in the Theatre: From Four Decades of the History of the Theatre in Hannover'. Reprints theatre reviews including **E11:66**, *Fadren*, **E41:1034** and **E41:1035**, *Ett drömspel*, **E49:185**, *Oväder*, and **E51:647**, *Spöksonaten*]

[D1:160] Freyhan, Max, *Das Drama der Gegenwart*, Berlin: Mittler Verlag, 1922, pp. 19-21. ['Contemporary Drama'. Primarily concerned with the Chamber Plays of 1907 and their relevance for recent German drama]

[D1:161] Fromell, Axel, *Stora Teatern i Göteborg, 1893-1929. Några blad ur dess historia*, Göteborg: A. Lindgren & Söners Boktryckeri, 1929. Illus. 509 pp. ['Gothenburg's Grand Theatre, 1893-1929. Some Pages from its History']

[D1:162] Gade, Svend Lauritz, *Mitt Livs Drejescene. 50 aar i teatrets og filmens tjenste*, København: Alfred G. Hassings Forlag, [1941]. Illus. 273 pp. ['My Life's Revolving Stage. 50 Years in the Service of Theatre and Film'. An informal theatrical autobiography of the Danish stage designer and director with several brief comments on his stagings of *Advent* (pp. 125-127) and *Ett drömspel* (p. 113), and the film version of *Brott och brott* with Asta Nielsen (pp. 131-132)]

[D1:163] Garton, H. F., *Modern German Drama*, London: Methuen, 1959, pp. 102-104. [Identifies *Till Damaskus* as the prototype of German expressionist drama fashioned by Sg long before the genre came into being]

[D1:164] Gassner, John [Waldhorn], *Directions in the Modern Theatre and Drama*, New York: Holt, Rinehart and Winston, Inc., 1965. 457 pp. [This expanded version of Gassner's *Form and Idea in Modern Theatre* (1956) gives an inaccurate account of Sg's career as a dramatist (pp. 16-17), comments briefly on the Preface to *Fröken Julie* (pp. 275-277), and reprints Marvin Rosenberg's essay, 'A Metaphor for Dramatic Form', **D1:665**, (pp. 341-351)]

[D1:165] Gassner, John [Waldhorn], *Form and Idea in Modern Theatre*, New York, Chicago and London: Holt, Rinehart and Winston, Inc., 1956. 289 pp. [Comments only intermittently on Sg in an overview of 'the modern theatre as an enterprise marked by instability, eclecticism, and a mélange of genres']

[D1:166] Gassner, John [Waldhorn], *Masters of the Drama*, New York: Random House, 1940, pp. 384-396. [Includes a chapter on 'Scandinavian Succession and Strindberg'. See **D1:167**]

[D1:167] Gassner, John [Waldhorn], *Masters of the Drama*, 3rd revised and enlarged ed., New York: Dover, 1954, pp. 388-395. [Describes Sg as 'a master of both naturalism and a forerunner of the "expressionism" of the post-war theatre…[he] lacked only one attribute that belongs to the greatest dramatists; he was deficient in balance and consistent rationality']

[D1:168] Gautier, Jean-Jacques, *Théâtre d'aujourd' hui*, Paris: Julliard, 1972. 389 pp. [Theatre reviews for the decade 1961-1971. Includes **E38:85** on *Karl XII* and **E41:465**, *Ett drömspel*]

[D1:169] Gierow, Carl-Olof, *Att se teater*, Verdandis skriftserie 12, Stockholm: Svenska bokförlaget, Bonniers, 1960. Illus. 137 pp. ['Seeing Theatre'. A guide to theatre going, with eleven references to Sg. Gierow uses *Fröken Julie* to exemplify the nature of realistic theatre]

[D1:170] Gilman, Richard, *The Making of Modern Drama: A Study of Büchner, Ibsen, Strindberg, Chekhov, Pirandello, Brecht, Beckett, Handke*, New York: Farrar, Strauss & Giroux, 1974, pp. 83-115. [A widely disseminated biographical reading of Sg as a writer who made his own life the experimental matter of his work in many genres, but whose histrionic personality found its natural expression in drama. According to Gilman, his so-called naturalist dramas of psychic and spiritual warfare go far deeper dramatically than the sociologically based works of Zola and Gerhart Hauptmann. Ultimately, *Fadren* 'is a modern legend of ancient despair whose subject is larger and more complex than the play's means of embodying it' while, in the Preface to *Fröken Julie*, Sg composed a manifesto for many future changes in the theatre, especially where the representation of character is concerned. Perhaps the most durable of his other plays in this vein are *Fordringsägare* and *Leka med elden*, but in *Till Damaskus* and *Ett drömspel* he goes much further in breaking up the unity and stability of his characters. His new dramaturgy, which gave access to the unconscious, 'meant that irrational material could now be presented throughout a play, as part of its very texture, instead of being confined as it had been in the past to *irrational characters*'. He thus foreshadows the surreal and absurd drama of our era. However, it is the Chamber Plays which represent Sg 'at his most complete, most unassailable; [in them] there isn't the slightest space...between his materials and his technical means']

[D1:171] Goldberg, Isaac, *The Drama of Transition: Native and Exotic Playcraft*, Cincinnati: Stewart & Kidd Co., 1922. 487 pp. [Makes four references to Sg, pp. 10, 31, 274, 276]

[D1:172] Goldman, Emma, *The Social Significance of Modern Drama*, New York: Applause Theatre Book Publishers, 1987, pp. 22-35. [Rpr. of **D1:173** with an introduction by Harry G. Carlson]

[D1:173] Goldman, Emma, *The Social Significance of Modern Drama*, Boston: R. G. Badger, 1914, pp. 43-68. [Includes analyses of *Fadren*, *Fröken Julie*, and *Kamraterna* by the eminent revolutionary anarchist and feminist, whose judgement of Sg as 'the spiritual conscience of the whole human family, and, as such, a most vital revolutionary factor' is largely favourable]

[D1:174] Goodman, Randolph G., *Drama on Stage*, 2nd ed., New York: Holt, Rinehart and Winston, 1978. Illus. XIII+658 pp. [Quotes the director, Andrei Serban, on *Spöksonaten*: 'It seems to me that Sg, writing this play towards the end of his life, was trying to see through everyday reality to reality of another sort so that, as in Shakespeare's final romances, the real and the unreal, the visible and the visible are present simultaneously. Here there is a special concern for, and inclination towards, something spiritual, for music and for art', p. 442. 1st ed. 1961, 475 pp.]

[D1:175] Gregor, Joseph, and Margret Dietrich, *Der Schauspielführer*, Stuttgart: Hiersemann, 10 Bde., 1953-76. ['The Playgoer's Guide'. A substantial number of Sg's plays are discussed with plot summaries in Volume Four]

[D1:176] Gregor, Joseph, *Weltgeschichtes des Theaters*, Zürich: Phaidon, 1933. Illus. 829 pp. ['A History of World Theatre']

[D1:177] Grevenius, Herbert, *Dagen efter. Premiärer och mellanspel 1944-1950*, Stockholm: C. E. Fritzes Bokförlag, 1951. Illus. 404 pp. ['The Day After. Premières and Interludes, 1944-1950'. Theatre reviews, including **E5:382**, *Mäster Olof*, **E13:461**, *Fordringsägare*, **E30:363**, *Erik XIV*, **E36:98**, *Kronbruden*, **E41:1041** and **E41:1045**, *Ett drömspel*, **E50:36**, *Brända tomten*, and **E53:152**, *Pelikanen*]

[D1:178] Grevenius, Herbert, *I afton klockan 8: Premiärer och Mellanspel*, Stockholm: C. E. Fritzes Bokförlag, 1940. Illus. 276+[29] pp. plates. ['This Evening at 8 O'Clock. Premières and Interludes'. Theatre reviews, including **D1:572**, **E5:379**, *Mäster Olof*, **E13:459**, *Fordringsägare*, **E25:505**, *Till Damaskus*, **E28:49**, *Folkungasagan*, **E31:98**, *Gustav Adolf*, **E34:374**, *Påsk*, **E36:80**, *Kronbruden*, **E41:357**, *Ett drömspel*, and **E49:86**, *Oväder*]

[D1:179] Grevenius, Herbert, *Offentliga nöjen. Premiärer och mellanspel 1939-1944*, Stockholm: Fritzes Bokförlag, 1946. Illus. 271+26 pp. plates. ['Public Pleasures. Premières and Interludes, 1939-1944'. Theatre reviews, including **E10:83**, *Kamraterna*, **E11:538**,

Fadren, **E12:508**, *Fröken Julie*, **E25:300**, *Till Damaskus*, **E29:67**, *Gustav Vasa*, **E38:63**, *Karl XII*, **E40:91**, *Kristina*, **E41:1043**, *Ett drömspel*, and **E51:271**, *Spöksonaten*]

[D1:180] Grzymała-Siedlecki, A[dam], *Świat aktorski moich czasów*, Warszawa, 1957. [Includes some discussion of Karol Adwentowicz as a Sgian actor, notably as the Captain in *Fadren*]

[D1:181] Gubernatis, Angelo De, *Storia del teatro drammatico*, Milano: Ulrico Hoepli, 1983, pp. 547-556.

[D1:182] Gustafson, Alrik, 'The Scandinavian Countries', in Barret H[arper] Clark and George Freedley, eds, *A History of Modern Drama*, New York: Appleton-Century-Crofts, Inc., 1947, pp. 20-44. [An informed overview of Sg's career as a dramatist in several genres]

[D1:183] Gustafson, Ragnar, *Anteckningar om Malmö teater 1809-1938. 1: Inledning, verkförteckning*, Malmö: Föreningen för scen och manegemuseum, 1986. 121 pp. [Lists the repertoire of plays performed in Malmö, 1809-1939. Vol. II, *Författarregister, sällskapens sejourer, artistregister, sakregister. Bihang: Cirkus Hippodromens teater 1902-1922*, gives details of the dramatists performed, companies, and performers, with an appendix on the Malmö Hippodrome, 1902-1922]

[D1:184] Gvozdev, A. A., *Zapadnoevropeiskii teatr na rubezhe XIX i XX stoletii*, Moscow and Leningrad: Iskusstvo, 1939. 378 pp. ['West European Theatre from the Late 19th to the Early 20th Century'. Discusses Sg, pp. 58, 84, 156-160, and 233 with comments on Zola's critique of *Fadren*, the staging of *Fröken Julie* by Antoine at the Théâtre Libre, Sg's work with the Intimate Theatre, and Max Reinhardt's production of *Samum* on tour at the Maly Theatre. E.947]

[D1:185] Hain, Mathilde, *Studien über das Wesen des frühexpressionistischen Dramas*, Frankfurter Quellen und Forschungen zur germanischen und romanischen Philologie 5, Hildesheim: Verlag d. H. A. Gerstenberg, 1973. 102 pp. ['Studies in the Nature of Early Expressionist Drama'. Considers that the German expressionists discovered in Sg a symbol for their society and time, a powerful exponent of the mood of the period. His drama is, in fact, nothing but a single great monologue spoken by the writer's ego. The various possibilities invested in his chaotic self are personified in dramatic characters, who appear as protagonists and antagonists and over whom one colossal being towers, the writer himself who in *Till Damaskus* speaks through the Stranger with an enormous pathos. A facsimile of the 1st edition published by Diesterweg, Frankfurt am Main,1933]

[D1:186] Hallingberg, Gunnar, *Radiodramat. Svensk hörspelsdiktning – bakgrund, utveckling och formvärld*, Stockholm: Sveriges Radios förlag, 1967. 344 pp. ['Radio Drama. Swedish Radio Plays – Background, Development, and Form'. Studies the background, development, and form of radio drama with reference mainly to playwriting for the medium in Sweden, but with nineteen references to Sg. English summary]

[D1:187] Hauser, Otto, *Das Drama des Auslandes seit 1800*, Leipzig: Voigtländer, 1913. 156 pp. ['Foreign Drama Since 1800'. Touches on late 19th-Century Scandinavian drama, including Sg]

[D1:188] Hedberg, Frans, *Svenska skådespelare. Karakteristiker och porträtter*, illustrerad av V. Andrén, Stockholm: Fritzes Bokförlag, 1884. Illus. 252 pp. ['Swedish Actors. Sketches and Portraits'. On Swedish actors at the time Sg made his debut by the dramaturge of the Royal Dramatic Theatre. Includes an account of Emil Hillberg as Gert Bokpräntare in the 1881 première of the prose *Mäster Olof*]

[D1:189] Hedberg, Tor, *Ett decennium: III: Teater*, Stockholm: Albert Bonniers Förlag, 1913. 335 pp. ['A Decade: III. Theatre'. Reprints theatre reviews previously published in *Svenska Dagbladet*, including **E5:137**, *Mäster Olof*, **E25:161**, *Till Damaskus*, **E27:55**, *Brott och brott*, **E28:19**, *Folkungasagan*, **E29:27**, *Gustav Vasa*, **E30:56**, *Erik XIV*, **E38:42**, *Karl XII*, **E39:8**, *Engelbrekt*, and **E41:219**, *Ett drömspel*]

[D1:190] Henderson, Archibald, *European Dramatists*, London: Grant Richards, 1914, pp. 3-72. [Presents a lurid account of Sg's life, which draws heavily upon his own autobiographical writings. Sg is 'tumultuous, passionate, unstable', his works are 'chiselled with the cold, merciless steel of the sculptor-analyst'. A gruesome naturalist, it is in plays like *Fadren*, *Fröken Julie*, *Den starkare*, and *Paria* that he is least foreign to American taste. He is 'the arch-subjectivist of our era', touched (like Nietzsche) with 'the blight of dementia', a passionate pessimist who ultimately 'sought refuge from the storms of life in the haven of mysticism and occultism'. His early plays are influenced by Ibsen and Bjørnson, and in *The Master Builder*, which was inspired by *Gillets hemlighet*, the former is influenced in turn by Sg. His characters are transitional beings in a transitional era, and though Henderson dwells on the sexual and psychological conflicts of the naturalist plays he also acknowledges the social pathos, as well as the dark humour and a strain of fantasy in Sg's writing (thus *Svanevit* might win popular success in a 'Juvenile Theatre' if produced by a Gordon Craig). 'The most astounding testimony to the versatile genius of Sg is that he, the most distinctive naturalist which the modern dramatic movement has furnished, could also write the marvellous fantasy entitled *The Dream Play* [which]...is assuredly one of the most marvellous dramatic achievements of modern times – unique, incomparable.' Otherwise, Henderson stresses Sg's experiments in the one-act form (in his Maeterlinckian 'soul interiors' from *Den starkare* to the Chamber Plays of 1907, he creates an intimate form as distinctive as the short stories of Poe and Maupassant), and recognises the theatrical vitality of *Brott och brott* and *Dödsdansen*]

[D1:191] Henderson, Archibald, *European Dramatists*, 4th ed., Cincinnati: Stewart & Kidd, 1918. 429 pp. [See **D1:190**]

[D1:192] Henderson, Archibald, *European Dramatists*, New York: D. Appleton & Co., 1926, pp. 3-72. Illus. [Rpr. of **D1:190** with two additional chapters]

[D1:193] Henderson, Archibald, *The Changing Drama: Contributions and Tendencies*, London: Grant Richards Ltd., 1914. XVI+321 pp. [What Sg described as mood ('Stimmung'), Henderson considers the clue to the art of the future, which Edward Gordon Craig, Max Reinhardt, Stanislavskii, and Granville Barker are also all seeking. Makes repeated exemplifying reference to Sg but includes no extended discussion]

[D1:194] Hensel, Georg, *Das Theater der siebziger Jahre. Kommentar, Kritik, Polemik*, Stuttgart: Deutsch Verlags-Anstalt, 1980. 367 pp. [Articles on the theatre, including **E12:739**, on *Fröken Julie*, together with five other references to Sg]

[D1:195] Hermann, Oscar, *Living Dramatists*, New York: Brentano's, 1905. Illus. 187 pp.

[D1:196] Hillebrand, Harold N., *Writing the One-Act Play: A Manual for Beginners*, New York: Alfred A. Knopf, pp. 31-32, 99-101.

[D1:197] Hilleström, Gustaf, *Swedish Theater During Five Decades*, Stockholm: Svenska Institutet, 1962. Illus. 15 pp. [A survey of recent Swedish theatre with some reference to prominent productions of Sg's plays]

[D1:198] Hinck, Walter, *Das moderne Drama in Deutschland. Vom expressionistischen zum dokumentarischen Theater*, Göttingen: Vandenhoeck & Ruprecht, 1973. 241 pp. ['Modern Drama in Germany. From Expressionism to Documentary Theatre']

[D1:199] Hjelm, Keve, *Dionysos och Apollon: tankar om teater*, red. Hannes Meidal, Teaterhögskolans i Stockholm skriftserie 1, Stockholm: Carlsson i samarbete med Teaterhögskolan, 2004. Illus. + 1CD. 246 pp. ['Dionysus and Apollo. Thoughts on the Theatre'. Reprints several short articles on Sg, brought together in a section entitled 'Varför kan vi inte spela Strindberg?' (Why can't We Act Strindberg?' Includes: 'Möten med Strindberg' (Encounter with Strindberg), pp. 81-90; 'Skådespelaren Strindberg' (Strindberg the Actor), pp. 92-94; 'Teaterns mord på August Strindberg' (The Theatre's Murder of August Strindberg), pp. 100-102; and 'Strindbergs dialog: rum för det oväntade' (Strindberg's Dialogue: Room for the Unexpected), pp. 103-115]

[D1:200] Homén, Olaf, *Från Helsingfors teatrar*, 3 vols, Helsingfors: Söderström & C:o Förlagsaktiebolag, 1915-1919. 259, 216, 209 pp. ['From Helsinki's Theatres'. Theatre reviews, including **E10:167**, *Kamraterna*, **E49:191**, *Oväder*, and **E53:350**, *Pelikanen*]

[D1:201] Hoy, Cyrus, *The Hyacinth Room: An Investigation into the Nature of Comedy, Tragedy, & Tragicomedy*, New York: Alfred A. Knopf; London: Chatto & Windus, 1964, pp. 281-294. [Focuses on tragicomic elements in *Till Damaskus*, *Påsk*, *Brott och brott* (which demonstrates Sg's comic manner at its most effective), *Ett drömspel*, *Spöksonaten* (where Sg's view of the world is at its most Jacobean), and *Stora landsvägen*. The need for punishment is the central fact in Sg's view of humanity; his characters 'dwell at the meeting place of tears and laughter', and the tragicomic view of human experience is most poignantly defined in the Hunter's words, 'I could not be the one I longed to be', from *Stora landsvägen*, a play which is related to Sg's earlier work much as *The Tempest* is to Shakespeare's]

[D1:202] Hughes, Glenn, *The Story of the Theatre: A Short History of Theatrical Art from its Beginnings to the Present Day*, London: Samuel French Ltd., 1928, pp. 258-260.

[D1:203] Huneker, James [Gibbons], 'August Strindberg', in *Iconoclasts: A Book of Dramatists*, New York: Charles Scribner's Sons, 1905, pp. 139-162. [Although under the impression that *Giftas* is a play and he reads Sg only in German, Huneker's pioneering study praises him as 'a prime creator of character', who introduced technical innovations as startling as Wagner's. Discussing Sg in mid career, Huneker regards his naturalistic one-acters as his finest achievement and reveals that Nietzsche's sister 'once assured me in Weimar that her brother enjoyed reading Sg's novels'. He comments on Sg's scientific investigations, which are full of flashes of divination, as well as the novels and autobiographical fictions of 'this erratic man [who] is beginning to reach the cooling period of his genius']

[D1:204] Huneker, James [Gibbons], 'August Strindberg', in *Iconoclasts: A Book of Dramatists*, New York: Greenwood Press, 1969, pp. 139-162. [Facsimile Rpr. of **D1:203**]

[D1:205] Ignatov, S. I., 'Avgust Strindberg', in *Istoriia zapadnoevropeiskogo teatra novogo vremeni*, Moscow and Leningrad, 1940, pp. 297-302. ['A History of Modern West-European Theatre'. E.952]

[D1:206] Ihering, Herbert, *Theater der produktiven Widersprüche, 1945-1949*, Berlin und Weimar: Aufbau-Verlag, 1967. [270] pp. ['Theatre of Productive Contradictions'. Includes thirteen references, mainly to Sg's relevance for the German theatre]

[D1:207] Ihering, Herbert, *Von Reinhardt bis Brecht. Vier Jahrzehnte Theater und Film*, Bd 1, 1909-1923, 1958, Berlin: Aufbau-Verlag. [Reprints articles on the theatre and film, including **D1:586**, together with several reviews of German productions of Sg's plays]

[D1:208] Ihering, Herbert, *Von Reinhardt bis Brecht. Eine Auswahl der Theaterkritiken von 1909-1932*, Hrsg. und mit einem Vorwoort von Rolf Badenhausen, Reinbek bei Hamburg: Rowohlt, 1967. 428 pp. ['From Reinhardt to Brecht. A Selection of Theatre Criticism, 1909-1923'. Collects Ihering's theatre reviews and articles from a period that coincides with the years when Sg was a significant presence in the German theatre. Includes reviews of *Kronbruden*, **E36:59**, *Advent*, **E26:52**, *Brott och brott*, **E27:169**, *Kristina*, **E40:80**, and Felix Bausch's film of *Fröken Julie*, **P5:134**]

[D1:209] Innes, Christopher, *Avant Garde Theatre 1892-1992*, London: Routledge, 1993, pp. 28-35. Illus. [Revised and augmented edition of **D1:210**]

[D1:210] Innes, Christopher, 'Dreams, Archetypes and the Irrational', in *Holy Theatre: Ritual and the Avant Garde*, Cambridge: Cambridge University Press, 1981, pp. 29-37. Illus. [Illustrates how the unitary characterisation and contrapuntal structure of *Till Damaskus* initiates an assault on the tenets of naturalism. In such a play, thematic pattern replaces conventional plot construction but given the play's stage history (or lack of it), it is difficult to see how it can have had the impact on the modern theatre that it is reputed to have had. It was the subtler and formally more integrated *Ett drömspel* and *Spöksonaten* that were really influential via Artaud and Max Reinhardt respectively]

[D1:211] Innes, Christopher, 'Modernism in Drama', in Michael Levenson, ed., *The Cambridge Companion to Modernism*, Cambridge: Cambridge University Press, 1999, pp. 130-156. [Situates the Sg of *Ett drömspel* cursorily within the development of modern drama, pp. 139-141]

[D1:212] Isaksson, Curt, *Pressen på teatern. Teaterkritik i Stockholms dagspress 1890-1941*, Stockholm: Stift. för utgivning av teatervetenskapliga studier, 1987. Illus. IX+286 pp. ['The Press on the Theatre. Theatre Criticism in Stockholm's Daily Newspapers, 1890-1941'. Contains little directly about Sg but affords an insight into theatre reviewing in Sweden and consequently into his reception there over a fifty-year period when his fortunes on the Swedish stage fluctuated widely. Includes an English summary. Doctoral dissertation]

[D1:213] Itschert, Hans, Hrsg., *Das amerikanische Drama von den Anfängen bis zur Gegenwart*, Darmstadt: Wissenschaftliche Buchgesellschaft, 1972. 449 pp. [A collection of essays on modern American drama. Includes **B3:181**, John Gassner, 'The Influence of Strindberg in the United States', and **C1:399**, Frederic Fleisher, 'Strindberg and O'Neill']

[D1:214] Jacobsohn, Siegfried, *Max Reinhardt*, Berlin: Erich Reiß, 4. und 5. völlig veränderte Auflage, 1921. Illus. 152 pp. [Takes account of Reinhardt's recent Sg productions, including *Spöksonaten*, which was appropriately musical in conception. Its high point was the 'ghost supper' in the second scene, which was both grimly humorous as well as dim and misty as in Maeterlinck, thus producing a terrifying image on the edge of credibility]

[D1:215] Jacobsohn, Siegfried, *Jahre der Bühne. Theaterkritische Schriften*, Hrsg. von Walther Karsch unter Mitarbeit von Gerhart Göhler, Reinbek bei Hamburg: Rowohlt Verlag, 1965. 276 pp. [Republishes many of Jacobsohn's influential theatre reviews, including **E9:46**, *Herr Bengts hustru*, **E26:56**, *Advent*, **E35:184**, *Dödsdansen*, and **E40:81**, *Kristina*]

[D1:216] Jameson, Storm, *The Modern Drama in Europe*, London: W. Collins Sons & Co. Ltd.; New York: Harcourt, Brace and Company, 1920, pp. 28-63. [Judges Sg's work to be one-sided and pessimistic in the highest sense of the term; although he has written several great dramas, it is difficult to call him a great dramatist. The historical plays are virile studies of real people but they lack the distinction of great national drama, *Till Damaskus* is marked by a total lack of dramatic power, and *Lycko-Pers resa* exaggerates all the worst features of his later symbolic plays. For Jameson, his great dramas are those of the 1880s like *Fadren* (the greatest in conception, and in execution not far short of greatness) and *Fröken Julie*, 'the terrible study of a neurotic woman', as well as *Dödsdansen*, in which naturalism in drama touches its highest point. These plays display a realism which transcends mere record and confirm Sg's drama as the summit of the naturalist movement. Some of the symbolic plays of his third phase, on the other hand, 'are almost as bad as they can be']

[D1:217] Jaron, Norbert, Renate Möhrmann, and Hedwig Müller, *Berlin – Theater der Jahrhundertwende. Bühnengeschichte der Reichshauptstadt im Spiegel der Kritik (1889-1914)*, Tübingen: Max Niemeyer Verlag, 1986. XVIII+814 pp. [A history of the Berlin stage as chronicled in numerous reprinted reviews. Includes reviews of the German premières of *Fadren*, pp. 138-151, *Fröken Julie*, pp. 201-209, a triple-bill of *Fordringsägare, Första varningen*, and *Inför döden*, pp. 233-244, and another of *Paria, Moderskärlek*, and *Debet och kredit*, 392-400, as well as *Bandet* and *Den starkare* at Max Reinhardt's Schall und Rauch, pp. 467-474, and *Brott och brott*, pp. 475-483]

[D1:218] Jaspers, Gertrude, *Adventure in the Theatre: Lugné-Poe and the Théâtre de 'Œuvre*, New Brunswick: Rutgers University Press, 1947. XV+355 pp. [Includes comments on Lugné-Poe's productions of Ibsen and Sg]

[D1:219] Jomaron, Jacqueline de, ed., *Le Théâtre en France*, Vol. II, *De la Revolution a nos jours*, Paris: Ed. Armand Colin, 1989. 614+28 pp. plates. [Discusses Sg in the context of a general survey of the French theatre, pp. 274-276. Includes seventeen other references to Sg]

[D1:220] Josephson, Ludvig, *Vigtiga teaterfrågor för dagen kristiskt belysta*, Stockholm, 1888. ['Important Theatre Questions of the Day Critically Illuminated'. Criticises Sg for not fulfilling the promise of early works like *Mäster Olof*; his naturalistic plays elevate man at woman's cost, and present his distasteful attacks on women in a new form]

[D1:221] Kayser, Rudolf, *Das junge deutsche Drama*, Volk und Kunst 2, Berlin: Volksbühnen Verlags-und Vertriebsgesellschaft, 1924. 42 pp. ['Recent German Drama'. Presents Sg as the iconoclastic precursor of the new, anti-naturalistic German drama]

[D1:222] Kayßler, Friedrich, *Gesammelte Schriften*, Bde 1-3, Leipzig: P. List Verlag; Berlin: Horen-Verlag, 1929. [Includes Kayßler's reflections on his engagement with Sg's plays as a director and performer, most notably with *Till Damaskus* at the Berlin Volksbühne in 1920-21. See **E25:68** and **E25:69**]

[D1:223] Kerr, Alfred, *Gesammelte Schriften* in Zwei Reihen, Ertse Reihe in fünf Banden: *Die Welt in Drama*, Berlin: S. Fischer Verlag, 1917. [Republishes Kerr's collected theatre reviews and essays on the modern, generally German, theatre. Includes several items on Sg, many of them subsequently reprinted in **D1:225** and **D1:227**]

[D1:224] Kerr, Alfred, *Die Welt im Drama*, Hrsg. von Gerhard F. Hering, 2. Auflage, Köln-Berlin: Kiepenheuer & Witsch, 1964. 627 pp. [Theatre reviews, including **D2:813**, **E11:434**, *Fadren*, and **E49:50**, *Oväder*. Earlier edition 1954]

[D1:225] Kerr, Alfred, *Mit Schleuder und Harfe. Theaterkritiken aus drei Jahrzehnten*, Hrsg. von Hugo Fetting, Berlin: Henschel Verlag, 1981. [668] pp. ['With Slingshot and Harp'. Theatre reviews, including **E12:491**, *Fröken Julie*, **E35:189**, *Dödsdansen*, **E40:84**, *Kristina*, and **E41: 1059**, *Ett drömspel*. Rpr. [East] Berlin: Severin und Siedler, 1982]

[D1:226] Kerr, Alfred, *Mit Schleuder und Harfe. Theaterkritiken aus 3 Jahrzehnten*, Hrsg. von Hugo Fetting, Ungekürzte Ausgabe, München: Deutscher Taschenbuch-Verlag, 1985. [668] pp. [Rpr. of **D1:225** in paperback]

[D1:227] Kerr, Alfred, "*Ich sage, was zu sagen ist*". *Theaterkritiken 1893-1919*, Hrsg. von Günther Rühle, Werke in Einselbänden 7:1, Frankfurt am Main: S. Fischer, 1998. 958 pp. ['"I Say What Needs Saying". Theatre Criticism 1893-1919'. Theatre reviews, including **E10:171**, *Kamraterna*, **E11:433**, *Fadren*, **E12:356**, *Fröken Julie*, **E25:336** and **E25:238** *Till Damaskus*, **E28:37**, *Folkungasagan*, **E35:190**, *Dödsdansen*, **E35:225**, *Dödsdansen*, **E44:31**, *Näktergalen i Wittenberg*, **E49:52**, *Oväder*, and **E53:20**, *Pelikanen*]

[D1:228] Kerr, Alfred, "'*So liegt der Fall*". *Theaterkritiken 1919-1933 und im Exil*, Hrsg. von Günther Rühle, Werke in Einselbänden 7:2, Frankfurt am Main: S. Fischer Verlag; Berlin: 2001. Illus. 1060 pp. ['"Such is the Case". Theatre Reviews 1919-1933 and in Exile'. Includes **E12:492** on *Fröken Julie*, **E27:172**, *Brott och brott*, **E36:147**, *Kronbruden*, **E40:85**, *Kristina*, and **E41: 1058**, *Ett drömspel*]

[D1:229] Kerr, Alfred, *Theaterkritiken*, Hrsg. von Jürgen Behrens, Stuttgart: Reclam, 1971. 174 pp. ['Theatre Criticism', including, **E34:73**, *Påsk*, and **E35:226**, *Dödsdansen*]

[D1:230] Kienzl, Hermann, *Dramen der Gegenwart*, betrachtet und besprochen von Hermann Kienzl, Graz: Leuschner & Lubensky, 1905. XXX+452 pp. ['Contemporary Drama']

[D1:231] Kindermann, Heinz, *Theatergeschichte Europas*, 10 Bde, Salzburg: Müller, 1959-71, Vol. 8, 'Naturalismus und Impressionismus: I. Teil, Deutschland-Österreich-Schweiz', Salzburg: Otto Müller Verlag, 1968. Illus 892 pp. [Includes a discussion of Max Reinhardt's 'definitive' productions of Sg', in particular of the post Inferno plays, pp. 545-550]

[D1:232] Kindermann, Heinz, *Theatergeschichte Europas*, Vol. 9, 'Naturalismus und Impressionismus. II Teil, Frankreich/Russland/England/Skandinavien', Salzburg: Otto Müller Verlag, 1970. Illus. 800 pp. [An authoritative theatre history which includes a discussion of the work of the Intimate Theatre, pp. 624-639, as well as of stagings of Sg's plays by Harald Molander and Gustaf Collijn, Max Reinhardt's Swedish production of *Ett drömspel* at Dramaten in 1921, and the Ballet Suédois *Fröken Julie*]

[D1:233] Kitchen, Laurence, *Drama in the Sixties: Form and Interpretation*, London: Faber and Faber Limited, 1966, pp. 45-53. [Identifies *Fadren* and *Dödsdansen* as the most powerful sources for the form of modern drama which Kitchen calls 'compressionism', as in Sartre's *Huis clos*]

[**D1:234**] Knapp, Bettina L., *The Reign of the Theatrical Director. French Theatre: 1887-1924*, Troy, New York: The Whitston Publishing Company, 1988, pp. 70-74, 140-142. [Includes brief accounts of Antoine's production of *Fröken Julie* (1893) and Lugné-Poe's staging of *Fordringsägare* (1894)]

[**D1:235**] Knudsen, Hans, *Deutsche Theatergeschichte*, 2., neu beartbeitete und erweiterte Auflage, Stuttgart: Alfred Kröner Verlag, 1970. 455 pp. ['A History of the German Theatre'. Includes several references to stagings of Sg's plays by the Berlin Freie Bühne and Residentztheater, and productions by Max Reinhardt and Josef Jarno]

[**D1:236**] Koblar, France, *Slovenska dramatika*, 2 vols, Ljubljana, 1972-73. [A history of Slovenian drama and theatre, which comments on the significance of Sg for the development of modern drama there]

[**D1:237**] Kosch, Wilhelm, *Das deutsche Theater und Dramen im 19.Jahrhundert. Mit ein Ausblick auf der Folgezeit*, Leipzig: Dyk Verlag, 1913. Illus. 237 pp. ['The German Theatre and Drama in the 19th Century with a Look at the Following Period']

[**D1:238**] Kragh-Jacobsen, Svend, and Kaj Christensen, *25 teatersæsoner: Københavnske Teatre i Billeder og Repertoire, 1931 til 1956*, København: Illustrationsforlaget, [1956]. Illus. 136 pp. ['25 Theatrical Seasons. Copenhagen's Theatre in Pictures and Repertoire, 1931 to 1956'. Republishes several of Kragh-Jacobsen's influential theatre reviews]

[**D1:239**] Kragh-Jacobsen, Svend, *Teateraftener. Anmeldelser fra fire årtier*, [København: Nyt Nordisk Forlag Arnold Busck A/S, 1980. Illus. 212 pp. ['Evenings in the Theatre. Reviews from Four Decades'. Reprints reviews originally published in the Copenhagen daily *Berlingske Tidende* during the period 1943-1980]

[**D1:240**] Krutch, Joseph Wood, *"Modernism" in Modern Drama: A Definition and an Estimate*, Ithaca, New York: Cornell University Press, 1953, pp. 23-42. [Concentrates on Sg's portrayal of sexual strife, in a section entitled 'Strindberg and the Irreconcilable Conflict', which makes passing reference to *Fadren* and *Fröken Julie*, as well as to Ibsen's treatment of the same issue. To Sg, the essence of man's tragic dilemma is that there is no rational solution such as Ibsen strives for, only an irrational one, and his standpoint is 'a kind of romanticism turned pessimistic'. No sort of consistency, either of thought or of method is to be expected of Sg, who is always violent and extreme. Krutch compares Sg with D. H. Lawrence, Bernard Shaw, Gerhart Hauptmann, and John Milton, and acknowledges his influence on Eugene O'Neill and Tennessee Williams, but there is no significant discussion of Sg's dramaturgy]

[**D1:241**] Krutch, Joseph Wood, *"Modernism" in Modern Drama: A Definition and an Estimate*, New York: Russell & Russell Inc., 1962, pp. 23-42. [Rpr. of **D1:240**]

[**D1:242**] Kubiak, Anthony, *Stages of Terror. Terrorism, Ideology, and Coercion as Theatre History*, Bloomington and Indianapolis: Indiana University Press, 1991, pp. 120-150. ['What we see in Sg's plays isn't so much the objectification and displacement of psychological terror in "realistic" or emblematic characters or naturalistic plot devices, as it is the movements or oscillations of psychosocial catastrophe itself.' Plays like *Fadren*, *Dödsdansen I*, and *Pelikanen* expose a solipsistic terror at the heart of culture, a terror that seems categorically causeless and empty but even Sg does not fully comprehend the coming catastrophe that is modernism. It is left to Artaud to complete the alchemical investigation started by Sg in Paris in the mid-1890s (wrongly dated by Kubiak here)]

[D1:243] Kuhns, David F., *German Expressionist Theatre: The Actor and the Stage*, Cambridge: Cambridge University Press, 1997, pp. 95-98. [Presents Sg as a forerunner of Expressionist 'Schrei' drama, particularly as realised in Max Reinhardt's productions of his later plays. The impact of *Till Damaskus*, *Ett drömspel*, and *Spöksonaten* on the development of Expressionist theatre cannot be overestimated; they filled German stages with the symbolic imagery of psycho-spiritual anguish and social alienation that seemed to capture so perfectly the young Expressionist generation's sense of its own historical situation. Particularly influential was Sg's revolutionary concept of dramatic space in which its cinema-like fluidity of spatio-temporal transformations illuminated the interior subjective space of the characters. Thus states of mind become (theatrical) spaces]

[D1:244] Kvam, Kela, 'To gæstespil', in Kela Kvam, Janne Rusum, and Jytte Wiingaard, eds, *Dansk Teaterhistorie*, Vol. 2, *Folkets, teater*, Copenhagen: Gyldendal, 1992, pp. 107-111. Illus. ['Two Visiting Companies'. The standard modern history of the Danish theatre. Includes an assessment of the impact which Sg's plays made on Denmark, in touring performances by the Intimate Theatre Company under August Falck and Max Reinhardt's Berlin troupe. Regular reference is made to Sg throughout, including the 1887 world première of *Fadren* at Copenhagen's Casino Theatre, the fortunes of Sg's own Scandinavian Experimental Theatre in the 1880s, and Staffan Valdemar Holm's production of *Fröken Julie* in 1992]

[D1:245] Lagerroth, Ulla-Britta, *Regi i möte med drama och samhälle. Per Lindberg tolkar Pär Lagerkvist*, Stockholm: Rabén & Sjögren, 1978. Illus. [416] pp. ['The Director's Encounter with Drama and Society. Per Lindberg Interprets Pär Lagerkvist'. A study of Lindberg's productions of Lagerkvist's plays, with some consideration of Sg's imporance for Lagerkvist's development as a dramatist, and Lindberg's views on Max Reinhardt and Sg, pp. 37-47 and index]

[D1:246] Lamm, Martin, *Det moderna dramat*, Stockholm: Albert Bonniers Förlag, 1948, pp. 147-163. ['Modern Drama'. An informed overview of Sg as the boldest and most poetic experimenter in modern drama by the (then) doyen of Sg studies. Concentrates on the two sets of plays which, for Lamm, impinge most directly on the development of modern drama as a whole, the naturalist dramas of the late-1880s and the series of autobiographical plays from *Till Damaskus* to *Stora landsvägen*, which foreshadow the work of O'Neill and Pirandello. What distinguishes Sg from his great contemporaries is his theatrical originality, and *Ett drömspel* is possibly his greatest contribution to world drama]

[D1:247] Lamm, Martin, *Modern Drama*, Translated by Karin Elliott, Oxford: Blackwell, 1952, pp. 135-151. [English edition of **D1:246**]

[D1:248] Lange, Sven, *Meninger om Teater*, Samlede og udgivne ved Oskar Thyregod, København: Gyldendalske Boghandel, 1929. 250 pp. [Includes reviews of *Fadren*, **E11:447**, *Dödsdansen*, **E35:1034**, and *Ett drömspel*, **E41:253**]

[D1:249] Laurin, Carl G., *Ros och ris från Stockholms teatrar, 1903-13*, Stockholm: P. A. Norstedt & Söners Förlag, 1913. Illus. 512 pp. [Reprints Laurin's regular reviews of the Stockholm theatres published in *Ord och Bild* over four decades. These include his frequently unsympathetic accounts of many Sg premières and early performances, among them **E13:147**, *Fordringsägare*, pp. 96-97; **E7:36**, *Gillets hemlighet*, pp. 124-125; **E12:377**, *Fröken Julie*, pp. 150-155; **E41:222**, *Ett drömspel*, pp. 176-178; **D3:89**, *Kronbruden*, *Mäster Olof*, pp. 197-200, and *Den starkare*, *Brända tomten*, and *Oväder*, pp. 179-186; **D3:90**, *Mäster Olof*, *Påsk*, *Bandet*, and *Paria*, pp. 214-216; **D3:91**, *Fadren*, 243-245, *Svanevit*, pp. 242-243, *Siste Riddaren*, pp. 256-258; **E57:15**, *Bjälbojarlen*, pp. 265-268; **E56:26**, *Riksföreståndaren*, pp. 310-314; and **E31:87**, *Gustav Adolf*, 418-420]

[D1:250] Laurin, Carl G., *Ros och ris från Stockholms teatrar, 1914-18*, Andra Samlingen, Stockholm: P. A. Norstedt & Söners Förlag, 1923. Illus. 360 pp. [Theatre reviews originally published in *Ord och Bild*, including **D3:92** *Svanevit*, pp. pp. 90-91, and *Leka med elden*, *Paria*, and *Den starkare*, pp. 92-94; **D3:93**, *Fadren*, *Fordringsägare*, and *Bandet*, pp. 103-106, and *Oväder*, pp. 113-115; **E35:210**, *Dödsdansen*, pp. 141-143; **E8:82**, *Lycko-Pers resa*, pp. 163-165; **E42:34**, *Gustav III*, pp. 189-193; **E10:65**, *Kamraterna*, pp. 224-227; **E12:423**, *Fröken Julie*, pp. 242-244; **E51:206**, *Spöksonaten*, pp. 262-267; and **E36:76**, *Kronbruden*, pp. 313-314]

[D1:251] Laurin, Carl G., *Ros och ris från Stockholms teatrar, 1919-23*, Tredje Samlingen, Stockholm: P. A. Norstedt & Söners Förlag, 1923. Illus. 348 pp. [Theatre reviews originally published in *Ord och Bild*, including **E38:155**, *Karl XII*, pp. 10-11; **E35:1035**, *Dödsdansen*, pp. 68-70; **E41:265**, *Ett drömspel*, pp. 195-198; **E23:208**, *Leka med elden*, p. 250; and **D3:95**, *Gustav Vasa* and *Pelikanen*, pp. 255-256, 268-270, and 279-281]

[D1:252] Laurin, Carl G., *Ros och ris från Stockholms teatrar, 1924-1928*, Fjärde Samlingen, Stockholm: P. A. Norstedt & Söners Förlag, 1928. Illus. 406 pp. [Theatre reviews originally published in *Ord och Bild*, including **E42:161**, *Gustav III*, pp. 145-146; **E26:66**, *Advent*, pp. 184-188; **E25:265**, *Till Damaskus*, pp. 236-241; *Bandet* and *Leka med elden*, pp. 330-331; **D3:94**, *Gustav III*, pp. 363-365, and *Kristina*, pp. 375-377]

[D1:253] Laurin, Carl G., *Ros och ris från Stockholms teatrar, 1929-1933*, Femte Samlingen, Stockholm: P. A. Norstedt & Söners Förlag, 1933. Illus. 435 pp. [Theatre reviews originally published in *Ord och Bild*, including **D3:96**, *Pelikanen*, pp.46-49, and *Erik XIV*, pp. 49-51; **E29:183**, *Gustav Vasa*, pp. 190-191; **D3:97**, *Bandet* and *Fröken Julie*, pp. 282-284; and **E5:386**, *Mäster Olof*, pp. 374-379]

[D1:254] Laurin, Carl G., *Ros och ris från Stockholms teatrar, 1934-1939*, Saml. 6., Stockholm: P. A. Norstedt & Söners Förlag, 1939. Illus. 464 pp. [Theatre reviews originally published in *Ord och Bild*, including **E41:360**, *Ett drömspel*, pp. 159-164; **D3:98**, *Till Damaskus* and *Dödsdansen*, pp. 283-287, 295-297; **E28:44**, *Folkungasagan*, pp. 317-318; and **D3:99**, on *Påsk*, *Fordringsägare*, and *Leka med elden*, pp. 418-420, 428-430]

[D1:255] Leaska, Mitchell A., *The Voice of Tragedy*, New York: Robert Speller & Sons, 1963, pp. 212-231. [Compares Sg with Ibsen, stressing the deeply personal nature of his psychological realism which is described here as sado-masochistic and profoundly neurotic. His characters are parts of a mosaic made up of the insights he gained sporadically through prolonged self-analysis, and it is the conflicts in his own disturbed mind that animate the conflicts between his characters. Nevertheless, so long before Freud his insight into the structure of the psyche was remarkable. Discusses only *Fadren* in any detail, with brief comments on *Brott och brott*, *Spöksonaten*, and *Ett drömspel*]

[D1:256] Leiser, Erwin, red., *Tidens teater*, 4 vols, Stockholm: Tiden, 1957-1960. Illus. 147, 156, 122, 113 pp. [Swedish theatre annuals, with details of selected productions]

[D1:257] Lemaître, Jules, 'August Strindberg', in *Impressions de théâtre*, Vol. 9, Paris: Lecène et Oudin, 1897, pp. 103-110.

[D1:258] Lewis, Allan, *The Contemporary Theatre: The Significant Playwrights of Our Time*, New York: Crown Publishers Inc., 1962, pp. 42-59. [Discusses Sg and especially his break with realism in *Spöksonaten* under the heading 'Realism and Beyond']

[D1:259] Lewisohn, Ludwig, *The Drama and the Stage*, New York: Harcourt, Brace and Company, 1922, pp. 53-71. [Considers Sg's contribution to modern drama, focusing almost exclusively on *Dödsdansen*. Rpr. 1968]

[D1:260] Lewisohn, Ludwig, *The Modern Drama: An Essay in Interpretation*, New York: B. W. Huebsch, 1915, pp. 27-33. [In Lewisohn's reading of Sg, 'The heart of his immense productivity lies…in his naturalistic period. His symbolism dislimns into mere phantasmagoria.…He lays bare his characters nerve by nerve and in each nerve laid bare is also the quiver of Sg's agony.' Although Sg's art is the most joyless in the world, he is to be praised for the economy of structure, exclusion of intrigue, seamless continuity of theme, and the effect of real speech variously displayed in *Fadren*, *Fröken Julie*, *Kamraterna*, *Fordringsägare*, and *Bandet*]

[D1:261] Liljenberg, Bengt, *100 spelår. Från 90-tal till 90-tal i svensk teater och film*, Stockholm: Carlssons, 1994. Illus. 297 pp. ['100 Years of Performance. From the 1890s to the 1990s in Swedish Theatre and Cinema'. An introduction, pp. 7-14, which surveys a century of Swedish theatre, deals mainly with Sg's preeminence at Dramaten, the Intimate Theatre, and in other private theatres. Liljenberg also provides production details of thirty-eight Swedish performances of Sg's plays together with brief extracts from contemporary reviews]

[D1:262] Lindberg, Per, *August Lindberg. Skådespelaren och människan: Interiörer från 80- och 90-talens teaterliv*, Stockholm: Bokförlaget Natur och Kultur, 1943, pp. 205-208, 217-224, 251-267, 395-402, 417-426. Illus. ['August Lindberg. Actor and Man: Interiors from the Theatrical Life of the 1880s and 1890s'. The Swedish actor and director's friendship with Sg as well as their theatrical collaboration at various periods, e.g. on the dramatisation of *Hemsöborna* in 1889 and during Sg's last years, are recounted here by Lindberg's son, who was himself a theatre director. Also describes Sg's life in Copenhagen at the end of the 1880s and his first attempt to found a Scandinavian Théâtre Libre. Includes Sg's correspondence with Lindberg on staging the history plays *Folkungasagan*, *Gustav Vasa*, and *Erik XIV*]

[D1:263] Lindberg, Per, 'Strindberg', in *Kring ridån. Studier i teaterns utveckling under femtio år*, Stockholm: Albert Bonniers Förlag, 1932, pp. 131-136. ['Around the Curtain. Studies in the Development of the Theatre over Fifty Years'. Includes a discussion of the expressionist dramaturgy of *Till Damaskus*, in which the *dramatis personae* appear to hover about the protagonist like broken shadows, and emerge as different sides of the author objectified, based on Lindberg's valuable experience as a director]

[D1:264] Lindberg, Per, and Sten af Geijerstam, *Anders de Wahl*, Stockholm: Wahlström & Widstrand, 1944. Illus. 306 pp. [A biographical study of an actor who knew Sg informally and performed in many of his plays, including the premières of the verse edition of *Mäster Olof*, *Folkungasagan*, *Gustav Vasa*, and *Erik XIV*]

[D1:265] Lindenberger, Herbert, *Historical Drama: The Relation of Literature and Reality*, Chicago: University of Chicago Press, 1975. XIV+194 pp. [Relates Sg's cycle of history plays briefly to the panoramic element of the genre]

[D1:266] Lindström, Göran, *Att läsa dramatik*, Lund: C. W. K. Gleerup, 1969. 188 pp. [A pedagogical introduction to the elements of drama, applied to texts by several dramatists including Sg, whose *Paria* is the subject of an exemplary analysis employing techniques outlined elsewhere in the book]

[D1:267] Ljungberger, Erik, *Harriet Bosse*, Sceniska konstnärer 5, Stockholm: Hasse W. Tullbergs, 1917. Illus. 43 pp. [A biographical account of Bosse's career as an actress to date, including her performances in the premières of *Påsk*, *Till Damaskus*, and *Ett drömspel*]

[D1:268] Löfgren, Lars, *Svensk teater*, Stockholm: Teater och Kultur, 2003. Illus. 487 pp. [A richly illustrated history of the Swedish theatre including an account of Sg's practical involvement, initially as an apprentice actor, as a naturalist author in *Fröken Julie*, a collaborator with Harriet Bosse, and his involvement in the venture of the Intimate Theatre, pp. 282-306]

[D1:269] Löfgren, Lars, *Theaterchefen bakom maskerna*, Stockholm: Albert Bonniers Förlag, 1987, pp. 35-37, 48-53, 97-101, 207-208. [Löfgren's memoirs covering the period he spent as artistic director of Dramaten. Includes regular, but only occasional, reference to Sg]

[D1:270] Longum, Leif, *Å lese skuespill: En innføring i dramanalys*, Oslo: Gyldendal Norsk, 1976. 206. pp. [A pedagogical guide to studying play texts, illustrated with some examples from Sg]

[D1:271] Longum, Leif, 'Strindberg og det moderne dramæt', in Bjarne Fidjestøl, red., *Norsk litteratur i tusen år: texthistoriske linjer*, Oslo: Landslaget for norskundervisning, 1994. Illus. 701 pp. ['Strindberg and Modern Drama'. A comment on Sg's influence on modern drama in a chapter entitled 'National konsolidering og nye signaler, 1905-1945' (National Consolidation and New Signals)]

[D1:272] Lorde, André de, *Théâtre de la peur*, Paris: Librairie théâtrale, 1924. 238 pp. ['Theatre of Fear'. Lorde accuses Ibsen and Sg of having created 'un théâtre médical', at odds with the boulevard theatre for which he himself writes. According to Lorde, the protagonists of *Fadren* and *Fordringsägare* are sick]

[D1:273] Lothar, Ernst, *Macht und Ohnmacht des Theaters: Reden, Regeln, Rechenschaft*, Ausgewählte Werke Band 6, Wien und Hamburg: Paul Zsolnay Verlag, 1968. 330 pp. [Includes reviews of *Fadren*, **E11:116**, and *Fröken Julie*, **E12:188**]

[D1:274] Loup, Kurt, Hrsg., *Das festliche Haus: das Düsseldorfer Schauspielhaus Dumont -Lindemann – Spiegel und Ausdruck der Zeit*, Köln: Kiepenheuer & Witsch, 1955. Illus. 339 pp. [A history of the Düsseldorf theatre, including its Sg productions]

[D1:275] Lüchou, Marianne, *Svenska teatern i Helsingfors. Repertoar, styrelser och teaterchefer. Konstnärlig personal 1860-1975*, Helsingfors: Stiftelsen för Svenska teatern, 1977. Illus. 327 pp. ['The Swedish Theatre in Helsinki'. A history of the Swedish Theatre in Helsinki with details of its repertoire. management, directors, and performers]

[D1:276] Lüchou, Nils, *Teaterstaden Helsingfors under tre decennier. Teaterrecensioner 1921-1949*, Inledning och repertoar förteckning 1920-50 redigerad av Marianne Lüchou, Helsingfors: Söderström, 1960. Illus. [465] pp. [Theatre reviews of performances in

Helsinki with an introduction and details of the repertoire of the major theatres over a thirty year period. Includes **E11:1011**, *Fadren*, **E27:277**, *Brott och brott*, **E29:185**, *Gustav Vasa*, **E30:370**, *Erik XIV*, **E35:1048**, *Dödsdansen*, **E36:81**, *Kronbruden*, **E41:1069**, *Ett drömspel*, and **E51:672**, *Spöksonaten*. Also published in a limited edition for Sällskapet Bokvännerna i Finland and Svenska Teaterklubben-Kammarteatern, Tammerfors, 1960]

[**D1:277**] Luft, Friedrich, *Berliner Theater 1945-1961: sechzehn kritische Jahre*, Hrsg. von Henning Rischbieter, Velber bei Hannover: Erhard Friedrich, 1961. 395 pp. [Reprints theatre reviews of performances in Berlin, 1945-1961, including **E11:576**, *Fadren*, **E38:157**, *Karl XII*, and **E41:400**, *Ett drömspel*]

[**D1:278**] Luft, Friedrich, *Stimme der Kritik. Berliner Theater seit 1945*, 3., neu bearb. und erw. Aufl., Velber bei Hannover: Friedrich, 1965. 414 pp. [A revised and enlarged edition of **D1:277**]

[**D1:279**] Luft, Friedrich, *Stimme der Kritik. Band I: Berliner Theater 1945-1965*, Ungekürzte Ausgabe, Frankfurt am Main – Berlin - Wien: Verlag Ullstein, 1982. 526 pp. [Theatre reviews, including **E11:577** and **E11:1012**, *Fadren*, **E38:158**, *Karl XII*, and **E41:401**, *Ett drömspel*]

[**D1:280**] Luft, Friedrich, *Stimme der Kritik. Theaterreigniße seit 1965*, Stuttgart: Deutsche Verlag-Anstalt, 1979. 333 pp. [Theatre reviews, including **E11:734**, *Fadren*, and **E35:602**, *Dödsdansen*]

[**D1:281**] Lugné-Poe, Aurélien François, *La Parade. Souvenirs et impressions de théâtre*, 4 vols, Paris: Librairie Gallimard, 1930-33, Vol. 2, 1894-1902, *Acrobaties*, pp. 91-97, 269, 271-272. [Cites a letter from Maeterlinck: 'It is good that you are staging Strindberg's *The Father*. I have just reread the play, and it is beautiful, very beautiful'. Lugné-Poe quotes from his correspondence with Sg and comments on the latter's theatre in general, as well as their contacts in Paris in 1894 when Lugné-Poe mounted the French premières of *Fadren* and *Fordringsägare*. He also confirms the importance of Herman Bang's role in persuading him to stage the latter, thus paving the way for his production of *Fadren* the following season]

[**D1:282**] Lukács, Georg, *Zur Soziologie des modernen Dramas*, in Georg Lukács, *Schriften zur Literatursoziologie*, Hrsg. von Peter Ludz, Neuwied, 1961, pp. 261-295. ['On the Sociology of Modern Drama'. New edition of **D1:618**]

[**D1:283**] Lukács, György, *A modern dráma fejlödésének története*, 2 vols, Budapest: Kisfaludy Társaság, Franklin, 1911. 496, 548 pp. ['A History of the Development of Modern Drama'. Comments on Sg's significance throughout, with an in-depth discussion of his dramatic techniques in Chapters 7 and 15. See **D1:284**]

[**D1:284**] Lukács, György, *A modern dráma fejlödésének története*, Budapest: Magvetö Kiadó, 1978. 635 pp. ['A History of the Development of Modern Drama'. Rpr. of **D1:282** in Hungarian. Discusses both Sg's naturalism and his post-Inferno dramaturgy in the context of an important study of the development of modern drama, pp. 326-337, 368-370, 567-570, with numerous other references. Lukács refers specifically to *Bandet, Brott och brott, Den starkare, Debet och kredit, Ett drömspel, Dödsdansen, Fadren, Fordringsägare, Fröken Julie, Gustav Adolf, I havsbandet, Paria, Påsk, Till Damaskus,* and *Svanevit*]

[D1:285] Lukács, György, *A drámaírás fobb iranyai a múlt század utolsó negyedében*, Budapest: Magvetö Kiadó, 1980. 275 pp. ['Principal Trends in Drama during the Final Quarter of the Last Century']

[D1:286] Lyman, Jane, ed., *Perspectives on Plays*, London and Henley: Routledge & Kegan Paul, 1976, pp. 143-160. [An Open University textbook, with readings for a course in drama that includes *Fröken Julie* and *Spöksonaten* (see **D2:280**). Includes extended extracts from commentary on the two plays by Robert Brustein, **D1:76**, Patrick Roberts, **D1:376**, Michael Elliott, **E12:83**, on *Fröken Julie*, and Milton A. Mays and Egil Törnqvist, on *Spöksonaten*, **E51:87**, **E51:138**]

[D1:287] MacCarthy, Desmond, *Theatre*, London: MacGibbon & Kee, 1954, pp. 84-93. [Includes reviews of *Fadren*, **E11:487**, pp. 84-88, and *Fröken Julie* and *Paria*, **E12:1392**, pp. 88-93. Previously published in *Portraits*, London, 1931. Rpr. 1949]

[D1:288] Macgowan, Kenneth, and Robert E. Jones, *Continental Stagecraft*, New York: Harcourt Brace and Company, 1922. [Refers to Sg, pp. 27-29, 31-32, 42, 51, and 107]

[D1:289] Macgowan, Kenneth, *The Theatre of Tomorrow*, New York: Boni and Liveright, 1921. [Brief mention of Sg, pp. 214, 225-226, and 247]

[D1:290] Mackay, Constance D'Arcy, *The Little Theatre in the United States*, New York: Henry Holt & Company, 1917. [Includes Sg's Scandinavian Experimental Theatre and the Intimate Theatre in a discussion of the Little Theatre Movement in Europe]

[D1:291] Macy, John Albert, 'Strindberg', in *The Critical Game*, New York: Boni and Liveright, [1922], pp. 135-142. [Within the dramatic forms in which he expressed every aspect of himself, Sg 'lies abroad on his times leviathan-like']

[D1:292] Mamroth, Fedor, *Aus der Frankfurter Theaterchronik (1889-1907)*, 2 Bde, Berlin: E. Flieschel Verlag, 1908. [Volume Two of Mamroth's chronicle covers the repertoire of the Frankfurt theatres in the period 1900-1907, including their first notice of Sg]

[D1:293] Manheim, Michael, *Vital Contradictions: Characterization in the Plays of Ibsen, Strindberg, Chekhov and O'Neill*, Bruxelles, Bern, Berlin, New York: P.I.E.-Peter Lang, 2002. 208 pp. [Believes that the major (and some minor) figures in modern drama are driven by the vital contradictions at the core of their natures, which govern how they think and behave, particularly in stressful situations. Examines the characters of the four named dramatists, in Sg's case with close – but nevertheless often superficial and poorly informed – reference to *Fröken Julie*, *Ett drömspel*, and (most interestingly) *Påsk*, pp. 61-99. Manheim frequently assumes too close an identification between the dramatist and his characters]

[D1:294] Marker, Frederick J., and Lise-Lone Marker, *A History of Scandinavian Theatre*, Cambridge: Cambridge University Press, 1996, pp. 193-223, 235-237, 252-262, 282-287. Illus. [Maintains that Sg's contribution to the emergence of modern theatre ranks alongside that of Adolphe Appia and Edward Gordon Craig. Contrary to received opinion, he was always attuned to new theatrical developments. Focuses on the ways he believed his plays might be staged (e.g. by adopting the conventions of the Munich Shakespeare Stage for his post-Inferno dramas) rather than on their literary aspect. Discusses Sg's own work with August Falck at the Intimate Theatre; Per Lindberg's stagings of his plays at the Lorensberg Theatre in Göteborg; Olof Molander's Craigian experiments with a fluid, supple theatre form that facilitated the staging of his associational, metamorphic later dramaturgy and led to a Sg renaissance in Sweden;

and Ingmar Bergman's ongoing dialogue with *Ett drömspel* and *Spöksonaten*, and the problems they pose in performance. Revised and expanded edition of **D1:298**]

[**D1:295**] Marker, Frederick J., and Lise-Lone Marker, *Ingmar Bergman. A Project for the Theatre*, New York: Frederick Ungar, 1983, pp. 1-45. Illus. [Includes the text of an interview with Bergman about his intentions in staging *A Doll's House*, *Fröken Julie*, and his own *Scenes from a Marriage* as a cycle at the Residenztheater in Munich, in 1981, together with 'Love without Lovers' in which the Markers discuss the productions, and a translation of the performance text which includes Bergman's stage directions as performed rather than those provided by Sg's original text. In spite of Bergman's observation that, 'Today...you ought never to cut Sg – but you should always cut Ibsen', he omits Julie's speech about hypnotism, believing that 'from the moment she decides, she becomes stronger than anyone else. She forces *him*'. Kristin's role is given greater prominence than normal since '[she] is the strongest of them all', while the six non-speaking servant figures that Bergman introduces heighten the 'fantastically brutal, cruel eroticism that runs beneath the surface of the play']

[**D1:296**] Marker, Frederick J., and Lise-Lone Marker, *Ingmar Bergman: Four Decades in the Theatre*, Cambridge: Cambridge University Press, 1982, pp. 54-130. Illus. [See **D1:297**]

[**D1:297**] Marker, Frederick J., and Lise-Lone Marker, *Ingmar Bergman: A Life in the Theatre*, Cambridge: Cambridge University Press, 1992, pp. 59-142. Illus. [An informed and valuably illustrated discussion of Bergman's stagings of Sg from *Pelikanen* at Malmö Stadstheater in 1945, still very much under the influence of Olof Molander, to *Ett drömspel* at Dramaten, in 1986. This latter play has had the profoundest influence on Bergman's search for a performance style for Sg, and he has staged it four times, but close attention is also paid to his productions of *Spöksonaten* (1954 and 1973), *Fröken Julie* (1981), and *Till Damaskus I-II* (1974). Bergman's approach to Sg is compared with Max Reinhardt's and Olof Molander's in what is an essential account of his work with Sg in the theatre. Revised and enlarged edition of **D1:296**]

[**D1:298**] Marker, Frederick J., and Lise-Lone Marker, *The Scandinavian Theatre: A Short History*, Oxford: Basil Blackwell, 1975, pp. 176-203, 213-217, 232-238, 270-273. Illus. [See **D1:294**]

[**D1:299**] Marker, Frederick J., and Christopher Innes, 'Introduction', in *Modernism in European Drama: Ibsen, Strindberg, Pirandello, Beckett. Essays from Modern Drama*, University of Toronto Press, 1998, pp. ix-xv. [Observes that, while Ibsen's influence on modern drama has been decisive and indisputable, it could be argued that both Pirandello and Beckett seem more closely related to Sg, both in spirit and technique. The volume also includes **D1:526**: Benjamin K. Bennett, 'Strindberg and Ibsen: Towards a Cubism of Time in Drama'; **E12:223**: Brian Parker, Strindberg's *Miss Julie* and the Legend of Salomé'; and **E25:45**: Diane Filby Gillespie, 'Strindberg's *To Damascus*: Archetypal Autobiography']

[**D1:300**] Marriott, J[ames] W[illiam], *Modern Drama*, London and New York: Thomas Nelson & Sons, Ltd., 1934, pp. 52-57, 231. [A superficial presentation of Sg as the pioneer of both naturalism and expressionism in the theatre]

[**D1:301**] Marschall, Brigitte, *Die Droge und ihr Double. Zur Theatralität anderer Bewußtseinszustände*, Literatur – Kultur – Geschlecht: Grosse Reihe 14, Köln und Wien: Böhlau

Verlag, 2000, pp. 91-178. ['The Drug and its Double. On the Theatricality of Different States of Consciousness'. Relates Sg to Walter Benjamin's *Passagearbeit*]

[D1:302] Marshall, Norman, *The Other Theatre*, London: John Lehmann, 1947, pp. 17-29. [Discusses James Bernard Fagan's Oxford Players and their performances of several of Sg's plays during the 1920s, including *Spöksonaten*, *Påsk*, and *Brott och brott*]

[D1:303] Martini, F. M., *Cronachi teatrali 1923*, Firenze: Barbèra, 1924, p.245. ['Theatre Chronicles']

[D1:304] Matthews, Honor, 'August Strindberg: The Appearance of Eastern Mythology', in *The Primal Curse: The Myth of Cain and Abel in the Theatre*, London: Chatto and Windus; New York: Schoken Books, 1967, pp. 123-136. Argues that 'The strife of opposites is an obsessive motif in Strindberg's work. He uses both Cain and Esau as types of the rejected man and identifies both with himself, but in spite of this use of Old Testament typology the version of the myth of the warring brothers which is most in tune with his own imagination is not that of Genesis but rather that of the Zoroastrian heresy of Zurvanism.' The Manichean hostility to both body and sex, which is often focused in the figure of a woman, is illustrated with reference to *Fadren*, *Fröken Julie*, *Till Damaskus*, *Påsk*, *Ett drömspel*, and *Spöksonaten*]

[D1:305] Megged, Matti, *Ha-drama ha-modernit: mevo'ot omekorot*, Tel Aviv: Masada Publishing House, 1976. 443 pp. ['The Modern Drama'. Megged suggests that 'There is a tight internal connection between Sg's "realistic" plays and the delirious "expressionist" ones...[He] could never have moulded his raw materials in formal structures without feeling or recognising the active presence and participation of the spectator'. Previous edition 1968]

[D1:306] Melchinger, Siegfried, *Theater der Gegenwart*, Fischer-Taschenbuch 118, Frankfurt am Main: S. Fischer Verlag, 1956, pp. 129-130. ['The Contemporary Theatre'. Includes Sg together with Ibsen, Wedekind, Gerhart Hauptmann, Shaw, and Pirandello, as one of the six figures responsible for creating a living drama for the modern stage]

[D1:307] Mezzanotte, Riccardo, Renato Simone, and R. Calzini, *Cronache di un grande teatro. Il Teatro Manzoni di Milano*, Milano: Edizioni BNL., 1952, pp. 151, 161. ['Chronicle of a Great Theatre: Milan's Manzoni Theatre'. Comments on productions by Renato Simone of *Fadren* and *Fröken Julie* at the Teatro Manzoni]

[D1:308] Miller, Anna Irene, 'Giants of the North', in *The Independent Theatre in Europe, 1887 to the Present*, New York: Long & Smith, 1932, pp. 7-11. [Couples Sg with Ibsen as a significant playwright in the development of the independent theatre movement. The staging of his plays at the Théâtre Libre, Freie Bühne, and elsewhere is subsequently the subject of brief comment in the course of a history of these theatres and their repertoire]

[D1:309] Miller, Nellie B[urget], *The Living Drama: Historical Development and Modern Movements Visualized*, New York and London: The Century Co., 1924. XX+437 pp.

[D1:310] Mittenzwei, Werner, *Gestaltung und Gestalten im modernen Drama. Zur Technik des Figurenaufbaus in der sozialistischen und spätbürgerlichen Dramatik*, Berlin und Weimar: Aufbau-Verlag, 1965, pp. 71-81. ['Structure and Characters in Modern Drama. On the Technique of Character Formation in Socialist and Late-Bourgeois Drama'. Presents Sg as the forerunner of psychological drama and a precursor of the theatre of the absurd. His central motif is the battle of the sexes while the protagonists of *Gustav Vasa* and *Erik XIV* are petty bourgeois in their meagre stature]

[D1:311] Moderwell, Hiram K., *The Theatre of To-Day*, London and New York: John Lane, 1914, pp. 200-203. [Regards Sg as a genius of great power who ploughed his own furrow and established not only a new dramatic type but a new domain of literary expression. Psychological condensation and a dialogue laden with introspective thought is a dramatic convention which Sg invented to carry his particular kind of play. The resulting sense of unreality prejudiced both reader and spectator against his plays]

[D1:312] Molander, Harald, *Harald Molander. Människan och konstnären, I. Ungdom och resor 1858-1886. Brev och anteckningar utgivna av Olof Molander*, Stockholm: Albert Bonniers Förlag, 1950. Illus. 366 pp. ['Harald Molander: Man and Artist, I. Youth and Travels 1858-1886. Letters and Memoranda Published by Olof Molander'. Includes some brief references to Sg and his works by the Swedish theatre director who staged important productions of *Mäster Olof* and *Erik XIV* (the première) in the 1890s, and with whom Sg corresponded over *Fadren* in 1887]

[D1:313] Molander, Olof, *Detta är jag...*, Stockholm: Albert Bonniers Förlag, 1961. 168 pp. ['This is Me'. The autobiography of one of the central figures in the development of the modern Swedish theatre, who was largely responsible for establishing an effective and distinctive performance style for Sg's post-Inferno plays in Sweden, one that contrasted strongly with Max Reinhardt's expressionist approach and complemented the critical approach of Martin Lamm where the works are read biographically in terms of Sg's life]

[D1:314] Möller, Kai, *Paul Wegener, sein Leben und sein Rollen*, Ein Buch von ihm und über ihn. Eingerichtet von Kai Möller, Hamburg: Rowohlt, 1954. Illus. 184 pp. ['Paul Wegener, His Life and Roles'. An account of Wegener's career and principal stage and film roles which included the Captain in *Fadren*, Edgar in *Dödsdansen*, the Justice in *Advent,* and Hummel in *Spöksonaten*]

[D1:315] Monteyne, Lode, *Kritische bijdragen over toneel*, Met een inleidend woord van Dr Maurits Sabbe, Antwerpen: Ruqouy, Delagarde & Van Uffelen, 1926. 258 pp. [Theatre reviews, including **E10:14**, *Kamraterna*; **E11:124**, *Fadren*; and **E12:199**, *Fröken Julie*]

[D1:316] Moses, Montrose Jonas, *Dramas of Modernism and their Forerunners*, edited with introductions and bibliographies by Montrose J. Moses; revised and supplemented with new plays by Oscar James Campbell, Boston: Little, Brown and Company, 1941. XVI+946 pp.

[D1:317] Moss, Leonard, *The Excess of Heroism in Tragic Drama*, Gainsville: University Press of Florida, 2000, pp. 85-99. [Includes a chapter entitled 'Nietzschean Dream Imagery in Strindberg and Kafka', which focuses on *Ett drömspel* as a play which 'might have been designed by Apollo working closely with Dionysus'. According to Moss, Sg presents 'the choric man's perplexity as outlined by the theory of flux, patented by Heraclitus and reinvented by Nietzsche'. Reproduces material from Moss's essay on *Ett drömspel*, **E41:117**]

[D1:318] Muller, Herbert J., *The Spirit of Tragedy*, New York: Alfred A. Knopf, 1956, pp. 274-283. [Discusses Sg in a section entitled 'Naturalistic Tragedy: Strindberg and Hauptmann'. Argues that, in its reduction of man to a mere creature of brute compulsion, the theory of naturalism is plainly disastrous for tragedy, and while there is a fierce concentration in Sg's dramatic technique as well as a greater profundity and originality in his work when compared with Ibsen's, who appears bourgeois by contrast, his Darwinian tragedy is not that of a great tragic dramatist. 'The neurotic Miss Julie is too mean to be a tragic figure; at most she stirs some pity – more than Sg intended, if we take him at his word.' Such characters are repulsive and, since everything he wrote was rooted in his own fixations, 'the chief objection to Sg's pathological dramas is that he himself was pathological']

[D1:319] Musil, Robert, *Theater. Kritisches und Theoretisches*, Hrsg. Marie-Louise Roth, Reinbek bei Hamburg: Rowohlt, 1965. 266 pp. [Theatre reviews, including **D3:131**, on *Fröken Julie* and *Fadren*; **E41:1079**, *Ett drömspel*; and **E51:678**, *Spöksonaten*]

[D1:320] Naeff, Top, *Dramatische Kroniek*, 4 vols, Amsterdam: Van Holkema & Warendorf, 1919-1923. [Theatre Reviews first published in *De Amsterdammer*, including **E11:451**, on *Fadren*, **E27:149**, *Brott och brott*, **E34:128**, *Påsk*, **E35:211** and **E35:1053**, *Dödsdansen*, **E41:310**, *Ett drömspel*, **E49:80**, *Oväder*, and **E53:105**, *Pelikanen*]

[D1:321] Naeff, Top, *Willem Royaards. De toneelkunstenaar in zijn tijd*, Haag: 's-Gravenhage: D. A. Daamen's Uitgeversmaatschappij, 1947. Illus. 368 pp. ['Willem Royaards: The Theatre Artist in His Time'. Discusses Royaards's productions of *Dödsdansen*, *Ett drömspel*, and *Brott och brott*, in which he also played the roles of Edgar and Maurice. Naeff also affirms the importance of Max Reinhardt's production of *Dödsdansen* on tour to Holland in 1916 for the development of a modern theatre in the Netherlands]

[D1:322] Naeseth, Henriette C. K., *The Swedish Theatre of Chicago, 1868-1950*, Rock Island, Illinois: Augustana Historical Society and Augustana College Library, 1951. Illus. XVI+390 pp.

[D1:323] Näslund, Erik, Elisabeth Sörenson, and Ingmar Bergman, red., *Kungliga dramatiska teater 1788-1988*, Hoganäs: Bra bok, 1988, Illus. 280 pp. [A popular illustrated history of Dramaten, which includes some reference to its major Sg productions by Olof Molander, Ingmar Bergman, and others]

[D1:324] Natanson, Wojciech, *Godzina teatru. Eseje o teatrze i literaturze*, Poznań: Wydawniczy Poznańskie, 1970. Illus. 277 pp. ['Contemporary Theatre. Essays on Theatre and Literature'. Includes a study of 'Strindberg and Modern Drama' entitled 'Cięrpie, więc jestem', pp. 255-261, in a collection of essays in Polish on the theatre and literature]

[D1:325] Natanson, Wojciech, *Karol Adwentowicz*, Warszawa, 1955. Illus. 49 pp. [A biographical study of the actor whose performances over four decades as the Captain in *Fadren* and Edgar in *Dödsdansen* did more than anything else to establish Sg's reputation as a dramatist in Poland]

[D1:326] Nedden, Otto C. A. zur, and Karl H. Ruppel, *Reclams Schauspielführer*, Stuttgart: Philipp Reclam Jun., 1963, pp. 603-616. ['Reclam's Theatre Guide'. Includes a short overview of Sg's career as a dramatist together with plot summaries of *Fadren, Fröken Julie, Till Damaskus, Ett drömspel, Påsk*, and *Spöksonaten*]

[D1:327] Nedden, Otto C. A. zur, *Drama und Dramaturgie im 20. Jahrhundert. Abhandlungen zum Theater und zur Theaterwissenschaft der Gegenwart*, 'Das Nationaltheater': Schriftenreihe des Theaterwissenschaftlichen Institute der Friedrich-Schiller Universität Jena 4, Würzburg: Konrad Triltsch Verlag, 1940. 137 pp. ['Drama and Dramaturgy in the 20th Century. Papers on the Modern Theatre and Theatre Studies'.

Includes six references to Sg, mainly in an essay on 'Das Drama der Nordländer und seine Bedeutung für das Theater des 20. Jahrhunderts' (The Drama of the Nordic Lands and their Importance for the Theatre of the 20th Century), pp. 17-42. 3rd edition, 1944]

[D1:328] Neudecker, Norbert, *Der "Weg" als strukturbildendes Element in Drama*, Deutsche Studien 11, Meisenheim: Hain, 1972. 211 pp. ['The "Path" as a Structural Element in Drama'. Discusses the notion of a journey, or pilgrimage, as a structuring device in drama with special reference to Goethe, Brecht, Sg, and Ibsen, the two last in a chapter entitled 'Skandinavisches Zwischenspiel: Ibsen und Strindberg', pp. 88-111. In Sg's case the discussion focuses mainly on *Till Damaskus* and *Stora landsvägen*]

[D1:329] Nicoll, Allardyce, *Dzieje dramatu, Od Ajschylosa do Anouilha*, 2 vols, Warszawa, 1962-65. [Polish edition of **D1:330**]

[D1:330] Nicoll, Allardyce, *World Drama. From Aeschylus to Anouilh*, London: George G. Harrap & Company Ltd., 1949, pp. 550-563. Illus. [Presents Sg as an intensely subjective dramatist who reduces the plot element, aiming in his naturalist dramas to present one unified action from start to finish, and stressing the passions and not the intrigue. His later history plays, which are 'among the most powerful plays of the kind produced in modern times', reveal the power of his dramatic conceptions and his technical mastery while the plays he wrote following the Inferno crisis may conveniently be divided into 'realistic' works, which here includes *Advent*, *Påsk*, *Oväder*, and *Brända tomten*, and 'dream' plays, in which Sg forges far ahead of Ibsen in vision and concept and reveals a power that is barely matched elsewhere in the 19th-Century theatre. 'There is no author whose range is wider or more provocative. In him the entire history of the stage from 1800 to the present day is epitomized']

[D1:331] Niemi, Irmeli, *Nykydraaman ihmiskuva. Analyyseja 1900-luvun eurooppalaisista näytelmistä*, Helsinki: Tammi, 1969. 253 pp. ['The Portrayal of Human Life in Modern Drama. Analyses of European Drama in the 20th Century'. A history of modern drama which argues that Sg is hardly surpassed in subjectivity by any other dramatist of this century. Discusses *Ett drömspel*, *Dödsdansen*, and *Spöksonaten*]

[D1:332] Nordensvan, Georg, *Svensk teater och svenska skådespelare. Från Gustav III till våra dagar*, 2 vols, Stockholm: Albert Bonniers Förlag, 1917-18, Vol. 2, 1842-1918. Illus. 504 pp. ['Swedish Theater and Swedish Actors. From Gustav III to Our Time'. Comments on early Swedish productions of many of Sg's plays, including *I Rom*, *Mäster Olof*, *Gillets hemlighet*, *Lycko-Pers resa*, *Fordringsägare*, *Till Damaskus*, *Gustav Vasa*, *Brott och brott*, *Påsk*, and the Chamber Plays]

[D1:333] Nygaard, Jon, *Teatrets historie i Europa*, 3 vols, [Norway]: Spillerom, 1992, Vol. 2, pp. 190-191. ['The History of European Theatre'. Discusses Sg's form of naturalism]

[D1:334] Nygaard, Jon, *Teatrets historie i Europa*, 3 vols, [Norway]: Spillerom, 1993, Vol. 3, pp. 59-61. ['The History of European Theatre'. Discusses Sg's dreamplay style and the Chamber Plays]

[D1:335] Oborski, Stanisław Marczak, *Życie teatralne w latach 1944-1964: kierunki rozwojowe*, Warszawa: Panstwowy Wydawniczy Naukowe, 1968. Illus. 306 pp. [A study of the Polish theatre in the period immediately after the Second World War which gives only brief consideration to Sg's place and influence during a period when the official doctrine of socialist realism was often vigorously promoted]

[D1:336] Obraztsova, A. G., '[*Bernard Shaw and the European Theatre*]', Moscow: Nauka, 1974, p. 16. [Comments on the principles informing Sg's Intimate Theatre and its conception of stage character. E.1069]

[D1:337] Ödeen, Mats, *Dramatiskt berättande. Om konsten att strukturera ett drama*, Stockholm: Carlssons, 1988. 341 pp. ['Dramatic Narration. On the Art of Dramatic Structure'. A dramaturgical handbook, with examples drawn from Sg's plays among many others]

[D1:338] Oehm, Heidemarie, *Subjektivität und Gattungsform im Expressionismus*, München: Fink Verlag, 1993. 294 pp. ['Subjectivity and Generic Form in Expressionism'. Discusses Sg's influence on the form of German expressionist Station Drama and the technique of presenting subjective experience on stage, pp. 129-137]

[D1:339] Olsoni, Eric, *Från Strindberg till Anouilh. Hundra teateraftnar i Helsingfors*, Helsingfors: Söderström & C:o Förlags AB., 1964. Illus. 320 pp. ['From Strindberg to Anouilh. One Hundred Evenings in the Theatres of Helsinki'. Theatre reviews, including **E11:606**, *Fadren*, **E25:287**, *Till Damaskus*, **E27:282**, *Brott och brott*, **E29:190**, *Gustav Vasa*, **E30:375**, *Erik XIV*, **E35:1066**, *Dödsdansen*, **E35:1067**, *Dödsdansen*, **E36:83**, *Kronbruden*, **E38:163**, *Karl XII*, **E41:1086**, *Ett drömspel*, and **E42:164**, *Gustav III*]

[D1:340] Orr, John, *Tragic Drama and Modern Society*, Basingstoke: Macmillan, 1981, pp. 50-53. [Argues that the profound thematic differences between the realist drama of Ibsen and the more reactionary Sg can be indirectly related to the different histories of Norway and Sweden. In *Fröken Julie*, Sg tries to subordinate social to sexual hierarchy while his switch to Expressionism obscured the limitations of his subjective approach, and led him to a pathological vision of the world]

[D1:341] Österling, Anders, *Tio års teater 1925-1935*, Stockholm: Albert Bonniers Förlag, 1936. 303 pp. ['Ten Years of Theatre, 1925-1935'. Theatre reviews, including **E26:68**, *Advent*, **E25:266**, *Till Damaskus*, and **E41:364**, *Ett drömspel*]

[D1:342] Palmer, D[avid] J., 'Drama', in C. B. Cox and A. E. Dyson, eds, *The Twentieth-Century Mind: History, Ideas, and Literature in Britain*, 3 vols, London: Oxford University Press, 1972, Vol. 1, pp. 456-460. [Sg's plays are the product of a mind too urgently involved in the modern moment of crisis, a sensibility too irreparably damaged by its suffering, for the achievement of a proper artistic poise and calm. Nevertheless, he constantly extended the expressive resources of the dramatic medium into new and unexplored territories, and both *Ett drömspel* and *Spöksonaten* continue the freely-moving rhythms typical of earlier works like *Fadren* and *Fröken Julie*]

[D1:343] Palmier, Jean-Michel, *L'Expressionisme et les arts, 2: Peinture-Théatre-Cinéma*, Paris: Payot, 1980, pp. 13-22. Illus. ['Expressionism and the Arts. 2. Painting-Theatre-Cinema'. Regards Sg's role as decisive for the change in perspective from naturalism to expressionism in the theatre, just as Munch was in painting. His comments on character in the Preface to *Fröken Julie* already foreshadow the later movement, and his post-Inferno plays abound with the kind of morbid elements that so fascinated his German successors. The Station Drama *Till Damaskus*, which resembles Munch's painting *The Scream*, perhaps comes closest to the often circular Ich-dramas of Georg Kaiser and Ernst Toller. Palmier argues that expressionist drama is inconceivable without the plays of Sg and their realisation on stage by Max Reinhardt]

[D1:344] Pandolfi, Vito, *Il teatro expressionista tedesco*, Bologna: Ugo Guanda editore, 1956, pp. v-xvi. ['German Expressionist Theatre'. Includes comments on Sg's role as a precursor of German expressionism]

[D1:345] Pardieri, Giuseppi, *Ermete Zacconi*, Bologna: Cappelli, 1960. Illus. 154 pp. [A theatrical biography of the actor manager (1857-1948) whose performances as the Captain in *Fadren* established Sg as a presence in the Italian theatre]

[D1:346] Patterson, Michael, *The Revolution in German Theatre 1900-1933*, London: Routledge, 1981. XXX+232 pp. [Notes the popularity of Sg in the years immediately preceding the First World War but wrongly attributes early productions of his plays to Edward Gordon Craig]

[D1:347] Perry, C[larence] A[rthur], *The Work of the Little Theatres: The Groups They Include, The Plays They Produce, Their Tournaments, and the Handbooks They Use*, New York: Russell Sage Foundation, 1933. 228 pp. [Sees in Sg a significant inspiration to the little theatre movement, pp. 71, 92, 94, 100, 137]

[D1:348] Peter, John, *Vladimir's Carrot: Modern Drama and the Modern Imagination*, London: André Deutsch, 1987. 372 pp. [Discusses *Fadren*, *Kamraterna*, *Fröken Julie*, *Till Damaskus*, *Ett drömspel*, and *Spöksonaten*, pp. 253-255, 281-282, 303-314, 336-341, in relation to Peter's central thesis that modern drama may be divided into 'open' forms, which move in a world that they share with that of their audience and tell a story, and more static, 'closed' compositions which, like Kafka's parables or Beckett's plays, leave nothing behind except the experience we have of them. For Peter, Sg's theatre, with its psychotic characters and the repetitive obsessions of the later plays that are manifest in their circular form as well as their content, is much closer to the latter than Ibsen's *Ghosts*. American edition published by the University of Chicago Press, 1987]

[D1:349] Petzet, Wolfgang, *Die Münchener Kammerspiele 1911-1972*, München-Wien-Basel: Kurt Desch Verlag, 1973. Illus. 630 pp. ['The Munich Kammerspiele 1911-1972'. Discusses the so-called 'Strindberg-Zyclus' (Sg Cycle) at the Munich Kammerspiele, where *Fröken Julie*, *Den starkare*, *Leka med elden*, *Fordringsägare*, *Kamraterna*, *Brott och brott*, *Pelikanen*, and *Spöksonaten* were all performed on successive evenings between 29 April and 3 June 1915]

[D1:350] Phelps, William Lyon, *Essays on Modern Dramatists*, New York: The Macmillan Company, 1926. 278 pp.

[D1:351] Polgar, Alfred, 'Strindberg', in *Ja und Nein. Darstellungen von Darstellungen*, Hrsg. von Wolfgang Drews, Reinbek bei Hamburg: Rowohlt, 1956, pp. 40-47. [Includes reviews of *Fröken Julie*, **E12:496**, and *Till Damaskus*, **E25:214**, together with comments on *Pelikanen* and Maria Orska as Berta in *Kamraterna*, p. 148]

[D1:352] Polgar, Alfred, *Kleine Schriften*, Hrsg. von Marcel Reich-Ranicki in Zusammenarbeit mit Ulrich Weinzierl, Band 5, 'Theater I', Reinbek bei Hamburg: Rowohlt Verlag, 1985. [XV]+[624] pp. [Theatre reviews, including, **E10:78**, *Kamraterna*, **E12:495**, *Fröken Julie*, **E19:35**, *Debet och kredit*, **E25:212**, *Till Damaskus*, **E27:286**, *Brott och brott*, **E30:379**, *Erik XIV*, **E35:231**, *Dödsdansen*, **E40:199**, *Kristina*, **E41:1092**, *Ett drömspel*, **E49:209**, *Oväder*, and **E53:377**, *Pelikanen*]

[D1:353] Polgar, Alfred, 'Strindberg', in *Kritisches Lesebuch*, Berlin, 1926, pp. 149-171. [Theatre reviews, including **E10:77**, *Kamraterna*, **E12:497**, *Fröken Julie*, **E25:213**, *Till Damaskus*,

E27:285, *Brott och brott*, **E30:380**, *Erik XIV*, **E35:232**, *Dödsdansen*, **E40:200**, *Kristina*, **E41:1093**, *Ett drömspel*, **E49:210**, *Oväder*, and **E53:378**, *Pelikanen*]

[D1:354] Pollak, Mimi, *Teaterlek. Memoarer*, Stockholm: Askild & Kärnekull, 1977. Illus. 242 pp. ['Theatre Games. Memoirs'. The autobiography of the first woman to direct at Dramaten with eleven references to Sg]

[D1:355] Pollow, Helmut, *Zur Dialektik von Kunst- und Geschichtesbewusstein: Interpretations- und Rezeptionserfahrungen unserer Bühnen mit Stücken von Wedekind, Strindberg, Kaiser, Wolf, Horvath und J. R. Becker*, Berlin: Verband der Theaterschaffenden der DDR, 1978. 111 pp.

[D1:356] Popov, Iva, *Minaloto na balgariskia teatar*, Vol. 5, Sofia, 1960, pp. 259-260. ['A History of the Bulgarian Theatre', including a single comment on Sg]

[D1:357] Poupeye, Camille, 'Le Théâtre Suédois. Auguste Strindberg', in *Les Dramaturges Exotiques*, Nouvelle série, Bruxelles: Editions de la Renaissance D'Occident, 1926, pp. 57-101. [Uses *Tjänstekvinnans son* and Sg's other autobiographical fictions to outline the life of a dramatist whose work has been slow in gaining acceptance in France, and then only by a minority. Poupeye surveys his career as a dramatist from *Den fredlöse* to *Stora landsvägen*, dwelling principally on *Fadren, Fröken Julie, Fordringsägare, Den starkare, Bandet, Brott och brott,* and *Dödsdansen,* but commenting on many other plays. Of the post-Inferno dramas, *Svanevit, Kronbruden, Ett drömspel*, and *Spöksonaten* compel greatest attention with comments on Sg's misanthropy, as well as the misogyny and kaleidoscopic incoherence of those late works in which he nevertheless enlarges the domain of the theatre to include the world of dreams. Although of limited value as criticism, Poupeye provides an unusually detailed account of Sg as a dramatist for the period where historical accounts in French are concerned, and he is also unusually sympathetic to the later plays. Thus, he applauds Sg's formidable powers of suggestion, for example in *Spöksonaten* where 'the reader [sic] is gripped from the outset']

[D1:358] Prince, Félix, *André Antoine et le renouveau du théâtre hollondais 1880-1900*, Amsterdam: Vermeulen, 1941, pp. 56-58. ['André Antoine and the Renewal of the Dutch Theatre, 1880-1900'. Comments on Antoine's production of *Fröken Julie*, which was given only a private press performance on its tour of Holland because of Dutch censorship]

[D1:359] Pruner, Francis, *Le Théâtre Libre d'Antoine: 1. Le Répertoire étranger*, Paris: Lettres Modernes, 1958, pp. 109-121. [Sg is discussed briefly as a Nietzschean in the wake of 'L'Ibsénisme' of the immediately preceding years. Pruner focuses mainly on Antoine's staging of *Fröken Julie* but also refers to *Fadren* and *Spöksonaten*, and confirms this ideological reading with quotations from *Tjänstekvinnans son* and the Preface to *Fröken Julie*. He also compares Sg's approach to characterisation with the precepts of Zola and Taine]

[D1:360] Quarnström, Ingrid, *Svensk teater i Finland: I. Rikssvensk teater*, Helsingfors: Holger Schildts Förlag, 1946. Illus. 301 pp. ['Swedish Theatre in Finland: I. Theatre from Sweden'. Provides data on early performances of Sg's plays in Finland prior to 1894, including Harald Molander's regime at Svenska Teatern in Helsinki between 1886 and 1893, *Fröken Julie* at the Vasa Theatre, directed by Konni Wetzer, and a series of Sg productions by his successor, Gustaf Nessler]

[D1:361] Quarnström, Ingrid, *Svensk teater i Finland: II. Finlandssvensk teater*, Helsingfors: Holger Schildts Förlag, 1947. Illus. 317 pp. ['Swedish Theatre in Finland: II. 'Finland-Swedish Theatre'. Provides data concerning performances of Sg's plays in post-1894 Finland, in both Helsinki and the provinces]

[D1:362] Quinn, Arthur H., *A History of American Drama from the Civil War to the Present Day*, London: Harper and Brothers, 1936, pp. 170, 181.

[D1:363] Ranft, Albert, *Min Repertoir 1892-1921*, Stockholm: P. A. Norstedt & Söners Förlag, 1921, 96 pp. [A largely bibliographical account of the repertoire of the theatres owned by Ranft in Stockholm during a significant part of Sg's career, where his work occasionally featured]

[D1:364] Reckert, Blandine M., *et al.*, ed., *A Library of Literary Criticism*, Vol. 2, 'Major Modern Dramatists', New York: The Ungar Publishing Company, 1986, pp. 32-56. [Reprints short extracts from letters, commentaries, books, and critical essays on Sg and his plays by Emile Zola, Georg Brandes, Gerhart Hauptmann, Eugene O'Neill, Pär Lagerkvist, Antonin Artaud, Karl Jaspers, James Huneker, Ashley Dukes, Arthur Henderson, Frank Wadleigh Lewisohn, Carl E. W. Dahlström, Barrett H. Clark, Eric Bentley, John Gassner, Maurice Gravier, Raymond Williams, Joseph Wood Krutch, Walter Sokel, Alrik Gustafson, George Steiner, Børge Gedsø Madsen, Walter Johnson, Maurice Valency, Robert Brustein, Göran Lindström, Gunnar Ollén, Morris Freedman, Carl-Olof Gierow, Birgitta Steene, Gunnar Brandell, Richard Gilman, John Ward, Harry G. Carlson, and Evert Sprinchorn]

[D1:365] Reinert, Otto, ed., *Drama, An Introductory Anthology*, Boston: Little, Brown, 1961. XXVIII+889 pp. [Comments on *Spöksonaten* and *Fröken Julie*, pp. 461-465]

[D1:366] Reinhardt, Gottfried, *The Genius: A Memoir of Max Reinhardt by His Son*, New York: Alfred A. Knopf, 1979, pp. 95-97. [An anecdotal account of 'the possum-like guile and quivering neurasthenia' displayed by Sg on his one and only, largely apocryphal, 'meeting' with Reinhardt. If Sg's plays 'had pumped fresh blood into Reinhardt's reformation of the theatre', Reinhardt was 'the Strindberg pioneer', and decisive in establishing his European reputation as a dramatist]

[D1:367] Reinhardt, Gottfried, *Der Liebhaber. Erinnerungen seines Sohnes*, München & Zürich: Droemer Knaur, 1973, pp. 76-83. [See **D1:366**]

[D1:368] Reinhardt, Max, *Briefe, Reden, Aufsätze, Interviews, Gespräche, Auszüge aus Regiebüchern*, Hrsg. von Hugo Fetting, Berlin: Henschelverlag Kunst und Gesellschaft, 1974. [528] pp. [Sg and his plays (*Fröken Julie, Näktergalen i Wittenberg, Pelikanen, Brott och brott, Dödsdansen, Ett drömspel*, and *Oväder* are recurring points of reference in this collection of Reinhardt's letters, talks, essays, and interviews]

[D1:369] Reinhardt, Max, *Ich bin nichts als ein Theatermann, Schriften: Briefe, Reden, Aufsätze, Interviews, Gespräche, Auszüge aus Regiebüchern*, Hrsg. von Hugo Fetting, Berlin: Henschelverlag Kunst und Gesellschaft, 1974. [618] pp. [Rpr. of **D1:368**]

[D1:370] Richardson, Gunnar, *Oscarisk teaterpolitik. De kungliga teatrarnas omvandling från hovinstitution till statliga aktiebolag*, Studia historica Gothoburgensis 5, Göteborg: Akademiförlaget, 1966. 156 pp. [A study of the transformation of Dramaten from a court theatre into a state-owned company, a change that was largely accomplished during Sg's lifetime]

[D1:371] Richter, Renate, *Das Deutsche Künstler-Theater unter Victor Barnowsky (1915-1924): eine Untersuchung unter Berücksichtigung der zeitgenössischen Kritik*, Theater und Drama 33, Berlin: Colloquium Verlag, 1970. Illus. 141 pp. ['The German Artistic Theatre under Victor Barnowsky (1915-1924): A Study Based on Contemporary Criticism'. Includes nothing of relevance regarding Barnowsky's major Sg productions]

[D1:372] Ringby, Per, *Författerens dröm på scenen. Harald Molanders regi och författarskap*, Acta Universitatis Umensis. Umeå Studies in the Humanities 84, Stockholm: Almqvist & Wicksell International, 1987. Illus. 476 pp. ['The Author's Dream on Stage. Harald Molander as Director and Writer'. A study of the Swedish author and theatre director Harald Molander (1858-1900). Ringby discusses his generally well-received pictorial staging of *Mäster Olof* in Helsinki (1897) as well as the premières of *Gustav Vasa* and *Erik XIV*, which he directed in Stockholm in 1899. He applies Patrice Pavis's concept of a *mise en scène* semiology in an attempt to achieve a dynamic image of the production of meaning in the realisation of the play text on stage, particularly in Molander's staging of Gerhart Hauptmann's *Die Weber*, which Ringby regards as his greatest achievement. English summary. Doctoral dissertation]

[D1:373] Ringdal, Nils Johan, *Nationaltheatrets historie 1899-1999*, Oslo: Gyldendal, 2000. Illus. 416 pp. ['The History of the National Theatre, 1899-1999'. Documents the modest place accorded Sg's plays, including *Mäster Olof*, *Brott och brott*, *Till Damaskus*, and *Oväder*, in the repertoire of the Norwegian National Theatre]

[D1:374] Ritchie, J. M., *German Expressionist Drama*, Boston: Twayne, 1976, pp. 24-26. [Maintains that, in seeking to move beyond the world of appearances and express an inner reality, both Sg's paintings and plays like *Till Damaskus* and *Ett drömspel* already employ the essence of the expressionist method]

[D1:375] Ritzu, Merete Kjøller, ed., *La Didascalia nella letteratura teatrale scandinava: Testo drammatico e sintesi scenica*, Atti del VII Convegno Italiano di Studi Scandinavi, Firenze 21-22-23 maggio 1987, Firenze: Bulzoni Editore, 1987. Illus. 256 pp. ['Stage Directions in the Theatrical Literature of Scandinavia: Dramatic Text and Stage Synthesis'. The proceedings of the 7th Italian Conference of Scandinavian Studies, held in Florence 21-23 May 1986. Includes **C4:22**: Anna Maria Segala, 'Tra testo apparente e testo latente: le didascalie nella *Notte delle Tribadi* (1) di Per Olov Enquist'; **D2:946**: Andrea Martini, 'Strindberg e la tentazione visionaria: un itinerario teatrale verso il cinema'; **D2:1035**: Birgitta Ottosson Pinna, 'Le "case viventi" di Strindberg'; **D2:1052**: Renzo Pavese, 'Istruzioni e "suggerimenti" scenici di Strindberg ad un attore'; **D2:1054**: Franco Perrelli, 'Il teatro di Asmodeo. Pessimismo e misticismo nella struttura e nella didascalia del dramma strindberghiano'; and **D2:1245**: Egil Törnqvist, 'Le didascalie di Strindberg in scena']

[D1:376] Roberts, Patrick, *The Psychology of Tragic Drama*, London: Routledge & Kegan Paul, 1975, pp. 54-68. [Like Freud, whose work he seems not to have known, Sg taps into primitive sources of violent energy that civilised man is supposed to have outgrown. He has an uncanny understanding of the satisfaction that can be obtained in the infliction and suffering of pain, and contrives to detach himself just enough from his own violent conflicts to write effective drama. Both *Fadren* and *Fröken Julie* demonstrate how brilliantly he turned his own neurotic illness to account in his art, demonstrating an uncannily accurate knowledge of the primitive constituents of the psyche and a remarkable insight into infantile sexuality and sexual fantasy. 'After sixty-odd years of modern drama, there has been no one to surpass Sg in intimate understanding of "the psychological process", especially in the vital sphere of the relations between the sexes']

[**D1:377**] Robichez, Jacques, *Le Symbolisme au théâtre: Lugné-Poe et les débuts de L'Œuvre*, Paris: L'Arche, 1957, pp. 281-283. ['Symbolism in the Theatre. Lugné-Poe and the First Performances at L'Œuvre'. Describes Sg's relations with Aurélien Lugné-Poe, who staged the French premières of *Fordringsägare* and *Fadren* at the Théâtre de l'Œuvre in 1894. In spite of the esteem these productions brought him, Sg failed to capitalise on the opportunity, and it was Bjørnson and Ibsen whose names were subsequently associated most immediately with Lugné-Poe's theatre]

[**D1:378**] Rock, Freddie [Rokem], *Tradition och förnyelse. Svensk dramatik och teater från 1914-1922*, Stockholm: Akademilitteratur, 1977. pp. 27-34. ['Tradition and Renewal. Swedish Drama and Theatre from 1914 to 1922'. Discusses Sg in performance in Sweden between 1914 and 1922, when positions adopted during the Sg Feud continued to influence the reception of his plays even after his death in 1912. Nevertheless, by 1922 a more balanced view of his life and work was emerging, particularly in response to the Chamber Plays, which had originally been received with incomprehension or hostility. Pär Lagerkvist's essay on 'Modern Drama', **D1:604**, was symptomatic of this development, even though reviews of Max Reinhardt's productions of the later plays still regarded them as pathological or abnormal. They are consequently a touchstone of what was possible in Swedish theatre at the time]

[**D1:379**] Rønneberg, Anton, *Nationalteatret gjennom femti år*, Oslo: Gyldendal Norsk Forlag, 1949. Illus. 514 pp. ['The National Theatre over Forty Years'. Surveys the repertoire of the Norwegian National Theatre, with comments on its own, and touring, productions of Sg's plays]

[**D1:380**] Rønneberg, Anton, *Nationalteatret 1949-1974*, Oslo: Gyldendal Norsk Forlag, 1974. Illus. 339 pp. ['The National Theatre, 1949-1974'. Continues the survey of the repertoire of the Norwegian National Theatre in **D1:379**]

[**D1:381**] Rosenberg, Tiina, *En regissörs estetik. Ludvig Josephson och den tidiga teaterregin*, Stockholm: Stiftelsen för utgivning av teatervetenskapliga studier, 1993. Illus. 211 pp. ['The Aesthetic Program of a Director. Ludvig Josephson and Early Theatrical Direction'. Focuses on the years 1850-1899 and includes an analysis of Josephson's staging of the première of *Mäster Olof* and the aesthetic which underlay it, pp. 146-164. English summary, pp. 176-180]

[**D1:382**] — Austin, John, *Scandinavian Studies* (Provo), 67:4 (1995), 556-558.

[**D1:383**] — Hägglund, Kent, *entré* (Norsborg), 20:3 (1993), 103-104.

[**D1:384**] Rosslyn, Felicity, *Tragic Plots: A New Reading from Aeschylus to Lorca*, Studies in European Cultural Transition 9, Aldershot: Ashgate Publishing Limited, 2000, pp. 173-195. [Couples Sg with Ibsen in an examination of four plays in which women's emancipation is the social shock that re-animates the tragic theatre in the bourgeois 19th Century. Sg is represented by *Fadren*]

[**D1:385**] Rostotskii, B. I., ed., V. E. Meierkhol'd, *Stat'i. Pis'ma. Rechi. Besedy: v dvukh tomakh*, 2 vols, Moscow: Iskusstvo, 1968. [Provides information on Meyerhold's productions of Sg, including *Fröken Julie* and *Brott och brott*, Vol. 1, p. 234, Vol. 2, pp. 596-597, 601. E.1025]

[D1:386] Rouché, Jacques, *L'Art théâtrale moderne*, Nouv. ed., Paris: Blond et Gay, 1924. ['Modern Theatrical Art'. 1st edition, 1910]

[D1:387] Ruberti, Guido, *Il Teatro contemporaneo in Europa*, 2 vols, Bologna: L. Capelli, 1920-21. ['Contemporary European Theatre'. Discusses Sg in Volume Two, pp. 80-88]

[D1:388] Rühle, Günther, *Theater für die Republik 1917-1933 im Spiegel der Kritik*, Frankfurt am Main: S. Fischer Verlag, 1967. [1264] pp. ['Theatre for the Republic, 1917-1933, as Reflected in Contemporary Criticism'. An extensive anthology of performance reviews by a range of critics in which Sg figures prominently, both as a subject and a point of reference, during a period when he made an extraordinary impact on the German theatre. See **E12:493** on *Fröken Julie*, **E26:45, E26:47,** and **E26:57,** *Advent*, **E27:170**, *Brott och brott*, **E40:86**, *Kristina*, and **E41:281, E41:283**, and **E41:290**, *Ett drömspel*]

[D1:389] Rydell, Gerda, *Adertonhundratalets historiska skådespel i Sverige före Strindberg*, Stockholm: P. A. Nordstedt & Söners Förlag, 1928. 312 pp. ['The 19th-Century History Play in Sweden before Strindberg'. Discusses the Swedish history play prior to *Mäster Olof*]

[D1:390] Saloni, J[anina] Kulczycka, ed., *Ku czci Karola Adwentowicza w 55-lecie pracy teatralnej*, Łódź-Warszawa, 1950. ['In Celebration of Karol Adwentowicz's 55 Years on the Stage'. Includes accounts his performances as the Captain in *Fadren* and Edgar in *Dödsdansen*]

[D1:391] Salten, Felix [Pseudonym of Sigmund Salzmann], *Schauen und Spielen. Studien zur Kritik des modernen Theaters*, 2 vols, Leipzig: Wiener literarische Anstalt, 1921. [Theatre reviews, including **E9:42**, *Herr Bengts hustru*, **E10:43**, *Kamraterna*, and **E34:50**, *Påsk*]

[D1:392] Sarrazac, Jean-Pierre, *Théâtres intimes*, Arles: Actes sud, 1989. 166 pp. [Includes several psychoanalytical readings of Sg as a dramatist, notably of *Till Damaskus*]

[D1:393] Sayler, Oliver M., *Max Reinhardt and his Theatre*, Translated from the German by Mariele S. Gudernatsch and Others, New York: Brentano's, 1924. Illus. XI+381 pp. [Contains numerous passing references to Sg, but no in-depth discussion of Reinhardt's Sg productions]

[D1:394] Sayler, Oliver M., *Max Reinhardt and his Theatre*, Translated from the German by Mariele S. Gudernatsch and Others, New York & London: Benjamin Blom, 1968. Illus. XI+381 pp. [Rpr. of **D1:393**]

[D1:395] Schiller, Harald, and Arne Lindenbaum, *En bok om Oscar Winge*, Stockholm: Victor Pettersons Bokindustriaktiebolag, 1944. Illus. 193 pp. ['A Book about Oscar Winge'. Surveys Winge's early career as an actor and director in *Till Damaskus*, pp. 55-56, *Karl XII*, pp. 48-49, Axel in *Kamraterna* and *Hemsöborna*, pp. 45-47, *Dödsdansen* and *Påsk*, pp. 36-37, as well as *Gillets hemlighet, Paria, Fordringsägare*, and *Inför döden*. The volume also documents discussions concerning his taking over the Intimate Theatre from Sg and August Falck in 1910]

[D1:396] Schiller, Harald, *Hundra nya premiärer på Hippodromteatern*, Malmö: Röhrs Boktryckeri, 1938. Illus. XV+135 pp. [The introduction discusses Oscar Winge's contacts with Sg when the latter wanted him to take over the Intimate Theatre, but the volume includes no reviews of Sg's plays in performance]

[D1:397] Schiller, Harald, *Thalia i Malmö och andra essayer*, Malmö: Sydsvenska Dagbladets Aktiebolag, 1948. Illus. [236] pp. ['Thalia in Malmö and Other Essays'. Theatre reviews and essays, including **B1:51**: 'Strindbergsforskning'; **B3:381**: 'Carl G. Laurin som teaterkritiker'; **D1:673**: 'Om teaterkritiken och teaterkritikerna'; **E8:90**, *Lycko-Pers resa*; **E41:162**; *Ett drömspel*; and **J:416** on Sg's correspondence]

[D1:398] Schings, Dietmar, *Über die Bedeutung der Rolle als Medium der Entpersonalisierung im Theater des XX. Jahrhunderts: Strindberg, Pirandello, Brecht, Ionesco*, München, Schön Verlag, 1969. 125 pp. ['Concerning the Importance of Roles as a Method of De-Personalisation in 20th-Century Theatre']

[D1:399] Schley, Gernot, *Die Freie Bühne in Berlin. Der Vorläufer der Volksbühnenbewegung. Ein Beitrag zur Theatergeschichte in Deutschland*, Berlin: Baude & Spener, 1967, pp. 96-99. ['The Berlin Freie Bühne. The Forerunner of the Volksbühne Movement. A Contribution to Theatre History in Germany'. An historical account of the Freie Bühne, including the German première of *Fröken Julie* in 1892, which departed from Sg's directions and divided the play into two acts]

[D1:400] Schneider, Manfred, *Der Expressionismus im Drama*, Stuttgart: Verlag von Julius Hoffmann, 1920. 32 pp. ['Expressionism in Drama'. Notes Sg's significance for the development of German expressionist theatre]

[D1:401] Schnetz, Diemut, *Der moderne Einakter. Eine poetologische Untersuchung*, Bern und München: Francke Verlag, 1967. 244 pp. ['The Modern One-Acter'. Frequent reference throughout to *Den starkare*, *Bandet*, *Fröken Julie*, *Fordringsägare* and *Leka med elden* in the course of an influential theoretical and dramaturgical discussion of the nature of the one-act play as a distinct and characteristic modern genre, one that establishes itself in the wake of Sg's theoretical debut in 1889 with 'On Modern Drama and Modern Theatre']

[D1:402] Schultes, Paul, *Expressionistische Regie*, Köln: Hundt Verlag, 1981. XI+609 pp. [Includes analyses of Ludwig Bergner's production of *Advent* in 1919 and Karlheinz Martin's staging of *Brända tomten* in 1920, both at the Kammerspiele des Deutsches Theater, Berlin]

[D1:403] Schumacher, Ernst, *Berliner Kritiken. Ein Theater-Dezennium 1964-1974*, 4 Bde, Berlin: Henschelverlag Kunst und Gesellschaft, 1975-86. ['Berlin Criticism. A Decade of Theatre, 1964-1974'. Theatre reviews written for the *Berliner Zeitung*, Vols 1-2, 1964-1974, Vol. 3, 1974-79, Vol. 4, 1979-1984]

[D1:404] Schumacher, Ernst, *Theater der Zeit – Zeit des Theaters. Thalia in den Fünfzigern*, [München]: Dobbeck Verlag, 1960. Illus. 312 pp.

[D1:405] Schwarz, Alfred, *From Büchner to Beckett: Dramatic Theory and the Modes of Tragic Drama*, Athens, Ohio: Ohio University Press, 1978, pp. 33-38, 123-132, 141-150. [Sg is discussed mainly with reference to *Fadren* but also *Fröken Julie*, *Bandet*, and *Dödsdansen*. Unlike Zola, Sg was aware that a thorough-going revision of dramatic method was required, and his poetics of naturalism, as outlined in the Preface to *Fröken Julie*, stresses the important mid-century shift 'from a historical and moral consciousness of human existence to a primarily sociological, psychological, and even biological interest.... The limitation of these plays is that they represent, not an action which defines the fate of the characters, but rather a series of ingeniously varied acts of mutilation, like a large canvas depicting damned souls tormenting each other without reprieve.' In *Fröken Julie*, where the antagonist is society itself, we witness not merely the psychological disintegration of an individual, but her destruction by the punitive force of the law, which does not tolerate the errant or defective personality. The play is thus comparable to Tennessee Williams's *A Streetcar Named Desire*, although greatly superior]

[D1:406] Schyberg, Frederik, *Ti Aars Teater (1929-1939)*, København: Gyldendalske Boghandel Nordisk Forlag, 1939. 226 pp.+10 pp. plates. ['Ten Years' Theatre, 1929-1939'. Theatre reviews, including **E31:94**, on *Gustav Adolf*, **E35:1093**, *Dödsdansen*, and **E41:366**, *Ett drömspel*]

[D1:407] Schyberg, Fredrik, *Teater i Krig: 1939-1948*, København, 1948. Illus. 358 pp. ['Theatre in Wartime: 1929-1948'. Includes reviews of the three plays by Sg performed in Copenhagen during the Second World War: *Ett drömspel* (1940), *Fröken Julie* (1941), and *Svanevit* (1942)]

[D1:408] Segel, Harold B., *Turn-of-the-Century Cabaret*, New York: Columbia University Press, 1987, pp. xxv-xxvii. [Places Frida Strindberg's cabaret, The Cave of the Golden Calf, in London's Regent Street within the context of the history of cabaret in the years immediately preceding the First World War. Assumes that her interest in this form of theatre derived from her relationship with Frank Wedekind rather than from Sg, who in fact shared his interest in Parisian cabaret with her during the mid-1890s]

[D1:409] Serreau, Geneviève, *Histoire du "nouveau théâtre"*, Paris: Éditions Gallimard, 1966, pp. 66-71. ['History of the "New Theatre"'. With his combination of poetry and realism, Sg was an inspiration to dramatists writing in French post-1945: 'Sg is one of the most attuned to this post-war period's search for a truth both poetic and realist, to its ways, and to its freedom in relation to theatrical forms'. Primarily concerned with Sg's influence on the early plays of Arthur Adamov]

[D1:410] Sharypkin, D[mitrii] M[ikhailovich], '[The Art of Drama in Norway and Sweden]', in *Istoriia zapadno-evropeiskogo teatra*, Vol. 5, Moscow, 1970, pp. 423-446. [Discusses Sg's Intimate Theatre, the stage history of his plays in Sweden, and his ideas about drama and the theatre in a standard *History of the European Theatre*, pp. 437-445. E.1043]

[D1:411] Siedhoff, Thomas, *Das Neue Theater in Frankfurt am Main 1911-135. Versuch der systematischen Würdigung eines Theater betriebs*, Studien zur Frankfurter Geschichte 19, Frankfurt am Main: Verlag Waldemar Kramer, 1985. 509 pp. ['The New Theatre in Frankfurt am Main, 1911-35. An Attempt at a Systematic Evaluation of a Working Theatre'. Discusses the staging of plays by Scandinavian authors pp. 88-96, and includes details of productions of thirteen plays by Sg in an extensive documentary catalogue of plays produced at Das Neue Theater]

[D1:412] Simonson, Lee, *The Stage is Set*, New York: Harcourt, Brace and Company, 1932. Illus. XVII+585 pp. [References to Sg, pp. 24, 67-68, 80-81]

[D1:413] Simonson, Lee, *The Stage is Set*, Plainview, New York: Books for Libraries Press, 1975. [Rpr. of **D1:412**]

[D1:414] Simons, L., *Het drama en het toonel in hun ontwikkeling*, Nederlandsche bibliotheek 585, Vol. 5, 1875-1930, Amsterdam: Maatschappij voor goede en goedkoope lectuur, 1932, pp. 275-324. [A Dutch history of drama and the theatre with an overview of Sg's career as a dramatist]

[D1:415] Siwertz, Margit, *Lars Hanson*, Stockholm: P. A. Norstedt & Söners Förlag, 1947. 341 pp. [A biographical study of the Swedish actor who was most closely identified with many of Sg's major roles during the early 20th Century, including *Mäster Olof*, *Fadren*, *Paria*, *Dödsdansen*, *Karl XII*, *Till Damaskus*, and *Stora landsvägen*, in the last of which he was directed by Olof Molander to resemble Sg's *alter ego*]

[D1:416] Sjöberg, Alf, *Teater som besvärjelse. Artiklar från fem decennier*, Antologi redigerad av Sverker R. Ek, Ulla Åberg, Elsa Sjöberg, and Katarina Sjöberg, Dramatens skriftserie nr 4, Stockholm: P. A. Norstedt & Söners Förlag, 1982. Illus. [320] pp. ['Theatre as Invocation. Articles from Five Decades'. A collection of Sjöberg's essays on the theatre and on individual plays which illustrates the place of Sg in his career, both as a theatre director and (with *Fröken Julie*) in the cinema. Includes a catalogue of all Sjöberg's productions at Dramaten. See **C1:1157**, Strindberg and Molière, **E5:82**, *Mäster* Olof, **E11:153**, *Fadern*, and **E50:17**, *Brända tomten*]

[D1:417] Sjögren, Henrik, *Ingmar Bergman på teatern*, Stockholm: Amqvist & Wicksell / Gebers Förlag, 1968. Illus. 316 pp. [A resumé of Bergman's work in the theatre to 1968, including his Sg productions. Frequently employs material from Sjögren's reviews in *Kvällsposten* and elsewhere, including **E30:168** on *Erik XIV*, **E36:111**, *Kronbruden*, **E51:312**, *Spöksonaten*, and **E53:392**, *Pelikanen*]

[D1:418] Sjögren, Henrik, *Lek och raseri. Ingmar Bergmans teater 1938-2002*, Stockholm: Carlssons, 2002. Illus. [VIII]+463 pp. ['Play and Fury. Ingmar Bergman's Theatre, 1938-2002'. Discusses Bergman's career as a theatre director with copious quotation from contemporary reviews in the daily press. Sjögren considers his stagings of *Lycko-Pers resa*, *Fadren*, *Fröken Julie*, *Pelikanen*, *Oväder*, *Till Damaskus*, *Ett drömspel*, *Spöksonaten*, *Kronbruden*, *Svarta handsken*, *Svanevit*, and *Erik XIV*, pp. 247-332. The volume also includes **E25:125**, a retrospective dialogue between Sjögren and Bergman about his productions of Sg in general, pp. 333-342]

[D1:419] Sjögren, Henrik, *Stage and Society in Sweden: Aspects of Swedish Theatre since 1945*, Translated by Paul Britten Austin, Stockholm: The Swedish Institute, 1979, pp. 10-12, 45-46, 49-53, 102-104, 149-153. Illus. [On Sg's plays in performance in Sweden, directed by Olof Molander, Ingmar Bergman, Per Verner-Carlsson, and Lennart Hjulström]

[D1:420] Sjögren, Henrik, *Teater i Sverige efter andra världskriget*, Stockholm: Natur och Kultur, 1982, pp. 14-16, 47-52, 95-97, 141-144. Illus. ['Theatre in Sweden after the Second World War'. Swedish edition of **D1:419**]

[D1:421] Sletbak, Nils, red., *Det Norske Teatret. Femti år 1913-1963*, Oslo: Det Norske Samlaget, 1963. Illus. [488] pp. [Includes brief details of works by Sg staged at the Norwegian National Theatre in Oslo. The relatively few plays listed (*Gillets hemlighet*, *Hemsöborna*, *Lycko-Pers resa*, *Fadren*, *Gustav Vasa*, *Dödsdansen*, and *Spöksonaten*), would seem to question rather than confirm the claim that Sg has become something of a 'house dramatist', and then only in the period after 1948]

[D1:422] Söderman, Sven, *Melpomene och Thalia. Från Stockholms teatrar: studier och kritiker*, Stockholm: Åhlén & Åkerlunds Förlag AB, 1919. Illus. 307 pp. ['Melpomene and Thalia. From Stockholm's Theatres: Studies and Reviews'. Includes **E11:444**, *Fadren*, **E12:449**, *Fröken Julie*, **E34:111**, *Påsk*, **E35:212**, *Dödsdansen*, and **E51:211**, *Spöksonaten*]

[D1:423] Sokel, Walter H., *Anthology of German Expressionist Drama: A Prelude to the Absurd*, New York, Anchor Books, 1963, pp. ix-xxxii. [Traces the influence of Sg's later dramaturgy, in which 'the old structural principle of causal interrelation between character, incident, and action gives way to a new structural pattern, closer to music than to drama – the presentation and variation of a theme', on German Expressionist playwrights]

[D1:424] Spaini, Alberto, *Il teatro tedesco*, Nuova ed., Il Teatro del Novecento 2, [Milano]: Garzanti, 1943. 332 pp. ['German Theatre'. Original edition 1937]

[D1:425] Stål, Sven, *Rep i hängd mans hus. Teaterkritiska artiklar*, Stockholm: Svenska Andelsförlaget, 1925. 165 pp. ['Rope in a Hanged Man's House. Theatre Critical Articles'. Discusses the role of Sg's Intimate Theatre in contemporary Swedish theatrical history and the subsequent fortunes of its performers, pp. 13-20. Stål also comments on Gösta Ekman as Erik in *Gustav Vasa*, pp. 63-64]

[D1:426] Stål, Sven, *Teater-nihilism? Teaterkritiska artiklar*, Stockholm: Svenska Andelsförlaget, 1926. 206 pp. [Compares Sg with Pirandello and discusses Inga Tidblad as *Svanevit*, pp. [87]-103, and Olof Molander's production of *Advent*, pp. 150-171]

[D1:427] Stanislavskii, K[onstantin] S., *Iz rabochikh tetradei: v 2 tomakh*, Revised and Edited by V. N. Prokof'ev, Vol. 1, Moscow: VTO, 1986. 608 pp. [Stanislavskii's notebooks including positive comments on Sg's essay 'Om modernt drama' and his inablity to work on a play that Sg had entrusted to him, pp. 124, 288-289, 478, 565. E.1778e]

[D1:428] Steiger, Edgar, *Das Werden des neuen Dramas, Zweiter Teil: Von Hauptmann bis Maeterlinck*, Berlin: F. Fontane & Co., 1898, pp. 301-303. ['The Development of the New Drama'. Discusses *Fadren* and *Fröken Julie* as expressions of Sg's misogyny]

[D1:429] Steiner, George, *The Death of Tragedy*, London: Faber and Faber, 1961, pp. 298-300. [For Steiner, 'Sg's characters are emanations from his own tormented psyche and his harrowed life. Gradually they lose all connection to a governing centre and are like fragments scattered from some great burst of secret energy.' *Ett drömspel* and *Spöksonaten* 'belong to a theatre of the mind and work inside us like remembered music. But what Sg achieved in depth, he lost in theatrical coherence. These ghost-plays are shadows of drama']

[D1:430] Streisand, Marianne, *Intimität: Begreffsgeschichte und Entdeckung der "Intimität" auf dem Theater um 1900*, Berlin: Wilhelm Fink Verlag, 2001. 375 pp. ['Intimacy: A History of the Concept and Discovery of "Intimacy" in the Theatre ca. 1900'. A study of the concept of intimacy and the idea of intimate theatre at the end of the 19th Century. Streisand makes the Preface to *Fröken Julie* and Sg's later comments on an intimate theatre in *Memorandum till Medlemmarne av Intima Teatern* the focus of a chapter on 'Das Programm des "intimen Gesamtkunstwerkes' (The Theory of the Intimate Total Work of Art), pp. 136-176. She also discusses the performance of *Fordringsägare* in a private house in Munich in 1895 with the Hungarian writer, Juliane Déry, as Tekla, Max Halbe (Adolf), and Julius Schaumberger (Gustav), pp. 273-278. See **E13:24**, **E13:35**, and **E13:59**]

[D1:431] Stuart, Donald Clive, *The Development of Dramatic Art*, London and New York: D. Appleton and Company, 1928, pp. 635-641. [Claims that in plays like *Fadren* and *Fröken Julie*, the action passes in a world as real as the devices of the naturalistic theatre can make it]

[D1:432] Stümcke, Heinrich, *Modernes theater. Eindrücke und Studien*, Berlin: Verlag 'Deutsche Bücherei', 1907. 186 pp. [Theatre reviews, including **E12:358** on the German première of *Fröken Julie*]

[D1:433] Stümcke, Heinrich, *Der vierte Wand. Theatralische Eindrücke und Studien*, Leipzig: Wigand, 1904. X+402 pp. [Theatre reviews, including **E27:108**, *Brott och brott*]

[D1:434] Stümcke, Heinrich, *Vor der Rampe. Neue dramaturgische Blätter*, Oldenburg und Leipzig: Schulz, 1915. VIII+314 pp. [Theatre reviews, including **E35:204**, *Dödsdansen*, **E36:71**, *Kronbruden*, **E44:40**, *Näktergalen i Wittenberg*, and **E53:84**, *Pelikanen*]

[D1:435] Styan, J. L., *Max Reinhardt*, Cambridge: Cambridge University Press, 1982, pp. 36-40. Illus. [Discussion of Reinhardt's Sg productions concentrates primarily on his 1915 staging of *Spöksonaten*]

[D1:436] Styan, J. L., *Modern Drama in Theory and Practice*, 3 vols, Cambridge: Cambridge University Press, 1981, Vol. 1, pp. 37-44. Illus. [Comments on Sg's contribution to theatrical realism in *Fadren* and *Fröken Julie*, a form that contains within itself the seeds of its own dissolution. Styan is under the illusion that *Giftas* is two plays rather than two collections of short stories]

[D1:437] Styan, J. L., *Modern Drama in Theory and Practice*, 3 vols, Cambridge: Cambridge University Press, 1981, Vol. 3, pp. 24-38. Illus. [Discusses *Till Damaskus*, *Ett drömspel*, and *Spöksonaten* as the forerunners of Expressionism; Sg's own ideas on how such plays might be staged at the Intimate Theatre and elsewhere; and subsequent productions by Max Reinhardt, Olof Molander, and Ingmar Bergman, especially the latter's 1973 staging of *Spöksonaten* at Dramaten. Styan insists that the kind of experience which is the basis of this play is so subjective as to preclude successful production]

[D1:438] Styan, J. L., *The Dark Comedy: The Development of Modern Comic Tragedy*, Cambridge: Cambridge University Press, 1962, pp. 76-82, 133-139. [Sg is a 'lunatic genius' who tried almost every theatrical style known to the modern theatre. The better known plays like *Fadren*, *Fröken Julie*, and *Dödsdansen* are not naturalistic at all. Lacking the restraints of naturalism and life's comic compensations, they suggest an incipient expressionism. Yet there is another Sg who sees with an ironic eye in, for example, *Fordringsägare*, *Debet och kredit*, and the 'far more interesting' *Brott och brott*, which anticipates the sardonic logic of feelings in the later dream plays. With their 'private surrealism', these plays abandon the laws of comedy and tragedy, but even though they make little effort to draw the spectator into the world of the play, we are aware at certain overwhelming moments that 'we move in vaguely recognisable regions on the fringe of our consciousness'. *Spöksonaten* in particular anticipates the Beckett of *Endgame*]

[D1:439] Styan, J. L., *The Elements of Drama*, Cambridge: Cambridge University Press, 1960. 306 pp. [Analyses *Fadren*, Act 2, Scene 5, to illustrate aspects of tempo and meaning in drama (pp. 158-162), and uses *Fröken Julie* to exemplify the creation and development of character (pp. 167-168, 176-177)]

[D1:440] Sukhanova, T. N., 'Strindberg', in Boiadzhieva, G. N., A. G. Obraztsova, and A. A. Iakubovskii, *Istoriia zarubezhnogo teatra, Tom II, Teatr zapadnoi Evropy XIX – nachala XX veka*, Moscow, 1984, pp. 182-186. [On Sg's relevance for the development of modern drama and theatre in a two-volume 'History of Foreign Theatre'. E.1777]

[D1:441] Surer, Paul, *Cinquante ans de théâtre*, Paris: Société d'édition et d'enseignement supérieur, 1969. Illus. VIII+443 pp. ['Fifty Years of Theatre'. Surveys recent French theatre with fifteen references to Sg]

[D1:442] Surer, Paul, *Le Théâtre français contemporain*, Paris: Société d'édition et d'enseignement supérieur, 1964. Illus. 516 pp. ['The Contemporary French Theatre'. Includes several passing references to Sg]

[D1:443] Svanberg, Johannes, *Kungl. Teatrarne under ett halft sekel 1860-1910. Personalhistoriska anteckningar*, 2 vols, Stockholm: Nordisk familjebok, 1917-1918. 204, 211 pp. ['The Royal Theatres During a Half Century, 1860-1910'. A reference work on the directors, designers, administrators, and other personnel associated with Dramaten and the Stockholm Royal Opera over a fifty year period]

[D1:444] Szondi, Peter, *Teoria del dramma moderno*, Introduzione di Cesare Cases, Torino: G. Enaudi, 1962. XXXVI+138 pp. [Italian translation of **D1:450**. Rpr. 1972 and 1982]

[D1:445] Szondi, Peter, *Teoria nowoczesnego dramatu*, przeł. Z niem. E. Misiołek, Warszawa, 1976. 169 pp. [Polish translation of **D1:450**]

[D1:446] Szondi, Peter, *The Theory of Modern Drama*, Translated by Michael Hays, Cambridge: Polity Press, 1987, pp. 22-31. [One of the most influential theoretical discussions of modern drama, in which the emergence of an epic form that emphasises the isolation of the individual and is clearly related to contemporary social processes, marks a radical departure from the conventions of classical drama. Szondi points out that Sg's subjective drama coincides with the development of the psychological novel. Even in *Fadren*, the action is constructed solely from the standpoint of the title figure and unfolds through his subjective point of view. Placing the ego of a single individual at the centre of a play takes Sg further and further away from traditional dramatic construction. The art form *par excellence* of dialogic openness and frankness is given the task of presenting secret psychic events which it achieves either by becoming monodrama or enclosing the other characters within the principal character's frame of reference, as in *Till Damaskus*, where unity of action is replaced by unity of the self. Continuity of action is replaced by a series of scenes which no longer generate one another, 'they seem to be isolated stones strung out along the path of the onward moving *I*'. Dialogue becomes self-communing and action gives way to stasis as the *dramatis personae* assume the roles of epic commentators and (like Hummel in *Spöksonaten*) comment on the condition of mankind from without. Thus, for Szondi, *Spöksonaten* presents 'the one source of modern epic dramaturgy'. English version of **D1:450**]

[D1:447] Szondi, Peter, *Det moderna dramats teori, 1880-1950*, Översättning av Kerstin Derkert, Stockholm: Wahlström & Widstrand, 1972. 137 pp. [Swedish edition of **D1:450**]

[D1:448] Szondi, Peter, *Théorie du drame moderne: 1880-1950*, Lausanne-Paris: L'Âge d'homme, 1983. 144 pp. [French edition of **D1:450**]

[D1:449] Szondi, Peter, *Theorie des modernen Dramas*, Frankfurt am Main: Suhrkamp, 1956, pp. 33-47. [See **D1:446**]

[D1:450] Szondi, Peter, *Theorie des modernen Dramas*, Revid. Ausgabe, edition Suhrkamp 27, Frankfurt am Main: Suhrkamp, 1965, pp. 40-57. [Revised ed. of **D1:449**. See **D1:446**]

[D1:451] Thalasso, Adolphe, *Le Théâtre libre. Essai critique, historique et documentaire*, Paris: Mercure de France, 1909. XVI+299 pp. ['The Théâtre Libre: A Critical, Historical, and

Documentary Essay'. The earliest standard history of Antoine's Théâtre Libre and its repertoire, including his production of *Fröken Julie* in 1893]

[D1:452] Thompson, Alan Reynolds, 'Strindberg and Expressionism', in *The Anatomy of the Drama*, 2nd ed., Berkeley and Los Angeles: University of California Press, 1946, pp. 341-356. [Also comments on the dreamplay mode, pp. 184-185. First edition 1942]

[D1:453] Torberg, Friedrich, *Das fünfte Rad am Thespiskarren. Theaterkritiken*, 2 vols, München und Wien: Albert Langen Georg Müller, 1966-67. 445 and 527 pp. ['The Fifth Row of Thespis' Wagon'. Theatre reviews, including **E11:668** on *Fadren*, **E12:1518**, *Fröken Julie*, **E25:343**, *Till Damaskus*, **E35:448**, *Dödsdansen*, and **E41:1110**, *Ett drömspel*, in Volume Two, pp. 425-429]

[D1:454] Törnqvist, Egil, *Between Stage and Screen. Ingmar Bergman Directs*, Amsterdam: Amsterdam University Press, 1995. Illus. 243 pp. [Includes chapters on Bergman's productions of *Ett drömspel* (1970), *Spöksonaten* (1973), and *Fröken Julie* (1985) for the theatre, *Oväder* for television (1960), and *Påsk* for radio (1952), often revised from earlier publications. Discussion of Bergman's films focuses attention on their affinity with Sg, e.g. the relevance of the Chamber Plays for *Autumn Sonata*, *Oväder* and *Stora landsvägen* for *Wild Strawberries*, *Spöksonaten*, and *Ett drömspel* for *Cries and Whispers*, and *Ett drömspel* for *Fanny and Alexander*, in which the final words are 'a tribute to the writer who has meant the most to Bergman, both ideologically and aesthetically']

[D1:455] Torsslow, Stig, *Dramatenaktörernas republik. Dramatiska teatern under associationstiden 1888-1907*, Dramatens skriftserie nr 2, Stockholm: Kungl. Dramatiska teatern, 1975. 346 pp. ['The Actors' Republic at Dramaten. The Royal Dramatic Theatre during the Association Period, 1888-1907'. Sg's relationship with Dramaten and its management is the subject of a specific chapter (pp. 280-290), but his various links with the theatre and many of those closely involved with it (including Erik af Edholm, Emil Hillberg, Gustaf Fredrikson, and Harriet Bosse), is a recurring subject throughout, as are the fortunes of his plays there (both staged and unstaged)]

[D1:456] Trolle, Constance af, *Teaterkonst signerad Per Verner-Carlsson*, Stockholm: Carlssons, 1995. Illus. 240 pp. ['Theatre Art Signed Per Verner Carlsson'. Analyses Verner-Carlsson's productions of *Pelikanen* in 1968 and 1978 (pp. 99-123, 172-189), and *Brott och brott* in 1980 (pp. 191-210), and discusses *Porträtt av en konstnär som ung man* (Portrait of an Artist as a Young Man), his dramatic collage based on Sg's correspondence (pp. 211-216). English summary, pp. 217-223]

[D1:457] Ulanov, Barry, *Makers of the Modern Theatre*, New York: McGraw Hill, 1961. 743 pp. [Includes introductory material on Sg, prefacing a translation of *Till Damaskus I* in an anthology of nineteen modern dramas]

[D1:458] Vaittinen, Pirjo, ed., *Teatterin vuosi. Turun kaupunginteatterin toiminta, ohjelmisto ja yleisö näytäntökaudella 1990-1991*, Helsingissä: VAPK-kustannus, 1992. Illus. 243 pp. ['A Year in the Theatre. Report on the Activities, Repertoire, and Audience at Turku City Theatre during the 1990-1991 Season'. Includes an account of Laura Jäntii's 1991 staging of 'Encounters According to Strindberg', which combines characters and material from *Spöksonaten*, *Dödsdansen*, and *Brända tomten*]

[D1:459] Verner-Carlson, Per, *Teater och teater. Artiklar 1950-1965*, Dramatens skriftserie nr 3, Stockholm: Kungl. Dramatiska Teatern, 1978. 261 pp. [Given the place of Sg in his work as a theatre director (most notably *2 x Pelikanen* (1968) and *Brott och brott* (1980)), Verner-Carlsson's essays contain surprisingly little discussion of Sg or his works, although he remains a recurring point of reference]

[D1:460] Viertel, Berthold, *Schriften zum Theater*, Hrsg. von Gert Heidenrich mit einem Geleitwort von Herbert Ihering, Berlin: Henschelverlag Kunst und Gesellschaft, 1970, pp. 150-151. ['Writings on Theatre'. Recognises Sg's accomplishment as a creator of myth and fairy tale as well as the writer of unsparing autobiographies. In his plays 'die Essenz "Strindberg"' is always recognisable]

[D1:461] Vilar, Jean, *Le Théâtre, service public et autres textes*, Présentation et notes d'Armand Delcampe, Paris: Éditions Gallimard, 1975. 562 pp. [Includes sixteen references to Sg, who is preferred by Vilar to Ibsen (p. 152)]

[D1:462] Visser, Edmond, *Eduard Verkade*, Onze tooneelkunstenaars. Amsterdam, [1922]. 48 pp. [Discusses Willem Royaards's staging of *Ett drömspel* and Eduard Verkade's Dutch language première of *Oväder*]

[D1:463] Vitti, Achille, *Storie e storielle del teatro di prosa*, Milano: Casa editoriale Vecchi, 1926. 238+49 pp. plates. ['Stories and Tales of the Theatre in Prose', Memoirs of the actor-manager who appeared in an early Italian staging of *Fadren*]

[D1:464] Viviani, Annalisa, *Das Drama des Expressionismus*, München: Winkler-Verlag, 1970. 190 pp. ['The Drama of Expressionism'. Presents Sg as a significant precursor of German expressionism in the theatre]

[D1:465] Viviani, Annalisa, *Dramaturgische Elemente im expressionistischen Drama*, Bonner Arbeiten zur deutschen Literatur 21, Bonn: H. Bouvier u. Co. Verlag, 1979. 187 pp. ['Dramaturgical Elements in Expressionist Drama'. Discusses Sg's influence on German expressionist drama with reference to *Fröken Julie, Till Damaskus, Ett drömspel,* and *Stora landsvägen*, pp. 24-27, 77-79, 85-87]

[D1:466] Vogel, Manfred, *...und neues Leben blüht aus den Kulissen. Theaterstreifzüge durch Deutschland*, Wien: Deutsch, 1963. Illus. 288 pp. ['...and new life blossoms out of the wings. Theatrical Explorations in Germany'. See **E25:528** on *Till Damaskus*]

[D1:467] Volkov, N. D., *Meierkhol'd: v 2 tomakh*, 2 vols, Moscow and Leningrad: Academia, 1929. [Includes material on Meyerhold's productions of *Fröken Julie* in Poltava (1906), Vol. 1, p. 245, and *Brott och brott* in Terioki (1912), Vol. 2, pp. 239-241. E.937]

[D1:468] Volkelt, Johannes, *Äesthetik des Tragischen*, Dritte neue bearbeitete Auflage, München: J. C. Beck'sche Verlagsbuchhandlung, 1917. XXIV+552 pp. [Includes no close analysis of Sg's dramaturgy but passing references to *Fadren, Fröken Julie, Fordringsägare, Brott och brott, Dödsdansen, Brända tomten, Spöksonaten,* and *Pelikanen*]

[D1:469] Wagner, Hans, *200 Jahre Münchner Theaterchronik 1750-1950*, München: R. Lerche Verlag, 1958. 263 pp. ['200 Years of Munich Theatre, 1750-1950, A Chronicle'. Dates the heyday of the Munich Kammerspiele from its staging of *Spöksonaten* as part of the so-called Strindberg Zyklus in 1915 (see **D1:349**)]

[D1:470] Wahlgren, Helge, *Anders de Wahl. En studie*, Publikens gunstlingar 5, Stockholm: Hökerberg, 1988. Illus. 88 pp. [A largely biographical study of the eminent Swedish actor, with comments on several of his performances in Sg's plays]

[D1:471] Wahlund, Per Erik, *Avsidesrepliker. Teaterkritik 1961-1965*, Stockholm: Bonniers, 1966. 270 pp. ['Asides. Theatre Criticism, 1961-1965'. Theatre reviews, including **E18:44**,

Himmelrikets nycklar, **E25:354**, *Till Damaskus*, **E29:118**, *Gustav Vasa*, **E38:80**, *Karl XII*, and **E42:98**, *Gustav III*]

[D1:472] Wahlund, Per Erik, *Ridåfall. Teaterkritik 1966-1968*, Stockholm: Bonniers, 1969. 209 pp. ['Curtain-Fall. Theatre Criticism, 1966-1968'. Theatre reviews, including **E11:678**, *Fadren*, **E35:554**, *Dödsdansen*, and **E41:455**, *Ett drömspel*]

[D1:473] Wahlund, Per Erik, *Scenväxling. Teaterkritik 1954-1960*, Stockholm: Natur och Kultur, 1962. Illus. 288 pp. ['Scene Change. Theatre Criticism, 1954-1960'. Theatre reviews, including **E5:223**, *Mäster Olof*, **E27:203**, *Brott och brott*, **E30:170**, *Erik XIV*, and **E41:394**, *Ett drömspel*]

[D1:474] Wahlund, Per Erik, *Sortirepliker. Teaterkritik i urval, 1970-1985*, Stockholm: Alba, 1986. 236 pp. ['Exit Lines. Theatre Criticism, 1970-1985'. Theatre reviews, including **E13:356**, *Fordringsägare*, **E27:302**, *Brott och brott*, **E29:149**, *Gustav Vasa*, **C4:59** on Per Olov Enquist's drama about Sg, *Tribadernas natt*, and **E35:728**, *Dödsdansen*]

[D1:475] Waith, Eugene M., ed., *The Dramatic Moment*, Englewood Cliffs, New Jersey: Prentice Hall, 1967. 505 pp.

[D1:476] Warburg, Karl, *Essayer*, Stockholm: Albert Bonniers Förlag, 1918. 293 pp. [Warburg's literary journalism, including several reviews of Sg's plays on publication and in performance]

[D1:477] Waxman, Samuel Montefiore, *Antoine and The Théâtre Libre*, Cambridge, Mass.: Harvard University Press, 1926, pp. 176-181. [An exposition of Sg's theories in the Preface to *Fröken Julie* rather than a presentation of Antoine's production of the play which 'created a considerable furore for the moment, but like all the other violent plays of its kind…was soon forgotten.' Nevertheless, more than any other foreign (i.e. non-French) dramatist, Waxman suggests that Sg follows Zola closely, both in theory and in practice]

[D1:478] Waxman, Samuel Montefiore, *Antoine and The Théâtre Libre*, New York: Benjamin Blom, Inc., 1964, pp. 176-181. [Facsimile Rpr. of **D1:477**]

[D1:479] Weigel, Hans, *Tausendundeine Premiere. Wiener Theater, 1946-1961*, Band 2, Wien: Im Wollzeilen Verlag, [1961]. 288 pp. ['One Thousand and One Premières. Viennese Theatre 1946-1961'. Theatre reviews, including **E12:1536**, *Fröken Julie*, **E35:450**, *Dödsdansen*, and **E41:204**, *Ett drömspel*]

[D1:480] Wellwarth, George E., *Modern Drama and the Death of God*, Madison: The University of Wisconsin Press, 1986, pp. 14-25. [Although clearly paranoid, Sg is nevertheless, for Wellwarth, the father of the modern drama of the self. He never wrote about anything except himself, even in the domestic dramas *Fröken Julie*, *Fadren*, *Dödsdansen*, and *Kamraterna*, where we are confronted by self-pity rather than psychological insight. Nevertheless, these plays are significant in assuming that the two institutions on which society is principally based – the family and distinctions of social rank – are carefully contrived fictions, especially in *Fröken Julie* which, unlike *Fadren* and *Dödsdansen*, Wellwarth considers a viable stage play. However, the later dramas of self-analysis, such as *Till Damaskus*, are self-indulgent and incomprehensible to anyone not familiar with the facts of Sg's personal life, but in *Ett drömspel* he is at least concerned with the outer world's effect upon the dreamer. Both thematically and technically, this is a remarkable, pioneering drama]

[D1:481] Wennerholm, Erik, *Anders de Wahl: Människan bakom maskerna*, Stockholm: Albert Bonniers Förlag, 1974. Illus. 230 pp. ['Anders de Wahl. The Man behind the Masks'. A biographical study of the eminent Swedish actor who first appeared as the schoolboy, Nils, in the 1890 première of the verse edition of *Mäster Olof*, made his breakthrough as Olof in Harald Molander's production in 1897 (pp. 47-50), and went on to give celebrated performances in numerous major Sg roles, several of which, like Erik XIV, he created. Wennerholm also comments on de Wahl's personal relationship with Sg (pp. 53-57). In all some twenty-one references to Sg]

[D1:482] Wennerholm, Erik, *Jag Kulle*, Stockholm: Albert Bonniers Förlag, 1977. [310] pp. Illus. ['I Kulle'. An artist biography of the actor, Jarl Kulle's career with twenty-two references to Sg, including an account of his performance as Gustav Vasa in Alf Sjöberg's 1951 production of *Mäster Olof*, pp. 86-88]

[D1:483] Wennerholm, Erik, Karl Ragnar Gierow, Akke Kumlien and Ragnar Svanström, red., *Carl G. Laurin sjuttio år. Festskrift*, Stockholm: P. A. Norstedt & Söners Förlag, 1938. 104 pp. [A Festchrift for the long-serving theatre critic of *Ord och Bild*, the author of many, often unsympathetic, reviews of Sg's plays. See e.g. **D1:249- D1:254**]

[D1:484] Wettergren, Erik, *Scenerier. Resor, konst, teater*, Stockholm: P. A. Norstedt & Söners Förlag, 1927. 292 pp. ['Settings. Travels, Art, Theatre'. Includes some theatre reviews, among them **E25:269** on *Till Damaskus* and **E26:71** on *Advent*]

[D1:485] Wettergren, Erik, and Ivar Lignell, red., *Teater i Sverige de sista 50 åren*, Svensk scenkonst och film 9, Stockholm: AB Svensk litteratur, 1940, pp. 523-646. Illus. ['Theatre in Sweden: The Last Fifty Years'. Surveys recent Swedish theatre, covering the final twelve years of Sg's life, as well as several subsequent performances of his plays. Wettergren makes numerous references to Sg but only in the context of assessments of performers such as Lars Hanson, Harriet Bosse, Maria Schildknecht, and others]

[D1:486] Whitaker, Thomas R., *Mirrors of Our Playing: Paradigms and Presences in Modern Drama*, Ann Arbor: The University of Michigan Press, 1999. [X]+309 pp. [Makes regular brief reference to Sg, notably to the post-Inferno plays represented by *Till Damaskus, Ett drömspel, Spöksonaten,* and *Stora landsvägen*]

[D1:487] Wikander, Matthew, 'Progress and Providence: Schiller and Strindberg', in *The Play of Truth and State: Historical Drama from Shakespeare to Brecht*, Baltimore: John Hopkins University Press, 1986, pp. 139-196. [Discusses Sg's acute interest in the relationship between recorded history and revealed truth, which reflects his own highly personal experience of providence in Paris during the mid-1890s, in relation to the essay 'Världshistoriens mystik', *En blå bok, Mäster Olof*, and the later history plays. Sg is the only major dramatist to devote as much of his attention to his nation's history as Shakespeare, and demands comparison with his English forbear. His historical dramas place Swedish history in a trans-national context, combine public and private worlds, and provide biblical parallels with worldly events, thus indicating a problematic relationship between his historical protagonists (e.g. Gustav Vasa, Erik XIV, Karl XII, or Gustav III) and providence. The plays are sometimes pervaded by a sense of repeated patterns, played off against each other. There is often an affinity between actors on the stage of history and in the theatre (as in *Erik XIV*, *Kristina*, and *Gustav III* in which theatrical metaphors abound), and the stagecraft of the later plays is influenced by Maeterlinck as well as by Shakespeare. In several of the later history plays, the providential model that informed *Gustav Vasa* and *Erik XIV* gives way to a vision of history as a game, thus substituting a basically comic vision for the tragic uncertainty about the relationship between hero and providence that characterises Sg's major achievements in the genre]

[D1:488] Wilde, Percival, *The Craftsmanship of the One-Act Play*, Boston: Little, Brown and Company, pp. 3, 47-49. [Quotes the preface to *Fröken Julie* in defence of the monologue as a legitimate dramatic device]

[D1:489] Williams, Raymond, *Drama from Ibsen to Eliot,* London: Chatto and Windus, 1952, pp. 98-125, 270-271. [Concludes that Sg's genius as a dramatist lay in his ability to find, against the grain of the dramatic methods of his time, viable forms of expression. Recognises the achievement of the history plays and *Lycko-Pers resa* but focuses mainly on 'the play[s] of violent action or declaration', like *Fadren*, *Fröken Julie*, or *Dödsdansen*, in which elemental characters engage, not with everyday experience but revealed truth. The virtue of these and Sg's other naturalist plays, is 'the intensity of the revealed experience, the unforgettable power of a savage insight into motive and situation. The limitation…is in the incongruity between the bared, elemental experience of crisis and the covering apparatus of seen and spoken normality.' Attempting to resolve this dilemma, Sg develops the new dramatic form of *Till Damaskus*, which is to be appreciated for the control with which it realises its central theme rather than quarried for material relating to its author's autobiographical obsessions. Nevertheless, the 19th-Century divorce between drama and literature means that it is a play more easily read than realised on stage. Of Sg's other later plays, *Påsk* 'is the nearest to Ibsen…a typical piece of naturalist theatre', *Dödsdansen* is inferior to *Fadren*, and *Ett drömspel* is 'an astonishing feat of virtuosity', but theatrically diffuse. On the other hand, in *Spöksonaten* 'he realises the persistent pattern in a powerfully concentrated and eminently dramatic form'. Subsequently published in a revised edition entitled *Drama from Ibsen to Brecht*]

[D1:490] Williams, Raymond, *Modern Tragedy*, London: Chatto and Windus, 1966, pp. 106-115. [Characterises the work of Sg as the most challenging single example of the kind of tragedy in which man's deepest and primary desires include destruction and self-destruction, and are barely tempered by society. Plays like *Fadren* and *Dödsdansen* enact a cruel vision, at once terrible and absurd which, even in *Fröken Julie*, whose sole virtue is its speed, passes beyond the struggle between social classes that is central to the liberal tragedy of Ibsen. Sg's power as a dramatist derives from the pitiless process in which his characters are caught up, the private tragedy of isolated individuals subject to malign forces that he himself partly comes to terms with in *Till Damaskus*, and often formulated in a manner that anticipates the plays of Eugene O'Neill and Tennessee Williams]

[D1:491] Williamson, Audrey, *Theatre of Two Decades*, London: Rockliff, 1951, pp. 229-230. [Observes that 'A psychological perversion seems to give the plays an additional and passionate intensity, but less universality as a portrayal of life']

[D1:492] Wilski, Zbigniew, *Stanisława Wysocka*, Warszawa, 1965. [A biographical study of the actress who helped establish Sg's name in Poland where she regularly played the role of the Mother in *Pelikanen* and Laura on tour opposite Karol Adwentowicz in *Fadren*, and directed a production of *Kamraterna* in 1918]

[**D1:493**] Winds, Adolf, *Der Schauspieler in seiner Entwicklung vom Mysterien- zum Kammerspiel*, Berlin: Schuster & Loeffler, 1919. 284 pp. ['The Development of the Actor from the Mystery to the Chamber Play'. Contains five occasional references to Sg]

[**D1:494**] Wirmark, Margareta, *Noras systrar. Nordisk dramatik och teater 1879-99*, Stockholm: Carlssons, 2000. Illus. 421 pp. ['Nora's Sisters. Nordic Drama and Theatre, 1879-99'. Presents Ibsen's and Sg's dramas on marriage and the role of women (in Sg's case *Herr Bengts hustru*, *Fadren*, *Leka med elden*, *Moderskärlek*, and *Kamraterna*) within the context of the Scandinavian theatre and drama of their period, comparing and contrasting their plays with the work of numerous contemporary dramatists, both female and male: Alfhild Agrell, Anne Charlotte Leffler, Edvard Brandes, Alexander Kielland, Otto Benzon, Amalie Skram, Bjørnstjerne Bjørnson, Gunnar Heiberg, Emma Gad, Victoria Benedictsson, Minna Canth, Mathilda Malling, Arne Garborg, Frida Stéenhoff, and Klara Johanson. This prompts an intriguing and nuanced revisioning of their work and its intertextual place in the ongoing contemporary debate on the role of women and marriage. Wirmark also studies these works in relation to the overall repertoire of the established theatres of Kristiania, Stockholm, Helsinki, and Copenhagen, and considers the consequences of their exposure to a form of semi-official censorship. Includes appendices cataloguing (a) published plays in Danish, Norwegian, and Swedish between 1879 and 1899, and (b) plays by Nordic writers staged in Copenhagen, Helsinki, Kristiania, and Stockholm during the same period. The book is also well and copiously illustrated]

[**D1:495**] Zacconi, Ermete, *Ricordi e battaglie*, Milano: Garzanti Editore 1946. Illus. VIII+232 pp. [The memoirs of the renowned Italian actor which include an account of performing *Fadren* with his company during the 1890s, and his notorious decision to give up performing the play. No mention is made of the other plays by Sg in which Zacconi also appeared – *Fröken Julie* and *Inför döden*]

[**D1:496**] Zamora, Juan Guerrero, *Historia del teatro contemporáneo*, Vol. 2, Barcelona: Juan Flors, Editor, 1961, pp. 3-55.

[**D1:497**] Zingerman, B[oris[I]saakevich], *Ocherki istorii dramy 20 veka: Chekhov, Strindberg, Ibsen, Meterlink, Pirandello, Brekht, Gauptman, Lorka, Anui*, Moscow: Izdat Nauka, 1979. 392 pp. ['A History of Drama During the Twentieth Century: Chekhov, Strindberg, Ibsen, Maeterlinck, Pirandello, Brecht, Hauptmann, Lorca, Anouilh'. Includes a Rpr. of **D2:1327**, 'On Sg's Theatre', pp. 148-182. E.1093]

(ii) Essays in Edited Books and Journals

[**D1:498**] A. B-s [August Brunius], 'Ny svensk dramatik', *Svenska Dagbladet* (Stockholm), 5 July 1918. ['New Swedish Drama'. A review of Pär Lagerkvist's one-act plays *Den svåra stunden* and his essay on modern theatre, **D1:604**, with its positive response to Sg's later dramaturgy. According to Brunius, where Sg's later plays are often pathological, Lagerkvist's works in this vein are distinguished by their macabre humour and fantasy]

[**D1:499**] Adamov, Arthur, 'De quelques faits', *Théâtre populaire* (Paris), No. 46 (1962), 46-60. ['A Few Facts'. Now committed to Marxism and a socially engaged literature, Adamov criticises his previous exemplar, Sg, so lauded in **D2:1**, for failing to fuse the socio-economic dimension implicit in *Spöksonaten* with its psycho-pathological elements. Also comments critically on *Ett drömspel*]

[D1:500] Adler, Henry, 'To Hell with Society', *The Tulane Drama Review* (New Orleans), 4:1 (1960), 53-76. [An attack upon Kenneth Tynan for his blinkered advocacy of a socially committed theatre, sometimes at the expense of good drama. Adler picks up on a disparaging remark of Tynan's about *Ett drömspel* and argues that, 'if ever there was a socially critical play, this is one'. He also compares Sg with Brecht and William Blake as well as with Ibsen and Freud, and argues the contemporary relevance of Sg's theatre]

[D1:501] 'Agathon' [Julien Leclerq?], 'Le Théâtre septentrionale', *Revue Encyclopédique* (Paris), 1 October 1894.

[D1:502] Åkerhielm, Helge, 'Förkunnaren Molander', *Svenska Dagbladet* (Stockholm), 8 March 1953. ['Preacher Molander'. A rare and eloquent Swedish critique of Olof Molander's approach to staging Sg. Not only are his profoundly Christian interpretations misguided; Åkerhielm maintains that he has also trivialised Sg's works by rooting them in the inconsequential circumstances of a thoroughly tangible Stockholm reality. He has reshaped the plays according to his own will rather than the author's intentions]

[D1:503] Arnold, Paul, 'From the Dream in Aeschylus to the Surrealist Theatre', *Journal of Aesthetics and Art Criticism* (Cleveland, Ohio), 7 (1949), 349-354. [Discusses *Ett drömspel* and *Till Damaskus I*, where Sg continues the impulse of Shakespeare in *The Tempest* and explores the modalities of dreaming]

[D1:504] Bab, Julius, 'Der neue Strindberg. (Im Theaterwinter 1913/1914)', in *Der Wille zum Drama*, Neue Folge der Wege zum Drama, Deutsches Dramenjahr 1911-1918, Berlin: Oesterheld & Co. Verlag, 1919, pp. 367-379. ['The New Strindberg'. Focuses on the post-Inferno Sg of the 'greater' mystery, dream, and chamber plays, rather than the naturalist works of the 1880s. According to Bab, *Ett drömspel* and *Till Damaskus* combine realism with symbolism to create a new scenic poetry, in which the playwright's soul is visible. This later Sg is perhaps the greatest phenomenon of the 19th Century]

[D1:505] Bab, Julius, 'Die Expressionisten und das Drama', *Die Schaubühne* (Berlin), 19 September 1916, pp. 266-270. ['The Expressionist and Drama']

[D1:506] Bab, Julius, 'Durch das Drama des Naturalismus und der Mystik', in *Der Mensch auf der Bühne. Eine Dramaturgie für Schauspieler*, Bd 3, Berlin: Oesterheld & Co., 1920, pp. 317-347. ['Through the Drama of Naturalism and Mysticism'. Discusses Chekhov, Maeterlinck, Hofmannsthal, and Sg, and the transition from naturalism to a more subjective, symbolist-inflected drama. The 1910 edition comments on Sg in a discussion of the state of German drama and the naturalist revolution in Volume Three, p. 68]

[D1:507] Bab, Julius, 'Expressionistisches Drama', *Die Schaubühne* (Berlin), 26 September 1916, pp. 286-289. ['Expressionist Drama']

[D1:508] Bachmann-Medick, Doris, 'Kulturelle Spielräume: Drama und Theater im Licht ethnologischer Ritualforschung', in Erika Fischer-Lichte, Hrsg., *Soziale und theatralische Konventionen als Probleme der Dramenübersetzung*, Forum modernes Theater, Schriftenreihe 1, Tübingen: Francke Verlag, 1988, pp. 117-128. ['Cultural Play Space: Drama and Theatre in the Light of Ethnological Research into Ritual'. Exemplifes the discussion of post-Shakespearean drama's relation to ritual with detailed reference to *Till Damaskus* and *Ett drömspel*, in which a stage play is endowed with something of the liminal nature of ritual]

[D1:509] Bark, Richard, 'Dramat – själens teater. Om litteratur i dramaanalysis', *Svensklärarförenings årsskrift* (Stockholm), 1985, pp. 174-183. ['Drama – The Theatre of the Soul. On Literature in Dramatic Analysis'. Uses Sg's post-Inferno dramas to illustrate ways of approaching the analysis of play texts]

[D1:510] Bayerdörfer, Hans-Peter, 'Der totgesagte Dialog und das monodramatische Experiment: Symptome der "Umsetzung" im modernen Schauspieltheater', in Erika Fischer Lichte, Hrsg., *TheaterAvantgarde: Wahrnehmung – Körper – Sprache*, Tübingen und Basel: Francke Verlag, 1995, pp. 242-290. ['Dialogue Spoken to Death and Monodramatic Experiment: Symptoms of "Transference" in Modern Theatre'. Comments on the tendency in Sg's dramaturgy to the one-act form and his increasing use of monologue in *Den starkare*, which may be linked to the psychoanalytical [sic] ideas of Théodule Ribot and Jean-Martin Charcot. The 'Ich-dramatik' of Sg's later plays with their restricted dramatic action has affinities with the theatre of Maeterlinck, as well as important consequences for expressionism and the plays of Eugene O'Neill]

[D1:511] Bayerdörfer, Hans-Peter, 'Dramatische Analyse und Ich-Dramatik. Ibsen und Strindberg', in Rolf Grimminger, Jurij Murasov and Jörn Stückrath, Hrsg., *Literarische Moderne. Europäische Literatur im 19. Und 20. Jahrhundert*, Reinbek bei Hamburg: Rowohlt Verlag, 1995, pp. 112-138. ['Dramatic Analysis and Ego-Drama. Ibsen and Strindberg']

[D1:512] Bayerdörfer, Hans-Peter, 'Eindringlinge, Marionetten, Automaten: Symbolistische Dramatik und die Anfänge des modernen Teaters', in Viktor Zmegac, Hrsg., *Deutsche Literatur der Jahrhundertwende*, Königstein: Verlagsgruppe Athenäum-Hain-Scriptor-Hanstein, 1981, pp. 191-216. ['Intruders, Marionettes, Automata: Symbolist Drama and the Origins of Modern Theatre'. Examines symbolist features in Sg's later dramas, including *Till Damaskus*, *Ett drömspel*, the Chamber Plays, and the dramatic fragment *Toten-Insel*, which were of significance for European drama as a whole, both influenced by, and mediating, the influence of Maeterlinck, pp. 201-202]

[D1:513] B. B-n [Bo Bergman], 'Pär Lagerkvist, *Teater*', *Dagens Nyheter* (Stockholm), 29 June 1918. [Apropos **D1:604**, with its generally positive response to Sg's later dramaturgy. Although Lagerkvist regards Sg's Chamber Plays as his greatest achievement, for Bergman they represent an 'artistic breakdown', however psychologically interesting and scenically effective they may be]

[D1:514] Beijer, Agne, 'Il teatro svedese', in *Svezia. Saggi sulla Svezia odierna*, Roma, 1945, pp. 119-127. ['The Swedish Theatre']

[D1:515] Beijer, Agne, 'Svensk teater efter sekelskiftet från Stockholms horisont', in Erik Wettergren and Ivar Lignell, red., *Teater i Sverige sista 50 åren*, Stockholm: Svensk litteratur, 1940, pp. 535-619. ['Swedish Theatre after the Turn-of-the-Century as seen from Stockholm'. A survey of the Swedish theatre during the first forty years of the 20th Century, adopting a metropolitan perspective]

[D1:516] Bennett, Benjamin K., 'Strindberg and Ibsen: Towards a Cubism of Time in Drama', *Modern Drama* (Toronto), 26:3 (1983), 262-281. [Suggests that, just as the painter gives the impression of planes situated behind the surface of his canvas, so the dramatist, by making his plot depend on events in the relatively distant past, gives the impression of a temporal continuum extending beyond the limits of what is performed. Although increasingly aware that this past is experienced variously by different characters (hence the proximity of his later plays to impressionism rather than naturalism), Ibsen always retains the conventions of the mimetic, in order that real contact (of dramatist with audience as well as character with character) remains a possibility. Sg fractures this contract. In his plays, time is often circular, not linear, even though the expressionist notion that our world is never anything but our own mental construction continues to exist in tension with the kind of ethical imperatives that concerned Ibsen. Hence Sg's development in *Spöksonaten* of what might be termed 'cubist tragedy', where past and present exist on the same plane, as full face and profile might be fused in a cubist painting. However, in Bennett's view, it is only in *Stora landsvägen* that Sg's destiny as a dramatist is finally fulfilled. An analysis of the play here suggests it is there that Sg achieves 'the perfect fusion of ethical and aesthetic']

[D1:517] Bennett, Benjamin K., 'Strindberg and Ibsen: Toward a Cubism of Time in Drama', in Frederick J. Marker and Christopher Innes, **D1:299**, *Modernism in European Drama: Ibsen, Strindberg, Pirandello, Beckett. Essays from Modern Drama*, Toronto: University of Toronto Press, 1998, pp. 69-91. [Rpr. of **D1:516**]

[D1:518] Bennett, Benjamin K., 'Strindberg and Ibsen. Cubism, Communicative Ethics, and the Theater of Readers', in *Theater as Problem: Modern Drama and its Place in Literature*, Ithaca: Cornell University Press, 1990, pp. 17-54. [Substantially the same as **D1:516**]

[D1:519] Bergman, Gösta M., 'Det nya scendramat', *Skådebanans årsbok* (Stockholm), 3 (1929-30). ['The New Form of Stage Play']

[D1:520] Bethke, Artur, 'Die Geste des Zeigens', in Bertil Nolin and Peter Forsgren, red., *The Modern Breakthrough in Scandinavian Literature*, Skrifter utgivna av Litteraturvetenskapliga institutionen vid Göteborgs universitet 17, Göteborg, 1988, pp. 187-190. ['The Gesture of Showing'. Discusses *Till Damaskus*, *Ett drömspel*, and *Spöksonaten* as exemplifications of a significant break with Aristotelian dramaturgy]

[D1:521] Beyer, Nils, 'Stjärnspel och regiteater', in Jan Cornell, Bengt Olof Vos, and Märtha Ängström-Wilson, red., *De 50 åren: Sverige 1900-1950*, Stockholm: Åhlen & Åkerlund, 1950, pp. 135-164. ['Star Performers and Director's Theatre'. Surveys Swedish theatre 1900-1950, defining it as dominated by star actors and dogmatic directors]

[D1:522] Beyer, Nils, 'Olof Molander 50 år', *Social-Demokraten* (Stockholm), 16 October 1942. ['Olof Molander at 50'. Stresses Molander's achievement as an interpreter of the later Sg]

[D1:523] Bjurström, Carl Gustaf, 'De la difficulté du dialogue: quelques auteurs dramatiques suédois de Strindberg à Norén', *Théâtre en Europe* (Paris), 5:1 (1985), 32-38. Illus. ['On the Difficulty of Dialogue: Some Swedish Dramatists from Strindberg to Norén'. Focuses on Sg's later 'théâtre onirique' as seen by Pär Lagerkvist in **D1:604**, and realised on stage by Max Reinhardt. Also stresses the shadow cast by Sg over Lagerkvist's own plays, as well as those of Hjalmar Bergman, Axel Strindberg, Stig Dagerman, Per Olov Enquist, and Lars Norén]

[D1:524] Blanchart, P., 'L'Inconscient au Théâtre', *Masques* (Paris), 15 (March 1947), pp. 75-82. ['The Unconscious in the Theatre']

[D1:525] Boborykin, P., *Stolitsy mira*, Moscow: Sfinks, 1911, pp. 198-199. [Comments on Sg's plays in the repertoire of the Théâtre Libre in Paris. E.819]

[D1:526] Böckmann, Paul, 'Wandlungen der Dramenform im Expressionismus', in Vincent J. Günther, Hrsg., *Untersuchungen zur Literatur als Geschichte*, Festschrift für Benno von Weise, Berlin: Schmidt, 1973, pp. 445-464. ['The Transformation of Dramatic Form in Expressionism'. Considers Sg's influence on German expressionist drama in a study of the transformation wrought by expressionist dramatists on traditional, Aristotelian dramatic form. Focuses primarily on *Ett drömspel*]

[D1:527] Bødtker, Sigurd, 'Svensk Teater', in *S. B. Kristiania-premierer gjennem 30 aar. Sigurd Bødtkers teaterartikler*, utvalget besørget av Einar Skavlan og Anton Rønneberg, 3 Bind, Kristiania: Aschehoug, 1923-1929, Bind 2, pp. 93-97. ['Swedish Theatre'. Rpr. of **D1:669**]

[D1:528] Bødtker, Sigurd, 'Harriet Bosse', in *S. B. Kristiania-premierer gjennem 30 aar. Sigurd Bødtkers teaterartikler*, utvalget besørget av Einar Skavlan og Anton Rønneberg, 3 Bind, Kristiania: H. Aschehoug & Co. (W. Nygaard), 1923-1929, Bind 2, pp. 215-218. [Characterises Bosse as an actress with reference to her performances as Viola in *Twelfth Night*, Hugo von Hofmannsthal's Elektra, and Agda in Tor Hedberg's *Johan Ulfstjerna*, as well as to her appearance as an ultra-Parisienne Henriette in *Brott och brott*]

[D1:529] [Bouquet, Michel], 'Faire de l'abstrait avec du réel. Entretien avec Michel Bouquet', *Théâtre/Public* (Gennevilliers), 73:4 (1986), 60-65. Illus. ['Create the Abstract with the Real. An Interview with Michel Bouquet'. Bouquet (who played Edgar in Claude Chabrol's staging of *Dödsdansen* at the Théâtre de l'Atelier in 1985) discusses acting in Sg. Draws comparisons with performing in Beckett and Pinter]

[D1:530] Brisson, Pierre, 'En retrouvant *Hedda Gabler*', in *Le Théâtre des années folles*, Geneva: Éditions du Milieu du monde, 1943, pp. 69-81. ['Meeting Hedda Gabler'. Argues with reference to Lugné-Poe's production of *Dödsdansen* at Théâtre de l'Œuvre that 'the true poet of the peninsular, Ibsen's contemporary, could be found on the other side of the frontier, in Sweden, and was called Strindberg…His work ignores dogma and reanimates the true spirit of tragedy']

[D1:531] Brown, John Mason, 'The Modern Theatre in Revolt', in *Dramatis Personæ: A Retrospective Show*, London: Hamish Hamilton, 1963, pp. 461-534. [Makes only brief reference to Sg]

[D1:532] Brunius, August, 'Max Reinhardt 1920. En karakteristik och värdering', *Ord och Bild* (Stockholm), 30:11 (1921), 58-64. ['A Characteristic and an Evaluation'. Assesses the theatre of Max Reinhart, but with little regarding his productions of Sg]

[D1:533] Buckman, Thomas R., 'Pär Lagerkvist and the Swedish Theatre', *Tulane Drama Review* (New Orleans), 6:2 (1961), 60-89. [Characterises Lagerkvist as the direct heir to Sg's dramatic expressionism in *Till Damaskus* and *Ett drömspel*, and the first in Sweden to recognise his revolutionary role in the development of modern drama. From the apparent confusion of his hallucinatory experiences, Sg evolved an entirely new dramatic form, akin to the most disciplined of all art forms, the musical fugue. His dramatic concepts initially repelled Swedish critics and could not be realised by contemporary actors or existing technical resources, but Olof Molander's production of *Ett drömspel* in 1935 initiated a new period in the stage history of Sgian drama, in which his characteristic fluctuation between fantasy and realism at last received adequate expression. Moreover, for the first time, the deep religious feeling of these plays was manifested with clarity and intensity. Buckman contextualises Sg's innovations and Lagerkvist's response to them, both in his early plays and the essay on modern theatre within an overview of 20th-Century Swedish theatre. According to Brunius, although it recalls *Spöksonaten*, a play like Lagerkvist's *Den svåra stunden III* does not share Sg's optimism, but sees the transition from life to death as a movement from darkness to darkness]

[D1:534] Buckman, Thomas R., 'Pär Lagerkvist and the Swedish Theatre', in *Pär Lagerkvist*, New Orleans: The Tulane Drama Review, 1961, pp. 60-89. [Rpr. of **D1:533**]

[D1:535] Buckman, Thomas R., 'Stylistic and Textual Changes in "Modern Theatre"', *Scandinavian Studies* (Lawrence, Kansas), 33:3 (1961), 137-149. [Pär Lagerkvist revised the 1918 text for the second edition of his manifesto on the modern theatre (1946) with its assessment of Sg's significance for the development of a new drama. This entailed a number of stylistic changes, the rewriting of several paragraphs, and the elimination of others entirely, but without materially altering the effect of the original. A further revision in 1956 removed a disparaging remark about Ibsen]

[D1:536] Carlson, Harry G[ilbert], and Susan Einhorn, 'Stockholm's Orion Theatre', *Western European Stages* (New York), 3:1 (1991). [Includes an account of Lars Rudolfsson's 1987 production of *Till Damaskus* and his staging of *Ett drömspel* in 1990]

[D1:537] Charpentier, J. L., 'A propos de la Décadence du Théâtre', *Akademos* (Paris), 15 December 1909. ['On the Decadence of the Theatre']

[D1:538] Chevrel, Yves, 'Ibsen et la rénovation de la scène française a la fin du XIXe siècle', in Bengt Novén, Lars-Göran Sundell, Gunilla Ransbo, and Maria Walecka-Garbalińska, eds, *Resonances de la recherche. Festskrift till Sigbrit Swahn*, Acta Universitatis Upsaliensis, Studia Romanic Upsaliensia 59, Uppsala: University of Uppsala, 1999, pp. 111-119. ['Ibsen and the Renewal of the French Theatre at the End of the 19th Century'. Although Ibsen may have been a primary inspiration, Chevrel also notes Sg's influence]

[D1:539] Coco, William, 'The Dramaturgy of the Dream Play. Breuer, Chaikin, Shepard', in [Roberto Alonge], ed., **D2:7**, *Alle origini della drammaturgia moderna Ibsen, Strindberg, Pirandello*, pp. 171-178. [Regards Sg's dreamplay dramaturgy as the precursor of (post)-modernity in the contemporary American theatre, e.g. in Lee Breyer's stage monologue *Hajj* and *The War in Heaven*, a monologue for radio co-authored through improvisation by Joseph Chaikin and Sam Shepard, which explores the notion of the 'characterless character'. New technologies exploited in these works permit the stage representation of an innovative idea of character, one only dreamt of by Sg]

[D1:540] Coco, Bill, 'The Dramaturgy of the Dream Play. Breuer, Chaikin, Shepard', in Enoch Brater, ed., *The Theatrical Gamut: Notes for a Post-Beckettian Stage*, Ann Arbor: University of Michigan Press, 1995, pp. 159-170. [See **D1:539**]

[D1:541] Codignola, Luciano, 'La crisi della struttura drammatica tradizionale in Strindberg e in Pirandello', *Studi Urbaniti di Storia, Filosofia e Letteratura* (Urbino), 48 (1974), 91-102. ['The Crisis of Traditional Dramatic Structure in Strindberg and Pirandello'. See **D1:542**]

[D1:542] Codignola, Luciano, 'La crisi della struttura drammatica tradizionale in Strindberg e in Pirandello', in [Roberto Alonge], ed., **D2:7**, *Alle origini della drammaturgia moderna Ibsen, Strindberg, Pirandello*, pp. 63-73. ['The Crisis of Traditional Dramatic Structure in Strindberg and Pirandello'. With reference mainly to *Fadren*, *Fordringsägare*, and *Spöksonaten*, Codignola describes how, after the experiences described in *Inferno*, Sg was compelled to develop radically new forms of dramatic structure which are open rather than closed, to which Pirandello subsequently responded in *Sei personaggi in cerca d'autore* (1921)]

[D1:543] Cohn, Ruby, 'Surrealism and Today's French Theatre', *Yale French Studies* (New Haven, Conn.), 31 (1964), 159-165. [Observes that Artaud's production of *Ett drömspel* in 1928 was a venture into the commercial theatre and hence brought about his break with the surrealists. Cohn also notes how Arthur Adamov's drama, *L'Aveu*, is indebted to Sg]

[D1:544] Currie, R. Hector, 'The Energies of Tragedy: Cosmic and Psychic', *Centennial Review* (East Lancing, Michigan), 11:2 (1967), 220-236. [Contrasts Shakespeare's 'psychic tragedy of stress' with the superior cosmic drama of Sophocles and Sg. Currie employs Jungian categories to locate tragedy's ultimate action as an integration of the hero in the cosmic energy of original chaos]

[D1:545] Defresne, A., 'Het expressionisme in de huidige Duitsche tooneelschrijfkunst', 1-4, *Groot Nederland* (Amsterdam), 23:1 (1925), pp. 293-312, 406-429, 513-530, 625-642. ['Expressionism in Contemporary German Drama'. Comments on Sg's significance for German expressionism]

[D1:546] d'Hoedt, P.-J., 'Tooneelschrijvers van betekenis', 1-2, *De Zaaier* (Flanders), 2 (1908), pp. 5-7; 3 (1909), p. 92. ['Playwrights of Consequence'. Comments on Sg as a naturalist dramatist in Part Two]

[D1:547] Diamond, Elin, 'Modern Drama/Modernity's Drama', *Modern Drama* (Toronto), 44:1 (2001), 3-15. [Discusses the Preface to *Fröken Julie* as a seminal text in the definition of modernity in the theatre. Also discusses Brecht and Aphra Benn]

[D1:548] Ek, Sverker R., 'Olof Molander – Sanningssökaren', in Claes Rosenqvist, red., *Den Svenska nationalscenen. Tradition och reform på Dramaten under 2000 år*, Höganäs: Wiken, 1988, pp. 390-394. ['Olof Molander – The Seeker after Truth'. Considers Olof Molander's role in establishing Dramaten as Sweden's national stage with Sg as its national dramatist, primarily with reference to his productions of *Ett drömspel* in 1955 and *Spöksonaten* in 1942 and 1946]

[D1:549] Erdmann, Nils, 'Pär Lagerkvist, *Teater*', 1-2, *Nya Dagligt Allehanda* (Stockholm), 15 and 22 June 1918. [Reviews Lagerkvist's play *Den svåra stunden* and his essay on modern theatre, **D1:604**, with its largely positive response to Sg's later dramaturgy. Erdmann, however, considers the latter pathological]

[D1:550] Esslin, Martin, 'Naturalism in Context', *Tulane Drama Review* (New Orleans), 13:2 (1968), 67-76. [Contextualises Sg's naturalism in terms of the theories of Taine and Zola, as well as the dramas of Ibsen, Chekhov, Gerhart Hauptmann, Maksim Gor'kii, and Henry Becque]

[D1:551] Esslin, Martin, 'Naturalism in Perspective', in *Brief Chronicles: Essays on the Modern Theatre*, London: Maurice Temple Smith, 1970, pp. 21-38. [Rpr. of **D1:550**]

[D1:552] Esslin, Martin, 'Naturalism in Perspective', in *Reflections: Essays on Modern Theatre*, New York: Doubleday & Company, Inc., 1969, pp. 11-27. [Rpr. of **D1:550**]

[D1:553] Ewbank, Inga-Stina, 'Scandinavia 1849-1912', in Claude Schumacher, ed., *Naturalism and Symbolism in European Theatre, 1850-1918*, Cambridge: Cambridge

University Press, 1996, pp. 259-320. Illus. [Includes annotated documentation on Sg's attitude to realism and naturalism, his correspondence with Zola in 1887, and material concerning the foundation of the Scandinavian Experimental Theatre in Copenhagen in 1888 and the creation of the Intimate Theatre in Stockholm in 1907-10, as well as on how to stage *Till Damaskus* and *Ett drömspel*]

[D1:554] Faludi, Iwan, 'Schwedisches Theater', *Das Blaue Heft* (Berlin), 9 (1927), 19-22. ['Swedish Theatre']

[D1:555] 'Fero', 'Die drei großen skandinavischen Dramatiker', *Die Schaubühne* (Berlin), 1 (1905), 221-222. ['The Three Great Scandinavian Dramatists'. Comments on Sg, Ibsen, and Bjørnstjerne Bjørnson]

[D1:556] Finney, Gail, 'Theater of Impotence: The One-Act Tragedy at the Turn of the Century', *Modern Drama* (Toronto), 28:3 (1985), 451-461. [Discusses Sg's ideas in the essay 'Om modernt drama och modern teater' (1889), which Finney regards as the first programmatic attempt to define a specifically modern form of one-act play. Sg commends the genre's rejection of complicated and unlikely external intrigue in favour of a concern with inner processes. Because of its compressed nature and its concentration on a single dramatic situation, the one-acter tends to depict extremes of experience and moments of crisis, very often the moment immediately preceding death, thus facilitating the tragic experience in plays like *Fröken Julie*, *Pelikanen*, and *Samum*, which Finney discusses alongside works by Oscar Wilde, Maeterlinck, John Millington Synge, and Arthur Schnitzler]

[D1:557] Flaxman, Seymour L., 'Hebbel, Ibsen, Strindberg and the Development of Dramatic Technique', in *Langue et Littérature. Actes du VIIIe Congrès de la Fédération Internationale des Langues et Littératures Modernes*, Paris, 1961, pp. 297-298.

[D1:558] Fuchs, Elinor, 'The Mysterium. A Modern Dramatic Genre', *Theatre Three* (Pittsburgh), 1 (1986), 73-88. [Defines the genre of the modern mystery play with reference to Georg Kaiser, Antonin Artaud, and Samuel Beckett, as well as to Sg in *Advent* and elsewhere]

[D1:559] Garibova, O., '[They Play Strindberg]', *Teatr* (Moscow), 1976:11, pp. 129-131. [On Ingmar Bergman's productions of *Ett drömspel*, *Spöksonaten*, and *Till Damaskus*. E.1092a]

[D1:560] Garten, H. F., 'Foreign Influences on German Expressionist Drama', in Ulrich Weisstein, ed., **C1:1360**, *Expressionism as an International Literary Phenomenon*, pp. 59-68. [Identifies Sg as the greatest single influence on expressionism in the theatre, especially with the dramaturgy of *Till Damaskus* and *Ett drömspel*, and most particularly in Germany. His ostensibly naturalistic plays already contain expressionistic elements and the Damaskus trilogy is the prototype of expressionist drama, both in terms of its external form (which anticipates Reinhardt Sorge's *Der Bettler*, 1912), and its spiritual substance (a man's transformation and regeneration, which becomes the dominant theme of German expressionist drama). Although the pessimism of *Ett drömspel* distinguishes it from genuine expressionist drama, Garten argues that the non-verbal aspects of this play, and especially the symbolic use of light, colour, music, and scenery to express states of mind, foreshadow the principles of expressionist staging]

[D1:561] Gerould, Daniel, and Jadwiga Kosicka, 'The Drama of the Unseen: Turn-of-the-Century Paradigms for Occult Drama', *New York Literary Forum*, 4 (1980), 3-42. Illus.

[Gerould and Kosicka believe that Sg's contacts with the occult are germane to an account of its relationship with drama that otherwise focuses mainly on the work of Bely, Przybyszewski, Miciński, Ciurlionis, and Maeterlinck. Sg in fact practiced several varieties of the historical occult, revealing the hand of invisible powers in the Swedish past in *Gustav Vasa* and *Erik XIV*, and interventions by the Unseen in contemporary life in *Till Damaskus* and *Brott och brott*. Here, cause-and-effect plot is subordinated to symmetrical patterning of events, which the author-hero sees as a manifestation of the invisible forces directing his life. His rejection of causality in favour of coincidence in *Inferno* violates common sense and the supposed logic of the theatre that is based upon it, but far from being a flaw, excessive use of coincidence is a crucial device in occult drama. Although concerned only briefly with Sg, this essay provides his post-Inferno dramaturgy with an interesting context in both contemporary drama and the undergrowth of *fin-de-siècle* culture]

[D1:562] Giannini, Clemente, 'Introdotto' and 'Commentato', in *Teatro Svedese*, a cura di Clemente Giannini, Milano: Nuovo Accademia Editrice, 1963. 515 pp. [The introduction and notes to Italian translations of *Dödsdansen*, *Svanevit*, *Pelikanen*, and *Ett drömspel*]

[D1:563] Gilman, Richard, 'The True and Only Crisis of the Theater: Notes for a Scenario on Drama, Movies, Acting, Illusion and Reality', in *The Confusion of Realms*, London: Weidenfeld and Nicolson, 1970, pp. 219-233. [Rpr. of **D1:564**]

[D1:564] Gilman, Richard, 'The True and Only Crisis of the Theater: Notes for a Scenario on Drama, Movies, Acting, Illusion and Reality', *New American Review* (New York), 4 (1968), 164-176. [Declares that, 'Almost all the interesting drama of our century has taken shape under Sg's auspices']

[D1:565] Goodman, Randolph G., 'Playwatching with a Third Eye', *Columbia University Forum* (New York), 10:1 (1967), 18-22.

[D1:566] Govekar, Fran, 'Drama ljubezni in zakona', *Jutro* (Ljubljana), 10 August 1922.

[D1:567] Gravier, Maurice, 'L'Expressionnisme dramatique en France entre les deux guerres', in Denis Bablet and Jean Jacquot, eds, **D1:33**, *L'Expressionnisme dans le théâtre européen*, pp. 287-298. Illus. ['Expressionist Drama in France Between the Two Wars'. Initially best known for the naturalist dramas premièred in France by Antoine and Lugné-Poe, Gravier illustrates how Sg's post-Inferno plays only made an impact on the French theatre between the two World Wars via the plays of H.-R. Lenormand, who had first encountered them in Max Reinhardt's productions of *Dödsdansen* and *Spöksonaten*. An analysis of Lenormand's plays reveals how he adopted many features of Sg's later dramaturgy. Other French dramatists influenced by Sgian expressionism were Simon Gantillon and Jean-Victor Pellerin, whose *Cris des cœurs* recalls the Chamber Plays. Gravier also comments on Artaud's staging of *Ett drömspel*]

[D1:568] Gravier, Maurice, 'Les Héros du drame expressionniste', in *Le Théâtre moderne: Hommes et tendances*, Entretiens d'Arras, 20-24 Juin 1957, Études réunies et présentés par Jean Jacquot, deuxième édition illustrée, Paris: Éditions du Centre National de la Recherche Scientifique, 1965, pp. 117-130. ['The Heroes of Expressionist Drama'. Defines the divided, unstable, and sometimes hysterical hero of expressionist drama with reference to the Preface to *Fröken Julie*, *Till Damaskus*, and *Ett drömspel*, as well as to Sg's overall impact on subsequent German drama in general. Gravier also compares Sg with Pirandello and Pär Lagerkvist, and treats Kafka as a declared disciple of Sg]

[D1:569] Gravier, Maurice, 'Strindberg and French Drama' / 'Strindberg et les dramaturges français', *World Theatre-Le Théâtre dans le monde* (Bruxelles), 11:1 (1962), 45-60. Illus. [Points out that several of those who, like Alexandre Dumas *fils*, Jean-Martin Charcot, the Sâr Péladan, and Louis Desprez, exerted a significant influence on Sg and his playwriting were French. But in spite of the early productions of his naturalist plays by Antoine and Lugné-Poe, it was as a woman-hater and alchemist that Sg enjoyed most renown in France during his lifetime. He only came to the fore with Boris's staging of *Dödsdansen* at the Théâtre de l'Œuvre in 1921, and again with the same play during the German occupation. Initially, it was Artaud, Jean-Victor Pellerin, and H.-R. Lenormand on whom Sg exerted a palpable influence, but following Jean Vilar's wartime productions of *Dödsdansen* and *Oväder*, both Jean Cocteau and Sartre eulogised him. To Gravier's mind, Sg was never a genuine naturalist and the scientific psychology of *Vivisektioner* and his best-known plays of the 1880s already display an affinity with magic and occult modes of thought. His dramatic dialogue, meanwhile, is striking because of its starkness, and if one strips a play like Jean Cocteau's *Parents terribles* to its essentials, one can discern the Sgian formula, just as one recognises *Dödsdansen* in both Jean Anouilh's *Valse des Toréadors* and Sartre's *Huis clos*, and *Till Damaskus* in Lenormand's *L'Homme est ses fantômes*]

[D1:570] Grevenius, Herbert, 'Sanningen är torr. Samtal om teater och religion', *Signum* (Uppsala), 14 (1988), 167-172. ['The Truth is Dry. A Conversation about the Theatre and Religion'. Sg discussed, pp. 168-169]

[D1:571] Grevenius, Herbert, 'Sekelvändan 1900', in Claes Hoogland and Gösta Kjellin, *Bilder ur svensk teaterhistoria*, Stockholm: Sveriges Radios förlag, 1970, pp. 227-250. Illus. ['The Turn-of-the-Century, 1900'. Places Sg's dramas in the context of turn-of-the-century Swedish theatre, with the première of *Till Damaskus I* commanding most attention. Recordings of the foremost actors of the period, sometimes in roles by Sg, are listed, pp. 268-276]

[D1:572] Grevenius, Herbert, 'Molanders insats', in **D1:178**, *I afton klockan 8: Premiärer och Mellanspel*, pp. 221-226. ['Molander's Contribution'. Rpr. of **D1:573**]

[D1:573] Grevenius, Herbert, 'Molanders insats', *Stockholms-Tidningen*, 13 June 1938. ['Molander's Contribution'. Olof Molander made Sg speak Swedish in contrast to the cosmopolitan Max Reinhardt by setting his production of *Pelikanen* in the turn-of-the century milieu in which it was written. His biographical approach has given us a Sg who is a Swede and a Stockholmer in whose pessimism and bitterness we can hear the green shores and open water of the archipelago. The international bohemian Sg with the neurotic gestures of a superman and his eternal poet's querulousness is foreign to a Swedish theatre audience]

[D1:574] Grevenius, Herbert, 'Den göteborgska talscenen', in Erik Wettergren and Ivar Lignell, red., *Teater i Sverige de sista 50 åren*, Stockholm: Svensk litteratur, 1940, pp. 620-629. ['The Dramatic Theatre in Gothenburg'. Includes performances of Sg's plays in a survey of fifty years of theatre in Göteborg]

[D1:575] Grimm, Reinhold, 'The Hidden Heritage: Repercussions of Nietzsche in Modern Theatre and its Theory', *Nietzsche Studien: Internationales Jahrbuch für die Nietzsche*

-Forschung (Berlin), 12 (1983), pp. 355-371. [Argues the centrality for the development of modern drama of Nietzsche's theory of tragedy, first articulated in *Die Geburt der Tragödie* (The Birth of Tragedy, 1872), although it has been consistently underestimated even in relation to writers like Sg, with whom Nietzsche had a known affinity]

[D1:576] Groff, Edward, 'Point of View in Modern drama', *Modern Drama* (Lawrence, Kansas), 2:3 (1959), 268-282. [Comments briefly on *Ett drömspel* and notes that, like Pirandello, Arthur Miller, Eugene O'Neill, Brecht, and Thornton Wilder, Sg seeks 'to make the playform more subjective by associating the dramatic events with the consciousness of individual characters who may participate in the action or merely narrate the story presented on the stage']

[D1:577] Halleux, Pierre, 'Le domaine Scandinavie', in Denis Bablet and Jean Jacquot, eds, **D1:33**, *L'Expressionnisme dans le théâtre européen*, pp. 299-310. Illus. [Halleux assesses the influence of Sg on Scandinavian dramatists between the two World Wars, a process that was often mediated by the impact of Max Reinhardt's productions of his plays. Pär Lagerkvist was the first to respond positively to the later Sg in **D1:604**, and several of his plays, including *Den osynlige*, betray Sg's influence. So, too, do the plays of the Swede, Hjalmar Bergman, the Norwegian, Tore Ørjasæter, and the Dane, Svend Borberg]

[D1:578] Hamilton, Clayton, 'Seen on the Stage', *Vogue* (New York), 47 (15 April 1916), pp. 68-69, 121. [Describes how 'the stormy mind of Sg rushes like a tempest through a vale of tears, blowing out all lights and leaving us agrope in darkness']

[D1:579] Hansen, Harald, '[Téâtre]', *Revue d'Art Dramatique* (Paris), 15 (1 July 1889), 37-45. [Recognises Sg as 'a Swedish author of unarguable genius who has recently been engaged in creating a Scandinavian Théâtre Libre in Copenhagen. M. Sg has written several powerful plays which are, however, inferior to those of Ibsen'. This notice in a reputable French journal was immediately seized upon and quoted by Sg himself in a letter to Ola Hansson (6 July 1889)]

[D1:580] Hasenkamp, Gottfried, 'Von Gerhart Hauptmann zu Paul Claudel. Ein Querschnitt durch das moderne Drama', *Literaturwissenschaftliches Jahrbuch der Görres-Gesellschaft* (Freiburg), 6 (1931), pp. 1-24. ['From Gerhart Hauptmann to Paul Claudel. A Cross-Section through Modern Drama']

[D1:581] Heiberg, Gunnar, 'Strindberg', in *Franske visitter*, Kristiania: H. Aschehoug & Co., 1919, pp. 56-66. [A discussion of *Mäster Olof*, *Fordringsägare*, and *Brott och brott* by the Norwegian Dramatist (1857-1929)]

[D1:582] Henning, Fenger, 'Det veldrejede og mondæne teater', in Christian Ludvigsen and Stephan Kehler, red., *Teatrets historie*, København: Politiken, 1962, pp. 219-70. ['The Well-Made and Fashionable Theatre'. Advances the claims of the well-made play as an influential precursor of the kind of naturalistic drama produced by both Ibsen and Sg]

[D1:583] Holm, Ingvar, 'Arvet från Strindberg', in Claes Hoogland and Gösta Kjellin, eds, *Bilder ur svensk teaterhistoria*, Stockholm: Sveriges Radios Förlag, 1970, pp. 279-301. Illus. ['The Legacy of Strindberg'. Surveys Sg's influence on modern Swedish drama, in the form of Pär Lagerkvist's *Himlens hemlighet* and Hjalmar Bergman's *Sagan*, and the continental theatre, most notably German expressionism, as in the plays of Wedekind and Toller, and the work of contemporary absurdists like Adamov, Beckett, and Ionesco]

[D1:584] Huneker, James [Gibbon], 'After Ibsen?', *Forum* (New York), 39 (1907), 248-254. [Identifies Sg as Ibsen's natural successor]

[D1:585] Hupperetz, Karel J., 'Scandinavian Authors on Dutch Stages', *Scandinavian Newsletter* (Groningen), 7 (1992-93), 23-25. Illus. [Reports on Dutch productions of plays by Ibsen, Sg, and Lars Norén]

[D1:586] Ihering, Herbert, 'Seltsames Zwischenspiel', in *Von Reinhardt bis Brecht. Vier Jahzehnte Theater und Film*, Vol. 2, 1924-1929, Berlin: Aufbau-Verlag, pp. 449-451. ['Strange Interlude'. On Ibsen and Sg. First published 5 November 1929]

[D1:587] Jacobsohn, Siegfried, 'Vignettes from Reinhardt's Productions', in Oliver M. Sayler, ed., *Max Reinhardt and His Theatre*, Translated by Mariele S. Gudernatsch and Others, New York/London: Benjamin Blom, 1968, pp. 323-326. [Describes how Max Reinhardt's ear hears all of Sg's music, even its dissonances, without attempting to make harmonies of them. 'He venerates the Sg who is tortured beyond measure...He carries the victims of this fanatic lover of the truth into an atmosphere so distorted, so gloomy, so full of fantastic life and motion, that it might be Van Gogh's'. Rpr. of the 1924 edition]

[D1:588] Jarc, Evgen, 'Moderna nemška drama (Literarna študija)', *Katoliški obzornik* (Ljubljana/Maribor), 7 (1904), pp. 14, 19, 326, 435.

[D1:589] Jollivet, Gaston, 'Le Théâtre Scandinave', *L'Éclair* (Paris), 14 November 1894. ['The Scandinavian Theatre']

[D1:590] Kerr, Alfred, 'Wegener', in *Das Welt in Drama*, 5 Bde, Bd 1, *Das Mimenreich*, Berlin: S. Fischer Verlag, 1917, pp. 437-439. [Comments on Paul Wegener as Edgar in *Dödsdansen* and Hummel in *Spöksonaten*]

[D1:591] Kerr, Alfred, 'Die Bertens', in *Das Welt in Drama*, 5 Bde, Bd 1, *Das Mimenreich*, Berlin: S. Fischer Verlag, 1917, pp. 452-453. [On Rosa Bertens who created the roles of Laura and Julie in the German premières of *Fadren* and *Fröken Julie* in 1892-93, and went on to play a significant part in securing Sg a preeminent place in the German theatre as the Mother in *Mäster Olof*, Mme X in *Den starkare*, the Baroness in the world première of *Bandet*, the Judge's Wife in *Advent*, and Alice in Max Reinhardt's staging of *Dödsdansen*. According to Kerr, 'For Sg her creativity was indispensable']

[D1:592] Kerr, Alfred, 'Die Orska', in *Das Welt in Drama*, 5 Bde, Bd 1, *Das Mimenreich*, Berlin: S. Fischer Verlag, 1917, pp. 454-458. [Comments on Maria Orska's performances as the Wife in *Kamraterna* and Judith in *Dödsdansen II*]

[D1:593] Kerr, Alfred, 'Die Eysoldt', in *Das Welt in Drama*, 5 Bde, Bd 1, *Das Mimenreich*, Berlin: S. Fischer Verlag, 1917, pp. 465-468. [Assesses Gertrud Eysoldt's qualities as an actress, including her celebrated performances in Sg's plays, in productions usually directed by Max Reinhardt]

[D1:594] Kerr, Alfred, 'Die Triesch', in *Das Welt in Drama*, 5 Bde, Bd 1, *Das Mimenreich*, Berlin: S. Fischer Verlag, 1917, pp. 468-471. [On Irene Triesch, who created the role of Kersti in the German première of *Kronbruden* (1913) and Indra's Daughter in Rudolf Bernauer's production of *Ett drömspel* (1916)]

[D1:595] Kesting, Marianne, 'Brecht und der Symbolismus. Verleugnete Zusammenhänge', in *Entdeckung und Destruktion. Zur Strukturumwandlung der Künste*, München: Wilhelm Fink Verlag, 1970, pp. 223-248. ['Brecht and Symbolism. A Repudiated Relationship'. Compares the dreamlike structure of *Der gute Mensch von Sezuan* with

Ett drömspel, to demonstrate a greater affinity between the dramaturgy of Brecht and the later Sg than is customarily assumed]

[D1:596] Kesting, Marianne, 'Der Abbau der Persönlichkeit. Zur Theorie der Figur im modernen Drama', in *Beiträge zur Poetik des Dramas*, Hrsg. von Werner Keller, Darmstadt: Wissenschaftliche Buchgesellschaft, 1976, pp. 211-235. ['The Deconstruction of Personality. On the Theory of Character in Modern Drama'. Surveys the destruction of traditional, realistic notions of personality and character in the modern theatre with reference to Sg's vivisection 'Le Caractere un role?' (1894) and the Preface to *Fröken Julie* (both written with the contemporary French psychologists Jean-Martin Charcot and Théodule Ribot in mind), as well as to his practice in *Dödsdansen*. Kesting also suggests that, with *Spöksonaten*, Sg anticipates and influences Pirandello's deconstruction of traditional characterisation into a series of roles in *Cosi é (se vi pare)* (1917) and *Sei personaggi in cerca d'autore* (1921), as well as the theatre of Samuel Beckett. Together with *Till Damaskus* and *Ett drömspel*, Kesting suggests that *Spöksonaten* exemplifies the way in which the modern theatre presents character as a series of roles, even including the work of Brecht, whose *Der gute Mensch von Sezuan* compares with *Ett drömspel* in this respect]

[D1:597] Kesting, Marianne, 'Musikalisierung des Theaters – Theatralisierung der Musik', in *Entdeckung und Destruktion. Zur Strukturumwandlung der Künste*, München: Wilhelm Fink Verlag, 1970, pp. [277]-302. ['The Musicalisation of Theatre – The Theatricalisation of Music'. Discusses Sg's dramaturgy in *Till Damaskus, Ett drömspel*, and his one-acters as, along with the plays of Chekhov and Maeterlinck, a major impetus in the introduction of musical form into modern drama, pp. 279-280]

[D1:598] Kobialka, Michal, 'Symbolist Drama and New Genesis: The Concept of the Suffering Demon as the Ordering Principle of Chaos', *Journal of Dramatic Theory and Criticism* (Lawrence, Kansas), 3:1 (1988), 31-46. [Describes how the theme of God versus the Devil which permeates much Symbolist theatre was inherited by Sg from Byron's *Cain* and first appeared in the Manichean 'Coram Populo' which concludes *Mäster Olof*, where Lucifer is depicted as the Bearer of Light who is dethroned by the evil spirit, God. In presenting the Devil as a suffering demon, Sg anticipates several symbolist plays including Oscar Panizza's *The Council of Love* (1894), and the paintings of Mikhail Vrubel]

[D1:599] Koltai, Tamás, 'Messages from the Past: Gyorgy Spiró: *Az imposztor* (The Imposter), Magda Szabó: *Béla király* (King Belaj), Gábor Görgey: *Galopp a Vérmezön* (Galloping on Vérmezön), Milhály Babits: *Leodameia*, Wedekind: *Lulu*, Schnitzler: *Anatol*, Strindberg: *Fadren*, Shaw: *Widower's Houses*, Shakespeare: *Hamlet*', *The New Hungarian Quarterly* (Budapest), 25 (1984), 193-199. [*Fadren* is one of several plays from the turn-of-the-century which features a *femme fatale* and is currently to be seen in the Hungarian theatre]

[D1:600] Kosovel, Stano, 'Kritika dramskega repertoarja', *Kritika* (Ljubljana?), 3 (1925), 35-37. ['A Critique of the Dramatic Repertoire']

[D1:601] Kralj, Vladimir, 'Sodobna antidrama', '*Problemi* (Ljubljana), 3:29 (1965), 597-610. ['Contemporary Anti-Drama']

[D1:602] Kraus, Karl, 'Josef Jarno', *Die Fackel* (Vienna), 10 February 1906, pp. 14-21. [Contains Kraus's unflattering view of Jarno's contribution to the contemporary

Viennese theatre, including his advocacy of Sg under his direction at the Theater in der Josefstadt and elsewhere]

[D1:603] Krauß, Rudolf, 'August Strindberg', in *Das Schauspielbuch*, 3 Aufl., Stuttgart, 1915, pp. 323-330. [Primarily concerned with the naturalistic Sg of *Fadren*, *Fröken Julie*, and *Fordringsägare*]

[D1:604] Lagerkvist, Pär, 'Modern teater. Synpunkter och angrepp', in *Teater*, Stockholm: Albert Bonniers Förlag, 1918. 183 pp. ['Modern Theatre: Points of View and Attack'. One of the definitive manifestos of the modern theatre, in which Sg's later plays are presented as models for a contemporary dramaturgy. Naturalism, including the drab psychological realism of Ibsen, curtails the possibilities of the theatre, and is an inadequate response to the age in which we live. But Sg's later plays, with their echoes of Shakespeare and the middle ages, provide a model for the modern theatre. In them, 'everything is directed to one end – the liberation of a single mood, a single feeling, whose intensity grows and grows unceasingly. Everything superfluous is excluded, even if it is of relevance to the context and the fidelity of the representation. Everything that happens is of equal importance. There are no minor roles…indeed, there are no "persons" in the normal, accepted meaning, no analysis, no psychological apparatus, or drawing of "characters". And yet, no abstractions, but images of man as he is when he is evil, when he is good, when he is sorrowful or full of joy. Simplification. And yet, richness. Richness, too, in the form itself: because everything plays its part, nothing is lifeless, everything is elevated and put into the drama as a living part of it, and because the theme is always shifting and suddenly broken off – to be continued on another plane. Confusion, but a confusion with meaning and order']

[D1:605] Lagerkvist, Pär, 'Modern teater. Synpunkter och angrepp (1918)', in *Dramatik*, Vols 1-3, Stockholm: Albert Bonniers Förlag, 1956, Vol. 1, pp. 5-50. [Revised version of **D1:604**]

[D1:606] Lagerkvist, Pär, 'Modern Theatre: Points of View and Attack', in Evert Sprinchorn, ed., *The Genius of the Scandinavian Theater*, New York: New American Library, 1964, pp. 604-637. [Rpr. of **D1:604** in Thomas Buckland's translation, first published as **D1:607**]

[D1:607] Lagerkvist, Pär, 'Modern Theatre: Points of View and Attack', Translated by Thomas R. Buckman, in Pär Lagerkvist, *Modern Theatre. Seven Plays and an Essay*, Lincoln: University of Nebraska Press, 1966, pp. 1-38. [Translation of **D1:604**, at Lagerkvist's request using the revised version of 1946]

[D1:608] Lagerkvist, Pär, 'Modern Theatre: Points of View and Attack', in *Pär Lagerkvist*, New Orleans: The Tulane Drama Review, 1961, pp. 3-31. [Rpr. of **D1:604** in Thomas Buckland's translation, first published as **D1:607**]

[D1:609] Lagerkvist, Pär, 'Strindberg and the Theater of Tomorrow', in Otto Reinert, **B1:371**, *Strindberg: A Collection of Critical Essays*, pp. 90-96 [An extract from **D1:604** in Thomas Buckland's translation]

[D1:610] Lagerkvist, Pär, 'Strindberg and the Theater of Tomorrow', *The Tulane Drama Review* (New Orleans), 6:2 (1961), 60-89 [**D1:604** in Thomas Buckland's translation]

[D1:611] Lagerkvist, Pär, 'Le Théâtre moderne', traduction C. G. Bjurström, *Revue Théâtrale* (Paris), 14:5 (1950), 29-50. [French translation of **D1:604**]

[D1:612] Lagerroth, Ulla-Britta, 'Pär Lagerkvist – dramatikern och teaterteoretikern', in *Pär Lagerkvist 100 år. Föreläsningar och anföranden i Växjö våren 1991 utgivna av Pär Lagerkvist-Samfundet*, Växjö, 1991, pp. 5-22. ['Pär Lagerkvist: The Dramatist and Theorist of the Theatre'. Surveys Lagerkvist's achievement as a dramatist and his ideas about the theatre, inspired in part by his appreciation of Sg's post-Inferno dramas]

[D1:613] Lämmerts, Eberhard, 'Das expressionistische Verkündigungsdrama', in Hans Steffen, Hrsg., *Das deutsche Expressionismus, Formen und Gestalten*, Göttingen: Vandenhoeck & Ruprecht, 1965, pp. 138-156. ['The Expressionist Prophecy Drama'. Discusses Sg's influence on expressionist dramaturgy; without adequate psychological motivation, it is difficult to find an appropriate motivation for the succession of stage images such plays present]

[D1:614] Lange, Sven, 'Omkring Reinhardt', *Teatret* (Copenhagen), 20 (1921-22), p. 38ff. ['About Reinhardt'. Discusses Max Reinhardt's productions of Sg]

[D1:615] Levi, C., 'Augusto Strindberg', in *Studi di teatro*, Palermo, 1923, pp. 277-287.

[D1:616] Lindström, Göran, 'De gamles form', *Samtiden* (Oslo), 61 (1952), 522-532. ['The Old Form'. On the traditional five-act form of drama, with reference to Shakespeare, Ibsen, Sg, and Lagerkvist]

[D1:617] Loraine, Winifred, *Robert Loraine. Soldier, Actor, Airman*, London: Collins, 1938. Illus. 390 pp. [A biography of Loraine by his wife, with an account of his appearances in *Fadren*, pp. 317-335, and *Dödsdansen*, pp. 344-348]

[D1:618] Lukács, György, *Zur Soziologie des modernen Dramas*, Archiv für Sozialwissenschaft und Socialpolitik (Tübingen), 38 (1914), pp. 303-345, 662-706. ['On the Sociology of Modern Drama'. German version of a substantial part of **D1:282**]

[D1:619] Lunacharskii, A[natoli] V., '[Contemporary Italian Drama]', *Novaia zhizn'* (St Petersburg) 1911:5, Sp. 142-146. [Discusses Sg in Sp. 151-152. E.822]

[D1:620] Lunacharskii, A[natoli] V., '[Contemporary Italian Drama]', in *Sobranie sochinenii*, Vol. 5, Moscow, 1964, pp. 156-169. [Rpr. of **D1:619**. E.822]

[D1:621] Lundgren, Henrik, 'Max Reinhardt in Dänemark', in Edda Leisler and Gisela Prossnitz, Hrsg., *Max Reinhardt in Europa*, Publikation der Max-Reinhardt-Forschungsstätte 4, Salzburg: Otto Müller Verlag, 1973, pp. 117-133. [Discusses Reinhardt's Sg productions (especially of *Spöksonaten*) on tour in Denmark. For a Danish public they were something of an unknown commodity]

[D1:622] Lutomski, Bołesław, 'Nowy temat w dramacie i now kobieta', *Echo Muzyczne, Teatralne i Artystyczne*, Nos 582-587 (1894), pp. 47-52. ['New Themes in Drama and the New Woman']

[D1:623] McMullen, Sally, 'Sense and Sensuality – Max Reinhardt's Earliest Productions', in Margaret Jacobs and John Warren, eds, *Max Reinhardt: The Oxford Symposium*, Oxford: Oxford Polytechnic, 1986, pp. 16-33. [Discusses Reinhardt's staging of *Brott och brott* with Gertrud Eysoldt as Henriette, 'a snakelike, disingenuous creature who conveyed the atmosphere of a latter-day Paradise Lost if anything rather too graphically'. This was one of five Reinhardt productions, including Maksim Gor'kii's *Lower Depths*, Hugo von Hofmannsthal's *Elektra*, and Frank Wedekind's *Erdgeist*, which contributed to a revolution in the history of the theatre and helped launch Reinhardt's spectacular career]

[D1:624] Malekin, Peter, 'The Perilous Edge: Strindberg, Madness and Other Worlds', in Patrick D. Murphy, ed., *Staging the Impossible: The Fantastic Mode in Modern Drama*, Contributions to the Sudy of Science Fiction and Fantasy, 54, Westport, CT.: Greenwood Press, 1992, pp. 44-55. [Explores the relationship of *Spöksonaten* and *Ett drömspel* to the fantastic in their concern with the theatrical representation of reality and appearance. To explain the late plays in terms of psychoanalytical theory or approach them merely as social or political comments is to explain them away. They are akin to the ontological decentring of language insisted upon by Derrida. Sg employs the doctrines of Swedenborg, Theosophy, and non-Western religion as interpretive models; they are part of a shifting, referential complementarity. which undermines conventional and erroneous ways of seeing and feeling, and opens the mind to new ways of experiencing]

[D1:625] Mann, Otto, 'Das Drama des Expressionismus', in Hermann Friedmann und Otto Mann, Hrsg., *Expressionismus. Gestalten einer literarischen Bewegung*, Heidelberg: Rothe Verlag, 1956, pp. 213-240. ['Expressionist Drama'. Confirms Sg's influence on Expressionist drama, particularly through *Till Damaskus* and *Ett drömspel*]

[D1:626] Marcus, Carl David, 'Ett besök hos Reinhardt. Vad han säger om Strindberg', *Dagens Nyheter* (Stockholm), 9 November 1915. ['A Visit to Reinhardt; What He has to Say about Strindberg'. An interview with Max Reinhardt on the eve of his first tour to Sweden. Fascinated by the way Sg delves so deeply into the mysteries of the inner life, Reinhardt wishes to make him the basis for theatrical renewal, and cannot understand why he is so neglected in his own country]

[D1:627] Marotti, Ferruccio, 'Il teatro svedese in Italia', *Il Veltro* (Rome), 10 (1966). ['Swedish Theatre in Italy']

[D1:628] Martin, Jacqueline, and Willmar Sauter, 'Postmodernism in the Theatre', *Nordic Theatre Studies* (Copenhagen), 5 (1992), 89-96. [Touches on *Fröken Julie* and *Till Damaskus* within an historically contextualised discussion of postmodernist theatre]

[D1:629] McNamara, Brooks, 'Scene Design: 1876-1965. Ibsen, Chekhov, Strindberg', *Tulane Drama Review* (New Orleans), 13:2 (1968), 77-91. [Includes production photos of *Brott och brott*, *Fadren*, *Moderskärlek*, and *Fröken Julie*, 1899-1965]

[D1:630] Mencken, H[enry] L[ouis], 'A Counterblast to Bunscombe', *The Smart Set* (New York), No. 39 (August 1913), pp. 153-160. [Concludes that Sg 'was a man of striking originality and unbounded courage, and always magnificently in earnest, most of all in his lunacies. But he was without the critical faculty. He lacked a feeling for form'. Mencken regards *Fadren* as Sg's masterpiece, followed by several 'extremely clever plays' – *Fröken Julie*, *Den starkare*, *Bandet*, and *Ett drömspel*]

[D1:631] Mencken, H[enry] L[ouis], 'Gerhart Hauptmann', *The Smart Set* (New York), No. 40 (March 1913), 153-158. [Dismisses both *Lycko-Pers resa* and *Påsk* as 'very silly stuff']

[D1:632] Mencken, H[enry] L[ouis], 'The Revival of the Printed Play', *The Smart Set* (New York), No. 33 (1911), 163-168. [In one of his earliest comments on Sg, Mencken observes that 'Sg knows how to write. For all his violence, he never grows ridiculous']

[D1:633] Mencken, H[enry] L[ouis], 'Synge and Others', *The Smart Set* (New York), No. 37 (October 1912), 147-152.

[D1:634] Mencken, H[enry] L[ouis], 'The Drama and Some Dramatists: Strindberg a Final Estimate', *The Smart Set*, No. 40 (1913). [Reviews recent translations of several prose works, including *Giftas*, as well as comments briefly on the plays. Mencken takes a less positive view of Sg than previously. 'He was a second rate artist....Over and over again he spoiled a good idea by treating it clumsily and superficially'. Rpr. in **B1:165**]

[D1:635] Michaelis, Rolf, 'Plaintes dans une vallée de larmes: Strindberg et la théâtre allemand', *Théâtre en Europe* (Paris), 5:1 (1985), 55-60. Illus. ['Lamentations in a Vale of Tears. Strindberg and the German Theatre'. Productions of *Dödsdansen* by Rudolf Noelte in Berlin (1971) and Barbara Bilabel in Hamburg (1982), *Gustav Adolf* by Hans-Günther Heyme in Wiesbaden (1965), *Ett drömspel* by Ingmar Bergman in Munich (1977), and *Fröken Julie* by B. K. Tragelehn in East Berlin, Werner Schröter in Bochum (1977), and at the Kammerspiele in Munich (1980) all testify to the German theatre's abiding interest in Sg. This interest also manifests itself in Peter Weiss's translation of *Fröken Julie* and Friedrich Dürrenmatt's *Play Strindberg*. Translated from the German by Olivier Mannoni]

[D1:636] Misiak, Tomasz, 'Dramat a myslenie mityczne', *Dialog* (Warsaw), 26:3 (1981), 94-99. ['Drama and Mythical Modes of Thinking']

[D1:637] Molander, Olof, 'Teater av i dag', Efterskrift to *Nordiska teaterkongressen i Stockholm*, 18-22 May 1937. ['Theatre Today'. Argues that only now has the time come to do justice to Sg's vision in plays where the dialogue conveys not only what people say but what they are thinking]

[D1:638] Mori, Mitsuya, *Hoku engeki ron. Horubea, Ipusen, Sutorindoberi, soshite gendai*, Tokyo: Tokai Daigaku shuppan-kai, 1980. Illus. 258 pp. [A Japanese assessment of Scandinavian Drama from Holberg, Ibsen, and Sg to the present]

[D1:639] Mortimer, John, 'The New Drama?', *The Spectator* (London), 3 January 1976. [Regards Sg as the precursor of much modern drama in its 'flight from reason into the terrifying abyss of Beckett, or the irrational fears of Pinter.' John Osborne's Jimmy Porter and Archie Rice are also the inhabitants of Sg's world which 'is not the voice of reason; but it is the true voice of experience hardly won, and it is the voice of modern drama']

[D1:640] Muhr, Michael, 'Max Reinhardt und Schweden', in Edda Leisler and Gisela Prossnitz, eds, *Max Reinhardt in Europa*, Publikation der Max-Reinhardt-Forschungsstätte 4, Salzburg: Otto Müller Verlag, 1973, pp. 134-168. Illus. ['Max Reinhardt and Sweden'. Contextualises the visits of Reinhardt's various companies to Sweden in 1911, 1915, 1917, and 1920 in terms of the contemporary Swedish theatre, and comments on his productions of *Dödsdansen* and *Spöksonaten*. Muhr also discusses Reinhardt's Swedish-language production of *Ett drömspel* in 1921 (pp. 152-154), and his impact on Swedish directors, including Olof Molander (pp. 161-167)]

[D1:641] Müller, Robert, 'Tektonik des Theaters', *Blätter des Burgtheaters* (Vienna), 1:4 (1919), 26-31. [Includes Sg in his programme for an activist and intellectually aristocratic theatre]

[D1:642] Munthe, Arne, 'Tre nordiska dramaturger: Holberg, Ibsen, Strindberg', in Carl and Julia Svedelius, red., *Kultur i Norden*, Stockholm: P. A. Norstedt & Söners Förlag, 1934, pp. 232-249.['Three Nordic Dramatists: Holberg, Ibsen, Strindberg'. Presents the major dramatists of Denmark, Norway, and Sweden, discussing Sg, pp. 243-249]

[D1:643] Naeseth, Henriette C. K., 'Drama in Swedish in Chicago', *Journal of the Illinois State History Society* (Chicago), 41:2 (1948), 159-170.

[D1:644] Neiiendam, Robert, 'Dagmarteatrets Oprindelse', *Vor Fortid*, København, 1918. ['The Origins of the Dagmar Theatre'. Includes recollections of the première of *Fadren* at Copenhagen's Dagmar Theatre]

[D1:645] Nolin, Bertil, 'Artonhundratalets teater', in Lars Lönnroth and Sven Delblanc, red., *Den svenska litteraturen*, 7 vols, Vol. 3, 'De liberala genombrotten 1830-1890', Stockholm: Bonniers, 1988, pp. 249-268. Illus. ['Nineteenth-Century Theatre'. Provides an overview of Swedish theatre during the 19th Century, concluding with a section on 'Strindberg – The Renewer of the Theatre', pp. 266-268]

[D1:646] Nolin, Bertil, 'Artonhundratalets teater', in Lars Lönnroth and Sven Delblanc, red., *Den svenska litteraturen*, Stockholm: Bonniers, 1999, pp. 249-268. Illus. [A revised edition of **D1:645** in three volumes]

[D1:647] Nordmark, Dag, 'Jaget och världen i det modernistiska dramat', *Tidskrift för litteraturvetenskap* (Lund), 6:3 (1977), 28-42. ['The Self and the World in Modernist Drama'. A response to the crisis in dramatic form identified by Peter Szondi in *Theorie des modernen Dramas*, **D1:450**, and evident in the way that Sg's post-Inferno plays depart from traditional forms of drama. The different scenes are no longer bound together by the causality of the action but through the identity of the protagonist. Sg's role is central to this development because of his influence on both German expressionism and Pär Lagerkvist]

[D1:648] Oesterheld, Erich, 'Vom Traum und Traumspiel', *Die Deutsche Bühne* (Berlin), 29 September 1919, pp. 458-459. ['Of Dream and Dreamplay'. Discusses the dreamplay as a genre, and *Ett drömspel* as a prime example]

[D1:649] Ollén, Gunnar, 'Svensk dramatik på dansk scen', *Studiekamraten* (Tollarp), 50 (1968), 25-28. ['Swedish Drama on the Danish Stage']

[D1:650] Ollén, Gunnar, 'Svensk dramatik på dansk scen', in Catharina Söderberg and Anna Bodin, red., **B1:347**, *Forskarliv – sex decennier med Strindberg*, pp. 87-95. [Rpr. of **D1:649**]

[D1:651] Osiński, Z., and W. Rzepka, 'Dwa sezony Teatru Narodowego i Teatru Nowego', *Pamiętnik Teatralny* (Warsaw), 1965:2. [Comments on visiting Russian productions of *Erik XIV* and *Kristina*]

[D1:652] Perrelli, Franco, 'Un "grande attore" svedese: August Lindberg', in *Il grande attore nell'Otto e Novecento*', 1 Quaderni de *Castello di Elsinore* (Torino), Supplemento al n. 41, 2001, pp. 123-144. ['A Great Swedish Actor: August Lindberg'. A study of Sg's friend and occasional collaborator (e.g. on staging the dramatisation of *Hemsöborna*), in which the emphasis is placed understandably on his performances as Hamlet and Osvald in Ibsen's *Ghosts*]

[D1:653] Petsch, Robert, 'Das Drama des 19.Jahrhunderts', *Zeitschrift für den deutschen Unterricht* (Leipzig), 27 (1913), 197-215. ['19th-Century Drama']

[D1:654] Pitches, Jonathan, 'Theatre, Science and the Spirit of the Time: Towards a Physics of Performance', in Anthony Frost, ed., *Theatre Theories*, Norwich: The Drama Studio, 2000, pp. 121-144. [Studies the relationship between science and the theatre, in which Sg's post-Inferno dramaturgy (notably *Ett drömspel*) breaks with the classic

Newtonian paradigm and is thus linked with the Quantum physics of Max Planck and the Uncertainty Principle of Werner Heisenberg]

[D1:655] Pregelj, Ivan, 'Iz poetike – moderna drama', *Mentor* (Ljubljana), 10:9-10 (1917-18), pp. 180, 214. ['For a Poetics of Modern Drama']

[D1:656] Pregelj, Ivan, 'Poezija *Mlade Poljske*', 1-2, *Ljubljanski zvon* (Ljubljana), 43:1 and 3 (1923), pp. 25, 154. ['The Poetics of Young Poland'. Comments on Sg's importance for the Young Poland group of writers, one of whom was Sg's Berlin companion, Stanisław Przybyszewski]

[D1:657] Rheiner, Walter, 'Expressionismus und Schauspiel', *Die neue Schaubühne* (Dresden), 1:1 (1919), 14-17. ['Expressionism and Drama'. Refers to *Ett drömspel* and *Spöksonaten* and their affinity with music, in an attempt to define expressionism in the theatre. Claims that, in his later dramas (and to a certain extent in his novels and poetry, too), Sg is an unconscious, but no less committed expressionist]

[D1:658] Rheiner, Walter, 'Expressionismus und Schauspiel', in Hans-Peter Bayerdörfer, Hrsg., **B3:85**, *Strindberg auf der deutschen Bühne*, pp. 295-297. ['Expressionism and Drama'. Rpr. of **D1:657**]

[D1:659] Robida, Adolf, 'Skica razvoja moderne dramatike', *Čas* (Ljubljana), 3:10 (1909), pp. 452-460. ['The Development of Modern Drama in Outline']

[D1:660] Rokem, Freddie, 'Der *Deus ex Machina* im Theater der historischen Avantgarde', in Erika Fischer Lichte, Hrsg., *TheaterAvantgarde: Wahrnehmung – Körper – Sprache*, Tübingen und Basel: Francke Verlag, 1995, pp. 324-368. ['The *Deus ex Machina* in the Theatre of the Historic Avante-Garde'. Discusses modernist forms of the traditional *Deus ex Machina*, in Sg's case as dream in *Ett drömspel*, considered here together with Ansky's *Ha-Dybbuk*, Pirandello's *Sei personaggi in cerca d'autore*, and Brecht's *Dreigroschenopfer*. Rokem also comments briefly on the Count's late appearance at the close of *Fröken Julie* and the ending of *Spöksonaten*]

[D1:661] Rokem, Freddie, '*Deus ex Machina* in the Modern Theatre', in **B1:388**, *Strindberg's Secret Codes*, pp. 103-122. [Revised version of **D1:660** in English]

[D1:662] Rokem, Freddie, '*Deus ex Machina* in the Modern Theatre', in Peter Holland and W. B. Worthen, eds, *Theorizing Practice: Redefining Theatre History*, Palgrave: Houndmills, Basingstoke, 2003, pp. 177-195. [Revised version of **D1:660** in English]

[D1:663] Romdahl, Axel L., 'Lorensbergsteatern 1919-1923', in *En bok om Per Lindberg*, Stockholm: Wahlström & Widstrand, 1944, pp. 37-82. [Discusses Lindberg's productions at the Lorensberg theatre in Göteborg]

[D1:664] Rosenberg, Marvin, 'A Metaphor for Dramatic Form', *The Journal of Aesthetics and Art Criticism* (Cleveland, Ohio), 17:2 (1958), 174-180. [Focuses on modernist features in the dramaturgy of *Ett drömspel*. Places Sg's use of montage and his representation of discontinuous psychic activity in a context that includes Schönberg, Pirandello, and Joyce]

[D1:665] Rosenberg, Marvin, 'A Metaphor for Dramatic Form', in John Gassner, **D1:164**, *Directions in the Modern Theatre*, New York: Holt, Rinehart and Winston, Inc., 1965, pp. 341-351. [Rpr. of **D1:664**]

[D1:666] Rossowski, S., 'Z literatury skandynawskiej (próba reformy dramatu)', *Przegląd Literacki* (Warsaw), 1889, No. 42, pp. 1-4. ['On Scandinavian Literature and the Reform of Drama'. Considers the reforms introduced into the form and style of modern drama primarily by Ibsen in *Ghosts* and other plays of contemporary life, but also by Bjørnson and by Sg in his naturalistic dramas of the 1880s, with particular reference to the Preface to *Fröken Julie*]

[D1:667] Sarcey, Francisque, 'August Strindberg', in *Quarante ans de théâtre*, Paris: Bibliothèque des Annales politiques et littéraires, 1902, pp. 400-407. [Sarcey observes that, 'Of all the Scandinavian authors who have been introduced to us with such fanfare over recent years, M. Auguste Strindberg seems to me, inasmuch as I can judge from translation, to be the one who has the best feel for theatre. His plays are clearly structured; they proceed with obvious logic; each scene is constructed and accomplished with art. M. Auguste Strindberg is much less distant than he and we might think from our melodramatists and producers of vaudeville. It is just his characters which often disconcert us: the exoticism sometimes pleases us; sometimes it is obscure or even unintelligible to us']

[D1:668] Sartorius, Ella, 'Der Traum und das Drama', *Wortkunst*, Neue Folge, 11, München, 1936. 79 pp. ['Dream and Drama'. Studies dreamplays by Shakespeare, Grillparzer, and Gerhart Hauptmann as well as Sg, whose *Till Damaskus* and *Ett drömspel* are nevertheless given pride of place. Dreams always take the form of a play within the play, have a different level of reality to the main action, increase the sense of illusion, and afford an insight into the dreamer's inner life. Yet in Sg, it is difficult to determine a distinction between 'dream scenes' and 'scenes of reality'; the Unknown is subsumed by the action he inhabits and the drama must thus become the spectator's dream, with the Unknown as his protagonist. In *Ett drömspel*, however, Sartorius argues that Agnes is partly outside the events of a play in which the visual elements are as significant as the verbal]

[D1:669] S. B. [Sigurd Bødtker], 'Svensk Teater', *Tidens Tegn* (Oslo), 16 June 1912. ['Swedish Theatre'. Comments on *Erik XIV*, with Anders de Wahl in the title role, which prompts reflections on the multifariousness of Sg's work, the vitality and immediacy of his language, and the essential unity in everything he wrote]

[D1:670] Schaefer, Hans Joachim, 'Grundprobleme des modernen Dramas. Versuch einer Orienterung', *Begegnung* (Koblenz), 22 (1967), 125-135. ['Fundamental Problems of Modern Drama. Attempt at a Compass Reading']

[D1:671] Schiller, L[eon], 'Pro domo nostra', *Pamiętnik Teatralny* (Warsaw), 1952:2-3, p. 345.

[D1:672] Schiller, Harald, 'Om teaterkritiken och teaterkritikerna', *Sydsvenska Dagbladet* (Malmö), 29 January 1947. ['On Theatre Criticism and Theatre Critics'. Uses *Fröken Julie* to illustrate issues in contemporary theatre criticism]

[D1:673] Schiller, Harald, 'Om teaterkritiken och teaterkritikerna', in **D1:397**, *Thalia i Malmö och andra essayer*, pp. 37-[42]. ['On Theatre Criticism and Theatre Critics'. Rpr. of **D1:672**]

[D1:674] Schulz, Gerhard, 'Zur Theorie des Dramas im deutschen Naturalismus', in Reinhold Grimm, Hrsg., *Deutsche Dramentheorien. Beiträge zu einer historischen Poetik des Dramas in Deutschland*, 2 vols, Frankfurt am Main: Athenäum Verlag, 1971. XXVIII+591 pp. ['On the Theory of Drama in German Naturalism']

[D1:675] Senelick, Laurence, 'Strindberg, Antoine and Lugné-Poe: A Study in Cross-Purposes', *Modern Drama* (Lawrence, Kansas), 15:2 (1972), 391-401. [Surveys the relationship between Sg and the French directors whose productions of his plays at the Théâtre Libre and the Théâtre de l'Œuvre in the mid-1890s helped establish his reputation as a dramatist outside Scandinavia, although Senelick maintains that he was never widely discussed as a playwright in Paris]

[D1:676] Sigaux, Gilbert, 'Théâtre dans un fauteuil', in *Preuves: Les Idées qui changent le monde*, 140 (1962), 86-90. ['Theatre in an Armchair'. On Sg's intimate form of theatre and Antoine's Théâtre Libre]

[D1:677] Shonami, Gidon, 'Mahaze Expressionisti be-Tzippui Naturalisti', *Bama: Educational and Theatre Review* (Jerusalem), 71 (1976), pp. 27-38. [Examines expressionist elements in ostensibly naturalist dramas such as *Fadren*]

[D1:678] Sjögren, Fredrik, '"Det är jävlar anamma inte så lätt...". Samtal med regissören Per Verner-Carlsson', *Musik & Teater* (Stockholm), 1981:9. ['"It's Not So Easy, Damn It...". Conversation with the Director Per Verner-Carlsson'. An interview apropos Verner-Carlsson's 1978 production of *Pelikanen* which considers Sg's influence on the theatre, especially in France, and most notably on Artaud: 'Generally, I don't know of any major dramatist or theatre practitioner who doesn't refer [back] to Sg in some way.... Unconsciously Artaud built a great deal of his theories about theatre...both formally and in terms of content on Sg. At any rate, one can't escape the fact that Sg was a pre-surrealist']

[D1:679] Sjögren, Henrik, 'Bergman i Malmö 1952-58. En höjdpunkt i vår modern teater-historia', in Margareta Wirmark, red., *Ingmar Bergman: Film och teater i växelverkan*, Stockholm: Carlssons, 1996, pp. 100-127. Illus. ['Bergman in Malmö, 1952-58. A Highpoint in Our Modern Theatre History'. Discusses Ingmar Bergman's stagings of *Kronbruden*, *Spöksonaten*, and *Erik XIV* during his residency at Malmö Stadsteater in the 1950s]

[D1:680] Sleusser, Ignacy, 'Ewolucje sceny nowozytnej', *Echo Muzyczne, Teatralne i Artystyczne* (Warsaw?), 1892, Nos 434-438. ['The Evolution of Modern Theatre'. Includes observations on the innovatory nature of Sg's drama by the first Polish translator of *Fadren* (1891) and *Fröken Julie* (1892)]

[D1:681] Sokhriakov, I, '[Disillusionment in Twentieth-Century Western Drama]', *Teatr* (Moscow), 1970:10, pp. 146-152. [A discussion in which Sg is linked together with Pirandello and O'Neill in an examination of the theme of identity in modern European drama. E.1046]

[D1:682] Sprinchorn, Evert, 'The Transition from Naturalism to Symbolism in the Theater from 1880-1900', *Art Journal* (New York), 45:2 (1985), 113-119. Illus. [Maintains that Symbolism is already present in Zola's novels as well as a play like Ibsen's *Ghosts*, but in understanding the new, *fin-de-siècle* artistic movements, Sg's career is more instructive than Ibsen's. Unlike Maeterlinck, Sg could translate the unconscious life of the soul into effective drama. In an *omnium gatherum* of symbolist techniques like *Till Damaskus*, he begins by evoking a dreamlike atmosphere, in which it is difficult to tell what is real and what is illusory, what is symbolic of something and what is the thing itself, and then proceeds to create an elaborate network of visions, intimations, and literary illusions that vibrates with suggestions. But in Sprinchorn's opinion, a comparison of *Till Damaskus* with *Ghosts* reveals the close connection between naturalism and symbolism]

[D1:683] Steene, Birgitta, 'Royal Dramatic Theatre', in Colby H. Kullman and William C. Young, eds, *Theatre Companies of the World*, Bridgeport, Conn.: Greenwood Press, 1986, pp. 491-494. [Notes the importance accorded Sg's plays in Dramaten's repertoire and performance tradition]

[D1:684] Stefanek, Paul, 'Zur Dramaturgie des Stationendramas', in *Beiträge zur Poetik des Dramas*, Hrsg. von Werner Keller, Darmstadt: Wissenschaftliche Buchgesellschaft, 1976, pp. 383-404. ['The Dramaturgy of the Station Drama'. Analyses the subjective Station Play as a structural technique and literary form, referring to *Lycko-Pers resa*, *Påsk*, *Stora landsvägen*, and *Till Damaskus*. Stefanek also considers the influence of Sg's dramaturgy on German drama, exemplified here by Wolfgang Borchert's *Draußen vor der Tür* (The Man Outside, 1947)]

[D1:685] Steiner, F., 'Das Theater und der Expressionismus', *Die deutsche Bühne* (Berlin), 12 (1919). ['The Theatre and Expressionism']

[D1:686] *Svenska scenen* (Stockholm), 1915-16:7. [The issue includes a resumé of the critical reception accorded Max Reinhardt's tour of Sweden in 1915 with productions of *Dödsdansen* and other plays]

[D1:687] Szondi, Peter, 'Teoria przemian stylu', prezkł. z jęz. niem. E. Misiołek, *Scena* (Warsaw), 1976:7, pp. 2-7. [Extract from the Polish translation of **D1:450**]

[D1:688] Taits, I . F., '[The Problem of Character in Late Nineteenth-Century European Drama]', in *Nekotorye voprosy istorii i teorii zarubezhoi literatury*, Papers of the Sverdlovsk State Pedagogical Institute, 149, Sverdlovsk, 1971, pp. 19-48. [Sg is discussed, pp. 22-23, 26, 30-32, in a volume devoted to 'Some Aspects of the History and Theory of Foreign Literature'. E.1051]

[D1:689] Tessari, Roberto, 'Il teatro, e l'altra metà della vita. Funzione del sogno nella drammaturgia e nelle ipotesi sceniche di Ibsen, Strindberg e Pirandello', in Roberto Alonge, ed., **D2:7**, *Alle origini della drammaturgia moderna Ibsen, Strindberg, Pirandello*, pp. 99-127. ['Theatre and the other Half of Life. The Function of Dreams in Dramaturgy and in the Hypothetical Scripts of Ibsen, Strindberg, and Pirandello'. On the place of dreams in the dramaturgy of Ibsen, Sg, and Pirandello, and their ideas on how those plays in which they focus on 'the other half of life' might be staged. In Sg's case, his notions on how to stage a play like *Ett drömspel* may be related to his experiments in photography and alchemy, the states of mind explored in *Ensam* and *Ockulta dagboken*, and the discussion of the irradiation and extension of the soul in *Inferno*, which Tessari finds as relevant here as his views on dematerialised staging in *Memorandum till Medlemmarne av Intima Teatern*]

[D1:690] Törnqvist, Egil, 'Das Drama in historischer Perspektiv', in Horst Bien, Hrsg., *Die nordischen Literaturen als Gegenstand der Literaturgeschichtsschreibung*, Beiträge zur 13. Studienkonferenz der Internationalen Assoziation für Skandinavische Studien (IASS), 10.-16. August 1980 an der Ernst-Moritz-Arndt-Universität Greifswald, Rostock: VEB Hinstorff Verlag, 1982, pp. 119-125. ['Drama in an Historical Perspective'. Employs Sg as an example in discussing the problems associated with writing the literary history of drama, a medium that is not confined to print]

[D1:691] Törnqvist, Egil, 'Då som nu. Det historiska dramat', in Hans Schottmann, Hrsg., *Arbeiten zur Skandinavistik* 11, Arbeitstagung der deutschsprachigen Skandinavistik 8-14 August 1993 in Sigtuna, Münster: Kleinheinrich, 1994, pp. 310-322. ['Then as

Now: The History Play'. Discusses the genre of the history play in general, with brief reference to Sg as an eminent practitioner. *Mäster Olof* combines the public sphere with the private as in Shakespeare's *Julius Caesar*, thus avoiding the danger that the protagonist of a history play will become the mere incarnation of an idea or principle. With Coleridge's precept that a proper historical drama should deal with the history of the people to whom it is addressed in mind, the national dimension of Sg's history plays (e.g. *Gustav Vasa*) is evident, but *Kristina* and *Erik XIV* have both held the stage outside Scandinavia, in the latter case because the power struggle it presents echoed contemporary experience in post-war Europe. Törnqvist notes that Sg has himself recently become the subject of a history play in the form of Per Olof Enquist's *Tribadernas natt*, which seeks to reflect the present in the received image of Sg]

[D1:692] Törnqvist, Egil, 'The Modern(ist) One-Act Play', in Janet Garton, ed., *Facets of European Modernism. Essays in Honour of James McFarlane presented to him on his 65th Birthday*, Norwich: [Norvik Press], 1985, pp. 175-198. [Compares Sg's conception of a truly modern drama in the Preface to *Fröken Julie* and 'Om modernt drama och modern teater' with other theories and practice, including plays by Maeterlinck, Sartre, Lagerkvist, and Ionesco. Offers a brief analysis of *Paria*]

[D1:693] Törnqvist, Egil, 'Monodrama: Term and Reality', in *Essays on Drama and Theatre: Liber Amicorum Benjamin Hunningher*, Amsterdam: Baarn, Mousault, 1973, pp. 145-159.

[D1:694] Torsslow, Stig, 'Strindberg och gamla Dramatiskan', *Dramaten* (Stockholm), 1971:12. ['Strindberg and the Old Dramaten'. Examines Sg's links with Dramaten prior to 1908]

[D1:695] T. Sh.-A [Tat'iana K. Shakh-Azizova], 'Strindberg', in *Teatral'naia entsiklopediia*, Vol. 4, Moscow, 1965, pp. 1114-1115. E.1009]

[D1:696] Tyrell, H., 'The Drama', *Forum* (New York), 38 (July 1906), pp. 69-85.

[D1:697] Vilar, Jean, *Bref* (Paris), February, 1960. [Discusses directing and acting in Sg. Notes that while he was responsible for formulating the laws of realism in the theatre, Sg continually broke them]

[D1:698] W. [W. Feldman], 'Teatr krakówski', *Krytyka* (Warsaw), 3 (1907), 273-274. ['Theatre in Kraków'. Presents Sg as Ibsen's 'demonic protegé']

[D1:699] Walch, L. J., 'Dramatisch Overzicht. Reinhardt en zijn Deutsches Theater', *Groot Nederland* (Amsterdam), 14:1 (1916), 649-656. ['Dramatic Survey. Reinhardt and His Deutsches Theater'. Identifies *Dödsdansen* as Max Reinhardt's finest directorial achievement, 'a joy forever']

[D1:700] Walzel, Oskar, 'Expressionistische Drama', *Internationale Monatschrift für Wissenschaft, Kunst und Technik* (München), August 1919, pp. 789-819. ['Expressionist Drama'. Identifies Sg as the movement's principal precursor]

[D1:701] Wegener, Paul, '[Intervju]', *Dagens Nyheter* (Stockholm), 3 May 1917. [Interviewed on tour to Sweden with Max Reinhardt, Wegener identifies Sg as the master of literary expressionism and expresses surprise at how he remains identified with naturalism in Sweden]

[D1:702] Wieczorkowski, Aleksander, 'Naturalistyczne jasnowidzenie', *Współczesność* (Warsaw), 1962:14, p. 5. ['Naturalist Clairvoyance']

[D1:703] Wieselgren, Oscar, 'Svensk teater från 1500-1900', in Einar Sundström, red., *Svenska konstnärer inom teaterns, musikens och filmens värld*, Stockholm: Mimer, 1943. 531 pp. ['Swedish Theatre from 1500-1900'. A panoramic overview of Swedish theatre history, referring only to Sg's early work]

[D1:704] Williams, Simon, 'Theater and Degeneration. Subversion and Sexuality', in *Degeneration. The Dark Side of Progress*, Edited by J[ohn] Edward Chamberlin and Sander L. Gilman, New York: Columbia University Press, 1985, pp. 241-262. [Relates Sg's experience of psychic formlessness and his inability to reconcile contradictory impulses located within himself to the late 19th-Century preoccupation with the Janus-faced coupling of development (evolution) and degeneration, which often centre on notions of sexuality, and form the nucleus from which his later dramaturgy derives. Sg abandoned linearity and conventional forms of stage representation. From being a place where an action is represented under the assumption that it has an objective existence, the stage became one in which personal psychic states are reproduced and dramatic action approaches 'a more static condition, closer in nature to the lyric poem', as in *Ett drömspel*]

[D1:705] Wirth, Andrzej, 'Expresjonizm niemiecki jako prąd literacki', *Dialog* (Warsaw), 1962, No. 6. ['German Expressionism as a Literary Movement'. Maintains that *Till Damaskus* was the first entirely expressionist drama in European literature, one that depicts the protagonist's inner life. Hence, the first German expressionist drama, Reinhard Sorge's *Der Bettler* (The Beggar, 1912), merely continues the dramaturgy which Sg had already employed in *Ett drömspel*]

[D1:706] Zadravec, Franc, 'Ekspresionizem v dramatiki', in *Upornik: Slovenska ekspresionistiăčna enodejanka in prizori*, Ljubljana, 1966, pp. 161-208. ['Expressionism and Drama' in a study of expressionism in Slovenia]

[D1:707] Zeij, Hanneke, 'Per l'esegesi del contenuto drammatico', *Biblioteca teatrale* (Rome), N.S., No. 2 (1986), pp. 1-21. ['For the Exegesis of Dramatic Content']

[D1:708] Žmegac, Viktor, 'Zur Poetik des expressionistischen Dramas', in Reinhold Grimm, Hrsg., *Deutsche Dramentheorien: Beiträge zu einer historischen Poetik des Dramas in Deutschland*, Athenaion Literaturwissenschaft 12, Wiesbaden: Athenaion Verlag, 1981, pp. 154-180. ['On the Poetics of Expressionist Drama'. Traces the influence of Sg's post-Inferno dramas on plays by Oskar Kokoschka, Walter Hasenclever, and Reinhard Sorge]

See also **C1:847, C1:1128, V:25, V:36, V:38, V:41, V:61, V:86, V:183, V:203, V:208, V:224**

D2: Drama General: B

B. Monographs, Collections of Essays and Reviews, and Longer Studies on Strindberg's Plays and Work in the Theatre.

[As well as book-length studies of the plays and Sg's engagement with theatre practice, this section also lists collections of essays or books which include several essays on more than one of the plays, with the exception of the four Chamber Plays of 1907. These are frequently discussed, and even staged, as a self-contained and thematically linked group. Consequently, books or

essays in which they are treated together are listed in a separate section, **E48**. *However, while the contents of the collections listed in this section are noted here and all their titles given, where they are concerned with a single drama, the essays themselves are annotated with their titles translated where necessary in the section in Volume 2 devoted to the drama in question*]

(i) Books

[D2:1] Adamov, Arthur, *August Strindberg*, Avec la collaboration de Maurice Gravier, Les grands dramaturges 6, Paris: L'Arche, 1955. Illus. 160 pp. [Adamov's influential study of a writer whose '*Dream Play* prompted me to write for the theatre', focuses on key scenes from *Fordringsägare, Ett drömspel, Till Damaskus, Pelikanen, Advent, Fadren, Fröken Julie, Dödsdansen*, and *Spöksonaten*, which are discussed thematically across periods and styles. He also relates these plays to Sg's exploration of similar themes in *Tjänstekvinnans son*. Although not without a number of factual errors, Adamov's book, which has enjoyed a wide circulation in France and elsewhere, is frequently illuminating about Sg's theatricality and its underlying drives. Republished 1982, 127 pp.]

[D2:2] — Ahlström, Stellan, 'Franskt pekoral om Strindberg', *Aftonbladet* (Stockholm), 24 May 1955. ['French Garbage about Strindberg']

[D2:3] — Brandell, Gunnar, *Svenska Dagbladet* (Stockholm), 16 May 1955.

[D2:4] — Gravier, Maurice, *Revue d'histoire du théâtre* (Paris), 7:2 (1955), 211-212.

[D2:5] — Linnuste, V., *Sydsvenska Dagbladet* (Malmö), 7 January 1960.

[D2:6] Adamov, Arthur, *August Strindberg*, Paris: Les Miroirs, 1982. 127 pp. [New edition of **D2:1**]

[D2:7] [Alonge, Roberto], ed., *Alle origini della drammaturgia moderna: Ibsen, Strindberg, Pirandello*, Atti del Convegno Internazionale Torino, 18-20 aprile 1985, Genova: Costa & Nolan, 1987. 251 pp. ['The Origins of Modern Dramaturgy'. The proceedings in Italian, French, and English of a conference held in Turin, 18-20 April 1985. Includes **B9:67**: Gunnar Brandell, 'Ibsen, Strindberg and the Emancipation Movement in 19th-Century Scandinavia'; **C1:24**: Roberto Alonge, 'Solitudine dei maschi e mitologemi femminili in Ibsen, Strindberg, Pirandello'; **C2:4**: Guido Aristarco, 'Fonti culturali di Bergman: da Kierkegaard a Strindberg'; **D1:539**: William Coco, 'The Dramaturgy of the Dream Play. Breuer, Chaikin, Shepard'; **D1:542**: Luciano Codignola, 'La crisi della struttura drammatica tradizionale in Strindberg e in Pirandello'; **D1:689**: Roberto Tessari, 'Il teatro, e l'altra metà della vita. Funzione del sogno nella drammaturgia e nelle ipotesi sceniche di Ibsen, Strindberg e Pirandello'; **D2:1082**: Paolo Puppa, 'I luoghi della notte'; **E12:226**: Renzo Pavese, '"Il gioco delle parti" in *Fröken Julie*'; **E25:47**: Maurice Gravier, 'Le Double ironique et provocant. D'Ulrik Brendel, de *Rosmersholm*, au Mendiant du *Chemin de Damas*'; **E48:40**: Ludovica Koch, 'Architetture sognate e mobili medianici nei "drammi da camera" di Strindberg'; and **T:438**: Jan Myrdal, 'Woman and Anti-Semitism in Strindberg']

[D2:8] Bandle, Oskar, Walter Baumgartner, and Jürg Glauser, Hrsg., *Strindbergs Dramen im Lichte neuerer Methodendiskussionen*, Beiträge zum IV. Internationalen Strindberg-Symposion in Zürich, Basel: Verlag Helbing & Lichtenhahn, 1981. 289 pp. ['Strindberg's Dramas in the Light of Recent Critical Approaches'. The proceedings in

German, French, and English of the 4th International Sg Conference, held in Zürich in 1979. Contains **C1:215**: Gunnar Brandell, 'Fragen ohne Antworten. Zum Dialog von Strindberg - und Ibsen'; **D2:518:** Regis Boyer, 'À la recherche d'un principe de composition dans cinq pièces "naturalistes" de Strindberg'; **D2:689**: Maurice Gravier, 'Comment étudier le dialogue de Strindberg?'; **D2:1019**: Otto Oberholzer, 'Strindberg und die Komödientheorie'; **E8:28**: Georges Ueberschlag, 'Le discours satirique dans le théâtre féerique de Strindberg. Un parallèle avec le modèle Voltairien'; **E11:30:** Artur Bethke, 'Strindbergs Dramenkonzeption in *Fadren*'; **E12:225**: Wolfgang Pasche, 'Dichtung im Unterricht am Beispiel von *Fräulein Julie*'; **E23:4**: Hans-Göran Ekman, 'Strindberg's *Leka med elden* as a Comedy'; **E25:135**: Göran Stockenström, 'His Former Dream Play *To Damascus*'; **E29:4**: Harry G. Carlson, 'Christian Ritual and Mythic Pattern in *Gustav Vasa*': **E44:11**: Helmut Müssener, 'Die trapsende *Nachtigall von Wittenberg.* Eine systemimmanente Interpretation'; **E51:112**: Nils Åke Sjöstedt, '*The Ghost Sonata*'; **E53:14**: Hilde Haider-Pregler, 'Szenische Dramaturgie und Rollenstruktur'; **E53:32**: Egil Törnqvist, 'The Structure of *Pelikanen*'; and **P5:68**: Birgitta Steene, 'Alf Sjöberg's Film *Fröken Julie*: Too Much Cinema, Too Much Theatre?']

[**D2:9**] — Ciesielski, Zenon, 'Dramaty Strindberga', *Dialog* (Warsaw), 1980:1, pp. 168-169. ['Strindberg's Dramas']

[**D2:10**] — Ciesielski, Zenon, *Studia Scandinavica* (Gdańsk), 4 (1982), pp. 103-105.

[**D2:11**] — Lide, Barbara, *Journal of English and Germanic Philology* (Urbana, Illinois), 83:3 (1984), 428-429.

[**D2:12**] — Paul, Fritz, *Skandinavistik* (Kiel), 12:2 (1982), 162-165.

[**D2:13**] — Scholl, G., *Referatedienst zur Literaturwissenschaft* (Berlin), 17 (1985), 463-464.

[**D2:14**] — Sokoll, G., *Nordeuropa* (Greifswald), 15 (1982), 175-177.

[**D2:15**] — Sprinchorn, Evert, *Scandinavian Studies* (Lawrence, Kansas), 55:4 (1983), 388-389.

[**D2:16**] — Stenström, Thure, *Scandinavica* (Norwich), 21:2 (1982), 195-196.

[**D2:17**] — Sundberg, Björn, *Svenska Dagbladet* (Stockholm), 17 August 1982.

[**D2:18**] — Uecker, Heiko, *Arcadia* (West Berlin), 23 (1988), 198-203.

[**D2:19**] — Vogelweith, Guy, *Etudes Germanistiques* (Paris), 37:4 (1982), 506-507.

See also **A4:11, A4:139**

[**D2:20**] Bark, Richard, *Strindbergs drömspelteknik – i drama och teater*, Lund: Studentlitteratur, 1981. Illus. 224 pp. ['Strindberg's Dream Play Technique in Drama and Theatre'. Surveys earlier discussions of Sg's post-Inferno dramas and examines how dreams have been represented on stage from antiquity to symbolism before focusing in more detail on *Till Damaskus I*, *Ett drömspel*, and *Spöksonaten*. Bark stresses their theatrical dimension, on the problematic premise that Sg's dreamplay technique entails the 'abolition of time and space' where '(1)...a character in a play is in a dream-like situation and on the same level as the dream-like, or (2) when a character in a play is in a dream-like situation but is not on the same level as the dream-like, but regards it as a spectator of a play within a play, or (3) when the reader/spectator is given the role of "dreamer" of the dream-like.' His study contains valuable comparative discussions of the plays' Swedish premières, and of the early German productions of Max Reinhardt, Victor Barnowsky, and Rudolf Bernauer, as well as later revivals by Olof Molander and Ingmar Bergman. Also includes selected cast lists and production details. English summary, pp. 212-217. Doctoral dissertation]

[D2:21] — Bellquist, John Eric, *Scandinavian Studies* (Lawrence, Kansas), 55:4 (1983), 394-396.

[D2:22] — Ollén, Gunnar, *Sydsvenska Dagbladet* (Malmö), 21 December 1981.

[D2:23] — Sundberg, Björn, *Samlaren* (Uppsala), 105 (1984), pp. 94-97.

[D2:24] — Törnqvist, Egil, *Scandinavica* (Norwich), 22:2 (1983), 226-227.

[D2:25] Berendsohn, Walter A[rthur], *August Strindberg. Ein geborener Dramatiker*, München: A. Langen-G. Müller Verlag, 1956. [91] pp. ['August Strindberg: A Born Dramatist'. Includes a chapter on the theatre-based Falander episodes in *Röda rummet* as well as introductory chapters on the plays in general and an account of Sg's practical experience of the theatre, with the stress throughout on his links with Germany. Berendsohn also republishes Sg's responses to Georg Bröchner's ubiquitous questionnaire (see **R:2119**)]

[D2:26] Börge [sic], Vagn Albeck, *Strindberg, Prometheus des Theaters*, Wien – München: Österreichische Verlagsanstalt und A. Schroll-Verlag, 1974. Illus. XVIII+500 pp. [Claims that Sg's drama is 'Welttheater' matching the theatre of Shakespeare and Molière and its theatrical dimension is recognised throughout a study which nevertheless reads his work biographically and is partly organised in terms of his marriages to Siri von Essen, Frida Uhl, and Harriet Bosse. Børge discusses other texts apart from the dramas in some detail, including e.g. *En blå bok*, and compares Sg with Goethe in a lengthy examination of 'Der schwedische Faust'. He also explores his interests in (variously) Kierkegaard, Swedenborg, Ibsen, Georg Brandes, Dante, and Hans Christian Andersen, as well as his fluctuating philosophical and scientific ideas. Børge makes considerable use of previously published material and his account of Sg's *oeuvre* is strongly inflected towards a German readership, with numerous references to Max Reinhardt, Nietzsche, Schopenhauer, Freud, and Kant. He also stresses the relationship between Goethe's *Faust* and the post-Inferno plays. The volume includes an extensive bibliography and an introduction by Algot Werin]

[D2:27] — Lindström, Göran, *Sydsvenska Dagbladet* (Malmö), 27 July 1975.

[D2:28] — Rinman, Sven, *Upsala Nya Tidning*, 12 August 1975.

[D2:29] Børge, Vagn Albeck, *Strindbergs mystiske Teater. Æstetisk–dramaturgiske Analyser med særlig Hensyntagen til Drömspelet*, København: Ejnar Munksgaard, 1942. Illus. 403 pp. ['Strindberg's Mystical Theatre. Aesthetic-Dramaturgical Analyses with Particular Attention to *A Dream Play*'. Børge endows 'Sg's "mystiske" theatre with a similar place in our time as Lessing granted Shakespeare in relation to his'. He approaches Sg's post-Inferno dramaturgy via a survey of previous scholarship (mainly Swedish and German) and the major post-Inferno dramas prior to *Ett drömspel*: i.e. *Till Damaskus, Advent, Brott och brott, Kronbruden, Påsk*, and *Dödsdansen*. But the core of the book is an extended, dramaturgical analysis of *Ett drömspel*, conducted with an awareness of the play's theatrical dimension and its place in theatre history, which opens the way for a final section on the dramas written in its wake, including the history plays, the posthumously published 'Kristus-Trilogie', the Chamber Plays of 1907, and *Stora landsvägen*. Contrary to Martin Lamm in **D2:169**, whose approach is defined here as 'literary', Børge stresses the Oriental as well as the theatrical aspects of *Ett drömspel* ('all Sg's plays are written with the stage space in his mind's eye'), and he makes numerous illuminating comparisons with contemporary music and literature while also relating these plays to Sg's non-dramatic works. But while he does not doubt that both *Till Damaskus* and *Ett drömspel* represent dreams (the whole of the former is dreamt by the Unknown and the latter by Agnes), Børge's terminology is sometimes imprecise, especially regarding the 'mystisk Aura' that supposedly permeates Sg's later dramas, that so-called 'spiritual substance which exists both in and outside the text, like a secret something that fills the whole space in which the mystical theatre plays'. Doctoral dissertation]

[D2:30] — Amenius, Ragnar, *Folklig kultur* (Stockholm), 8 (1943), p. 245.

[D2:31] — Bergström, C. O., *Nya Dagligt Allehanda* (Stockholm), 28 January 1943.

[D2:32] — Brandell, Gunnar, *Bonniers Litterära Magasin* (Stockholm), 12 (1943), 167-169.

[D2:33] — Linneballe, P., 'Mystikeren paa Scenen', *Berlingske Aftenavis* (Copenhagen), 28 October 1942. ['The Mystic on the Stage']

[D2:34] — Ollén, Gunnar, *Dagens Nyheter* (Stockholm), 21 February 1943.

[D2:35] — Platen, Gustaf von, *Afton-Tidningen* (Stockholm), 23 March 1943.

[D2:36] — Pl. [K. F. Plesner], *Nordisk Tidskrift* (Stockholm), 18:8 (1942), p. 617.

[D2:37] — Schultz, H. J., '*Strindbergs mystiske Teater*', 1-2, *Flensborg Avis*, 31 December 1942 and 2 January 1943.

See also **A4:30, A4:67**

[D2:38] Brun, Inger, *August Strindberg: Ein presentasjon av författaren og hans dramatiske diktning*, [Oslo]: Riksteatret, [1979]. 7 pp. ['August Strindberg: A Presentation of the Writer and His Dramatic Works']

[D2:39] Campos, Armando de Maria y, *Manuel Acuña en su teatro, seguido de una breve historia del teatro en Suecia y de la aventura dramática de Augusto Strindberg*, Mexico: Compañia de Ediciones Poplares, S.A. 1952. Illus. 104 pp. ['Manuel Acuña and His Theatre, Followed by a Short History of the Swedish Theatre and the Dramatic Endeavour of August Strindberg'. Includes a brief history of the theatre in Sweden and a somewhat more detailed discussion of Sg, pp. 63-91. Described here as both a romantic and a realist, Campos describes the latter's works as reflecting the entire intellectual history of his epoch which he had experienced with passion. He comments briefly on a wide range of plays and prose works, but most specifically on centennial stagings of *Dödsdansen* and *Fröken Julie*]

[D2:40] Carlson, Harry G., *Strindberg and the Poetry of Myth*, Berkeley: University of California Press, 1982. X+240 pp. [Maintains that Sg's life-long preoccupation with mythology affords an alternative to the familiar biographical approach to his writing. Sg possessed a profoundly mythopoeic imagination and wove Norse, Greek, and Indic mythology together with material from numerous legends, sagas, fairy tales, the Bible, and other non-European religious texts. Myth offered him parallels for recuperating his own experience and he used its structures as blueprints in the search for self-realisation which underlay so much of his writing, thus anticipating the research of Carl Gustav Jung, Erich Neumann, and Joseph Campbell, He also utilised Johan Jakob Bachofen's *Das Mutterecht* (1841) and Viktor Rydberg's writings on Germanic mythology, as well as Gunnar Olof Hyltén-Cavallius's *Wärend och wirdarne* on Scandinavian ethnology and folklore. What Carlson calls this polyphonic approach to myth is exemplified in readings of *Mäster Olof*, *Fadren*, *Fröken Julie*, *Fordringsägare*, *Till Damaskus I*, *Påsk*, *Ett drömspel*, and *Spöksonaten*. *Fröken Julie* evokes the fairy tale of 'The Princess in the Tree' and Adam's encounter with Eve in Genesis; in a seemingly ordinary house, *Fadren* entraps the spirit of the culture hero, Hercules, within the sacral precinct of the Great Mother; in *Påsk* Sg evokes Persephone and the underworld as well as many overt analogies with Christ's Passion; and in *Ett drömspel* his polyphonic mythology attains a kind of intensity which blends elements drawn from 'Hindu, Greek, and Biblical mythology, Mahayana Buddhism, Gnosticism, the chivalric tradition of the quest of the knight errant, and tales from the Arabian nights.' See Bellquist's critique of Carlson's interpretation of myth in **D2:447**]

[**D2:41**] — Anon, *Modern Drama* (Toronto), 26 (1983), 572-573.

[**D2:42**] — Taraba, A.-S., *World Literature Today* (Norman, Oklahoma), 57 (1983), 303-304.

[**D2:43**] — Westman, N., *Stockholms-Tidningen*, 19 January 1983.

[**D2:44**] Carlson, Harry G., *Strindberg och myterna*, Förord av Olof Lagercrantz, Översättning från engelskan av Sven Erik Täckmark, Stockholm: Författarförlaget, 1979. 286 pp. [Previously published Swedish edition of **D2:40**]

[**D2:45**] — Aggestam, R., *Nya Norrland* (Härnösand), 23 May 1979.

[**D2:46**] — Backman, P. O., *Barometern* (Kalmar), 7 June 1979.

[**D2:47**] — Bergengren, Kurt, *Aftonbladet* (Stockholm), 24 May 1979.

[**D2:48**] — Berman, Nils, *Norrköpings-Tidningar-Östergötlands Dagblad*, 7 June 1979.

[**D2:49**] — Blackwell, Marilyn Johns, *Scandinavian Studies* (Lawrence, Kansas), 52:1 (1980), 95-97. [Suggests that the author's critical model does not fit the pre-Inferno plays; the later dramas lend themselves much better to a mythological or archetypal treatment]

[**D2:50**] — Bladh, Curt, *Sundsvalls Tidning*, 25 April 1979.

[**D2:51**] — Boëthius, Ulf, 'Sjuttitalets Strindberg', *Bonniers Litterära Magasin* (Stockholm), 48:4 (1979), 284-285. ['1970s Strindberg']

[**D2:52**] — Boström, H., *Folkbladet* (Eskilstuna), 8 May 1979.

[**D2:53**] — Brevinge, V., *Örebro Kuriren*, 18 May 1979.

[**D2:54**] — C. E. [Claes Englund], *entré* (Norsborg), 6:3 (1979), p. 36.

[**D2:55**] — Ekman, Hans-Göran, *Upsala Nya Tidning*, 27 October 1979.

[**D2:56**] — Franzén, Lars-Olof, 'Strindberg, ännu en väg till förståelsen', *Dagens Nyheter* (Stockholm), 7 May 1979. ['Yet another Way of Understanding Strindberg']

[**D2:57**] — Green, C.-G., *Sydsvenska Dagbladet* (Malmö), 8 May 1979.

[**D2:58**] — Hesslander, Ingrid, *Jönköpings-Posten*, 9 May 1979.

[**D2:59**] — Janzon, Åke, 'Nytt sätt att älska Strindberg', *Svenska Dagbladet* (Stockholm), 26 April 1979. ['A New Way to Love Strindberg']

[**D2:60**] — Johannesson, H.-E., *Vår lösen* (Sigtuna), 72 (1981), 139-140.

[**D2:61**] — Lång, Helmer, *Skånska Dagbladet* (Malmö), 27 April 1979.

[**D2:62**] — Lindström, Göran, *Sydsvenska Dagbladet* (Malmö), 24 April 1979.

[**D2:63**] — Magnusson, Bo, *Eskilstuna Kuriren*, 30 April 1979.

[D2:64] — Muradian, K. E., *Obschchestvennye nauki za rubezhom. RZh. Seriia 7, Literaturovedenie*, 4, Moscow, 1984, pp. 109-112. [A synopsis rather than a review]

[D2:65] — Ollén, Gunnar, *Kvällsposten* (Malmö), 23 April 1979.

[D2:66] — Randver, Gunnel Widel, *Östgöta Correspondenten* (Linköping), 9 May 1979.

[D2:67] — Robinson, Michael, *Scandinavica* (Norwich), 19:1 (1980), 81-82.

[D2:68] — Rönnerstrand, T., *Göteborgs-Tidningen*, 12 November 1979.

[D2:69] — Rundqvist, V., *Blekinge Läns Tidning* (Karlskrona), 24 July 1979.

[D2:70] — Schöier, Ingrid, *Västerbottens-Kuriren* (Umeå), 6 June 1979.

[D2:71] — Stolpe, Sven, *Nya Wermlands Tidningen* (Karlstad), 12 May 1979.

[D2:72] — Svenson, Lars, *Helsingborgs Dagblad*, 28 May 1979.

See also **A4:93, A4:106, A4:122**

[D2:73] Catalogue, *Strindberg på scen. Teaterfotografier 1882-1998. Strindbergsmuseet 21 augusti-4 oktober 1998*, Stockholm: Strindbergsmuseet, 1998. 7 pp. ['Strindberg on Stage. Theatre Photographs 1882-1998'. The catalogue for an exhibition of photographs of Sg's plays in performance together with an essay, 'Strindberg på scen' (Strindberg on Stage) by Erik Höök]

[D2:74] Dahlström, Carl Enoch William Leonard, *Strindberg's Dramatic Expressionism*, University of Michigan Publications in Language and Literature 7, Ann Arbor: University of Michigan, 1930. 242 pp. [See **D2:81**]

[D2:75] — Marcus, Carl David, *Zeitschrift für Ästhetik* (Stuttgart), 25 (1931), 391-394.

[D2:76] — Neckel, Gustav, *Deutsche Literaturzeitung* (Berlin), 53 (1932), Sp. 1846-1848.

[D2:77] — Palmblad, Harry V. E., *Germanic Review* (New York), 6 (1931), 205-207.

[D2:78] — Richter, Helene, *Archiv für das Studium der neueren Sprachen und Literatur* (Braunschweig), 87 (1932), 247-249.

[D2:79] — Rose, William, *Modern Language Review* (London), 27 (1932), 111-112.

[D2:80] — Uppvall, Axel J., *Scandinavian Studies* (Menasha, Wisconsin), 12:1 (1932-1933), 24-28.

[D2:81] Dahlström, Carl Enoch William Leonard, *Strindberg's Dramatic Expressionism*, Second ed., with the author's essay "Origins of Strindberg's Expressionism", New York: Benjamin Blom, Inc., 1968. XXI+264 pp. [For many years, and for both good and ill, this remained one of the most influential statements on Sg's dramas in English. Dahlström adopts a systematic approach which judges Sg's texts in the light of previous definitions of expressionism, focusing on the notion of an 'Ausstrahlungen des Ichs', and testing these theories against a selection of Sg's plays – the 'so-called naturalistic dramas', *Fadren*, *Fröken Julie*, and *Fordringsägare*, as well as *Till Damaskus*, *Brott och brott*, *Påsk*, *Midsommar*, *Svanevit*, *Kronbruden*, *Ett drömspel*, the Chamber Plays of 1907, and the dramatic fragments *Holländaren* and *Toten-Insel*. Dahlström anticipates a later tendency in Sg criticism that sees expressionist elements in the naturalistic dramas, but he also reads aspects of German expressionism back into Sg's earlier plays. Includes **B2:108**]

[D2:82] Drei Masken Verlag Berlin, *August Strindberg und die deutschen Bühnen*, Zusammengestellt und Hrsg. vom Drei Masken-Verlag, Berlin, 1915. 23 pp. ['August Strindberg and the German Stage'. Contains Carl Hagemann, **D2:734**, and Julius Bab,

D3:14, as well as a survey of the plays in performance in Germany, 1913-1915, pp. 17-18, edited by Max Schievelkamp]

[D2:83] Ekman, Hans-Göran, *Klädernas magi*, Värnamo: Gidlunds, 1991. Illus. 206 pp. ['The Magic of Clothes'. Analyses the importance of costume in Sg's plays, both in its ordinary, theatrical sense and, more significantly, as a deeply personal symbolic and structural device, pertinent both to the individual plays studied (*Herr Bengts hustru*, *Marodörer*, *Fröken Julie*, *Advent*, *Brott och brott*, *Ett drömspel*, *Abu Casems tofflor*, and *Svarta handsken*), and for an understanding of Sg's psychology. Given Ekman's interest in the private associations that certain items of clothing held for Sg (e.g. the fetishistic preoccupation with shoes revealed in *Fröken Julie*, which remains just this side of pathological), J. C. Flugel's *The Psychology of Clothes* (1930) is more relevant here than theatre semiotics. But these private associations rarely make themselves understood across the footlights, and it is the dramatic function of clothes as integral to the action of the plays (e.g. the strait-jacket and Laura's shawl in *Fadren* or the scarf and gloves that Jeanne sends Maurice in *Brott och brott*), on which this study ultimately concentrates, and where it frequently sheds new light]

[D2:84] — Anderberg, Rolf, *Göteborgs-Posten*, 1 November 1991.

[D2:85] — Bark, Richard, *Samlaren* (Uppsala), 112 (1991), pp. 131-132.

[D2:86] — Bolinder, Jean, *Skånska Dagbladet* (Malmö), 12 March 1992.

[D2:87] — Fraser, Catherine, *Scandinavian Studies* (Madison), 64:3 (1992), 471-473.

[D2:88] — Hultsberg, Peter, *Skånska Dagbladet* (Malmö), 28 June 1991.

[D2:89] — [Huss, Pia], 'Strindberg och kostymen', *entré* (Norsborg), 19:4 (1992), p. 85.

[D2:90] — Linnér, Sture, 'Plagg med psykisk laddning', *Allt om böcker* (Göteborg), 1992:4, pp. 46-47. ['Garments with a Psychic Charge']

[D2:91] — Ohlson, Per-Ove, *Borås Tidning*, 13 August 1991.

[D2:92] — Ollén, Gunnar, *Sydsvenska Dagbladet* (Malmö), 1 July 1991.

[D2:93] — Robinson, Michael, *Scandinavica* (Norwich), 30:2 (1991), 253-255.

[D2:94] — Rubin, Birgitta, 'Skon symboliserar det sensuella. Hans-Göran Ekman förklarar dräktens roll i Strindbergs dramatik', *Dagens Nyheter* (Stockholm), 11 July 1991. ['Shoes Symbolise the Sensual. Hans-Göran Ekman Explains the Role of Clothing in Strindberg's Plays']

[D2:95] — Schöier, Ingrid, *Svenska Dagbladet* (Stockholm), 19 June 1991.

[D2:96] — Steinick, K., *Helsingborgs Dagblad*, 13 June 1991.

[D2:97] — Wiingaard, Jytte, *Nordic Theatre Studies* (Copenhagen), 6:1-2 (1993), 80-81.

[D2:98] — Wittrock, Ulf, *Upsala Nya Tidning*, 2 January 1993.

[D2:99] Englund, Claes, and Gunnel Bergström, eds, *Strindberg, O'Neill and the Modern Theatre*: Addresses and Discussions at a Nobel Symposium at Dramaten, Norsborg: Entré/Svenska riksteatern, 1990. 79 pp. [The often highly subjective proceedings of a symposium that includes **C1:490**: Lars Gyllensten, 'Opening Address'; **C1:1297**: Egil Törnqvist, 'Strindberg, O'Neill and their Impact on the Dramatists of Today'; and **D2:546** Harry G. Carlson, 'In Search of the Dionysian Actor'; but which otherwise pays more attention to the work of Heiner Müller and Chinese Yan drama than to Sg and O'Neill. As well as Müller, contributors also discuss the work of Peter Sellars, Robert Wilson, and Joshua Sobel]

[D2:100] — Martin, Jacqueline, *Nordic Theatre Research* (Copenhagen), 4 (1991), 192-193.

[D2:101] Evelein, Johannes F., *August Strindberg und das expressionistische Stationendrama: eine Formstudie*, Studies on Themes and Motifs in Literature 13, New York: Peter Lang, 1996. XI+218 pp. ['August Strindberg and Expressionist Station Drama. A Study in Form'. An analysis of nearly thirty German station plays demonstrates that Sg was the source of a genre exemplified by *Till Damaskus I* and *Stora landsvägen*. In terms of structure, these plays are the paradigms of the non-classical dramatic form that he developed with reference to late medieval models, in order to facilitate the inward turn made by drama at the end of the 19th Century. This new drama, in which the world is seen from the perspective of the central figure and traces his journey through life, stressed the isolation of the individual better than its Aristotelian counterpart. Such plays are theme-centred and, in their German progeny, essentially Oedipal in conflict; their form often foregrounds repetition, with circularity replacing linearity; and their structure resembles music in its formal use of leitmotif. Hence the analysis which Evelein offers here of the leitmotifs and colours that function as unifying devices. The protagonists, meanwhile, frequently evokes archetypal associations (with Cain and Ahasueras as well as with Adam, Jacob, and Christ) while the secondary characters are aspects of the central figure and conversation with them is thus a form of monologue. Evelein also considers the significance of these plays for the development of German expressionist drama, and reflects on the extent to which the latter differs from its Sgian model. Doctoral dissertation]

[D2:102] — Behschnitt, Wolfgang, *Referatedienst zur Literaturwissenschaft* (Berlin), 29 (1997), 627-628.

[D2:103] — Hupperetz, Karel J., *TijdSchrift voor Skandinavistiek* (Groningen), 18:1 (1997), 120-122.

[D2:104] — Mazellier-Grünbeck, C., Etudes Germanistiques (Paris), 54:1 (1999), p. 126.

[D2:105] — Vonhoegen, Corrina, *Skandinavistik* (Kiel), 27:2 (1997), 149-150.

[D2:106] Falck, August, 'Cinq ans avec Strindberg', Traduit de suédois par Pernille Jourde, in Elena Balzamo, ed., **B1:7**, *August Strindberg*, Paris: L'Herne, 2000, pp. 82-104. ['Five Years with Strindberg'. French translation of material extracted from **D2:107**]

[D2:107] Falck, August, *Fem år med Strindberg*, Stockholm: Wahlström & Widstrand, 1935. Illus. 363 pp. ['Five Years with Strindberg'. Although not always entirely reliable on factual grounds, this copiously illustrated account of Falck's collaboration with Sg at the Intimate Theatre by his co-director remains a key source of information, both about the theatre itself and the plays performed there. For many years, Sg's letters and memoranda to Falck and other members of the company were only readily accessible in the often partial form in which they are cited here, sometimes in facsimile, and Falck's narrative provides a basis for assessing Sg's practical involvement with the theatre and the extent to which he was part of the modern theatre movement in the early 20th Century. The account is also an important contribution to Swedish theatre history as well as a deeply engaging portrait of Sg who, according to Falck, 'gave many of us, perhaps me most of all, a meaning in life'. As such, it has frequently influenced many subsequent accounts]

[D2:108] — B. B-m [Birger Bæckström], *Göteborgs Handels- och Sjöfartstidning*, 2 December 1935.

[D2:109] — B. B-n [Bo Bergman] *Dagens Nyheter* (Stockholm), 26 November 1935.

[D2:110] — Beyer, Nils, *Social-Demokraten* (Stockholm), 7 December 1935.

[D2:111] — D. R. [D. Rydsjö], *Svensk lärartidningen* (Stockholm), 55 (1936), p. 208.

[D2:112] — E. C. [E. Colliander], *Åbo Underrättelser*, 15 December 1935.

[D2:113] — Edfelt, Johannes, *Bonniers Litterära Magasin* (Stockholm), 5:3 (1936), 237-238.

[D2:114] — Elfelt, Kjeld, *Ti Aar*, København, 1942, pp. 59-62.

[D2:115] — Erdmann, Nils, *Nya Dagligt Allehanda* (Stockholm), 26 November 1935.

[D2:116] — Grevenius, Herbert, *Stockholms-Tidningen*, 26 November 1935.

[D2:117] — Hj. L [Hjalmar Lenning], *Hufvudstadsbladet* (Helsingfors), 20 December 1935.

[D2:118] — Landquist, John, *Aftonbladet* (Stockholm), 29 November 1935.

[D2:119] — 'Strindberg och Intima teatern', in Solveig Landquist, red., **B1:248**, *John Landquist om Strindberg personen och diktaren*, pp. 155-158. [Rpr. of **D2:118**]

[D2:120] — Mörn, Kaj, *Granskaren* (Alingsås), 7 (1936), 28-29.

[D2:121] — Olsson, Hagar, *Tidevarvet* (Stockholm), 14:1 (1936), p. 3.

[D2:122] — Österling, Anders, *Svenska Dagbladet* (Stockholm), 27 November 1935.

[D2:123] — Schiller, Harald, *Sydsvenska Dagbladet* (Malmö), 13 January 1936.

[D2:124] — Vedel, Valdemar, *Dagens Nyheder* (Copenhagen), 5 June 1935.

[D2:125] — Wahlgren, Helge, *Ord och Bild* (Stockholm), 45 (1936), 218-222.

[D2:126] Falck, August, 'Strindberg och teater', in *Bref till medlemmar af Gamla Intima teatern från August Strindberg*, Stockholm, 1918. Unpaginated. ['Strindberg and Theatre'. Introduces a collection of Sg's writings on the theatre, several in facsimile, edited with a commentary by his co-director at the Intimate Theatre]

[D2:127] Florin, Magnus, red., *i ljuset av Strindberg*, Dramatens skriftserie 4, Stockholm: 1980-81. Illus. 64 pp. ['In the Light of Strindberg'. Includes forty-six statements about Sg by actors, directors, and others connected with performing his dramas, plus a richly illustrated record of productions of many of the plays staged at Dramaten, compiled by Herbert Grevenius]

[D2:128] Gravier, Maurice, *Strindberg et le théâtre moderne, I. L'Allemagne*, Lyon/Paris: Bibliothèque de la Société des Etudes Germaniques, 1949. 185 pp. ['Strindberg and the Modern Theatre. I. Germany'. An examination of Sg's impact on German literature as well as theatre, organised in three parts: (1) Sg and Naturalism, covering Sg's reception in the German theatre 1889-1914, when the marriage question (in *Giftas* as well as *Kamraterna*, *Fadren*, *Fröken Julie*, and *Fordringsägare*), the female vampire, and 'Le meurtre psychique' were seen as his main themes and exerted a major impact on contemporary German and Austrian writing (e.g. Gerhart Hauptmann, Hermann Bahr, Johannes Schlaf, and Max Halbe); (2) Sg and Wedekind (particularly the Lulu plays and *König Nicolo*); and (3 - the most useful section) Sg and Expressionism, which examines *Till Damaskus* and its influence on German expressionist drama (including plays by Franz Werfel, Walter Hasenclever, Reinhard Sorge, and Ernst Toller). Gravier explores issues relevant to the nature of dramatic expressionism generally in chapters on 'Le caractère et l'âme', 'Le moi et ses fantômes', and 'Le théâtre du rêve'. Includes material from **D2:688**, **D2:701**, **D2:702**, **D2:703**, **D2:704**, and **D2:705**. No other parts published, although 'II. Pays Scandinaves, Anglo-Saxons et Latins' is listed as forthcoming]

[D2:129] — Ahlström, Stellan, *Samtid och framtid* (Stockholm), 7 (1950), p. 441.

[D2:130] — Bang, Carol C., *Modern Language Notes* (Madison, Wisconsin), 66:2 (1951), 110-112.

[D2:131] — Fehrman, Carl, *Sydsvenska Dagbladet* (Malmö), 5 October 1950.

[D2:132] — Jolivet, A[lfred], *Revue d'histoire du théâtre* (Paris), 2:1 (1950), p. 98.

[D2:133] — Maury, Lucien, *Mercure de France* (Paris), 307 (1949), 540-543.

[D2:134] — Minder, Robert, *Revue de littérature comparée* (Paris), 25:4 (1951), 373-378.

[D2:135] Gravier, Maurice, *Strindberg, père du théâtre moderne*, Stockholm: Institut Suédois, 1962. 64 pp. ['Strindberg, Father of the Modern Theatre'. A Swedish Institute booklet for the general reader which places the emphasis on Sg's work as a dramatist and its significance for the development of the modern theatre rather than his biography]

[D2:136] Hedvall, Yngve, *Strindberg på Stockholmsscenen 1870-1922. En teaterhistorisk översikt*, Stockholm: N. S. Lundströms förlag, 1923. 191 pp. ['Strindberg on the Stockholm Stage, 1870-1922. A Theatre-Historical Survey'. An invaluable survey of the early fortunes of Sg's plays in performance in Stockholm during his lifetime and the decade following his death in 1912. Hedvall provides details of their casts, directors, and designers, notes their critical reception, with frequent quotation from the daily press, and comments on their place in the repertoire as a whole. In accord with their early popularity in Sweden, he allots most attention to *Mäster Olof* and *Lycko-Pers resa*, and comparatively little to several major works which had sometimes received only a very few performances by 1922. Published in a limited edition of 450 numbered copies]

[D2:137] — A. B-s [August Brunius], *Göteborgs Handels- och Sjöfartstidning*, 20 June 1923.

[D2:138] Heise, Wilhelm, *August Strindberg*, I-IV, in *Das Drama der Gegenwart. Analysen zeitgenössischer Bühnenwerke*, Reclams Universalbibliothek Nos 6846, 6866, 6939, 6979, Leipzig: Reclam, 1928-29. [Comprises four concise pamphlets containing analyses of Sg's major dramas, organised on a generic basis. Taken together they form a substantial early monograph on his playwriting. The plays discussed are: Vol. I. *Das Vater*, pp. 5-21. *Fräulein Julie*, pp. 22-37, *Kameraden*, pp. 39-45, *Gläubiger*, pp. 45-48, and *Totentanz*, pp, 49-66; Vol. II. *Nach Damaskus*, pp. 3-44, and *Ein Traumspiel*, pp. 45-65; Vol. III. *Kammerspiele*: *Wetterleuchten*, pp. 7-14, *Die Brandstätte*, pp. 15-22, *Gespenstersonate*, pp. 22-33, *Scheiterhaufen*, pp. 33-42; and *Märchendramen*: *Advent*, pp. 46-56, *Ostern*, pp. 57-66, *Schwanenweiss*, pp. 66-68, and *Kronbraut*, pp. 68-76; Vol. IV. *Historische Dramen*: *Meister Olaf*, pp. 5-23, *Gustav Vasa*, pp, 24-40, *Erik XIV*, pp. 40-46, *Gustav Adolf*, pp. 47-59, and *Näktergalen i Wittenberg*, pp. 59-73.]

[D2:139] Johnson, Walter [Gilbert], *Strindberg and the Historical Drama*, Seattle: University of Washington Press, 1963. X+326 pp. [Confirms the importance of Sg's history plays, both as theatre and literature. Johnson maintains that at least seven of them have stood the test of frequent stage production and twelve remain of interest to the educated reader. With their individualised, complex, and dynamic characters, they represent a unique achievement in terms of time span and literary quality, and form the single most important body of such work in European drama after Shakespeare, whose history plays, from *Henry IV* to *Julius Caesar*, Sg so greatly admired. He discusses each play in turn as well as the early dramas, *Den fredlöse*, *Gillets hemlighet*, and *Herr Bengts hustru*, the three World-Historical Plays, and his abiding, but changing, interest in history in general. Johnson concludes that the cycle of dramas devoted to Swedish monarchs stamps Sg as the major modern practitioner of the genre; indeed, these plays represent a unique contribution, not only to Swedish literature and the Swedish stage, but also to world literature. Johnson's study remains the standard overview of this aspect of Sg's playwriting]

[D2:140] — Berendsohn, Walter A[rthur], *Erasmus* (Darmstadt), 16 (1964), Sp. 464-465.

[D2:141] — Carlson, Harry G., *Players Magazine* (DeKalb, Illinois), 40:7 (1964), 222-223.

[D2:142] — Günther, Helmut, *Welt und Wort* (Bad Wörishofen), 19 (1964), p. 221.

[D2:143] — Johannesson, Eric O., *Scandinavian Studies* (Lawrence, Kansas), 35:4 (1963), 347-349.

[D2:144] — Landquist, John, 'Strindberg näst Shakespeare säger Amerika', *Aftonbladet* (Stockholm), 8 August 1963. ['Strindberg next to Shakespeare Says America']

[D2:145] — Landquist, John, 'Strindberg näst Shakespeare säger Amerika', in Solveig Landquist, red., **B1:248**, *John Landquist om Strindberg personen och diktaren*, pp. 193-196. ['Strindberg next to Shakespeare says America'. Rpr. of **D2:144**]

[D2:146] — Lindström, Hans, *Samlaren* (Uppsala), 87 (1966), pp. 205-207.

[D2:147] — Poulenard, Elie, *Bulletin de la Faculté des lettres de Strasbourg*, 43:2 (1965), 219-221.

[D2:148] — Smedmark, Carl Reinhold, *Scandinavica* (London), 3:1 (1964), 67-70.

[D2:149] — Wayne, Wonderley A., *Germanic Review* (New York), 47:4 (1972), 305-306.

See also **A4:62**

[D2:150] Jolivet, Alfred, *Le Théâtre de Strindberg*, Bibliothèque de la Revue des Cours et Conférences, Paris: Boivin & cie, Éditeurs, 1931. 356 pp. [Adopts a chronological approach in keeping with the assumption that everything Sg wrote contributed to a continuous account of his own life. Like Sg's naturalism, *Gillets hemlighet*, *Lycko-Pers resa*, and *Herr Bengts hustru* are given equal weight with many of the post-Inferno dramas which are, however, sometimes treated more selectively, even if their significance for modern drama is nevertheless recognised. Apart from *Mäster Olof*, the history plays are despatched in a dozen pages. For its period, this was a useful volume based on primary sources, in which the plays are discussed in relation to the French dramatic tradition. Their impact on the German theatre is also acknowledged, but not examined in detail]

[D2:151] — Einarsson, Stefán, *Modern Language Notes* (Baltimore), 48:2 (1933), 122-123.

[D2:152] — Erdmann, Nils, *Nya Dagligt Allehanda* (Stockholm), 6 March 1932.

[D2:153] — Robertson, J[ohn] G[eorge], *Modern Language Review* (London), 27 (1932), p. 233.

[D2:154] Karnick, Manfred, *Rollenspel und Welttheater: Untersuchungen an Dramen Calderóns, Schillers, Strindbergs, Becketts und Brechts*, München: Fink, 1980, pp. 81-198, 321-348. ['Role Play and World Theatre. Studies in the Dramas of Calderón de la Barca, Schiller, Strindberg, Beckett, and Brecht'. Includes a section on Sg entitled 'Universale Rollenbedingtheit und sozialer Rollenprotest: Die strukturelle Einheit im Werk August Strindbergs' on the tension between social protest and conditioning in an often metatheatrical theatre that, contrary to received notions, enjoys a large measure of unity. Focuses mainly on *Fröken Julie*, *Inferno*, *Mäster Olof*, and *Till Damaskus*]

[D2:155] Kesting, Marianne, 'Einleitung', in August Strindberg, *Über Drama und Theater*, Aus dem Schwedischen von Verner Arpe, Collection Theater Werkbücher 6, Köln: Kiepenheuer & Witsch, 1966, pp. 13-32. [Introduces a frequently cited collection of Sg's writings on drama and the theatre in German translation, including the various memoranda which he addressed to members of the Intimate Theatre]

[D2:156] — Baer, Volker, *Die Bücherkommentare* (Stuttgart), 15 (1966), p. 132.

[D2:157] — Beckmann, Heinz, *Rheinischer Merkur* (Koblenz), 21:39 (1966), p. 37.

[D2:158] Kvam, Kela, ed., *Strindberg's Post-Inferno Plays*, København: Munksgaard-Rosinante, 1994. Illus. 216 pp. [The proceedings of the 11th Sg conference in Copenhagen, 7-12 April 1992, with a short introduction by the editor, pp. 7-8. Contains **A3:38**: Lars Dahlbäck, 'The National Edition. A Presentation'; **C1:233**: Thomas Bredsdorff, 'Three Post-Inferno Strindberg Plays which Strindberg did not Write: Bergman's *Wild Strawberries* and *Persona* and Enquist's *The Night of the Tribades*'; **C2:83**: Egil Törnqvist, 'Long Day's Journey into Night: Bergman's TV-Version of *Oväder* Compared to *Smultronstället*'; **D2:549**: Harry G. Carlson, 'Medieval Themes and Structures in Strindberg's Post-Inferno Drama'; **D2:607**: Hans-Göran Ekman, 'Death Angst, Death Wish. Aspects of Death in Strindberg's Post-Inferno Plays'; **D2:774**: Barry Jacobs, 'Strindberg and the Myth of the Androgyne: Christ Figures in *Påsk* and *The Bridal Crown*'; **D2:897**: Barbara Lide, 'Strindberg as "medveten spefågel": Post-Inferno Irony'; **D2:1009**: Bertil Nolin, 'Strindberg as Director. His Theories on Staging and Acting in *Öppna brev till Intima Teatern*'; **D2:1194**: Evert Sprinchorn, 'Strindberg and the Decline of the Drama of Ideas'; **D2:1263**: Pirjo Vaittinen, 'Autumn Encounters'; **E40:13**: Margaretha Fahlgren, 'Kristina – The Public Woman'; **E26:4**: Klaus van den Berg, 'Spatial Consciousness and Theatrical Image: *Advent* at the Deutsches Theater, Berlin 1919'; **E26:15**: Jan Esper Olsson, 'Strindberg's Use of "The Macabre" and "The Sweet" as Means of Expression in the Penance Play *Advent*'; **E30:45**: Margareta Wirmark, 'Vakhtangov's Production of *Erik XIV*, Moscow Arts Theatre, First Studio, 1921'; **E41:7**: Richard Bark, 'Humanity's Imprisonment in Matter and the Annulment of Time and Space. The Lars Rudolfsson Production of *A Dreamplay* at Orionteatern, Stockholm 1990'; **E51:9**: Knut Ove Arntzen, '"Das Nilpferd ist ein Text": *Spöksonaten* According to Transformtheater and Heiner Müller'; and **D2:1119**: Freddie Rokem, 'Strindberg's "Optical Unconscious"']

[D2:159] — Blackwell, Marilyn Johns, *Scandinavian Studies* (Provo), 67:2 (1995), 261-264.

[D2:160] — Lagerroth, Ulla-Britta, *Nordica* (Odense), 11 (1994), 306-311.

[D2:161] — Lewin, Jan, 'Fortsatt forskning kring August', *entré* (Norsborg), 21:2 (1994), p. 90. ['Continued Research about August']

[D2:162] — Petherick, Karin, *Scandinavica* (Norwich), 34:1 (1995), 145-147.

[D2:163] — Robinson, Michael, *Theatre Research International* (Oxford), 19 (1994), 274-275.

[D2:164] — Sauter, Willmar, *Samlaren* (Uppsala), 115 (1994), pp. 152-155.

[D2:165] — Syréhn, Gunnar, *Nordic Theatre Studies* (Copenhagen), 8 (1995), 89-91.

[D2:166] Kvam, Kela, *Max Reinhardt og Strindbergs visionære dramatik*, Theatervidenskabelige Studier 3, København: Akademisk Forlag, 1974. Illus. 170 pp. ['Max Reinhardt and Strindberg's Visionary Drama'. An important contribution to the performance history of Sg's plays and to theatre history in general. Kvam analyses Reinhardt's productions of *Oväder*, *Pelikanen*, *Spöksonaten*, *Dödsdansen*, and *Ett drömspel* in the general context of the wave of enthusiasm for Sg's dramas in Germany during the second two decades of the 20th Century. She establishes the importance of Reinhardt's readings of the plays in performance for a modern understanding of Sg and the central role which Sg's dramaturgy played in the development of the modern European theatre. She also discusses both the impact of Reinhardt's tours to Sweden in 1915, 1916, 1917, and 1920 on the hitherto often indifferent Swedish response to Sg's later plays, and his staging of *Ett drömspel* with Swedish actors at Dramaten in 1921]

[D2:167] — Larsson, B., *Samlaren* (Uppsala), 95 (1974), pp. 237-238.

[D2:168] — Lindström, Göran, *Sydsvenska Dagbladet* (Malmö), 31 July 1974.

[D2:169] Lamm, Martin, *Strindbergs dramer I-II*, Stockholm: Albert Bonniers Förlag, 1924-1926. 413, 448 pp. [Written by the foremost Sg scholar of his generation and based in part on many previously unpublished or unexamined sources, this survey of the plays in chronological order inaugurated serious Sg scholarship, and includes numerous reflections on his life and work as a whole. Later studies have extended, revised, and rethought many of Lamm's conclusions, but even if its biographical approach has rightly been questioned (for Lamm, Sg's entire output 'is really nothing but a gigantic self-incarnation'), this overview remains a considerable achievement, not least for the way in which it sought to make serious sense of the Inferno crisis and its significance for the plays which succeeded it. Lamm's study set the tone and the agenda for the largely positivistic nature of Swedish Sg studies for some four decades, and exerted a powerful influence on the, often biographical, staging of Sg's plays in Sweden, particularly in the productions of Olof Molander]

[D2:170] — Anon, 'New Foreign Books', *The Times Literary Supplement* (London), 1 October 1925. [I]

[D2:171] — B. B. [Birger Bæckström], *Göteborgs Handels- och Sjöfartstidning*, 8 January 1925. [I]

[D2:172] — B. B. [Birger Bæckström], *Göteborgs Handels- och Sjöfartstidning*, 6 December 1928. [II]

[D2:173] — Berendsohn, Walter A[rthur], *Deutsche Literaturzeitung* (Berlin), 48 (1927), Sp. 1860-1863. [I-II]

[D2:174] — Berendsohn, Walter A[rthur], *Zeitschrift für deutsche Philologie* (Berlin), 52 (1927), 235-237. [I-II]

[D2:175] — Böök, Fredrik, *Hufvudstadsbladet* (Helsingfors), 21 November 1924. [I]

[D2:176] — Castrén, Gunnar, *Nya Argus* (Helsingfors), 18 (1925), 4-6. [I]

[D2:177] — Clausen, Julius, *Tilskueren* (Copenhagen), 44:1 (1927), 350-352. [I-II]

[D2:178] — Erdmann, Nils, *Nya Dagligt Allehanda* (Stockholm), 12 December 1928. [II]

[D2:179] — Hagberg, K., *Sydsvenska Dagbladet* (Malmö), 18 December 1924. [I]

[D2:180] — Hedén, Erik, *Tiden* (Stockholm), 17 (1925), 287-296. [Discusses Volume One. Hedén comments on the profound difference in temperament between Sg and Lamm, and maintains that the latter entirely misunderstands *Mäster Olof*. Nevertheless, he regards this as the best critical study of Sg to date, and considers Lamm is right to emphasise the significance played by the Inferno crisis in Sg's development as a period of literary rebirth]

[**D2:181**] — Hedén, Erik, 'Martin Lamm. *Strindbergs dramer I*', in *Valda skrifter*, 5 vols, Stockholm: Tiden, 1927, Vol. 5, pp. 375-387. [Rpr. of **D2:180**]

[**D2:182**] — Hedvall, Yngve, 'Solid Offerings in the Swedish Book Market', *American Scandinavian Review* (New York), 15 (1927), 282-302. [I-II]

[**D2:183**] — Hgr. O. [Hagar Olsson], *Svenska Pressen* (Helsingfors), 17 January 1925. [Olsson stresses the vitality and boldness of Sg's plays. His naturalist and symbolist dramas initiate a line of development that leads to the most recent form of collective drama. Vol. I]

[**D2:184**] — Hgr. O. [Hagar Olsson], *Svenska Pressen* (Helsingfors), 9 March 1927. [II]

[**D2:185**] — Holmberg, Olle, *Nya Dagligt Allehanda* (Stockholm), 2 December 1924. [I]

[**D2:186**] — J. L. [John Landquist], *Aftonbladet* (Stockholm), 5 January 1925. [I]

[**D2:187**] — 'Professor Lamm om Strindberg', in Solveig Landquist, red., **B1:248**, *John Landquist om Strindberg personen och diktaren*, pp. 137-141. [Rpr. of **D2:186**]

[**D2:188**] — J. L. [John Landquist], *Aftonbladet* (Stockholm), 14 December 1926. [II]

[**D2:189**] — 'Professor Lamm om Strindberg', in Solveig Landquist, red., **B1:248**, *John Landquist om Strindberg personen och diktaren*, pp. 142-147 [Rpr. of **D2:188**]

[**D2:190**] — Jolivet, A[lfred], *Litteris* (Lund), 5 (1928), 211-222. [II]

[**D2:191**] — Kj. Sg [Kjell Strömberg], *Stockholms-Tidningen*, 7 December 1924. [I]

[**D2:192**] — Krog, Helge, in *Meninger om bøker og forfattere*, Oslo, 1929, pp. 167-170. [I]

[**D2:193**] — Montelin, G., *Orfeus* (Stockholm), 1927, pp. 34-35. [I-II]

[**D2:194**] — O. H. [Olle Holmberg], *Dagens Nyheter* (Stockholm), 25 November 1928. [II]

[**D2:195**] — Olsson, Oscar, *Bokstugan* (Djursholm), 9 (1925), 81-89. [I]

[**D2:196**] — Österling, Anders, *Svenska Dagbladet* (Stockholm), 26 November 1928. [II]

[**D2:197**] — Palmblad, Harry V. E., *Scandinavian Studies* (Menasha, Wisconsin), 10:4 (1928), 115-117. [I-II]

[**D2:198**] — Robertson, J[ohn] G[eorge], *Modern Language Review* (London), 22 (1927), 354-356. [I-II]

[**D2:199**] — Selander, Sten, *Stockholms Dagblad*, 21 November 1926. [I-II]

[**D2:200**] — T. F-t [Torsten Fogelqvist], *Dagens Nyheter* (Stockholm), 30 May 1925. [I]

[**D2:201**] — Werin, Algot, *Lunds Dagblad*, 23 December 1924. [I]

[**D2:202**] — Wieselgren, Oscar, *Tidskrift* (Stockholm), 15 (1925), 279-285. [I]

[**D2:203**] Lewko, Marian, *Studia o Strindbergu*, Lublin: Redakcja Wydawnictw, Katolickiego Uniwersytetu Lubelskiego, 1999. Illus. 351 pp. ['Studies on Strindberg'. Contains six studies of Strindberg as a dramatist: (1) 'The Intimate Theatre of August Strindberg', which discusses the structure of his dramas from *Fadren* to the dream plays and considers the practical experience he gained as a failed actor in 1869 as well as with the Scandinavian Experimental Theatre in Copenhagen in 1889 and the Intimate Theatre in 1907-1910; (2) 'The Christian Contexts of August Strindberg's Dramaturgy', which reviews both the legacy of his early pietism and the Catholicism he became acquainted with through Frida Uhl's family in Austria; and (3) 'About the Semantics and the Function of Properties in *Erik XIV*', which explores how, in Sg's theatre, stage properties are often substituted for language and are given a complementary function in the text. Further chapters compare (4) Ibsen's *When We Dead Awaken* with *Stora landsvägen* as autobiographical dramas; (5) surveys the early reception of Sg in Poland in the modernist period, focusing primarily on the plays in performance; and (6) charts the performance history of his plays in the Polish theatre. Lewko also documents the reception of the plays in productions for both television and the stage with details of casts and directors as well as reviews and reviewers. Summary in English, pp. 343-345]

[D2:204] Liljenberg, Bengt, *Svenska stycken efter Strindberg – Anteckningar kring den svenska scendramatiken och dess författare 1910-1960*, Stockholm: Carlssons, 1990. Illus. 271 pp. ['Swedish Plays After Strindberg. Observations on Swedish Stage Plays and Their Authors, 1910-1960'. Focuses primarily on the place accorded contemporary Swedish drama in the Swedish theatre and its critical reception in the daily press and weekly journals. Discusses Sg's Intimate Theatre, pp. 31-36]

[D2:205] Lunin, Hanno, *Strindbergs Dramen*, Die Schaubühne. Quellen und Forschung zur Theatergeschichte 60, Emsdetten: Verlag Lechte, 1962. [VI]+323 pp. ['Strindberg's Plays'. A structural analysis of selected plays, one for each genre studied: Naturalism: *Fadren*; Fairy-Tale Play: *Himmelrikets nycklar*; Historical Drama: *Gustav Adolf*; Dream Play: *Ett drömspel*; and Chamber Play: *Spöksonaten*, where Lunin agrees with Peter Szondi in *Theorie des modernen Dramas*, **D1:450**, that Hummel has the role of a narrator in a drama which represents a crucial break with the rules of the classical Aristotelian theatre]

[D2:206] Madsen, Børge Gedsø, *Strindberg's Naturalistic Theatre: Its Relation to French Naturalism*, Seattle: University of Washington Press; Copenhagen: Munksgaard, 1962. 192 pp. [Examines Sg's naturalistic dramas in the light of Zola's dramatic theories, Henry Becque's plays, and Antoine's theatrical practice at the Théâtre Libre. Madsen traces Sg's contacts with French naturalism between 1876 and 1887 and analyses *Kamraterna*, *Fadren*, *Fröken Julie*, *Fordringsägare*, and the one-acters of the late 1880s and early 1890s, in order to define Sg's 'Nouvelle Formule'. Madsen explores his links with the theories of suggestion and the self of the French psychologists Jean-Martin Charcot, Théodule Ribot, and Hippolyte Bernheim, as well as with the work of French writers (e.g. the Goncourt brothers, Alphonse Daudet, Villiers de l'Isle Adam, and Guy de Maupassant). To some extent each of Sg's major naturalistic dramas embodies the principles of Zola's formula – 'faire grande, faire vrai, et faire simple', but not necessarily in quite the manner that Zola envisaged. Thus, while *Fröken Julie* reveals Sg's indebtedness to doctrinaire naturalism to a greater extent than any of his other plays, *Fadren* was too grand for Zola's liking and *Fordringsägare* deficient in the determining scenic décor on which Zola placed such stress. Together with *Leka med elden* and *Bandet*, the *quart d'heure* plays that follow are even more concise than the latter; in many of them, Sg's debt to the French *comédie rosse* as the genre was sometimes practiced at the Théâtre Libre is frequently apparent. Doctoral dissertation] .

[D2:207] — Johnson, Walter [Gilbert], *Scandinavian Studies* (Lawrence, Kansas), 35:1 (1963), 86-87.

[D2:208] — Jolin, C., *Barometern* (Kalmar), 6 September 1962.

[D2:209] — Poulenard, Elie, *Scandinavica* (London), 2:1 (1963), 59-60.

[D2:210] — Raphael, Robert, *American-Scandinavian Review* (New York), 52:1 (1964), p. 97.

[D2:211] — Rinman, Sven, *Göteborgs Handels- och Sjöfartstidning*, 27 October 1962.

[D2:212] Madsen, Børge Gedsø, *Strindberg's Naturalistic Theatre: Its Relation to French Naturalism*, New York: Russell and Russell, 1973. [Facsimile Rpr. of **D2:206**]

[D2:213] Marcus, Carl David, *Strindbergs Dramatik*, Mit Abbildungen nach Svend Gade, Ernst Stern und [Leo] Pasetti, München: Georg Müller, 1918. Illus. 479 pp. ['Strindberg's Dramas. With Illustrations by Svend Gade, Ernst Stern, and Leo Pasetti'. A popular but, for its period, fairly well-informed, treatment of Sg's achievement as a dramatist, one which demonstrates an interest in the dramaturgic rather than the biographical aspects of the plays. The latter are classified by genre and according to both their form and the assumed source of their inspiration rather than discussed in strict chronological order. Thus, chapters on the historical dramas from *Mäster Olof* to *Gustav III* (i.e. excluding the final three history plays of 1908-09), the romantic plays (*Gillets hemlighet*, *Herr Bengts hustru*, and *Lycko-Pers resa*), and the naturalistic dramas of the late-1880s and early 1890s, which here includes *Himmelrikets nycklar*, are followed by a more detailed discussion of four of the plays that impacted most immediately upon Germany (*Till Damaskus*, *Ett drömspel*, *Brott och brott*, and *Dödsdansen*). Meanwhile, *Advent*, *Påsk*, and *Midsommar* are grouped together and discussed as 'Jahresfestspiele', and there are separate chapters on the Märchenspiele (*Kronbruden* and *Svanevit*), the Chamber Plays of 1907, and the verse dramas (*Abu Casems tofflor*, *Svarta handsken*, and *Stora landsvägen*)]

[D2:214] — Bolander, C. A., *Dagens Nyheter* (Stockholm), 26 November 1919.

[D2:215] — Coffrin, Assaf, 'Literarwißenschaftliche Rundschau', *Nord und Süd* (Breslau), 167 (1918), 328-332.

[D2:216] — El. [Richard Elsner], *Das deutsche Drama* (Berlin), 2 (1919), 119-120.

[D2:217] — G. W. [Georg Witkowski], *Zeitschrift für Bücherfreunde* (Leipzig), NF, 10:2 (1918-19), Sp. 428-429.

[D2:218] — Katann, Oscar, 'Literarische Umschau. Neue ästhetische Erkenntnisse des Wesens der Bühne', *Der Gral* (Trier), 15 (1920-21), 364-367.

[D2:219] — Knudsen, Hans, *Die schöne Literatur* (Leipzig), 22 (1921), p. 75.

[D2:220] — Nilsson, Albert, *Göteborgs Handels- och Sjöfartstidning*, 28 May 1920.

[D2:221] — Stern, Julius, 'Literaturforschung und Verwandtes. II. Literaturgeschichte', *Zeitschrift für Deutschkunde* (Leipzig), 35 (1921), 209-210.

[D2:222] — Strömberg, K. R. G., *Forum* (Stockholm), 5 (1918), 480-481.

See also **A4:7, A4:61, A4:63, A4:66, A4:129**

[D2:223] Marker, Frederick J., and Lise-Lone, *Strindberg and Modernist Theatre: Three Major Post-Inferno Plays in Performance*, Cambridge: Cambridge University Press, 2002. Illus. 188 pp. [Studies the issues raised, and the technical problems presented, in staging Sg's post-Inferno plays, which are exemplified here with detailed analysis of *Till Damaskus, Ett drömspel*, and *Spöksonaten* in productions by Max Reinhardt, Olof Molander, and Ingmar Bergman. The Markers comment more briefly on productions by Evgenii Vakhtangov, Per Lindberg, Victor Barnowsky, Erwin Axer, Robert Lepage, and Robert Wilson, and they also examine the effect which Sg's allusive (and elusive) dramaturgic method has had on the changing nature of the theatrical experience and the spectator's relationship to it. This innovatory dramaturgy is initially implemented in *Till Damaskus*, a work that foreshadows both Joyce's *Ulysses* and the Cubism of

Picasso and Braque, and thus becomes 'one of the truly seminal works of modernist art'. But the authors also suggest that *Spöksonaten* represents yet another significant shift in style for Sg, one that is as radical and experimental as the stylistic transformation which occurred in his work at the start of the post-Inferno period in 1898. Appositely illustrated]

[D2:223a] — Blackwell, Marilyn Johns, *Scandinavian Studies* (Provo), 77:1 (2005), 152–155.

[D2:224] — *Scandinavian Review* (New York), 91:1 (2003), p. 73.

[D2:225] Meidal, Björn, 'A Strindberg Forgery: Carl Öhman's *August Strindberg and the Origin of Scenic Expressionism*', *Scandinavica* (Norwich), 34:1 (1995), 61-69. [Establishes the spuriousness of many of the sources on which Öhman based his thesis in **D2:233**. These include not only bibliographical and other references but numerous forged quotations attributed to Sg and others, all of them designed to provide unambiguous proof that Sg was well informed about the most up-to-date theories of the theatre of the period, including the work of Adolphe Appia, Otto Brahm, and Julius Bab, as well as Edward Gordon Craig and Georg Fuchs. However, as Meidal points out, whatever value the book loses as a work of scholarship, it ought rapidly to recover as a rare piece of Sgiana]

[D2:226] Meidal, Björn, 'Ett Strindbergsfalsarium: Carl Öhmans *August Strindberg and the Origin of Scenic Expressionism*', *Samlaren* (Uppsala), 116 (1995), pp. 142-148. [A more detailed exposure of **D2:233** than Meidal's original article, **D2:225**]

[D2:227] Melmpergk, Margarita, ed., *Ho Strintmperg kai he synchrone dramaturgia*, Atena: Hestia, 1997. 324 pp. ['Strindberg and Modern Drama'. The proceedings of a conference held in Greece, 7-12 May 1988. Text in Greek, New Greek, and English]*

[D2:228] Morgan, Margery, *August Strindberg*, Basingstoke: Macmillan, 1985. Illus. XI+198 pp. [Surveys Sg's writing for the theatre in its entirety in a popular series on modern dramatists, although the argument is too brief in places. Unusually in England, Morgan places the emphasis on the post-Inferno plays, with chapters on the historical dramas, *Till Damaskus*, *Dödsdansen*, *Ett drömspel*, and the Chamber Plays, and makes a particularly interesting case for *Advent* as a much under-estimated play and one of the inspirations for Kafka's *Der Prozeß*. She also stresses the importance accorded the visual dimension in Sg's plays and the role which his often overlooked knowledge of the practical theatre had for his writing for the stage, where he thought as a director as well as a dramatist]

[D2:229] — Muradian, K[atarin], '[Against Madness and Delusions]', *Obshchestvennye nauki za rubezhom. RZh. Seriia 7. Literaturovedenie* (Moscow), 4, (1987), 109-113.

[D2:230] — Robinson, Michael, *Scandinavica* (Norwich), 25:1 (1986), 84-85. [Considers the attempt to rehabilitate *Advent* as a stage-worthy play to be the book's most interesting feature]

[D2:231] — *The Times Educational Supplement* (London), 6 June 1986, p. 28.

[D2:232] Nolin, Bertil, *Intima Teatern. Strindbergs teater 1907-1910*, Stockholm: Strindbergsmuseet, 1995. Illus. 22 pp. ['The Intimate Theatre. Strindberg's Theatre, 1907-1910'. The catalogue for an exhibition at the Sg Museum. Includes an abbreviated English version of Nolin's essay, 'Strindberg och idén om en intim teater' (Strindberg and the Idea of an Intimate Theatre), **D2:1012**]

[D2:233] Öhman, Carl, *August Strindberg and the Origins of Scenic Expressionism*, Michigan Studies in the Theatre, Shortened Edition, Helsingfors: Mercators tryckeri, 1961. 235 pp. [This purports to be the abridged version of a North American doctoral thesis and supports its argument that Sg advocated a complete renewal of dramatic form and performance not only as a dramatist but also as a theatre practitioner and theoretician with reference to a great deal of previously unknown material, both published and unpublished, Unfortunately, much of the latter has subsequently proved to be fictitious (see the articles by Björn Meidal, 'A Strindberg Forgery: Carl Öhman's *August Strindberg and the Origin of Scenic Expressionism*', **D2:225** and 'Ett Strindbergsfalsarium: Carl Öhmans *August Strindberg and the Origin of Scenic Expressionism*', **D2:226**), as has the thesis on which the book is based. Thus, cleverly assembled and intriguingly written, this remains one of the curiosities of Sg scholarship, its attractive, almost plausible, thesis emerging as partly its author's wish-fulfilment, partly a scholastic documentary novel, and partly a thesis concerning Sg's relationship with other theatrical innovators of the period, such as Edward Gordon Craig, which could almost be argued by other means. Like several of the cleverly written letters that Öhman attributes to Sg and others and cites here, the diary of the Swedish theatre director Emil Grandinson, which provides much of the supporting evidence for his argument, has never been traced. Nor have either the Michigan series, of which this volume claims to be a part, or the 1961 doctoral thesis from which it supposedly derives]

[D2:234] — H. K. [Hans Kutter], *Hufvudstadsbladet* (Helsingfors), 20 January 1962.

See also **A4:61, U1:166, U1:514, U1:515, U1:866, U1:867**

[D2:235] Ollén, Gunnar, *August Strindberg*, Translated from the original German by Peter Tirner, World's Dramatists Series, New York: Frederick Ungar Publishing Co., 1972. Illus. VII+150 pp. [English version of **D2:236**]

[D2:236] Ollén, Gunnar, *August Strindberg*, Friedrichs Dramatiker des Welttheaters 54, Velber bei Hannover: Friedrich Verlag, 1968. Illus. 128 pp. [Briefly contextualises Sg and his plays in terms of his life and times, then summarises and comments on each play in order of composition. Ollén concludes with a skeleton stage history, giving the date and place of their premières and of a few other notable performances, mainly in Scandinavia and Germany]

[D2:237] — Baldus, Alexander, *Welt und Wort* (Bad Wörishofen), 24 (1969), p. 226.

[D2:238] Ollén, Gunnar, *August Strindberg*, Übertragung und Bearbeitung der vorliegenden Kurzfassung von Verner Arpe, 2. Aufl., München, 1975. Illus. 128 pp. [An introduction to Sg's career as a dramatist. New edition of **D2:236**]

[D2:239] Ollén, Gunnar, *Strindbergs dramatik. En handbok*, Stockholm: Radiotjänst, 1948. Illus. 445 pp. [The first edition of what has become the standard reference work on Sg's dramas, their genesis and production history. See **D2:266**]

[D2:240] — Ahlström, Stellan, *Samtid och framtid* (Stockholm), 6 (1949), p. 28.

[D2:241] — Blanck, Anton, *Göteborgs Handels- och Sjöfartstidning*, 21 January 1949.

[D2:242] — Fredén, Gustaf, *Svenska Morgonbladet* (Stockholm), 23 December 1948.

[D2:243] — Grevenius, Herbert, *Stockholms-Tidningen*, 12 January 1949.

[D2:244] — Groothoff, Otto, *Sydsvenska Dagbladet* (Malmö), 12 January 1949.

[**D2:245**] — Johnson, Walter [Gilbert], *Scandinavian Studies* (Menasha, Wisconsin), 22:1 (1950), 28-30.

[**D2:246**] — Kula, Kauko, *Valvoja-Aika* (Helsinki), 27 (1949), p. 210.

[**D2:247**] — O. H. [Olle Holmberg], *Dagens Nyheter* (Stockholm), 15 January 1949. [Elicits a comment by Ollén and a reply by Holmberg, 20 January 1949]

[**D2:248**] — Smedmark, Carl Reinhold, *Bonniers Litterära Magasin* (Stockholm), 18:1 (1949), p. 72.

[**D2:249**] — T. B-s [Teddy Brunius], *Upsala Nya Tidning*, 18 December 1948.

[**D2:250**] — Zennström, Per-Olof, *Vår Tid* (Stockholm), 5:1 (1949), 11-12.

[**D2:251**] Ollén, Gunnar, *Strindbergs dramatik*, Omarb. och utvidgad upplaga, Stockholm: Sveriges Radio Förlag, 1961. Illus. 546 pp. [Enlarged edition of **D2:232**. See **D2:266**]

[**D2:252**] — Berendsohn, Walter A[rthur], *Erasmus* (Darmstadt), 14 (1961), Sp. 628-630.

[**D2:253**] — Beyer, Nils, *Stockholms-Tidningen*, 15 September 1961.

[**D2:254**] — Hamberg, Lars, *Nya Pressen* (Helsingfors), 5 January 1949.

[**D2:255**] — Holm, Ingvar, *Dagens Nyheter* (Stockholm), 13 November 1961.

[**D2:256**] — Janzon, Åke, *Svenska Dagbladet* (Stockholm), 12 February 1962.

[**D2:257**] — Landquist, John, *Aftonbladet* (Stockholm), 3 June 1962.

[**D2:258**] — Näslund, N. Sture, *Dagbladet Nya Samhället* (Sundsvall), 5 October 1961.

[**D2:259**] — N. L. Olsson [Nils Ludvig Olsson], *Nyaste Kristianstadsbladet*, 7 October 1961.

[**D2:260**] — Northam, J[ohn] R., *Scandinavica* (London), 2:1 (1963), 57-59. [Finds that Ollén places us in debt to him for the copiousness of his information, but he writes too much about Sg himself, and not enough about the plays as plays]

[**D2:261**] — Osbornson, Harry, *Falu-Kuriren* (Falun), 4 January 1962.

[**D2:262**] — Rinman, Sven, *Göteborgs Handels- och Sjöfartstidning*, 7 December 1961.

[**D2:263**] — Sjögren, Henrik, *Kvällsposten* (Malmö), 23 September 1961.

[**D2:264**] — Svenson, Lasse, *Smålands Folkblad* (Vaxjö), 12 February 1962.

[**D2:265**] Ollén, Gunnar, *Strindbergs dramatik. En handbok*, Stockholm: Bokförlaget Prisma, 1966. Illus. [293] pp. [Abridged paperback Rpr. of the 2nd (1961) edition. See **D2:266**]

[**D2:266**] Ollén, Gunnar, *Strindbergs dramatik*, Stockholm: Sveriges Radios Förlag, 1982. Illus. 614 pp. [Revised and expanded 4th edition of what remains the standard survey of the genesis of all of Sg's plays and their later performance history. Ollén contextualises each work in terms of its place in Sg's life, comments on its biographical and other sources, and then charts its fortunes in performance, primarily on stage, but also on radio and television, with the emphasis on Sweden but highlighting many European and North-American productions as well. Ollén's biographical approach often stifles a textually responsive dramaturgic analysis and promotes some questionable (or at least quite partial) readings, but where the fortunes of Sg's plays on stage are concerned, this remains an indispensable work of reference, one which rightly gives precedence to the theatrical rather than the purely literary dimension of each of the dramas]

[**D2:267**] — Sundberg, Björn, 'Strindbergs dramer på scen', *Upsala Nya Tidning*, 8 January 1983. ['Strindberg's Plays on Stage']

[D2:268] Pennington, Michael, and Stephen Unwin, *A Pocket Guide to Ibsen, Chekhov, and Strindberg*, London: Faber & Faber, 2004. 288 pp. [Includes a short appraisal of Sg's life and his significance for the modern theatre together with plot summaries and commentary on five of the plays: *Fadren, Fröken Julie, Dödsdansen, Ett drömspel*, and *Spöksonaten* (this amounts to less than half the number of works discussed by Ibsen and fewer even than those by Chekhov). The authors' conclusion that 'the forbidding nature of so much of Sg's work has meant that his influence has been more marginal' suggests a British rather than a European perspective, although that seems not to be their intention]

[D2:269] Perrelli, Franco, *August Strindberg. Sul dramma moderno e il teatro moderno*, Teatro studi e testi 6, Firenze: Leo S. Olschki Editore, 1986. 137 pp. ['August Strindberg. On Modern Drama and the Modern Theatre'. Discusses Sg's theatrical theories as well as the non-dramatic works (*Röda rummet, Giftas*, and the two collections of *Vivsektioner*) where pertinent, includes annotated translations of 'Själamord (Apropå *Rosmersholm*)', the Preface to *Fröken Julie*, 'Om modernt drama och modern teater', together with extracts from the *Memorandum till Medlemmarne av Intima Teatern*, and situates Sg's naturalism in relation to the psychological theories of Hippolyte Bernheim, Eduard von Hartmann, and Théodule Ribot, as well as to the literary templates of Zola and Louis Desprez's *L'Évolution naturaliste*. Also includes a discussion of the achievement of the Intimate Theatre]

[D2:269a] — Tiozzo, E., *Dagens Nyheter* (Stockholm), 16 March 1986.

[D2:270] Petri, Sten Magnus, '"*Blås upp vind och gunga bölja...*". *August Strindbergs sagospel Lycko-Pers resa, Himmelrikets nycklar, Abu Casems tofflor: sago- och sägen-motiv, narrativa grundmönster och mytisk initiationssymbolik*, Uppsala: the Author, 2003. 459 pp. ['"Blow Wind and Billow Wave..."'. August Strindberg's Fairy-Tale Plays *Lucky Peter's Journey, The Keys of Heaven, and Abu Casem's Slippers. Fairy-Tale and Traditional Motifs, Primal Narrative Patterns and Mythical Initiation Symbolism*'. An academic thesis which stresses the role of Sg's fairy-tale plays in his dramatic production as a whole. Petri focuses primarily on *Lycko-Pers resa* as the first of his 'journey' plays and draws attention to the motifs and ideas that it shares with *Gillets hemlighet* and *Herr Bengts hustru*. *Lycko-Per* can thus be seen as both representative of the dramas of the 1880s and a herald of the later fairy-tale plays, *Svanevit* and *Svarta handsken*. Moreover, somewhat formlessly and at length, Petri maintains that an analysis of these plays in accordance with 20th-Century structural techniques confirms that, on the syntagmatic and morphologic planes, they have a close affinity with the verbal traditions of the folk tale as well as narrative patterns, motifs, and the symbolism of folklore in general. See also the associated discussion of *Svanevit* in **E37:13**. English summary. Doctoral dissertation]

[D2:270a] — Ek-Nilsson, Katarina, *Samlaren*, 126 (2005), pp. 306-310.

[D2:271] Peukert, Ester, *Strindbergs religiöse Dramatik. Versuch einer historischen und systematischen Bestimmung ihrer religiösen motive*, Hamburg, 1929. 142 pp. ['Strindberg's Religious Dramas. An Attempt at an Historical and Systematic Classification of their Religious Motifs'. Relates Sg to Carl von Linnaeus's notion of a Nemesis Divina as well as to Kierkegaard and Swedenborg, and analyses Sg's religious drama in relation to two pre-Inferno plays, *Fritänkaren* and *Mäster Olof*, and four from the following period, *Till Damaskus I, Advent, Påsk*, and *Ett drömspel*. Peukert also discusses the

Inferno crisis as depicted in *Inferno* for the light it sheds on Sg's changing attitude to religion as well as on those dramas in which religious motifs are prominent, and which raise religious questions of a psychological and philosophical nature. Written from a Christian perspective. See **V:165**]

[D2:272] Roger, Pascale, *La Cruauté et le théâtre de Strindberg: du "meurtre psychique" aux maladies de l'âme*, Paris, Budapest, Torino: L'Harmattan, 2004. Illus. 278 pp. ['Cruelty and Strindberg's Theatre: From Psychical Murder to Sicknesses of the Soul']

[D2:273] Rokem, Freddie, in *Theatrical Space in Ibsen, Chekhov and Strindberg*, Michigan: UMI Research Press, 1986. XIII+105 pp. [The chapter on Sg, 'Strindberg: The Camera and the Aesthetics of Repetition', focuses mainly on *Fröken Julie*, *Ett drömspel*, and *Spöksonaten*, and seeks to establish how he represents the private and the irrational on stage. His late plays are metaphorical explorations of the vast inner landscapes of the mind, place the reliability of any information we receive in question, gradually abandon the proscenium arch, and constantly manipulate our vision and point of view, which in many respects resembles the function of the narrator in the novel or even the camera in film. The latter is a useful analogy to the way in which Sg used techniques that resemble cinematic zoom, montage, and cut, and which are not only of technical significance but are also central to the meaning of plays in which the spectator joins the protagonist as an increasingly active participant in the process of perception and interpretation]

[D2:274] — Carlson, Marvin, *Genre* (Chicago), 19:2 (1986), 197-198.

[D2:275] — Garner, S., *Theatre Journal* (Baltimore), 41 (1989), 259-261.

[D2:276] — Kowzan, Tadeusz, *Revue d'histoire du théâtre* (Paris), 39:3 (1987), 341-342.

[D2:277] — Norwood, James, *Theatre Research International* (Oxford), 12:2 (1987), 177-178.

[D2:278] — Robinson, Michael, *Scandinavica* (Norwich), 28:1 (1989), 89-90.

[D2:279] — Sprinchorn, Evert, *Scandinavian Studies* (Lawrence, Kansas), 58:4 (1986), 438-440.

[D2:280] Rothwell, Brian, *Miss Julie* and *The Ghost Sonata*, Milton Keynes: Open University Press, 1977. Illus. 34 pp. [Affords an introduction to each play in turn, together with a comparison of their respective dramatic styles. A booklet designed to accompany additional material broadcast by the Open University]

[D2:281] Schmidt, Franz Werner, *August Strindberg und seine Besten Bühnenwerke. Eine Einführung*, Schneiders Bühnenführer 5, Berlin: Franz Schneider Verlag, 1922. [213] pp. ['August Strindberg and his best Stage Works. A Guide'. Contains synopses of what Schmidt considers are Sg's best plays – forty-four in all, including the three parts of *Till Damaskus* and both parts of *Dödsdansen*]

[D2:282] — Groß, Edgar, *Das literarische Echo* (Berlin), 25 (1922-23), Sp. 1221.

[D2:283] — Hesse, O. E., *Die Schöne Literatur* (Leipzig), 24 (1923), p. 275.

[D2:284] — Tacke, O[tto], *Bücherei und Bildungspflege* (Leipzig), 4 (1924), p. 255.

[D2:285] [Smedmark, Carl Reinhold], *Strindberg and Modern Theatre*, Published by the Strindberg Society, Sweden, Stockholm: Strindbergssällskapet, 1975. [162] pp. [Contains the text of contributions to a symposium hosted by the Sg Society in Stockholm, 3-6 September 1973, with a brief preface by Smedmark, p. [7]. Contains **B3:99**: Ileana Berlogea, 'Strindberg and the Romanian Modern Theatre'; **B3:232**: Walter Johnson,

'Strindberg and the American University Audience'; **B3:264**: Marian Lewko, 'Rezeption der theatralischen Theorie Strindbergs in Polen'; **C3:23**: Timo Tiusanen, '"Strindmatt or Dürrenberg?" Dürrenmatt's *Play Strindberg*'; **C1:290**: Luciano Codignola, 'Two Ideas of Dramatic Structure: Strindberg's Last Period and Pirandello's Third Period, a Confrontation'; **C1:476**: Maurice Gravier, 'Strindberg et Ionesco'; **C1:1167**: Irena Sławińska, 'Strindberg and Early Expressionism in Poland'; **E25:139**: Egil Törnqvist, 'Strindberg and the Drama of Half-reality. An Analysis of *To Damascus I*'; and **M:165**: Evert Sprinchorn, 'The Zola of the Occult']

[**D2:286**] — Skuncke, Marie-Christine, *Zeszyty Naukowe Wydziału Humanistycznego Uniwersytety Gdańskiego, Studia Scandinavica* (Gdańsk), 2 (1979), 111-112.

[**D2:287**] — Sokół, Lech, *Pamiętnik Teatralny* (Warsaw), 1979:3-4, pp. 571, 575-579. [Also reviews the proceedings of the 3rd International Sg Conference held in Paris and published in **B7:35**]

[**D2:288**] Stockenström, Göran, ed., *Strindberg's Dramaturgy*, Minneapolis: University of Minnesota Press, 1988. Illus. XXII+375 pp. [The proceedings in English of the 6th International Strindberg Conference, held at the University of Minnesota in 1983. Arranged in four sections: (I) 'Strindberg's Dramas: Historical Dimensions'; (II) 'Strindberg and the Modern Theater: Dramatic Form and Discourse'; (III) 'The Naturalistic or Supernaturalistic Plays: Dramatic Discourse and Stagings'; and (IV) 'The Dream Plays: Dramatic Discourse and Stagings'. Contains **B2:79**: Harry G. Carlson, 'Strindberg and the Dream of the Golden Age: The Poetics of History'; **B2:116**: Sven Delblanc, 'Strindberg and Humanism'; **C1:1205**: Evert Sprinchorn, 'Strindberg and the Superman'; **D2:425**: Richard Bark, 'Strindberg's Dream-Play Technique'; **D2:520**: Gunnar Brandell, 'Macro-Form in Strindberg's Plays: Tight and Loose Structure'; **D2:697**: Maurice Gravier, 'Strindberg and the French Drama of His Time'; **D2:810**: Manfred Karnick, 'Strindberg and the Tradition of Modernity: Structure of Drama and Experience'; **D2:926**: James McFarlane, 'Strindberg's Vision: Microscopic or Spectroscopic?'; **D2:1117**: Freddie Rokem, 'The Camera and the Aesthetics of Repetition: Strindberg's Use of Space and Scenography in *Miss Julie*, *A Dream Play*, and *Spöksonaten*'; **E12:191**: Frederick J. Marker and Lise-Lone Marker, 'Love Without Lovers: Ingmar Bergman's *Julie*'; **E25:42**: Elinor Fuchs, 'Strindberg "Our Contemporary": Constructing and Deconstructing *To Damascus I*'; **E25:59**: Barry Jacobs, 'Titanism and Satanism in *To Damascus* (I)'; **E25:130**: Göran Söderström, '*To Damascus* (I): A Dream Play?'; **E25:138**: Timo Tiusanen, 'Expressionistic Features in *To Damascus* (I)': **E35:19**: Susan Brantly, 'Naturalism or Expressionism: A Meaningful Mixture of Styles in *The Dance of Death* (I)'; **E38:27**: Göran Stockenström, '*Charles XII* as a Dream Play'; **E38:28**: Göran Stockenström, '*Charles XII* as Historical Drama'; **E41:36**: Susan Einhorn, 'Directing *A Dream Play*: A Journey through the Waking Dream'; **E41:66**: Ingvar Holm, 'Theories and Practice in Staging *A Dream Play*'; **E41:195**: Egil Törnqvist, 'Staging *A Dream Play*'; **E51:20**: Jon Berry, 'Discourse and Scenography in *The Ghost Sonata*'; **E51:23**: Sarah Bryant-Bertail, '"The Tower of Babel": Space and Movement in *The Ghost Sonata*'; **E53:36**: and Paul Walsh, 'Textual Clues to Performance Strategies in *The Pelican*'; as well as a Preface (pp. ix-xviii) in which the editor examines Sg's impact on the modern theatre, starting with Eugene O'Neill's response to the Provincetown Playhouse's staging of *Spöksonaten*]

[D2:289] — Bellquist, John Eric, *Theater Journal* (Baltimore), 42:2 (1990), 274-277. [Also discusses the monograph on *Fröken Julie* by Egil Törnqvist and Barry Jacobs, **E12:274**]

[D2:290] — Ollén, Gunnar, *Sydsvenska Dagbladet* (Malmö), 14 April 1989.

[D2:291] — Robinson, Michael, *Scandinavica* (Norwich), 28:2 (1989), 203-207.

[D2:292] — Rosenberg, Tina, *Nordic Theatre Studies* (Copenhagen), 5 (1992), 156-157.

[D2:293] — Uecker, Heiko, *Skandinavistik* (Kiel), 20:2 (1990), 149-150.

[D2:294] — Warme, Lars G., *World Literature Today* (Norman, Oklahoma), 64 (1990), p. 137.

[D2:295] — Westling, Barbro, *entré* (Norsborg), 17:4 (1990), p. 111.

See **A4:45a**

[D2:296] Szewczyk, Grażyna, *Strindberg jako prekursor ekspresjonizmu w dramacie*, Katowice: Uniwersytet Slaski, 1984. Illus. 147 pp. ['Strindberg as a Forerunner of Expressionist Drama'. Presents Sg as the immediate and necessary forerunner of European expressionism in the theatre with chapters on expressionist elements in his naturalistic dramas (especially *Fadren*) and the shift in Sg's theatrical aesthetic during the Inferno period, as well as specific discussions of *Till Damaskus*, *Ett drömspel*, and the Chamber Plays of 1907]

[D2:297] — Chojecki, Andrzej, 'Polska systematyka twórczości Strindberga', *Zeszyty Naukowe Wydziału Humanistycznego. Studia Scandinavica* (Uniwersytet Gdański), 9 (1985), 71-73.

[D2:298] — Drzyzga, Marianna, *Opole* (Opole), 1985:4, pp. 20-22.

[D2:299] — Greń, Zygmunt, *Życie Literackie* (Kraków), 1984:43, p. 6.

[D2:300] — J. C. [Justyna Csató], *Le Théâtre Polonaise* (Warsaw), 1985:11-12, p. 33.

[D2:301] — Jarosz, Ewa, *Tak i Nie* (Katowice), 1985:5, p. 13.

[D2:302] — Koprowski, Jan, *Tu i Teraz* (Warsaw), 1984, No. 51, p. 10.

[D2:303] — Sprusiński, Michal, *Trybuna Ludu* (Warsaw), 1984, No. 240, p. 5.

[D2:304] Thompson, Vance C., *Strindberg and His Plays*, Studies in Personality I, New York: McDevitt-Wilson's Inc., 1921. Illus. [38] pp. [Purports to build on personal acquaintaince with Sg during the mid-1890s in Paris, and is written in a sentimental, impressionistic style with more about the women he married than the plays of the title]

[D2:305] Thormann, Werner E., *August Strindberg*, Literatur- und Musikgeschichte in Einzelheften für Theaterbesucher, Reihe 3, Hefte 4, Frankfurt am Main, 1918.

[D2:306] Thormann, Werner E., *August Strindberg*, Augsburg, 1921. 16 pp. [Rpr. of **D2:305**]

[D2:307] Törnqvist, Egil, *Det talade ordet. Om Strindbergs dramadialog*, Stockholm: Carlssons, 2001. 262 pp. ['The Spoken Word. On Strindberg's Dramatic Dialogue'. Törnqvist notes Sg's insistence that the spoken word is the core of drama and therefore seeks to redress the surprising lack of attention paid by previous studies of the plays to Sg's dialogue and his use of language in general. Enlisting the aid of several literary and linguistic theorists from Aristotle to Peter Szondi, John Searle, Keir Elam, and Manfred Pfister, and engaging in close textual analysis of a wide range of Sg's plays (but most frequently *Bandet, Brända tomten, Dödsdansen, Ett drömspel, Fadren,*

Fröken Julie, Oväder, Pelikanen, Påsk, Spöksonaten, and *Till Damaskus*), this is a much needed study of Sg's style, his written text in action (what Pirandello called 'azione parlata'), and his sentence structure, as well as of his use of silence, metaphor, dramatic irony, characterisation through language, and the relationship between dialogue and action, subtext, and intertextual elements. In two substantial appendices Törnqvist discusses Sg's language in modern stagings via a comparison of the printed texts of *Fadren, Första varningen*, and *Oväder* with their verbal transposition in performances directed by Bo Widerberg and Ingmar Bergman, and he also considers issues raised by the translation of dramatic texts, with examples drawn from several English versions of *Fröken Julie, Ett drömspel, Oväder*, and *Pelikanen*]

[D2:308] — Ekman, Hans-Göran, *Samlaren* (Uppsala), 123 (2002), pp. 410-412.

[D2:309] — Robinson, Michael, *Scandinavica* (Norwich), 41:1 (2002), 98-100.

[D2:310] Törnqvist, Egil, *Strindbergian Drama: Themes and Structure*, Stockholm: Almqvist & Wiksell International, 1982. 259 pp. ['Törnqvist's collection of interrelated essays is a cornerstone of Sg scholarship which brings together an essential series of newly written or revised analyses of eleven plays, together with an assessment of the modernity of Sgian drama as a whole and a study of English translations of *Spöksonaten*. He stresses the artistry with which Sg composed his plays and the formal characteristics of his increasingly non-Aristotelian drama. The approach is structural and applied to a range of genres (naturalism, dreamplay, history play, monodrama, and chamber play). Characteristic of Sg, particularly of the post-Inferno plays, is the way in which the spectator or reader is included in Sg's own sphere and *experiences* the life they project: as the sequence develops, there is a gradual progression from letter to spirit, from outward to inward reality, from the singular to the universal. Taken as a whole, these studies give proper critical substance to the hitherto vague and subjective adjective 'Strindbergian' when applied to Sg's plays, and confirm his pivotal role in the development of modern drama. See the commentary elsewhere on the individual essays on *Fadren*, **E11:164**, *Fröken Julie*, **E12:270**, *Den starkare*, **E14:20**, *Första varningen*, **E20:6**, *Till Damaskus*, **E25:140**, *Erik XIV*, **E30:42**, *Dödsdansen*, **E35:120**, *Ett drömspel*, **E41:193**, *Brända tomten*, **E50:19**, *Spöksonaten*, **E51:148**, *Pelikanen*, **E53:33**, and translating *Spöksonaten* into English, **B4:183**]

[D2:311] — Muradian, K. E., *Obschchestvennye nauki za rubezhom. RZh. Seriia 7, Literaturovedenie*, 1, Moscow, 1984, pp. 109-112.

[D2:312] — Rinman, Sven, *Upsala Nya Tidning*, 2 September 1982.

[D2:313] — Steene, Birgitta, *Scandinavian Studies* (Lawrence, Kansas), 55:3 (1983), 273-274.

[D2:314] — Sundberg, Björn, *Samlaren* (Uppsala) 103 (1982), pp. 175-176.

[D2:315] Valency, Maurice [Jaques], *The Flower and the Castle: An Introduction to Modern Drama*, New York: Macmillan, 1946. VII+460 pp. [The first of three volumes which offer a survey of the major figures of early modern drama. Valency couples Sg yet again with Ibsen, but while the repetitious source of the plays in Sg's neuroses is over-emphasised, the result is far more subtle, sympathetic, and well informed about the theatrical dimension of the plays than F. L. Lucas's anti-Sgian diatribe in **C1:812**. Valency relates the post-Inferno dramas to the medieval theatre of allegory and exemplum, focuses in considerable detail on *Ett drömspel* as Sg's most ambitious attempt to formulate the passion of the artist in modern conceptual terms, and explores the naturalism of *Fadren*, *Fröken Julie*, and *Fordringsägare*, although the overriding biographical approach obscures discussion of their dramaturgical aspects. Ignores the history plays]

[D2:316] — Johnson, Walter [Gilbert], *Scandinavian Studies* (Lawrence, Kansas), 37:4 (1965), 384-386.

[D2:317] Vogelweith, Guy, *Le Psychothéâtre de Strindberg. Un auteur en quête de métamorphose*, Paris: Librairie C. Klincksieck, 1972. 303 pp. ['Strindberg's Psychotheatre. An Author in Search of Metamorphosis'. Vogelweith explores similarities between Freud's psychoanalytical method and Sg's psycho-dramaturgical techniques, above all in *Till Damaskus I*, *Erik XIV*, and *Ett drömspel*, but also with substantial sections on *Mäster Olof*, *Fadren*, *Fröken Julie*, *Bandet*, *Folkungasagan*, *Dödsdansen*, *Karl XII*, and *Stora landsvägen*. Vogelweith argues that catharsis and therapy are aspects of both drama and psychoanalysis, and in Sg's autobiographical dramaturgy it is apparent how he establishes mental space for himself and creates his own double by projecting his experiences onto an imaginary setting in which the stage is located somewhere between the reflection provided by a piece of white paper and the boards of an ideal theatre. He also reckons that the new understanding of character developed by Sg's theatre is initially informed by the example of Kierkegaard, to whom Sg had responded in the 1870s, but it is subsequently reformulated under the influence of late 19th-Century French psychology (most notably the theories of Théodule Ribot concerning the multiple nature of the self), as well as through his own self-analyses in *Tjänstekvinnans son*, *En dåres försvarstal*, and *Inferno*. See **V:230**]

[D2:318] Vogelweith, Guy, *Strindberg*, Théâtre de tous les temps 26, Paris: Seghers, 1973. Illus. 190 pp. [A concise introduction to Sg and his theatre which discusses *Mäster Olof* and the impact on Sg in his early years of Kierkegaard, Georg Brandes, and Shakespeare, the psychological realism of *Fadern* and *Fröken Julie*, the pivotal role of the Inferno crisis, the relationship of *Till Damaskus* and *Ett drömspel* to psychoanalysis and expressionism, and three of the history plays, *Folkungasagan*, *Gustav Vasa*, and *Karl XII*. Vogelweith also sketches Sg's intellectual development and includes several extracts from the works in French translation, as well as a collection of critical comments, mostly from French sources, a Chronology, List of Works, and Bibliography]

[D2:319] Volk, Majam *Poetika Augusta Strindberg*, Beograd: Institut za pozoriste, film, radio i televiziju, 1992. 198 pp. ['August Strindberg's Poetics'. Examines Sg's views expressed in his writings about the theatre and drama on the assumption that there is a continuity between them and the form, subject, and poetics of his theatre. Volk contends that Sg's writings on the theatre display a more rational approach than is suggested in his autobiographical writings. His modern approach, reflected particularly in the choice of psychological subjects, leads to a total reorganisation of dramatic form. This becomes open and places the audience in an active relationship to the play. Character becomes central, with a stress on the inner life; time and space become active and changeable, dialogues are fragmentary and incomplete, and conflict transfers to the inner world and becomes a battle of souls – a struggle between reason and intuition. Total freedom of expression and structure is a prerequisite for the development of modern drama. Plays referred to in support of this argument are principally *Fadren, Fröken Julie, Lycko-Pers resa, Leka med elden, Möderskärlek, Till Damaskus I-III, Kristina, Spök-*

sonaten, *Pelikanen*, *Ett drömspel*, and *Stora landsvägen*. An appendix includes details of Sg's plays performed on the Yugoslavian stage]

[D2:320] Volz, Ruprecht, *Strindbergs Wanderungsdramen: Studien zur Episierung des Dramas mit einer Edition unveröffentlicher Entwürfe zu 'Till Damaskus IV'*, München: TUDUV-Verlagsgesellschaft, 1982. 187 pp. ['Strindberg's Pilgrim Plays: Studies in the Epicisation of Drama with an Edition of Unpublished Sketches for *To Damascus IV*'. Surveys earlier research on 'Pilgrim', or 'Station', drama and places Sg's post-Inferno experiments in this genre in the context of his recourse to imagery in which life (particularly his own) is represented in terms of a journey and linked to figures from literature and myth who are often condemned to lives of wandering and travail, like Ahasueras, the Flying Dutchman, Hercules, and Faust. Volz discusses the form and language of Sg's contributions to the genre in some detail and identifies his post-Inferno works, and their frequent medieval trappings, as typical of turn-of-the-century European drama in general. He also includes extensive extracts from Sg's literary remains which might be considered drafts for a fourth part of *Till Damaskus*. Doctoral Dissertation]

[D2:321] — Oberholzer, Otto, *Scandinavica* (Norwich), 23:2 (1984), 181-182.

[D2:322] — Reinke-Engbert, Ingrid, *Skandinavistik* (Kiel), 15:1 (1985), 67-69.

[D2:323] — Sundberg, Björn, *Samlaren* (Uppsala), 103 (1982), pp. 177-178.

[D2:324] — Tindemans, C., *Streven* (Amsterdam & Antwerp), 52 (1984-85), 983-984.

[D2:325] Ward, John, *The Social and Religious Plays of Strindberg*, London: Athlone Press, 1980. XI+337 pp. [Offers a general account of each of Sg's translated social and religious plays in terms of his principal ideas and dramatic themes, and places him in the context of 19th and 20th-Century drama by examining his sources and influence. Ward discusses the pre-Inferno plays chronologically in relation to naturalism, misogyny, and the intellectual impulses they took from Nietzsche, Max Nordau, Schopenhauer, Darwin, Jean-Martin Charcot, and Hippolyte Bernheim, and the post-Inferno plays in relation to Schopenhauer, Kierkegaard, Swedenborg, German Expressionism, Maeterlinck, and the Symbolists. Much of the discussion is based confessedly on non-Swedish secondary material, but it sometimes foregrounds a generally overlooked work (e.g. *Himmelrikets nycklar*), and there is a useful, if brief, concluding statement regarding Sg's enduring influence on modern drama]

[D2:326] — Johnson, Walter [Gilbert], *Scandinavian Studies* (Lawrence, Kansas), 53:2 (1981), 236-237.

[D2:327] — Kaufman, Michael, *Comparative Drama* (Kalamazoo, Michigan), 15:2 (1981), 173-175.

[D2:328] — McFarlane, James, 'Strindberg for the English', *The Times Higher Education Supplement* (London), 3 October 1980. ['The product of a mind anxious above all to maintain a very English sense of fair play towards a writer [seen as] essentially unwholesome and distasteful']

[D2:329] — Thomas, D[avid], *Modern Language Review* (London), 77:1 (1982), 249-250.

[D2:330] — Tindemans, C., *Streven* (Amsterdam & Antwerp), 49 (1981-82), 88-89.

[D2:331] Weaver, Donald K., ed., *Strindberg on Stage*, Stockholm: Strindberg Society, 1983. Illus. 175 pp. [Contains the proceedings of a symposium held in Stockholm, 18-22 May 1981. Includes **B2:81**: Harry G. Carlson, 'Strindberg's Biblical Imagery'; **B3:389**: Shi

Qin'er, 'August Strindberg in China'; **B4:70**: Maurice Gravier, 'Traduire Strindberg'; **B4:73**: Group Report, 'Translating Strindberg' with Supplement: 'Existing Translations of Strindberg's Dramas'; **B4:120**: Mitsuya Mori, 'Japanese Translations of Strindberg'; **B9:159**: Kela Kvam, 'Strindberg and the Roles of the Sexes'; **C1:1176**: Lech Sokół, 'The Drama of Initiation: Villiers de l'Isle-Adam, Strindberg and S. I. Witkiewicz'; **C1:1311**: Jouko Turkka, 'A Line Strindberg – Salama?'; **D2:714**: Group Report, 'Performing Strindberg – Problems of Role Interpretation'; **D2:715**: Group Report, 'Stage Design'; **D2:716**: Group Report, 'Dramaturgy and Ideology I'; **D2:717**: Group Report, 'Dramaturgy and Ideology II'; **D2:939**: Charles Marowitz, 'Approaching Strindberg by Passing Him By'; **D2:1174**: Göran Söderström, 'Strindberg's Scenographic Ideas'; **E11:76:** Group Report, 'Symbolic Language and Myths'; and **E12:221**: Gunilla Palmstierna-Weiss, 'A Hundred Years after *Miss Julie*'; together with a brief Preface by Carl Reinhold Smedmark (p. 5) and a 'Panel Discussion' on performing Sg (pp. 64-83) with the actors Keve Hjelm, Sven Wollter, and Irma Christenson, the then director of Dramaten, Jan-Olof Strandberg, and the theatre's dramaturge, Niklas Brunius]

[**D2:332**] Wirmark, Margareta, *Den kluvna scenen. Kvinnor i Strindbergs dramatik*, Stockholm: Gidlunds, 1989. Illus. 260 pp. ['The Split Stage. Women in Strindberg's Plays'. Basing her analysis on a study of thirteen of the plays with female protagonists who are often, as in *Kronbruden*, *Påsk*, and *Ett drömspel*, portrayed as far stronger and more independent than it has been the custom to represent women on stage, Wirmark employs Anne Ubersfeldt's actant model of dramatic structure from *Lire le Théâtre* (1977) in order to achieve a thoroughgoing revision of our understanding of the female figures in Sg's plays. Reference is also made to the contemporary legal status of women, and to more recent research in ethnology, sociology, and theology, including a comparison of Agnes in *Ett drömspel* with the beliefs and practice of the Shakers, with which Wirmark assumes Sg was familiar. She associates them with more general *fin-de-siècle* notions of a female Messiah and to a new morality that can be of relevance to the portrayal of Judith in *Dödsdansen II*, Kersti in *Kronbruden*, and the eponymous heroine of *Svanevit*. Each of the characters analysed is related to one or other of the primary functions that women may assume within the patriarchal family, as wife, widow, daughter, mother, or sister. Wirmark concludes with a discussion of the role that women play in the emergence of Sg's later experimental dramaturgy, where they sometimes come to represent mankind. She also discusses *Den sjunkande Hellas, Herr Bengts hustru, Fröken Julie, Den starkare, Moderskärlek, Påsk, Dödsdansen, Kristina*, and *Pelikanen*]

[**D2:333**] — Bladh, Curt, *Sundsvalls Tidning*, 8 February 1989.

[**D2:334**] — Fischer, W., *Horisont* (Vasa), 37:6 (1990), 94-96.

[**D2:335**] — Fischer, W., *Västerbottens-Kuriren* (Umeå), 28 March 1989.

[**D2:336**] — Forsås-Scott, Helena, *Samlaren* (Uppsala), 110 (1989), pp. 158-160. [In spite of the simplifications she introduces into Anne Ubersfeld's actant model of theatrical analysis and the questionable way in which the dramas are classified, this ambitious study opens new and rewarding perspectives on Sg's plays]

[**D2:337**] — Granberg, Nils, *LO-tidningen* (Stockholm), 1989:40, p. 50.

[**D2:338**] — Gustafsson, Lars, *Nerikes Allehanda* (Örebro), 11 February 1989.

[**D2:339**] — Levander, Hans, *Svenska Dagbladet* (Stockholm), 14 July 1989.

[**D2:340**] — Ollén, Gunnar, *Sydsvenska Dagbladet* (Malmö), 21 February 1989.

[**D2:341**] — Ollfors, Anders, *Nya Wermlands Tidningen* (Karlstad), 13 May 1989.

[**D2:342**] — Sommar, Carl Olof, *Östgöta Correspondenten* (Linköping), 26 May 1989.

[**D2:343**] — Ström, B., *Kvinnobulletinen* (Stockholm), 19:3 (1989), p. 50.

[**D2:344**] — Sund, Lars, *Upsala Nya Tidning*, 18 January 1989.

[**D2:345**] — Svenson, Lars, *Helsingborgs Dagblad*, 12 May 1989.

[**D2:346**] — Westling, Barbro, 'Strindbergs kvinnor', *entré* (Norsborg), 16:2 (1989), 113-114. ['Strindberg's Women']

[**D2:347**] — Wittrock, Ulf, *Upsala Nya Tidning*, 7 February 1989.

[**D2:348**] Witalec, Janet, ed., 'Strindberg', in *Drama Criticism*, Volume 18, Detroit, Gale, 2003, pp. 149-341. [Reprints a range of recent Anglo-Saxon criticism in the form of general discussions of Sg as a dramatist as well as studies of specific plays. Also includes several performance reviews. Includes an extract from Harry G. Carlson **D2:40**, on Sg's naturalism, as well as Richard Bark, **D2:437**; Marilyn Johns Blackwell, **D2:501**; Barry Jacobs, **D2:776**; Barbara Lide, **D2:895**; Freddie Rokem, **D2:1121**; Barbro Ståhle Sjönell, **D2:1203**; Egil Törnqvist, **D2:1254**; and Margareta Wirmark, **D2:1310**, on different aspects of Sg's playwriting; Simon Grabowski, **C1:472**, on *Ett drömspel*; and Lorelei Lingard, **C1:797**, on *Fröken Julie* and *Hedda Gabler*. The volume also contains the following studies of individual dramas: John Eric Bellquist, **E11:28**, and Arnold Weinstein, **E11:175**, on *Fadren*; Charles Spencer, **E12:1192**, Edward S. Franchuk, **E12:96**, John L. Greenway, **E12:114**, on *Fröken Julie*, Daniel Davy, **E27:12**, on *Brott och brott*; Harry G. Carlson, **E34:8**, Jeffrey B. Loomis, **E34:33**, and Stephen Mitchell, **E34:40**, on *Påsk*; Ben Brantley, **E35:873**, Charles Spencer, **E35:888**, and D.J.R. Bruckner, **E35:960**, on *Dödsdansen*; Jeremy Kingston, **E37:91**, on *Svanevit*; Susan Brantley, **E38:15**, and Egil Törnqvist, **E38:33**, on *Carl XII*; Margareta Wirmark, **E40:46**, on *Kristina*; Matthew Wikander, **E42:24** and **E42:26**, on *Gustav III*; Lynn R. Wilkinson, **E48:69**, on the Chamber Plays; Ron Jenkins, **E51:599**, on *Spöksonaten*; Paul Walsh, **E53:37**, on *Pelikanen*; Hans-Göran Ekman, **E55:4**, on *Abu Casems tofflor*, Freddie Rokem, **E58:11**, on *Svarta handsken*, and Erik Näslund, **P4:47**, on Birgit Cullberg's ballet, *Fröken Julie*]

D2. Drama General: B

(ii) Essays, Articles, and Reviews Devoted Wholly or Substantially to Strindberg's Plays and Place in Theatre History, or to Two or More of the Plays as Dramatic Texts.

[**D2:349**] ***SV* 64** (Stockholm: Norstedts, 1999 – *Teater och Intima teatern*), Texten redigerad och kommenterad av Per Stam, 'Kommentarer' and 'Ordförklaringar', pp. 247-462, 473-561. Illus. [Contains the text of Sg's five *Memorandum till Medlemmarne av Intima Teatern*, together with several other items, both published and unpublished, in the form of notes, letters, articles, and other contributions to the press on theatrical topics and the state of the contemporary Swedish theatre, all written during the period 1910-11]

[D2:350] A. B-s [August Brunius], 'August Strindbergs teaterprinciper', *Svenska Dagbladet* (Stockholm), 5 December 1908. ['August Strindberg's Theatrical Principles'. A critical comment on the Intimate Theatre. Sg may be on firmer ground in thinking that an audience comes to the theatre to listen rather than (as Edward Gordon Craig believes) to see, but he has realised none of the reforms outlined in the Preface to *Fröken Julie*. Moreover, his ideas are of variable worth, and require a very specialised form of theatre; they are not generally applicable]

[D2:351] A. B-s [August Brunius], '*Hamlet. Ett minnesblad*', *Svenska Dagbladet* (Stockholm), 24 November 1908. [Comments critically on Sg's pamphlet on *Hamlet* and acting, published to mark the first anniversary of the Intimate Theatre]

[D2:352] A. B-s [August Brunius], 'Den litterära teatern', *Svenska Dagbladet* (Stockholm), 17 January 1907. ['The Literary Theatre'. Questions the grounds on which Sg and August Falck intend to found the Intimate Theatre. It may have some virtue as a recruiting ground for new talent, but theatre is for the many, not the few; a small, exclusively literary, theatre of this kind might have a role in a period of theatrical decadence, but that is not the case today, when the new national theatre currently under construction should engage all energies]

[D2:353] A. B-s [August Brunius], '*Plays by Strindberg*', *Svenska Dagbladet* (Stockholm), 5 April 1916. [Reviews Volume Four in Edwin Björkman's English translations of Sg's plays]

[D2:354] A. B-s [August Brunius], 'Strindberg', *Svenska Dagbladet* (Stockholm), 14 October 1910. [Discusses Sg's fifth *Memorandum till Medlemmarne av Intima Teatern*, remarking on its heterogeneous combination of polemic and dramatic criticism]

[D2:355] A. B-s [August Brunius], 'Strindbergsteatern in memoriam', *Svenska Dagbladet* (Stockholm), 10 November 1910. ['Strindberg's Theatre In Memoriam'. A valedictory article on the Intimate Theatre, which would give its final performances (of *Kristina*, *Fadren*, and *Fröken Julie*) on 11 December 1910. 'Sg has been the capital on which the Intimate Theatre has lived, its guiding principle and raison d'être'. Successes such as *Fröken Julie* and *Påsk* have to be balanced against failures like the Chamber Plays and the 'historical-fantastic chaos of *Kristina*']

[D2:356] A. B-s [August Brunius], 'Teaterskrifveri af "Titulärregissören"', *Svenska Dagbladet* (Stockholm), 21 December 1908. ['Theatre Scribbles of the "Titular Director"'. Reviews the third of Sg's *Memorandum till Medlemmarne av Intima Teatern*, which are in danger of becoming a permanent plague]

[D2:357] A. B-s [August Brunius], 'Intima teatern och pieteten', *Svenska Dagbladet* (Stockholm), 12 October 1910. ['The Intimate Theatre and Piety'. Questions the respect with which Sg's Intimate Theatre is often treated]

[D2:358] Adamov, Arthur, 'Strindberg en la cocina', *Primer Acto* (Madrid), No. 154 (1973), pp. 34-35. ['Strindberg in the Kitchen']

[D2:359] 'Adin', 'Teatr Strindberga', 1-3, *Rampa i zhizn'* (Moscow), 1912:18, pp. 3-4; 1912:19, pp. 3-3; 1912:20, pp. 3-4. [A three-part survey of Sg's plays following his recent death. E.867]

[D2:360] A. K., 'Teater konst och litteratur', *Dagens Nyheter* (Stockholm), 24 November 1908. [Reviews Sg's reflections on *Hamlet* and acting in *Memorandum till Medlemmarne av Intima Teatern*]

[D2:361] A. K. [Axel Krook], '*Tryckt och otryckt I*', *Göteborgs-Posten*, 23 March 1890. [An uncharacteristically positive review of *Fordringsägare*, *Paria*, and *Samum* on publication. Praises the psychological subtlety of the dialogue and the ironic humour in *Paria*]

[D2:362] Alldahl, Thomas, '*Ett drömspel* och *Spöksonaten*, det konkreta språkets teater', *Meddelanden från Strindbergssällskapet* (Stockholm), 53-54 (1974), pp. 22-41. ['*A Dream Play* and *The Ghost Sonata*: The Theatre of Concrete Language'. Studies the theatrical significance of Artaud's staging of *Ett drömspel* at the Théâtre Alfred Jarry and his perception of its concrete theatrical language as part of the lost dimension of the theatre that he was himself seeking to recover. Alldahl also discusses his plans for staging *Spöksonaten* and those aspects of Sg's Chamber Play that may be related to the theories which Artaud articulated in *Le Théâtre et son double*]

[D2:363] Alten, M., 'Teatr obcy', *Nasz Kraj* (Warsaw), 3:20 (1907). [Reports the founding of the Intimate Theatre by Sg and Falck in Stockholm]

[D2:364] Alvarez, A., 'Domesticity', *The New Statesman* (London), 10 May 1963. [Reflects on Sg's genius, which is 'directly related to the rawness of his nerves', apropos Michael Meyer's recently published translations of twelve of the plays. 'He seems to have invented what now passes for the avant-garde theatre, and a great deal of what we take for granted in the cinema']

[D2:365] Ambjörnson, Ronny, 'Lockelse och äckel', *Bonniers Litterära Magasin* (Stockholm), 56:1 (1987), 20-27. Illus. ['Attraction and Revulsion'. Studies the paradoxes of masculinity in *Fadren* and *Fordringsägare*, in both of which man is identified as the head and woman as the body, and where, for the man, mother and wife merge in a conflict between nature and culture, in which the Captain's intellect is overcome by madness and Tekla contravenes the patriarchal order by appearing as a public woman]

[D2:366] Anderberg, Rolf, '*Ungdomsdramer 2*', *Göteborgs-Posten*, 11 January 1992. [Reviews Volumes 3 and 39 in *Samlade Verk*, containing *I Rom*, *Den fredlöse*, and *Anno fyrtioåtta*, and *Till Damaskus* respectively]

[D2:367] Andersson, Ragnar, 'Strindberg som dramatiker', *Studiekamraten* (Tollarp), 19:8-9 (1937), 129-133. ['Strindberg as a Dramatist']

[D2:368] André, Robert, 'Strindberg et les puissances des ténèbres', *Les Lettres Françaises* (Paris), No. 1139 (1966). ['Strindberg and the Power of Shadows']

[D2:369] Andreas-Salomé, Lou, 'Ibsen, Strindberg, Sudermann', *Freie Bühne für modernes Leben* (Berlin), 4 (1893), 149-172. [Discusses Sg in conjunction with the German première of *Fordringsägare* at the Berlin Freie Bühne. Presents the play as a case study of pathological individuals and, like many other German articles from this period, concentrates on Sg's misogyny. Also discusses *Inför döden* and *Första varningen*]

[D2:370] Anker, Øyvind, 'To Strindberg-Oppförelser i Christiania i 1890-årene', *Nordisk Tidskrift* (Stockholm), 41:1 (1965), 1-9. Illus. ['Two Strindberg Productions in Oslo in the 1890s'. On *Inför döden* and *Första varningen* at Centralteatret and Christiania Theater in Christiania (Oslo) in 1897 and 1893 respectively. The former gave Harriet Bosse her first Sg role as the Young Girl. Includes a correspondence between Sg and Christiania Theater]

[D2:371] Anon [A. Falkman], 'Om Forsøgsteatret', *Nationaltidende* (Copenhagen), 15 December 1888. ['On the Experimental Theatre'. Discusses Sg's attempt to found an experimental theatre in Copenhagen on the lines of Antoine's Théâtre Libre in Paris]

[D2:372] Anon [A. Falkman], '*Tre Skuespil*', *Nationaltidende* (Copenhagen), 30 April 1889. ['Three Plays'. Reviews *Mäster Olof*, *Gillets hemlighet*, and *Herr Bengts hustru*, translated into Danish by Peter Hansen]

[D2:373] Anon, 'A New Series of Strindberg's Translated Plays', *The Dial* (Chicago), No. 56 (1 January 1914), p. 27. [Reviews Volumes One and Two of Edwin Björkman's translations]

[D2:374] Anon, 'August Strindberg om sina historiska dramer', *Dagens Nyheter* (Stockholm), 5 December 1903. ['Strindberg on his History Plays'. Reports on an article in *Berliner Tageblatt* in which Sg offers an overview of his historical dramas, the impulse behind their writing, and his ideas about Gustav Adolf, Kristina, Karl XII, and Gustav III as historical figures]

[D2:375] Anon, 'August Strindberg, *Plays*', *The Outlook* (New York), 20 April 1912, pp. 877-878. [Reviews Edwin Björkman's translations of *Ett drömspel*, *Bandet*, and *Dödsdansen*. With Sg, pessimism reaches its ultimate conclusion. 'Poe is almost commonplace as compared with him. If this volume of plays be taken as an interpretation of the great body of his work, nothing could be more misleading as an interpretation of life']

[D2:376] Anon, 'August Strindberg, *Plays*', *The Nation* (New York), No. 96 (23 January 1913), 88-89. [Reviews recent translations of *Fordringsägare*, *Paria*, and *Påsk* by Edwin Björkman and Velma S. Howard]

[D2:377] Anon, 'August Strindbergs öppna bref', *Stockholms-Dagblad*, 15 October 1910. ['August Strindberg's Open Letters'. Discusses the fifth of Sg's *Memorandum till Medlemmarne av Intima Teatern*, citing extended extracts. This article is also published almost verbatim in *Göteborgs Handels- och Sjöfartstidning*, *Arbetet*, and *Göteborgs Aftonblad*]

[D2:378] Anon [Carl David af Wirsén?], 'Litteratur', *Post- och Inrikes Tidningar* (Stockholm), 30 September 1893. [Reviews *Debet och kredit*, *Första varningen*, *Moderskärlek*, and *Inför döden* on publication]

[D2:379] Anon, '*Dramatik*', *Dagens Nyheter* (Stockholm), 29 September 1893. [Reviews *Debet och kredit*, *Första varningen* (which is the volume's weak point), *Moderskärlek*, and *Inför döden* on publication. The latter is 'a real one-act tragedy, a kind of pocket *King Lear*']

[D2:380] Anon [Edvard Brandes], 'Strindbergs to Skuespil: *Fröken Julie* og *Kreditorer*', *Politiken* (Copenhagen), 3 March 1889. ['Strindberg's Two Plays'. Reviews *Fröken Julie* and *Fordringsägare* on publication in Denmark. Although he considers the conclusion to be artificial, Brandes regards *Fröken Julie* as a major contribution to modern Scandinavian literature. *Fordringsägare*, which is improperly called a tragi-comedy, since the author treats it with deadly seriousness, he finds less interesting. See **D2:524**]

[D2:381] Anon [Edvard Brandes], 'Tre Skuespil', *Politiken* (Copenhagen), 15 May 1889. ['Three Plays'. Reviews *Mäster Olof*, *Gillets hemlighet*, and *Herr Bengts hustru*, in Danish translations by Peter Hansen]

[D2:382] Anon [Edvard Brandes], '*Tryckt och otryckt I*', *Politiken* (Copenhagen), 10 April 1890. [Reviews *Fordringsägare*, *Paria*, and *Samum* on publication]

[D2:383] Anon [Edvard Brandes], '*Dramatik*', *Politiken* (Copenhagen), 8 October 1893. [Reviews the one-acters *Inför döden*, *Första varningen*, *Debet och kredit*, and *Moderskärlek* on publication]

[D2:384] Anon, 'En Strindbergsteater i Stockholm? August Falck och August Strindberg – Strindberg som inspicient', *Svenska Dagbladet* (Stockholm), 15 January 1907. ['A Strindberg Theatre in Stockholm? August Falck and August Strindberg – Strindberg as Theatre Manager'. Reports plans for the opening of a new intimate theatre in Stockholm by Sg and Falck]

[D2:385] Anon, 'Ett intimt memorandum från August Strindberg', *Svenska Dagbladet* (Stockholm), 23 August 1907. ['An Intimate Memorandum from August Strindberg'. On the first of Sg's *Memorandum till Medlemmarne av Intima Teatern,* which is of relevance to others besides the small circle to which it is addressed]

[D2:386] Anon, 'Ett regissörsprogram af August Strindberg. Författaren till sin personal', *Nya Dagligt Allehanda* (Stockholm), 22 August 1907. ['A Director's Statement from August Strindberg. The Author to his Personnel'. Comments on the first of Sg's *Memorandum till Medlemmarne av Intima Teatern*. 'It will be interesting to see Sg turn his directorial theory into practice']

[D2:387] Anon, '*Hamlet. Ett minnesblad*', *Dagens Nyheter* (Stockholm), 24 November 1908. [A positive review of Sg's pamphlet on *Hamlet* and acting, published to mark the first anniversary of the Intimate Theatre]

[D2:388] Anon, '*Hamlet. Ett minnesblad*', *Nya Dagligt Allehanda* (Stockholm), 23 November 1908. [Reviews Sg's pamphlet on *Hamlet* and acting, published to mark the first anniversary of the Intimate Theatre]

[D2:389] Anon, '*Hamlet. Ett minnesblad*', *Stockholms-Dagblad*, 24 November 1908. [See **D2:388**]

[D2:390] Anon [Harold Hannyngton Child], 'Three Plays by Strindberg', *The Times Literary Supplement* (London), 13 June 1912. [Discusses Edwin Björkman's translations of *Bandet*, *Dödsdansen*, and *Ett drömspel*. As a play, the strongest of these is the latter, exactly like a dream and enormous in scope. 'Of reality Sg is a master. It is in the "more than reality" that he proves himself a poet']

[D2:391] Anon, 'Hur fyller vår Strindbergteater sin funktion?', *Ridå* (Stockholm), 1909:12. ['How does our Strindberg Theatre fulfil its Function?' Criticises the running of the Intimate Theatre and questions its artistic policies]

[D2:392] Anon, 'Hur skall Strindberg spelas?', *Sydsvenska Dagbladet* (Malmö), 6 July 1912. ['How should Strindberg be Performed?']

[D2:393] Anon, 'Intima teatern', *Hvar 8 Dag* (Stockholm), 24 November 1909. [Discusses the founding of the Intimate Theatre, stressing its novel intimacy and 'unpretentious yet distinguished milieu']

[D2:394] Anon [James W[alter] McFarlane], 'From the Swedish', *The Times Literary Supplement* (London), 28 June 1963 [Reviews Elizabeth Sprigge's 'always readable' translations of twelve of the plays]

[D2:395] Anon, 'Jubileumslitteraturen', *Dagens Nyheter* (Stockholm), 22 January 1910. [Reviews publications related to the 60th anniversary of Sg's birth, including the fourth of his *Memorandum till Medlemmarne av Intima Teatern*, on *Macbeth* and other Shakespeare plays]

[D2:396] Anon, 'Konst och litteratur', *Aftonbladet* (Stockholm), 22 August 1907. [Reviews the *Memorandum till Medlemmarne av Intima Teatern*]

[D2:397] Anon, 'Litteratur: *I högre rätt*', *Svenska Dagbladet* (Stockholm), 26 June 1899. ['Before a Higher Court'. Reports Nils Kjær's most appreciative comments in his review of *Brott och brott* and *Advent* on publication. See **D2:827**]

[D2:398] Anon, 'Nya öppna bref af Aug. Strindberg. En vidräkning med kritiken', *Nya Dagligt Allehanda* (Stockholm), 30 September 1910. ['New Open Letters by August Strindberg. An Attack on the Critics'. Comments in advance of publication on the fifth of Sg's *Memorandum till Medlemmarne av Intima Teatern*, including his essay on *Faust*, his critique of Viktor Rydberg's translation, and a polemical defence of his theatre's practice]

[D2:399] Anon, '*Öppet brev* från August Strindberg', *Öresunds-Posten* (Ängelholm), 28 October 1909. [Reviews Sg's *Memorandum till Medlemmarne av Intima Teatern*]

[D2:400] Anon, 'Pessimistic Plays', *The Independent* (New York), 5 December 1912. [Reviews translations of *Fadern*, *Fröken Julie*, *Den Fredlöse*, and *Den starkare* by Edwin Björkman and Warner and Edith Oland]

[D2:401] Anon, '*Plays by Strindberg*', *Stockholms Dagblad*, 21 May 1916. [Reviews Volume Four of Edwin Björkman's English translations of Sg's plays]

[D2:402] Anon, 'Prolific Dramatist', *The Times* (London), 30 January 1964. [Reviews Volume One of Michael Meyer's 'convincing' translations of Sg's plays]

[D2:403] Anon, 'Schwedische Strindberg-Darstellerinnen über ihre Rollen', *Theater-Courier* (Berlin), 23 (1916), 275-276. ['Swedish Strindberg Actresses on their Roles']

[D2:404] Anon, '[Strindberg on the Theatre]', *Vestnik teatra* (Moscow), No. 89-90 (1 May 1921), p. 21. [Comments on the publication of Sg's *Memorandum till Medlemmarne av Intima Teatern*. E.904]

[D2:405] Anon, 'Strindberg, Plays', *American Playwright* (New York), 15 May 1912, pp. 178-179. [Reviews Edwin Björkman's translations of *Ett drömspel*, *Dödsdansen*, and *Bandet*. Concludes that Sg is unoriginal, his 'philosophy a comic supplement of modernity']

[D2:406] Anon, 'Strindberg, *Plays*', *The Athenaeum* (London), 23 August 1913. [Reviews *Kamraterna*, *Inför döden*, *Paria*, and *Påsk* in translations by Edith and Warner Oland]

[D2:407] Anon, 'Strindberg, *Plays*', *The Athenaeum* (London), 22 November 1913. [Reviews *Den starkare*, *Brända tomten*, *Advent*, and *Svanevit* in Edwin Björkman's translations. It is unfair to emphasise their indebtedness to Nietzsche, Edgar Allan Poe, Maeterlinck, or Swedenborg. Their diversity brings into sharp relief features that are entirely Sg's own]

[D2:408] Anon, 'Strindberg Plays', *The Independent* (New York), 11 April 1912. [Reviews Edwin Björkman's translations of *Bandet, Ett drömspel*, and *Dödsdansen*: 'So heavy with symbolism that we are not sure we get the author's meaning; though we are quite sure, if we did get it, we did not like it']

[D2:409] Anon, 'Strindberg, *Plays*', *The Outlook* (New York) 4 January 1913. [Reviews Edwin Björkman's translations of *Fordringsägare* and *Paria*]

[D2:410] Anon, 'Strindbergs försöksteater', *Dagens Nyheter* (Stockholm), 11 March 1889. ['Strindberg's Experimental Theatre'. Reports on the positive reception accorded Sg's Scandinavian Experimental Theatre at the Dagmar Theatre, Copenhagen]

[D2:411] Anon, 'Strindberg's Plays', *The Athenaeum* (London), 22 June 1912, p. 714. [Reviews Edwin Björkman's translations of *Ett drömspel*, *Bandet*, and *Dödsdansen* and identifies an affinity between Sg and both Thomas Hardy and the Greek tragedians]

[D2:412] Anon, 'Strindberg's Plays: A New Translation'', *The Times* (London), 26 March 1929. [Reviews the first of four volumes of translations of the plays sponsored by the Anglo-Swedish Literary Foundation]

[D2:413] Anon, 'Strindberg, Plays', *The Nation* (New York), 8 March 1913. [Reviews Edith and Warner Olands' English translations of *Kamraterna*, *Inför döden*, *Paria*, and *Påsk*]

[D2:414] Anon, 'Strindberg, *Samlade Verk*', *Aftonbladet* (Stockholm), 9 September 1984. [Reviews Volume 27 of *Samlade Verk*, containing *Fadren*, *Fröken Julie*, and *Fordringsägare*]

[D2:415] Anon, 'Strindberg som regissör. Hans memorandum till Intima teaterns skådespelare', *Dagens Nyheter* (Stockholm), 23 August 1907. ['Strindberg as Director. His Memorandum to the Actors of the Intimate Theatre'. A positive review of the first of Sg's *Memorandum till Medlemmarne av Intima Teatern*, where the experienced man of the theatre is in evidence throughout]

[D2:416] Anon [Harold Hannyngton Child], 'Tchekoff and Strindberg, *Plays*', *The Times Literary Supplement* (London), 29 June 1916. [Reviews Edwin Björkman's translations of *Spöksonaten* and *Kronbruden*. 'Sg at his best has so powerful and poetic a genius that it is a pleasure to find him at his best']

[D2:417] Anon, 'Teatr Strindberga', *Kurier Lwowski* (Lwów [Lemberg]), 1907, No. 198. ['Strindberg's Theatre'. Reports on the founding of the Intimate Theatre in Stockholm by Sg and Falck]

[D2:418] Anon, 'Ur dagskrönikan', *Ridå* (Stockholm), 1907:2. [Reports on August Falck's 'Strindbergsteater' (i.e. the Intimate Theatre) for which Sg had sketched the designs for several of his as yet unperformed plays]

[D2:419] Arrufat, Antón, 'Prologo', in Augusto Strindberg, *Teatro*, Cuba: La Habana, 1964, pp. 9-20. [Introduces a volume containing translations into Spanish of *Fadren, Fröken Julie, Den starkare, Dödsdansen, Ett drömspel*, and *Spöksonaten*]

[D2:420] Artaud, Antonin, 'States of Mind: 1921-1945', *Tulane Drama Review* (New Orleans), 8:2 (1963), 30-73. [Includes Artaud's production notes for his 1928 staging of *Ett drömspel* as well as his sketches for a production of *Spöksonaten* that never reached the stage]

[D2:421] Astroh, Michael, 'Strindbergs theatralischer Naturalismus', in Walter Baumgartner and Thomas Fechner-Smarsly, Hrsg., **B1:19**, *August Strindberg: Der Dichter und die Medien*, pp. 156-192. ['Strindberg's Theatrical Naturalism'. A wide-ranging philosophical examination of Sg's engagement with naturalism both in the dramas of the 1880s and the more inwardly focused later plays. As well as discussing specific plays, Astroh compares naturalism with earlier modes of representation based on mythical and realistic forms, with reference to Homer, Ovid, and Aristotle, examines the consequences of Darwinian biology for 19th-Century aesthetics as exemplified in the poetry of Tennyson, and compares Zola's conception of naturalism with Strindberg's more flexible form in *Giftas* and *Fröken Julie*. The notion of metamorphosis is seen as crucial to the form of theatre which Sg develops in *Till Damaskus, Ett drömspel*,

Dödsdansen, and *Pelikanen* where, as in *Fadren*, the focus is on the development of a single central character. Astroh links this dramaturgy to the theories of aleatory creation in the essay 'Des arts nouveaux! Du hasard dans la production artistique' (1894) and relates them to Sg's interest in *laterna magica*, the kaleidoscope, and *camera obscura*]

[D2:422] 'Attis' [Astrid Ljungström], 'Öst och väst ser Strindberg i Wien', *Svenska Dagbladet* (Stockholm), 1 November 1953. ['East and West see Strindberg in Vienna']

[D2:423] Aumont, Arthur, 'Strindberg'ske skuespil opførte paa Kjøbenhavns Teatre', *Politiken* (Copenhagen), 15 May 1912. ['Strindbergian Plays Performed in Copenhagen's Theatres'. Surveys the performance history of Sg's plays on the Copenhagen stage, including the contribution made by his own Scandinavian Experimental Theatre during his residence there in 1888-89]

[D2:424] Austin, John, '"En reform? Falck har verkat!" Intima teaterns betydelse i Stockholms teaterliv', *Strindbergiana* (Stockholm), 13 (1998), pp. 49-77. Illus. ['"A Reform? Falck has had an Effect!" The Significance of the Intimate Theatre in Stockholm's Theatrical Life'. Contextualises the founding of the Intimate Theatre in relation to the Swedish theatrical establishment of the period and the development of a modern, experimental, or intimate, theatre in Europe as a whole. Austin assesses the response of contemporary Swedish critics to its size and repertoire, and considers both its public and the working conditions of its performers]

[D2:425] Autrusseau-Adamov, Jacqueline, 'De la femme à la scène. Portrait du dramaturge en personnage bisexuel', *Théâtre/Public* (Gennevilliers), 73:4 (1986), 7-10. Illus. ['Of Woman on Stage. Portrait of the Dramatist as a Bisexual'. Compares Sg with Daniel Schreber as a supposedly bisexual dramatic author, with reference to *Herr Bengts hustru*, *Kamraterna*, *Fröken Julie*, *Brott och brott*, and *Ett drömspel*]

[D2:426] b., 'Spostrzeżnie A. Strindberga. Teatr religijny', *Scena i Sztuka* (Warsaw), 1908, No. 4. ['August Strindberg's Religious Theatre']

[D2:427] B. [Ferdinand Bauditz], 'Forsøgsteatrets Repertoire', *Dagbladet* (Copenhagen), 2 March 1889. ['The Experimental Theatre's Repertoire'. Comments critically on the repertoire of Sg's Scandinavian Experimental Theatre in Copenhagen in 1889]

[D2:428] B. [Ferdinand Bauditz], 'Tre Skuespil', *Dagbladet* (Copenhagen), 27 March 1889. ['Three Plays'. Reviews *Mäster Olof*, *Gillets hemlighet*, and *Herr Bengts hustru*, translated into Danish by Peter Hansen]

[D2:429] Bab, Julius, 'August Strindberg', *Die Gegenwart* (Berlin), 81 (1912), 324-326. [Comments on Sg's life and work following his recent death]

[D2:430] Bab, Julius, 'Der neue Strindberg', *Die Schaubühne* (Berlin), 1-2, 11:2 (1915), pp 33-38, 56-58. ['The New Strindberg'. Focuses mainly on *Ett drömspel* and the 'fairy-tale' plays *Kronbruden* and *Svanevit*]

[D2:431] Bab, Julius, 'Strindberg', in *Der Mensch auf der Bühne* (Berlin), 1923:10, pp. 340-347.

[D2:432] Bab, Julius, 'Strindbergs Dramaturgie', *Das literarische Echo* (Berlin), 14 (1911-12), Sp. 1336-1341. [Uses a review of Emil Schering's translation of Sg's writings on the theatre, including his essays on Shakespeare, *Faust* and the history play as a genre exemplified by his own works, to discuss and challenge his concept of drama]

[D2:433] Bab, Julius, 'Strindbergs Totenfeier', *Die Gegenwart* (Berlin), 82 (1912), 636-637. ['Strindberg's Burial Ceremony'. On *Påsk* and *Dödsdansen*]

[D2:434] Bajić, Stanislav, 'August Strindberg (1849-1912)', in August Strindberg, *Gospoìdica Julija, Otac*, Beograd, 1960, pp. 173-178. [Introduces a Serbo-Croat translation of *Fröken Julie* and *Fadren* and presents Sg's overall achievement as a dramatist. R.499]

[D2:435] Bang, Herman, 'Skandinavisk Théâtre Libre', *Göteborgs Handels- och Sjöfarts-tidning*, 29 November 1888. [Discusses Sg's plans for a Scandinavian 'free' theatre, modelled on Antoine's Théâtre Libre in Paris and designed to foster a new drama]

[D2:436] Banville, Charles, 'Strindberg', *Revue des Revues* (Paris), 6 (1893), 139-141. [Presents Sg's essay 'Om modernt drama och modern teater' and comments on his opinions regarding contemporary French drama, not least his derogatory comments about Henry Becque's play *Les Corbeaux* (premièred 1892)]

[D2:437] Bark, Richard, 'Strindberg's Dream-Play Technique', in Göran Stockenström, ed., **D2:288**, *Strindberg's Dramaturgy*, pp. 98-106. [Summarises the gist of **D2:20** (*Strindbergs drömspelteknik – i drama och teater*), with reference mainly to *Till Damaskus, Ett drömspel*, and *Spöksonaten*]

[D2:438] Bark, Richard, 'Strindberg's Dream-Play Technique', in Janet Witalec, ed., **D2:348**, *Drama Criticism*, Volume 18, pp. 157-161. [Rpr. of **D2:437**]

[D2:439] Barone, Rosangela, 'Alla ricerca di August Strindberg: Stretta strada verso il profondo nord', in Franco Perrelli, ed., **B1:365**, *Omaggio a Strindberg. Strindberg nella cultura moderna*, pp. 165-172. Illus. ['In Search of August Strindberg. A Narrow Road to the Deep North'. Analyses the one-acters *Moderskärlek, Den starkare*, and *Inför döden*, translated by Franco Perrelli and staged by Giancarlo Nanni under the collective title *Strindberg di Strindberg*. In performance they represent a transition from Sg's earlier naturalism to the post-Inferno dramaturgy of the subjective theatre of the mind as realised in the Chamber Plays. They thus anticipate the work of Samuel Beckett and betray affinities with the closet dramas of Swinburne and the plays of William Butler Yeats]

[D2:440] Barr, Richard L., 'Perfect and Imperfect Illusions: Coercive and Collaborative Communities in Strindbergian Theatre', in Karelisa V. Hartigan, ed., *From the Bard to Broadway*, The University of Florida Department of Classics Comparative Drama Conference Papers, Vol. VII, Lanham, Md.: University Press of America, 1987, pp. 1-10. [Uses the Preface to *Fröken Julie* and the various *Memorandum till Medlemmarne av Intima Teatern* to demonstrate how Sg's 'closely conjoined social and aesthetic theory shifts from a *coercive* to a *collaborative* conception of community', taking the modern theatre out of 'the fully particularised rooms of naturalism to the spare, suggestive realms of expressionism.' An early exploration of ideas developed in Barr's monograph, **D1:35**]

[D2:441] Basch, Hermann, '*Der Vater*; *Gläubiger*', *Die Schöne Literatur* (Leipzig), 7 (1906), Sp. 280. ['*The Father, Creditors*']

[D2:442] Baude, Hans, 'Strindbergs teaterteorier och Intiman', *Ord och Bild* (Stockholm), 66:11 (1957), 499-505. ['Strindberg's Theatre Theories and the Intimate Theatre'. Considers Sg's theories of drama in performance and their realisation or adaptation in response to the practical exigencies of the Intimate Theatre]

[D2:443] B. B-n [Bo Bergman], '*Samlade otryckta skrifter. Del 1. Dramatiska arbeten*', *Dagens Nyheter* (Stockholm), 5 December 1918. [Reviews the plays and dramatic fragments published in Volume One of Vilhelm Carlheim-Gyllensköld's two-volume edition of Sg's collected unpublished works]

[D2:444] Bécsy, Tamás, 'Sorsábrázolás Strindberg korai drámáiban', *Színház* (Budapest?), 1982:1. ['The Representation of Fate in Strindberg's Early Dramas']

[D2:445] Begović, Milan, 'Strindberg: *Gospođica Julija* i *Materinska ljubav*, in *Kritike i prikazi*, Zagreb: Izd. Hrvatskog izdavalackog bibiografskog zavoda, 1943, pp. 60-62. ['Strindberg, *Fröken Julie* and *Moderskärlek*'. R.495]

[D2:446] Bellini, Pasquale, 'Giancarlo Nanni: il *suo* Strindberg', in Franco Perrelli, ed., **B1:365**, *Omaggio a Strindberg. Strindberg nella cultura moderna*, pp. 173-177. Illus. ['Giancarlo Nanni's Strindberg'. An account of Giancarlo Nanni's triple-bill of *Moderskärlek*, *Den starkare*, and *Inför döden* under the collective title *Strindberg di Strindberg*, using translations by Franco Perrelli]

[D2:447] Bellquist, John E., 'On Myth and Myth-Making in Strindberg', *Scandinavica* (Norwich), 23:1 (1984), 51-52. [A critique of Harry G. Carlson's conception of myth and its application to Sg's plays in **D2:40**, *Strindberg and the Poetry of Myth*]

[D2:448] Bennich-Björkman, Bo, 'Strindberg och kasperteatern. Några fakta och en probleminventering', *Tidskrift för litteraturvetenskap* (Lund), 13:2-3 (1984), 37-89. Illus. ['Strindberg and Punch and Judy Theatre. Some Facts and an Inventory of Problems'. A finely documented study of Sg's abiding interest in popular fairground, or Punch and Judy, theatre, which is already manifest in *Gamla Stockholm* and again apparent in the post-Inferno dramas *Kaspers fettisdag* and *Midsommar*. Both *Lycko-Pers resa* and *Gillets hemlighet* may reflect this interest too. Bennich-Björkman also comments on the importance which the satirical Stockholm journal *Kasper* had for Sg]

[D2:449] Benston, Alice, 'From Naturalism to the *Dream Play*: A Study of the Evolution of Strindberg's Unique Theatrical Form', *Modern Drama* (Lawrence, Kansas), 7:4 (1965), 382-398. [For Benston, the formal evolution of Sg's theatre exemplifies the contemporary dramatist's rejection of realism and a return to stylised theatre. His naturalistic plays (here *Fadren*, *Fröken Julie*), which are patterned on classic models (e.g. *Othello*), lack universality and do not achieve proper tragic representation since they are both too personally particularised and refer only to the rational world. With *Brott och brott*, however, he discovers a way of combining a realistic with a symbolic plot, and in the dreamplay dramaturgy of *Till Damaskus* and *Ett drömspel* 'he found a theatricality that completely merges with his message'. See **V:23**]

[D2:450] Bentley, Eric Russell, 'August Strindberg (Reconsiderations: No. IV)', *Kenyon Review* (Gambier, Ohio), 7:1-4 (1945), 540-560. [An alternative version of the chapter on Sg in **D1:48**]

[D2:451] Bentley, Eric, 'The Ironic Strindberg', in Evert Sprinchorn, ed., *The Genius of the Scandinavian Theater*, New York: New American Library, 1964, pp. 599-603. [Describes *Brott och brott* as a 'fake melodrama' and suggests that, as a playwright, Sg represents a later cultural phase than Ibsen. An extract from **D1:48**, *The Playwright as Thinker*]

[D2:452] Bentley, Eric, 'On Strindberg', in *Six Plays*, Translated by Elizabeth Sprigge, Garden City, N.Y.: Doubleday Anchor, 1955, pp. v-vi.

[D2:453] Bentley, Eric, 'Strindberg in 1985', in *Thinking About the Playwright*, Evanston, Illinois: Northwestern University Press, 1987, pp. 13-18. [Examines the affinities between Sg and Wagner regarding their mutual sexism and racism. The starting point for Bentley's essay is Michael Meyer's Sg biography, **R:1516**, which is criticised here for its inadequate understanding of Sg as a writer]

[D2:454] Bentley, Eric, 'Strindberg, the One and the Many', in *In Search of Theater*, New York: Alfred A. Knopf, 1953, pp. 134-143. [Discovers that France is experiencing a Sg revival resembling the one in Germany a generation ago, stimulated in part by the current interest in Artaud. Of three recent French Sg productions, Jean Vilar's version of *Dödsdansen* was especially valuable for demonstrating that, unlike Ibsen, Sg's naturalistic tragedies can only be adequately rendered by actors who can project great emotional intensity with great immediacy. 'An Ibsenite actor has to present a man at war with himself. A Sgian actor is at war with someone else, often his wife. His emotions come right out of him with no interference whatsoever.' The problems of staging Sg are manifold, in particular the post-Inferno plays, which are sometimes reduced to kitsch, but the most beautiful and satisfying Strindberg production Bentley has seen is one of *Kronbruden* in Vienna, directed by Berthold Viertel with a discreet balance of realism and fantasy]

[D2:455] Bentley, Eric, 'Strindberg, the One and the Many', in *In Search of Theater*, London: Dennis Dobson, 1954, pp. 134-143. [English edition of **D2:454**]

[D2:456] Bentley, Eric, 'Strindberg, the One and the Many', in *In Search of Theater*, New York: Vintage, 1957, pp. 126-134. [Rpr. of **D2:454**]

[D2:457] Bentley, Eric, 'Strindberg, the One and the Many', in Otto Reinert, ed., **B1:371**, *Strindberg: A Collection of Critical Essays*, pp. 97-104. [Rpr. of **D2:454**]

[D2:458] Berendsohn, Walter A[rthur], 'August Strindbergs Dramær', in *Nordisk Digtning af Verdensry, 5 Foredrag*, København: Det Schönbergske forlag, 1942, pp. 103-141. ['August Strindberg's Dramas'. Unlike Berendsohn's later stylistic criticism in **B1:25** and elsewhere, here he provides some biographical data as a basis for interpretation (e.g. *Fadren* makes a greater impression when we know Sg wrote it on the brink of madness). He also explores Sg's stylistic and temperamental affinity with Hans Christian Andersen and quotes extensively from *Ensam*, *Påsk*, and *Ett drömspel*]

[D2:459] Berendsohn, Walter A[rthur], 'A, Strindbergs Dramær', *Tidens Stemme* (Copenhagen), 9 September 1935, pp. 7-8.

[D2:460] Berendsohn, Walter A[rthur], 'August Strindbergs Dramen', *Der Vorspruch. Blätter de Volksbühne Groß-Hamburg*, 2:1 (1926), pp. 4-7.

[D2:461] Berendsohn, Walter A[rthur], 'August Strindbergs skådespel ur svenska historien', *Värld och vetande* (Göteborg), 1-4, 9 (1959), pp. 268-274, 303-310, 340-348, 377-382. ['August Strindberg's Plays from Swedish History'. A mainly stylistic, four-part survey of Sg's Swedish history plays, which focuses on his artistry rather than their relationship to his life or, as was often a concern in Sweden, the authenticity or otherwise of their treatment of historical detail. Revised and reprinted in **B1:25**, *August Strindbergs skärgårds och Stockholmsskildringar. Struktur- och stilstudier*]

[D2:462] Berendsohn, Walter A[rthur], 'En tysk skåderspelerska om Strindbergs dramer', *Samlaren* (Uppsala), 31 (1950), pp. 115-118. ['A German Actress on Strindberg's Dramas'. Contains previously unpublished extracts from ten letters about Sg addressed by

Gertrud Eysoldt to his German translator, Emil Schering, mainly concerning *Påsk*, *Brott och brott*, and the Chamber Plays, about which her comments are particularly positive. Berendsohn prefaces Eysoldt's remarks by an account of her many performances in Sg's plays, often directed by Max Reinhardt]

[D2:463] Berendsohn, Walter A[rthur], 'Nachwort', in August Strindberg, *Ein Traumspiel. Die Brandstätte*, Aus dem Schwedischen übersetzt von Willi Reich, Frankfurt am Main: Fischer Bücherei, 1963. 141 pp. [The Afterword to a widely available translation of *Ett drömspel* and *Brända tomten*]

[D2:464] Berendsohn, Walter A[rthur], 'August Strindbergs Dramen', in August Strindberg, *Meisterdramen*, in der Übers. von Willi Reich, München: Langen & Müller, 1973, pp. 423-434. ['Strindberg as Dramatist'. An assessment of Sg's achievement as a dramatist accompanying German translations of *Fadren*, *Fröken Julie*, *Dödsdansen*, *Till Damaskus*, *Ett drömspel*, and *Spöksonaten*]

[D2:465] Berendsohn, Walter A[rthur], 'Strindberg als Dramatiker', in *August Strindberg: Meisterdramen*, München: Dtv Weltliteratur, 1981. 440 pp. ['Strindberg as Dramatist']

[D2:466] Berendsohn, Walter A[rthur], 'Strindberg och teatern', in **B1:42**, *Strindbergsproblem*, pp. 191-201. ['Strindberg and the Theatre'. Comments on Sg's practical experience of the theatre and the potential importance of his comments on how his plays should be performed]

[D2:467] Berg, G., 'Den tyska Strindbergstilen', *Figaro* (Stockholm), 29 January 1921. ['The German Strindberg Style'. Comments on the German manner of performing Sg's post-Inferno plays, which is represented here primarily by Max Reinhardt, and compares it with Swedish approaches]

[D2:468] Berg, Valter, 'August Strindbergs sista dramatik', 1-2, *Växjöbladet*, 21 and 22 February 1968. ['August Strindberg's Last Plays']

[D2:469] Bergman, Gösta M. 'Strindberg and the Intima Teatern', *Theatre Research* (Glasgow), 9:1 (1967), 14-47. Illus. [Discusses Sg's ideas for staging his plays as well as on acting and production values in general. Bergman suggests that his attempt to implement them at the Intimate Theatre in Stockholm should be seen as part of the contemporary avant-garde movement, exemplified elsewhere by Edward Gordon Craig, Georg Fuchs, and Max Reinhardt. Sg was particularly receptive to ideas that would facilitate the dematerialised staging he sought after in his most experimental plays, and Bergman's essay remains an essential initial source for any study of the development of his thinking in this respect, as well as for the history and significance of the Intimate Theatre in general]

[D2:470] Bergman, A. Gunnar, 'Kring Strindbergs dramatik', *Folklig kultur* (Stockholm), 14:1 (1949), 10-13. ['On Strindberg's Plays']

[D2:471] Bergmann, Sven-Arne, 'Strindberg's Symbolic Drama', *The Norseman* (Liverpool), 15 (1957), 133-143. [Discusses *Till Damaskus I* and *Ett drömspel* as two of only three plays by Sg (the other is *Spöksonaten*) which both make use of symbols and are symbolic through and through, 'each of them aspiring to form one great dramatic symbol'. Bergmann observes that Sg's later works exhibit a new complexity of feeling rather than of ideas]

[D2:472] Bernardini-Sjöstedt, L[éonie], 'August Strindberg. Le Théâtre Intime', *Feuilleton du Le Temps* (Paris), 29 August 1910. [Presents the repertoire of Sg's Intimate Theatre to French readers. Discusses *Fröken Julie* as well as *Spöksonaten*]

[D2:473] Bergengren, K., '*August Strindbergs dramer*, Vol. 4', *Aftonbladet* (Stockholm), 8 February 1971. [Reviews Volume Four in Carl Reinhold Smedmark's incomplete text-critical edition of Sg's plays containing *Paria, Den starkare, Samum, Leka med elden, Debet och kredit, Första varningen, Inför döden, Moderskärlek, Hemsöborna, Himmelrikets nycklar*, and *Bandet*]

[D2:474] Bethke, Artur, 'Die Geste des Zeigens', in Bertil Nolin and Peter Forsgren, eds, *The Modern Breakthrough in Scandinavian Literature*, Skrifter utgivna av Litteraturvetenskapliga institutionen vid Göteborgs universitet 17, Göteborg, 1988, pp. 223-227. ['The Gesture of Showing'. Discusses Sg's post-Inferno dramaturgy in *Till Damaskus, Ett drömspel*, and *Spöksonaten*, and the general move towards epic theatre in European drama, of which these are early examples]

[D2:475] Bethke, Artur, 'Nachwort' and 'Anmerkungen', in August Strindberg, *Ausgewählte Dramen in drei Banden*, Bd 3, Rostock: VEB Hinstorff Verlag, 1983, pp. 470-508, 509-522. [The Afterword and Commentary to an East German edition of the plays in Three Volumes, which offers a chronological survey of Sg's career as a dramatist and places his dramas in their intellectual and theatrical context]

[D2:476] Beyer, Nils, 'Strindberg som teaterkritiker', *Bonniers Litterära Magasin* (Stockholm), 15:3 (1946), 217-225. ['Strindberg as a Theatre Critic'. Documents and cites the theatre criticism which Sg contributed to *Dagens Nyheter*, *Svalan*, and *Göteborgs Handels- och Sjöfartstidning* between 1873 and 1875, as well as his report on a performance of Alexandre Parodi's *Rome vaincue* which he saw at the Odéon in Paris in 1876. Although largely ignored in *Tjänstekvinnans son*, which offers surprisingly little evidence of Sg's early regard for the theatre, these reviews are of considerable interest in tracing the development of his ideas on drama in performance]

[D2:477] Beyer, Nils, '*August Strindbergs dramer*, Vol. 1', *Stockholms-Tidningen*, 21 January 1964. [Reviews Volume One of Carl Reinhold Smedmark's incomplete text-critical edition, containing *Fritänkaren, Hermione, I Rom, Den fredlöse, Anno Fyrtioåtta*, and *Gillets hemlighet*]

[D2:478] Beyer, Nils, '*August Strindbergs dramer*, Vol. 4', *Arbetet* (Malmö), 7 November 1970. [Reviews Volume Four of Carl Reinhold Smedmark's incomplete text-critical edition, containing *Paria, Den starkare, Samum, Leka med elden, Debet och kredit, Första varningen, Inför döden, Moderskärlek, Hemsöborna, Himmelrikets nycklar*, and *Bandet*]

[D2:479] Beyer, T[homas] P[ercival], 'The Plays of Strindberg', *The Dial* (Chicago), No 54 (16 January 1913), pp. 52-54. [An overview of existing American translations of the plays by Björkman (*Den starkare, Brott och brott, Fordringsägare*, and *Paria*), Velma S. Howard (*Påsk* and *Lycko-Pers resa*), and Warner Oland (*Fadren, Fröken Julie, Den starkare*, and *Den fredlöse*). 'No one can read a play of Sg's without receiving an intellectual jolt. There comes the startling conviction that here is the transcript of a great mind.... Nowhere else have I come upon such utter desolate pessimism; but it is an earnest pessimism...biological, and so complete.' Beyer claims that *Fröken Julie* is a symptom of the fact that 'our age has been sex-mad']

[D2:480] Beyer, Thomas P[ercival], 'The Plays of Strindberg', in *The Integrated Life: Essays, Sketches, and Poems*, Minneapolis: University of Minnesota Press; London: Geoffrey Cumberlege – Oxford University Press, 1948, pp. 109-113. [Rpr. of **D2:479**]

[D2:481] Beyer, W., 'Strindberg Heritage, *Father* and *Creditors*', *School and Society* (Lancaster, Philadelphia), 71 (14 January 1950), 23-24.

[D2:482] Biberi, Ion, 'De la drama de constiinta la elaborarea artistica: Strindberg', *Steaua* (Transylvania), 26:9 (1975), 36-38. ['From Drama of Conscience to Artistic Creation']

[D2:483] Biernacki, Jerzy, '*Dramaty*', *Nasz Klub* (Warsaw), 1962:37, p. 4. [Reviews recent Polish translations of *Mäster Olof*, *Fadren*, *Fröken Julie*, *Ett drömspel*, and *Spöksonaten* by Zygmunt Łanowski]

[D2:484] Billington, Michael, 'Swede's Corner', *The Guardian* (London), 18 January 1995. [Observes that, with four revivals of Sg's work now running in London, it is clear that the dramatist who was once regarded as an obsessional neurotic was not only the midwife of modern drama but a psychological pioneer, whose vision of sex and marriage is one we all too readily understand today]

[D2:485] Bisicchia, Andrea, ed., 'Lo spazio nel teatro di August Strindberg', in August Strindberg, *Tutti il teatro*, a cura di Andrea Bisicchia, trad., Rosella Lanari *et al.*, Vol. 1, 1869-1887, Milano: Mursia Editore, 1984. XLVII+623 pp. ['Space in the Theatre of August Strindberg'. Introduces a volume containing Italian translations of *Hermione, I Rom, Fritänkaren, Den Fredlöse, Mäster Olof, Anno Fyrtioåttio, Gillets hemlighet, Herr Bengts hustru, Lycko-Pers resa, Fadren,* and *Kamraterna,* with introductions and notes]

[D2:486] Bisicchia, Andrea, ed., 'Per una storia della messinscena strindberghiana in Italia', in August Strindberg, *Tutti il teatro*, a cura di Andrea Bisicchia, trad., Rosella Lanari *et al.*, Vol. 2, 1888-1899, Milano: Mursia Editore, 1985, pp. X-XXXIX. ['For a History of Strindberg's Plays on Stage in Italy'. Introduces a volume containing Italian translations of *Fordringsägare, Fröken Julie, Den starkare, Paria, Samum, Himmelrikets nycklar, Leka med elden, Bandet, Debet och kredit, Första varningen, Inför döden, Moderskärlek, Till Damaskus I-II, Advent*, and *Brott och brott*, with short introductions and notes, in all LXIV+597 pp.]

[D2:487] Bisicchia, Andrea, ed., 'Introduzione', in August Strindberg, *Tutti il teatro*, a cura di Andrea Bisicchia, trad., Rosella Lanari *et al.*, Vol. 3, 1899-1901, Milano: Mursia Editore, 1985. XL+615. [Introduces a volume containing Italian translations of *Folkungasagan, Gustav Vasa, Erik XIV, Dödsdansen I-II, Påsk, Engelbrekt*, and *Karl XII*, with short introductions and notes]

[D2:488] Bisicchia, Andrea, ed., 'Introduzione', in August Strindberg, *Tutti il teatro*, a cura di Andrea Bisicchia, trad., Rosella Lanari *et al.*, Vol. 4, 1901-1904, Milano: Mursia Editore, 1985. XLI+528 pp. [Introduces a volume containing Italian translations of *Svanevit, Midsommar, Kronbruden, Ett drömspel, Gustav III, Till Damaskus III, Kristina*, and *Näktergalen i Wittenberg*, with introductions and notes]

[D2:489] Bisicchia, Andrea, ed., 'Introduzione', in August Strindberg, *Tutti il teatro*, a cura di Andrea Bisicchia, trad., Rosella Lanari *et al.*, Vol. 5, 1907-1909, Milano: Mursia Editore, 1985. XXXIV+491 pp. [Introduces a volume containing Italian translations of *Oväder, Brända tomten, Spöksonaten, Pelikanen, Abu Casems tofflor, Siste riddaren,*

Riksförståndaren, *Bjälbo-Jarlen*, *Svarta handsken*, and *Stora landsvägen*, with introductions and notes]

[D2:490] Björkman, Edwin, 'Introduction', in *Plays by August Strindberg: Third Series*, London: Duckworth & Co., 1913, pp. 3-9. [Introduces the author's own translations of *Svanevit*, *Samum*, *Debet och kredit*, *Advent*, *Oväder*, and *Brända tomten*]

[D2:491] Björkman, Edwin, 'Introduction', in *Plays by August Strindberg, Fourth Series, The Bridal Crown, The Spook Sonata, The First Warning, Gustavus Vasa*, London: Duckworth & Co., 1916, pp. 3-17. [Introduces the author's own translations of *Kronbruden*, *Spöksonaten*, *Första varningen*, and *Gustav Vasa*]

[D2:492] Björkman, Edwin, 'Introduction', in August Strindberg, *Plays: The Dream Play, The Link, The Dance of Death Part I, The Dance of Death Part II*, London: Duckworth & Co.; New York: Charles Scribner's Sons, 1913, pp. 3-20. [A (for the period) relatively informed biographical introduction which draws upon Sg's own reading of his life in *Tjänstekvinnans son* and elsewhere. A prefatory note to these translations of *Ett drömspel*, *Bandet*, and *Dödsdansen* states that 'This translation is authorised by Mr. Sg, and he has also approved the selection of the plays included in this volume']

[D2:493] Björkstén, Ingmar, 'Strindberg på amerikanska', *Scen och Salong* (Stockholm), 48:11 (1963), 22-24. ['Strindberg in American']

[D2:494] Bjurström, Carl Gustaf, 'Notes', in August Strindberg, *Théâtre complet*, Vol. 1, Paris: L'Arche, 1982, pp. [529]-558. [Contains *I Rom, Hermione, Anno '48, Den fredlöse, Fritänkaren, Fritänkaren, Mäster Olof*, and *Gillets hemlighet*]

[D2:495] Bjurström, Carl Gustaf, 'Notes', in August Strindberg, *Théâtre complet*, Vol. 2, Paris: L'Arche, 1982, pp. [535]-579. [Contains *Herr Bengts hustru, Lycko-Pers resa, Kamraterna, Fadren, Fröken Julie, Fordringsägare, Den starkare, Paria, Samum*, Sg's own dramatisation of *Hemsöborna*, and *Himmelrikets nycklar*]

[D2:496] Bjurström, Carl Gustaf, 'Notes', in August Strindberg, *Théâtre complet*, Vol. 3, Paris: L'Arche, 1983, pp. [555]-585. [Contains *Moderskärlek, Inför döden, Debet och kredit, Första varningen, Leka med elden, Bandet, Till Damaskus, Advent, Brott och brott*, and *Folkungasagan*]

[D2:497] Bjurström, Carl Gustaf, 'Notes', in August Strindberg, *Théâtre complet*, Vol. 4, Paris: L'Arche, 1984, pp. [565]-596. [Contains *Gustav Vasa, Erik XIV, Gustav Adolf, Dödsdansen, Påsk, Kaspers fettisdag*, and *Midsommar* with Bjurström's comments]

[D2:498] Bjurström, Carl Gustaf, 'Notes', in August Strindberg, *Théâtre complet*, Vol. 5, Paris: L'Arche, 1986, pp. [551]-590. [Contains *Kronbruden, Svanevit, Karl XII, Engelbrekt, Kristina, Ett drömspel, Gustav III, Holländaren*, and *Näktergalen i Wittenberg* with Bjurström's comments]

[D2:499] Bjurström, Carl Gustaf, 'Notes', in August Strindberg, *Théâtre complet*, Vol. 6, Paris: L'Arche, 1986, pp. [503]-540. [Contains *Oväder, Brända tomten, Spöksonaten, Toten-Insel, Pelikanen, Siste riddaren, Riksföreståndaren, Abu Cassems tofflor, Svarta handsken, Bjälbo-Jarlen*, and *Stora landsvägen* with Bjurström's comments]

[D2:500] Blackwell, Marilyn Johns, 'Strindberg's Early Dramas and Lacan's "Law of the Father"', *Scandinavian Studies* (Provo), 71:3 (1999), 311-324. [Claims that Sg and Lacan are central figures in the discussion engendered by the erosion of European patriarchal structures, and maintains that they render certain gender related issues in strikingly similar ways. This is borne out by an analysis of *Fadren* and *Fröken Julie* in terms of Lacan's theories about the Symbolic phase of human development, in which the primary goal is a separation from the mother and an identification with the name, or law, of the father. Blackwell concludes that both plays conform to a Lacanian framework, the one defining women in terms of their biology, the other ending in 'the re-establishment, after this night of misrule', of the '"right" rule of the father']

[D2:501] Blackwell, Marilyn Johns, 'Strindberg's Early Dramas and Lacan's "Law of the Father"', in Janet Witalec, ed., **D2:348**, *Drama Criticism*, Volume 18, pp. 215-222. [Rpr. of **D2:500**]

[D2:501a] Bladh, Curt, 'Strindberg, Enaktare', *Sundsvalls Tidning*, 10 December 1984. [Reviews Volume 33 in *Samlade Verk* containing nine one-acters from the late 1880s]

[D2:502] Blanchart, Paul, 'Autour de Strindberg', *Le Soir* (Paris), 4 August 1931. [A generally unsympathetic response to a dramatist whose art is described here as 'painful and morbid']

[D2:503] Blau, Herbert, 'The Soul-Complex of Strindberg: Suffocation, Scopophilia, and the Seer', *Assaph: Studies in the Theatre* (Tel-Aviv), 16 (2000), pp. 1-12.

[D2:504] Bleibtrau, Karl, '*Vor höherer Instanz*', *Neue Bahnen* (Vienna), 1 (1901), p. 264. [Reviews *Advent* and *Brott och brott* translated into German by Emil Schering]

[D2:505] Bleijenberg, Gerrie, 'Strindberg is Quasi-Modern: Strindberg spelen', *Toneel teatraal* (Amsterdam), 1985:3, pp. 12-14.

[D2:506] Block, Haskell M., 'Strindberg and the Symbolist Drama', *Modern Drama* (Lawrence, Kansas), 5:3 (1962), 314-322. [Observes that Sg's symbolist affinities in the 1890s are primarily mystical and religious rather than literary in origin. Of symbolist writers, the Wagnerian Joséphin [Sâr] Péladan (1859-1918) may have been the most important to him as a dramatist, but a play like *Påsk* is also imbued with the suggestive mystery of Maeterlinck, whose dramaturgy, free from 'the violence of anecdote', has evident links with Sg's post-Inferno theatre. There are symbolist elements even in the history plays (e.g. *Karl XII*) while *Kronbruden* and *Svanevit* are his most deliberate attempts at writing symbolist drama. However, Block concludes that Sg's 'energy and turbulence as well as his relentless probing into the recesses of individual motivation and action are all essentially foreign to symbolist preoccupations']

[D2:507] Blok [sic], Haskell, 'Doprinos Strindberga modernom teatru', *Nedeljne informativne novine* (Belgrade), 24 February 1963. ['Strindberg's Contribution to the Modern Theatre'. R.589]

[D2:508] Blümner, Rudolf, 'August Strindberg', *Das Nationaltheater* (Berlin), 3 (1930-31), 241-248.

[D2:509] B-nr. [Otto Groothoff], 'Oskrivna Strindberg-dramer', *Göteborgs Handels- och Sjöfartstidning*, 15 January 1949. ['Unwritten Plays by Strindberg']

[D2:510] Boas, Guy, 'The Plays of August Strindberg', *English* (Reigate, Surrey), 6 (1946-47), 111-117. [Seeks to rehabilitate Sg's 'precarious and alarming' reputation in Britain where a just estimate cannot be based on only a few of his more lurid studies of marriage. Boas focuses initially on *Brott och brott*, *Ett drömspel*, and *Spöksonaten*, but it is *Påsk*, *Advent*, *Midsommar*, *Kronbruden*, *Svanevit*, and *Lycko-Pers resa* that will prove the real corrective to received notions. He also stresses the imaginative truth of the history plays, in an article whose emotive tone does little to remedy the wrong it is seeking to redress]

[D2:511] Bøgh, Ole, 'Strindbergs Forsøgsteater', *Den Danske Tilskuer* (Copenhagen), 1 (1990), 125-172. Illus. [Offers a well-documented account of the history, repertoire, and theatrical (as well as personal) politics of Sg's Experimental Theatre in Copenhagen in 1888-89]

[D2:512] Bolin, W., 'Aug. Strindberg som dramatiker', *Finsk Tidskrift* (Åbo), 9 (1880), 353-362. ['Strindberg as Dramatist'. One of the earliest assessments of Sg's abilities as a dramatist. Bolin discusses *Mäster Olof*, which he considers more suited to reading than to the theatre, and especially *Gillets hemlighet*, with what he calls its masterly characterisation. He also comments on *I Rom*, *Den fredlöse*, and *Hermione*]

[D2:513] Borchsenius, Otto, '*Strindberg och teater*', *Nationaltidende* (Copenhagen), 30 April 1919. [Reviews August Falck's edition of Sg's letters and the latter's *Memorandum till Medlemmarne av Intima Teatern*]

[D2:514] Børge, Vagn Albeck, 'Ingvar Holm und das Strindbergdrama auf der Bühne', in Fritz Paul, Hrsg., *Akten der Vierten Arbeitstagung der skandinavisten des deutschen Sprachgebiets*, 1. bis 5. Oktober 1979 in Bochum, Hattingen: Scandica Verlag, pp. 85-114. ['Ingvar Holm and Strindberg's Dramas on the Stage'. Maintains that the genuine, often tragi-comic, Sg is only fully realisable on stage, as Johannes Poulsen's performance in the role of Erik XIV demonstrated. Holm's current, Lund-based research into Sg's dramas on stage provides a valid academic approach to the study of these works in their appropriate environment]

[D2:515] Børge, Vagn Albeck, 'Johannes Poulsen og Strindberg', *Teatret* (Copenhagen), 1938:5. [On the Danish actor and his performances in Sg's plays, including Olof in *Mäster Olof*, Vasa in *Gustav Vasa*, Erik XIV, and the Son in *Pelikanen*]

[D2:516] Børge, Vagn [Albeck], 'Strindberg, o del teatro mistico', *Il Dramma* (Rome), May 1970. ['Strindberg, Or the Mystical Theatre'. Summarises ideas developed in **D2:29** in an issue published in conjunction with Michael Meschke's staging of *Ett drömspel* at the Teatro Stabile di Torino]

[D2:517] Borie, Monique, 'Strindberg, de pouvoir des ombres et la puissance de doubles', in *Le Fantôme ou le théâtre qui doute*, Arles: Actes Sud, 1997, pp. 193-209. ['Strindberg, the Power of Shadows and the Puissance of Doubles']

[D2:518] Boyer, Regis, 'À la recherche d'un principe de composition dans cinq pièces "naturalistes" de Strindberg', in Oskar Bandle, Hrsg., **D2:8**, *Strindbergs Dramen im Lichte neuerer Methodendiskussionen*, pp. 51-68. ['In Search of a Principle of Composition in Five "Naturalistic" Plays by Strindberg'. Argues that *Fadren*, *Fröken Julie*, *Fordringsägare*, and *Dödsdansen I-II* demonstrate how all the important themes and images in Sg's plays are to be found in the first act. These images direct Sg's creative process and the characters become the 'slaves' of their images (thus 'Laura is the straitjacket of power, Jean is the razor, Tekla the statue, and Alice the vampire or the wolf), to the same extent as the characters of the Eddas or the Icelandic sagas become victims to their fate in the metaphorical shape of the 'hamingja', 'fyglia', or 'valkyrja']

[D2:519] Bradbrook, M[uriel] C[lara], 'First Inklings of the Absurd', *The Times Literary Supplement* (London), 19 November 1976. [Reviews Volume Two of Michael Meyer's translations of nine of the plays and Walter Johnson's translations of *Dödsdansen*, *Advent*, *Påsk*, and *Brott och brott*. 'At last Sg is shown [in English] in the astounding range of his masterpieces']

[D2:520] Brandell, Gunnar, 'Macro-Form in Strindberg's Plays: Tight and Loose Structure', in Göran Stockenström, ed., **D2:288**, *Strindberg's Dramaturgy*, pp. 87-97. [Draws a distinction between those plays which are tightly composed, like *Fadren*, *Fröken Julie*, *Dödsdansen*, and *Fordringsägare*, the last of which possesses a formal classicism that is reminiscent of Racine, and the more loosely composed works like *Lycko-Per's resa*, *Till Damaskus* and *Ett drömspel*, which correspond to a different side of his personality. Brandell omits the history plays from the discussion]

[D2:521] Brandell, Gunnar, 'Strindberg as Dramatist', *Zeszyty Naukowe Wydziału Humanistycznego. Studia Scandinavica* (Gdańsk), 9 (1985), 7-12. [Discusses the formal variety of Sg's plays where the element of routine is less important than the element of improvisation, in part because he was never a professional playwright or exclusively devoted to a single field. His plays are therefore often flawed, but there are compensations in the form of a unique dramatic intensity, the frequent reduction of scenic elements, and a quite distinct form of dialogue, which is rarely structured in a logical way. With Sg, action is always interaction and situation is a constantly changing set of relations between characters]

[D2:522] Brandell, Gunnar, 'Strindberg och scentekniken', *Tidskrift för litteraturvetenskap* (Lund), 13:2-3 (1984), 33-36. ['Strindberg and Dramatic Technique'. Contrasts the 'tight' technique of *Fröken Julie*, *Fordringsägare*, and *Dödsdansen* with the 'loose' compositional method of *Till Damaskus*, *Ett drömspel*, and *Stora landsvägen*]

[D2:523] Brandes, Edvard, 'Strindberg', *Politiken* (Copenhagen), 15 January 1900. [Reviews *Folkungasagan*, *Gustav Vasa*, and *Erik XIV* on publication]

[D2:524] Brandes. Edvard, 'Strindberg: *Fröken Julie* og *Kreditorer*', in **D1:68**, *Edv. Brandes om Teater: Anmeldelser og Erindringer fra henved 50 Aar*, pp. 43-49. [Rpr. of **D2:380**]

[D2:525] Brandes, Edvard, 'Teater-besök i Stockholm', *Ur dagens krönika* (Stockholm), 1889, pp. 887-901. ['Theatre Visit in Stockholm'. Reports that Sg has been side-lined in Stockholm even though his plays (*Mäster Olof*, *Herr Bengts hustru*, *Gillets hemlighet* and perhaps, in future, even *Fadren*) are classics of Swedish literature. A consequence of this neglect is that Sg is now writing plays far less suited for the stage, like *Fröken Julie*]

[D2:526] Brantly, Susan, *August Strindberg's Use of Scenic Elements*', Madison: University of Wisconsin. htt://pocahontus.doit.wisc.edu [A web site devoted to Sg's pioneering use of scenic elements in stage design, using voice-over narrative, digitised images, and illustrated with dialogue from the plays]

[D2:527] Brasil, Assis, 'Introdução', in August Strindberg, *Senhorito Júlia e A Mais forte*, Rio de Janeiro: Editora Tecnoprint, [1994]. Illus. 100 pp. [Introduces a Portuguese translation of *Fröken Julie* and *Den starkare*]

[D2:528] Brausewetter, Ernst, 'Strindberg als historischer Dramatiker. Eine litterarische Studie', *Bühne und Welt* (Hamburg), 4 (1901-02), 829-838. ['Strindberg as a Writer of History Plays. A Literary Study'. Contains comments on Sg's recent historical dramas by one of his first German translators]

[D2:529] Brejcha, Gun, 'Tre förgrundsgestalter i nordisk dramatik', 3-4, *Nya Wermlands Tidningen* (Karlstad), 29 and 31 July 1963. ['Three Prominent Figures in Nordic Drama'. The third and fourth of four articles on the 'major' Nordic dramatists, Holberg, Ibsen, and Sg]

[D2:530] Brion, Marcel, 'Le théâtre de Strindberg', *Vie intellectuelle* (Paris), 13:2 (1931).*

[D2:531] Brisson, Pierre, 'Une épopé de la détresse humaine', *Figaro Littéraire* (Paris), 22 January 1949. ['An Epic of Human Distress'. Brisson acclaims Sg as a tragic poet *par excellence* and observes that 'two figures dominate the times which have forgotten them: Becque on the one hand, Sg on the other']

[D2:532] Broman, Walter E., 'Selected Plays by August Strindberg', *Philosophy and Literature* (Baltimore, Maryland), 12:1 (1988), 151-152. [Reviews English translations of twelve of Sg's plays by Evert Sprinchorn]

[D2:533] Brunel, Pierre, 'Strindberg et Artaud', *Revue d'histoire du théâtre* (Paris), 30:3 (1978), 346-358. [Considers the importance of Sg for the development of Artaud's ideas about a Theatre of Cruelty via a discussion of the latter's staging of *Ett drömspel* and his production plan for staging *Spöksonaten*. When he came to write 'Position de la chair' (1925) Artaud had evidently absorbed Sg's 'supra-naturalisme', but it is important to distinguish between Artaud's notion of a theatre of cruelty and Sg's psychological cruelty in a naturalistic drama like *Fordringsägare*. Nevertheless, Sg's impact on Artaud amounts to more than what has sometimes been termed merely an 'episode']

[D2:534] Brunius, August, 'Något om Strindbergs dramatiska figurer', in *Ansikten och masker. Modern litteratur, konst och teater*, Stockholm: P. A. Norstedt & Söners Förlag, 1917, pp. 147-152. ['On Strindberg's Dramatic Characters'. The striving for simplification and energy which dominates Sg's dramaturgy is integral to his characterisation, and many of his figures only acquire human warmth on stage. Brunius singles out Jacques in *Gillets hemlighet*, Mäster Olof, and the protagonist of *Gustav Vasa* as three of Sg's most achieved stage characters]

[D2:535] Brunius, August, 'Något om Strindbergs dramatiska personligheter', *Bonniers månadshäften* (Stockholm), 1909:1, pp. 26-31. ['On Strindberg's Dramatic Characters'. See **D2:534**]

[D2:536] Brunius, Teddy, 'C. Grabow, A. Strindberg och 8000 skisser', *Kulturens Värld* (Stockholm), 9:4 (1994). ['C. Grabow, A. Strindberg and 8,000 Sketches'. Presents the Swedish stage designer Carl Ludvig Grabow's many designs for productions of Sg's plays at Dramaten, including his important contribution to the world première of *Till Damaskus*]

[D2:537] Brustein, Robert [Sandford], 'August Strindberg', in Otto Reinert, ed., **B1:371**, *Strindberg: A Collection of Critical Essays*, pp. 27-47. [Rpr. of the chapter on Sg in **D1:75**]

[D2:538] Brustein, Robert [Sandford], 'Introduction', in August Strindberg, *Selected Plays and Prose*, New York: Holt, Rinehart and Winston, Inc., 1964, pp. [ix]-lxiii. [Rpr. of the chapter on Sg in *The Theatre of Revolt*, **D1:75**]

[D2:539] Brustein, Robert [Sandford], 'Male and Female in August Strindberg', *Tulane Drama Review* (New Orleans), 7:2 (1962), 130-174. [A version of the chapter on Sg published, in a slightly revised form, in *The Drama of Revolt*, **D1:75**]

[D2:540] Brustein, Robert [Sandford], 'Male and Female in August Strindberg', in Travis Bogard and William I. Oliver, eds, *Modern Drama: Essays in Criticism*, New York: Oxford University Press, 1965, pp. 313-354. [Rpr. of **D2:539**]

[D2:541] Brustein, Robert [Sandford], 'Strindberg: The Victor and the Vanquished', *The New Republic* (Washington, D.C.), 19 February 1962.

[D2:542] Bry, Carl Christian, 'Das Drama des Auslandes. Die deutschen Theater nach dem Kriege 5. Die nordischen Dramatiker – Strindberg', *Die christliche Welt* (Marburg), 39 (1925), 513-515. ['Foreign Drama. German Theatre after the War. 5. The Nordic Dramatists – Strindberg'. An unsympathetic response to the 'monomaniac' Sg and the place accorded him in the post-war German theatre]

[D2:543] Burkhard, Arthur, 'August Strindberg and Modern German Drama', *German Quarterly* (Philadelphia), 6 (1933), 163-174. [Clarifies Sg's importance as one of the main foreign influences on a generation of German expressionist dramatists who were selective in the use they made of his work in several genres, much of it still unknown in the United States. Like Goethe and Rousseau, though far more shameless than either, he was an autobiographical writer and, as well as his confrontational stance, Burkhard argues that it was the subjective, confessional element in his writing that exerted so powerful an influence on these younger German writers]

[D2:544] Burton, R., 'August Strindberg, *Plays*', *The Bellman* (Minneapolis), 12 (1912), p. 435. [Reviews Edwin Björkman's translations of *Ett drömspel*, *Bandet*, and *Dödsdansen*]

[D2:545] Cahn, Alfredo, 'Prefacio', in Augusto Strindberg, *Obras teatrales*, Prefacio y versiones castellanas por Alfredo Cahn, Córdoba: Univ. Nacional, 1962. 223 pp. [Introduces annotated Spanish translations of *Dödsdansen*, *Spöksonaten*, and *Oväder*]

[D2:546] Carlson, Harry G., 'In Search of the Dionysian Actor', in Claes Englund and Gunnel Bergström, eds, **D2:99**, *Strindberg, O'Neill and the Modern Theatre*, pp. 48-56. [On the failure to perform Sg adequately in the United States and elsewhere, and the need for a new, 'Dionysian' actor, resembling Laurence Olivier in *Dödsdansen*, if his plays are to be successfully realised on stage]

[D2:547] Carlson, Harry G., 'Introduction', in *Strindberg: Five Plays*, Berkeley and London: University of California Press, 1983, pp. 1-13. [Introduces the author's own translations of *Fadren, Fröken Julie, Dödsdansen, Ett drömspel,* and *Spöksonaten*]

[D2:548] Carlson, Harry G., 'Introduction', in *Strindberg: Five Plays*, New York: Signet, 1984, pp. ix-xx. [Rpr. of **D2:547**]

[D2:549] Carlson, Harry G., 'Medieval Themes and Structures in Strindberg's Post-Inferno Drama', in Kela Kvam, ed., **D2:158**, *Strindberg's Post-Inferno Plays*, pp. 19-31. [Acclaims the post-Inferno Sg as a major renewer of the ritual drama of the Middle Ages. Instead of the future intersecting with the past at a final crossroads, as in the plays of the Sophoclean Ibsen, they now commingle, as the dividing line between the two dimensions becomes unstable. Sg had demonstrated an awareness of the evocative poetic power of medieval themes and the expressive, flexible nature of medieval staging as early as *Mäster Olof*; he now responded to impulses in *fin-de-siècle* Paris and the theatrical revolution associated with e.g. William Poel and Vsevolod Meyerhold. Carlson suggests that in the ritual structure of the morality play and the place afforded allegory and typology in medieval drama, Sg found new ways of dramatising his own experience in a form of drama that was at once individual and universal]

[D2:550] Carlson, Harry G., 'Strindberga wyobrażenia mityczne', *Ład* (Warsaw?), 1985:2, p. 5. ['Strindberg's Conception of Myth'. Summarises Carlson's notion of Sg's mythological imagination, which is presented in detail in **D2:40**]

[D2:551] Carlsson, K., '*Kammarspel*', *Norrländska Socialdemokraten* (Luleå), 4 November 1991. [Reviews Volumes 39 and 58 in *Samlade Verk*, containing *Till Damaskus* and the Chamber Plays respectively]

[D2:552] Car-Mihec, Adriana, 'Menipejska tradicija i dramsko stvaralastvo August Strindberg', *Fluminensia: Casopis za Filoloska Istrazivanja* (Zagreb?), 5:1-2 (1993), pp. 71-81. ['The Menippean Tradition in the Dramatic Works of August Strindberg'. A Bakhtinian study of Sg's plays in Croatian with an Italian summary]

[D2:553] Casanove, Charles de [Bignault], 'Auguste Strindberg', 1-3, *Revue d'art dramatique* (Paris), 1 March, 1 April, and 15 July 1892. [The first significant presentation of Sg as a dramatist in France. Casanove points out, with some prompting from Sg, that Laura in *Fadren* and Tekla in *Fordringsägare* antedate *Hedda Gabler* by several years. He also stresses the socialist dimension of *Fröken Julie*, which is entirely absent from *Fordringsägare*, quotes Zola's letter to Sg about *Fadren* in full, and compares the terror evoked in *Fadren* to the horror engendered by the stories of Edgar Allan Poe]

[D2:554] Castrén, Gunnar, 'August Strindberg, *Kronbruden*, *Svanevit*, *Drömspel*', *Euterpe* (Helsinki), 1902, p. 10. [Review on publication]

[D2:555] C. D. W. [Carl David af Wirsén], 'Litteratur', *Post- och Inrikes Tidningar* (Stockholm), 1 May 1897. [Discusses *Leka med elden* and *Bandet* on publication in *Tryckt och otryckt IV*: 'they are more or less equally unpleasant and painful']

[D2:556] C. D. W. [Carl David af Wirsén], 'Litteratur', *Post- och Inrikes Tidningar* (Stockholm), 2 December 1899. [Reviews *Folkungasagan*, *Gustav Vasa*, and *Erik XIV* on publication. *Vasa* betrays some dramatic talent but the other two works are repulsive. Indeed, the psychology in *Erik XIV* is superficial, and its coarseness breaks all bounds]

[D2:557] C. D. W. [Carl David af Wirsén], 'Litteratur', *Vårt Land* (Stockholm), 5 May 1899. [Reviews *Advent* and *Brott och brott* on publication. However horrible the volume may be in its sick desire not merely to engage with, but openly to indulge in, the unpleasant, it indicates a greater seriousness than his earlier works, as well as a rich talent and new view of life]

[D2:558] C. D. W. [Carl David af Wirsén], 'Litteratur', *Vårt Land* (Stockholm), 13 June 1902. [Reviews *Kronbruden*, *Svanevit*, and *Ett drömspel* on publication. The former is monotonous in its symbolism and the latter indulgent, since it requires no method to write like this; it lacks depth, even if many naïve souls will convince themselves there is some profound meaning in its empty imagery. However, *Svanevit* is somewhat better – a bright intermezzo in an *œuvre* that 'has otherwise become increasingly bizarre, arbitrary, and discordant']

[D2:559] C. E. [C. E. Jensen], 'Strindbergs Teater I. Et Forord', *Social-Demokraten* (Copenhagen), 28 February 1889. [The first of three articles on the plays which Sg wrote in Copenhagen during the 1880s. See also **E12:54** and **E13:9**]

[D2:560] Cerkvenik, Angelo, 'Nekaj o Strindberg', *Maska* (Ljubljana?), 1:5 (1920-21), 65-67.

[D2:561] Cheshikhin, V., '[Plays by Strindberg]', *Artist* (Moscow), No. 38 (June 1894), pp. 51-59. [The first extended discussion of Sg as a dramatist in Russian, dealing with *Fadren*, *Fröken Julie*, and *Fordringsägare*. To Cheshikhin he is neither an original author nor a significant psychologist. In *Fadren* his characters are pale shadows and merely mouthpieces for certain ideas; *Fröken Julie* likewise lacks psychological credibility; and *Fordringsägare* displays his misogyny most openly. This is rooted in his harsh upbringing and inferiority complex as well as in the widespread predilection of Nordic literature for Nietzsche. Cheshikhin prophesies that Sg's future, if he has one, will be as a thinker rather than an artist. E.698]

[D2:562] Ciesielski, Zenon, '*Wybór dramatów*', *Pamiętnik Teatralny* (Warsaw), 1978:4, pp. 612-614. [Apropos a collection of Sg's plays, translated into Polish by Zygmunt Łanowski and introduced by Lech Sokół, **D2:1176**]

[D2:563] Claesson, Åke, 'Strindberg som rollinstrukör', *Meddelanden från Strindbergs-sällskapet* (Stockholm), 8 (1950), pp. 3-8, 11. ['Strindberg as a Director of Actors'. Introduces Sg's letters to the actor Ivar Nilsson, with advice on how to play the roles of Olof in the verse edition of *Mäster Olof* and Sten Sture the Younger in *Siste Riddaren*]

[D2:564] Clark, Barrett H[arper], 'Strindberg, Reinhardt, and Berlin', *Drama* (New York), May 1914, pp. 270-279.

[D2:565] Clark, J., 'Work of August Strindberg', *Colonnade* (Georgia College & State University), 7 (1914), 262-268. [Reviews ongoing editions of Sg's plays in English translation]

[D2:566] Clausen, Julius, 'Strindbergs Memorandum til Skuespillerne', *Berlingske Tidende* (Copenhagen), 10 July 1919. ['Strindberg's Memorandum to the Actors'. Reviews Sg's practical advice to his actors in the various memoranda that he addressed to members of the Intimate Theatre]

[D2:567] Codignola, Luciano, 'Il teatro contemporaneo parte da Strindberg', *Il Dramma* (Rome), 1978:6-8. ['Strindberg's Role in the Contemporary Theatre']

[D2:568] Codignola, Luciano, 'Introduzione', in August Strindberg, *Teatro naturalistico*, a cura di L[uciano] Codignola, 2 vols, Milano: Adelphi, 1978-1982. 156 and 219 pp. [Introduces the author's own Italian translations of *Fadren, Fröken Julie,* and *Fordringsägare*]

[D2:569] 'Cognitus' [Otto Sjögren], 'Strindbergs nya bok: *Tryckt och otryckta*', *Ur dagens krönika* (Stockholm), 1890, pp. 235-238. ['Strindberg's New Book: *Published and Unpublished*'. Reviews *Fordringsägare*, *Paria*, and *Samum* on publication]

[D2:570] Cohn, Helge, 'Strindberg och Intima Teatern', *Falu-Kuriren* (Falun), 22 March 1967. ['Strindberg and the Intimate Theatre']

[D2:571] Cohn, Helge, 'Strindberg och Intima Teatern', *Scen och salong* (Stockholm), 47:4 (1962), 30-32. ['Strindberg and the Intimate Theatre']

[D2:572] Coolus, Romain, 'Notes Dramatiques: Auguste Strindberg', *La Revue Blanche* (Paris), 8 (1895), 88-91. [A presentation of Sg by the author of *Le ménage Brésil*, which was performed in a double-bill with *Fröken Julie* at the Théâtre Libre in 1893. Lugné-Poe's current staging of *Fadren* at the Théâtre de l'Œuvre now draws from Coolus the conclusion that Sg is one of the greatest writers in Europe]

[D2:573] Corrigan, Robert W., 'Strindberg and the Abyss', in August Strindberg, *A Dream Play and Spöksonaten*, trans. Carl Richard Mueller, San Francisco: Chandler Publishing Co., 1966, pp. ix-xx. [Judges Sg's whole career to have been an unending quest to create a form that was capable of expressing his profoundly subjective concerns]

[D2:574] Corrigan, Robert, W., 'Strindberg and the Abyss', in *The Theatre in Search of a Fix*, New York: Delacorte Press, 1973, pp. 111-124. [Rpr. of **D2:573**]

[D2:575] Craig, Edward Gordon, '*Mäster Olof and Other Plays*', *The Spectator* (London), 24 October 1931 (Literary Supplement), pp. 537-539. [Reviews Volume Three in the

Anglo-Swedish Literary Foundation series of translations of Sg's plays, to which it contributes four historical dramas. Craig also recalls visiting Sg in Stockholm in 1908 and insists that '[Sg's] plays are not photographic; they are things heard and seen, felt and experienced, drawn and etched as well as written...never photographed']

[D2:576] Cullberg, Johan, 'Kvinnohat och manšångest', *Bonniers Litterära Magasin* (Stockholm), 56:1 (1987), 13-19. Illus. ['Misogyny and Male Anxiety'. Discusses the paradoxes of masculinity as represented in *Fadren* and *Fordringsägare*, which Cullberg reads psychoanalytically in order to demonstrate that, in the former, Sg dramatises a male fear of being consumed by both wife and mother and, in the latter, how an Oedipal triangle is established on stage, with Gustav the father figure against whom both Tekla and Adolf are in revolt]

[D2:577] Cyprian, M. F., 'Das Drama Strindbergs', *Hochland* (München), 16 (1918-19), 178-184. ['Strindberg's Dramas'. Considers the possible rebirth of religious drama in Sg, with reference to Otto Kaus, **B3:241**, *Strindberg. Eine Kritik*, and C. D. Marcus, **D2:213**, *Strindbergs Dramatik*. As opposed to Ibsen, Sg 'rediscovered tragedy exactly where it had its real home – in human beings themselves']

[D2:578] Czerny, R[udolf], '*Das Geheimnis der Gilde*; *Ritter Bengts Gattin*', *Österreichisches Litteraturblatt* (Vienna), 5 (1896), 63-64. [Reviews the first German translations of *Gillets hemlighet* and *Herr Bengts hustru*]

[D2:579] Dahlström, Carl E[noch] W[illiam] L[eonard], 'August Strindberg, The Father of Dramatic Expressionism', *Papers of the Michigan Academy of Science, Arts and Letters* (Ann Arbor), 10 (1928-29), 261-272. [One of the earliest essays to argue that Sg's naturalistic plays have many features in common with his expressionist, post-Inferno dramas]

[D2:580] Dahlström, Carl E[noch] W[illiam] L[eonard], 'Strindberg and Naturalistic Tragedy', *Scandinavian Studies* (Lawrence, Kansas), 30:1 (1958), 1-18. [Whether or not Sg's naturalism followed Zola's formula precisely, if everything is determined mechanically and there can be no free will, no individuality, no options, choices, or responsibility, the cultural context of *Fadren* inhibits the achievement of tragedy, even though the play responds to an Aristotelian analysis and there are parallels between it and *Othello*. Likewise, the *dramatis personae* in *Fröken Julie* are flawed and Sg regarded Julie's fall as tragic, although scientific determinism robs her of genuine individuality. The play falls short as a tragedy 'because the author failed to give it adequate tragic substance']

[D2:581] Dahlström, Carl E[noch] W[illiam] L[eonard], 'Strindberg and the Problems of Naturalism', *Scandinavian Studies* (Menasha, Wisconsin), 16:6 (1941), 212-219. [Seeks to establish the extent to which Sg's plays may or may not conform to the criteria of literary naturalism as defined by Zola]

[D2:582] Dahlström, C[arl] E[noch] W[illiam] L[eonard], 'August Strindberg, *The Last of the Knights*, *The Regent*, *Earl Birger of Bjälbo* and *Gustav Adolf*. Translations and Introductions by Walter Johnson', *Scandinavian Studies* (Lawrence, Kansas), 29:2 (1957), 94-97. [A positive review of two volumes which 'will help to correct the distorted picture of Sg that exists in the minds of too many American readers. Not only was Sg a significant artist during his lifetime, he also persists as a potent cultural force in the present']

[D2:583] Dahlström, C[arl] E[noch] W[illiam] L[eonard], '[Strindberg, August] *Strindberg's Kristina, Charles XII, Gustav III*. Translations and Introductions by Walter Johnson', *Scandinavian Studies* (Menasha, Wisconsin), 27:4 (1955), 203-206. [A positive review of three plays in which 'Sg exhibits a remarkable capacity to create strikingly different living figures from the historical dead']

[D2:584] Dahlström, C[arl] E[noch] W[illiam] L[eonard], 'August Strindberg. *The Vasa Trilogy: Mäster Olof, Gustav Vasa, Erik XIV*' and August Strindberg. *Folkungasagan; Engelbrekt*. Translations and Introductions by Walter Johnson', *Scandinavian Studies* (Lawrence, Kansas), 31:3 (1959), 139-141. [Reviews two volumes in the University of Washington Press edition of Sg's plays. 'Professor Johnson has done his job so well that it is now possible for those who do not read Swedish to grasp Sg's significance']

[D2:585] Dahms, W., 'Strindbergs Dramaturgie', *Neue Preussische Kreuzzeitung* (Berlin), 8 September 1918. ['Strindberg's Dramaturgy']

[D2:586] Damiens, Claude, 'Auguste Strindberg: l'enfer du théâtre au-delà au naturalisme', *Paris-Théâtre*, No. 185 (1962). ['August Strindberg: The Hell of Theatre Beyond Naturalism']

[D2:587] De Decker, Jacques, 'Un auteur: August Strindberg', *Clés pour le spectacle* (Bruxelles), April 1978.

[D2:588] Deer, Irving, 'Strindberg's Dream Vision: Prelude to the Film', *Criticism* (Detroit), 14:3 (1972), 253-265. [Deer seeks to demonstrate how some of Sg's plays 'show an inclination toward a cinematic conception of form'. He stresses the fluidity of Sg's experimental drama, its dissolution of character, mingling of illusion and reality, interdependence of time and space, and breakdown of fixed moral coordinates. Deer draws on Susanne Langer's definition of the dream mode in *Feeling and Form* and compares Sg's later work with the cinema of Fellini and Bergman]

[D2:589] Diebold, Bernhard, 'Szenische Mimik', *Die Scene* (Berlin), 11:2-3 (1921), 40-42. [An extract on Sg from *Anarchie im Drama*, **D1:108**]

[D2:590] Diebold, Bernhard, 'Szenische Mimik', in Hans-Peter Bayerdörfer, Hrsg., **B3:85**, *Strindberg auf der deutschen Bühne*, pp. 316-320. [Rpr. of **D2:589** on poetry of the theatre exemplified by a discussion of the creation of the heightened atmosphere in Sg's post-Inferno dramas with reference to *Advent, Till Damaskus, Kronbruden*, and the Chamber Plays, the last of which display an affinity with the work of Edgar Allan Poe and E. T. A. Hoffmann]

[D2:591] Diebold, Bernhard, 'Strindberg der Führer?', *Die Scene* (Berlin), 11:2-3 (1921), 36-37. ['Strindberg the Leader?' Questions the extent to which the younger generation of German dramatists has been led by someone who 'was the performer of his own life situation: how could this poor man become the leader of an entire nation's youth?' Diebold maintains that Sg was weak of will and wisdom, and without the war, which brought with it the mystic of the Chamber Plays rather than the naturalist of *Fröken Julie*, the hold he subsequently gained in Germany would not have been possible]

[D2:592] Diebold, Bernhard, 'Strindberg der Führer?', in Hans-Peter Bayerdörfer, Hrsg., **B3:85**, *Strindberg auf der deutschen Bühne*, pp. 312-316. [Rpr. of **D2:591**]

[D2:593] Diebold, Bernhard, 'Strindberg und die heutige deutsche Jugund', *Das Deutsche Buch* (Leipzig), 1:4 (1921), 3-7. ['Strindberg and German Youth Today'. An extract from **D1:108**, *Anarchie im Drama*]

[D2:594] Dodd, L. W., 'Strindberg's Plays', *Yale Review* (New Haven, Conn.), New Series, 1 (1912), 690-693. [Reviews Edwin Björkman's latest volume of translations, including *Ett drömspel*, and outlines the divisions in Sg's work between the quasi-romantic, the naturalistic, and his autumnal renaissance, in which his motto has become "Erase and pass on!"]

[D2:595] Donnér, Jarl W., 'Göran Lindström: *Att läsa dramatik*; Göran Lindström: *Strindberg om drama och teater*', *Samlaren* (Uppsala), 91: (1970), pp. 201-202. [Reviews **D1:266** and an anthology of Sg's writings on drama and the theatre]

[D2:596] Donnér, Jarl W., '*Spöksonaten* och *Fröken Julie*', *Sydsvenska Dagbladet* (Malmö), 10 April 1964. [Reviews annotated student editions of *The Ghost Sonata* and *Miss Julie*: **E51:76** and **E12:184**]

[D2:597] Donnér, Jarl W., '[Strindberg]', *Sydsvenska Dagbladet* (Malmö), 6 July 1984. [Reviews Volume 27 in *Samlade Verk*, containing *Fadren, Fröken Julie*, and *Fordringsägare*]

[D2:598] Drews, Wolfgang, 'Der neurotische Faust in der Götterdämmerung. Randbemerkungen zu Strindbergs Werk und Wirkung', *Theater und Zeit* (Wuppertal), 10 (1962-63), 121-128. ['The Neurotic Faust in the Twilight of the Gods. Marginalia on Strindberg's Work and Impact'. One of many characterisations which identify the restlessly intellectual Sg with Faust]

[D2:599] Dünwald, Willi, 'Strindberg', *Die Schaubühne* (Berlin), 8 (1912), 237-242.

[D2:600] Duvignaud, Jean, 'Strindberg nell'orizzonte del teatro europeo. La distruzione del personaggio', *Il Dramma* (Rome), May 1970. ['Strindberg and Horisons of the European Theatre: The Destruction of Character']

[D2:601] E. A. [Edvard Alkman], 'August Strindberg, *Vid högre rätt*', *Dagens Nyheter* (Stockholm), 6 June 1899. [Reviews *Advent* and *Brott och brott* on publication. The latter is one of Sg's most surely composed pieces, but its refined dialectic may be too complex for the theatre, and prove more compelling on the page]

[D2:602] E. A. [Edvard Alkman], 'August Strindberg, *Tryckt och otryckt IV*', *Dagens Nyheter* (Stockholm), 29 April 1897. [Reviews *Leka med elden* and *Bandet* on publication]

[D2:603] E. H., 'Die Welt August Strindberg...und weitere Texte internationaler Dramatik', *Die andere Zeitung* (Hamburg), 12 (1966), No. 43, p. 13. [Reviews the 1964-65 German edition of Sg's plays translated by Willi Reich in three volumes]

[D2:604] Egri, Peter, 'A naturalizmustól az expresszionizmus felé: A drámatötenet strindbergi fordulója', *Filológiai Közlöny* (Budapest), 26:3 (1980), 313-332. ['From Naturalism to Expressionism: The History of Drama in Strindberg's Stage Directions'. Primarily a discussion of Sg's role in the development of modern drama from naturalism to expressionism]

[D2:605] Eklund, Torsten, 'Fordringsägaren Strindberg', *Teatern* (Stockholm), 22:2 (1955), pp. 5-6, 10. ['Strindberg the Creditor'. Provides autobiographical contexts for both *Oväder* and *Fordringsägare*, which confirm that the theatre is where Sg settles his accounts with friends and enemies alike]

[D2:606] Eklund, Torsten, 'Strindberg och Intima teatern', *Studiekamraten* (Tollarp), 18:6 (1936), 111-114. ['Strindberg and the Intimate Theatre']

[D2:607] Ekman, Hans-Göran, 'Death Angst, Death Wish. Aspects of Death in Strindberg's Post-Inferno Plays', in Kela Kvam, ed., **D2:158**, *Strindberg's Post-Inferno Plays*, pp.

32-51. Illus. [Establishes that death is one of the dominant themes in Sg's post-Inferno dramas. From *Till Damaskus* to *Gustav III* its main function seems to be to frighten, sometimes even physically to torment, the protagonist into penitence and pilgrimage. In the Chamber Plays and those written after them, it becomes a beguiling escape from the tribulations of life. Ekman explores Sg's virtuoso treatment of the theme in *Inferno*, *Till Damaskus*, *Brott och brott*, *Folkungasagan*, *Gustav Adolf*, *Ett drömspel*, the Chamber Plays, and *Stora landsvägen*, with an emphasis on its visual representation on stage]

[D2:608] Ekman, Hans-Göran, 'La Magie des vêtements', Traduit du suédois par Régis Boyer, *Europe* (Paris), No. 858 (October 2000), pp. 107-119. ['The Magic of Clothes'. Describes the magic properties that Sg invested in clothes. Summarises the arguments of **D2:83**, with examples drawn from *Herr Bengts hustru*, *Fadren*, *Fröken Julie*, *Brott och brott*, *Svanevit*, and *Ett drömspel*]

[D2:609] Ekman, Hans-Göran, 'Strindbergova postinfernální dramatická tvorba', in August Strindberg, *Hry II*, Edice Divadelní hry 6, Praha: Divadelní ústav, 2004, pp. 559-567. ['Strindberg's Post-Inferno Dramas', Translated by Zbyněk Černík. The Afterword to Volume Two of a Czech edition of Sg's plays, translated by Zbyněk Černík (*Dödsdansen I and II, Påsk, Oväder, Spöksonaten* and *Toten-Insel*), František Fröhlich (*Till Damaskus I and II*), Azita Haidarová (*Ett drömspel*), and Dagmar Hartlová (*Holländaren, Brända tomten, Pelikanen*). Ekman clarifies the relevance of Sg's intellectual and emotional crisis in the mid-1890s for the innovatory form of drama he produced in *Till Damaskus, Ett drömspel*, and the Chamber Plays, and stresses their structural originality and visual qualities. *Spöksonaten* is Sg's most original play, not least because it is unique among them in being extremely difficult to interpret]

[D2:610] Ekman, Hans-Göran, 'Strindberg's Use of Costume in *Carl XII* and *Kristina*', in Birgitta Steene, ed., **B1:434**, *Strindberg and History*, pp. 165-175. Illus. [Indicates how costume in Sg's history plays has functions other than to provide local colour or to locate the action to a particular time and place. As in his drama generally, clothes have a symbolic import and an emblematic role in advancing the moral and psychological conflicts of the plays. At times fetishistic and erotic, as in *Fröken Julie* and *En dåres försvarstal*, they indicate shifts in gender role play and figure in the motif of unmasking, or disrobing, that is a recurring theme throughout Sg's career]

[D2:611] Ekman, Hans-Göran, 'Teatermannen', in Margareta Brundin, red., **B1:86**, *August Strindberg. Diktare som mångfrestare*, pp. 56-58. Illus. pp. 59-62. ['The Man of the Theatre'. A comment on Sg's involvement with the practicalities of theatre as manager of the Intimate Theatre, which prompted the ideas about acting and stagecraft recorded in his Memoranda to its members]

[D2:612] Ellehauge, Martin, 'Ekko fra Strindberg i Verdensteatret', *Edda* (Oslo), 31 (1931), 313-327. ['Echoes of Strindberg in World Theatre'. Examines the influence of Sg's dramas on world theatre, including the plays of Wedekind, O'Neill, Shaw, Schnitzler, and Sudzuki. Ellehauge identifies three main themes in his work: the conflict between the sexes, an everlasting struggle between religion and materialism, and, in history plays like *Folkungasagan* and *Erik XIV*, the principles of nationality and humanity]

[D2:613] Elers-Jarleman, Agneta, 'Varför Strindberg?', in Anita Persson and Barbara Lide, red., **B1:366**, *Ja, må han leva!*, pp. 71-80. ['Why Strindberg?' On the author's stagings of several of Sg's plays. His attraction lies in his circular, rather than linear, dramaturgy, his childishness, and the musical way in which his themes repeat themselves]

[**D2:614**] Elsberga, Solveiga, in Augusts Strindbergs, *Tevs, Naves deja*, no zviedru valodos tulkojusi Solveiga Elsberga, Riga: Daugava, 1996. Illus. 224 pp. [A Latvian edition of *Fadren* and *Dödsdansen*, edited and translated by Elsberga]

[**D2:615**] Em. F., 'Strindberg', *Social-Demokraten* (Stockholm), 18 October 1910. [Discusses the Fifth of Sg's *Memorandum till Medlemmarne av Intima Teatern*, attacking August Brunius's critical remarks in **D2:356**]

[**D2:616**] Ephra, Minni, 'Die Frauen in Strindbergs Dramen', *Die Deutsche Bühne* (Berlin), 6:48 (1914), 595-597. ['Women in Strindberg's Dramas'. Discusses the representation of women in Sg's naturalistic plays]

[**D2:617**] Erdmann, Nils, '*Samlade otryckta skrifter. Del 1. Dramatiska arbeten*', *Nya Dagligt Allehanda* (Stockholm), 8 December 1918. [Reviews the plays and dramatic fragments published in Volume One of Vilhelm Carlheim-Gyllensköld's edition of Sg's collected unpublished works]

[**D2:618**] Erdmann, Nils, '*Strindberg och teater*', 1-3, *Nya Dagligt Allehanda* (Stockholm), 16, 19, and 20 January 1919. [Discusses Sg's ideas about the theatre apropos August Falck's recently published edition of Sg's letters and his memoranda to members of the Intimate Theatre]

[**D2:619**] Erdmann, Nils, 'Strindbergsdramer', *Nya Dagligt Allehanda* (Stockholm), 23 February 1909. ['Strindberg's Dramas']

[**D2:620**] Erichsen, Svend, 'Fra Strindberg til de absurde', *Aktuelt* (Copenhagen), 14 May 1962. ['From Strindberg to the Absurd'. Recognises in Sg a significant precursor of the theatre of the absurd]

[**D2:621**] Erichsen, Svend, 'Strindberg och teatret', *Social-Demokraten* (Copenhagen), 22 January 1949. ['Strindberg and the Theatre']

[**D2:622**] Erickson, Jon, 'The *Mise en Scène* of the Non-Euclidean Character: Wellman, Jenkin and Strindberg', *Modern Drama* (Toronto), 41:3 (1998), 355-370. [On the difficulties of characterisation and inter-personal contact in theatrical situations that may elude our spatial and temporal grasp, and where obstacles have been placed in the way of communication, with reference to *Fröken Julie* and *Ett drömspel*]

[**D2:623**] Eustachiewicz, Lesław, 'Strindberga gra snów i koszmarów', *Dialog* (Warsaw), 1963:11, pp. 71-74. ['Strindberg's Dream and Nightmare Plays'. Discusses the development of Sg's dreamplay technique from *Fadren* which, unlike a conventional naturalistic drama, could be performed on a bare stage, to the almost operatic qualities of *Ett drömspel* and *Spöksonaten*. Concerned primarily with the latter]

[**D2:624**] Evelein, Johannes F., 'Drama Turning Inward: Strindberg's Station Play and its Expressionist Continuum', *TijdSchrift voor Skandinavistiek* (Groningen), 19:1 (1998), 163-184. [Essentially an essay-length resumé of the thesis presented in **D2:101**, *August Strindberg und das expressionistische Stationendrama: eine Formstudie*]

[**D2:625**] Even-Zohar, Itamar, 'Ha-zman shel ha-drama, izuvo u-bituyo be-*Ha-av* u-be-*Mahaze halom* le-August Strindberg', *Ha-sifrut* (Tel Aviv), 1:3-4 (1969), pp. 538-568, 770-771. ['Correlative Positive and Correlative Negative: Time in August Strindberg's *The Father* and *A Dream Play*'. Examines the patterning of time in Sg's plays with reference to European theories of time and a definition of dramatic time which assumes that there is a correlation between the time of presentation and presented time in the action of a play. English summary]

[D2:626] Everard, William R., 'August Strindberg: Staging a Broken Dream', in *The First Moderns: Profiles in the Origins of Twentieth-Century Thought*, Chicago and London: University of Chicago Press, 1997, pp. 251-264. [An anecdotal and banal outline of Sg's career, which focuses entirely on the plays. Stresses his modernity]

[D2:627] Ewbank, Inga-Stina, 'The Intimate Theatre: Shakespeare Teaches Strindberg Theatrical Modernism', *Theatre Journal* (Baltimore), 50:2 (1998), 165-174. [Considers how Sg learnt from Shakespeare to be his own contemporary, thus replacing an outworn naturalism with modern(ist) dramatic forms and modes of theatrical expression. Shakespeare was central to Sg's thinking about drama and theatre in his Intimate Theatre years and helped him develop his own ideas that were in turn crucial to international modernist developments. Sg knew Shakespeare in Hagberg's translations, and read him biographically, in keeping with much contemporary criticism (e.g. Edward Dowden). He followed the contemporary experiments in staging his plays by Jocza Savits at the Munich 'Shakespearebühne', but was sceptical of Edward Gordon Craig's ideas. The drapery stage he used for the première of *Kristina* at the Intimate Theatre pursued ideas derived from Savits, and in Shakespeare he also found confirmation both for a form of staging which reflects the sense that identity is not something given but something searched for and maybe never found, and (in *Hamlet*) an appreciation that so-called inconsistent characters on stage are in fact only being represented, Picasso-like, from different sides, as inconsistent, self-contradictory, fragmented, and forever fragmenting, conflicting, and ultimately unfathomable]

[D2:628] Felner, Karl von, 'August Strindbergs Dramaturgie', *Der Merker* (Vienna), 8 (1917), 722-727. ['August Strindberg's Dramaturgy']

[D2:629] 'Femo' [Otto Groothoff], 'Strindbergs försöksteater i Köpenhamn och Malmö. Några plock ur gamla kollegor', *Maj. Skånejournalisternas vårtidning*, 1921, pp. 19-21. ['Strindberg's Experimental Theatre in Copenhagen and Malmö'. Presents a selection of early critical responses to performances of Sg's naturalistic plays performed by his Scandinavian Experimental Theatre in Copenhagen and on tour to Malmö in 1889]

[D2:630] Fischer, Hans, 'Neue Dramen von August Strindberg', *Die christliche Welt* (Marburg), 16 (1902), Sp. 225-229. ['New Plays by August Strindberg'. Examines the Christian elements in Sg's recent plays *Påsk*, *Gustav Vasa*, and *Gustav Adolf*]

[D2:631] Fischer, Heinrich, 'Briefe ans Intime Theater', *Die Weltbühne* (Berlin), 19:1 (1923), p. 344. ['Letters to the Intimate Theatre'. Reviews the German translation of Sg's *Memorandum till Medlemmarne av Intima Teatern*]

[D2:632] Fischer, Lotte, 'Der Dramatiker Strindberg', *Osten* (Breslau), 43:11-12 (1917), pp. 14-15. ['Strindberg the Dramatist']

[D2:633] Fleury, René [Pseudonym of Lucien Muhlfeld], 'Un Théâtre Libre scandinave', *Revue d'Art Dramatique* (Paris), 15 (15 September 1889), 361-368. [Reports that Sg, who is the only dramatist of note in Sweden, has just founded an experimental theatre in Copenhagen. He is a true naturalist, seemingly inspired by the Médan School, and his three tragedies (*Fadren*, *Fröken Julie*, and *Fordringsägare*, in which one encounters 'something of the fear of being') exemplify a more daring kind of naturalism and are thus material for Antoine's Théâtre Libre. Fleury quotes Zola's letter to Sg which the latter used as a Preface to the French edition of *Fadren* and summarises both this play and *Fordringsägare* at some length. He observes that *Fröken Julie* is thought by its author to be his best work; it is thoroughgoing in its naturalism and no actress in Scandinavia will play the title role, which is why it was performed by the author's wife. Fleury includes an extract in order to give the reader an idea of this singularly powerful drama, and praises Sg's psychology at the expense of Zola and his school]

[D2:634] Fogelqvist, T[orsten], '*Samlade otryckta skrifter. Del 1. Dramatiska arbeten*', *Afton-Tidningen* (Stockholm), 15 December 1918. [Reviews the plays and dramatic fragments published in Volume One of Vilhelm Carlheim-Gyllensköld's edition of Sg's collected unpublished works]

[D2:635] Fors, Hans, 'Med Strindberg genom medeltiden', *Hufvudstadsbladet* (Helsingfors), 29 October 1972. ['With Strindberg through the Middle Ages'. Introduces Sg's history plays apropos their performance on Finnish radio]

[D2:636] Fraenkel, Pavel, 'August Strindberg og verdensdramatikkens utviklingshistorie, 1912-14 mai 1962: Et teaterhistorisk perspektiv', *Samtiden* (Oslo), 71 (1962), 280-296. ['August Strindberg and the Development of World Drama, 1912 to 14 May 1962: From the Perspective of Theatre History'. Surveys Sg's impact on the development of modern drama on the 50th anniversary of his death. His major contribution is in the psychological sphere, where he dissolves Ibsen's conflict-ridden individuals into fluid, multiple personalities and somnambulistic pilgrims, who anticipate the characters of Kafka and Joyce. The power struggle between these characters is conducted in a thematically organised language that resembles music, much of which takes the form of an inner monologue. His influence on 20th-Century European drama is evident in terms of technique and composition, but more important than his ideas or view of life is his understanding of what the function of drama can be in a fragmented society]

[D2:637] Franck, Hans, 'August Strindberg', *Bühne und Volk* (Leipzig), 1:4 (1919-20), pp. 138-149. [Largely a sketch of Sg's life conducted in terms of the plays]

[D2:638] Franck, Hans, 'August Strindberg', *Dramaturgische Blätter* (Meiningen), 2 (1920-21), 86-95.

[D2:639] Franck, Hans, 'August Strindberg', *Masken* (Düsseldorf), 11 (1915-16), 291-306.

[D2:640] Freeberg, Debra L., 'Fem generationer Dramatenskådespelerskor talar om Strindberg', Översättning Kerstin Trowbridge, in Anita Persson and Barbara Lide, red., **B1:366**, *Ja, må han leva!*, pp. 185-203. ['Five Generations of Actresses at Dramaten Talk about Strindberg'. Includes reflections on performing in Sg's plays by the Swedish actresses Anita Björck, Sif Ruud, Marie Göranzon, and Stina Ekblad]

[D2:641] Freedman, Morris, 'Strindberg's Positive Nihilism', *Drama Survey* (Minneapolis), 2:3 (1963), 288-296. [Examines *Fadren*, *Fröken Julie*, and *Ett drömspel* in order to demonstrate that Sg's characters develop from those who are 'unable to bear the requirements of reality' to those who can bind their nature and accept resignation. This development represents a progression in his work from destructive despair to positive nihilism]

[D2:642] Freedman, Morris, ed., 'Strindberg's Positive Nihilism', in *Essays in the Modern Drama*, Boston: Heath, 1964, pp. 56-63. [Rpr. of **D2:641**]

[D2:643] F[ritz], G[ottlieb], '*Die Nachtigall von Wittenberg; Totentanz*', *Blätter für Volksbibliotheken* (Leipzig), 8 (1907), p. 108. [Introduces *Dödsdansen* and *Näktergalen i Wittenberg* to a German readership]

[D2:644] Fröding, Gustaf, '*Dramatik*', *Karlstadstidningen*, 14 October 1893. [A mainly descriptive review of *Debet och kredit*, *Första varningen*, *Moderskärlek*, and *Inför döden* on publication]

[D2:645] Fröding, Gustaf, 'Strindbergs dramatik', in *Samlade Skrifter*, Vol. 9, Stockholm: Albert Bonniers Förlag, 1923, pp. 147-150. [Rpr. of **D2:644**]

[D2:646] Frost, Lucia Dora, 'Strindberg', *Theater und Zeit* (Wuppertal), 8 (1960-61), 44-53.

[D2:647] Fuchs, Robert, 'Vampir statt Pelikanen: Blutsaugerei in Strindbergs Dramen', *Norrøna* (Kiel), 17 (1993), 69-74. ['Vampire, not Pelican. Bloodsucking in Strindberg's Dramas'. On the portrayal of women in Sg's dramas as vampires who suck the blood of their male partners. Fuchs discusses the motif with reference to *Kamraterna*, *Fröken Julie*, *Fordringsägare*, and *Spöksonaten*]

[D2:648] F. V. [Fredrik Vetterlund], '*Samlade otryckta skrifter. Del 1. Dramatiska arbeten*', *Aftonbladet* (Stockholm), 13 December 1918. [Reviews the plays and dramatic fragments published in Volume One of Vilhelm Carlheim-Gyllensköld's edition of Sg's collected unpublished works]

[D2:649] F. Z. K. [Ryszard Marek Groński], '*Drammaty*', *Szpilki* (Warsaw), 1984:34, p. 6. [Reviews Polish translations of *Mäster Olof*, *Kamraterna*, *Påsk*, *Första varningen*, and *Brott och brott*]

[D2:650] Gabrieli, Inselin Maria, 'Strindberg il precursore', *Aion-n. Studi nederlandesi – studi nordici*, Annali dell'Instituto Universtitario Orientale, Napoli, 21 (1978), pp. 279-313. ['Strindberg the Precursor'. Presents Sg as a dramatist via his correspondence and biography. Gabrieli considers Sg's own, sometimes psychotic, lack of balance to be frequently evident in the characters of his plays; his innovative theatrical experiments are undermined by his eclecticism and although his dialogue is often incisive and his characterisation brilliant, even his most achieved work, like *Fadren*, lacks the cathartic power of Greek tragedy and Shakespeare]

[D2:651] Gabrieli, Mario, 'Appunti per uno studio del teatro di Strindberg', *Studi Germanici* (Napoli), 4:3-4 (1940), 255-266. ['Notes for a Study of Strindberg's Theatre']

[D2:652] Gabrieli, Mario, 'Il naturalismo di Strindberg', *Studi Germanici* (Napoli), 3:4-5 (1938), 363-401. ['Strindberg's Naturalism'. Seeks to define the particular qualities of Sg's naturalism]

[D2:653] Gade, Svend, 'Strindberg i Danmark', *Politiken* (Copenhagen), 17 February 1917. ['Strindberg in Denmark'. A comment on the fortunes of Sg's plays in Denmark by the Danish director and designer]

[D2:654] Garrett, George, 'Strindberg, Pioneer of Realism', *Theatre Magazine* (New York), 51 (1930), pp. 38-39, 60-61. [Discusses the establishment of the Anglo-Swedish Literary Fund and the publication of the first volume of an English edition of Sg's plays]

[D2:655] 'Gasparone' [Erik Thyselius], 'Strindberg som dramatiker', *Afton-Tidningen* (Stockholm), 14 May 1912 (Extra-nr.). ['Strindberg as a Dramatist'. Part of a special issue marking Sg's death]

[D2:656] Gassner, John [Waldhorn], 'General Introduction and Prefaces to the Plays', in August Strindberg, *Seven Plays*, Translated by Arvid Paulson, New York: Bantam

Books, 1960, pp. vii-xviii. [An unoriginal introduction which compounds many old clichés regarding what Gassner calls this 'psychopathic Don Quixote of the bedroom'. The volume also includes prefatory comments on *Fadern*, pp. 3-5, *Fröken Julie*, pp. 59-61, *Kamraterna*, pp. 118-119, *Den starkare*, pp. 172-173, *Bandet*, pp. 183-184, *Brott och brott*, pp. 219-221, and *Påsk*, pp. 286-287]

[D2:657] Gassner, John [Waldhorn], 'Strindberg the Expressionist', in August Strindberg, *Eight Expressionist Plays*, Translated and with Prefaces to The Pilgrimage Plays by Arvid Paulson, New York: New York University Press, 1972 [1945], pp. 1-12. [Considers Sg 'the chief originator of the "modernist" drama, if we mean by this term the drama that represents a renewal of imagination after the triumph of 19th-Century realism.' In seeking to come closer than realism could to reality, he developed a new dramatic style, now known as expressionism, but in one respect he remained a 19th-Century man: 'he treasured a beam of optimism in the Cimmerian night of his world picture'. See **B1:91**]

[D2:658] Gassner, John [Waldhorn], 'Strindberg and the Twentieth Century', in *The Theatre in Our Times. A Survey of the Men, Materials and Movements in the Modern Theatre*, New York: Crown Publishers, 1954, pp. 170-176. [Considers that any influence Sg may once have had on the American theatre seems to have evaporated and we shall probably have to cede him to history, where his place as a moulder of modern drama is impregnable. He is antithetical to the American spirit on several grounds and yet, for all his failure to achieve classical outline and wholeness, in his later expressionist plays, as in the more communicable pieces that preceded them, he is a major figure in 20th-Century drama]

[D2:659] Gassner, John [Waldhorn], 'Strindberg, Ibsen and Shaw', in *The Theatre in Our Times. A Survey of the Men, Materials and Movements in the Modern Theatre*, New York: Crown Publishers Inc., 1954, pp. 208-211. [Regards Sg's later experimental plays as intense expressions of personal experience and classics of modern drama, but even in earlier plays like *Fadren* and *Fordringsägare* he falls short of being one of the greatest of playwrights because 'he discharged his feelings directly instead of subjecting them to a process of sublimation']

[D2:660] Gassner, John [Waldhorn], 'Strindberg in America', *Theatre Arts Monthly* (New York), 33:5 (1949), 49-52. Illus. [It is difficult to gauge Sg's stature from a few samples of his work in anthologies and the occasional performance; in fact there are several Sgs, not all of them irrationally anti-feminist and impossibly vindictive. 'There is *Easter*, as tender a play as any play written in modern times. There is the vivid folk-drama *The Bridal Crown*; there are those dream fugues *The Dream Play* and *The Spook Sonata* and those mordant comedies *Comrades* and *There are Crimes and Crimes*. There is that curious trilogy of human error and search for salvation, *To Damascus*; and finally, there are seven or eight plays drawn from Swedish history that make him the greatest writer of historical drama since Shakespeare.... Both by choice and inner compulsion Strindberg became an uncanny exponent of our century. He is the dramatist of our division']

[D2:661] Gassner, John [Waldhorn], 'Strindberg: 1950 Centenary Productions', in *The Theatre in Our Times. A Survey of the Men, Materials and Movements in the Modern Theatre*, New York: Crown Publishers Inc., 1954, pp. 177-181. [Observes that none of the centennial productions of Sg's plays was as satisfying as Elizabeth Sprigge's new biography, **R:2066**, in explaining a neurotic artist who cured himself through his work. With the exception of Eugene O'Neill, 'the American theatre has evinced no understanding or appreciation of Sg's playwriting in any field other than that of naturalistic drama']

[D2:662] Gdowska, Marianna, 'Les pièces de Strindberg dans les theatrales polonais de 1905 à 1983', *Le Théâtre Polonais* (Warsaw), 1984:8-9, pp. 14-15. ['Strindberg's Plays in the Polish Theatre from 1905 to 1983'. English and French parallel texts]

[D2:663] Gerard-Arlberg, Gilles, '*Erik XIV* och *Fröken Julie*', *Svenska Dagbladet* (Stockholm), 1 August 1959. [Reviews Volumes One and Two of Carl Gustaf Bjurström's edition of Sg's plays in French translation, as well as two Swedish student editions of *Erik XIV* and *Fröken Julie*]

[D2:664] Giannini, Clemente, 'Prefazione', in August Strindberg, *Svanevit: saga drammatica, Il sogno: una fantasmagoria*, Milano: Alpes Edizione, 1927. 193 pp. [Introduces an Italian translation of *Svanevit* and *Ett drömspel*]

[D2:665] Gierow, Carl-Olof, 'Strindberg och fransk scen', *Meddelanden från Strindbergssällskapet* (Stockholm), 39 (1967), pp. 11-27. Illus. ['Strindberg and the French Stage'. Considers Sg's knowledge of the French theatre and the impact it had on him, with an account of Sarah Bernhardt's acting style initiated by Sg's comments on her performance as Posthumia in Alexandre Parodi's *Rome vaincue*, and the stress he placed on individuality and naturalness, generally preferring Swedish acting to French. Gierow comments more briefly on the five performances he witnessed in France during his second stay there in the 1880s (during the 1890s he seems not to have attended any) and concludes that Sg took surprisingly little from his direct contacts with French theatre]

[D2:666] Gilman, Richard, 'Strindberg's Invention', *A.R.T. News* (New York), 10:2 (1990), p. iii.

[D2:667] Gitel'man, Lev, 'A. Strindberg i A. Antuan', in L[ev] Gitel'man and V[alentina] Dianova, eds, **B1:148**, *Avgust Strindberg i mirovaia kul'tura. Materialy mezhvyzovskoi nauchnoi konferentsii. Stat'i. Soobshcheniia*, pp. 14-18. [Primarily concerned with Antoine's staging of *Fröken Julie* at the Théâtre Libre in 1893]

[D2:668] G-g N [Georg Nordensvan], 'August Strindberg, *Tryckt och otryckt IV*', *Aftonbladet* (Stockholm), 29 April 1897. [Reviews *Leka med elden* negatively and *Bandet* more positively on publication. In the former the way in which the characters bare their feelings in public renders them common]

[D2:669] G-g N [Georg Nordensvan], 'Strindbergs tre sagospel', *Dagens Nyheter* (Stockholm), 11 June 1902. ['Strindberg's Three Fairy-Tale Plays'. Reviews *Kronbruden*, *Svanevit*, and *Ett drömspel* on publication. The latter is without doubt the most captivating of the three and one of the most important works of Sg's latest period. *Svanevit* is quite enchanting with its fairy-tale tone, naïveté, and confidence in the victory of young, pure, and unselfish love over evil, but it will certainly prove hard to stage. *Kronbruden* is powerfully atmospheric and is reminiscent of music]

[D2:670] Gnudtzmann, A., 'August Strindberg og Scenen', *Masken* (Düsseldorf), 26 May 1912.

[**D2:671**] Goebel, Heinrich, 'Strindberg und das Theater', *Die Scene* (Berlin), 11:12 (1921), 202-205. ['Strindberg and the Theatre'. An assessment of Sg and August Falck's Intimate Theatre]

[**D2:672**] Goebel, Heinrich, 'Strindberg und das Theater', *Deutsche Allgemeine Zeitung* (Berlin), 22 September 1920. ['Strindberg and the Theatre']

[**D2:673**] Goebel, Heinrich, 'Strindbergs Repertoire', *Berliner Börsen-Courier,* Beilage, 4 September 1920.

[**D2:674**] Goldfeld, Karl, 'Strindberg und seine Einakter', *Allgemeine Künstlerzeitung* (Berlin), 8 (1918), No. 65-66. ['Strindberg and His One-Acters']

[**D2:675**] [Goldman, Emma], 'The 1914 Mystery Critic: Strindberg from an American Perspective', *Swedish Book Review* (Lampeter), 1986 (Supplement), pp. 3-4. [Reprints extracts from **D1:172**, *The Social Significance of Modern Drama*]

[**D2:676**] Goodman, E., 'Another View Point on Symbolism and Naturalism', *New York Times Book Review*, 1 December 1912. [Reflections based largely on Edwin Björkman's translations of the plays]

[**D2:677**] Górski, Ryszard, 'August Strindberg na scenach polskich', *Program Teatru Ludowego* (Warsaw), 23 November 1957. ['August Strindberg on the Polish Stage'. Programme essay reviewing the performance history of Sg's plays in Poland in conjunction with the first significant post-1945 production of *Fröken Julie* there, directed by Irena Grywińska-Adwentowicz with Krystyna Ciechomska as Julie at the Teatr Ludowy, Mała Scena, Warsaw, 23 November 1957]

[**D2:678**] Gosse, Edmund, 'Strindberg', *The Sunday Times* (London), 30 January 1921. [Comments on Edwin Björkman's translations of the plays. Sg was one of several late 19th-Century geniuses, who were either mad or afflicted with monomania. 'If nations receive the authors they deserve, Sweden ought to feel morally uncomfortable in the possession of the author of the *Inferno*'. Although 'a squalid tale of today', *Dödsdansen* is one of his ablest and most characteristic productions, superior to both *Till Damaskus* and the stupendous, beautifully written, but incoherent *Ett drömspel*]

[**D2:679**] Gosse, Edmund, 'Strindberg', *The Living Age* (London), 26 February 1921, pp. 555-557. [Rpr. of **D2:678**]

[**D2:680**] Grabe, Inga, 'Röster från Strindbergs teater', *Teatervetenskap* (Stockholm), No. 23 (1981), pp. 16-19. ['Voices from Strindberg's Theatre'. Describes sound recordings of Sg's texts by actors from the Intimate Theatre, including the 88-year-old Maria Schildknecht as Miss Julie]

[**D2:681**] Gran, Ulf, 'Strindberg "regissör". En översikt över hans inställning till skådespeleri', in Ulf Gran and Ulla-Britta Lagerroth, red., *Perspectiv på teater*, Stockholm: Rabén & Sjögren, 1971, pp. 31-50. ['Strindberg "Director". An Outline of his Views on Acting'. Provides an overview of Sg's opinions on acting, from his own failure to become an actor himself in the 1870s to his work with the Intimate Theatre. Gran bases his discussion on Sg's correspondence and his comments on acting in the memoranda to members of the Intimate Theatre and elsewhere]

[**D2:682**] Granberg, Nils, *LO-tidningen* (Stockholm), 1989:46, p. 26. [Reviews Volume 61 in *Samlade Verk*, containing *Siste riddaren, Riksföreståndaren*, and *Bjälbo-Jarlen*]

[**D2:683**] Grandinson, Emil, 'En regissör om August Strindberg', *Thalia* (Stockholm), 3:3 (20 January 1912), p. 25. ['A Director on August Strindberg'. Reflections on Sg and the theatre by the eminent Swedish theatre director who staged the première of *Till Damaskus* in 1900]

[D2:684] Gravier, Maurice, 'Introduction', in August Strindberg, *Théâtre cruel et théâtre mystique*, traduit du suèdois par Mlle Diehl, Paris: Gallimard, 1964. pp. 7-32. Illus. [Introduces a useful anthology of Sg's theoretical and critical writings about the theatre in French translation. Discusses his relationship to French naturalism in both theory and practice, and notes the emergence in his later works of a drama that evokes Proust and Bergson as well as German expressionism]

[D2:685] — Lachnitt, J.-C., *La Revue de Paris*, 72:1 (1965), p. 156.

[D2:686] — Poulenard, Elie, *Études Germaniques* (Paris), 20:3 (1965), 468-469.

[D2:687] Gravier, Maurice, 'Harriet Bosse et la théâtre mystique', *Obliques. Littérature-Théâtre* (Paris), 1:1 (1972), 20-21. ['Harriet Bosse and the Mystical Theatre'. Describes Bosse as a catalyst for much of Sg's later theatre, particularly in *Ett drömspel* where Sg had her in mind when creating the character of Indra's Daughter]

[D2:688] Gravier, Maurice, 'The Character and the Soul', in Otto Reinert, ed., **B1:371**, *Strindberg: A Collection of Critical Essays*, pp. 79-89. [English version of Chapter Seven in **D2:128**]

[D2:689] Gravier, Maurice, 'Comment étudier le dialogue de Strindberg?', in Oskar Bandle, Hrsg., **D2:8**, *Strindbergs Dramen im Lichte neuerer Methodendiskussionen*, pp. 1-27. ['How should One Study Strindberg's Dialogue?' Believes that Sg's dialogue may best be approached following his own hint in the Preface to *Fröken Julie* that the dramatist works in the manner of a musical composer, thematically and with repetition, in a medium that combines word with movement. Silence is likewise relevant, as is the indirectly audible interior dialogue which the characters conduct with themselves. Includes two diagrams: (1) detailing the themes and key words of *Herr Bengts hustru*, *Första varningen*, and *Fadren*; (2) outlining the links or breaks in the thematic progression of the first major theme between Jean and Julie in *Fröken Julie*, and linking them with character and theme. Gravier also analyses several exchanges from *Till Damaskus*]

[D2:690] Gravier, Maurice, 'La Dramaturgie de Strindberg', *Les Langues modernes* (Paris), 41 (1947), 156-165. ['Strindberg's Dramaturgy'. Introduces Sg's writings on drama and the theatre, with reference to the Preface to *Fröken Julie*, the essay 'Om modernt drama och modern teater', and the *Memorandum till Medlemmarne av Intima Teatern*, illustrating the discussion with examples from *Fröken Julie*, *Fordringsägare*, *Ett drömspel*, and the Chamber Plays, the last of which Gravier relates to Max Reinhardt's Kleines Theater]

[D2:691] Gravier, Maurice, 'Introduction', in August Strindberg, *Théâtre complet*, 1, Paris: L'Arche, 1982, pp. 7-54. [Introduces the six-volume French edition of Sg's collected plays, translated by Carl Gustaf Bjurström and others. See **D2:494**]

[D2:692] Gravier, Maurice, 'Karaktären och själen', Översättning av Karin Norström, in Gunnar Brandell, red., **B1:82**, *Synpunkter på Strindberg*, Stockholm: Aldus/Bonnier, 1964, pp. 209-221. ['Character and the Soul'. Swedish version of **D2:688**]

[D2:693] Gravier, Maurice, 'Le Théâtre naturaliste de Strindberg. Réalité et poésie', in *Réalisme et poésie au théâtre*, Entretiens d'Arras 5, juin 1958, réunies et présentées par Jean Jacquot, Paris, 1960, pp. 99-117. ['Strindberg's Naturalistic Theatre: Reality and

Poetry'. Focuses primarily on *Kamraterna* and, less fully, on the three plays performed in Paris during the 1890s, *Fadren, Fröken Julie,* and *Fordringsägare*. Contrasts Sg's practice with that of the French naturalists, Alexandre Dumas *fils*, and Ibsen, and comments on several prose works from the 1880s, including *Giftas, Tjänstekvinnans son*, and 'Tschandala'. Gravier draws an interesting comparison between Sg's dramatic technique in *Kamraterna* and Alexandre Dumas *fils*' drama *Le demi-monde* (1855), contrasts his practice in *Fröken Julie* with Molière's, and analyses the psychological poetry of his naturalistic dialogue, but the essay touches only with relative brevity on the later 'poetic' works represented here by *Till Damaskus, Dödsdansen, Ett drömspel,* and *Spöksonaten*]

[D2:694] Gravier, Maurice, 'Les Drames oniriques (Drömspel) de Strindberg et leur représentation en France', in Gunnel Engwall, red., **B1:121**, *Strindberg et La France*, pp. 71-82. ['Strindberg's Dreamplays and their Performance in France'. Discusses Sg's early fortunes in France with productions of his naturalist plays at the Théâtre Libre and the Théâtre de l'Œuvre before establishing that it was in 1921, with *Dödsdansen*, that he made his breakthrough there. Gravier also considers Antonin Artaud's staging of *Ett drömspel* in 1928 and Raymond Rouleau's production of Maurice Clavel's free translation at the Comédie Française in 1970]

[D2:695] Gravier, Maurice, 'Mises en scène de Strindberg', in *La Mise en scène des œuvres du passé*, Études réunies et présentées par Jean Jacquot et André Veinstein, Entretiens d'Arras, 15-18 Juin 1956, Paris: Editions du centre national de la recherche scientifique, 1957, pp. [41]-51. Illus. ['Stage Productions of Strindberg'. Includes discussion of Sg's practical experience of the theatre and his familiarity with the innovatory ideas of Edward Gordon Craig and others, as well as the issues posed in staging both his materialised naturalism and his dematerialised post-Inferno dramaturgy. Notes the directorial achievements of Max Reinhardt and Olof Molander]

[D2:696] Gravier, Maurice, 'Strindberg', *Revue de la société d'histoire de théâtre* (Paris), 7 (1958), 211-212.

[D2:697] Gravier, Maurice, 'Strindberg and the French Drama of His Time', in Göran Stockenström, ed., **D2:288**, *Strindberg's Dramaturgy*, pp. 141-151. [Indicates how Eugene Scribe and the well-made play, including the 'theatre of ideas' of Émile Augier and Alexandre Dumas *fils*, impacted strongly on Scandinavia. Like *A Doll's House*, Sg's first major play with a contemporary setting, *Kamraterna*, is a refinement on their dramatic aesthetics, if not as well-made. Even though Sg knew the work of Zola and Henry Becque, he did not rate their plays highly, and his own major dramas from the 1880s, in each of which he seemed to be creating a new genre, are naturalist in name only. Of these, *Fordringsägare* is a masterpiece of rigour, logic, and economy and, evoking as it does both the dramaturgy of the *pièce bien faite* and the play-within-a-play of vaudeville, it is hardly surprising that it has been much admired in France. Sg kept abreast of developments in the French theatre and recognised his affinity with the dramaturgy of Maeterlinck, but he imitated little of what he had read or seen in Paris. The translation of this essay (by Sarah Bryant-Bertail) contains a number of misleading inadvertencies, e.g. the suggestion that Maupassant and Freud (rather than Charcot) lectured at the Salpêtrière]

[D2:698] Gravier, Maurice, 'Strindberg auteur comique', *Maske und Kothurn* (Vienna), 30:1-2 (1984), 131-139. ['Strindberg as a Writer of Comedy'. Discusses both *Kamraterna* in detail and *Hemsöborna* more briefly as comic dramas. Gravier regards Act One of *Kamraterna* as genuinely comic, but Sg rarely achieves the necessary distance between the writer and his comic subject: 'In Sg's work, the polemicist's vigour and the satirist's sarcasms dominate too easily and distract quickly from the finesses of the truly comic writer']

[D2:699] Gravier, Maurice, 'Strindberg auf der Bühne unserer Zeit', *Maske und Kothurn* (Vienna), 14 (1968), 29-43. ['Strindberg on Today's Stage'. Surveys responses to Sg and productions of his plays in several European countries, including England, France, and Germany. Gravier also identifies a number of departures from the Swedish performing tradition and asks whether Sg's primary text is sacrosanct or adaptable, as well as to what extent it remains specifically Swedish]

[D2:700] Gravier, Maurice, 'Strindberg, dramaturge naturaliste ou poète du cauchemar', *Bref* (Paris), No. 10 (1955). ['Strindberg, Naturalist Playwright or Poet of the Nightmare']

[D2:701] Gravier, Maurice, 'Strindberg et le théâtre naturaliste allemand', *Études Germaniques* (Paris), 2:2 (1947), 201-211. ['Strindberg and the German Naturalist Theatre'. See **D2:128**]

[D2:702] Gravier, Maurice, 'Strindberg et le théâtre naturaliste allemand', *Études Germaniques* (Paris), 2:3 (1947), 334-348. [See **D2:128**]

[D2:703] Gravier, Maurice, 'Strindberg et le théâtre naturaliste allemand. Le problem du mariage', *Études Germaniques* (Paris), 3:1 (1948), 25-36. ['Strindberg and German Naturalist Theatre. The Problem of Marriage'. See **D2:128**]

[D2:704] Gravier, Maurice, 'Strindberg et le théâtre naturaliste allemand. Le femme vampire', *Études Germaniques* (Paris), 3:4 (1948), 383-396. ['Strindberg and German Naturalist Theatre. The Female Vampire'. See **D2:128**]

[D2:705] Gravier, Maurice, 'Strindberg et le théâtre naturaliste allemand: Le meurtre psychique,' *Études Germaniques* (Paris), 4:1 (1949), 13-26. ['Strindberg and German Naturalist Theatre. The Psychic Death'. See **D2:128**]

[D2:706] Grén, Zygmunt, 'Strindberg, *Dramaty królewskie. Dramaty liryczne*', *Życie Literackie* (Kraków), 1988, No. 48, p. 7. [Reviews translations of *Erik XIV, Karl XII, Gustav III, Till Damaskus I, Ett drömspel*, and *Stora landsvägen* by Zygmunt Łanowski, with an introduction by Lech Sokoł]

[D2:707] Greń, Zygmunt, 'Strindberg i my', *Dziennik Polski* (Kraków), 1962, No. 187, pp. 3-4. [Reviews Polish translations of *Mäster Olof, Fadren, Fröken Julie, Ett drömspel*, and *Spöksonaten* by Zygmunt Łanowski]

[D2:708] Grimm, Reinhold, 'Strindbergs Wiederkehr: Notizen zu seiner Wirkungsgeschichte am Beispiel der *Gespenstersonate*', *Jahresring 81-82: Literatur und Kunst der Gegenwart*, Stuttgart: Deutsche Verlags-Anstalt, 1981, pp. 40-47. ['Strindberg's Return. Observations on the History of his Influence as Shown by *The Ghost Sonata*'. Grimm asks if one must always play off Sg against Brecht, as is the custom? Sg was well represented in Brecht's library, and his *Arbeitsjournal* indicates that he was preoccupied with Sg's novels as well as many of the plays. He produced a film script based on *Dödsdansen* and offered to furnish a complete prompt and model book for *Karl XII*. In fact, Sg has had a profound influence on virtually all modern Western drama, and none of the plays has been more influential than *Spöksonaten*. Productions by Otto Falckenberg (1915) and Max Reinhardt (1916) impacted powerfully on Rilke, as well as the younger expressionists, and both Kafka and Kurt Tucholsky responded positively to his work as, in recent years, have Friedrich Dürrenmatt and Peter Weiss. Sg has also had a profound influence on dramatists writing in French, among them Adamov, Beckett, Ionesco, and Ghelderode. The article represents an implicit polemic against the cult of Brecht, whose contribution to the modern theatre is seen here as less significant than Sg's]

[D2:709] Grimm, Reinhold, '*Spöksonaten* and Strindberg's Influence on Modern European Theatre', in Anna K. Kuhn and Barbara D. Wright, eds, *Playing for Stakes: German-Language Drama in Social Context: Essays in Honor of Herbert Lederer*, Oxford / Providence, USA: Berg, 1994, pp. 65-74. [English version of **D2:708**]

[D2:710] Gripenberg, Bertel, 'August Strindberg, *Bjälbojarlen*, *Siste riddaren*, *Riksföreståndaren*', *Finsk Tidskrift* (Åbo), 67:2 (1909), 470-472. [Reviews Sg's last three historical dramas on publication. They testify to his extraordinary creativity; Sg stands alone, without an equal in contemporary literature]

[D2:711] Groothoff, Otto, 'Strindberg på landsortscenen. Kompletterande anteckningar till en nyutkommen Strindbergsbok', *Scenen* (Stockholm), 9 (1923), 192-195. ['Strindberg on the Provincial Stage. Supplementary Information to a Recently Published Book on Strindberg'. Augments Hedvall's study of Sg in the theatre, **D2:136**, with details of productions of his plays outside Stockholm]

[D2:712] Groothoff, Otto, 'Strindbergsteatern', *Sydsvenska Dagbladet* (Malmö), 26 November 1957. ['Strindberg's Theatre'. Marks the 50th anniversary of the founding of the Intimate Theatre by Sg and August Falck]

[D2:713] Groothoff, Otto, 'Strindbergsteatern – ett femtioårsminne', *Studiekamraten* (Tollarp), 39 (1957), 212-216. ['Strindberg's Theatre: A Fifty-Year-Old Memory'. Includes recollections of the Intimate Theatre in performance]

[D2:714] Group Report, 'Performing Strindberg – Problems of Role Interpretation', in Donald Weaver, ed., **D2:331**, *Strindberg on Stage*, pp. 160-166. [Discusses the interpretation of roles in five of today's most frequently performed Sg plays: *Fröken Julie*, *Fadren*, *Kamraterna*, *Ett drömspel*, and *Brott och brott*, drawing attention to the way Sg sometimes turns the stage space into an enlarged ear or evil spirit]

[D2:715] Group Report, 'Stage Design', in Donald Weaver, ed., **D2:331**, *Strindberg on Stage*, pp. 172-175. [Discusses issues raised by Gunilla Palmstierna-Weiss in **E12:221**: 'A Hundred Years after *Miss Julie*']

[D2:716] Group Report, 'Dramaturgy and Ideology I', in Donald Weaver, ed., **D2:331**, *Strindberg on Stage*, pp. 148-155. [Discusses the ideological choices which performing Sg today entails, apropos current productions of *Brott och brott* at Dramaten and *Fadren* at Stockholm's Stadsteater]

[D2:717] Group Report, 'Dramaturgy and Ideology II', in Donald Weaver, ed., **D2:331**, *Strindberg on Stage*, pp. 156-159. [Discusses ideological issues raised in performing Sg today, focusing on current productions of *Brott och brott* at Dramaten and *Fadren* at Stockholm's Stadsteater]

[D2:718] Grumman, P. H., 'August Strindberg (Modern European Dramatists, 5)', *Poet Lore* (Philadelphia), 1913, pp. 42-52.

[D2:719] Gullfoss, Per Henrik, 'August Strindberg og hans dramatik', *Astrologisk forum* (Oslo), 7:1 (1989), pp. 8-9, 15. ['August Strindberg and His Dramas']

[D2:720] Gumpenburg, Hanns von, 'Strindberg in München', *Der Kunstwart* (München), 29:1 (1916-17), 103-104. ['Strindberg in Munich']

[D2:721] G. W. [Georg Witkowski], 'Bühnenwerke', *Zeitschrift für Bücherfreunde* (Leipzig), NF, 12 (1920), Beibl., Sp. 251-253. [Reviews the German edition of Sg's works for the stage, published in 1919]

[D2:722] Hagemann, Carl, 'Strindberg als Dramatiker', *Propyläen* (München), 10 (1912-13), 500-502. ['Strindberg as a Dramatist']

[D2:723] Hagemann, Carl, 'Strindberg als Dramatiker', *Der Stadt-Anzeiger* (Mannheim), 27 (1929), No. 27. ['Strindberg as a Dramatist']

[D2:724] Hagemann, Carl, 'Strindberg als Dramatiker', in *August Strindberg und die deutschen Bühnen*, Zusammengestellt und herausgegeben vom Drei Masken-Verlag, Berlin, 1915, pp. 3-9. ['Strindberg as a Dramatist']

[D2:725] Hamsun, Knut, 'Dramaturg Strindberg', *Die Volksbühne* (Hamburg), 12 (1961-62), 204-205. ['Strindberg the Dramatist']

[D2:726] Hansson, Ola, 'Skandinavische Litteratur', 1-3, *Das Magazin für die Literatur des In- und Auslandes* (Leipzig), 59 (1890), pp. 305-306, 337-338, 404-405. [Includes some of the earliest commentary on *Fröken Julie* and *Fordringsägare* in a continental forum]

[D2:727] Harris, Alan, 'Introduction', in August Strindberg, *Eight Famous Plays*, New York: Charles Scribner's Sons; London: Gerald Duckworth & Co., Ltd., 1949, pp. 7-15. [Provides a perfunctory sketch of Sg's career in order 'to throw a little light on the genesis of certain works in virtue of which he is a name of power to the Western world'. Harris refers only to the dramatic works, except for three of the autobiographical fictions, and shirks the critical challenge his later plays pose, Thus, of *Spöksonaten*, 'it is useless to ask what it "means", and each man must make what he can of it']

[D2:728] Harrison, Austin, 'Strindberg's Plays', *The English Review* (London), No. 13 (1912), pp. 80-97. [One of the best informed, early English-language evaluations of Sg's plays, claiming that '*Erik XIV* is one of the great historical plays of the world', and that, in range, variety, passion, and quality, 'even the most prejudiced mind must fain admit the greatness of his achievement'. Harrison is almost unique among early critics in English in concentrating on the technical originality of Sg's dramaturgy]

[D2:729] Harvey, Anne-Charlotte Hanes, 'Strindbergs scenografi', *Strindbergiana* (Stockholm), 5 (1990), pp. 56-86. Illus. ['Strindberg's Scenography'. Discusses scenographic solutions to the problems of staging Sg's plays, including how he saw his plays with his 'inner eye', both in retrospect, when they were staged, and in his original stage directions. Examples are taken from throughout his dramatic production, but mainly from the post-Inferno period, and in particular from *Oväder*. In each case it is necessary to reconstruct 'the virtual milieu', using both 'Haupt' and 'Neben' texts, paying attention to six elements: significant objects or scenic elements, sound, time of day/year and the weather, scenic image, design, and the progression of scenic images. A detailed, practical, and suggestive approach which builds on Harvey's doctoral thesis (**V:85**: *Strindberg's Symbolic Room: Commanding Form for Set Design in Selected Strindberg Scripts 1887-1907*). Here she concludes that, while Sg insisted that 'In the beginning was the word: Yes, the spoken word is all', a complete understanding of the true meaning of the word demands a close study of the system of scenic signs with which he supports and completes the spoken text]

[D2:730] Hasse, Else, 'Streifzuge durch die dramatische Saisonliteratur', *Die Frau* (Berlin), 11 (1903-04), 79-86. ['A Brief Survey of the Season's Dramatic Literature'. Discusses *Fröken Julie* and *Brott och brott* along with plays by other dramatists currently being performed in Germany]

[D2:731] Hatvany, Ludwig, 'Der Sechziger Strindberg', *Pan* (Berlin), 1 (1910-11), 235-240. ['The Sexagenarian Strindberg'. Discusses the Chamber Plays of 1907 (primarily *Spöksonaten* and *Pelikanen*), which are concerned with 'the tragedy of family houses']

[D2:732] Hatvany, Ludwig, 'Der Sechziger Strindberg', in Hans-Peter Bayerdörfer, Hrsg., **B3:85**, *Strindberg auf der deutschen Bühne*, pp. 185-190. [Rpr. of **D2:731**]

[D2:733] Hatvany, Paul, 'Strindbergs historische Dramen', *Der Merker* (Vienna), 6 (1915), 378-382. ['Strindberg's Historical Dramas']

[D2:734] Haugen, Einar I., 'Strindberg the Regenerated: A Study of the Moral Personality in a Group of his Later Plays', *Journal of English and Germanic Philology* (Urbana, Illinois), 29 (1930), 257-270. [Maintains that Sg's later plays portray the inevitability of sin and human suffering in personal relationships as well as the redemption of the sin and hatred of Sg's earlier dramatic world by Christian charity, humility, and resignation. Sg is 'a man who did not passively accept, but achieved Christianity; and who after a life of struggle against his exaggerated sensibilities found in its gospel of love the only balm which could minister to a mind diseased.' In arguing his thesis, Haugen focuses primarily on *Till Damaskus III*, *Påsk*, and *Spöksonaten*]

[D2:735] Hauptman, Ira, 'Strindberg's Realistic Plays', *Yale Theatre* (New Haven, Conn.), 5:3 (1974), 87-94. [Compared with *A Doll's House*, there is no real dialectic with opposite truths in *Fadren* and *Fröken Julie*. Such plays possess a ritualistic power which makes Sg's realism more assertive and less exploratory than Ibsen's. But in them there is a progressive shrinking of the dramatic universe: placed in generalised settings, the characters have 'nothing objective over which to fight, and no sense of an objectified society in which victory can have more than purely personal implications'. Ultimately, it is a universe that Sg will be able to carry around entirely inside his own head]

[D2:736] Hedberg, Tor, 'Litteratur', *Svenska Dagbladet* (Stockholm), 10 June 1902. [A largely positive review of *Kronbruden*, *Svanevit*, and *Ett drömspel* on publication. The latter, in which Sg has succeeded in imitating the confusing, disconnected, but so natural life of the dreamer, is the strangest and most remarkable of the three. It is one of his most original works and should make a strange and powerful effect in performance. *Kronbruden* has its *longeurs* but with its often delightful fairy-tale tone and atmosphere, and a dialogue full of poetry, imagination, and playfulness, the Maeterlinckian *Svanevit* comes from the hand of a master – a Sunday-child of poetry and Swedish Aladdin, whom the spirit is always ready to serve, even if he himself is not always willing to polish his lamp]

[D2:737] Hedberg, Tor, '*Kronbruden, Svanehvit, Drömspelet*', in **B1:167**, *Ett decenium, I: Litteratur*, pp. 15-21. [Rpr. of **D2:736**]

[D2:738] Hedvall, Yngve, 'Strindberg på scenen under 10 år. En översikt med anledning av tioårsminnet av vår främste dramatikers död', *Stockholms-Tidningen*, 7 May 1922. ['Ten Years of Strindberg in the Theatre. A Survey in Respect of the Tenth Anniversary of

Our Foremost Dramatist's Death'. A survey of the fortunes of Sg's plays on the Swedish stage during the ten years since his death]

[D2:739] Hedvall, Yngve, 'Strindberg på våra teatrar', *Stockholms Dagblad*, 14 May 1917. ['Strindberg in Our Theatres'. On the repertoire of plays by Sg performed on the Stockholm stage]

[D2:740] Held, Berthold, 'Zum Problem der Strindberg-Regie', *Die Scene* (Berlin), 11:2-3 (1921), 38-40. ['On the Problem of Directing Strindberg']

[D2:741] Henderson, Archibald, 'August Strindberg: Universalist', *South Atlantic Quarterly* (Durham, North Carolina), 13:1 (1914), 28-42. [Reviews translations of thirteen plays by Edwin Björkman, Nelly Erichsen, Velma Swanston Howard, Edith and Warner Oland, and Charles Recht]

[D2:742] Hennings, Lennart, 'Strindberg, *Tryckt och otryckt*', *Upsala Nya Tidning*, 8 May 1897. [Reviews *Bandet* and *Leka med elden* on publication. Singles out Sg's language in the former for special praise]

[D2:743] [Henry, A. S.], 'Strindberg, *Plays*', *The Bookman* (New York), 37 (June 1913), p. 371. [Contains factually inaccurate comments on new translations of *Kamraterna*, *Inför döden*, *Paria*, and *Påsk*, which Henry insists are all 'based on Sg's own experiences']

[D2:744] Hering, Gerhard F., 'Das Datum: 26. 11. 1907. Strindbergs "Intimes Theater" in Stockholm eröffnet', *Theater heute* (Hannover), 6:2 (1965), 26-27. [On the opening of Sg's Intimate Theatre on 26 November 1907 and its significance for the development of modern drama]

[D2:745] Herzog, Wilhelm, 'August Strindbeg und unserer Zeit', *Das Forum* (München), 1 (1914), 65-69. ['August Strindberg and Our Time'. Reflects on the stylistic variety of Sg's plays in the wake of recent productions of *Svanevit*, *Kronbruden*, *Oväder*, *Till Damaskus I*, and *Pelikanen* in Berlin]

[D2:746] H. H., '*Comrades, Facing Death, Easter, Pariah*', *New York Times*, 27 April 1913. [Reviews Werner Oland's translations of the four plays]

[D2:747] Hjärne, Harald, 'Nysvenska historiedramer', in *Blandade spörsmål*, Stockholm: Albert Bonniers Förlag, 1903, pp. 317-327. ['New Swedish History Plays'. Rpr. of **D2:748**]

[D2:748] Hjärne, Harald, 'Strindbergs historiska skådespel', *Svenska Dagbladet* (Stockholm), 15 November 1900. ['Strindberg's History Plays'. Discussion of Sg as a historical dramatist in *Folkungasagan*, *Gustav Vasa*, *Erik XIV*, and *Gustav Adolf*, by an eminent Swedish professor of history who considers it might be interesting to see what happens to the ('true') historical material when it falls into the hands of a 'lost' (förtappat) genius like Sg, with little respect for established traditions. While he may not have set out to desecrate the nation's dearest memories, Sg has distorted many of the historical figures whom he has portrayed and the plays contain numerous anachronisms. But historical inaccuracies are not in themselves fatal. What condemns these plays is that their protagonists are not portrayed as statesmen, but rather merely as individuals, preoccupied by their own private problems. Hence they are concerned only in name with Sweden's kings. Sg's poetic imagination is unpolitical and asocial, and these figures who dwell in the realm of private and subjective feeling, all talk about politics like amateurs, as of something strange to them. Hjärne also compares Sg as a person with his fellow revolutionaries and supermen, Tolstoi, Ibsen, and Nietzsche]

[D2:749] Hj. Sdg [Hjalmar Sandberg], '*Dramatik*', *Svenska Dagbladet* (Stockholm), 21 October 1893. [Reviews *Debet och kredit*, *Första varningen*, *Moderskärlek*, and *Inför döden* on publication, preferring the latter in which 'the nine scenes are charged with a dramatic life of which no other of our writers for the stage is capable, to the same degree as Sg']

[D2:750] Hoedt, P. J. d', 'Strindberg', *De Zaaier* (Sammelsdijk), 3 (1909), p. 92. [Presents Sg as No. 9 in a series of articles on modern dramatists]

[D2:751] Holm, Erich [Pseudonym of Mathilde Präger], 'Drei Ehedramen von August Strindberg', *Die Gegenwart* (Berlin), 41 (1892), 309-313. ['Three Marriage Dramas by August Strindberg'. Considers *Fadren*, *Kamraterna*, and *Fordringsägare* as plays about the institution of marriage. By one of Sg's earliest German translators with whom he corresponded between 1885 and 1895]

[D2:752] Holm, Erich [Pseudonym of Mathilde Präger], 'Strindbergfeier am Josefstädter-theater', *Die Wage* (Vienna), 15:1 (1912), 83-84.

[D2:753] Holm, Ingvar, 'Strindberg and the Theatre', in John M. Weinstock and Robert T. Rovinsky, eds, *The Hero in Scandinavian Literature. From Peer Gynt to the Present*, Austin and London: University of Texas Press, 1975, pp. 145-155. Illus. [Considers the stylistic features in Sg's plays which relate them to expressionism, paying some attention in a loosely argued essay to the different ways in which Sg has been performed in Germany and Sweden]

[D2:754] Entry cancelled.

[D2:755] Holmqvist, Bengt, 'August Strindberg, *Théâtre*', *Dagens Nyheter* (Stockholm), 9 March 1959. [Reviews Volumes One and Two in C. G. Bjurström's French edition of Sg's collected plays. See **D2:494** and **D2:495**]

[D2:756] Holmström, Kirsten Gram, 'Teatermannen', in Folke Ollson, red., **B1:348**, *Strindberg*, pp. 50-55. Illus. ['The Man of the Theatre'. Rather than re-examine the extent of Sg's knowledge of the contemporary theatrical avant-garde, Holmström seeks an answer to the question, 'How well was Sg acquainted with the artistic, technical, and administrative basis of the 'everyday' theatre of the time?' with reference to his work with the Intimate Theatre where (as regards *Till Damaskus* and *Ett drömspel*), he was caught between the production techniques of Baroque theatre and the just emerging methods of theatrical 'dematerialisation', advocated by Edward Gordon Craig and others]

[D2:757] 'Homo Novus' [A. P. Kugel], 'Strindberg', *Teatr i iskusstvo* (St Petersburg), 1912:19 (6 May 1912), pp. 402-404. [An assessment of Sg's career as a dramatist in the shape of an obituary. E.851]

[D2:758] Hood, Arthur, '"Plant Nettles, or Sow Lettuce". Strindberg, Chekhov and Others', *Poetry Review* (London), 30 January 1930, pp. 196-200. [Reviews Volume Four of the Anglo-Scandinavian Literary Foundation series of translations of Sg's plays, containing *Lycko-Pers resa*, *Bandet*, *Fröken Julie*, and *Fadren*: 'We should have preferred to see [the Captain] free himself of that abominable strait-waistcoat and rise up and thrash Laura until she sued for mercy!']

[D2:759] Hoogland, Claes, 'How to Produce Strindberg?', *World Theatre-Le Théâtre dans le monde* (Bruxelles), 11:1 (1962), 67-79. Illus. [On the emergence of a performance tradition for Sg in Sweden, originating in the work of Olof Molander and variously continued by Alf Sjöberg, Ingmar Bergman, Per Axel Branner, Rune Carlsten, and Bengt Ekerot. Text in both English and French]

[D2:760] Höök, Erik, '"Rädda Dig i tid på utlandet! Du har ju Freie Bühne i Berlin!"', *Strindberg i Berlin*, Strindbergsmuseet, Stockholm, 1998, pp. 13-20. Illus. ['"Save Your Self in Time by going Abroad! After all, You have the Freie Bühne in Berlin!"' Charts Sg's fortunes in the Berlin theatre, from *Fadern* at the Freie Bühne in 1890 to *Gustav III* at the Theater in der Königgrätzerstraße in 1927. Concentrates mainly on productions by Max Reinhardt, Victor Barnowsky, and Rudolf Bernauer]

[D2:761] Horch, Franz, 'Zu Strindbergs historischen Bühnendichtungen', *Die Scene* (Berlin), 11:2-3 (1921), 46-47. ['On Strindberg's History Plays']

[D2:762] Horsnell, Horace, 'Unhappy Strindberg', *Outlook* (London), 60 (July 1927), p. 19.

[D2:763] H. S-r, 'Strindberg', *Vårt Land* (Stockholm), 22 August 1908. [Reviews Sg's *Memorandum till Medlemmarne av Intima Teatern*]

[D2:764] Humpál, Martin, 'Koneãnû Strindberg', *Tvar* (Prague), 12:6 (22 March 2001), pp. 21-22. [Reviews Volume One of a Czech edition of Sg's plays. See **D2:1028**]

[D2:765] Huneker, James [Gibbons], 'August Strindberg and His Plays', *Theatre Magazine* (New York), 5 (1905), 89ff.

[D2:766] Huneker, James Gibbons], 'August Strindberg, the Swedish Dramatist', *New York Sun*, 8 March 1903. [The earliest significant North-American notice of Sg as a dramatist whose play, *Fröken Julie*, is 'an emotional bombshell' and displays 'the writer's deep, almost abysmal knowledge of human nature']

[D2:767] Huneker, James [Gibbons], 'Sueden no gesakusha August Strindberg', Translated by Osanai Kaoru, *Shinshōsetsu*, 1906:2. [Japanese translation of Chapter Two of *Iconoclasts*, **D1:203**. The first published notice of Sg's work in Japan]

[D2:768] Ihering, Herbert, 'Strindbergs dramaturgi', *Die Schaubühne* (Berlin), 8:2 (1912), 465-466. ['Strindberg's Dramaturgy']

[D2:769] Isaksson, Curt, 'Strindberg gör entré', *Teatervetenskap* (Stockholm), No. 23 (1981), 29-32. ['Strindberg makes his Entrance'. Considers the relevance for his development as a dramatist of Sg's experience as an apprentice actor at Dramaten where he had a small role in Bjørnstjerne Bjørnson's *Maria Stuart* in 1869]

[D2:770] Iwaszkiewicz, Jarosław, '*Dramaty*', *Życie Warszawy* (Warsaw), 1962, No. 227, p. 4. [Reviews translations of *Mäster Olof*, *Fadren*, *Fröken Julie*, *Ett drömspel*, and *Spöksonaten* by Zygmunt Łanowski]

[D2:771] Jacob, Heinrich Eduard, 'Strindberg, der Angreifer', *Blätter des Deutschen Theaters* (Berlin), 3 (1913-14), 753-755. ['Strindberg the Assailant']

[D2:772] Jacobbi, Ruggero, 'Discendiamo tutti dalla costola di Strindberg', *Il Dramma* (Rome), 1969:6. ['We all Descend from Strindberg's Rib'. On Sg as fhe fount of modern theatre]

[D2:773] Jacobs, Barry, 'Introduction', in *Strindberg's One-Act Plays*, Translated by Arvid Paulson, New York: Simon and Schuster, 1969, pp. vii-xxxii. [An informative introduction, dividing Sg's playwriting into five periods and tracing his abiding interest in a concentrated one-act form of drama, which ranges from the *quart d'heure* plays of the later 1880s to the approximately ninety minutes which *Fröken Julie* and *Pelikanen* take to perform, Jacobs relates Sg's theatre to contemporary developments in France

(Antoine, Brunetière, Maeterlinck) and argues that, although he created fine roles for actors, he 'really wrote for directors']

[D2:774] Jacobs, Barry, 'Strindberg and the Myth of the Androgyne: Christ Figures in *Påsk* and *The Bridal Crown*', in Kela Kvam, ed., **D2:158**, *Strindberg's Post-Inferno Plays*, pp. 92-105. [Both plays reveal that the myth of the androgyne occupies a central position in Sg's thought around the turn of the century, when he was also concerned with the moral significance and redemptive power of suffering. 'Though Elis (in *Påsk*) falsely identifies himself with Christ, Eleonora is truly Christ-like. Kersti [in *Kronbruden*] represents Sg's attempt to integrate these two figures. If Eleonora is innocence singing a song of experience, Kersti is experience singing a song of innocence']

[D2:775] Jacobs, Barry, 'Strindberg's *Advent* and *Brott och brott*: *Sagospel* and Comedy in a Higher Court', in Michael Robinson, ed., **B1:373**, *Strindberg and Genre*, pp. 167-187. [Examines the importance of the *féerie*, or fairy-tale play, for Sg's post-Inferno dramaturgy. It is closely related to the idea of the 'Nemesis' play, which is represented in its Coleridgean form by *Advent* and its Wordsworthian guise by *Brott och brott*, both of which are analysed at length. Jacobs also discusses *Lycko-Pers resa* and the influence on Sg of both Hans Christian Andersen and Rudyard Kipling]

[D2:776] Jacobs, Barry, 'Strindberg's *Advent* and *Brott och brott*: *Sagospel* and Comedy in a Higher Court', in Janet Witalec, ed., **D2:348**, *Drama Criticism*, Volume 18, pp. 175-186. [Rpr. of **D2:775**]

[D2:777] Jacobs, Barry, 'Strindberg and the Dramatic Tableau: *Master Olof* and *Charles the Twelfth*', *Scandinavica* (Norwich), 43:1 (2004), 53-95. [Studies Sg's history plays where his occasional use of the term 'tablå' (tableau) sets him apart from other dramatists of the period as regards post-Diderot pictorial drama and Sg's own painterly interests and practice. Georg von Rosen's painting 'Erik XIV and Karin Månsdotter' about which Sg had written critically in *Stockholms Aftonpost* in 1872. It failure to achieve the complex narrative energy of drama, something he realises in his own best work, as Jacobs's analysis of *Mäster Olof* sets out to confirm. With the Inferno crisis, when Sg was convinced that the visible world is interpenetrated by an invisible one peopled with good and evil, or corrective, spirits, he came to experience works of pictorial art in a different way, and to 'distort familiar [literary] genres almost beyond recognition', as is the case with *Karl XII*. There, the scenic elements do not simply create an appropriate historical atmosphere but become pointers to the world beyond. It is best understood as what Sg called a 'Nemesis play' like *Advent* with a metaphysical dimension that draws upon elements of his dream play technique. This explains the incomprehension with which it was greeted by contemporary critics and the conventional nature of Sg's next history play, *Gustav III*, in which he abandons the metaphysical dimension of *Karl XII* in favour of the traditional Scribean conspiracy play]

[D2:778] Jacobsen, Harry, 'Den skandinaviske Forsøgsteaters Historie', in **R:1044**, *Strindberg i Firsernes Köbenhavn*, pp. 79-164. ['The History of the Scandinavian Experimental Theatre'. For its period a well-documented account of Sg's attempt to set up an experimental theatre in Copenhagen on the lines of Antoine's Théâtre Libre, the reception it received in the Danish press, and the sometimes farcical events surrounding its personnel's attempts at staging *Fröken Julie*, *Den starkare*, and *Fordringsägare*]

[D2:779] Jacobsohn, Siegfried, 'Strindberg i Tyskland', *Thalia* (Stockholm), 3:3 (1912), pp. 27-28. ['Strindberg in Germany'. Surveys Sg's presence in the German theatre to date. Jacobsohn also suggests that the post-Inferno Sg is the real Sg]

[D2:780] 'Jacqueline' [Jacobine Ring], '*Tryckt och otryckt IV*', *Nya Dagligt Allehanda* (Stockholm), 29 April 1897. ['Published and Unpublished IV'. Reviews *Leka med elden* and *Bandet* on publication. Praises Sg for the dramatic tension and harrowing power of the latter, as well as for bringing so topical a subject to the stage]

[D2:781] 'Jacqueline' [Jacobine Ring], 'Strindbergs Nemesis-dramer', *Nya Dagligt Allehanda* (Stockholm), 20 June 1902. ['Strindberg's Nemesis Plays'. Reviews *Kronbruden*, *Svanevit*, and *Ett drömspel* on publication. The latter is the most illogical and flawed of the three but also 'the most captivating and, above all, psychologically interesting'. *Kronbruden* lacks any overall unity but *Svanevit* possesses all the clear and powerful poetry of an old folk song]

[D2:782] 'Jacqueline' [Jacobine Ring], 'Strindberg. *Vid högre rätt*', *Nya Dagligt Allehanda* (Stockholm), 23 June 1899. ['Strindberg. Before a Higher Court'. An enthusiastic review of *Advent* and *Brott och brott* on publication. The former is unique in Swedish literature, an incomparable work that combines elements from the old medieval mystery plays with the logical form of modern drama. *Brott och brott* is not its equal, but its abrupt dialogue and concentrated action ought to be highly effective in performance]

[D2:783] Jaensch, Wilfrid, 'Die soziale Funktion des Theaters I. Von Strindberg zu Brecht', *Polemos* (Basel), 1963, No. 2. ['The Social Function of the Theatre, I. From Strindberg to Brecht']

[D2:784] Jalkanen, Hugo, 'August Strindbergin näytelmiä', *Uusi Suomi* (Helsinki), 1948, No. 75. ['Plays by August Strindberg']

[D2:785] Janicki, W., 'Reformatorzy sceny. Cz. 1: Juliusz Strindberg', *Echo Muzyczne, Teatralne i Artystyczne* (Warsaw?), 1893, No. 505-507, pp. 22-24. ['Reformers of the Stage'. One of the earliest comments in Polish on Sg as a (naturalistic) dramatist]

[D2:786] Janzén, Assar, 'Walter Johnson. Strindberg's *Kristina, Charles XII, Gustav III*', *Modern Language Quarterly* (London) 16:4 (1955), 365-367. [Reviews Johnson's authoritative English translations and his introductions to three of Sg's history plays]

[D2:787] Janzon, Åke, 'En teaterkritikers syn på Strindberg', *Bonniers Litterära Magasin* (Stockholm), 34:9 (1965), 510-516. ['A Theatre Critic's View of Strindberg'. On how a practicing theatre critic sees Sg and the importance in understanding him of understanding theatre as a medium for something that can only be expressed through theatre. Stresses Sg's ability at creating atmosphere, his break with conventional characterisation, and his use of the theatre as an instrument of discovery]

[D2:788] [Jarno, Josef], '[Memories of Strindberg]', *Obozrenie teatrov* (Moscow), 6-7 May 1912, pp. 6-7. [E.841]

[D2:789] [Jarno, Josef], '[Memories of Strindberg]', *Rampa i zhizn'* (Moscow), 1912:21, pp. 10-11. [Identical with **D2:788**. E.841]

[D2:790] 'Jarro' [Giulio Piccinni], 'Augusto Strindberg', 1-3, *La Nazione* (Rome), 29 August, 26 September, 3 October 1892. [The first of three articles on contemporary dramatists in which Sg in *Fadren* is regarded sympathetically as an anti-Ibsenite anti-naturalist. Also discusses *Kamraterna*, *Den starkare* and the Preface to *Fröken Julie* in the second essay, and *Fröken Julie*, *Paria*, and *Fordringsägare*, in the third]

[D2:791] Jcs, 'Från parkett', *Scenisk konst* (Stockholm), 1903:2, pp. 5-12. [Discusses Harriet Bosse as an actress, with reference to her performances in Sg's plays]

[D2:792] Jensen, Astrid, 'Ibsens og Strindbergs søstre', in Britta Lundqvist, red., *Teatrets Kvinder*, Gråsten: Drama, 1984, pp. 9-33. ['Ibsen's and Strindberg's Sisters']

[D2:793] Johnson, B. S., 'Martyr at the Winch', *The Spectator* (London), 24 May 1963. [Considers Sg as the dramatist of married life, with reference to Elizabeth Sprigge's newly published translations of twelve of the plays and *Marriage and Genius*, John Stewart Collis's account of Sg's three marriages, **R:526**]

[D2:794] Johnson, Walter [Gilbert], '*August Strindbergs dramer I, II, II.* Utgivna med inledningar och kommentarer av Karl [sic] Reinhold Smedmark', *Scandinavian Studies* (Lawrence, Kansas), 38:1 (1966), 76-77. [Reviews the first three volumes of Carl Reinhold Smedmark's incomplete text-critical edition of Sg's plays]

[D2:795] Johnson, Walter [Gilbert], 'Introduction to the One-Act Plays', in August Strindberg, *Plays from the Cynical Life*, Seattle and London: University of Washington Press, 1983, pp. 3-6. [Introduces a volume containing the author's own English translations of *Leka med elden, Debet och kredit, Moderskärlek, Första varningen, Inför döden, Paria,* and *Samum*]

[D2:796] Johnson, Walter [Gilbert], 'Introduction' and 'Notes', in August Strindberg, *Open Letters to the Intimate Theatre*, Translations and Introductions by Walter Johnson, London: Peter Owen, 1967, pp. vii-ix, 3-15, 55-57, 160-166, 235-245, 307-317.

[D2:797] Johnson, Walter [Gilbert], 'Introduction' and 'Notes', in August Strindberg, *Open Letters to the Intimate Theatre*, Translations and Introductions by Walter Johnson, Seattle and London: University of Washington Press, 1966. [XIII]+323 pp. [The North-American edition of **D2:796**]

[D2:798] — Johannesson, Eric O., *Scandinavian Studies* (Lawrence, Kansas), 39:2 (1967), 193-194.

[D2:799] — Lundbergh, H., *American Swedish Review* (New York), 61:5 (1967), p. 20.

[D2:800] — Vowles, Richard B., *Modern Drama* (Lawrence, Kansas), 10:2 (1967), 219-220.

[D2:801] Jolivet, Alfred, 'Les Drames de Strindberg. Cours 1-24', *Revue des cours et conférences* (Paris), 29 (1927-28), No. 1, pp. 193-204, 432-449, 549-554, 577-591, 689-701; No. 2, pp. 163-176, 406-415, 577-594; 30 (1928-29), No. 1, 44-58, 140-153, 213-222, 455-467, 549-564; No. 2, pp. 71-82, 183-192, 352-362, 409-417, 564-576, 621-631; 31 (1929-30), No. 1, pp. 186-192, 360-371; No. 2, pp. 155-162, 521-535, 717-726. [A study of Sg's dramas in twenty parts, which constitutes the greater part of Jolivet's book, **D2:150**. Comprises: (1) Introduction; (2) Débuts littéraires; (3-4) *Maître Olof*; (5) *Maître Olof* (le drame en vers); (6) *Le secret de la Guilde – Le voyage de Pierre-Bonheur*; (7) *La femme de Sire Bengt*; (8) Les drames naturalistes. Première ébauche de la théorie; (9) Les drames naturalistes (suite); (10) *Le père*; (11) *Mademoiselle Julie*; (12) *Créanciers*; (13) Petits drames en une scène; (14) Inferno; (15) Inferno (suite); (16) *Le chemin de Damas* (1re partie); (17) *Le chemin de Damas* (2e partie) - *Avent*; (18) *Crime et crime - Paques*; (19) *La Saint Jean – La danse de mort*; (20) *La couronne de la mariée*; (21) *Svanevit – Le Songe*; (22) *Le chemin de Damas* (3e partie); (23) Les pièces intimes. Epilogue dramatique; (24) Les drames historiques]

[D2:802] 'Jörgen' [Georg Lundström], 'Med tvål och borste', *Figaro* (Stockholm), 27 April 1901. ['With Soap and Brush'. Offers a positive review of *Påsk* on publication, but a negative response to both *Midsommar* and *Kaspers fettisdag*]

[D2:803] Jungmannová, Leka, 'Nedotažený Strindberg', *Mladá fronta Dnes* (Prague), 26 January 2001. [Reviews Volume One of a Czech edition of Sg's plays, with translations by František Fröhlich, Dagmar Hartlová, Irena Kunovská, Libor Stukavec, and Josef Vohryzek. See **D2:1028**]

[D2:804] K., 'Strindberg als Dramatiker', *Der Schleswig-Holsteiner* (Schleswig), 7:4 (1926), p. 5. ['Strindberg as a Dramatist']

[D2:805] Kabell, Aage, '*Påsk* og det mystiske teater', *Edda* (Oslo), 54 (1954), 158-235. ['*Easter* and the Mystic Theatre'. Attempts to see Sg's post-Inferno dramas as a whole in order to provide an individual play like *Påsk*, which draws on numerous aspects of Sg's psychological and religious crisis, with a context. The Book of Job provides a correlative for the problems of guilt, suffering, and atonement that Sg explores while his later plays are offprints of the primary autobiographical version of this material originally presented in *Inferno*, with its evident literary debts to Edgar Allan Poe, Balzac, E. T. A. Hoffmann, *et al.* The idea of Nemesis and the Swedenborg-inflected theme of sleeping, dreaming, blindness, and sight recur throughout the period, but Sg has difficulty reconciling the mystic dimension with the naturalistic, and some plays, like *Advent* and *Brott och brott*, are too stylised. Kabell also discusses *Till Damaskus*, *Dödsdansen*, *Karl XII*, *Svanevit*, *Kronbruden*, *Ett drömspel*, and the application of the Inferno 'theodicy' to history plays like *Folkungasagan* and *Engelbrekt*]

[D2:806] 'Kaifas', 'Intima teatern', *Scenisk konst* (Stockholm), 1907 (Julnummer), pp. 22-24. [An assessment of the Intimate Theatre's first season]

[D2:807] [Kalff, Jan], 'Théâtre de l'Œuvre – August Strindberg', *Het Tooneel* ('s Gravenage), 18 February 1893, pp. 74-76. [The first Dutch discussion of Sg's work to recognise his importance as a dramatist, but Kalff comments on *Röda rummet* as well as *Mäster Olof*, *Fadren*, the Preface to *Fröken Julie*, and Lugné-Poe's production of *Fordringsägare*]

[D2:808] Kalischer, Siegfried, 'Strindberg und die deutsche Bühne', *Deutsche Theater-Zeitschrift* (Berlin), 2 (1909), 219-220. ['Strindberg and the German Stage']

[D2:809] Kalnacs, Benedikts, 'Strindberga pleejamiba', *Karogs* (Riga), 1 (January 1999), 187-196. [Surveys Sg's career, focusing primarily on his work as a dramatist]

[D2:810] Karnick, Manfred, 'Strindberg and the Tradition of Modernity: Structure of Drama and Experience', in Göran Stockenström, ed., **D2:288**, *Strindberg's Dramaturgy*, pp. 59-74. [Asks what it is that makes Sg's work so profoundly representative and therefore important even today, with reference to *Fadren*, *Till Damaskus*, *Ett drömspel*, and drawing possible parallels between Sg's theatre and the baroque *teatrum mundi* of Calderón de la Barca. Karnick confirms Sg's central role in the development of modernist drama]

[D2:811] Karnick, Manfred, 'Strindberg und die Tradition des Modernen: Über Dramen- und Bewußtseinsformen', in Gerhard Buhr, Friedrich A. Kittler and Horst Turk, Hrsg., *Das Subjekt der Dichtung. Festschrift für Gerhard Kaiser*, Würzburg: Königshausen & Neumann, 1990, pp. 579-594. [German version of **D2:810**]

[D2:812] Kerr, Alfred, 'Sternheim. [2.] Sybil. Sternheim. Schnitzler. Tolstoi. Strindberg', in *Ewigskeitszug. Die Welt im Drama*, Bd 2, Berlin: S. Fischer Verlag, 1917, pp. 116-123.

[D2:813] Kerr, Alfred, 'Strindberg', *Der Tag* (Berlin), 14 March 1902. [A critical discussion of *Fröken Julie*, which is 'just as naturalistic as all naturalistic plays, namely not naturalistic at all'; everything becomes a living symbol. Kerr, for whom Sg is a monomaniac who depicts man as helpless and his works as suffused in a cold fire, also comments on *Fadren* and *Bandet*]

[D2:814] Kerr, Alfred, 'Strindberg', in *Das neue Drama*, Berlin: S. Fischer Verlag, 1904, pp. 246-250. [Rpr. of **D2:813**]

[D2:815] Kerr, Alfred, 'Strindberg', in *Das Welt im Drama*, 5 Bde, Bd 1, *Das neue Drama*, Berlin: S. Fischer Verlag, 1917, pp. 357-363. [Rpr. of **D2:813**]

[D2:816] Kerr, Alfred, 'Strindberg', in *Die Welt im Drama*, Hrsg. von Gerhard F. Hering, Köln und Berlin: Kiepenheuer & Witsch, 1964, pp. 51-53. [Rpr. of **D2:813**]

[D2:817] Kerr, Alfred, 'Strindberg', in Hans-Peter Bayerdörfer, Hrsg., **B3:85**, *Strindberg auf der deutschen Bühne*, pp. 151-156. [Rpr. of **D2:813**]

[D2:818] Kerr, A[lfred], 'Vedekind i Strindberg', Translated from the German by E. K., *Biblioteka Teatr i Iskusstvo* (St Petersburg), No. 7, 1908, pp. 31-41. ['Wedekind and Strindberg'. A translation of several short pieces by Kerr into Russian, where Sg and Wedekind are presented under the heading 'New Dramatists'. E.780]

[D2:819] Kesting, Marianne, 'Strindberg und die Folgen', in *Vermessung des Labyrinths. Studien zur modernen Ästhetik*, Fischer doppelpunkt 20, Frankfurt am Main: S. Fischer, 1965, pp. 126-138. ['Strindberg and After'. Presents Sg as a forerunner of the theatre of the absurd. Discusses *Dödsdansen* in relation to Sartre's *Huis Clos*, Vauthier's *Capitaine Bada*, Beckett's *Endgame*, and Ionesco's *Amédée*, compares the Chamber Plays (wrongly dated 1906) with Maeterlinck, and *Ett drömspel* and *Till Damaskus* with Tennessee Williams]

[D2:820] Kesting, Marianne, 'Welttheater des Ichs: Strindberg-Artaud-Ionesco', in Peter Csobádi, *et al.*, Hrsg., *Welttheater. Mysterienspiel, Rituelles Theater: "Vom Himmel durch die Welt zur Hölle". Gesammelte Vorträge des Salzburger Symposions 1991*, Anif / Salzburg: Verlag Ursula Müller-Speiser, 1992, pp. 41-52. ['The World Theatre of the Self: Strindberg-Artaud-Ionesco'. Kesting focuses her comparison on Sg's search for a dramatic language with which to stage the self and his dramatisation of subjectivity and inward, ordinarily concealed, experience in *Till Damaskus, Ett drömspel, Spöksonaten,* and *Stora landsvägen*]

[D2:821] Kilian, Eugen, 'Strindberg-Dramaturgie', *Die Schaubühne* (Berlin), 14:11* (1918), 247-249. [Reflects on Sg's dramaturgy and his writings about drama]

[D2:822] Kilian, Eugen, 'Strindberg-Inszenierungen', *Die Scene* (Berlin), 8:7-8 (1918), 79-81. ['Performing Strindberg'. Considers how best to stage Sg's plays, primarily *Till Damaskus*]

[D2:823] Kilian, Eugen, 'Strindberg-Dramaturgie', *Allgemeine Zeitung* (München), 1919, No. 111.* ['Strindberg's Dramaturgy']

[D2:824] Kilian, Eugen, 'Strindbergs dramaturgische Bekenntnisse, auf Grund seiner Briefe', *Weser-Zeitung* (Bremen), 1921, No. 101, pp. 48-49. ['Strindberg's Dramaturgical Confession on the Basis of His Letters']

[D2:825] Kivimaa, Arvi, 'August Strindberg, maailmandramatiikan uusija', *Uusi Suomi* (Helsinki), 1950:10. ['August Strindberg, the Renewer of World Drama']

[D2:826] Kivimaa, Arvi, 'August Strindberg, maailmandramatiikan uudistaja', in *Näyttämön lumous*, Helsingissä: Otava, 1952, pp. 18-23. ['August Strindberg. The Renewer of World Drama', in *The Charm of the Theatre*. Rpr. of **D2:825**]

[D2:827] Kjær, Nils, '*Vid högre rätt*', *Verdens Gang* (Oslo), 22 June 1899. [Reviews *Advent* and *Brott och brott* on publication. 'I know of no play in the whole of modern literature as simple, as rich, as convincing and yet so new, so powerful and manly as this (*Brott och brott*); the second act above all seems to me to represent the highpoint of modern dramatic art']

[D2:828] Kjær, Nils, 'Strindbergsteater. En norsk kritiker har ordet', *Stockholms Dagblad*, 12 October 1910. ['Strindberg's Theatre. A Norwegian Critic gives his Opinion'. Comments on the aims and achievement of the Intimate Theatre]

[D2:829] 'Klabund' [Pseudonym of Alfred Henschke], 'Eine Fahne des Triumphs...', *Das Programm. Blätter der Münchener Kammerspiele*, 1915:1, pp. 10-11. ['A Banner of Triumph'. Presents the staging of eight of Sg's plays as a cycle at the Munich Kammerspiele between 29 April and 3 June 1915. Maintains that 'Sg was inwardly connected with this war', and that his 'banner also fights in this war.' Nor is this surprising since 'Sg thinks bloodthirsty thoughts']

[D2:830] Klabund [Alfred Henschke], 'Eine Fahne des Triumphs...', in Hans-Peter Bayerdörfer, Hrsg., **B3:85**, *Strindberg auf der deutschen Bühne*, pp. 235-236. [Rpr. of **D2:829**]

[D2:831] Klemensiewiczowa, Józefa, 'Intima Teatern Augusta Strindberga', *Prawda* (Warsaw), 1908, No. 12. ['August Strindberg's Intimate Theatre'. Reports on the founding of the Intimate Theatre by Sg and August Falck]

[D2:832] Knapp, Bettina L., '*Dramas of Testimony* by August Strindberg, translated and introduced by Walter Johnson', *Comparative Drama* (Kalamazoo, Michigan), 11:2 (1977), 181-183. [Reviews Johnson's English translations of *Dödsdansen I-II*, **E35:50**]

[D2:833] Knudsen, Hans, 'Bühnenwerke', *Die schöne Literatur* (Leipzig), 21 (1920), 176-177. [Reviews the 1919 German edition of Sg's works for the stage]

[D2:834] Koch, Max, 'Ausländische Dramen', *Literarisches Centralblatt für Deutschland* (Leipzig), 52 (1901), 1204-1208. [Reviews *Gustav Adolf* and *Påsk* on publication]

[D2:835] Kökeritz, Helge, 'Strindberg's Greatest Dramatist: August Strindberg, 1849-1912', *Bulletin of the American Institute of Swedish Arts, Literature and Science* (Minneapolis), 4:1 (1949), 11-18. [Published in conjunction with the centenary of Sg's birth]

[D2:836] Kulundzić, Josip, 'Simbolika naturalizma', in August Strindberg, *Otac, Gospodîca Julija*, Zagreb, 1921, pp. 3-5. ['Symbolist Naturalism'. Introduces a Croatian edition of *Fröken Julie* and *Fadren*. R.489]

[D2:837] Kumakova, D., '[The Musical Structure of Strindberg's "Late Sonatas"]', in L[ev] Gitel'man and V[alentina] Dianova, eds, **B1:148**, *Avgust Strindberg i mirovaia kul'tura. Materialy mezhvyzovskoi nauchnoi konferentsii. Stat'i. Soobshcheniia*, pp. 42-50. [Discusses the musical form and thematic organisation employed by Sg in the four Chamber Plays of 1907]

[D2:838] Kurth, Dietrich, 'August Strindberg. Vom Naturalismus zum Symbolismus', *Volksbühnenspiegel* (West Berlin), 5:7-8 (1959), pp. 17-19. ['August Strindberg. From Naturalism to Symbolism']

[D2:839] Kurth, Dietrich, 'Die unbekannte Strindberg', *Volksbühnenspiegel* (West Berlin), 5 (1959), No. 10, pp. 17-19. ['The Unknown Strindberg']

[D2:840] Kvam, Kela, 'Inledet', in August Strindberg, *Memorandum til medlemmerne af Intima Teatern fra instruktøren*, 'København: Hasselbach, 1968. 87 pp. [Introduces a Danish edition of *Memorandum till Medlemmarne av Intima Teatern*]

[D2:841] Kvam, Kela, 'Margareta Wirmark, *Kampen med döden*; *Den kluvna scenen*; Egil Törnqvist, *Transposing Drama*', *Nordic Theatre Research* (Copenhagen), 4 (1991), 190-192. [Reviews **E35:129** and **D2:332**]

[D2:842] Kvam, Kela, 'Max Reinhardt und Strindberg. Die Bedeutung der Inszenierungen der "Kammerspiele" und des "Traumspiels" für den deutschen Expressionismus', in Wilhelm Friese, Hrsg., **B3:168**, *Strindberg und die deutschsprachigen Länder*, pp. 265-288. Illus. ['Max Reinhardt and Strindberg. The Significance of His Productions of the Chamber Plays and *A Dream Play* for German Expressionism'. Kvam maintains that Reinhardt's stagings of *Pelikanen* (1914), *Spöksonaten* (1916), and *Ett drömspel* (1921) were of importance not only in transforming the image of Sg in Germany from that promoted by the naturalistic dramas of the 1880s, but also for the emergence of German expressionism]

[D2:843] Kvam, Kela, 'Om August Strindberg', in *Sceneskift; det 20.århundredes teater i Europa: en antologi*, redigeret af Alette Scavenius and Stig Jarl, København: Multivers, 2001, pp. 11-27. Illus. ['On August Strindberg']

[D2:844] Kvam, Kela, 'Strindberg and French Symbolist Theatre', in Michael Robinson, ed., **B1:379**, *The Moscow Papers*, pp. 57-62. [Points out that, although Sg turned away from playwriting in 1894 and broke the links he had forged with contemporary French theatre through the directors Antoine and Lugné-Poe, he drew on the cultural climate in 1890's Paris for his return to literature at the turn of the century. He was particularly responsive to the ideas of Wagner, which exerted a profound influence on the symbolist theatre, and which were mediated to Sg via the works of Maeterlinck and Joséphin [Sâr] Péladan. Sg was interested in dreams and monodrama, and Wagner's *leitmotiv* technique and the notion of a *Gesamtkunstwerk* are certainly relevant to the dramaturgy of his post-Inferno dramas in which these interests are realised]

[D2:845] Kvam, Kela, 'Strindberg as an Innovator of Dramatic and Theatrical Form', in Michael Robinson, ed., **B1:373**, *Strindberg and Genre*, pp. 108-118. [Unlike Ibsen, Sg remained an avant-garde artist throughout his career. *Till Damaskus*, *Ett drömspel*, and the Chamber Plays are all attempts to escape the prevailing dramaturgy of the well-made play; they have something in common with the dramas of Péladan and Maeterlinck but also look back to the pre-realistic theatre of Shakespeare and Goethe's *Faust*. Kvam also examines the common ground between Sg and Edward Gordon Craig in their innovatory ideas regarding a dematerialised theatre production]

[D2:846] K. W-g [Karl Warburg], 'Bokvärlden', *Göteborgs Handels- och Sjöfartstidning*, 8 April 1890. [Reviews *Fordringsägare*, *Paria*, and *Samum* on publication. The former is too one-sided while the others lack *Fadren*'s tragic power. The influence of 'Nietschke' (sic) is apparent in *Paria* while the accompanying essay, 'Om modernt drama och modern teater', promotes an all-too monotonous form of drama, one entirely lacking in the variety and life necessary for the stage]

[D2:847] K. W-g [Karl Warburg], 'Bokvärlden', *Göteborgs Handels- och Sjöfartstidning*, 12 May 1897. [Reviews *Tryckt och otryckt IV*, including *Leka med elden* and *Bandet*, on publication. Warburg takes exception to the fact that 'The characters speak openly about their most intimate circumstances and actions whereas in life one normally talks about these things in other, more muted, tones']

[D2:848] K. W-g [Karl Warburg], 'Bokvärlden', Göteborgs Handels- och Sjöfartstidning, 17 May 1899. [Reviews *Advent* and *Brott och brott* on publication, and is highly critical of the former]

[D2:849] K. W-g [Karl Warburg], 'Bokvärlden', *Göteborgs Handels- och Sjöfartstidning*, 30 September 1893. [Reviews *Debet och kredit, Första varningen, Moderskärlek*, and *Inför döden* on publication, questioning their highly concentrated format. They are 'abruptly written dramatic sketches' in which the psychology with which Sg has imbued them does not have the time to make an effect. *Inför döden* is 'the only one which has any real literary importance']

[D2:850] K. W-g [Karl Warburg], 'Bokvärlden', *Göteborgs Handels- och Sjöfartstidning*, 25 June 1902. [Reviews *Kronbruden, Svanevit*, and *Ett drömspel* on publication. With its powerful, poetic atmosphere, Warburg judges the former to be the finest of these plays. In *Svanevit*, meanwhile, Sg captures the tone of a genuine fairy tale, but *Ett drömspel* demands too much of the reader (sic): its clever representation of the dream world is ultimately an impossibly confusing muddle]

[D2:851] K. W-g [Karl Warburg], 'Bokvärlden: Aug. Strindbergs *Kristina- Gustaf III*', *Göteborgs Handels- och Sjöfartstidning*, 12 October 1904. [Criticises both plays on publication, the former for its characterisation and anachronistic dialogue, the latter, which gives the impression of being a set of variations on a theme, for the absence of a dramatically effective structure. Gustav's unhappy situation is treated by Sg with some sensitivity, but he is not endowed with any tragic depth, while Schröderheim and his wife provide the opportunity for a new variation on the marriage question]

[D2:852] Laestadius, Lars-Levi, 'Varför tar Strindberg så högtidligt?', *entré* (Norsborg), 2:6 (1975), 12-13. ['Why take Strindberg so Solemnly?']

[D2:853] Lagerkvist, Pär, 'Strindberg och Intima teatern', *Svenska Dagbladet* (Stockholm), 27 January 1919. ['Strindberg and the Intimate Theatre'. Reviews August Falck's edition of Sg's letters and his memoranda to members of the Intimate Theatre. Lagerkvist stresses the expressionist elements in Sg's later plays but sees the miniature format of the Intimate Theatre as artistically limiting]

[D2:854] Lamm, Martin, 'Strindberg and the Theatre', *Tulane Drama Review* (New Orleans), 6:2 (1961), 132-139. [As an experimental dramatist, Sg was a liberating influence on modern drama, which was becoming fixed in rigid forms. Lamm concentrates mainly on the staging of the Chamber Plays and their relevance for later playwrights, including Pär Lagerkvist]

[D2:855] Lamm, Martin, 'Strindberg and the Theatre', in *Pär Lagerkvist*, New Orleans: The Tulane Drama Review, 1961, pp. 90-97. [Rpr. of **D2:854**]

[D2:856] Lamm, Martin, 'Strindberg i jego teatr', *Dialog* (Warsaw), 1062:2, pp. 139-142. ['Strindberg and the Theatre'. Polish translation of **D2:854**. Rpr. in **E51:356**]

[D2:857] Landau, Paul, 'Strindberg als Dramatiker des Expressionismus', *Die Deutsche Bühne* (Berlin), 12:21-22 (24 May 1920), 371-374. ['Strindberg as an Expressionist

Dramatist'. Published apropos new German translations of the plays which shine a clearer light on 'the great Sg...the mightiest personality World Literature has known'. Landau bases his discussion mainly on *Till Damaskus*, *Advent*, *Påsk*, *Ett drömspel*, *Brända tomten*, and the musical and Hoffmanesque *Spöksonaten*, and defines Sg's expressionism as one which presents subjective states of mind rather than objective reality, achieved via characters who are 'Ausstrahlungen seines Ichs'. Time and place are of little importance in this form of drama. Each scene portrays an inner state of mind. Even when presenting the everyday, the atmosphere is dreamlike. Structurally there is often an analogy with music, and the typification of many of the characters arises from the predominant subjective view of the world. Sg's form is sometimes contrapuntal, sometimes cubist, but these plays are 'genuine expressionist art']

[**D2:858**] Landau, Paul, 'Strindberg als Dramatiker des Expressionismus', in Hans-Peter Bayerdörfer, Hrsg., **B3:85**, *Strindberg auf der deutschen Bühne*, pp. 307-312. ['Strindberg as an Expressionist Dramatist'. Rpr. of **D2:857**]

[**D2:859**] Landau, Paul, 'Strindberg als Dramatiker des Expressionismus', *Vorwärts* (Hannover), 17 May 1920. [See **D2:857**]

[**D2:860**] Landauer, Gustav, 'Strindberg', *Blätter des Deutschen Theaters* (Leipzig), 2 (1912), 321-324.

[**D2:861**] Landquist, John, 'Strindberg och hans härskargestalter', in Gunnar Brandell, red., **B1:82**, *Synpunkter på Strindberg*, pp. 175-181. ['Strindberg and His Rulers'. Discusses Sg's creative process and his relationship to his fictional portraits of three strong rulers, Gustav Vasa, Karl XII, and Gustav III. Excerpted from Landquist's *Människokunskap*, 1920]

[**D2:862**] Landquist, John, 'Strindbergs postuma dramer', in Solveig Landquist, red., **B1:248**, *John Landquist om Strindberg personen och diktaren*, pp. 217-221. ['Strindberg's Posthumous Dramas'. Rpr. of **D2:863**]

[**D2:863**] Landquist, John, 'Strindbergs postuma dramer', *Litteraturen* (Copenhagen), 1 (1918-19), pp. 716-719. ['Strindberg's Posthumous Dramas'. Reviews the plays and dramatic fragments published in Volume One of Vilhelm Carlheim-Gyllensköld's edition of Sg's collected unpublished works]

[**D2:864**] Landquist, John, 'Gustav III:s och Strindbergs teater 175 år: Dramaten', *Aftonbladet* (Stockholm), 17 May 1963. ['The 175th Anniversary of Gustav III's and Strindberg's Theatre: Dramaten'. Reviews Gösta M. Bergman and Niklas Brunius, red., *Dramaten 175 år. Studier i svensk scenkonst*]

[**D2:865**] Lång, Helmer, '*Samlade Verk*', *Skånska Dagbladet* (Malmö), 17 May 1984. [Reviews Volume 27 in *Samlade Verk*, containing *Fadren*, *Fröken Julie*, and *Fordringsägare*]

[**D2:866**] Lång, Helmer, '*Samlade Verk*', *Skånska Dagbladet* (Malmö), 23 December 1992. [Reviews Volume 43 in *Samlade Verk*, containing *Midsommar*, *Kaspers fettisdag*, and *Påsk*]

[**D2:867**] Lång, Helmer, *Skånska Dagbladet* (Malmö), 2 September 1989. [Reviews Volume 61 in *Samlade Verk*, containing *Siste riddaren*, *Riksföreståndaren*, and *Bjälbo-Jarlen*]

[**D2:868**] Łanowski, Zygmunt, 'Euripides XIX wieku. W 50-lecie smierci Augusta Strindberga', *Teatr* (Warsaw), 1962: 14, pp. 16-18. ['The Euripides of the 19th Century. On the 50th Anniversary of August Strindberg's Death'. Łanowski, Sg's main Polish translator, stresses the autobiographical aspects of his work, as well as his extreme sensitivity and personal suffering, but offers an overview of his development as a dramatist from naturalism to symbolism and expressionism, and indicates how he also anticipates the theatre of the absurd]

[D2:869] Larreta, Antonio, 'Actores en busca de estilo', *Marcha* (Montevideo), 23 June 1950. ['Actors in Search of a Style'. Larreta argues that their preoccupation with realism renders contemporary Uruguayan actors unable to perform Sg. By the director of the Uruguayan première of *Påsk*, 19 November 1951, who also staged *Fordringsägare* in 1969]

[D2:870] Lawson, Stephen R., 'Strindberg's *Dream Play* and *Ghost Sonata*', *Yale Theatre* (New Haven, Conn.), 5:3 (1974), 95-102. [In studying dreams, Freud and Sg were both compelled by identical forces; the latter was also encouraged by Maeterlinck to develop a form of drama in which the purpose of dialogue was to reveal the soul, not advance the situation on stage, and these later plays are characterised by an omnipresent dualism. Contains numerous generalisations, several factual errors, and a brief comment on *Advent* as well as the named plays No references are given for its numerous quotations]

[D2:871] Lazarević, Branko, 'Dramaturske ideje A. Strindberga', *Srpski knjizevni glasnik* (Novi Sad), 28:2 (1912), 141-145. ['August Strindberg's Dramaturgical Theories'. R.472]

[D2:872] Lebourg-Oule, Anne-Marie, 'Les didascalies para-textuelles chez Strindberg', *Litteratures* (Toulouse), 1992, (Supplément), pp. 85-93. ['Strindberg's Paratextual Stage Directions'. An analysis of Sg's use of the dramatic *Nebentext*]

[D2:873] Lebourg-Oule, Anne-Marie, 'Les didascalies para-textuelles chez Strindberg mise en cadre', in André Mansau et Jean-Louise Cabanès, eds, *Textes, images, musique. Travaux du Centre de recherche Textes, images, musique*, Toulouse: Le Mirail University Press, 1992, pp. 89-93. ['Framing Strindberg's Paratextual Stage Directions']

[D2:874] Leino, Eino, *Maailmankirjailijoita: Homeros, Dante, France, Strindberg: Esseitä, arviointeja, arvosteluja kirjallisuuden ja näyttämötaiteen aloilta*, Toimittanut Aarre M. Peltonen, Suomalaisen Kirjallisuuden Seuran toimituksia 342, Helsinki: Suomalaisen Kirjallisuuden Seura, 1978, pp. 311-358. ['Writers of the World: Homer, Dante, France, Strindberg. Essays, Judgments, Criticisms in Literature and Drama'. A wide-ranging discussion of Sg's plays by the eminent Finnish *fin-de-siècle* lyric poet and critic (1878-1926)]

[D2:875] Lemarchand, Jacques, '[Strindberg]', *Figaro littéraire* (Paris), 21 September 1963. [Observes that plays like *Fröken Julie*, *Spöksonaten*, *Fadren*, *Fordringsägare*, and *Dödsdansen* have been instrumental in creating a new theatre. The latter, which Jean Vilar staged in 1945 at the time of Sartre's *Huis Clos* and Camus's *Le Malentendu*, showed that, whether we were aware of it then or not, a new theatre was possible]

[D2:876] Levander, Hans, 'Strindberg, *Samlade Verk*', *Svenska Dagbladet* (Stockholm), 19 December 1989. [Reviews Vols 49 and 61 in *Samlade Verk*, containing *Näktergalen i Wittenberg* and *Siste riddaren, Riksföreståndaren*, and *Bjälbo-Jarlen* respectively]

[D2:877] Levertin, Oscar, 'August Strindbergs neue Dramen', *Wiener Rundschau* (Vienna), 3 (1898-99), 334-337. ['August Strindberg's New Dramas'. Rpr. of Levertin's reflections on *Advent* and *Brott och brott* in German translation]

[D2:878] Levertin, Oscar, 'Litteratur', *Svenska Dagbladet* (Stockholm), 3 May 1899. [Reviews *Advent* and *Brott och brott* on publication. The former is 'among the most repulsive things Sg has ever written', wallowing in crime and punishment with little love or understanding. However, Levertin finds (the more traditional) *Brott och brott* 'the most artistically accomplished and spiritually well-thought-out piece that Sg has written during his most recent phase'. This may mark a return to health, and hopefully the end of the Inferno period]

[D2:879] Levertin, Oscar, '*Vid högre rätt*. Två dramer', in *Samlade Skrifter*, 24 vols, Stockholm: Albert Bonniers Förlag, 1908, Volume 13, 'Svensk litteratur I', pp. 5-13. [Rpr. of **D2:878**]

[D2:880] Levertin, Oscar, '*Vid högre rätt*. Två dramer', in *Project Runeberg*, http: //www.lysator.liu.se/runeberg/olrecens/hogrerat.html. [Rpr. of **D2:878** in electronic form]

[D2:881] Levy, Louis, 'Strindberg og Teatret', *Tilskueren* (Copenhagen), 35:2 (February 1918), 176-180. ['Strindberg and the Theatre'. On Sg's inexorable conquest of the theatre. 'Our [Danish] poets worship a plenitude of soul. Strindberg's spirit and fire']

[D2:882] Levy, Louis, 'Teater-Dagbog', *Tilskueren* (Copenhagen), 32:1 (1915), 108-112. [Reviews the Intimate Theatre on tour to Denmark with *Fröken Julie*, comments on Sg's impact on Denmark, and considers Harriet Bosse in *Pygmalion* at Copenhagen's Dagmarteatret]

[D2:883] Lewin, Jan, 'De gamla spelen om envar', *entré* (Norsborg), 19:4 (1992), p. 88. ['The Old Play about Everyman'. Reviews Volumes 39 and 58 in *Samlade Verk*, containing *Till Damaskus* and the Chamber Plays respectively]

[D2:884] Lewin, Jan, 'Kungadramer värda omvärdering', *entré* (Norsborg), 20:1 (1993), pp. 105-106, 108. ['Royal Dramas Worthy of a Revaluation'. Reviews Volumes 41 and 43 in *Samlade Verk*, containing *Folkungasagan, Gustav Vasa*, and *Erik XIV*, and *Midsommar, Kaspers fettisdag*, and *Påsk* respectively]

[D2:885] Lewin, Jan, 'Ny drive för August', *entré* (Norsborg), 16:4 (1989), 55-57. ['New Drive for August'. Reviews six volumes of Sg's plays in *Samlade Verk*. There is a danger that the National Edition of his works will turn Sg into a national monument. Where the theatre is concerned, it is good to have dependable texts, but these must be seen as no more than scores for future productions]

[D2:886] Lewin, Jan, 'Strindberg', *entré* (Norsborg), 18:1 (1991), 150-151. [Reviews Volume 45 in *Samlade Verk*, containing *Svanevit* and *Kronbruden*]

[D2:887] Lewin, Jan, 'Strindberg', *entré*, (Norsborg), 18:2 (1991), 105-106. [Reviews Volume 1 in *Samlade Verk*, containing *Fritänkaren, Det sjunkande Hellas*, and *Hermione*]

[D2:888] Lewin, Jan, 'Strindberg', *entré* (Norsborg), 18:4 (1991), 73. [Reviews Volume 3 in *Samlade Verk*, containing *I Rom, Den fredlöse*, and *Anno Fyrtiåtta*]

[D2:889] Lewin, Jan, 'Värderingar som står sig', *entré* (Norsborg), 21:3 (1994), p. 100. [Reviews Volume 47 in *Samlade Verk*, containing *Karl XII* and *Engelbrekt*]

[D2:890] Lewko, Marian, 'Biblijne konteksty dramaturgii August Strindberg', *Zeszyty Naukowe* (Lublin), 1988:4, pp. 29-40. ['Biblical Contexts in the Plays of August Strindberg'. See **D2:203**]

[D2:891] Lewko, Marian, 'Chrześcijańskie konteksty dramaturgii Augusta Strindberga', *Roczniki Humanistyczne – Annales de Lettres et Sciences Humaines / Annals of Arts* (Lublin), 42:1 (1994), 85-121. ['The Role of Christianity in August Strindberg's Dramas'. In Polish with an English summary. See **D2:203**]

[D2:892] Lewko, Marian, 'O dramacie i teatrze Strindberga', *Biuletyn Polonistyczny* (Warsaw), 1985:1-2, pp. 75-80. ['On Strindberg's Dramas and Theatre']

[D2:893] Lewko, Marian, 'O semantyce i funkcji rekwizytów w dramatach Augusta Strindberga', *Akcent* (Lublin), 1991:1, pp. 170-177. ['On the Semantics and Function of the Stage Properties in the Dramas of August Strindberg'. Based primarily on an analysis of *Erik XIV*. See **D2:203**]

[D2:894] Lide, Barbara, 'Perspectives on a Genre: Strindberg's *Comédies rosses*', in Michael Robinson, ed., **B1:373**, *Strindberg and Genre*, pp. 148-166. [Suggests that previous critical accounts of *Första varningen* and *Leka med elden* have often failed to establish their genre and appreciate their humour; they are fully executed one-acters of the kind that Sg discussed in his essay 'Om modernt drama och modern teater', and may be related to the often cynical French form of *comédies rosses*, a genre which emerged in France in the heyday of the Théâtre Libre. As such, they are to be compared with plays by Octave Feuillet and Henry Becque, containing dialogue of the kind that Jules Lemaitre called 'an essentially jovial pessimism'. Unlike their French counterparts, however, Lide observes that Sg's plays are never hypocritical in their portrayal of human relationships, but are similarly ironic and exhibit both a straightforward eroticism and a decidedly sceptical attitude towards both love and marriage. Above all, they confirm 'Sg's wonderfully incisive, cynical, comic spirit']

[D2:895] Lide, Barbara, 'Perspectives on a Genre: Strindberg's *Comédies rosses*', in Janet Witalec, ed., **D2:348**, *Drama Criticism*, Volume 18, pp. 186- 195. [Rpr. of **D2:894**]

[D2:896] Lide, Barbara, 'Stations of Expressionism: Stora landsvägen from *Till Damaskus* to Contemporary Performance', in Michael Robinson and Sven Hakon Rossel, eds, **B1:387**, *Expressionism and Modernism*, pp. 101-110. [Examines Sg's station dramas, from *Lycko-Pers resa* to *Stora landsvägen*, their transposition to the stage by Max Reinhardt and others, their influence on expressionist cinema, and several more recent stagings of the naturalist plays, including Staffan Valdemar Holm's 1992 production of *Fröken Julie* in Copenhagen, Emil Graffman's 1996 *Brott och brott*, and Teater Les Enfants's version of *Fordringsägare*, all of which are far removed from realism, and reflect the legacy of expressionistic theatre]

[D2:897] Lide, Barbara, 'Strindberg as "medveten spefågel": Post-Inferno Irony', in Kela Kvam, ed., **D2:158**, *Strindberg's Post-Inferno Plays*, pp. 52-70. Illus. ['Strindberg as a "Conscious Jester"'. Suggests that if we are to achieve a more comprehensive understanding of Sg, we should be willing to examine his use of irony. Lide analyses both the verbal irony that arises when the superficial meaning of the signifier does not correspond to the true, or essential, meaning of the signified, as well as instances of dramatic, or situational, irony that result from a character's displayed ignorance of her situation, illustrated here by reference to *Inferno*, *Gillets hemlighet*, and *Brott och brott*. She also considers a third form of irony that results from the fragmentation of the ego in plays like *Till Damaskus* or *Ett drömspel*, which are designedly repetitious in nature, and where a character is split into two or more persons. These manifestations of a single ego may be observed from a detached, often ironic, perspective which is related to that of superior, or cosmic, irony]

[D2:898] Lide, Barbara, 'Strindberg på scenen i dag. Postmoderna parodier', *Strindbergiana* (Stockholm), 13 (1998), pp. 82-91. Illus. ['Strindberg on Stage Today. Postmodern Parodies'. Identifies elements of postmodernist parody of Sg's style and form in contemporary stagings of his plays with reference to Sven Valdemar Holm's production of *Fröken Julie*, Teater Les Enfants's version of *Fordringsägare*, and Emil Graffman's production of *Brott och brott*]

[D2:899] Light, James, 'Why Strindberg?', *Provincetown Playbill*, 1925-26, No. 3.

[D2:900] Lindau, Paul, 'Strindberg als Dramatiker des Expressionismus', *Die Deutsche Bühne* (Berlin), 12:21-22 (24 May 1920), pp. 371-374. ['Strindberg as an Expressionist Dramatist']

[D2:901] Linde, Ebbe, 'Strindbergs dramatik', in Lars Ardelius and Gunnar Rydström, red., *Författarnas litteraturhistoria*, Den andra boken, Stockholm: Författarförlaget, 1978, pp. 55-77. ['Strindberg's Plays'. Linde offers a personal response to Sg's dramas, placing *Ett drömspel* highest as his 'richest and most consummate work', but he also discusses *Fröken Julie*, *Till Damaskus*, *Dödsdansen*, *Spöksonaten*, *Stora landsvägen*, and the history plays (of which *Erik XIV* is the finest, followed by *Karl XII*, and *Mäster Olof*, even if the latter is more diffuse in structure). Linde also comments on the importance of Sg's post-Inferno dramaturgy for German expressionism and many later dramatists, including Luigi Pirandello, Pär Lagerkvist, Nikolai Evreinov, Eugene O'Neill, Stanisław Witkiewicz, Samuel Beckett, and Boris Vian]

[D2:902] Lindenbaum, Arne, 'Strindberg på landsortsscenen', *Afton-Tidningen* (Stockholm), 2 February 1949. ['Strindberg in the Provincial Theatre']

[D2:903] Lindenbaum, Arne, 'Strindbergs scen fyller 50 år', *Dala-Tidningen* (Falun), 27 November 1957. ['The 50th Anniversary of Strindberg's Theatre'. On the founding of the Intimate Theatre by Sg and August Falck]

[D2:904] Lindenbaum, Arne, 'Strindbergs ungdomsteater', *Afton-Tidningen* (Stockholm), 25 January 1949. ['Strindberg's Youthful Theatre']

[D2:905] Lindenbaum, Arne, 'Strindbergsscenen vid Bantorget', *Afton-Tidningen* (Stockholm), 26 February 1949. ['The Strindberg Theatre at Bantorget'. Commemorates the Intimate Theatre founded by Sg and August Falk]

[D2:906] Lindenbaum, Arne, 'Teaterhöst för 50 år sen: Strindberg fick egen teater i Stockholm', *Aftonbladet* (Stockholm), 1 December 1957. ['The Autumn Theatre Season 50 Years Ago: Strindberg got his own Theatre in Stockholm'. Comments on the founding of the Intimate Theatre by Sg and August Falck]

[D2:907] Lindenberger, Herbert, 'Experiencing History', *Scandinavian Studies* (Madison), 62:1 (1990), 7-23. [The opening address to the 9th International Strindberg Conference on Sg and History. Provides a theoretical backdrop for a consideration of Sg's history plays by examining the historicity implicit in 19th-Century thinking]

[D2:908] Lindenberger, Herbert, 'Experiencing History', in Birgitta Steene, ed., **B1:434**, *Strindberg and History*, pp. 11-27. [Rpr. of **D2:907**]

[D2:909] Linder, Eric Hjalmar, 'Strindberg, ung dramatiker', *Göteborgs-Posten*, 14 May 1962. ['Strindberg, Young Dramatist'. Reviews Volume One of Carl Reinhold Smedmark's incomplete text-critical edition of the plays]

[D2:910] Lindström, Göran, 'August Strindbergs dramer, Vol. 4', *Sydsvenska Dagbladet* (Malmö), 17 December 1970. [Reviews Volume Four in Carl Reinhold Smedmark's incomplete text-critical edition of the plays]

[D2:911] Lindström, Johan, 'Strindberg. *Tryckt och otryckt I*', *Arbetet* (Malmö), 8 April 1890. [Reviews *Fordringsägare*, *Paria*, and *Samum* on publication. The first of these is 'gripping' and a complete exemplification of Sg's theories on a new form of drama in the accompanying essay 'Om modernt drama och modern teater']

[D2:912] Livadić, Branimir, 'Dramaturške ideje A. Strindberga', *Ilustrirani kazališni list sa dnevnim programom* (Zagreb), 2:22 (1911-12), 3-6. [Discusses Sg's ideas on dramaturgy. R.471]

[D2:913] Loewenberg, Karl, 'Strindberg als Expressionist', *Die Scene* (Berlin), 11:2-3 (1921), 44-46. ['Strindberg as an Expressionist'. Notes that the transition to expressionism which Sg achieved in *Ett drömspel*, *Till Damaskus*, and *Stora landsvägen* is already implicit his remarks on characterisation in the Preface to *Fröken Julie*, but it is as an expressionist rather than a naturalist that he has been most influential for the development of the modern theatre and later dramatists]

[D2:914] Loewenberg, Karl, 'Strindberg als Expressionist', in Hans-Peter Bayerdörfer, Hrsg., **B3:85**, *Strindberg auf der deutschen Bühne*, pp. 321-324. ['Strindberg as an Expressionist'. Rpr. of **D2:913**]

[D2:915] Loiseau, Georges, 'Introduction', in Auguste Strindberg, *Créanciers*, *Le Lien*, *On ne joue pas avec le feu*, Paris: Paul Ollendorff, 1894. 342 pp. [Introduces the first French edition of *Fordringsägare*, *Bandet*, and *Leka med elden*, translated by Loiseau in consultation with Sg]

[D2:916] Loiseau, Georges, 'Introduction', in Auguste Strindberg, *Père*, *Le paria*, Paris: Paul Ollendorff, 1895. IX+247 pp. [Introduces the author's own translations of *Fadren* and *Paria*, undertaken in consultation with Sg after the latter had himself produced a French version of *Fadren*]

[D2:917] Lucas, Craig, 'The Disturbing Truths Told by Strindberg', *New York Times*, 7 October 2001. [An appraisal of Sg and his 'disturbing truths'. Lucas considers him more compassionate towards his female figures than his male, and only Shakespeare is comparable to him in his ability to renew both form and content. Published in conjunction with the staging of *Dödsdansen* on Broadway with Ian McKellen as Edgar and Helen Mirren as Alice]

[D2:918] [Lugné-Poe, Aurélian], 'Lugné-Poe om Strindbergs dramer', *Göteborgs Handels- och Sjöfartstidning*, 6 June 1928. ['Lugné-Poe on Strindberg's Plays'. An interview with the theatre director who staged the French premières of *Fordringsägare* and *Fadren*, about his opinion of Sg as a dramatist]

[D2:919] Lundberg, E., 'Strindberg, *Samlade Verk*', *Hallandsposten* (Halmstad), 26 February 1985. [Reviews Volume 33 in *Samlade Verk*, containing nine one-acters from the late 1880s and 1890]

[D2:920] Lundberg, E., 'Strindberg, Pjäser', *Hallandsposten* (Halmstad), 13 September 1989. [Reviews Volumes 49 and 61 in *Samlade Verk*, containing *Näktergalen i Wittenberg* and *Siste riddaren*, *Riksföreståndaren*, and *Bjälbo-Jarlen* respectively]

[D2:921] Lundgren, Lars O., 'Två Athendramer av August Strindberg', *Platonselskabet. Symposium* (Lund), 16 (2003), 187-196. ['Two Athenian Dramas by August Strindberg'. Discusses *Hermione* and *Hellas*, two plays on Athenian subjects written at widely different periods of Sg's career. Summary in English]

[D2:922] m- [J. A. Runström], 'Konst och litteratur', Aftonbladet (Stockholm), 6 June 1902. [Reviews *Kronbruden*, *Svanevit*, and *Ett drömspel* on publication. All three plays have something of the dream play about them, even the first in which Sg's prodigious imagination repeatedly breaks the frame of the folk play. However, this last judgement piece which recalls *Advent*, is nevertheless the best of the three: *Svanevit* is subjective in the extreme and *Ett drömspel* crosses the boundary of the arbitrary. But even someone who finds the whole thing bizarre cannot help admiring the intensity of Sg's imagination, projected through images that combine to present a fragmentary and kaleidoscopic picture of the great misery of existence]

[D2:923] m- [J. A. Runström], 'Konst och litteratur', *Aftonbladet* (Stockholm), 8 December 1904. [Reviews *Till Damaskus III*, *Kristina*, and *Näktergalen i Wittenberg* on publication. Although Luther is portrayed with a certain robust power, there is nothing here of his burning faith. The dialogue contains numerous coarse expressions while the play as a whole testifies to Sg's febrile way of working and his almost total lack of artistic responsibility for, as in other of his recent history plays, he has given us a first draft rather than a fully composed drama. Part III of *Till Damaskus* is a gripping work and superior to its predecessors; this is a domain where Sg stands alone, without predecessors or competitors. In *Kristina*, however, both the characterisation and the dialogue are poor]

[D2:924] McCarthy, Justin Huntly, 'August Strindberg såsom dramatiker. Ur en uppsats i *The Fortnightly Review*', in Gustaf Fröding, red., **B1:142**, *En bok om Strindberg*, pp. 37-48. ['August Strindberg as a Dramatist. From an Essay in *The Fortnightly Review*'. Swedish translation of part of McCarthy's pioneering English appreciation of Sg in **B2:264**]

[D2:925] McCarthy, Justin Huntly, 'Pages on Plays', *The Gentleman's Magazine* (London), 49 (1892), 205-210. [Presents Sg's theories on drama as set forth in the Preface to *Fröken Julie* to English readers for the first time]

[D2:926] McFarlane, James [Walter], 'Strindberg's Vision: Microscopic or Spectroscopic?', in Göran Stockenström, ed., **D2:288**, *Strindberg's Dramaturgy*, pp. 131-140. [Demonstrates with reference to *Fadren*, Georg Brandes's essay 'Om "Det uendeligt Sma" og "Det uendeligt Store" i Poesien', and Adalbert Stifter's *Bunte Steine* (1853) that Sg's 'astonishing capacity for prefiguring the fundamental patterns of modern scientific and philosophical enquiry' is related to 'his conviction – which grew progressively stronger in the last twenty years of his life – that many of the smaller and seemingly inconsequential things of modern living are unexpectedly found to be charged with high-intensity meaning']

[D2:927] McKinney, George W., 'Projecting Strindberg', *Players Magazine* (DeKalb, Illinois), 34:2 (1957), 32-33.

[D2:928] Madsen, Børge Gedsø, 'Strindberg as a Naturalistic Theorist: The Essay "Om modernt drama och modern teater"', *Scandinavian Studies* (Lawrence, Kansas), 30:2 (1958), 85-92. [A descriptive account of Sg's essay, placing it in relation to the contemporary discussion of naturalism in France, the repertoire and aims of the Théâtre Libre, Zola's theories, and Henry Becque's plays]

[D2:929] Magnusson, Bo, '*Påsk* och *Drömspelet*', *Eskilstuna-Kuriren*, 11 April 1968.

[D2:930] Magnusson, Bo, '*Samlade Verk*', *Eskilstuna-Kuriren*, 22 April 1986. [Reviews Volume 27 in *Samlade* Verk, containing *Fadren, Fröken Julie*, and *Fordringsägare*]

[D2:931] Magnusson, Bo, '*Samlade Verk*', *Eskilstuna-Kuriren*, 5 August 1986. [Reviews Volume 33 in *Samlade Verk*, containing nine naturalistic one-acters]

[D2:932] Mahen, Jiří, 'Sopechny duch', in *Pfied oponou*, Brno, 1920, pp. 9-16. ['Before the Curtain'. An introduction to Sg's work as a dramatist entitled 'A Vulcanic Spirit' which originally introduced a translation of *Oväder* into Czech, performed at the Reduta Theatre, Brno, in 1919-1920. Mahen describes Sg as a transitional figure between the 19th and the 20th Centuries, a dramatist without compare in the whole of European literature. 'He creates his figures out of his own being and his plays resemble Munch's paintings. Physically, they are almost unendurable and yet they convey the circumstances of our lives with a shattering reality']

[D2:933] Maillefer, Jean-Marie, 'Un précurseur du théâtre de l'absurde', *Europe* (Paris), No. 858 (October 2000), pp. 60-77. ['A Forerunner of the Theatre of the Absurd'. Traces the emergence of Sg as a precursor of the theatre of the absurd and identifies passages in *Erik XIV, Gustav Adolf, Ett drömspel, Karl XII, Kaspers fettisdag, Näktergalen i Wittenberg*, and *Stora landsvägen* which express a view of the world in keeping with Camus's definition of the absurd, as well as with the absurdist theatre of Ionesco, Adamov, and Beckett. Maillefer observes that, 'If Sg ushers in the general mood and the tragic dimension so characteristic of the contemporary theatre of the absurd, it is even more astonishing to note that he also prepares the way for the techniques and the dramaturgical procedures of the absurd']

[D2:934] Marchand, J., 'Strindberg, *Plays*, Third Series', *The Bookman* (New York), 38 (December 1913), 435-437. [Reviews Volume Three of Edwin Björkman's translations of the plays]

[D2:935] Marcus, Carl David, 'Svensk dramatik', *Ord och Bild* (Stockholm), 18:5 (1909), 279-284. [Reviews *Sista Riddaren, Riksföreståndaren*, and *Abu Casems tofflor* on publication. The first of these demonstrates once again Sg's ability to bring the past to life on stage, and is imbued with something of his own, ever-changing and universally vital soul; the second has obviously been thrown together in haste and 'lacks both a hero and a plot'; while the verse in the third, and Sg's use of rhyme, is praiseworthy. If he had only bathed the work in the kind of fairy-tale mood with which he previously endowed *Svanevit*, it would have assumed an even higher lustre]

[D2:936] Marcus, Carl David, 'Strindbergs naturalistiska skådespel', *Tiden* (Stockholm), 15 (1923), 443-464. ['Strindberg's Naturalistic Plays']

[D2:937] Marken, Amy Van, 'Strindbergnotities', 1-2, *Bzzlletin* (Amsterdam), Nos 86 and 88 (May and September 1981), pp. 85-93, 29-33. [Comments on *Ett drömspel, Stora landsvägen, Gustav III, Pelikanen*, and Mina Mezzadri's production of *Fadren* with Il Carro dei Comici]

[D2:938] Marken, Amy van, 'Strindbergs Koningsdramas', in *Het laatste Woord: Bijzondere uitgave van de Sticjting 'Kroniek van Kunst en Kultuur'*, Amsterdam: P.N. van Kampen & Zoon, 1968, pp. 74-85. Illus. ['Strindberg's Royal Dramas'. Discusses *Gustav Vasa, Erik XIV, Karl XII*, and *Gustav III*, relating them as historical dramas to his other plays, and maintaining their theatrical potential. Although less frequently performed abroad than his naturalistic or expressionist works, there is no reason why they should prove any less effective on stage than Shakespeare's history plays]

[D2:939] Marowitz, Charles, 'Approaching Strindberg by Passing Him By', in Donald Weaver, ed., **D2:331**, *Strindberg on Stage*, pp. 53-63. [When Sg wrote he created dream imagery, in the naturalist plays just as in the post-Inferno dream plays: 'exaggeration and distortion, obsessiveness and hallucination were his very grammar', and his plays are not performed today in an appropriate style. His language is 'often gauche, turgid and stodgy'. We should not 'doodle' in his works, as actors and directors continue to do, but develop an experimental style of production which will make manifest the inner world concealed beneath the surface of his plays]

[D2:939a] Marowitz, Charles, 'Om a nærme sig Strindberg ved å styre unna ham', *Arena* (Trondheim), 4:3 (1980-81), pp. 13-15, 17-19, 21-22. ['Approaching Strindberg by Passing Him By'. Norwegian translation of **D2:939**]

[D2:940] Marowitz, Charles, 'Pristupati Strindbergu zaodilazeci ga', *Prolog* (Zagreb), 55-56 (1983), pp. 32-37. Illus. [Translation of **D2:939**]

[D2:941] Marschall, Brigitte, 'Higher States of Consciousness in August Strindberg's "Inferno Dramas"', in Michael Robinson and Sven Hakon Rossel, eds, **B1:387**, *Expressionism and Modernism*, pp. 111-120. [Suggests that Sg's dream plays *Till Damaskus*, *Ett drömspel*, and *Spöksonaten* express the universal correspondences, double images, and transition mechanisms of an all-embracing philosophy of life as experienced under the influence of drugs, of which he had direct experience with his chemical experiments and the exploration of heightened states of consciousness in the prose piece 'Sensations detraquées' (1894)]

[D2:942] Märker, Friedrich, 'Zum Problem Strindberg', *Das deutsche Drama* (Berlin), 4 (1921), 10-15. ['On the Strindberg Problem'. An unsympathetic view of Sg's current importance for the German theatre]

[D2:943] Märker, Friedrich, 'Zum Problem Strindberg', *Theater Rundschau* (Hamburg), 2:9 (1922), pp. 2-3. [See **D2:942**]

[D2:944] Martersteig, M., 'Das Strindberg-Bild und die Kommenden', *Das deutsche Theater* (Bonn), 1 (1922-23). ['The Image of Strindberg and the Future']

[D2:945] Martin, Joe, 'Introduction: Strindberg – A Revaluation', in *Strindberg – Other Sides. Seven Plays*, New York: Peter Lang, 1997, pp. [1]-56. [Introduces Martin's own translations of *Den starkare, Paria, Samum, Dödsdansen, Karl XII, Spöksonaten*, and *Pelikanen*, with comments on each of the plays and an informative overview of Sg's life and work, including several of his non-dramatic texts]

[D2:946] Martini, Andrea, 'Strindberg e la tentazione visionaria: un itinerario teatrale verso il cinema', in Merete Kjøller Ritzu, ed., **D1:375**, *La didascalie nella letteratura teatrale Scandinava. Testo drammatico e sintesi scenica*, pp. 173-182. ['Strindberg and the Visionary Temptation: A Theatrical Journey towards Cinema'. Discusses the increasingly cinematic aspects of Sg's theatre as it develops from the naturalistic plays of the 1880s to *Till Damaskus*, *Ett drömspel*, and the Chamber Plays, with their pronounced Artaudian elements]

[D2:947] Martinus, Eivor, 'Introduction', in August Strindberg, *The Father, Lady Julie, Playing with Fire*, Charlbury, Oxon: Amber Lane Press, 1998, pp. 7-16. [A biographically framed introduction to the author's own translations]

[**D2:948**] Martinus, Eivor, 'Strindberg Indirect', in Kirsten Wechsel, Hrsg., **B1:473**, *Strindberg and His Media*, pp. 213-222. [Discusses the transposition of Sg's published play texts to their other medium on the stage in the light of their further translation from Swedish into another language]

[**D2:949**] Martinus, Eivor, 'Margareta Wirmark, *Den kluvna scenen*; *Kampen med döden*', *Swedish Book Review* (Lampeter), 2002:1, pp. 65-67. [Reviews **D2:332** and **E35:129**]

[**D2:950**] Martynova, O. S., 'Kartina "faustovskoi dushi" v Ich-Drama A. Strindberga i nemetskogo ekspressionizma', *Filologicheskie Nauki*, 1 (1996), 46-54. [Studies the relationship between Sg's post-Inferno plays and both Goethe's *Faust* and German expressionist 'ich-drama']

[**D2:951**] Masát, Andras, 'Vom Nutzen und Nachteil des historischen Dramas. Zu Ibsens und Strindbergs historischen Dramen', in Hans Schottmann, Hrsg., *Arbeiten zur Skandinavistik* 11, Arbeitstagung der deutschsprachigen Skandinavistik 8-14 August 1993 in Sigtuna, Münster: Kleinheinrich, 1994, pp. 323-333. ['On the Advantages and Drawbacks of the Historical Drama'. Concerning the History Plays of Ibsen and Strindberg'. Whereas Ibsen's historical dramas represent an early stage of his development towards *Peer Gynt* and *Brand*, on the one hand, and the dramas of contemporary life, on the other, Sg's are an integral part of his *œuvre* as a whole, and invested with many of the same personal concerns and formal experimentation as his other works for the stage. From the outset, *Mäster Olof* introduces the modern notion of relativity that Ibsen would only approach in his later plays, from *The Wild Duck* onwards, and the protagonists of *Gustav Adolf*, *Gustav Vasa*, and *Kristina* have no real antagonist but, like the protagonists of Sg's other post-Inferno dramas, are their own adversaries]

[**D2:952**] Mathieu, André, 'Un pas nouveau dans la connaissance de Strindberg', *Cahiers Littéraires O.R.T.F.* (Paris), 1970:12. ['A New Step in the Knowledge of Strindberg']

[**D2:953**] Mattsson, Margareta, 'Strindberg, August. *Dramas of Testimony*, Translations and Introductions by Walter Johnson, *Scandinavian Studies* (Lawrence, Kansas), 49:2 (1977), 277-278. [Reviews Johnson's translations of *Dödsdansen I-II*, **E35:50**. Mattsson suggests that these 'authoritative' volumes are becoming '*the* scholarly English edition' of the plays]

[**D2:954**] Mattsson, Margareta, 'Strindberg, August. *Apologia and Two Folk Plays. The Great Highway, The Crownbride* and *Swanwhite*', *Scandinavian Studies* (Lawrence, Kansas), 54:3 (1982), 270-271. Illus. [Reviews Walter Johnson's translations of *Stora landsvägen*, *Kronbruden*, and *Svanevit*]

[**D2:955**] Mattsson, Margareta, '*Strindberg. Three Experimental Plays*, Translated with an introduction by F. R. Southerington', *Scandinavian Studies* (Lawrence, Kansas), 48:1 (1976), 111-112. [A rightly critical review of a poorly translated and badly edited volume containing English versions of *Fröken Julie, Den starkare*, and *Ett drömspel*]

[**D2:956**] Mattsson, Margareta, 'August Strindberg. *Pre-Inferno Plays*, Translations and Introductions by Walter Johnson', and 'August Strindberg. *A Dream Play* and *Four Chamber Plays*', *Scandinavian Studies* (Lawrence, Kansas), 46:4 (1974), 444-447. [A positive review of two volumes in Johnson's University of Washington Press series of translations which only queries his choice of 'Lady Julie' as an English title for *Fröken Julie*. Otherwise, 'it is precisely because of his inspired and informed adherence to a strict literalness whenever possible that Johnson's translations are so valuable and unique']

[D2:957] Maximov, Vadim, 'Strindberg and the French Symbolist Tradition in the Theatre', in Michael Robinson, ed., **B1:379**, *The Moscow Papers*, pp. 49-56. [Traces Sg's links with Parisian symbolism and considers the importance of his later works for Antonin Artaud's concept of the theatrical double]

[D2:958] Mazzini, M., 'Fugure materne nella dramaturgia europea del primo novecento: Strindberg, Pirandello, Witkacy', *Acta Universitatis Wratislaviensis* (Wroclaw), 34 (1991), pp. 55-61. ['Maternal Figures in European Dramaturgy in the Early 20th Century: Strindberg, Pirandello, and Witkiewicz']

[D2:959] M., D. L., 'Plays, Fourth Series, On Romantic Scandinavia', Boston Evening Transcript, 1 March 1916. [Concentrates on Edwin Björkman's translation of the folkloric *Kronbruden* rather than the other plays in the volume (*Spöksonaten*, *Gustav Vasa*, and *Första varningen*)]

[D2:960] M., D. L., '*Plays*, Fourth Series', *American Review of Reviews* (New York), 53 (1916), 376. [Reviews *Kronbruden*, *Spöksonaten*, *Första varningen*, and *Gustav Vasa* as in **D2:959**]

[D2:961] Mehring, Walter, 'Zu Strindbergs Traumspielen', *Blätter des Deutschen Theaters* (Berlin), 8:7 (1921-22), pp. 5-6. ['On Strindberg's Dream Plays']

[D2:962] Meidal, Björn, 'Köket – det mest dramatiska av alla strindbergska rum', in Heidi von Born, red., **U1:149**, *Med himlen till tak...och Drottninggatan som golv. Femton balkongtal till Strindberg*, pp. 57-60. ['The Kitchen – The Most Dramatic of all Strindbergian Rooms'. Argues with reference to *Fröken Julie*, *Ett drömspel*, *Fadren*, and the Chamber Plays that the kitchen where the food that sustains or poisons life is prepared is the most dramatic location in Sg's plays]

[D2:963] Meidal, Björn, 'Punk- och plockepinn-teater? Thorsten Flincks uppsättningar av *Fadren* och *Paria*', *Strindbergiana* (Stockholm), 16 (2001), pp. 43-[53]. Illus. ['Punk and Spillikins Theatre? Thorsten Flinck's Productions of *The Father* and *Pariah*'. Discusses Flinck's stagings of *Fadren* at the Teater Plaza and *Paria* at the Intimate Theatre, both of which turn Sg's naturalism on its head. In the former, where Flinck himself plays the Captain, death and sexuality are made immediately and physically concrete. Both the principal characters are present as at once adults and children throughout much of the play, in a production that recalls absurdism by the way it renders the language of Sg's text literally, in the form of stage images. In *Paria*, meanwhile, Flinck plays both roles as a conflict between two sides of the same person. Sg's Nietzschean battle of the brains thus becomes an act for Siamese twins, as Naturalism evolves into metatheatre]

[D2:964] Melchinger, Siegfried, 'Strindberg heute', *Nationaltheater Mannheim. Bühnenblätter für die 182. Spielzeit*, 1960-61, Hefte 80 (1960-61). ['Strindberg Today'. An assessment of Sg's current standing as a dramatist]

[D2:965] Mencken, H[enry] L., 'Plays by August Strindberg', *The Book Buyer* (New York), 37:3 (1912), 34-35. [Reviews Edwin Björkman's English translations of *Ett drömspel*, *Bandet*, and *Dödsdansen*, including a foreword to the first of these which Sg wrote as an afterthought in 1910 [sic] and placed at Björkman's disposal, thus permitting the latter to publish it here for the first time]

[D2:966] Mencken, H[enry] L., 'The Terrible Swede', *The Smart Set* (New York), 37:2 (June 1912), 153-158. [Comments mainly on the naturalistic plays (here including *Dödsdansen*) which are the work of 'a metaphysical realist who has carried the search for motives and causes to its uttermost limit'. Mencken stresses the element of personal, lived experience in Sg's drama ('Sg, indeed, has lived more stories than even Sg could invent') and his preoccupation with gender conflict as the force that informs his best work. See **B1:368**]

[D2:967] Mencken, H[enry] L., 'Strindberg – A Final Estimate', in *H. L. Mencken's Smart Set Criticism*, Selected and Edited by William H. Nolte, Ithaca, New York: Cornell University Press, 1968, pp. [64]-68. [Rpr. of the discussion of Sg in **D1:630**]

[D2:968] Menter, Leon, 'Strindberg, Kortner und wir', *Die Weltbühne* (Berlin), 5 (1951), 193-195. ['Strindberg, Kortner and Us'. Published in conjunction with Fritz Kortner's staging of *Fadren* in West Berlin]

[D2:969] Mesarić, Kalman, 'August Strindberg', *Komedija* (Zagreb), 3:35 (1936), 1-2. [R.569]

[D2:970] Messer, Max, 'Vor höherer Instanz', *Die Gesellschaft* (München), 16:2 (1900), p. 126. ['Before a Higher Court'. Reviews *Advent* and *Brott och brott* on publication]

[D2:971] Michel, Wilhelm, 'Über Strindberg', *Die Schaubühne* (Berlin), 3:1 (1907), 265-266. [Discusses *Påsk*, which is absolutely a tragedy, and *Till Damaskus*, which would make a fine project for a puppet theatre]

[D2:972] Michel, Wilhelm, 'Über Strindberg', in Hans-Peter Bayerdörfer, Hrsg., **B3:85**, *Strindberg auf der deutschen Bühne*, pp. 177-179. [Rpr. of **D2:971**]

[D2:973] Milekic, Gudrun, 'Television och film som strukturer i *Vasasagans* dramaturgi', *Strindbergiana* (Stockholm), 17 (2002), pp. 93-[106]. Illus. ['The Dramaturgy of the *Vasa Saga* is Structured by Film and Television'. Presents Staffan Valdemar Holm's conflation of seven of Sg's history plays as a six-hour cycle in chronological order of the events they depict, performed in Malmö in 1997-98. Draws attention to the televisual and cinematic techniques adopted in both the staging and dramaturgy]

[D2:974] Milton, John R., 'The Esthetic Fault of Strindberg's "Dream Plays"', *Tulane Drama Review* (New Orleans), 4:3 (1960), 108-116. [Contends that plays like *Till Damaskus*, *Ett drömspel*, and *Spöksonaten* fail to combine subjectivity with the correct dramatic techniques to arrive at the proper aesthetic distance essential for the creation of effective theatre. The 'dreamer' is not established as an element *within* the plays but remains associated with the author, thus alienating the spectator]

[D2:975] Mitchell, Christopher Joseph, 'Gender and Marriage Constructions Across the "Inferno": August Strindberg's *The Father* and *Dödsdansen I*', in Michael Robinson and Sven Hakon Rossel, eds, **B1:387**, *Expressionism and Modernism*, pp. 121-128. [Mitchell contends that, in both his pre- and post-Inferno periods, Sg was equally disposed to championing and questioning the elements and implications of both sides in the struggle between the dominant patriarchal order and its female opposition]

[D2:976] Molander, Harald, 'Modern dramatisk konst VII och IX', *Aftonbladet* (Stockholm), 4 June, and 26 August 1892. ['Modern Dramatic Art, VII and IX'. Mentions Sg's recent plays with approval in the course of a discussion of modern dramatic art]

[D2:977] Molander, Olof, 'August Strindberg', *Hörde ni? Månadstidskrift för Sveriges Radio* (Stockholm), 2 (1949), 212-215.

[D2:978] Molander, Olof, 'En svensk regissör om Reinhardtspelen', *Scenen* (Stockholm), 1 January 1921. ['A Swedish Director on Reinhardt's Theatre'. Records Olof Molander's initially enthusiastic response to Max Reinhardt's productions of *Ett drömspel* and *Pelikanen*, over which Reinhardt's spirit presided more powerfully, more vitally, more brilliantly than ever]

[D2:979] Molander, Olof, 'Möten med Strindberg', *Svenska Dagbladet* (Stockholm), 21 January 1949. ['Encounter with Strindberg'. Molander distances himself from Max Reinhardt's 'romantic expressionism', which he considers completely alien to Sg's surrealistic dreamplay dramaturgy. The latter is concerned with the nightmares of everyday life rather than any more extreme nightmare. The characters in *Pelikanen* may certainly appear strange, but they are not grotesques out of Daumier. Performed in this way, *à la* Reinhardt, the post-Inferno plays become unpalatable]

[D2:980] Molander, Olof, 'Strindbergska scenerier', in Sigurd Nauckhoff, red., *Harald Nordenson. En samling uppsatser tillägnade Harald Nordenson på 60-årsdagen den 10 augusti 1946*, Stockholm, 1946, pp. 241-250. ['Strindbergian Settings'. On designs for Sg's plays]

[D2:981] Monteyne, Lode, 'August Strindberg', *Het Tooneel* ('s-Gravenhage), 6 October 1923.

[D2:982] Morburger, Carl, 'Das "Strindberg Theater"', *Blätter des Deutschen Theaters* (Berlin), 3 (1913-14), 625-627.

[D2:983] Morburger, Carl, 'Das Kind in Strindbergs Dramen', *Blätter des Deutschen Theater* (Berlin), 3 (1913-14), 757-760. ['The Child in Strindberg's Plays']

[D2:984] Morgenstern, Christian, 'Zum Thema Strindberg', *Schwäbische Thalia* (Stuttgart), 8 (1926-27), 257-258. ['On the Subject of Strindberg']

[D2:985] Morgenstern, Christian, 'Strindberg', *Freiburger Theaterblätter*, 1929-30, pp. 286-287.

[D2:986] Mortensen, Johan [Martin], 'August Strindberg', *Thalia* (Stockholm), 3:3 (1912), 18-20. [An overview of Sg's work as a whole, in commemoration of his 63rd birthday, in which Mortensen places the stress on his work as a dramatist. According to Mortensen, 'There was no Swedish drama before *Mäster Olof*...Sg is the first to combine a significant content with a not only secure but often masterly technique'. See also **U4:39**]

[D2:987] Mortensen, Johan Martin, 'August Strindberg', in *Likt och olikt. Studier och kritiker*, Stockholm: Albert Bonniers Förlag, 1908, pp. [269]-297. [Rpr. of reviews of *Till Damaskus*, **E25:99**, *Vid högre rätt*, **D2:991**, and the history plays, **D2:988**]

[D2:988] Mortensen, Johan [Martin], 'Ett och annat om Strindbergs senaste historiska dramer', *Ord och Bild* (Stockholm), 10:1 (1901), 61-64. ['One Thing and Another about Strindberg's Latest History Plays'. Focuses principally on the representation of the central characters and finds the eponymous hero of *Gustav Vasa* to be the very finest combination of historical and poetic characterisation in Swedish literature]

[D2:989] Mortensen, Johan Martin, 'Ett och annat om Strindbergs senaste historiska dramer', in *Likt och olikt. Studier och kritiker*, Stockholm: Albert Bonniers Förlag, 1908, pp. 288-297. ['One Thing and Another about Strindberg's Latest History Plays'. Rpr. of **D2:988**]

[D2:990] Mortensen, Johan [Martin], '*Samlade otryckta skrifter. Del 1. Dramatiska arbeten*', *Forum* (Stockholm), 6 (1919), 7-9. [Reviews the plays and dramatic fragments published in Volume One of Vilhelm Carlheim-Gyllensköld's two-volume edition of Sg's collected unpublished works]

[**D2:991**] Mortensen, Johan [Martin], 'Ur bokmarknaden', *Ord och Bild* (Stockholm), 8:9 (1899), 494-495. [Reviews *Advent* and *Brott och brott* on publication. Although so unlike one another, these plays are characterised by a mood of reconciliation which suggests a milder view of people and of life than in Sg's previous works Mortensen emphasises the childlike qualities of the former, which is strikingly at odds with Sg, the feared revolutionary, and summarises the plot of the second which, unlike *Advent*, is rooted in the writer's lived experience]

[**D2:992**] Mortensen, Johan Martin, 'Vid högre rätt', in *Likt och olikt. Studier och kritiker*, Stockholm: Albert Bonniers Förlag, 1908, pp. [283]-287. ['Before a Higher Court'. Rpr. of **D2:991**]

[**D2:993**] 'Mr Gray', 'Strindbergs-teatern', *Ridå* (Stockholm), 1907:3. [Discusses the newly-founded Intimate Theatre, which will probably be devoted exclusively to staging Sg's plays]

[**D2:994**] Mudford, P. G., 'The Theatre of Trance: A View of the Consistency of Strindberg's Dramatic Craft', *Theatre Research International* (Oxford), 11:2-3 (1971), 133-140. [Identifies common features in Sg's theatre extending from *Fadren* and *Fröken Julie* to *Spöksonaten*. His greater naturalism presupposes a trance-like struggle between characters who are driven by their unconscious impulses, and is enacted in an intimate space that involves the audience in the action in an often discomforting manner]

[**D2:995**] Munthe, Arne, 'Strindberg på scenen', *Studiekamraten* (Tollarp), 10 (1928), pp. 3-4. ['Strindberg on Stage']

[**D2:996**] Müssener, Helmut, 'Auktorität und Sinnlichkeit in Strindbergs Dramen um die Jahrhundertwende', in Karol Sauerland, Hrsg., *Auktorität und Sinnlichkeit. Studien zur Literatur- und Geistestgeschichte zwischen Nietzsche und Freud.* Eine internationale Tagung veranstaltet vom Österreichischen Kulturinstitut in Bachotek Polen, Oktober 1984, Frankfurt am Main: Akten internationaler Kongresse auf den Gebieten der Ästhetik und der Literaturwissenschaft, 1986, pp. 129-155. ['Authority and Sensuality in Strindberg's Turn-of-the-Century Dramas']

[**D2:997**] Natanson, Wojciech, 'August Strindberg', *Twórczość* (Warsaw), 1962:5, pp. 77-86. [Stresses the importance of Sg's naturalism in the history of modern drama, and his influence on dramatists from Frank Wedekind to Max Frisch and Jean Anouilh. *Ett drömspel* may be compared with the role dreams play in Kafka's diaries; the outlook of both authors is a projection of a subjective reality made up of dreams, fantasies, and nightmare visions. Sg also anticipates psychoanalysis and works like *Fröken Julie* and *Ett drömspel* are full of motifs such as the inferiority complex or persecution mania that have become the commonplaces of psychoanalysis, and influenced recent American dramatists like Eugene O'Neill and Tennessee Williams. Natanson also describes the impact in Poland of Karol Adwentowicz's performance as Edgar in *Dödsdansen*, places Sg at the heart of modern European culture, where he has rightly been admired by Kafka, Thomas Mann, Camus, and Pirandello, and provides an overview of the stage history of Sg's plays in the Polish theatre]

[**D2:998**] Natanson, Wojciech, 'Wstęp', in A. Strindberg, *Dramaty*, Translated by Zygmunt Łanowski, Warsaw: Panstwowy Instytut Wydawniczy, 1962. 440 pp. [Rpr. of **D2:997** as the introduction to a collection of Sg's plays in Polish translation which contains *Fadren, Fröken Julie, Mäster Olof, Ett drömspel*, and *Spöksonaten*]

[D2:999] Nathan, George Jean, 'Strindberg', in *Materia Critica*, New York: Alfred A. Knopf, 1924. [245] pp. [When his mind was still blessed with reason, Sg wrote excellent drama, some of it with enduring life. Occasionally a genius, he was also an absurdly unconscious quack]

[D2:1000] Nathan, George Jean, 'Strindberg', in *Materia Critica*, New Introduction by Charles Angoff, Rutherford-Madison-Teaneck: Fairleigh Dickinson University Press, 1971, pp. 67-69. [Rpr. of **D2:999**]

[D2:1001] N. E-nn [Nils Erdmann], 'Strindberg Memorandum', *Nya Dagligt Allehanda* (Stockholm), 22 January 1910. [Reviews the Fourth of Sg's memoranda to members of the Intimate Theatre, which comments on *Macbeth* and other Shakespeare plays. These essays teach us little about Shakespeare but, with their sudden shifts between the inspired and the ridiculous, they remain of interest for what they have to say about Sg]

[D2:1002] Netland, Anna Karolina, 'Virkelighet og illusjon i August Strindbergs *Till Damaskus I* og *Spöksonaten*', *NORskrift* (Oslo), No. 107 (2004), pp. 69-86. ['Reality and Illusion in August Strindberg's *To Damascus I* and *The Ghost Sonata*'. Examines the dramatic devices whereby Sg has problematised the notion of an evident distinction between reality and illusion with considerable reference to earlier critics (Dahlström, Lamm, Bark, Törnqvist, and Blackwell). Moreover, although they both avail themselves of aspects of Sg's dreamplay technique, the two plays demonstrate a distinct change in the way in which objective reality is perceived. In *Till Damaskus* the characters have both a subjective and an objective existence, thus illustrating how reality is partly subjective, whereas in *Spöksonaten* objective reality is depicted as far more problematic, as is the extent to which the characters may be judged either objective or subjective]

[D2:1003] Neuweiler, A., 'Strindberg-Inszenierungen', *Die Scene* (Berlin), 11:2-3 (1921), p. 59. ['Staging Strindberg']

[D2:1004] Neumann-Hofer, Otto, 'Theater-Rundschau', *Nord und Süd* (Breslau), 143 (1912), 259-262.

[D2:1005] Nightingale, Benedict, 'Truths torn from a tortured heart of darkness', *The Times* (London), 15 February 2005. [Comments on the kind of realism that Sg brought to the stage, whose source was the ugly depths of his self-loathing and paranoia]

[D2:1006] Nilsson, Albert, 'Strindbergs dramatiska kvarlåtenskap', *Göteborgs Handels- och Sjöfartstidning*, 10 December 1918. ['Strindberg's Dramatic Literary Remains'. Reviews the plays and dramatic fragments published in Volume One of Vilhelm Carlheim-Gyllensköld's edition of Sg's collected unpublished works. These late works are imbued with a primitive mystical outlook, reminiscent of older forms of religion. Consequently, they have little to offer educated people today, although the passionate, demonic strength of *Holländarn* possesses a terrible suggestive power that is even more gripping than his earlier prose narrative, 'Tschandala']

[D2:1007] Nilsson, Albert, 'Strindbergs dramatiska kvarlåtenskap', in *Ur diktens värld*, Stockholm: Albert Bonniers Förlag, 1926, pp. 172-178. ['Strindberg's Dramatic Literary Remains'. Rpr. of **D2:1006**]

[D2:1008] Nilsson, Nils Åke, 'Strindberg och Konstnärliga Teatern i Moskva', *Meddelanden från Strindbergssällskapet* (Stockholm), 21 (1957), pp. 23-25. ['Strindberg and the Moscow Arts Theatre'. Documents known contacts between Sg and the MAT which were mediated by his German translator, Emil Schering. The latter suggested that Sg should write a play on Peter the Great to be directed by Stanislavskii, whom Schering thought might also stage *Abu Casems tofflor*]

[D2:1009] Nolin, Bertil, 'Strindberg as Director. His Theories on Staging and Acting in *Öppna brev till Intima Teatern*', in Kela Kvam, ed., **D2:158**, *Strindberg's Post-Inferno Plays*, pp. 119-128. Illus. [Sg wanted to extend his control to all stages of producing theatre; hence his practical interventions at the Intimate Theatre, both as a director during its second season and in his memoranda on acting and drama. Also includes brief comments on his understanding of the director's role and ideas on voice and tempo, setting, and casting]

[D2:1010] Nolin, Bertil, 'Strindberg – teaterns förnyare', in Lars Lönnroth and Sven Delblanc, red., *Den svenska litteraturen*, 7 vols, Vol. 3: 'De liberala genombrotten: 1830-1890', Stockholm: Bonniers, 1988, pp. 266-268. Illus. ['Strindberg – The Renewer of the Theatre'. Comments on Sg's role in Swedish theatre]

[D2:1011] Nolin, Bertil, 'Strindberg – teaterns förnyare', in Lars Lönnroth and Sven Delblanc, red., *Den svenska litteraturen*, Vol. 2, Stockholm: Bonniers, 1999, pp. 266-268. Illus. [Revised edition of **D2:1010** in three volumes]

[D2:1012] Nolin, Bertil, 'Towards a Concept of an Intimate Theatre', *Nordic Theatre Studies* (Copenhagen), 6:1-2 (1993), 71-78. Illus. [Nolin charts a line of development in Sg's views on theatre which ends quite logically in the establishment of the Intimate Theatre and the writing of the Chamber Plays through which (as in the Preface to *Fröken Julie* and his founding of the Scandinavian Experimental Theatre in Copenhagen in 1888-89) he becomes closely associated with the Independent Theatre movement]

[D2:1013] Nordensvan, Georg, 'Strindbergs drei Märchenspiele', *Das Magazin für die Litteratur des In- und Auslandes* (Leipzig), 72:2 (1903), 269-271. ['Strindberg's Three Fairy-tale Plays'. Reviews *Kronbruden*, *Svanevit*, and *Ett drömspel* on publication]

[D2:1014] Norlin, Marianne, 'Strindbergs-föreställningar i Stockholm 1870-1912', *Teatervetenskap* (Stockholm), No. 23 (1981), 25-28. ['Performances of Strindberg in Stockholm, 1870-1912'. During his lifetime, Sg's plays failed to be performed at the major Stockholm theatres for long periods; his definitive breakthrough came only with Max Reinhardt's productions in Germany, which were the first to take account of the musical rhythm and tone of Sg's texts, and sometimes toured Scandinavia. Also contains a catalogue of plays with details concerning the length of their runs]

[D2:1015] Norlin, Marianne, 'Sven Erik Skawonius 1908-1981', *Teatervetenskap* (Stockholm), No. 23 (1981), 20-21. Illus. [A note on the Swedish stage-designer, which documents his professional links with Sg's work]

[D2:1016] Normann, J., 'Strindberg och Teatrene', *Nationaltidende* (Copenhagen), 22 August 1924. ['Strindberg and the Theatres']

[D2:1017] -o-, '*Gläubiger*, *Das Band*, *Vor dem Tod*, *Herbstzeichen*, *Mit dem Feuer spielen*', *Deutsche Dichtung* (Berlin), 18 (1895), p. 102. [Reviews *Fordringsägare*, *Bandet*, *Inför döden*, *Första varningen*, and *Leka med elden*]

[D2:1018] Oberholzer, Otto, 'August Strindbergs Komödien. Perspektiven aus der Sieht der modernen Komödientheorie', *Neue Zürcher Zeitung* (Zürich), No. 102. (1980). ['August Strindberg's Comedies. Perspectives in the Light of Modern Theory of Comedy'. Analyses Sg's stage comedies in the light of comic theory, from Peter Haida to Fritz Martini and Karl Guthke]

[D2:1019] Oberholzer, Otto, 'Strindberg und die Komödientheorie', in Oskar Bandle, Hrsg., **D2:8**, *Strindbergs Dramen im Lichte neuerer Methodendiskussionen*, pp. 97-118. ['Strindberg and the Theory of Comedy'. Identifies ten of Sg's plays, from *Anno fyrtioåtta* to *Kaspers fettisdag*, as possible comedies, and discusses them in the light of modern theories of comedy, which are in turn indebted to recent plays by Ionesco and other dramatists who have prompted new conceptions of the comic. Includes detailed discussions of *Kamraterna*, *Fordringsägare*, *Brott och brott*, and *Midsommar*]

[D2:1020] Ofrat, Gideon, 'The Structure of Ritual and Mythos in the Naturalistic Plays of August Strindberg', *Theatre Research International* (Oxford), 4:2 (1979), 102-116. [Uses the theories of Claude Levi-Strauss and Northrop Frye to trace the mythological and ritualistic structures which underlie *Fadren*, *Fröken Julie*, and *Fordringsägare*. Viewed through the lens of archetypes, these apparently naturalistic plays emerge as variations on the Oedipal myth, although in contrast to the latter, 'which rejects the origin of man from the earth, Sg affirms that origin.' According to Ofrat, Sg rejects the duality of male and female, foregrounds the notion of androgyny, and, along with the traditional dramatic patterns underlying the realism of these plays (thus *Fadren* embodies the classic comic archetype of the *Miles Gloriosus*), he organises them in terms of both Christian and Dionysian myth and ritual, a dualistic conflict between Christ and Antichrist in which the encounter of tragedy with comedy is often deeply ironic]

[D2:1021] Oland, Edith and Warner Oland, 'Foreword', in August Strindberg, *Plays*, Vol. II, Translated by Edith and Warner Oland, London: Frank Palmer, 1913, pp. v-ix. [Introduces translations of *Inför döden*, *Paria*, and *Påsk*]

[D2:1022] Oland, Edith and Warner, 'Foreword', in August Strindberg, *Plays*, Vol. IV, Translated by Edith and Warner Oland, London: Frank Palmer, 1913, pp. v-xiii. [Introduces the authors' translations of *Svanevit*, *Advent*, and *Oväder*]

[D2:1023] Ollén, Gunnar, 'Introduction', in August Strindberg, *World Historical Plays*, Translated from the Swedish by Arvid Paulson, The Library of Scandinavian Literature 6, New York: Twayne Publishers, Inc., and The American Scandinavian Foundation, 1970, pp. 1-9. [Introduces a volume containing translations of *Näktergalen i Wittenberg, Moses, Sokrates,* and *Kristus*]

[D2:1024] Ollén, Gunnar, 'Strindberg 1962', *World Theatre-Le Théâtre dans le monde* (Bruxelles), 11:1 (1962), 4-20. Illus. [Comments on Sg's personality and life, as well as on his contribution to world drama on the 50th anniversary of his death. English and French text]

[D2:1025] Ollén, Gunnar, 'Strindberg and Dramaten/Strindberg et Dramaten', *Swedish Theatre* (Stockholm), 1986:2, pp. 5-8. Illus. [Traces Sg's association with Dramaten, both during his life and afterwards. Parallel text in English and French]

[D2:1026] Ollén, Gunnar, 'Strindberg och Dramaten', *Kungliga dramatiska teatern. Stora scenen. Strindbergsjubileet 1949* (Stockholm), pp. 25-56. Illus. ['Strindberg and the Royal Dramatic Theatre'. Surveys Sg's turbulent relationship with Dramaten during his lifetime and considers its subsequent staging of his plays to date. Contains details of several premières and other major productions, illustrated by some striking photographs]

[D2:1027] Ollén, Gunnar, 'Strindberg och Dramaten', in Catharina Söderberg and Anna Bodin, red., **B1:347**, *Forskarliv – sex decennier med Strindberg*, pp. 58-76. [Rpr. of **D2:1026**]

[D2:1028] Ollén, Gunnar, 'Strindberg dramatik', in August Strindberg, *Hry*, Praha: Divadelní ústav, 2000, pp. 737-751. [The Afterword to Volume One of a new Czech edition of Sg's plays, translated by František Fröhlich (*Fröken Julie, Fordringsägare, Den starkare*), Dagmar Hartlová (*Fadren*), Irena Kunovská (*Erik XIV*), Libor Štukavec (*Mäster Olof, Gustav Vasa*), and Josef Vohryzek (*Leka med elden, Bandet, Kristina*)]

[D2:1029] Ollén, Gunnar, 'Strindberg som dramatiker', in Catharina Söderberg and Anna Bodin, red., **B1:347**, *Forskarliv – sex decennier med Strindberg*, pp. 119-121. ['Strindberg as a Dramatist']

[D2:1030] Ollén, Gunnar, 'Strindberg som skådespelare', in Råland Ginsburg, red., *Världens klassiker*, Stockholm: Utbildningsradion, 1990, pp. 92-95. ['Strindberg as Actor']

[D2:1031] Ollén, Gunnar, 'Strindberg sulle scene del mondo', in *Strindberg. Il meglio del teatro per la prima volta*, Torino:SET, 1951, pp. xlvii-lv. ['Strindberg on the World Stage'. A survey of Sg's place in world theatre in a volume of Italian translations of eighteen of his plays]

[D2:1032] Olofgörs, Gunnar, 'Livet, kärleken och döden: Tre Strindbergdramer', in *Scenografi och kostym: Gunilla Palmstierna-Weiss*, Stockholm: Carlsson Bokförlag, 1995, pp. 175-220. Illus. ['Life, Love, and Death. Three Strindberg Dramas'. Discusses productions of *Dödsdansen* at Dramaten in 1967, 1976, and 1978, as well as at the Düsseldorf Schauspielhaus in 1981; *Fadren* at the Munich Residenztheater in 1979 and Stockholms Stadsteater in 1981; and *Fröken Julie* at the Residenztheater in 1981 and Dramaten in 1985, all with designs by Gunilla Palmstierna Weiss. Summary in English and German]

[D2:1033] Oreglia, Giacomo, 'Strindberg', in *Strindberg. Il meglio del teatro per la prima volta*, I capolavori 6, Torino: SET, 1951, pp. xi-xxxvii. [Introduces a collection of eighteen of Sg's plays in Italian translation]

[D2:1034] Ostrowska Róża, 'Strindberg – teatr nieznany', *Głos Wybrzeża* (Gdańsk), 22-23 April 1967, pp. 4-5. ['Strindberg – An Unknown Art of the Theatre'. Discusses *Dödsdansen* and the role of Sg's theatre as the precursor of much modern drama in the course of a review of Piotr Paradowski's production of of *Dödsdansen I* at the Teatr Wybrzeża in Gdańsk, 22 April 1967, with Andrzej Szaławski as Edgar and Wanda Stanisławska-Loth as Alice. Ostrowska also stresses the play's evident affinities with Edward Albee's *Who's Afraid of Virgina Woolf*]

[D2:1035] Ottosson Pinna, Birgitta, 'Le "case viventi" di Strindberg', in Merete Kjøller Ritzu, ed., **D1:375**, *La didascalie nella letteratura teatrale Scandinava. Testo drammatico e sintesi scenica*, pp. 161-173. ['The "Living House" of Strindberg'. On the recurring image of the 'living house' in Sg's works, which culminates in the Chamber Plays (notably *Oväder, Spöksonaten*, and *Svarta handsken*), and the associated images of the 'red' house, 'blue' tower, and 'black' glove, with their possible Freudian associations]

[D2:1036] Ozaki, Yoshi, '[Introduction]' in August Strindberg, *Fukkatsu-sai hoka*, Tokyo, 1954. [Comments on *Påsk*, *I Rom*, and *Samum* in the author's own Japanese translation]

[D2:1037] Palmqvist, Bertil, '*Samlade Verk*', *Arbetet* (Malmö), 26 May 1984. [Reviews Volume 27 of *Samlade Verk*, containing *Fadren*, *Fröken Julie*, and *Fordringsägare*]

[D2:1038] P. A. R. [P. A. Rosenberg], 'Tre Skuespill', *Litteratur og Kritik* (Copenhagen), 1889, pp. 218-219. ['Three Plays'. Reviews Peter Hansen's Danish translations of *Mäster Olof*, *Gillets hemlighet*, and *Herr Bengts hustru*]

[D2:1039] Paracho, Ana Maria, and Fernando Midões, 'Introduction', in August Strindberg, *Tempestada, A casa queimada, A menina Júlia*, Lisboa: Editorial Presença, 1963. 311 pp. [Introduces Portuguese translations of *Oväder*, *Brända tomten*, and *Fröken Julie*]

[D2:1040] Paul Fritz, 'Ahnvater der Moderne. Strindbergs Dramen', *Deutsch Zeitung. Christ und Welt* (Stuttgart), 1973:34, p. 13. ['Forefathers of the Modern. Strindberg's Plays'. Recognises Sg as a major precursor of modern drama, and of modernity in general]

[D2:1041] Paul, Fritz, 'Episches Theater bei Strindberg?', *Germanistisch Romanische Monatsschrift* (Heidelberg), New Series, 24:3 (1974), 323-339. ['Strindberg's Epic Theatre?' Explores to what extent Sg may have prepared the way for Brecht's epic theatre with the station technique of *Till Damaskus*, the post-Nietzschean musical compositional principal in *Påsk*, and the new form of the Chamber Plays, as analysed by Peter Szondi in *Theorie des modernen Dramas*, **D1:450**. Although numerous striking correspondences exist, there is no direct correlation but, from his post-Inferno plays and theoretical writings, Paul suggests that one may deduce several ways in which Sg prepared the ground for Epic theatre. These include the way in which the station drama technique anticipates the loose sequence of 'Bildern' in Epic theatre, as does the revue structure of *Ett drömspel*; how the dissolution of time and space and the fracturing of the real through surreal and absurd moments in the sometimes cinematic Chamber Plays facilitates a break with the theatre of illusion; and, finally, the way in which Sg's post-Inferno plays question conventional notions of mimesis, sometimes including a narrative, epic, element in the form of a character who comments on, and links together, the actions performed by the more traditionally conceived *dramatis personae*. Paul concludes that breaking the illusion, the concept of *gestus*, and the dramatic independence of scenes are already present in Sg's plays, but without Brecht's political intent]

[D2:1042] Paul, Fritz, 'Idealismus und Realismus. Strindbergs erste Versuche zu einer dramatischen Theorie (1871-1882)', *Etudes Germaniques* (Paris), 32:4 (1977), 365-379. ['Idealism and Realism. Strindberg's First Attempt at a Theory of Drama (1871-1882)'. Examines Sg's theoretical comments on drama and aesthetics from his student paper on Oehlenschläger's play *Hakon Jarl* (1871) to the essay 'Om Realism' (1882), including comparisons with his practice as evidenced by the plays he wrote during this period]

[D2:1043] Paul, Fritz, 'Im Grenzbereich der Gattungen: Strindbergs monodramatische Experimente', in L. Forster and H.-G. Roloff, Hrsg., Akten des V. Internationalen Germanisten-Kongresses Cambridge 1975, *Jahrbuch für Internationale Germanistik* (Bad Homburg), 2:3 (1976), pp. 384-400. ['At the Frontiers of Genre: Strindberg's Monodramatic Experiments'. Studies Sg's experimentation with theatrical genres and the development of a modern, monodramatic form, focusing mainly on *Den starkare*,

Paria, and *Stora landsvägen* but also taking account of earlier works like Rousseau's 'scène lyrique', *Pygmalion*, the Benda-Brandes *Ariadne auf Naxos*, and Goethe's *Prosperina*. Paul identifies the 'microscopic' basis of Sg's approach to the one-act form with the aid of a passage in *Götiska rummen* and the impulse that his writing received from the French *quart d'heure* dramas staged at Antoine's Théâtre Libre, a genre which Sg radically renewed. *Den starkare* invites comparison with a form of theatre subsequently encountered in Jean Cocteau's *La Voix humaine* and Samuel Beckett's *Krapp's Last Tape*, but the apparently monodramatic voice of its single speaker assumes the presence of a second figure, and it is in fact not the speaker but the silent character who is the protagonist of Sg's play. It is thus impossible to speak of *Den starkare* as a strict monodrama. However, the technique of this kind of play, which represents the extreme reduction of an analytical drama in several acts and presents its essentially epic material in dramatic form, *is* relevant to the dramaturgy of *Till Damaskus* and *Ett drömspel*, in which the accumulation of individual scenes is related to a single consciousness. The epic qualities inherent in this approach are visible in *Stora landsvägen*, which presents the audience with the voice of a single, endlessly divisible but unifying character, and is thus, for all its numerous secondary figures, 'a covert form of monodrama']

[**D2:1044**] Paul, Fritz, 'Motivverfremdung im antimimetischen Drama am Beispiel von August Strindbergs Nachinfernodramatik', in Theodor Wolpers, Hrsg., *Ergebnisse und Perspektiven der literaturwissenschaftlichen Motiv- und Themenforschung*, Göttingen: Vandenhoeck und Ruprecht, 2002, pp. 225-250. [See **D2:1046**]

[**D2:1045**] Paul, Fritz, 'Strindberg og monodramaet', *Edda* (Oslo), 76:5 (1976), 283-295. ['Strindberg and Monodrama'. Norwegian version of **D2:1043**]

[**D2:1046**] Paul, Fritz, 'Strindbergs antimimetiska teater', Översättning Thommy Andersson, in Ulf Olsson, red., **B1:357**, *Strindbergs förvandlingar*, pp. 137-167. ['Strindberg's Anti-Mimetic Theatre'. An investigation into how Sg's post-Inferno plays demonstrate the way in which drama that mimetically reproduces the world which it takes as its subject is problematised when there are fundamental doubts concerning the reality of this world and the possibility of its representation. Paul examines the consequences of this change in scope for a public art like drama through analyses of key scenes from *Till Damaskus I* and *II* and *Spöksonaten*, in which the boundary between the assumed 'real' world and the world as represented on stage is displaced]

[**D2:1047**] Paul, Fritz, 'Strindbergs Nachinfernodramatik und das lyrische Drama des Fin de Siècle', in Hans Bekker-Nielsen, Hans Anton Koefoed, and Johan de Mylius, red., *Nordisk Litteraturhistoria – en bog til Brøndsted*, Odense: Odense Universitetsforlag, 1978, pp. 263-276. ['Strindberg's Post-Inferno Plays and the Lyrical Drama of the Fin de Siècle'. Considers that with *Till Damaskus* Sg broke the hegemony of Aristotelian drama, but the historical situation of European drama between 1898 and 1910 meant that he was unable to achieve the kind of absolute autonomy over generic criteria that Mallarmé acquired in poetry. Discusses *Stora landsvägen* in light of a series of listed criteria concerning a *théâtre statique*, which is based on a subjective, monologic structure, and concerned with the *vie intérieur* of an isolated character's visions and dreams. Its dialogue is organised in terms of *leitmotiv* and governed by memory, and the form is also to be discerned in the move towards lyrical monodrama in the work of Holger Drachmann (*Melodrama*), Sigbjørn Obstfelder (*Esther*), and

Knut Hamsun (*Livets spil*), as well as the plays of the internationally better known Maeterlinck and Hofmannsthal. According to Paul, lyric drama is the characteristic form of the period, and Sg's work as a poet in *Ordalek och småkonst* (1905) is relevant to his experimentation with dramatic genres in *Ett drömspel* and the Chamber Plays, including *Svarta handsken*, but these works are only touched on in the discussion of *Stora landsvägen* here]

[D2:1048] Paul, Fritz, 'Strindbergs Nachinfernodramatik und das lyrische Drama des Fin de Siècle', in **B1:361**, *Kleine Schriften zur Nordischen Philologie*, Hrsg. von Joachim Grage, Heinrich Detering, Wilhelm Heizmann, und Lutz Rühling. [Rpr. of **D2:1047**]

[D2:1049] Paulson, Arvid, 'Strindberg's Pilgrimage Dramas', 1-3, *The Chronicle* (New York), 1 (Winter, 1954-55), pp. 12-18; 2 (Spring, 1955), pp. 12-16; 3 (Summer, 1955), pp. 7-11. [Principally concerned with *Till Damaskus* and *Stora landsvägen*]

[D2:1050] Pavese, Renzo, 'Introduzione', in August Strindberg, *La signorina Julia, Il padre, Il pellicano*, traduzione di Franco Moccia, Teatro e cinema 48, Milano: Mondadori Editore, 1988. 185 pp. [Introduces Italian translations of *Fadren*, *Fröken Julie*, and *Pelikanen*]

[D2:1051] Pavese, Renzo, 'August Strindberg e la tragedia classica', *Classiconorroena* (Perugia), 13 (1999), 1-5. ['August Strindberg and Classical Tragedy'. Focuses on the early dramas, including *Fritänkaren*]

[D2:1052] Pavese, Renzo, 'Istruzioni e "suggerimenti" scenici di Strindberg ad un attore', in Merete Kjøller Ritzu, ed., **D1:375**, *La didascalie nella letteratura teatrale Scandinava. Testo drammatico e sintesi scenica*, pp. 153-159. ['Strindberg's Instructions and Scenic "Advice" to an Actor'. On Sg's practical advice to actors as conveyed in the *Memorandum till Medlemmarne av Intima Teatern*, including his instructions concerning tone, speech, gesture. Pavesi also reflects in general on the actor's contribution to the realisation of a dramatic text]

[D2:1053] Pelka, K., 'August Strindberg – twórca dramatu naturalistycznego', *Kurier Literacko-Naukowy*, 14 June 1937. ['August Strindberg – Two Naturalist Dramas'. Considers Strindberg's form of naturalism in *Fadren* and *Fröken Julie*]

[D2:1054] Perrelli, Franco, 'Il teatro di Asmodeo. Pessimismo e misticismo nella struttura e nella didascalia del dramma strindberghiano', in Merete Kjøller Ritzu, ed., **D1:375**, *La didascalia nella letteratura teatrale scandinava. Testo drammatico e sintesi scenica*, pp. 141-152. ['Asmodeus's Theatre. Pessimism and Mysticism in the Structure and in the Stage Directions of Strindberg's Dramas'. Relates Sg's revelatory theatrical aesthetic in the post-Inferno dramas to the anecdote of Asmodeus in one of the intertexts of *Spöksonaten*, Alain-René Lesage's novel *Le Diable boiteux* (1707), where the devil exposes what is concealed behind the house facades of Madrid to a young Student. He also links the reversals, unmaskings, and revelations inherent in Sg's plays with the influence of Swedenborg and Schopenhauer, as well as with ideas presented in *Inferno*, *Legender*, and *En blå bok*. The discussion draws mainly on *Fröken Julie*, *Kristina*, *Ett drömspel*, *Spöksonaten*, and *Pelikanen*]

[D2:1055] Perrelli, Franco, 'Il critico teatrale August Strindberg', *Teatro e Storia (Annali 1)*, 9 (1994), 331-350. ['The Theatre Criticism of August Strindberg']

[D2:1056] Perrelli, Franco, 'Introduzione', in August Strindberg, *Il padre, Signorina Julie*, Introduzione e note di Franco Perrelli, Milano: Biblioteca Universale Rizzoli, 1993, pp. 5-22. [The introduction with notes to Italian translations of *Fadren* and *Fröken Julie*]

[D2:1057] Perrelli, Franco, 'Un piccolo breviario di estetica teatrale di August Strindberg', *Quaderno*, No. 18, del Teatro Stabile del Friuli-Venezia Giulia, February 1981. ['A Brief Compendium of August Strindberg's Theories of the Theatre'. Introduces a collection of Sg's statements about the nature of theatre]

[D2:1058] Perrelli, Franco, 'Strindberg e la Stoccolma dei teatri, in *Ombre metropolotane: Città e spettacolo nel Novecento*, a cura di Giaime Alonge e Federica Mazzocchi, Torino: Università degli Studi, 2002, pp. 155-177. ['Strindberg and the Stockholm Theatres'. Surveys Sg's responses to Stockholm's theatres, their managers and repertoire, and considers both the role of the Intimate Theatre and his place in the development of the Swedish cinema]

[D2:1059] Perrelli, Franco, 'Tre atti unici di Strindberg', in **B1:365**, *Omaggio a Strindberg. Strindberg nella cultura moderna*, pp. 155-163. ['Three One Act Plays by Strindberg'. In fact surveys the majority of the plays with which Sg developed the genre of the modern one-acter between 1888 and 1891]

[D2:1060] Persson, Anna Lena, 'Vasasagan skall provocera publiken', *Svenska Dagbladet* (Stockholm), 18 March 1998. ['The *Vasa Saga* should Provoke the Audience'. An interview with Staffan Valdemar Holm about his production of an amalgamation of seven of Sg's history plays performed as a six-hour drama in order of the events they depict in chronological sequence]

[D2:1061] Persson, K., '*Memorandum till Medlemmarne af Intima Teatern från regissören*', *Borås Tidning*, 10 September 1975. [Reviews a new edition]

[D2:1062] P. H-m [Per Hallström], 'August Strindberg, *Samlade dramatiska arbeten*', *Dagens Nyheter* (Stockholm), 30 October 1904. [Reviews *Till Damaskus III* and *Gustav III*. The former is among Sg's most remarkable achievements. Hallström also comments favourably on *Ett drömspel*, which is compared with Calderón de la Barca's *La Vida es sueño*]

[D2:1063] [Photographic Essay], 'Strindberg, le temps et l'espace', *Théâtre en Europe* (Paris), 5:1 (1985), 19-31. Illus. ['Time and Space in Strindberg'. A collection of photographs from a range of French, Swedish, Polish, and North-American productions of *Spöksonaten*, *Till Damaskus*, *Kronbruden*, *Gustav Vasa*, *Erik XIV*, *Dödsdansen*, *Fadren*, *Karl XII*, *Påsk*, *Oväder*, *Brända tomten*, *Pelikanen*, and *Stora landsvägen*]

[D2:1064] Picchio, Carlo, 'Prefazione', in August Strindberg, *Teatro*, 1, Traduzione di Alfhild Paulucci di Caboli, Milano: Mursia Editore, 1966. 171 pp. [Introduces Italian translations of *Fadren*, *Fröken Julie*, and *Fordringsägare*]

[D2:1065] Pirk, Robert, 'Strindberg als Dramatiker', *Die Scene* (Berlin), 11:2-3 (1921), 22-35. ['Strindberg as a Dramatist']

[D2:1066] Pirk, Robert, 'Strindbergs als Dramatiker', *Baltische Blätter für Theater und Kunst* (Bielefeld), I (1918), 59-62. ['Strindberg as a Dramatist']

[D2:1067] Pirk, Robert, 'Strindberg-Stil', *Die Scene* (Berlin), 8:2-3 (1918), 20-24.

[D2:1068] Pirk, Robert, 'Strindbergs als Dramatiker', *Die Rampe* (Hamburg), September 1919. ['Strindberg as a Dramatist']

[D2:1069] Pirk, Robert, 'Strindbergs als Dramatiker', *Blätter für Theater und Kunst* (Bielefeld), 1:1-2 (1919), 14-16. ['Strindberg as a Dramatist']

[D2:1070] Pirk, Robert, 'Strindbergs und das Kammerspiel', *Der Zuschauer* (Leipzig), 1:1 (1919-20), 1-3. ['Strindberg and the Chamber Play']

[D2:1071] Piwińska, Marta, 'Nie taki straszny Strindberg', *Teatr* (Warsaw), 1965:15. ['Strindberg is not so Dangerous']

[D2:1072] P. L., 'Strindberg e la drammaturgia dell' io', *Arcoscenico* (Rome), March-April 1977. ['Strindberg and the Dramaturgy of the Self']

[D2:1073] Planck Johnson, Kristi, 'Strindberg: Selected Plays', *European Studies Journal* (Cedar Falls, Ohio), 5:1 (1988), 60-61.

[D2:1074] Pleijel, Agneta, and Lennart Hjulström, 'Han gör allt till dramatik', in Folke Olsson, red., **B1:348**, *Strindberg*, pp. 40-49. Illus. ['He Turns Everything into Drama'. A discussion between author and critic, Pleijel, and theatre director, Hjulström, on Sg as an instinctive dramatist, who possessed both an extraordinary ability to hear the subtext in a situation and a Shakespearean sense of theatrical structure, which was already clearly developed when he wrote *Mäster Olof*, where he portrayed social contradictions that are embedded deep within the psychological structure of the individual]

[D2:1075] Polet, Sybren, 'Inleiding', in August Strindberg, *Droomspel, Schuldeisers, Met vuur spelen*, Vertaling Sybren Polet and Cora Polet, Amsterdam: De Bezige Bij, 1965, pp. 9-12. [Introduces Dutch translations of *Ett drömspel, Fordringsägare*, and *Leka med elden*. Polet complains about the 'indigestible' poetry in *Ett drömspel* and suggests that the director or translator may amend Sg here and there when he is careless]

[D2:1076] Polet, Sybren, 'Nawoord', in August Strindberg, *Dodendans 1, Dodendans 2, Pasen*, Vertaling Cora and Sybren Polet, Amsterdam: De Bezige Bij, 1967. 223 pp. [The Afterword to Dutch translations of *Dödsdansen* and *Påsk*]

[D2:1077] Powell, Anthony, 'Three Plays by August Strindberg: *The Father, Miss Julia, Påsk*', *Punch* (London), 234 (1958), 787-788. [Reviews Peter Watt's translations for Penguin Classics]

[D2:1078] Powell, Jocelyn, 'Demons that Live in Sunlight: Problems in Staging Strindberg', *Yearbook of English Studies* (London), 9 (1979), 116-134. Illus. [A valuable discussion of the difficulties inherent in staging plays which shift rapidly between the illusion of reality and the unravelling of reality, where the dialogue proceeds by association rather than intention, and which demand an arresting combination of physical detail and continuous fluidity. Concentrates primarily on *Ett drömspel* and *Till Damaskus I* and their realisation in productions by Ingmar Bergman and Mike Ockrent respectively. Powell identifies 'inconsistency and incongruity' as 'the principal subjects of Sg's art', which challenges a director and actor in awkward ways. He also refers to *Fröken Julie*, *Brott och brott*, and *Påsk*]

[D2:1079] Pruner, Francis, 'Strindberg et Antoine', in Gunnel Engwall, ed., **B1:121**, *Strindberg et La France*, pp. 109-120. [Documents Sg's contacts with the director of the Théâtre Libre and the staging there of *Fröken Julie* in 1893, which Pruner contextualises in terms of French naturalism]

[D2:1080] Pryce-Jones, Alan, 'The Openings: Hullabaloo and Strindberg Too', *Theatre Arts* (Chicago), 44:11 (1960), 8-9.

[D2:1081] -pt- [Hans Emil Larsson], 'August Strindberg. *Tryckt och otryckt I*', *Sydsvenska Dagbladet* (Malmö), 22 April 1890. [Reviews *Fordringsägare, Samum*, and *Paria* on publication. 'Apart from its rather odd characterisation, [*Fordringsägare*] is composed with great skill and carries extraordinary power. It is excellent proof of the new form of drama for which Sg argues in the accompanying essay, 'Om modernt drama och modern teater']

[D2:1082] Puppa, Paolo, 'I luoghi della notte', in Roberto Alonge, ed., **D2:7**, *Alle origini della drammaturgia moderna Ibsen, Strindberg, Pirandello*, pp. 140-154. ['Domains of the Night'. Presents Ibsen, Strindberg, and Pirandello as the portal figures of modern drama, focusing in Sg's case on *Till Damaskus* and *Oväder*]

[D2:1083] 'Qvidam Qvidamsson' [Pseudonym of Nils Peter Svensson], 'Strindberg i et Par af hans sidste Arbejder', *Politiken* (Copenhagen), 19 January 1918. ['Strindberg in some of His Last Works'. Reviews the plays and dramatic fragments published in Volume One of Vilhelm Carlheim-Gyllensköld's edition of Sg's collected unpublished works]

[D2:1084] 'Qvidam Qvidamsson' [Pseudonym of Nils Peter Svensson], 'Strindberg i Danmark', *Svenska scenen* (Stockholm), 3 (1917). ['Strindberg in Denmark']

[D2:1085] 'Qvidam Qvidamsson' [Pseudonym of Nils Peter Svensson], 'Strindberg og Teatret', *Politiken* (Copenhagen), 29 April 1919. ['Strindberg and the Theatre'. Reviews August Falck's edition of Sg's letters and memoranda to members of the Intimate Theatre]

[D2:1086] 'Qvidam Qvidamsson' [Pseudonym of Nils Peter Svensson], 'Strindberg i København', *Hver 8 Dag* (Stockholm), 13 August 1925. ['Strindberg in Copenhagen']

[D2:1087] 'Qvidam Qvidamsson' [Pseudonym of Nils Peter Svensson], 'Strindberg paa Københavns Teatre', *Politiken* (Copenhagen), 4 May 1918. ['Strindberg in Copenhagen's Theatres']

[D2:1088] 'Qvidam Qvidamsson' [Pseudonym of Nils Peter Svensson], '*Samlade otryckta skrifter*', *Scenen* (Stockholm), 5 (1919), 42-44. [Reviews Volume One of Vilhelm Carlheim-Gyllensköld's edition of Sg's *Samlade otryckta skrifter*]

[D2:1089] 'Qvidam Qvidamsson' [Pseudonym of Nils Peter Svensson], 'Strindberg og teatret', *Tidens Tegn* (Oslo), No. 121, 1919. ['Strindberg and the Theatre']

[D2:1090] Racaciuni, Isaia, 'Premergatorii. August Strindberg', *Premiera* (Bucureşti?), Nos 11-12, 13 (1929). ['Forerunners'. Discusses Sg as a forerunner of modern drama at a time when his plays were unperformed in the Romanian theatre]

[D2:1091] Rangström, Ture, 'Strindbergs Intima teater. En ny teater med en gammal historia', *Strindbergiana* (Stockholm), 18 (2003), pp. 10-25. Illus. ['Strindberg's Intimate Theatre. A New Theatre with an Old History'. An account of the architecture, décor, and format of Sg's Intimate Theatre at Norra Bantorget, Stockholm, and its recent restoration and revival]

[D2:1092] Rangström, Ture, 'Intima teatern', Prijevod sa svedskoga Mirko Rumac, *Prolog* (Zagreb), 55-56 (1983), pp. 49-63. Illus. [An historical account of Sg and Falck's Intimate Theatre]

[D2:1093] Rawiżski, Marian, 'Oniryczny teatr wizjonerski od Strindberga do Artauda', *Akcent* (Lublin), 1983:1, pp. 137-151. ['Visionary Dream Theatre from Strindberg to Artaud'. Compares Sg's later conception of the theatre as no longer concerned with reproducing everyday reality on stage with that of Antonin Artaud]

[D2:1094] R. B., 'Strindberg', *Vårt Land* (Stockholm), 23 November 1908. [Reviews Sg's reflections on *Hamlet* in his *Memorandum till Medlemmarne av Intima Teatern*]

[D2:1095] Reichardt, Konstantin, 'Strindberg Agonistes', *Yale Review* (New Haven, Conn.), 39 (1949), 153-155. [Reviews August Strindberg, *Eight Famous Plays*, translated by Edwin Björkman and Nellie Erichsen, with an introduction by Alan Harris. See **D2:727**]

[D2:1096] Reicher, Emanuel, 'Wie spielt man Strindberg?', *Der Strom* (Vienna and Berlin), 2 (1912-13), 118-120. ['How does One Perform Strindberg?' Reflections on performing Sg by the actor who played the Baron in the première of *Bandet* (1902), the Captain in the German première of *Fadren* in 1890, and Maurice in Max Reinhardt's production of *Brott och brott* in 1902]

[D2:1097] Reicher, Emanuel, 'Wie spielt man Strindberg?', *Theater und Zeit* (Wuppertal), 6 (1958-59), 194-195. ['How Does One Perform Strindberg?' Rpr. of **D2:1096**]

[D2:1098] Reinke-Engbert, Ingrid, 'Zum Verhältnis von Haupt- und Nebentext in Strindbergs Nachinfernodramatik', in Heiko Uecker, Hrsg., *Akten der Fünften Arbeitstagung der Skandinavisten des deutschen Sprachgebiets* 16-22 August 1981 in Kungälv, St. Augustin: Verlag Dr. Bernd Kretschmer, 1983, pp. 269-273. ['On the Relationship between the Primary Text and Secondary Text in Strindberg's Post-Inferno Dramas'. Outlines a research project into the relationship in Sg's later plays between what Roman Ingarden defined as the '*Haupttext*' (everything that is verbalised in the performance text of a play, i.e. the dialogue) and the '*Nebentext*' (that which is verbalised only in the drama text, i.e. the stage- and acting directions), with special reference to *Spöksonaten* and employing a theoretical approach derived from the Prague structuralists, Jan Mukařovský and Jiri Veltrusky]

[D2:1099] 'René' [Anna Branting], 'Skådebanan', *Skådebanan* (Stockholm), No. 2 (1907), pp. 1-4. [An editorial comment on contemporary Stockholm theatre which concludes that 'This whole Intimate Theatre cult is deplorable and strange, it is a sign of degeneration of a piece with religious brooding']

[D2:1100] 'René' [Anna Branting], 'Skådebanan', *Skådebanan* (Stockholm), No. 12 (1908), pp. 1-4. [Compares *Fadren* with *Pelikanen* and *Spöksonaten*. Whereas the former is 'a masterpiece from a time when the author's suffering was still new and striking', the trivial concerns of the latter prove that 'sorrow over questionable fatherhood rates more highly than irritation over a little pilfered gravy']

[D2:1101] R. F-r [Ragnar Fehr], 'Litteratur och konst'. *Göteborgs Handels- och Sjöfartstidning*, 17 December 1908. [Reviews Sg's comments on *Julius Caesar* and Shakespeare's history plays in his series of *Memorandum till Medlemmarne av Intima Teatern*]

[D2:1102] Rhodes, Russel, 'August Strindberg, *Eight Famous Plays*', *Saturday Review of Literature* (New York), 32:34 (1949), 17-18. [Reviews August Strindberg, *Eight Famous Plays*, translated by Edwin Björkman and Nellie Erichsen, with an introduction by Alan Harris. See **D2:727**]

[D2:1103] *Ridå* (Stockholm), 'August Strindberg. Skådespelarna ha ordet', No. 1 (1909). ['August Strindberg. The Actors Speak'. Comments on Sg by Bror Ohlson, Augusta Lindberg, Nils Personne, Alrik Kjellgren, Ella Widercrantz, and Agnes Symra, on the 60th anniversary of his birth]

[D2:1104] Rischbieter, Henning, and Ernst Wendt, 'Noch zwei Jubiläen: Hauptmann und Strindberg', *Theater heute* (Hannover), 3 (1962), 62-63. ['Two More Jubilees:

Hauptmann and Strindberg'. Reflections on Sg's place in the modern theatre on the 50th anniversary of his death]

[D2:1105] Rismondo, Piero, 'Strindberg und das moderne Theater', *Wort und Wahrheit* (Freiburg im Breisgau), 11 (1956), 68-69. ['Strindberg and the Modern Theatre']

[D2:1106] Roberts, Peter, 'Sweden's Mad Genius', *Plays and Players* (London), 6:5 (1959), p. 5. [Believes that 'The unbalanced, urgent quality of Sg's work seems to chime more appropriately with our own insecure, troubled times' than Ibsen's does]

[D2:1107] Robertson, J[ohn] G[eorge], 'Introduction', in August Strindberg, *Mäster Olof and Other Plays*, The Anglo-Swedish Literary Foundation, London: Jonathan Cape, 1931, pp. 7-14. [Claims that 'Sg's historical plays are a modern contribution to the great paradox of historical art; that the truth of poetry cannot be the truth of history. History is not the end of historical drama. Sg would have it point up circularity within the history of events – Allt går igen (Everything repeats itself) – an attitude not different from that of the dramatic poets who wrote before the vaunted realism was thought of. Sg's historical dramas hold easy balance with the modern problem plays inspired by the personal woes of his complex-ridden life']

[D2:1108] Robertson, J[ohn] G[eorge], 'Introduction', in August Strindberg, *Easter and Other Plays*, London: Jonathan Cape, 1929, pp. 5-12. [Introduces the first of four volumes of translations in an incomplete English edition of the plays sponsored by the Anglo-Swedish Literary Foundation]

[D2:1109] Robida, Adolf, 'Ekstrem ekstremov Strindberg', *Dom in svet* (Maribor), 24 (1911), p. 43.

[D2:1110] Robichez, Jacques, 'Strindberg et Lugné-Poe', *Revue d'histoire du théâtre* (Paris), 30:3 (1978), 287-290. [Describes how Sg cultivated Lugné-Poe's acquaintance, using his French translator, Georges Loiseau, as an intermediary, and documents their brief working relationship in Paris during 1894, when Lugné-Poe staged both *Fordringsägare* and *Fadren*]

[D2:1111] Robinson, Michael, 'History and His-Story', in *Studies in Strindberg*, **B1:380**, pp. 55-71. [Rpr. of **D2:1113**]

[D2:1112] Robinson, Michael, 'History and His-Story', in Birgitta Steene, ed., **B1:434**, *Strindberg and History*, pp. 45-59. Illus. [Rpr. of **D2:1113**]

[D2:1113] Robinson, Michael, 'History and His-Story', *Scandinavian Studies* (Madison), 62:1 (1990), 53-66. [Examines the links between autobiographical and historical discourse in the 19th Century, and considers how Sg sometimes emplots his own experience in terms provided by historical grand narrative, even as he was also dismantling drama's dependence on conventional plot-making. Writing the history of his own life in *Tjänstekvinnans son* led him to question the notion of history as a meaningful sequence of events, yet he also saw it as offering a series of plots or scenarios through which he might establish the contours of his life, even as he was living it. History provided both a parallel series of fates, figurations of plot, and patterns of relationship, in which he could read his own life and locate himself, not least when it appeared to him as something already composed and 'staged', a ready-made play, 'satt i scen' by some higher power, as he came to feel his own life had been. Exemplified with reference to *Fordringsägare*, *Erik XIV*, *Kristina*, *Karl XII*, *Gustav III*, and the essay 'Världshistoriens mystik' (The Mysticism of World History)]

[**D2:1114**] Robinson, Michael, 'Introduction' and 'Notes', in August Strindberg, *Miss Julie and Other Plays*, Oxford: Oxford University Press, 1998, pp. vii-xxxvi, 286-313. [An introduction to Sg's development as a dramatist, focusing primarily on the five plays in the volume: *Fadren*, *Fröken Julie*, *Dödsdansen I*, *Ett drömspel*, and *Spöksonaten* with notes]

[**D2:1115**] Rochwicz, Jan, 'Strindberg walczył o prawa skrzywdzonych', *Wieczory Teatralne* (Katowice), 1950:13-14.

[**D2:1116**] Rokem, Freddie, 'Det filmiska som visuell struktur och metafor i Strindbergs teater', *Strindbergiana* (Stockholm), 12 (1997), pp. 81-99. Illus. ['The Cinematic as Visual Structure and Metaphor in Strindberg's Theatre'. Considers how Sg employed photographic and cinematic means of expression in his later plays, thus reformulating the visual language which had formed the basis of the more traditional kind of realistic theatre. He employs both technical ideas like zoom, montage, and cut, and incorporates photographic and cinematic terms in his own visual and verbal imagery. Rokem examines the 'photographic stage space' of *Fröken Julie*, the 'cinematic mirror structure' of *Ett drömspel*, and the 'metaphysics of flowers and light' in *Spöksonaten*]

[**D2:1117**] Rokem, Freddie, 'The Camera and the Aesthetics of Repetition: Strindberg's Use of Space and Scenography in *Miss Julie*, *A Dream Play*, and *Spöksonaten*', in Göran Stockenström, ed., **D2:288**, *Strindberg's Dramaturgy*, pp. 107-128. [A cogently argued investigation into how the visual information, based primarily on our perception of the scenographic elements in some of Sg's major plays, is 'narrated' by the dramatist through the manner and order of its presentation to us, in large part because of the way it is mediated by Sg's cinematic method of directing the attention of the reader/ spectator]

[**D2:1118**] Rokem, Freddie, 'Scenography and the Camera: *Miss Julie*, *A Dream Play*, and *The Ghost Sonata*', in **B1:388**, *Strindberg's Secret Codes*, pp. 11-38. [Revised version of **D2:1117**]

[**D2:1119**] Rokem, Freddie, 'Strindberg's "Optical Unconscious"', in Kela Kvam, ed., **D2:158**, *Strindberg's Post-Inferno Plays*, pp. 71-84. Illus. [Studies the relationship between the life of the individual character and the aesthetic framework into which it has been inscribed, focusing particularly on the development of this aesthetic framework into a photographic image, where the art of photography serves as an expression of moments of heightened significance. *Stora landsvägen* exemplifies the way Sg formulated new rules for the dynamics of dramatic and theatrical images, as he seeks to liberate the narrative from its deterministic patterns of causality. Rokem elucidates Sg's theatrical practice in comparisons with his photographic experiments and reflections on photography by Roland Barthes and Walter Benjamin]

[**D2:1120**] Rokem, Freddie, 'Strindbergs Optical Unconscious', in **B1:388**, *Strindberg's Secret Codes*, pp. 39-57. [Revised version of **D2:1119**]

[**D2:1121**] Rokem, Freddie, 'The Camera and the Aesthetics of Repetition: Strindberg's Use of Space and Scenography in *Miss Julie*, *A Dream Play*, and *Spöksonaten*', in Janet Witalec, ed., **D2:348**, *Drama Criticism*, Volume 18, pp. 161-172. [Rpr. of **D2:1117**]

[**D2:1122**] Rolander, J., 'Strindberg na polskiej scenie', *Ziemia i Morze* (Szczecin), 1957, No. 10. ['Strindberg on the Polish Stage']

[D2:1123] Rørdam Olesen, Ragnhild, 'Omkring to Strindberg-skuespil', *Aarhus Stiftstidende*, 8 November 1961. ['Concerning Two Plays by Strindberg']

[D2:1124] Rosenberg, P. A., 'August Strindberg: Tre Skuespil', *Litteratur og Kritik* (Copenhagen), 1889, p. 218. ['August Strindberg: Three Plays'. Reviews *Mäster Olof*, *Gillets hemlighet*, and *Herr Bengts hustru*, translated into Danish by Peter Hansen]

[D2:1125] Roth, Marc A., 'Strindberg's Historical Role-Players', *Scandinavica* (London), 18:2 (1979), 123-140. [Applies the notion of character as a conglomeration of roles developed in Sg's vivisections and the Preface to *Fröken Julie* to the history play, whose self-conscious theatricality as a variation on a known theme he recognised. Roth discusses *Gustav Vasa*, *Erik XIV*, and *Karl XII* (in which the protagonist is a player divorced from his role and thus anticipates the alienation of Pirandello's *Enrico IV*), as well as *Gustav III*, in which the king is, like the dramatic poet himself, 'characterless' and a consummate actor]

[D2:1126] Rothenberg, Albert, 'Autobiographical Drama: Strindberg and O'Neill', *Literature and Psychology* (Teaneck, New Jersey), 17:2-3 (1967), 95-114. [A reductively biographical comparison of *Fadren* with *Long Day's Journey into Night* as examples of autobiographical drama, on the assumption that any piece of literature is drawn from fantasies that preoccupy a writer at the time of writing, and that this work will bear a definite thematic relationship with other works from the same period (*En dåres försvarstal*, *Hemsöborna*, *Kamraterna*, and *Tjänstekvinnans son*)]

[D2:1127] Ruest, Anselm, '*Ostern, Kameraden*', *Bücherei Maiandros* (Berlin-Wilmersdorf), 2 (1912), pp. 15-16. ['*Easter* and *Comrades*']

[D2:1128] Ruest, Anselm, 'Strindbergs Entwickelung als dramatischer Dichter', *Saale-Zeitung*, Kriegsunterhaltungsbeil., 20 (1916). ['Strindberg's Development as a Dramatist']

[D2:1129] Ruhe, Algot, 'Auguste Strindberg et son œuvre dramatique', *Revue d'Art dramatique* (Paris), 13 (January 1898). ['Strindberg and His Dramatic Works'. Suggests that *En dåres försvarstal* and Sg's other naturalistic prose works confirm that he always writes about himself; thus, *Inferno* takes the form of a brutally revealing diary. Discusses *Kamraterna* in some detail and comments on *Lycko-Pers resa*, *Fröken Julie*, *Inför döden*, *Leka med elden*, and *Bandet*]

[D2:1130] Ruhe, Algot, 'Strindberg som skådespelsförfattare', *Stormklockan* (Stockholm), 23 January 1909. ['Strindberg as a Playwright'. Apropos his 60th birthday]

[D2:1131] Rung, Otto, 'Det klg. Teaters Strindberg-Forestilling', *Teatret* (Copenhagen), 17 (1917), 1-6. ['The Royal Theatre's Strindberg Performance'. Concludes that 'Sg should be permanently included in the spiritual sustenance of every age']

[D2:1132] R. v. W. [Reinhold Felix von Willebrand], '*Tryckt och otryckt IV*', *Finsk Tidskrift* (Åbo), 43 (1897), 230-231. [A disdainfully hostile review of *Bandet* and *Leka med elden* on publication]

[D2:1132a] Sabzevari, Hanif, 'Varför tiger du? Expositionen i Strindberg's *Den starkare*, *Paria*, och *Samum*', *Samlaren*, 127 (2006), pp. 178-231. ['Why are you silent? The Exposition in Strindberg's *The Stronger, Pariah*, and *Simoon*'. [Considers how Sg organises expository material in the three play following a presentation of the Théâtre Libre in Paris and the development of one-act drama. Sg's expository technique is designed to illustrate the battle of the brains, a theme that is common to all three plays, and he complicates traditional approaches by letting one of the two characters remain silent, thus confusing boundaries between truth and lie, reality and fiction. A brief comparison with Pirandello's *Sei personaggi in cerca d'autore* establishes that Sg raises similar questions about drama and reality as Pirandello. In fact, he is already dissolving naturalistic form and creating a metadramatic mood of considerable intensity. English summary]

[D2:1133] Sabbatini, Adriana, and Luciano Codignolo, 'Strindberg passaggio obbligato', *Ridotto: Rassegna Mensile di Teatro* (Rome), 3:12 (December 1980), 5-6. ['Strindberg's Fixed Path']

[D2:1134] Salotti, M., 'August Strindberg sulla scena italiana', in *Il Padre*, E. Teatro di Genova, No. 45, November 1983, pp. 59-64. ['August Strindberg on the Italian Stage'. An historical survey in a programme book accompanying a production of *Fadren*]

[D2:1135] Samuelson, Sven, 'Något om Strindbergsföreställningar i Wien 1899-1923', *Meddelanden från Strindbergssällskapet* (Stockholm), 16 (1954), pp. 3-7. ['On Performances of Strindberg in Vienna, 1899-1912'. Documents the staging of Sg's plays in Vienna, where Josef Jarno was his principal apostle. A range of works were presented at the Theater in der Josefstadt, Volkstheater, and Burgtheater, which mounted 91, 42, and 44 performances respectively, mainly of the naturalistic works. Samuelson scans their critical reception, quoting from reviews in the *Neue Feie Presse*]

[D2:1136] Sandberg, K.-H., '*Memorandum till Medlemmarne af Intima Teatern från regissören*', *Arbetarbladet* (Gävle), 27 August 1975. [Reviews a new edition]

[D2:1137] 'Sandr.' [A. V. Tavaststjerna], '[Historical Dramas by Strindberg]', *Vestnik vsemirnoi istorii*, No. 1 (1900), pp. 168-176. [E.710]

[D2:1138] Sandstroem, Yvonne L., '*The Plays of Strindberg, Volume II*, Introduced and translated from the Swedish by Michael Meyer', *Scandinavian Studies* (Lawrence, Kansas), 50:1 (1978), 129-131. [Reviews Meyer's translations which are characterised by a 'pervasive carelessness and insensitivity' regarding Sg's text]

[D2:1139] Sandstroem, Yvonne L., 'Strindberg, August. *World Historical Plays*. Translated by Arvid Paulson with an introduction by Gunnar Ollén', *Scandinavian Studies* (Lawrence, Kansas), 44:1 (1972), 146-147. [Reviews **E45:3**]

[D2:1140] Sarrazac, Jean-Pierre, 'Dramaturgie de l'autoportrait', *Théâtre/Public* (Gennevilliers), 73:4 (1986), 11-16. Illus. ['Dramaturgy of the Self-Portrait'. An essay which largely conflates extracts from **D2:1142** and **D2:1144**, focusing firstly on the 'model' marriage scene of Sg's 'théâtre conjugale' of the 1880s, and then on the way in which the dramaturgy of this scene is supplanted by a dramaturgy of 'le tableau', in such post-Inferno dramas as *Till Damaskus*, *Oväder*, and *Spöksonaten*. Sarrazac concludes that 'the Sgian dramaturgy of the tableau is apparently "private", to the extent that it proceeds directly from the Imaginary of the author; in reality, it is completely public, since the Symbolic, *all culture*, is inscribed therein']

[D2:1141] Sarrazac, Jean-Pierre, 'Dramaturgie de l'impersonnel', in Elena Balzamo, ed., **B1:7**, *August Strindberg*, pp. 54-64. ['Dramaturgy of the Impersonal'. Counters the accusation that Sg's dramaturgy is too subjective with a Deleuzean reading of the naturalist plays (primarily *Fordringsägare*) and an analysis of Sg's post-Inferno dreamplay style in which we are at once the dreamer and the dream, and where the actor is also the spectator. Within a kind of tableau, or symbolic, internal landscape in which silence triumphs over hateful words, and the will to appeasement and reconciliation prevails over confrontation, the dramaturgy of the "dream play" becomes a theatre of meditation']

[D2:1142] Sarrazac, Jean-Pierre, 'Strindberg: dramaturgia do auto-retrato', Desenhos de Alain Gauvin, *Ada'gio* (Evora), No. 17 (December 1996), pp. [5]-21. Illus. ['Strindberg: Dramaturgy of the Self-Portrait'. Portuguese version of **D2:1143**]

[D2:1143] Sarrazac, Jean-Pierre, 'Strindberg, dramaturgie de l'autoportrait', in *Dramaturgies, langages dramatiques: mélanges pour Jacques Scherer*, publié avec le concours du Centre national des lettress et de l'Université de la sorbonne nouvelle, Paris: Nizet, 1986, pp. [217]-224. [See **D2:1141**]

[D2:1144] Sarrazac, Jean-Pierre, 'Strindberg: dramaturgie de l'autoportrait', in *Théâtres Intimes: essai*, Arles: Actes Sud, 1989, pp. 31-[45]. [Rpr. of **D2:1143**]

[D2:1145] Sarrazac, Jean-Pierre, 'Strindberg, la scène', *Théâtre en Europe* (Paris), 5:1 (1985), 15-17. Illus.

[D2:1146] Sauter, Willmar, 'Eine verschrumpfte Avantgarde: Das Intima Teatern des August Strindberg', in Erika Fischer Lichte, Hrsg., *TheaterAvantgarde: Wahrnehmung – Körper – Sprache*, Tübingen und Basel: Francke Verlag, 1995, pp. 291-323. ['A Shrivelled Avante Garde: August Strindberg's Intimate Theatre'. A detailed study of the Intimate Theatre as an aborted venture in the context of avant-garde drama and theatre elsewhere in Europe during the first decade of the 20th Century. Sauter concentrates on the 1907 production of *Fadren*, the reception accorded a series of its productions in the Swedish press (*Kristina*, *Dödsdansen*, *Påsk*, *Fröken Julie*, and *Svanevit*) by influential critics (August Brunius, Bo Bergman, Sven Söderman), and the ideological and theoretical premises outlined in the series of *Memorandum till Medlemmarne av Intima Teatern*. He also considers Intiman's place in the structural context of Swedish theatre of the period and the model of theatrical communication within which it was constrained]

[D2:1147] Sauter, Wilmar, 'Strindberg's Words Versus the Actor's Action', in Michael Robinson, ed., **B1:379**, *The Moscow Papers*, pp. 187-192. [Examines Sg's ideas on acting as outlined in his memoranda to his colleagues at the Intimate Theatre. According to Sauter, his concept of theatrical performance as initiated by the dramatist, with the actors merely intermediaries between the author and the audience, was conventionally linear and ignored the encoded actions that actors bring to their encounter with the spectator, which is the true theatrical event. Sauter focuses primarily on *Påsk* and *Svanevit*, and considers why they should have been the most successful of the Intimate Theatre's productions]

[D2:1148] Scheib, M. E., 'August Strindberg as He Appears in some of His Plays', *Southern Speech Journal* (Tuscaloosa, Alabama), 31:2 (1965), 106-107.

[D2:1149] Scherek, Jacob, 'Elf Einakter', *Das literarische Echo* (Berlin), 5 (1902-03), Sp. 859-860. ['Eleven One-Acters']

[D2:1150] Schering, Emil, 'Vor höherer Instanz', *Die Zukunft* (Berlin), 29 (1899), p. 225. ['Before a Higher Court'. Reviews *Advent* and *Brott och brott* on publication]

[D2:1151] Schering, Emil, 'Vor höherer Instanz', in Hans-Peter Bayerdörfer, Hrsg., **B3:85**, *Strindberg auf der deutschen Bühne*, p. 128. ['Before a Higher Court'. Rpr. of **D2:1150**]

[D2:1152] Schering, Emil, 'Elf Einakter', *Die Zukunft* (Berlin), 41 (1902), 86-87. ['Eleven One-Acters']

[D2:1153] Schering, Emil, 'Strindbergs Traumbühne', *Theater* (Morgenstern), 1 (1903-04), 178-180. ['Strindberg's Dream Stage'. Discusses Sg's ideas on staging his dream plays and the inspiration that he derived from developments in the contemporary German theatre]

[D2:1154] Schering, Emil, 'August Strindberg und sein Dialog von der Liebe', *Aus fremden Zungen* (Stuttgart), 16:2 (1906), p. 780. ['August Strindberg and his Dialogue on Love']

[D2:1155] Schildknecht[-Wahlgren], Maria, 'Strindberg och Intima teatern', *Hörde Ni? Månadstidskrift för Sveriges Radio* (Stockholm), 5:9 (1952), 633-638. ['Strindberg and the Intimate Theatre'. Introduces a broadcast of the author's recollections of the Intimate Theatre, where she performed in several of Sg's plays]

[D2:1156] Schildknecht-Wahlgren, Maria, 'Strindberg som regissör', *Göteborgs Handels- och Sjöfartstidning*, 16 January 1953. ['Strindberg as a Director'. Recollections of working with Sg as an actress at the Intimate Theatre]

[D2:1157] Schimmelpfennig, Carl von, 'Strindbergs schwedische Königs-Dramen', *Nord und Sud* (Breslau), 114 (1905), 245-258. ['Strindberg's Plays about the Kings of Sweden'. Discusses Sg's recent plays on subjects from Swedish history, up to and including *Gustav III*]

[D2:1158] Schwarz, Hans, 'Zum Verständnis des Werkes', in August Strindberg, *Dramen*, neu übertragung von Willi Reich, Reinbek bei Hamburg: Rowohlt Verlag, 1960. 343 pp. ['Towards an Understanding of the Works'. Introduces a volume containing Willi Reich's translations of *Fadren, Fröken Julie, Till Damaskus, Dödsdansen, Ett drömspel*, and *Spöksonaten*]

[D2:1159] Sebrecht, Friedrich, 'Strindberg und der "Expressionismus"', *Die Scene* (Berlin), 11:2-3 (1921), 42-44. ['Strindberg and "Expressionism"'. Presents *Dödsdansen* as an important precursor of German expressionism in the theatre]

[D2:1160] Sénart, Phillipe, 'Strindberg, Maupassant, Courteline', *Revue des Deux Mondes* (Paris), (July-August 1988), 216f.*

[D2:1161] Sergeeva, A., and E. Solov'eva, 'Kommentarii', in Avgust Strindberg, *Slovo bezumtsa v svoiu zashchitu*, Moscow: Khudozhestvennaia literatura, 1997. 560+24 pp. Illus. [Includes commentary and other editorial material accompanying translations of *Fröken Julie, Till Damaskus, Dödsdansen, Ett drömspel, Oväder, Spöksonaten*, and *Pelikanen*, together with *En dåres försvarstal* and *Ensam*]

[D2:1162] Sevander, S. M., '[A. Strindberg and Naturalistic Drama]', in *Zarubezhnaia dramaturgiia: Metod i zhanr: Sbornik nauchykh trudov*, Sverdlovsk, 1985, pp. 118-128. [Research Papers on modern drama, primarily concerned here with *Fröken Julie, Fadren*, and the nature of naturalism in the theatre. E.1778a]

[D2:1163] Sever, Alexandru, 'August Strindberg. Ideile unui dramaturg', in *Eseuri critice*, Bucureşti: Cartea Românească, 1982, pp. 309-379. ['August Strindberg: A Dramatist's Ideas'. A study in Romanian of Sg's ideas about drama and dramaturgy]

[D2:1164] Sever, Alexandru, 'Prefată', in August Strindberg, *Teatru. Tatăl, Domnişoara Julie, În faţa morţii, Nu vă jucaţi cu focul, Dansul morţii, Un joc al visului. Kristina. Fulger fără*, in românește de Valeriu Munteanu, Bucureşti: Editura Univers, 1973, pp. 5-46. [Introduces Romanian translations of nine of Sg's plays: *Fadren, Fröken Julie, Leka med elden, Dödsdansen, Ett drömspel, Kristina, Oväder, Spöksonaten*, and *Pelikanen*.

Stresses Sg's revolutionary dramatic technique and his use of symbols and images in order to express a desire for harmony and the salvation of mankind, which is obsessed with its loneliness]

[D2:1165] — Lombard, A., 'August Strindberg, *Teatru*', *Sydsvenska Dagbladet* (Malmö), 18 February 1974.

[D2:1166] Shakh-Azizova, Tat'iana, 'Naturalism and Symbolism: The Shadow of Fate in Strindberg's Plays', in Michael Robinson, ed., **B1:379**, *The Moscow Papers*, pp. 63-68. [Explores Sg's ambiguous position in relation to naturalism, expressionism, and symbolism. Links him with Aleksandr Blok and compares *Ett drömspel* with the latter's symbolist drama *The Stranger*. Shakh-Azizova considers the paradox of his humanity vis-à-vis his ruthlessness, and contrasts the way in which fate is treated in *Fröken Julie, Dödsdansen,* and *Ett drömspel*. She concludes that 'the constantly perceptible presence of fate may be at the root of Sg's integrity, with all his complexity and protean tendency to change, the source of the profound humanity of his cruel plays, when the unseemly story of petty family conflicts takes on a tragic dimension that is Shakespearean in scale']

[D2:1167] Skácelik, František, 'O Strindbergove dramaturgii', 1-2, *Lumír* (Prague), 50 (1923), pp. 435-442, 475-478. ['On Strindbergian Dramaturgy'. An early Czech essay which sees Sg as a revolutionary spirit who can assist the Czech theatre in making the transition from an outmoded form of naturalism to a higher, more modern art of the stage]

[D2:1168] Sławińska, Irena, and Marian Lewko, 'Strindberg och den polska teatern', Translation by Tore Wretö, *Meddelanden från Strindbergssällskapet* (Stockholm), 44 (1970), pp. 2-8. ['Strindberg and the Polish Theatre'. Surveys the history of Sg in performance on the Polish stage from 1905 to 1967]

[D2:1169] Sławińska, Irena, 'Strindberg i teatr wspólczesny', *Dialog* (Warsaw), 1974:1, pp. 169-171. ['Strindberg in the Polish Theatre']

[D2:1170] Šmeralová, Eva, 'Strindberg stálým hostem českých scén jeho *Sonáta duchů* v *Divadle Komedie*', *Haló noviny* (Prague), 4 October 1995, p. 8. [Discusses performances of *Spöksonaten* and *Leka med elden* in the Czech theatre]

[D2:1171] Smith, Molly, 'Strindberg's Dramatic Art as Search for Self. *The Father, Miss Julie*, and *A Dream Play*', *Journal of Evolutionary Psychology* (Pittsburgh), 9:1-2 (1988), 43-51. [Regards all Sg's creations as reflections of the chaotic ambivalences in his own life; they are thus intimately linked with his experiences as well as intended to provide both biographical and literary glosses on each other. Driven by the unsatisfied wishes of Freudian theory, the early naturalistic plays seek to resolve his dilemmas by manipulating outer reality whereas in *Ett drömspel* he turns towards an exploration of his own psyche and achieves a more optimistic resolution. Discusses *Fadren* and *Fröken Julie* in relation to *En dåres försvarstal* and *Ett drömspel* as a descent into the subconscious with reference to C. G. Jung and the story of Cupid and Psyche in Apuleius's *Golden Ass*]

[D2:1172] Söderhjelm, Werner, '*Samlade otryckta skrifter. Del 1. Dramatiska arbeten*', *Svenska Dagbladet* (Stockholm), 17 December 1918. [Reviews the plays and dramatic fragments published in Volume One of Vilhelm Carlheim-Gyllensköld's edition of Sg's collected unpublished works]

[D2:1173] Söderman, Sven, 'Saga och dröm', in **B1:413**, *Böcker och författare. Kritiker och studier (1894-1914)*, pp. 15-23. ['Saga and Dream'. Rpr. of **D2:1200**]

[D2:1173a] Söderström, Göran, 'Mary Stuart: a scenography', in Olle Granath, *August Strindberg: Painter, Photographer, Writer*, London: Tate Publishing, 2005, pp. 139-141. Illus [Comments on Sg's conception of stage design with reference to Bjørnstjerne Bjørnson's play in which he made his debut as an actor at Dramaten in 1869]

[D2:1174] Söderström, Göran, 'Strindberg's Scenographic Ideas', in Donald Weaver, ed., **D2:331**, *Strindberg on Stage*, pp. 33-52. Illus. [Surveys both published and unpublished material in the form of letters, essays, sketches, notes, and stage directions in which Sg considers how his plays should be staged, with particular attention to *Till Damaskus* and *Stora landsvägen*. Sg's visual imagination is evident in the interest he took in the scenography of his plays, which he visualised in his mind before writing, something that is frequently confirmed by this material]

[D2:1175] Söderström, Göran, 'Strindbergove ideje o scenografiji', Prijevod sa svedskoga Mirko Rumac, *Prolog* (Zagreb), 55-56 (1983), pp. 80-88. Illus. ['Strindberg's Scenographic Ideas'. Serbo-Croat translation of **D2:1174**]

[D2:1176] Sokół, Lech, 'Wstęp', in August Strindberg, *Wybór dramatów*, Przekląd i przypisy Zygmunt Łanowski, Narodowa. Seria 2, No. 185, Wrocław: Ossolineum, 1977. Illus. CXXV+1097 pp. [A substantial (pp. III-CXXV) introduction to a collection containing *Fadren*, *Fröken Julie*, *Fordringsägare*, *Den starkare*, *Leka med elden*, *Till Damaskus*, *Erik XIV*, *Dödsdansen*, *Ett drömspel*, *Oväder*, *Spöksonaten*, and *Pelikanen*, as well as a selection from the *Memorandum till Medlemmarne av Intima Teatern*, all translated into Polish by Zygmunt Łanowski. Sokół also offers an overview of Sg's life in the context of the political, social, and cultural circumstances of 19th-Century Sweden, a general account of his overall production, and the reception accorded his plays in France, England, and Germany, as well as Poland. Includes a bibliography, pp. [CXXII]-CXXV]

[D2:1177] — Greń, Zygmunt, 'Strindberg' na tle', *Życie Literackie* (Kraków), 1977:47, pp. 8-9.

[D2:1178] — Kasiewicz, Alicja, *Wiadomości* (Wrocław), 1978:2, p. 13.

[D2:1179] — Litwinowicz, Aniela, '*Wybór dramatów*', *Tygodnik Powszechny* (Kraków), 1978:18, p. 7.

[D2:1180] — 'Quas' [Bogdan Bąk], '*Wybór dramatów*', *Gazeta Robotnicza* (Wrocław), No. 226 (1977), p. 5.

[D2:1181] — Szweczyk, Grażyna, *Nowe Książki* (Warsaw), 1977:24, pp. 48-50.

[D2:1182] Sokół, Lech, 'Wstęp', in August Strindberg, *Dramaty królewskie; Dramaty liryczne*, wybrał i przełozyl ze szwedzkiego Zygmunt Łanowski poslowiem opatrzył Lech Sokół, Seria dziel pisarzy skandynawskich, Poznań: Wydawnictwo Poznańskie, 1988. [Introduces a volume containing Zygmunt Łanowski's translations of *Erik XIV*, *Karl XII*, *Gustav III*, *Till Damaskus I*, *Ett drömspel*, and *Stora landsvägen*]

[D2:1183] Soliman, Aziz, 'Introduction', in August Strindberg, *Miss Julie and The Ghost Sonata*, Cairo: Anglo Egyptian Bookshop, [1967], pp. vii-lii. [A substantial introduction to Sg's career as a dramatist, using the two translated plays in order to elaborate a comparison between naturalism and expressionism. Includes references to English, German, and French secondary sources]

[D2:1184] Sörenson, Elisabeth, 'Sann Strindbergstolkning existerar inte', *Svenska Dagbladet* (Stockholm), 30 June 1983. ['A True Interpretation of Strindberg doesn't Exist'. Interviews Johan Bergenstråhle and Kjell Grede on interpreting Sg in performance today. Both maintain that there is no single, or 'true', way of performing his plays]

[D2:1185] Sörenson, Margareta, 'Swedish Theater after Strindberg', *American-Scandinavian Review* (New York), 76:1 (1988), 153-[159]. Illus.

[D2:1186] Sosnosky, Theodor von, 'Litterarische Revue', *Deutsche Revue* (Berlin), 18:3 (1893), 371-377. [Discusses *Fordringsägare*, *Den starkare*, *Bandet*, and *Första varningen*. Also comments on *I havsbandet*]

[D2:1187] Southerington, F. R., 'Introduction', in August Strindberg, *Three Experimental Plays*, Charlottesville: University Press of Virginia, 1975, pp. xi-xxii. [Introduces the author's own translations of *Fröken Julie*, *Den starkare*, and *Ett drömspel*]

[D2:1188] Spivack, C. K., 'The Many Hells of August Strindberg', *Twentieth Century Literature* (Hempstead, N.Y.), 9 (1963), 10-16. [Identifies three forms of hell in Sg's plays: 'The Swedenborgian hell of *Crimes and Crimes*; the existentialist hell of *The Dance of Death*; and the biblical hell of *The Great Highway*']

[D2:1189] Sprigge, Elizabeth, 'Introduction', in August Strindberg, *Twelve Plays*, Translated from the Swedish by Elizabeth Sprigge, London: Constable/Chicago: Aldine, 1962, 1964, pp. vii-xiv. [Introduces a volume of the author's own translations]

[D2:1190] Sprinchorn, Evert, 'Strindberg (1849-1912)', in Sprinchorn, ed., *The Genius of the Scandinavian Theater*, New York: New American Library, 1964, pp. 267-277. [On Sg's achevement as a dramatist, prefacing the anthologised texts of *Brott och brott* and *Till Damaskus I*]

[D2:1191] Sprinchorn, Evert, 'Vändpunkten', översatt av Marianne Eyre, *Dramaten* (Stockholm), Program 1, (1983), pp. 19-23, 28-33. ['The Turning Point'. A translation of Chapter 7 from *Strindberg as Dramatist*, **B1:421**, on Sg's change of direction during the Inferno crisis]

[D2:1192] Sprinchorn, Evert, 'Hell and Purgatory in Strindberg', *Scandinavian Studies* (Lawrence, Kansas), 50:4 (1978), 371-380. [Describes how Swedenborg's concept of 'vastation', a process in which our external state is stripped away and our internal self made visible, provides Sg with a dramatic device, whereby he can depict the experience of spiritual conversion on stage, which otherwise is without external action and difficult to convey dramatically. Discusses *Inferno*, *Till Damaskus*, *Dödsdansen*, and *Spöksonaten*]

[D2:1193] Sprinchorn, Evert, 'Introduction', in August Strindberg, *Selected Plays*, 2 vols, Minneapolis: University of Minnesota Press, 1986, pp. ix-xvi. [Introduces the author's own translations of *Mäster Olof, Fadren, Fröken Julie, Fordringsägare, Den starkare, Leka med elden, Till Damaskus I, Brott och brott, Dödsdansen I, Ett drömspel, Spöksonaten,* and *Pelikanen*]

[D2:1194] Sprinchorn, Evert, 'Strindberg and the Decline of the Drama of Ideas', in Kela Kvam, ed., **D2:158**, *Strindberg's Post-Inferno Plays*, pp. 204-215. [Considers how the new literary and theatrical devices that Sg invented in order to put the supranatural on stage in *Till Damaskus*, *Dödsdansen*, and *Karl XII* have been appropriated by later playwrights while the intellectual and moral scheme that gave birth to them is now ignored. Sprinchorn maintains the continuing relevance and superiority of Maeterlinck and Sg to their epigones, Brecht, Ionesco, and Beckett. Both the epic theatre and the theatre of the absurd emanate from the 19th Century but have failed to go beyond it and engage with the underlying conflicts of our times. Placing Sg's plays 'against the best of both the epic theatre and the theatre of the absurd shows how far the drama of thought has declined in the last eighty years']

[D2:1195] Sprinchorn, Evert, 'Strindberg and the Greater Naturalism', *Tulane Drama Review* (New Orleans), 13:2 (1968), 119-129. [Discusses the nature of Sg's naturalism, focusing on *Fadren*, *Fröken Julie*, and 'Hjärnornas kamp' (1887), as well as on Sg's differences with Zola and his reaction against the 'lesser', or photographic, form of naturalism]

[D2:1196] Sprinchorn, Evert, 'August Strindberg, *Dramas of Testimony*, Translated by Walter Johnson', *American-Scandinavian Review* (New York), 64:3 (1976), 71–72. [Reviews Johnson's translations of *Dödsdansen I-II*, **E35:50**]

[D2:1197] S. S-n [Sven Söderman], 'Intima teatern', *Stockholms Dagblad*, 24 November 1907. [Questions the decision of the recently founded Intimate Theatre to devote itself exclusively to Sg's plays: he is without doubt our most gifted dramatist, but also the most uneven]

[D2:1198] S. S-n [Sven Söderman], 'Literatur och konst: August Strindbergs sista dramatik samling. *Kronbruden, Svanevit, Drömspelet*', *Stockholms Dagblad*, 15 June 1902. ['August Strindberg's most Recent Collection of Plays'. Reviews the three plays, which have an affinity with German new romanticism, on publication. Praises *Svanevit* for its beauty and theatricality but dismisses *Kronbruden* as an unsuccessful blend of reality and fantasy. However, *Ett drömspel* is a successful experiment, and an astonishing example of Sg's genius. It ranks among his most remarkable works]

[D2:1199] S. S-n [Sven Söderman], '*Samlade otryckta skrifter. Del 1. Dramatiska arbeten*', *Stockholms Dagblad*, 15 December 1918. [Reviews the plays and dramatic fragments published in Volume I of Vilhelm Carlheim-Gyllensköld's edition of Sg's collected unpublished works]

[D2:1200] S. S-n [Sven Söderman], 'Strindbergs senaste damatik', *Stockholms Dagblad*, 20 November 1904. ['Strindberg's Latest Plays'. Reviews *Gustaf III* and *Näktergalen i Wittenberg* on publication. Söderman criticises Sg for the irresponsible way in which he travesties the events of Swedish history, even though, compared with *Kristina*, *Gustav III* is at least relatively seemly. As a play, however, it is a farce, with little pretension to effective drama even if one or two scenes are occasionally witty. Meanwhile, Sg's portrait of Luther in *Näktergalen i Wittenberg* presents him as unnecessarily coarse and his psychological development as a whole is shallow. Only the odd scene has any dramatic power]

[D2:1201] Ståhle Sjönell, Barbro, 'The Plans, Drafts and Manuscripts of the Historical Plays in Strindberg's "Green Bag"', in Birgitta Steene, ed., **B1:434**, *Strindberg and History*, pp. 95-101. Illus. [Rpr. of **D2:1202**]

[D2:1202] Ståhle Sjönell, Barbro, 'The Plans, Drafts and Manuscripts of the Historical Plays in Strindberg's "Green Bag"', *Scandinavian Studies* (Madison, Wisconsin), 62:1 (1990), 69-75. [Describes the development of *Karl XII*, *Kristina*, and *Gustav III* from the notes and drafts among Sg's extant papers, and the creative process this entailed]

[D2:1203] Ståhle Sjönell, Barbro, 'The Plans, Drafts and Manuscripts of the Historical Plays in Strindberg's "Green Bag"', in Janet Witalec, ed., **D2:348**, *Drama Criticism*, Volume 18, pp. 172-175. [Rpr. of **D2:1202**]

[D2:1204] Stam, Per, '"Alltså Teater", svarade Strindberg', *Strindbergiana* (Stockholm), 20 (2005), pp. 129-137. ['"And so the Theatre!", Strindberg Replied'. Discriminates between the alternative titles for the five pamphlets on drama and the theatre which Sg addressed to his colleagues at the Intimate Theatre between 1907 and 1909. Stam considers his relationship with his co-director, August Falck, and the publisher, Börjesson]

[D2:1205] Steene, Birgitta, 'August Strindberg. *Selected Plays I and II.* Trans. by Evert Sprinchorn', *Scandinavian Studies* (Urbana, Illinois), 60:3 (1988), 407-408. [A polite review of Sprinchorn's translations which merely questions the basis on which the selection has been made and the sometimes 'overdone' defence of Sg in the introduction]

[D2:1206] Steene, Birgitta, 'Shakespearean Elements in the Historical Plays of Strindberg', *Comparative Literature* (Eugene, Oregon), 11:3 (1959), 209-220. [Steene compares the techniques of two dramatists who both used their historical sources according to their artistic purposes; their respective views of history were an integral part of their world views in general. *Folkungasagan* is Sg's most Shakespearean history play, after which his wish to portray his historical figures 'realistically' and to stress the purely personal led him away from Shakespeare: 'the scope of his individual plays narrowed down to a living-room perspective, so that many of his historical dramas convey, not a uniform and homogeneous view of the past, but "partial perspectives of the modern theatre"'. In its diversity and epic scope, *Folkungasagan* is reminiscent of *Henry VI* and combines the personal with the public and panoramic, but both *Gustav Vasa* and *Erik XIV* are increasingly personal, and in the latter, the protagonist has a modern dissecting mind which anticipates several later history plays. These isolated and independent works often adhere to a simplified, non-Shakespearean structure. Sg's historical cycle thus breaks into fragments and, in spite of what he writes in the *Memorandum till Medlemmarne av Intima Teatern*, the continuous encroachment of the modern analytic temper upon a providential attitude towards history, in which the king is a public man whose identity is his public office, makes the plays less and less Shakespearean in character]

[D2:1207] Steene, Birgitta, 'Shakespearean Elements in the Historical Plays of Strindberg', in Otto Reinert, ed., **B1:371**, *Strindberg: A Collection of Critical Essays*, pp. 125-136. [Rpr. of **D2:1206**]

[D2:1208] Stern, Julius, 'Neue Dramen. II', *Ethische Kultur* (Berlin), 9 (1901), 253-255. [Examines *Advent* and *Brott och brott* as moral dramas]

[D2:1209] Sterner, Jan, 'Strindberg och skådespelarkonsten', *Gefle Dagblad* (Gävle), 18 June 1999. ['Strindberg and the Art of Acting']

[D2:1210] Stockenström, Göran, 'August Strindberg: A Modernist in Spite of Himself', *Comparative Drama* (Kalamazoo, Michigan), 26:2 (1992), 95-123. [Sg's painful and bizarre psychic experiences between 1894 and 1897 undermined the shared sense of reality underlying the naturalistic works and the attempt to re-compose the fragments of reality into an infinite order that he sought in science, occultism, mythology, and religion, as well as in psychological introspection, produced a new outlook which was enriched by an eclectic complex of ideas and proved fruitful in terms of renewed artistic creation in proto-modernist forms. As a result, he evolved a new form of theatre that is apparent in a history play like *Karl XII* as well as in *Till Damaskus*, *Dödsdansen*, *Ett drömspel*, and *Spöksonaten*. In virtually all his later plays Sg introduced new forms of theatre practice, in which the physical and the spiritual are constantly translated into one another's language in ever new, more complicated relationships. However, their artistic modernity was a consequence of Sg's attempt to resolve his personal dilemma rather than the result of any deliberate artistic strategy. Stockenström also discusses the prose texts *Svarta fanor*, *En blå bok*, and *Inferno*]

[D2:1211] Stolpe, Sven, 'Onko August Strindberg Surri draamakirjailija?', *Uusi Suomi* (Helsinki), 30 March 1960. ['Is August Strindberg a Great Dramatist?']

[D2:1212] Stommel, Gottfried, 'Strindberg', 1–2, *Theater-Courier* (Berlin), 23 (1916), pp. 241-242, 252, 266-267. [On Sg's plays in general and *Brott och brott* and *Dödsdansen* in particular]

[D2:1213] Stonier, G. W., 'August Strindberg, *Mäster Olof and Other Plays*', *The New Statesman* (London), 12 March 1932.

[D2:1214] Strecker, Karl, 'Strindberg und die Bühne', *Tägliche Rundschau* (Berlin), 11 March 1918. ['Strindberg and the Stage']

[D2:1215] Strecker, Karl, 'August Strindbergs Dramaturgie', *Tägliche Rundschau* (Berlin), Unterhaltungsbeilage Nr. 7 vom 20. Januar 1912. ['August Strindberg's Dramaturgy']

[D2:1216] Streisand, Marianne, 'Strindbergs Entwurf einer "Aesthetik der Intimität" und ihre Realiserung bei Max Reinhardt', in Kirsten Wechsel, Hrsg., **B1:473**, *Strindberg and His Media*, pp. 147-172. ['Strindberg's Design for an 'Aesthetic of Intimacy" and its Realisation by Max Reinhardt'. Examines the idea of a theatre presented in the Preface to *Fröken Julie* and compares his theories with those of Wagner and Kandinsky, as well as in relation to contemporary discourses on intimacy with reference to Ferdinand Tönnies, Gustave Le Bon, Ernst Mach, and Nietzsche]

[D2:1217] Strel'tsov, R., '[The Plays of August Strindberg]', *Zaprosy zhizni* (St Petersburg), 5 May 1912, Sp. 1099-1104. [E.866]

[D2:1218] Stubbs, P. C., 'That Man Strindberg and His Plays', *Green Book Magazine* (New York), 8 (September, 1912), 518-526.

[D2:1219] 'Suecus' [Erik Löfgren], 'Svensk historia och Strindbergs dramatik', *Dagsposten* (Stockholm), 21 January 1949. ['Swedish History and Strindberg's Plays]

[D2:1220] *The Sunday Times* (London), 'August Strindberg, *The Plays*, Vols 1 and 2', 23 November 1975. [Reviews sixteen of Michael Meyer's translations. Concludes that 'the lesser known plays are as gripping as the more famous']

[D2:1221] Sundberg, Björn, '"Guds hands menniskor" – Ett stråkdrag genom Strindbergs historiedramatik', in Bengt Landgren, red., *Att välja sin samtid. Essäer om levande svensk litteratur från Birgitta till Karlfeldt*, Stockholm: Norstedts, 1986, pp. 199-210. ['"Those Touched by the Hand of God"' – A Survey of Strindberg's History Plays'. Focuses on *Bjälbo-Jarlen* and the final history plays, which reflect Sg's serious and conscious attempt to establish himself as a national poet in 1908-09. But Sundberg also examines the tension in his historical cycle as a whole between discrete events, human passions, and a deepening conviction that the course of history is shaped by an invisible, guiding hand]

[D2:1222] Sundberg, Björn, 'Strindberg på jakt efter guds hand i historien', in *Ibsen-Strindberg seminar på Voksenåsen 15-17 september 1997*, Oslo: Voksenåsen, 1997, pp. 25-40. ['Strindberg in Search of God's Hand in History'. Although they were generally well received at the time, Sg's last three history plays (*Siste riddaren, Riksföreståndaren*, and *Bjälbo Jarlen*) have seldom been performed again, and have often been the object of critical censure as loosely constructed and circumstantial works populated by numerous, poorly characterised secondary figures. Acknowledging this, Sundberg compares Sg's historical dramaturgy with Ibsen's and the nationalist aspects of such plays, relating them to contemporary political conflicts in Sweden in the early years of the century, as well as to Sg's philosophy of history as developed in the essay 'Världs-historiens mystik'. Such an analysis suggests that Sg's achievement in these plays is at variance with the preconceived ideas that most critics normally bring to them]

[D2:1223] Sundberg, Björn, 'Strindbergs sena historiedramatik', *Tidskrift för litteraturvetenskap* (Lund), 13:2-3 (1984), 90-95. Illus. ['Strindberg's Late History Plays'. Considers the grounds for an examination of Sg's later history plays in relation to the ideas on history developed in 'Världhistoriens mystik', the cultural (mainly theatrical) context, and the dramaturgy of the Chamber Plays and *Stora landsvägen*. The essay focuses almost exclusively on *Siste riddaren*]

[D2:1224] Svenson, Lars, '*Memorandum till Medlemmarne af Intima Teatern från regissören*', *Helsingborgs Dagblad*, 27 August 1975. [Reviews a new edition]

[D2:1225] Svenson, Lars, 'Strindberg', *Helsingborgs Dagblad*, 19 December 1989. [Reviews Volume 61 in *Samlade Verk*, containing *Siste riddaren, Riksföreståndaren*, and *Bjälbo-Jarlen*]

[D2:1226] Swortzell, Lowell, 'Strindberg's Legacy to Drama for Young People', *Children's Literature Association Quarterly* (El Paso, Texas), 9:3 (1984), 119-121.

[D2:1227] Szalczer, Eszter, 'August Strindberg's Dramatic Expressionism and the Discourse of the Self', in Michael Robinson and Sven Hakon Rossel, eds, **B1:387**, *Expressionism and Modernism*, pp. 197-204. [Sg's later characters are often unable to break the confines of their masks or escape the compulsion of play-acting. Szalczer establishes how Sg contrived to retain and reconstitute the endangered self with reference to the theosophical ideas of Helena Blavatsky and Annie Besant, which draw in turn on Indian philosophy and the ideas of Schopenhauer and Carl du Prel. She uses *Till Damaskus, Ett drömspel, Spöksonaten*, and *Stora landsvägen* to exemplify this. But whereas both Blavatsky and du Prel offer 'the notion of a unified subject whose perplexing fragmentation is but a temporary illusion, in Sg's plays the desired single subject is revealed only through the veils of a dream world or as a stage illusion']

[D2:1228] Szalczer Eszter, 'Främmande röster. Besatthet och exorcism i Strindbergs dramatik', Översättning Birgitta Steene, *Strindbergiana* (Stockholm), 19 (2004), pp. 30-41. ['Alien Voices. Possession and Exorcism in Strindberg's Dramas'. Uses Sg's description of himself as writing in a state of unconscious possession, as a kind of medium, and yet tongue-tied and almost mute when speaking in public to examine how his plays represent conflicts between different discourses and forms of representation with reference especially to *Fadren, Fröken Julie*, and *Ett drömspel*. This demonstrates how, as the unified consciousness gives way to a polyphonic stream of numerous voices, Sg's plays reflect a crisis in dramatic and linguistic conventions]

[D2:1229] Szalczer, Eszter, 'Nature's Dream Play: Modes of Vision and August Strindberg's Re-Definition of the Theatre', *Theatre Journal* (Baltimore), 53:1 (2001), 33-52. Illus. [Demonstrates how Sg's photography, and his life-long interest in science and modes of vision, informs not only his naturalistic plays but also his dramatic experiments of the post-Inferno period, thereby expanding the domain of the European theatre in general. Closely linked to Sg's scientific speculations in the 1890s, in e.g. *Antibarbarus*, Szalczer argues that his experimental photography raises issues of objectivity and subjectivity that are explored in 'Sensations détraquées' (1894) and underlie the scenic experiments of *Till Damaskus* and *Ett drömspel*, where we are taken metaphorically inside the theatre of the mind. For Szalczer, 'The optical-photographic experiments and reflections of the 1890s indicate a transition from the masquerade of nature towards the theatre of the mind', thus confirming that we live in a world of illusion that consists of purely cerebral phenomena]

[D2:1230] Szalczer, Eszter, 'Theosophy as Catalyst – Strindberg's Theatre of the Self and the Other', in Poul Houe, *et al.*, ed., **B1:170**, *August Strindberg and the Other*, pp. 101-114. [The theatrical metaphor in which life is seen as an elusive theatre piece and the identity of the speaker dissolves into a plurality of roles is central to Sg's writing. Moreover, in his texts the authorial self acts numerous parts, 'appearing simultaneously as actor and spectator, agent and observer of the action'. The inherent theatricality of his project has affinities with the ideas of the contemporary theosophical movement, an affinity explored here with primary reference to the knowledge of Theosophy that Sg displayed in *Svarta fanor*, 'Genvägar' (Short Cuts), and *Giftas*, and especially his correspondence with Torsten Hedlund]

[D2:1231] Szewczyk, Grażyna Barbara, 'August Strindberg's Influence on the Drama of German Expressionism', in Michael Robinson and Sven Hakon Rossel, eds, **B1:387**, *Expressionism and Modernism*, pp. 205-211. [Considers the extent to which Sg influenced the nature of expressionist drama in general and Reinhard Sorge, Franz Werfel, and Ernst Toller in particular. But Szewczyk reckons that many of his dramatic motifs and ideas were of no interest to these playwrights, who did not imitate him and, in spite of a feeling of spiritual kinship, went their own way]

[D2:1232] Szweczyk, Grażyna, 'Strindberg i niemiecki ekspresjonizm', *Przegląd humanistyczny* (Warsaw), 29:9-10 (1985), 63-73. ['Strindberg and German Expressionism']

[D2:1233] Taurman, Howard, 'Neglected Dramatist', *New York Times*, 4 December 1960.

[D2:1234] *Teatr* (Warsaw), 'August Strindberg', 1983:2, pp. 2, 4-10. [A photographic essay, illustrating Sg's plays on the Polish stage, 1961-1982]

[D2:1235] Terzakes, Angelos, 'Prologos', in Augoustou Strintmpergk, *Despoinis Tzoulia*; *He pio dynate*, Athena: Vivliopoleio 'Dodone', 1977. [Introduces modern Greek translations of *Fröken Julie* and *Den starkare* by Pelos Katseles]

[D2:1236] Thompson, V[ance C.], 'Strindberg and His Plays', *The Bookman* (New York), 47:1 (June 1918), 361-369. [Maintains that Sg was the greatest dramatist of his age and the most important figure in the intellectual evolution of Europe in recent times]

[D2:1237] Thormann, Werner E., 'Strindberg', *Blätter der Württenbergischen Volksbühne* (Stuttgart), 6 (1924-25).

[D2:1238] Thormann, Werner E., 'August Strindberg', in *Dichter und Bühne*, Reihe 3: Unsere Zeit, Augsburg, 1921.

[D2:1239] 'Tigram' [Margit Siwertz], 'Strindberg och skådespelarna', 1-6, *Svenska Dagbladet* (Stockholm), 7, 9, 13, 16, and 31 December 1948, and 28 January 1949. ['Strindberg and the Actors'. Six interviews with the Swedish actors Anna Flygare, Lars Hanson, Märta Ekström, Inga Tidblad, Anders de Wahl, and Karin Kavli, on acting in Sg. Flygare, who worked directly with Sg at the Intimate Theatre, observes that 'he felt a pin-prick as others felt a blow with an axe']

[D2:1240] Törnqvist, Arne, 'Enaktarna', *Dagens Nyheter* (Stockholm), 2 May 1985. ['The One-Acters']

[D2:1241] Törnqvist, Egil, 'De bewerking van de realiteit: het Historie-drama', in *Scenarium*, Zutphen: De Walburg Pers, 1980, pp. 9-21. ['The Adaptation of Reality: The History Play']

[D2:1242] Törnqvist, Egil, 'Den ongespeelde Strindberg', *Vooys: Tijdschrift voor Letteren* (Utrecht), 19:1 (2001), 48-53. ['The Unperformed Strindberg'. On the limited repertoire of Sg's plays regularly performed in the Netherlands]

[D2:1243] Törnqvist, Egil, 'Den Strindbergska enaktaren', in Bertil Nolin and Peter Forsgren, eds, *The Modern Breakthrough in Scandinavian Literature*, Skrifter utgivna av Litteraturvetenskapliga institutionen vid Göteborgs universitet 17, Göteborg, 1988, pp. 261-266. ['The Strindbergian One-Act Play'. Swedish version of **D2:1252**]

[D2:1244] Törnqvist, Egil, 'Inleiding', in August Strindberg, *Freule Julie en andere eenakters*, Amsterdam: International Theatre Bookshop, 1986, pp. 7-22. [Introduces a Dutch translation of *Miss Julie* and several of the one-act plays from the late-1880s]

[D2:1245] Törnqvist, Egil, 'Le didascalie di Strindberg in scena', Traduzione di M. Cristina Lombardi, in *La didascalie nella letteratura teatrale Scandinava. Testo drammatico e sintesi scenica*, a cura di Merete Kjøller Ritzu, Roma: Bulzoni, 1987, **D1:375**, pp. 111-126. Illus. ['Strindberg's Stage-Directions on Stage'. Studies Sg's stage-directions in *Fröken Julie, Ett drömspel*, and *Spöksonaten*, and examines the way in which their demands have been resolved in productions by Olof Molander, Max Bigneu, Max Reinhardt, and Ingmar Bergman]

[D2:1246] Törnqvist, Egil, 'Questions without Answers? An Aspect of Strindberg's Drama Dialogue', in Göran Rossholm, Barbro Ståhle Sjönell, and Boel Westin, eds, **B1:389**, *Strindberg and Fiction*, pp. 33-40. [Examines the 'complex' relationship between question(er) and answer(er) in Sg's plays with particular reference to *Fröken Julie, Spöksonaten*, and *Pelikanen*. In Sg, questions are sometimes left unanswered or are only answered enigmatically, although in order to determine for whom requires us to discriminate between those on stage and the audience. These are issues which scholars have generally ignored whereas actors and directors obviously cannot]

[D2:1247] Törnqvist, Egil, 'Strindberg and Subjective Drama', in Michael Robinson, ed., **B1:373**, *Strindberg and Genre*, pp. 97-107. [Uses Peter Szondi's distinction between 'Dramatik' and 'Drama' in *Theorie des modernen Dramas*, **D1:450**, to trace Sg's development from a more objective form of inter-human conflicts associated with traditional dramatic forms to the intra-human, psychologically interiorised conflicts of the – often static – form of subjective modern drama. In Sg's case this is based on conclusions about the nature of the self and subjectivity that he drew from his own self-analysis in *Tjänstekvinnans son* and subsequently formulated in his statements on character and its fictional representation in the Prefaces to *Fröken Julie* and *Ett* *drömspel*. As a novelist as well as dramatist, Sg was familiar with issues of focalisation and point-of-view, and many of his plays, including several of the most experimental, are concerned with the personal angle from which the dramatised events are seen, one which problematises in turn the way these events are apprehended by the audience. Törnqvist establishes common and changing features in Sg's subjective dramaturgy via a comparison of two pre-Inferno dramas (*Den starkare* and *Fadren*) and one later play (*Ett drömspel*), as well as by way of briefer references to *Till Damaskus*, *Karl XII*, *Dödsdansen*, *Spöksonaten*, *Stora landsvägen*, and *En dåres försvarstal*]

[D2:1248] Törnqvist, Egil, 'Strindberg is quasi modern', *Toneel teatraal* (Amsterdam), March 1985, pp. 12-14.

[D2:1249] Törnqvist, Egil, 'Strindberg's Secondary Text', *Modern Drama* (Toronto), 33:4 (1990), 486-493. [English version of **D2:1250**]

[D2:1250] Törnqvist, Egil, 'Strindbergs bitext', *Strindbergiana* (Stockholm), 3 (1988), pp. 15-33. Illus. ['Strindberg's Secondary Text'. Törnqvist uses Roman Ingarden's distinction between a play's 'Haupttext' and 'Nebentext' to determine how the non-verbalised elements in Sg's play texts may, or may not, contribute to an understanding of the verbalised text and its realisation on stage. He identifies twelve possible such elements, not all of which are necessarily present in every drama, and examines their role with reference, among others, to *Mäster Olof*, *Fadren*, *Fröken Julie*, *Till Damaskus*, *Karl XII*, *Ett drömspel*, and *Spöksonaten*]

[D2:1251] Törnqvist, Egil, 'Strindbergs dramatik i Sveriges Radio 1925-2000', *Strindbergiana* (Stockholm), 17 (2002), pp. 140-[164]. ['Strindberg's Plays Broadcast on Swedish Radio, 1925-200'. A useful check list of performances of Sg's dramas on Swedish Radio with details of the director, producer, and performers]

[D2:1252] Törnqvist, Egil, 'The Strindbergian One-Acter', in Winfried Herget and Brigitte Schultze, Hrsg., *Kurzformen des Dramas. Gattungspoetische, epochenspezifische und funktionale Horizonte*, Mainzer Forschungen zu Drama und Theater 16, Tübingen-Basel: Francke Verlag, 1996, pp. 133-143. [Surveys Sg's role in launching the genre of the modern one-act play as a serious and independent form of drama. He wrote fourteen mainly naturalistic such plays, which sought maximum illusion (the playing time is often identical with their scenic time), in which characters were frequently more types than individuals, and which leant themselves to parabolic situations. Nevertheless, these plays vary greatly in length, as well as the number and kind of characters. Törnqvist uses *Den starkare* and *Inför döden* to exemplify the characteristics of the genre and indicates how these plays anticipate major themes in post-Inferno dramas like *Ett drömspel* and *Spöksonaten*]

[D2:1253] Törnqvist, Egil, 'The Strindbergian One-Act Play', *Scandinavian Studies* (Provo), 68:3 (1996), 356-369. [Rpr. of **D2:1252**]

[D2:1254] Törnqvist, Egil, 'The Strindbergian One-Act Play', in Janet Witalec, ed., **D2:348**, *Drama Criticism*, Volume 18, pp. 209-215. [Rpr. of **D2:1252**]

[D2:1255] Törnqvist, Egil, 'Unreliable Narration in Strindbergian Drama', *Scandinavica* (Norwich), 38:1 (1999), 61-79. [Points out that Sg's plays frequently raise issues of narrative reliability in what characters have to say about events that are not enacted in the presence of the audience. Traditionally, most such information has to be taken on trust if the play is to remain credible, but in Sg's case an audience is frequently confronted with dramaturgically unstable and unreliable data that is not included merely in the interests of the intrigue but as an integral part of the issues and actions his plays are exploring. In *Spöksonaten* such unreliable information is included even in the secondary text (e.g. the list of *dramatis personae*), thus extending it beyond the characters' words to the authorial apparatus. Törnqvist examines cases of unreliable narration in *Fadren*, *Fröken Julie*, *Den starkare*, *Inför döden*, *Påsk*, *Oväder*, and *Pelikanen*. These demonstrate that, 'as long as he was adjusting to relatively traditional, plot-oriented drama, Sg was forced to adhere to...the dramaturgical law of reliability and its rather rigid insistence that while narrative statements early in the play may well prove (retrospectively) unreliable, late statements should be truthful – so that in the course of the play we experience a sense of gradual revelation. This dramaturgic law is clearly at odds with the growing awareness...of the complexity of the human psyche and the subjectivity and relativity of what we call truth', and the frequently enigmatic nature of 'factual' detail in Sg's later plays reflects this change]

[D2:1256] Torsslow, Stig, 'Strindberg och teatercensuren', *Svenska Dagbladet* (Stockholm), 24 August 1970. ['Strindberg and the Theatre Censor']

[D2:1257] Trekman, Borut, 'Popotnik skozi inferno', in August Strindberg, *Tri drame*, Ljubljana, 1977, pp. 134-153. ['Wanderer through Inferno'. The Afterword to a collection of Slovenian translations of *Fröken Julie*, *Ett drömspel*, and *Spöksonaten*]

[D2:1258] Triesch, Irene, 'August Strindberg', *Deutsch-nordisches Jahrbuch für Kulturaustausch und Volkskunde* (Jena), 1914, pp. 67-69. [Reflections on Sg by an actress who gave notable performances as Kersti in *Kronbruden* (1913), Indra's Daughter in *Ett drömspel* (1916), and Alice in *Dödsdansen* (1922)]

[D2:1259] Uggla, Andrzej N[ils], 'W poszukiwaniu humoru Strindberga', *Teatr* (Warsaw), 1983:2, pp. 6-8. ['In Quest of Strindberg's Humour']

[D2:1260] Ugglas, Carl R. af, 'Svensk dramatisk litteratur', *Ord och Bild* (Stockholm), 20:7 (1911), 435-442. [Reviews *Svarta handsken* and *Stora landsvägen* on publication. Identifies crime and its atonement, a fall and subsequent rehabilitation, and the heavy wandering 'per aspera ad astra' as recurring themes in Sg's post-Inferno drama. *Svarta handsken*, with its questionable realism in which external events have no psychological relationship to what occurs within the heroine, is largely a failure. In an abstract drama of ideas like *Stora landsvägen*, on the other hand, Sg achieves a kind of unity in which the familiar themes are successfully explored]

[D2:1261] Ulmanová, Martina, 'Strindberg poprvé', *Svět a divadlo* (Prague), 12:2 (2001), pp. 166-169.

[D2:1262] Uriz, Francisco J., 'Pròlogo', in August Strindberg, *Teatro escogido*, versiòn española de Francisco Uriz, Madrid: Alianza editorial, 1999. 352 pp. [Introduces a collection of Sg's plays in the author's own Spanish translation]

[D2:1263] Vaittinen, Pirjo, 'Autumn Encounters', in Kela Kvam, ed., **D2:158**, *Strindberg's Post-Inferno Plays*, pp. 171-185. [An account of Laura Jäntii's staging of 'Encounters According to Strindberg', which combines characters and material from *Spöksonaten*, *Dödsdansen*, and *Brända tomten*, at the Turku City Theatre in 1991]

[D2:1264] Valk, Sonja van der, 'Voorbij de psychologie, naar de paradox: Strindberg spelen', *Toneel teatraal* (Amsterdam), 1985:3, pp. 4-9. ['Beyond Psychology to Paradox: Strindberg's Plays']

[D2:1265] Vegesack, Siegfried von, 'Strindberg in Kopenhagen', *Die Weltbühne* (Berlin), 18:13 (1922), 321-324. ['Strindberg in Copenhagen']

[D2:1266] Viertel, Berthold, 'Strindberg-Feier', *März* (München), 6:1 (1912), 239-240. ['Strindberg Celebration']

[D2:1267] Viertel, Berthold, 'Der produktive Hass', *Der Strom* (Vienna und Berlin), 2 (1912-13), 127-128. ['Productive Hatred'. An attempt to define Sg's qualities as a dramatist shortly after his death. According to Viertel, 'He was the cruellest of playwrights. His method was to vivisect the hero. He wrote pamphlets against individuals – both living and dead – against intellectual trends, against religions, and against women…and the life work of Sg the moralist, the sociologist, and the philosopher is so rich in results that nations could live off them']

[D2:1268] Viertel, Berthold, 'Der produktive Hass', in Hans-Peter Bayerdörfer, Hrsg., **B3:85**, *Strindberg auf der deutschen Bühne*, pp. 209-211. [Rpr. of **D2:1267**]

[D2:1269] Vogelweith, Guy, 'Attente et intuition de la psychanalyse dans le théâtre de Strindberg', *Scandinavica* (London), 12:1 (1973), 1-16. ['The Prospect and Intuition of Psychoanalysis in Strindberg's Theatre'. Discusses anticipations of Freudian psychoanalysis in Sg's post-Inferno theatre which emerged from the descent into himself that he undertook during the Inferno crisis. Sg dramatised the mechanisms of the unconscious in ways which Freud was shortly to make familiar in his analytical work. Vogelweith focuses on *Till Damaskus*, which dramatises the interplay of the ego, id, and super-ego, and *Ett drömspel*, in which the play of dreams exemplifies Freud's notions of desire and the conflict between the principles of pleasure and reality]

[D2:1270] Vogelweith, Guy, 'Le Théâtre Intime de Strindberg: un dramaturge en attente du 7e art', *Théâtre en Europe* (Paris), 5:1 (1985), 69-74. Illus. ['Strindberg's Intimate Theatre: A Playwright Awaiting the 7th Art'. Regards the Intimate Theatre as a natural development of the ideas expressed in the Preface to *Fröken Julie* and the practice of the Théâtre Libre, as well as the theories formulated in Sg's *Memorandum till Medlemmarne av Intima Teatern*. Vogelweith also considers Sg's influence on Ingmar Bergman]

[D2:1271] Vowles, Richard B., 'Strindberg's Plays', *Modern Language Journal* (Madison, Wisconsin), 48:1 (1964), 60-61. [Reviews recent English translations]

[D2:1272] Vowles, Richard B., 'Strindberg's *Kristina*, *Charles XII*, *Gustav III*, Translated by Walter Johnson', *American-Scandinavian Review* (New York), 43:3 (1955), 300-301.

[D2:1273] V.v.K. [Vera von Kraemer], 'Strindbergs Memorandum', *Social-Demokraten* (Stockholm), 22 January 1910. [Reviews the fourth of Sg's *Memorandum till Medlemmarne av Intima Teatern*, devoted to *Macbeth* and other plays by Shakespeare]

[D2:1274] Wachler, E., 'Betrachtungen über die Strindberg-Bühne', *Deutsche Tageszeitung*, 11 April 1916. ['Reflections on the Strindberg Stage']

[D2:1275] Waern, Carina, 'Strindberg', *Dagens Nyheter* (Stockholm), 7 August 1989. [Reviews Volumes 49 and 61 in *Samlade Verk*, containing *Näktergalen i Wittenberg* and *Siste riddaren, Riksföreståndaren*, and *Bjälbo-Jarlen* respectively]

[D2:1276] Wagner, Ernst, 'Der später Strindberg', *Weimarer Blätter* (Weimar), 4 (1922), 213-221. ['The Later Strindberg'. Discusses Sg's post-Inferno dramaturgy, exemplified here by *Till Damaskus* and *Spöksonaten*]

[D2:1277] Wahlgren, Helge, 'Strindberg som teaterägare och regissör', *Svenska Scenen* (Stockholm), 2:29-30 (1916), 222-224. ['Strindberg as a Theatre Owner and Director'. Contains recollections of Sg's participation in the practical work of the Intimate Theatre by one of the company's actors]

[D2:1278] Wahlgren, Helge, 'Strindbergs egen teater', *Ord och Bild* (Stockholm), 37:1 (1928), 45-56. Illus. ['Strindberg's Own Theatre'. An account of the Intimate Theatre and its significance for the Swedish theatre in general by one of its permanent members, who created several important Sg roles there, including the Student in *Spöksonaten*]

[D2:1279] Wallinder, J., 'August Strindberg och hans historiska dramatik', *For Kirke og Kultur* (Oslo), 1902, pp. 397-415. ['August Strindberg and His History Plays']

[D2:1280] Warburg, Karl, 'Strindbergs nya historiedramer', *Nordisk Tidskrift* (Stockholm), 13:2 (1900), 85-100. ['Strindberg's New History Plays'. On *Folkungasagan*, *Gustav Vasa*, and *Erik XIV* in which Warburg is pleased to see that Sg has abandoned the *idées fixes* and labyrinthine subjectivism of his recent works in favour of more objective subjects. However, he often renders history unrecognisable by rewriting it, recreating historical figures in his own image. Because this tendency is less pronounced in *Gustav Vasa*, the latter is a considerable achievement, and far superior to its companions]

[D2:1281] Ward, John, 'The Neglected Dramas of August Strindberg', *Drama* (London), 92 (1969), 30-35. [Seeks to rehabilitate several of the plays which are rarely performed in England]

[D2:1282] Watts, Peter, 'Introduction', in August Strindberg, *Three Plays*, Harmondsworth: Penguin Classics, 1958, pp. 7-19. [Introduces the author's own translations of *Fadren*, *Fröken Julie*, and *Påsk*]

[D2:1283] Wecker, H., 'Bühnenwerke', *Das deutsche Drama* (Berlin), 3 (1920), p. 281. [Reviews the 1919 German edition of Sg's dramatic works]

[D2:1284] [Wegener, Paul], 'Strindberg i tysk belysning. Den litterära expressionismens mästare enligt Paul Wegener', *Dagens Nyheter* (Stockholm), 3 May 1917. ['Strindberg in German Eyes. Paul Wegener on the Master of Literary Expressionism'. An interview with the actor, who identifies Sg as the source of German expressionism]

[D2:1285] Weivers, Margreth, 'Ett möte med Anna Flygare – aktris vid Intima teatern', *Strindbergiana* (Stockholm), 16 (2001), pp. 62-[70]. Illus. ['A Meeting with Anna Flygare – Actress at the Intimate Theatre'. An interview which includes recollections of rehearsals at the Intimate Theatre (especially of *Dödsdansen* when Flygare played Alice), and provides details of her contacts with Sg]

[D2:1286] Wendriner, Richard, 'Die neue Strindberg', *Die Zukunft* (Berlin), 1901:34, pp. 433-438. ['The New Strindberg'. Discusses the post-Inferno Sg of *Brott och brott* and *Påsk*, with their palpable Christian dimension]

[D2:1287] Wendriner, Richard, 'Die neue Strindberg', *Strindberg blätter* (Dresden), No. 3 (1901), pp. 33-40. ['The New Strindberg'. Identifies the Faust-like attributes of the later Sg of *Inferno, Till Damaskus*, and *Brott och brott*, and his affinity with E. T. A. Hoffmann or Maupassant in his short story 'L'Horla'. Like Dante, he is seeking the right path, and in so doing explores various aspects of Christianity, Theosophy, and other beliefs. Wendriner focuses primarily on *Brott och brott*]

[D2:1288] Wendt, Ernst, 'Mit dem Feuer spielen, sich verbrennen. Anmerkungen zu August Strindberg', *Teater heute* (Hannover), 25:2 (1984), 37-41. Illus. ['Playing with

Fire, Burning Yourself. Observations on August Strindberg'. Argues for a more comprehensive, less clichéed image of Sg than currently prevails in Germany]

[D2:1289] Wendt, Ernst, 'Mit dem Feuer spielen, sich verbrennen. Über den Dramatiker August Strindberg', in *Wie es euch gefällt geht nicht mehr. Meine Lehrstücke und Endspiele*, Edition Akzente, München: C. Hanser Verlag, 1985. 351 pp. ['Playing with Fire, Burning Yourself. Observations on August Strindberg'. Includes a Rpr. of **D2:1298**]

[D2:1290] West, Rebecca, 'Literary Pulp: A Comment on Strindberg', *Daily News* (London), 7 August 1916. [On the fourth collection of Edwin Björkman's translations of plays by the 'unattractive' Sg. According to the Ibsenite West, 'All the characters are moral imbeciles'; although *Kronbruden* is a better play than *Spöksonaten*, 'over which one can do nothing but ring one's hands in wonder', it is nevertheless 'inchoate and fantastic']

[D2:1291] West, Rebecca, 'Literary Pulp: A Comment on Strindberg', in *The Young Rebecca. Writings of Rebecca West 1911-1917*, ed. Jane Marcus, London: Virago, 1983, pp. 320-322. [Rpr. of **D2:1290**]

[D2:1292] Westholm, Carl Axel, 'Strindbergs *Samlade Verk*', *Vestmanlands Läns Tidning* (Västerås), 26 September 1989. [Reviews Volumes 49 and 61 in *Samlade Skrifter*, containing *Näktergalen i Wittenberg* and *Siste riddaren, Riksföreståndaren*, and *Bjälbo-Jarlen* respectively]

[D2:1293] Wetzer, Konni, 'Strindberg och teatern', *Åbo Underrättelser* (Åbo), 16 May 1937. ['Strindberg and the Theatre']

[D2:1294] W. F. H. de, 'Life and Works of August Strindberg', *The Nation* (New York), No. 94 (23 May 1912), 522-524. [Discusses Edwin Björkman's translations of *Ett drömspel*, *Bandet*, and *Dödsdansen*, as well as Sg's recent death. Compares him with John Donne and sees *Ett drömspel* as emblematic of his life's tragedy in which a 'passionate desire to know and help mankind resolved itself into a brutal jest'. In general, however, 'his work is instinct with futility']

[D2:1295] Whitby, Charles, 'Strindberg', *The Theosophist* (London), 43:8 (1922), 119-129. [Sketches Sg's career as a dramatist, focusing mainly on the post-Inferno works *Gustav Vasa, Dödsdansen, Ett drömspel, Påsk, Kronbruden, Spöksonaten*, and (anachronistically) *Bandet*]

[D2:1296] Widfors, Karl, 'Strindberg som teaterfilosof', *Ridå* (Stockholm), 1909:1, p. 3. ['Strindberg as a Philosopher of the Theatre'. Reviews the first three of Sg's *Memorandum till Medlemmarne av Intima Teatern*. Concludes that, although designed for a specific readership, they are also of more general relevance and interest]

[D2:1297] Wien, Alfred, 'August Strindberg als Dramaturg', *Bühne und Welt* (Hamburg), 14:2 (1911-12), 138-143. ['August Strindberg as a Dramaturge']

[D2:1298] Wiese [und Kaiserwaldau], Leopold von, 'Über Strindberg', *Die Deutsche Bühne* (Berlin), 11:5 (1919), 37-38. ['On Strindberg']

[D2:1299] Wieselgren, Oscar, '*Samlade otryckta skrifter. Del 1. Dramatiska arbeten*', *Svenska Tidskrift* (Uppsala), 9 (1919), 51-53. [Reviews the plays and dramatic fragments published in Volume One of Vilhelm Carlheim-Gyllensköld's edition of Sg's collected unpublished works]

[D2:1300] Wieselgren, Oscar, 'Strindberg och den praktiska teatern. Ett minne från ett sammanträffande med Emil Grandinson', *Stockholms-Tidningen*, 10 April 1924.

['Strindberg and the Practice of Theatre. A Recollection of an Encounter with Emil Grandinson'. Reflects on Sg's experience of practical theatre following a discussion with the director of the world première of *Till Damaskus I*]

[D2:1301] Wieselgren, Oscar, 'Strindberg's Significance for the Swedish Theatre', *Theatre Arts* (New York), 24 (1940), 575-578. [Confirms that Sg's plays have exerted a profound and decisive influence on the Swedish theatre. From *Mäster Olof*, which inaugurated a new epoch in the history of the Swedish theatre with its demand for a Meininger-like realism in historical drama, to *Ett drömspel*, with its novel portrayal of the workings of the unconscious mind, Sg has compelled Swedish actors and directors to a revolution in stage-techniques]

[D2:1302] Wilkinson, Lynn R[osellen], 'Strindberg, Peter Szondi, and the Origin of Modern (Tragic) Drama', *Scandinavian Studies* (Provo), 69:1 (1997), [1]-28. [A critical analysis of Szondi's 'cryptic' presentation of Sg in his influential *Theorie des modernen Dramas*, **D1:450**, where his radical dissolution of 'absolute drama' makes him the great formal innovator in turn-of-the-century playwriting. Wilkinson relates Szondi's theories and Sg's plays to both modernism and notions of bourgeois tragedy, with its roots in the 18th Century]

[D2:1303] Williams, Raymond, 'Strindberg and the New Drama in England', *World Theatre-Le théâtre dans le monde* (Bruxelles), 11:1 (1962), 61-66. Illus. [Ponders Sg's reception in England and his influence, or lack of it, on English writers, including D. H. Lawrence and John Osborne. Any advances beyond naturalism in the European theatre in general are likely to be associated with Sg]

[D2:1304] Williams, Raymond, 'Private Tragedy: Strindberg', in Otto Reinert, ed., **B1:371**, *Strindberg: A Collection of Critical Essays*, pp. 48-56. [Reprints part of the chapter on Sg from *Modern Tragedy*, **D1:490**]

[D2:1305] Williams, Raymond, 'Strindberg and Modern Tragedy', in Carl Reinhold Smedmark, ed., **B1:405**, *Essays on Strindberg*, pp. 7-18. [Substantially the same text as **D2:1304**. Williams maintains that Sg anticipates the theatre of O'Neill and Tennessee Williams in which the family has become a destructive entity and life an even fiercer animal struggle than it already is in Sg]

[D2:1306] Williams, Raymond, 'Strindberg i moderna tragedija', *Pozoriste* (Belgrade), 10:6 (1968), p. 635. ['Strindberg and Modern Tragedy'. See **D2:1305**. R.595]

[D2:1307] Winge, Stein, 'Strindberg – en förförare i helvetet', *Strindbergiana* (Stockholm), 14 (1999), pp. 34-38. ['Strindberg – A Seducer in Hell'. Reflections on directing Strindberg's plays with reference to *Fadren*, *Fröken Julie*, *Dödsdansen*, *Ett drömspel*, and *Spöksonaten*]

[D2:1308] Wiren, Göran, 'Strindberg et Jean Vilar', *Revue d'histoire du théâtre* (Paris), 30:3 (1978), 359-369. [At first sight it appears strange to associate a psychological dramatist whose plays generally require an intimate theatre with the socially and politically committed director of the TNP and the Avignon Festival. But while it is true that Vilar mounted only one Sg production with the TNP (*Erik XIV* in 1960), he began his career with *Dödsdansen*, a play he directed three times in the 1940s. *Oväder* in 1943 was also his first notable success. Sg was associated in Vilar's mind with the claustrophobic post-war dramatic discourse of Sartre's *Huis clos* as well as with the theatre of the absurd, and he remains a hidden presence in Vilar's work with the TNP, surfacing in *Erik XIV*, a play that is more concerned with the absurdity of life than with politics]

[D2:1309] Wirmark, Margareta, 'Strindberg's History Plays: Some Reflections', in Michael Robinson, ed., **B1:373**, *Strindberg and Genre*, pp. 200-206. [Points out that Sg's history plays do not all share the same generic characteristics; *Gustav Vasa* is a relatively conventional conflict drama while *Karl XII* is both a history play and a modern drama, whose protagonist resembles Samuel Beckett's Vladimir and Estragon]

[D2:1310] Wirmark, Margareta, 'Strindberg's History Plays: Some Reflections', in Janet Witalec, ed., **D2:348**, *Drama Criticism*, Volume 18, pp. 195-198. [Rpr. of **D2:1309**]

[D2:1311] Wirmark, Margareta, 'Vasadrama blev en stor framgång. August Strindbergs historiska pjäser aktuella på nytt', *Populär historia* (Lund), 1998:2, pp. 34-38. Illus. ['Vasadrama was a Great Success. August Strindberg History Plays Topical Again'. Reflects on the successful staging of several of Sg's history plays, performed as a cycle at Malmö Stadsteater]

[D2:1312] Wirsén, Carl David af, '*Vid högre rätt*', in *Kritiker*, Stockholm: P. A. Norstedt & Söners Förlag, 1901, pp. 377-381. ['Before a Higher Court'. Rpr. of **D2:557**]

[D2:1313] Wittrock, Ulf, 'Strindbergs *Memorandum till Medlemmarne af Intima Teatern från regissören*', *Upsala Nya Tidning*, 6 December 1975. [Reviews a new edition]

[D2:1314] W. L. H., 'August Strindberg, *Plays*', *New York Times*, 3 March 1912. [Reviews Edwin Björkman's translations of *Ett drömspel*, *Bandet*, and *Dödsdansen*]

[D2:1315] Woodbridge, Homer, '*Plays*, Fourth Series', *The Dial* (Chicago), 62 (1917), 99-100. [Reviews Edwin Björkman's translations of *Kronbruden*, *Spöksonaten*, *Första varningen*, and *Gustav Vasa*. The latter is the strongest work in the volume, a history play of extraordinary quality. Woodbridge suggests that its nearest analogue is possibly Shaw's *Anthony and Cleopatra*]

[D2:1316] Woolf, Leonard, 'The World of Books. The Drama', *The Nation and Athenaeum* (London), 45:2 (13 April 1929), p. 45. [Reviews an English translation of *Easter and Other Plays*. Concludes that *Påsk* is 'a very poor play…weak and sentimental', and *Ett drömspel* 'must also be counted a failure…never quite big enough to bear the colossal burden of pessimism which Sg tries to impose on it'. *Spöksonaten*, however, is rather better and *Dödsdansen* 'has claims to be included among great modern dramas'. Provokes a dissenting response about *Ett drömspel* from Eskel Sundström in **E41:187**]

[D2:1317] W-r, 'August Strindberg, *Tryckt och otryckt I*', *Finsk Tidskrift* (Åbo), 28 (1890), pp. 317-319. [Reviews *Fordringsägare*, *Paria*, and *Samum* on publication]

[D2:1318] W. S[öderhjelm], '*Samlade otryckta skrifter. Del 1. Dramatiska arbeten*', *Nya Argus* (Helsingfors), 11 (1918), 177-178. [Reviews the plays and dramatic fragments published in Volume One of Vilhelm Carlheim-Gyllensköld's edition of Sg's collected unpublished works]

[D2:1319] -x-n [Arvid Axelsson], 'Den naturalistiska dramatiken och Aug. Strindbergs nya bok', *Nya Dagligt Allehanda* (Stockholm), 5 April 1890. ['Naturalist Drama and August Strindberg's Latest Book'. Reviews *Tryckt och otryckt* 1-3, with *Paria*, *Samum*, and *Fordringsägare*. The latter is full of cynical expressions and unsuitable for family reading while Sg's ideas about the theatre in the essay 'Om modernt drama och modern teater' are untenable. Naturalistic drama, which treats the abnormal, preferably in the form of criminals, murderers, idiots, and disturbed or deranged creatures, is neither entertaining nor true to reality]

[D2:1320] Y - - r [Yngve Hedvall], 'Strindberg på våra teatrar. En liten öfversikt med anledning af 5-årsminnet af hans bortgång', *Stockholms Dagblad*, 14 May 1917. ['Strindberg in Our Theatres. A Brief Survey on the 5th Anniversary of His Decease']

[D2:1321] Young, Vernon, 'Strindberg's Ghosts', *The New Criterion* (New York), 31:7 (1985), 71-79.

[D2:1322] Zern, Leif, 'Därför skulle diktaren inte ha någon grav', *Strindbergiana* (Stockholm), 16 (2001), pp. 9-[24]. ['Therefore the Writer should not have a Grave'. Discusses the manner of staging Sg in Sweden and considers different aspects of the performance tradition exemplified by Ingmar Bergman and Alf Sjöberg, each of whom has displayed an affinity with different plays in the canon. Consequently, Zern argues that there is no single continuous tradition of Sg in performance]

[D2:1323] Zern, Leif, 'The Devil Being Exorcised. Dialogue with Leif Zern', *Scandinavian Review* (New York), 64:3 (1976), 17-24. Illus. [Comments on contemporary Swedish opinions of Sg apropos Per Olov Enquist's portrait of him in *Tribadernas natt*, and considers the Swedish approach to performing his plays with special reference to four directors, Lennart Hjulström, Alf Sjöberg, Olof Molander, and Ingmar Bergman]

[D2:1324] Zern, Leif, 'Det meningslösa sökandet efter Strindbergs kärna', *Moderna tider* (Stockholm), No. 100 (February 1999), pp. 44-[46], [48]-49. ['The Meaningless Search for Strindberg's Essence'. Discusses various 20th-Century productions of Sg's plays and insists that it is futile to seek some essential Sg among the variety of his work]

[D2:1325] Zickel, Reinhold, 'Zur Kritik der Dramen Strindbergs', *Der Zuschauer* (Leipzig), 1:19-20 (1919–20). ['On the Criticism of Strindberg's Plays']

[D2:1326] Ziegler, Francis J., 'August Strindberg', *Poet Lore* (Philadelphia), 17 (1906), p. 46. [Introduces a translation of *Svanevit*, made from the German, with a general comment on Sg as a dramatist 'whose characters are real, despite their neuroticism. They speak the language of real life and never that of literature']

[D2:1327] Zingerman, B[oris] I[saakevich], 'O teatre Strindberga', *Teatr* (Moscow), 1976:5, pp. 97-111. ['On Strindberg's Theatre'. A significant study of Sg's contribution to the development of modern drama and the European theatre. Zingerman discusses his plays in relation to both naturalism and symbolism, and argues that he is not to be identified entirely with either one or the other. E.1093]

[D2:1328] Zupan, Vinko, 'Avgust Strindberg', *Ljubljanski zvon* (Ljubljana), 32:7 (1912), 370-375. [A survey of Sg's achievement as a dramatist following his recent death]

[D2:1329] Zupančić, Mirko, 'Poglavje o naturalizmu: August Strindberg I-III', *Sodobnost* (Ljubljana), 29:4 (1981), pp. 446-454; 29:11 (1981), pp. 1088-1095; 31:1 (1983), pp. 97-104. [A three-part study of Sg as a dramatist, with the emphasis on the naturalist plays and *Dödsdansen*]

[D2:1330] Zupančić, Mirko, 'August Strindberg in naturalizem', in *Problematika tragedije*, Maribor, 1987, pp. 107-148. ['Strindberg and Naturalism']

See also **B5:27, C1:250, C1:864, D1:480, D1:487, P5:29, S:188, V:4, V:12, V:21, V:23, V:25, V:62, V:67, V:68, V:85, V:99, V:106, V:111, V:131, V:133, V:138, V:142, V:150, V:151, V:153, V:163, V:165, V:173, V:174, V:179, V:183, V:186, V:188, V:189, V:208, V:213, V:216, V:227, V:230, V:231, V:233, V:239, V:249**

D3. Surveys of Two or More of Strindberg's Plays in Performance

[D3:1] Ahlenius, Holger, 'Från Stockholms teatrar', *Ord och Bild* (Stockholm), 58:7 (1949), 338-352. [Reviews five of Sg's plays, all staged at Dramaten in commemoration of the centenary of his birth: 1. *Stora landsvägen* (Dir. Olof Molander; Hunter: Lars Hansen); 2-3. a double-bill comprising *Den starkare* and *Fröken Julie* (Dir. Alf Sjöberg; Julie: Inga Tidblad; Jean: Ulf Palme); 4. *Leka med elden* (Dir. Mimi Pollack with Gunnar Björnstrand as Axel and Gunnel Broström as Kerstin); and 5. *Lycko-Pers resa* (Dir: Per Oscarsson). Ahlenius also discusses performances of *Brott och brott* at Boulevard teatern, *Dödsdansen* at Blancheteatern, and *Paria*, again at Dramaten, with Anders Henrikson as Herr X and Lars Hanson as Herr Y. This last play emerges here as at once a razor-sharp game of chess and a subdued chamber play with an intensely concentrated mood, in which voices are never raised, and only small shifts in atmosphere, tone, rhythm, and tempo indicate the movement of the action and the changing phases of this battle of the brains. However, in realistic plays like *Leka med elden*, one notices that Sg's language, which was once so vital and contemporary, is now beginning to assume the patina of the time in which these dramas were written]

[D3:2] Aigner, Hans, '*Fräulein Julie* und *Mit dem Feuer spielen*', *Die Rampe* (Hamburg), 1 (1919-20). [Reviews performances of '*Miss Julie* and *Playing with Fire*']

[D3:3] A. M. [Artur Möller], 'Strindbergs vecka', *Figaro* (Stockholm), 11 September 1915. ['Strindberg's Week']

[D3:4] Andersson, Gunder, 'En marknad för smågrupper. Strindberg festivalen ett eldorado för ambitiösa färskingar', LOT, 76:26 (1997), p. 19. ['A Market for Small Groups. The Strindberg Festival: An Eldorado for Ambitious Fresh Faces'. Surveys the productions of Sg's plays in performance at the 1997 Sg Festival]

[D3:5] Anon, '[Germany]', *Sovremennyi zapad* (Petersburg), 1923:3, p. 228. [On the premières of the trilogy of world-historical plays *Sokrates, Moses,* and *Kristus* in Berlin and Hannover. E.917]

[D3:6] Anon, '[Germany]', *Teatr* (Petersburg), 1923:3, p. 22. [See **D3:5**. E.918]

[D3:7] Anon, '*Dödsdansen* och *Fröken Julie*', *Helsingborgs Dagblad*, 1 February 1915.

[D3:8] Anon, '*Fadren* och *Fröken Julie*', *Helsingborgs Dagblad*, 5 March 1915.

[D3:9] Anon, 'Strindbergs-premiärer i Berlin', *Göteborgs Handels- och Sjöfartstidning*, 7 October 1912. ['Strindberg Premières in Berlin']

[D3:10] Antropp, Theodor, 'Wiener Theater', *Österreichische Rundschau* (Vienna), 43 (1915), 317-319. [Discusses productions of *Fröken Julie, Leka med elden, Fordringsägare, Brott och brott, Den starkare,* and *Dödsdansen I* at the Vienna Stadttheater]

[D3:11] A. Ö. [Anders Österling], 'Strindbergs minne hyllat på fem scener', *Svenska Dagbladet* (Stockholm), 23 January 1928. ['Strindberg's Memory Honoured on Five Stages'. Includes comments on productions of *Bandet* and *Leka med elden* in Stockholm to mark the anniversary of Sg's birth]

[D3:12] A. Ö. [Anders Österling], 'Bodil Ipsen i Strindbergsprogram', *Svenska Dagbladet* (Stockholm), 29 November 1931. ['Bodil Ipsen in a Strindberg Programme'. Reviews the Danish actress on tour to Stockholm with *Fröken Julie* and *Bandet* at Konserthuset. The former revealed 'a vital force which exceeded that of *Fadren*']

[D3:13] Bab, Julius, 'Deutsche Bühnenkunst', *Die Hilfe* (Berlin), 20 (1914), 30-31. [Reviews the German première of *Kronbruden* at the Theater in der Königgrätzerstraße with Irene Triesch as Kersti, and Max Reinhardt's production of *Oväder* with Gertrud Eysoldt as Gerda and Albert Bassermann as the Gentleman]

[D3:14] Bab, Julius, 'Strindberg im Kriegsjahr', in *August Strindberg und die deutschen Bühnen*, Zusammengestellt und herausgegeben vom Drei Masken-Verlag, Berlin, 1915, pp. 9-12. [Rpr. of **D3:15**]

[D3:15] Bab, Julius, 'Strindberg im Kriegsjahr', *Das Programm. Blätter der Münchener Kammerspiele*, 1915:1, pp. 1-4. ['Strindberg in Wartime'. Discusses the so-called Munich 'Strindberg Cycle' when *Fröken Julie*, *Den starkare*, *Fordringsägare*, *Kamraterna*, *Leka med elden*, *Brott och brott*, *Pelikanen*, and *Spöksonaten* were all performed at the Kammerspiele between 29 April and 3 June 1915]

[D3:16] Bab, Julius, 'Strindberg im Kriegsjahr', in Hans-Peter Bayerdörfer, Hrsg., **B3:85**, *Strindberg auf der deutschen Bühne*, pp. 232-235. ['Strindberg in Wartime'. Rpr. of **D3:15**]

[D3:17] Bark, Richard, 'Strindbergsuppsättningar i Skandinavien 1987-1990', *Strindbergiana* (Stockholm), 6 (1991), pp. 140-172. Illus. ['Productions of Strindberg in Scandinavia, 1987-1990'. Focuses mainly on performances in Sweden, including *Till Damaskus* (Orion Teater, Stockholm, directed by Lars Rudolfsson), *Kronbruden* (Dramaten), *Mäster Olof* (Dramaten), *Hemsöborna* (Angeredsteatern), *Stora landsvägen* (Dramaten), and *Spöksonaten* (Teater 9, Stockholm), as well as some performances in Denmark and Norway, and Milan's Piccolo Theatre on tour to Stockholm with *Pelikanen*]

[D3:18] Bark, Richard, 'Strindbergsuppsättningar 1990-1993', *Strindbergiana* (Stockholm), 9 (1994), pp. 133-164. Illus. ['Strindberg Productions, 1990-1993'. Reports on forty-five different Swedish productions of eighteen of the plays (most notably of *Ett drömspel*, *Oväder*, *Folkungasagan*, *Karl XII*, and *Fröken Julie*), Nyt Skandinavisk Forsøgsteater's staging of *Fröken Julie* in Copenhagen, a dramatisation of *En dåres försvarstal*, and five operas based on works by Sg, including Margareta Hallin's settings of *Fröken Julie*, *Ett drömspel*, and *Den starkare*]

[D3:19] Bark, Richard, 'Strindbergsuppsättningar 1993-1996', *Strindbergiana* (Stockholm), 12 (1997), pp. 122-145. Illus. ['Strindberg Productions, 1993-1996'. Focuses on performances in Sweden, quoting selectively from reviews of several among the thirty-nine productions of twenty of the plays listed, including *Mäster Olof*, *Pelikanen*, *Dödsdansen*, *Erik XIV*, *Spöksonaten*, *Fröken Julie*, *Fadren*, *Gustav Vasa*, *Svanevit*, *Fordringsägare*, *Ett drömspel* (directed by Robert Lepage), and *Leka med elden*. Bark also comments on dramatisations of *En dåres försvarstal* and *Inferno*]

[D3:20] Bark, Richard, 'Svenska Strindbergsuppsättningar 1996-2001', *Strindbergiana* (Stockholm), 17 (2002), pp. 113-[139]. Illus. ['Swedish Strindberg Productions, 1996-2001'. Reports on sixty-six productions of thirty of the plays, all mounted in Sweden, as well as dramatisations of *Svarta fanor* and *En dåres försvarstal*, the latter at Svenska Teatern, Helsinki. Bark quotes selectively from reviews of *Kamraterna*, *Gustav III*, *Ett drömspel* (Dir. Robert Wilson), *Pelikanen*, *Fadren*, *Fröken Julie*, *Spöksonaten* (Dir. Ingmar Bergman), and *Dödsdansen*]

[D3:21] Bark, Richard, 'Svenska Strindbergsuppsättningar 2001-2004', *Strindbergiana* (Stockholm), 20 (2005), pp. 139-[157]. Illus. ['Swedish Strindberg Productions, 2001-

2004'. Reports on twenty professional productions of thirteen of the plays, none of which were history plays. Bark quotes selectively from reviews of Katie Mitchell's staging of *Påsk* at Dramaten, a site-specific performance of *Hemsöborna*, a musical version of *Fröken Julie*, and productions of *Fordringsägare, Brott och brott* (at Dramaten), *Leka med elden, Fritänkaren* (the première at Strindbergs Intima Teater, 134 years after it was written), *Till Damaskus I* and *Till Damaskus I-III* (Teater Kaos), and two stagings of *Fröken Julie*, as well as Reine Brynolfsson in a collage of texts from *En blå bok*, entitled *Paralysie Généralet*]

[D3:22] B. B-n [Bo Bergman], 'Festspelen på teatrarna', *Dagens Nyheter* (Stockholm), 23 January 1909. ['Festival in the Theatres'. Reports on performances of *Gustav Vasa* at Svenska Teatern, *Lycko-Pers resa* at Östermalmsteatern, *Brott och brott* at Intima teatern, and *Svanevit* in Uppsala, all staged in honour of Sg's 60th birthday. Bergman also reviews the première of *Siste riddaren*, see **E54:11**]

[D3:23] Besnehard, Daniel, 'Guirlande', *Théâtre/Public* (Gennevilliers), 73:4 (1986), 94-95. [Considers five recent French productions of *Dödsdansen* (Dir. Claude Chabrol), *Fordringsägare* (Dir. Charles Tordjman), *Pelikanen* (Dir. Henri Ronse (1972) and Alain Françon (1984)), and *Fadren* (Dir. Ottomar Krejca)]

[D3:24] Besnehard, Daniel, and Tristan Valès, 'Strindberg aux Ateliers de Formation et de Recherche', *Théâtre/Public* (Gennevilliers), 73:4 (1986), 45-53. Illus. [Documents several experimental French productions of Sg's plays as staged by the Ateliers de Formation et de Recherche. Comments by Besnehard and the plays' directors are illustrated with performance photographs of *Kamraterna*, *Fordringsägare*, and *Till Damaskus* by Valès]

[D3:25] Beyer, Nils, 'Strindbergs minne hyllat på scenen och genom radio', *Social-Demokraten* (Stockholm), 15 May 1942. ['Strindberg's Memory Honoured on Stage and Radio'. Surveys productions mounted to mark the 30th anniversary of Sg's death, including a version of *Brott och brott* for radio directed by Olof Molander with Harriet Bosse as Henriette and Anders de Wahl as Maurice]

[D3:26] Björkman, Rudolf, 'Två Strindbergs dramer', *Scenisk konst* (Stockholm), 1912:2, pp. 21-24. ['Two Dramas by Strindberg'. Reviews commemorative performances of *Gustav Vasa* and *Erik XIV* at Dramaten]

[D3:27] Børge, Vagn Albeck, 'Strindberg-Renaissance i Oslo', *Berlingske Aftenavis* (Copenhagen), 24 October 1924. ['Strindberg Renaissance in Oslo']

[D3:28] Børge, Vagn, 'Strindbergs Jubilæumssæson i Sverige', *Teatret* (Copenhagen), 28 (1928). ['The Strindberg Jubilee in Sweden']

[D3:29] Brøgger, Niels Chr., 'Norsk Teater Sesongen', *Ord och Bild* (Stockholm), 58:12 (1949), 497-505. [Reviews *Dödsdansen* with Tordis Marstrad and Lars Tvinde as Alice and Edgar, and *Pelikanen* at Nationaltheatret, directed by Olafr Harrevold]

[D3:29a] Buchner, Heribert, 'Münchener Schauspielbericht', *Der Aar* (Regensberg), 3:1 (1912-13), 282-283. [Reviews *Moderskärlek* and *Oväder* in Munich]

[D3:30] Carlson, Harry G., 'Strindberg and Bergman at the Strindberg Festival', *Western European Stages* (New York), 6:3 (1994).

[D3:31] Carlson, Harry G., 'Strindberg and O'Neill at the Stockholm Cultural Year Festival: Revisionism and Eroticism', *Western European Stages* (New York), 10:3 (1998), 5-[12].

[D3:32] Centerwall, Julius, 'Utländska Strindbergs-föreställningar', *Teatern* (Stockholm), 16:2 (1949), pp. 8, 15. ['Strindberg Productions Abroad'. Surveys productions staged outside Sweden in commemoration of the centenary of Sg's birth]

[D3:33] Döblin, Alfred, 'Einakter von Strindberg', *Der Sturm* (Berlin), 3 (1912-13), 170-71. ['One-Acters by Strindberg'. An enthusiastic response to the psychological naturalism of Sg's theatre during the late 1880s derived from recent performances of *Fordringsägare* and *Leka med elden*. Compares Sg with Dostoevskii]

[D3:34] Döblin, Alfred, 'Einakter von Strindberg', in *Die Zeitlupe. Kleine Prosa*, Olten und Freiburg im Breisgau: Walter-Verlag, 1962, pp. 15-16, 264. [Rpr. of **D3:33**]

[D3:35] Döblin, Alfred, 'Einakter von Strindberg', in Hans-Peter Bayerdörfer, Hrsg., **B3:85**, *Strindberg auf der deutschen Bühne*, pp. 206-208. [Rpr. of **D3:33**]

[D3:36] Dukore, Bernard F., 'Strindberg: The Real and the Surreal', *Modern Drama* (Lawrence, Kansas), 5:3 (1962), 331-334. [Discusses recent Californian productions of *Dödsdansen I* and *Fordringsägare*, and advocates the creation of 'a uniquely Strindbergian style…[with] a mutual transformation of the real and the surreal']

[D3:37] -er, 'Intima teatern', *Idun* (Stockholm), 5 December 1907. [Reviews productions of *Pelikanen* and *Fröken Julie* in Intima teatern's inaugural season]

[D3:38] Falk, Bertil, '[Strindberg i Indien]', *Kvällsposten* (Malmö), 2 April 1985. ['Strindberg in India'. A news report on versions of *Fadren* and *Fröken Julie* performed in Hindi, directed by Emmanuel Alkazi at the National School of Drama, New Delhi. According to Falk, the caste system in India makes *Fröken Julie* as relevant as ever there]

[D3:39] Felner, Karl von, 'Berliner Theater', *Der Merker* (Vienna), 7 (1916), 373-379. [Covers productions of *Kamraterna*, *Kristina*, *Fadren*, *Brott och brott*, and *Ett drömspel* at various Berlin theatres]

[D3:40] Feuchtwanger, Lion, 'Strindberg-Zyklus in München', *Die Schaubühne* (Berlin), 11:1 (1915), 517-524. ['Strindberg Cycle in Munich'. Comments on *Fröken Julie*, *Den starkare*, *Leka med elden*, *Fordringsägare*, *Kamraterna*, *Brott och brott*, *Pelikanen*, and *Spöksonaten* at the Munich Kammerspiele, where they were all performed between 29 April and 3 June 1915. Feuchtwanger reports that 'despite the war the city was shaken to the core by the Sg cycle at the Munich Kammerspiele. I cannot recall any theatre productions in Munich that have ever resonated so powerfully']

[D3:41] Feuchtwanger, Lion, 'Strindberg-Zyklus in München', in Hans-Peter Bayerdörfer, Hrsg., **B3:85**, *Strindberg auf der deutschen Bühne*, pp. 236-242. [Rpr. of **D3:40**]

[D3:42] Florin, Magnus, 'Strindberg Dramaten 93', *Strindbergiana* (Stockholm), 9 (1994), pp. 165-175. Illus. [Discusses a production of *Pelikanen*, a series of dramatisations of *En blå bok*, *Kvarstadsresan*, and *Han och hon*, and a programme of adaptations or explorations of Sgian material entitled variously 'Strindbergbarnet' (The Strindberg Child), 'Strindbergs kvinnor' (Strindberg's Women), 'Stadsresan' (The City Journey), 'Hôtel Orfila', 'Strindbergs Kymmendö', and 'Bussresan' (The Bus Journey), all staged by actors from Dramaten during 1993]

[D3:43] Freeberg, Debra L., 'Strindberg in Malmö, Sweden', *Western European Stages* (New York), 10:3 (1998), 13-20. [A report on Malmö Dramatiska Teater's 'Strindberg Year', which included productions of *Advent*, *Kamraterna*, *Ett drömspel*, and *Leka med elden*, as well as Staffan Valdemar Holm's conflation of extracts from seven of the history plays over a single, six-hour, production, entitled *Vasasagan* (see **D3:235**)]

[D3:44] Frerking, Johann, 'Hannoverscher Schauspielkalender', *Das hohe Ufer* (Hannover), 1 (1919), 82-84. [On *Fröken Julie* and *Fordringsägare* at the Deutsches Theater]

[D3:45] Frerking, Johann, 'Theater-Frühling', *Das hohe Ufer* (Hannover), 2 (1920), 92-96. [Reviews *Fröken Julie* and *Pelikanen* at the Hamburg Kammerspiele]

[D3:46] 'Gasparone' [Erik Thyselius], 'Från parkett', *Ur Dagens Krönika* (Stockholm), 1890, pp. 405-407. ['From the Stalls'. The belated première of the verse edition of *Mäster Olof* prompts some bitter reflections, not least regarding the long-standing opinion that Sg should be criticised for the historical inaccuracy of his history plays. This production confirms his importance as a dramatist, and it is only to be regretted that the performance does not measure up to the play. Also discusses the Swedish première of *Fordringsägare* which made a powerful impression with its passionate but artistically controlled address, inspired dialogue, and vital characters, among whom the female protagonist is more substantial than the corresponding figure (Laura) in *Fadren*. Those who criticise Sg's naturalistic theatre are misguided: its time will come]

[D3:47] Gasteren, Louis van, 'August Strindberg in Holland', *Tooneel-Leven* (Amsterdam), November-December 1918, pp. 6-8. [Discusses performances of Sg's plays in Holland, including Max Reinhard's staging of *Dödsdansen*, on tour in 1916. This was 'the most brilliant Sg production ever seen' in the Netherlands]

[D3:48] Geijerstam, Sten af, 'Från Stockholms teatrar', *Ord och Bild* (Stockholm), 52:7 (1943), 335-347. Illus. [Discusses Olof Molander's first production of *Spöksonaten* at Dramaten with Lars Hanson as Hummel and Märta Ekström as the Mummy (see **E51:265**). 'As a Sg interpreter Molander has no equal, and as such, he has made theatre history'. Geijerstam also comments on productions of *Svanevit* with Nini Löfberg, *Fröken Julie* with Karin Kavli and Stig Järrel, and *Fadren* at Blancheteatern with Harry Roeck Hansen (Captain), Linnéa Hillberg (Laura), and Anna-Lisa Baude (Nurse) – see **E11:536**]

[D3:49] G. O. [Gunnar Ollén], 'Radio och film', *Meddelanden från Strindbergssällskapet* (Stockholm), 15 (1953), p. 10.

[D3:50] G. O-n [Gunnar Ollén], 'Strindbergspremiärer', *Meddelanden från Strindbergssällskapet* (Stockholm), 15 (1953), pp. 10-12. [Ollén is mainly concerned with Gösta Folke's production of *Gustav III* in Uppsala with Hans Strååt as the King and *Fröken Julie* in Malmö, with Gun Arvidsson as 'the most convincing Miss Julie I have ever seen, and the list includes Karin Kavli, Inga Tidblad, and Anita Björck....For the first time one saw a Miss Julie whose fate seemed decided. Abandoned to her powerful emotions, striking and recklessly young, but nevertheless as hysterically proud as a Spanish noble – one could see from the beginning that, were her honour to be besmirched, she would remove the mark with death']

[D3:51] Grieco, Agnese, 'Progetto Strindberg', *Sipario* (Milano), No. 490 (1989), p. 54. ['Project Strindberg'. Reviews productions of *Fröken Julie* and *Fordringsägare* at the Teatro dell'Elfo, Milan, in which the directors (Nanni Garella and Elio De Capitani) and their actors exchanged roles]

[D3:52] 'Hafniensis' [Otto Borchsenius], 'Strindbergs föreställningarna i Köpenhamn', *Sydsvenska Dagbladet* (Malmö), 13 April 1913. ['Strindberg Performances in Copenhagen'. Reports on productions of *Fröken Julie* and *Dödsdansen*]

[D3:53] Halpren, Julie, 'August in January', *Off Off Broadway Review* (New York), 11 February 1999. [Reviews Outlet Theatre Company's staging of the 'Coram Populo' afterpiece to *Mäster Olof*, *Den starkare*, and *Fordringsägare*, all in translations by Harry G. Carlson]

[D3:54] Hartung, Hugo, 'Der große Besenversuch. Einer wahren Berliner Strindberg-Begebenheit nacherzählt', *Theater-Rundschau für Bühnen* (Bonn), 16:6 (1970), p. 7. ['The Great Attempt at a Sweep-Out. A Real Berlin Strindberg Event Retold']

[D3:55] Havemann, Julius, 'Strindberg, *Fräulein Julie mit dem Feuer spielen*', *Lübeckische Blätter*, 66 (1924), p. 397. [On a double-bill, directed by Karl Heidmann at the Stadttheater, Lübeck]

[D3:56] Hedberg, Karl, 'Från Stockholms teatrar', *Ord och Bild* (Stockholm), 9:1 (1900), 56-61. Illus. [Reviews the premières of *Gustav Vasa* and *Erik XIV* at Svenska Teatern. The latter is less secure than the former, and its material inferior, but where dramatic life as a whole is concerned, there are few plays which can hold their own with *Erik XIV*, which contains no trace of a *longeur*. As for *Gustav Vasa*: here, for the first time, the central theme of Sg's later works, namely the intervention of the unseen powers in the life of the individual, comes over really strongly, free for once from the many purely superstitious and abnormal aspects with which it is endowed elsewhere in his work. Hedberg concludes with a jibe at Ibsen: 'At present there is no one, even in Norway, with so accomplished a dramatic technique as Sg']

[D3:57] H. H. [Hanna Hellmann], 'Drei Einakter von Strindberg', *Neue Blätter für Kunst und Literatur* (Frankfurt am Main), 1 (1918-19), 23-24. ['Three One-Acters by Strindberg'. Reviews performances of *Bandet*, *Leka med elden*, and *Brott och brott* in Frankfurt]

[D3:58] H. H. [Hanna Hellmann], 'Strindberg. Notizen zu den Strindberg-Abenden der Frankfurter Theater 1918-19', *Neue Blätter für Kunst und Literatur* (Frankfurt am Main), 2 (1919-20), 43-45. ['Strindberg. Comments on the Strindberg Evenings at the Frankfurt Theatre, 1918-19'. Discusses productions of *Bandet*, *Brända tomten*, *Leka med elden*, and *Brott och brott*]

[D3:59] Hermann-Neiße, Max, 'Berliner Theater', *Die neue Schaubühne* (Dresden), 2 (1920), 191-193. [Reviews *Påsk* and *Leka med elden*, the latter directed by Rudolf Bernauer at the Theater in der Königgrätzerstraße]

[D3:60] Hilleström, Gustaf, 'Strindberg på svenska scener just nu', *Studiekamraten* (Tollarp), 31:1-2 (1949), 15-19. ['Strindberg on the Swedish Stage Today'. Reviews productions of Sg's plays mounted in 1949 to mark the centenary of his birth]

[D3:61] H. J. M[ehler], '*Julie* en *Gläubiger*', *De Amsterdammer*, 29 January 1893. [Reports on the success of *Juffrouw Julie* in Antoine's staging at the Théâtre Libre and the German première of *Fordringsägare* at the Residenztheater, Berlin]

[D3:62] Högman, Ernst, 'Stockholmsscenens honnör för August Strindberg', *Scenisk konst* (Stockholm), 1909:3, pp. 4-7. ['The Stockholm Stages' Tribute to August Strindberg'. Surveys productions of *Siste riddaren, Gustav Vasa, Brott och brott*, and *Lycko-Pers resa*, all mounted in Stockholm to mark Sg's 60th birthday. Högman also reports on the Intimate Theatre's tour of the provinces with *Herr Bengts hustru, Svanevit*, and *Påsk*]

[D3:63] Hultman, Harald S., 'Strindberg i Paris', *Gefle Dagblad* (Gävle), 15 January 1997. ['Strindberg in Paris'. A résumé of productions of Sg's plays in Paris post-1945, including Luc Bondy's staging of *Leka med elden* with Emmanuelle Béart as Kerstin]

[D3:64] Huppert, Rudolf, 'Uraufführungen und Erstaufführungen', *Die schöne Literatur* (Leipzig), 6 (1905), 219-222. ['World Premières and Premières'. Discusses new productions of *Leka med elden* and *Första varningen*, both of which received their German premières in 1893]

[D3:65] Ihering, Herbert, 'Deutsches Schauspielhaus', *Die Schaubühne* (Berlin), 8:2 (1912), 386-388. [Reviews productions of *Påsk*, *Fordringsägare*, and *Leka med elden*]

[D3:66] Ihering, Herbert, 'Von Cohn bis Strindberg', *Die Schaubühne* (Berlin), 9 (1913), 322-323. ['From Cohn to Strindberg'. Reviews productions of *Första varningen*, *Debet och kredit*, and *Den starkare*]

[D3:67] Jacobsohn, Siegfried, 'Von Strindberg', *Das Jahr der Bühne*, Bd III: 1913-14, Berlin: Verlag der Weltbühne, 1914, pp. 176-182. ['Of Strindberg'. Reprinted reviews of Max Reinhardt's production of *Pelikanen* with Rosa Bertens as the Mother and the German première of *Till Damaskus I*, directed by Victor Barnowsky with Friedrich Kayßler as The Unknown and Lina Lossen as The Lady]

[D3:68] Jacobsohn, Siegfried, 'Strindberg-Aufführungen', in *Das Jahr der Bühne*, Bd 7: 1917-18, Berlin: Verlag der Weltbühne, 1918, pp. 88-91. ['Strindberg Performances'. Reviews *Brott och brott*, Dir. Ernst Welisch, and *Fordringsägare* at the Trianon-Theater, Dir. Max Jungk]

[D3:69] Jacobi, Johannes, 'Unbekannter Strindberg', *Die Zeit* (Hamburg), 24 (1969), No. 9, p. 24. ['Unknown Strindberg'. Here, in 1969, 'unknown' refers to *Paria* and *Fordringsägare*, although both plays (and especially the latter) had been frequently performed in Germany prior to the Third Reich]

[D3:70] Jäger, Gerd, 'Frankfurt und Berlin: Einakter von August Strindberg', *Theater heute* (Hannover), 16:2 (1975), 6-9. ['One-Acters by August Strindberg'. Reviews productions of *Fordringsägare*, *Den skarkare*, and *Leka med elden* in Frankfurt and Berlin]

[D3:71] Janzon, Åke, '*Leka med elden*, *Fordringsägare*', *Bonniers Litterära Magasin* (Stockholm), 26:9 (1957), 804-805. [Reviews *Leka med elden* (Dir. Stig Torsslow; Friend: Jarl Kulle) and *Fordringsägare* (Dir. Rune Carsten; Adolf: Olof Widgren; Gustav: Ulf Palme; Tekla: Eva Dahlbäck), both at Dramaten]

[D3:72] Janzon, Leif, 'Strindberg – vår samtida', *entré* (Norsborg), 8:3 (1981), p. 16. ['Strindberg – Our Contemporary'. Comments on the plays performed at the 1981 Sg Festival]

[D3:73] Johnsson, Sigfrid, 'Teater', *Ridå* (Stockholm), 1909:3. [Reviews *Brott och brott* at Intima teatern, and the première of *Siste riddaren* at Dramaten]

[D3:74] Josephson, Lennart, 'Strindbergspremiärer i Stockholm', *Sydsvenska Dagbladet* (Malmö), 1 February 1949. ['Strindberg Premières in Stockholm'. Surveys productions of Sg's plays mounted in Stockholm in 1949 to commemorate the centenary of his birth]

[D3:75] Kässens, Wend, 'Dämonen, Dichter, Doppelspiele', *Teater heute* (Hannover), 28:5 (1987), 35-36. ['Demons, Poets, Double Games'. Reviews *Fordringsägare* and *Den starkare* in Cologne (Dir. Peter Löscher; Tekla: Susanne Barth), and *Brott och brott* in Bremen (Dir. Werner Schroeter; Henriette: Traute Hoess)]

[D3:76] Kienzl, Hermann, 'Der Zweck und das Mittel', *Der Türmer* (Stuttgart), 16:2 (1913-14), 380-383. ['Ends and Means'. Reviews the German première of *Till Damaskus I*, directed byVictor Barnowsky with Friedrich Kayßler as The Unknown and Lina Lossen as The Lady at the Lessing Theater, Berlin, and *Oväder* at Max Reinhardt's Kammerspiele with Albert Basserman as the Gentleman]

[D3:77] Kienzl, Hermann, 'Bekenntniss-Dramen', *Der Türmer* (Stuttgart), 14:1 (1911-12), 859-863. ['Confessional Drama'. Discusses *Den starkare* and *Fordringsägare*]

[D3:78] Kienzl, Hermann, 'Mehr Spreu als Weizen', *Der Türmer* (Stuttgart), 15:2 (1912-13), 92-94. ['More Chaff than Wheat'. Reviews a triple-bill comprising *Den starkare*, *Första varningen*, and *Debet och kredit*]

[D3:79] Kienzl, Hermann, 'Profan?', *Der Türmer* (Stuttgart), 16:1 (1913-14), 434-442. ['Profane?' Reviews *Brott och brott* with Maria Orska as Henriette and *Kronbruden* with Irene Triesch as Kersti, both at the Theater in der Königgrätzerstraße, Berlin]

[D3:80] Kilian, Eugen, '*Mutterliebe* und *Wetterleuchten*. Zu ihrer Inszenierung', *Die Scene* (Berlin), 11 (1921), 54-55. ['*Motherly Love* and *The Pelican*. On their Production']

[D3:81] Kjellander, Ann-Marie, 'Strindberg', *Kvällsposten* (Malmö), 18 December 1982. [Comments on *Fröken Julie*, *Dödsdansen*, two productions of *Pelikanen*, and *Moderskärlek* with *Inför döden* and *Den starkare* in a triple-bill, all running simultaneously at five theatres in Rome]

[D3:82] Klotz, Volker, 'Zweimal Strindberg. Schwedisch. *Traumspiel* im Stockholmer Dramaten, *Das rote Zimmer* im Fernschen', in *Bühnen-briefe. Kritiken und Essays zum Theater*, Frankfurt am Main: Athenäum Verlag, 1972, pp. 124-131. ['Twice Strindberg. Swedish *Dream Play* at Stockholm's Dramaten, *The Red Room* in Fernschen'. Discusses Ingmar Bergman's staging of *Ett drömspel* with Dramaten and a German dramatisation of *Röda rummet*]

[D3:83] Knudsen, Hans, '*Folkungersage*; *Nach Damaskus 2 und 3*', *Die schöne Literatur* (Leipzig), 19 (1918), 99-100. [Reviews *Folkungasagan* at the Theater in der Königgrätzerstraße, Dir. Rudolf Bernauer, as well as *Till Damaskus II-III* at the Lessingtheater, Berlin, directed by Victor Barnowsky with Theodor Loos as The Unknown]

[D3:84] Koch, Max, 'Ausländische Dramen', *Literarisches Centralblatt für Deutschland* (Leipzig), 52 (1901), Sp. 1204-1208. ['Foreign Drama'. Reviews the world première of *Påsk* in Frankfurt, 9 March 1901, and *Brott och brott*, which was given its German première, directed by Alfred Halm, at the Neues Sommertheater, Breslau, 19 August 1900, and revived at the Munich Schauspielhaus, 22 December 1900]

[D3:85] Kraeger, H[einrich], 'Theater', *Bühne und Welt* (Hamburg), 16:2 (1913-14), 137-138. [Reviews the one-acters *Första varningen*, *Den starkare*, and *Moderskärlek*]

[D3:86] Krafft, Erich, 'Das Spiel der Zeit. Berlin', *Hellweg* (Essen), 2 (1922), p. 930. [Reviews a triple-bill comprising *Första varningen*, *Bandet*, and *Inför döden* in Berlin, as well as Richard Levy's production of *Näktergalen i Wittenberg* at the Großes Schauspielhaus, Berlin, with Werner Kraus as Luther]

[D3:87] Kutter, Hans, 'Strindberg på våra scener', *Hufvudstadsbladet* (Helsingfors), 22 January 1949. ['Strindberg on Our Stages'. Surveys productions of Sg's plays in Finland in 1949, staged to commemorate the centenary of his birth]

[D3:88] Landsberg, Hans, 'Theater. Berlin', *Masken* (Düsseldorf), 3 (1907-1908), 563-564. [On *Leka med elden*, *Den starkare*, and *Inför döden*]

[D3:89] Laurin, Carl G., 'Från Stockholms teatrar', *Ord och Bild* (Stockholm), 17:2 (1908), 120-128. [Reviews *Mäster Olof* at Svenska Teatern with Ivan Hedqvist as Olof and Emil Hillberg as Gert, *Kronbruden* (this 'mishmash of false psychology and backwood's superstition') with Harriet Bosse as Kersti, *Den starkare*, and the premières of *Brända tomten* and *Oväder* at the Intimate Theatre. Laurin concludes that 'Two natures are inseparably bound together in this great and strange writer, the pietist's and the devil's'. He also comments on what he regards is Sg's pathological development and compares him with the German publicist, Maximilian Harden]

[D3:90] Laurin, Carl G., 'Från Stockholms teatrar', *Ord och Bild* (Stockholm), 17:6 (1908), 327-336. [Reviews *Mäster Olof* at Dramaten and *Paria*, *Bandet*, and the 'sickly' *Påsk* at Intima teatern with Anna Flygare (Eleonora), August Falck (Lindqvist), Anton de Verdier (Elis), Karin Alexandersson (Fru Heyst)]

[D3:91] Laurin, Carl G., 'Från Stockholms teatrar', *Ord och Bild* (Stockholm), 18:2 (1909), 118-126. [Reviews *Fadren* with August Falck and Karin Alexandersson (from the first line to the last, this masterly drama is intensely compelling and full of suspense), and *Svanevit* with Fanny Falkner (an unsuccessful work by a great writer who appears here in small format), both presented at Intima teatern. Laurin also covers the première of *Siste riddaren* at Dramaten with August Palme as Sten Sture. In the latter, it would seem that, as so often before, Sg soon lost interest in its dramatic form. 'There was nothing…of the unity of action that makes *Fadren* a technical masterpiece']

[D3:92] Laurin, Carl G., 'Från Stockholms teatrar', *Ord och Bild* (Stockholm), 24:2 (1915), 113-127. [Reviews Tora Teje and Gösta Ekman in *Svanevit* at Svenska Teatern, Doris Nelson as the incarnation of Sg's 'unwholesomely curious, ice-cold, but nevertheless enticing little wife', in *Leka med elden* (which Laurin regards as 'one of Sg's best plays'), Einar Fröberg and Lars Hansson in *Paria*, and Seelig Sandberg as Fru X in *Den starkare*, all at Gustaf Collijn's Nya Intima teatern]

[D3:93] Laurin, Carl G., 'Från Stockholms teatrar', *Ord och Bild* (Stockholm), 24:7 (1915), 379-393. [Comments on *Fadren* with Emil Hillberg as the Captain and Jessie Wessel as Bertha, *Fordringsägare* with Maria Schildknecht exuding triumphant cynicism and a powerful sensuality as Tekla, *Bandet* with Gösta Hillberg and Maria Schildknecht as the Baron and Baroness, all in productions at Dramaten, and *Oväder* ('one of the most peaceful of Sg's plays. It has something of the stillness of a sick-room'), directed by Mauritz Stiller with Lars Hanson as the Gentleman at Stockholm's Nya Intima Teatern]

[D3:94] Laurin, Carl G., 'Från Stockholms teatrar', *Ord och Bild* (Stockholm), 37:8 (1928), 440-448. [Reviews *Gustav III* at Oscarsteatern (directed by Rune Carlsten with Lars Hanson as Gustav) and *Kristina* at Konserthusteatern]

[D3:95] Laurin, Carl G., 'Från Stockholms teatrar', *Ord och Bild* (Stockholm), 32:2 (1923), 109-125. [Reviews a revival of *Gustav Vasa* with Gunnar Klintberg as Vasa and Gösta Ekman as Erik at Svenska Teatern and *Pelikanen*, directed by Olof Molander at Dramaten with Tecla Sjöblom as the Mother]

[D3:96] Laurin, Carl G., 'Från Stockholms teatrar', *Ord och Bild* (Stockholm), 38:7 (1929), 387-411. [Reviews *Erik XIV* with Anders de Wahl and Märta Ekström as Karin and *Pelikanen*, directed by Olof Molander with Hilda Borgström as the Mother and Lars

Hanson as the Son, in a double-bill with Anders de Wahl's reading of the poem 'Stadsresan' (The City Journey), to music by Ture Rangström, all at Dramaten]

[D3:97] Laurin, Carl G., 'Från Stockholms teatrar', *Ord och Bild* (Stockholm), 41:2 (1932), 109-128. [Reviews *Fröken Julie* and *Bandet* at Konserthusteatern, Stockholm, in guest performances by the Danish actress Bodil Ipsen with Uno Henning as the Baron and Gunnar Olsson as Jean]

[D3:98] Laurin, Carl G., 'Från Stockholms teatrar', *Ord och Bild* (Stockholm), 46:7 (1937), 399-415. [Reviews *Till Damaskus I* at Dramaten with Lars Hanson as the Unknown. Olof Molander interprets the play biographically: it is a nightmare, and while this staging is artistically accomplished, it contains so much of mankind's sick, dark underworld that one is in no hurry to repeat the experience. Laurin also discusses *Dödsdansen*, again at Dramaten where Poul Reumert as Edgar and Tora Teje as Alice resembled a pair of tigers, growling and spitting in their circular prison]

[D3:99] Laurin, Carl G., 'Från Stockolms teatrar', *Ord och Bild* (Stockholm), 48:7 (1939), 388-400. [Reviews *Påsk* with Signe Hasso as Eleonora at Dramaten and a double-bill of *Fordringsägare* and *Leka med elden* at Blancheteatern, Stockholm, with Mimi Pollak and Esther Roeck Hansen as the respective Sgian wives. Full of energy and snake-like poison, no one has surpassed the latter's interpretation of the Sgian woman]

[D3:100] *Le Théâtre en Pologne* (Warsaw), 1967:12, p. 11. [Discusses *Fadren* on Polish Television (see **E11:695**) and Part I of *Dödsdansen* at the Teatr Wybreże, Gdańsk, directed by Piotr Paradowski with Andrzej Szalawski as Edgar and Wanda Stanisławska-Lothe as Alice (see **E35:518**)]

[D3:101] Lemm, Alfred, '*Der Scheiterhaufen, Nach Damaskus*', *Die schöne Literatur* (Leipzig), 15 (1914), p. 191. [*Pelikanen* and *Till Damaskus* at the Berlin Kammerspiele and the Lessingtheater, Dir. Max Reinhardt and Victor Barnowsky respectively]

[D3:102] Lerch, Paul, 'Berliner Kunstbrief', *Der Aar* (Regensberg), 3:1 (1912-13), 278-281. [Reviews *Påsk* and *Dödsdansen*, the latter directed by Max Reinhardt at the Deutsches Theater with Paul Wegener as Edgar and Gertrud Eysoldt as Alice]

[D3:103] Lewin, Jan, 'Nationalmonument på gott och ont', *entré* (Norsborg), 22:4 (1995), 28-31. Illus. ['National Monument for Good and Ill'. Surveys productions of fourteen of Sg's plays performed during the second Sg festival in Stockholm]

[D3:104] Linde, Ebbe, 'Teaterkrönika', *Bonniers Litterära Magasin* (Stockholm), 18:2 (1949), 132-137. [Reviews *Stora landsvägen* at Dramaten (Dir. Olof Molander; Hunter: Lars Hanson); *Gustav Vasa* at Malmö Stadsteater (Dir. Gösta Folke; Vasa: Oscar Winge); two productions of *Dödsdansen* (by Riksteatern, with Anders Henrikson and Sif Ruud as Edgar and Alice, and at Blancheteatern, with Stig Järrel and Esther Roeck Hansen); two productions of *Leka med elden* (in Linköping, Dir. Hans Dahlin, and at Dramaten, Dir. Mimi Pollak); and *Den starkare*, also at Dramaten, with Märta Ekström as Fru X and Eva Dahlbeck as Mlle Y. Linde criticises Olof Molander who, as a Catholic, has introduced too many Christian symbols into the staging of *Stora landsvägen*, for there has scarcely ever been a more brilliant example of an anti-Christian individual than the old titan who wrote this play, desiring at the last not grace but his rights]

[D3:105] Linde, Ebbe, 'Teaterkrönika', *Bonniers Litterära Magasin* (Stockholm), 18:3 (1949), 223-227. [Further reflections on centennial stagings of *Fröken Julie*, *Brott och brott*, *Pelikanen*, and *Lycko-Pers resa*]

[D3:106] Linzer, Martin, 'Rostocker Theaterfesttage 1960. Strindberg-Festival als Auftakt', *Theater der Zeit* (East Berlin), 15:9 (1960), 49-50. [Reviews Sg's own dramatisation of *Hemsöborna* and a production of *Brott och brott* at the 1960 Rostock Festival]

[D3:107] Löffler, Sigfrid, 'Märchenkinder im Leissen frost- und fahle Gespenster', *Theater heute* (Hannover) 29:7 (1988), 46-48. ['Fairytale Children in the Silent Frost, and Pale Ghosts'. Discusses *Pelikanen* (Dir. Arie Zinger) in Hamburg, and *Spöksonaten* at the Wiener Akademietheater (Dir. Cesare Lievi: Mummy: Gusti Wolf: Hummel: Walter Reyer)]

[D3:108] Löfgren, Lars, 'Strindberg på Dramaten 1988', *Strindbergiana* (Stockholm), 4 (1989), pp. 9-12. [Comments on productions of *Fröken Julie* and *Ett drömspel* by Ingmar Bergman, *Kronbruden* by Peter Stormare, and *Svarta handsken* by Wilhelm Carlsson, all at Dramaten]

[D3:109] Lupi, Paoli, 'Bari: Dedicato a Strindberg', *Ridotto: Rassegna Mensile di Teatro* (Rome), 12 (December 1982), 20-24. [Surveys recent performances of Sg's plays in Italy]

[D3:110] Lyche, Hans, 'Oslo-teatrene i sesongen 1951-52', *Ord och Bild* (Stockholm), 61:7 (1952), 400-408. ['Oslo Theatres in the 1951-52 Season'. Reviews *Oväder* at Nationaltheatret with Olafr Havrevold as the Gentleman and Ada Kramm (Gerda), and *Fröken Julie* with Tordis Maurstad at Det Norske Teatret]

[D3:111] Marcus, Carl David, 'Nordiska teaterkväller i Berlin', *Ord och Bild* (Stockholm), 26:5 (1917), 263-270. ['Nordic Theatre Evenings in Berlin'. Reports on performances by Maria Orska as Agnes in *Ett drömspel* and Friedrich Kayßler as The Unknown in *Till Damaskus*, Paul Wegener and Gertrud Eysoldt in Max Reinhardt's production of *Spöksonaten*, and *Mäster Olof* at the Volksbühne with Ferdinand Gregori as Olof]

[D3:112] Marcus, Carl David, 'Den nya tyska regi', *Ord och Bild* (Stockholm), 31 (1922), 611-624. ['The New German Theatre Directing'. Primarly concerned with the theatre work of Max Reinhardt, and comments briefly on his productions of *Ett drömspel, Dödsdansen*, and *Spöksonaten*]

[D3:113] Marcus, C[arl] D[avid], '*Pelikanen* och *Till Damaskus*', *Dagens Nyheter* (Stockholm), 6 May 1914. [Discusses Max Reinhardt's production of *Pelikanen* at the Kammerspiele in Berlin with Rosa Bertens and Alexander Moissi as the Mother and Son, and the German première of *Till Damaskus I*, directed by Victor Barnowsky at the Lessingtheater, Berlin, with Friedrich Kayssler as The Unknown and Lina Lossen The Lady]

[D3:114] Marcus, Carl David, 'Reinhardts Strindberg-Darstellung', *Das junge Deutschland* (Berlin), 1 (1918), 56-58. ['Reinhardt's Strindberg Method'. Offers impressionistic responses to Reinhardt's productions of *Pelikanen, Oväder, Spöksonaten*, and *Dödsdansen*]

[D3:115] Marcus, Carl David, 'Reinhardts Strindberg-Darstellung', in Hans-Peter Bayerdörfer, Hrsg., **B3:85**, *Strindberg auf der deutschen Bühne*, pp. 266-270. ['Reinhardt's Strindberg Method'. Rpr. of **D3:114**]

[D3:116] Marcus, Carl David, 'Strindbergs *Schwanenweiß* und *Kronbraut*', *Die Scene* (Berlin) 3 (1913-14), 86-87. [Discusses the German premières of *Svanevit* at the Köngliches Schauspielhaus, Berlin, with Helene Thimig, and *Kronbruden* at the Theater in der Königgrätzerstraße, with Irene Triesch as Kersti]

[D3:117] Matson, M. N., 'The Theatre's Approach to Strindberg: Four Productions in the Strindberg Festival, Stockholm, May, 1981', *Scandinavian-Canadian Studies* (Ottawa), 1 (1983), 97-105. [Discusses *Brott och brott* at Dramaten, directed by Per Verner-Carlsson with Jan Malmsjö as Maurice and Solveig Ternström as Henriette (see **E27:213**); Mina Mezzadri's variations on *Fadern* with the Teatro di Porta Romana (see **E11:785**); the Stockholm Stadsteater production of *Fadren* with Keve Hjelm as the Captain and Lena Grandhagen as Laura (see **E11:771**); and William Runström's operatic setting of the same play]

[D3:118] Merbach, Paul Alfred, 'Berliner Theater. II', *Bühne und Welt* (Hamburg), 16:1 (1913-14), 84-86. [Reviews a performance of *Fröken Julie* and the German première of *Svanevit* with Helene Thimig in the title role (see **E37:41**)]

[D3:119] Meyer, Michael, 'Strindberg Productions in Britain in the Eighties', *Swedish Book Review* (Lampeter), 1986 (Supplement), pp. 29-30.

[D3:120] Meyer, Michael, 'Strindberg Productions in Great Britain 1974', *Meddelanden från Strindbergssällskapet* (Stockholm), 55 (1975), pp. 10-12. ['The outstanding Sg event in Great Britain in 1974 was undoubtedly Mike Ockrent's production of *A Dream Play* at the Traverse Theatre, Edinburgh'. Meyer also comments on productions of *Kamraterna,* directed by Barry Kyle for the Royal Shakespeare Company, *Kronbruden,* and *Erik XIV* (the two last on BBC Radio)]

[D3:121] Meyer, Michael, 'Strindberg Productions in Great Britain 1975', *Meddelanden från Strindbergssällskapet* (Stockholm), 56 (1976), pp. 13-15. [Reports on eleven British and Irish productions mounted during 1975. Particularly notices Mike Ockrent's staging of *Till Damaskus* in Edinburgh (see **E25:403**)]

[D3:122] Meyer, Michael, 'Strindberg Productions in Great Britain 1976', *Meddelanden från Strindbergssällskapet* (Stockholm), 57-58 (1977), pp. 12-13.

[D3:123] Meyer, Michael, 'Strindberg Productions in Great Britain 1978', *Meddelanden från Strindbergssällskapet* (Stockholm), 61-62 (1979), pp. 17-20. [Meyer is especially critical of the Royal Shakespeare Company's production of *Dödsdansen* in what has been 'a thin year' for Sg in England]

[D3:124] Meyer, Michael, 'Strindberg Productions in Great Britain 1979', *Meddelanden från Strindbergssällskapet* (Stockholm), 63-64 (1980), pp. 11-12. [Meyer notes only four professional productions of Sg in Great Britain during 1979]

[D3:125] Meyer, Michael, 'Strindberg Productions in Great Britain 1980', *Meddelanden från Strindbergssällskapet* (Stockholm), 65 (1981), pp. 10-12. [Focuses primarily on 'two outstanding Sg productions', *Spöksonaten* on BBC Television, directed by Philip Saville with Robert Helpmann as Hummel and Beatrix Lehmann as the Mummy; and *Fordringsägare* with Heather Sears as Tekla at Leicester Haymarket and then in London (see **E13:297**)]

[D3:126] Meyer, Michael, 'Strindberg Productions in Great Britain 1982', *Meddelanden från Strindbergssällskapet* (Stockholm), 67 (1983), pp. 33-34. [Reports on only three productions (*Dödsdansen* and *Fröken Julie* in the theatre and *Ett drömspel* on the radio)]

[D3:127] Meyer, Michael, 'Strindberg Productions in Great Britain 1983', *Meddelanden från Strindbergssällskapet* (Stockholm), 68 (1984), pp. 15-17. [Reports only two professional stagings of Sg in Britain during the past year: *Fröken Julie* with Cheryl Campbell at the Lyric Theatre, Hammersmith (see **E12:843**), and Kenneth MacMillan's production of

Dödsdansen at the Royal Exchange in Manchester with Edward Fox as Edgar and Jill Bennett as Alice (see **E35:730**)]

[D3:128] Meyer, Michael, 'Strindberg Productions in Great Britain 1984-86', *Strindbergiana* (Stockholm), 2 (1987), pp. 48-53. [Surveys three years of British Sg, dominated by numerous productions of *Fröken Julie*, and with disappointing versions of *Ett drömspel* and *Fordringsägare* from the Royal Shakespeare Company]

[D3:129] Musil, Robert, 'Wiener Theater', in **D1:319**, *Theater. Kritisches und Theoretisches*, Hrsg. von Marie-Louise Roth, pp. 71-72. [Rpr. of **D3:131**]

[D3:130] Musil, Robert, 'Wiener Theater', in *Gesammelte Werke*, 9 vols, *Kritik*, Vol. 9, Hrsg. von Adolf Frisé, Reinbek bei Hamburg: Rowohlt Verlag, 1978, pp. 1545-1548. [Rpr. of **D3:131**]

[D3:131] Musil, Robert, 'Wiener Theater', *Prager Presse* (Prague), 5 February 1922. ['Theatre in Vienna'. Reviews Heinrich George's production of *Fröken Julie* at the Burgtheater with Rosa Albach-Retty as Julie and George himself as Jean, which highlights the limits of Sg's naturalism and *Fadren* at the Neue Wiener Bühne with Paul Wegener as the Captain, where the play's affinity with Nietzsche is evident]

[D3:132] Musil, Robert, 'Wiener Theater', in Hans-Peter Bayerdörfer, Hrsg., **B3:85**, *Strindberg auf der deutschen Bühne*, pp. 328-329. [Rpr. of **D3:131**]

[D3:133] Nagel, Alfred, 'Strindberg-Inszenierungen', *Hamburger Theater-Zeitung*, 1:8 (1919), pp. 1-3.

[D3:134] Nordgren, Elisabeth, 'Strindberg är pop i Växjö', *Hufvudstadsbladet* (Helsingfors), 27 May 2001. [On productions of *Fadren, Till Damaskus,* and *Erik XIV* at the Swedish Theatre Festival in Växjö]

[D3:135] Oberlaender, L[eopold] G[ustav], 'Bühnen- und Musikrundschau. Strindbergstücke', *Allgemeine Rundschau* (München), 18 (1921), p. 482. [Reviews productions of *Fadren* and *Kristina*, the latter at the Munich Schauspielhaus]

[D3:136] Oberlaender, L[eopold] G[ustav], 'Strindbergzyklus', *Allgemeine Rundschau* (Munich), 12 (1915), 336. [Discusses the so-called 'Strindberg Cycle' at the Munich Kammerspiele when eight plays, including *Spöksonaten* directed by Otto Falckenberg, were performed over six evenings at the Munich Kammerspiele in 1915]

[D3:137] Ollén, Gunnar, 'Divers Strindbergsnytt', *Meddelanden från Strindbergssällskapet* (Stockholm), 10 (1951), p. 8.

[D3:138] [Ollén, Gunnar], 'På scen och i radio', *Meddelanden från Strindbergssällskapet* (Stockholm), 4 (1948), pp. 8-9. ['On Stage and Radio'. Surveys recent Swedish productions including Olof Molander's staging of *Ett drömspel* in Göteborg and Ingmar Bergman's radio version of *Leka med elden*]

[D3:139] [Ollén, Gunnar], 'Strindberg i radio', *Meddelanden från Strindbergssällskapet* (Stockholm), 2 (1946), p. 12.

[D3:140] [Ollén, Gunnar], 'Strindberg i radio', *Meddelanden från Strindbergssällskapet* (Stockholm), 3 (1947), p. 31.

[D3:141] Ollén, Gunnar, 'Strindberg på teatrarna', *Meddelanden från Strindbergssällskapet* (Stockholm), 9 (1950), pp. 1-2. [Reports on Swedish productions of *Oväder* (Dir. Alf Sjöberg), *Brända tomten, Gustav Vasa, Fadren,* and *Fröken Julie* (Birgit Cullberg's ballet)]

[D3:142] Ollén, Gunnar, 'Strindbergspremiärerna', *Meddelanden från Strindbergssällskapet* (Stockholm), 7 (1949), pp. 5-7, 10. [Reports on performances in Sweden, Mexico, Denmark, Norway, Finland, USA, Germany, and London]

[D3:143] Ollén, Gunnar, 'Strindbergspremiär', *Meddelanden från Strindbergssällskapet* (Stockholm), 12 (1952), pp. 1-3. [Reports on Swedish productions of *Advent, Dödsdansen,* and *Ett drömspel*]

[D3:144] [Ollén, Gunnar], 'Strindbergspremiärer', *Meddelanden från Strindbergssällskapet* (Stockholm), 13-14 (1953), pp. 1-2. [Reports on performances in Sweden, including Ingmar Bergman's staging of *Kronbruden* in Malmö (see **E36:87**)]

[D3:145] Ollén, Gunnar, 'Strindbergspremiärer', *Meddelanden från Strindbergssällskapet* (Stockholm), 16 (1954), pp. 1-2, 7. [Comments on *Spöksonaten* (Dir. Ingmar Bergman), *Gustaf III* in Göteborg with Curt Masreliez as the king, a double-bill of *Paria* and *Fröken Julie* in Odense, and *Herr Bengts hustru* (Dir. Hans Dahlin) and *Kaspers fettisdag* on Swedish Radio]

[D3:146] Ollén, Gunnar, 'Strindbergspremiärer', *Meddelanden från Strindbergssällskapet* (Stockholm), 18 (1955), pp. 1-5. [Reports on productions of *Kristina* in Helsingborg and *Ett drömspel* (Dir. Olof Molander) at Dramaten (see **E41:369**)]

[D3:147] Ollén, Gunnar, 'Strindbergspremiärer', *Meddelanden från Strindbergssällskapet* (Stockholm), 19 (1956), pp. 1-3, 11-12. [Reports on Swedish productions of *Gustav Vasa, Advent* (Dir. Olof Molander), and Anders Henrikson's film of *Giftas*]

[D3:148] Ollén, Gunnar, 'Strindbergspremiärer', *Meddelanden från Strindbergssällskapet* (Stockholm), 21 (1957), pp. 22-23. [Primarily concerned with Ingmar Bergman's 'unforgettable' staging of *Erik XIV* at Malmö Stadsteater (see **E30:157**)]

[D3:149] Ollén, Gunnar, 'Strindbergspremiärer', *Meddelanden från Strindbergssällskapet* (Stockholm), 22 (1958), pp. 1-4, 16. [Reports on recent Swedish productions, as well as Alf Sjöberg's production of *Fröken Julie* in Copenhagen and Erwin Piscator's staging of *Dödsdansen* in Hamburg]

[D3:150] Ollén, Gunnar, 'Strindbergspremiärer', *Meddelanden från Strindbergssällskapet* (Stockholm), 24 (1959), pp. 12-15. [Reports on Swedish productions of *Leka med elden, Mäster Olof,* and *Dödsdansen*]

[D3:151] Ollén, Gunnar, 'Strindbergspremiärer', *Meddelanden från Strindbergssällskapet* (Stockholm), 25 (1959), pp. 1-3. [Reports on recent productions, including *Ett drömspel* (Dir. Bengt Ekerot) in Malmö]

[D3:152] Ollén, Gunnar, 'Strindbergspremiärer', *Meddelanden från Strindbergssällskapet* (Stockholm), 26 (1960), pp. 1-4, 10. [Includes a report on *Brott och brott* at Dramaten, and Alf Sjöberg film's of *Fröken Julie*, following its screening in Cannes]

[D3:153] Ollén, Gunnar, 'Strindbergspremiärer', *Meddelanden från Strindbergssällskapet* (Stockholm), 28 (1961), pp. 1-6. [Includes reports on Swedish productions of *Fröken Julie* and *Kristina* (with Inga Tidblad)]

[D3:154] Ollén, Gunnar, 'Strindbergspremiärer', *Meddelanden från Strindbergssällskapet* (Stockholm), 30-31 (1962), pp. 11-13. [Surveys Swedish productions of *Fröken Julie, Gustav Vasa, Fadren, Erik XIV, Karl XII, Påsk,* and *Mäster Olof,* all commemorating the 50th anniversary of Sg's death]

[D3:155] Ollén, Gunnar, 'Strindbergspremiärer', *Meddelanden från Strindbergssällskapet* (Stockholm), 32 (1962), pp. 3-5. [Surveys productions in Sweden and (mainly) abroad, marking the 50th anniversary of Sg's death]

[D3:156] Ollén, Gunnar, 'Strindbergspremiärer', *Meddelanden från Strindbergssällskapet* (Stockholm), 34 (1964), pp. 1-4. [Reports on Swedish productions, including *Ett drömspel* (Dir. Ingmar Bergman), *Gustav III*, and *Påsk*, as well as *Karl XII*, directed by Gabriel Garran at the Théâtre de l'Ouest Parisien, and *Fadren* with Trevor Howard as the Captain at the Piccadilly Theatre, London]

[D3:157] Ollén, Gunnar, 'Strindbergspremiärer', *Meddelanden från Strindbergssällskapet* (Stockholm), 36 (1964), pp. 1-4. [Includes reports on Swedish productions of several of the plays, as well as Heinz Kindermann's reworking of *Till Damaskus* in Vienna]

[D3:158] Ollén, Gunnar, 'Strindbergspremiärer 1966-67', *Meddelanden från Strindbergssällskapet* (Stockholm), 39 (1967), pp. 1-5. [Includes reports on Swedish productions of *Karl XII, Gustav III* and *Kristina*, as well as Laurence Olivier as Edgar in *Dödsdansen* at the National Theatre, London, and Fritz Kortner's production of *Fadren* in Hamburg]

[D3:159] Ollén, Gunnar, 'Strindbergspremiärer 1967-68', *Meddelanden från Strindbergssällskapet* (Stockholm), 40-41 (1968), pp. 1-8. [Includes reports on Swedish productions of *Pelikanen*, directed by Per Verner-Carlsson at Dramaten, *Fröken Julie*, and *Dödsdansen*, as well as Fritz Kortner's staging of *Fröken Julie* in Hamburg with Ingrid Andree as Julie and Rolf Boysen as Jean]

[D3:160] Ollén, Gunnar, 'Strindbergspremiärer 1968-69', *Meddelanden från Strindbergssällskapet* (Stockholm), 42-43 (1969), pp. 1-4. [Includes reports on Swedish productions of *Fadren* (Dir. Alf Sjöberg), *Påsk*, and *Dödsdansen*, and of *Spöksonaten* in Denmark]

[D3:161] Ollén, Gunnar, 'Strindbergspremiärer 1969-70', *Meddelanden från Strindbergssällskapet* (Stockholm), 45 (1970), pp. 1-10. [Includes reports on Swedish productions of *Ett drömspel* (Dir. Ingmar Bergman), *Fröken Julie, Dödsdansen, Mäster Olof*, and *Spöksonaten*]

[D3:162] Ollén, Gunnar, 'Strindbergspremiärer 1970-71', *Meddelanden från Strindbergssällskapet* (Stockholm), 47-48 (1971), pp. 1-8. [Includes reports on Swedish productions of *Brända tomten* (Dir. Alf Sjöberg), *Gustav Vasa* (Dir. Lennart Hjulström), and *Ett drömspel* at the Comédie-Française. Dir. Raymond Rouleau. Ollén also discusses the reception accorded Herbert Grevenius's nine-part adaptation of *Röda rummet* on Swedish Television]

[D3:163] Ollén, Gunnar, 'Strindbergspremiärer 1971-72', *Meddelanden från Strindbergssällskapet* (Stockholm), 50 (1972), pp. 1-7. [Includes reports on Swedish productions of *Herr Bengts hustru* (Dir. Alf Sjöberg at Dramaten), *Lycko-Pers resa, Fordringsägare, Leka med elden, Paria, Stora landsvägen*, and *Dödsdansen*, as well as a dramatisation of *I havsbandet* for Swedish Television and stagings of *Fadren* in Copenhagen and *Pelikanen* in Paris]

[D3:164] Ollén, Gunnar, 'Strindbergspremiärer 1972-73', *Meddelanden från Strindbergssällskapet* (Stockholm), 51-52 (1973), pp. 8-18.

[D3:165] Ollén, Gunnar, 'Strindbergspremiärer 1973-74', *Meddelanden från Strindbergssällskapet* (Stockholm), 53-54 (1974), pp. 1-9. [Includes reports on Swedish productions of *Till Damaskus* (Dir. Ingmar Bergman), *Brott och brott, Erik XIV, Dödsdansen*, and

Gustav III, as well as *Fadren* on Danish Television and *Fröken Julie* at the Théâtre du Tertre in Paris]

[D3:166] Ollén, Gunnar, 'Strindbergspremiärer 1974-75', *Meddelanden från Strindbergssällskapet* (Stockholm), 55 (1975), pp. 1-9. [Includes reports on Swedish productions of the history plays on Swedish Television, *Brända tomten, Fröken Julie,* and *Fordringsägare,* as well as *Erik XIV* in Helsinki and Copenhagen]

[D3:167] Ollén, Gunnar, 'Strindbergspremiärer 1975-76', *Meddelanden från Strindbergssällskapet* (Stockholm), 56 (1976), pp. 1-12. [Includes reports on Swedish productions of *Gustav Vasa, Kristina, Mäster Olof, Folkungasagan,* and *Ett drömspel,* as well as several of the one-acters. Ollén also comments on Danish productions of *Fadren, Fordringsägare, Fröken Julie,* and *Herr Bengts hustru,* as well as performances of *Dödsdansen II* in Helsinki, *Spöksonaten* in Paris, and *Fadren, Fröken Julie,* and *Pelikanen* in Germany]

[D3:168] Ollén, Gunnar, 'Strindbergspremiärer 1976-77', *Meddelanden från Strindbergssällskapet* (Stockholm), 57-58 (1977), pp. 1-11. [Includes reports on Swedish productions of Kjell Grede's television series based on Sg's life, illustrating its reception in Sweden with numerous quotations from the daily press, *Erik XIV* (Dir. Alf Sjöberg at Dramaten), *Ett drömspel, Dödsdansen, Fadren,* and *Kronbruden,* as well as *Ett drömspel* in Copenhagen.

[D3:169] Ollén, Gunnar, 'Strindbergspremiärer 1977-78', *Meddelanden från Strindbergssällskapet* (Stockholm), 59-60 (1978), pp. 1-14. [Includes reports on Swedish productions of *Ett drömspel* (Dir. Ingmar Bergman), *Fordringsägare,* and *Fröken Julie, Leka med elden* in Copenhagen, and *Ett drömspel* and *Dödsdansen* in Vienna. Also includes a listing of Sg premières in Germany for 1977 by Ruprecht Volz]

[D3:170] Ollén, Gunnar, 'Strindbergspremiärer 1978-79', *Meddelanden från Strindbergssällskapet* (Stockholm), 61-62 (1979), pp. 1-13. Illus. [Includes reports on numerous Swedish productions, including *Pelikanen* (Dir. Per Verner-Carlsson), *Påsk,* and *Till Damaskus, Bandet* in Copenhagen, *Dödsdansen* in Hamburg, *Pelikanen* (Dir. Achim Benning) in Vienna, and *Ett drömspel* in Tokyo]

[D3:171] Ollén, Gunnar, 'Strindbergspremiärer 1979-80', *Meddelanden från Strindbergssällskapet* (Stockholm), 63-64 (1980), pp. 1-10. [Includes reports on Swedish productions of *Brott och brott* (Per Verner-Carlsson), *Folkungasagan, Ett drömspel, Dödsdansen, Leka med elden, Paria,* and an adaptation of *Inferno* as a ballet]

[D3:172] Ollén, Gunnar, 'Strindbergspremiärer 1980-81', *Meddelanden från Strindbergssällskapet* (Stockholm), 65 (1981), pp. 1-9. [Includes reports on Swedish productions of *Ett drömspel, Leka med elden,* and *Lycko-Pers resa,* as well as *Fröken Julie* and *Pelikanen* in Amsterdam and *Oväder* (Dir. Giorgio Strehler) in Milan]

[D3:173] Ollén, Gunnar, 'Strindbergsföreställningar 1981', *Meddelanden från Strindbergssällskapet* (Stockholm), 66 (1982), pp. 1-13. [Includes reports on Swedish productions of *Erik XIV, Ett drömspel, Fadren, Fordringsägare,* and *Påsk, Fröken Julie* in Munich (Dir. Ingmar Bergman), *Den starkare* in Belgium and New York, *Pelikanen* in Milan, and *Spöksonaten* on BBC Television with Donald Pleasance as Hummel and Lily Kedrova as the Mummy]

[D3:174] Ollén, Gunnar, 'Strindbergspremiärer 1982', *Meddelanden från Strindbergssällskapet* (Stockholm), 67 (1983), pp. 13-23. [Includes reports on Swedish productions including *Pelikanen, Kamraterna, Mäster Olof, Spöksonaten,* and *Fröken Julie,* as well as *Fadren* in Paris, *Gustav III* in Finland, *Dödsdansen* in Denmark, *Den starkare* in Calcutta, and *Ett drömspel* in Seattle]

[D3:175] Ollén, Gunnar, 'Strindbergspremiärer 1983', *Meddelanden från Strindbergssällskapet* (Stockholm), 68 (1984), pp. 1-11. [Includes reports on Swedish productions of *Fordringsägare, Mäster Olof, Dödsdansen, Oväder*, and *Fröken Julie*, as well as *Fadren* and *Påsk* in Copenhagen, *Fröken Julie* in Paris, *Brott och brott* in Milan, *Fadren* in Genoa, and *Kristina* in Rome]

[D3:176] Ollén, Gunnar, 'Strindbergspremiärer 1984-85-86', *Strindbergiana* (Stockholm), 2 (1987), pp. 5-42. [Surveys numerous Swedish productions on both stage and television, including Per Olov Enquist's six-part dramatisation of Sg's life for television, Ingmar Bergman's productions of *Ett drömspel* and *Fröken Julie* at Dramaten, *Pelikanen* and *Leka med elden* in Göteborg, and versions of *Kristina* (Dir. Ernst Günther), *Advent* (Dir. Lars Svenson), and *Ett drömspel* (Dir. Per Oskarsson). Ollén also discusses Per Olov Enquist's production of *Fröken Julie* in Copenhagen, Claude Chabrol's staging of *Dödsdansen* in Paris, and performances of *Fröken Julie* in Tokyo, Catania, and West Germany]

[D3:177] Ollén, Gunnar, 'Strindbergspremiärer 1986-87', *Strindbergiana* (Stockholm), 3 (1988), pp. 130-140. [Documents a range of productions, including *Ett drömspel* in Vasa, *Påsk* in Oslo, *Spöksonaten* in Århus, *Pelikanen* in Poland, and *Fröken Julie* as a musical in Tokyo]

[D3:178] Ostojić, Karlo, 'A. Strindberg: *Gospođica Julija* i *Igra snova*', *Nedeljne informativne novine* (Belgrade), 13 December 1953. ['A. Strindberg: *Miss Julie* and *A Dream Play*'. R.457]

[D3:179] Paulin, Hillewi, 'Borgerlig dramatik och politiska tidsdramer. Ur höstens teaterrepertoar', *Perspektiv* (Stockholm), 15:1 (1964), 36-37. ['Bourgeois Plays and Contemporary Political Dramas. From this Autumn's Repertoire in the Theatres']

[D3:180] Paulin, Hillewi, 'Diktarvisioner mot verklighetsfond. Ur årets teaterrepertoar', *Perspektiv* (Stockholm), 15:6 (1964), 259-263. ['Poetic Visions against a Backdrop of Reality. From the Year's Repertoire in the Theatres']

[D3:181] Paulin, Hillewi, 'Strindbergsteater i modern svensk tolkning', *Horisont* (Vasa), 13:3 (1966), 87-91. ['Strindberg's Theatre in Modern Swedish Interpretations'. Discusses productions of *Till Damaskus, Påsk, Marodörer*, and *Fröken Julie*]

[D3:182] Polgar, Alfred, 'Einakter von Strindberg', *Die Schaubühne* (Berlin), 3:1 (1907), 455-458. ['One-Acters by Strindberg'. On *Bandet, Den starkare*, and *Moderskärlek*]

[D3:183] Polgar, Alfred, 'Strindberg in Wien', *Die Schaubühne* (Berlin), 11:2 (1915), 290-292. [Discusses productions of *Kristina* and *Brott och brott* in Vienna]

[D3:184] Polgar, Alfred, 'Strindberg in Wien', *Die Weltbühne* (Berlin), 15:2 (1919), 168–169. [Discusses productions of *Bandet* (at the Vienna Burgtheater), and *Fordringsägare* and *Inför döden*, also in Vienna]

[D3:185] Polgar, Alfred, 'Strindberg in Wien', *Der neue Tag* (Berlin), 4 May 1919. [As **D3:184**]

[D3:186] Prellwitz, Gertrud, 'Theater-Korrespondenz', *Preußische Jahrbücher* (Berlin), 155 (1914), pp. 167-177. [On the German premières of *Svanevit* at the Königliches Schauspielhaus, Berlin, with Helene Thimig, and *Kronbruden* at the Theater in der Königgrätzerstraße, with sets by Svend Gade and Irene Triesch as Kersti]

[D3:187] 'Qvidam Qvidamson' [Pseudonym of Nils Peter Svensson], 'Från Göteborgs-scenerna', *Scenisk konst* (Stockholm), 1912:6-7, pp. 78-80. [Reviews productions of *Fordringsägare* and *Leka med elden* in Göteborg]

[D3:188] -r, 'Två Strindbergs föreställningar', *Skånska Social-Demokraten* (Malmö), 27 January 1910. ['Two Strindberg Performances'. Of *Kronbruden* and *Svarta handsken*, performed by the so-called Strindberg Touring Company with Greta Sg and Erland Colliander as Kersti and Mats in the former, and the same two actors as the Wife and the Taxidermist in the latter]

[D3:189] Rauscher, Ulrich, 'Berliner Theater', *Süddeutsche Monatshefte* (München and Leipzig), 11:1 (1913-14), 668-670. [Reviews *Svanevit* at the Königliches Schauspielhaus in Berlin with Helene Thimig in the title role and the German première of *Kronbruden* at the Theater in der Königgrätzerstraße with Irene Triesch as Kersti]

[D3:190] 'René' [Anna Branting], 'Skådebanan', *Skådebanan* (Stockholm), No. 8 (1908), pp. 8-9. [On *Kristina* ('this peculiar play') and *Påsk* at the Intimate Theatre. 'Theoretically I have no love for this play whose morality smacks of the nursery and the cane, but the powerful mood that tormented Sg when he wrote it certainly transmits itself to the spectator']

[D3:191] 'René' [Anna Branting], 'Teaterrevy', *Puck* (Stockholm), 1901 (Julnummer), pp. 11-13. [A sometimes supercilious and generally critical account of the largely unsuccessful world premières of *Påsk*, with Harriet Bosse as Eleonora, *Kaspers fettisdag*, *Midsommar*, and *Folkungasagan*, all staged to often little acclaim in Stockholm]

[D3:192] Rokem, Freddie, 'Mörka ljusstrålar. Strindberg på scenen 1987-1988', *Strindbergiana*, 6 (1991), pp. 121-139 ['Dark Rays of Light. Strindberg on Stage, 1987-1988'. Rokem studies one Finnish and eleven Swedish productions of ten of Sg's plays (among them Ingmar Bergman's staging of *Fröken Julie* at Dramaten). He also comments on a parody of his work and a theatrical collage which draws on extracts from several works]

[D3:193] R. P. [Rudolf Pechel], 'Berliner Theater', *Deutsche Rundschau* (Berlin), 49:2 (1922-23), 197-202. [Reviews *Näktergalen i Wittenberg* with Werner Krauß, *Kristina* with Elisabeth Bergner, *Bandet*, and *Inför döden*, all staged in Berlin during 1923. Muses that 'we [Germans] may have taken on the immortal quality of Sg's personality too strongly as an integral part of our mental and spiritual nature']

[D3:194] Ruhe, Algot, 'Courrier de Stockholm', *Revue d'Art dramatique* (Paris), 9:1 (Janvier-Juillet 1900), 92-96. [Discusses the world premières of *Gustav Vasa* and *Erik XIV* in Stockholm]

[D3:195] Ruhe, Algot, 'Från Stockholms teatrar', *Ord och Bild* (Stockholm), 11:11 (1902), 607-611. [Reviews the world première of *Karl XII* at Dramaten, which was a grave disappointment; however, the première of *Samum* with Harriet Bosse as Biskra was a shattering experience]

[D3:196] Ruhe, Algot, 'Théâtre à l'Etranger', *Revue d'Art dramatique* (Paris), 11:12 (December 1901), 308-311. [Comments critically on the world premières of *Engelbrekt*, *Midsommar*, and *Karl XII* in Stockholm, but remains deeply impressed by *Samum* at Dramaten with Harriet Bosse as Biskra]

[D3:197] Scharrer, Eduard, 'Das Spiel der Zeit. München. Wegener als Strindbergsspieler', *Hellweg* (Essen), 2 (1922), p. 731. [On Paul Wegener's acting style as Edgar in *Dödsdansen* and the Captain in *Fadren*]

[D3:198] Schievelkamp, Max, 'Strindberg in Berlin', *Zeit im Bild* (Berlin), 16 January 1916, pp. 39-40.

[D3:199] Schmidt, Konrad, 'Strindberg-Aufführungen', *Die Neue Zeit* (Stuttgart), 32:2 (1913-14), 274-278. [Surveys the German première of *Till Damaskus I* directed by Victor Barnowsky, *Dödsdansen*, directed by Max Reinhardt, and performances of several one-acters]

[D3:200] Schneider, Isidor, 'Theatre: Odets, Strindberg, Anderson', *Masses and Mainstream* (New York), 3:1 (1950), 93-96. [Comments positively on the Raymond Massey staging of *Fadren* at the Cort Theatre, New York, and the off-Broadway On Stage Company's production of *Fordringsägare* at the Cherry Lane Theatre. 'The writing of few playwrights has shown such sustained and unrhetorical brilliance']

[D3:201] Siwertz, Sigrid, 'Från Stockholms teatrar', *Ord och Bild* (Stockholm), 70 (1961), 451-459. [Reviews *Gustav Vasa* at Stockholm's Stadsteater (Dir. Lars Levi Læstadius; Gustav: Kolbjörn Knudsen; Erik: Keve Hjelm), and *Kristina* with Inga Tidblad as a royal diva at Dramaten]

[D3:202] Siwertz, Sigrid, 'Från Stockholms teatrar', *Ord och Bild* (Stockholm), 67:2 (1958), 53-63. [Reviews *Leka med elden* with Doris Svedlund and Jarl Kulle at Dramaten, and Ulf Palme as Gustav with Eva Dahlbäck (Tekla) and Olof Widgren (Adolf) in *Fordringsägare*, again at Dramaten]

[D3:203] S. J. [Jacobsohn, Siegfried], 'Strindberg-Aufführungen', *Die Schaubühne* (Berlin), 14:1 (1918), 64-65. [Reviews *Rausch* (i.e. *Brott och brott*), directed by Ernst Welisch in Berlin, 1918, and *Gläubiger*, directed by Max Jungk at the Trianon-Theater, Berlin, 1917]

[D3:204] Sjödin, K. E., 'På parkett i Paris: Strindberg och Ibsen', *Perspektiv* (Stockholm), 15 (1964), 165-167.

[D3:205] Smith, Ejnar, 'Sjuttiofemårsminnet av Strindbergs födelse hyllat på en rad scener', *Svenska Dagbladet* (Stockholm), 7 February 1924. ['The Seventy-Fifth Anniversary of Strindberg's Birth Celebrated on a Number of Stages'. Surveys plays staged to commemorate the anniversary of Sg's birth in January 1849]

[D3:206] Söderberg, Hjalmar, 'Teaterkrönika', *Ord och Bild* (Stockholm), 10:7 (1901), 385-394. [Reviews the world premières of *Folkungasagan* and *Midsommar*. The latter is painfully bad, but *Folkungasagan* is 'the best of this author's history plays since *Mäster Olof*...despite the fact that it is – fortunately – more poetry than history and here and there more feverish fantasy than poetry...it exerts a strong grip not only on the spectator's nerves but on his whole soul, and it is rich in episodes of an unusual and moving beauty, rich too in figures that etch themselves firmly into one's memory and provide rewarding assignments for the actors']

[D3:207] Stahl, Ernst Leopold, 'Das Theaterjahr 1922 im Reich', *Velhagen und Klasings Monatshefte* (Bielefeld and Leipzig), 37:2 (1922-23), 217-224. [Surveys productions of Sg's plays in Germany throughout 1922, pp. 222-223]

[D3:208] Stahl, Ernst Leopold, 'Das Theaterjahr im Reich', *Velhagen und Klasings Monatshefte* (Bielefeld und Leipzig), 39:2 (1924-25), 337-345. [Includes comments on productions of Sg's plays in Germany during 1923-24]

[D3:209] Steene, Birgitta, 'Strindberg Productions in America: Glimpses from the 1980s', *Swedish Book Review* (Lampeter), 1986 (Supplement), pp. 26-29.

[D3:210] Szalczer, Eszter, 'Spring Stages in Stockholm: Two Strindberg Productions', *Western European Stages* (New York), 9:3 (1997), 43-46.

[D3:211] Szalczer, Eszter, 'The 1996 Strindberg Festival in Stockholm', *Western European Stages* (New York), 9:2 (1997), 43-46. [Discusses Bibi Andersson's Sg programme *Var tog du elden?* (Where did you get your Fire From?) and a production of all three parts of *Till Damaskus* by Teater Lam, *Den starkare* directed by Yuu Komaki, and Teater Infernetto's experimental staging of *Brott och brott*]

[D3:212] 'Teater-Nisse', 'Teaterbref', *Söndags-Nisse* (Stockholm), 28 April 1901. [Reviews the premières in Stockholm of *Midsommar* and *Kaspers fettisdag*. The former is undoubtedly far inferior to *Lycko Pers resa* while the latter spoils a good idea]

[D3:213] *Theater heute* (Hannover), 'Strindberg-Inszenierungen in Bochum und Hannover', 3:2 (1962), 16ff. ['Productions of Strindberg in Bochum and Hannover']

[D3:214] Thyselius, Erik, 'Från några Strindbergsföreställningar', *Thalia* (Strindberg), 3:3 (1912), pp. 25-27. ['From some Strindberg Performances'. Surveys performances of Sg's plays, given in honour of his 63rd birthday]

[D3:215] Thyselius, Erik, 'Strindbergs vecka', *Göteborgs Handels- och Sjöfartstidning*, 6 September 1915. ['Strindberg's Week']

[D3:216] Tian, Renzo, 'De *La Contessa* au *Sogno*', *Théâtre en Europe* (Paris), 5:1 (1985), 61-64. Illus. ['From *Miss Julie* to *A Dream Play*'. Discusses Italian productions of *Fröken Julie, Till Damaskus*, and *Ett drömspel*, directed by Luchino Visconti, Mario Missiroli, and Luca Ronconi respectively]

[D3:217] Tsimbal, Irina, '[An Autumn Sonata]', *Interval* (St Petersburg) 2 (1994), p. 5. [Surveys the current Stockholm theatre scene, including productions of *Pelikanen* and *Mäster Olof*]

[D3:218] Vas-ii [L. Vasilevskii], '[New Scandinavian Dramas]', *Rech'* (St Petersburg), No. 223 (18 September 1908), p. 2. [Notices performances of *Siste riddaren* at Dramaten (the première) and *Påsk*, *Fröken Julie*, and *Fadren* at the Intimate Theatre. E.773]

[D3:219] 'Virgo', 'Zur Strindberg-Aufführung im Deutschen Schauspielhaus', *Die Aktion* (Berlin), 2 (1912), Sp. 1300-1301. ['On Performances of Strindberg in German Theatres'. Discusses productions of *Fordringsägare* and *Påsk*. Together with Ibsen, Sg is the dramatist of the hysterical woman, and hence of her true nature]

[D3:220] Volli, Ugo, 'Strindberg: motivi di un'attualità', in Franco Perrelli, ed., **B1:365**, *Omaggio a Strindberg. Strindberg nella cultura moderna*, pp. 141-145. ['Strindberg: Motifs of the Present. Discusses contemporary Italian productions of *Oväder* by Giorgio Strehler (see **E49:113**), *Fadren* by Mina Mezzadri, *Fröken Julie* by Pier'Alli, and *Till Damaskus* by Mario Missiroli and Glauco Mauri, which confirm Sg's modernity as the precursor of Eugene O'Neill, Edward Albee, and Harold Pinter]

[D3:221] Volz, Ruprecht, 'Strindbergspremieren in Deutschland 1978', *Meddelanden från Strindbergssällskapet* (Stockholm), 61-62 (1979), pp. 15-16. [Reports on eight German productions of plays by Sg during 1978]

[D3:222] Volz, Ruprecht, 'Strindbergspremieren in Deutschland 1979', *Meddelanden från Strindbergssällskapet* (Stockholm), 63-64 (1980), pp. 13-16. [Reports on twelve German productions, the most interesting being *Till Damaskus I-III* directed by Frank-Patrick Steckel in Bremen. *Till Damaskus* was also staged in Münster by Rolf Michaelis while

Jens Pesel's production of *Kamraterna* in Augsburg was another exception to the usual narrow choice of *Fadren*, *Fröken Julie*, or *Fordringsägare*]

[D3:223] Volz, Ruprecht, 'Strindbergspremieren in Deutschland 1980', *Meddelanden från Strindbergssällskapet* (Stockholm), 65 (1981), pp. 13-17. [Half the German productions of Sg's plays in 1980 (which was 'a moderate Sg year on the German stage') were of *Fadren*]

[D3:224] Volz, Ruprecht, 'Strindbergspremieren in Deutschland 1981', *Meddelanden från Strindbergssällskapet* (Stockholm), 66 (1982), pp. 14-16. [Reports on thirteen German productions of Sg's plays, including *Fräulein Julie*, directed by Ingmar Bergman at the Residenztheater, Munich]

[D3:225] Volz, Ruprecht, 'Strindbergspremieren in Deutschland 1982', *Meddelanden från Strindbergssällskapet* (Stockholm), 67 (1983), pp. 30-32. [Reports on fifteen German productions]

[D3:226] Volz, Ruprecht, 'Strindbergspremieren in Deutschland 1983', *Meddelanden från Strindbergssällskapet* (Stockholm), 68 (1984), pp. 12-14. [On six German productions, including *Fröken Julie*, directed by Daniel Karasek in Tübingen, and *Till Damaskus I*, directed by Erwin Axer in Munich. Volz also comments on Hans Falár's two-hour version of the brief one-acter, *Den starkare*, in Mannheim]

[D3:227] Volz, Ruprecht, 'Strindberg-Premieren in Deutschland 1984-85', *Strindbergiana* (Stockholm), 2 (1987), pp. 54-60. [Notes that fifty procent of the stagings of Sg's plays during this period were of *Fröken Julie*, including productions in Munich (Dir. Ernst Wendt), Mönchengladblach (Dir. Wolfram Fuchs), the Rheinisches Landestheater (Dir. Eckhart Neuberg), Bremerhaven (Dir. Hans-Rüdiger Berbalk), and the Hannover Landesbühne (Dir. Ulf Reher). Volz also provides details of productions of *Fadren* in both Dortmund and Rostock, *Påsk* in Gauting, *Dödsdansen* in Frankfurt, and *Pelikanen* in Freiburg]

[D3:228] Walden, Herwarth, 'Kinder. Kinder – Schlenthrian', *Der Sturm* (Berlin), 6 (1915-16), 82-83. [Reviews *Fadren* and *Fordringsägare*, the latter directed by Felix Hollaender at the Berlin Kammerspiele]

[D3:229] Weigel, Hans, 'Autoren und Stücke. 14. Strindberg', in *Tausendundeine Premiere*, Graz: Styria, [1961], pp. 31-32. [Reviews productions of *Dödsdansen* and *Ett drömspel* in Austria]

[D3:230] Weiglin, Paul, 'Berliner Bühnen', *Velhagen und Klasings Monatshefte* (Bielefeld and Leipzig), 34:2 (1919-20), 205-216. [Reviews productions of *Advent*, *Fröken Julie*, and *Ett drömspel*]

[D3:231] Weiglin, Paul, 'Berliner Bühnen', *Velhagen und Klasings Monatshefte* (Bielefeld and Leipzig), 35:1 (1920-21), 527-540. [Reviews *Brända tomten* (Dir. Karlheinz Martin), *Till Damaskus* at the Volksbühne with Friedrich Kayßler as The Unknown, and *Brott och brott*]

[D3:232] Wendt, Ernst, 'Strindberg – von heute aus gesehen', *Teater heute* (Hannover), 3:2 (1962), 17-18. ['Strindberg Seen from Today's Perspective'. Discusses productions of *Till Damaskus* in Hannover and *Spöksonaten* in Bochum]

[D3:233] Winter, Hanns, 'Wildgans und Strindberg. Die großen Wiener Bühnen', *Wort in der Zeit* (München), 2 (1956), 364-366. [On productions of *Fadren* and *Fröken Julie*]

[**D3:234**] Ziegler, Theobald, '*Die Kronbraut*; *Königin Christine*', *Bühne und Welt* (Hamburg), 16:2 (1913-14), 362-363. [Reviews the German première of *Kronbruden* in Berlin with Irene Triesch and Paul Wegener, and *Kristina*, also with Irene Triesch (see **E36:39**)]

Vasasagan, Malmö Dramatiska Teater, 20 March 1998. Dir. Staffan Valdemar Holm. (A six-hour production comprising scenes from* Siste riddaren, Riksföreståndaren, Mäster Olof, Gustav Vasa, Erik XIV, Gustav Adolf, *and* Kristina, *performed in chronological sequence of the events depicted)

[**D3:235**] Berglund, Jonny, *Borås Tidning*, 22 March 1998.

[**D3:236**] Carlsson, Larsolof, *Helsingborgs Dagblad*, 22 March 1998.

[**D3:237**] Franzon, Johan, *Göteborgs-Posten*, 24 March 1998.

[**D3:238**] Gerell, Boel, *Kvällsposten* (Malmö), 22 March 1998.

[**D3:239**] Granath, Sara, *Svenska Dagbladet* (Stockholm), 22 March 1998.

[**D3:240**] Håkanson, Jan S., *Hallandsposten* (Halmstad), 27 March 1998.

[**D3:241**] Karlsson, Jan, *Östgöta Correspondenten* (Linköping), 25 March 1998.

[**D3:242**] Lång, Helmer, *Skånska Dagbladet* (Malmö), 22 March 1998.

[**D3:243**] Larsson, Lisbeth, *Expressen* (Stockholm), 27 March 1998.

[**D3:244**] Larsson, Stellan, *Expressen* (Stockholm), 27 March 1998.

[**D3:245**] Palmqvist, Bertil, *Arbetet* (Malmö), 22 March 1998.

[**D3:246**] Sjögren, Henrik, *Arbetet* (Malmö), 8 January 1999. [On Swedish Television]

[**D3:247**] Vinterhed, Kerstin, *Dagens Nyheter* (Stockholm), 23 August 1998. [On Swedish Radio]

[**D3:248**] Waaranperä, Ingegärd, *Dagens Nyheter* (Stockholm), 28 December 1998. [On Swedish Television]

[**D3:249**] Waaranperä, Ingegärd, '"Vasasagan" en lysande bragd', *Dagens Nyheter* (Stockholm), 22 March 1998. ['"The Vasa Saga" a Brilliant Feat']

[**D3:250**] Wahlin, Claes, *Aftonbladet* (Stockholm), 22 March 1998.

[**D3:251**] Smiding, Birgitta. *Den stora mekanismen – i Holm/Møllers Vasasagan*, Lund: Centre for Languages and Literature, 2006. Illus. 254 pp. ['The Great Mechanism in Holm/Møller's Vasasagan'. Summary in English. Doctoral dissertation]

See also **D2:1060, D2:1311**

www.ingramcontent.com/pod-product-compliance
Lightning Source LLC
Chambersburg PA
CBHW060424100426
42812CB00030B/3296/J

* 9 7 8 0 9 4 7 6 2 3 8 1 4 *